for Windows™: A Multi-Simulation Approach

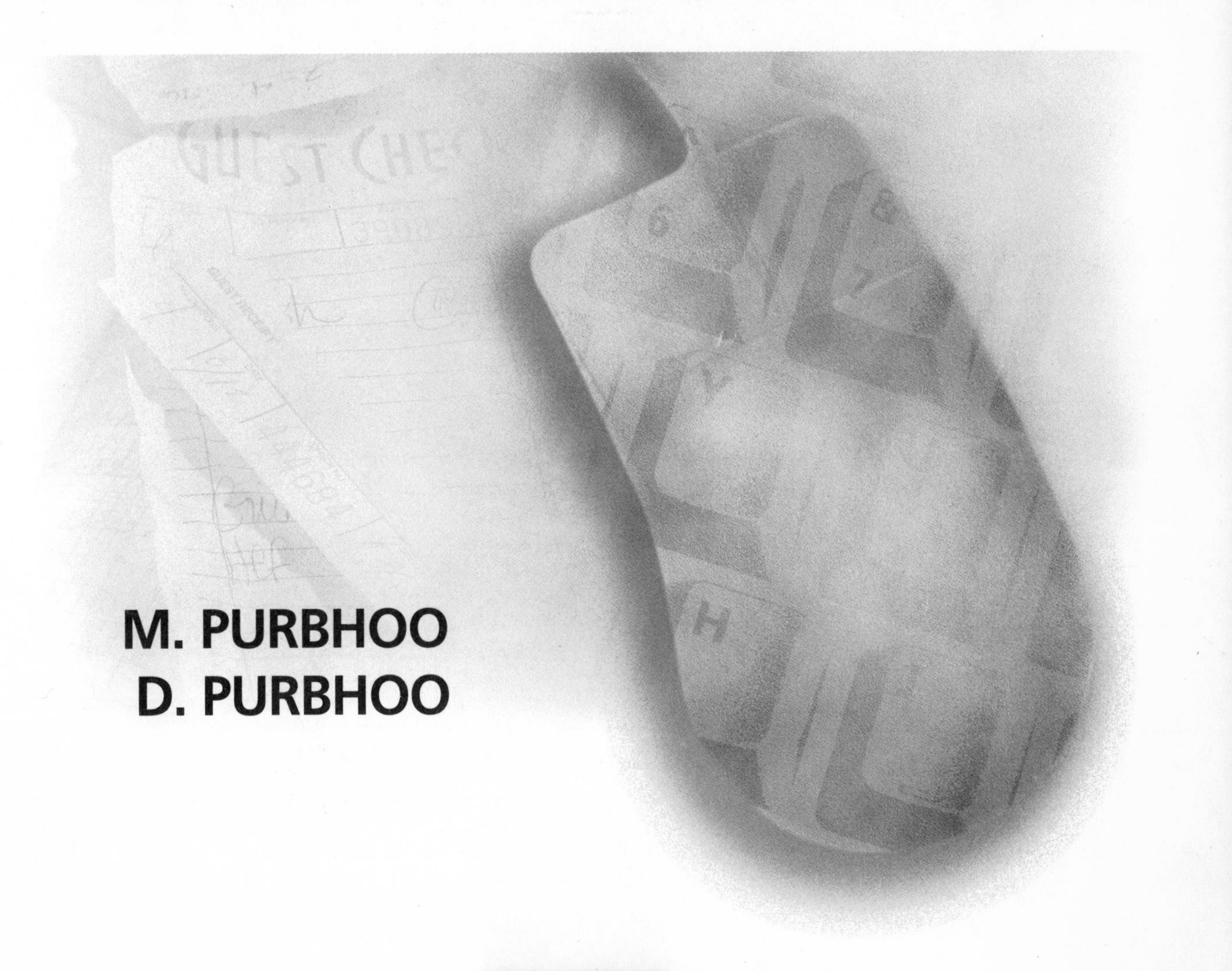

M. PURBHOO
D. PURBHOO

Toronto

National Library of Canada Cataloguing in Publication Data

Purbhoo, Mary, 1949-
Using Simply Accounting versions 8.0 and 8.5 for Windows: a multi-simulation approach

Includes index.
Issued also as trade ed. under title: Teach yourself Simply Accounting versions 8.0 and 8.5 for Windows. The title on the trade ed. is found on separate bellyband on monograph.
ISBN 0-201-74916-5 (college) - ISBN 0-201-75835-0 (trade ed.)

1. Simply Accounting for Windows (Computer file) 2. Accounting - Computer programs. I. Purbhoo, D. (Dhirajlal) II. Title

HF5679.P895 2002 657'.0285'5369 C2001-900782-5

0-201-74916-5 (college)
0-201-75835-0 (trade)

Vice President, Editorial Director: Michael Young
Acquisitions Editor: Samantha Scully
Marketing Manager: Cas Shields
Developmental Editor: Laurie Goebel
Production Editor: Marisa D'Andrea
Copy Editor: Dawn Hunter
Production Coordinator: Patricia Ciardullo
Page Layout: Mary Purbhoo
Art Director: Mary Opper
Cover Design: Anthony Leung
Cover Image: EyeWire Inc.

This edition is also published as Teach Yourself Simply Accounting Versions 8.0 and 8.5 for Windows: A Multi-Simulation Approach.

5 06 05 04 03 02

Printed and bound in Canada.

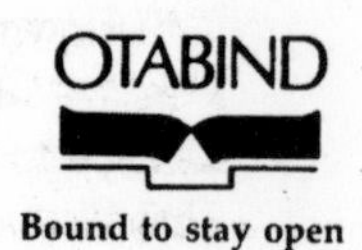

CONTENTS

ACKNOWLEDGEMENTS

As usual, many people helped this project come to fruition. We had the additional advantage this time of working with a familiar team. When timelines are short, knowing that you can trust everyone to do their part, do it well and do it on time, makes the author's job easier.

We want to extend a special thank you to Mary Watson at ACCPAC International for giving us timely access to new versions of Simply Accounting and information about upcoming changes. These made it possible to complete this book in preparation for the fall school semester. And, as always, working with Mary is a pleasure.

Although no formal reviews were conducted this time, we value the informal feedback we receive from users over the years. A cumulation of this feedback helps us to meet our goals of continual improvement as suggestions from past reviews find their way into our books.

Joanna Severino-Souto and Irene Mota, teachers with the Toronto District School Board and Dufferin-Peel Catholic District School Board respectively, assisted us once again with the critical task of independently checking all keystroke instructions and transactions. Despite busy teaching schedules, they put in their usual careful effort of checking the keystrokes for accuracy. In addition, their perspective as classroom teachers led to changes that we hope will make it even easier for students to learn to use Simply Accounting from our books.

A good copy editor can change a few outdated or awkward words and create a smoothly flowing sentence. Dawn Hunter accomplished this, as well as eliminating many stylistic inconsistencies. Again, her rapid turnaround time and high quality work are greatly appreciated. Commas do make a difference.

It has been two years since the Addison Wesley and Prentice Hall merger. Although we sometimes still miss our Addison Wesley friends, we are getting used to the new name, Pearson Education, and with each project, our working relationship with the Pearson staff keeps getting better. Anthony Leung, whose creative talents have produced many of our book covers and designs, performed his magic once again. Samantha Scully, Laurie Goebel, Marisa D'Andrea and Trish Ciardullo — always calm and professional — have been great to work with. Even though all handle several projects at once, they succeed in making us feel that ours is the most important one.

The two real companies in this book deserve a special note. One of the authors has been involved with CISV (Children's International Summer Villages) for over 10 years and has enjoyed participating in the growth of the Toronto Chapter. This is a landmark year for CISV as Doris Allen, the organization's founder, celebrates her 100th birthday and CISV marks its 50th year of providing international programs for children. We also want to thank our nephew, David Manga, owner of Outset Media Corporation and creator of The All Canadian Board Game, for his permission to profile his board games and business in our book. We are pleased to contribute to the promotion of these two organizations in our own small way.

PREFACE

Using Simply Accounting Versions 8.0 and 8.5 for Windows: a Multi-Simulation Approach updates our previous multi-simulation book. As in previous versions, we cover both the basics and the latest features of this popular accounting software from ACCPAC INTERNATIONAL, INC.

Shortly after publishing *Using Simply Accounting Version 8.0: An Integrated Simulation* in 2000, we decided to update the multi-simulation book for Version 8.0. Almost immediately after this decision, the Pro Version was released. The principal differences in the Pro Version — the multi-user and multi-currency features — do not affect the way accounting transactions are entered. Therefore, we chose to combine the two versions into a single book. With the release in the spring of Version 8.5 (non-Pro), we chose to cover this version in the book as well because many of our users in educational settings likely have Version 8.5 rather than Pro 8.5.

notes

The data CD has separate ready-to-use data sets for the different versions of the program so that no conversions are required for any users. Refer to Using This Book, pages xiii–xiv, and Chapter 1, pages 12–13, for instructions on installing the correct data set for your system.

This book is the result of those decisions. Both Versions 8.5 and Pro 8.5 are covered comprehensively in the main body of the text. Version 8.0 differs from these two (mainly in the way menus are organized) and these differences are described in detail in a separate section of the text, Part Three: Using Version 8.0. Extensive cross-referencing between the main text and Part Three makes it easy to find the details required to work through the application setups and transactions. We added Version 8 sidebars to point you to Part Three, and sidebar page numbers in Part Three refer back to the main text. In addition, Part Three pages are edged with a blue stripe so that you can find them quickly. We also believe that, in most cases, once you have read Part Three, the small differences between versions will often make it unnecessary to return to this section.

Some of the new features that we cover in this text include the use of foreign currencies for sales, purchases, inventory prices and bank accounts; automatic application of import duties; optional reduced inventory prices for preferred customers; and adjusting General Journal entries after posting.

Realism is one of our goals when writing these workbooks. Since our users live in all parts of Canada and work in a variety of companies, the 13 accounting applications in the workbook represent a wide variety of business types and settings.

- Two of the applications in this workbook are based on real companies — the Toronto Chapter of Children's International Summer Villages (CISV), an international non-profit organization, and Outset Media Corporation, creator of The All Canadian Trivia Board Game.
- To enhance the feel of a real small business, we include a company profile for each application.
- We familiarize our users throughout Canada with a broad range of Canadian tax requirements by covering the Harmonized Sales Tax (HST), GST using the quick and regular methods, and QST (Quebec Sales Tax). Quebec's approach to sales tax is a variation of the HST model.
- We deal with various payroll tax requirements by including Employer Health Tax (EHT) for Ontario as well as examples for other provinces.
- Several applications include foreign transactions because, today, the global economy is a fact of life even for small businesses.

To offer this variety, we include many shorter applications rather than follow a single company throughout the workbook.

As the Simply Accounting program is updated, the alternative methods of inputting data and using the program are increasing. When possible, we choose optional settings that reduce the likelihood of errors and increase the controls that are an essential part of good accounting practices. For example, we hide unused modules to prevent error messages when users try to access them, and we do not allow future dates so that dates cannot be advanced in error. In setup applications we show how these settings can be changed. We provide alternative ways of entering data. For example, we include different keystrokes or the choice between using menu bars and tool buttons. We also offer different methods of setting up new company files. For each method, we show and explain all the settings and setup options rather than use the setup wizard shortcuts. Once you learn to complete a setup from scratch, using Simply Accounting's setup wizards on your own and modifying the built-in templates for future setups will be easier because you will already understand the different settings and options. Again, we hope that our users will learn some alternative methods and use the ones best suited to their new applications or the ones they prefer.

Much thought and discussion has gone into the organization of the material, specifically the order of keystroke instructions and source documents within each chapter. A certain amount of page-flipping is inevitable in a book of this nature because the description or instructions for any type of transaction invariably occupy more than one page. We believe that keeping all the source documents together and all the keystroke instructions together makes it easy to see the whole picture of what you are accomplishing. The rule of order that we have chosen is simple:

- When keystrokes refer to a setup that must be completed before entering transactions, we place them before the source documents;
- If the keystrokes refer to the transactions, they follow the source documents.

As much as possible, we try to present new keystroke transactions first. However, we are cautious about sacrificing realism. Employees are not paid on their first day of work and recurring transactions are recalled only after the recurring interval has passed.

We continue to search for ways to improve the workbook and make it easier for you to find your way around the book:

- Beside every source document or transaction that has keystroke instructions, we have added the page number where those instructions begin. These transactions have ✔ beside them in the check box.
- All other transactions have a blank check box for you to mark once you have completed the entry.
- We also provide a bookmark that we hope will serve a dual purpose: use it to mark your place as you move back and forth between transactions and keystrokes, and use the index listed on it as a quick reference to find the beginning page for the keystrokes for all major kinds of transactions.

The accounting applications in the workbook follow the same approach as our other workbooks. We introduce each of the six ledgers of the Simply Accounting program (General, Payables, Receivables, Payroll, Inventory and Project) in six separate applications, with a detailed demonstration of keystrokes and matching screens for each new type of sample transaction. Three more applications explain additional features: budgeting, account reconciliation procedures, and advanced Receivables and Payables features (credit cards, discounts, tax remittances, sales to foreign customers and Internet linkages). These nine applications are set up in advance.

Three applications provide a comprehensive introduction to setting up a computerized accounting system using Simply Accounting. Detailed instructions are given for each setup. We walk you through each step as you learn to convert, design and implement a complete accounting system.

- The first setup introduces an actual non-profit organization that uses only the General Ledger. The application describes the accounting for a program in the Toronto chapter of the international organization.
- The second setup is for a service organization using the General, Payables and Receivables Ledgers.
- The third setup application describes a comprehensive retail organization and covers the General, Payables, Receivables, Payroll and Inventory Ledgers, and Projects.

The final application in the workbook offers a fourth opportunity to convert a manual accounting system to a computerized one. This time you are asked to enter accounting transactions using descriptive and realistic source documents to give you the "feel" of actual company transactions.

At the end of each application, you will find one or more case problems. These are provided to supplement and extend the principles covered in the applications.

A new section, Part Three, covers all the differences between Version 8.0 and Versions 8.5 and Pro 8.5.

A number of appendices have been included for reference or further study:

- Appendix A provides complete descriptions and screen displays for reversing entries or correcting errors after posting.
- Appendix B describes system security — entering and removing users, access rights and passwords.
- Appendix C provides additional case problems.
- The systems approach is illustrated in Appendix D with discussions on how Simply Accounting reports can be integrated with other software for analysis and decision making. We cover exporting reports to Microsoft Access, linking through Dynamic Data Exchange, exporting financial reports to Canada Customs and Revenue Agency (GIFI reports) and finally, importing data into the Simply Accounting program from data files or from online bank, customer and vendor connections.
- Appendix E shows the equivalent accounting and non-accounting terms that you will see in Simply Accounting.

Using This Book

The accounting applications in this workbook were prepared using **Version 8.0B, Version 8.5A and Pro Version 8.5A** of the Simply Accounting for Windows software published by ACCPAC INTERNATIONAL, INC. If you are using a subsequent version of the software, you may find some changes in screens and keystrokes. Always refer to your user's guides, readme files and update notices when you work with later versions of the software.

We assume that you are using an IBM PC or compatible with a hard disk and CD-ROM drive, or a network system with Windows installed. You will need a copy of the licensed Simply Accounting software or access to that software through a network environment. Each user must have a formatted data disk or a pseudo data disk on a network system, with the correct attributes and permissions for each user. For network systems, we recommend that you work with the site-administrator of the network.

In addition, you should have a standard accounting text for reviewing accounting principles. The workbook does provide some accounting principles and procedures, but it is not intended to replace the breadth and depth of all the principles covered in most standard accounting texts. You should also consult the built-in Help features or have access to the Simply Accounting user's manuals.

notes

Instructor's packages to accompany this workbook should be ordered from your Pearson Education Canada sales representative.

Instructors can order an instructor's package that includes a solutions CD with Simply Accounting files for each application after all transactions are completed, and an instructor's manual that has answers for all the cases in the workbook as well as additional teaching resources and testing material.

The workbook is as simple and straightforward as we could make it, but you will still need some familiarity with computers before you work through it. Your life will be easier still if you have acquired some of the fundamentals of troubleshooting.

The Data CD

We have tried to make the differences between the versions of the program as explicit as possible so that no one will be confused about what to do or what they will see at each stage. In addition, we provide separate data sets for the three versions of the software. All are ready to use without data conversions. We also provide separate installation programs for the three data sets to help you install the right data set for your computer setup. All company files are set up without passwords for maximum flexibility of access.

To choose the correct data set for your program installation, you must know what version of the program you are using. You can get this information from the package that the program came in, from the program CD or by starting the program and reading the version number from the introductory screen that shows temporarily, just before the Select Company window appears. You can also find the program version number once you start the program. (Select one of the Sample companies.) In the Home window, choose the Help menu and click About Simply Accounting. The information window shows the program name, version, serial or key code number and ACCPAC INTERNATIONAL company information.

Use the following chart to help you install the data set you need.

For Program Version	Use Install Program	Data Set (Folder on CD)
Version 8.0	Load80	Data80
Version 8.5	Load85	Data85
Pro Version 8.5	LoadPro	DataPro

All three Load programs create a data folder named Simdata on Drive C. If you need to work with another location for your data files, refer to page 14. If you need to install data sets for more than one version, run the Load program for the first data set you want. Then, using Windows Explorer, change the name of the Simdata folder (e.g., to Simdata8). Run the second Load program you need and rename the Simdata folder so that you will not confuse the two data sets.

If you are working with other data sets that include users and passwords, you must enter your user name and password before you can open the data files. Ask your instructor or site administrator for the user name and password that you should use. Refer to Appendix B for instructions on working with passwords.

Order of Working Through the Applications

Before all the modules are covered, setup applications are introduced. Advanced users should have no difficulty working through the applications in the order given and may even choose to skip some applications. However, at a minimum, we recommend working through all keystroke transactions (the ones with a ✔ beside them) so that you become familiar with all the journals before starting the more comprehensive applications.

We realize that in some classrooms the workbook is used first at a basic or introductory level in one course and then at an advanced level for a different course. In this case, the instructor may wish to deviate slightly from the order given. Completing all six ledgers before beginning the setup applications will provide additional practice before beginning the more complex setup procedures. A recommended order for these situations would be:

1. Read and work through the two *Getting Started* chapters in Part 1.
2. Complete the ledger applications in order: Reliable Roofing (General), Java Jean's (Payables), Grandeur Graphics (Receivables), Outset Media Corp. (advanced features of the first three ledgers), Carnival Catering (Payroll), Meteor Mountain Bikes (Inventory) and Puretek Paving & Stoneworks (Project).
3. Complete the account reconciliation (HSC School Store) and budgeting (Bonnie Brides) applications.
4. Complete the three setup applications in order: CISV (General), Maverick Micro Solutions (three ledgers) and Hearth House (six ledgers).
5. Complete the Serene Sailing setup application with realistic source documents. Users may want to attempt this setup with the help of the setup wizard from the Setup menu in the Home window.

This order is shown graphically in the following chart:

notes

Another approach to the applications is to complete the source document transactions for every application (except Serene Sailing), then return to complete the three keystroke setup applications and Serene Sailing. This, of course, means setting up an application that you are already familiar with from the source documents and accounts.

AN ALTERNATIVE SEQUENCE FOR WORKING THROUGH THE APPLICATIONS

Getting Started	Ledger Applications	Advanced Features	Setup Applications	Challenge Application
Getting Started (**1**)				
GST (**2**) → →	Reliable Roofing (**3** General)			
	↓ Java Jean's (**4** Payables)			
	↓ Grandeur Graphics (**5** Receivables) → →	Outset Media Corporation (**7** Advanced A/P & A/R)		
	Carnival Catering (**8** Payroll) ← ← ← ←	↓		
	↓ Meteor Mtn Bike (**9** Inventory)			
	↓ Puretek Paving & Stoneworks (**11** Project) → →	Bonnie Brides (**12** Budgeting) HSC School Store (**14** Account Reconciliation) → →	CISV Village (**6** General)	
			↓ Maverick Micro Solutions (**10** General, Payables, Receivables)	
			↓ Hearth House (**13** General, Payables, Receivables, Payroll, Inventory, Project) → →	Serene Sailing & Boating (**15**)

notes

- Each box includes the chapter or application title, the chapter number and the topic or ledger introduced.
- Applications within the same box may be completed in any order.

Part One
Getting Started

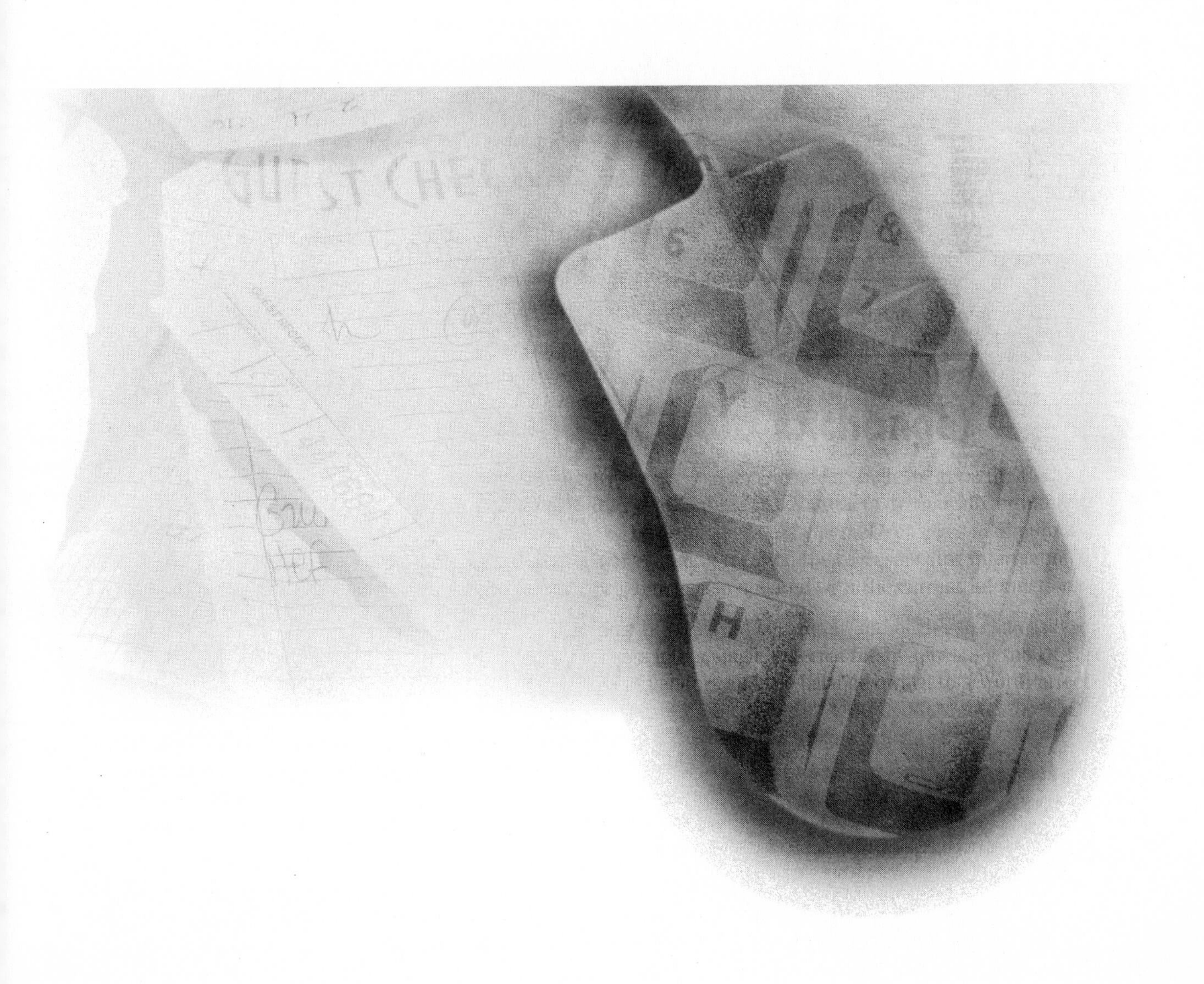

CHAPTER ONE

Getting Started

OBJECTIVES

After completing this chapter, you should be able to

- *install* the Simply Accounting program under Windows
- *access* the Simply Accounting program
- *access* the data files for a business
- *understand* Simply Accounting's help features
- *save* your work
- *back up* your data files
- *finish* your session
- *change* default date format settings

DATA FILES AND ABBREVIATIONS

notes

The instructions in this chapter for installing the program, starting the program and copying files refer to Windows 98 procedures. If you are using a different version of Windows, please refer to Windows and Simply Accounting Help and manuals for assistance with these procedures.

The applications in this workbook were prepared using Windows 98 and the Simply Accounting Pro Version 8.5 and the non-Pro Version 8.5 software packages produced by ACCPAC INTERNATIONAL, INC. Subsequent versions of the software may have changes in screens or keystrokes. Income tax tables change regularly; the most recent ones will be used in later versions of the software.

The instructions in this workbook have been written for a stand-alone IBM PC or compatible computer, with a hard disk drive and a CD-ROM disk drive. Windows should be correctly installed on your hard drive. Your printers should be installed and accessible through the Windows program. Refer to Windows Help and manuals for assistance with these procedures.

This workbook reflects the authors' approach to working with Simply Accounting. There are alternative approaches to setting up company accounts and to working with the software. Refer to Simply Accounting and Windows Help and manuals for further details.

Warning!

Before using your data files, you should make backup copies of all the files. Always work with this working backup copy, so that you can use the original to restore the files if later you have data errors. Refer to page 13 and your Windows manuals for complete instructions.

notes

The Serene Sailing file is not set up in advance for you. You must create that file on your own.

DATA APPLICATION FILES

Company	Folder\File name	Chapter
Reliable Roofing	reliable\reliable.sdb	3
Java Jean's Coffee Emporium	java\java.sdb	4
Grandeur Graphics	grandeur\grandeur.sdb	5
CISV Toronto Village	setup\cisv\cisv.sdb	6
Outset Media Corporation	outset\outset.sdb	7
Carnival Catering	carnival\carnival.sdb	8
Meteor Mountain Bike Shop	meteor\meteor.sdb	9
Maverick Micro Solutions	setup\maverick\maverick.sdb	10
Puretek Paving & Stoneworks	puretek\puretek.sdb	11
Bonnie Brides	brides\brides.sdb	12
Hearth House	setup\hearth\hh-oct.sdb	13
	setup\hearth\hh-nov.sdb	13
	setup\hearth\hh-dec.sdb	13
HSC School Store	hsc\hsc.sdb	14
Serene Sailing and Boating	user setup	15

The applications increase in complexity, with each one introducing new ledgers, setups or features as shown in the following chart.

DATA APPLICATION	GL	AP	AR	PAY	INV	PROJ	OTHER
Reliable Roofing	*						
Java Jean's	*	*					
Grandeur Graphics	*	*	*				
CISV Toronto	*						1
Outset Media Corp.	*	*	*				2, 5
Carnival Catering	*	*	*	*			
Meteor Mountain Bike	*	*	*		*		2, 5
Maverick Micro	*	*	*				1, 2, 5
Puretek Paving	*	*	*	*	*	*	2, 5
Bonnie Brides	*	*	*	*	*		2, 3, 5
Hearth House	*	*	*	*	*	*	1, 2, 5
HSC School Store	*	*	*		*		4
Serene Sailing	*	*	*	*			2, 6

Ledgers:
GL = General Ledger
AP = Accounts Payable
AR = Accounts Receivable
PAY = Payroll
INV = Inventory
PROJ = Project (Jobcosting)

Other: 1 Setup application with keystrokes
2 Credit cards, Internet links
3 Budgeting
4 Account reconciliation
5 Foreign currency transactions
6 Setup application without keystrokes

Some Windows and Mouse Basics

Skip this section if you are already familiar with Windows and the use of a mouse.

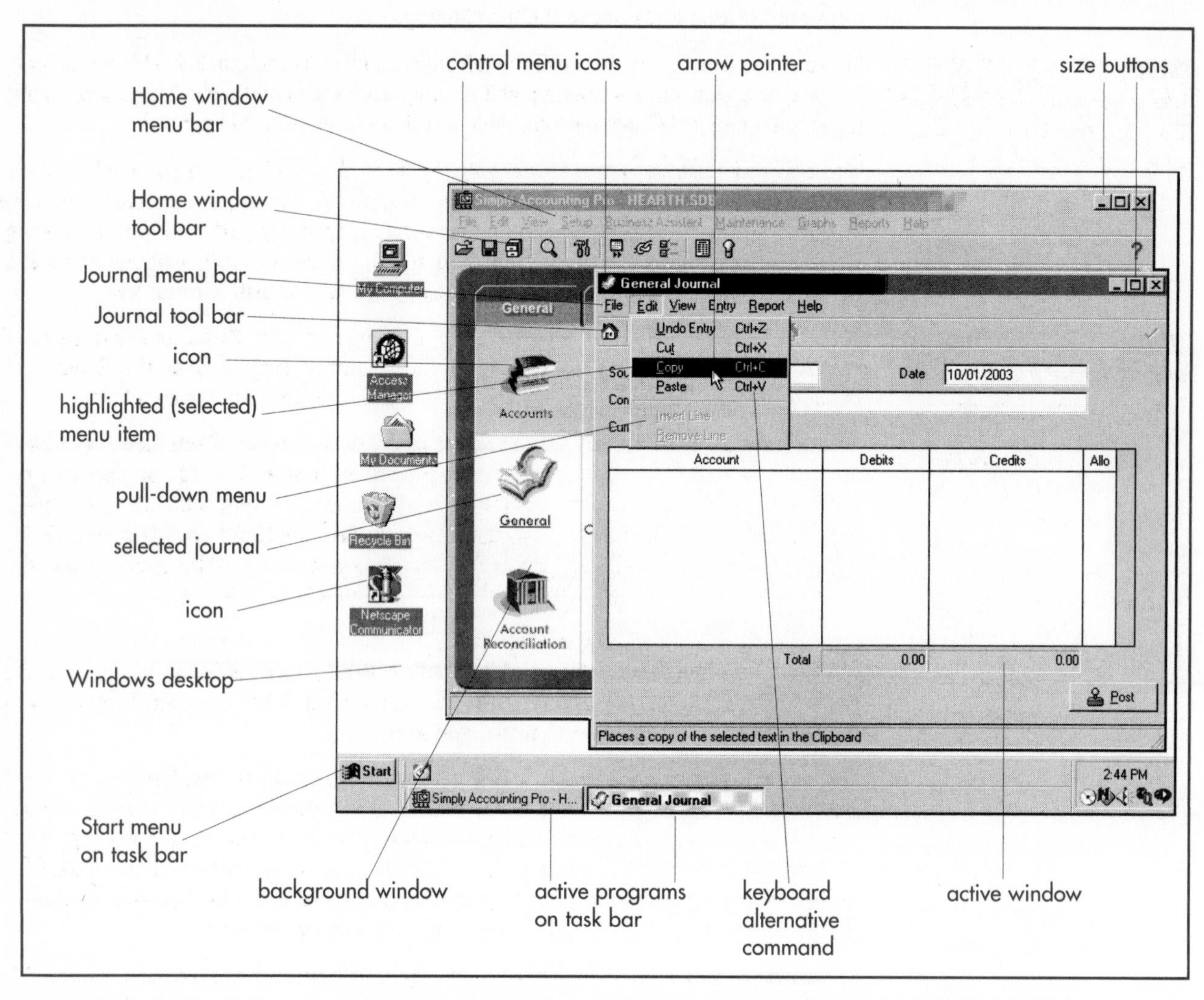

In the illustration above, the Simply Accounting program is open on the Windows 98 desktop. The General Journal is open and active with the Home window in the background. The Journal's Edit menu is pulled down and Copy is selected.

notes

Your windows may look different from those shown in this chapter if you have a different computer setup or if you have selected different display options.

The **mouse** is used to move the cursor. When you move the mouse, an **arrow** or **pointer** moves to indicate the cursor placement. If you **click** (press) the left mouse button, the cursor will move to the location of the arrow (if this is a legitimate place for the cursor to be at the time). That is, you use the mouse to **click** (point to and click) a screen location, item on a list, command or icon.

The arrow or pointer changes shape, depending on what actions you may perform. When you are moving the mouse, it appears as an arrow or pointer. When you are in a field that can accept text, it appears as a long **I bar**. Clicking will change it to an insertion point — a flashing vertical line in a text field. When the computer is processing information and you are unable to perform any action, you will see an **hourglass**. This is your signal to wait.

Dragging refers to the method of moving the mouse while holding the left button down. As you drag through the options in a menu, each one will be successively highlighted or darkened. Dragging through text will highlight it. Point to the beginning of the text to be highlighted. Then click and hold the mouse button down while moving through the entire area that you want to highlight. Release the mouse button at the end of the area you want to highlight. You can highlight a single character or the entire contents of a field. The text will remain highlighted and can be edited by typing new text. Delete text by pressing the Backspace key or del. Clicking a different location will remove the highlighting.

notes

The Simply Accounting files are set up to open journals and windows with a single click instead of a double click.

To **double click** means to press the left mouse button twice quickly. This action can be used as a shortcut for opening and closing windows. Double clicking an icon or file name will open it. Double clicking the control icon will close the window.

The **active window** is the one that you are currently working in. If you click an area outside the active window that is part of a background window, that window will move to the foreground. To return to a previous window, click any part of it that is showing. If the window you need is completely hidden, you can restore it by clicking its button on the task bar. Click to reduce an active window to a task bar button.

notes

Often a program will include dialogue boxes that look like windows but do not have menu bars. Usually they require you to make a choice, such as answering a question, before you can proceed. You cannot make a dialogue box into a background window; you must click one of the options such as Yes, No, OK, Proceed, Cancel and so on to continue. Closing the dialogue box without making a choice is like choosing Cancel.

An **icon** is a picture form of your program, file name or item. **Buttons** are icons or commands surrounded by a box frame. In Simply Accounting, clicking the Home window button will bring the Home window to the front and make it active.

The **menu bar** is the line of options at the top of each window. Each menu contains one or more commands or selections (the **pull-down menu**) and can be accessed by clicking the menu name. Each window may have different menu selections, and the options in the pull-down menu may differ. To choose an option from the menu, click the menu name and then click the option you want in order to **highlight** and **select** it. If an option is dimmed, you will be unable to highlight or select it.

Some menus are **cascading menus**. When the menu option you want has an arrow, , it has a second level of menu choices. To select from a cascading menu, click the menu bar name and point to the first-level menu option. When the next level of the menu appears, click the selection that you need.

You can **select multiple items** from a screen or list. Click the first item to select it. Then press and hold ctrl while you click each of the other items you want to select. The items previously selected will remain selected. If the items are in a list and you want to select several items in a row, click the first item and then press and hold shift while clicking the last item that you want to include. All the items between the two will also be selected. To change a selection, click somewhere else.

The **control menu icon** is situated in the upper left-hand corner of each window. The icon is different for different programs and windows. It has its own pull-down menu, including the Close and size commands. To close windows, you can double click this icon, choose Close from its pull-down menu or click the **Close button** in the upper right-hand corner of the window.

Size buttons are located in the upper right-hand corner of the window. Use them to make a window larger (**maximize** to full screen size) or to reduce the window to a task bar button (**minimize**). If the window is full screen size, reduce it to its normal smaller size with the (**restore**) button.

You can also change the size of a window by dragging. Point to a side. When the pointer changes to a two-sided arrow, drag the window frame to its new size.

When a window contains more information than can fit on the screen at once, the window will contain **scroll arrows** (, , , or) in any corner or direction next to the hidden information (bottom or right sides of the window). Click the arrow and hold the mouse button down to scroll the screen in the direction of the arrow you are on.

Input fields containing data may have a **drop-down** or **pop-up list** from which to select. A **list arrow** beside the field indicates that a list is available. When you click the arrow, the list appears. Click an item on the list to add it to the input field directly.

USING THE KEYBOARD INSTEAD OF A MOUSE

All Windows software applications are designed to be used with a mouse. However, there may be times when you prefer to use keyboard commands to work with a program because it is faster. There are also times when you need to know the alternatives to using a mouse, as when the mouse itself is inoperative. It is not necessary to memorize all the keyboard commands. A few basic principles will help you to understand how they work, and over time you will use the ones that help you to work most efficiently. Some commands are common to more than one Windows software program. For example, ctrl + C (press and hold the Control key while you press C) is commonly used as the copy command and ctrl + V as the paste command. Any selected text will be copied or pasted.

The menu bar and the menu choices can be accessed by pressing alt. The first menu bar item will be highlighted. Use **arrow keys**, ↑ and ↓, to move up and down through the pull-down menu choices of a highlighted menu item or ← and → to go back and forth to other menu items. Some menu choices have direct keyboard alternatives or shortcuts. If the menu item has an underlined letter, pressing alt together with the underlined letter will access that option directly. For example, alt + F (press alt, and while holding down alt, press F) accesses the File pull-down menu. Then pressing O (the underlined letter for Open) will give you the dialogue box for opening a new file. Some tool buttons in Simply Accounting have a direct keyboard command and some menu choices also have a shortcut keyboard command. When available, these direct keystrokes are given with the button name or to the right of a menu choice. For example, alt + f4 is the shortcut for closing the active window or exiting from the Simply Accounting program.

To cancel the menu display, press esc.

In the Simply Accounting Home window, you can use the **arrow keys** to move among the ledger and journal icons. Press alt, alt and → to highlight the Accounts icon, and then use the arrow keys to change selections. Each icon is highlighted or selected as you reach it and deselected as you move to another icon.

To choose or open a highlighted or selected item, press enter.

When input fields are displayed in a Simply Accounting window, you can move to the next field by pressing tab or to a previous field by pressing shift and tab together. The tab key is used frequently in this workbook as a quick way to accept input, advance the cursor to the next field and highlight field contents to prepare for immediate editing. Using the mouse while you input information requires you to remove your hands from the keyboard, while the tab key does not.

INSTALLING SIMPLY ACCOUNTING

notes

Skip this section if your Simply Accounting program is already installed.

Start your computer and the Windows program.

Insert the program CD in the CD-ROM drive. Installation from CD-ROM drives often begins immediately. Proceed to the opening Simply Accounting installation options screen (page 8). Otherwise, you can install the program from the Windows opening screen or desktop.

Double click the **My Computer icon** My Computer. The screen that follows will show the drives and devices on your system.

The computer configuration screen shown here has one 31/2″ floppy drive (A:); a hard drive partitioned into C:, D:, E:, and F:; a zip drive, G:; and two CD-ROM drives (H: and I:):

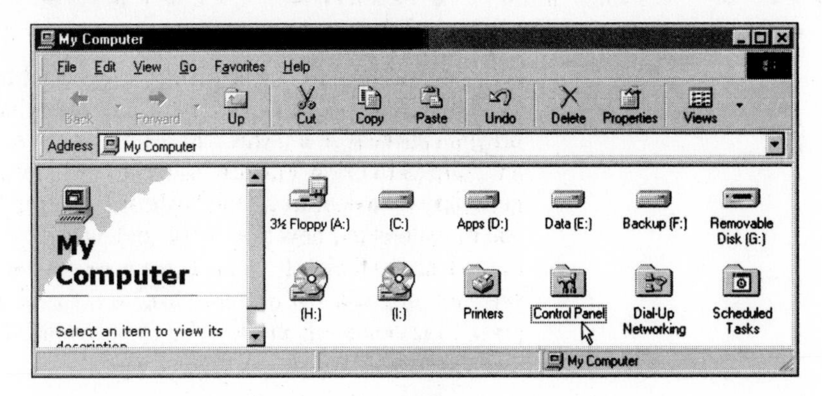

Warning!

Remember that the screens on your computer may look different from the ones we show if you have different components, programs or settings.

Double click the **Control Panel icon** to see the components that are installed on your computer:

notes

- You can also access the Control Panel from the Start menu. Choose Settings and click Control Panel. Then choose Add/Remove Programs.
- You can install programs from the Run menu. (Choose Start and then click Run). Type d:\launch in the Open field and click OK. (For d: in the example, substitute the drive letter for your CD-ROM drive.)

Double click the **Add/Remove Programs icon**. The installation may begin immediately at this stage. If it does not,

Click Install to proceed.

Click Next to continue.

Click the **Command line field** to move the cursor if necessary.

Type `d:\launch` (where d:\ is your CD-ROM drive)

Click Finish

notes

If programs that are part of the installation procedure are encountered, you may be asked whether you want to replace them or not. You should choose not to replace the individual programs if the existing version is more recent.

notes

In Versions 8.0 and 8.5, the program is named Simply Accounting (Pro is not added) and the EFT program is not included.

The following installation options screen appears, to begin the installation:

If you have any other programs running, click ✕ (Exit), close the other programs and start again. Otherwise,

Click Install Simply Accounting to advance to the Welcome screen:

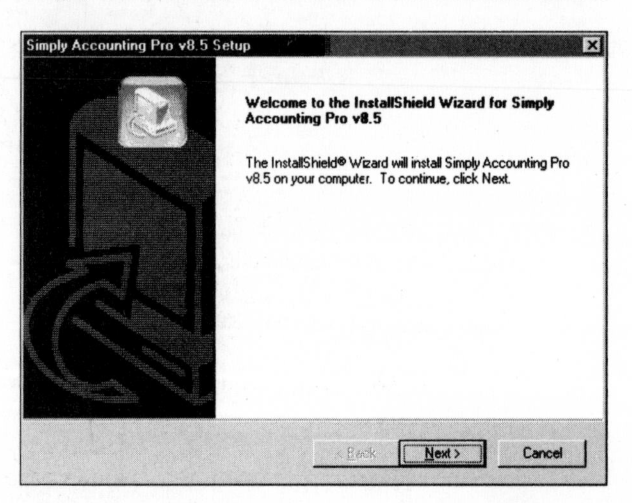

Click Next to advance to the licence agreement. Read the agreement, and if you accept the agreement,

Click Yes to begin installing the program.

notes

Your name and company name may appear by default if you entered them for other Windows programs. You can edit them if they are wrong.

The next screen prompts you to enter your name, company name and the key code from the software package. You must enter the key code correctly before you can continue (be careful to distinguish between the alpha and numeric characters in the key code):

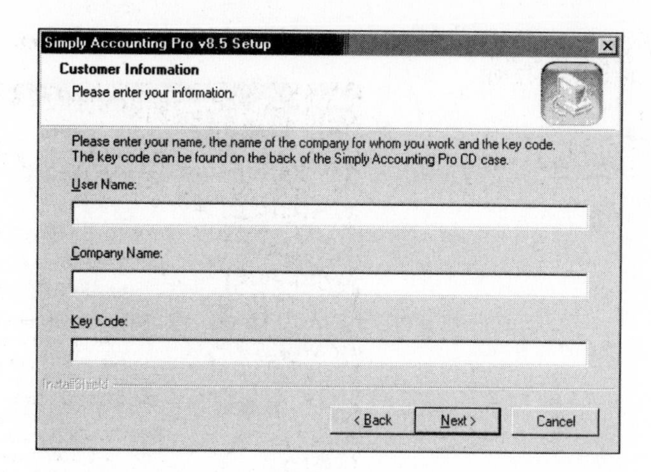

Type the required information. Press tab to advance to the next field.

Click Next. When prompted on the next screen, confirm that you entered the information correctly. If there are errors, click No and make corrections.

Click Yes to continue with the installation.

notes

This screen will not be displayed if you are installing Version 8.0 or 8.5 (non-Pro).

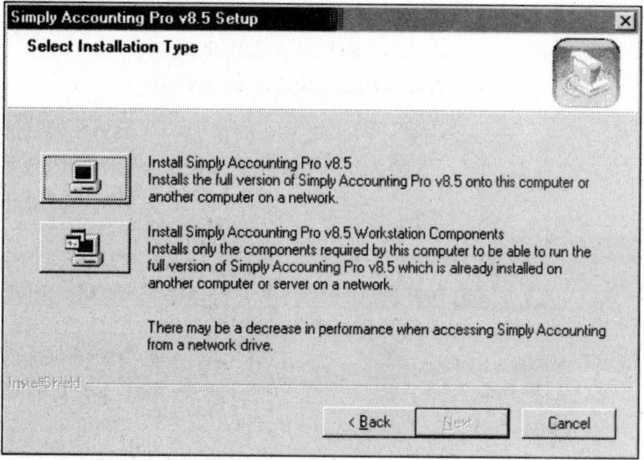

You can install the Pro version on an individual computer or on a workstation for a network.

Click Install Simply Accounting Pro v8.5 (the first option) for stand-alone computers.

Click Next

Your next decision concerns the location of your program files as shown:

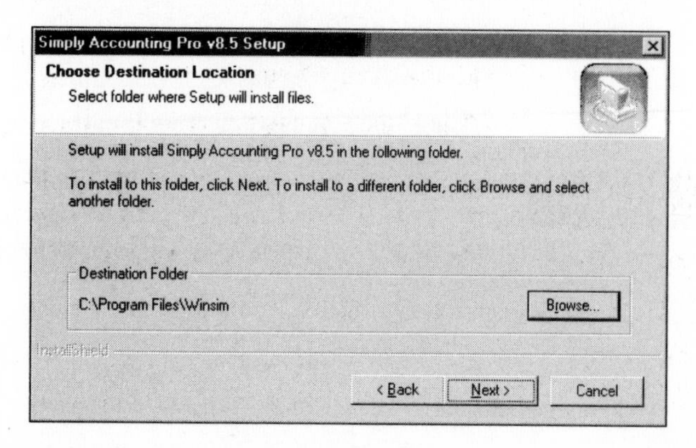

You can accept the default location. You can also choose another folder from the pop-up window provided when you click Browse, or you can type an alternative location in the Browse window and click OK.

Click Next to continue with the selection of program components to install:

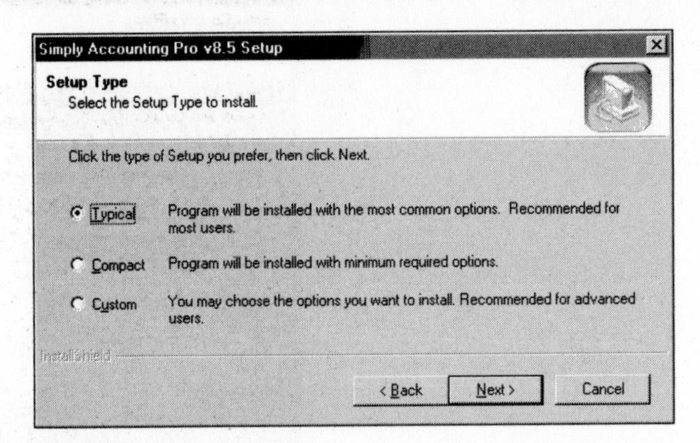

Accept the Typical installation option to have all the program elements included.

If you are updating an earlier version of Simply Accounting, there may be changes you have made that you want to keep. The next message advises you that the new program will overwrite these customizations:

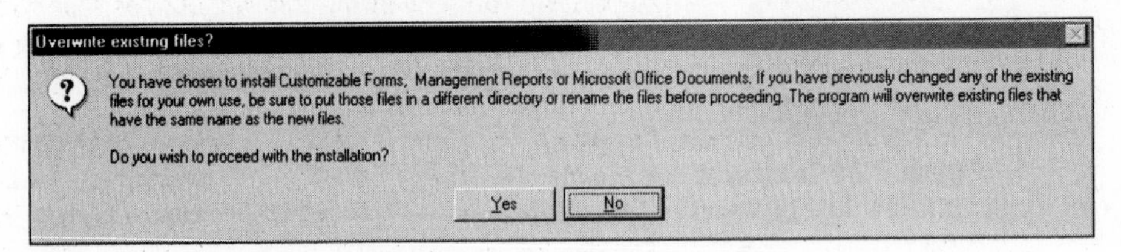

notes

If you choose No, you should copy your customized forms to another folder before continuing with the installation.

Click Yes if you do not want to keep your earlier modifications.

Click Next to select a name for Simply Accounting in your Programs folder:

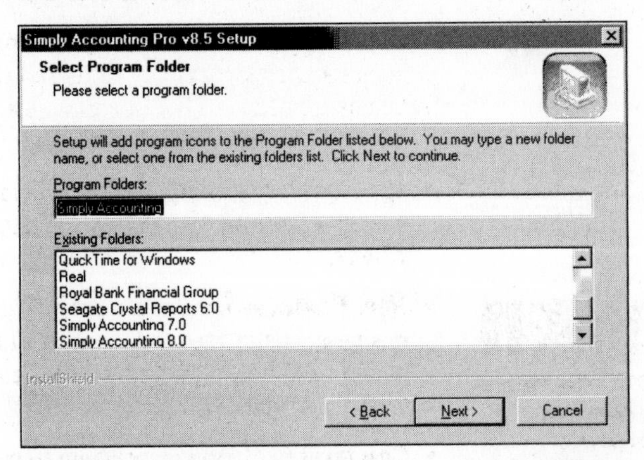

The name you enter here will be the name that appears on the Programs list. You can accept the default name, Simply Accounting, or type a different name such as Simply Accounting Version 8.5.

Click Next to proceed to the confirmation screen:

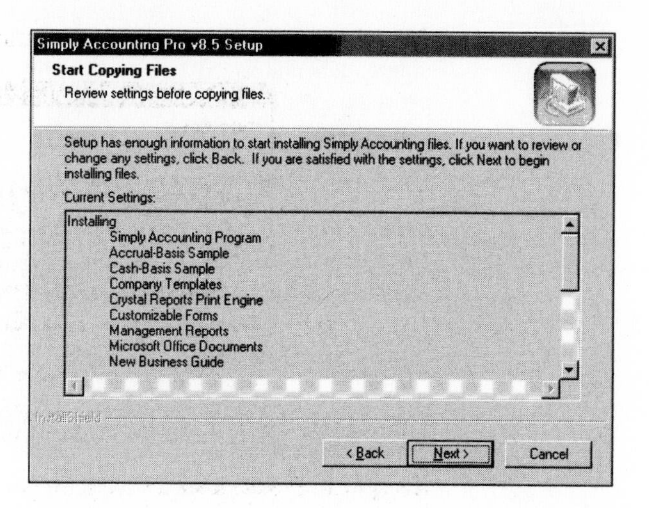

notes

To omit any of these components, click Back to return to the previous screens and choose the Custom Installation option.

By default, all components are selected for installation, as follows:

- **Simply Accounting Program**: the Simply Accounting program that you will need to perform the accounting transactions for your company. It will be placed in the main Winsim folder under the Program Files folder or the folder location you selected.
- **Samples**: complete company records for both accrual-basis and cash-basis accounting methods for two sample companies — Universal Construction and Universal Crustacean Farm. They will be placed in the folder under Winsim called Samdata if you install them.
- **Templates**: predefined charts of accounts and settings for a large number of business types. These files will be stored in a folder under Winsim called Template. Two starter files with only charts of accounts also appear in this folder.
- **Crystal Reports Print Engine**, **Forms** and **Management Reports**: a variety of commonly used business forms and reports that you can customize to suit your own business needs and the program to access and print them. They will be placed in a folder under Winsim called Forms.
- **Microsoft Office Documents**: a variety of MS Office documents designed for integrated use with Simply Accounting. They are placed in an Office folder under Winsim.
- **New Business Guide**: a number of checklists of steps to follow in setting up a new business, customized for a variety of business types in different provinces; guides include addresses, phone numbers and Web addresses that you can contact for further information.
- **Conversion Utility**: a program to convert accounting records that were created using DOS versions of the program into a Windows version of Simply Accounting. Data files in older Windows versions of the program are updated automatically. The conversion program is placed in the main Winsim folder.

notes

Access the business guides from the Start menu on the desktop (choose Start, then point to Programs and Simply Accounting and click New Business Guide). You can also access the business guides from Simply Accounting's Home window (choose the Business Assistant menu and click New Business Guide).

Click Next

Follow the instructions to proceed with the installation.

The Install program creates the folders for all the components described above. There is an additional folder, Winsim\Data, that is empty initially. We will use this folder to store the data files for the applications in the workbook.

In addition, the installation procedure adds names in the Programs list for the Simply Accounting program, for the Conversion program if it is installed and for the New Business Guide.

After the installation is complete, you will be asked whether you want to register online immediately or register the program later. Choose Yes to start the registration procedure (you may need to start your Internet connection before clicking so that you can register) or choose No to register later by mail or online.

The next option is to view the Readme file or start the program.

Click Finish to see the Readme file, which may announce recent program changes. You can print this file. Please read this information. After you have read the file, click ☒ to close the Readme window.

If you have previously installed versions of the software, you may be asked whether you want to replace individual program files. You can choose to replace them all, or decide on a one-by-one basis.

Click (Exit), or continue by installing manuals, other information or programs from the program CD.

Click ☒ to close the Control Panel window.

BACKING UP YOUR DATA CD

Before you begin the applications, you must copy the data files to your hard disk drive. You cannot work from the CD because Simply Accounting will not open Read Only files, and all CD-ROM files are Read Only files. Next, you should make a working backup copy of all the files so that you can keep the original for future use if you want to begin again without returning to the CD. The following instructions will copy all the files to your hard disk, create the necessary new folders and remove the Read Only file attributes or properties.

Warning!

Each application has more than one file containing different parts of the accounting information. All files must be contained in the same folder. If any file is missing, you will be unable to access the information. By copying folders and not the individual files, you will correctly keep the necessary files together.

Installing Your Data Files

The Data CD contains programs that will automatically copy the data files to a new SimData folder on your hard drive (drive C:). If you want to use a different location for your data files, proceed to page 14. You can copy the data files for Version 8.0 using the **load80** program, the files for Version 8.5 using the **load85** program and for Pro Version 8.5 using the **loadpro** program.

Choose the **Start menu** on the desktop and **click Run** as shown:

Warning!

We strongly recommend using the Load programs on the CD to create your data set, unless you are experienced at copying files from a CD and changing properties.

The Run window opens:

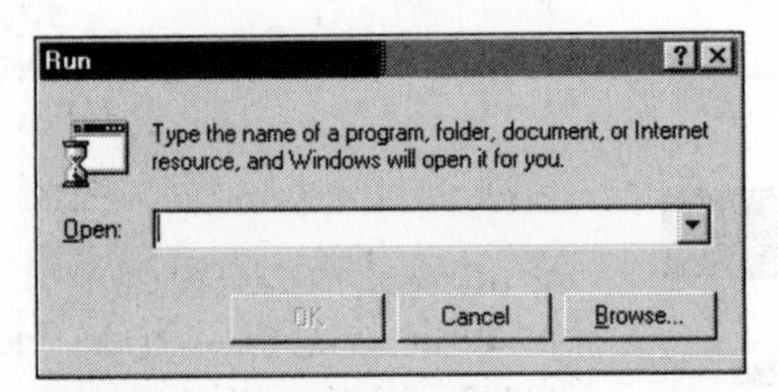

version 8

If you are using Version 8.0, refer to Part Three (beginning on page 560) for detailed notes on the differences between Version 8.0 and 8.5. These pages have a blue stripe at the edge.

You must work with the correct version of the data set. You cannot open Version 8.5 files with the Version 8.0 program, or open Pro files with Version 8.5. In addition, there are payroll changes for Version 8.5 that are not included in the data for Version 8.0. If you are working with Version 8.0, you must install the data for Version 8.0 using the load80 program. If you are working with Version 8.5, you must install Version 8.5 data using the load85 program. By using the loadpro program for the Pro Version 8.5, you will not have to convert the regular Version 8.5 files.

Type `d:\load80` (to copy the data set for Version 8.0), **or**

Type `d:\load85` (to copy the data set for Version 8.5) **or**

Type `d:\loadpro` (to copy the data set for the Pro Version 8.5)

Click OK

Click [X] to close the DOS program window after the messages "Done!" and "The data files are in c:\SimData" appear.

All the data files for the book are now located in the new SimData folder in drive C:.

You should now copy or back up the files to your working folder.

Warning!

Simply Accounting writes directly to the file you are using throughout your working session. If you do not back up your original data files before using them, you may be unable to access them if you make an unrecoverable error.

Copying Data Files on the Hard Disk

To copy the data files to another folder on your hard disk, use the Windows Explorer program.

Click Start (on the desktop task bar).

Choose (point to) **Programs** and then **click Windows Explorer** (at or near the bottom of the list of programs).

Click SimData, the new data folder you just created so that the contents — the 10 folders — appear on the Contents side of the window. (Scroll down [▼] if necessary to include SimData in the list of Folders.)

Click Brides, the first folder in the Contents list. Now **press** [shift] and **click Setup**, the last folder in the Contents list. Or, you can choose the Edit menu and click Select All. This will highlight all 10 folders in SimData as shown:

notes

Your screen may look different if you have selected different viewing options. We show folders and files listed with details rather than by icon. This selection is changed from the Explorer View menu.

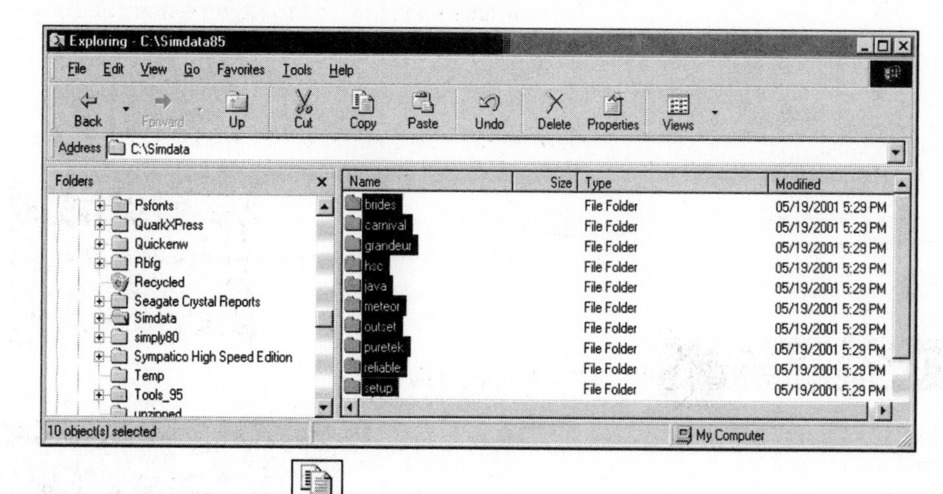

Click the **Copy button** [Copy] or choose the Edit menu and click Copy.

Scroll up [▲] the Folders list to the **Program Files folder** in drive C:. **Click** the [+] beside the folder to see the folders under Program Files. Now **click** the [+] beside the Winsim folder to list the folders under Winsim. The Data folder should be visible.

notes

You can choose a different destination folder for your data files if you want.

Click the **Data folder** so that it is open. The Contents side of the Explorer window should be empty.

Click the **Paste button** [Paste] or choose the Edit menu and click Paste.

Warning!

Unless you are experienced at working with Windows folders and file attributes, we recommend using the Load program on the data CD to install your data set and remove the Read Only file properties for all files at once.

Your screen will show the files being copied. When the copying is complete, all the folders and files from SimData will be copied to the Data folder under Winsim that was created during installation. When you click the new ⊞ icon beside Data, you will see the new list of data folders.

Click ☒ to close Windows Explorer.

If you want to copy only the files for a single application, click the folder for the application you want (e.g., Reliable) under SimData to highlight it. Complete the copy as you would for the entire set of folders — use the copy command, open the destination folder and then paste the folder.

Working with Other File Locations

You can copy the files to a different location if you want. Copy the data folders you want from the CD just as you would copy the files from one folder to another on your hard disk drive. Be careful to choose the correct version of the data set and copy a complete folder, choosing Data80, Data85 or DataPro.

After copying the folders and files, you must remove the Read Only attribute from all the data files before you can open them with Simply Accounting. If you do not, you will receive an error message like the following when you try to open the file:

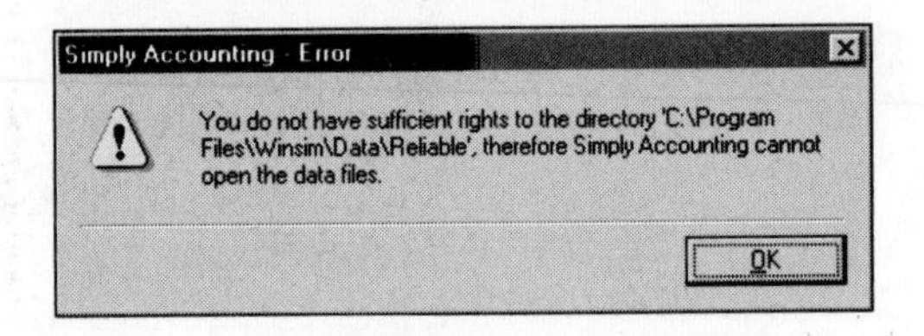

Warning!

If you are working on a network, the site administrator should change the attributes of the master copy before copying the files to individual workstations because, for security reasons, some networks do not allow individual users to change attributes.

If you try to open a data file from the data CD, you will see a similar message:

Removing Read Only Attributes

File attributes must be changed for the files in one folder at a time. This means that the attributes for each data application must be changed individually because each application is in a separate folder. Changing the attributes of a folder does not change the attributes for the files inside the folder but all files in an open folder can be changed at once.

You can change the file properties in Windows Explorer.

Open Windows Explorer and find the folder that contains your data set.

Double click Brides, the **first data folder** to open it.

Some data folders contain only two files, others may have more.

Click the **first file in the folder**, **press** shift and **click the last file in the folder** to select all the Simply Accounting data files.

Choose the **File menu** and **click Properties** or right-click and choose Properties from the pop-up menu. The files remain selected while the Properties window is open.

Click Read-only to remove the ✓.

Repeat this procedure for the remaining folders and files.

Starting Simply Accounting and Accessing Data Files

From your Windows desktop,

Click Start (on the task bar) so that the pop-up menu appears.

Point to Programs. Hold the mouse on Programs until the list of programs appears.

Point to Simply Accounting (or the name you entered for the Simply Accounting program when you installed it. Hold the mouse on Simply Accounting until its cascading menu list of programs appears.

Click Simply Accounting (or Simply Accounting Pro). You should follow the path illustrated here:

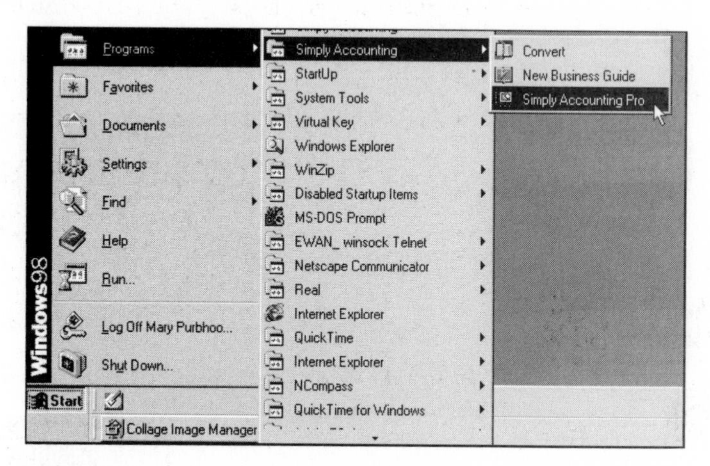

version 8 notes

- Pro will not appear as part of the program name for Version 8.0 or 8.5.
- Your previously used data files will appear under the option to Open the last company you worked on. This option provides a useful shortcut when you are working with the same data set for several work sessions. You will bypass the Open Company window.
- In Chapter 6, we explain how to restore the Select Company window if it has been turned off.

You will see the Simply Accounting - Select Company screen:

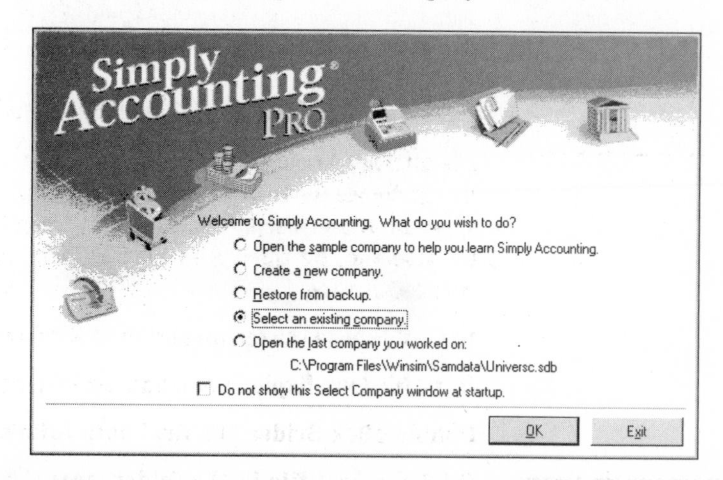

The opening window gives the options of working with the sample company files, creating new company files, restoring backup files or working with existing data files. The option to Open the last company you worked on does not appear the first time you use the program.

Click Select an existing company.

Click OK

The Simply Accounting Open File window appears next with the most recently used file selected. Therefore, the File name you see on your screen may be different from the one shown below.

> **notes**
>
> The next time you start the Simply Accounting program, the name of the file that you used most recently will be selected for you to accept or to change.

Click the **Look in field list arrow** to see the folder path for the file selected:

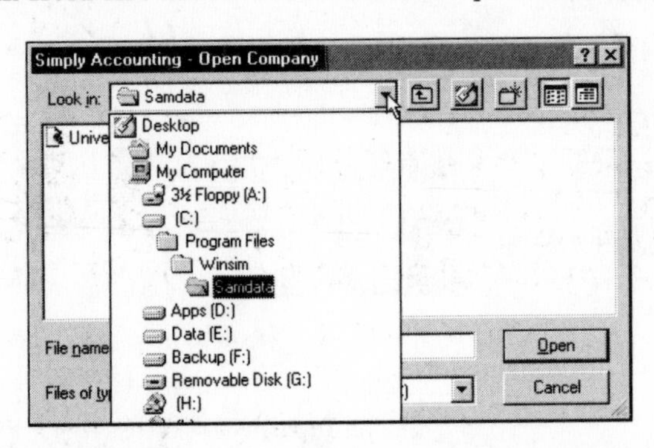

The path shown here is for the sample company in Program Files\Winsim\Samdata in drive (C:). The following instructions will access data stored in the Winsim\Data folder.

> **notes**
>
> If your starting point is different from the one shown here, click drive C: in the Look in field list. Then in the folders/files section, double click the Program Files folder to open it and then double click the Winsim folder to display its six folders.

Click the **Winsim folder** to list the six folders under Winsim in the large files/folders list in the centre of the window. The Look in field now displays Winsim as the folder name:

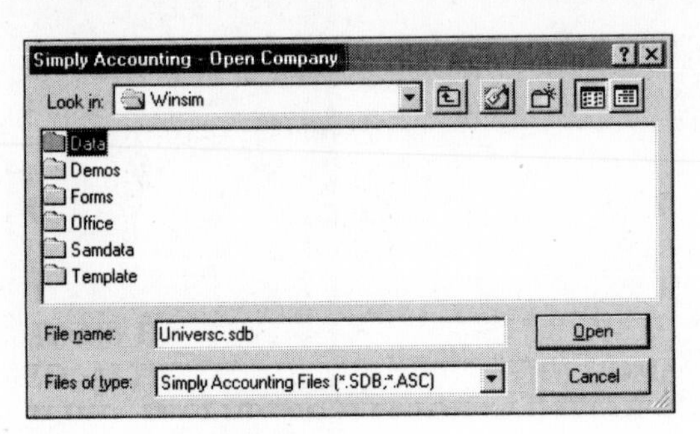

Click the **Data folder** to select it as shown above.

> **notes**
>
> You can gain access to the company records only through the *.sdb file. This is the file extension that Simply Accounting recognizes as a Simply Accounting format file. Other files that are part of the data set must be located in the same folder. They will be listed in the Windows Explorer program when you open the data folder.

Click Open to list the 10 folders containing your workbook data. The folder name Data now appears in the Look in field.

Click the **Reliable folder** to select it.

Click Open to list the Simply Accounting data files contained in this folder and to display the folder name Reliable in the Look in field. There should be just one file listed, Reliable (or Reliable.sdb — we have selected to show file name extensions).

Click Reliable to select it and add this name to the File name field as shown:

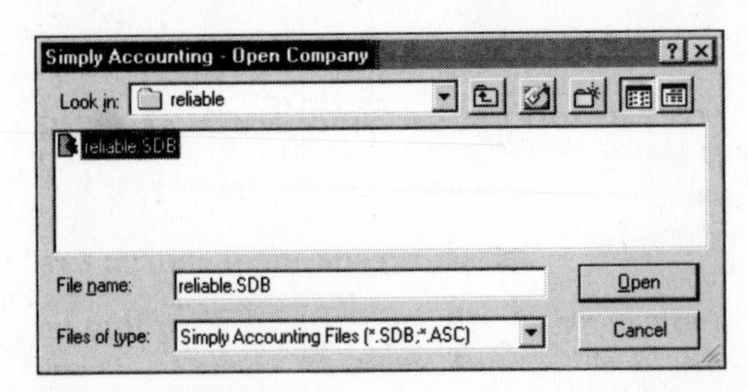

Substitute the appropriate drive and path or folders for your own setup to access the Simply Accounting Home window.

If you are using Pro Version 8.5, you may see a screen advising you that the data has been used in a newer version of the program. **Click Yes** to proceed.

notes

If you see a screen that asks for a user name and password, ask your instructor or site administrator for the name and password you should use (see page 593).

notes

The session date is explained in the Reliable Roofing application, where you will also learn how to change the session date.

Click Open to see the following screen prompting you for the session date:

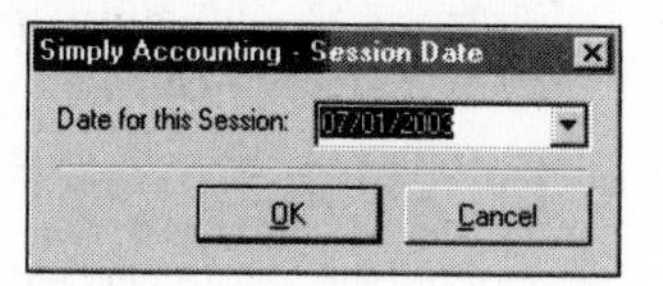

Many date fields in Simply Accounting have a list arrow beside them. The dates in the drop-down list show the range of dates that you can enter for the data file in use.

For now you should accept the date shown.

Click OK and you will see the Simply Accounting Home window.

For other applications, substitute the appropriate folder and file name for Reliable above.

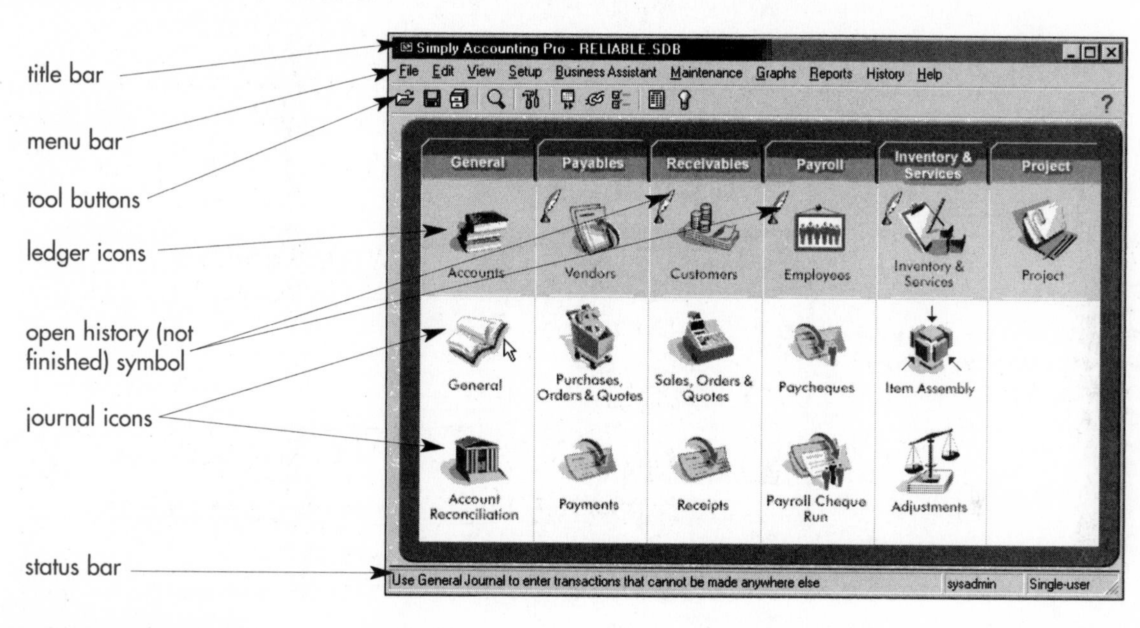

version 8

notes

- Pro will not appear as part of the program name in the title bar for Version 8.0 or 8.5. In Version 8.5, the status bar will show sysadmin, the user, but not Single-user.
- Many Simply Accounting windows include a Home window button that brings the Home window to the front without closing the other windows.

Your Reliable Home window will have icons only for the General Ledger. The unused ledgers are hidden because they are not set up. We show them here to illustrate the open history symbol.

The Home window is organized as follows: the title bar is on top with the program and file names, control menu icon and size buttons; the main menu bar comes next with the tool bar buttons below. Tool buttons permit an alternative and quick access to commonly used menu items. Different Simply Accounting windows have different buttons on the tool bar. The six ledger or module names come next with their respective icons filling up the major part of the window — six ledgers in the top row below the ledger or module name, journal icons under their respective ledgers in the last two icon rows of the window. Below the journal icons, the status bar describes the purpose of the General Journal because the pointer is on the General icon.

Hold the mouse on a tool button for a few seconds to see the name or function of the tool button and the keyboard shortcut if there is one. Hold the mouse over an icon to see its description or function in the status bar at the bottom of the window.

SIMPLY ACCOUNTING HELP FEATURES

Simply Accounting provides program assistance in several different ways. You can display or print **Help** information on many topics in Simply Accounting. General accounting information, advice topics and Simply Accounting software assistance are included. You can access Help from the menu bar in the Home window, from the Help tool button [?] in the Home window or by pressing (f1).

version 8

The most immediate form of help comes from the **status bar** at the bottom of many program windows. It offers a one-line description of the icon or field that the mouse is pointing to. As you move the mouse around the screen, the status bar information changes accordingly. The message in the status bar is connected to the mouse position only. This may not be the same as the position of the cursor or insertion point, which is located wherever the mouse was when you last clicked the mouse button. The status bar can be turned off from the View menu (User Preferences) in the Home window if it is not needed, but we recommend leaving it on.

The general help menu can be accessed in several ways: by pressing (f1), by choosing the Help menu and clicking Contents, or by clicking the Help button [?].

Click the **Help button** [?].

The Contents tab "book" menu is shown here:

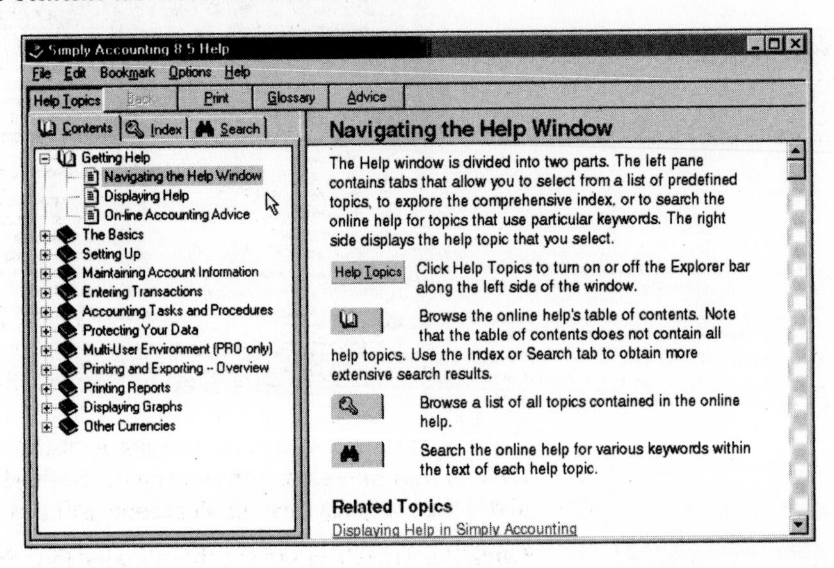

Click ⊞ beside a "book" title to see the list of topics under that heading (or double click the book). Click a topic to get the complete information on that subject on the right-hand side of the Help window. The first title, "Getting Help," is a good place to begin if you have not previously used the Help features in Windows programs. Navigating the Help Window is selected, so this is the topic displayed. Click any underlined text in the display area to get further information on that topic.

notes

Double click a book title or click the boxed minus sign beside it to close the book and hide the list of topics.

Double click Entering Transactions, then **click Reversing Entries** to view the procedures for reversing a journal entry:

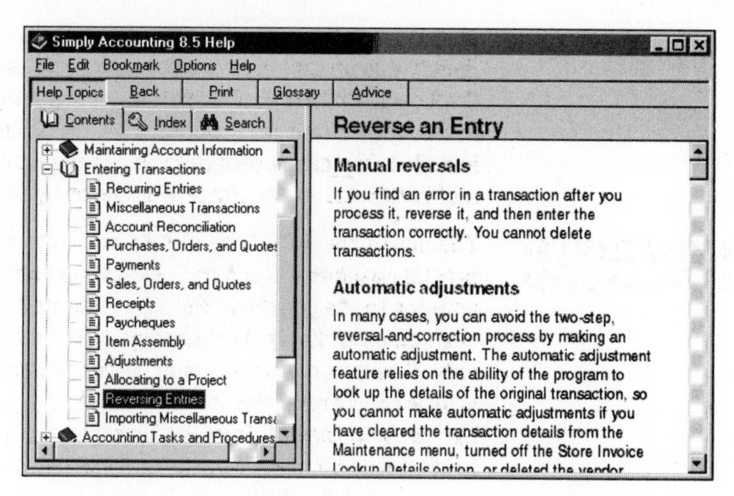

Click the **Index tab** to see an alphabetic list of entries as shown here:

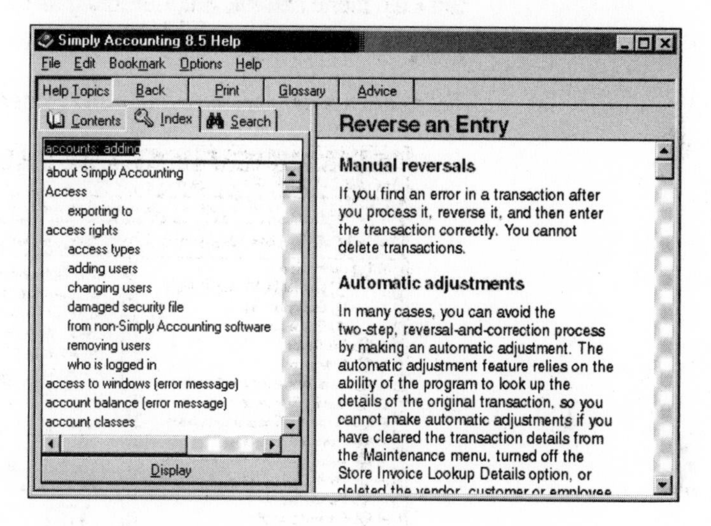

Notice that the previous topic remains on display until you select a new topic. Click a topic to read the help information on the selected topic. Type a letter in the field above the list to advance the alphabetic list quickly.

Click the **Search tab** to see the following Find Setup Wizard database setup screen (if this is the first time you are using this feature):

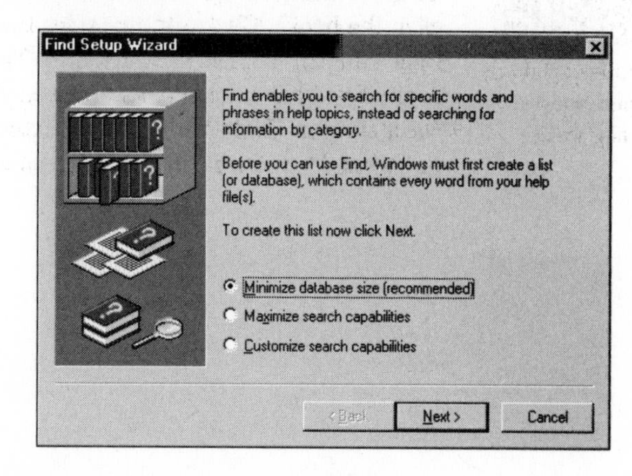

Click the **database setup option** you prefer, and follow the instructions to complete the setup. The opening Search screen looks like the one shown here:

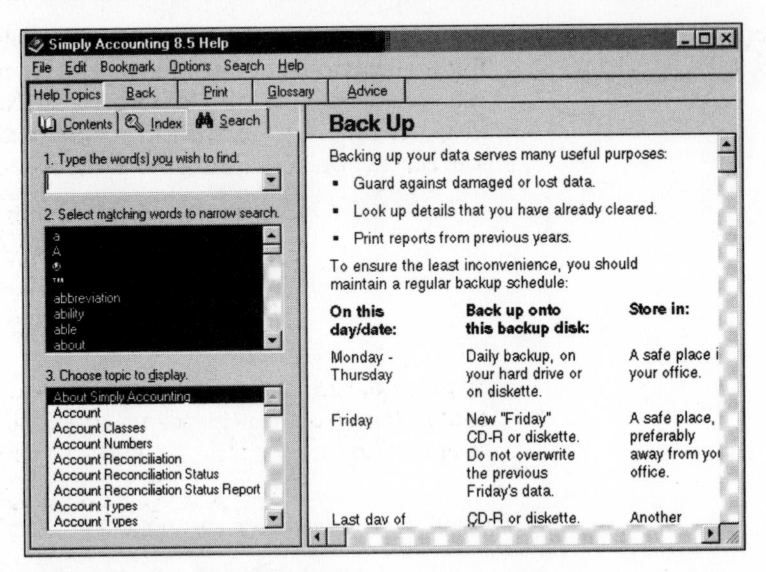

Again, the previous topic remains displayed until you select a new one. You can search for a topic that you define by typing it in part one and using the second part to narrow the search, or by selecting a topic directly from part three.

Many windows in Simply Accounting have a Help button that provides help related to that specific ledger or window.

Also available from the Help window on any topic is an extensive glossary of general accounting and Simply Accounting terms. Click the Glossary button and then click a glossary topic to see the explanation or definition. Continue by exploring other topics and features. Close the Help windows when you have finished.

notes

The Advice tab in the Help window provides another means to access the General Advice topics described below.

Click the **Advice tool button** in Simply Accounting's Home window to access the main Advice menu shown here:

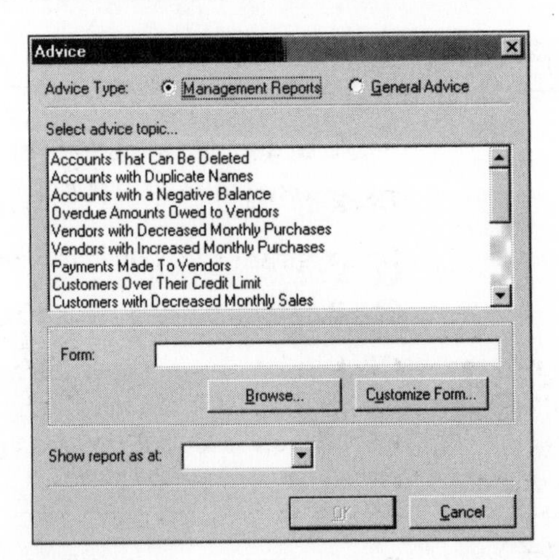

The default list of topics is the list of Management Reports. Click the report or advice topic you want, and then click OK to see the report (or double click the topic). Rather than providing general information, these reports relate specifically to the company data set that is in use at the time. Management reports are available only for ledgers that are not hidden, so the list you see may be smaller. The reports combine the company data with forms and reports provided through Crystal. If you have not installed Crystal Report Engine and the customizable Forms, these reports will not be available.

notes

General management advice topics are also available from the Business Assistant menu under the Business Advice option.

Click General Advice to see the list of topics that provide other suggestions about general accounting practices. Close the advice report windows when finished.

version 8

A final source of general assistance is available as automatic advice. Again, this is a feature that can be turned off from the View menu (User Preferences) in the Home window if it is not needed. We recommend leaving it on. When it is turned on, the Simply Accounting program will provide warning statements as, for example, when a sale causes inventory to drop below the re-order point:

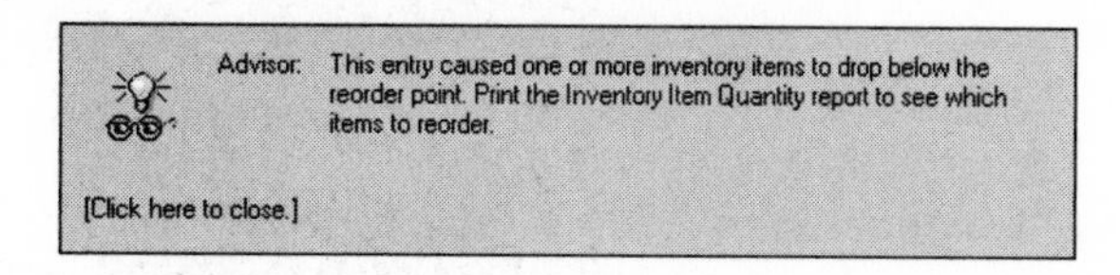

To proceed, you must close an advice screen. Close the type of message above by clicking the advisor icon as indicated (Click here to close). The following screen shows a sample of an advice screen warning that a customer has exceeded the credit limit:

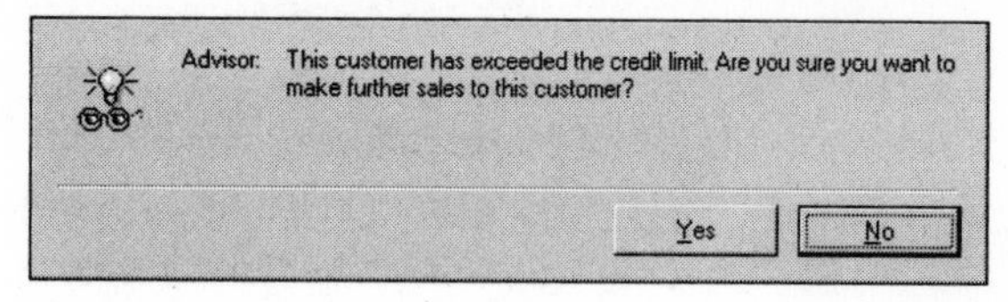

In the example shown here, you can click Yes if you want to proceed with the sale, or No if you want to make a change (perhaps asking for a deposit). The program also warns when year-end is approaching and it is time to complete year-end adjustments or when a bank account is overdrawn.

Saving and Backing up Your Work

Simply Accounting saves your work automatically at various stages when you are working with the program. For example, when you display or print reports, Simply Accounting writes all the journal transactions to your file to compile the report you want. When you exit from the program properly, Simply Accounting also saves all your work. At any time while working in Simply Accounting, you can also save your work.

Click the Save button on the tool bar, or **choose** the File menu and **click** Save.

On a regular basis, you should also make a backup copy of your files.

The Backup command is described in detail in Chapter 3.

Click the Backup button or choose the File menu and click Backup to start the Backup Wizard. The Wizard will create a separate backup folder inside your current working folder so that the backup will remain separate from your working copy. If you prefer, you can use floppy disks for your backups. However, you can store only one backup file on a floppy disk when you use the Backup command.

notes

To save several backups on a single floppy disk, first back up to your hard disk drive then copy the backups to a floppy disk. You can restore the files from the floppy disk.

Save As is different from the Backup command in Simply Accounting. Backup creates a compressed copy of the files that must be restored with the Restore command before you can use them. Save As creates a complete working copy of your files. Remember to return to your original working copy before entering any transactions if you use the Save As command.

Because the data files are very large, we recommend using the Backup procedure described in Chapter 3 rather than Save As for your regular backups.

You can also back up all your data files at the same time by using Windows Explorer Copy and Paste commands as described earlier in this chapter. In this way, you can save the files to a different folder on your hard drive.

Finishing a Session

Choose the **control menu icon** and **click Close** or click ☒ to close the journal input form or display window you are working in.

You will return to the main Home window.

Choose the **control menu icon** and **click Close**, or click ☒ or choose the File menu and click Exit to close the Home window.

Your work will be saved again automatically when you complete this step.

You should now be in the Windows desktop.

Creating New Folders

notes

Simply Accounting windows that allow you to create new folders have a New Folder tool button. You can also use the right-click pop-up menu in these windows to select New and then Folder.

You will need to make folders to work with the applications in this workbook. The four setup applications — CISV, Maverick, Hearth House and Serene Sailing — will require new folders. In addition, you may want to make folders for backing up individual applications. You can make folders from Windows Explorer or from the Save As, Open Company and Create Company windows in Simply Accounting. The method is the same in all Simply Accounting windows and is described in Chapter 6.

We will describe the Windows Explorer approach here.

Choose the **Start menu** on the desktop and **click Windows Explorer**.

Double click the **drive you want to use** and then **double click** the **folder** in the drive where you want to place the new folder (or you can create the new folder at the root of the disk drive).

Choose the **File menu** and then **choose New** and **click Folder** (or right-click the mouse and choose New and Folder from the pop-up menu):

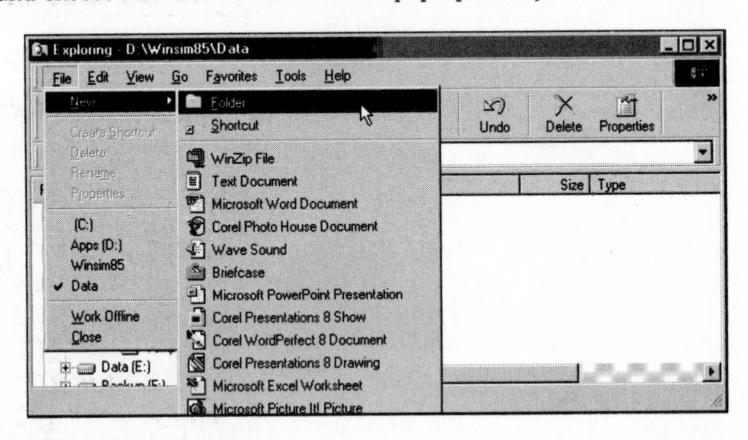

The new folder is placed inside the folder or drive that is open. Its name, New Folder, will be selected so you can type a new folder name immediately.

Type a new name and then click somewhere else on the screen to save the name change. You can create several new folders in the same session by repeating these steps. Close Windows Explorer when you have finished.

Date Formats and Settings

notes

Fortunately, Simply Accounting allows you to enter dates as text if you are unsure of the date settings. Thus, you may type June 7, 2003, in a date field.

Before shutting down your computer you should check the date formats set up on your computer. Simply Accounting will interpret and display dates according to your Windows settings. When you enter dates using a series of two digits for month, day and year, it is important to know how these will be interpreted because many entries are ambiguous. For example, when you type 06-07-03, this may be June 7, July 6, July 3 or March 7 in the year 2003, 1903, 1906 or 2006, depending on whether month, day or year comes first and whether your computer defaults to 1900 dates or is preset for 2000 dates.

Double click the **My Computer icon** on the Windows desktop.

Double click the **Control Panel icon**. (Or choose the Start menu, then choose Settings and click Control Panel.)

Double click the **Regional Settings icon** to open the settings control window:

Click the **Date tab** to open the Date settings window:

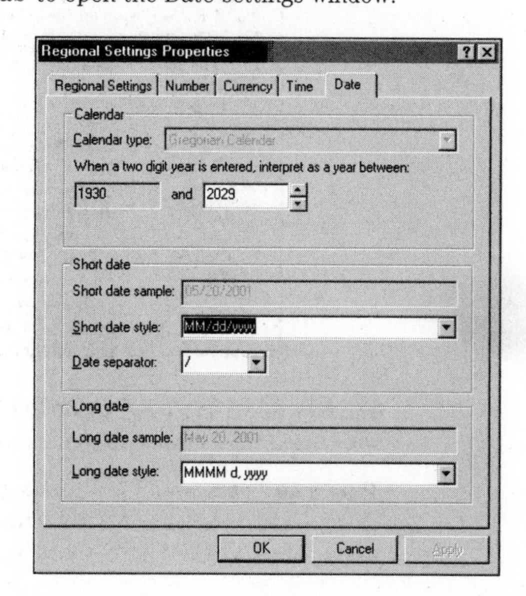

Windows 98 has a special setting for interpreting a two-digit year code. Windows 95 does not have this option so you must type a four-digit year to indicate year 2000 dates.

The Short date style shows whether month, day or year comes first. Throughout this book, we use the order of month followed by day and year. You can change your date control setting to match this book or always use the text style of entering dates. To change the setting,

Click the **Short date style field list arrow**.

Click MM/dd/yyyy (Showing a four-digit year will ensure that you see whether you are using 1900 or 2000 year dates.)

Click OK to save the changes and return to the Control Panel window.

Close the **Control Panel window** and then **close** the **My Computer window**.

Click Start

Click Shut Down

Click OK to confirm your choice.

You may now turn off your computer.

CHAPTER TWO The Goods and Services Tax

OBJECTIVES

After completing this chapter, you should be able to

- *understand* the terms relevant to the federal Goods and Services Tax
- *understand* the different methods of calculating the GST
- *understand* how to file for remittance or refund
- *understand* Harmonized Sales Tax and other provincial taxes in relation to GST

GENERAL ACCOUNTING INFORMATION

Definition of GST

The Goods and Services Tax is a compulsory tax levied by the federal government on most goods and services in Canada. The tax rate of 7 percent applies at all levels of sales. Retailers pay the GST to wholesalers and other vendors but are allowed to deduct any GST they pay from the GST they collect from customers. Retailers remit the difference, GST owing, to the Receiver General of Canada or claim a refund on a monthly or quarterly basis.

Provinces may or may not include GST in the price on which they calculate provincial sales tax (PST). Provincial tax rates vary from province to province.

GST Registration

A business with annual sales exceeding $30 000 per year **must** register for GST collection and must collect Goods and Services Tax on all applicable sales. Registration is optional for businesses whose annual sales are less than $30 000. Businesses that are not registered for GST do not charge GST on sales to their customers, but they also cannot recover the GST they pay on business-related purchases.

Collecting the GST

The business must collect GST for those goods and services sold that are not zero-rated or tax exempt. GST collected on sales is reduced by the GST on sales returns. The business must remit GST at regular intervals, filing GST returns monthly, quarterly or annually with quarterly instalments paid, depending on annual income and GST owing.

Zero-Rated Goods and Services

Zero-rated goods and services are those on which the tax rate is zero. These goods include basic groceries, prescribed medical instruments and devices, prescribed drugs, exported goods and services, agricultural products and fish products. A business selling only zero-rated goods and services does not collect GST from customers, but it can still claim a refund for GST paid for any purchases made for selling these zero-rated goods and services.

Tax-Exempt Goods and Services

Tax-exempt goods and services are those on which tax is not collected. These goods and services include health care, dental care, daycare services and rents on residences. Most educational and financial services are also included in this group. These businesses are not able to claim refunds for GST paid for business purchases related to selling tax-exempt goods and services.

Paying the GST

A business must pay GST for purchases made specifically for business purposes, unless the goods or services purchased are zero rated or tax exempt. The business can use the GST paid as an **input tax credit** by subtracting the amount of GST paid from the amount of GST collected and remitting GST owing or claiming a refund. The input tax credit is reduced by the amount of GST for purchases returned. GST paid on purchases for personal use do not qualify as input tax credits.

Bank and Financial Institution Services

Most bank products and services are not taxable. Exceptions include safety deposit box rentals, custodial and safekeeping services, personalized cheques, fees for self-administrated registered savings plans, payroll services, rentals of night depository, rentals of credit card imprinters and reconciliation of cheques. Banks must remit the full amount of GST they collect from customers. Because most bank services are not GST taxable, banks cannot claim input tax credits for GST they pay on business-related purchases.

notes

Visitors to Canada can request a GST refund for GST paid on goods purchased in Canada that they are taking home with them. They cannot claim a refund for goods and services they consumed in Canada, such as entertainment, dining and hotels.

GST on Imported and Exported Goods

GST is not charged on exported goods. Customers in other countries who import goods from Canada do not pay GST.

Businesses in Canada must pay GST on the items they import or purchase from other countries. The GST is collected by Canada Customs and Revenue Agency when the goods enter Canada based on the purchase price (plus import duty) and current exchange rates. Businesses must pay this GST and other import duties before the goods are released to them.

Administering the GST

The federal government has approved different methods of administering the GST; the regular method and the quick method are the most common.

The Regular Method

The regular method of administering the GST requires the business to keep track of GST paid for all goods and services purchased from vendors (less returns) and of GST collected for all goods and services sold to customers (less returns). It then deducts the GST paid from the GST collected and files for a refund or remits the balance owing to the Receiver General on a monthly or quarterly basis.

Accounting Examples Using the Regular Method (without PST)

SALES INVOICE

Sold goods to customer for $200 plus $14 GST collected. Invoice total, $214.

Date	Particulars	Debit	Credit
xx/xx	Accounts Receivable	214.00	
	GST Charged on Sales		14.00
	Revenue from Sales		200.00

notes

GST Paid on Purchases is a contra-liability account because it normally has a debit balance while most liability accounts have a credit balance. Therefore, GST Paid on Purchases reduces the total GST liability to the Receiver General.

PURCHASE INVOICE

Purchased supplies from vendor for $300 plus $21 GST paid. Invoice total, $321.

Date	Particulars	Debit	Credit
xx/xx	Supplies	300.00	
	GST Paid on Purchases	21.00	
	Accounts Payable		321.00

The GST owing is further reduced by any GST adjustments — for example, GST that applies to bad debts that are written off. If the debt is later recovered, the GST liability is also restored as an input tax credit adjustment.

Simplified Accounting Methods

notes

The streamlined accounting method of calculating GST is not used in the applications in this workbook. The quick method is used in Chapter 4.

Certain small businesses may be eligible to use a simplified method of calculating their GST refunds and remittances that does not require them to keep a separate record for GST on each individual purchase or sale.

The streamlined accounting method is available only to some grocery and convenience stores. The quick method is available to a wider range of businesses.

The Quick Method

Some small businesses may choose to remit a flat tax payment ranging from 1 percent to 5 percent of their sales. This simplified system is available to manufacturers and retailers with sales up to a maximum of $200 000 per year, to grocery and convenience stores with sales up to $500 000 per year and to some service businesses. The GST is calculated by multiplying the total sales, including GST, for the filing period (monthly or quarterly) by the flat tax rate for the type of business under consideration. A business is still able to deduct any GST paid on **capital expenditures** from the GST liability calculated using the flat tax rate. Capital expenditures include purchases of plant and equipment such as cash registers, furniture, computers and other depreciable assets.

The quick method described above is not available to legal, accounting or financial consulting businesses. Businesses allowed by Canada Customs and Revenue Agency to use the quick method may change methods from year to year.

Accounting Examples Using the Quick Method (without PST)

CASH SALES OVER THE COUNTER

Cash register tapes in a café for one week total $3 200 including GST collected for goods and services.

Date	Particulars	Debit	Credit
xx/xx	Cash in Bank	3 200.00	
	Revenue from Services		3 200.00

PURCHASE INVOICES

1. Food Inventory
   Purchased basic groceries for café services from vendor for $1 000 on account. Basic groceries are zero-rated goods.

Date	Particulars	Debit	Credit
xx/xx	Food Inventory	1 000.00	
	Accounts Payable		1 000.00

2. Non-Capital Expenditures
   Purchased gasoline, oil and repair services for delivery van from vendor on account for $428, including $28 GST.

Date	Particulars	Debit	Credit
xx/xx	Van Maintenance	428.00	
	Accounts Payable		428.00

3. Capital Expenditures
   Purchased pizza oven for café from vendor on account for $2 000 plus $140 GST paid. Invoice total, $2 140.

Date	Particulars	Debit	Credit
xx/xx	Cafeteria Equipment	2 000.00	
	GST Paid on Capital Goods	140.00	
	Accounts Payable		2 140.00

Calculating GST Refunds or Remittances

The following examples apply to a retailer who is filing quarterly and has maximum annual sales of $200 000.

The Regular Method

Quarterly Total Sales (including GST)	$50 000.00	
Quarterly Total Purchases	29 700.00	
GST Charged on Sales		$3 500.00
Less: GST Paid on Purchases		
Cash Register (cost $1 000)	70.00	
Inventory (cost $25 000)	1 750.00	
Supplies (cost $500)	35.00	
Payroll Services (cost $200)	14.00	
Store Lease (cost $3 000)	210.00	
Total GST Paid		– 2 079.00
GST Remittance		$1 421.00

The Quick Method with a Flat Rate of 3 Percent

Quarterly Total Sales (including GST)	$50 000.00	
Multiply by 3%		$1 500.00
Less: GST Paid on Capital Goods		
Cash Register (cost $1 000)		– 70.00
GST Remittance		$1 430.00

notes

The flat tax rate is reduced by 1 percent on the first $30 000 in sales.

Generally the flat rate is set so that there is very little difference between using the regular and quick methods. The quick method can save time if the business has a large number of purchases for small amounts.

GST Remittances and Refunds

GST Collected on Sales	>	GST Paid on Purchases	=	GST Owing
GST Collected on Sales	<	GST Paid on Purchases	=	GST Refund

The business must file a statement periodically that summarizes the amount of GST it has collected and the amount of GST it has paid. The business may file monthly, quarterly or yearly with quarterly instalments paid.

Accounting Examples for Remittances and Refunds

Remittances

notes

The rules concerning the Goods and Services Tax may change periodically. Always refer to current GST guidelines.

Most of the time a business will make GST remittances since sales usually exceed expenses — the business operates at a profit. The example below shows how the GST accounts are cleared and a liability (*Accounts Payable* account) is set up to remit GST owing to the Receiver General of Canada. In this case, the usual one, the Receiver General becomes a vendor for the business so that the liability can be entered and the payment made.

Date	Particulars	Debit	Credit
03/31	GST Charged on Sales	2 500.00	
	GST Paid on Purchases		700.00
	A/P - Receiver General		1 800.00
03/31	A/P - Receiver General	1 800.00	
	Cash in Bank		1 800.00

Refunds

The example below shows how the GST accounts are cleared and a current asset account (*Accounts Receivable* account) is set up for a GST refund from the Receiver General of Canada. In this case, the Receiver General owes money to the business; that is, it acts like a customer. A customer record is set up for the Receiver General to record and collect the amount receivable.

Date	Particulars	Debit	Credit
03/31	GST Charged on Sales	1 500.00	
	A/R - Receiver General	500.00	
	GST Paid on Purchases		2 000.00
04/15	Cash in Bank	500.00	
	A/R - Receiver General		500.00

GST and Provincial Sales Taxes

The rules governing provincial sales taxes vary from province to province, in terms of the rates of taxation, the goods and services that are taxed, and whether PST is applied to the GST as well as to the base purchase price. The examples that follow assume that the item sold has both GST and PST applied.

notes

If a business purchases inventory for resale but uses the inventory within the business instead, it must remit PST on this internal transaction as it would if buying the items from another vendor.

Although GST is applied at each level of sale, resale and manufacturing, PST is paid only by the final consumer of a product or service. Thus, a business purchasing inventory to sell to customers will not pay PST on these purchases. When the same business buys supplies or services for its use in conducting business, it must pay PST because it has become the final consumer of these goods or services.

PST applies only to sales within a province, not to sales to customers in a different province or in a different country.

Alberta has no provincial sales tax. Thus, the examples provided above, without PST, illustrate the application of GST for Alberta.

PST in Ontario, Manitoba, Saskatchewan and British Columbia

The provinces west of Quebec apply PST to the base price of the sale, the amount without GST included.

ONTARIO

Sold goods on account to customer for $500. GST charged is 7% and PST charged is 8%.

GST = (0.07 × 500) = $35
PST = (0.08 × 500) = $40
Total amount of invoice = $500 + $35 + $40 = $575

Date	Particulars	Debit	Credit
xx/xx	Accounts Receivable	575.00	
	GST Charged on Sales		35.00
	PST Payable		40.00
	Revenue from Sales		500.00

The full amount of PST collected on sales is remitted to the provincial Minister of Finance (less any applicable sales tax compensation).

Harmonized Sales Tax — Nova Scotia, Newfoundland, New Brunswick and Labrador

notes

The Harmonized Sales Tax model adopted in these Atlantic provinces is the one that the federal government would like to apply across all provinces in Canada. HST is covered in Chapter 5.

In these Atlantic provinces, the GST and PST are harmonized at a single rate of 15 percent. The full 15 percent Harmonized Sales Tax (HST) operates much like the basic GST, with HST remittances equal to HST collected on sales less HST paid on purchases. Prices shown to customers may have the HST included (tax-inclusive pricing), but they must show either the amount of HST included in the price or the HST rate.

NEW BRUNSWICK

Sold goods on account to customer for $575, including HST at 15% ($500 base price).

HST = (0.15 × 500) = $75
Total amount of invoice = $575

Date	Particulars	Debit	Credit
xx/xx	Accounts Receivable	575.00	
	HST Charged on Sales		75.00
	Revenue from Sales		500.00

A single remittance for the full 15 percent is made to the Receiver General; the provincial portion of the HST is not remitted separately. The administration of the HST may be taken over by the provincial governments in the future.

Quebec Sales Tax (QST)

notes

Quebec was the first province to introduce a Harmonized Sales Tax. It differs from the model in the Atlantic provinces in that the GST and QST components are administered separately by the federal and provincial governments respectively. QST is covered in Chapter 12.

Provincial sales taxes in Quebec (QST) are also combined with the GST. The provincial tax rate is applied to a broader base of goods and services than PST in Ontario, like the base that has GST applied. The QST is calculated on the base amount of the sale plus the GST. That is, QST is applied to GST — a piggy-backed tax or a tax on a tax.

QUEBEC

Sold goods on account to customer for $500. GST charged is 7% and QST charged is 7.5%.

GST = (0.07 × 500) = $35
QST = (0.075 × 535) = $40.13
Total amount of invoice = $500.00 + $35.00 + $40.13 = $575.13

Date	Particulars	Debit	Credit
xx/xx	Accounts Receivable	575.13	
	GST Charged on Sales		35.00
	QST Charged on Sales		40.13
	Revenue from Sales		500.00

QST is remitted to the ministre du Revenu du Québec, separately from GST. However, part of the QST is refundable and businesses can deduct some of the QST they pay on their purchases from the QST they collect on sales. The QST paid on some items, such as raw materials or inventory that are inputs to the business, is refundable, the rest is not. Therefore, QST paid must be designated as refundable or non-refundable at the time of the purchase and when the purchase is recorded.

PST in Prince Edward Island

Provincial sales taxes in PEI (PST) are applied to the base sale price plus GST. However, unlike Quebec, and like Ontario, some items have only GST applied, and some have both GST and PST applied.

PRINCE EDWARD ISLAND

Sold goods on account to customer for $500. GST charged is 7% and PST charged is 10%.

GST = (0.07 × 500) = $35
PST = (0.10 × 535) = $53.50
Total amount of invoice = $500.00 + $35.00 + $53.50 = $588.50

Date	Particulars	Debit	Credit
xx/xx	Accounts Receivable	588.50	
	GST Charged on Sales		35.00
	PST Payable		53.50
	Revenue from Sales		500.00

The full amount of PST collected on sales is remitted to the provincial Minister of Finance (less any applicable sales tax compensation).

Part Two
Applications

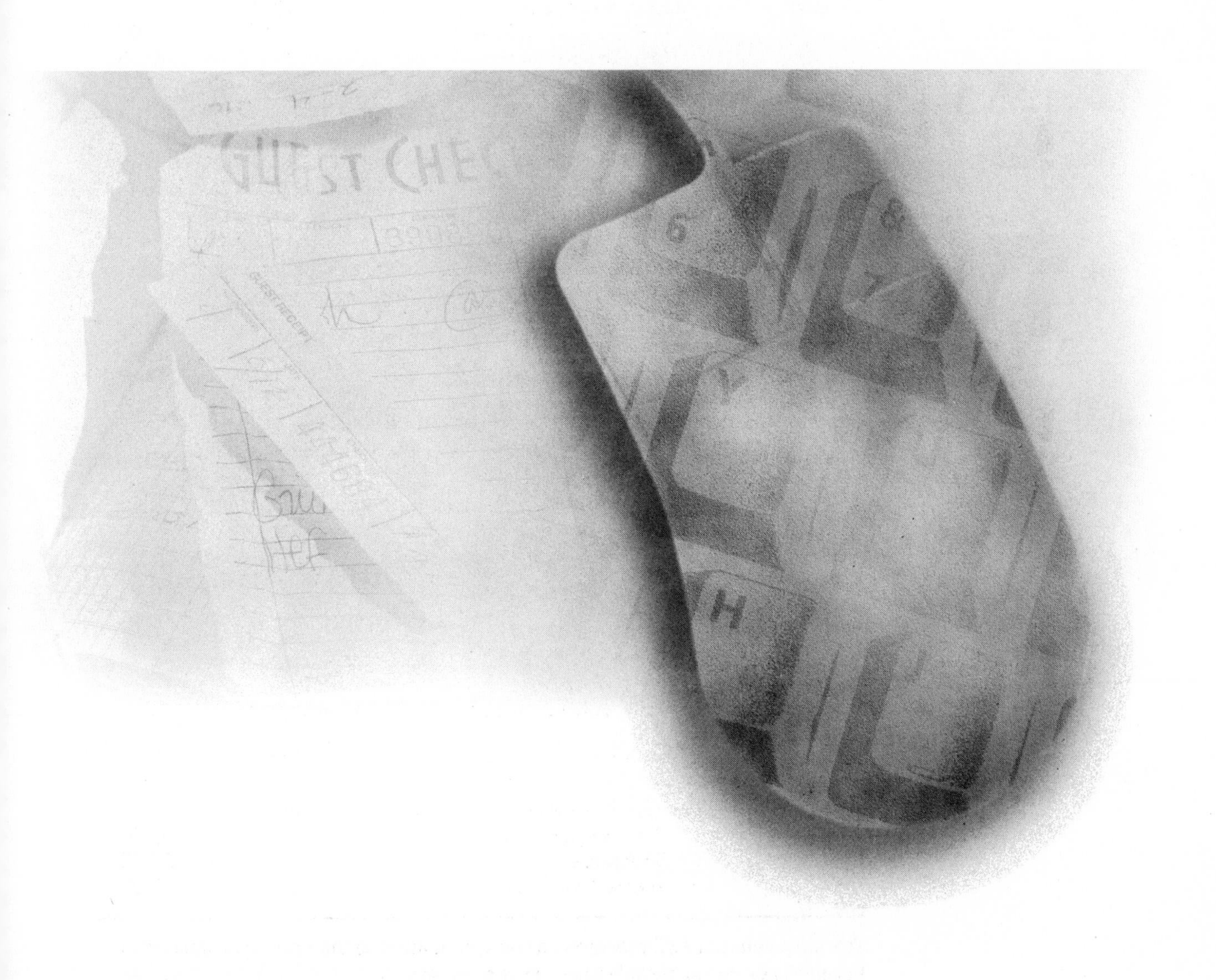

CHAPTER THREE

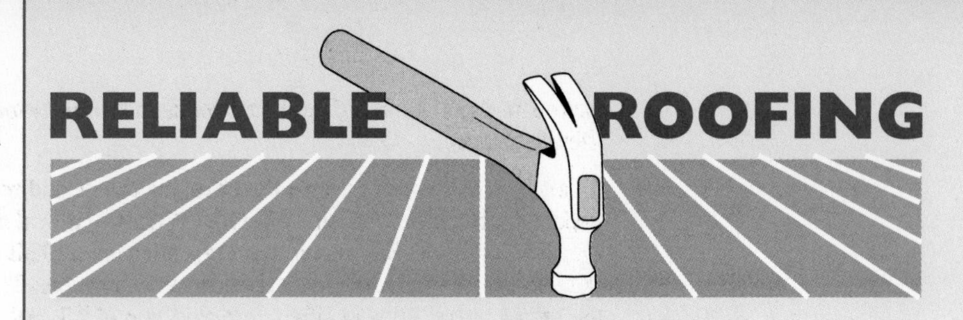

OBJECTIVES

After completing this chapter, you should be able to

- *access* the Simply Accounting program
- *access* the data files for the business
- *open* the General Journal
- *enter* transactions in the General Journal
- *edit* and *review* General Journal transactions
- *post* transactions
- *create* new General Ledger accounts
- *adjust* journal entries after posting
- *display* General Ledger and General Journal reports
- *print* General Ledger and General Journal reports
- *graph* General Ledger reports
- *display* and *print* comparative financial reports
- *back up* your data files
- *advance* the session date
- *finish* an accounting session

COMPANY INFORMATION

Company Profile

Reliable Roofing, owned by Albert Dresden, has operated successfully in Red Deer, Alberta, for the past six years. Dresden works alone most of the time, replacing and repairing roofs in the Red Deer area. For larger projects, or for tighter deadlines, he hires an assistant on a day-to-day contractual basis. Dresden's friendly manner and his work guarantees — five years for roof replacement work and one year for repair work — have given him a community reputation for reliability, honesty and friendly service.

Albert Dresden keeps up with the changing trends and roof styles. The majority of Reliable Roofing's customers still request the traditional asphalt roof shingles. However, an increasing number are replacing old asphalt shingle roofs with cedar or slate shingles, with Marlee or clay tiles or with copper. These homeowners believe that the greater expense is justified because the roof will last longer and make their house more attractive to potential buyers. Dresden's mobile unit is specially equipped for working with traditional as well as specialty roofing materials.

Since Dresden is on a job most of the time, he relies on his answering machine, pager and cellular telephone to arrange appointments for work estimates or to schedule work. Individual homeowners, most of Reliable Roofing's customers, generally settle their accounts as soon as the work is completed, but Dresden sometimes extends the payment period for up to one month. When Dresden replaces or repairs roofs on townhouse and apartment complexes, he deals directly with the property management companies rather than the owners or tenants. These companies have set up accounts with Reliable Roofing and are expected to pay for completed work within 30 days.

For an annual fee, Peter Lacklustre, an accountant, records and manages all the financial transactions for Reliable Roofing. Mr. Lacklustre is gradually converting the accounts for all his clients to Simply Accounting, because the program is well suited to small businesses. He converted the accounts for Reliable Roofing on July 1, 2003, using the following information:

- Chart of Accounts
- Trial Balance
- Accounting Procedures

notes

The Chart of Accounts includes only postable accounts and the Net Income or Current Earnings account. Simply Accounting uses the Net Income account for the Income Statement to calculate the difference between revenue and expenses before closing the books.

RELIABLE ROOFING
CHART OF ACCOUNTS

ASSETS
1080 Cash in Bank
1200 A/R - Toller Properties
1220 A/R - Lakeside Co-op
1240 A/R - M. DeZwager
1320 Prepaid Insurance
1340 Supplies: Computer
1360 Supplies: Roofing
1540 Portable Computer
1550 Computer Peripherals
1560 Power Tools
1580 Mobile Roofing Unit

LIABILITIES
2100 A/P - Space for You
2120 A/P - Ads On-Line
2130 A/P - Alberta Hydro
2140 A/P - Alberta Telephone
2160 A/P - Dominion Building Supplies
2190 A/P - Summit Scaffold
2650 GST Charged on Services
2670 GST Paid on Purchases

EQUITY
3100 A. Dresden, Capital
3150 A. Dresden, Drawings
3600 Net Income

REVENUE
4100 Revenue from Roofing
4200 Interest Revenue

EXPENSES
5050 Advertising
5080 Bank Charges
5130 Hydro Expense
5150 Interest Expense
5200 Mobile Unit Maintenance
5250 Rent
5280 Telephone Expense
5500 Wages Expense

RELIABLE ROOFING
TRIAL BALANCE
June 30, 2003

Account	Debit	Credit
1080 Cash in Bank	$16 250.50	
1200 A/R - Toller Properties	3 210.00	
1240 A/R - M. DeZwager	1 070.00	
1320 Prepaid Insurance	1 200.00	
1340 Supplies: Computer	500.00	
1360 Supplies: Roofing	2 800.00	
1540 Portable Computer	800.00	
1550 Computer Peripherals	2 000.00	
1560 Power Tools	3 200.00	
1580 Mobile Roofing Unit	35 000.00	
2160 A/P - Dominion Building Supplies		457.50
2650 GST Charged on Services		560.00
2670 GST Paid on Purchases	105.00	
3100 A. Dresden, Capital		59 700.00
3150 A. Dresden, Drawings	750.00	
4100 Revenue from Roofing		8 000.00
5050 Advertising	75.00	
5080 Bank Charges	32.00	
5200 Mobile Unit Maintenance	175.00	
5250 Rent	1 000.00	
5280 Telephone Expense	50.00	
5500 Wages Expense	500.00	
	$ 68 717.50	$ 68 717.50

Accounting Procedures

GST Remittances

notes

- All bank and other financial institution services used in this application are exempt from GST charges.
- Alberta does not levy a provincial sales tax.

Dresden has chosen the regular method for remittance of the Goods and Services Tax (GST). He records the GST collected from customers as a liability (credit) in the *GST Charged on Services* account. He records GST that he pays to vendors in the *GST Paid on Purchases* account as a decrease (debit) to his liability to Canada Customs and Revenue Agency. His GST remittance or refund is calculated automatically in the *GST Owing (Refund)* subgroup total. You can see these accounts when you display or print the Balance Sheet. Dresden files his GST remittances or requests for refunds with the Receiver General of Canada on the last day of each fiscal quarter. (For details, please read Chapter 2 on the Goods and Services Tax.)

INSTRUCTIONS

1. Using the Chart of Accounts and Trial Balance for Reliable Roofing, enter the source documents for July using the General Journal in Simply Accounting. The procedures for entering each new type of transaction for this application are outlined step by step in the keystroke section following the source documents. These transactions have a ✔ in the check box and, immediately below the check box, the page number on which the relevant keystrokes begin.
2. After you have completed your entries, print the reports and graphs indicated on the printing form below. Keystrokes for reports begin on page 51.

REPORTS

Lists

- ☐ Chart of Accounts

Financials

- ☑ Comparative Balance Sheet
  dates: July 1 and July 13
  with percent difference
- ☑ Income Statement
  from July 1 to July 13

Management Reports

- ☐ General

Journals

- ☑ General (by posting date)
  from July 1 to July 13
  from July 14 to July 31 (after completing Case Two)
- ☑ Trial Balance
  date: July 13
- ☑ General Ledger
  accounts: 1080 2650
  3100 4100
  from July 1 to July 13

GRAPHS (after completing Case Two)

- ☐ Revenues by Account
- ☑ Expenses and Net Profit as % of Revenue
  All expenses from July 1 to July 31
- ☐ Expenses by Account
- ☐ Current Revenue vs Last Year

SOURCE DOCUMENTS

notes

Remember that the ✔ and the number beneath it indicate that keystroke instructions for this entry begin on page 39.

notes

☑ **45** Create new Group account 2200 Bank Loan. (See Keystrokes on page 45.)

SESSION DATE – July 6

☑ 39 Purchase Invoice #DBS-7643
Dated July 2, 2003
From Dominion Building Supplies, $850 for roofing supplies (tar paper and shingles) plus GST paid $59.50. Purchase invoice total $909.50. Terms: 2/15, net 30 days.

☐ Bank Credit Memo #WCU-2264
Dated July 3, 2003
From Workers' Credit Union, $8 000 bank loan deposited in bank account.

☐ Sales Invoice #RR-1001
Dated July 3, 2003
To Georg Johanssen, $650 for replacement of garage shingle roof plus GST charged $45.50. Sales invoice total $695.50. Payment received in cash on completion of work.

☐ Sales Invoice #RR-1002
Dated July 3, 2003
To Maryke DeZwager, $380 for roof repair work completed plus GST charged $26.60. Sales invoice total $406.60. Terms: net 30 days.

☑ 48 Memo #1
Dated July 4, 2003
The loan from Workers' Credit Union was entered incorrectly. The actual loan amount deposited was $8 500. Make the correction in the General Journal.

- [ ] Cheque Copy #501
  Dated July 4, 2003
  To Dominion Building Supplies, $457.50 in payment of invoice #DBS-6199.

- [ ] Purchase Invoice #AOL-431
  Dated July 5, 2003
  From Ads On-Line Inc., $1 800 to design a Web page for advertising of roofing services plus GST paid $126. Purchase invoice total $1 926. Terms: net 20 days.

- [ ] Bank Debit Memo #WCU-3181
  Dated July 5, 2003
  From Workers' Credit Union, $35.50 for bank service charges.

- [ ] Cash Receipt #45
  Dated July 6, 2003
  From Toller Properties, $3 210 in full payment of account.

- [ ] Cash Receipt #46
  Dated July 6, 2003
  From Maryke DeZwager, $1 070 in payment of account.

notes

See Keystrokes on Advancing the Session Date, page 49.

SESSION DATE – July 13

- [ ] Purchase Invoice #AT-44318
  Dated July 9, 2003
  From Alberta Telephone, $240.00 for office and cellular telephone services plus GST paid $16.80. Purchase invoice total $256.80. Terms: cash on receipt of invoice.

- [ ] Cheque Copy #502
  Dated July 10, 2003
  To Alberta Telephone, $256.80 in full payment of account.

- [ ] Purchase Invoice #DBS-8763
  Dated July 10, 2003
  From Dominion Building Supplies, $250 for roofing supplies (tar, tar paper and nails) plus GST paid $17.50. Purchase invoice total $267.50. Terms: 2/15, net 30 days.

- [ ] Bank Credit Memo #WCU-7101
  Dated July 11, 2003
  From Workers' Credit Union, $312 for interest earned on bank account.

- [ ] Sales Invoice #RR-1003
  Dated July 12, 2003
  To Toller Properties Management, $3 000 for reshingling roof on two townhouse units plus GST charged $210. Sales invoice total $3 210. Terms: 50% due on completion of work, balance in 30 days.

- [ ] Cash Receipt #47
  Dated July 12, 2003
  From Toller Properties Management, $1 605 in payment of account.

notes

- [ ] Create new Group account, 2170 A/P - Micron Equipment. See Keystrokes on page 45.

- [ ] Purchase Invoice #ME-64299
  Dated July 13, 2003
  From Micron Equipment, $4 800 for Pentium 800 MHZ Micron portable computer with active matrix screen, plus GST paid $336. Purchase invoice total $5 136. Terms: COD.

- [ ] Cheque Copy #503
Dated July 13, 2003
To Micron Equipment, $5 136 in full payment of account.

KEYSTROKES

Opening Data Files

Using the instructions for accessing a data file in Chapter 1, page 15, open the Reliable Roofing application.

The following screen appears, asking (prompting) you to enter the session date for this work session:

Simply Accounting - Session Date
Date for this Session: 07/01/2003
OK Cancel

notes

Many screens include a cancel button. If you click Cancel, you will return to your previous screen without entering any changes.

notes

- The drop-down list for any date field shows the range of dates that will be accepted based on the settings chosen for the company files. These settings are discussed in Chapter 6.
- The section Advancing the Session Date on page 49 will explain how to work with later dates.
- The format of the date that shows on your screen is controlled by the Regional Settings in the Control Panel of your Windows program, not by the format you use to enter the date. Refer to Chapter 1, page 23, and Windows Help for further information.

The session date is the date of your work session, the date on which you are recording the accounting transactions on the computer. A business with a large number of transactions may record these transactions at the end of each day. One with fewer transactions may enter them once a week. In this workbook, transactions are entered once a week so the session date is updated by one week at a time. The session date may or may not be the same as the date on which the transaction actually took place.

The session date for your session is July 6, 2003. Since this date is not shown by default on the screen, you must change the date. You can enter dates using the following alternative formats. Note that they all use the same order of month, day and year. You must enter the year at this stage of opening the file.

- 07-06-03
- 07/06/03
- 07 06 03
- July 6, 2003
- 7-6-03
- 7/6/03
- 7 6 03
- jul 6 03
- other non-alpha or non-numeric separating characters may also be accepted by the program
- after you open the file, you may enter dates without the year

We will use a variety of date formats throughout this workbook. If you are uncertain about how the date format is set for your computer, using a text version of the date will prevent an incorrect date entry and show you how the format is set. Refer to Chapter 1, page 23, for instructions on checking and changing date format settings.

version 8

Type `july 6, 2003`

Click OK

notes

Only the General Ledger and Journal can be accessed for this file. Maximize the Home window if necessary.

version 8

Your screen shows the following Home window:

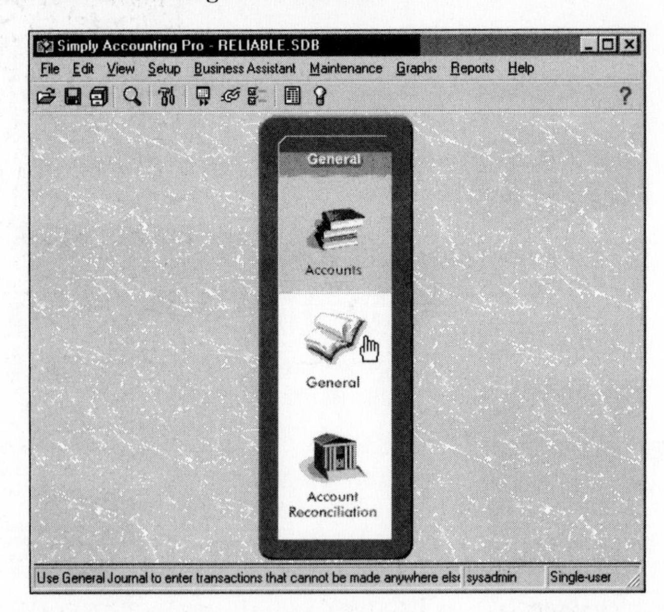

notes

If you are using Simply Accounting 8.0 or the regular single-user version of 8.5 (instead of the Pro version), you will not see the Single-user tag in the status bar line, or Pro in the title bar.

Click [maximize button] to maximize the window if necessary. The Home window is divided as follows: the title bar is on top with the program and file names, control menu icon and size buttons; the main menu bar comes next; the tool bar follows, with tool buttons that permit alternative and quick access to commonly used menu items. The Home window tool buttons from left to right (with their alternative pull-down menu locations) are Open Company, Save and Backup (File menu), Find record (Edit menu), Setup (Setup menu), Change session date (Maintenance menu), To-Do Lists and Checklists (Business Assistant menu), Display reports (Reports menu), Advice and Help (Help menu).

notes

When ledger icons are hidden, all main menu options related to those ledgers are also hidden or unavailable.

The ledger names with their respective icons occupy the major part of the window — ledgers in the top row below the ledger or module name, and journal icons below the line under their respective ledgers in the next two icon rows of the window. Ledgers contain the records for accounts, customers, vendors, employees, inventory items and their balances. Journals are used to enter accounting transactions. Only the General or Accounts Ledger is set up for Reliable Roofing, so it is the only ledger displayed. The remaining ledgers are hidden.

Below the journal icons, the status bar describes the purpose of the General Journal because the hand-shaped pointer is on the General icon. Point to different parts of the Home window to observe the changes in the status bar message. The Home window icons change as you pass the mouse over them.

Entering General Journal Transactions

notes

Notice that the status bar describes the position of the pointer, not the position of the cursor or insertion point, which is usually in an input field.

All transactions for Reliable Roofing are entered in the General Journal, indicated by the pointer in the following screen:

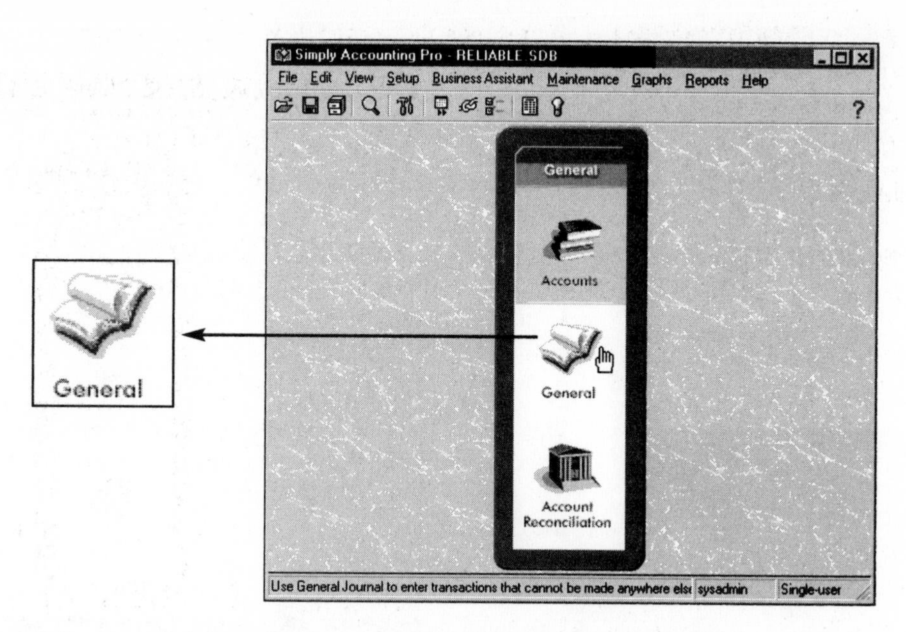

Click the **General icon** from the middle portion of the Home window to open the General Journal. The General Journal input form shown below appears on your screen:

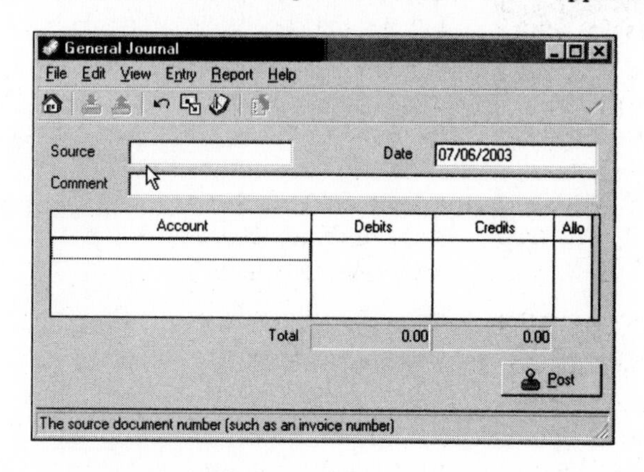

notes

- The buttons in the tool bar are different from those in the Home window. The General Journal tool buttons are Home window, Store, Recall, Undo, Customize journal, Adjust posted entry on the left and Allocate on the right. The Pro version also has a Refresh lists tool for its multi-user option that is not used in Version 8.0 or 8.5. Tools are explained as they are used. Buttons that are dimmed cannot be selected.
- Move the mouse over the tool buttons and journal input fields and watch the changes in the status bar message.

You are now ready to enter the first transaction in the General Journal input screen. The cursor, a flashing vertical line, is blinking in the Source field, ready to receive information. The Source field identifies the reference document from which you obtain the information for a transaction. In this transaction, the source is the invoice number. Source codes can contain up to 13 characters, including spaces.

Type `DBS-7643`

Press tab

The cursor advances to the next field, the Date field. Here you should enter the transaction date. The program enters the session date by default. It is highlighted, ready to be accepted or changed. Because the work was completed on July 2, 2003, the session date of July 6 is incorrect and must be changed.

notes

- If your journal displays the date as 06-07 (or 6/7, etc.), your computer has the date order as day, month, year. If you are unsure, enter the date as text (July 6). Refer to page 23.
- Unless you change the date, the session date will become the posting date for the entry.
- Remember that you can use any of the date formats listed on page 39 and you may also omit the year.

Type `07-02`

Press tab

The year is added to the date. The cursor advances to the Comment field, where you can enter a description of the transaction to make the permanent record more meaningful. You may enter up to 39 characters, including spaces.

Type `Dominion Building Supplies (2/15, n/30)`

Press tab

The cursor moves forward to the first line of the Account field, creating a dotted box for the first account.

Simply Accounting organizes accounts into sections or categories using the following boundaries for numbering:

- 1000–1999 Assets
- 2000–2999 Liabilities
- 3000–3999 Equity
- 4000–4999 Revenue
- 5000–5999 Expense

notes

You can also double click the dotted box in the Account column to display the list of accounts.

This system makes it easy to remember the first digit of an account. Pressing enter when the cursor is in the Account field will display the list of accounts. By typing the first digit of an account then pressing enter while the cursor is flashing in any account field, the program will advance the list to the accounts beginning with that digit.

Press enter

The following list of accounts appears on your journal screen:

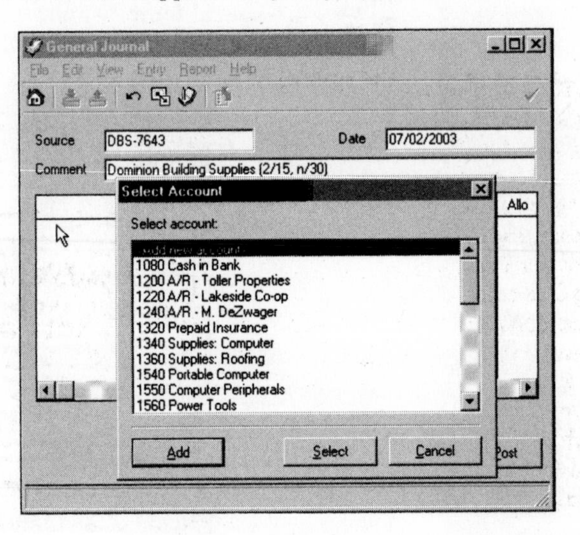

notes

You can also double click a selected account or press enter to add it directly to your journal entry form.

The beginning of the account list is displayed. The list includes only postable accounts, those that can be debited or credited in journal entries. Following usual accounting practice, we enter the account to be debited first.

Click 1360 Supplies: Roofing to select this asset account.

Click the **Select** button. (The darker box framing the button indicates it is selected.) Notice that the account number and name have now been added to your input form, so you can easily see whether you have selected the correct account. If the screen does not display the entire account title, you can see the rest of the account title by clicking anywhere on the part that is showing.

notes

- Decimals are not required when you enter whole numbers. Non-numeric characters are ignored by the program in amount fields.

Your cursor is now positioned in the Debits field. The amount is selected, ready to be changed. Type amounts without dollar signs.

Type 850

Press tab

notes

Instead of using the selection list, you can find the number in the Chart of Accounts, type it in and then press tab.

Your input form should now appear as follows:

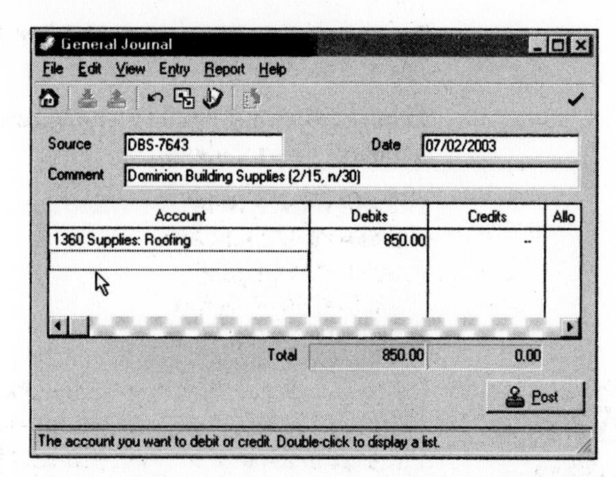

The cursor has advanced to the next line of the Account field, creating a new dotted box so you can enter the next account for this transaction: the liability account *GST Paid for Purchases*. Remember, liability accounts start with 2. However, we will type 3 to advance to the end of the 2000 level accounts.

Type 3

notes

If you know that the account you need is closer to the end of its numbered section, typing the next higher number advances you to the end of the section you want. For example, typing 3 advances to 3100 and includes 2670 in the display. In this way, your account is more likely to be included in the display. Typing 2 will show the list with 2100 at the end and you will have to scroll down to include 2670.

Press enter to advance your list to the 3000 accounts as shown:

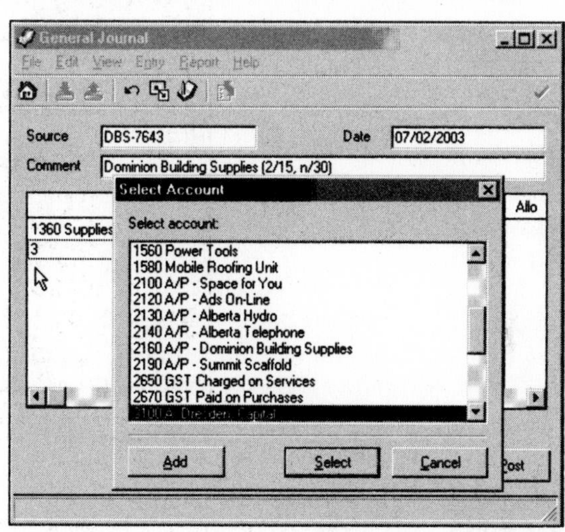

version 8

Click 2670 GST Paid on Purchases from the displayed list to highlight it. If necessary, click the scroll arrow to move through the account list to include 2670 in the display.

Press enter

Again, the account number and name have been added to your transaction form. The cursor has advanced to the Credits field, which shows $850.00 as the default amount because this amount will balance the entry. The amount is highlighted to indicate that you may edit it. This is a compound entry. You must change the amount to separate the GST, and you must delete the credit entry because the GST account is debited.

Press del to delete the credit entry.

Click the **Debits field** on the second journal line to move the cursor.

Type `59.50`

Press tab

The cursor moves to the next line in the Account field.

Type 2

Press enter to advance your list to the 2000 accounts. The liability account, *2100 A/P - Space for You*, is selected because it is the first 2000 level account.

Click ▾ (down scroll arrow) or **press** ↓ until the remaining liability accounts are in view.

Double click 2160 A/P - Dominion Building Supplies to select it and return to the journal.

The cursor advances to the Credits field again, where the amount that will now balance the entry is shown. The amount is correct, so you can accept it. The total for the Credits column is still displayed as zero.

Press tab to update the totals.

The cursor advances to the next line in the Account field. Your completed input form should appear as follows:

Don't post the transaction until you make sure that it is correct. Once you post an entry, you cannot change it without making a reversing entry. Always review a transaction before posting it.

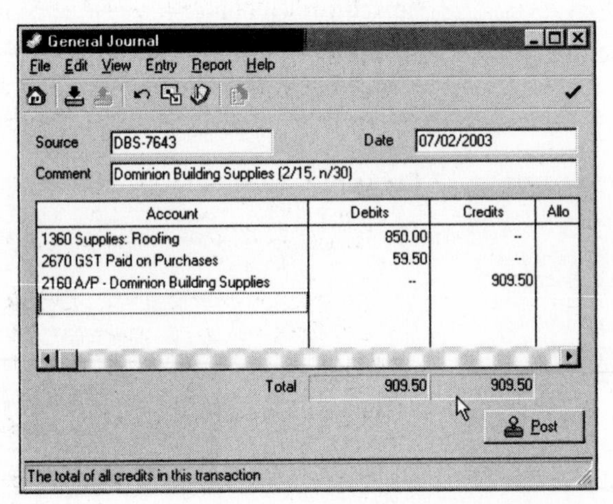

Until the debits and credits of a transaction are equal, you cannot post an entry. Once the entry is complete and balanced, it can be posted. The Store button, for recurring entries, is also darkened. We will use the Store button in the following application, Java Jean's (Chapter 4). Before you store or post an entry, you should review the transaction.

Reviewing the General Journal Entry

Choose the **Report menu** and then **click Display General Journal Entry** as shown:

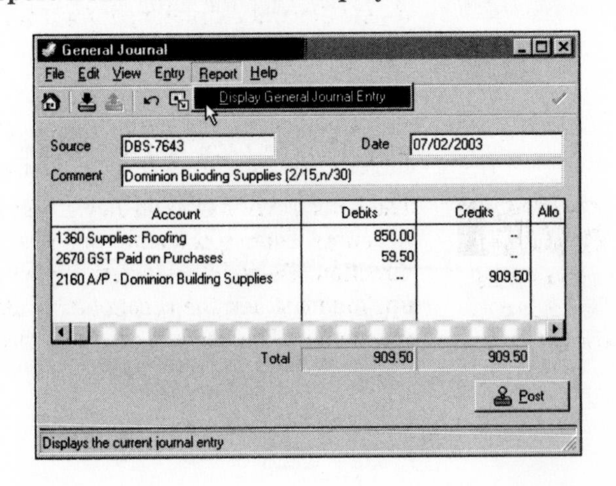

notes

The refresh tool appears in all Pro Version 8.5 report screens, not in Version 8.5 or Version 8.0.

version 8

The transaction is displayed as follows:

General Journal Entry

File Options Help

07/02/2003 (J1)	Debits	Credits	Project
1360 Supplies: Roofing	850.00	-	
2670 GST Paid on Purchases	59.50	-	
2160 A/P - Dominion Building Supplies	-	909.50	
	909.50	909.50	

Click the maximize button [□] to change your display to full screen size or use the scroll arrows to see more of the display if your transaction does not fit completely on the screen. To return to your input form,

Click [X] or **choose** the **control menu icon** and **click Close**.

notes

Refer to page 48 and Appendix A for assistance with correcting errors after posting.

CORRECTING THE GENERAL JOURNAL ENTRY BEFORE POSTING

Press tab to advance to the field that has the error. To move to a previous field, **press** shift and tab together (that is, while holding down shift, **press** tab). The field will be highlighted, ready for editing. **Type** the correct information and **press** tab to enter it.

You can also use the mouse to point to a field and drag through the incorrect information to highlight it. You can highlight a single number or letter or the entire field. **Type** the correct information and **press** tab to enter it.

To correct an account number, **click** the incorrect account number (or name) to select the field. **Press** enter to display the list of accounts. **Click** the correct account. **Click Select**. **Press** tab to advance to the next line and enter the correction.

Click an incorrect amount to highlight it. **Type** the correct amount and **press** tab.

To discard the entry and begin again, **click** [X] to close the Journal or **click** [↶] (on the tool bar) to open a blank Journal window. When Simply Accounting asks whether you want to discard the entry, **click Yes** to confirm your decision.

Posting

Once you are sure that all the information is correct, you are ready to post the entry.

Click the **Post button** [Post] in the lower right corner of the General Journal (the one that looks like a stamp) or **choose** the **Entry menu** and then **click Post**.

A new General Journal input form appears for you to enter the next transaction for this session date.

Adding a New Account

notes

You can also add accounts in the Accounts Ledger. The Accounts Ledger is explained in Chapter 6.

The bank credit memo on July 3 uses an account that is not listed in your Chart of Accounts. Often a company will need to create new accounts as it expands or changes direction. These future needs are not always foreseen when the accounts are first set up. You must add the account *2200 Bank Loan* to enter the bank credit memo transaction. You can add accounts directly from the Account field in any journal.

notes

The date of the previous journal entry becomes the default date until you close the journal. Then the session date becomes the default again.

version 8

Type `WCU-2264` (as the source). **Press** tab to advance to the Date field.

Type `07-03` **Press** tab to advance to the Comment field.

Type `Workers' Credit Union bank loan` **Press** tab to move to the Account field.

Choose the *Cash in Bank* account and **type** `8000`, the amount of the loan, as the debit part of the transaction. **Press** tab to advance to the Account field on the second journal line.

Press enter to see the Select account list.

Click Add new account, the first entry in the list, if it is not already selected.

Click Add to begin the wizard for adding a General Ledger account:

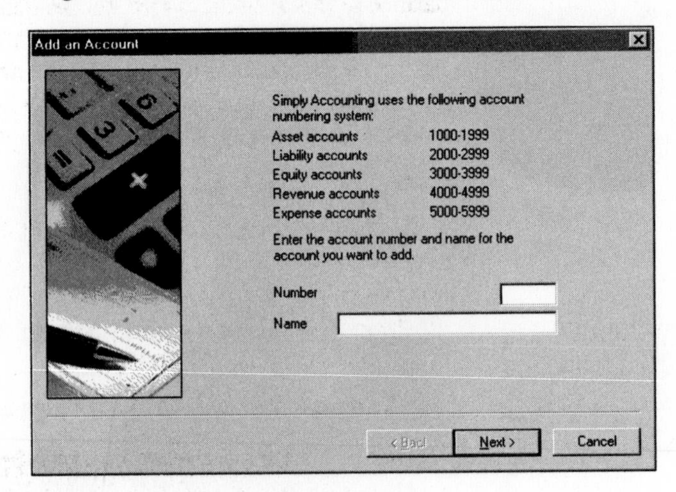

The first screen prompts you for the account number and name. The cursor is in the Number field.

Type `2200`

Press tab

Type `Bank Loan`

Click Next to continue. The next screen asks for the GIFI code. This is the four-digit account number assigned by Canada Customs and Revenue Agency for this category of account for use with electronically filed business returns. GIFI codes are not used in this workbook. They are described in Appendix D.

notes

Each screen shows the selections you made, on the left side.

Click Next to skip this screen and continue. The next screen asks whether this account is to be used as a Heading or Total in the financial statements. *Bank Loan* is an ordinary postable account that has a balance so the default selection, No, is correct.

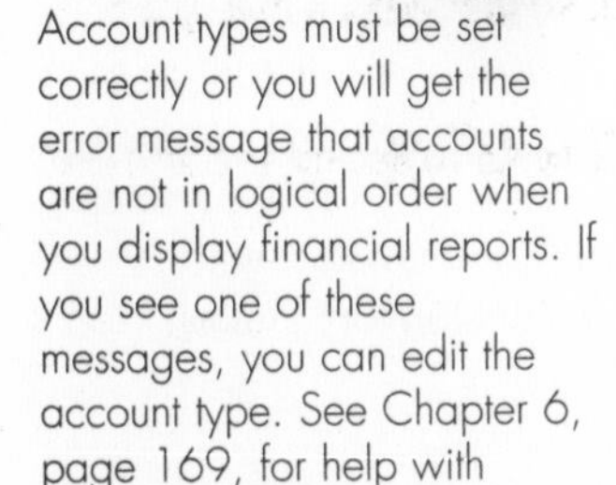

Account types must be set correctly or you will get the error message that accounts are not in logical order when you display financial reports. If you see one of these messages, you can edit the account type. See Chapter 6, page 169, for help with creating and editing accounts.

Click Next to accept the default and continue.

The following screen deals with another aspect of the account type. Accounts may be subtotalled within their group of accounts. For example, if you have several bank accounts, you will want your Balance Sheet report to include the total cash deposited in all of them together. The use of different account types will be explained fully in the CISV application (Chapter 6), where you will set up the accounting records for a company from scratch.

Bank Loan is a Group account. It is not subtotalled with any other account so the default selection, No, is correct.

Click Next to continue. The next wizard screen refers to the account class. Account classes are explained in Chapter 10. The default selection is the name of the section. Therefore, for account 2200, Liability is the section and the default class. Generally, you can accept the default selection.

Click Next to continue.

Now you are being asked whether you want to allocate the balance of the account to different projects. Since we do not have any projects set up for Reliable Roofing, the default setting is correct at No.

Click Next to continue.

The next setting screen asks whether you want to include or omit this account in all financial statements when it has a zero balance. Choosing Yes means that if the balance in this account is zero, the account will not be included in your financial statements. If you choose No, the account will be printed, even if it has a balance of zero. Some accounts, such as *Cash in Bank*, should always be printed in financial statements. In Chapter 6 we explain this setting. The default setting, not to omit the account, is never wrong and errs on the side of caution.

Click Next to continue.

In the Pro Version 8.5 only, you will next see a screen asking whether there are statements for the account that are to be reconciled against the General Ledger account entries and balances. That is, will you be performing account reconciliation for the account? The default is correct at No. This screen will not appear for Version 8.0 or 8.5. Click Next to continue.

Your final screen should look like the one shown here:

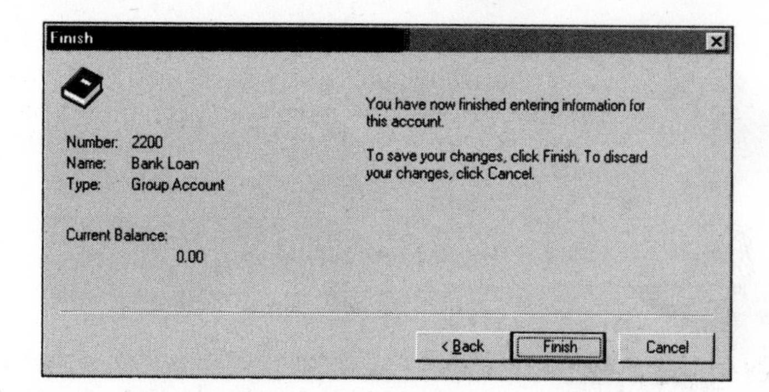

This final screen shows the selections you have made. Check your work. Make any corrections necessary by **clicking Back** till you reach the screen with the error. Make the correction and **click Next** until you reach this final screen again. When all the information is correct, you need to save the new account information.

Click Finish

You will return to the General Journal window with the new account added to the account field. Notice that the cursor has not yet advanced, so you can change your account selection if you need to.

Press tab twice to advance to the Credits field. **Press** tab again to accept the amount.

Display the journal entry to see whether it is correct.

Click Post [Post] to save the information.

Enter the next two sales transactions.

Adjusting a Posted Entry

Sometimes you discover after posting a journal entry that it had an error. You can make these corrections directly in the General Journal by adjusting the previously posted transaction. Simply Accounting allows you to make the correction by adjusting the entry without completing a reversing entry. The program fills in the reversing and correcting journal entries after you post the correction so that the audit trail is complete. The bank credit memo on July 3 was posted with an incorrect amount.

The General Journal should still be open.

version 8

Click the **Adjust a previously posted entry tool** (or choose the Entry menu and click Adjusting Entry) to open the Adjust an Entry screen:

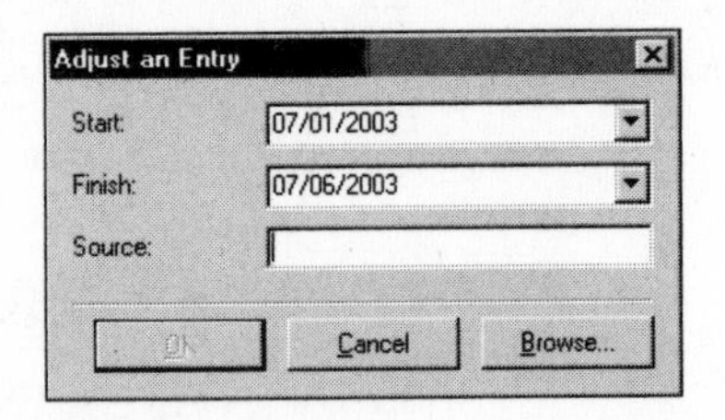

You may now select a range of dates for the journal entries you want to browse through so that you may choose one. The earliest transaction date, the date we converted the data files to Simply Accounting, and the session date are the default start and finish dates for the list. If you know the Source number for the entry, you can enter it and see the journal entry directly.

We can accept the default dates because we are certain that they include the transaction we need.

Click Browse to display the journal entries:

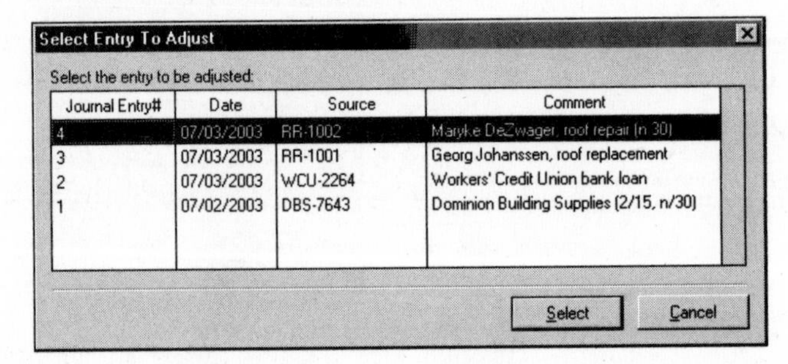
Select Entry To Adjust

Select the entry to be adjusted:

Journal Entry#	Date	Source	Comment
4	07/03/2003	RR-1002	Maryke DeZwager, roof repair (n 30)
3	07/03/2003	RR-1001	Georg Johanssen, roof replacement
2	07/03/2003	WCU-2264	Workers' Credit Union bank loan
1	07/02/2003	DBS-7643	Dominion Building Supplies (2/15, n/30)

Select Cancel

All journal entries are listed with the most recent one at the top of the list.

Click WCU-2264 (Journal entry # 2) to select it.

notes

You can also double click anywhere on the line for a journal entry to open the Adjusting General Journal screen.

Click Select or **press** enter to open the journal entry as it was posted:

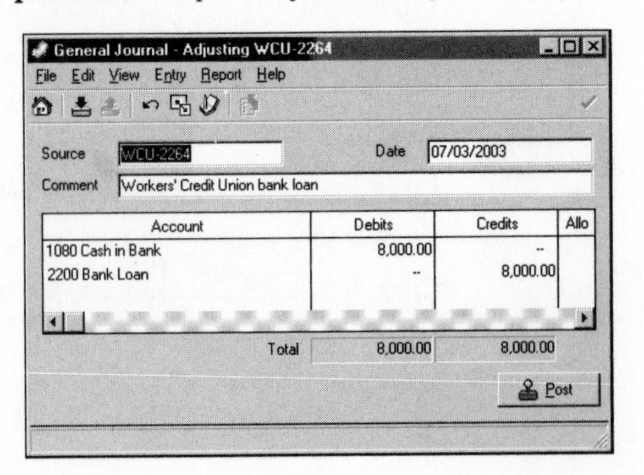

All fields may now be edited, just as if you had not yet posted the transaction.

Click 8,000.00, the amount in the Debit column for *Cash in Bank*, to select it for editing.

Type 8500

Click 8,000.00, the amount in the Credit column for *Bank Loan*.

Type 8500

Press tab to update the totals with the correct amounts.

We will also modify the source so that this entry is recognized as the correction for the bank memo.

Click the **Source field** before the current entry (before W).

Type (COR)

Review the entry to see the correct transaction and close the display.

Make corrections if necessary.

Click Post Post

notes

The adjusting and correcting entries are posted with the date of the original transaction.

When you review the General Journal, you will see three entries for the bank memo. The original incorrect entry, a reversing adjusting entry created by the program (ADJWCU-2264) and the correct entry (COR)WCU-2264. Thus, a complete audit trail exists for the transaction and the correction.

Advancing the Session Date

notes

The data files for Reliable Roofing are set up not to allow postdated transactions.

When you have finished all the entries for the July 6 session date, the date for the next transaction is later than July 6. Therefore, you must advance the session date before you can continue. Before taking this step, however, save and back up your work because you have already completed one week of transactions. Although Simply Accounting saves automatically each time you display a report or exit the program, it is important to know how to save and back up your work directly to a separate file and location or disk because your working disk may become damaged and unusable.

Click ☒ or **choose** the **control menu icon** for the journal and **click Close** to close the General Journal.

Click (**Save button**) on the tool bar or **choose** the **File menu** and **click Save**.

The data files for this workbook have been prepared with the default warning to back up your work weekly. Since we also advance the session date by one week at a time, you will be reminded to back up each time you advance the session date. You are now ready to advance the session date to July 13.

version 8

Choose the **Maintenance menu** and **click Change Session Date as** shown:

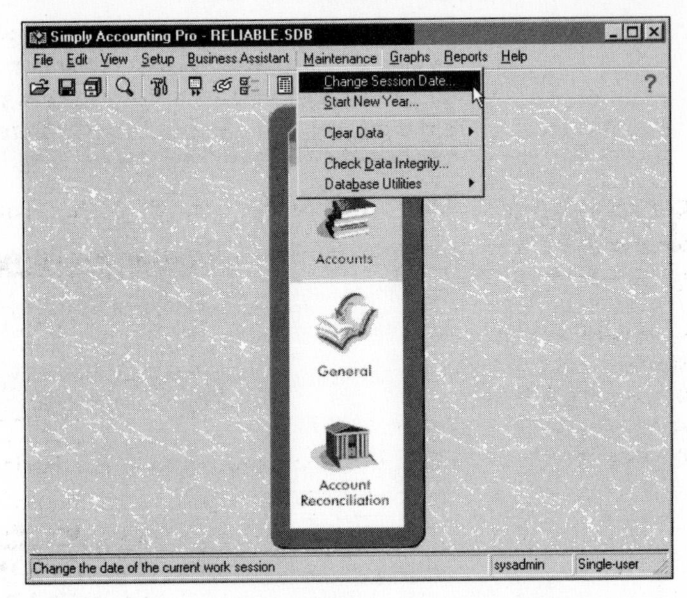

Warning!

Be sure to back up each time you are prompted to do so or each time you advance the session date. If your files are damaged, your work will be lost unless you have a backup.

The following dialogue box appears, advising you that you have not yet backed up your work:

notes

The next time you back up your files, Simply Accounting will tell you the date of your most recent backup and will provide the same location that you used before. The backup number in the comment will be updated.

Click Yes to proceed with the backup. The next screen asks for a file name for the backup:

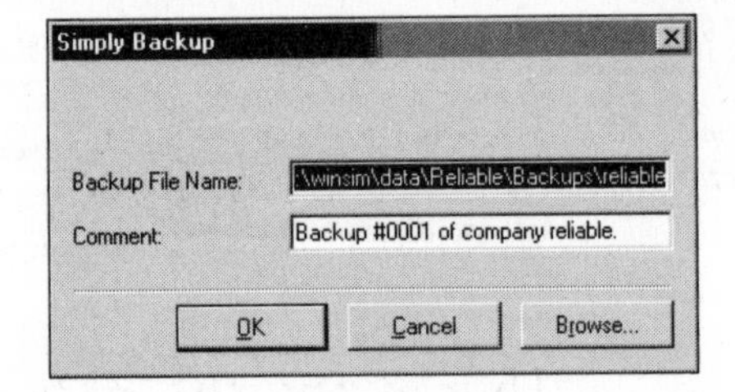

Simply Accounting will create a default directory named Backup in the folder that contains your working data files. You can edit the file name and comment if you want. If you want to change the location of the backup, click Browse, select a folder and file name and click Save.

Click OK to proceed.

When you name a new folder, you will see the following advisory message:

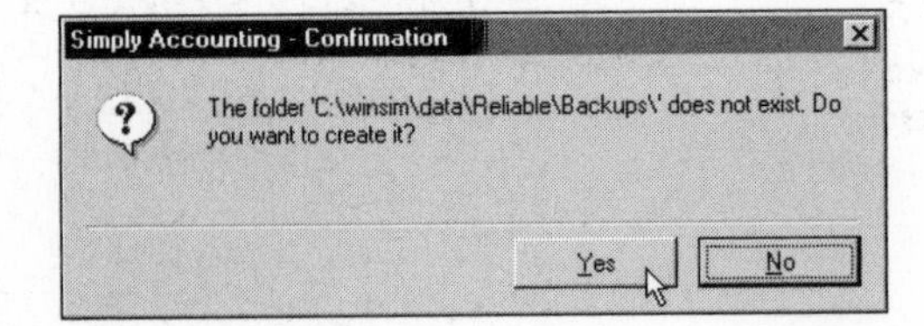

The program recognizes that the name is new and offers to create the folder. If you have typed the correct location,

Click Yes to accept the information and continue.

The backup file is different from the one you create by copying or using the Save As command. The Copy and Save As commands create a complete working copy of your data that you can access with the Simply Accounting program directly. Backup creates a compressed file that must first be restored before you can use it to enter transactions.

notes

If your working files are lost or damaged, you can restore the backup files by choosing Restore from backup from the Select Company opening window. Follow the on-screen instructions to locate the backup and choose a file name for the restored data files.

After a brief interval, you will see the following message that the backup is complete:

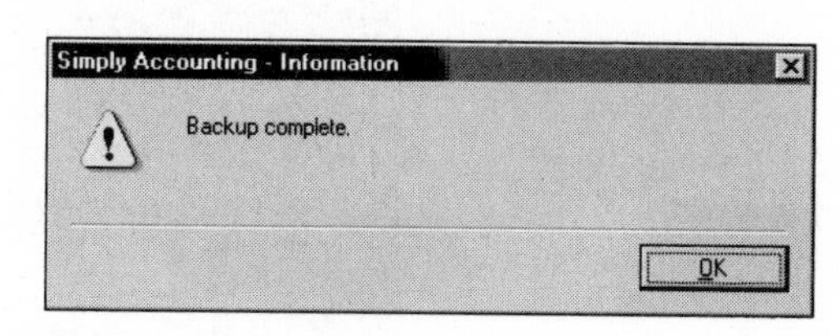

Click OK to proceed to the Change Session Date dialogue box with the current session date highlighted:

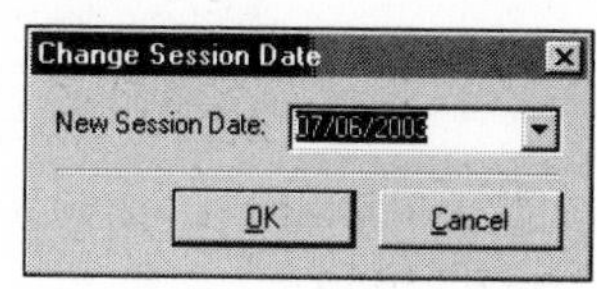

Type `07-13-03`

Click OK to accept the new date. You may now enter the remaining transactions for this exercise.

Displaying General Reports

notes

When the Accounts window is open, all General Reports are available from the Reports menu. Click the Accounts icon in the Home window to open the Accounts window.

A key advantage to using Simply Accounting rather than a manual system is the ability to produce financial reports quickly for any date or time period. Reports that are provided for a specific date, such as the Balance Sheet, can be produced for any date from the time the accounting records were converted to the computerized system up to the most recent session date. Reports that summarize a financial period, such as the income statement, can be produced for any period between the beginning of the fiscal period and the session date.

Displaying the Balance Sheet

notes

- When you are entering a transaction, the only report available is the review of the transaction being entered.
- The Home window Reports menu shows only the General Ledger reports because the other ledgers are hidden.

You can display the Balance Sheet at any time except when you are entering a transaction. In the Home window,

Choose the **Reports menu**, then **choose** (point to) **Financials** and **click Balance Sheet** as shown:

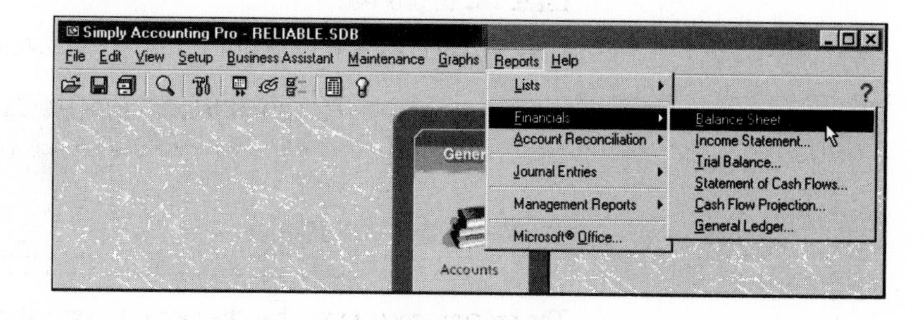

Your screen now includes the following Balance Sheet Options window:

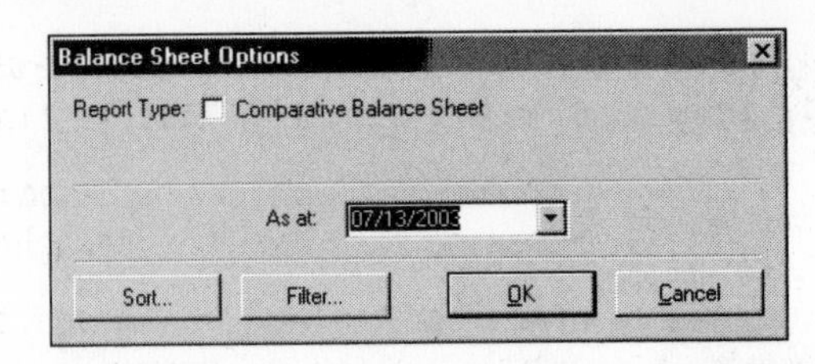

One option is to show the balance sheet for two different dates at the same time, the Comparative Balance Sheet.

Click Comparative Balance Sheet to select this style of report and expand the report options as follows:

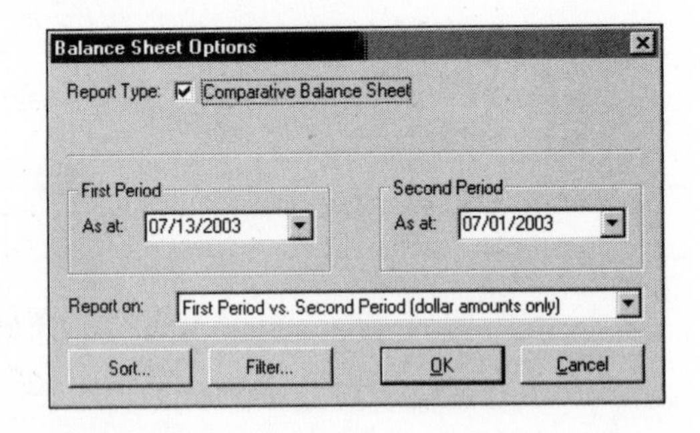

notes

- If you want a single Balance Sheet only, do not click Comparative Balance Sheet (the check box does not have a ✔ in it). Your most recent session date is displayed by default and highlighted. Choose from the list of dates or type in the date you want. Click OK to display the Balance Sheet.
- If you have accounting data for more than one fiscal period, you can display reports for the previous period as well as for the current period.

Your most recent session date is displayed in the first date field. The second date is the date on which the files were converted to Simply Accounting. Press tab to highlight the first date if you want to change it. If you click ▼, the list arrow to the right of the Date (As at) field, you can see the range of dates that you can choose for the Balance Sheet. Choose from this list or type the date you want using one of the accepted formats given earlier.

Press tab

Type the second date or choose from the list.

Click the **Report on field** to display the report types in the drop-down list as shown:

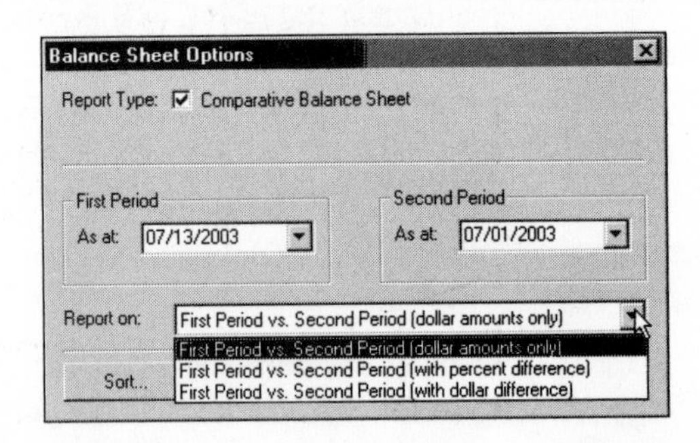

Choose dollar amounts if you want only the dollar balances for both dates. Choose with percent difference if you want the dollar balances as well as the percentage increase from the second, earlier period amount to the first; choose with dollar difference if you want the dollar balances together with the difference between them in dollars. The second period amount is subtracted from the first to calculate the difference.

Click the **report contents** you want.

Click OK to display the Balance Sheet.

Click ☒ when you have finished to return to the screen or window you were last working with.

Displaying the Trial Balance

> **notes**
>
> The Trial Balance is also available as a comparative report with the same options as the Balance Sheet. Click Comparative Trial Balance, enter the first and second dates, choose the report contents from the Report on list and click OK.

You can display the Trial Balance at any time while working with the software, except when you are actually entering a transaction.

Choose the **Reports menu**, then choose **Financials** and click **Trial Balance**. The session date is once again highlighted.

Type the date for which you want the Trial Balance or choose from the options given with the drop-down list arrow.

Click OK to display the Trial Balance.

Click ☒ to leave the display and return to the previous screen or window.

Displaying the Income Statement

You can view the Income Statement at any time, except when you are actually entering a transaction.

Choose the **Reports menu**, then **choose Financials** and **click Income Statement** to display the Income Statement Options window with Start and Finish date fields:

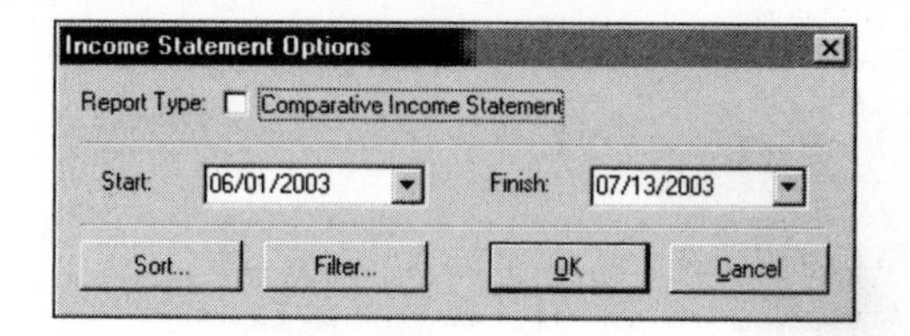

> **notes**
>
> Later applications use comparative statements for analysis purposes.

The Income Statement also has a comparative report option, allowing comparisons between two different periods. You might want to compare the income for two different months, quarters or years. For the comparative report content, you have the same amount and difference options as for the Balance Sheet.

Click Comparative Income Statement to select this option.

By default, the beginning of the fiscal period and the current session date are provided as the start and finish dates (for both periods if you have selected the comparative report). You must enter the beginning and ending dates for the period (or periods) you want your Income Statement to cover. Again, you may choose one of the dates offered from the drop-down list or you may type in the dates.

Type the date on which your Income Statement period begins.

Press tab

Type the date on which your Income Statement period ends.

Type the start and finish dates for the second period and choose the report content if your report is comparative.

Click OK

Close the display window when you have finished.

Displaying the General Ledger Report

You can display the General Ledger at any time unless you are entering a transaction.

Choose the **Reports menu**, then **choose Financials** and **click General Ledger** to display the following report options:

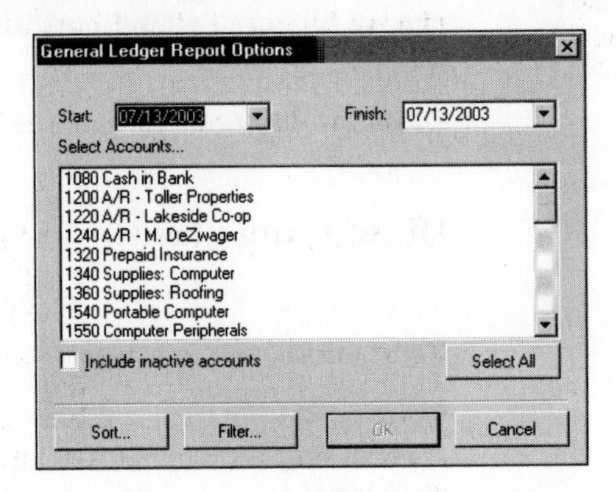

Type the starting date for your General Ledger report, or choose a date from the drop-down list selections.

Press tab

Type the ending date for your General Ledger report.

Click the account or press and hold ctrl and click the accounts you want to display. Use the scroll arrows to see more accounts if the one you want is not visible. If you want to include all accounts in the display, **click Select All**.

Click OK to view the report.

Close the display window when you have finished viewing it.

notes

To select more than one account from the list, press and hold ctrl and click the accounts you want. To select several accounts in a row, click the first one and then press shift and click the last one you want to include in the list.

Tool Bar Display Button

The Display button on the tool bar provides a shortcut to displaying reports that are related directly to ledger and journal icons in the Home window. These include lists related to the ledgers such as the Chart of Accounts, and customer, vendor and employee lists as well as all journal reports. The Display button works in three different ways.

1. If a ledger or journal icon is highlighted or selected but not open, the report for that item or its options window is displayed immediately when you click the Display button.
2. If no icon is highlighted, clicking the Display button produces the Select Report window that lists all journal reports and ledger lists. Click the list arrow and choose from this list. Click Select to display the report or its options window.
3. When the Accounts window is open, clicking the Display button provides a Select a Report window that lists all the reports for the General Ledger. Click the list arrow and choose from this list to display the report or its options window. From other ledger windows, the report list will include the reports related to that ledger.

Displaying the Chart of Accounts

Right-click the **Accounts icon** to select it.

Click the **Display button** on the tool bar or **choose** the **Reports menu,** then **choose Lists** and **click Chart of Accounts**. The report will be displayed immediately.

Close the display when you have finished.

notes

The label for the Display button changes to name the report for a selected icon.

Displaying the General Journal

Right-click the **General icon** 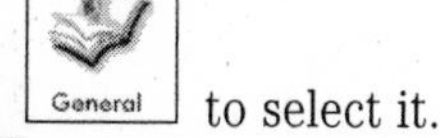 to select it.

Click the **Display button** on the tool bar or **choose** the **Reports menu,** then **choose Journal Entries** and **click General**. The following report options will be displayed:

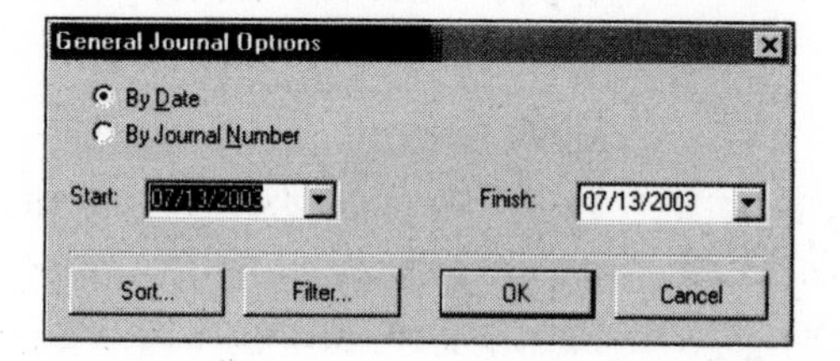

All report options windows include Sort and Filter buttons, although not all reports may be sorted and filtered. Sorting changes the order in which data are presented, while filtering selects the records to include in the report according to the data fields used as selection criteria. Journal reports may be filtered and sorted. We will first sort the journal according to the transaction date.

notes

When a report is displayed, you can sort or filter it by clicking the Sort and Filter tools (Versions 8.5 and Pro 8.5) or by making these choices from the Options menu.

Sorting Reports

You may display journals either by the posting date of the journal entries or by journal entry number. All reports in this workbook are requested by posting date — the default setting — so leave this option unchanged.

notes

When you choose By Journal Number, you must enter the first and last numbers for the entries you want to display. If you do not know the journal numbers, the posting date method is easier. Furthermore, your journal entry numbers might not match the ones we use if you have made any additional or correcting journal entries.

The latest session date is given by default for the period of the report because normally a business will print journal reports each day as part of the audit trail. The starting date is highlighted for editing.

Type `07-01` (to enter the Start date for the journal entries you want to print)

Accept July 13 as the ending date for your journal report. (You can edit this date to any date between the fiscal start and the last journal entry, including postdated entries.)

Click Sort to open the Sort Report window:

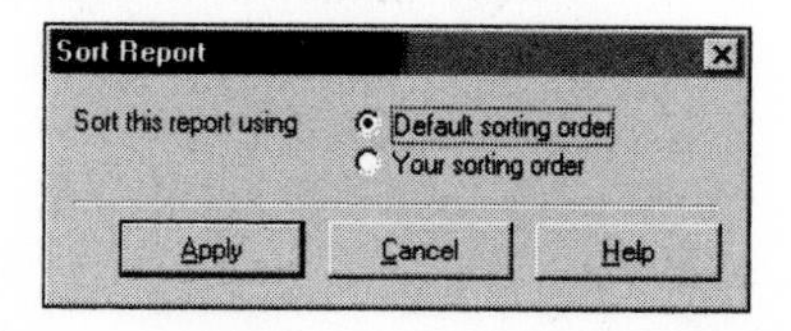

Click Your sorting order to expand the window and see the report options.

Click the first **Sort by field list arrow** to see the criteria that you may select:

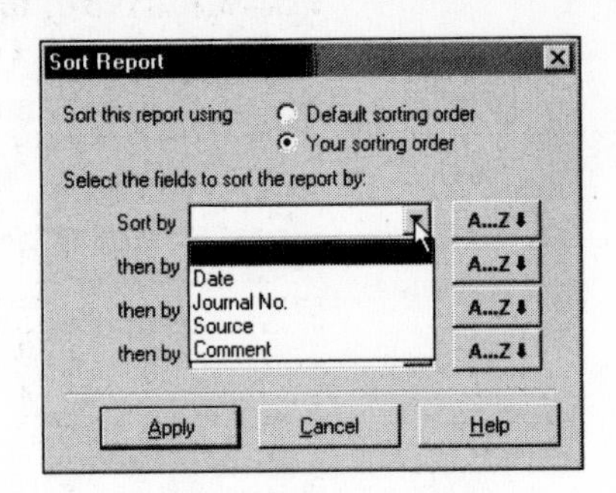

You can sort by four criteria for each report, applying each one in order. For journals, you may choose to sort by date, by journal entry number, by source number or by comment. The sorting is by chronological or alphanumeric order. You can also reverse the order with the A...Z button.

To display the journal report with the most recent entries first,

Click Date from the first Sort by field list.

Click A...Z beside this field. The button label changes to Z...A.

Click Apply to return to the General Journal Options window.

Click OK to see the report with the new order. The July 13 transactions are listed first and the July 2 transactions are at the end of the report. The sorting criteria remain in effect until you remove them or change them.

Close the display when you have finished.

To restore the default order, click the Display tool again (the General icon should still be selected), click Sort and then click Default sorting order. To remove your selection, click Date in the Sort by field and then click the blank entry at the top of the list. Click Z...A to restore the normal order. Click Default sorting order and then click Apply. You cannot delete the criteria by pressing del.

Close the display when you have finished.

Filtering Reports

To filter the report, **click** the **Display tool** again to see the General Journal Options window.

version 8

Click Filter to access the Report Filter screen:

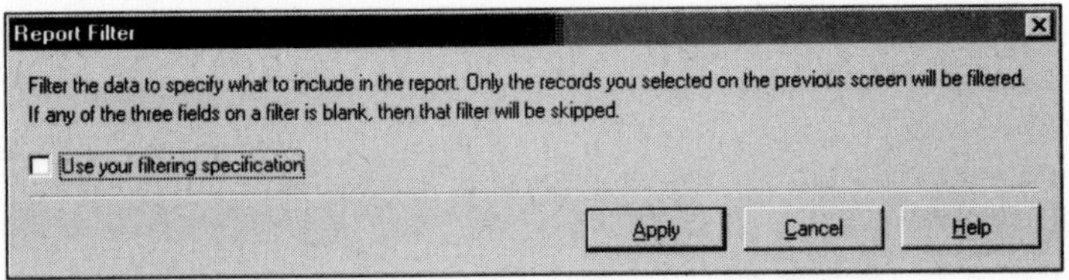

Click Use your filtering specification to access the filter options:

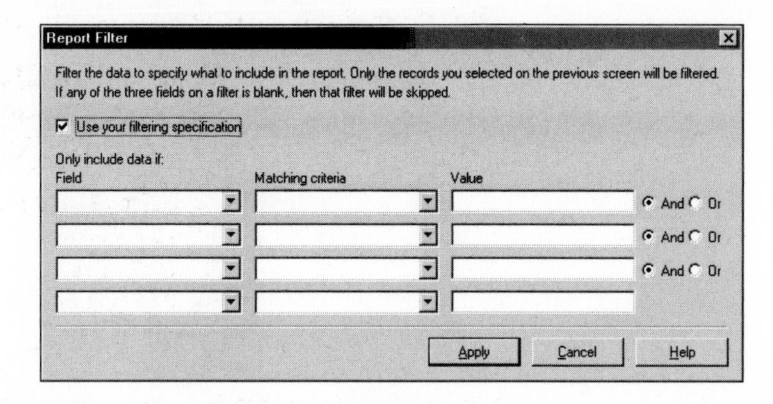

Journal reports may be filtered by the same criteria or fields you use for sorting. For each criterion, you must enter the matching criteria (greater than, equal to or less than, starting character, etc.) and a value for comparison. You can add three more criteria for the report, selecting And if you want the data to meet both criteria at the same time. Choose Or if you want to include data that meet either criterion. For example, the following steps will generate a report with only sales invoices (if you began the Source with RR... for these entries).

Click the first **Field list arrow** and **choose Source**.

Choose Starts with from the Matching criteria drop-down list.

Click the **Value field**.

Type RR

Click Apply to return to the General Journal Options screen.

Choose 07/01/2003 from the Start field drop-down list.

Click OK to see the report of sales entries. (If any other source documents began with RR, they will also be included.)

Close the display when you have finished.

The filters will remain in effect so you should remove them. Click the Display tool. Click Filter. Click Source and then click the blank at the top of the Field list. Click Starts with and then click the blank at the top of this list. Double click RR in the Value field and press del. Click Use your filtering specification to remove the checkmark. Click Apply. Click OK to see the normal journal reports. Close the display when you have finished.

Displaying Management Reports

Management reports provide accounting information that is specific to the company data file. When the other ledgers are used, the menu also includes management reports for these ledgers.

Choose the **Reports menu,** then **choose Management Reports** and **click General** to see the display of available reports:

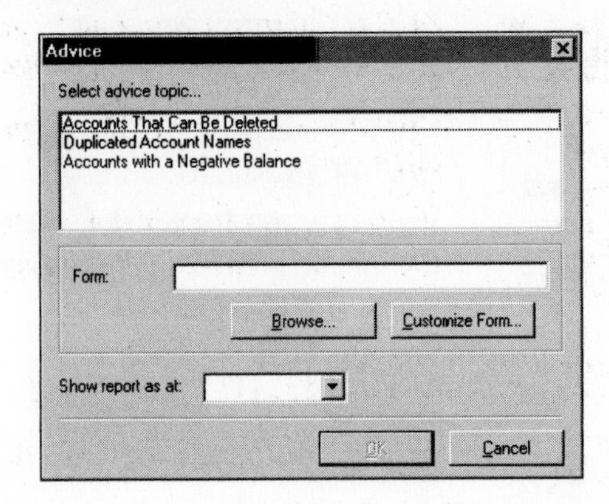

To see a report, click a topic to select it. The date field may de dimmed, depending on the topic selected. If it is not, type the date for the report in the Show report as at field. The program will select a default report form from the ones you installed with the program. Generally this is the best choice. You can click Browse to see other report forms available and select the one you need. If you have the appropriate software program, you may customize the report form. Click OK to display the report.

For example, click the advice topic Accounts with a Negative Balance. Click OK. Your report should include the *GST Paid on Purchases* and the *A. Dresden, Drawings* accounts because these contra-accounts normally have negative balances.

Close the display when you have finished.

Drill-Down Reports

notes

When the other ledgers are used, detailed customer, vendor and employee reports are also available from the General Ledger Report and from the General Journal.

notes

Transactions by Account is the non-accounting term for the General Ledger Report. Refer to Appendix E for a complete list of non-accounting terms.

Some reports can be accessed from other reports that you have opened or displayed. These are cross-referenced or drill-down reports.

Whenever the pointer changes to (a magnifying glass icon with a plus sign inside it) the additional reports can be displayed. As you move the mouse pointer over various items in the first report, the type of second report available may change. The name of the second report will appear in the status bar. Double click while the magnifying glass icon is visible to display the second report immediately. The first report stays open in the background.

The General Ledger Report is always named Transactions by Account in the status bar drill-down message. The General Ledger Report for a specific account can be accessed from the Balance Sheet, Income Statement, Trial Balance, Chart of Accounts or General Journal when you double click an account number, name or balance amount. The General Ledger record for an account can be accessed from the General Ledger Report.

While you have the additional drill-down report displayed, you may print it or drill down to additional reports. (See Printing General Reports on the next page.)

Close the second report and then close the first report when you have finished viewing them.

Printing General Reports

Display the report you want to print by following the instructions in the previous section on Displaying General Reports.

Click the **Print tool** or **choose** the **File menu** in the report window then **click** **Print**.

Printing begins immediately. Wait for the printing information displayed to clear from the screen, then close the displayed report.

notes

If the printer you need is not selected, minimize the report, then choose the Setup menu and click Reports & Forms. Be sure that the Reports tab is selected because you can choose different printers for different printing needs. Click the printer name to see the available printers. Click the one you need. You can change the font (typeface) and font size as well as the report margins in this window. Click OK and then restore your report.

Graphing General Reports

Graphs are available only from the Home window.

Expenses and Net Profits as % of Revenue

Choose the **Graphs menu,** then **click** **Expenses and Net Profit as % of Revenue** to display the following report options:

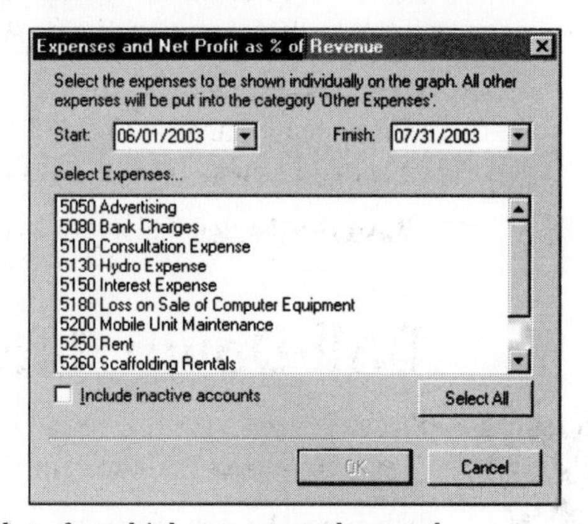

Type the beginning date for which you want the graph.

Press tab

Type the ending date of the period for your graph.

Press ctrl and **click** **each expense account you want included in the graph** or **click** **Select All** to include all the accounts in the graph.

Click **OK**

The graph will be displayed. The pie chart graph shown here, including all accounts for the period from June 1 to July 31, is a form of the Income Statement:

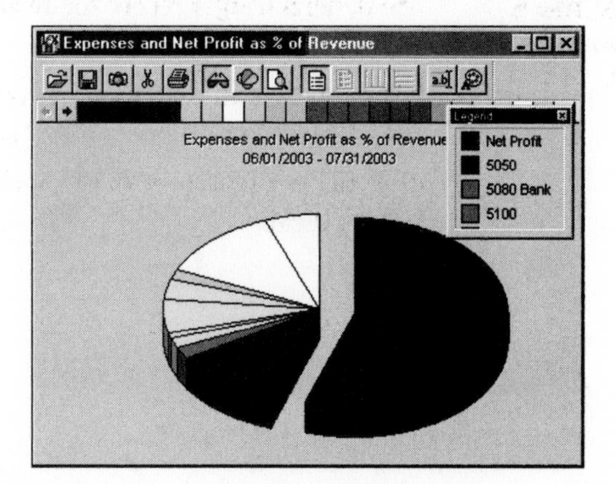

notes

- Double click a portion of the graph to see the name of the account, the dollar amount and the percentage of the total.
- Double click the legend to make it larger and to add the account names. Double click the expanded legend to reduce it.
- Right-click the legend title to view a set of options for positioning the legend on the graph page. To move the legend to the new position, click the new legend position option. Double click the legend to restore the original size and position.

You have several options regarding the graph at this stage. The tool bar options are the same for all graphs. By selecting the appropriate button on the tool bar, you can import a graph, export the displayed graph, copy it to the clipboard as a bitmap or a text file, print the graph, change the view from 3-D to 2-D, hide the legend, edit or add titles, etc. Hold the mouse pointer over a tool button for a few seconds to see a brief description of the tool's purpose. Most tool buttons lead to an additional option or control window requiring your input.

In addition, you can change colours by dragging the colour you want to the pie section you want to change; expand or shrink the legend by dragging its bottom border down or up respectively; or pull out a section of the pie chart by dragging it away from the rest of the chart. The graph displayed has the Net Profit portion pulled out for emphasis.

Close the graph when you have finished.

Revenues by Account

Choose the **Graphs menu,** then **click Revenues by Account** to display the following report options:

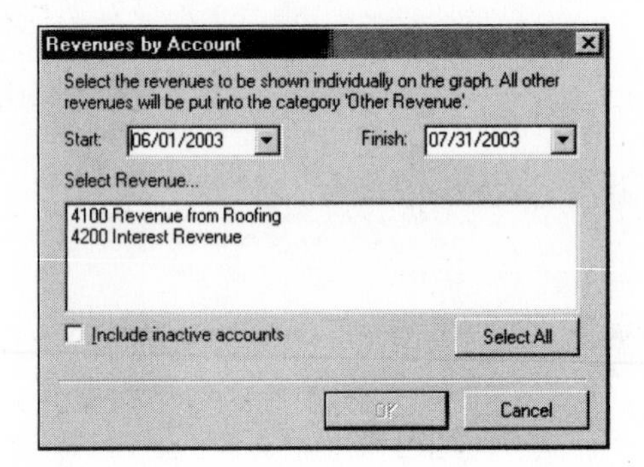

Type the beginning date for which you want the graph.

Press *tab*

Type the ending date of the period for your graph.

Press *ctrl* and **click each revenue account you want included in the graph** or **click Select All** to include all the accounts in the graph.

Click OK to display the pie chart graph as shown:

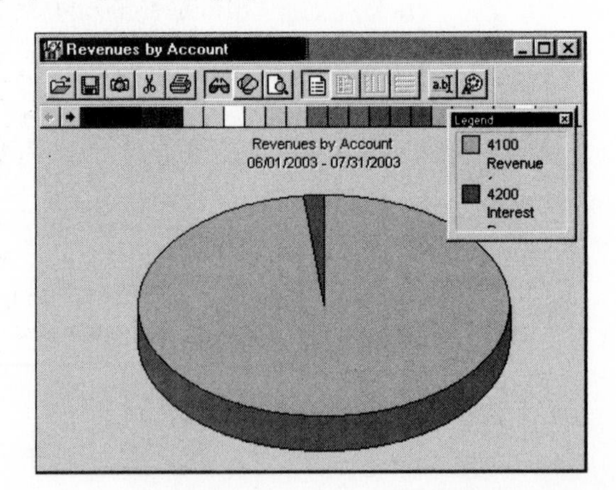

The pie chart graph has each revenue account represented by a different piece of the pie. You can see that most of the revenue comes from roofing work.

You have the same options for the graph as you did for the Expenses and Net Profit as % of Revenue.

Close the graph when you have finished.

Expenses by Account

Choose the **Graphs menu,** then **click Expenses by Account** to display the following report options:

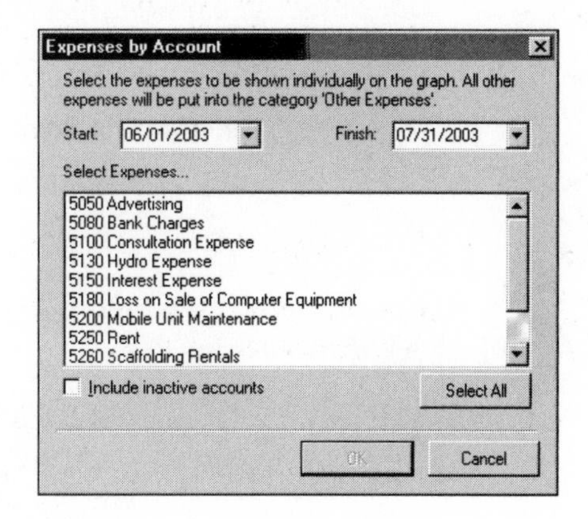

Type the beginning date for which you want the graph.

Press tab

Type the ending date of the period for your graph.

Press ctrl and **click each expense account you want included in the graph** or **click Select All** to include all the accounts in the graph.

Click OK to see the pie chart graph:

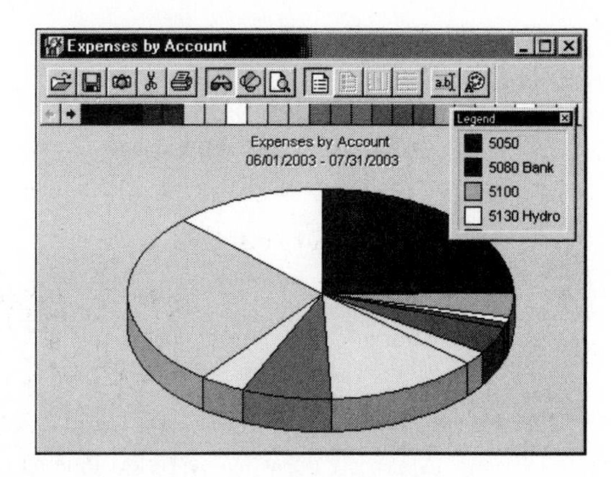

Each expense account that was selected is represented as a separate piece of the pie. The accounts not selected are grouped together in the Other category. The expenses graph makes it easy to identify at a glance the items that make up the largest share of expenses.

Close the graph when finished.

Finishing a Session

notes

Alternatively, you could choose the File menu and click Exit to close the program.

Finish the last transaction you are working on for this session.

Click ☒ to close the transaction window (such as journal input or display) to return to the Home window.

Click ☒ to close the Home window. The Simply Accounting program will automatically save your work when you finish your session and exit properly.

Click Start in the Windows opening screen.

Click Shut Down

Be sure that the option to Shut Down the Computer is selected.

Click OK to confirm your intention to turn off the computer.

CASE PROBLEMS

Case One

At the end of March 2003, after paying several bills, Dresden completed the following manual journal entries to record the transactions (cheque numbers are in brackets):

Date	Ref.	Accounts	Debit	Credit
Mar. 31	rent (#434)	Expenses	800.00	
		GST	56.00	
		Bank		856.00
Mar. 31	hydro (#435)	Expenses	100.00	
		GST	7.00	
		Bank		107.00
Mar. 31	telephone (#436)	Expenses	90.00	
		GST	6.30	
		Bank		96.30
Mar. 31	printer cable (#437)	Supplies	20.00	
		GST	1.40	
		Bank		21.40
Mar. 31	rewritable CDs (#437)	Supplies	40.00	
		GST	2.80	
		Bank		42.80

Manually show the detailed journal entries that record these transactions as they would appear in a Simply Accounting journal report. (You may want to print a General Journal Report for reference to see the details that Simply Accounting provides.)

How is the Simply Accounting method of entering journal transactions different from the manual accounting procedures? What are the advantages of using Simply Accounting?

Case Two

notes

- You will need to create the following new Group accounts to complete these realistic source documents:
  - 5180 Loss on Sale of Computer Equipment
  - 5100 Consultation Expense
  - 2180 A/P - InfraRed Diagnostics
  - 5260 Scaffolding Rentals
  - 2185 A/P - Prairie Roof Equipment
  - 1250 A/R - Premier Ballet School
  - 5300 Supplies Used

Enter the following source documents using the General Journal in Simply Accounting. Advance the session date to July 20, July 27 and July 31 as required.

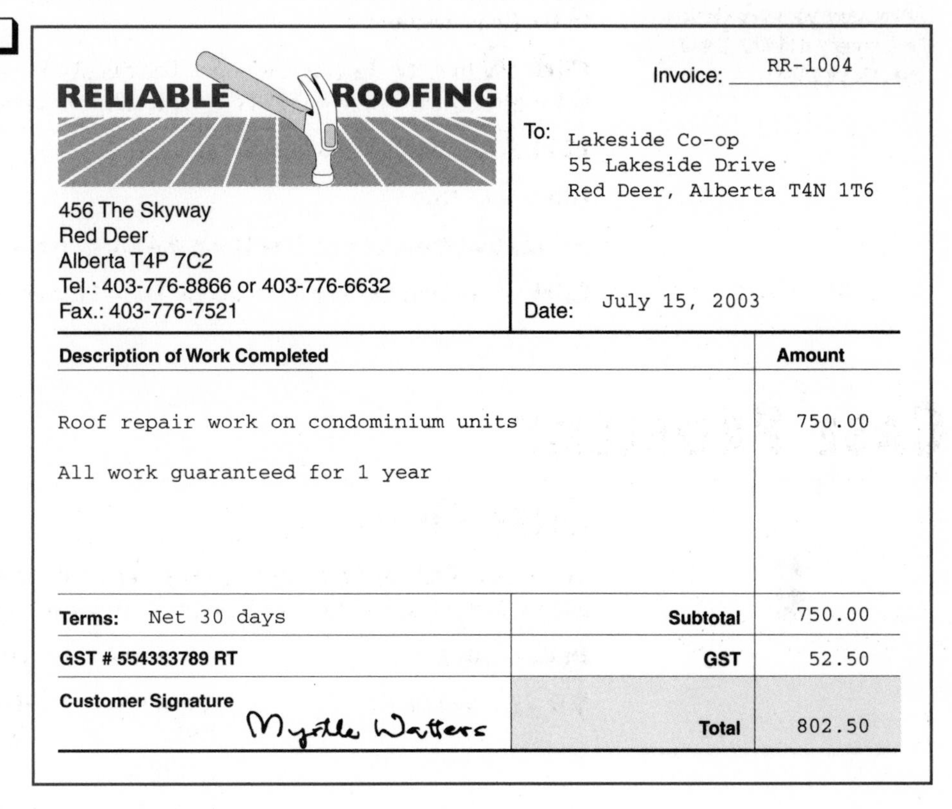

RELIABLE ROOFING

456 The Skyway
Red Deer
Alberta T4P 7C2
Tel.: 403-776-8866 or 403-776-6632
Fax.: 403-776-7521

Invoice: RR-1004

To: Lakeside Co-op
55 Lakeside Drive
Red Deer, Alberta T4N 1T6

Date: July 15, 2003

Description of Work Completed	Amount
Roof repair work on condominium units	750.00
All work guaranteed for 1 year	

Terms: Net 30 days	Subtotal	750.00
GST # 554333789 RT	GST	52.50
Customer Signature: Myrtle Watters	Total	802.50

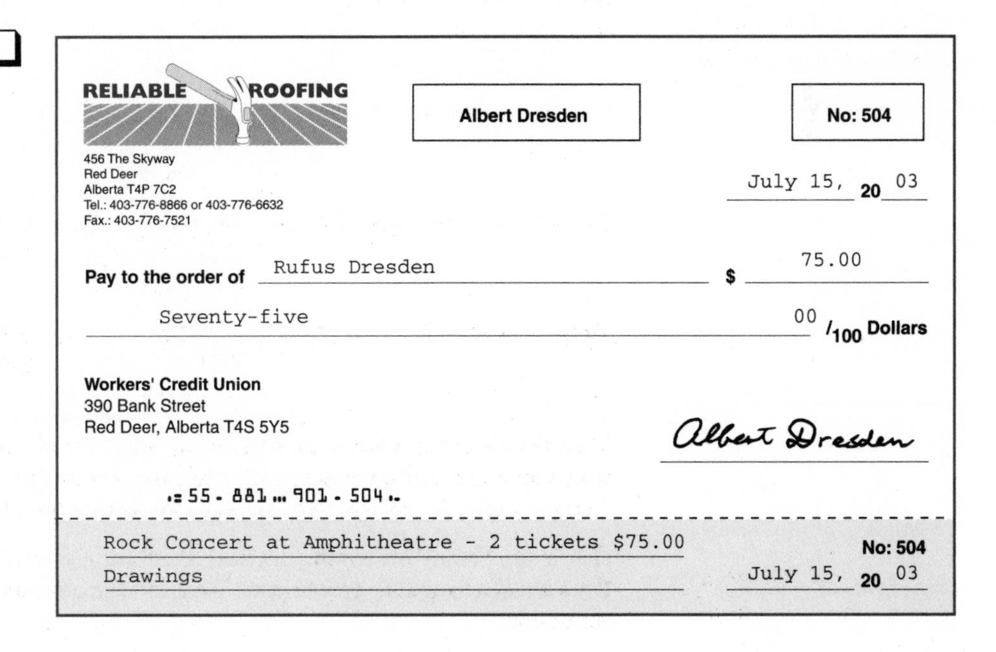

RELIABLE ROOFING

456 The Skyway
Red Deer
Alberta T4P 7C2
Tel.: 403-776-8866 or 403-776-6632
Fax.: 403-776-7521

Albert Dresden

No: 504

July 15, 20 03

Pay to the order of Rufus Dresden $ 75.00

Seventy-five 00/100 Dollars

Workers' Credit Union
390 Bank Street
Red Deer, Alberta T4S 5Y5

Albert Dresden

⑆55-881⑈901-504⑆

Rock Concert at Amphitheatre - 2 tickets $75.00
Drawings

No: 504
July 15, 20 03

notes

Remember that the book value of the old computer was $800.

❑

Student Credit Union
110 College Street
Red Deer
Alberta T4P 4T7

No: 250

July 16, **20** 03

Pay to the order of Reliable Roofing **$** 500.00

Five hundred 00 /100 **Dollars**

Lynn Roth
McKinley Hall, U of C
Calgary, Alberta T1Y 5H6

Lynn Roth

⑆ 449-7 ⑈ 8811-250 ⑈

Purchase used portable computer from
Reliable Roofing for $500

No: 250

July 16, **20** 03

❑

InfraRed Diagnostics
340 Rouge Valley Road
Red Deer
Alberta T4R 9J1
Tel.: 403-465-1751
Fax.: 403-465-1755

No: ID 61086

To: Reliable Roofing
456 The Skyway
Red Deer
Alberta T4P 7C2

Date: July 17, 2003

Description of Service	**Amount**
Roof consultation on building requiring roof work. Use of infra-red heat-seeking device to estimate thermal efficiency.	300.00
Terms: Cash on Receipt — **Subtotal**	300.00
GST # 561066631 RT	21.00
Signature Albert Dresden — **Total**	321.00

❑

RELIABLE ROOFING

456 The Skyway
Red Deer
Alberta T4P 7C2
Tel.: 403-776-8866 or 403-776-6632
Fax.: 403-776-7521

Albert Dresden

No: 505

July 18, 20 03

Pay to the order of InfraRed Diagnostics $ 321.00

Three hundred twenty-one 00/100 Dollars

Workers' Credit Union
390 Bank Street
Red Deer, Alberta T4S 5Y5

Albert Dresden

⑈55-881⑈901-505⑈

InfraRed Diagnostics - Consultation Service
roof consultation $300 + $21 GST

No: 505
July 18, 20 03

❑

Dominion Building Supplies

800 Ash Avenue, Red Deer, Alberta T4N 4V2. Tel: 403-349-5176 Fax: 403-344-5910

No: DBS 9541 Date: July 18, 2003

Sold To:

Reliable Roofing
456 The Skyway
Red Deer
Alberta T4P 7C2

Deliver to:

same

Deliver Date:

Customer pick up

Qty	Description	Amount
	Roofing supplies	400.00
Terms: 2/15, Net 30	**Subtotal**	400.00
GST # 461877290	**GST**	28.00
Signed Albert Dresden	**Total**	428.00

❑

Summit Scaffold

56 Hilife Cres., Red Deer, Alberta T4S 8B5 Tel:(403)752-8861 Fax:(403)752-8888

No: SS 66312 Invoice Date: July 19, 2003

To:	rental period:
Reliable Roofing 456 The Skyway Red Deer Alberta T4P 7C2	July 19 - July 26

description	amt
scaffolding: frames, braces, guardposts, platforms & wheels	600.00
terms: Net 30 days — **#: 442197610** — **gst**	42.00
Customer: *Albert Dresden* — **total**	642.00

❑

Invoice: 3-61247

Date: July 22, 2003

Prairie Roof Equipment

8500 Cannon Heights, Red Deer, Alberta T4R 1P8 Tel: (403) 556-3491 Fax: (403) 556-4980

Customer: Albert Dresden - Reliable Roofing

Address: 456 The Skyway
Red Deer
Alberta T4P 7C2

Item Description	Qty	Amount
Mobile Roofing Unit Equipment	1	2100.00
Terms: Net 30 days	**Sub**	2100.00
Reg#: 410277188 RT	**GST**	147.00
Customer: *Albert Dresden*	**Total**	2247.00

❑

Lakeside Co-op
55 Lakeside Drive
Red Deer, Alberta T4N 1T6

No: 308

July 24, 20 03

Pay to the order of Reliable Roofing $ 802.50

Eight hundred two 50 /100 **Dollars**

Royalty Trust
1201 Queen Street
Red Deer, Alberta T4P 3M3

Myrtle Watters

⑆3331-3366⑈97112-308⑈

Payment of invoice # RR 99004
Reliable Roofing -$802.50

No: 308
July 24, 20 03

❑

ALBERTA HYDRO

No: 6119961

444 GENERATOR COURT, RED DEER, ALBERTA T4R 1S7

Account: 2290 000 91000 1 Statement Date: July 25, 2003

Reliable Roofing
456 The Skyway, Red Deer, Alberta T4P 7C2

Description	**Billing Period**	**Rate/KwH**	**Energy Consumption**	**Amount**
Minimum Business rate	20/05-20/07			60.00
GST (#220876177)				4.20
			Total due	64.20
Business office: (403) 777-6193			**If paid after 01/08/03**	70.20

456 The Skyway
Red Deer
Alberta T4P 7C2
Tel.: 403-776-8866 or 403-776-6632
Fax.: 403-776-7521

Invoice: RR-1005

To: Premier Ballet School
106 Classic Blvd.
Red Deer,
Alberta T4P 3L5

Date: July 26, 2003

Description of Work Completed		Amount
Replace school roof - shingle		4000.00
All work guaranteed for 5 years		
Terms: Net 30 days	Subtotal	4000.00
GST # 554333789 RT	GST	280.00
Customer Signature Nadia Kammanski	Total	4280.00

RELIABLE ROOFING
456 The Skyway
Red Deer
Alberta T4P 7C2
Tel.: 403-776-8866 or 403-776-6632
Fax.: 403-776-7521

Albert Dresden

No: 506

July 26, 20 03

Pay to the order of Alberta Hydro $ 64.20

Sixty-four 20 /100 Dollars

Workers' Credit Union
390 Bank Street
Red Deer, Alberta T4S 5Y5

Albert Dresden

⑆55-881⑈901-506⑈

Alberta Hydro $64.20
Hydro expense (ref#6119961)

No: 506
July 26, 20 03

❑

RELIABLE ROOFING

456 The Skyway
Red Deer
Alberta T4P 7C2
Tel.: 403-776-8866 or 403-776-6632
Fax.: 403-776-7521

Albert Dresden

No: 507

July 30, 20 03

Pay to the order of Sal Skywalker $ 500.00

Five hundred 00/100 Dollars

Workers' Credit Union
390 Bank Street
Red Deer, Alberta T4S 5Y5

Albert Dresden

⑆55 - 881 ⑈ 901 - 507 ⑆

Sal Skywalker re: wages $500
Assist-Premier Ballet School

No: 507
July 30, 20 03

❑

Bank Debit Memo
8319

Workers' Credit Union
390 Bank Street
Red Deer, Alberta T4S 5Y5

July 31, 2003

Account 55 881 901
Reliable Roofing
456 The Skyway, Red Deer, Alberta T4P 7C2

Particulars

Interest charged on outstanding loan $80.00

Authorization: Jim Yu

❑

MEMO

From: A. Dresden
Date: July 31/03

Roofing supplies used for work completed in July were valued at $2 100. This amount should be charged to expense account, 5300 Supplies Used. Asset account 1360 Supplies: Roofing should be reduced (credited) by this amount.

CHAPTER FOUR

OBJECTIVES

After completing this chapter, you should be able to

- *open* the General and Payables journals
- *enter* vendor-related purchase transactions
- *enter* vendor-related payment transactions
- *enter* partial payments to vendors
- *enter* cash purchase transactions
- *store* recurring purchase transactions
- *add* a new vendor account
- *edit* and *review* transactions in the journals
- *recall*, *use* and *edit* stored purchase transactions
- *place* and *fill* purchase orders and quotes
- *post* transactions in each of the journals
- *adjust* purchase invoices after posting
- *understand* Payables Ledger linked accounts
- *display* and *print* payables transactions and reports
- *graph* payables reports

COMPANY INFORMATION

Company Profile

Java Jean's Coffee Emporium is a small coffee and pastry shop owned and operated by Jean Yankelovich. Since opening the store two years ago, Jean has expanded her business by buying an adjacent store, using the additional space to create a seating area for about 20 customers. Situated in the busy downtown business and entertainment section of Calgary, Alberta, most of the take-out business comes from clients on their way to work, while the in-store customers enjoy the stimulating atmosphere at lunchtime or after theatre events.

Although she offers a large selection of teas and hot chocolate, Jean's specialty coffees — roasted directly in the store — and her home-baked pastries are the main sources of the Emporium's success. To provide this variety, she has fully equipped the store with coffee makers, espresso machines and cappuccino makers, as well as coffee roasting ovens and regular baking ovens. She also sells an assortment of specialty coffees in 500-gram packages and a selection of coffee mugs designed by Canadian artists.

Her latest expansion project is the outdoor patio. Sliding patio doors will connect the patio to the indoor seating area and a retractable awning will ensure that, even on most rainy days, customers can sit comfortably outdoors. She has obtained the permit and the renovations have begun.

All food and merchandise sales are cash only; weekly summary entries are made from cash register tapes. A few vendors make regular deliveries — coffee and chocolate every second week and baking supplies weekly. Jean has set up accounts with these suppliers as well as other regular vendors.

Jean employs four university students, including her eldest daughter Judy, part-time to help run the store. Judy, a business student, plans to open her own coffee emporium, Java Judy's, after she graduates next year. With her business and computer training, her experience in her mother's store and her mother's guidance, she is well prepared for the entrepreneurial experience. She is currently managing all the accounting records for the Emporium and has just finished converting the manual records to Simply Accounting using the following:

- Chart of Accounts
- Post-Closing Trial Balance
- Vendor Information
- Accounting Procedures

JAVA JEAN'S COFFEE EMPORIUM
CHART OF ACCOUNTS

ASSETS
1080 Bank Account
1220 Packaged Coffee
1240 Coffee Mugs
1260 Coffee & Chocolate
1280 Tea
1300 Baking Goods
1330 Cappuccino Maker
1350 Chairs & Tables
1370 Computerized Cash Register
1390 Coffee Makers
1410 Coffee Roasting Oven
1430 Coffee Mill/Grinder
1450 Cutlery & Dishes
1470 Espresso Machine
1490 Kitchen Equipment
1600 Coffee Emporium

LIABILITIES
2100 Bank Loan
2200 Accounts Payable
2650 GST Charged
2670 GST Paid on Capital Expenditures
2850 Mortgage Payable

EQUITY
3100 J. Yankelovich, Capital
3200 J. Yankelovich, Drawings
3600 Net Income

REVENUE
4100 Revenue from Sales

EXPENSES
5100 Baking Goods
5120 Coffee & Chocolate
5140 Cost of Goods Sold
5160 Tea
5200 Advertising & Promotion
5220 Bank Charges
5240 Hydro Expense
5260 Loan Interest Expense
5280 Maintenance & Repairs
5300 Miscellaneous Expenses
5350 Mortgage Interest
5380 Telephone Expense
5500 Wages Expense
5600 Washroom Supplies Expense

JAVA JEAN'S COFFEE EMPORIUM
POST-CLOSING TRIAL BALANCE

May 31, 2003

Account	Debit	Credit
1080 Bank Account	$10 250.00	
1220 Packaged Coffee	2 500.00	
1240 Coffee Mugs	1 500.00	
1260 Coffee & Chocolate	600.00	
1280 Tea	200.00	
1300 Baking Goods	400.00	
1330 Cappuccino Maker	800.00	
1350 Chairs & Tables	2 000.00	
1370 Computerized Cash Register	3 000.00	
1390 Coffee Makers	1 200.00	
1410 Coffee Roasting Oven	900.00	
1430 Coffee Mill/Grinder	500.00	
1450 Cutlery & Dishes	2 000.00	
1470 Espresso Machine	800.00	
1490 Kitchen Equipment	15 000.00	
1600 Coffee Emporium	50 000.00	
2100 Bank Loan		$ 5 000.00
2200 Accounts Payable		3 700.00
2650 GST Charged		700.00
2670 GST Paid on Capital Expenditures	210.00	
2850 Mortgage Payable		45 000.00
3100 J. Yankelovich, Capital		37 460.00
	$91 860.00	$91 860.00

JAVA JEAN'S COFFEE EMPORIUM
VENDOR INFORMATION

Vendor Name (Contact)	Address	Phone No. Fax No.	Terms
AA Cleaning Services (Katie Klenzer)	10 Bleech Circle Calgary, AB T2M 7Y1	Tel: 712-5611 Fax: 712-6481	n/1 (Pay on Receipt of Invoice)
Alberta Telephone (Kiepa Tokkin)	556 Connexion Blvd. Calgary, AB T2P 1X2	Tel: 834-7120 Fax: 834-7668	n/1
Baking Supplies Wholesalers (Alix Fuda)	7 Cherry Lane Calgary, AB T2R 6B2	Tel: 611-4423 Fax: 611-6892	n/15
Blue Mountain Mugs (Art Isan)	699 Pottery Rd. Beaumont, AB T4X 4V3	Tel: 403-779-6188	n/30
Ceylon Tea Co. (Bev Ridges)	200 Tannin Ave. Vancouver, BC V5L 4L8	Tel: 1-800-662-8619	n/15
Columbia House (Lax Kaffine)	111 Rue Hautbois Montreal, PQ H6T 9B2	Tel: 1-800-552-9641	n/30
Equipment Suppliers	28 Coolcrest Rd. Calgary, AB T2G 8N8	Tel: 529-7624 Fax: 529-8261	n/30
International Coffee (I. M. Porter)	688 Colonial Ct. Halifax, NS B3R 7Y1	Tel: 1-800-618-6173	n/30

JAVA JEAN'S COFFEE EMPORIUM
VENDOR INFORMATION CONTINUED

Vendor Name (Contact)	Address	Phone No. Fax No.	Terms
Maintenance Services Inc. (Ken Fixet)	92 Carpenter St. Calgary, AB T2S 2R3	Tel: 881-8811 Fax: 719-7700	n/30
Western Hydro (Les Power)	45 Uranium Cres. Calgary, AB T3P 3X1	Tel: 771-9911 Fax: 778-8800	n/1

JAVA JEAN'S COFFEE EMPORIUM
OUTSTANDING VENDOR INVOICES

Vendor Name	Date	Inv/Chq No.	Terms	Amount	Total
Baking Supplies Wholesalers	05/26/03	BS-1121	n/15	$200.00	$200.00
Blue Mountain Mugs	05/25/03	BM-411	n/30	$800.00	$800.00
Columbia House	05/06/03	CH-505	n/30	$450.00	
	05/20/03	CH-512	n/30	$450.00	
			Balance		$900.00
Equipment Suppliers	05/05/03	ES-133	n/30	$1 800.00	
	05/05/03	CHQ#623	Payment	–$1 000.00	
	05/31/03	ES-169	n/30	$1 000.00	
			Balance		$1 800.00
			Grand Total		$3 700.00

Accounting Procedures

The Goods and Services Tax (GST)

Java Jean's uses the **quick method** for calculating and remitting the GST. All items sold in the café are priced to include GST, and a sign is posted so that customers are aware that they are paying GST. At the end of each quarter, a flat tax rate of 5 percent on revenue from sales will be calculated and charged to *GST Charged*. This flat rate GST liability to the Receiver General is reduced by any GST paid to vendors on capital expenditures, such as equipment, cash registers, capital improvements to the emporium, and furniture and fixtures. These amounts are input tax credits recorded in *GST Paid on Capital Expenditures*. GST paid on supplies and services is not included as a decrease in the GST liability to the Receiver General under the quick method. GST is included in the purchase price for these non-capital items. Java Jean's *GST Owing (Refund)* subgroup total account shows the amount of GST that is to be remitted to the Receiver General of Canada on the last day of each quarter. (For details please read Chapter 2 on the Goods and Services Tax.)

Open-Invoice Accounting for Payables

The open-invoice method of accounting for invoices issued to a business allows a business to keep track of each individual invoice and partial payment made against the invoice. This is in contrast to methods that keep track only of the outstanding balance by combining all invoice balances owed to a vendor. Simply Accounting uses the open-invoice method. When an invoice is fully paid, you can either retain the invoice or remove (clear) it.

notes

- In some source documents that follow, such as purchase invoices for non-capital expenditures and cash receipts from cash register tapes, GST is included in the total amount. Do not record GST separately for these source documents.
- Beverages and food items are zero-rated goods.
- Most bank and other financial institution services are exempt from GST charges. Bank payroll services are subject to GST charges.
- Provincial sales tax is not levied in Alberta. It will be introduced in a later application.

Purchase of Inventory Items
Inventory items purchased are immediately recorded in the appropriate inventory or supplies asset account. The items in stock are also manually recorded on inventory cards for periodic updating.

Cost of Goods Sold
Periodically, the food inventory on hand is counted. The manager then calculates the cost price of the inventory or food supplies sold and issues a memo to reduce the inventory or supplies asset account and to charge the cost price to the corresponding expense account. For example, at the end of each month, the *Coffee & Chocolate* asset account (*1260*) is reduced (credited) and the *Coffee & Chocolate* expense account (*5120*) is increased (debited) by the cost price of the amount sold.

INSTRUCTIONS

1. Using the Chart of Accounts, Trial Balance, Vendor Information and Accounting Procedures for Java Jean's, enter the source documents for the month of June using Simply Accounting. The procedures for entering each new type of transaction for this application are outlined step by step in the keystroke section following the source documents. These transactions have a ✔ in the check box and below the box is the page number where the related keystrokes begin.
2. Print the reports and graphs indicated on the printing form below after you have completed your entries. Instructions for reports begin on page 102.

REPORTS

Lists
- ☐ Chart of Accounts
- ☐ Vendors

Financials
- ☐ Balance Sheet
- ☑ Income Statement
  from June 1 to June 30
- ☑ Trial Balance
  date: June 30
- ☑ General Ledger
  accounts: 1300 4100 5100
  from June 1 to June 30

Mailing Labels
- ☐ Labels

Journals
- ☐ All Journals
- ☑ General (by posting date)
  from June 1 to June 30
- ☑ Purchases (by posting date)
  from June 1 to June 30
- ☑ Payments (by posting date)
  from June 1 to June 30

Payables
- ☑ Vendor Aged
  Detail Report for June 30
- ☐ Aged Overdue Payables
- ☐ Pending Purchase Orders

Management Reports
- ☐ Ledger

GRAPHS

- ☑ Payables by Aging Period
- ☐ Revenues by Account
- ☐ Expenses and Net Profit as % of Revenue
- ☐ Payables by Vendor
- ☐ Expenses by Account
- ☐ Current Revenue vs Last Year

SOURCE DOCUMENTS

notes

Remember that the ✔ and the number below it indicate that keystroke instructions are provided beginning on the page number shown.

SESSION DATE – June 7

✔ 79
Purchase Invoice #BS-1274
Dated June 1/03
From Baking Supplies Wholesalers, $200 for regular weekly supplies of baking goods. Terms: n/15. Store this entry because it is a recurring weekly entry.

✔ 84
Cheque Copy #638
Dated June 2/03
To Equipment Suppliers, $800 in payment of account. Reference invoice #ES-133.

✔ 87
Purchase Quote #7822
Dated June 2/03
From Outdoor Contractors (new vendor), $3 000 for granite patio stones for coffee emporium's outdoor patio, plus $210 GST Paid on Capital Expenditures. Patio stones to be shipped and installed on June 9. Purchase invoice total $3 210. Terms: net 30 days.

notes

✔ **87** Outdoor Contractors
(Contact Pierre Slate)
is located at
447 Stones Ave.
Calgary, AB T3N 8J5
Tel: 291-8907
E-mail: pslate@stonework.ca
Terms: net 30 days
Vendor collects GST

☐ Purchase Invoice #CH-601
Dated June 3/03
From Columbia House, $450 for bi-weekly purchase of coffee and hot chocolate. Store as recurring bi-weekly entry. Terms: net 30 days.

✔ 93
Purchase Order #1
Dated June 4/03
Confirmation that the patio stones will be ordered from Outdoor Contractors as described in Purchase Quote #7822. Change the quote to an order.

☐ Cheque Copy #639
Dated June 4/03
To Columbia House, $900 in payment of account. Reference invoices #CH-505 and CH-512.

☐ Cheque Copy #640
Dated June 4/03
To Blue Mountain Mugs, $400 in partial payment of account. Reference invoice #BM-411.

☐ Cheque Copy #641
Dated June 7/03
To Baking Supplies Wholesalers, $200 in payment of account. Reference invoice #BS-1121.

☐ Cash Receipt #31
Dated June 7/03
From cash register tapes (no. 3491 to 4193), $3 600 including GST collected for sale of food and merchandise. Amount deposited in bank.

notes

Enter the cash sales in the General Journal because the Receivables Ledger is not set up.

SESSION DATE – June 14

✔ 94
Purchase Invoice #BS-1396
Dated June 8/03
From Baking Supplies Wholesalers, $200 for weekly baking supplies delivery. Recall stored entry. Terms: n/15.

☑ 95
Cash Purchase: Utility Statement #WH-611
Dated June 9/03
From Western Hydro, $149.50 for hydro service including GST. Terms: cash on receipt of invoice. Issued cheque #642 in full payment.

☑ 97
Purchase Invoice #6127-OC
Dated June 9/03
Filled purchase order #1 from Outdoor Contractors, installation of granite patio stones for coffee emporium's outdoor patio completed. Purchase invoice total $3 210. Terms: net 30 days.

☑ 99
Memo #100
Dated June 10/03
From store manager, adjust invoice from Outdoor Contractors to include $200 plus $14 GST for additional services requested by store manager to complete the job.

❑ Purchase Invoice #IC-642PC
Dated June 10/03
From International Coffee, $400 for pre-packaged flavoured coffees for resale (Packaged Coffee merchandise). Terms: net 30 days.

❑ Bank Credit Memo #AT-75119
Dated June 11/03
From Alberta Trust, $5 000 loan secured for upcoming purchase of new refrigeration unit.

notes

❑ Patio Warehouse
(Contact Patti Owens)
is located at
1100 Flagstone Ct.
Calgary, AB T1P 1T2
Tel: 712-8611
www.patios.com/orders
Terms: net 30
Vendor collects GST

❑ Purchase Order #2
Dated June 12/03
From Patio Warehouse (choose Full Add for new vendor), $400 for 40 new patio chairs and $400 for 10 patio tables (Capital Expenditure: Chairs & Tables account) plus $56 GST paid. Invoice total $856. All items to be shipped on June 16. Terms: net/30.

❑ Memo #101
Dated June 13/03
From store manager, $55 cash plus coupon book to compensate customer for soiled shirt — employee spilled coffee. Charge to Miscellaneous Expenses. (Enter as Other Payment in the Payments Journal. Choose One-time vendor and Cash as the method of payment.)

❑ Cash Purchase Invoice #KR-53196
Dated June 13/03
From Koolhouse Refrigeration (use Quick Add), $4 800 for new outdoor refrigeration unit (Capital Expenditure: Kitchen Equipment) for patio, plus $336 GST paid. Invoice total $5 136. Terms: cash on receipt and installation. Issued cheque #643 in full payment.

❑ Cash Receipt #32
Dated June 14/03
From cash register tapes (no. 4194 to 5124), $3 500 including GST collected for sales of food and merchandise. Amount deposited in bank.

SESSION DATE – June 21

☑ 102
Purchase Invoice #BS-1739
Dated June 15/03
From Baking Supplies Wholesalers, $250 for weekly baking supplies delivery. Recall the stored entry and edit the amount. Terms: n/15.

- [ ] Purchase Quote #388
Dated June 16/03
Shipping Date June 20/03
From Western Highlights (use Quick Add for the new vendor), for preparation of advertising flyers for coffee house, $121.40, including GST. Terms: n/30.

notes

- [ ] Prairie Advertising (Contact Lila Adze) is located at 150 Flatland Blvd. Calgary, AB T2P 6F4 Tel: 775-6109 Fax: 771-7111 Terms: net 1 Vendor does not collect GST

- [ ] Purchase Quote #PA-Q211
Dated June 16/03
Shipping Date June 21/03
From Prairie Advertising (use Full Add), for advertising flyers for coffee house, $107 including GST. Terms: cash on receipt.

- [ ] Cash Purchase Invoice #PA-472
Dated June 16/03
From Prairie Advertising to accept quote #PA-Q211, for advertising flyers, $107 including GST. Terms: cash on receipt. Issued cheque #644 in full payment. (Enter the purchase in the Purchases Journal so that you can fill the quote. Choose Cheque as the method of payment.)

- [ ] Purchase Invoice # PW-710
Dated June 16/03
Filled purchase order #2 from Patio Warehouse for 40 patio chairs and 10 tables. Invoice total $856. Terms: n/30.

- [ ] Purchase Order #3
Dated June 17/03
Shipping Date June 24/03
Ordered from Blue Mountain Mugs, $500 for 100 designer mugs. Terms: n/30.

- [ ] Cheque Copy #645
Dated June 17/03
To Baking Supplies Wholesalers, $200 in payment of account. Reference invoice #BS-1274.

- [ ] Purchase Invoice #CH-825
Dated June 17/03
From Columbia House, for bi-weekly purchase of coffee and hot chocolate supplies, $450. Recall stored entry. Terms: n/30.

- [ ] Purchase Invoice #CTC-614
Dated June 19/03
From Ceylon Tea Co., for the purchase of a variety of teas, $100. Terms: n/15.

- [ ] Cash Receipt #33
Dated June 21/03
From cash register tapes (no. 5125 to 5998), $3 750 including GST collected for sales of food and merchandise. Amount deposited in bank.

SESSION DATE – June 28

- [ ] Purchase Invoice #BS-2136
Dated June 22/03
From Baking Supplies Wholesalers, $250 for weekly baking supplies delivery. Recall stored entry. Terms: n/15.

- [ ] Cheque Copy #646
Dated June 23/03
To Baking Supplies Wholesalers, $200 in payment of account. Reference invoice #BS-1396.

- [ ] Purchase Invoice #BM-599
Dated June 24/03
From Blue Mountain Mugs, to fill Purchase Order #3, $500 for designer mugs. Terms: n/30.

- [ ] Cash Purchase - Utility Statement #ATC-311904
Dated June 25/03
From Alberta Telephone, $73 for monthly telephone services, including GST. Terms: cash on receipt. Issued cheque #647 in full payment.

- [ ] Cheque Copy #648
Dated June 26/03
To Ceylon Tea Co., $100 in full payment of account. Reference invoice #CTC-614.

- [ ] Bank Debit Memo #AT-5295
Dated June 28/03
From Alberta Trust, $3 250 for wages to part-time employees, including GST on payroll services.

- [ ] Cash Receipt #34
Dated June 28/03
From cash register tapes (no. 5999 to 7011), $3 800 including GST collected for sales of food and merchandise. Amount deposited in bank.

SESSION DATE – June 30

- [ ] Cash Purchase Invoice #AA-191
Dated June 29/03
From AA Cleaning Services, $428 for cleaning services provided during June, GST included. Terms: cash on receipt. Issued cheque #649 in full payment.

- [ ] Purchase Invoice #BS-2416
Dated June 29/03
From Baking Supplies Wholesalers, $250 for weekly baking supplies delivery. Recall stored entry. Terms: n/15.

- [ ] Bank Debit Memo #AT-6125
Dated June 30/03
From Alberta Trust, $72 for interest expense on bank loan.

- [ ] Memo #102
Dated June 30/03
From store manager: Based on end-of-the-month inventory count, make adjusting entries to account for supplies used and inventory sold in June.

From (Inventory)	To (Expense)	Amount Used/Sold
Baking Goods (1300)	Baking Goods (5100)	$1 025
Coffee & Chocolate (1260)	Coffee & Chocolate (5120)	$875
Tea (1280)	Tea (5160)	$150
Packaged Coffee (1220)	Cost of Goods Sold (5140)	$1 100
Coffee Mugs (1240)	Cost of Goods Sold (5140)	$800

KEYSTROKES

Opening Data Files

Using the instructions for accessing data files in Chapter 1, page 15, open the data files for Java Jean's. You are prompted to enter the first session date, June 7, 2003, for this application.

Type `06-07-03` (or **type** `June 7 03`)

Click OK to enter the first session date for this application. The familiar Home window appears.

Accounting for Purchases

notes

The icons for the Receivables, Payroll, Inventory and Project ledgers are hidden because these ledgers are not set up or ready to use.

Purchases from vendors are entered in the Purchases Journal, indicated by the Purchases, Orders & Quotes icon as shown here:

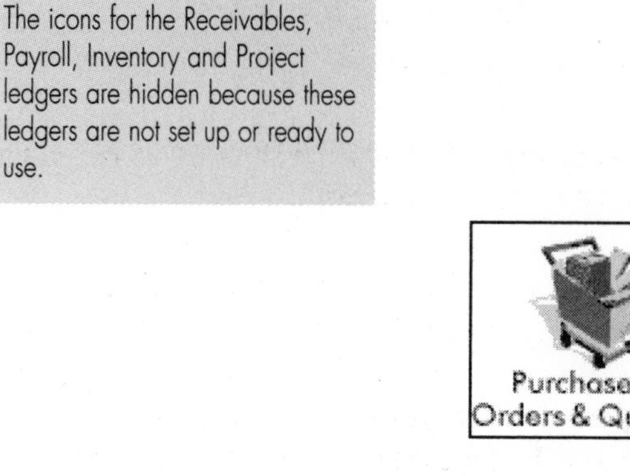

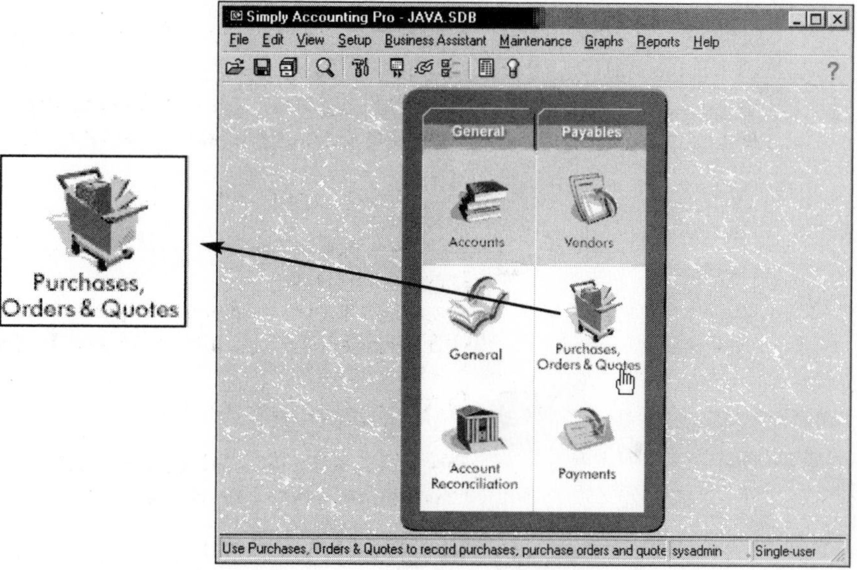

notes

Observe the status bar messages as you move the mouse pointer across the various tool buttons and input fields.

Click the **Purchases icon (Purchases, Orders & Quotes)** to open the Purchases Journal. The Purchases Journal input form appears on the screen:

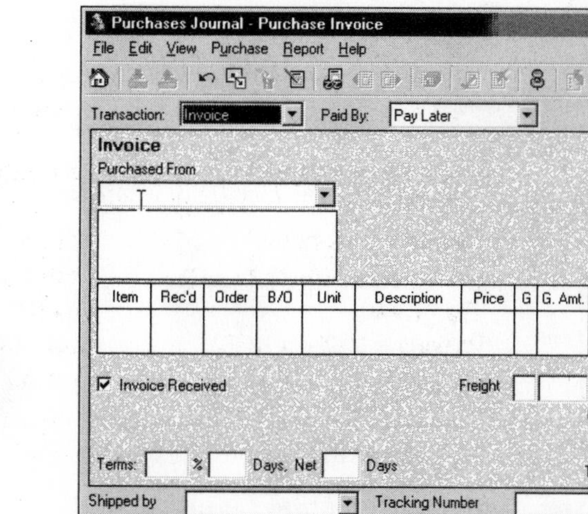

notes

Transaction types also include quotes and purchase orders. Payment methods include cheque, cash and credit cards (when these are set up). When more than one bank account is set up, an additional drop-down list for bank accounts appears for cheque transactions.

Invoice, selected initially by default, is correct as the Transaction because this is a normal purchase invoice. The option to Pay Later is also correct because this is a credit purchase.

Several tool buttons have been added to the Purchases Journal window: Remove quote or order, Look up an invoice, Look up Previous and Next invoice, Track shipments, Fill backordered quantities, Cancel backordered quantities, Use the same vendor next time, E-mail and Print. Each tool is discussed when it is used.

Click the **Vendor field (Purchased From) list arrow** to obtain the list of vendors as shown:

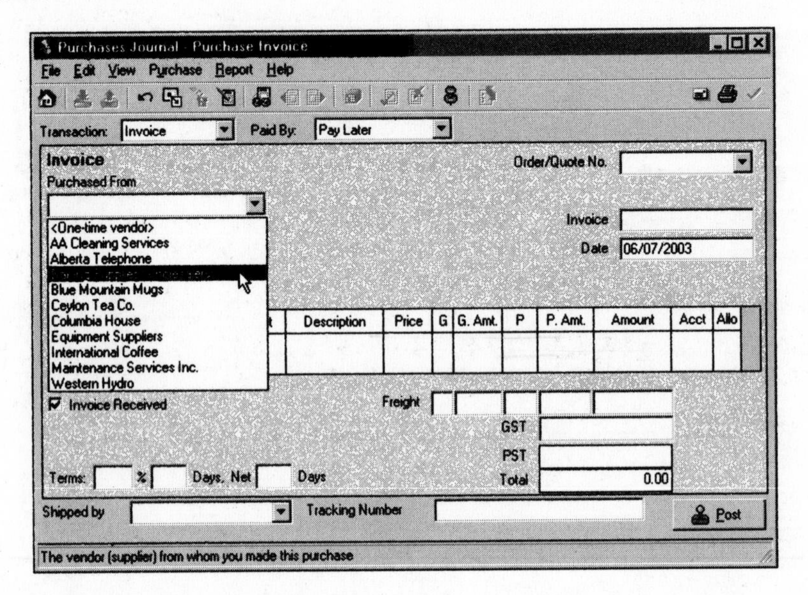

Whenever you see this arrow ▼ beside a field, a selection list is available to choose from. You can type the first letter to advance to the names beginning with that letter.

notes

When you type in the Purchased From field, the program fills in a name from the vendor list by trying to match the letters you type.

Click **Baking Supplies Wholesalers**, the vendor for this purchase, to select and enter it.

Notice that the vendor's name and address have been added to your input form, making it easy to check whether you have selected the correct vendor. The payment terms for the vendor are also included. If you have made an error in your selection, click the Vendor field and start again. If you have selected correctly,

Press tab

notes

Purchase order numbers are used when the goods purchased will be received at a later date. Vendors offer quotes to guarantee purchase prices for a limited time.

The cursor moves to the Order/Quote No. field, where you would type the number from Java's purchase order form or from the vendor's quote. This field does not apply to invoices, so you should skip it.

Press tab

The cursor moves to the Invoice field, where you should type the alphanumeric invoice number.

notes

You can also click the Invoice field directly to move to the cursor.

Type `BS-1274`

Press tab

The cursor moves to the Date field. Enter the date on which the transaction took place, June 1, 2003. The session date appears by default. It is highlighted, ready to be accepted or changed. You need to change the date.

Type `06-01` (or **type** `jun 1`)

Press tab

The cursor advances to the Item field. The next fields pertain to inventory items. Because we are not using the Inventory Ledger for this application, you can ignore the inventory-related fields. Any information you type in these fields does not appear in the journal report or on the printed cheque/invoice.

notes

You will use the tax fields when you enter the next purchase, and the inventory-related fields will be explained in a later application.

Click the **first line of the Amount field**, where you will enter the total amount for this purchase. Because the business is using the quick method for administering the GST, purchases of non-capital expenditures, such as supplies and services, will be recorded with the GST included. Since food inventory is zero rated, it will not include any GST. PST is not charged in Alberta. Review the Accounting Procedures section on page 73 for more information if necessary.

Type 200

Press tab

notes

Typing negative amounts will generate a credit entry with a debit for Accounts Payable.

The cursor moves to the Account field. The Account field for this purchase refers to the debit part of the journal entry, normally the acquisition of an asset or the incurring of an expense. It could also be used to decrease a liability or to decrease equity if the purchase were made for the owner's personal use. When you work in the subsidiary Payables journal, your *Accounts Payable* control account in the General Ledger will automatically be credited for the purchase. In fact, you cannot access the *Accounts Payable* account directly when the Payables Ledger is set up and linked.

notes

Double clicking the dotted box in the Account field also provides the list of accounts. Notice that you cannot access the Accounts Payable account from this list. Simply Accounting completes this portion of the journal entry automatically.

In this example, the business has acquired an asset, so you need to enter the asset account to which the purchase should be debited.

Type 1

Press enter

The familiar list of accounts appears. Notice that you can also add a new account.

Click 1300 Baking Goods to highlight it.

notes

The account name may not fit in the account column if the column is very narrow. To change the width of a column, point to the line beside the column title. When the pointer changes to a double-sided arrow, drag the line to the new location. Make a journal window wider by dragging the side frame. You can also maximize a journal window.

Click Select to enter the account to your Purchases Journal form. Your screen should now resemble the following:

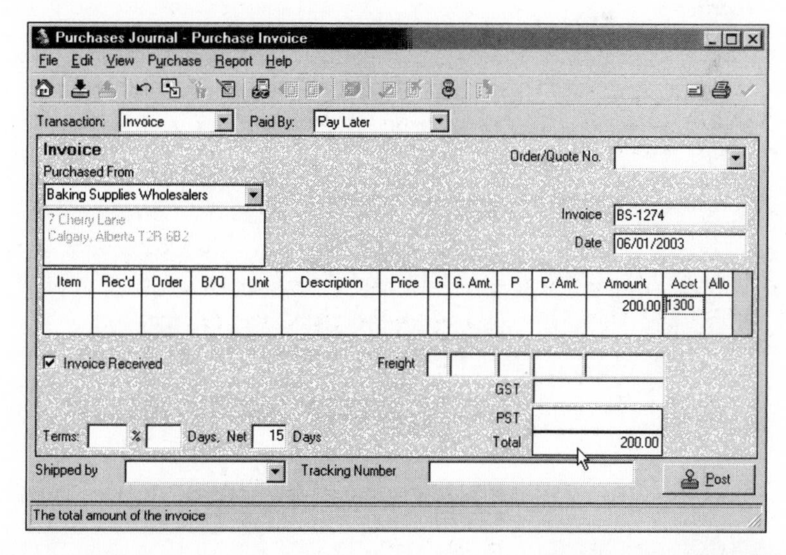

notes

Shipment tracking is covered in Chapter 7.

You can enter additional purchases from this vendor if there are any. Press tab to advance the cursor to the next invoice line. The payment terms have been set up as defaults for this vendor and are entered automatically. They can be edited if necessary for specific purchases, but in this case they are correct. There is no discount and full payment is due in 15 days. The entries for this transaction are now complete, so you are ready to review your transaction.

Reviewing the Purchases Journal Entry

Choose the **Report menu** and **click Display Purchases Journal Entry** to display the transaction you have entered on the screen:

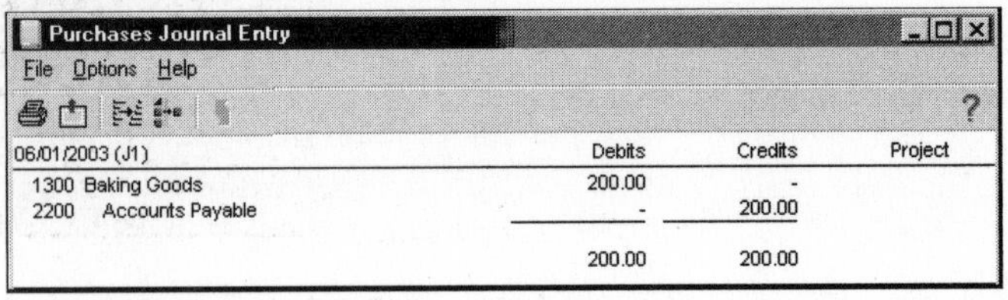

Purchases Journal Entry

File Options Help

06/01/2003 (J1)	Debits	Credits	Project
1300 Baking Goods	200.00	-	
2200 Accounts Payable	-	200.00	
	200.00	200.00	

notes

Other linked accounts for the Payables Ledger include a GST Paid account, a bank account, a freight expense account and a purchase discounts account. Each linked account will be explained when it is used in this workbook.

By reviewing the journal entry, you can check for mistakes. Note that the Simply Accounting program automatically updates the *Accounts Payable* control account because the Payables and General Ledgers are linked or fully integrated. Even though you did not enter account 2200, Simply Accounting uses it because it is defined as the linked account to which all purchases should be credited. Using the Purchases Journal instead of the General Journal to enter purchase transactions is faster because you need to enter only half the journal entry, the program provides a credit directly to the account of the selected vendor and it prevents you from choosing an incorrect payables account. In the next purchase, you will see that the GST account is also linked.

Close the display to return to the Purchases Journal input screen.

CORRECTING THE PURCHASES JOURNAL ENTRY BEFORE POSTING

Move to the field that has the error. **Press** *tab* to move forward through the fields or **press** *shift* and *tab* together to move back to a previous field. This will highlight the field information so you can change it. **Clicking** the amount or account fields will highlight the contents of these fields. **Type** the correct information and **press** *tab* to enter it.

You can also use the mouse to point to a field and drag through the incorrect information to highlight it. **Type** the correct information and **press** *tab* to enter it.

If the vendor is incorrect, re-select from the vendor list by **clicking** the arrow beside this field. **Click** the name of the correct vendor.

Click, or double click, if necessary, an incorrect amount to highlight it. Then type the correct amount and **press** *tab* to enter the change.

To correct an account number, **double click** the incorrect number to display the list of accounts. **Click** the correct account number to highlight it, then **click Select** and **press** *tab* to enter the change.

To discard the journal entry, **click** ☒ to close the journal or **click** ↶ (or **select** the **Edit menu** and **click Undo Entry**) to leave the journal open. **Click Yes** when you are asked to confirm that this is what you want to do.

Storing the Recurring Journal Entry

notes

The procedure for storing entries is the same for all journals when the option is available. Choose Store, assign a name to the entry, then choose a frequency.

Businesses often have transactions that are repeated on a regular basis. For example, loan payments, bank charges and rent payments usually occur on the same day each month; supplies may be ordered more frequently; insurance payments may occur less frequently but nonetheless regularly. Java Jean's has food supplies delivered on a regular basis. By storing the entry, and indicating the frequency, the entry can be recalled the next time it is needed, without re-entering all the information.

Click the **Store button** on the tool bar or choose the Purchase menu and click Store to open the following Store Recurring Transaction dialogue box:

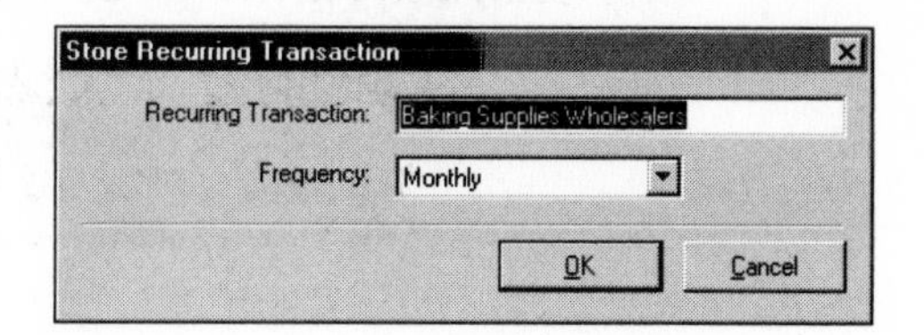

Simply Accounting enters the vendor and Monthly as the default name and frequency for the entry. The name is highlighted, so it can be changed by typing another descriptive name. Be sure to use one that you will recognize easily as belonging to this entry. The default frequency is incorrect since the food items are purchased weekly.

notes

The frequency options are Random (for irregular purchases) Weekly, Bi-Weekly, Semi-Monthly, Monthly, 13 times per year, Bi-Monthly, Quarterly, Semi-Annually and Annually.

Click Monthly to display the list of choices for the recurring frequency:

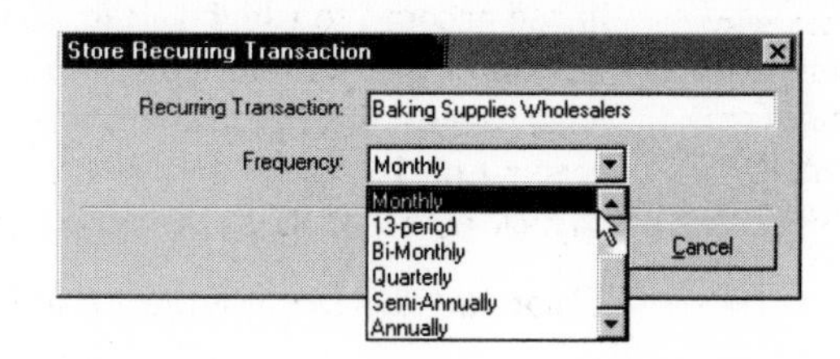

Scroll (click ▲) if necessary so that the frequency Weekly is included in the viewing area.

Click Weekly

Simply Accounting will advance the default journal date when you recall the stored entry according to the frequency selected. The session date is entered if the random frequency is chosen.

Click OK to return to the Purchases Journal window. Notice that (the Recall button) is now darkened and can be selected because you have stored a journal entry.

If you notice an error in the stored journal entry before posting, you must first correct the journal entry in the Purchases Journal window, then click Store. When asked to confirm that you want to overwrite or replace the previous version, click Yes.

Posting

notes

If you edit the journal entry after storing it, Simply Accounting will warn you that the entry has changed. Click Yes to proceed.

When you are certain that you have entered all the information correctly, and you have stored the entry if it is a repeating one, you must post the transaction to save it.

Click the **Post button** Post or choose the Purchase menu and click Post to save your transaction.

A new blank Purchases Journal form appears on the screen. Our next transaction is a payment, however, not a purchase.

Close the Purchases Journal window to return to the Home window.

Accounting for Payments

Payments are made in the Payments Journal indicated by the hand pointer in the following screen:

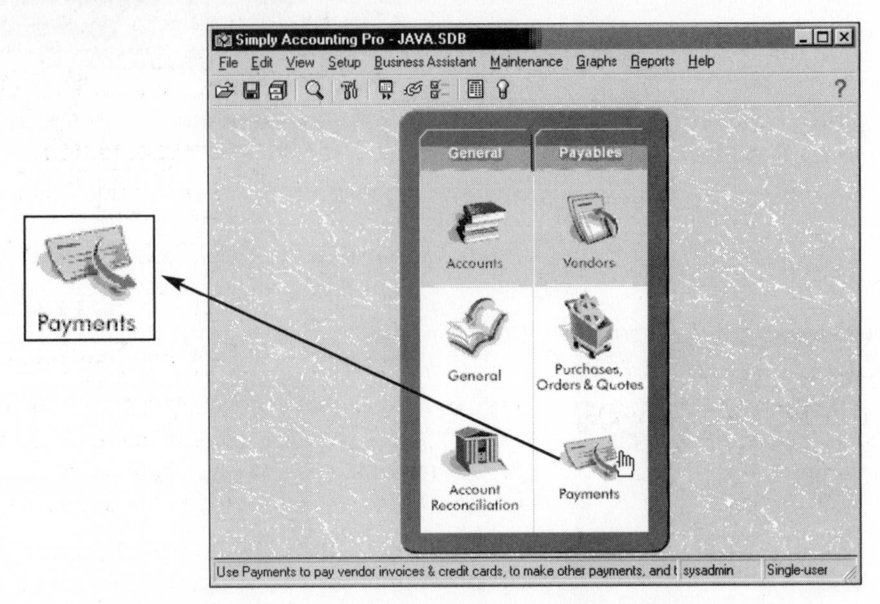

Click the **Payments Journal icon** to open the journal. The following blank Payments Journal input screen appears:

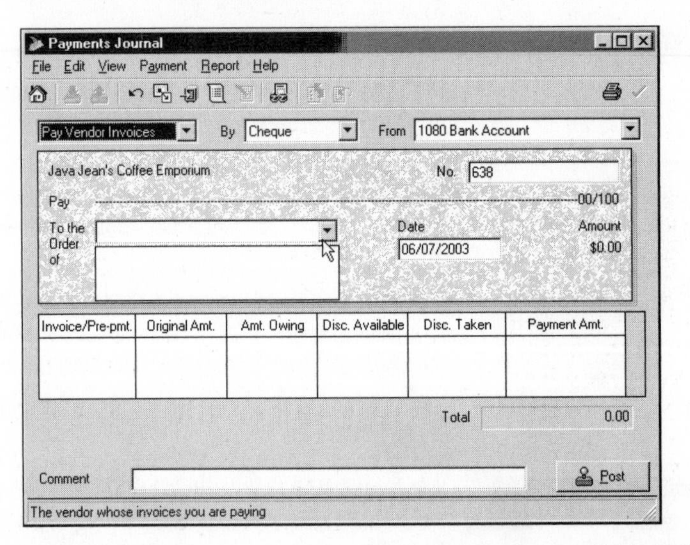

Pay Vendor Invoices is selected as the type of payment in the Pay field, and Cheque appears as the method of payment in the By field. These defaults are correct.

Click the **Vendor (To the Order of) field list arrow** to see the familiar list of vendors displayed in alphabetical order.

Click Equipment Suppliers to choose and enter the vendor to whom the payment is made. As shown, the vendor's name, address and outstanding invoice(s) have been added automatically to your input form, making it easy to see whether you have selected correctly:

notes

When more than one bank account is set up, you can select the bank from the drop-down list that appears in the Payments Journal. In Chapter 7, you will use these upper fields to work with credit card payments and multiple bank accounts. The Pro version has a Refresh invoices tool button in the journal.

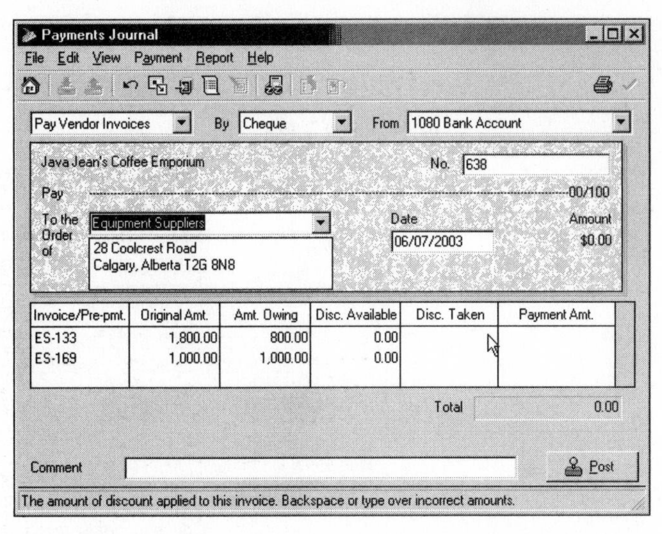

> **notes**
>
> Normally the cheque number should be correct. It can be edited, if necessary, for reversing or correcting entries.

If you need to change the vendor, click the Vendor field arrow again to select from the vendor list. The cheque number is entered in the number field. The next cheque number appears according to the settings for the company. It is correct, so you can accept it. When you have selected the correct vendor,

Double click the **Date field**, where the session date appears by default. Because it is highlighted, you can change it as required for this transaction.

Type `6 2` (or **type** `June 2`)

Press *tab*

The cursor moves to the Invoice/Pre-pmt. field. All outstanding invoices, including both the amount of the original invoice and the balance owing for the selected vendor, are listed on the screen.

Press *tab*

> **notes**
>
> Click the Include fully paid invoices tool if you need to make a reversing entry for a payment that was posted incorrectly. The Payments Journal will then display all paid and unpaid invoices for the selected vendor.

The cursor advances to the Disc. Taken (Discount Taken) field. Since there is no discount available, skip this field.

Press *tab*. The amount outstanding for the selected invoice is highlighted as the payment amount. You can accept a highlighted amount, or type an exact amount for a partial payment. To confirm that this invoice is being paid,

Press *tab* to advance the cursor to the Discount Taken field for the next invoice.

The amount for the next invoice should not be highlighted since this invoice is not being paid. If its amount is highlighted or entered, you must delete it by **pressing** *del* and then **pressing** *tab* to correct the total cheque amount.

notes

Notice that you cannot enter any account numbers in the Payments Journal. You only need to enter the amount of the payment on the appropriate invoice line.

Your completed Payments Journal form should now appear as follows:

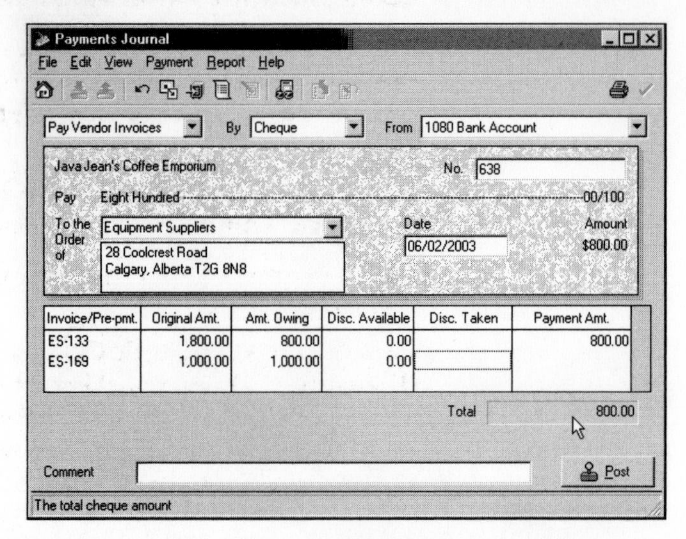

Notice that the upper cheque portion of the form is also complete.

notes

If you want to print the cheque, you should do this before posting the journal entry. Be sure that the information is correct before you print and that you have selected the correct printer and forms for printing cheques (see Chapter 6, page 158). Turn on your printer and then click the Print button.

As you pay invoices in the subsidiary Payments Journal, you do not enter any accounts. Simply Accounting chooses the default linked accounts defined for the Payables Ledger to create the journal entry. The *Accounts Payable* control account in the General Ledger will automatically be debited for the payment and *Bank Account* will be credited.

The entries for this transaction are complete, so you are ready to review and post your transaction.

Reviewing the Payments Journal Entry

Choose the **Report menu** and **click Display Payments Journal Entry** to display the transaction you have entered:

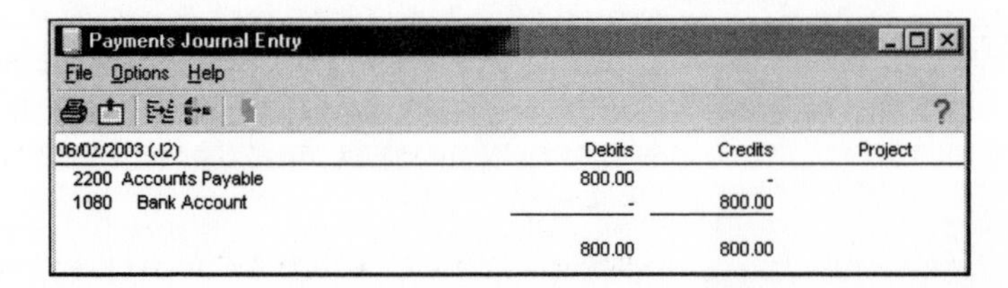

You can see that the Simply Accounting program automatically creates a related journal entry when you complete a Payments Journal entry. The program updates the *Accounts Payable* and *Bank Account* accounts because the Payables and General Ledgers are fully linked. *Bank Account* has been defined as the default Payables linked account to which payments are credited. The payment is also recorded to the vendor's account to reduce the balance owing.

Close the display to return to the Payments Journal input screen.

notes

To correct errors after posting, refer to Appendix A.

CORRECTING THE PAYMENTS JOURNAL ENTRY BEFORE POSTING

Move to the field that has the error. **Press** tab to move forward through the fields or **press** shift and tab together to move back to a previous field. This will highlight the field information so you can change it. **Type** the correct information and **press** tab to enter it.

You can also use the mouse to point to a field and drag through the incorrect information to highlight it. **Type** the correct information and **press** tab to enter it.

Click an incorrect amount to highlight it. **Type** the correct amount or **press** del if this invoice is not being paid.

If the vendor is incorrect, **click** [undo] to undo the entry or reselect from the vendor list by **clicking** the vendor list arrow. **Click** the name of the correct vendor. You will be asked to confirm that you want to discard the current transaction. **Click Yes** to discard the incorrect vendor entry and display the outstanding invoices for the correct vendor. Re-enter the payment information for this vendor.

Posting

When you are certain that you have entered all the information correctly, you must post the transaction to save it.

Click the **Post button** [Post] or choose the Payment menu and click Post to save your transaction.

Close the Payments Journal to return to the Home window.

notes

To complete transactions involving the General Journal, you must exit to the Home window and follow the keystroke instructions for the General Journal from the Reliable Roofing application.

Entering a Purchase Quote

The next transaction on June 2 is a purchase quote from Outdoor Contractors. The quote is an offer to install patio stones the following week. A quote usually provides a fixed price for some work or products. Often the offer is limited to a stated time period. If the business chooses to accept the offer, the quote may be filled as a purchase invoice for immediate delivery or converted to a purchase order for future delivery. Purchase quotes are entered and filled in the Purchases Journal. When the goods are received, or the work is completed, the quote is filled and the purchase is completed.

Since this transaction involves a company that is not listed as a vendor, you must add *Outdoor Contractors* to the vendor list in order to record the transaction.

Vendors can be added from the Payables Ledger or directly from the vendor field in the Purchases Journal or the Payments Journal. We will add the new vendor from the Journal.

Adding a New Vendor Record

Click the **Purchases icon** 

to open the Purchases Journal.

Click the **Transaction field list arrow** ▾ to see the types of transactions:

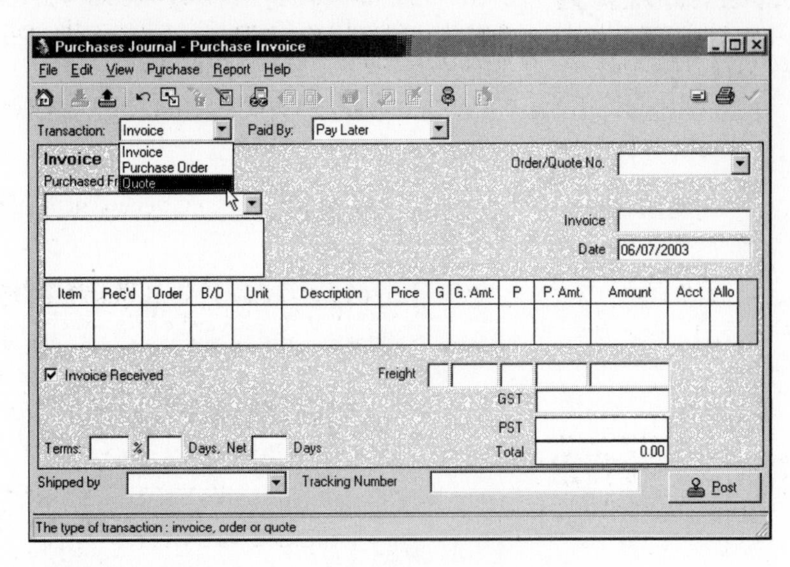

Click Quote to select purchase quote as the transaction type.

The Quote screen replaces the Purchase Invoice screen:

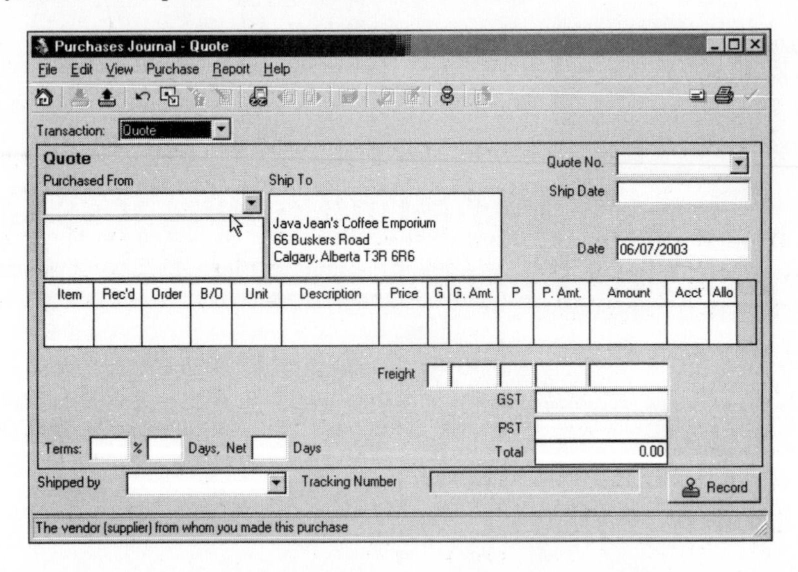

Click the **Purchased From field** to move the cursor (or press tab).

Type `Outdoor Contractors`

Press tab

The program recognizes that this is a new name and displays the following message:

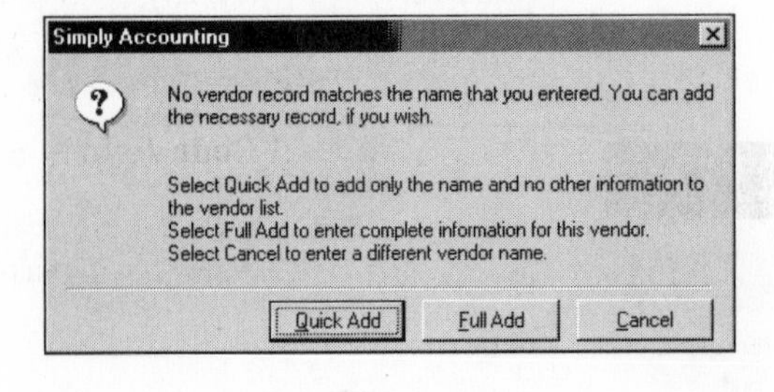

notes

If you choose One-time vendor for new vendors, the default settings will apply to include the GST codes and will add the transaction to the GST report. The vendor's name will not appear in the vendor lists.

notes

If you choose Quick Add for a new vendor, enter the payment terms in the Terms fields on the invoice, quote or order. When you add a new vendor from an invoice screen, you have the added option to Continue, that is to add the name to the invoice without creating a vendor record or adding the vendor to the Payables reports. This is similar to choosing One-time vendor from the vendor list.

version 8

Your options are: Quick Add — add only the Vendor's name and apply the default settings for the ledger; Full Add — open a new ledger record for the vendor and add complete details; or Cancel — return to the journal and type or choose another name if the one you typed was incorrect.

We want to add a complete record for the new vendor.

Click Full Add

The Ledger opens with the new vendor name already entered as you typed it in the Vendor field:

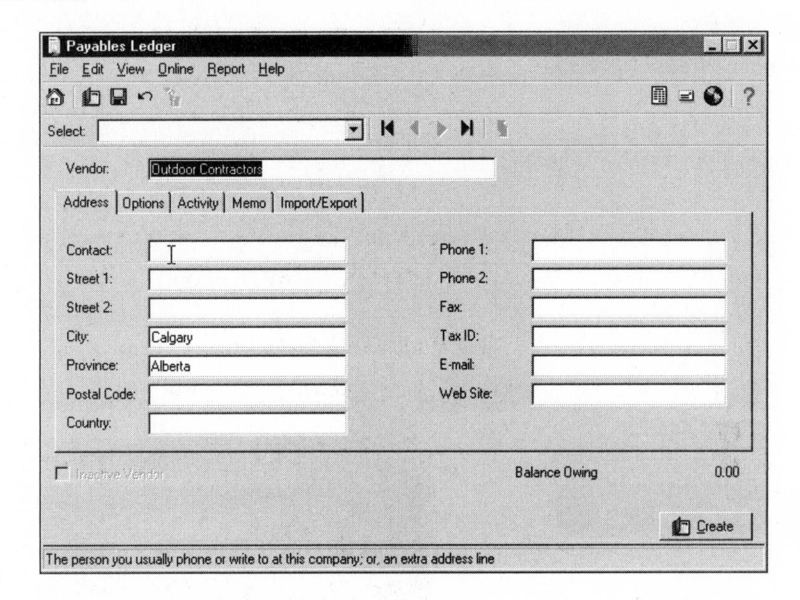

notes

To edit a stored vendor record, click the Vendors icon in the Home window. Select the vendor by clicking its icon. Then click the Edit tool button (the pencil icon) or choose the Edit menu and click Edit to open the Payables Ledger record for the selected vendor. (Or, you can double click the vendor's icon in the Vendors window to open the ledger.) Make the necessary changes. Close the Payables Ledger and the Vendors window.

You are ready to enter the new vendor. The Vendor Address tab information screen appears first. The vendor's name has been added to the Vendor field and the name is highlighted so you can edit it if necessary.

Press tab

The cursor advances to the Contact field, where you enter the name of Java Jean's contact person at Outdoor Contractors. This field can also be used to enter a third address line if two street lines are insufficient. It may be left blank by **pressing** tab.

Type `Pierre Slate`

Press tab

The cursor moves to the Street 1 field.

Type `447 Stones Ave.`

The Street 2 field can be used for a second address line, if there is one. By default, the program has entered the name of the city and province in which Java Jean's is located. If the vendor is in a different city or province, type the correct information before continuing. Double click the contents of a field to prepare for editing. You can accept the defaults because they are correct for Outdoor Contractors.

Click the **Postal Code field** to move the cursor.

notes

If you are missing any information for a vendor, you can leave the field blank and enter the details later by editing the record.

You do not need to use capital letters, nor do you need to leave a space within the postal code. The program will make these adjustments for you.

Type `t3n8j5`

Press tab

Notice that the format of the postal code has been corrected automatically. The cursor moves to the Country field.

Type `Canada`

Press tab

The cursor moves to the Phone 1 field. You do not need to insert a dash when you enter a telephone number.

Type `2918907`

Press tab

notes

Telephone and fax numbers may be entered with or without the area code.

Notice that the format for the telephone number has been corrected automatically. The cursor advances to the Phone 2 field where you can enter a second phone number for the vendor. Outdoor Contractors does not have a fax number, so you can leave the Fax field blank. The Tax ID number refers to the business federal tax or GST registration number. Adding e-mail address and Web site information permits sending purchase orders by e-mail and connecting to the vendor's Web site directly from Simply Accounting. Type e-mail and Web addresses just as you enter them in your Internet program. You do not need the http portion for Web sites.

Click the **E-mail field**.

Type `pslate@stonework.ca`

Click the **Options tab** to open the next vendor information screen:

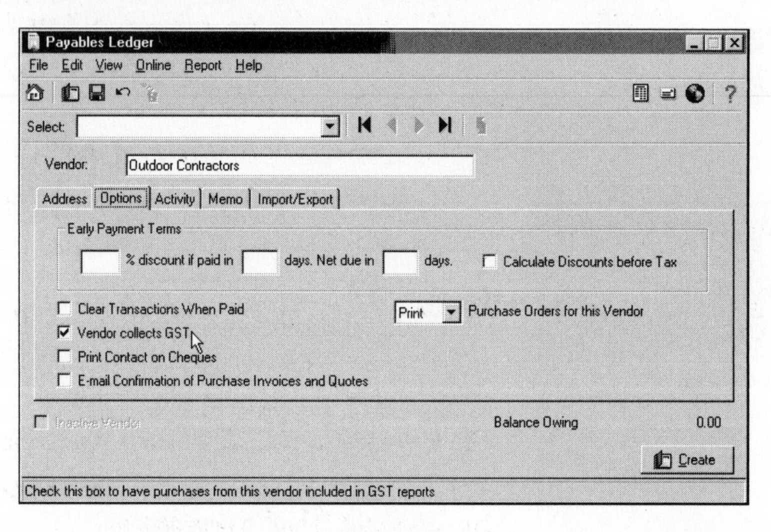

The Options screen has several important fields.

In the Early Payment Terms section of the ledger, you can enter the discount for early settlement of accounts and the term for full payment. According to the source document, the terms are net 30 days with no discount for early payment.

Click the **Net due in ___ days field** (Early Payment Terms section).

Type `30`

The next fields appear as check boxes: Calculate Discounts before Tax, Clear Transactions When Paid, Vendor collects GST, Print Contact on Cheques and E-mail Confirmation of Purchase Invoices and Quotes.

There are no discounts for this vendor. Refer to Chapter 2 for further information about taxes and discounts. The Clear Transactions option is used to remove invoices that are fully paid. Choose not to clear the invoices so that you can keep a record of all purchases and payments. Leave both boxes unchecked.

Selecting Print Contact on Cheques will add the name of the contact person to the cheque written to the vendor. If the contact field contains address information, check this box, otherwise leave it unchecked.

notes

- Unless you have checked Vendor collects GST, you will be unable to enter GST amounts in the Purchases Journal for that vendor.
- To turn off the GST option, click the field to remove the ✔.

Any vendor supplying goods or services that qualify as input tax credits should be marked as collecting GST by having this box checked. Since Java Jean's uses the quick method, only vendors supplying capital goods would fall into this category. Outdoor Contractors does supply capital goods, so you should leave the option on.

The final option allows you to choose between printing purchase orders and e-mailing them as the default setting. With either selection, you may still use the other method in the purchase order screen. If you choose to e-mail the orders, you should check the confirmation option by clicking it.

There are three additional input screens for vendor information: the Activity tab screen stores cumulative historical purchases and payments, the Memo tab screen allows you to add messages to the To-Do lists and the Import/Export tab allows you to specify the corresponding inventory item codes for your business and your supplier's. We can skip these fields. They will be introduced in a later application.

Check your work before saving the information because the options details will affect the invoices directly.

CORRECTING A NEW VENDOR ACCOUNT

Move to the field that contains the error by **pressing** tab to move forward or shift and tab to go back to the previous field. **Type** the correct information.

You can also highlight the incorrect information by dragging the cursor through it. You can now **type** the correct information.

After a field has been corrected, **press** tab to enter the correction.

To open a different tab screen, click the tab you want.

Saving the New Vendor and Completing the Quote

When you are certain that all the information is correct, you must save the newly created vendor.

Click Create [Create] to save the vendor information and return to the Quote.

The new vendor has been added to the Purchased From field. Java Jean's address appears as the shipping destination.

Click the **Quote No. field** to advance the cursor and skip the address fields.

Type `7822`

Press tab to advance to the Ship Date field. This is the date on which the work is to be completed or the order is to be received.

notes

Sometimes we use the term delivery date instead of shipping date because it is more appropriate for quotes and orders for services.

Type `06-09-03`

Press tab to advance to the Date field where you should enter the date that the quote was received.

Type `6-2`

The Item field refers to the code for inventory items and the Rec'd (quantity received with this purchase) field can also be skipped because this is not a purchase and no goods are received. However, you must enter the number of units that are ordered. You cannot leave the Order field blank.

Click the **Order field**. Since this is a contract job order, we will enter one as the quantity.

Type `1`

Press tab to advance to the Unit field that also applies to inventory purchases.

Press tab to advance to the Description field.

Type `Granite Patio Stones`

Press tab to advance to the Price field. This field refers to the unit price of the items.

Type `3000`

Press tab to advance to the G (GST code) field. Here you must enter the GST code for the purchase because this is a capital expenditure. Notice that the program has calculated and entered the amount of the purchase as the number of items ordered times the price.

Press enter to see the following list of available GST codes provided by the program:

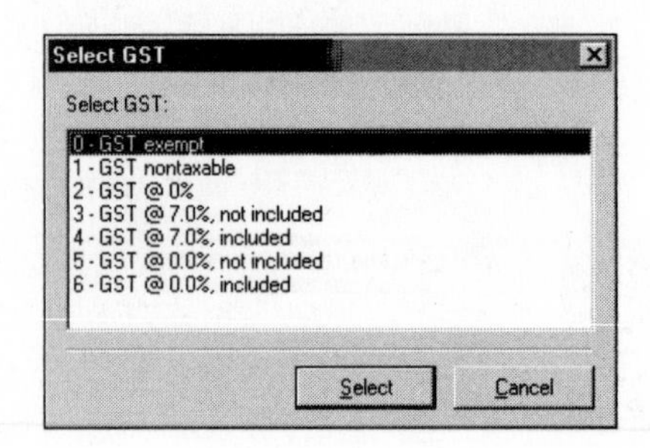

Some goods and services are tax exempt or zero rated and will not have GST applied. You would select **Codes 0** or **2** respectively for these items. **Code 1** applies to non-taxable items. You would use this code for discounts or for purchase allowances and credits. **Code 3** is used if the GST is not already included in the price. This option is used for most applications in this workbook. **Code 4** would be selected if the GST were already included in the price, as it is in the next application, Grandeur Graphics.

Click 3 - GST @ 7.0%, not included because GST has not yet been included in the purchase price.

Click Select

The code is added to the purchase order form, and the amount of GST is calculated and added to the G. Amt. (GST Amount) field.

Because Alberta has no provincial sales tax, the next two fields for the retail sales tax rate (P) and the amount of sales tax (P. Amt.) do not apply to purchases for Java Jean's.

Click the **Acct (Account) field** to advance the cursor.

Press enter to see the list of accounts.

Click 1600 Coffee Emporium (Scroll down if necessary to see this account number.)

Click Select to add the account number to the order form. The cursor advances to the next invoice line.

Your order form is now complete. Check your work carefully and make any corrections necessary. Refer to page 82 if you need help correcting the entry. When you try to display the Purchases Journal entry, you will see that there is no journal entry

notes

In a purchase order, the B/O (backordered quantity) field is filled in automatically with the order quantity.

notes

- GST Codes 5 and 6 refer to a second GST rate, should the government decide to apply a separate rate for different items. The second rate is set to zero and does not apply here. Chapter 7 uses the second GST rate (HST) for interprovincial sales.
- If the Vendor collects GST option was not selected in the Vendor Ledger, you will see only GST Codes 0 and 1.

notes

When retail or provincial sales tax is applied, type the tax rate in the P field. For example, if the sales tax rate is 8%, you would type 8 in the P field. The program will calculate the amount of the tax.

associated with the quote. The related journal entry will be completed when the quote is filled, when the purchase is completed.

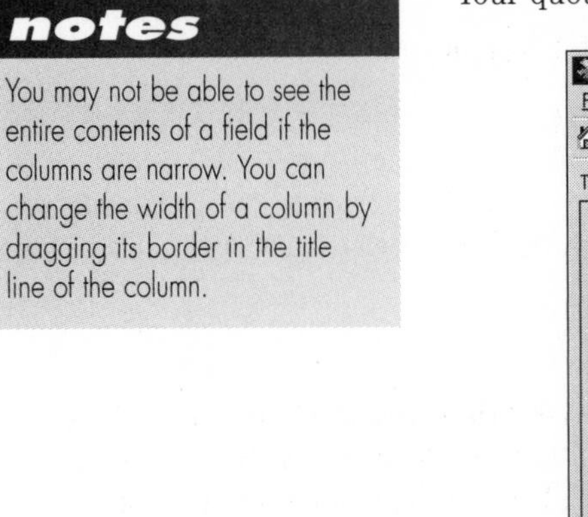

notes
You may not be able to see the entire contents of a field if the columns are narrow. You can change the width of a column by dragging its border in the title line of the column.

Your quote screen should now look like the following:

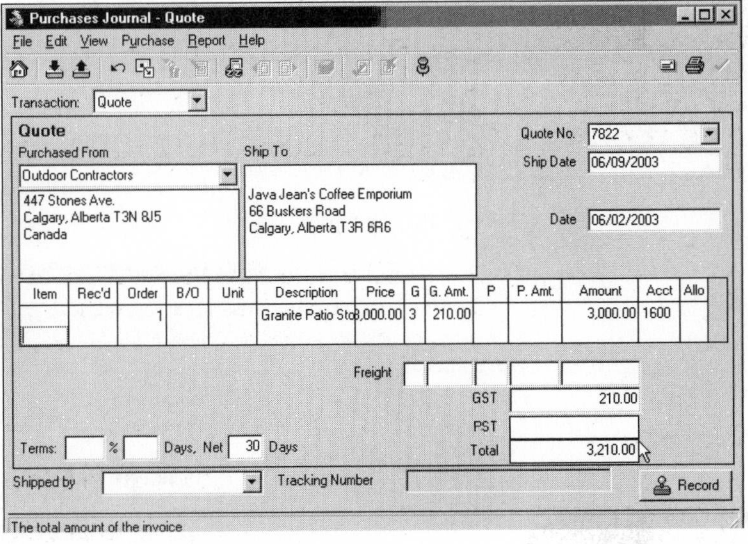

When you are sure that the entry is correct,

Click the **Record button** [Record] or choose the Purchase menu and click Record to save your transaction. Keep the journal open for the next transaction. Remember to select Invoice as the transaction for the purchase.

notes

The Post button label changes to Record for quotes and orders.

Placing a Purchase Order from a Quote

Click the **Transaction list arrow**.

Click Purchase Order as the transaction type and change the screen to an order form.

Click the **Quote/Order No. field** to view the list of all unfilled purchase quotes and purchase orders. The quote entered above — #7822 — is on the list.

Click 7822 to select it.

Press tab to select the quote and place it on-screen as a purchase order:

notes

Entering a purchase order directly, without the quote, is the same as entering a purchase quote except that you choose Purchase Order as the type of transaction.

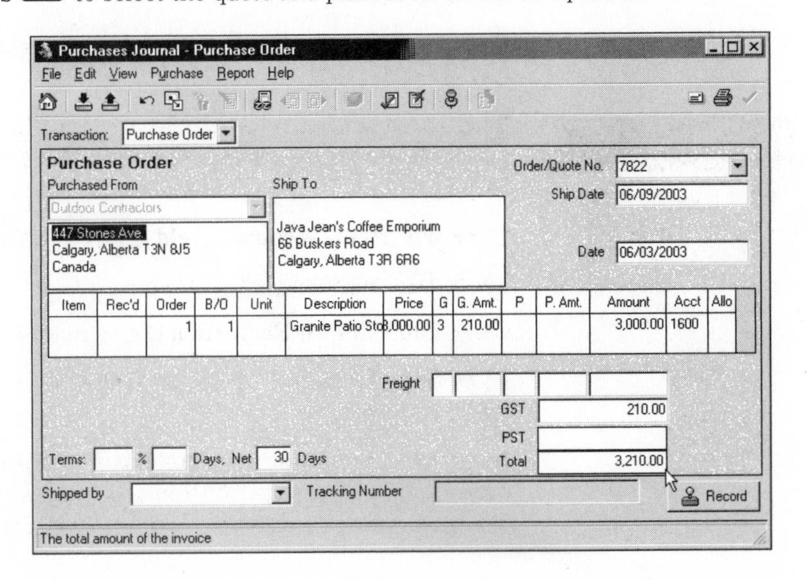

The date and the order number need to be changed.

Click the **Order/Quote No. field**.

Type 1

Double click the **Date field**.

Type 6-4-03 (or **type** jun 4)

Press tab

Click the **Record button** 

.

The program displays the warning message:

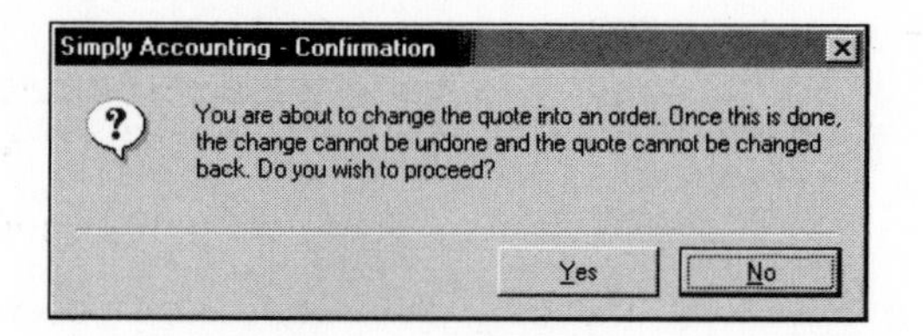

Since we want to convert the quote to an order, you can proceed.

Click Yes

A second warning will appear if you did not change the Quote number because this number was larger than the next automatic sequence number for purchase orders:

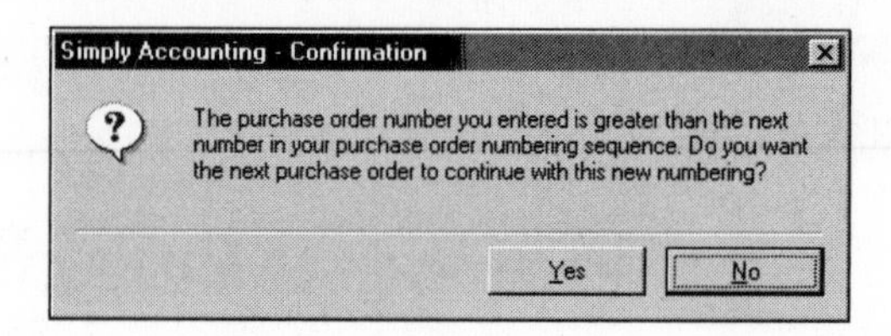

Click No because we do not want to reset the automatic sequence to this higher number. The higher purchase order number will still be recorded but the automatic counter will not be changed. A blank purchase order screen appears.

Complete the remaining transactions for the June 7 Session date. Back up your data set and then advance the session date to June 14.

We will change the quote number so that we can retain the purchase order sequence. The program updates this number automatically.

Recalling a Stored Entry

The first journal entry for the June 14 session date is the recurring purchase from Baking Supplies Wholesalers. Since we have stored this purchase, we do not need to re-enter all the information.

Click the **Purchases icon** 

in the Home window to open the Journal.

notes

- From the Recall Stored Entry dialogue box, you can remove an entry that is incorrect or no longer needed. Click an entry to select it. Click Remove and then click Yes to confirm that you want to delete the entry.
- The stored entries are listed in order according to the next date that they will be repeated.

Click the **Recall button** in the tool bar or choose the Purchase menu and click Recall to display the Recall Recurring Transaction dialogue box as shown here:

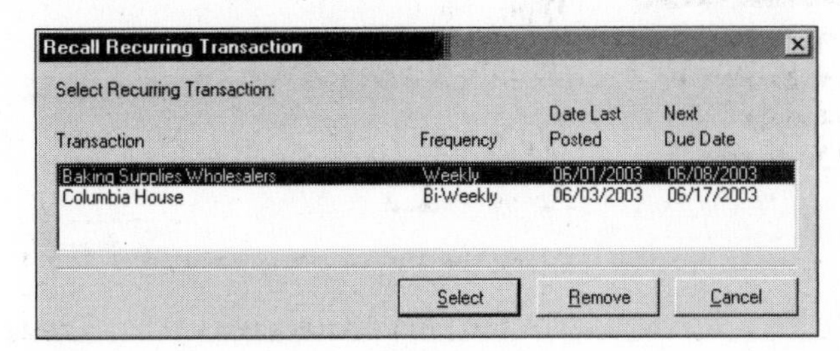

Baking Supplies Wholesalers, the name of the entry we want to use, should be selected because it is the next recurring entry that is due. (If it is not already selected, click Baking Supplies Wholesalers.)

Click Select to return to the Purchases Journal.

The entry we stored is displayed just as we entered it the first time, except that the date has been changed to one week past the previous posting date, as needed, and the Invoice field is blank so we can enter the new invoice number. Remember that Simply Accounting does not accept duplicate invoice numbers.

Click the **Invoice field** to move the cursor.

Type `BS-1396`

The entry is now complete. You should review it before posting.

Choose the **Report menu** and click **Display Purchases Journal Entry**.

Close the display when finished and make any necessary corrections.

Click the **Post button** Post. **Close** the Purchases Journal.

Entering Cash Purchases

The hydro statement on June 9 is to be paid immediately on receipt of the invoice. Instead of recording a separate payment in the Payments Journal, you can record the payment with the purchase in the Payments Journal.

Click the **Payments icon** to open the Payments Journal.

Click Pay Vendor Invoices to see the transaction choices for the journal:

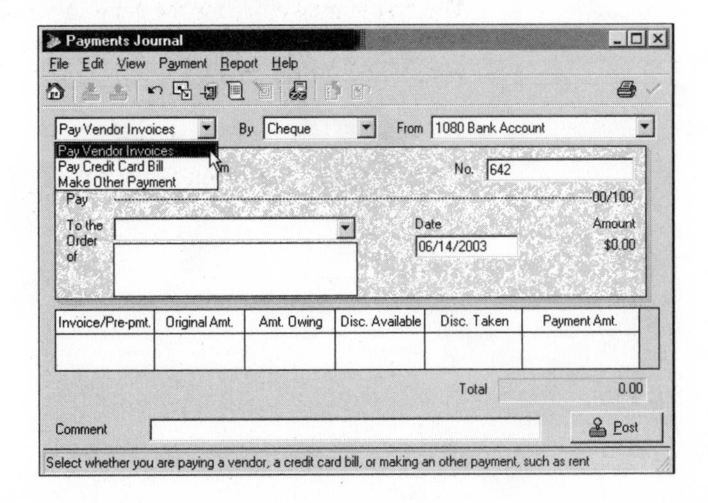

Click Make Other Payment

Choose Western Hydro from the vendor list (the To the Order of field).

The journal now resembles an invoice with journal input fields:

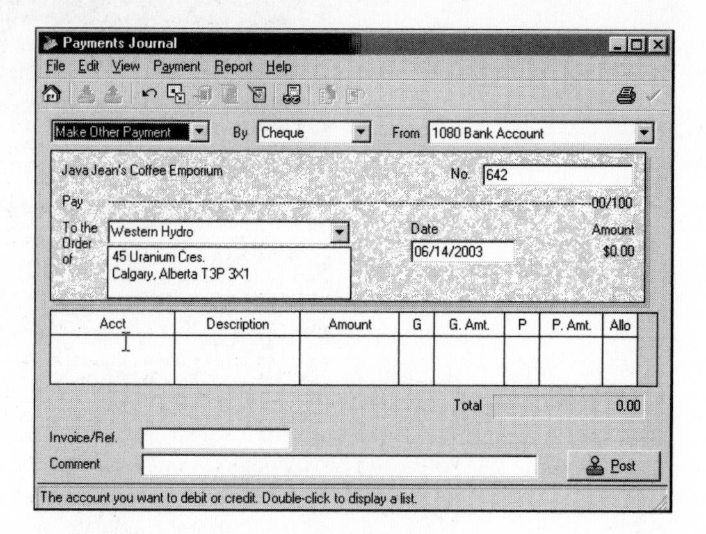

The next available cheque number is entered by default and the bank account is selected for the payment. Cheque numbers are updated in sequence for both payment journal entries and cash purchases.

Double click the **Date field**.

Type 6/9

Press tab to advance to the Acct (Account) field.

As usual, you must enter the expense account that is debited for the transaction.

Type 5

Press enter and scroll down the account list.

Double click 5240 Hydro Expense to select the account and add it to the journal. The cursor advances to the Description field.

Type **May hydro service**

Press tab to advance to the amount field.

Type 149.50

Click the **Invoice/Ref. field** where you should enter the invoice number for the purchase.

Type WH-611 **Press** tab to advance to the Comment field.

The comment will become part of the journal record so you should include it.

Type WH-611, hydro service for May

notes

If you will not be making additional purchases from a vendor for a cash purchase, you can choose One-time vendor from the Vendor list. Type the vendor's name and address on the invoice in the text box area below the To the Order of field. The default settings for the ledger will apply to the invoice.

notes

Sometimes a business uses more than one bank account. If these multiple accounts are set up, all bank accounts will be listed in the From drop-down list. You can choose the appropriate bank account from the list for purchases by cheque and for payments. Credit cards and multiple bank accounts are used in later applications.

notes

When we tested the keystrokes, the Invoice/Ref. field contents were not included in the journal record and the Comment was included. Therefore, we repeat the invoice number in the Comment field to be sure that it will be included in the journal reports.

The journal entry is complete as shown:

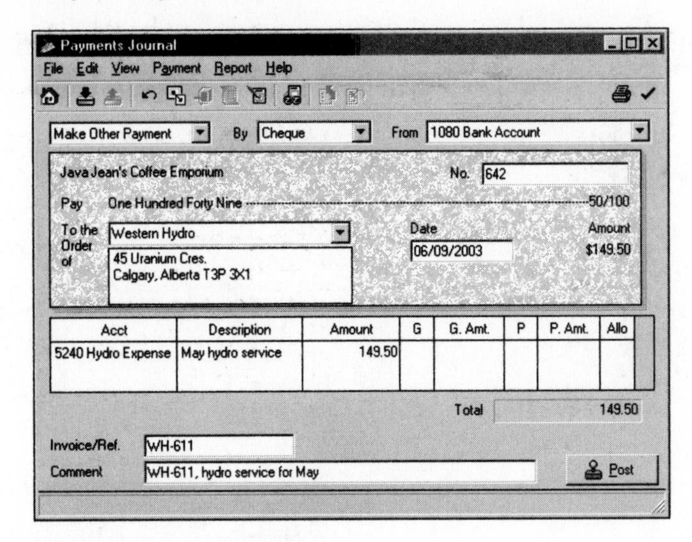

When you have finished, review the entry.

Choose the **Report menu**, then **click Display Payments Journal Entry**. Your display should look like the following:

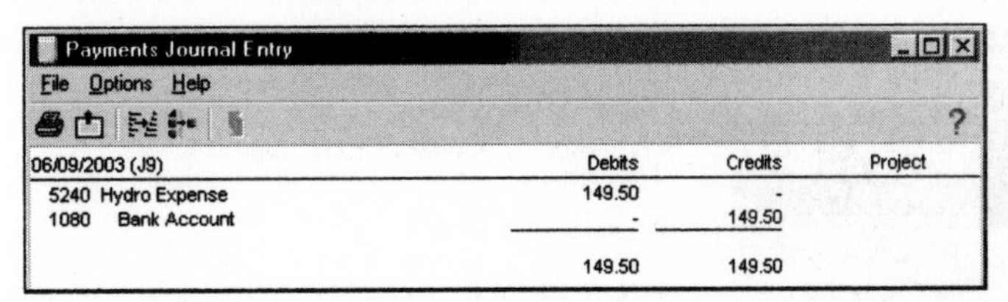

Notice that the program has automatically credited *Bank Account*, the Payables linked bank account, instead of *Accounts Payable* for this cash purchase.

Close the display when you have finished and make any corrections necessary. Double click an incorrect entry and type the correct details.

Post the entry when you are certain that it is correct. **Close** the Payments Journal.

Filling a Purchase Order

When an ordered item is received, or work is completed, you must complete a purchase invoice entry to record the transaction.

Click the **Purchases icon** to open the journal.

The default selections, Invoice as the Transaction and Pay Later as the Paid By selection are correct because this is credit purchase.

Click the **Order/Quote No.** list arrow to display the numbers for all unfilled quotes and orders.

Click 1 (It is the only order number available at this time.)

notes

After you enter the order number, the purchase order will not appear until you press tab or advance to another field.

Press (tab). You will see the following purchase order that was placed on June 4:

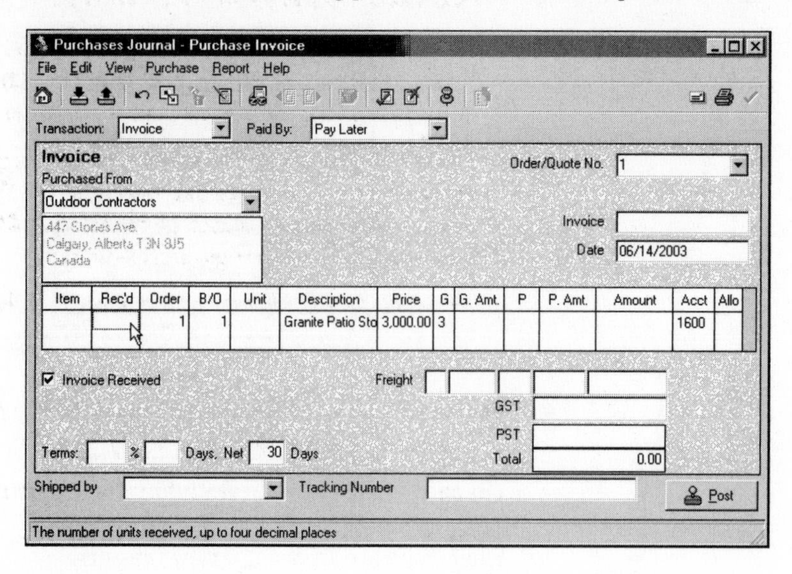

The cursor is in the Invoice field.

Type `6127-OC`

Press (tab) to advance to the Date field.

Type `6-9`

The invoice is still incomplete because the quantity displays as backordered. We need to "fill" the order.

Click the **Fill backordered quantities button** in the tool bar or choose the Purchase menu and click Fill Purchase Order. Your invoice now is completed as shown:

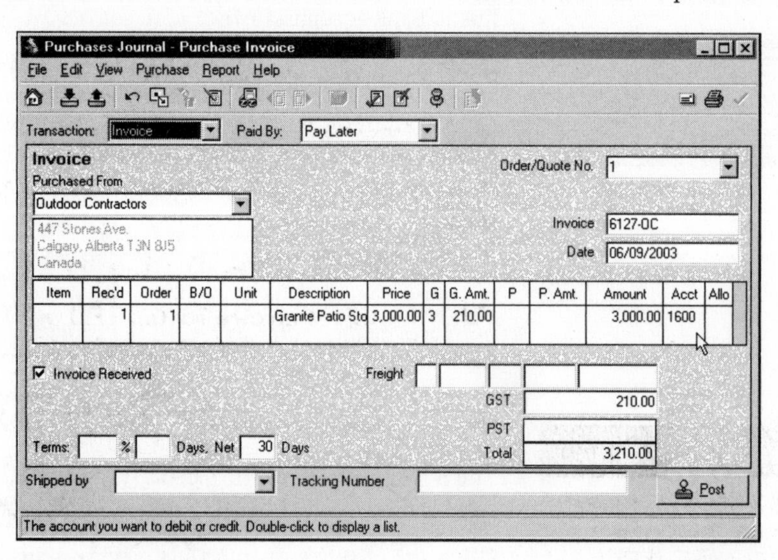

The B/O quantity has been moved to the Rec'd column to reflect the completion of the order. Check the entry carefully to be sure that it is correct.

notes

Filling a purchase quote is the same as filling an order. Choose Invoice, select the quote number and press (tab) to place the quote on-screen as an invoice. You do not need to choose Fill backordered quantities.

Warning!

Be sure to complete the step of filling the order. If, instead, you complete the invoice manually, the purchase order will remain unfilled and continue to show in the list of available orders.

CORRECTING A PURCHASE ORDER

If the purchase invoice is not correct, undo the journal entry (click [undo]). Confirm that you want to discard the entry by **clicking Yes**. **Choose Purchase Order** as the Transaction. Enter the purchase order number in the Order/Quote No. field. **Press** tab to recall the order.

Click the **Adjust purchase order tool** [tool]. You can now edit the purchase order as needed. **Post** the revised purchase order. **Click Yes** when asked to confirm that you want to overwrite the original purchase order.

Then complete a purchase invoice entry to fill the purchase order.

Choose the **Report menu** and **click Display Purchases Journal Entry**. You can see that this is a normal journal entry.

Close the display. When the information is correct,

Click the **Post button** [Post] or choose the Purchase menu and click Post.

You will see the following message:

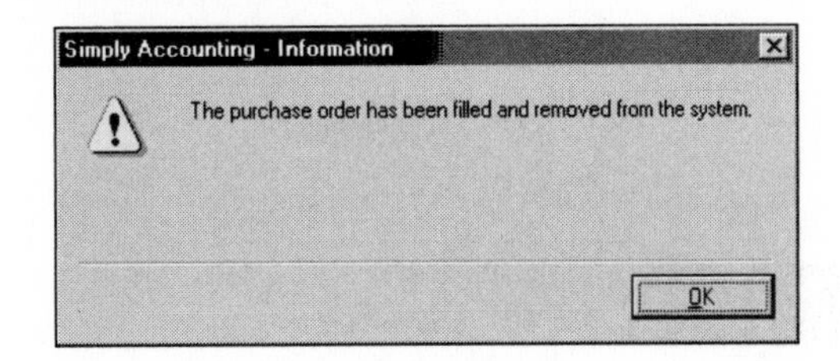

Click OK to display a new Purchases Journal invoice form.

Adjusting a Posted Invoice

In the same way that you can correct or adjust a previously posted entry in the General Journal, you can edit a Purchases Journal invoice after posting. Simply Accounting will provide the necessary reversing entry when you post the revised invoice.

The Purchases Journal should still be open.

Click the **Adjust invoice button** [button] or choose the Purchase menu and click Adjust Invoice to open the Adjust an invoice screen:

notes

If you know the invoice number, you can enter it in the Invoice Number field and click OK to select the invoice directly.

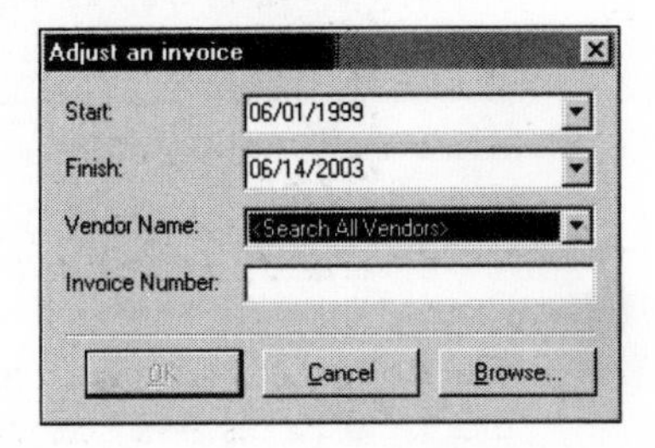

This is similar to the Adjust invoice screen for the General Journal, but you have the additional option of searching for invoices by the name of the vendor. The program enters default start and finish dates. These dates can be edited like any other date fields or you can choose a date from the drop-down lists.

Choose 06/01/2003 (June 1) from the Start date list.

We will search all invoices by choosing the default to Search All Vendors.

Click Browse to see the requested list of Purchases Journal invoices:

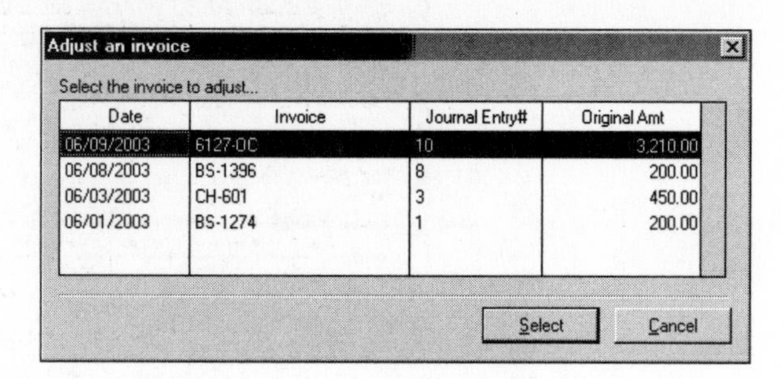

Invoices are presented in order with the most recent one listed first and selected. This is the invoice from Outdoor Contractors that we need.

Click Select or **press** (enter) to recall the selected transaction:

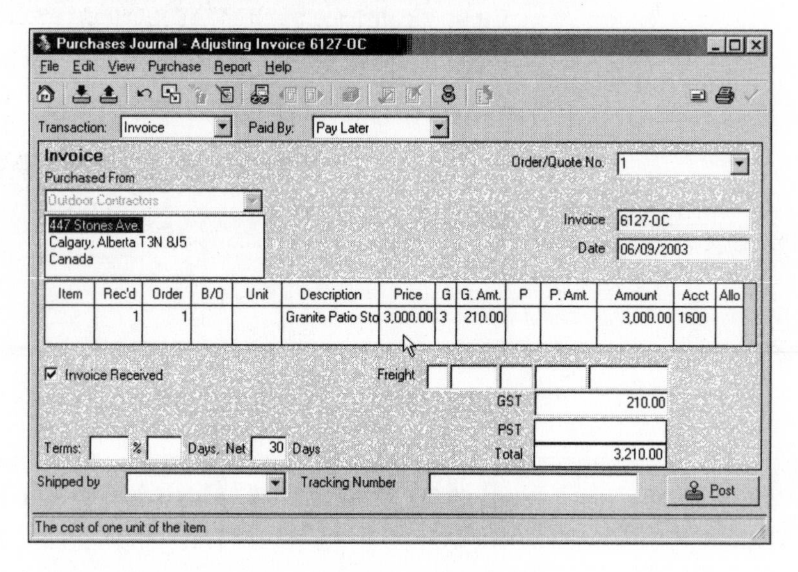

All fields are available for editing, except the vendor. We need to enter a second invoice line for the additional services not initially ordered.

> **notes**
>
> To correct the vendor, you must complete a reversing entry. See Appendix A for instructions.

Click the **Description field** below the current entry. (Be certain to click on the second line for the following steps or you will select the previous information instead.)

Type `Additional installation service`

Click the **G field** and **press** (enter) to see the codes.

Double click GST Code 3 to add it to the invoice.

Click the **Amount field**.

Type `200` **Press** (tab) to advance to the Acct field.

Press (enter) and **double click** account **1600** to add it to the invoice.

> **notes**
>
> An alternative approach would be to edit the amount initially entered on the invoice.

Your completed entry should now resemble the following:

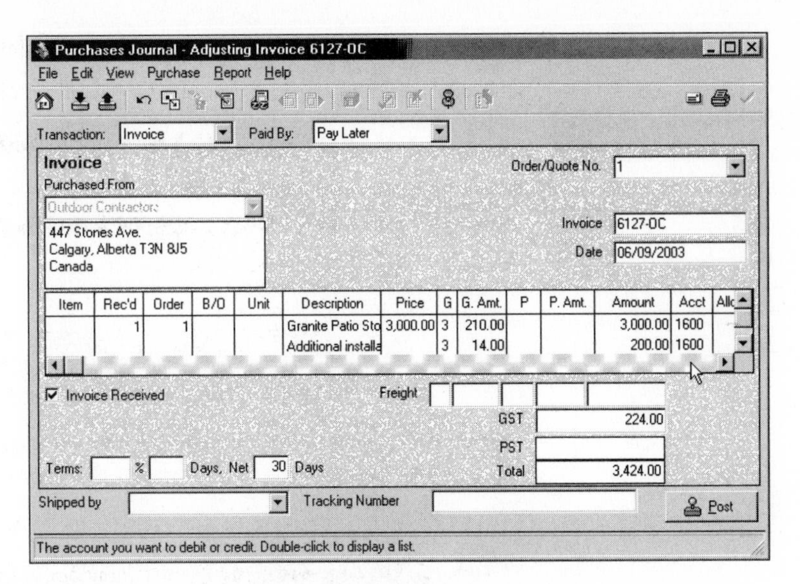

Before posting the revised transaction, review it for accuracy.

Choose the **Report menu** and **click Display Purchases Journal Entry**:

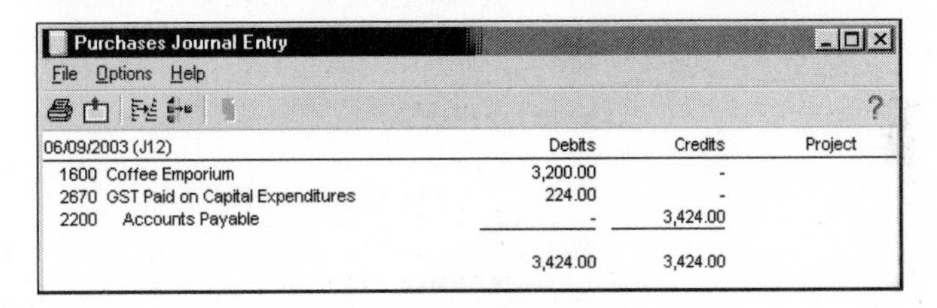

06/09/2003 (J12)	Debits	Credits	Project
1600 Coffee Emporium	3,200.00	-	
2670 GST Paid on Capital Expenditures	224.00	-	
2200 Accounts Payable	-	3,424.00	
	3,424.00	3,424.00	

Although you see only one journal entry at this stage, there are in fact three entries connected with this transaction — the first one that was incorrect, the second one created by Simply Accounting to reverse the incorrect entry and the final correct one you see in this display. All use the original posting date.

Close the report display when you have finished and make additional corrections if necessary.

Click the **Post button** Post.

Correcting Cash Purchases from the Payments Journal

Purchases entered as Other Payments in the Payments Journal do not appear on the Select an Invoice list from the Purchases Journal. You can, however, adjust these other payments from the Payments Journal as follows:

- Click the Payments Journal icon to open the journal.
- Click Make Other Payment from the transaction list.
- Click the Adjust a previously posted entry tool.
- Select your search parameters, the date range, vendor or cheque number.
- Click Browse (or click OK if you entered the cheque number).
- Click the invoice you want to adjust and press enter (or click Select).
- Make the corrections and review your entry to see the changes.
- Post the revised transaction.

Continue with the transactions for the June 14 session date.

notes

The Adjust tool is not available until you choose Make Other Payments because you cannot adjust regular credit invoice payments.

Changing a Stored Entry

notes

If the change is for a single purchase and will not be repeated, edit the entry after recalling it but do not store the entry again.

The first entry on the June 21 session date is the weekly purchase from Baking Supplies Wholesalers. The amount of the purchase has changed, however, and we need to update the stored entry.

Click the **Purchases icon** in the Home window to open the Purchases Journal.

Click the **Recall button** on the tool bar or choose the Purchase menu and click Recall to display the Recall Recurring Transaction dialogue box.

Click Baking Supplies Wholesalers, the name of the entry we want to use (if it is not already highlighted).

Click Select to display the purchase journal entry with the new date.

Click the **Invoice field**.

Type `BS-1739` (to add the new invoice number)

Click the **Amount** to highlight it so that you can edit it.

Type `250`

Press tab to enter the change.

Review the journal entry as usual to make sure that it is correct before proceeding.

Click the **Store button** or choose the Purchase menu and click Store.

Click OK to accept the name and frequency without changes. The following warning appears:

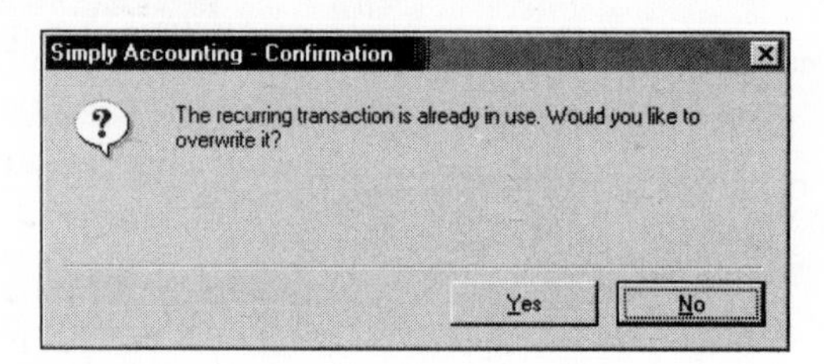

Click Yes to confirm that you want to replace the previous stored version and return to the Purchases Journal.

Click the **Post button** Post to save the journal entry.

Displaying Vendor Reports

All vendor-related reports can be displayed or printed from the Vendors window.

Click the **Vendors icon** Vendors in the Home window to open the Vendors window. The Reports menu now lists only vendor reports. You can select the report you want from this list and follow the instructions below to choose report options.

Close the Vendors window.

Displaying Vendor Lists

> **notes**
>
> - The label for the Display button changes to name the report for the selected icon.
> - You can drill down to Vendor Aged Reports from the Vendor List.

Right-click the **Vendors icon** in the Home window to select it.

Click the **Display button** on the tool bar or choose the Reports menu, then choose Lists and click Vendors. The report will be displayed immediately. Maximize the display and scroll as necessary to see vendors outside the screen viewing area.

Close the display when you have finished viewing the report.

Displaying Vendor Aged Reports

> **notes**
>
> If you chose One-time vendor or Continue for Koolhouse Refrigeration, it will not be included by name on the list of vendors for reports and graphs. If you used Quick Add, it will be included.

You can display Vendor Aged reports at any time except when you are entering a transaction.

Choose the **Reports menu** in the Home window, then **choose Payables** and **click Vendor Aged**. The following window appears with options for your display:

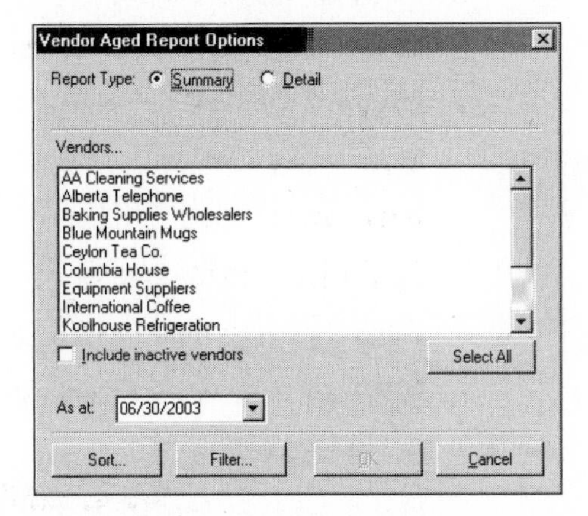

The **Summary** option provides the total balance owing to each vendor. It displays an alphabetic list of vendors with outstanding total balances organized into aged columns. By default, the program selects this option.

Select the **Detail** option if you want to see individual outstanding invoices and payments made to vendors. This more descriptive report is also aged. Management can use it to make payment decisions. Click Detail to choose this option. With the Detail option, you can also choose to add vendor payment terms by clicking Include Terms.

You can sort and filter the reports by the name of the vendor or by the balance owing.

> **notes**
>
> From the Vendor Aged Detail report, you can drill down to look up invoices and to Vendor Ledgers. From the Summary report, you can drill down to the Detail report.

Click the **name** or **press** ctrl and **click** the **names in the vendor list** to select the vendors for whom you want to see the report. If you want the report to include all vendors, **click Select All**.

Type the date you want for the report or accept the session date given by default. After you have indicated all of the options,

Click OK to see the report.

Close the displayed report when you have finished.

Displaying Aged Overdue Payables Reports

You can display Aged Overdue Payables reports at any time except when you are entering a transaction.

notes

You can drill down to look up invoices and to the Vendor Aged Reports from the Aged Overdue Payables Report. From the Summary report, you can drill down to the Detail report.

Choose the **Reports menu** in the Home window, then **choose Payables** and **click Aged Overdue Payables**. The following report options window appears:

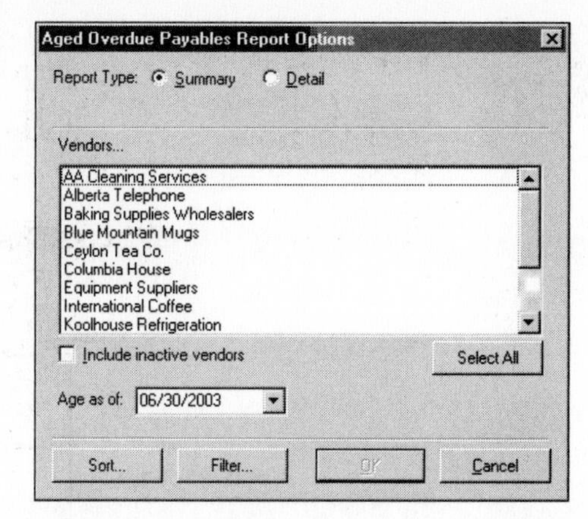

The Aged Overdue Payables report includes the same information as the Vendor Aged report but it adds a column for the invoice amounts that are overdue. Vendor name and balance owing may be selected as the criteria for sorting and filtering.

Choose Summary or **Detail**.

notes

Press and hold ctrl and click the names if you want to include more than one vendor.

Press ctrl and **click** the **names in the vendor list** to select the vendors for whom you want to see the report. If you want to include all vendors, **click Select All**.

Type the date you want for the report, or accept the session date given by default. After you have indicated all the options,

Click OK to see the report. One invoice from Blue Mountain Mugs is overdue.

Close the displayed report when you have finished.

Displaying Pending Purchase Orders Reports

notes

The Vendor Purchases report deals mainly with inventory. It will be introduced in a later application.

You can display Pending Purchase Orders reports at any time except when you are entering a transaction.

Choose the **Reports menu** in the Home window, then **choose Payables** and **click Pending Purchase Orders**. The report options window appears:

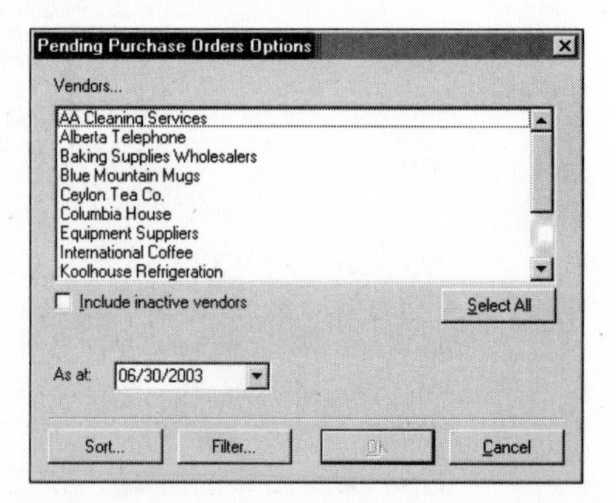

Press ctrl and **click** the **names in the vendor list** to select the vendors for whom you want to see the report of unfilled purchase orders, organized by the selected vendors. If you want the report to include all vendors, **click Select All**.

Click OK to see the report. There are no unfilled orders so there is no report (no data to report).

Close the displayed report when you have finished.

Displaying the Purchases Journal

Right-click the **Purchases icon** in the Home window to select it.

Click the **Display button** on the tool bar or choose the Reports menu, then choose Journal Entries and click Purchases. You will see the report options screen:

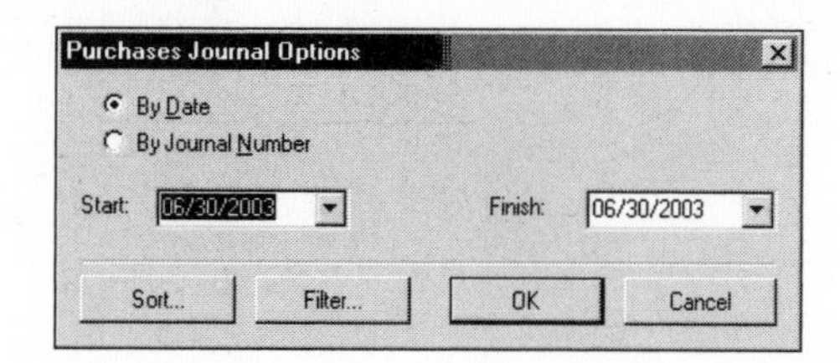

notes

If no icons are selected in the Home window, Purchases and Payments Journal reports are available from the list when you click the Display tool button.

The Purchases Journal can be displayed by posting date or by journal entry number. By default, the By Date option is selected. Since all reports in this workbook use this option, leave the selection unchanged. All journal reports may be sorted and filtered by date, journal number, source or comment.

Type the beginning date for the journal transactions you want to display.

Press tab

Type the ending date for the transaction period you want to see.

Click OK to see the report.

Close the display when you have finished.

notes

You can drill down to look up invoices, to the Vendor Aged Reports and to the General Ledger Reports from the Purchases Journal or the Payments Journal Report.

Displaying the Payments Journal

Right-click the **Payments icon** in the Home window to select it.

Click the **Display button** on the tool bar or choose the Reports menu, then choose Journal Entries and click Payments to see the report options screen:

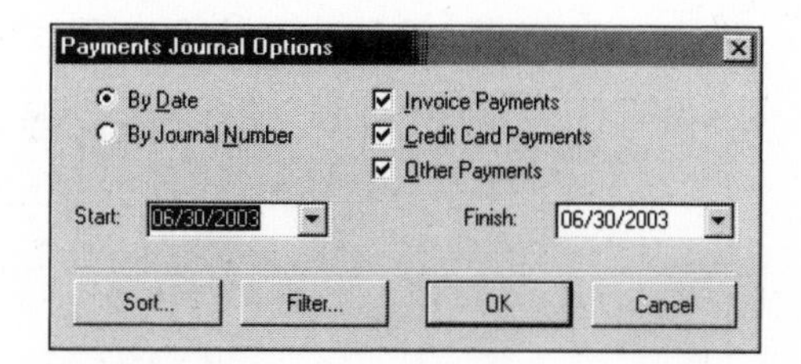

notes

To view the entries for all journals in a single report, choose the Reports menu, then choose Journal Entries and click All.

The Payments Journal has the same choices as the Purchases Journal report. You can display the report by posting date, the default setting, or by journal entry number. In addition, you can choose the type of payment for the report — invoice payments, credit card payments, and other payments. All are selected initially and any one can be omitted from a report by clicking it.

Type the beginning date for the journal transactions you want to display.

Press tab

Type the ending date for the transaction period you want to display.

Click OK to see the report.

Close the display when you have finished.

Displaying Management Reports

Management Reports are available for each ledger.

Choose the **Reports menu** in the Home window, then **choose Management Reports** and **click Payables**. The report options window appears:

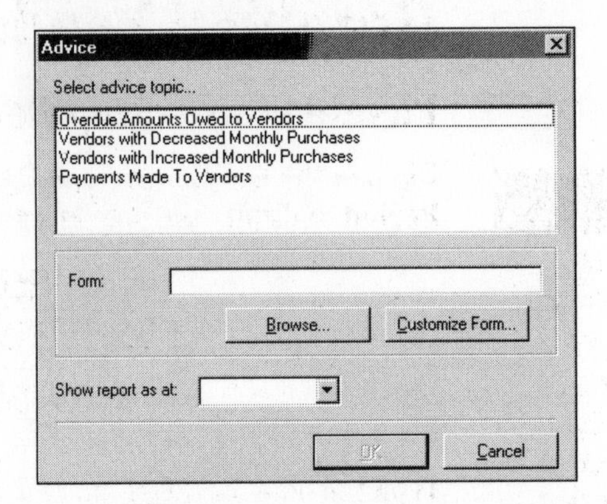

Sometimes management reports can reveal patterns in the business more directly than the regular financial reports. For example, the report for overdue accounts lists only the invoices that are overdue, with complete vendor and invoice details and the number of days that the account has been outstanding. The reports for increased or decreased monthly purchases show changes in purchase patterns over the previous year that an aged detail report may not.

When you click a topic, the appropriate form will be selected from those installed with the program. Unless you have the programs required to customize the forms, accept the default. If appropriate, enter a date for the report and click OK. Print the report and then close the display.

Printing Vendor Reports

To print vendor reports, display the report you want to print.

Click the **Print tool** or **choose** the **File menu** and **click Print**. Make sure that the print options have been set correctly before you print.

Printing Mailing Labels

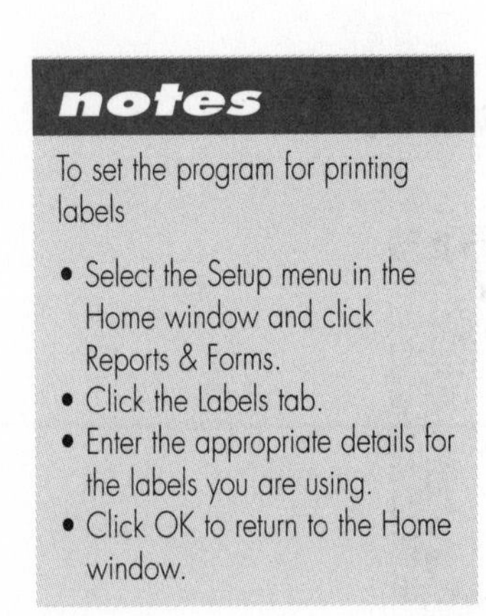

Choose the **Reports menu** in the Home window, then **choose Mailing Labels** and **click Vendors**:

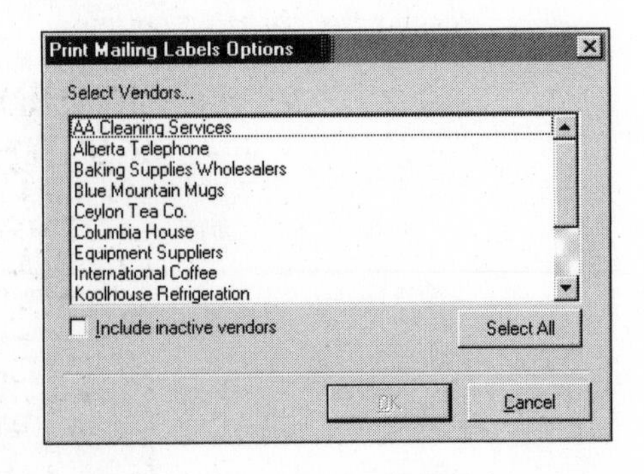

Press ctrl and **click** the **names of the vendors** to include in your list, or **click Select All** to include all vendors.

Make sure that the print options have been set correctly before you print and that your printer is turned on and has the correct labels paper.

Click OK

Graphing Vendor Reports

Payables by Aging Period Charts

notes

- Double click a portion of a graph to see the aging period, the dollar amount and the percentage of the total.
- Double click the legend to make it larger and to add the account names. Double click the expanded legend to reduce it.

Choose the **Graphs menu** in the Home window, then **click Payables by Aging Period** to display the date entry screen:

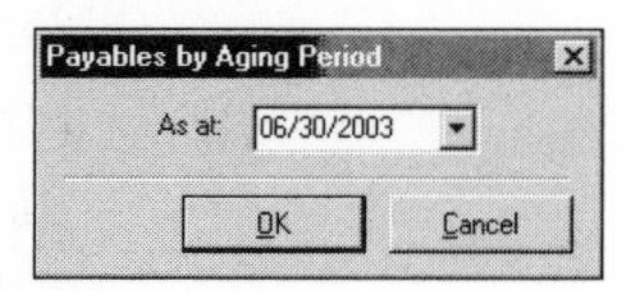

Type the date for the graph or accept the default session date.

Click OK to display the pie chart graph:

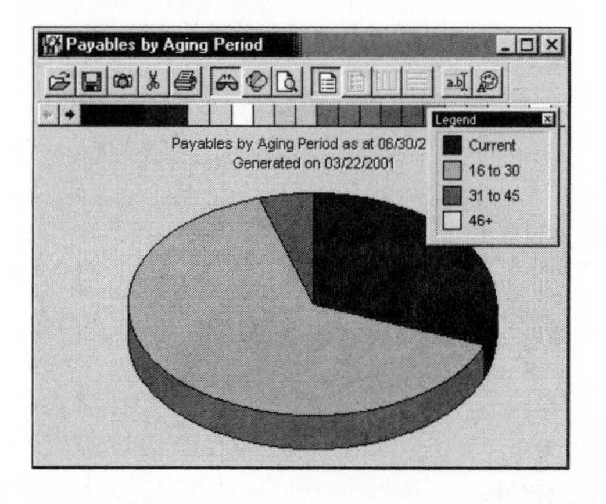

notes

The tool bar options, and the control of the colour and the legend, are the same for all graphs. Refer to page 60 for a review of these features.

Your graph will show all vendors combined with the aging periods selected in the company setup options to provide a quick visual reference of payment obligations.

Close the graph when you have finished.

Payables by Vendor Charts

Choose the **Graphs menu** in the Home window, then **click Payables by Vendor** to display the pie chart options:

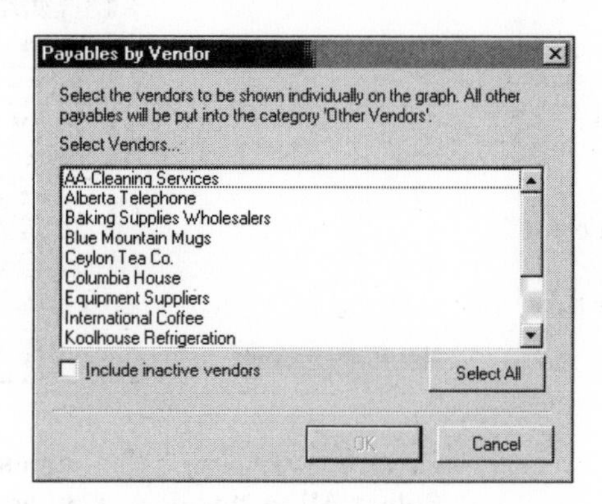

Press ctrl and **click** the **names of the vendors** to include in your pie chart, or **click Select All** to include all the vendors.

Click OK to display the graph:

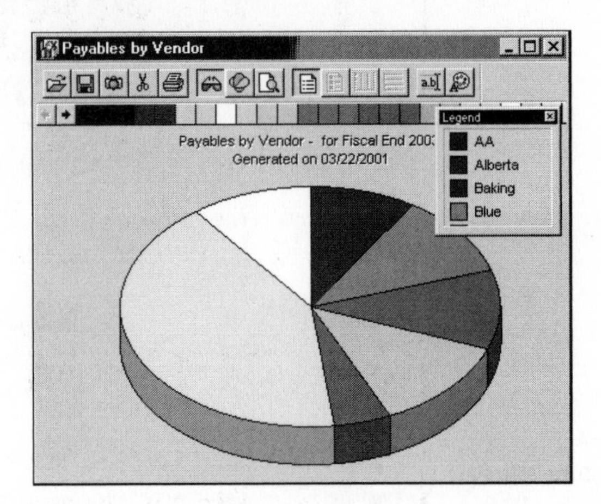

The graph shows the proportion of the total payables that is owed to each selected vendor. The tool bar options, and the control of the colour and the legend, are the same as for the other graphs.

Close the graph when finished.

CASE PROBLEMS

Case One

On July 14, Java Jean's purchased additional dishes for the new patio from a new vendor, Eternal Porcelains. Judy entered the purchase incorrectly as a purchase from Equipment Suppliers. She did not discover the error until two weeks later when the invoice was due. When she tried to make the payment in the Payments journal, Eternal Porcelains did not appear in the vendor list, so she could not make the payment. At that time, Judy was certain that she had entered the purchase, but did not remember exactly how she had entered it.

How can she find the original entry? In detail, describe how she would make the necessary corrections to complete the payment.

Case Two

At the end of September 2003, Java Jean's has the following balances for the quarter:

Revenue from Sales	CR		$58 600
GST Paid on Capital Goods	DR	$670	

Manually show the journal entries to reflect the GST liability incurred from Java Jean's sales for the quarterly period and the remittance of the balance owing to the Receiver General. Assume that the flat tax rate is 5 percent.

CHAPTER FIVE

OBJECTIVES

After completing this chapter, you should be able to

- *enter* cash and account sale transactions
- *enter* customer payment transactions
- *enter* transactions including Harmonized Sales Tax (HST)
- *store* and *recall* recurring entries
- *enter* and *fill* sales quotes and orders
- *enter* partial payments made by customers
- *add* new customer accounts
- *handle* an NSF cheque from a customer
- *edit* and *review* journal transactions
- *post* transactions in the Sales and Receipts journals
- *display*, *print* and *graph* customer reports
- *understand* linked accounts for the Receivables Ledger

COMPANY INFORMATION

Company Profile

Grandeur Graphics, owned and operated by Kathy Grandeur, provides a wide range of graphics, design and desktop publishing services to the business community in Halifax, Nova Scotia. After completing a graphics design program at a community college in Montreal and working for a large publishing company in Toronto, Grandeur decided to return to Halifax, her hometown, to start her own business. Building on her old connections and her reputation for creativity and reliability, she steadily acquired more work and made her business successful.

Grandeur now employs two full-time assistants. The senior designer assists with magazine layouts and the designs for advertising and promotional material. The recently hired junior designer inputs material for text-intensive projects, such as newspapers or company training manuals, and assists with layout on some other projects. Grandeur herself prepares initial design sketches and business proposals and oversees all the work. Since she particularly enjoys creative design, she sometimes completes projects by herself, but when working with others, she is careful to delegate not only the more routine assignments but also the interesting and challenging work. Over time she wants to increase the number of repeat customers or regular contracts and hire additional assistants.

In the past few months, Grandeur has completed accounting for small business courses, including an introduction to Simply Accounting. She is now ready to use the software for her business needs. She will continue to use the bank's payroll services for the time being, knowing that she can easily add her employees to the accounting files when she is more familiar with the program. She has gathered the following records to convert her manual accounting system:

- Chart of Accounts
- Post-Closing Trial Balance
- Vendor Information
- Customer Information
- Accounting Procedures

GRANDEUR GRAPHICS
CHART OF ACCOUNTS

ASSETS
1080 Cash in Bank
1200 Accounts Receivable
1240 Software Library
1280 Office Supplies
1300 Desktop Supplies
1340 Prepaid Insurance
1380 Computers
1400 Monitors
1420 Fax
1440 Scanner
1480 Laser Colour Printers
1500 LCD Projector
1610 Furniture & Equipment
1650 Automobile
1690 Office Condominium

LIABILITIES
2100 Bank Loan
2200 Accounts Payable
2650 HST Charged on Services
2670 HST Paid on Purchases
2850 Mortgage Payable

EQUITY
3560 K. Grandeur, Capital
3600 Net Income

REVENUE
4100 Revenue from Design
4140 Revenue from Desktop Services
4180 Revenue from Consulting
4200 Sales Allowances

EXPENSES
5200 Advertising
5250 Bank Charges
5300 General Expense
5360 Interest Expense
5400 Hydro Expense
5425 Payroll Service Charges
5450 Salaries
5610 Telephone Expense
5650 Wages

GRANDEUR GRAPHICS
POST-CLOSING TRIAL BALANCE

March 31, 2003

Account	Debit	Credit
1080 Cash in Bank	$ 22 310.00	
1200 Accounts Receivable	2 000.00	
1240 Software Library	3 600.00	
1280 Office Supplies	600.00	
1300 Desktop Supplies	450.00	
1340 Prepaid Insurance	840.00	
1380 Computers	6 400.00	
1400 Monitors	3 200.00	
1420 Fax	500.00	
1440 Scanner	1 600.00	
1480 Laser Colour Printers	4 200.00	
1500 LCD Projector	2 100.00	
1610 Furniture & Equipment	4 200.00	
1650 Automobile	25 000.00	
1690 Office Condominium	175 000.00	
2100 Bank Loan		$ 8 000.00
2200 Accounts Payable		4 000.00
2850 Mortgage Payable		150 000.00
3560 K. Grandeur, Capital		90 000.00
	$252 000.00	$252 000.00

GRANDEUR GRAPHICS
VENDOR INFORMATION

Vendor Name (Contact)	Address	Phone No. Fax No.	Terms
Custom Office Furniture (Tori Carpenter)	22 Sawdust Rd. Halifax, NS B3R 7T1	Tel: (902) 661-3412 Fax: (902) 661-5910	n/30
Eastern Bell (Ella Tokmore)	600 Seaforth St. Halifax, NS B3L 1E3	Tel: (902) 662-3998 Fax: (902) 662-4120	n/1 (Payment on Receipt of Invoice)
Expressions Inc. (Yvan Temper)	75 Agricola Lane Halifax, NS B3J 9P1	Tel: (902) 486-5127 Fax: (902) 486-9125	n/15
Language Resources Inc. (Foorin Tung)	510 White Dove Crt. Halifax, NS B3N 8N2	Tel: (902) 598-8227 Fax: (902) 598-5101	n/15
Nova Scotia Hydro (Thor Lektrik)	59 Wildwood Ave. Halifax, NS B3N 6W9	Tel: (902) 596-5197 Fax: (902) 596-5100	n/1
Sentinel Software Insurance (Chip Garde)	1 Sentinel Sq. Halifax, NS B3K 2F5	Tel: (902) 662-6197 Fax: (902) 662-7100	n/15
Telecompute Inc. (Ram Gazer)	45 Terminal Rd. Halifax, NS B3J 4D3	Tel: (902) 664-6619 Fax: (902) 664-6699	n/30

GRANDEUR GRAPHICS
OUTSTANDING VENDOR INVOICES

Vendor Name	Date	Inv/Chq No.	Terms	Amount	Total
Custom Office Furniture	3/10/03	CF-15981	n/30	$2 500.00	
	3/10/03	Chq 588	Payment	−1 000.00	
			Balance		$1 500.00
Telecompute Inc.	3/16/03	TI-673	n/30	$3 000.00	
	3/16/03	Chq 592	Payment	−500.00	
			Balance		$2 500.00
			Grand Total		$4 000.00

GRANDEUR GRAPHICS
CUSTOMER INFORMATION

Customer Name (Contact)	Address	Phone No. Fax No.	Terms
Atlantic Business Cards (Sandi Beech)	33 Pacific St. Halifax, NS B3K 7Y4	Tel: (902) 488-9137 Fax: (902) 488-8120	n/15
Cabot Trail Guides (Amy Walker)	1200 Clearview St. Halifax, NS B3R 3F3	Tel: (902) 662-9484 Fax: (902) 662-9400	n/15
Coastal Corporation (Crystal Waters)	48 Heron Walk Halifax, NS B3K 5R2	Tel: (902) 598-1123 Fax: (902) 598-1000	n/15
Fundy Corporation (Rocky Shore)	29 Herring Cove Rd. Halifax, NS B3R 6T9	Tel: (902) 662-7291 Fax: (902) 662-7900	n/15
Halifax Gazette (Lois Lane)	6 Jubilee Rd. Halifax, NS B3H 8U5	Tel: (902) 594-6199 Fax: (902) 594-5200	n/15
Nova Publishing House (Jill Harlequin)	70 Drumdonald Rd. Halifax, NS B3P 1M2	Tel: (902) 666-1299 Fax: (902) 666-1111	n/15

GRANDEUR GRAPHICS
OUTSTANDING CUSTOMER INVOICES

Customer Name	Date	Inv/Chq No.	Terms	Amount	Total
Atlantic Business Cards	3/15/03	GG-1201	n/15	$ 450.00	$ 450.00
Halifax Gazette	3/5/03	GG-1179	n/15	$1 500.00	
	3/15/03	Chq 87	Payment	−1 000.00	
			Balance		$ 500.00
Nova Publishing House	3/21/03	GG-1269	n/15	$ 800.00	
	3/24/03	GG-1275	n/15	250.00	
			Balance		$1 050.00
			Grand Total		$2 000.00

Accounting Procedures

Open-Invoice Accounting for Receivables

The open-invoice method of accounting for invoices issued by a business allows the business to keep track of each individual invoice and of any partial payments made against it. In contrast, other methods only keep track of the outstanding balance by combining all invoice balances owed by a customer. Simply Accounting uses the open-invoice method. When an invoice is fully paid, you can either retain the invoice or remove (clear) it.

NSF Cheques

If a cheque is deposited from an account that does not have enough money to cover it, the bank may return it to the depositor as NSF (non-sufficient funds). The treatment of an NSF cheque from a customer requires a reversing entry in the Receipts Journal. (See Keystrokes, page 135.) In most companies, the accounting department notifies the customer who wrote the NSF cheque to explain that the debt remains unpaid. Many companies charge an additional fee to the customer to recover their bank charges for the NSF cheque. A separate sales invoice should be prepared for the additional charge.

notes

- The name of the tax has been changed from GST to HST in the default settings for this application.
- The Harmonized Sales Tax as used in the Atlantic provinces is the tax model the federal government would like all provinces to adopt.

The Harmonized Sales Tax (HST)

Grandeur Graphics is a service business using the regular method of calculating HST, the Harmonized Sales Tax. The HST combines and replaces the separate GST and PST at a single rate of 15%. HST is included in all prices quoted to customers. HST charged and collected from customers will be recorded as a liability in *HST Charged on Services*. HST paid to vendors will be recorded in *HST Paid on Purchases* as a decrease in tax liability. Like the GST, the balance owing is the difference between the HST charged and HST paid.

The harmonized tax is administered by the federal government, and the balance to be remitted or the request for a refund will be sent to the Receiver General of Canada by the last day of the month for the previous quarterly period. The federal government forwards to the province the provincial sales tax portion of the amount remitted by the business. Refer to Chapter 2 for further details.

Cash Sales of Services

Cash transactions for services rendered are a normal occurrence in most service businesses. The Simply Accounting program's Sales Journal has Paid By options to handle cash transactions. (See Keystrokes, page 134.) When you choose Paid By Cash or Cheque, the program will debit *Cash in Bank* instead of the *Accounts Receivable* control account. All other accounts for this transaction will be debited or credited in the same way as they would be for credit sale transactions.

notes

The sales tax rules for credits, allowances and discounts are complex and may vary from province to province and for federal taxes. Adjusting General Journal entries may be required to adjust the amount of tax owing and calculate the tax remittance. Usually when discounts and allowances are made after the sale, GST/HST is charged on the full sales amount.

Sales Allowances and Credits

When a customer is dissatisfied with the service provided, Grandeur Graphics may offer a reduction in the price paid for the work. If the customer has not yet paid for the work, you can issue a negative sales invoice. Enter the allowance as a *negative* amount in the amount field and use the *Sales Allowances* account. Treat the allowance as non-taxable by entering the HST non-taxable code (Code 1) in the HST field. When payment is received, remember to "pay" the allowance invoice. If the customer has paid for the work, make a Payments Journal entry (Other Payment) to provide the refund. Again, the allowance should be non-taxable.

Purchases with Down Payments

When a purchase is accompanied by a partial payment, or a down payment, you should post a Purchases Journal entry for the full amount of the invoice followed by a Payments Journal entry for the amount of the down payment. Thus, two separate entries are required.

INSTRUCTIONS

1. Using the Chart of Accounts, Vendor Information, Customer Information and Accounting Procedures for Grandeur Graphics, record entries for the source documents in Simply Accounting. The procedures for entering each new type of documents in Simply Accounting. The procedures for entering each new type of transaction in this application are outlined step by step in the keystroke section following the source documents. These transactions are indicated with a ✔ in the completion box beside the source document. The page on which the relevant keystrokes begin is printed immediately below the check box.
2. After you have finished making your entries, print the reports and graphs indicated on the following printing form. Instructions for reports begin on page 138.

REPORTS

Lists
- ❑ Chart of Accounts
- ❑ Vendors
- ❑ Customers

Financials
- ☑ Balance Sheet
  date: April 30
- ☑ Income Statement
  from April 1 to April 30
- ❑ Trial Balance
- ☑ General Ledger
  accounts: 1200 2650 4100 4140
  from April 1 to April 30
- ❑ Cash Flow Projection

HST
- ☑ HST Summary Report

Mailing Labels
- ❑ Labels

Management Reports
- ❑ Ledger

Journals
- ☑ All Journals (by posting date)
  from April 1 to April 30
- ❑ General
- ❑ Purchases
- ❑ Payments
- ☑ Sales (by posting date)
  from April 1 to April 30
- ☑ Receipts (by posting date)
  from April 1 to April 30

Payables
- ❑ Vendor Aged
- ❑ Aged Overdue Payables
- ❑ Pending Purchase Orders

Receivables
- ☑ Customer Aged
  Detail Report dated April 30
- ❑ Aged Overdue Receivables
- ☑ Customer Statement
  for Halifax Gazette dated April 30

GRAPHS

- ❑ Payables by Aging Period
- ☑ Receivables by Aging Period
- ☑ Sales vs Receivables (all revenue accts)
- ❑ Revenues by Account
- ❑ Expenses and Net Profit as % of Revenue
- ❑ Payables by Vendor
- ❑ Receivables by Customer
- ❑ Receivables Due vs Payables Due
- ❑ Expenses by Account
- ❑ Current Revenue vs Last Year

SOURCE DOCUMENTS

SESSION DATE – April 8

> **notes**
> Refer to Keystrokes, page 120.

☑ 120

Sales Invoice #GG-1300
Dated April 2/03
To Coastal Corporation, $1 380 for completion of desktop publishing services contract. 15% HST included. Terms: net 15 days.

☑ 125

Cash Receipt #101
Dated April 3/03
From Halifax Gazette, cheque #121, $500 in full payment of account. Reference invoice #GG-1179.

☐

Sales Invoice #GG-1301
Dated April 3/03
To Artworks Inc. (new customer), $1 725 for designing toy box lid. 15% HST included. Terms: net 15 days.

> **notes**
> ☑ Artworks Inc.
> **128** (Contact Joan Miro)
> is located at
> 33 Abinaki Rd.
> Truro, NS B2N 8T1
> Tel: 902-771-9831
> Fax: 902-771-8136
> Credit Limit: $2 000
> E-mail: miro@artworks.com
> Web: www.artworks.com

☑ 131

Sales Quote #SQ-100
Dated April 3/03
To Halifax Gazette: The price for providing weekly desktop publishing services to weekly paper is $460. 15% HST is included in this price. Terms: net 15 days. This quote will be valid until April 15, 2003.

☑ 133

Sales Invoice #GG-1302
Dated April 4/03
To Halifax Gazette, acceptance of (filling) quote # SQ-100, $460 for desktop publishing services for weekly paper. 15% HST included. Store as recurring weekly entry. Terms: net 15 days.

☑ 134

Cash Sales Invoice #GG-1303
Dated April 4/03
To David Manga, $460 for design work for The All Canadian Trivia Game. 15% HST included. Full payment received in cash.

☑ 135

Bank Debit Memo #SB-7911
Dated April 4/03
From Scotia Bank, $500 for NSF cheque from Halifax Gazette. Reference invoice #GG-1179 and cheque #121. The Gazette has been notified of the unpaid account.

☐

Cash Receipt #102
Dated April 5/03
From Halifax Gazette, certified cheque #255 for $500 with letter of apology in full payment of account. Reference Bank Debit Memo #SB-7911 and invoice #GG-1179.

☐

Cheque Copy #601
Dated April 5/03
To Custom Office Furniture, $1 500 in full payment of account. Reference invoice #CF-15981.

> **notes**
> Use Quick Add for Cash Sales customers.

☐

Cash Sales Invoice #GG-1304
Dated April 5/03
To Malin Andersson, $287.50 for consulting services. 15% HST included. Received money order #3121.

notes

To edit a customer record, click the Customers icon in the Home window. Click the icon for the customer to select the customer. Click the Edit tool icon or choose the Edit menu and click Edit to open the Receivables Ledger record for the selected customer. (Or, double click the customer's icon in the Customers window to open the ledger.) Click the Activity tab to access the Credit Limit field. Make the necessary changes. Close the Receivables Ledger and the Customers window.

- [ ] Memo #1
Dated April 5/03
From Owner: Edit all existing customer records to include a credit limit of $5 000. The credit limit for new customers will be $2 000.

- [ ] Purchase Invoice #EI-4172
Dated April 5/03
From Expressions Inc., $690 for advertising in graphics magazine including $90 HST. Charge to advertising expense. Terms: n/15.

- [ ] Sales Invoice #GG-1305
Dated April 6/03
To Nova Publishing House, $3 450 for design on three book covers. 15% HST included. Terms: net 15 days.

- [ ] Cash Receipt #103
Dated April 8/03
From Nova Publishing House, cheque #884 for $800 in payment of account. Reference invoice #GG-1269.

- [ ] Sales Order #CT-821
Dated April 8/03
Shipping date April 15/03
To Cabot Trail Guides, $1 265 for desktop publishing work. 15% HST included. Terms: net 15 days.

- [ ] Purchase Quote #121
Dated April 8/03
Shipping date April 23/03
From Sentinel Software Insurance, $1 104 for insurance on software for one year including $144 HST. Terms: net 15 days. This quote remains valid for 15 days.

- [ ] Purchase Order #208
Dated April 8/03
Shipping date April 12/03
From Vision Camera (use Full Add), $2 760 for a new digital camera (new account) including $360 HST. Terms: n/30.

notes

- [ ] Vision Camera (Contact Polly Lenz) is located at 390 Kodak Cres. Halifax, NS B3P 5T4 Tel: (902) 668-7191 Fax: (902) 668-7109 Vendor collects GST Terms: net 30
- [ ] Create new Group account: 1390 Digital Cameras

SESSION DATE – April 14

- [ ] Cheque Copy #602
Dated April 9/03
To Telecompute Inc., $2 500 in full payment of account. Reference invoice #TI-673.

- [ ] Purchase Invoice #SS-14219
Dated April 10/03
From Sentinel Software Insurance, to fill purchase quote #121, $1 104 for software insurance, including $144 HST. Terms: net 15 days.

- [ ] Sales Invoice #GG-1306
Dated April 10/03
To Cabot Trail Guides, to fill sales order #CT-821, $1 265 for desktop publishing work. 15% HST included. Terms: net 15 days.

- [ ] Bank Credit Memo #SB-62514
Dated April 10/03
From Scotia Bank, $3 000 six-month loan granted to purchase LCD projector.

Sales Invoice #GG-1307
Dated April 11/03
To Halifax Gazette, $460 for weekly desktop publishing assignment. 15% HST included. Recall recurring weekly entry. Terms: net 15 days.

Purchase Invoice #VC-411
Dated April 11/03
From Vision Camera to fill purchase order #208, $2 760 for a new digital camera including $360 HST. Terms: n/30.

notes

The computer purchase with partial payment requires two journal entries — first a purchase and then a payment. Refer to Accounting Procedures.

Purchase Invoice #TI-818
Dated April 11/03
From Telecompute Inc., $5 750 including $750 HST for a new LCD projector that hooks up to a computer for workshops and demonstrations. Paid $3 000 with cheque #603, and balance on terms. Terms: net 30 days.

Cash Receipt #104
Dated April 12/03
From Nova Publishing House, cheque #1007 for $250 in payment of account. Reference invoice #GG-1275.

notes

We use the terms Shipping date and Delivery date interchangeably.

Sales Order #ABC-29
Dated April 12/03
Delivery date April 15/03
To Atlantic Business Cards, Inc., $575 for design work. This price includes 15% HST. Terms: net 15 days.

Sales Quote #101
Dated April 12/03
Shipping date April 22/03
To Fundy Corporation: The desktop work on the training manual for the corporation employees will cost $4 830 including 15% HST. Terms: net 15 days. This quote will remain in effect for 15 days.

Cash Receipt #105
Dated April 13/03
From Coastal Corporation, cheque #73 for $1 380 in full payment of account. Reference invoice #GG-1300.

notes

Remember to use Quick Add for Cash Sales customers.

Cash Sales Invoice #GG-1308
Dated April 14/03
To Swedish Design Inc., $575 for consulting services. 15% HST included. Received cheque #4321.

SESSION DATE – April 21

Sales Invoice #GG-1309
Dated April 15/03
To Atlantic Business Cards, Inc., to fill Sales Order #ABC-29, $575 for design work. 15% HST included. Terms: net 15 days.

notes

Enter the sales allowance as a cash purchase because the original invoice has been fully paid. Enter a positive amount.

Memo #2
Dated April 15/03
From Owner: Give Coastal Corporation (use Quick Add) an allowance of $100 for errors that required corrections by Coastal Corporation staff. Issued cheque #604 together with a letter of apology.

notes

Lobster Hut
(Contact Toby Fisher)
is located at
100 Atlantic St.
Halifax, NS B3H 3R3
Tel: (902) 596-1862

notes

Use the Same Customer tool for the second sale to Goodbar to pre-select the customer.

notes

When you post the changed recurring entry, the program will warn you that the entry has changed. Click Yes to proceed.

- [ ] Sales Invoice #GG-1310
Dated April 15/03
To Lobster Hut (use Full Add), $690 for design of menu for restaurant. 15% HST included. Terms: net 15 days.

- [ ] Cash Sales Invoice #GG-1311
Dated April 16/03
To Goodbar Law Firm (use Quick Add), $460 for desktop publishing task. 15% HST included. Payment by cheque #444. (Click the Use same customer tool.)

- [ ] Cash Sales Invoice #GG-1312
Dated April 16/03
To Goodbar Law Firm, $115 for designing business cards for paralegals. 15% HST included. Payment by cheque #445. Click the Use same customer tool to deselect it for the next transaction.)

- [ ] Cash Utility Purchase Invoice #NSH-33437
Dated April 16/03
From Nova Scotia Hydro, $230 for hydro services including $30 HST. Terms: cash on receipt. Issued cheque #605 in full payment.

- [ ] Cheque Copy #606
Dated April 17/03
To Expressions Inc., $690 in full payment of account. Reference invoice #EI-4172.

- [ ] Sales Invoice #GG-1313
Dated April 18/03
To Halifax Gazette, $920 for weekly desktop publishing assignment plus work on annual supplement. 15% HST included. Edit the recurring weekly entry but do not store the changes. Terms: net 15 days.

- [ ] Cash Utility Purchase Invoice #EB-67212
Dated April 18/03
From Eastern Bell, $172.50 for telephone services, including $22.50 HST. Terms: cash on receipt. Issued cheque #607 in full payment.

- [ ] Cash Receipt #106
Dated April 18/03
From Artworks Inc., cheque #312 for $1 725 in full payment of account. Reference invoice #GG-1301.

- [ ] Purchase Invoice #TI-982
Dated April 19/03
From Telecompute Inc., $345 for two rechargeable *ni-cad* batteries for portable computer including $45 HST. Terms: net 30 days. (Use Computers asset account.)

- [ ] Cash Sales Invoice #GG-1314
Dated April 20/03
To Carol Andonova, design artist, $287.50 for consultation services. 15% HST included. Payment by cash.

- [ ] Cash Receipt #107
Dated April 20/03
From Atlantic Business Cards, Inc., cheque #387 for $450 in payment of account. Reference invoice #GG-1201.

SESSION DATE – April 28

- [ ] Sales Invoice #GG-1315
Dated April 22/03
To Fundy Corporation, to fill sales quote #101, $4 830 for desktop work on training manual. 15% HST included. Terms: net 15 days.

- [ ] Bank Debit Memo #SB-10901
Dated April 23/03
From Scotia Bank, $46 for bank service charges, including charge for NSF cheque.

- [ ] Purchase Invoice #LR-679
Dated April 23/03
From Language Resources Inc., $345 for language fonts (Software Library account) required for special publishing project, including $45 HST. Terms: n/15.

- [ ] Bank Debit Memo #SB-11004
Dated April 24/03
From Scotia Bank, $80 interest charges on outstanding loan.

- [ ] Cheque Copy #608
Dated April 24/03
To Sentinel Software Insurance, $1 104 in full payment of account. Reference invoice #SS-14219.

notes

- [ ] Maritime Biscuit Co.
(Contact Ivan McCain)
is located at
80 Strawberry Hill
Halifax, NS B3K 6G6
Tel: (902) 488-7199
Fax: (902) 488-7001

- [ ] Sales Invoice #GG-1316
Dated April 24/03
To Maritime Biscuit Co. (use Full Add), $1 725 for cookie box design. 15% HST included. Terms: net 15 days.

- [ ] Sales Invoice #GG-1317
Dated April 25/03
To Halifax Gazette, $460 for weekly desktop publishing assignment. 15% HST included. Use recurring weekly entry. Terms: net 15 days.

- [ ] Purchase Invoice #CF-16213
Dated April 26/03
From Custom Office Furniture, $920 for new design table required for extra workload, including $120 HST. Terms: net 30 days.

- [ ] Cash Sales Invoice #GG-1318
Dated April 27/03
To Terry Geroche, $460 for design work. 15% HST included. Paid in cash.

- [ ] Cash Sales Invoice #GG-1319
Dated April 28/03
To Lila Read, $287.50 for consulting services. 15% HST included. Cheque #332 received in payment.

SESSION DATE – April 30

- [ ] Bank Debit Memo #SB-13129
Dated April 29/03
From Scotia Bank, monthly payroll and payroll services

Wages	$2 100.00
Salaries	3 200.00
Payroll Services	150.00
HST @ 15%	22.50
Total	$5 472.50

notes

❑ Halifax Art School (Contact Joyce Kane) is located at 5000 Gainsborough Pl. Halifax, NS B3K 2K8

❑❑ Sales Invoice #GG-1320
Dated April 30/03
To Halifax Art School (use Full Add), $1 380 with taxes included for sale of old LCD projector valued at $2 100. Sale price of projector is $1 200. Charge loss to new Group account, 5390 Loss on Sale of Peripherals. Terms: n/15. (Complete a Sales Journal entry for the sale and a General Journal entry for the loss.)

KEYSTROKES

Opening Data Files

Using the instructions for accessing data files in Chapter 1, page 15, open the data files for Grandeur Graphics. Enter the first session date, April 8, 2003, for this application.

Type `April 8 2003`

Click OK

You are shown the following warning statement:

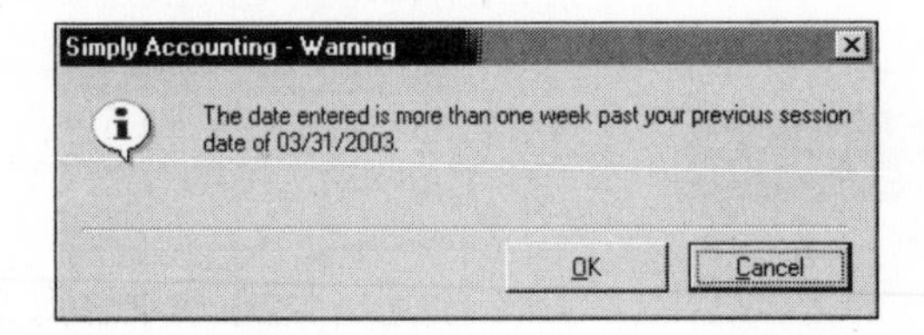

Normally a business would update its accounting records more frequently. If you have entered the correct date,

Click OK to accept the date entered and display the familiar Home window.

Accounting for Sales

notes

The icons for the Payroll, Inventory and Project ledgers are hidden because these ledgers are not set up.

Sales are entered in the Sales Journal indicated by the Sales, Orders & Quotes icon as shown in the following screen:

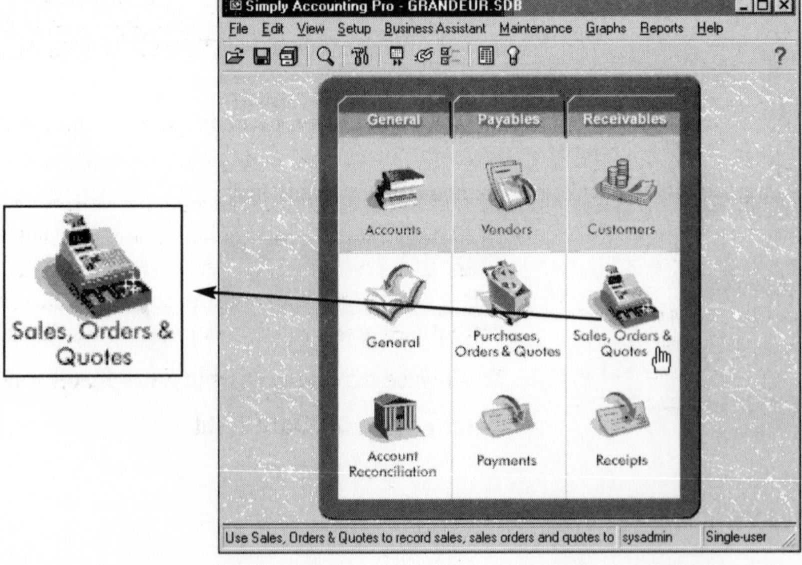

notes

Many of the tool bar buttons in the Sales Journal are familiar from other journals — Home window, Store, Recall, Undo, Customize journal and Allocate. Print and E-mail buttons allow you to print or e-mail the invoice before posting to provide a customer or store copy of the sales invoice. You can use tool buttons to remove, fill or cancel an order, to adjust a posted invoice and to continue using the same customer. Invoice lookup and the track shipments buttons will be explained in a later application.

Click the **Sales, Orders & Quotes icon** to open the Sales Journal. The Sales Journal input form appears on the screen as follows:

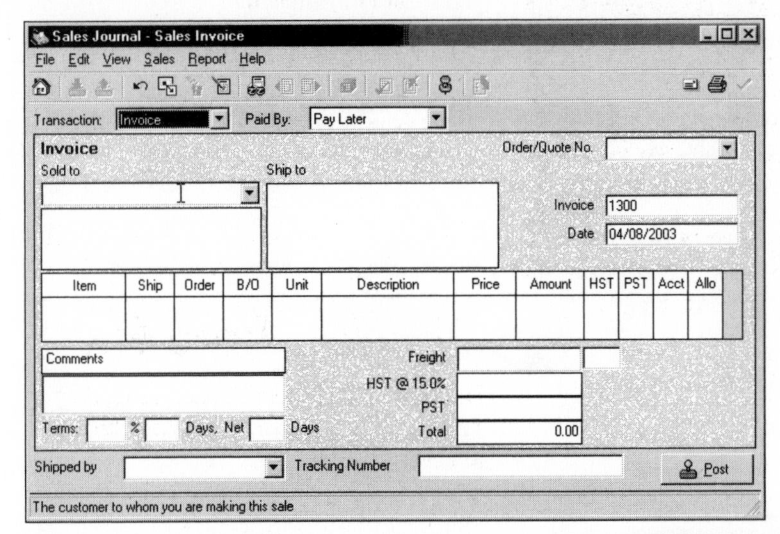

The Invoice option is selected as the default Transaction Type and Pay Later as the payment option. Since this is a regular sale, leave these selections unchanged.

Click the **Customer (Sold to) field list arrow** to obtain the list of customers as shown on the following screen:

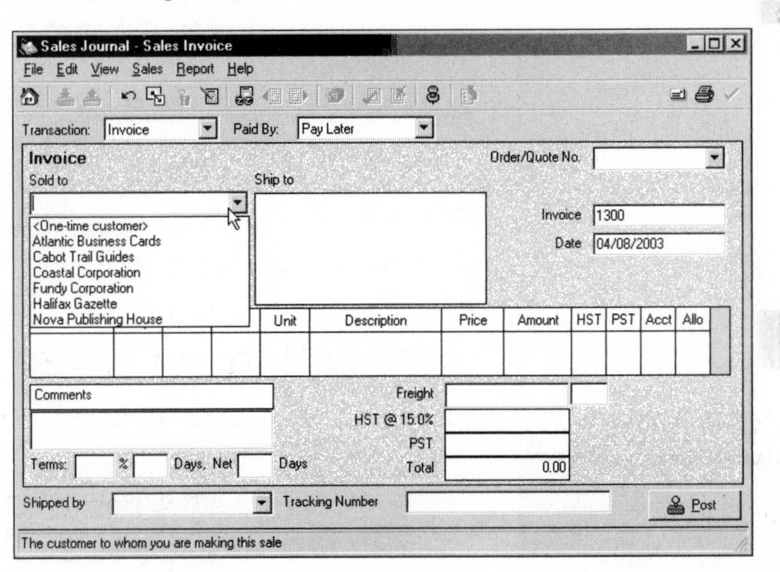

notes

We have set up invoice numbers to update automatically by omitting the GG portion. If you want to include GG with the numbers, you must type the entire invoice number for each sale because the alphanumeric code cannot be updated automatically.

Click Coastal Corporation, the customer in the first source document, to select and enter it.

Notice that the customer's name and address have been added to your input form. If you have made an error in your selection, click the customer list arrow and start again. By default, the Sold to and the Ship to fields are completed from the customer's ledger record. You can edit the shipping address if necessary. If you have selected the correct customer, you can skip over the shipping information.

The invoice number is entered and updated automatically by the program.

Double click the **Date field**.

notes

- You can also press (tab) repeatedly to move to the field you need next.
- If you want, you can enter the quantity (one for services, in this case), enter the price per unit in the price field and let the program calculate the amount by multiplying the two together. You can use this method if you are selling more than one item that is not an inventory item.

The session date appears by default. It is highlighted, ready to be accepted or changed. You need to change the date. Enter the date on which the transaction took place, April 2, 2003.

Type 4-2

Press (tab)

The cursor advances to the Item field. Because we are not using the Inventory Ledger for this application, skip this field and the next four.

Click the first line of the **Description field**. The Description field is used to enter a description or comment concerning the sale.

Type `Desktop services contract`

Press (tab)

The cursor is now in the Price field. The Price field also refers to unit prices; it is not needed for the service contract.

Press (tab)

notes

Entering a negative amount will generate a debit entry for the sale with a credit to Accounts Receivable.

The cursor should now be positioned in the Amount field, where you will enter the total amount for this invoice, with the HST included.

Type 1380

Press (tab)

The cursor is now positioned in the HST field. We will use this field to enter the HST, which replaces GST in Nova Scotia.

Press (enter) to display the following HST codes on your screen:

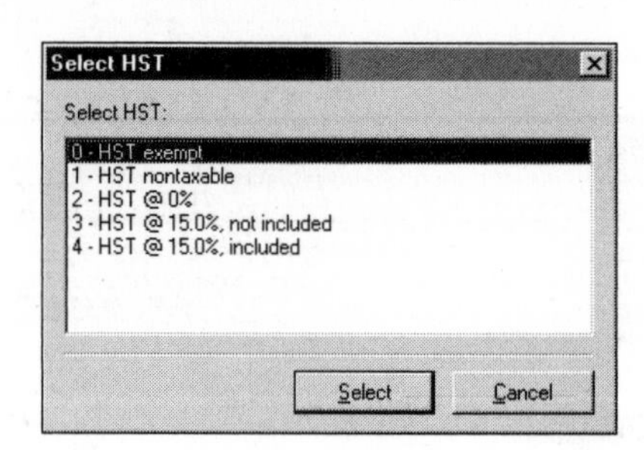

notes

- For this application, the sales tax rate is set to 15%, the harmonized single tax rate for Nova Scotia. For non-Atlantic provinces, the rate is set at 7% and GST codes will display as GST at 7%.
- Code 3, HST not included, is used when HST must be added to the sale price. HST Codes 0, 1 and 2 are used for exempt, non-taxable and zero-rated goods.

You may select from this list the appropriate HST code for the company. Since the invoice amount already includes the HST, you should choose Code 4 - HST @ 15%, included.

Click 4 - HST @ 15.0%, included to highlight it.

Click Select to enter the code.

Since the provincial and federal retail sales taxes are harmonized, and there is no separate entry for PST, the PST rate is set at 0% (customers are not charged PST) and the cursor skips over this field. When PST is applicable and is set up in the defaults for the company, the program will not skip over the PST field.

The Account field in a sales invoice refers to the credit portion of the journal entry, usually a revenue account. Again, you cannot access the *Accounts Receivable* linked account directly. The software will automatically debit the *Accounts Receivable* control account in the General Ledger.

In the Account field, you can see the list of accounts. To see revenue accounts, type the first digit for the revenue accounts.

Type 4

Press (enter)

Scroll down until the other revenue accounts are included in the viewing area.

Click 4140 Revenue from Desktop Services to highlight it.

Click Select to add it to your input form.

Press (tab) to advance the cursor to line 2 in the Item field, ready for additional sale items if necessary.

The Comments box can be used for a default comment set up for the business so that it appears on all invoices, or you can enter a comment at the time of the sale. You can add to or change a default comment if you want. We will add the comment that HST is included in all prices.

Click the **Comments field**.

Type `HST @15% is included in all prices.`

The transaction is now complete, and your invoice should resemble the following:

notes

The payment terms are set by default as net 15 days. They can be modified for individual customers in the Receivables Ledger. You can also edit the terms for individual sales in the Sales Journal.

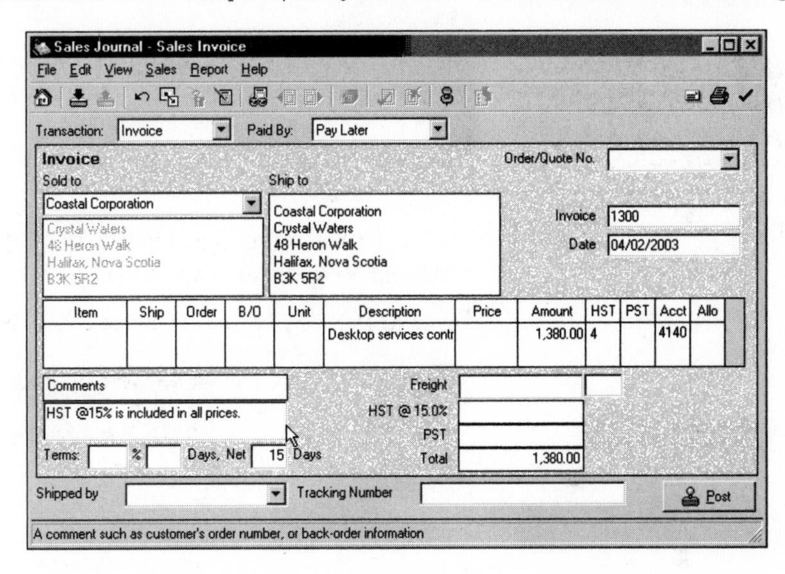

The payment terms have been set up as defaults for all customers as net 15 days. There is no discount. Terms can be changed for individual customers or on individual sales invoices.

notes

If you set up shippers and enter tracking numbers, you can access the shipper's Web site to trace goods shipped to customers.

Before storing, posting or printing a sales journal entry, you should review it carefully.

Reviewing the Sales Journal Entry

Choose the **Report menu** and **click Display Sales Journal Entry** to display the transaction you have entered as shown:

notes

This is not a recurring entry, so it will not be stored.

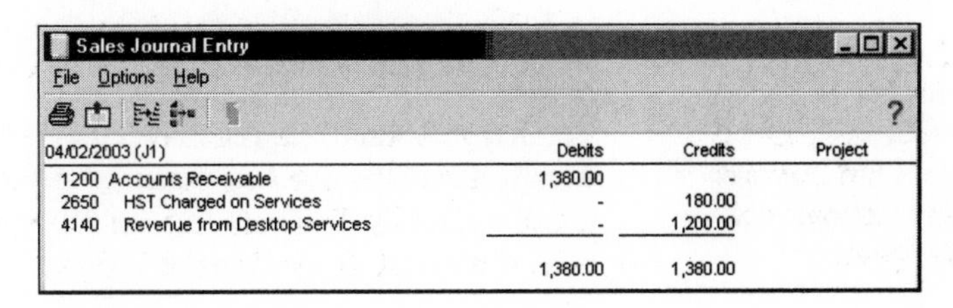
Sales Journal Entry
File Options Help

04/02/2003 (J1)	Debits	Credits	Project
1200 Accounts Receivable	1,380.00	-	
2650 HST Charged on Services	-	180.00	
4140 Revenue from Desktop Services	-	1,200.00	
	1,380.00	1,380.00	

notes

Other Receivables Ledger linked accounts will be used and explained later. These are the Receivables bank account, provincial sales tax account, freight revenue account and sales discount account.

Review the journal entry to check for mistakes. You can see that *Accounts Receivable*, the control account, has been updated automatically by the Simply Accounting program because the Receivables and General Ledgers are fully integrated. All credit sales are debited to *Accounts Receivable*, the default linked account for the Receivables Ledger. *HST Charged on Services* has also been updated correctly because of the HST code you entered and because *HST Charged on Services* was defined as the HST linked account for the Receivables Ledger. You did not need to enter either of these two accounts directly in the Sales Journal. The balance owing by this customer is also directly updated as a result of the Sales Journal entry.

Close the display to return to the Sales Journal input screen.

notes

If you selected the wrong customer, refer to Appendix A for instructions on making reversing entries.

CORRECTING THE SALES JOURNAL ENTRY BEFORE POSTING

Move to the field that has the error. **Press** tab to move forward through the fields or **press** shift and tab together to move back to a previous field. This will highlight the field information so you can change it. **Type** the correct information and **press** tab to enter it.

You can also use the mouse to point to a field and drag through the incorrect information to highlight it. **Type** the correct information and **press** tab to enter it.

If the customer is incorrect, re-select from the customer list by **clicking** the customer field list arrow. **Click** the name of the correct customer.

Click an incorrect description, HST code, amount or account to highlight the incorrect entry. **Type** the correct information and **press** tab. Or, in the HST and Account fields, **press** enter to display the selection list. **Click** the correct entry, **click Select**, then **press** tab to enter the change.

You can discard the entire entry. **Click** [undo] to leave the Sales Journal open or **click** [X] to close the Sales Journal. Simply Accounting will prompt you to confirm that you want to discard the entry.

Posting

notes

If you print or e-mail invoices through the Sales Journal, you must do this before posting. Turn on your printer with the forms you need. (For practice, you can use ordinary printer paper.) Click the Print button. You can print as many copies of the invoice as you want before posting. To e-mail invoices, you need Internet access and an e-mail account. Click the E-mail button.

When you are certain that you have entered all the information correctly, you must post the transaction to save it.

Click the **Post button** [Post] on the tool bar or choose the Sales menu and click Post to save your transaction. A new blank Sales Journal form appears on the screen.

CORRECTING THE SALES JOURNAL ENTRY AFTER POSTING

If you discover a Sales Journal transaction error after posting an entry, you can adjust the sales invoice from the Sales Journal window. The steps are the same as for the Purchases Journal. Refer to page 99 for a complete description of these steps.

Click the **Adjust invoice tool** [icon] or choose the Sales menu and click Adjust Invoice. Enter the search parameters (dates and customers) and **click Browse**. From the list of invoices, **click** the one with the error and **click Select**. The invoice will be displayed. Make corrections and then post the revised entry. Simply Accounting creates the appropriate reversing entry.

The next transaction is a receipt so we must exit from the Sales Journal.

Close the Sales Journal input form to return to the Home window.

Accounting for Receipts

Receipts are entered in the Receipts Journal indicated by the hand pointer as follows:

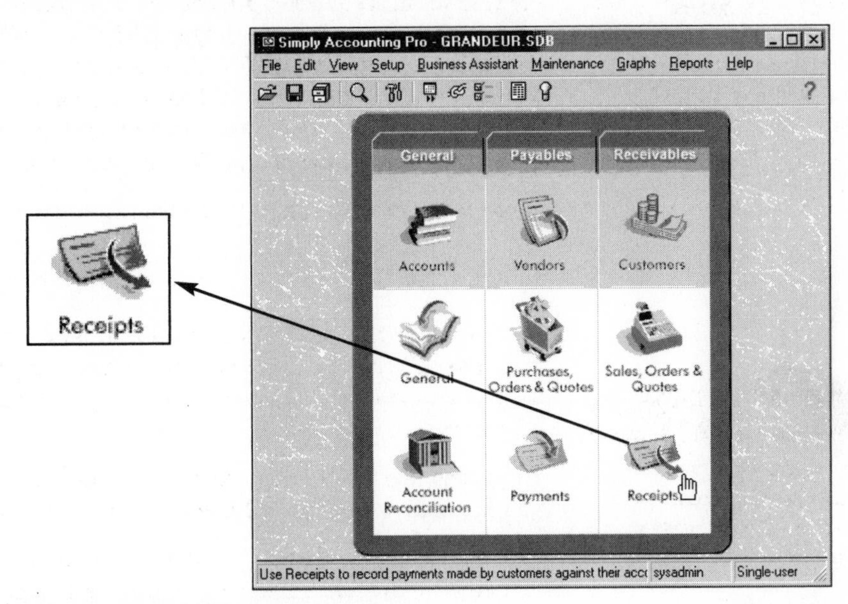

Click the **Receipts icon** to open the Receipts Journal. The following blank Receipts Journal input screen appears:

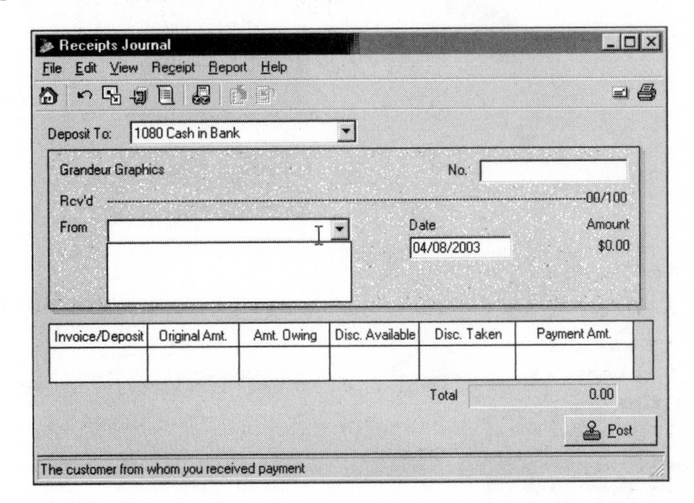

notes

Simply Accounting allows you to set up more than one bank account. If more than one bank account is set up, choose the account from the Deposit To drop-down list.

The Customer (From) field is ready to receive information.

Click the **Customer field list arrow** to display the familiar customer list as shown:

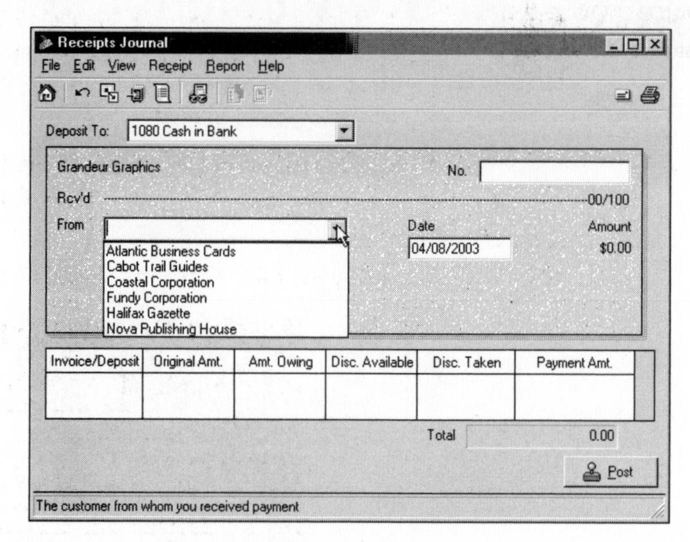

Click Halifax Gazette to choose this customer. As shown, the customer's name and address have been added to your input form, together with all outstanding invoices for Halifax Gazette:

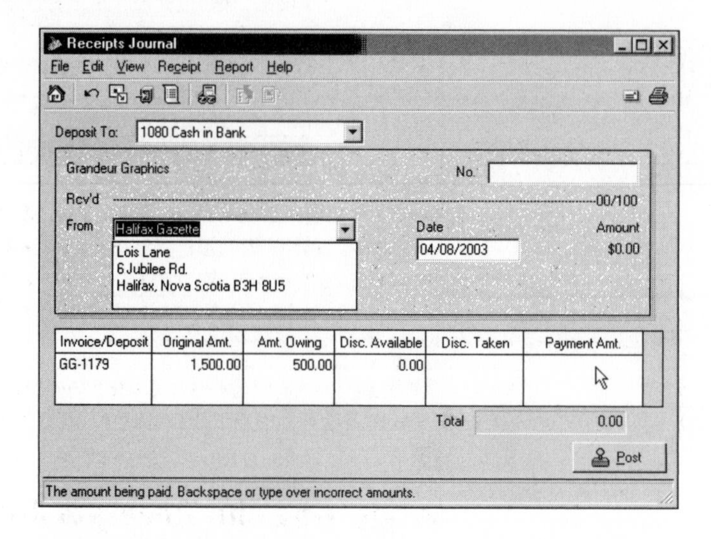

Grandeur Graphics has a single bank account so it is correctly selected in the Deposit To field. If you have chosen the wrong customer, display the list again and click the correct customer. If you have selected correctly,

Click the **No. field** and enter the customer's cheque number.

Type `121`

Press *tab*

The cursor moves to the Date field. Replace the session date with the date for this transaction.

Type `Apr 3`

Press *tab*

The cursor moves to the Invoice/Deposit field.

Press *tab* to advance to the Disc. Taken field. Since Grandeur Graphics does not offer customer discounts, we can skip this field.

notes

- As with payments to vendors, you cannot enter account numbers in the Receipts Journal. You need only enter the amount paid on the appropriate invoice line. The program automatically creates the journal entry.
- The No. field may also be used to record the business receipt number. Receipt numbers can be set up to increase automatically.

Warning!

When an invoice amount is highlighted and it is not being paid, press del to remove the amount from the total, and press tab to update the total.

Press tab to advance to the Payment Amt. field. By default, the amount owing on the first invoice is shown and highlighted. All outstanding invoices are listed on the screen. You can accept a highlighted amount, or type an exact amount for a partial payment. In this case, there is only one invoice and the full amount is being paid so you can accept the default.

Press tab to accept the amount in the Payment Amt. field. When there is more than one outstanding invoice, the cursor will advance to the Disc. Taken field for the next invoice.

The completed Receipts form should now appear as follows:

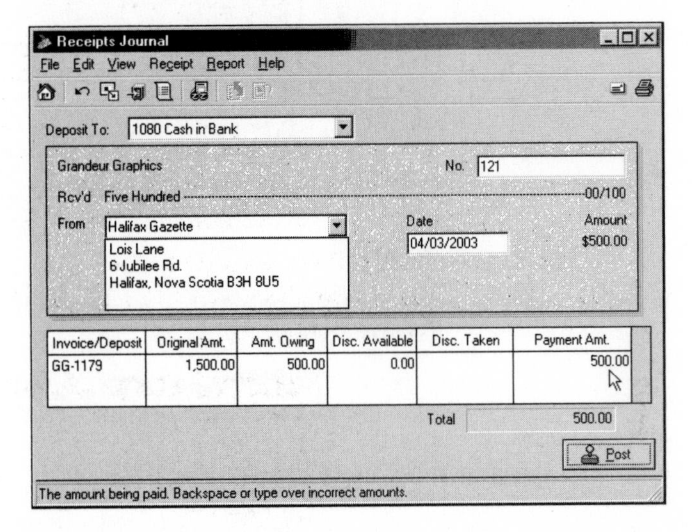

Notice that the upper cheque portion of the form has also been completed. In making Receipts Journal entries, you do not need to enter any accounts because Simply Accounting chooses the linked accounts defined for the Receivables Ledger to create the journal entry. *Cash in Bank* will be debited automatically and *Accounts Receivable* will be credited.

You have made all the entries for this transaction, so you are ready to review and post your transaction.

Reviewing the Receipts Journal Entry

Choose the **Report menu** and **click Display Receipts Journal Entry** to display the transaction you have entered as follows:

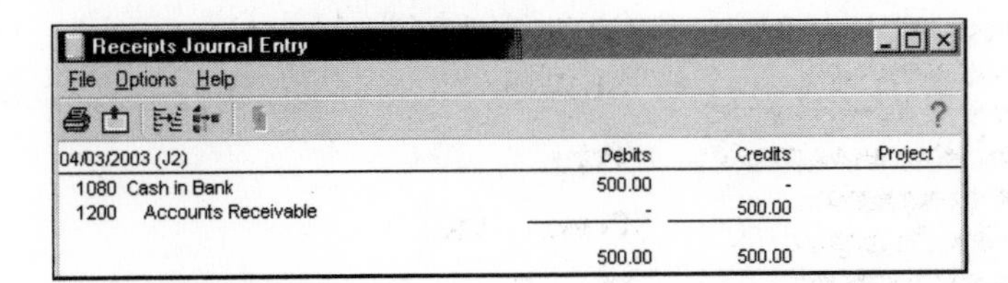

Here you can see the related journal entry created by Simply Accounting when you complete a Receipts Journal transaction. The program updates the *Accounts Receivable* control account in the General Ledger and *Cash in Bank* because the Receivables and General ledgers are fully integrated. *Cash in Bank* is defined as the default linked bank account for the Receivables Ledger as well as for the Payables Ledger because Grandeur Graphics has only one bank account. The receipt will also be credited directly to the customer's account in the Receivables Ledger to reduce the balance owing.

Close the display to return to the Receipts Journal input screen.

CORRECTING THE RECEIPTS JOURNAL ENTRY BEFORE POSTING

Move to the field that has the error. **Press** tab to move forward through the fields or **press** shift and tab together to move back to a previous field. This will highlight the field information so you can change it. **Type** the correct information and **press** tab to enter it.

You can also use the mouse to point to a field and drag through the incorrect information to highlight it. **Type** the correct information and **press** tab to enter it.

If the customer is incorrect, re-select from the customer list by **clicking** the list arrow beside this field. **Click** the name of the correct customer. You will be asked to confirm that you want to discard the current transaction. **Click Yes** to discard the incorrect entry and display the outstanding invoices for the correct customer. **Type** the receipt information for this customer.

You can also discard the entry. **Click** ☒ or ↶ and then **click Yes** to confirm.

Posting

When you are certain that you have entered all the information correctly, you must post the transaction to save it.

Click the **Post button** Post on the tool bar or choose the Receipt menu and click Post to save your transaction.

Close the Receipts Journal after confirming that the date is correct.

Adding a New Customer

You can add new customers from the Receivables Ledger. Return to the Home window. Double click the Customers icon. Then click the Create tool button to open a new ledger input form.

On April 3, a new customer is named in the source documents and must be added to your files. We will add the customer directly from the Sales Journal just as we added new vendors from the Purchases Journal.

Click the **Sales Journal icon** Sales, Orders & Quotes to open the Sales Journal.

Be sure that Invoice and Pay Later are selected as the transaction and payment options.

Click the **Sold to (Customer) field** to place the cursor.

Type `Artworks Inc.`

Press tab to display the warning that you have typed a name that is not on the list:

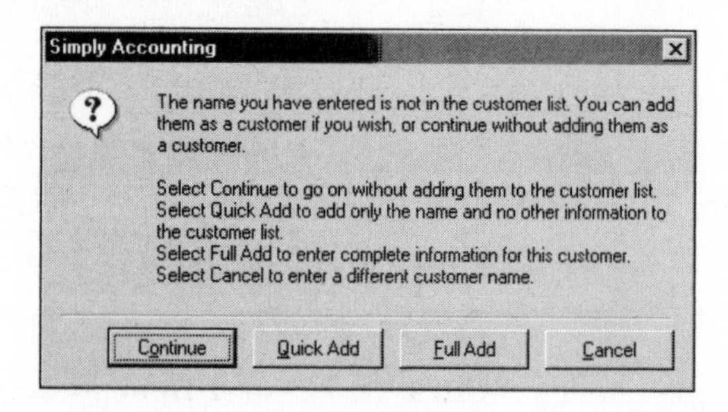

Simply Accounting
The name you have entered is not in the customer list. You can add them as a customer if you wish, or continue without adding them as a customer.
Select Continue to go on without adding them to the customer list.
Select Quick Add to add only the name and no other information to the customer list.
Select Full Add to enter complete information for this customer.
Select Cancel to enter a different customer name.
Continue
Quick Add
Full Add
Cancel

If you typed an incorrect name, click Cancel to return to the journal and start again. If you typed the name correctly, you can choose to add the customer's name only — Quick Add — or to add a full customer record with the Full Add option. If you need to change any defaults, you must choose the Full Add option. You can still skip customer fields that you do not need. The third option, Continue, will add the customer's name to the journal entry but will not create a ledger record for the customer or add the customer to the other Receivables Ledger reports.

Click Full Add to open the Customer Ledger at the Address information screen:

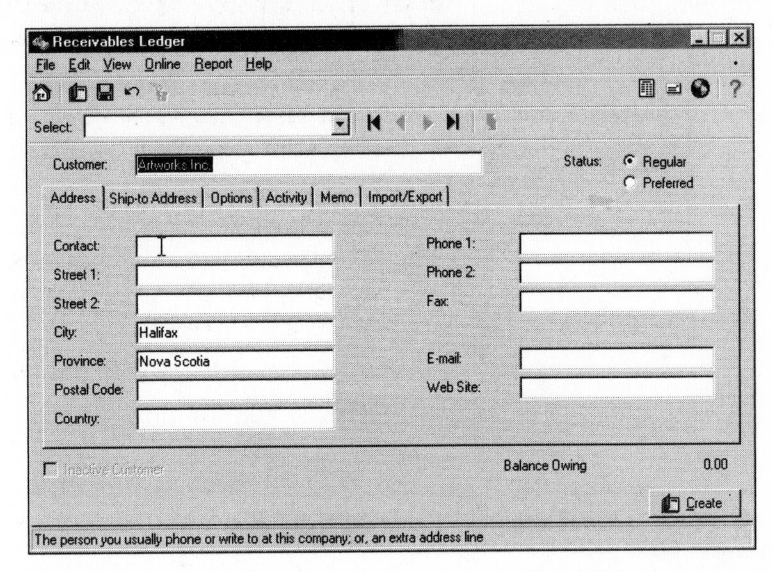

You are ready to enter your new customer. The Customer field is completed with the new name highlighted for editing if necessary.

Click the **Contact field**. If Grandeur Graphics normally deals with a particular individual at Artworks Inc. (e.g., the owner or the accountant), enter that person's name here.

Type `Joan Miro`

Press tab

The cursor moves to the Street 1 field.

Type `33 Abinaki Rd.`

Press tab

The cursor moves to the Street 2 field. If the address requires a second line, you would enter it here.

Press tab to move to the City field. Notice that the city and province in which Grandeur Graphics is located have been entered by default. The province is correct but you must change the city.

Type `Truro`

Press tab to advance to the Province field.

Press tab to skip the Province field.

The cursor moves to the Postal Code field. You do not need to use capital letters or to leave a space within the postal code. The program will make these adjustments.

Type `b2n8t1`

Click the **Phone 1 field**. Notice that the format of the postal code is corrected automatically. Since all Grandeur's customers and vendors are in the same country as the business, you can leave the Country field blank.

You do not need to insert dashes or brackets when you enter a telephone number.

Type `9027719831`

notes

If you need to edit a customer record, click the Customers icon in the Home window. Click the customer's icon in the Customers window to select the customer. Then click the Edit tool icon or choose the Edit menu and click Edit to open the Receivables Ledger record for the selected customer. (Or, double click the customer's icon in the Customers window to open the ledger.) To access the Credit Limit field, click the Activity tab. Make the necessary changes and click the Next customer tool to move to the Activity tab screen for the next customer on the list. Close the Receivables Ledger and the Customers window when you are finished.

version 8

notes

The customer Status — Regular — refers to the pricing of inventory items and will be introduced in Chapter 9.

notes

Telephone and fax numbers may be entered with or without the area code.

Click the **Fax field** to skip the second phone number field.

Type `9027718136`

Press tab to advance to the E-mail field. Notice that the format for the telephone and fax numbers is corrected automatically.

Type `miro@artworks.com`

Press tab

Type `www.artworks.com`

E-mail and Web addresses are typed exactly as you would type them in your regular Internet and e-mail access programs. You can also add these details later when you actually want to use them. When you click the Web or E-mail buttons, you will be prompted to enter the addresses if they are not part of the customer's record already.

The Shipping Address is the same as the business address.

Click the **Ship-to Address tab**.

Click Same as mailing address so that the customer's address will be entered as the shipping location on all invoices, orders and quotes.

Click the **Options tab**:

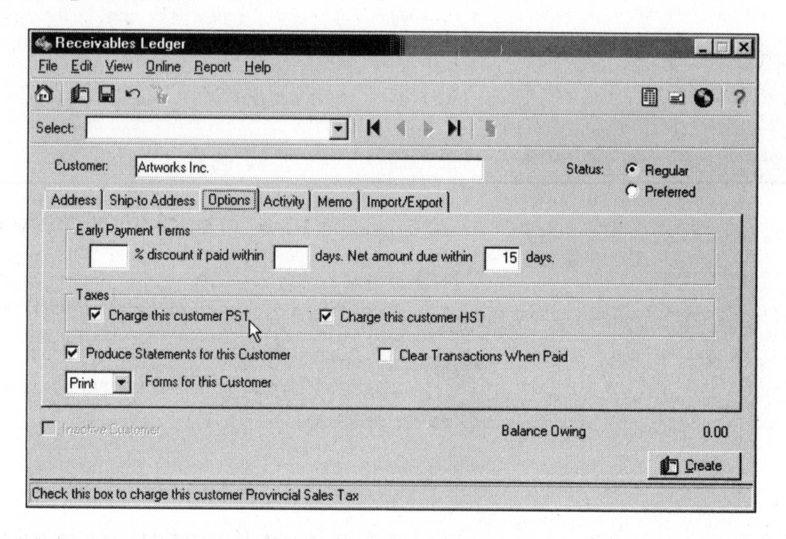

notes

Unless you have checked *Charge this customer HST*, the HST fields and codes will not be available in the Sales Journal for that customer. Applications for other provinces will display this option as Charge this customer GST.

The Options tab contains payment terms details. The payment terms for Artworks Inc. are the same as those for other customers and are entered by default. The customer is charged PST and GST/HST by default, allowing all the GST/HST codes to be active for sales transactions and for transactions to be included in GST/HST reports. However, PST is not charged separately in Nova Scotia so this option should be changed.

Click Charge this customer PST to remove the ✓.

The Clear Transactions When Paid option removes invoices that are fully paid. Choose not to remove paid invoices by leaving this box empty. This way you can keep a record of all purchases and payments made by this customer.

You may also choose to Produce Statements for this Customer, and you may choose to print or e-mail invoices and quotes. You should use the correct forms, but you can also print statements on ordinary printer paper.

You can change these settings at any time.

notes

When a customer exceeds the credit limit, the program will warn you before you can post the sale. You can accept the over-the-limit sale, or ask for a deposit to avoid exceeding the credit limit. Customers should be notified of changes in policy.

Click the **Activity tab** to open the next screen to which we need to add information:

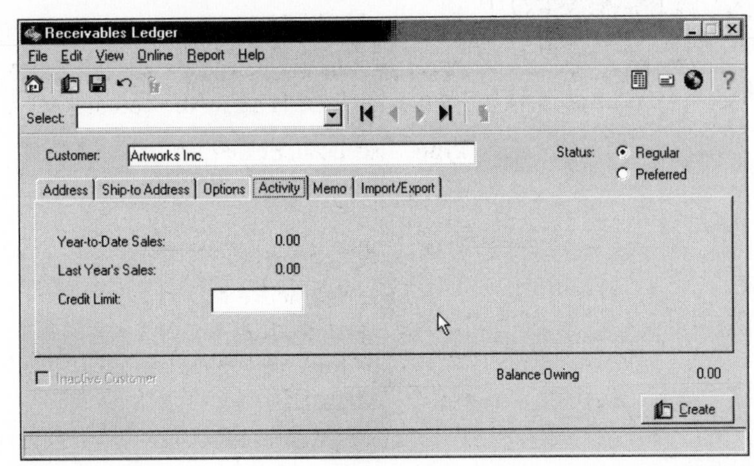

The Activity screen has a summary of the sales to the customer and the balance owing. These fields are updated from sales and receipts transactions. In the Credit Limit field, you can enter the upper credit limit for a particular customer to help keep bad debts to a minimum. Customers who have previously defaulted on making their payments could be placed on a cash-only basis by setting their credit limits at zero. Grandeur Graphics is presently analyzing customer payment trends to add this feature. The limit will be set at $2 000 on a trial basis.

Click the **Credit Limit field** to position the cursor.

Type 2000

CORRECTING A NEW CUSTOMER ACCOUNT

Click the appropriate tab to see the information for the customer. Move to the field that contains the error by **pressing** tab to move forward or shift and tab to go back to the previous field. **Type** the correct information.

You can also highlight the incorrect information by dragging the cursor through it. You can then **type** the correct information.

Saving a New Customer Account

When you are certain that all the information is correct, you must save the newly created customer account and add it to the current list.

Click Create Create to save the new customer information.

You will return to the Sales Journal. Enter the sale for the new customer by following the procedures outlined earlier. Remain in the Sales Journal for the next transaction.

Entering a Sales Quote

Sales quotes are like purchase quotes. They offer a customer a guaranteed price for a limited time for merchandise or for work to be completed. The customer may choose to accept or reject the offer.

Choose Quote from the Transaction drop-down list.

The invoice screen changes to the form for a sales quote:

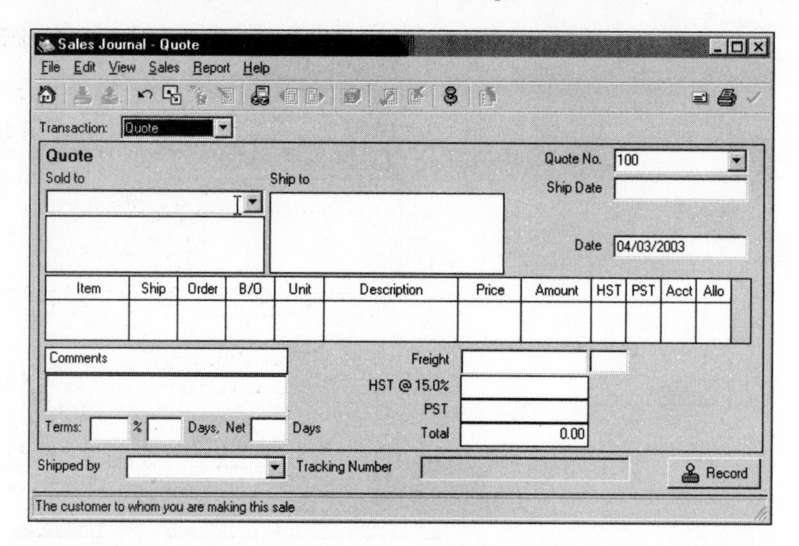

The quote is completed in much the same way as the sales invoice. However, you must enter a quantity in the Order field, just as you did for purchase quotes and orders. The quote number is updated automatically from the defaults for the Receivables Ledger.

Choose **Halifax Gazette** from the Customer (Sold to) list.

Click the **Ship Date field** to move the cursor because the shipping address and quote number are correct.

Type `4 15`

The transaction date, April 3, is correct from the previous invoice, unless you have closed the journal.

Click the **Order field**.

Type `1`

Click the **Description field**.

Type `Weekly Desktop contract`

Press tab to move to the Price field.

Type `460`

Press tab to advance to the Amount field. The program enters the amount correctly as the quantity times the price.

Press tab to move to the HST field.

Press enter to view the codes.

Double click code **4 - HST @ 15% included**

The cursor moves to the Account field.

Type 5 (to ensure that all revenue accounts will appear on the account list)

Press enter to view the list of postable accounts.

Double click account **4140 Revenue from Desktop Services** to add it to the quote.

Click the **Comments field**.

Type `HST is included in all prices quoted.` (or some other appropriate comment)

Your completed quote should look like the following:

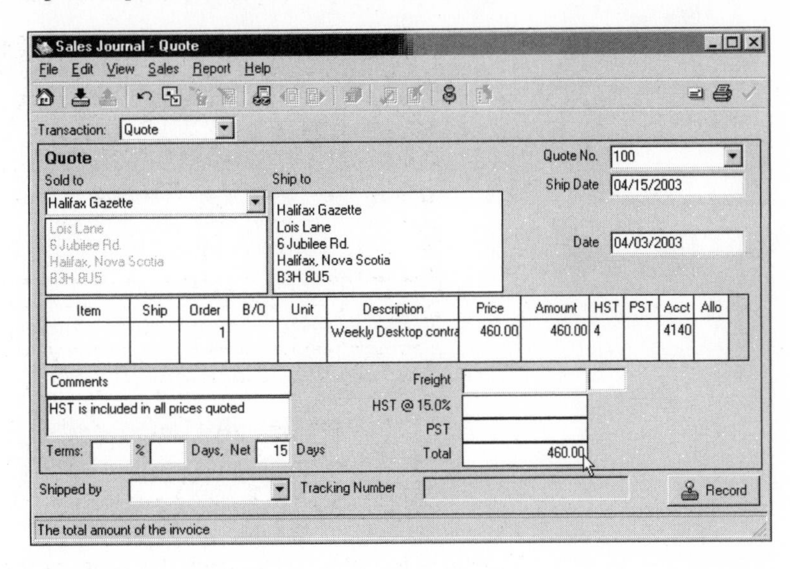

Check the quote carefully and correct mistakes just as you do in sales invoices. There is no journal entry to display. When a quote is filled by making a sale, the journal entry is completed.

Click Record [Record] to save the quote.

Leave the Sales Journal open for the next transaction, filling the quote.

Filling a Sales Quote

Filling a sales quote is similar to filling a purchase or a sales order. The Sales Journal should still be open with a blank quote screen displayed.

Choose Invoice as the Transaction type to change the screen to the invoice form. Pay Later should be selected as the payment option.

Click the **Quote/Order No. list arrow** to see the available quotes.

Click 100

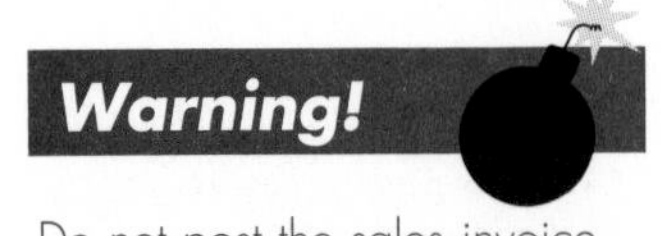

Do not post the sales invoice until you have stored it.

Press (tab) to display the quote on the invoice screen as shown:

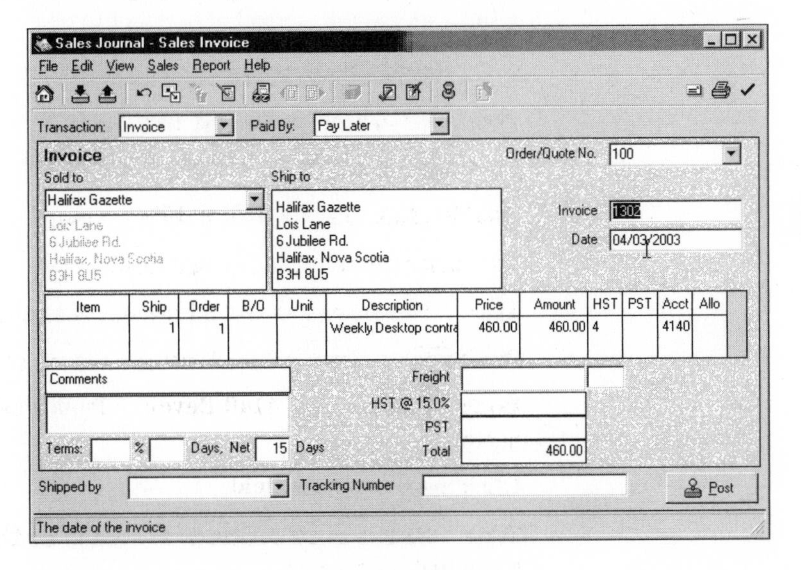

notes

It is necessary to choose Fill Backordered Quantities when filling sales orders but not when filling sales quotes.

notes

Refer back to page 82 if you need further help with storing an entry.

Enter the transaction date, April 4, and type an appropriate comment in the Comment field to complete the invoice. Check your work carefully.

Choose the **Report menu** and **click Display Sales Journal Entry** to review the entry. **Close** the display and return to the sales invoice. Make corrections if necessary.

Storing a Recurring Entry

Completing and storing a recurring entry in the Sales Journal is similar to storing a Purchases Journal entry.

Click the **Store button** or choose the Sales menu and click Store.

The familiar Store Recurring Transaction window appears:

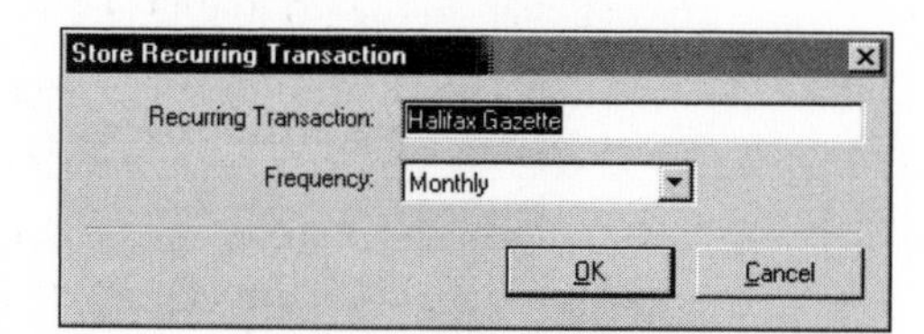

The customer name appears as the entry name, and the default frequency, Monthly, is selected. If you want, you can change the entry name to a more descriptive one that will help you to identify the entry when you need to recall it.

Click Monthly to display the frequency options.

Click the **up scroll arrow** until Weekly is in view.

Click Weekly to select this frequency.

Click OK to save the entry and return to the Sales Journal. Notice that the Recall button is now available.

Click Post Post to save the journal entry. Leave the Sales Journal open for the next transaction.

Entering Cash Sales

Click the **Paid By list arrow** to view the payment options.

Click Cash as the method of payment to change the invoice screen as shown here:

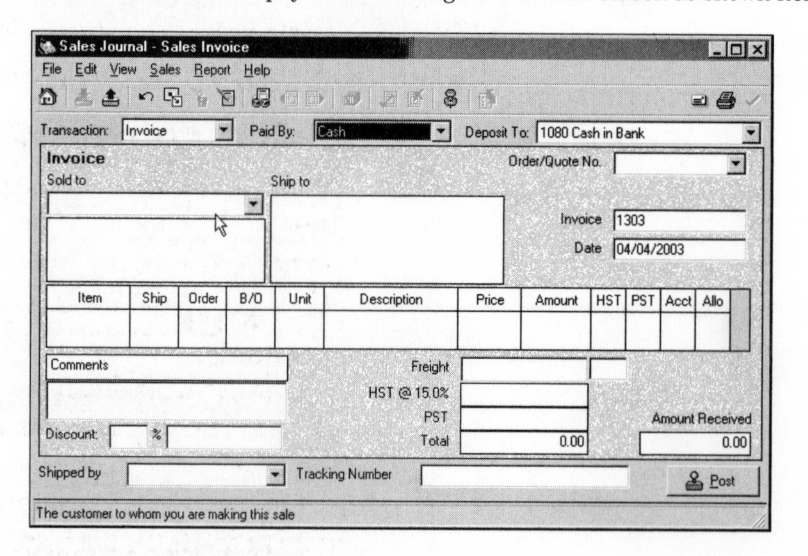

notes

When you choose Cheque as the method of payment, a cheque number field is added to the invoice so that you can add the customer's cheque number.

In the payment terms section, the Net days field has been removed and an Amount Received field has been added.

Click the **Customer (Sold to) field**.

Type `David Manga`

Press tab

The option to add a ledger record for the new customer appears. Because Manga is paying in cash, there is no need to keep a complete record.

Click Quick Add to return to the sales invoice.

The new customer's name appears in the Sold to and in the Ship to fields. You can type the customer's name and address in the Ship to address field so that it will appear on the printed invoice.

Complete the rest of the invoice in the usual manner. Refer to the keystroke instructions on page 120 if you need help. Enter "Thank you" as the Comment.

Choose the **Report menu** and **click Display Sales Journal Entry**. Your display should look like the one shown here:

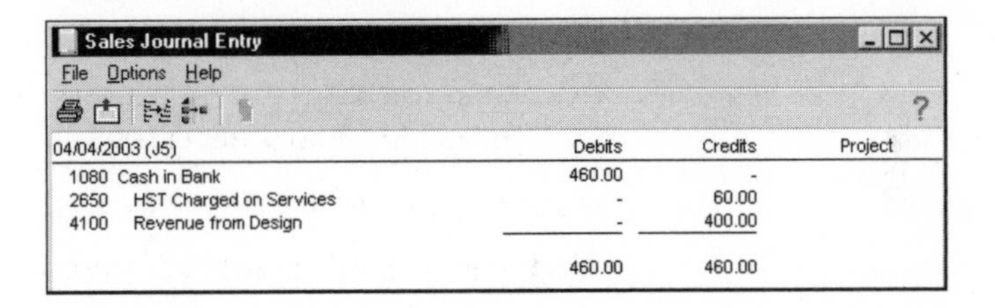

Notice that *Cash in Bank* is debited automatically instead of *Accounts Receivable* because we selected Cash as the method of payment. Close the display when you have finished. Make corrections if necessary.

Click Post  to save the entry. **Close** the Sales Journal.

Reversing a Payment (NSF Cheques)

When a cheque is returned by the bank as NSF, you need to record the fact that the invoice is still outstanding. You can do this in the Receipts Journal by entering a negative payment.

Click the **Receipts icon** Receipts to open the Receipts Journal.

Choose Halifax Gazette from the customer list to display the unpaid invoices:

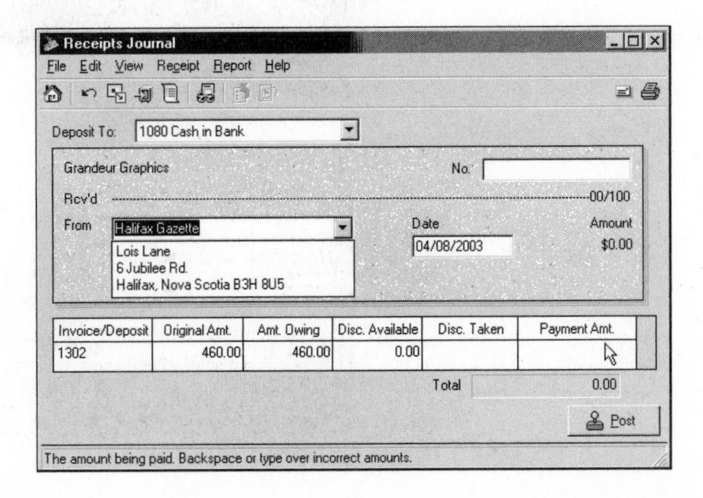

The only invoice displayed is the recurring entry just posted.

Click the **No. field** to move the cursor. To indicate that the original cheque is NSF and is being reversed, add NSF to the cheque number, or enter the bank memo number for reference.

Type `NSF-121`

Press (tab). In the Date field, enter the date of the bank memo.

Type `04-04-03`

Click Include fully paid invoices/deposits tool or choose the Receipt menu and click Include Fully Paid Invoices/Deposits. This will include the invoice that was paid as shown here:

notes

The Include tool remains selected until you click it again, even after you close the Receipts Journal.

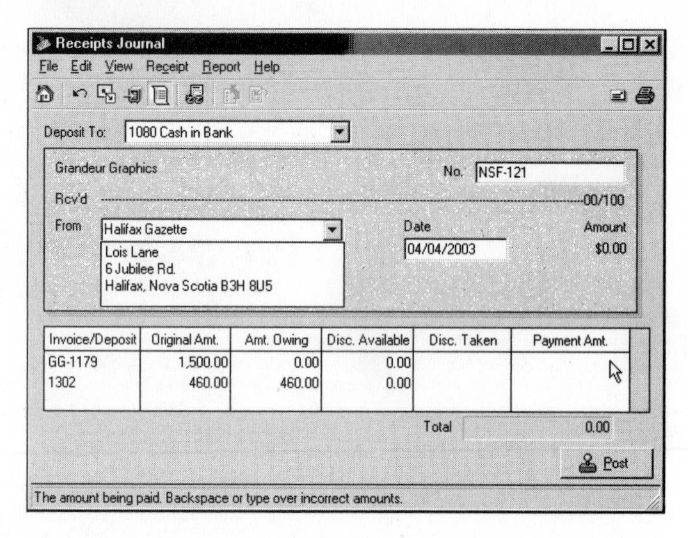

Click invoice number GG-1179, the one that the NSF cheque was issued against.

Press (tab) twice to advance to the Payment Amt. field for this invoice line.

notes

Or, you can click the Payment Amt. field on the line for invoice GG-1179.

Notice that the Payment Amount field is still blank because no balance is owing. Enter the cheque amount as a negative amount to reverse the original payment.

Type `-500`

Press (tab)

The cursor advances to the Discount Taken field for the next invoice.

Choose the **Report menu** and **click Display Receipts Journal Entry** to review the Receipts Journal entry. It should look like the one shown here:

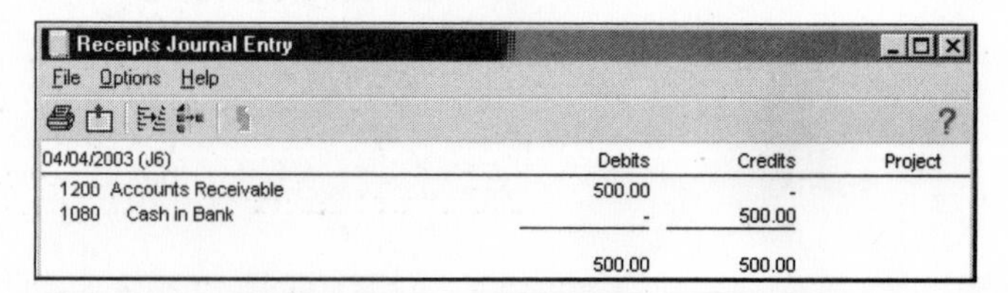

Receipts Journal Entry
File Options Help
04/04/2003 (J6) | Debits | Credits | Project
1200 Accounts Receivable | 500.00 | -
1080 Cash in Bank | - | 500.00
500.00 | 500.00

Notice that the same two linked accounts are used to create the reversing journal entry as the regular Receipts Journal entry. However, this time, *Cash in Bank* is credited and *Accounts Receivable* is debited because we entered a negative amount instead of a positive amount for the payment. This is a reversing entry of the payment.

Close the display when you have finished and make corrections if necessary.

Click the **Post button** [Post] to display a new Payments Journal.

Click Include fully paid invoices/deposits tool to turn off the option. Including paid invoices in the journal can make it more difficult to find the invoice that you are paying.

Choose Halifax Gazette from the Customer list. The unpaid invoice is added to the outstanding invoices and you can proceed with the payment.

Recalling a Stored Entry

On April 11, Grandeur Graphics completed the second of its weekly jobs for Halifax Gazette.

Click the **Sales icon** to open the Sales Journal from the Home window.

Click the **Recall button** or choose the Sales menu and click Recall to display the Recall Recurring Transaction window:

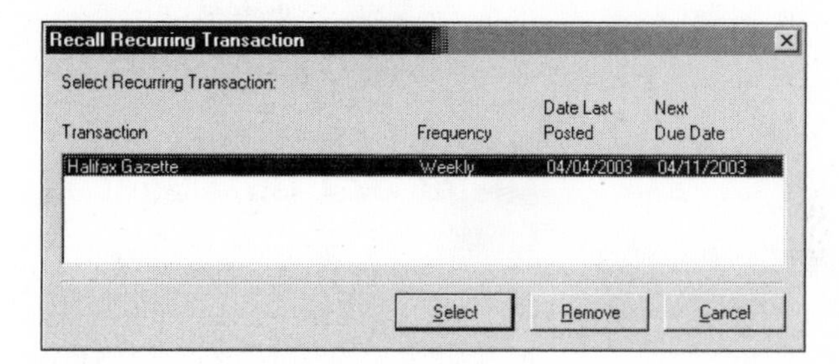

Since only one entry — the one for Halifax Gazette — is stored, it is selected.

Click Select to display the following copy of the entry posted on April 4:

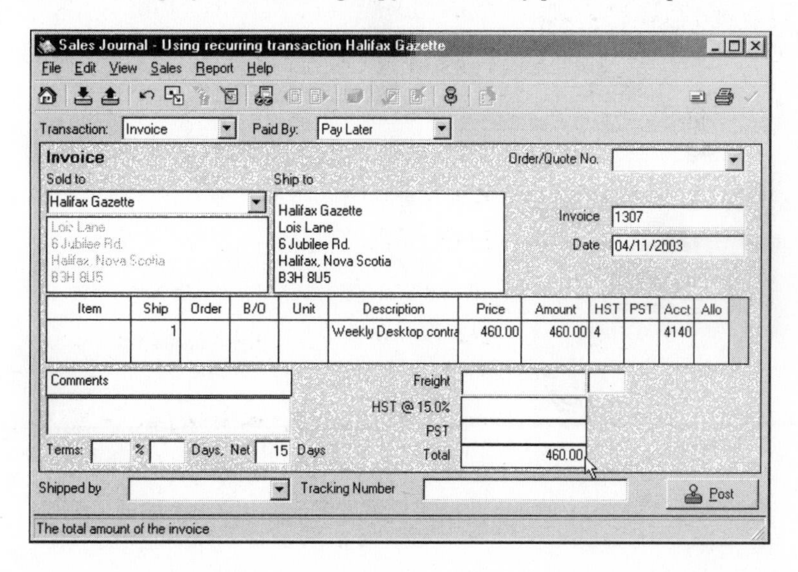

The default date is exactly one week past the previous posting date because we chose Weekly as the frequency. The invoice number is updated automatically so the entry is complete.

Review the entry to be certain that it is correct.

Click the **Post button** to save the entry.

notes

This warning will appear if you have made any changes to the entry before posting, although the message is a generic one referring only to the posting date.

Simply Accounting may display the following warning:

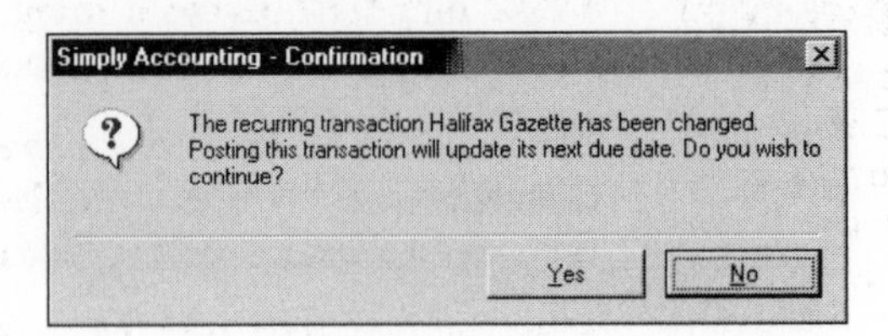

Click Yes to accept the change and continue with posting the journal entry.

Displaying Customer Reports

All customer-related reports can be displayed or printed from the Home window or the Customers window.

Click the **Customers icon** in the Home window to open the Customers window. The Reports menu list now contains only customer reports. You can select the report that you want from this list and follow the instructions below to choose report options. Customer-related graphs are not available from the Customers window.

Displaying Customer Lists

notes

You can drill down to the Customer Aged Report from the Customer List.

You should be in the Home window.

Right-click the **Customers icon** to select it.

Click the **Display button** on the tool bar, or choose the Reports menu, then choose Lists and click Customers. The report will be displayed immediately. Maximize the display and scroll as necessary to see customers outside the screen viewing area.

Close the display when you have finished viewing it.

Displaying Customer Aged Reports

notes

New customers you entered using Quick Add will appear on the lists of customers in the report options windows. Sales for One-time customers and customers for whom you chose the Continue option will not appear because these were cash transactions that did not create an entry for Accounts Receivable.

Choose the **Reports menu** in the Home window, then **choose Receivables** and **click Customer Aged**. You may view the customer reports at any time except when you are entering a transaction. The following window will appear, showing the options for your display:

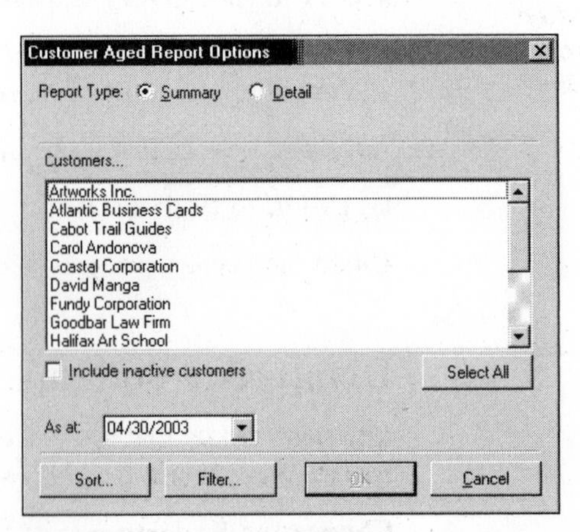

Type the date for the report, or accept the default session date.

Press ctrl and **click** the appropriate names in the customer list. If you want the report to include all customers, **click Select All**.

notes

You can drill down to look up invoices and to the Customer Ledger from the Customer Aged Report. From the Summary Report, you can drill down to the Detail Report.

notes

The Customer Aged and Aged Overdue reports can be sorted and filtered by name and total balance owing.

The **Summary** option will display an alphabetic list of the selected customers with outstanding total balances owing, organized into aging period columns, according to the defaults set up for the company. By default, the program selects this option.

Click the **Detail** option if you want to see individual outstanding invoices and payments made by customers. This more descriptive report is also aged. Management can use it to make credit decisions. You can add payment terms to the Detail Report.

After you have indicated the options you want,

Click OK to see the report.

Close the displayed report when you have finished.

Displaying Aged Overdue Receivables Reports

Choose the **Reports menu** in the Home window, then **choose Receivables** and **click Aged Overdue Receivables**. The following window will appear, showing the options for your display:

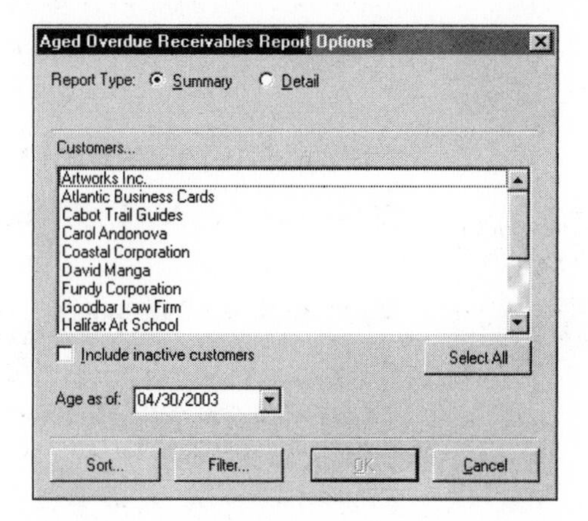

Type the date for the report, or accept the default session date.

Press ctrl and **click** the **names** in the customer list. If you want the report to include all customers, **click Select All**.

notes

You can drill down to look up invoices and to the Customer Aged Report from the Aged Overdue Receivables Report. From the Summary Report you can drill down to the Detail Report.

The **Summary** option will display an alphabetic list of the selected customers with outstanding total balances owing, organized into aging period columns, with an additional column for the overdue amount.

Click the **Detail** option to see individual outstanding invoices, due dates, payments and overdue amounts for the selected customers.

After you have indicated the options you want,

Click OK to see the report.

Close the displayed report when you have finished.

Displaying Pending Sales Orders

Any sales orders that are not yet filled can be displayed in the Pending Sales Orders report. You can also use this report to check for orders that should be removed.

Choose the **Reports menu** in the Home window, then **choose Receivables** and **click Pending Sales Orders**.

The following window shows the report options:

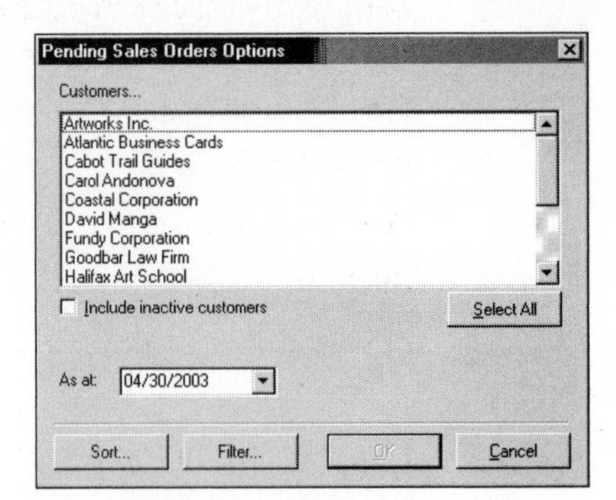

Press ctrl and **click** the names of the customers to include in the report, or **click Select All** to select all customers.

Enter a date for the report or accept the session date.

Click OK to view the report. (There are no sales orders pending.)

Close the display when you have finished.

notes

The Pending Sales Order report can be sorted and filtered by Order No., Order Date, Ship Date and Amount.

Displaying the Sales Journal

Right-click the **Sales icon** in the Home window.

Click the **Display button** or choose the Reports menu, then choose Journal Entries and click Sales to see the report options for the Sales Journal:

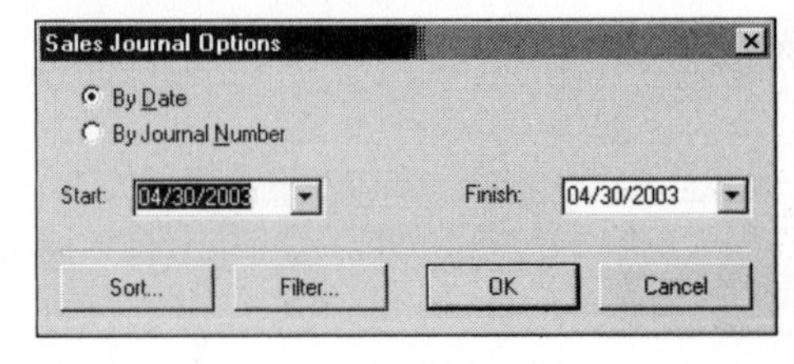

You can display the Sales Journal by posting date or by journal entry number. The default setting, By Date, is the option used for all reports in this workbook, so leave the selection unchanged.

Type the beginning date for the journal transactions you want to display.

Press tab

Type the ending date for the transaction period you want to see.

Click OK to see the report.

Close the display when you have finished.

notes

- To see the transactions for all journals in a single report, choose the Reports menu, then choose Journal Entries and click All.
- Sales and Receipts Journal reports are also available from the Select Report list when you click the Display tool button if no icon is selected in the Home window.

notes

- You can drill down to look up invoices and to the Customer Aged Report and the General Ledger Report from the Sales and the Receipts Journal Reports.
- Journal reports can be sorted and filtered by Date, Journal No., Source and Comment.

Displaying the Receipts Journal

Right-click the **Receipts icon** in the Home window.

Click the **Display button** or choose the Reports menu, then choose Journal Entries and click Receipts to see the report options for the Receipts Journal.

The Receipts Journal, like the Sales Journal, can be displayed by posting date or by journal entry number. The default setting, By Date, is the option requested for all reports in this workbook, so leave the selection unchanged.

Type the beginning date for the journal transactions you want to display.

Press tab

Type the ending date for the transaction period you want to see.

Click **OK** to see the report.

Close the display when you have finished.

Displaying the HST (GST) Report

Choose the **Reports menu** in the Home window and **click** **HST**. The following dialogue window appears:

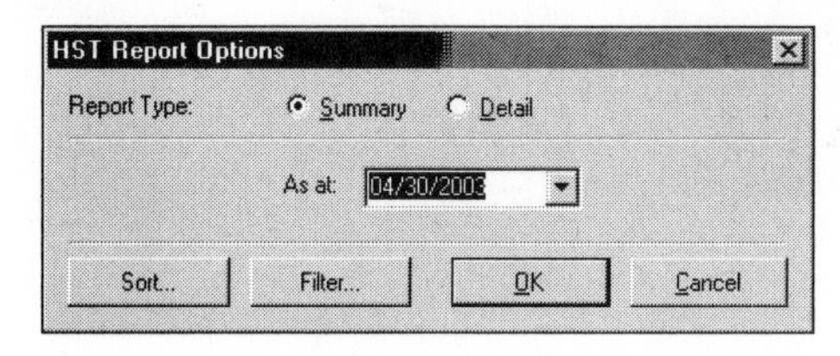

Type the date for which you want the report.

The default setting at **Summary** includes only the totals for the purchases, GST/HST Paid on Purchases, taxable sales and GST/HST Charged on Services. **Click** **Detail** if you want a detailed breakdown of individual customer and vendor transactions that included GST/HST. Totals are also provided. The HST/GST Report can be sorted and filtered by Name, Invoice No., Date, Invoice Amount Per Transaction and Tax Amount Per Transaction.

Once you have set the options as you want,

Click **OK** to see the report.

Close the display window when you have finished.

notes

In applications for other provinces, the report is named GST report. Only the GST/HST transactions that were entered through the Sales Journal or the Purchases Journal will be included in this report. Furthermore, only customers and vendors for whom *Charge/Collect...GST/HST* was checked will be included. GST/HST-related transactions completed in the General Journal will not be included. Therefore, the amounts shown in the GST report may differ from the balances in the General Ledger GST/HST accounts that include all GST/HST transactions. You should use the General Ledger accounts to determine the balance owing (or refund) and then make adjustments in the report as necessary.

Displaying Management Reports

Choose the **Reports menu** in the Home window, then **choose** **Management Reports** and then **click** **Receivables** to see the reports and options:

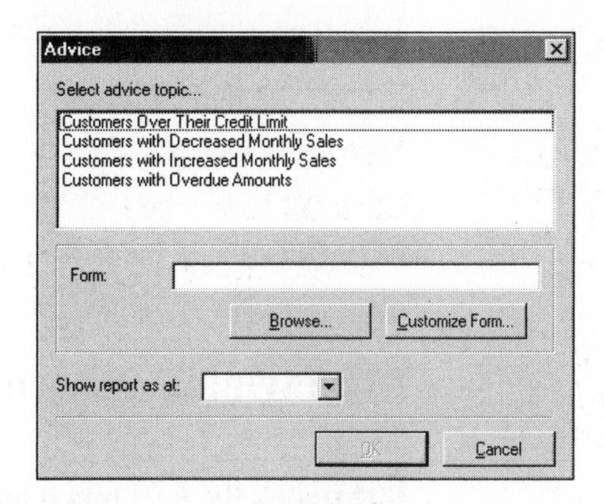

You can produce four different reports for the Receivables Ledger: a list of all customers who have exceeded their credit limits, purchase amounts for customers who have decreased their purchases since the previous year, amounts for customers who have increased purchases, and customers whose payments are overdue.

Click the **topic** for the report. The program will add a date, if appropriate, and a form for the report. Change the date if you need to, but leave the default report form unless you have the programs required to modify these forms.

Click OK to display the report and **print** it if you want. **Close** the display.

Displaying Cash Flow Projection Reports

Cash Flow Projection Reports predict the flow of cash in and out of an account — usually a bank account — over a specific future period based on current information.

Sorting and filtering do not apply to the Cash Flow Projection Report or to the Statement of Cash Flows.

Choose the **Reports menu** in the Home window, then **choose Financials** and **click Cash Flow Projection** to see the report options:

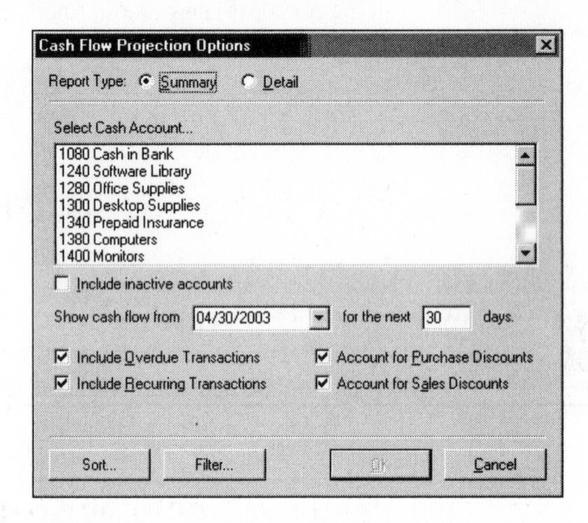

Click 1080 Cash in Bank, the account for which you want the report.

Click the **Date field**. **Type** the date at which you want the projection to start.

Press tab and **type** the number of days in the future for which the report should project the cash flow. Usually you will include only the number of days for which you have reasonable information, such as the number of days in which net payment is due. The session date and 30 days are useful periods. Accept the defaults.

Select the additional categories for which you want details. For example, you may choose to include discounts in the amounts to be received or paid, and you may include overdue transactions or omit them if you expect them to remain unpaid. By default, all details are included and clicking a detail will remove it from the report.

The report projects the account balance based on receivables and payables due and recurring transactions coming due within the time frame specified. The **Summary** Report shows the totals for the specified report period while the **Detail** report shows the individual transactions that are expected.

Click Detail

Click OK to view the report.

Close the display when you have finished.

Displaying the Statement of Cash Flows

version 8

The Cash Flow Statement summarizes sources (income, investments, etc.) and uses of cash (purchase of assets, etc.) and changes in liabilities during the designated period.

Choose the **Reports menu** in the Home window, then **choose Financials** and **click Statement of Cash Flows** to see the report options:

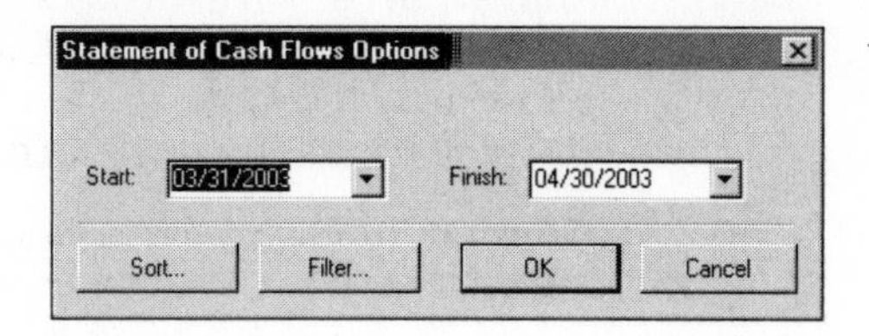

Type the Start and Finish dates for the report. The fiscal start and session date are the defaults.

Click OK to view the report.

By organizing the transactions involving cash, net changes in cash positions, as well as changes in liabilities, the statement allows the owner to judge how efficiently cash is being used for the business and to see potential problems resulting from increases in liabilities.

Close the display when you have finished.

Printing Customer Reports

To print customer reports, first display the report.

version 8

Click the **Print tool** or choose the File menu in the report window, and then click Print. Since printing will begin immediately, make sure that you have set the print options correctly. **Close** the display when finished.

Printing Customer Statements

notes

You can e-mail all customer statements or print them, or you can choose e-mail and print on a customer-by-customer basis according to the setting (preference) in the customer's ledger record.

Choose the **Reports menu** in the Home window, then **choose Receivables** and **click Customer Statements** to see the following options:

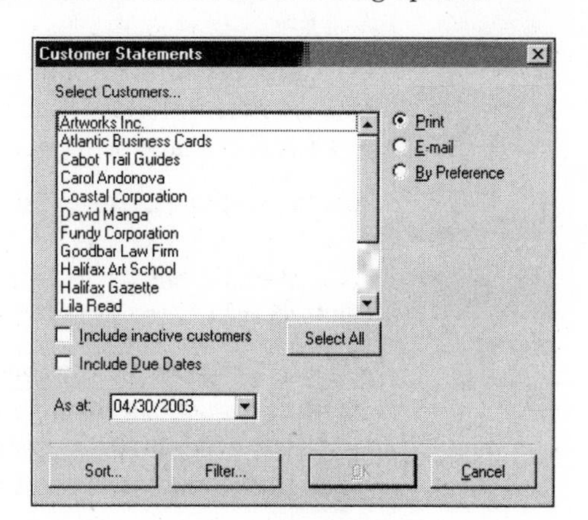

notes

Sorting and filtering do not apply to Customer Statements or Mailing Labels.

Press ctrl and **click** the customers for whom you want to print statements, or click **Select All** to include all customers.

Click Include Due Dates if you want to add the payment due date for invoices.

Click OK

Printing will begin immediately, so be sure your printer is set up with the correct forms before you begin.

Printing Customer Mailing Labels

notes

To set the program for printing labels

- Choose the Setup menu in the Home window and click Reports & Forms.
- Click the Labels tab.
- Enter the appropriate details for the labels you are using.
- Click OK to return to the Home window.

Choose the **Reports menu** in the Home window, then **choose Mailing Labels** and **click Customers** to see the following options:

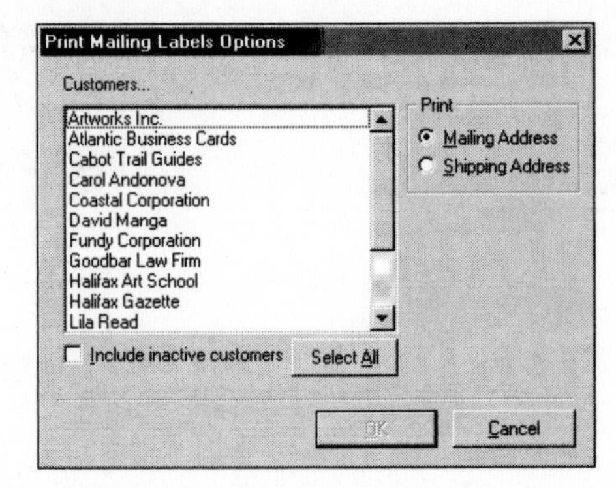

You may print labels for the business mailing addresses or for the shipping addresses.

Press ctrl and **click** the customers for whom you want to print the labels, or **click Select All** to include all customers.

Click OK

Printing will begin immediately, so before you print be sure that the print options have been set correctly and that your printer is turned on and has the correct labels paper.

Graphing Customer Reports

The customer-related graphs are available from the Home window.

Receivables by Aging Period Graph

notes

- Double click a portion of a graph to see the aging period, the dollar amount and the percentage of the total.
- Double click the legend to make it larger. Double click the expanded legend to reduce it.

Choose the **Graphs menu** and **click Receivables by Aging Period** to see the options screen:

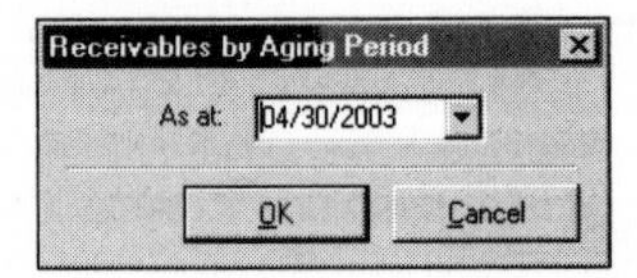

Enter a date for the graph.

Click OK

The pie chart shows the total receivables divided according to the aging intervals set up in the company defaults. The chart is the customer equivalent of the Payables by Aging Period Graph. You have the same tool bar options and colour and legend control choices that you have for the Expenses and Net Profit as % of Revenue graph. Refer to page 60 for a review of these features if you need further assistance.

Close the graph when you have finished.

Receivables by Customer Graph

Choose the **Graphs menu** in the Home window and **click Receivables by Customer** to see the following options:

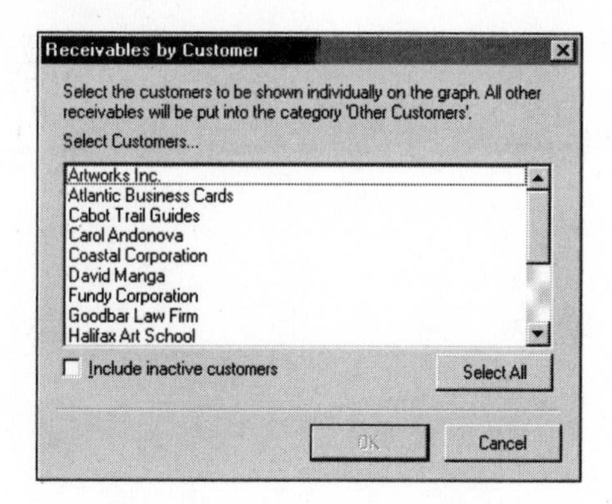

Press ctrl and **click** the customers you want individually on the chart, or **click Select All** to include all customers.

Click OK to display the chart:

notes

- Double click a portion of a graph to see the customer, the dollar amount and the percentage of the total.
- Double click the legend to make it large and add the customer names. Double click the expanded legend to reduce it.

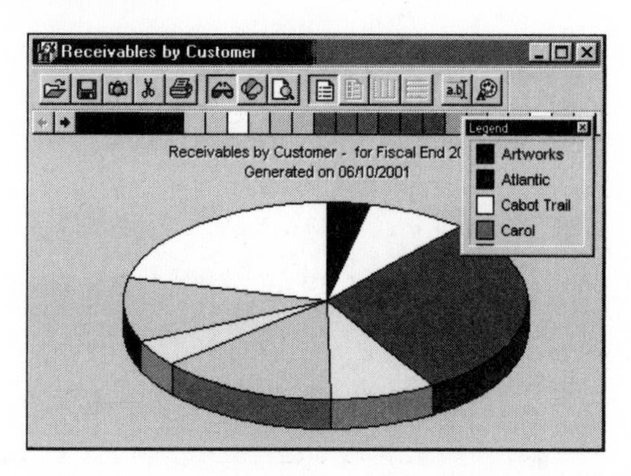

The amount owed by each customer, represented by a different colour in the pie chart, is shown as a proportion of the total receivables. Again the options for displaying, editing, printing and exporting the graph are the same as for other graphs.

Close the display when you have finished.

Sales vs Receivables Graph

Choose the **Graphs menu** and **click Sales vs Receivables** to see the options:

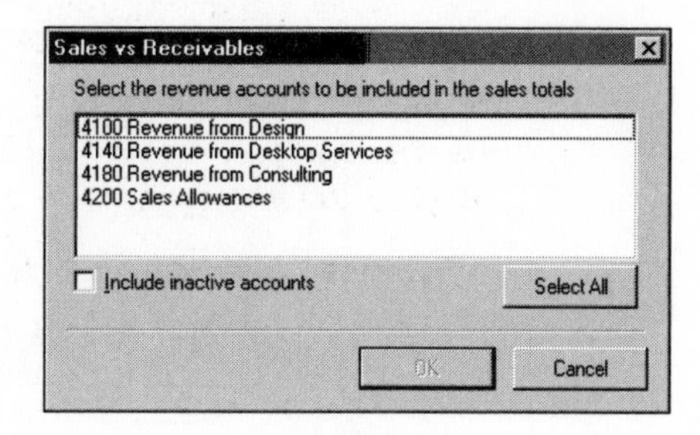

Click the revenue accounts that you want to include in the graph or **click Select All** to include all revenue accounts.

notes

Double click a portion of a graph to see the period, the category (Sales or Receivables) and the dollar amount.

Click OK to display the following bar chart for the end of April:

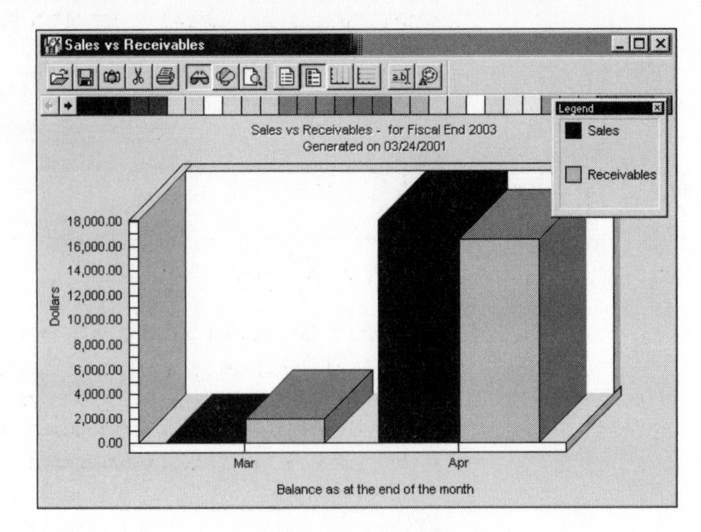

Although this is not a pie chart, you have the same options for exporting, copying, changing the display, and so on that you do for other graphs.

Close the graph when you have finished.

Receivables Due vs Payables Due Graph

Choose the **Graphs menu** and **click Receivables Due vs Payables Due** to see the following options:

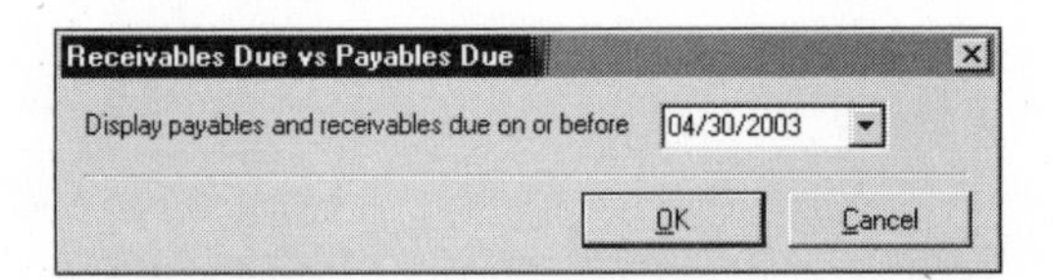

Type the date that you want the graph to include. All Receivables and Payables that are due by this date will be added to the chart totals.

Click OK to display the bar chart:

notes

Double click a portion of a graph to see the period, the category (Payables or Receivables) and the dollar amount.

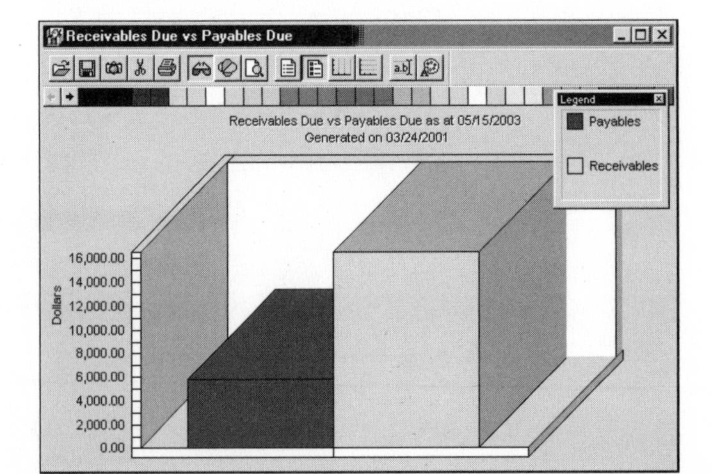

The graph shows the total amounts for receivables and payables due in the 15 days beyond the session date.

For this bar chart too, you have the same options for exporting, copying, changing the display and so on that you do for other graphs.

Close the graph when you are finished.

CASE PROBLEMS

Case One

For one of the regular customers, a credit sale of $230 was recorded with the HST Code 3 - HST not included in price. Therefore, the customer was overcharged by 15%. The error was not noticed until after the customer had made the full payment for the overcharged amount. What options does Grandeur Graphics have to correct this error, if the payment has not yet been recorded? If the payment has been recorded?

Case Two

Entering a purchase with a deposit requires a Purchases Journal entry together with a separate Payments Journal entry. Does a sale with a down payment require separate Sales and Receipts Journal entries? Explain why or why not. (Hint: You may want to try to enter the transaction in the Sales Journal to observe how the software treats the information.)

CHAPTER SIX

OBJECTIVES

After completing this chapter, you should be able to

- *plan* and *design* an accounting system for a nonprofit organization
- *prepare* a conversion procedure from manual records
- *understand* the objectives of a computerized accounting system
- *create* company files using the skeleton starter file for a nonprofit organization
- *set up* the organization's accounts
- *enter* historical account information
- *finish* entering accounting history to prepare for transactions
- *customize* journals
- *enter* transactions using the General Journal
- *display* and *print* reports

COMPANY INFORMATION

Company Profile

Children's International Summer Villages (CISV) is a worldwide organization promoting international peace, education and cross-cultural friendship. Doris Allen created CISV in 1951 because she believed that helping the world's young people "to live amicably with one another as friends" would contribute to a peaceful future. Today, more than 70 countries are members of CISV. In Canada alone there are 10 Chapters with more than 3 000 members. In 2001 CISV will celebrate its 50th anniversary and Doris Allen's 100th birthday!

notes

CISV Toronto's address is:
North Toronto PO Box 38172
Toronto, Ontario M5N 3A8
Business No.: 5643 87694
Tel: (416) 488-7711
Fax: (416) 489-8812
Web: www.cisv.ca.

To accomplish its goals, CISV offers a number of programs for children between the ages of 10 and 18. Eleven-year-old boys and girls from 12 different countries come together for four weeks in "Villages" to share their cultures through sports, social activities and cooperative games, learning to communicate even without a common language. Twelve- to 15-year-olds can participate in Summer Camps, a village-like experience for older children, or in family-oriented Interchanges with a single other country. All groups of children who travel are accompanied by an adult leader. Older children (16 through 18) have many opportunities to develop their leadership skills in the organization. They can serve as Junior Counsellors, assisting leaders in the planning and running of Villages. They can also participate in Seminar Camps and Youth Meetings where international and intercultural issues are explored through activities and discussion. And finally, on an ongoing basis, they plan and organize year-round educational and social activities for all junior members of their local Chapter — the Junior Branch. Through these and planned local work programs, the whole family can participate in the CISV experience.

notes

CISV is a real organization. Its goals and programs are as described in this chapter. The accounting information, although realistic, has been simplified for this application and the source documents are simulated.
CISV International is independent of any government, political party, religious organization or umbrella organization. It is administered by an International Board of Directors and has a permanent international office in England. Similarly, CISV Canada is administered by a National Board of Directors and has a permanent national office in Ottawa. CISV is a nonprofit charitable organization.

As a nonprofit, volunteer organization, CISV relies strongly on its members to volunteer for its regular activities as well as a variety of fundraising events. Member fees, donations that are fully receipted for income tax purposes, support the day-to-day operational expenses of the Chapter. Money from fundraising activities is used to support operations, programs and special events. Each Chapter is expected to host a Village every two or three years in return for sending delegates to Villages elsewhere. All the costs of running the Toronto Village, except for the travel expenses of the children and leaders attending, are borne by CISV Toronto. Similarly, a Chapter will periodically host a Summer Camp or a Seminar Camp. Interchanges are generally paid for by the members who participate in them, with the interchange group itself, rather than the entire Chapter, organizing special fundraising activities.

A separate bank account is set up for the Village funds. When the Village is in operation, it sets up its own accounting system, and the summary expense is consolidated into the Chapter's books. It operates as if it were a wholly owned subsidiary company. The Junior Branch also has its own accounting records and supports its own activities financially.

This application deals with the accounting for a four-week Village.

notes

Participants in each program pay international and national fees. Similarly, each Chapter pays fees to the national office to cover insurance, administration and other expenses.

The Toronto Chapter has decided to use Simply Accounting to keep the accounting records for the Village in July 2003, midway through their current fiscal year. The Village requires only General Ledger accounts, while the Chapter as a whole uses the Receivables Ledger to keep track of memberships and the Payables Ledger for regular vendor accounts. To set up the accounts using the General Ledger, the Chapter will use the following information:

- Chart of Accounts
- Income Statement
- Balance Sheet
- Trial Balance
- Accounting Procedures

notes

The Chart of Accounts is based on the Toronto Villages hosted in previous years and includes all accounts. Account types are marked in brackets for subgroup Accounts [A], Subgroup totals [S], Headings [H], Totals [T] and Current Earnings [X]. All unmarked accounts are postable Group [G] accounts. The explanation of account types begins on page 164.

CISV TORONTO VILLAGE
CHART OF ACCOUNTS

ASSETS
1000 CURRENT ASSETS [H]
1020 Cash in Bank - Village [A]
1100 Cash on Hand [A]
1150 Total Cash [S]
1200 Arts & Crafts Supplies
1300 Food Supplies
1320 Office Supplies
1360 Village T-shirts for Sale
1390 TOTAL CURRENT ASSETS [T]
1400 EQUIPMENT [H]
1450 Computer
1500 Fax/Answering Machine
1590 TOTAL EQUIPMENT [T]

LIABILITIES
2000 CURRENT LIABILITIES [H]
2200 A/P - Designs U Wear
2300 A/P - Quiq Kopy
2350 A/P - Sleeptight Cots
2400 A/P - Travel in Comfort
2670 GST Paid on Purchases
2690 TOTAL CURRENT LIABILITIES [T]

CISV EQUITY
3000 CISV EQUITY [H]
3560 Surplus Funds
3600 Net Income
3690 TOTAL CISV EQUITY [T]

REVENUE
4000 REVENUE [H]
4020 Revenue from Bingo
4080 Interest Revenue
4120 Other Revenue
4390 TOTAL REVENUE [T]

EXPENSE
5000 OPERATING & ADMIN EXPENSES [H]
5020 Caretaking Expense
5050 Cost of T-shirts
5080 Cots & Linen Rental
5180 Food Expense
5200 General Expense
5250 Office Supplies Used
5280 Non-refundable GST
5300 Postage Expense
5320 Printing & Copying
5350 Publicity
5400 Telephone Expense
5420 Wages - Cook
5440 TOTAL OPERATING & ADMIN EXPENSES [T]
5450 PROGRAM & ACTIVITY EXPENSES [H]
5500 Crafts Supplies Used
5550 Entertainment Expenses
5600 Transportation
5690 TOTAL PROGRAM & ACTIVITY EXPENSES [T]

notes

Because the Village has not yet started, most of the expenses are still at zero. Villages are not usually held each year because of the large cost involved. The Chapter will spend three or four years fundraising to prepare for a Village and the Income Statement at the end of the Village will show a net loss for the year.

CISV TORONTO VILLAGE: INCOME STATEMENT

For the Six Months Ending June 30, 2003

Revenue	
4000 REVENUE	
4020 Revenue from Bingo	$9 200.00
4080 Interest Revenue	240.00
4120 Other Revenue	100.00
4390 TOTAL REVENUE	$9 540.00
TOTAL REVENUE	$9 540.00
Expense	
5000 OPERATING & ADMIN EXPENSES	
5080 Cots & Linen Rental	$6 100.00
5300 Postage Expense	70.00
5320 Printing & Copying	150.00
5440 TOTAL OPERATING & ADMIN EXPENSES	$6 320.00
5450 PROGRAM & ACTIVITY EXPENSES	
5600 Transportation	$ 200.00
5690 TOTAL PROGRAM & ACTIVITY EXPENSES	$ 200.00
TOTAL EXPENSE	$6 520.00
NET INCOME (LOSS)	$3 020.00

CISV TORONTO VILLAGE
BALANCE SHEET

July 1, 2003

Assets		
1000 CURRENT ASSETS		
1020 Cash in Bank - Village	$49 550.00	
1100 Cash on Hand	1 000.00	
1150 Total Cash		$50 550.00
1200 Arts & Crafts Supplies		500.00
1300 Food Supplies		2 300.00
1320 Office Supplies		400.00
1360 Village T-shirts for Sale		800.00
1390 TOTAL CURRENT ASSETS		$54 550.00
1400 EQUIPMENT		
1450 Computer		$ 1 500.00
1500 Fax/Answering Machine		500.00
1590 TOTAL EQUIPMENT		$ 2 000.00
TOTAL ASSETS		$56 550.00
Liabilities		
2000 CURRENT LIABILITIES		
2200 A/P - Designs U Wear		$ 800.00
2300 A/P - Quiq Kopy		150.00
2350 A/P - Sleeptight Cots		3 050.00
2400 A/P - Travel in Comfort		200.00
2670 GST Paid on Purchases		–385.00
2690 TOTAL CURRENT LIABILITIES		$ 3 815.00
TOTAL LIABILITIES		$ 3 815.00
Equity		
3000 CISV EQUITY		
3560 Surplus Funds		$49 715.00
3600 Net Income		3 020.00
3690 TOTAL CISV EQUITY		$52 735.00
TOTAL EQUITY		$52 735.00
LIABILITIES AND EQUITY		$56 550.00

CISV TORONTO VILLAGE: TRIAL BALANCE		
July 1, 2003		
1020 Cash in Bank - Village	$49 550.00	
1100 Cash on Hand	1 000.00	
1200 Arts & Crafts Supplies	500.00	
1300 Food Supplies	2 300.00	
1320 Office Supplies	400.00	
1360 Village T-shirts for Sale	800.00	
1450 Computer	1 500.00	
1500 Fax/Answering Machine	500.00	
2200 A/P - Designs U Wear		$ 800.00
2300 A/P - Quiq Kopy		150.00
2350 A/P - Sleeptight Cots		3 050.00
2400 A/P - Travel in Comfort		200.00
2670 GST Paid on Purchases	385.00	
3560 Surplus Funds		49 715.00
4020 Revenue from Bingo		9 200.00
4080 Interest Revenue		240.00
4120 Other Revenue		100.00
5080 Cots & Linen Rental	6 100.00	
5300 Postage Expense	70.00	
5320 Printing & Copying	150.00	
5600 Transportation	200.00	
	$63 455.00	$63 455.00

Accounting Procedures

GST

As a registered charity, CISV has two options with respect to the GST. Like regular for-profit businesses, it can register to apply the GST, charge members GST on membership fees and claim all GST paid as input tax credits to reduce the liability to the Receiver General. Not wanting to subject the members to an increase in fees, CISV has chosen instead a second option that does not require registration or collection of GST but permits a partial rebate of GST paid. CISV submits an application for refunds quarterly, listing the total of all GST paid toward its operating expenses. Fifty percent of this amount is eligible for the rebate. Therefore, CISV records all purchases as compound General Journal entries, separating the amount paid for GST from the total and entering this amount to *GST Paid on Purchases*. Periodically, this account is cleared as the application for a rebate is submitted. The remaining 50 percent of the GST paid is charged to the *Non-refundable GST* expense account.

Bank Accounts

The proceeds from the weekly Bingo night fundraising event are entered into the Village bank account. They are reserved exclusively for the Village expenses and are not used for operational expenses of the Chapter as a whole. A separate bank account, not included here, is used for Chapter expenses. During the Village, a *Cash on Hand* account is set up for day-to-day expenses incurred by the Village staff. Regular transfers are made from the *Cash in Bank - Village* account to *Cash on Hand*.

Chapter Operating Expenses

All day-to-day operational expenses for the Chapter as a whole are itemized separately from the Village expenses. Membership fees are deposited in the main Chapter bank account to support the operational expenses. A summary of Village expenses is recorded in the main Chapter statements after the Village has ended.

Instructions

notes

If you prefer to enter the source documents before setting up the data files, you can use the CISV\CISV.sdb file in the Setup folder inside your Data folder. In this way, you will become familiar with the account structure and the setup may be easier to complete.

1. Using all the information provided in this application, set up the company accounts for CISV Toronto using only the General Ledger. Detailed keystroke instructions follow.
2. Using the Chart of Accounts and other information provided, enter the source documents that begin on page 175 using the General Journal in Simply Accounting.
3. After you have completed your entries, print the following reports:

   a. General Journal from July 1 to July 31
   b. Balance Sheet as at July 31, 2003
   c. Income Statement for the period Jan. 1, 2003, to July 31, 2003

Keystrokes for Setup

notes

Using subsequent versions of the Simply Accounting program may result in different screens and keystrokes from those described in this application.

There are five key stages in preparing the Simply Accounting program for use by a company:

1. creating company files
2. preparing the system
3. preparing the ledgers
4. printing reports to check your work
5. backing up your files and finishing the company history

The following keystroke instructions are written for a stand-alone IBM PC or compatible with a hard disk drive. The keystroke instructions provided in this application demonstrate one approach to setting up company accounts. Always refer to the Simply Accounting and Windows manuals and Help for further details

Creating Company Files

notes

- When working through this application, save your work frequently by choosing the File menu and clicking Save. You will also save your work by finishing your session properly. You may finish your session at any time while completing the setup. Simply open the CISV data file again, accept the session date and continue from where you left off.
- Use Backup frequently while setting up your files to update your backup files.

The following instructions assume that you have the Simply Accounting program correctly installed on your hard disk in drive **C:** in the **Program Files\Winsim** folder.

Simply Accounting provides both templates and starter files to make it easier to create files for a new company. These files contain different sets of accounts that match the needs of different kinds of businesses. By starting with one of these files, you eliminate the need to create all the accounts for your business from scratch.

There are many templates that work with the setup wizards to define not only accounts but also a number of settings for the different ledgers. These settings and accounts are suited to the type of business named by the files.

In addition, Simply Accounting includes two starter files — inteplus.sdb (Integration Plus) and skeleton.sdb. The starter files contain only a set of basic accounts. Starter accounts are opened like any other company files. You should work with a copy of these files so that you can use the original files for future applications.

The Skeleton starter has only General Ledger accounts whereas the Integration Plus starter is suitable for a variety of business types because it has the basic linked accounts for all the ledgers.

notes

We want to illustrate different ways of creating company files. Therefore, the method of creating your company files from scratch is described in the Maverick Micro Solutions setup application, Chapter 10.

You will have to customize any of these starter files to your particular company. Rarely are accounts identical for any two businesses. The files that most closely match the Chart of Accounts for CISV are the Skeleton starter files (skeleton.sdb). These files contain only a few General Ledger accounts, headings and totals. They contain no linked accounts that link General Ledger accounts to the subsidiary ledgers. This is appropriate for the CISV Village because they use only the General Ledger.

The starter files are located in the folder named Template in the Winsim folder — the folder that contains your Simply Accounting program. If you accepted the default installation location, the Skeleton starter file has the path C:\Program Files\Winsim\Template\Skeleton.sdb. The starter files were created when you installed the program.

Start the Simply Accounting program to access the Select Company window.

Choose Select an existing company to access the Open Company window.

If you were previously working with files in the Data folder under Winsim, it will be the active or selected folder.

Click the **Up One Level icon** beside the Look in field to go the Winsim folder level. (Click Up One Level twice if necessary.) You should see the folders under Winsim:

notes

If you were working with files in another drive, directory or folder, you would use the following steps to switch to Template:

- Click the drop-down list arrow beside the Look in field to see your data path.
- Double click (C:).
- Double click Program Files.
- Double click Winsim.
- Double click Template.
- Depending on your starting location, you may skip one or more of the above steps.

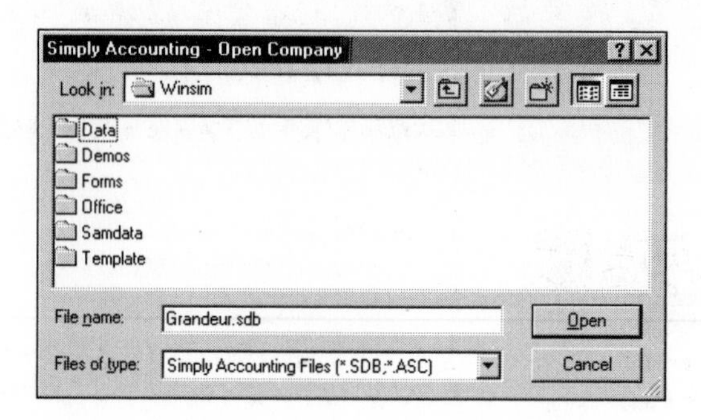

Double click Template to open it or click Template to highlight it and click Open.

You should now see the list of starter files as shown:

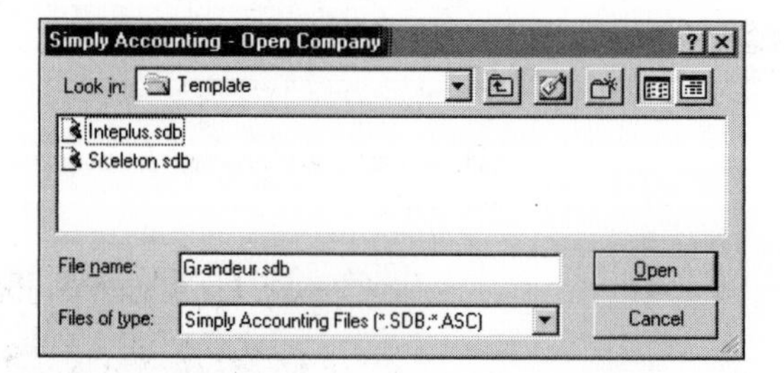

notes

The Template files with Simply Accounting 8.5 are Pro version files and cannot be opened with the regular Version 8.5 program. Instead, you should open a template from an earlier version of the program (e.g. V 8.0 or earlier) with Version 8.5 to convert it. Or download the correct template files from www.pearsoned.ca/text/purbhoo85.

Click Skeleton (or **Skeleton.sdb**)

Click Open to access the files.

The Session date window appears with January 1, 2000, as the session date.

Click OK to accept the date and open the Home window.

The familiar Home window appears with the file name Skeleton in the title bar.

notes

Icons for all ledgers appear in the Home window so that you can set them up.

You are now ready to make a copy of these files to store your records for CISV. Always work with a backup copy of the starter files so that you will have the original to use when creating other company records.

Choose the **File menu** and **click Save As** to open the Save As window:

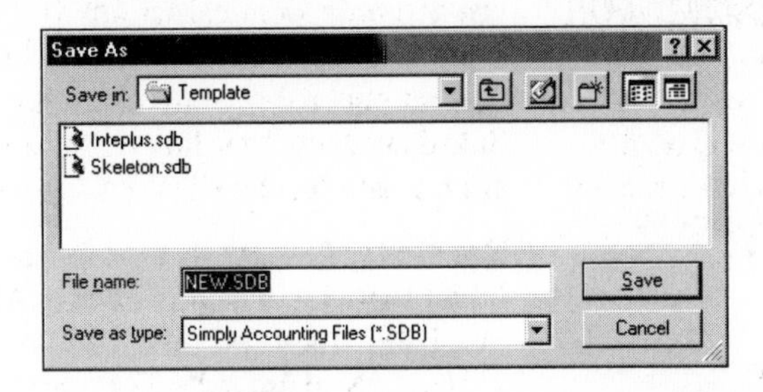

Click the **Up One Level icon** to return to the Winsim folder level.

notes

Substitute the appropriate data path, including the drive and folder where your data files are stored (e.g., D:\simplydata\cisv\cisv.sdb). Refer to Chapter 1, page 22, for more help with making folders.

Double click the **Data folder** to open it (or the folder on the hard drive that you are using for your data).

Click the **New Folder icon** (or **click** the **right mouse button**, **choose New** and then **Folder** from the displayed menu) to create a new folder. The folder name, New Folder, is selected for editing.

Type `CISV` (to rename the new folder CISV)

Double click the **CISV folder** to open it. CISV should appear in the Save in field.

Double click NEW (or **NEW.SDB**), the file name, to prepare the field for entering the new file name.

notes

- The program will add the .sdb file extension because the correct file type is contained in the Save as type field.
- Alternative methods of copying files are described in Chapter 1.

Type `cisv`

Click Save

You have now created a copy of the Skeleton starter files in a new folder and under the new name in the Data folder (or on the floppy disk) where you stored your other data files. Two files were copied in this procedure; both are necessary to work in Simply Accounting. The .sdb file is the one that you open to get started. The .sdb extension for the file name may not appear on the screen, depending on your Windows version and preferences. If all the files for the company are not in the same folder, you will not be able to access your data. Using the Save As command automatically puts all the necessary files together.

When you return to the Home window, the name CISV (or CISV.SDB) appears in the title bar:

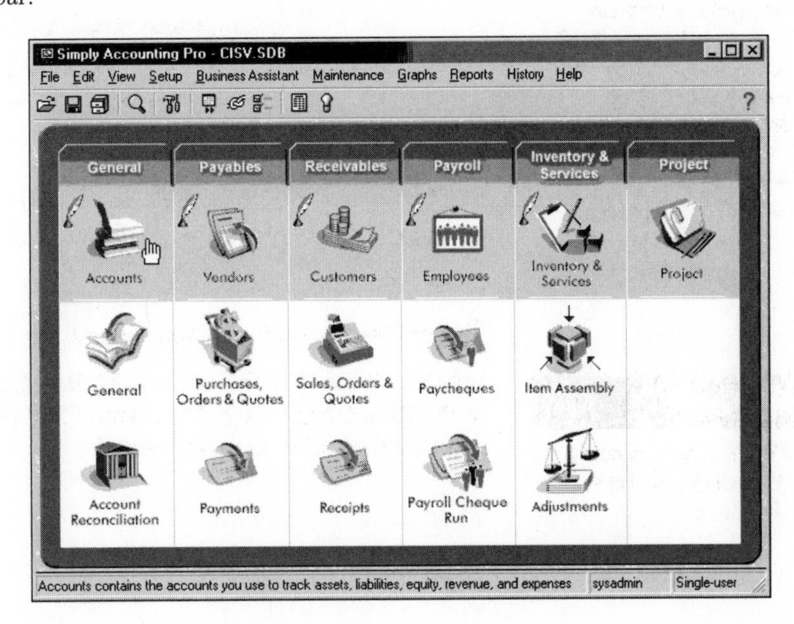

All ledgers are currently not set up. An open history (quill pen) symbol appears with each ledger icon, indicating that you can enter historical data for the ledger. You should enter all the necessary company information and finish entering the history before you enter journal transactions.

Preparing the System

notes

Simply Accounting includes a Setup Wizard that guides you through the company setup step by step with instructions. The Wizard is not used in this application. To access the Setup Wizard, choose the Setup menu then choose Wizards and click Settings.

Before entering financial records for a new company, you must prepare the system for operation. This involves changing the defaults that were set up when the CISV company files were created. For the General Ledger, these defaults include the company name and address, fiscal dates, screen display preferences and the Chart of Accounts. When you set up other ledgers, there will be additional default information. Some of the defaults will not be suitable for CISV. You must also provide other information, such as the printer(s) that you will be using and the printing formats. This process of adding, deleting and modifying information is called *customizing the system*.

You should change the defaults to suit your own work environment, such as choosing a printer or adding information for a second printer.

Changing Company Default Settings

Entering Company Information

version 8

Choose the **Setup menu**, then **choose System Settings** and **click Company Information**. You will see the following screen:

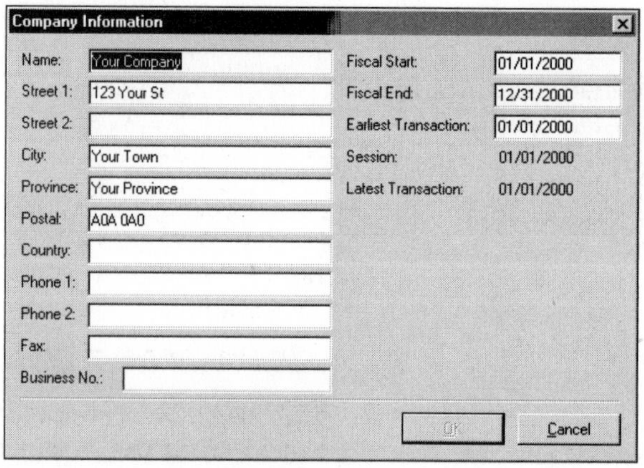

Company Information

Name: Your Company | Fiscal Start: 01/01/2000
Street 1: 123 Your St | Fiscal End: 12/31/2000
Street 2: | Earliest Transaction: 01/01/2000
City: Your Town | Session: 01/01/2000
Province: Your Province | Latest Transaction: 01/01/2000
Postal: A0A 0A0
Country:
Phone 1:
Phone 2:
Fax:
Business No.:
OK | Cancel

The cursor is in the Name field. This field contains the information "Your Company" to let you know that this is where you should enter the name of your company. The contents of the field are highlighted so that you can enter the name of the business. (If Your Company is not highlighted, drag through the text to select it.)

notes

You can personalize your files by adding your own name to this field (e.g., CISV Toronto - Purbhoo) so that all reports printed will include your own name for easy identification.

Type `CISV Toronto`

Press tab

The cursor moves to the Street 1 field, the first address field. You can enter the address immediately because the current contents are already highlighted.

Type `North Toronto`

Press tab to advance to the second street address line.

Type `PO Box 38172`

Press tab

The cursor advances to and highlights the contents of the City field.

Type `Toronto`

Press tab

The cursor advances to the Province field. It, too, is ready for editing.

Type `Ontario`

Press tab

The cursor is now placed at the highlighted Postal (postal code) field. Remember that you do not have to type the capitals or spaces in postal codes. The program automatically corrects the postal code format.

Type `m5n3a8`

Because all addresses will be in Canada, we can leave the Country field blank. Now enter the telephone and fax numbers for the business. There is only one phone number so the Phone 2 field will remain blank.

Click the **Phone 1 field**.

Type `4164887711`

Click the **Fax field**.

Type `4164898812`

Press tab to move to the Business No. field. All companies must use a single Canada Customs and Revenue Agency business number that also serves as the GST registration number.

Type `564387694`

notes

Enter all four digits for the year to be certain that the program recognizes the year correctly as 2003 and not 1903. Once you have entered the fiscal start, end, and earliest transaction dates, the program will correctly fill in the year when you type in the last two digits or leave out the year because the date must fall between the earliest transaction and end dates.

Simply Accounting will accept dates between January 1, 1900, and December 31, 2027. Since you can store up to two years of accounting records, you should not start with dates past the year 2025.

Press tab to advance to the Fiscal Start field. This date field contains the date at which the current fiscal year begins. This is usually the date used to define the beginning of the fiscal year for income tax purposes. As usual, the date format is mm-dd-yy (month, day, year).

Type `01-01-2003`

Press tab. The cursor moves to the Fiscal End field. This is the date at which the company closes its books, usually one year after the fiscal start, and the end of the fiscal year used for income tax reporting purposes.

Type `12-31-2003`

Press tab

notes

It is possible for a company to use a fiscal period shorter than one year for reporting purposes and to close its books more frequently, but the most common period is one year.

The cursor is now placed in the Earliest Transaction Date field. This is the date on which the company converts its manual accounting records to the computerized system. Entries before this date are historical entries. The earliest transaction date must not be earlier than the fiscal start and not later than the fiscal end. The earliest transaction date will be the first session date when you are ready to enter journal transactions. Simply Accounting automatically advances the earliest transaction date when you start a new fiscal year.

Type `07-01-2003`

The session date and the latest transaction date will change as you complete journal entries and advance the session date from the Home window. The latest transaction date shows if you have any postdated journal transactions.

notes

When you view the Company Information again, the session and latest transaction dates will have been updated to match the new fiscal dates.

Check your work. The earliest transaction date cannot be changed once you have finished entering history and have started to enter journal transactions. Return to any field with errors and correct the mistakes. The company name and address can be edited at any time.

Click OK to save the new company information.

Changing the Printer Defaults

version 8

notes

The default printer for your other Windows programs will be selected initially. Normally the printer selection is correct.

Choose the **Setup menu** and **click Reports & Forms** to show this screen:

Warning!

You should view the additional printer control screens but do not change the settings. The printer control screens will vary from one printer to another. Usually the default settings are correct.

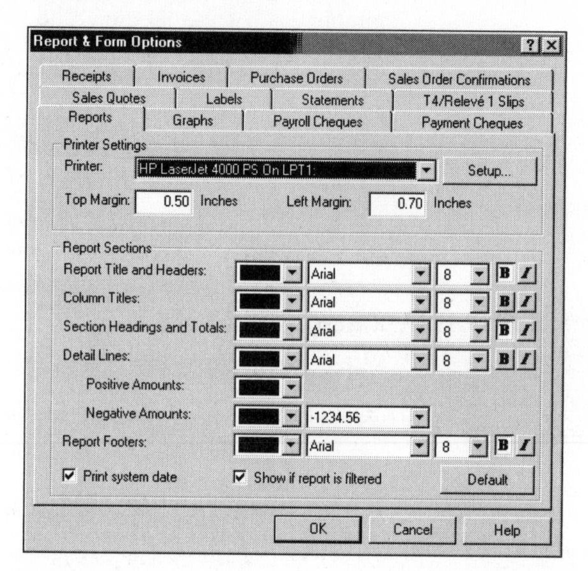

You can see that Simply Accounting allows you to set different printers for reports, graphs, cheques, invoices, labels, purchase, T4 slips, and so on. Many companies use one printer for their reports and another for various preprinted forms and invoices. Once you choose printer settings, Simply Accounting will apply them to all your Simply Accounting files.

notes

- Even if you use one printer, you may want to adjust fonts, margins and form sizes for each type of printed report or statement.
- Your default margin settings may be different from those shown here.

The printer setting options for reports are given. Choose the printer you will be using for reports from the list provided using the arrow beside the field. All printers that are attached to your computer and were installed under Windows should be on the list. Change the page margins if necessary. For each part of the report, choose a font and type size from the lists available when you click the arrows beside these fields. You may have to experiment with fonts and type sizes to find the combination that will fit the reports neatly on the page. By default, reports include the computer system date and a message indicating whether filtering is applied.

To modify the printer setup for other outputs, click the relevant tab at the top of the settings screen. You can modify printer setup information any time by returning to this screen.

The specific options vary from one printer to another.

Click Setup to display the following screen for additional printer settings:

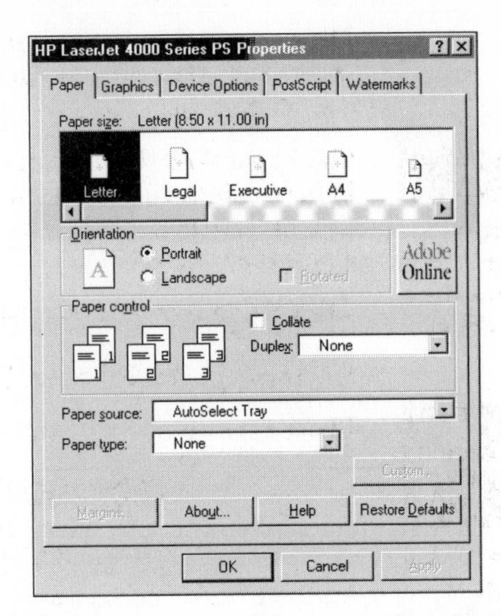

At this stage, you can modify the source of the paper, the paper size and orientation.

Additional control over your printed copy may be available from this screen by clicking the tabs for Graphics, Device Options, PostScript or Watermarks. Each one will give you additional printing options. The sequence of screens, options and tabs will vary from printer to printer.

Click OK to leave each dialogue box and save the changes or

Click Cancel to exit without making changes and return to the Home window.

Changing Ledger Default Settings

Setting System Defaults

version 8

notes

- If a Home window ledger icon is selected when you choose Settings, you will see the settings for that ledger. Click the System tab to see the System Settings.
- The Names option in the Setup menu refers to other ledgers. It will be introduced in a later application.

Choose the **Setup menu**, then **choose System Settings** and **click Settings**. Options that apply to all ledgers are available from the System settings:

Settings
Project | Forms | Comments | E-mail
System | Sales Taxes | General | Payables | Receivables | Payroll | Inventory & Services
Cash-Basis Accounting
Use Cash-Basis Accounting   Cash Accounting Date:
Store invoice lookup details
Use Cheque No. as the source code for cash purchases and sales
Allow transactions in previous year
Allow transactions in the future (beyond the session date)
Warn if transactions are 7 days in the future
Warn if accounts are not balanced when entering a new month
Backup frequency: Daily
OK | Cancel | Help

notes

The cash basis of accounting records revenues and expenses on the date the money is paid or received. In the accrual method, revenues and expenses are recorded on the transaction date (matching principle).

There are several important switches and settings in this screen. The first refers to whether the business is using the cash basis of accounting instead of the default, accrual-based accounting. To indicate the change, click the check box and enter the date on which the change is to take effect. This workbook uses the accrual basis. Do not change this setting for CISV.

The option to Store invoice lookup details allows you to display, print, store and adjust invoices that have already been posted. The option is turned on, or selected, when the ✔

appears in the check box. CISV does not need these features because they refer to Sales and Purchases Journal invoices.

notes

Invoice Lookup is used in the Outset Media Corporation application.

Click Store invoice lookup details to turn off this option.

The next option relates to the use of the cheque number as the source code for cash purchases and sales in account reconciliation. Since CISV uses only the General Ledger, this does not apply. When you are using the Payables and Receivables Ledgers, you should turn on the option.

The dimmed option, to Allow transactions in a previous year, becomes available when you have more than one fiscal period in your data file. You can post transactions to a previous fiscal period when the feature is selected. The feature should be turned on only for specific transactions and then turned off again so that you do not post in error with an incorrect date. Similarly, you should not generally allow posting to future periods, beyond the session date, unless you are entering a series of postdated transactions. You can activate the feature for specific transactions when needed so that you do not post with incorrect future dates. You can add a warning for dates beyond a certain period as well.

Click Allow transactions in the future to remove the ✓ and not allow postdating.

Since Versions 8 and 8.5 of Simply Accounting allow journal entries before the company setup details are completed, you can add a reminder warning as you continue to work with an incomplete and unbalanced account history. If you choose to post journal entries before completing the history, you should turn on the warning.

The final option refers to the frequency with which you back up your data. Since we advance the session date weekly, we will choose Weekly as the backup frequency as well. The program prompts you to back up according to the entry here.

Click the **Backup frequency field list arrow** and **choose Weekly**. If you want, you can choose a specific number of days as the interval between backups by choosing Other and typing the number in the Number of days field that opens with this choice.

Setting General Defaults

To change the settings for the General Ledger for CISV,

notes

You can click the Setup tool bar button in the Home window and select Accounts to access the General Settings window. If the Accounts icon is already selected, you will access the General Settings directly when you click the Setup button.

Click the **General tab** from the top of the Settings screen.

You will see a warning that invoice details will be removed:

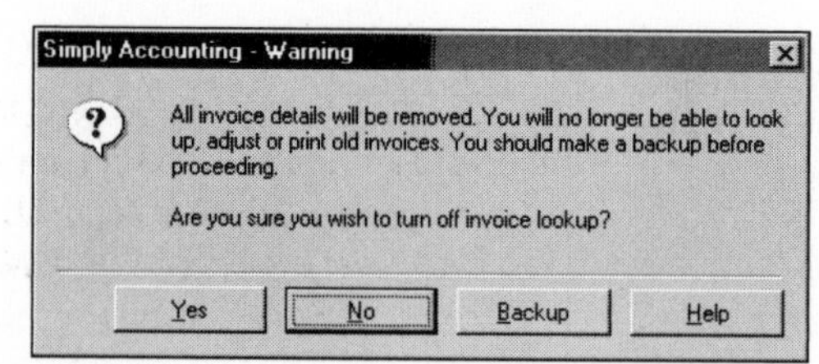

We do not need these details.

Click Yes to continue to the General Ledger Settings screen:

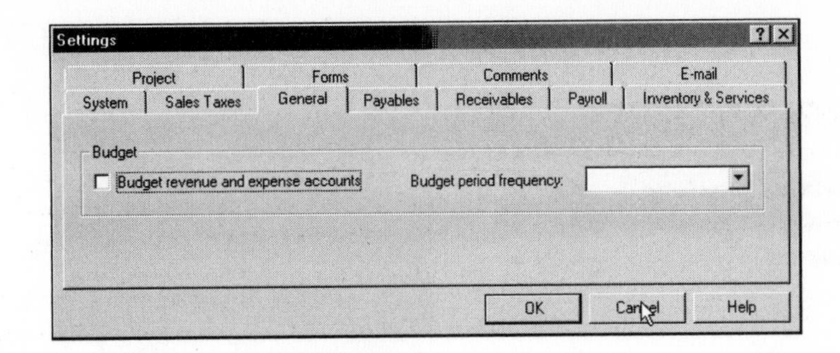

notes

The budgeting feature is explained in the Bonnie Brides application.

If you want the Simply Accounting program to prepare budget reports, click *Budget revenue and expense accounts* and choose the budget period from the drop-down list. Each revenue and expense ledger account window will include a *Budget* tab. Click this tab and then enter budget amounts for the account to include the account automatically in budget reports.

You can activate budgeting at any time.

Since the other ledgers are not used by CISV, you do not need to change their settings.

version 8

Click OK to save the changes and leave the Settings dialogue box and return to the Home window.

Changing User System Settings

Choose the **Setup menu**, then **choose User Preferences** and **click Settings**. The options are shown:

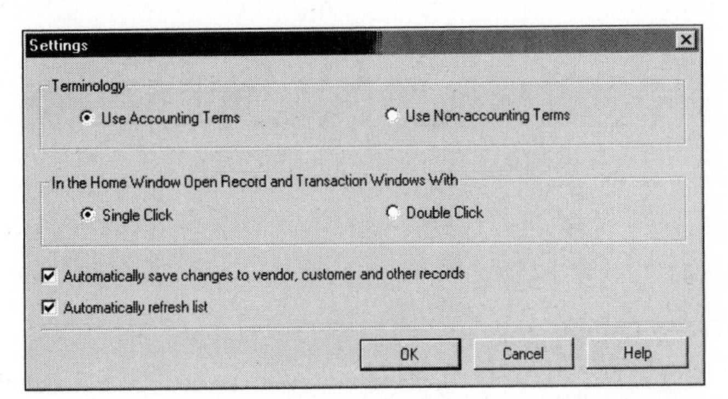

notes

Appendix E lists all equivalent accounting and non-accounting terms.

The first feature refers to the language used by the program. We have used accounting terminology throughout this workbook because most people who use accounting programs are familiar with it. If you choose non-accounting terms, the General Journal will be labelled Miscellaneous Transactions, the Payables Ledger will be named Vendors and Purchases in menus, and so on. To follow the instructions we provide, you should use accounting terms.

The next choice is about how you open the ledger (Record) and journal (Transaction) windows. The default setting is to open them with a single mouse click and select them without opening by right-clicking. This is the approach we used in previous chapters. If you choose double click to open the ledgers and journals, a single click action will select the icon.

The remaining selections are to save the changes to ledger records automatically when you close a record window and, for the Pro Version 8.5, to refresh the lists continually.

The default settings are correct. These settings can be changed at any time by clicking the option.

Click OK to return to the Home window.

Changing the View Settings

Several important display or appearance options are controlled from the View menu in the Home window.

version 8

Choose the **View Menu**, then **choose System Settings** and its submenu arrow ▸ :

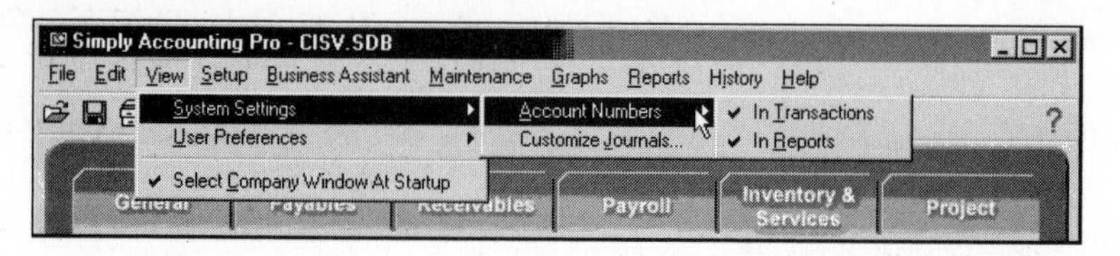

The system view settings control showing account numbers and customizing journals. If you choose to display accounts without account numbers in transactions and reports, accounts are displayed alphabetically. Do not change the setting.

Each journal has optional fields that can be hidden if they are not required by the program and the business. To customize the General Journal,

version 8

Choose the **View Menu**, then **choose System Settings** and **click Customize Journals**:

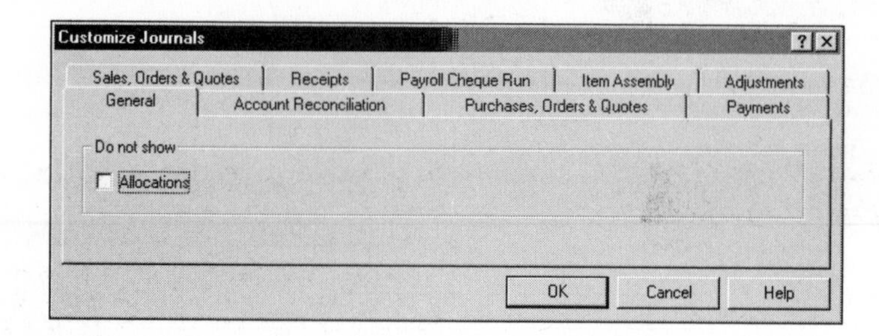

All journals may be customized from this window by choosing the tab for the journal.

The Customize journal tool in each journal provides the same options as the View menu System Settings screen. CISV does not require the project allocation feature so we can remove this column from the journal.

Click Allocations to remove this column from the General Journal window.

Hidden fields may be restored at any time by clicking their names again.

Click OK to save the changes and return to the Home window.

The final choice on the main View menu refers to the Select Company window that appears when you first start Simply Accounting. There are advantages to showing this window. If you use the same data file as in your previous session, you can open it with a single step. Similarly, you can restore a backup file from this window without first opening another data file. Again, the setting acts as a toggle switch and you can change it at any time.

version 8

Choose the **View Menu**, then **choose User Preferences** and its submenu arrow ▸ :

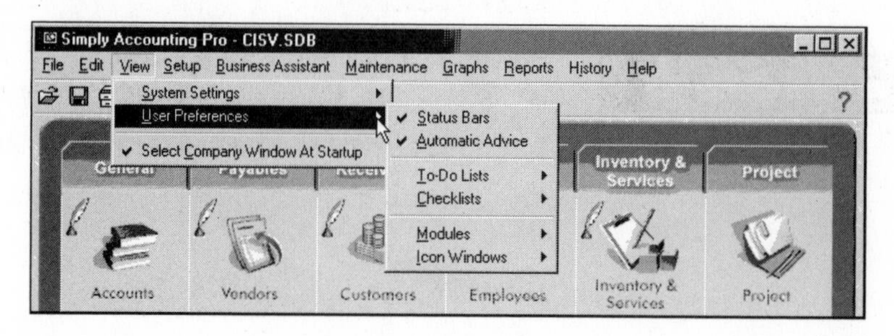

Several more display options are available at this stage. You can turn off the status bars at the bottom of many windows by clicking the Status Bars menu option. The status bar explains the role of the field containing the mouse pointer. Leave the status bars turned on.

Automatic advice shows advisory messages automatically while you are entering transactions, as, for example, when customers exceed credit limits. Clicking the menu option removes the ✓ and the feature. Leave advice turned on.

Simply Accounting offers reminders about upcoming activities such as payments that are due, discounts available and recurring entries. You can choose to be reminded of these activities through the To-Do Lists and Checklists each time you start the program, each time you advance the session date, or both. CISV does not use these lists.

version 8

Choose the **View menu**, then **choose User Preferences** and **To-Do Lists** and **click After Changing Session Date**. Repeat this step for Checklists to remove the ✓.

You can hide, that is, not display, the icons for ledgers that you are not using. The General Ledger and Journal icons cannot be removed. We must hide the remaining ledgers because they are not used.

version 8

Choose the **View menu**, **choose User Preferences** and **Modules** and then **click Payables** to remove the ✓.

Warning!

If you do not hide the remaining modules, you will be unable to complete the final setup step of finishing the history.

Repeat this step for the remaining modules so that all ✓ are removed. With each step, there will be one less set of icons in the Home window until your window looks like this:

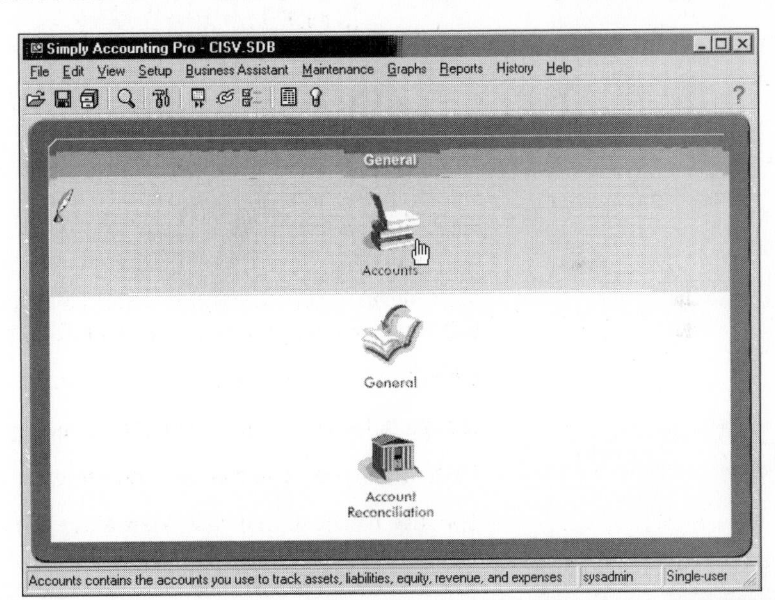

Warning!

Do not choose to skip the Accounts Icon Window before completing the company setup because you need to see which accounts you have already created.

Icon Windows, the last View menu, User Preferences option allows you to skip the accounts Icon Window for one or more ledgers. When you select the Home window Accounts icon (or other ledger icon) with this option turned on, account information for the first account will be displayed instead of the list of accounts. Do not skip the icon window.

version 8

You can also change the design and colour of Simply Accounting windows by choosing the Setup menu, then choosing User Preferences and clicking Colour Scheme.

You are now ready to make the necessary changes in the General Ledger.

Preparing the Ledgers

> **notes**
> Print the Chart of Accounts before you begin and compare it with the Chart of Accounts for CISV. Refer to page 55 for help with printing the Chart of Accounts if necessary.

The third stage in setting up an accounting system involves preparing each ledger for operation. For CISV, this important stage involves the following steps:

1. organizing all accounting reports and records (this step has already been completed for you)
2. modifying some existing accounts (you will not need to delete any accounts for CISV)
3. creating new accounts
4. entering historical account balance information.

Defining the Skeleton Starter Files

Print the **Chart of Accounts**. When you created the company files for CISV in stage one, Creating Company Files (page 153), these preset startup accounts were provided.

The initial Skeleton Chart of Accounts is shown here:

		Account Class
ASSETS		
1000 CURRENT ASSETS	H	
1020 Bank	G	Asset
1200 Accounts Receivable	G	Asset
1390 TOTAL CURRENT ASSETS	T	
LIABILITIES		
2000 CURRENT LIABILITIES	H	
2200 Accounts Payable	G	Liability
2690 TOTAL CURRENT LIABILITIES	T	
EQUITY		
3000 EARNINGS	H	
3560 Retained Earnings	G	Retained Earnings
3600 Current Earnings	X	Current Earnings
3690 TOTAL EARNINGS	T	
REVENUE		
4000 REVENUE	H	
4020 General Revenue	G	Revenue
4390 TOTAL REVENUE	T	
EXPENSE		
5000 EXPENSES	H	
5020 General Expense	G	Expense
5390 TOTAL EXPENSES	T	

> **notes**
> Account classes will be explained in Chapter 10 when you set up the files for Maverick Micro Solutions. For now you can accept the default class settings.

Accounts are organized by section: Assets, Liabilities, Equity, Revenue and Expense. The chart also shows the account type, such as Heading (**H**), Subgroup total (**S**), Total (**T**), subgroup Account (**A**), Group account (**G**) and Current Earnings (**X**). Account type is a method of classifying and organizing accounts within a section or subsection of a report.

Initial account numbers for each account are also shown on the Chart of Accounts. The accounts in this chart follow the sectional boundaries as follows:

- 1000 – 1999 Assets
- 2000 – 2999 Liabilities
- 3000 – 3999 Equity
- 4000 – 4999 Revenue
- 5000 – 5999 Expense

The Format of Financial Statements

When setting up the complete Chart of Accounts for CISV, it is important that you understand the composition and format of financial statements that Simply Accounting will accept.

The Balance Sheet is organized and divided into three sections, each with headings: **Assets**, **Liabilities** and **Equity**. The Income Statement is divided into two sections with headings: **Revenue** and **Expense**.

Each section of the financial statements can be further subdivided into groups. Assets can be divided into groups such as **CURRENT ASSETS**, **INVENTORY ASSETS** and **PLANT AND EQUIPMENT**. Liabilities can be divided into groups titled **CURRENT LIABILITIES** and **LONG TERM DEBT**. Equity, Revenue and Expense sections can also be divided.

Simply Accounting requires that all accounts, including group headings, subgroup totals and group totals, be assigned numbers. This is quite different from a manual accounting system, in which numbers are assigned only to postable accounts. Predefined section headings and section totals (e.g., ASSETS, TOTAL ASSETS and LIABILITIES), however, are not assigned numbers by the program.

The following chart illustrates the rules for organizing accounts in Simply Accounting:

ORGANIZATION OF ACCOUNTS

BALANCE SHEET

Type	Account Description	Amount	Amount
ASSETS [section heading]			
H	**CURRENT ASSETS**		
A	Cash in Bank — Village	xxx	
A	Cash on Hand	xxx	
S	Total Cash		xxx
G	Arts & Crafts Supplies		xxx
G	Food Supplies		xxx
	—		
	—		
T	**TOTAL CURRENT ASSETS**		**xxx**
H	**EQUIPMENT**		
G	Computer		xxx
G	Fax/Answering Machine		xxx
	—		
T	**TOTAL EQUIPMENT**		xxx
TOTAL ASSETS [section total]			xxx
LIABILITIES [section heading]			
H	**CURRENT LIABILITIES**		
G	A/P — Designs U Wear		xxx
G	A/P — Quiq Kopy		xxx
	—		
	—		
T	**TOTAL CURRENT LIABILITIES**		**xxx**
TOTAL LIABILITIES [section total]			xxx
EQUITY [section heading]			
H	**CISV EQUITY**		
G	Surplus Funds		xxx
X	Net Income		xxx
	—		
T	**TOTAL CISV EQUITY**		**xxx**
TOTAL EQUITY [section total]			xxx
TOTAL LIABILITIES & EQUITY			xxx

INCOME STATEMENT

Type	Account Description	Amount	Amount
REVENUE [section heading]			
H	**REVENUE**		
G	Revenue from Bingo		xxx
G	Interest Revenue		xxx
	—		
	—		
T	**TOTAL REVENUE**		**xxx**
TOTAL REVENUE [section total]			xxx
EXPENSE [section heading]			
H	**OPERATING & ADMIN EXPENSES**		
G	Caretaking Expense		xxx
G	Cost of T-shirts		xxx
	—		
	—		
T	**TOTAL OPERATING & ADMIN EXPENSES**		**xxx**
H	**PROGRAM & ACTIVITY EXPENSES**		
G	Craft Supplies Used		xxx
G	Entertainment Expenses		xxx
	—		
	—		
T	**TOTAL PROGRAM & ACTIVITY EXPENSES**		**xxx**
TOTAL EXPENSE [section total]			xxx
NET INCOME			xxx

Financial Statement Groups

The following are the Simply Accounting rules concerning financial statement **groups**:

1. Each group must start with a **group Heading (H)**, which will be printed in boldface type. A heading is not considered a postable account, cannot be debited or credited through transaction entries, and cannot have an amount assigned to it.
2. Each group must contain at least one **postable account** and can contain more. Postable accounts are those that can be debited or credited through journal transaction entries. Postable accounts may have an opening balance.
3. Postable accounts may be **subgroup Accounts (A)** or **Group accounts (G)**. Subgroup account balances appear in a separate column to the left of the group account balances, which are in the right column.
4. Postable subgroup accounts must be followed by a **Subgroup total (S)** account. A subgroup total is not a postable account and cannot be given an opening balance. The program automatically calculates a subgroup total by adding all preceding subgroup postable account balances that follow the last group, subgroup total or heading account. Subgroup total balances always appear in the right column. For example, in the previous applications, *GST Charged on Sales* and *GST Paid on Purchases* are subgroup accounts followed by the subgroup total *GST Owing (Refund)*. For CISV, the two cash accounts are subtotalled.
5. Each group must end with a **group Total (T)**. All accounts in the right column, both postable and subgroup total accounts, are added together to form the group total. A group total is not a postable account. The program automatically calculates it and prints it in boldface type.

Financial Statement Sections

The following are the Simply Accounting rules for financial statement **sections**:

1. Each financial statement section described above has a **total**. A section total is the total of the individual group totals within that section. The five section totals are

   TOTAL ASSETS
   TOTAL LIABILITIES
   TOTAL EQUITY
   TOTAL REVENUE
   TOTAL EXPENSE

   You cannot change the titles of the section totals; the program will automatically calculate and print them in the financial statement reports.
2. The Liabilities and Equity section totals are also automatically added together. **LIABILITIES AND EQUITY** is the sum of TOTAL LIABILITIES and TOTAL EQUITY. You cannot change this title.
3. In the Income Statement, the difference between TOTAL REVENUE and TOTAL EXPENSE is automatically calculated as **NET INCOME** and listed under TOTAL EXPENSE. You cannot change this title.

The Current Earnings (X) Account

There are two linked accounts for the General Ledger — *Retained Earnings* and *Current Earnings*. Both accounts appear under the EQUITY section in the Balance Sheet. You do not need to change the links for these accounts. Their titles will be modified later (see Editing Accounts in the General Ledger, page 170).

It is easy to identify the *Current Earnings* account because it is the only account in the Chart of Accounts whose type is X. This account is calculated as follows:

Current Earnings = Total Revenue – Total Expense

Current Earnings is not a postable account but it appears in the right column with the group accounts. It cannot be removed, but its title can be modified. *Current Earnings* is updated from any transactions that change revenue and expense account balances. At the end of the fiscal period when closing routines are performed, the balance of this account is added to *Retained Earnings* (or a renamed account for *Retained Earnings*) and then it is reset to zero.

For CISV, a charitable organization, the *Retained Earnings* account will be renamed *Surplus Funds*. The *Current Earnings* account will be renamed *Net Income*.

Omitting Zero Account Balances

At times, it may be appropriate to print an account with a zero balance, although zero balance accounts usually do not need to be printed. You have the option in Simply Accounting to omit accounts with zero balances from financial statements. You may select this option in the General Ledger.

Preparing the General Ledger

Compare the Skeleton Chart of Accounts you printed with the CISV Chart of Accounts, Balance Sheet and Income Statement provided in this application. You will see that some accounts are the same and some accounts you need are not yet in the program. You have to customize the accounts specifically for CISV.

Changing the Skeleton Accounts

The first step, that of identifying the changes needed in the Skeleton preset accounts to match the accounts needed for CISV, is a very important one. The changes that must be made to these preset accounts are outlined below:

1. Some starter accounts provided by the program require no changes. The account title, the initial account number and the account type are the same as those given in the financial statements. Those accounts not requiring changes follow:

CURRENT ASSETS	1000	Type H
TOTAL CURRENT ASSETS	1390	Type T
CURRENT LIABILITIES	2000	Type H
TOTAL CURRENT LIABILITIES	2690	Type T
REVENUE	4000	Type H
TOTAL REVENUE	4390	Type T

2. The following accounts have account titles that need to be changed. You must also change the account type for *Bank 1020*. (Account numbers are correct.)

FROM (SKELETON ACCOUNTS)			**TO (CISV ACCOUNTS)**
Account Name	**Number**	**Type**	**Account Name (Type)**
Bank	1020	Type G	Cash in Bank - Village (Type A)
Accounts Receivable	1200	Type G	Arts & Crafts Supplies
Accounts Payable	2200	Type G	A/P - Designs U Wear
EARNINGS	3000	Type H	CISV EQUITY
Retained Earnings	3560	Type G	Surplus Funds
Current Earnings	3600	Type X	Net Income
TOTAL EARNINGS	3690	Type T	TOTAL CISV EQUITY
General Revenue	4020	Type G	Revenue from Bingo
EXPENSES	5000	Type H	OPERATING & ADMIN EXPENSES
General Expense	5020	Type G	Caretaking Expense

notes

You will not need to delete any of the preset accounts for CISV.

3. The following account requires changes in both the account title and the number as follows:

FROM (SKELETON)			TO (CISV)	
Account Name	Number	Type	Account Name	Number
TOTAL EXPENSES	5390	Type T	TOTAL OPERATING & ADMIN EXPENSES	5440

Creating New Accounts

After identifying the modifications that must be made to the Skeleton accounts, the next step is to identify the accounts that you need to create or add to the preset accounts. Again, you should refer to the company Chart of Accounts on page 150 to complete this step.

The chart that follows shows the accounts that you will need to create. The chart includes account titles, account numbers, account types and the option to omit printing zero balances. It lists both postable (group and subgroup) and non-postable accounts (subgroup totals, group headings and group totals).

CHART OF ACCOUNTS TO BE CREATED

Account:	Number	Description	Type	Omit	GIFI	Allocate
	1100	Cash on Hand	A	No	NA	No
	1150	Total Cash	S			
	1300	Food Supplies	G	Yes	NA	No
	1320	Office Supplies	G	Yes	NA	No
	1360	Village T-shirts for Sale	G	Yes	NA	No
	1400	EQUIPMENT	H			
	1450	Computer	G	No	NA	No
	1500	Fax/Answering Machine	G	No	NA	No
	1590	TOTAL EQUIPMENT	T			
	2300	A/P - Quiq Kopy	G	Yes	NA	No
	2350	A/P - Sleeptight Cots	G	Yes	NA	No
	2400	A/P - Travel in Comfort	G	Yes	NA	No
	2670	GST Paid on Purchases	G	Yes	NA	No
	4080	Interest Revenue	G	No	NA	No
	4120	Other Revenue	G	No	NA	No
	5050	Cost of T-shirts	G	Yes	NA	No
	5080	Cots & Linen Rental	G	Yes	NA	No
	5180	Food Expense	G	Yes	NA	No
	5200	General Expense	G	Yes	NA	No
	5250	Office Supplies Used	G	Yes	NA	No
	5280	Non-refundable GST	G	Yes	NA	No
	5300	Postage Expense	G	Yes	NA	No
	5320	Printing & Copying	G	Yes	NA	No
	5350	Publicity	G	Yes	NA	No
	5400	Telephone Expense	G	Yes	NA	No
	5420	Wages - Cook	G	Yes	NA	No
	5450	PROGRAM & ACTIVITY EXPENSES	H			
	5500	Crafts Supplies Used	G	Yes	NA	No
	5550	Entertainment Expenses	G	Yes	NA	No
	5600	Transportation	G	Yes	NA	No
	5690	TOTAL PROGRAM & ACTIVITY EXPENSES	T			

Account Types: A = Subgroup Account S = Subgroup Total G = Group Account H = Heading T = Group Total

You are now ready to enter the account information into the CISV files.

Entering General Ledger Accounts

Click the **Accounts icon** under the General heading in the Home window to open the main Accounts window:

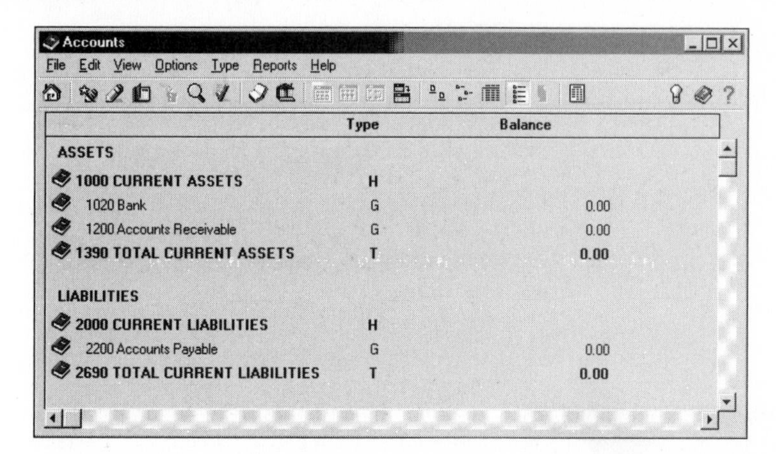

notes

Maximize the Accounts window to fill up the entire screen. This will allow you to display more accounts and keep the Accounts window in view in the background while you are creating or editing accounts. Return to the normal size window by restoring its size (Restore button).

The preset accounts should be displayed in the Type format.

Your settings may be different. You may see the accounts window in the Icon format with icons representing each account like this:

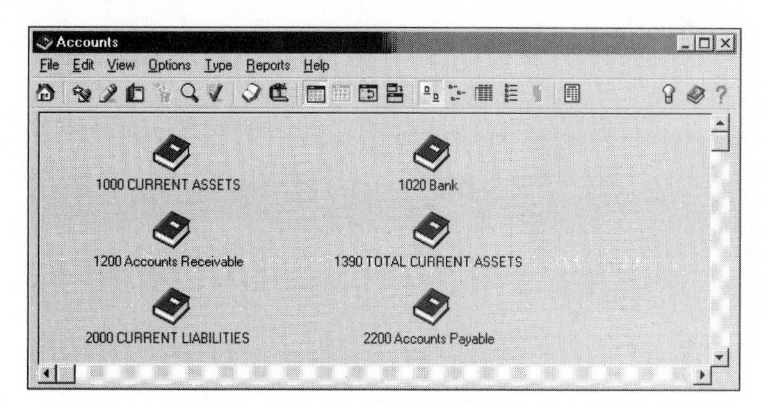

In the Icon view, the icons can be rearranged by dragging so that frequently used accounts appear on top for easier access. New accounts are added at the end but can be moved to the desired location. The same option of moving accounts is available for the small icon view. In small icon viewing mode, more accounts can be displayed at the same time.

Another format is available with the Name view:

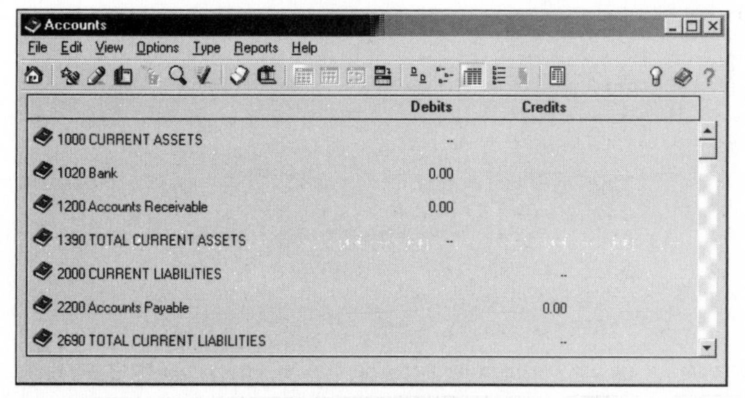

Viewing accounts by name shows the account numbers, names and balances in debit and credit columns. Accounts remain in numerical order as new accounts are added.

For entering new accounts and editing a large number of existing accounts, it is easier to work with the accounts listed in numerical order. New accounts are inserted in their correct order, providing a better view of the progress during the setup phase. The addition of account type in the Type view is helpful for checking the logical order of accounts as they are added. You can change the Accounts window view at any time.

If your screen does not show the accounts by Type, you should change the way accounts are displayed.

Click the **Display by type button** or **choose** the **View menu** and **click Type**.

Editing Accounts in the General Ledger

We will change the first account that requires editing, *1020 Bank*.

The Accounts window should be open with the preset accounts displayed.

Click the **icon** or **name of the account 1020 Bank** to highlight or select it.

Click the **Edit button** on the Accounts window tool bar or **choose** the **Edit menu** and click **Edit** to display the account information as shown:

notes

- Alternatively, you can double click the account's icon or name to open the account.
- If you choose to skip the Accounts icon window from the View menu, you will see the General Ledger window for CURRENT ASSETS, the first account, when you click the Accounts icon. You can use the Select field drop-down list of accounts to find the Bank account.

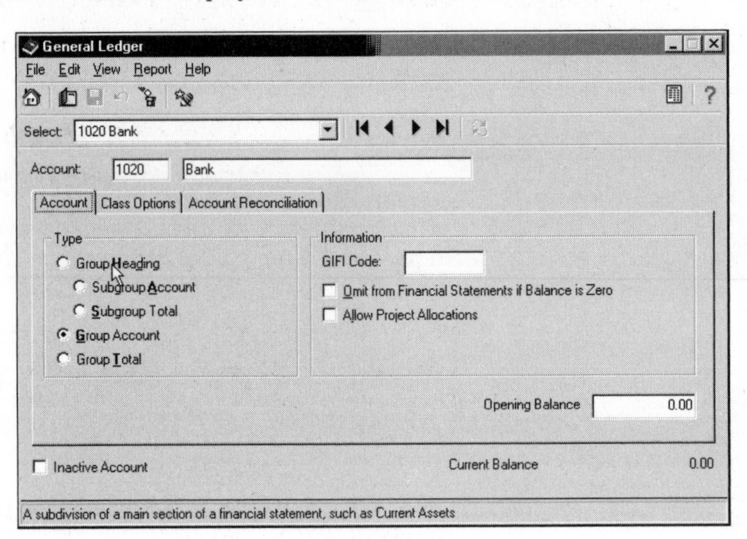

The Account information tab screen is displayed. This is the screen we use to edit the account name and type. For the bank account, the account number is correct. The balance of this account should always be displayed, so do not change the option to Omit from Financial Statements if Balance is Zero.

Press tab to advance to the name of the account and highlight it.

Type `Cash in Bank - Village`

notes

You can close the bank account window to return to the main Accounts window and select the next account to be changed; choose the Edit menu and then Edit to open the account ledger window.

We are not using GIFI codes (Canada Customs and Revenue Agency's account numbering system for electronic report filing) or project allocations, so we can leave these fields empty. The current balance is dimmed because it is updated from journal entries. The opening account balance will be added in the next step, Entering Historical Account Balances. We are not using Account Reconciliation and we do not need to change the account class, so we can skip these tab screens.

Click Subgroup Account to change the account type. The two cash accounts together will be subtotalled. You can now advance to the next account for editing.

Click the **Next Account tool** to open the ledger record for the next account in numerical sequence, or,

Click the **Select field** to show the list of all accounts as shown:

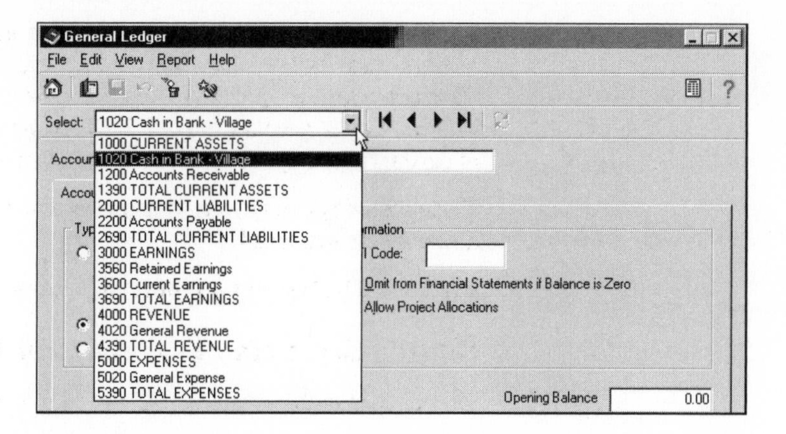

notes

Because you chose to save ledger record changes automatically (page 161) you do not need to save an account record (Save tool or File menu, Save option) after each change.

Click 1200 Accounts Receivable to display the ledger record.

Edit the remaining accounts shown on pages 167–168 as required. You may choose to print zero balances or to omit them.

Close the General Ledger window to return to the Accounts window.

Click [icon] or **choose** the **Edit menu** and click **Check the Validity of accounts**. You should see the following information screen at this stage:

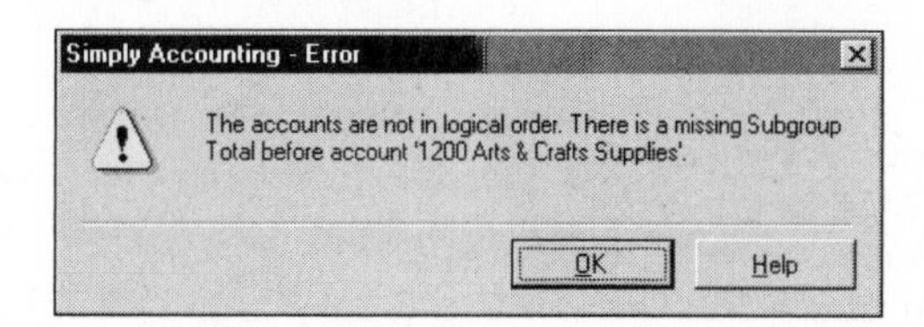

Without the second subgroup account and subgroup total, we have not followed the rules for Groups (page 166, rule 4) so the accounts are not in logical order. You can periodically check the validity of accounts while you are adding accounts to see whether you have made errors in your account type sequence that will prevent you from finishing the account history.

Click Help to see a more detailed explanation of the error and possible solutions. You can print the Help window details. Close the Help window when you have finished.

Click OK to return to the Accounts window. When we add the remaining accounts, the accounts should be in logical order and the error will be corrected.

Creating New Accounts in the General Ledger

You are now ready to enter the information for the first new account, *Cash on Hand*, using the chart on page 168 as your reference. The following keystrokes will enter the account title, number, type and option to include or omit zero balance accounts.

The Accounts window should still be open.

notes

You can also create accounts from any ledger window. Click the Create tool or choose the File menu and then Create.

version 8

Click the **Create button** on the Accounts window tool bar or **choose** the **File menu** and **click Create** to display the new account information window shown below:

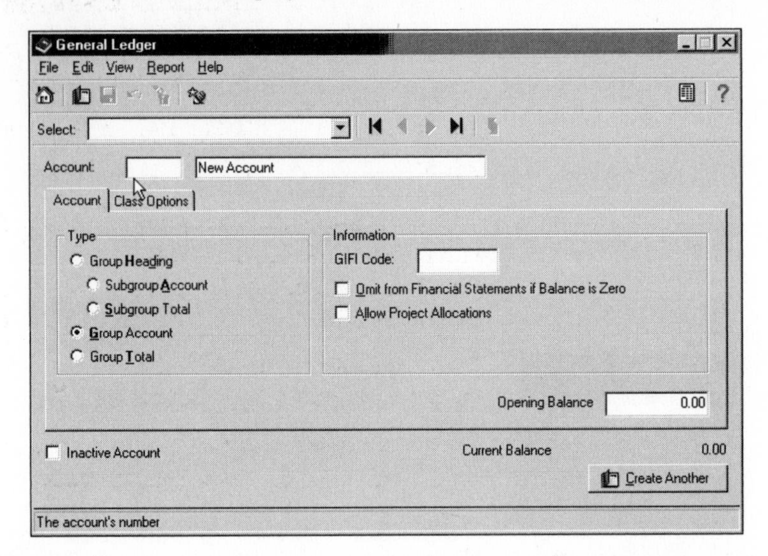

notes

The default account type depends on the account record you used most recently.

The tabs that appear in the ledger depend on the account section as defined by the account number. Since no number is entered initially, only the two tabs that apply to all accounts appear. We will create the first CISV account that was not in the Skeleton Chart of Accounts, *Cash on Hand*. The account type is selected as the most likely option for logical account order. Group total accounts are often followed by a group account. The cursor is in the Account number field.

notes

The Simply Accounting program will not allow you to enter duplicate account numbers.

Type `1100`

Press tab to advance the the Account title field and highlight the selection.

Type `Cash on Hand`

Click Subgroup Account to change the account type if necessary.

Leave the option to Omit from Financial Statements turned off. Skip the GIFI field and the project allocations check box.

Check your work. Make any necessary corrections by pressing tab to return to the incorrect field, typing the correct information, and pressing tab if necessary. When the information has been entered correctly, save your work.

notes

Remember that subgroup totals, group headings and group totals — the non-postable accounts — will have the balance field removed when you choose these account types.

Click Create Another [Create Another] to save the new account and to advance to another new account information window.

Create the remaining accounts on page 168.

Display or print the Chart of Accounts to check the accuracy of your work. If you find mistakes, edit the account information as described above in the section Editing Accounts in the General Ledger.

Entering Historical Account Balances

notes

If you want to end your session, close the General Ledger window and close the Accounts window to return to the Home window.

Before completing this step, we will create one more account that will be used as a test account for our Trial Balance. If you close the General Ledger before entering all the account balances, or if the total debits and credits are not equal, the program forces the Trial Balance to balance by adding the required debit or credit amount to another account. You will see a screen like the following:

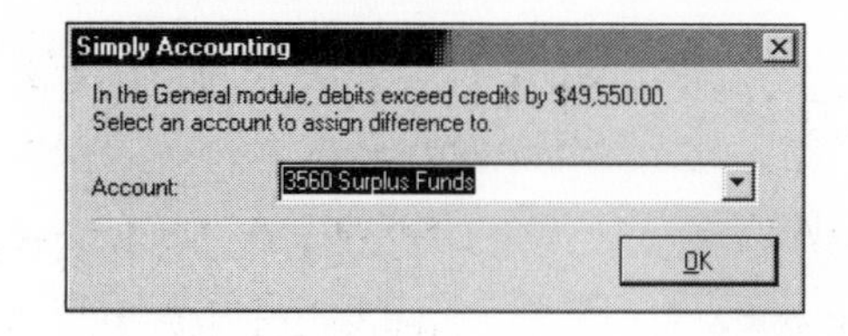

You can choose any account from the drop-down list, or accept the default.

Click OK to continue.

This automatic adjustment may compensate for other errors that you have made in entering amounts. To avoid this problem, we will create a **test account** and put all the adjustments into it. If all the balances are entered correctly, the test account will have a zero balance and we can remove the account.

Create the new Group account *1005 Test Account*. If you see the above warning, choose account *1005 Test Account* from the drop-down list.

You are now ready to enter the opening historical account balances for all postable (type G or A) accounts. The opening balances for CISV can be found in the Trial Balance on page 152.

notes

Before you finish the history, the opening balance can be edited. The Current Balance is dimmed because you cannot edit it. Initially, it is the same as the opening balance but it changes when you add journal entries. Because you can enter journal transactions before finishing the history, this distinction is very important. The balance in the Accounts window is the current balance, which may not be the same as the opening balance.

Click the **Select field** or **list arrow** and **choose 1020 Cash in Bank - Village** to open its ledger window:

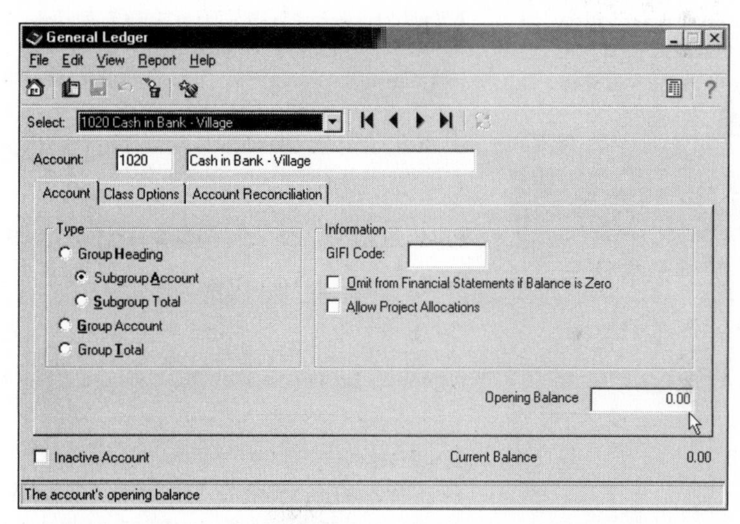

The Current Balance field dimmed. Simply Accounting updates this balance automatically from journal entries.

Click the **Opening Balance field** and highlight it.

Type 49550

notes

Remember to enter the amount for GST Paid on Purchases with a minus sign to create a debit entry.

Click the **Next tool** to advance to the next ledger account window.

Enter the balances for the remaining accounts.

notes

After entering all the accounts and balances, display or print the Trial Balance, Balance Sheet and Income Statement to check the accuracy of your work.

Remember that if you close the Ledger window before entering all the account balances, you will see the dialogue box asking for the account you want to use for the difference, an adjusting, balancing entry that will place the Trial Balance in balance. Choose *Test Account* from the drop-down list of accounts.

Be sure to check all your opening balances before finishing the history. The balance for *Test Account* should be zero.

Close the Ledger window to return to the Accounts window.

Check your work carefully by comparing your reports with the information on pages 150–152 to be sure that all account numbers, names and balances are correct. Make corrections if necessary.

Close the Accounts window to return to the Home window.

Warning!

Back up the not finished CISV files before proceeding. See Chapter 3 if you need further assistance.

Finishing the General Ledger History

Making a Backup Copy

By having a backup copy of your files before finishing the history, you will be able to make changes easily if you find an error, without having to repeat the entire setup from scratch. After the ledger history is finished, the program will not permit you to make certain changes, such as opening account balances and fiscal dates. You cannot change the account number for an account after making a journal entry to the account.

You should back up your unfinished open history files in a different folder so that they can be easily identified (e.g., NFCISV).

Choose the **File menu** and **click Backup**.

Follow the instructions to create the backup copy. Refer to page 50 if you need help.

Warning!

You can finish entering the history when the Trial Balance is in balance. Afterwards, you cannot change opening balances, even if they are incorrect. Simply Accounting always keeps the Trial Balance balanced. Therefore, checking for a zero balance in the test account can stop you from proceeding with incorrect account balances.

Finishing the General Ledger History

You should be in the Home window.

Choose the **History menu**, then choose **Finish Entering History**.

The following caution appears:

notes

If your accounts are out of order, you cannot finish entering the history. If you did not hide the unused modules, you cannot finish entering the history because some essential linked accounts for these modules are not defined. Read the error description very carefully, make corrections and try again.

If you see a different screen at this stage, like the following one, you have errors that must be corrected before you can continue:

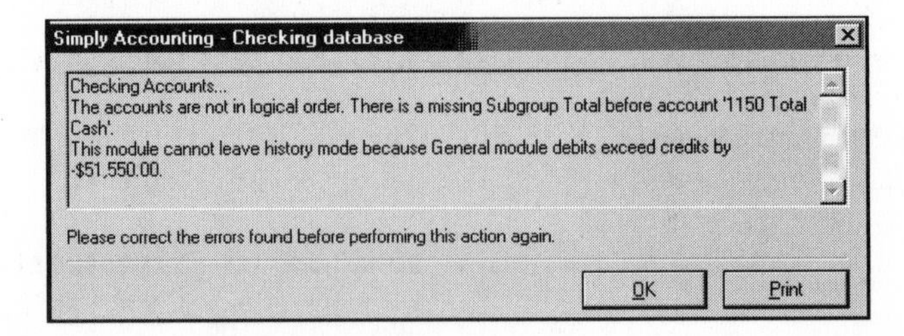

The message describes the mistakes. Read the message carefully or print the message so that you can make corrections. Click OK to return to the Home window. Make the necessary corrections and then try again to finish the history.

If you have not made a backup copy yet, click Backup and do so before proceeding. If you have made your backup copy, you should continue.

Click Proceed

Notice that the General Ledger Accounts icon no longer has the open history quill pen symbol on it.

You can now exit the program or continue by entering the source documents for July. Remember to advance the Session Date. Enter all transactions for CISV in the General Journal.

SOURCE DOCUMENTS

SESSION DATE — July 7

- ❑ Purchase Invoice #QK-2252
  Dated July 2/03
  From Quiq Kopy, $216 (including PST) for photocopying of Village participant packages and Village open day invitations, plus $14 GST. Invoice total $230. Terms: net 25 days.

notes

❑ Create new Group account: 2100 A/P - Bell Canada

- ❑ Purchase Invoice #BC-10116
  Dated July 2/03
  From Bell Canada, $324 (including PST) for rental of cellular telephone equipment, plus $21 GST. Invoice total $345. Deposit required and balance due at end of month or rental period.

- ❑ Cheque Copy #167
  Dated July 2/03
  To Bell Canada, $100 deposit on rental of telephone equipment. Reference invoice #BC-10116.

- ❑ Memo #1
  Dated July 2/03
  From Village Director to Treasurer: Give T-shirt to each Village participant. Cost of T-shirts given out is $500. Reduce T-shirt asset account and increase Cost of T-shirts expense account.

notes

In most businesses, the Cash on Hand balance is usually small and is used only for paying small amounts. In this application, we are using the Cash on Hand account to pay for any purchases that normally would require cash payments. In reality, the Village director, or another staff member, receives cash advances to cover these costs.

- ❑ Cash Purchase Invoice #CP-1
  Dated July 4/03
  Postage for mailing out Open House invitations to all members, $60 plus $4.20 GST. Invoice total $64.20. Amount paid from Cash on Hand.

- ❑ Funds Raised Form: #FR-03-13
  Dated July 5/03
  Collected $830 net from bi-weekly Bingo night. Amount deposited in bank (Cash in Bank - Village).

- ❑ Cash Purchase Invoice TTC-1
  Dated July 5/03
  From TTC, $350.00 for bus tickets for transportation for camp field trips (to Science Centre, beach and CN Tower). Paid from Cash on Hand.

- ❑ Cash Purchase Invoice #OSC-662
  Dated July 5/03
  From Science Centre, $450 for admission of all participants to Science Centre, plus $31.50 GST. Invoice total $481.50. Paid from Cash on Hand.

- ❑ Memo #2
  Dated July 7/03
  From Village Director to Treasurer: Issue cheque #168 for $3 000 to transfer funds to Cash on Hand for Village food purchases, and for bus and entertainment expenses for the next two weeks.

☐ Cash Purchase Invoice #SF-2168
Dated July 7/03
From SuperFoods, $1 616 for food for Village participant meals. Paid from Cash on Hand.

SESSION DATE — July 14

☐ Purchase Invoice #TC-10986
Dated July 8/03
From Travel in Comfort, $600 for bus rental for trip to Niagara Falls, plus $42 GST. Invoice total $642. Terms: net 30 days.

☐ Cash Purchase Invoice #MM-55231
Dated July 9/03
From Niagara Tours Inc., $320 for group rates on Misty Maid tour, plus $22.40 GST. Invoice total $342.40. Paid from Cash on Hand.

☐ Cheque Copy #169
Dated July 12/03
To Sleeptight Cots, $3 050 in full payment of account. Reference invoice #SC-606.

☐ Cash Purchase Invoice #CSS-5566
Dated July 14/03
From City Schools, Permits Department, $3 600 for caretaking expenses on Village site plus $252 GST. Invoice total $3 852. Terms: cash on receipt of invoice. Paid by cheque #170.

☐ Cash Purchase Invoice #QAS-4632
Dated July 14/03
From Quarts Arts Supplies, $216 (including PST) for craft supplies plus $14 GST. Invoice total $230. Paid from Cash on Hand.

SESSION DATE — July 21

☐ Cheque Copy #171
Dated July 15/03
To Designs U Wear $800, in full payment of account.

☐ Purchase Invoice #TC-14913
Dated July 16/03
From Travel in Comfort, $800 for bus rental for trip to Algonquin Park, plus $56 GST. Invoice total $856. Terms: net 30.

☐ Cheque Copy #172
Dated July 16/03
To Travel in Comfort, $1 698 in full payment of account. Reference invoices #TC-14913, #TC-10986 and previous balance owing.

☐ Cash Purchase Invoice #OP-988
Dated July 16/03
From Ontario Parks, $70.10 for park admission for Village participants, plus $4.90 GST. Invoice total $75. Paid from Cash on Hand.

☐ Funds Raised Form: FR-03-14
Dated July 18/03
Collected $980 net from bi-weekly Bingo night. Amount deposited in bank (Cash in Bank - Village).

- [ ] Memo #3
Dated July 21/03
From Village Director to Treasurer: Issue cheque #173 for $1 500 to transfer funds to Cash on Hand for Village food purchases and entertainment expenses for the week.

- [ ] Cash Purchase Invoice #SF-5217
Dated July 21/03
From SuperFoods, $1 022 for food for Village participant meals and Open House hors d'oeuvres. Paid from Cash on Hand.

SESSION DATE — July 28

- [ ] Purchase Invoice #QK-5306
Dated July 22/03
From Quiq Kopy, $108 (including PST) for photocopying of visitor handouts for Village Open House, plus $7 GST. Invoice total $115.00. Terms: net 15 days.

- [ ] Funds Raised Form #FR-0314A
Dated July 22/03
From sale of T-shirts at Open House, $600 revenue received in cash and deposited in bank. The cost of the T-shirts sold was $300. Reduce the Village T-shirts for Sale asset account and increase the Cost of T-shirts expense account for the cost of T-shirts sold.

- [ ] Cash Purchase Invoice #CNTower
Dated July 25/03
From CN Tours Inc., $420.56 for admissions to CN Tower, plus $29.44 GST. Invoice total $450. Paid from Cash on Hand.

- [ ] Cash Purchase Invoice #CinOd-1
Dated July 26/03
From Cineplex Odeon theatre, $300 for admissions to movie, plus $21 GST. Invoice total $321. Paid from Cash on Hand.

- [ ] Cheque Copy #174
Dated July 28/03
To Sophia Waterman, Village cook, $3 000 for wages for four weeks.

- [ ] Cash Purchase Invoice #Gifts-1
Dated July 28/03
From Gifts For All Occasions, $162.00 (including PST) for honorarium gifts for Village staff, plus $10.50 GST. Invoice total $172.50. Paid from Cash on Hand. Charge to General Expense.

SESSION DATE — July 31

- [ ] Purchase Invoice #QK-6732
Dated July 29/03
From Quiq Kopy, $129.60 (including PST) for colour copies of group Village photo to send to all participants, plus $8.40 GST. Invoice total $138. Terms: net 15 days.

- [ ] Cheque Copy #175
Dated July 31/03
To Quiq Kopy, $633 in full payment of account. Reference invoice #QK-6732, QK-5306, QK-2252 and previous balance owing.

❑ Cash Purchase Invoice #CP-2
Dated July 31/03
From Canada Post, $40 for postage to mail photographs, plus $2.80 GST. Invoice total $42.80. Paid from Cash on Hand.

❑ Memo #4
Dated July 31/03
From Village Director to Treasurer: Small quantities of supplies were left at the end of the Village. Leftover food supplies have been donated to food banks; craft and office supplies have been donated to the Junior Branch. Reduce the following asset accounts to zero and increase the corresponding expense accounts to reflect supplies used during Village:

Reduce Food Supplies and increase Food Expense by $4 938.
Reduce Arts & Crafts Supplies and increase Crafts Supplies Used by $716.
Reduce Office Supplies and increase Office Supplies Used by $400.

❑ Memo #5
Dated July 31/03
From Village Director to Treasurer: Deposit $332.60 balance of Cash on Hand to bank.

❑ Cheque Copy #176
Dated July 31/03
To Bell Canada, $245, in full payment of account. Reference invoice #BC-10116 and cheque #167.

❑ Bank Credit Memo #CT-53197
Dated July 31/03
From Canada Trust, $63 interest paid on bank account.

❑ Bank Debit Memo #CT-3881
Dated July 31/03
From Canada Trust, $21.50 in bank charges for cheques and statement preparation.

❑ Memo #6
Dated July 31/03
From Treasurer: Apply for GST rebate of $463.07. Record 50% of GST Paid on Purchases as GST Refund Receivable, the other 50% as the Non-refundable GST expense.

notes

At the time of writing this book, CISV Canada had chapters in the following cities:

Fredericton, NB
St. Gregoire, PQ
Ottawa, ON
Toronto, ON
Waterloo, ON
London, ON
Saskatoon, SK
Calgary, AB
Vancouver, BC
Victoria, BC

If you want more information about CISV, or to locate the Chapter nearest you, you can contact the national office at
CISV Canada
5 Dunvegan Road
Ottawa, ON K1K 3E7
1-877-472-2478

— or the international office at
CISV International
MEA House, Ellison Place
Newcastle Upon Tyne
NEI 8X5 England

notes

❑ Create new Group accounts:
5010 Bank Charges
1180 GST Refund Receivable

CASE PROBLEMS

1. A friend who has extensive experience using Simply Accounting advised the Treasurer for CISV to number the accounts with gaps between successive accounts (e.g., 1000, 1020, 1040, 1060, etc.).

   a. Explain why this system may be helpful.
   b. How is this system different from a manual accounting system?

2. Some time later, two new accounts were needed to represent more accurately the list of expenses. Unfortunately, to maintain the correct sequence of accounts and to have the correct subgroup total, the new accounts had to be placed between the accounts that were presently numbered 5050 and 5051. Discuss ways that you could resolve this problem.

CHAPTER SEVEN

OBJECTIVES

After completing this chapter, you should be able to

- *enter* credit card sale and purchase transactions
- *make payments* toward credit card accounts
- *enter* discounts for early payments to vendors and from customers
- *make* GST and PST remittances
- *apply* sales taxes to interprovincial sales
- *understand* linked accounts for discounts and credit cards
- *enter* sales and receipts for foreign customers
- *enter* deposits from customers and prepayments to vendors
- *access* vendor or customer Web sites
- *e-mail* invoices to customers
- *look up* invoices after posting them
- *track* shipments to customers
- *complete* closing routines at the end of a fiscal period
- *advance* the session date to begin a new fiscal period

COMPANY INFORMATION

Company Profile

Outset Media Corporation is owned and operated by David Manga out of a small office in Victoria, British Columbia. After graduating from the commerce program at Ottawa University, Manga created The All Canadian Trivia Board Game. Manga believed that many Canadians shared his enjoyment of trivia games and his frustration from learning more about American than Canadian history and culture as a result of playing the games. (Although the first Trivial Pursuit game was created by a Canadian, its content is largely American.)

notes

The information in this chapter is based on the real Canadian company Outset Media, but financial information has been created to illustrate various features of the Simply Accounting software.

Based on careful research of many Canadian sources — magazines, books, newspapers and encyclopedias — David wrote the questions for his first game, The All Canadian Trivia Board Game. The production, design and manufacturing were all completed by Canadian companies. Manga financed the production of the original game with capital borrowed from family and friends. He pursued business aggressively from his office by faxing and telephoning department, game, toy, gift and specialty stores across Canada. Within a few months, his game was available in more than 100 small gift, book and game stores. Within two years, he had added a Junior Edition of the game, supplementary questions, a French version and a special limited edition Millennium version. In 2000, Manga produced three more games: bird watching and hockey trivia games and Conjecture (charades with sculpting clay). Since then, he has created even more games. As his product list continued to grow, he opened a manufacturing division and warehouses in both Canada and the United States.

Gradually, the larger stores started to carry the games, including some in the United States. Manga relies on a variety of channels for selling the games. He still sells directly to some small businesses, to individuals who order directly from his Web site, <www.CanadianTrivia.com>, and to a publisher who handles bookstore sales and a toy distribution company that specializes in toy store sales. The business is seasonal, as it is for most games and toys. Most stores buy in late summer and early fall to prepare for the holiday season. There is a small sales peak for Canada Day on July 1. Individual sales are concentrated in the pre-holiday period. Manga works with companies across Canada to produce the game. To reduce unit production costs, he makes a large number of games in each production run and then pays modest storage costs.

notes

You can learn more about The All Canadian Trivia Board Game by visiting the Web site for the game at <www.CanadianTrivia.com> and for Outset Media at <www.outsetmedia.com>.

Manga converted his accounting records to Simply Accounting after a brief lesson and demonstration from his aunt. The following company information summarizes the conversion after the first nine months of the current fiscal period:

- Chart of Accounts
- Trial Balance
- Vendor Information
- Customer Information
- Accounting Procedures

OUTSET MEDIA CORP.
CHART OF ACCOUNTS

ASSETS
1020 Bank: Savings Account
1040 Bank: Chequing Account
1060 Bank: Visa
1080 Bank: MasterCard
1100 Bank: AMEX
1120 Bank USD
1200 Accounts Receivable
1280 Office Supplies
1300 Games Inventory
1340 Prepaid Expenses
1410 Computers
1420 Accum Deprec: Computers
1450 Furniture & Equipment
1480 Accum Deprec: Furn & Equip
1500 Automobile
1520 Accum Deprec: Automobile

LIABILITIES
2100 Bank Loan
2200 Accounts Payable
2260 Visa Payable
2460 PST Payable
2650 GST Charged on Sales
2660 HST Charged on Sales
2670 GST Paid on Purchases
2850 Long Term Loan

EQUITY
3560 D. Manga, Capital
3600 Current Earnings

REVENUE
4100 Revenue from Sales
4180 Sales Discounts
4200 Freight Revenue
4250 Interest Revenue
4280 Sales Tax Compensation
4300 Exchange Rate Differences

EXPENSES
5100 Advertising & Publicity
5150 Bank Charges & Card Fees
5200 Depreciation Expense
5220 Freight & Shipping Expenses
5260 Purchase Discounts
5280 Interest Expense
5300 Internet & Web Site Expenses
5340 Games Storage Expense
5360 Production & Assembly Costs
5380 Cost of Games Sold
5400 Office Rent
5500 Office Supplies Used
5520 Research Expenses
5560 Telephone Expenses
5580 Travel Expenses

OUTSET MEDIA CORP.
TRIAL BALANCE

June 30, 2003

Account	Debit	Credit
1020 Bank: Savings Account	$100 000.00	
1040 Bank: Chequing Account	66 500.00	
1060 Bank: Visa	900.00	
1080 Bank: MasterCard	1 100.00	
1100 Bank: AMEX	400.00	
1120 Bank USD ($400 USD)	600.00	
1200 Accounts Receivable	16 050.00	
1280 Office Supplies	400.00	
1300 Games Inventory	315 000.00	
1340 Prepaid Expenses	4 400.00	
1410 Computers	7 500.00	
1420 Accum Deprec: Computers		1 100.00
1450 Furniture & Equipment	8 000.00	
1480 Accum Deprec: Furn & Equip		1 500.00
1500 Automobile	10 500.00	
1520 Accum Deprec: Automobile		5 000.00
2100 Bank Loan		10 000.00
2200 Accounts Payable		1 610.00
2260 Visa Payable		505.00
2460 PST Payable		450.00
2650 GST Charged on Sales		4 900.00
2660 HST Charged on Sales		600.00
2670 GST Paid on Purchases	2 900.00	
2850 Long Term Loan		200 000.00
3560 D. Manga, Capital		127 360.00
4100 Revenue from Sales		410 000.00
4180 Sales Discounts	8 200.00	
4200 Freight Revenue		5 500.00
4250 Interest Revenue		4 800.00
4280 Sales Tax Compensation		45.00
5100 Advertising & Publicity	25 600.00	
5150 Bank Charges & Card Fees	1 350.00	
5220 Freight & Shipping Expenses	4 500.00	
5260 Purchase Discounts	750.00	
5280 Interest Expense	12 600.00	
5300 Internet & Web Site Expenses	180.00	
5340 Games Storage Expense	1 800.00	
5380 Cost of Games Sold	175 000.00	
5400 Office Rent	4 500.00	
5500 Office Supplies Used	600.00	
5520 Research Expenses	2 200.00	
5560 Telephone Expenses	890.00	
5580 Travel Expenses	950.00	
	$773 370.00	$773 370.00

OUTSET MEDIA CORP.
VENDOR INFORMATION

Vendor Name (Contact)	Address	Phone No. Fax No.	E-mail Web Site	Tax ID Terms
BC Tel (Manny Voyses)	45 Nexus Ave. Victoria, BC V7R 3D1	Tel: (250) 679-1011 Fax: (250) 679-1000	www.bell.ca	n/1
Box It (Able Wrapp)	80 Cubit Road Richmond Hill, ON L5R 6B2	Tel: (905) 881-7739 Fax: (905) 881-7000		63452 9125 1/5, n/30
Federal Express (DayLee Runner)	59 Effex Road Victoria, BC V7F 6X2	Tel: (800) 488-9000 Fax: (250) 488-1230	www.fedex.com	n/1
Game Makers (Marc Jeunot)	45 Rue de Jeux Montreal, PQ H3P 5N6	Tel: (514) 882-6252 Fax: (514) 882-1100		12964 6733 1/10, n/30
Grandeur Graphics (Kathy Grandeur)	26 Drawing Way Halifax, NS B5T 3D1	Tel: (902) 665-3998 Fax: (902) 665-3900	www.wedesignit.com	45911 2341 2/20, n/30
Let 'm Know (Jabber Jaws Lowder)	599 Broadcast Rd. Vancouver, BC V2F 7J8	Tel: (604) 604-6040 Fax: (604) 604-4660	www.wetellit.com	45392 5376 2/10, n/30
Miles 'R on Us (N. Gins)	522 Drivers St. Victoria, BC V6T 5E3	Tel: (800) 592-5239 Fax: (250) 591-4929		n/1
Minister of Finance	55 Munificence St. Victoria, BC V7P 2B5	Tel: (250) 529-7292	www.fin.gov.bc.ca	n/1
Purolator (Speedy Carriere)	46 Shipping Mews Victoria, BC V7H 6S2	Tel: (800) 355-7447 Fax: (250) 355-7000	www.purolator.com	n/1
Receiver General of Canada	Summerside Tax Centre Summerside, PE C1N 6L2	Tel: (902) 821-8186	www.ccra-adrc.gc.ca	n/1
Space Unlimited (Toller Wyder)	4500 Dundas St. W. Toronto, ON M8T 3G5	Tel: (416) 789-0123 Fax: (416) 729-7751	www.leaveitwithus.com	28899 5438 2/20, n/30

OUTSET MEDIA CORP.
OUTSTANDING VENDOR INVOICES

Vendor Name	Date	Inv/Chq No.	Terms	Pretax Amount	Tax	Total
Grandeur Graphics	6/28/03	GG-1304	2/20, n/30	$ 400.00	$ 60.00	$ 460.00
Space Unlimited	6/29/03	SU-692	2/20, n/30	$1 000.00	$150.00	$1 150.00
			Grand Total			$1 610.00

OUTSET MEDIA CORP.
CUSTOMER INFORMATION

Customer Name (Contact)	Address	Phone No. Fax No.	E-mail Web Site	Terms Credit Limit
Best Games (Michelle Young)	230 Old Young Blvd. Toronto, ON M6R 9K4	Tel: (416) 498-6189 Fax: (416) 498-6000	myoung@playtime.com www.bestgames.ca	3/30, n/60 $20 000
Internet Customers				Credit Card
It's All Canadian (Leaf Mapleston)	39 Federation Ave. Victoria, BC V8W 7T7	Tel: (250) 598-1123 Fax: (250) 598-1000	www.cangames.com	3/30, n/60 $20 000
Let's Have Fun (Chuck Trickster)	399 Playtime Blvd. Vancouver, BC V4E 5T6	Tel: (604) 557-5438 Fax: (604) 557-5550	chuck@playtime.com	3/30, n/60 $30 000
Mapleaves M. Porter	10 Red Rock Canyon Sedona, Arizona 86336 USA	Tel: (520) 678-4523 Fax: (520) 678-4500	mporter@mapleaves.com www.mapleaves.com	3/30, n/60 $10 000 USD
The Canada Store (X. Pats)	46 Ontario St. Tampa, Florida 33607 USA	Tel: (813) 930-4589 Fax: (813) 930-7330	XPats@canstore.com www.canstore.com	3/30, n/60 $20 000 USD
Toys 'N More (Patty Kaik)	93 Waterside Rd. Fredericton, NB E3B 4F4	Tel: (506) 455-7746 Fax: (506) 455-7000	patty@playtime.com www.toys.com	3/30, n/60 $50 000
Trivyal & Associates (Ken Trivyal)	50 Rue des Bagatelles Montreal, PQ H4S 9B3	Tel: (514) 487-2936 Fax: (514) 488-1500	ktrivyal@istar.ca	3/30, n/60 $150 000

OUTSET MEDIA CORP.
OUTSTANDING CUSTOMER INVOICES

Customer Name	Date	Inv/Chq No.	Terms	Pretax Amount	Tax	Total
Best Games	6/25/03	1991	3/30, n/60	$9 000.00	$630.00	$ 9 630.00
It's All Canadian	6/6/03	1989	3/30, n/60	$6 000.00	$420.00	$ 6 420.00
			Grand Total			$16 050.00

Accounting Procedures

GST

Outset Media Corporation uses the regular method of calculating GST. The GST charged and collected from customers is recorded as a liability in the *GST Charged on Sales* account. Customers in Nova Scotia, New Brunswick and Newfoundland (participating provinces) pay HST at the rate of 15% instead of GST. Manga has set up GST charged at rate 2 to record HST for these sales. GST paid to vendors is recorded in the *GST Paid on Purchases* account as a decrease in tax liability. The balance owing is the difference between the GST plus HST charged and GST paid.

Cash Sales of Services

Cash transactions for Manga are limited to credit card sales since most of his business is with wholesale customers who have accounts. He has set up merchant Visa, MasterCard and American Express (Amex) arrangements with three different financial institutions. Outset Media pays a percentage of each sale directly to the credit card companies (the fee is withheld from the sale amount). To simplify the entering of transactions, we provide summaries of these credit card sales as if they were to a single customer called Internet Sales.

Manga uses a Visa gold card for some business purchases and pays an annual user fee for this card.

notes

The sales tax rules for discounts are complex and may vary from province to province and for federal taxes. Simply Accounting calculates sales discounts as before or after tax but applies the same formula to GST and retail sales taxes. Adjusting General Journal entries may be required to adjust the amount of tax owing and calculate the tax remittance. We have omitted the tax adjustments for sales discounts.

Discounts

Discounts are calculated automatically by the program when the discount terms are entered as part of the invoices. If the payments are made before the discount terms have expired, the discount appears in the Payments and Receipts Journals automatically. All discounts are calculated on before-tax amounts. Manga offers a 3% discount to wholesale customers to encourage them to pay their accounts on time. Internet customers pay by credit card and do not receive discounts.

Some vendors offer discounts to Outset Media as well. These discount terms are set up in the vendor and customer records.

PST

Wholesale customers do not pay PST on merchandise they buy for resale. Thus when Manga sells directly to stores, he charges only GST. He does not charge PST to stores because they are not the final consumers of the product. When individual customers buy directly from Manga, he charges PST to customers in British Columbia but not to customers in other provinces. All customers pay GST at 7% or HST at 15%. PST and GST are also paid on all freight or shipping charges. When Outset Media makes the PST remittance, it reduces the amount of the remittance by 3.3%, the amount of the sales tax compensation.

Freight

Customers who order through the Internet pay a flat rate of $5 per game for shipping. Wholesale customers pay the actual shipping costs. GST and PST are charged on freight in British Columbia. Manga has accounts set up with his three regular shippers so that he can track shipments online. Their Web site addresses are included in the shipping setup data.

Sales Orders and Deposits

When a customer places a sales order, Manga requests a deposit as confirmation of the order. Deposits are entered in the Receipts Journal (page 209).

Sales to Foreign Customers

Customers outside Canada do not pay GST or PST on goods imported from Canada. Therefore, these sales outside the country do not have taxes applied to them.

INSTRUCTIONS

1. Using the Chart of Accounts, Vendor Information, Customer Information and Accounting Procedures for Outset Media, record entries for the source documents in Simply Accounting. The procedures for entering each new type of transaction in this application are outlined step by step in the keystroke section following the source documents. These transactions are indicated with a ✔ in the completion box beside the source document. The number for the page on which the relevant keystrokes begin is printed immediately below the check box.
2. After you have finished making your entries, print the reports for the end of the fiscal period suggested by the Simply Accounting checklists. Refer to the Keystrokes section, page 216.

SOURCE DOCUMENTS

SESSION DATE – July 15

notes

Refer to Keystrokes, page 193.

Credit Card Sales Invoice #1993
Dated July 2/03
193 To various Internet customers, for games sold during previous 3 months

BC	$2 200	plus 7% GST and 7% PST
Ontario	2 400	plus 7% GST
HST provinces	1 000	plus 15% HST
Shipping	600	plus 7% GST and 7% PST

(Shipped by Purolator #PCU773XT)
Invoice total $6 910. Paid by Visa.

notes

You do not need to enter shippers for the remaining Internet sales.

Credit Card Sales Invoice #1994
Dated July 2/03
To various customers, for games sold via Internet during previous 3 months

BC	$1 600	plus 7% GST and 7% PST
HST provinces	600	plus 15% HST
Other provinces	2 600	plus 7% GST
Shipping charges	480	plus 7% GST and 7% PST

Invoice total $5 843.20. Paid by MasterCard.

Credit Card Sales Invoice #1995
Dated July 2/03
To various customers, for games sold via Internet during previous 3 months

BC	$800	plus 7% GST and 7% PST
HST provinces	200	plus 15% HST
Other provinces	600	plus 7% GST
Shipping charges	220	plus 7% GST and 7% PST

Invoice total $2 034.80. Paid by Amex.

notes

Because the rental is purchased and used in Ontario, the Ontario Provincial Sales Tax rate applies.

Visa Purchase Invoice #MR-1301
Dated July 2/03
196 To Miles 'R on Us, $240 for six-day car rental while attending Game Trade Show in Toronto plus 7% GST and 8% PST. Invoice total $276. Paid by Visa.

Cheque Copy #501
Dated July 2/03
198 To Visa, $606.40 in payment of account, including $505 for purchases charged from May 1 to June 15, $95 for annual renewal fee and $6.40 in interest charges on unpaid balance from previous statement.

Cash Receipt #103
Dated July 3/03
201 From It's All Canadian, cheque #884 for $6 240 in payment of account including $180 discount taken for early payment. Reference invoice #1989.

Memo #36
Dated July 3/03
203 From D. Manga: Access the Web site for Canada Customs and Revenue Agency to see whether any recent announcements about GST affect the business.

notes

Wholesale customers who will be selling the product to their own customers do not pay PST.

☐ Sales Order #LHF-04
Dated July 5/03
Shipping date July 10/03
From Let's Have Fun, $16 300 plus 7% GST for 800 games. Shipping by Purolator for $110 plus GST and PST. Invoice total $17 566.40. Terms 3/30, n/60.

☑ 204 Memo #37
Dated July 5/03
From D. Manga: Refer to June 30 General Ledger balances to remit GST and HST to the Receiver General. Issue cheque #502 for $2 600 from Chequing Account.

☑ 206 Memo #38
Dated July 5/03
From D. Manga: Refer to the June 30 General Ledger balance to remit PST Payable to the Minister of Finance. Reduce the payment by the sales tax compensation of 3.3% of the balance owing. Issue cheque #503 for $435.15 from Chequing Account.

☑ 207 Sales Invoice #1996
Dated July 5/03
To The Canada Store, $1 070 (USD) for games. Shipped by Federal Express (#F19YTR563) for $200 plus 7% GST and 7% PST. Invoice total $1 298 (USD). Terms 3/30, n/60. The exchange rate is 1.54.

☑ 209 Cash Receipt #104
Dated July 6/03
From Let's Have Fun, cheque #911 for $2 000 as deposit #14 to confirm sales order #LHF-04.

☐ Sales Invoice #1997
Dated July 10/03
To Let's Have Fun, to fill sales order #LHF-04, $16 300 plus 7% GST for games. Shipped by Purolator (#PCU899XT) for $110 plus GST and PST. Invoice total $17 566.40. Terms 3/30, n/60. (Enter the shipper so you can track the shipment.)

☐ Sales Invoice #1998
Dated July 11/03
To Mapleaves, $428 (USD) for games. Shipped by Federal Express (#F27CGB786) for $100 plus 7% GST and 7% PST. Invoice total $542 (USD). Terms 3/30, n/60. The exchange rate is 1.535.

☑ 211 Cash Receipt #105
Dated July 15/03
From The Canada Store, cheque #2397 for $1 259.90 USD in payment of account less $38.10 discount for early payment. Reference invoice #1996. The exchange rate for July 15 is 1.549.

☑ 213 Memo #39
Dated July 15/03
From D. Manga: Let's Have Fun called to inform you that they have not received their shipment of games. Look up invoice #1997, e-mail a copy of the invoice to the customer and check the delivery status.

SESSION DATE – July 31

- ☐ Cheque Copy #504
  Dated July 16/03
  To Grandeur Graphics, $452 in full payment of account, including $8 discount for early payment. Reference invoice #GG-1304.

- ☐ Cheque Copy #505
  Dated July 16/03
  To Space Unlimited, $1 130 in full payment of account, including $20 discount for early payment. Reference invoice #SU-692.

- ☐ Cash Receipt #106
  Dated July 20/03
  From Best Games, cheque #28653 for $9 360 in payment of account including $270 discount taken for early payment. Reference invoice #1991.

notes

Record the advertising as a prepaid expense.

- ☐ Purchase Invoice #LMK-2303
  Dated July 30/03
  From Let 'm Know, $1 500 plus 7% GST and 7% PST for series of ads to run for the next 5 months. Invoice total $1 710. Terms: 2/10, n/30.

- ☐ Cash Purchase Invoice #BCT-6632
  Dated July 30/03
  From BC Tel, $135 plus 7% GST and 7% PST for telephone services for two months. Invoice total $153.90. Terms: payment on receipt of invoice. Paid by cheque #506.

- ☐ Cash Purchase Invoice #PE-49006
  Dated July 30/03
  From Purolator, $1 400 plus 7% GST and 7% PST for shipping services used from May 25 to July 25. Invoice total $1 596. Terms: payment on receipt of invoice. Paid by cheque #507.

notes

Use Quick Add for new vendors. Include gasoline costs with Travel Expenses. Use GST code 4.

- ☐ Visa Purchase Invoice #PC-34992
  Dated July 30/03
  From Petro Canada, $53.50 including 7% GST for gasoline for business use. Paid by Visa.

SESSION DATE – August 15

- ☐ Purchase Order #204
  Dated Aug. 1/03
  Shipping date Aug. 15/03
  To Game Makers, $180 000 plus 7% GST for game boards and pieces for 20 000 games. Invoice total $192 600. Terms: 1/10, n/30. (Use Production & Assembly Costs account.)

- ☐ Purchase Order #205
  Dated Aug. 1/03
  Shipping date Aug. 15/03
  To Box It, $60 000 plus 7% GST for boxes and for packaging 20 000 games. Invoice total $64 200. Terms: 1/5, n/30. (Use Production & Assembly Costs account.)

notes

Prepayments to vendors are entered in the same way as customer deposits. Use the Payments Journal, choose the Enter Prepayments to Vendors tool and enter the amount in the Prepayment Amount field. Type Re: PO #204 as the comment to add a comment to the journal entry.

- ❑ Cheque Copy #508
  Dated Aug. 2/03
  To Game Makers, $10 000 as down payment for purchase order #204.

- ❑ Cheque Copy #509
  Dated Aug. 2/03
  To Box It, $5 000 as down payment for purchase order #205.

- ❑ Cheque Copy #510
  Dated Aug. 2/03
  To Visa, $276 in payment of balance shown on Visa account statement for purchases before July 15, 2003.

- ❑ Cheque Copy #511
  Dated Aug. 8/03
  To Let 'm Know, $1 680 in full payment of account, including $30 discount for early payment. Reference invoice #LMK-2303.

- ❑ Cash Receipt #107
  Dated Aug. 9/03
  From Mapleaves, cheque #8531 for $526.16 USD in payment of account less $15.84 discount for early payment. Reference invoice #1998. The exchange rate for Aug. 9 is 1.530. Deposit to Bank: USD account.

notes

Remember to mark Deposit #14 as paid by clicking its amount in the Payment Amount field.

- ❑ Cash Receipt #108
  Dated Aug. 9/03
  From Let's Have Fun, cheque #1144 for $15 074.10 in payment of account including $492.30 discount taken for early payment. Reference invoice #1997 and deposit #14. Deposit to Bank: Chequing Account.

- ❑ Sales Order #TA-05
  Dated Aug. 9/03
  Shipping date Aug. 22/03
  To Trivyal & Associates, $111 000 plus 7% GST for 6 000 games purchased by major toy store chain. Shipping charges $400 plus GST and PST. Invoice total $119 226.00. Terms 3/30, n/60.

notes

Remember to use GST code 5 for the HST.

- ❑ Sales Invoice #1999
  Dated Aug. 10/03
  To Toys 'N More, $4 000 plus 15% HST for games. Shipping charges $80 plus GST and PST. Invoice total $4 691.20. Terms 3/30, n/60.

- ❑ Cash Receipt #109
  Dated Aug. 11/03
  From Trivyal & Associates, cheque #502 for $10 000 as down payment, deposit #15, to confirm sales order #TA-05.

- ❑ Visa Purchase Invoice #CA-7998
  Dated Aug. 12/03
  To Cars for All (use Quick Add for new vendor), $20 000 for new automobile less trade-in allowance on old car $5 000 plus 7% GST and 7% PST. Invoice total $17 100. Paid by Visa. The entry to write off the old car will be made at year-end.

- ❑ Purchase Invoice #GM-8823
  Dated Aug. 15/03
  From Game Makers, to fill purchase order #204, $180 000 plus 7% GST for game boards and pieces for 20 000 games. Invoice total $192 600. Terms: 1/10, n/30.

notes

When you advance the session date to Aug. 31, you may see an advice statement that it is time to prepare for year-end. Read and then close the advisory statement to proceed.

SESSION DATE – August 31

- ❑ Purchase Invoice #BI-3719
  Dated Aug. 18/03
  From Box It, to fill purchase order #205, $60 000 plus 7% GST for boxes and for packaging 20 000 games. Invoice total $64 200. Terms: 1/5, n/30.

- ❑ Memo #40
  Dated Aug. 20/03
  From D. Manga: Owner invests $100 000 personal capital to finance production of new games. Amount deposited to Bank: Chequing Account. (Check that CAD is selected as the currency.)

- ❑ Sales Invoice #2000
  Dated Aug. 21/03
  To Trivyal & Associates, to fill sales order #TA-05, $111 000 plus 7% GST for games purchased by major toy store chain. Shipping charges $400 plus GST and PST. Invoice total $119 226.00. Terms 3/30, n/60.

- ❑ Cheque Copy #512
  Dated Aug. 23/03
  To Game Makers, $180 800 in full payment of account, including $1 800 discount for early payment. Reference invoice #GM-8823 and prepayment with cheque #508.

- ❑ Cheque Copy #513
  Dated Aug. 23/03
  To Box It, $58 600 in full payment of account, including $600 discount for early payment. Reference invoice #BI-3719 and prepayment with cheque #509.

- ❑ Memo #41
  Dated Aug. 23/03
  From D. Manga: Transfer $75 000 CAD from Bank: Savings Account to Bank: Chequing Account to cover cheques because the chequing account is overdrawn.

- ❑ Visa Purchase Invoice #PC-49986
  Dated Aug. 30/03
  From Petro Canada, $53.50 including 7% GST for gasoline for business use. Paid by Visa.

SESSION DATE – September 15

- ❑ Cheque Copy #514
  Dated Sep. 2/03
  To Visa, $17 153.50 in payment of account for purchases before August 15, 2003.

- ❑ Sales Invoice #2001
  Dated Sep. 5/03
  To The Canada Store, $3 000 (USD) for games. Shipped by Federal Express (#F36FYT863) for $300 plus 7% GST and 7% PST. Invoice total $3 342 (USD). Terms 3/30, n/60. The exchange rate is 1.535.

- ❑ Cash Receipt #110
  Dated Sep. 5/03
  From Toys 'N More, cheque #2491 for $4 568.80 in payment of account including $122.40 discount taken for early payment. Reference invoice #1999. Deposit to Bank: Chequing Account.

❑ Sales Invoice #2002
Dated Sep. 11/03
To Mapleaves, $1 500 (USD) for games. Shipped by Federal Express (#F97HRP632) for $200 plus 7% GST and 7% PST. Invoice total $1 728 (USD). Terms 3/30, n/60. The exchange rate is 1.545.

SESSION DATE – September 29

notes

When you advance the session date to Sep. 29, you may see an advice statement about the year-end adjustments required. Read and then close the advisory statement to proceed.

❑ Cash Receipt #111
Dated Sep. 18/03
From Trivyal & Associates, cheque #574 for $105 884 in payment of account including $3 342 discount taken for early payment. Reference invoice #2000 and deposit #15. Deposit to Bank: Chequing Account.

❑ Visa Purchase Invoice #PC-59128
Dated Sep. 29/03
From Petro Canada, $53.50 including 7% GST for gasoline for business use. Paid by Visa.

❑ Credit Card Sales Invoice #2003
Dated Sep. 29/03
To various customers, for games sold via Internet during previous 3 months

BC	$1 800	plus 7% GST and 7% PST
HST provinces	200	plus 15% HST
Other provinces	2 100	plus 7% GST
Shipping charges	350	plus 7% GST and 7% PST

Invoice total $4 928. Paid by Visa.

❑ Credit Card Sales Invoice #2004
Dated Sep. 29/03
To various customers, for games sold via Internet during previous 3 months

BC	$600	plus 7% GST and 7% PST
HST provinces	150	plus 15% HST
Other provinces	480	plus 7% GST
Shipping charges	210	plus 7% GST and 7% PST

Invoice total $1 609.50. Paid by Amex.

❑ Credit Card Sales Invoice #2005
Dated Sep. 29/03
To various customers, for games sold via Internet during previous 3 months

BC	$1 400	plus 7% GST and 7% PST
HST provinces	500	plus 15% HST
Other provinces	1 900	plus 7% GST
Shipping charges	360	plus 7% GST and 7% PST

Invoice total $4 614.40. Paid by MasterCard.

❑ Cash Purchase Invoice #BCT-9810
Dated Sep. 29/03
From BC Tel, $140 plus 7% GST and 7% PST for telephone services for two months. Invoice total $159.60. Terms: payment on receipt of invoice. Paid by cheque #515.

❑ Cash Purchase Invoice #PE-62331
Dated Sep. 29/03
From Purolator, $1 200 plus 7% GST and 7% PST for shipping services used from July 25 to Sep. 25. Invoice total $1 368. Terms: payment on receipt of invoice. Paid by cheque #516.

- ❑ Cash Purchase Invoice #FE-46678
  Dated Sep. 29/03
  From Federal Express, $1 100 plus 7% GST and 7% PST for shipping services. Invoice total $1 254. Terms: payment on receipt of invoice. Paid by cheque #517.

SESSION DATE – September 30

notes

Read the keystroke section on Finishing a Fiscal Period on page 216 before completing the entries for September 30.

- ❑ Memo #42
  Dated Sep. 30/03
  From D. Manga: Refer to the Sep. 30 General Ledger balance to remit PST Payable to the Minister of Finance. Reduce the payment by the sales tax compensation of 3.3% of the balance owing. Issue cheque #518 for $842.14 from Bank: Chequing Account.

- ❑ Memo #43
  Dated Sep. 30/03
  From Owner: Prepare for closing the books by completing the year-end depreciation entries for all fixed assets as follows:

Furniture & Equipment	$650
Computers	$1 900
Automobile	$3 900

- ❑ Memo #44
  Dated Sep. 30/03
  From Owner: Complete adjusting entries for prepaid expenses and supplies used:

Office Supplies	$280
Prepaid Internet Expenses (3 months)	$60
Prepaid Storage (3 months of 6)	$600
Prepaid Rent (3 months of 6)	$1 500
Prepaid Advertising (2 months of 5)	$642

- ❑ Memo #45
  Dated Sep. 30/03
  From Owner: Complete an adjusting entry for $107 000 of inventory sold during the quarter. Reduce the Games Inventory asset account and increase Cost of Games Sold expense.

notes

Manga pays only interest on the loans. Both amounts are deducted from the Bank: Chequing Account.

- ❑ Memo #46
  Dated Sep. 30/03
  From Owner: Received debit memo from Western Trust regarding preauthorized withdrawals from Bank: Chequing Account for quarterly interest payments on loans. Complete adjusting entries for interest paid during the quarter:

on Bank loan	$200
on Long term loan	$4 000

- ❑ Memo #47
  Dated Sep. 30/03
  From Owner: Complete an adjusting entry to transfer $240 000 in completed games from production and assembly to games inventory. (Debit Games Inventory and credit Production & Assembly Costs.)

version 8

Enter the bank account transfers as four separate journal entries because you can use an account only once in a transaction. Enter Memo 48A, 48B, 48C and 48D in the Source field.

- ❑ Memo #48
  Dated Sep. 30/03
  From Owner: the following transfers of funds were completed.
  $75 000 from Bank: Chequing Account to Bank: Savings Account
  $10 000 from Bank: Visa to Bank: Chequing Account
  $10 000 from Bank: MasterCard to Bank: Chequing Account
  $3 000 from Bank: AMEX to Bank: Chequing Account

❑ Memo #49
Dated Sep. 30/03
From Owner: Record Interest Revenue as follows:

Bank: Savings Account	$1 500
Bank: Chequing Account	$150
Bank: Visa	$40
Bank: MasterCard	$25
Bank: AMEX	$5

✓ 216 Memo #50
Dated Sep. 30/03
From Owner: Review the year-end checklists. Print all reports for the fiscal period ended. Back up the data files. Check data integrity. Advance the session date to October 1, the first day of the next fiscal period.

KEYSTROKES

Opening Data Files

notes

Session dates are advanced two weeks at a time for Outset Media.

Using the instructions for accessing data files in Chapter 1, page 15, open the data files for Outset Media Corp. Enter the session date, July 15, 2003, for this application to open the Home window.

Accounting for Credit Card Sales

notes

The icons for the Payroll, Inventory and Project ledgers are hidden because these ledgers are not set up.

Click the **Sales Journal icon** [Sales, Orders & Quotes] to open the Sales Journal.

Choose Internet Customers from the Sold to list. Leave the transaction type as Invoice.

Click the **Paid By list arrow** as shown to see the payment options:

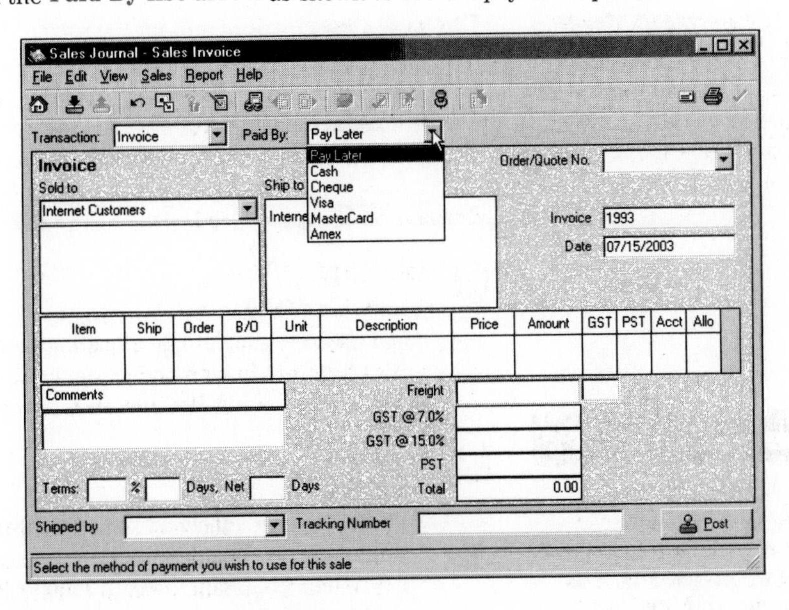

Click Visa as the method of payment.

The Net Days field is removed to match the immediate payment selection. Internet Customers have been set up with no discount so the discount fields are blank.

Type `July 2` (as the transaction date)

Click the **Description field**.

Type `BC sales`

Click the **Amount field**.

Type `2200`

Press tab to advance to the GST field.

Press enter to see the GST codes:

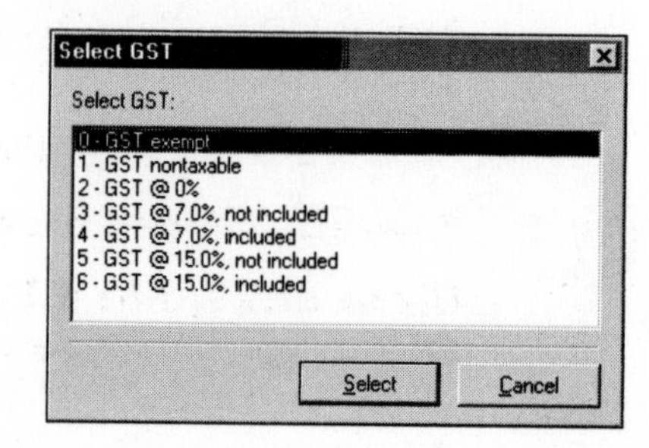

Notice that we have added a second GST rate (Codes 5 and 6 with GST @ 15%) to accommodate interprovincial sales to customers in the participating Atlantic provinces who pay HST. The first sale is to BC customers, so the GST rate is 7%.

Click 3 - GST @ 7% not included

Click Select to return to the sales invoice and advance to the PST field. The provincial tax rate in British Columbia is 7%.

Type `7`

Press tab

Press enter to display the account list.

Double click 4100 Revenue from Sales to add it to the invoice.

Click the **Description field** on the second invoice line.

Type `Ontario sales`

Click the **Amount field**.

Type `2400`

Press tab

Press enter to see the GST code list. The GST rate for Ontario is 7%.

Double click 3 - GST @ 7% not included to add the code and advance to the PST field. Since the PST rate applies to BC, customers outside the province do not pay this tax.

Press tab to skip the PST field and advance to the Account field.

Type `4100`

Click the **Description field** on the next invoice line.

Type `HST province sales`

Click the **Amount field**.

Type 1000

Press tab

Press enter to see the GST code list. The HST rate at 15% applies to these sales.

Double click 5 - GST @ 15% not included to add the code and advance to the PST field. Again PST is not applied to these sales because it is harmonized with the GST.

Press tab to skip the PST field and advance to the Account field.

Type 4100

Click the **first Freight field.**

Type 600

Because GST is paid on freight you must enter GST information if the customer pays freight.

Press tab to advance to the GST on Freight code field.

Press enter to display the list.

Double click 3 - GST @ 7% not included to add the GST amount. You do not need to enter an amount for the tax; it is calculated as soon as you enter the amount of freight charged and the code.

In British Columbia, PST is applied to freight. Therefore, PST is set up to apply automatically to freight charges for Outset Media and you do not not need to enter additional PST information.

To use the shipment tracking feature, you must have an account with the shipper and a PIN (personal identification number) to access the account.

We will now enter the shipping information so that the shipments can be traced if they are not delivered within the expected time.

Click the **Shipped by list arrow** to see the list of shippers used regularly:

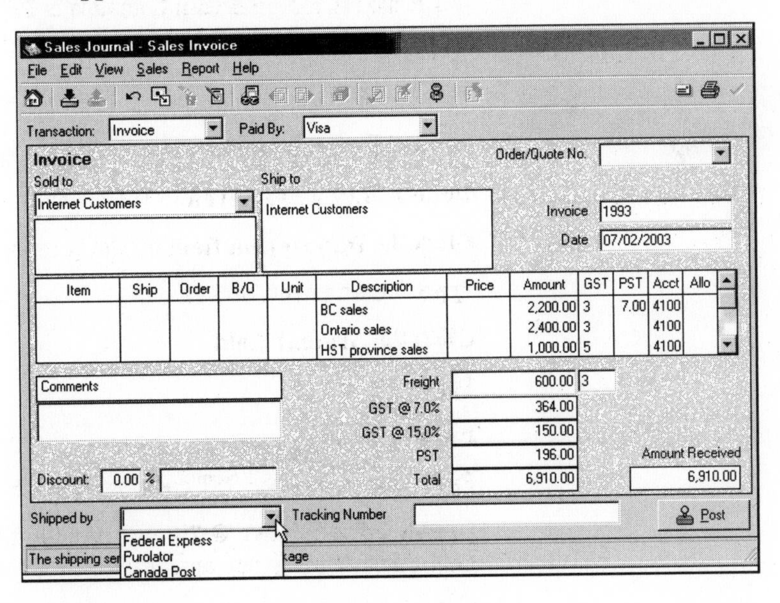

Click Purolator

Press tab to advance to the Tracking Number field.

Type PCU773XT

Your completed invoice should now look like the one shown here:

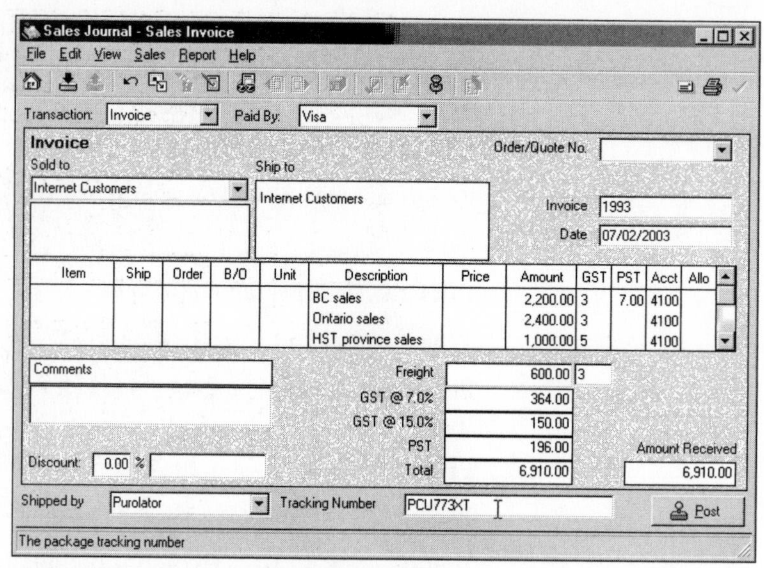

Before posting the entry, you should review it.

Choose the **Report menu** and **click Display Sales Journal Entry**:

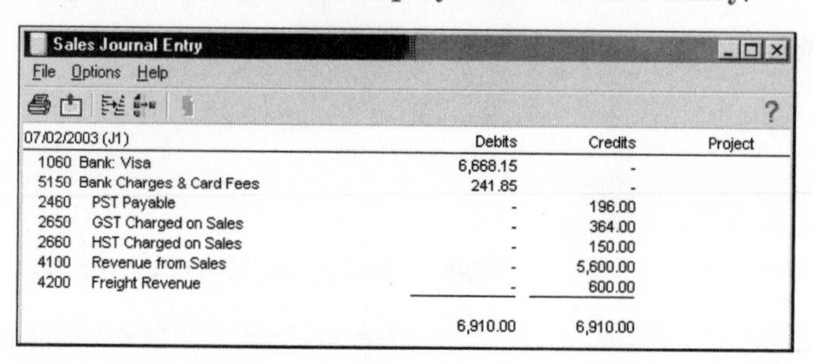

notes

When an invoice for these shipments is received from the shipper, it will be entered as a purchase to record the expense to Outset Media.

Notice the additional linked accounts used for this transaction. The credit card account — *Bank: Visa* — is debited for the total invoice amount minus the transaction discount fees withheld by the credit card company. These fees are debited to the linked fees expense account — *Bank Charges & Card Fees*. Both the *GST* and *HST Charged on Sales* accounts are credited to show the increase in the tax liability to the Receiver General. PST collected from customers is credited to the *PST Payable* account to show the increased liability to the Minister of Finance for BC. Freight charged to customers is credited automatically to the linked *Freight Revenue* account.

Close the display to return to the Sales Journal input screen.

Make corrections if necessary, referring to page 124 for assistance.

Click the **Post button** [Post].

Enter the following two credit card sale transactions.

Close the Sales Journal to return to the Home window.

Entering Credit Card Purchases

notes

Credit card purchases can be entered as Other Payments in the Payments Journal.

Credit card purchases are similar to other purchases paid by cash or by cheque.

Click the **Purchases Journal icon** [Purchases, Orders & Quotes] to open the Purchases Journal.

Invoice is the correct transaction type.

Click the **Paid By list arrow** to see the payment options:

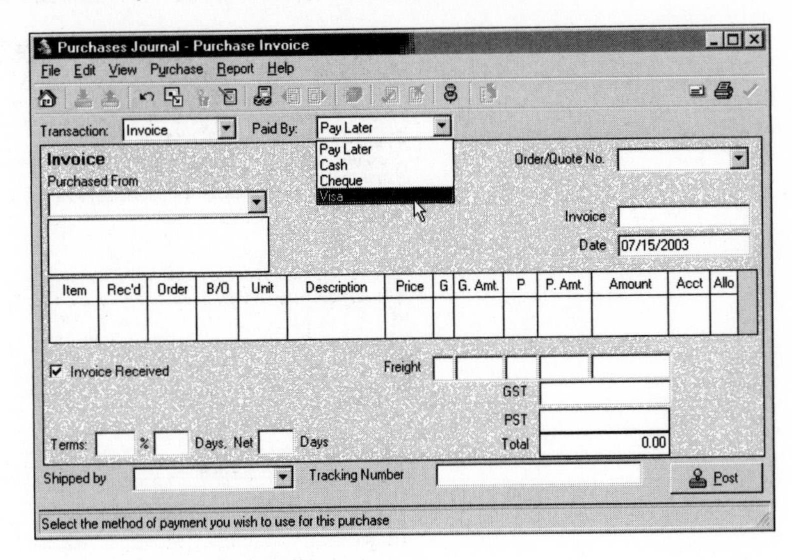

Click **Visa** as the method of payment.

The rest of the entry is the same as other purchase transactions.

Choose **Miles 'R on Us** as the vendor.

Click the **Invoice field**.

Type `MR-1301`

Press tab

Type `July 2` (to enter the date of the transaction)

Click the **Description field**.

Type `car rental`

Click the **G field**.

Press enter to see the GST codes.

Double click GST code **3**.

notes

Because the rental took place in Ontario, the 8% PST rate for Ontario applies.

Click the **P field** for the PST rate.

Type `8`

Click the **Amount field**.

Type `240`

Press tab to advance to the Account field.

Press enter to see the Account list.

Double click **5580 Travel Expenses** to enter the expense account.

Your completed journal entry should look like the following:

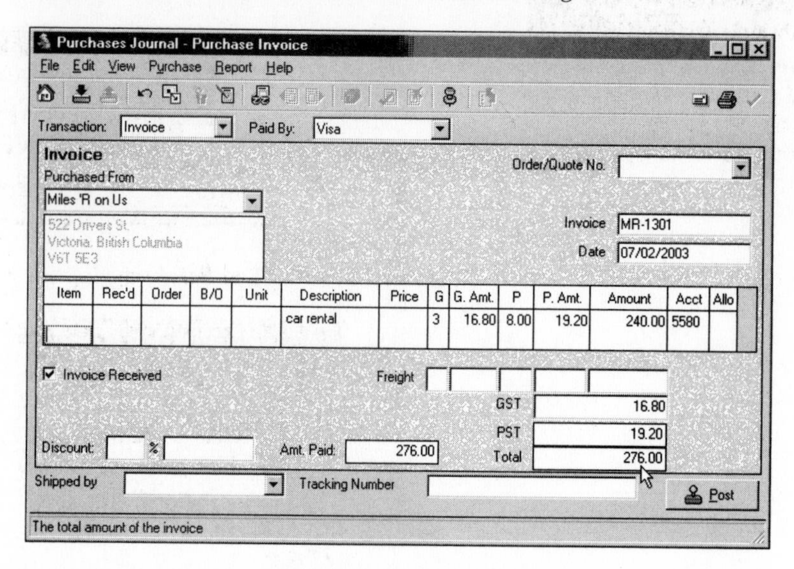

You should review the journal entry before posting it.

Choose the **Report menu** and **click Display Purchases Journal Entry** to see the transaction:

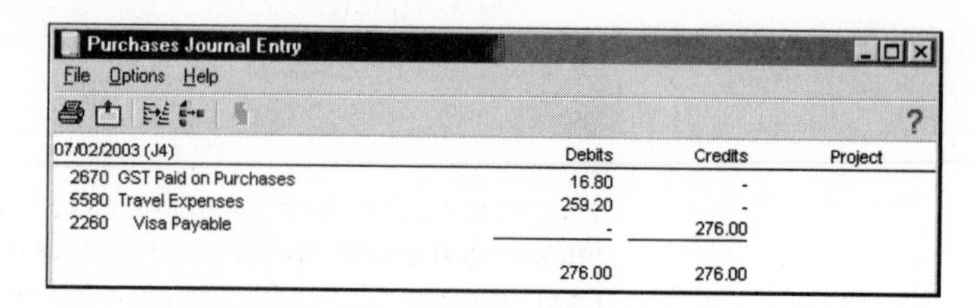

07/02/2003 (J4)	Debits	Credits	Project
2670 GST Paid on Purchases	16.80	-	
5580 Travel Expenses	259.20	-	
2260 Visa Payable	-	276.00	
	276.00	276.00	

The main difference between the Visa purchase transaction and other cash transactions is that *Visa Payable* is credited instead of the bank account. *Visa Payable* is defined as the linked account for the credit card used for purchases rather than for the Payables Ledger as a whole because a business may have more than one credit card and have separate accounts linked to them. As usual, PST paid is added to the expense part of the journal entry and *GST Paid on Purchases* is debited to show that the liability to the Receiver General is reduced.

Close the display when you have finished to return to the journal screen.

Make corrections as you would for any other purchase invoice, referring to page 82 for assistance if necessary.

Click the **Post button** Post.

Close the Purchases Journal to return to the Home window.

Entering Credit Card Payments

Click the **Payments icon** Payments to open the Payments Journal.

We will use the options in the upper part of the Payments Journal. Because Credit Cards are set up, the Pay list allows you to choose between paying a vendor and paying a credit card bill. The By field (method of payment) has the same options as the Purchases Journal — payment by cash, cheque or credit card. The From field allows you to select a bank account from which to pay because more than one bank account is defined as a Bank class account.

notes

All accounts defined as Bank class accounts are on the From list. Bank class is explained in Chapter 10.

notes

When you choose a different Bank class account from the From list, the cheque number changes to match the numbering sequence set up for that account.

Click the **Pay field list arrow** as shown:

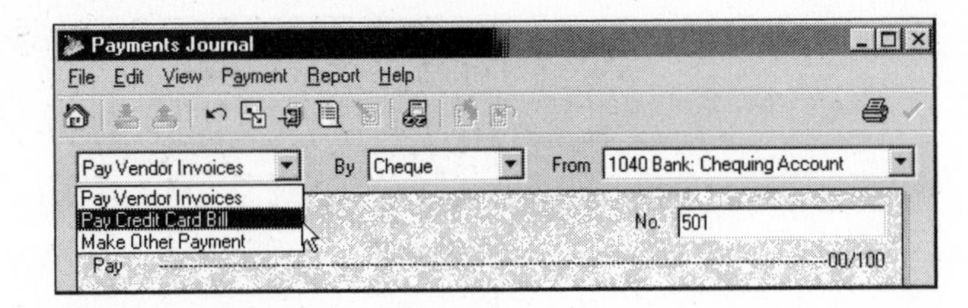

Click Pay Credit Card Bill to modify the journal for credit card payments as shown:

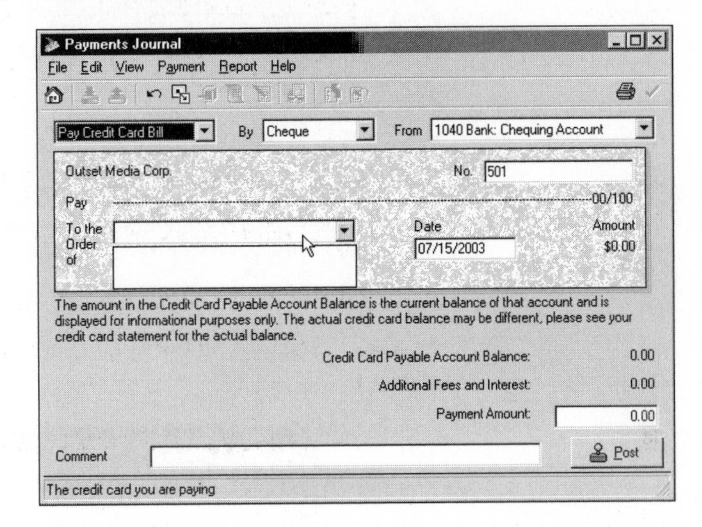

The default payment is by cheque. The bank account is correct and the cheque number is the next one in the sequence for this bank account. The From list has three bank accounts. The default account is the one we need for this payment.

Click the **To the Order of field list arrow** to access the list of credit cards set up for purchases. Only the Visa account is set up and listed.

Click Visa to select this account and update the journal with the Visa account information:

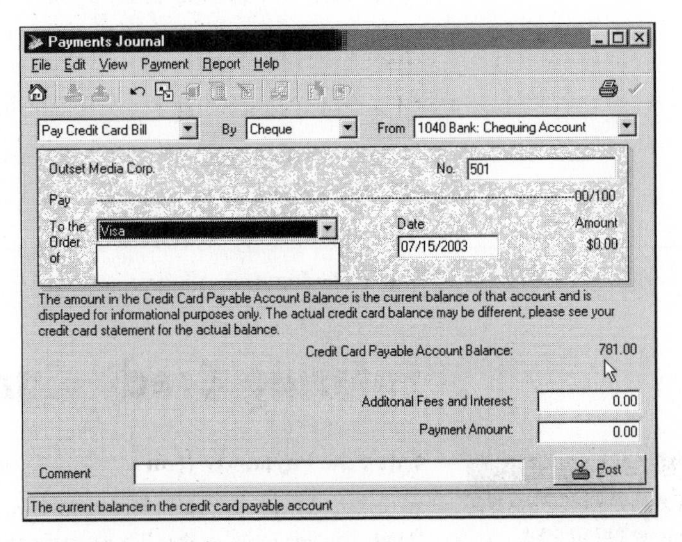

The balance shows the accumulation of all unpaid purchases to date according to the General Ledger *Visa Payable* account balance. This amount is not usually the same as the balance that appears on the credit card statement. Purchases after the statement date will not appear on the statement and interest charges or renewal fees are not included in the General Ledger account balance.

Double click the **Date field**, skipping the cheque number because it is correct.

Type `Jul 2`

Press tab to advance to the Additional Fees and Interest field.

This field is used to record interest charges on previous unpaid amounts as well as other fees associated with the use of the card. These amounts usually appear on the statement. You must add these amounts together and enter the total in the Additional Fees and Interest field. Outset Media owes $95 for the annual card renewal fee and $6.40 in accumulated interest for a total of $101.40.

Type `101.40`

Press tab to advance to the Payment Amount field.

notes

The remaining balance in the General Ledger Visa Payable account reflects current charges or purchases that will be included in the balance owing on the next statement and paid at that time.

In this field you should enter the amount of the cheque that is written in payment, the balance owing on the statement if the full amount is being paid, or some other amount if this is a partial payment.

Type `606.40`

Press tab to update the journal and complete the cheque amount in the upper portion of the journal.

You can add a comment to the journal entry in the Comment field if you want.

The journal is now complete and should look like the following:

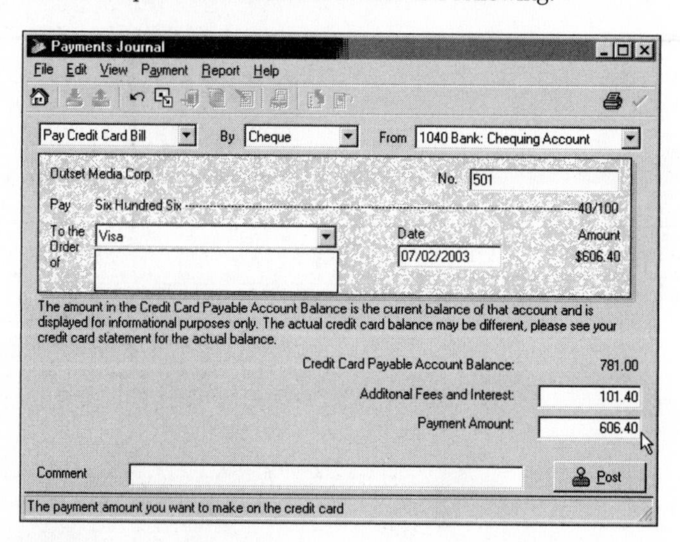

You should review the journal entry before proceeding.

Choose the **Report menu** and **click Display Payments Journal Entry** to display the transaction:

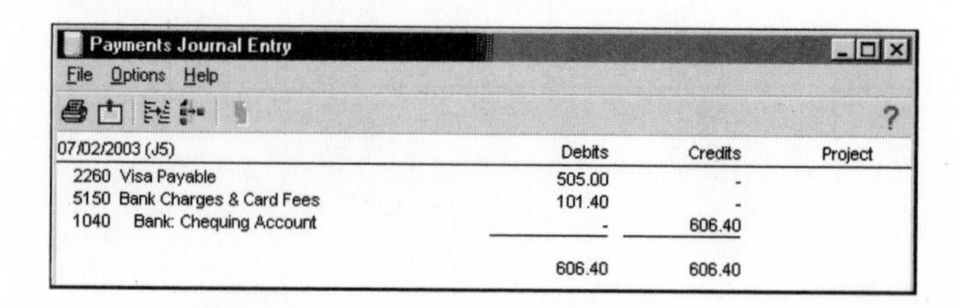

Notice that the linked bank account is credited for the full amount of the payment. The payment amount is divided between the debit to *Visa Payable* to reduce the liability and the debit to *Bank Charges & Card Fees*, the linked expense account for credit card expenses.

Close the display when you have finished reviewing it to return to the Payments Journal.

Make corrections by re-selecting from a drop-down list or by highlighting an incorrect entry and typing the correct amount. Press tab after changing an amount to update the totals.

Click the **Post button** Post.

Close the Payments Journal to return to the Home window.

Entering Discounts for Early Payment

Click the **Receipts icon** Receipts to open the Receipts Journal.

Choose It's All Canadian from the customer list to display the outstanding invoices for this customer:

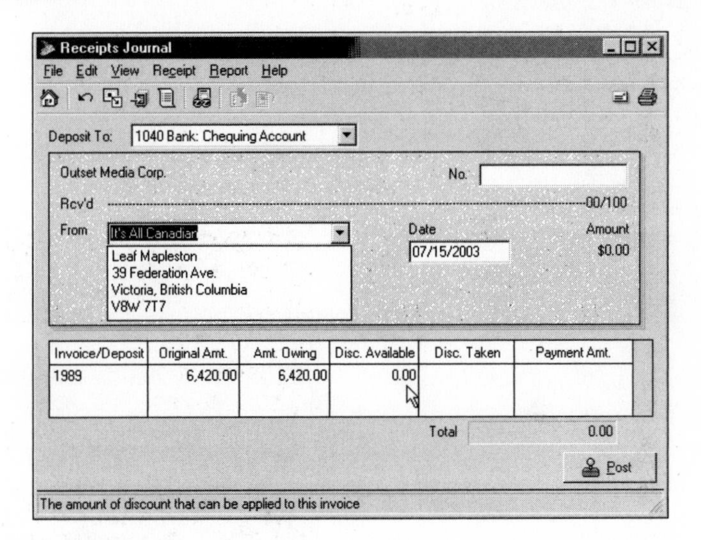

Notice that there is no discount available. Because the session date is more than 30 days past the invoice date, the discount period has elapsed and the discount shows as unavailable.

Click the **No. field**. As usual, we record the customer's cheque number.

Type `884`

Press tab to enter the customer's cheque number and advance to the Date field.

Type `July 3` (to enter the date of the customer payment)

Press (tab) to update the journal as shown:

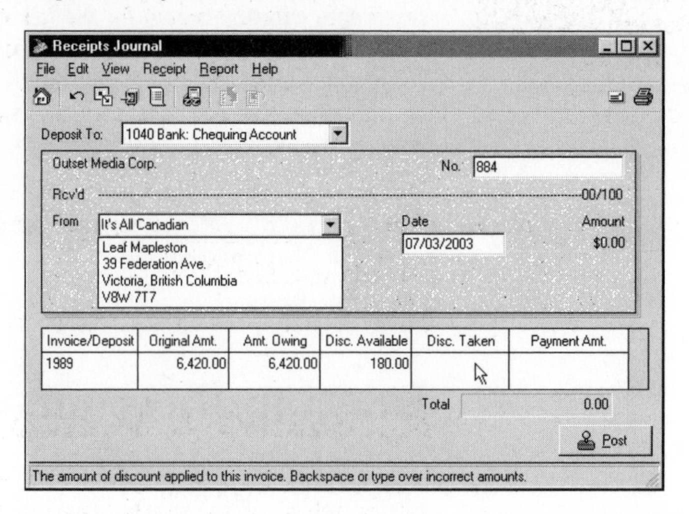

notes

No discount is allowed for partial payments. To omit a discount from an invoice, click the Payment Amt. field directly without tabbing across or clicking the Disc. Taken field. Once a discount amount shows in the Disc. Taken field, you can remove it by clicking the amount and then pressing (del) to remove it. Then press (tab) to update the totals. Review the journal entry to be sure that you have made the change correctly.

Because the cheque date is now within the 30-day discount period, calculated from the invoice date, the discount is available and appears in the Disc. Available field.

Press (tab) to advance to the Disc. Taken field and enter the discount amount. The discount is calculated on the pretax amount — 3% of $6 000 — according to the settings for the Receivable Ledger.

Press (tab) to advance to the Payment Amt. field and enter the amount. Notice that the discount amount has been subtracted from the invoice amount.

Press (tab) to accept the amount in the Payment Amt. field and update the total and the cheque portion of the journal.

The completed receipt should now appear as follows:

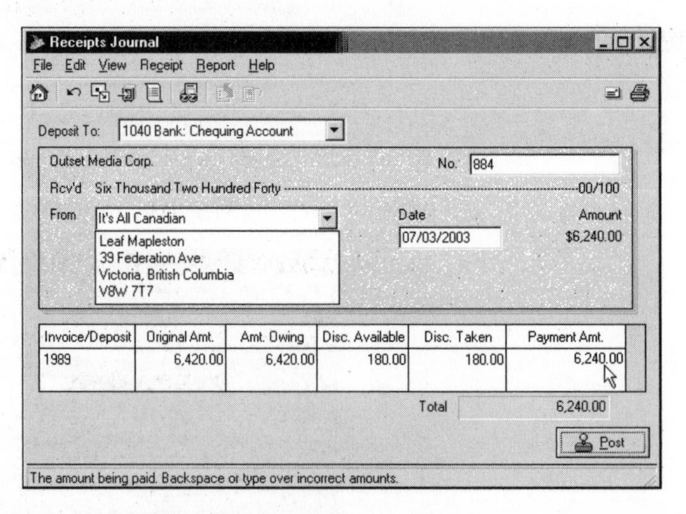

You are ready to review the transaction before posting it.

Choose the **Report menu** and **click Display Receipts Journal Entry** to display the transaction you have entered as follows:

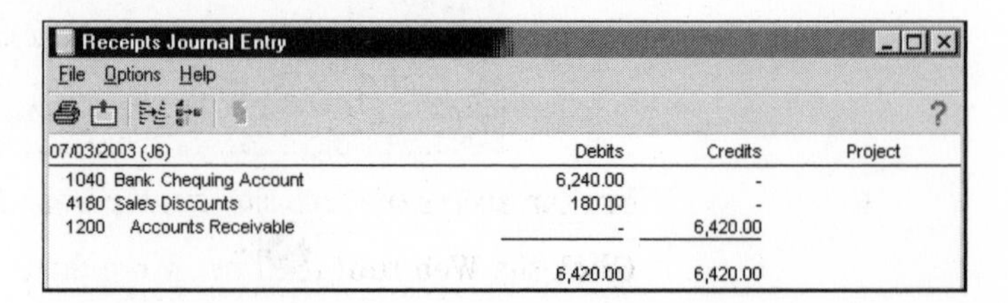

Receipts Journal Entry

07/03/2003 (J6)	Debits	Credits	Project
1040 Bank: Chequing Account	6,240.00	-	
4180 Sales Discounts	180.00	-	
1200 Accounts Receivable	-	6,420.00	
	6,420.00	6,420.00	

notes

Sales Discounts is a contra-revenue account. It has a debit balance and reduces total revenue.

In the related journal entry, the program has updated the General Ledger *Accounts Receivable* control account for the full amount of the invoice and reduced the customer's balance owing by the same amount. The amount deposited to *Bank: Chequing Account* is the actual amount of the payment, taking the discount into consideration. The discount amount is automatically debited to the linked *Sales Discounts* account.

Close the display to return to the Receipts Journal input screen and correct your work if necessary. Refer to page 128 for assistance if needed.

Click Post [Post].

Close the Receipts Journal to return to the Home window.

Accessing a Vendor's Web Site

Before making the GST Remittance, we will search the Canada Customs and Revenue Agency Web site to see whether there are any recent changes that we should be aware of.

Click the **Vendors icon** [Vendors] in the Home window to open the Vendors window:

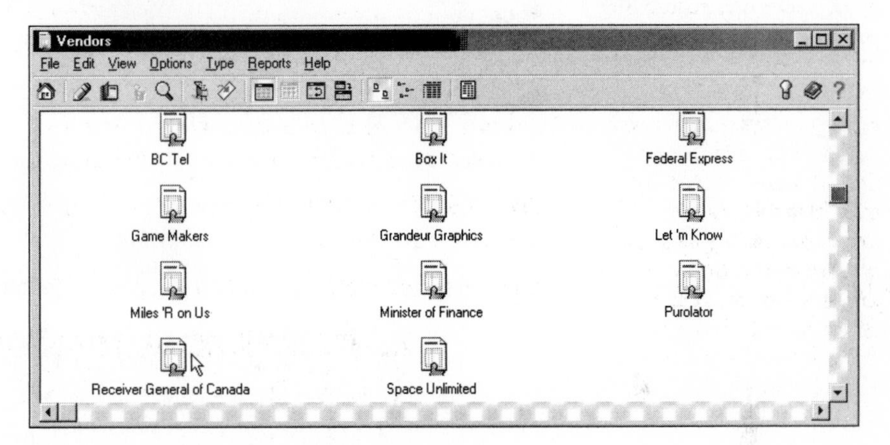

Each vendor record is represented by an icon.

Double click the **Receiver General of Canada icon** to open the vendor's ledger:

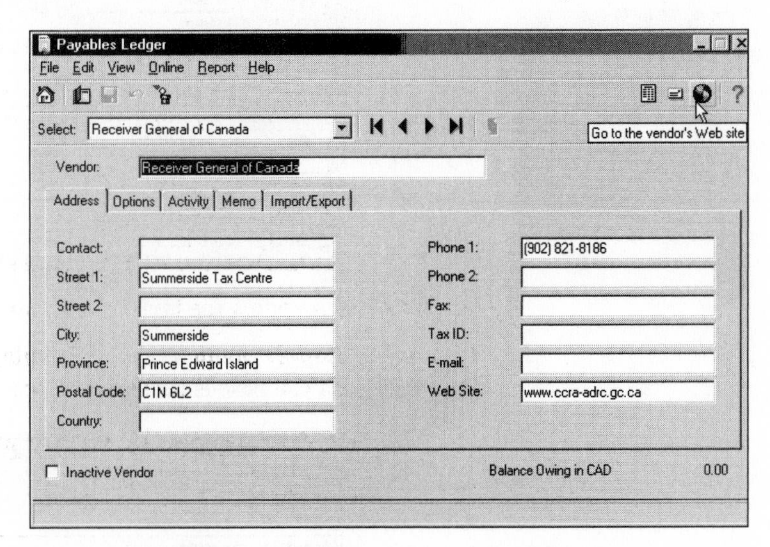

You can access the Web site directly from this vendor ledger page.

Click the **Web tool** or choose the Online menu and click Web Site.

Depending on how your Internet connection is set up, you may access the Web site directly or you may see a screen asking you to connect at this stage. You may need to enter the user ID and password for your Internet provider (if they are not set up to be saved and allow automatic connection). Again, your setup may be different. If you have a network connection to access the Internet, such as for high-speed access, you must start your Internet connection before clicking the Web tool in the Payables Ledger window.

You should see the Home page for the Canada Customs and Revenue Agency.

Choose your **language preference** and then **click** the **Search menu option**.

Click the **Search field**.

Type GST

Click **Search**

You should see a list of recent publications. Select the one you want and read it.

Close your Internet connection when you have found the information that you need or when you have finished. You will return to the vendor's ledger page.

Close the Ledger window and then **close** the Vendors window to return to the Home window.

Tax Remittances

Tax remittances are entered in the Purchases Journal as non-taxable purchase invoices with payment by cheque, or as Other Payments in the Payments Journal. There are two parts to a GST remittance — accounting for the GST (and HST) collected from customers and accounting for the GST paid for purchases. The first is owed to the Receiver General while the second part is refunded or used to reduce the amount owing. Refer to Chapter 2 for further details. The GST report can be used to help prepare the GST return, but the ledger account balances for the date of the filing period should be used as a final check in case there are amounts that were not entered in the Purchases and Sales Journals. For Outset Media, the opening or historical balance is needed. These amounts were not entered through journal transactions so we cannot use the GST Report.

PST remittances also have two parts — accounting for the PST collected from customers and reducing the tax remitted by the sales tax compensation for filing the return on time.

notes

The General Ledger balances are the GST and PST amounts in the Trial Balance on page 182. You can also display or print the Trial Balance or Balance Sheet for June 30 to see the amounts for the tax accounts.

Display or **print** the **General Ledger Report** for the following tax accounts for June 30, 2003, to see the amounts you must enter. (See page 54 if you need assistance.)

2460 PST Payable
2650 GST Charged on Sales
2660 HST Charged on Sales
2670 GST Paid on Purchases

Making GST Remittances

Click the **Payments Journal icon** Payments to open the Payments Journal.

Choose **Make Other Payment**

Choose **Receiver General of Canada** as the vendor.

Type July 5 (the transaction date)

Click the **Account field**.

Press (enter) to display the account list and **choose 2650 GST Charged on Sales**.

Press (tab) to advance to the Description field.

Type `Debiting GST Charged on Sales`

> **notes**
>
> You may skip the tax fields or enter the non-taxable code.

Press (tab) to advance to the Amount field.

Type `4900`

Click the **Account field** on the next journal line.

Press (enter) to display the account list and **choose 2660 HST Charged on Sales**.

Press (tab) to advance to the Description field.

Type `Debiting HST Charged on Sales`

> **notes**
>
> You may skip the tax fields or enter the non-taxable code.

Press (tab) to advance to the Amount field.

Type `600`

Click the **Account field** on the next journal line.

Press (enter) to display the accounts and **choose 2670 GST Paid on Purchases**.

Press (tab) to move to the Description field.

Type `Crediting GST Paid`

Press (tab) to go to the Amount field.

Type `-2900` (use a minus sign)

> **notes**
>
> The minus sign is necessary to create a credit for the liability account.

Click the **Invoice/Ref. field**.

Type `Memo 37`

Press (tab)

Type `Memo 37, GST remittance for June` (to complete your entry as shown here:)

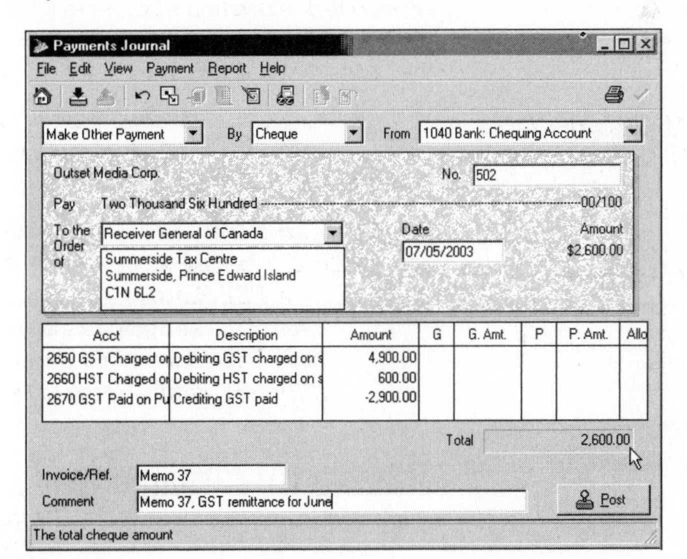

A review of the journal entry will help to clarify the transaction.

Choose the **Report menu** and **click Display Payments Journal Entry**:

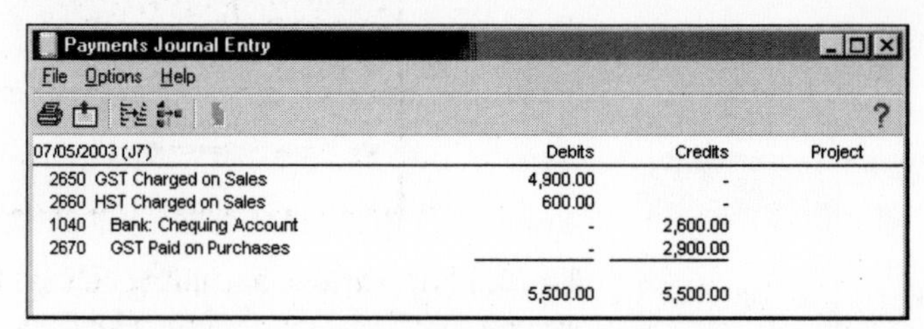

Payments Journal Entry

File Options Help

07/05/2003 (J7)	Debits	Credits	Project
2650 GST Charged on Sales	4,900.00	-	
2660 HST Charged on Sales	600.00	-	
1040 Bank: Chequing Account	-	2,600.00	
2670 GST Paid on Purchases	-	2,900.00	
	5,500.00	5,500.00	

Normally a positive amount will create a debit entry in the Purchases Journal for an expense or an asset purchase. *GST/HST Charged on Sales* are GST payable accounts with a credit balance. To reduce the GST payable balance we must enter a positive amount, or a debit, as we did for the GST and HST collected from customers. The negative entry or credit for *GST Paid on Purchases* will offset the debit balance in the ledger and will reduce the total amount that is paid to the Receiver General.

Close the display window when you have finished. Make corrections if necessary.

Click Post [Post]. You are now ready to make the PST remittance.

Making a PST Remittance

You should still be in the Payments Journal with Make Other Payment as the type of transaction selected.

Choose Minister of Finance as the vendor. Accept the default bank account.

Accept July 5 as the transaction date.

Click the **Account field**.

Press (enter) to display the account list and **choose 2460 PST Payable**.

Press (tab)

Type `Debiting PST Payable`

Press (tab) to move the cursor to the Amount field.

Type `450`

You are now ready to enter the revenue from sales tax compensation, 3.3% of the *PST Payable* amount.

Click the **Account field** on the second Journal line.

Press (enter) to display the accounts and **choose 4280 Sales Tax Compensation**.

Press (tab)

Type `Sales Tax Compensation`

Press (tab)

Type `-14.85` (use a minus sign)

notes

The minus sign will reduce the total amount that is paid to the Minister of Revenue.

Click the **Invoice/Ref. No. field**.

Type `Memo 38`

Press (tab) to advance to the Comment field.

Type `Memo 38, PST remittance for June`

Choose the **Report menu** and **click Display Payments Journal Entry** to review your journal entry:

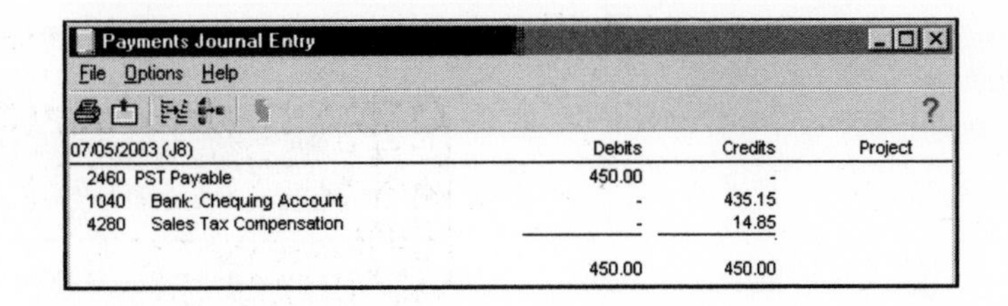
Payments Journal Entry

File Options Help

07/05/2003 (J8)	Debits	Credits	Project
2460 PST Payable	450.00	-	
1040 Bank: Chequing Account	-	435.15	
4280 Sales Tax Compensation	-	14.85	
	450.00	450.00	

The full PST Payable amount is debited to reduce the liability by crediting the bank account for the amount of the cheque and the *Sales Tax Compensation* revenue account for the amount of the tax reduction.

Close the display when you have finished.

Click Post [Post]. **Close** the Payments Journal.

Entering Sales to Foreign Customers

Click the **Sales Icon** [Sales, Orders & Quotes] to open the Sales Journal. Accept Invoice and Pay Later, the default selections for Transaction and Paid By.

Choose The Canada Store as the customer from the Sold to drop-down list. The invoice is modified for the foreign customer:

version 8

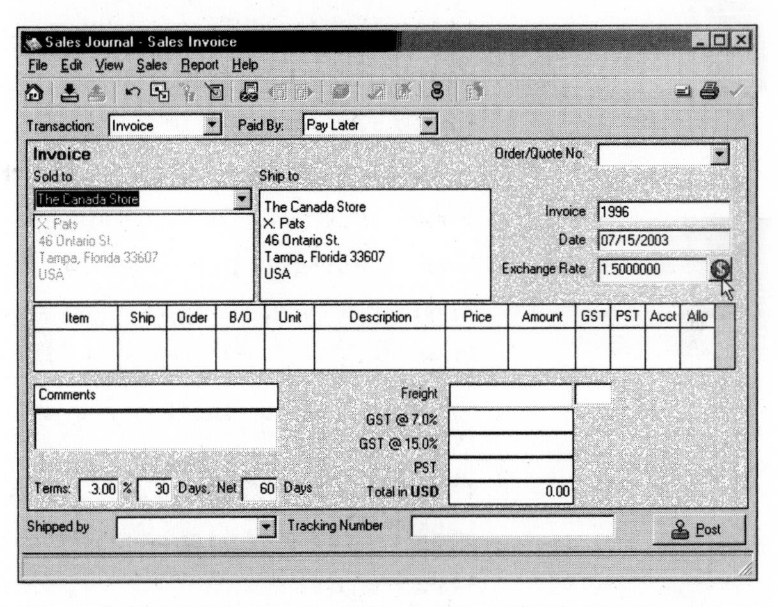

A field for the exchange rate appears below the Date and the Total is expressed in USD (United States dollars) rather than in Canadian dollars. An exchange rate button provides a list of exchange rates already entered for various dates. There is no rate for July 5.

Double click 07/15/2003 (the date).

Type `July 5`

Press (tab)

notes

The Exchange Rate setting for the company file is to warn when the exchange rate on record is more than one day old so that an incorrect old rate is not accepted in error.

The Exchange Rate screen opens because the exchange rate on record is more than one day old and no exchange rate is on record for this date:

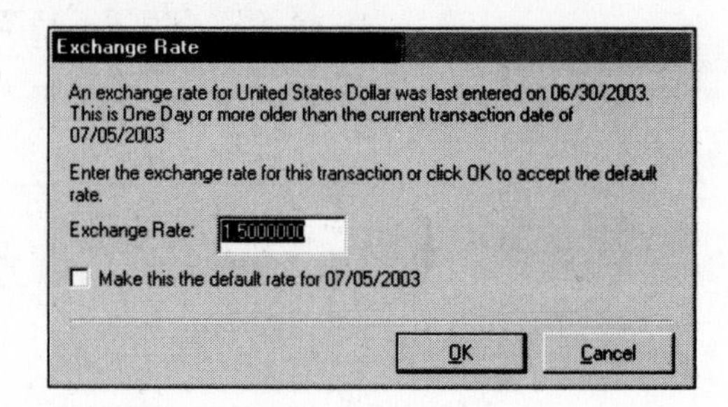

The most recent exchange rate is entered and selected for editing. You can also edit the exchange rate directly in the journal screen just as you edit any other field.

Type `1.54`

Click **Make this the default rate for 07/05/2003**

Click **OK** to return to the Sales Journal.

Click the **Description field**.

Type `games`

Click the **Amount field**.

Type `1070`

Exported goods are not taxable because they are "consumed" outside Canada. You can leave the tax fields blank or enter code 0 (tax exempt) for the GST field.

Click the **Acct field**.

Press *enter* and **select** account **4100** from the Select Account list to return to the Journal.

Click the **Freight field**.

Type `200`

Press *tab* to advance to the Freight GST code field. Freight has both GST and PST applied.

Press *enter* and **select** **code 3**.

Press *tab* to update the totals.

Choose **Federal Express** as the shipper from the Shipped by drop-down list.

Press *tab* to advance to the Tracking Number field.

Type `F19YTR563`

Your completed journal entry, ready for review, should look like the one shown here:

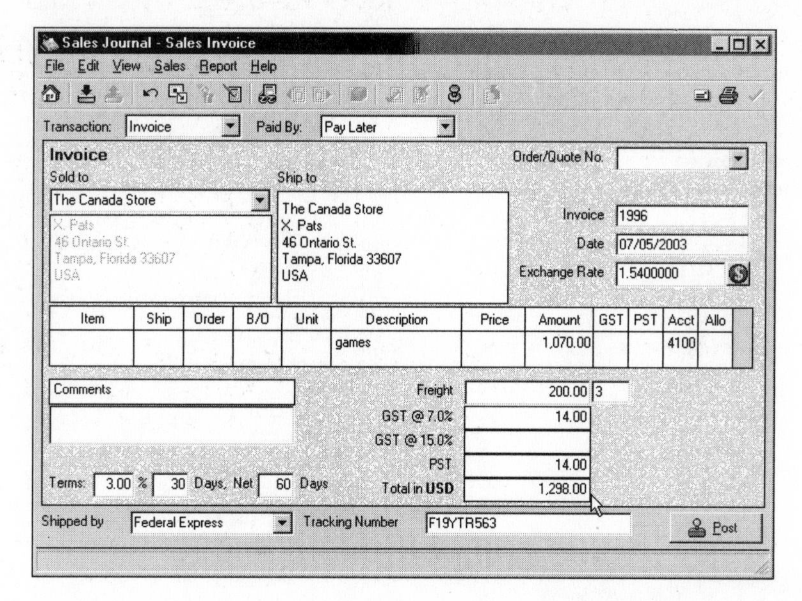

Choose the **Report menu** and **click Display Sales Journal Entry** to see the display:

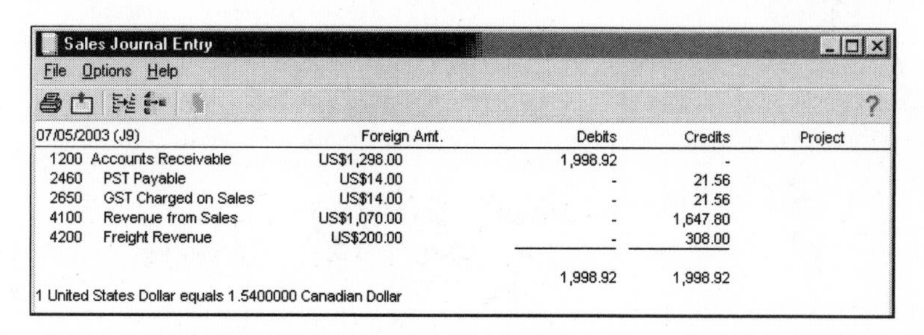

Sales Journal Entry

07/05/2003 (J9)	Foreign Amt.	Debits	Credits	Project
1200 Accounts Receivable	US$1,298.00	1,998.92	-	
2460 PST Payable	US$14.00	-	21.56	
2650 GST Charged on Sales	US$14.00	-	21.56	
4100 Revenue from Sales	US$1,070.00	-	1,647.80	
4200 Freight Revenue	US$200.00	-	308.00	
		1,998.92	1,998.92	

1 United States Dollar equals 1.5400000 Canadian Dollar

Although the journal itself shows the amounts only in US dollars, the journal entry has both the Canadian amounts and the US amounts. The remainder of the entry is the same as it would be for sales to Canadian customers.

Close the display when finished and make corrections if necessary.

Click Post [Post] to save the transaction.

Close the Sales Journal.

Entering Deposits from Customers

Click the **Receipts icon** [Receipts] to open the Receipts Journal.

Click the **Enter customer deposits tool** or choose the Receipt menu and click Enter Deposits.

This button/menu option acts as a switch that opens the fields for deposits:

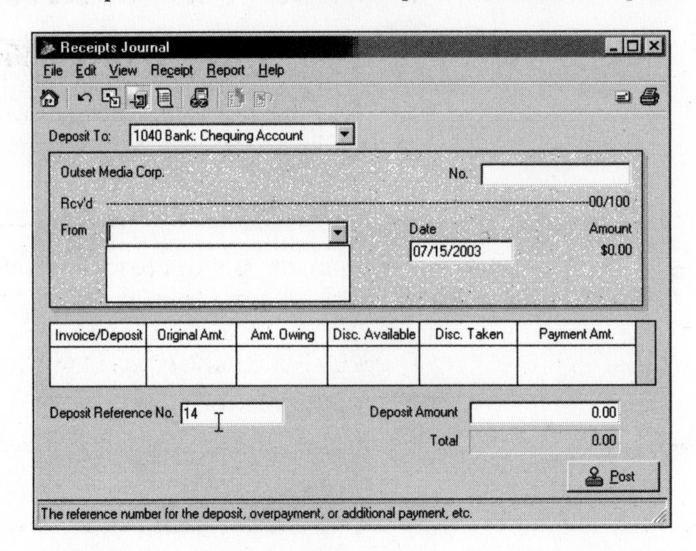

notes

Outstanding invoices, if there are any, will be included in the journal. If an outstanding invoice is paid with the same cheque, enter the payment in the usual way in addition to the deposit amount.

Two new fields are added to the journal, one for the deposit reference number, and one for the amount. The deposit number is updated automatically by the program. The rest of the journal is the same as before, but the invoice payment lines are not used for deposits.

Choose Let's Have Fun as the customer from the drop-down list.

Click the **No. field**.

Type `911` (to enter the customer cheque number)

Press tab

Type `July 6` (to enter the date)

Click the **Deposit Amount field**.

Type `2000`

Press tab to update the Total.

The deposit entry is complete and the journal looks like the one shown here:

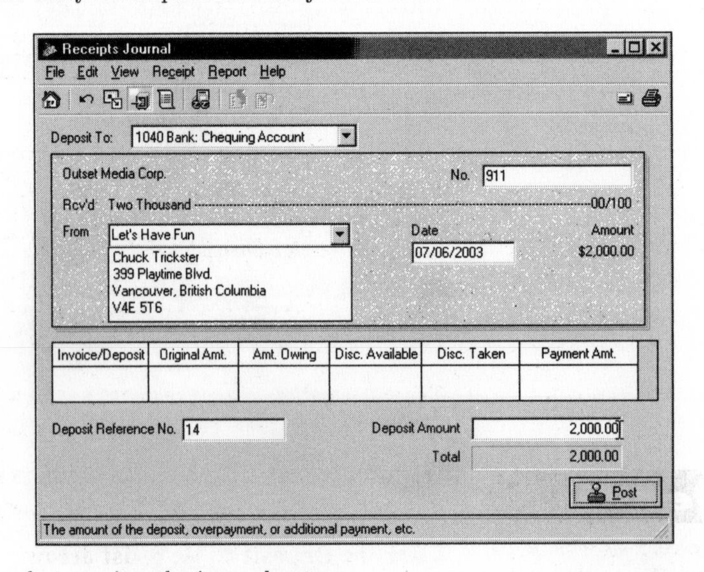

You are ready to review the journal entry.

Choose the **Report menu** and **click Display Receipts Journal Entry**:

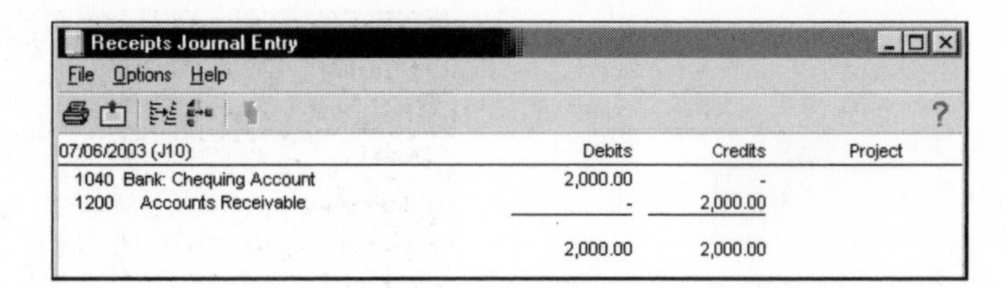

The journal entry is the same as the one for other receipts — the bank account is debited and *Accounts Receivable* is credited. If the customer has no previous balance, the deposit creates a credit entry for the account. After the sale, when the customer pays the invoice in full, the deposit will be displayed in red under the heading "Deposits" and you "pay" it by accepting its amount, just as you do to pay the invoice itself.

Close the display when you have finished and make corrections to the journal entry if necessary.

Click Post to save the transaction.

Click the **Enter customer deposits tool** again to close the deposit fields.

Close the Receipts Journal and enter the sales transactions for Let's Have Fun and Mapleaves.

Entering Foreign Customer Receipts

Click the **Receipts icon** to open the Receipts Journal.

Choose The Canada Store from the customer list to modify the journal for the foreign customer:

version 8

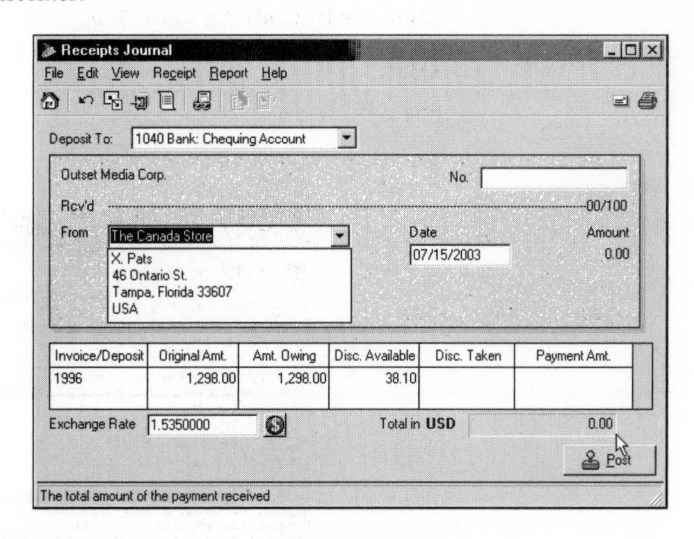

The outstanding invoice appears on the screen and the currency is marked as USD. An Exchange Rate field also becomes available.

notes

In later applications, we set up the foreign bank account as the default bank account for foreign currency transactions.

Deposits from US customers are made to the USD bank account, so we must select this account from the Deposit to list of bank accounts.

Click the **Deposit to field list arrow**.

Click 1120 Bank: USD to select the US currency account.

Click the **No. field**.

Type 2397 (to enter the customer's cheque number)

Press tab to advance to the Date field. The Session date is correct as the transaction date.

Press tab again to open the Exchange Rate screen.

notes

If the rate has not changed, you can accept it by clicking Make this the exchange rate for 07/15/2003 and click OK.

Again, because the last exchange rate we entered was for July 10, the rate is out of date and we can enter a new one. The previous rate is highlighted.

Type 1.549

Click Make this the default rate for 07/15/2003

Click OK to return to the Receipts Journal. The cursor is in the Invoice/Deposit field.

Press tab to advance to the Disc. Taken field.

Press tab to accept the discount because the full invoice is being paid. The cursor advances to the Payment Amt. field.

Press tab again to accept the amount and complete the entry as shown:

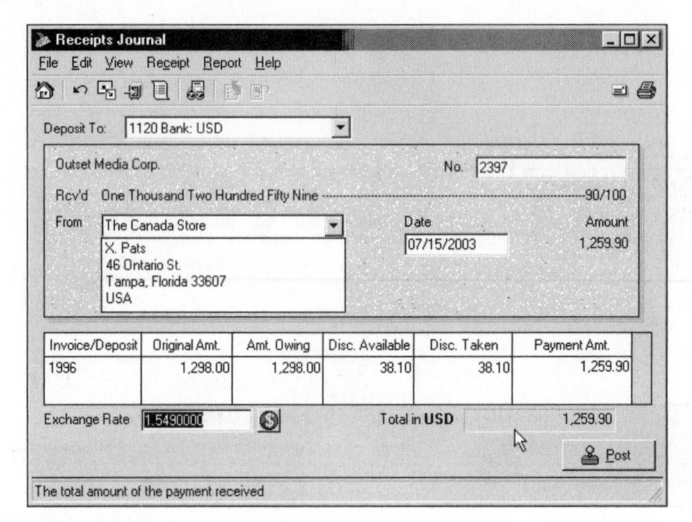

You should review the journal entry.

notes

In both Versions 8 and 8.5, the foreign currency label USD Amount appears as the column heading instead of with the individual amounts.

Choose the **Report menu** and **click Display Receipts Journal Entry**:

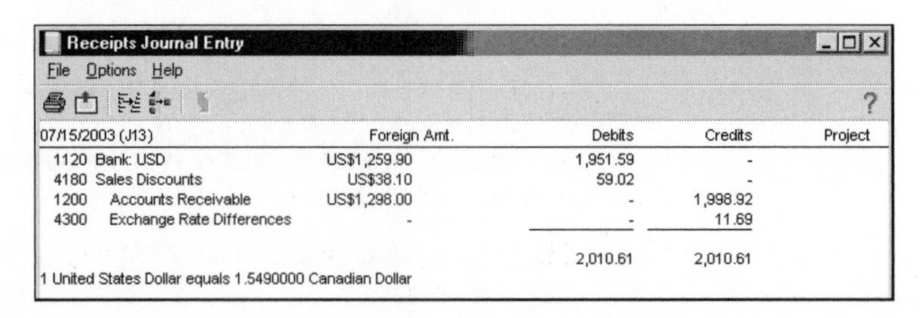

In addition to the usual linked accounts for receipts, an entry for *Exchange Rate Differences* appears. Because the exchange rate was lower on the day of the sale, the date the revenue was recorded, than on the day of the receipt, there has been a credit to the account. Outset Media has earned money on the lag in payment. If the rate had decreased, there would be a loss. As they were for foreign customer sales, amounts are given in both currencies.

Close the display to return to the journal and make corrections if necessary.

Click Post Post to save the transaction.

Close the Receipts Journal.

Looking up Invoices to Track Shipments

> **notes**
>
> You can also look up sales invoices from the Receipts Journal window. You can look up purchase invoices from the Purchases Journal and from the Payments Journal (choose Pay Vendor Invoices). You can look up Other Payment transactions only from the Payments Journal (choose Make Other Payment).

Lookup provides an exact copy of the posted invoice that you can store, print or e-mail if you have forgotten to do so before posting. This feature can also be useful if a customer has an inquiry about a purchase or needs a copy of the invoice. Once a sales or purchase invoice is posted with details about the shipping company, you can also look up the invoice to track the shipment to see when delivery is expected.

Click the **Sales icon** 

to open the Sales Journal.

Click the **Look up an invoice button** or choose the Sales menu and click Look up Invoice to display the following dialogue box:

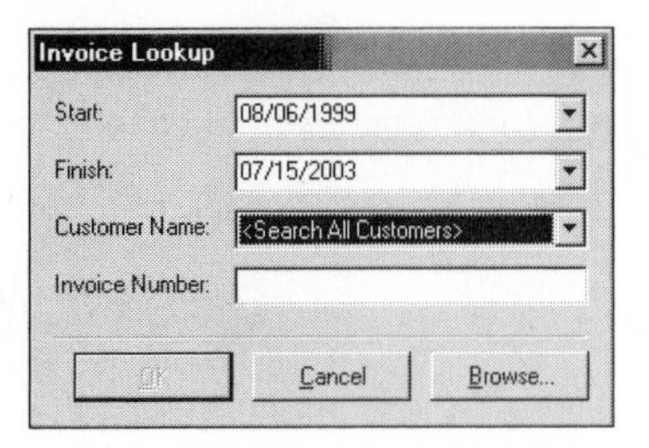

> **notes**
>
> If you know the invoice number, enter it in the Invoice Number field and click OK.

You can search through all invoices for the fiscal year to date (or for the previous year if you have not cleared the transactions and lookup data) or enter a narrower range of dates; you can search through invoices for all customers or for a specific customer, or you can search for a specific invoice number. Your search strategy will depend on how much information you have before you begin the search and how many invoices there are altogether.

The default displayed Start date may be the start of the fiscal period, the calendar date, or the date you created the company files. The Finish date is the most recent session date. You can change these dates to narrow the search, just as you would edit any other date fields, or you can choose dates from the lists.

The Customer Name option allows you to Search All Customers, the default setting, or a specific Customer's invoices.

Click 10/01/2002, the fiscal start date, from the Start drop-down list of dates to be certain that all invoices are included in the search.

Click the **Customer Name field** or its **drop-down list arrow** to display the list of customers and click the name you need. Notice that you can also look up the invoices for one-time customers. In this case we will look at all invoices so choose the default to Search All Customers.

Click Browse to display the list of invoices that meet the search conditions of date and customers:

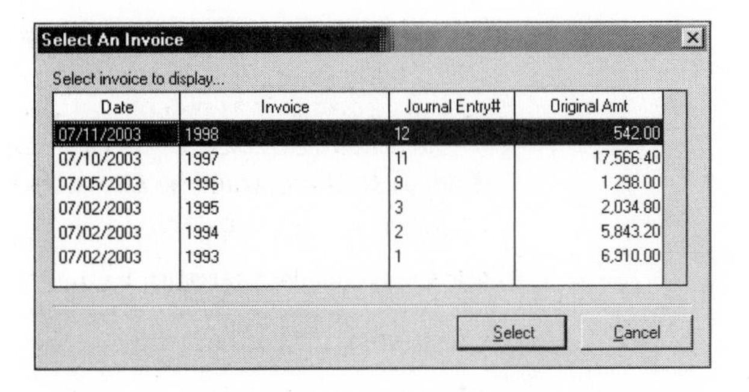

Date	Invoice	Journal Entry#	Original Amt
07/11/2003	1998	12	542.00
07/10/2003	1997	11	17,566.40
07/05/2003	1996	9	1,298.00
07/02/2003	1995	3	2,034.80
07/02/2003	1994	2	5,843.20
07/02/2003	1993	1	6,910.00

Click Invoice number **1997**, for $17 566.40 to select it. Click anywhere on the line.

Click Select. The requested invoice will be displayed as follows:

notes

If this is not the correct invoice, click the Look up next invoice or the Look up previous invoice tool buttons or choose the Previous or Next Invoice from the Sales menu to display other invoices. You can browse through the invoices in this way until you find the one you need. You should practise viewing other invoices by clicking the Look up next and previous invoice buttons.

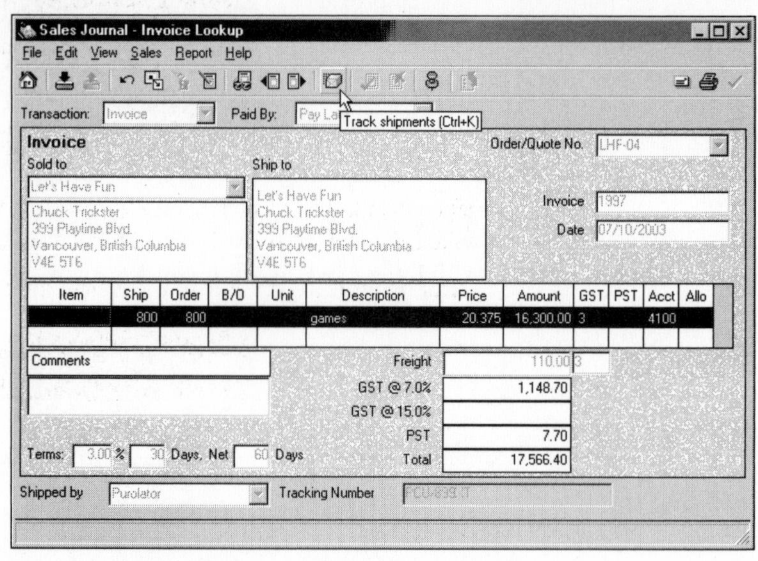

Notice that this is an exact copy of the original invoice, except that you cannot edit or post it. You can, however, store it, e-mail it or print it.

notes

Although you cannot adjust an invoice from the lookup window directly, the Adjust Invoice button is available. When you click Adjust Invoice, the journal screen changes to the Adjust Invoice form. You can use the Lookup method to locate the invoice you need to adjust.

Click Look up next invoice or Look up previous invoice if you want to access other invoices from this one. If there are no invoices in one or both directions, the corresponding button or buttons will be dimmed.

Click the **Track shipments tool** or choose the Sales menu and click Track Shipments to see the following question:

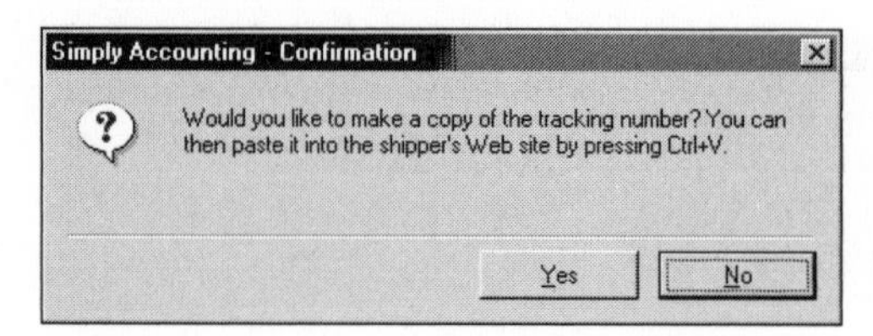

If you have set up a shipping account and have entered the actual number, you can choose Yes. However, we do not have an account with Purolator.

Click No to continue to the Internet connection.

Your screen at this stage will depend on your Internet setup — you may connect and access the Web site directly, or you may need to enter your account and password first. If you have a Network connection, such as for high-speed access, you must start the Internet connection before clicking the Track shipments button.

Continue as you would for your usual Internet connection.

You will access the Web site for Purolator.

Click Quick Track and follow the instructions provided to proceed with tracking the shipment.

Close the Internet connection when you have finished to return to the Lookup screen.

We are now ready to e-mail a copy of the invoice to the customer as notice of the shipping date and carrier.

Click the **E-mail tool** or choose the File menu and click E-mail.

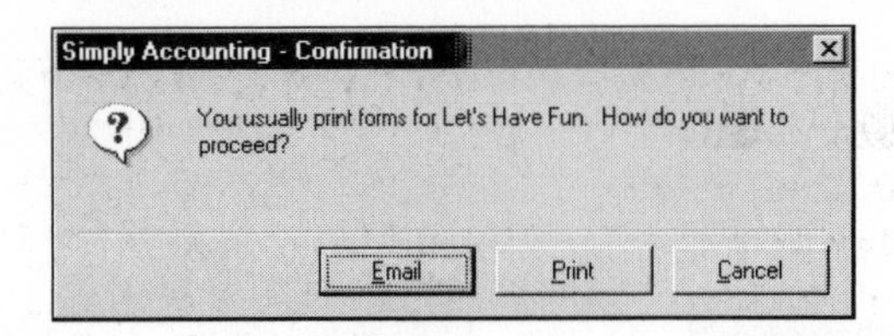

Since printing invoices is the default setting in the customer's ledger record, you are asked if you want to continue, just in case you clicked the wrong button by mistake.

Click E-mail to continue to the E-mail information screen:

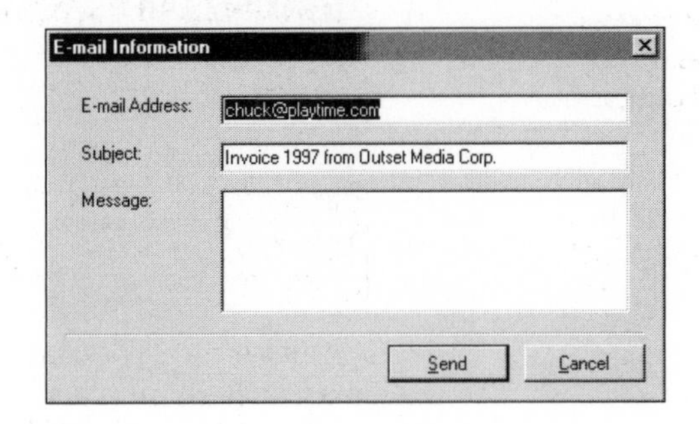

If there is no address in the ledger record, you can enter it here. You could also edit the default ledger record entry if needed.

Click the **E-mail address field**.

Type (Type your own e-mail address in this field, or that of a classmate.)

You can add the message in the Message field with shipment tracking information to inform the customer about the expected delivery date.

Click Send

You will see another advisory screen asking whether you want to update the e-mail address in the ledger record.

Click Yes to proceed.

You will see the Profile option screen:

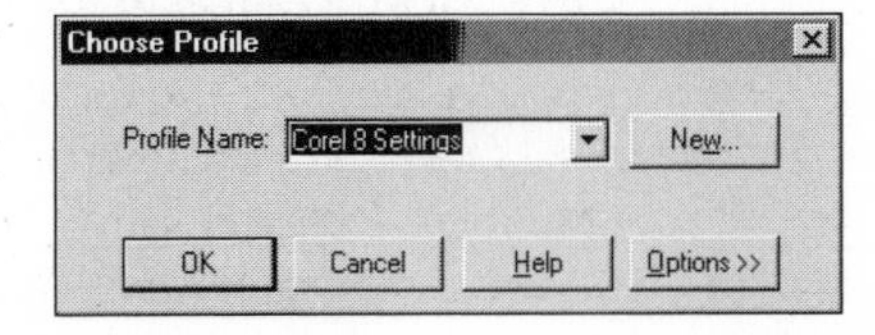

At this stage, your screens may look different, depending on your e-mail and Internet setup. MS Outlook profiles are commonly used for e-mail messages. Choose the profile you need. If you have already entered the profile settings, you will skip this screen.

Click OK. You should be connected to your Internet provider, or you may have to enter your ID and password first.

Close your e-mail and Internet programs to return to the Sales Journal - Invoice Lookup window.

Close the Lookup window to return to the Home window.

You can look up purchase invoices in the same way as you look up sales invoices. Open the Purchases or Payments Journal, click Look up an invoice, decide whether you want to restrict the search dates or vendors, and click Browse. Choose an invoice from the displayed list and click Select. Again, if you know the invoice number you can enter it directly, click OK and display the requested invoice immediately.

Ending a Fiscal Period

Warning!

You should advance to the new fiscal period in two steps. First advance to the last day of the current fiscal period and then advance to the first day of the new fiscal period. This control feature prevents you from advancing by mistake and losing important data or forgetting year-end adjusting entries.

When you advance the session date to about one month before the end of the fiscal period, Simply Accounting advises you to prepare for the year-end with the following warning:

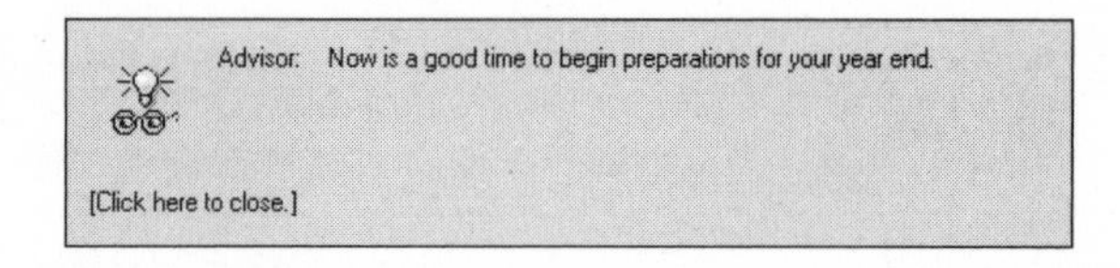

Close the advisor to continue with the transactions for the session date you have entered.

When you advance the session date further to a date very close to the end of the fiscal period, September 29 in this case, you receive another warning about the types of adjusting entries required at the end of the year:

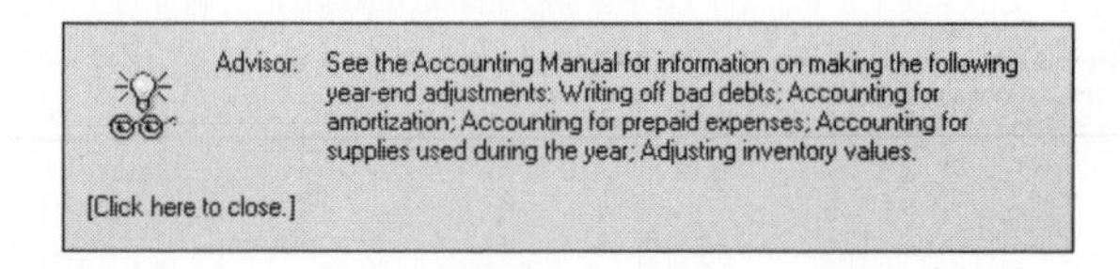

Close the advisor window to continue. The required adjusting entries are listed for September 30 with the source documents. They include depreciation entries, inventory adjustments, adjustments for prepaid expenses that have expired, and so on. Most adjusting entries do not have an external source document that reminds you to complete them, and most of them are General Journal entries.

notes

The Change Session Date dialogue box includes the last day of the fiscal period and the first day of the next fiscal period in the date drop-down list.

version 8

Enter the remaining transactions for September 30, and then close the journal to return to the Home window.

There are a few other steps to complete before beginning the new year. Simply Accounting provides assistance with these steps in its checklists.

Choose the **Business Assistant menu** (in the Home window) and **click Checklists** to see the lists available:

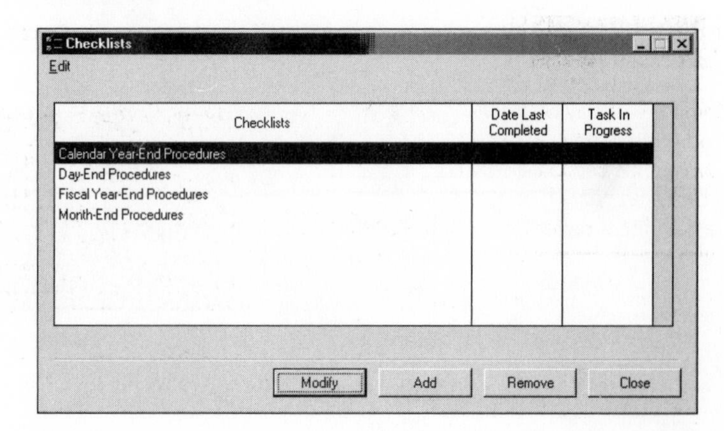

Several checklists are available for different periods — end of a fiscal period, end of a business day, end of a month and end of a calendar year for payroll. You can also create your own checklists.

notes

To add an item to a list, open the list, click the point where you want to add details and type. You can insert or remove lines and items by choosing these tool buttons or selecting these options from the Edit menu.

version 8

Double click Fiscal Year-End Procedures to see the checklist we need:

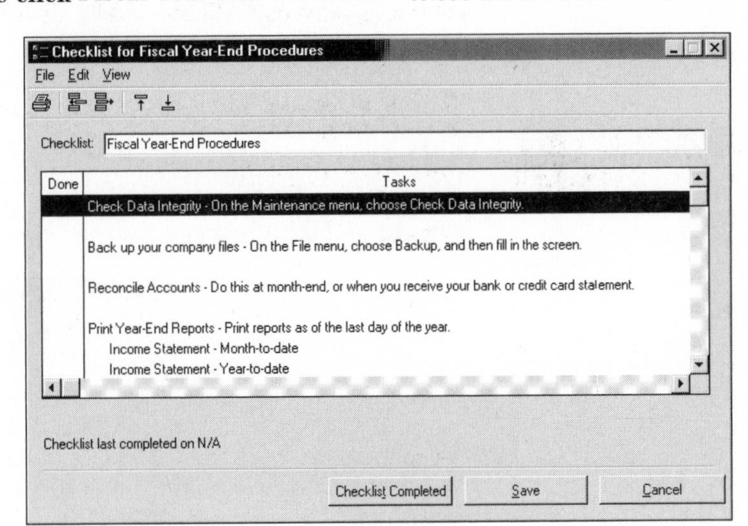

notes

Do not print reports for Payroll, Inventory, Projects or Budgets. Click the Done column after completing a task.

Each checklist can be customized for a company by using the tool buttons to insert activities, delete them or rearrange them.

You may want to print the checklist for reference by clicking the Print button, or keep it in the background for reference while you complete the activities on the list.

The most important elements on this list are backing up the data files and printing reports. Do not attempt to reconcile accounts yet. This will be explained in Chapter 14.

As you complete each activity, click the Done column for it. Click Save to leave the list and return later.

Complete all the activities listed, except account reconciliation and printing the reports for the modules that are not used. After finishing all the activities, click Checklist Completed.

Close the checklist window when you have finished.

There are two methods for beginning a new fiscal year. The first is the method we have been using to change the session date.

Choose the **Maintenance menu** and **click Change Session Date**.

Type `October 1, 2003`

Click OK. You will see a warning that allows you to back up the files or to cancel if you have made mistakes:

Warning!

Initially, from the last day of the fiscal period ending, you cannot advance the session date past October 1, the first day of the new fiscal period.

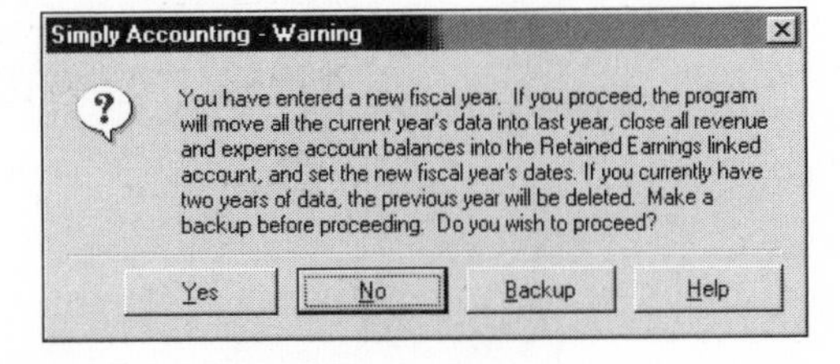

At this stage you can choose to back up the data files, continue with the date change or cancel the date change by clicking No.

notes

In Chapter 14, we describe how to clear data from company files.

The warning describes the changes about to take place in the data set. All revenue and expense accounts are reset to zero at the start of the new fiscal year. Their balances are closed out to the linked *Retained Earnings* account and the linked *Current Earnings* account is reset to zero to begin a new income statement. All previous year entries that are not cleared are stored as data for the previous year. Most reports offer comparisons with the previous year as an option. The program also updates the fiscal date for the company by one year. The new fiscal end date becomes the final date allowed as a session date.

Click No to cancel the procedure and then **click Cancel** to close the Change Session Date screen. We will use the second method to change to a new fiscal year.

Choose the **Maintenance menu** and **click Start New Year**:

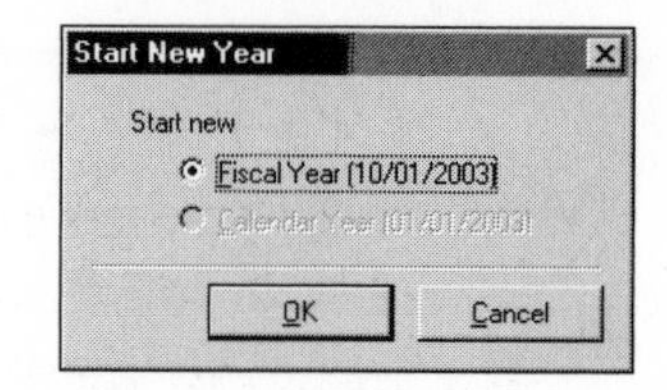

You can start a new calendar year, if the timing is appropriate, or a new fiscal year. A fiscal year of one year is assumed so the new fiscal end will be advanced by 12 months. Since we cannot start a new calendar year at this stage — the fiscal end is earlier than the start of a new year — the option is dimmed and the default is to begin a new fiscal year.

Click OK to continue. You will see a warning similar to the one on page 217 for changing the Session date:

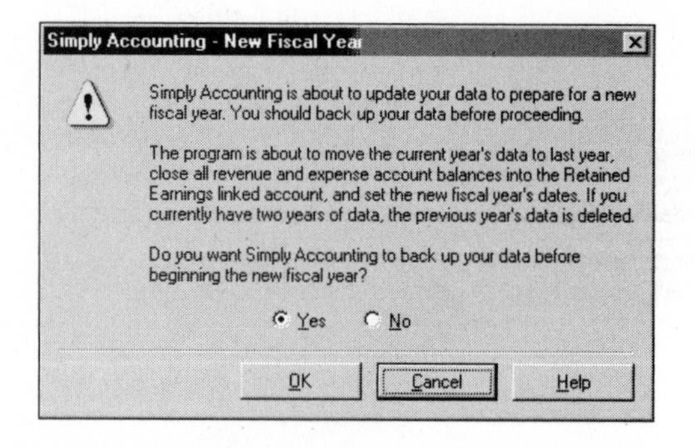

The default setting is to make a backup before continuing. If you have not yet made a backup, do so now. If you do not want to begin a new year, you can click Cancel and the old dates will remain in effect.

Warning!

If you have cleared journal entries or paid invoices, these details will be unavailable for reports. Comparative Income Statements and Balance Sheets are always available for the two fiscal periods.

Click No because you have already backed up your files.

Click OK to begin the new fiscal period.

Print the Comparative Trial Balance and Balance Sheet for September 30 and October 1. Notice the changes in the capital accounts on the Balance Sheet. The *Current Earnings* balance for September 30 has been added to the *D. Manga, Capital* account to create the October 1 balance in the *D. Manga, Capital* account.

Print the Comparative Income Statement for the previous year (Oct. 1, 2002, to Sep. 30, 2003) and the current fiscal year-to-date (Oct. 1, 2003, to Oct. 1, 2003). The Income Statement for the current year shows no income or revenue. All accounts have a zero balance because you have not recorded any transactions for the new fiscal year.

The files are now ready for transactions in the new fiscal period.

CASE PROBLEMS

Case One

At the end of September, Outset Media can file for a GST refund. How can you tell whether a business qualifies for a refund or a remittance?

1. Explain why GST refunds are processed through the Sales Journal instead of the Purchases Journal.
2. Describe the steps in completing the entry for a GST refund using Simply Accounting.
3. Why can you not enter a GST refund as a cash sale although you can enter the remittance as a cash purchase?
4. If a business consistently files for GST refunds, what could this tell you about the business?
5. Refer to the September 30 General Ledger balances for the three GST/HST accounts to claim the GST refund from the Receiver General. Using the Simply Accounting data file for Outset Media Corp., create a Customer record for the Receiver General (do not include in GST reports). Enter a Sales Journal pay later invoice to record the request for a refund.

Case Two

At the end of September, there is one adjusting entry that must still be made: accounting for the purchase of the new automobile to replace the old one. Assume that the old car was traded in at book value. Create the General Journal entry to adjust the accumulated depreciation value to reflect the disposal of the old car.

CHAPTER EIGHT

OBJECTIVES

After completing this chapter, you should be able to

- *open* the Payroll Journal
- *enter* employee-related payroll transactions
- *understand* automatic payroll deductions
- *post* payroll transactions
- *understand* Payroll Ledger linked accounts
- *edit* and *review* payroll transactions
- *adjust* Payroll Journal invoices that have been posted
- *complete* payroll runs for a group of employees
- *release* vacation pay to employees
- *display* and *print* payroll reports
- *use* To-Do Lists to make journal entries

COMPANY INFORMATION

Company Profile

Carnival Catering, owned and managed by Susie Sardinha in the city of Victoria, British Columbia, provides a variety of menus for all occasions. Sardinha's excellent international cuisine appeals to people from different cultures so that her reputation and business have grown steadily. She now handles weddings, anniversaries, retirements, funerals, birthdays, business meetings, conferences or any other special event for any size group.

Sardinha started a catering business alone two years ago, occasionally bringing in assistants when needed. Recently she has consistently been getting larger contracts and has bought out an old catering business from a friend who wanted to retire. She took over some of the old assets, purchased additional equipment including a computer, and hired a full-time staff to work with her.

Sardinha manages the business but also takes an active role in the day-to-day work. She actively seeks out new business and negotiates the contracts with her clients, basing the price on the size of the group, the complexity of the menu and the number of hours involved in the actual event. She then works out the menu details with the chef, gets final client approval and obtains an advance from the client. The advance is used to purchase food for the special event. The chef and sous chef then purchase all the food required from the city market, butcher shops, delicatessen and supermarkets. With some of these stores, Sardinha has arranged for weekly deliveries. The two full-time cooks, under the supervision of the chefs, complete most of the food preparation. Three waiters make up the rest of the staff, setting up the tables at the catered events, serving food and cleaning up afterwards.

Sardinha's business and food sciences education have prepared her not only for the menu-planning part of her job, but also for the business management aspects. Her solid grasp of accounting principles has enabled her to set up all her accounting records in Simply Accounting using the following:

- Chart of Accounts
- Post-Closing Trial Balance
- Vendor Information
- Customer Information
- Employee Information
- Employee Profiles and TD1 Information
- Accounting Procedures

CARNIVAL CATERING
CHART OF ACCOUNTS

ASSETS
1080 Cash
1200 Accounts Receivable
1240 Advances Receivable
1260 Food Inventory
1280 Liquor & Wine Inventory
1300 Catering Supplies
1360 Appliances & Equipment
1380 Chairs & Tables
1400 Computers & Peripherals
1420 Cutlery & Dishes
1460 Delivery Truck
1480 Shop

LIABILITIES
2100 Bank Loan
2200 Accounts Payable
2300 Vacation Payable
2310 EI Payable
2320 CPP Payable
2330 Income Tax Payable
2400 Medical Payable
2410 RRSP Payable
2460 WCB Payable
2640 PST Payable
2650 GST Charged on Services
2670 GST Paid on Purchases
2940 Mortgage Payable

EQUITY
3560 S. Sardinha, Capital
3580 S. Sardinha, Drawings
3600 Net Income

REVENUE
4020 Revenue from Catering

EXPENSES
5020 Advertising & Promotion
5040 Bank Charges
5060 Hydro Expense
5080 Telephone Expense
5100 Truck Expenses
5200 Food Used for Catering
5220 Liquor Used for Catering
5240 Catering Supplies Used
5300 Wages
5310 EI Expense
5320 CPP Expense
5330 WCB Expense

CARNIVAL CATERING
POST-CLOSING TRIAL BALANCE
June 1, 2003

Account	Debit	Credit
1080 Cash	$ 21 000.00	
1260 Food Inventory	1 500.00	
1280 Liquor & Wine Inventory	5 000.00	
1300 Catering Supplies	200.00	
1360 Appliances & Equipment	24 000.00	
1380 Chairs & Tables	2 500.00	
1400 Computers & Peripherals	4 000.00	
1420 Cutlery & Dishes	4 000.00	
1460 Delivery Truck	30 000.00	
1480 Shop	250 000.00	
2100 Bank Loan		25 000.00
2200 Accounts Payable		6 450.00
2670 GST Paid on Purchases	450.00	
2940 Mortgage Payable		225 000.00
3560 S. Sardinha, Capital		86 200.00
	$342 650.00	$342 650.00

CARNIVAL CATERING
VENDOR INFORMATION

Vendor Name (Contact)	Address	Phone No. Fax No.	Terms
Caterers Suppliers (Sue Plyers)	62 Providence Ave. Victoria, BC V9U 8H1	Tel: (250) 883-7735 Fax: (250) 883-1922	Net 30
Coastal Fish Wholesalers (Marina Pesce)	21 Salmon Ave. Victoria, BC V8T 2R4	Tel: (250) 888-7163 Fax: (250) 888-7299	Net 15
Commercial Cutlery Ltd. (Mac LeCouteau)	88 Ontario St. Vancouver, BC V7U 1A2	Tel: (604) 266-9013 Fax: (604) 266-9001	Net 30
David's Fresh Produce (David Appleton)	44 Pears Ave. Victoria, BC V8M 6M1	Tel: (250) 892-7844 Fax: (250) 892-5611	Net 15
European Smoked Meats (Antoine Jambon)	6 Alpine Court Victoria, BC V8B 2T7	Tel: (250) 891-7199 Fax: (250) 891-5191	Net 15
House of Spirits (Al Cool)	91 Moonshine Lane Victoria, BC V8T 5R2	Tel: (250) 896-6639 Fax: (250) 896-0111	(Payment with Purchase)
Hydro BC (Manny Lighter)	67 Energy Rd. Victoria, BC V8R 1H4	Tel: (250) 896-2345	Net 1
Ideal Equipment (Ivory Range)	181 Brunswick Rd. Vancouver, BC V7U 2D4	Tel: (604) 775-6370 Fax: (604) 775-6666	Net 30
Pacific Telephone (M.A. Bell)	55 Signal Rd. Victoria, BC V9P 3K9	Tel: (250) 895-5617 Fax: (250) 895-5600	Net 1
Reliable Food Supplies (Thon Visser)	366 Orange Grove Victoria, BC V8S 4L5	Tel: (250) 889-7190 Fax: (250) 889-7199	Net 15
Valu Petroleum (Val Petro)	79 Gasoline Alley Victoria, BC V8D 7B2	Tel: (250) 893-5286 Fax: (250) 893-5211	Net 1

CARNIVAL CATERING
OUTSTANDING VENDOR INVOICES

Vendor Name	Date	Inv/Chq No.	Terms	Amount	Total
Commercial Cutlery Ltd.	May 28/03	CC-4321	Net 30	$1 150.00	$1 150.00
Ideal Equipment	May 29/03	IE-6374	Net 30	$5 350.00	$5 300.00
			Grand Total		$6 450.00

CARNIVAL CATERING
CUSTOMER INFORMATION

Customer Name (Contact)	Address	Phone No. Fax No.	Terms Credit Limit
Coastal Corporation (Emery Lighthouse)	33 Seaside Cr. Victoria, BC V9X 2E7	Tel: (250) 882-8166 Fax: (250) 882-6210	Net 1
Ministry of Environment (Vicki Greene)	BC Government 660 Parliament Rd. Victoria, BC V9B 6R6	Tel: (250) 884-7182 Fax: (250) 884-7110	Net 1
Victoria Ladies Bridge Club (Victoria Bridge)	54 Gambler Rd. Victoria, BC V8C 7E3	Tel: (250) 896-8610 Fax: (250) 896-8011	Net 30 $3 000

CARNIVAL CATERING
EMPLOYEE INFORMATION SHEET

	Susie Sardinha	Louie Perch	Peter Terkee	Sera Suflay
Position	Owner/Exec. chef	Chef	Sous Chef	Cook
Social Insurance Number	419 910 989	477 732 754	469 412 407	571 628 643
Address & Telephone	31 Bawssey Cres. Victoria, BC V8R 1S4 (250) 882-7100	711 Bass Rd. Victoria, BC V7P 2R1 (250) 883-6108	60 Fowler Blvd. Victoria, BC V9Z 3M2 (250) 895-8262	53 Omlet St. Victoria, BC V8M 4B3 (250) 892-6173
Date of Birth (mm-dd-yy)	6-14-67	2-21-61	12-25-69	10-1-73
TD1 Tax Exemption Federal (BC)				
Basic Federal (BC)	$7 412 ($8 000)	$7 412 ($8 000)	$7 412 ($8 000)	$7 412 ($8 000)
Spouse		$6 294 ($6 850)	$6 294 ($6 850)	$6 294 ($6 850)
Caregiver				$3 500 ($2 424)
Total Claim Amount	$7 412 ($8 000)	$13 706 ($14 850)	$13 706 ($14 850)	$17 206 ($17 274)
Employee Earnings				
Regular Wage Rate				$18.00/hour
Overtime Wage Rate				$27.00/hour
Regular Salary	$2 000.00/month	$4 000.00/month	$3 200.00/month	
Commission		1% catering revenue	1/2% catering revenue	
Vacation		4 weeks	3 weeks	6%
Employee Deductions				
Medical/pay period	$64.00	$72.00	$72.00	$16.60
RRSP/pay period	$200.00	$200.00	$200.00	
Additional Income Tax/pay period		$80.00		

CARNIVAL CATERING
EMPLOYEE INFORMATION SHEET CONTINUED

	Ben Branjil	Sylvia Mellon	Adrian Poppi	Aziz Atta
Position	Cook	Waiter	Waiter	Waiter
Social Insurance Number	721 971 638	618 932 636	552 846 826	492 746 540
Address & Telephone	47 Aubergine St. Victoria, BC V7N 2L2 (250) 889-6291	9 Orchardview Ct. Victoria, BC V8K 4K2 (250) 893-7595	50 Seed St. #322 Victoria, BC V9B 4C1 (250) 881-8138	63 Peppertree Ave. Victoria, BC V8U 1X3 (250) 888-6353
Date of Birth (mm-dd-yy)	7-31-72	8-15-78	11-3-75	8-6-65
TD1 Tax Exemption Federal (BC)				
Basic Federal (BC)	$7 412 ($8 000)	$7 412 ($8 000)	$7 412 ($8 000)	$7 412 ($8 000)
Total Claim Amount	$7 412 ($8 000)	$7 412 ($8 000)	$7 412 ($8 000)	$7 412 ($8 000)
Employee Earnings				
Regular Wage Rate	$18.00	$10.00	$10.00	$10.00
Overtime Wage Rate	$27.00	$15.00	$15.00	$15.00
Regular Salary				
Commission				
Vacation	6%	4%	4%	4%
Employee Deductions				
Medical/pay period	$16.60	$16.60	$16.60	$16.60
RRSP/pay period	$25.00			
Additional Income Tax/pay period		$20.00		

Calculations for EI, CPP and income tax are built into the Simply Accounting program.

Employee Profiles and TD1 Information

Susie Sardinha is the owner and executive chef for Carnival Catering. She negotiates all contracts with clients, plans menus, hires the staff and performs general management duties. In addition to the company's profits, she draws a monthly salary of $2 000. She is married but claims a single tax exemption. Through the payroll, she pays the medical premiums for herself and spouse and makes regular RRSP contributions. As an owner, she is not eligible for EI and does not make EI contributions.

Louie Perch, the chef at Carnival Catering, works closely with the owner, planning and writing menus and scheduling the work of other staff for all events. He is also responsible for food purchases. Perch receives $4 000 per month in salary plus a 1 percent commission on the revenue from catering. He is entitled to take four weeks of vacation each year. Perch is married and fully supports his wife and two children who have no income, and, therefore, he pays the family rate for medical premiums. In addition, he has elected to make RRSP contributions through payroll deductions and to pay additional income tax each month to offset the tax on his investment income.

Peter Terkee, the sous chef, assists the chef in all aspects of the work, carries out his orders with respect to food preparation and supervises the cooks. His monthly salary of $3 200 is supplemented by a commission of 0.5 percent of the revenue from catering. His vacation entitlement is three weeks per year. Terkee fully supports his wife and two children who have no income. His regular pay deductions include the family rate for medical insurance premiums and RRSP contributions.

Sera Suflay works as one of the two cooks for Carnival Catering. Her primary responsibility is to prepare food for the catered events. She is paid weekly at the rate of $18 per hour for regular work and $27 per hour for overtime work. Her vacation pay is calculated at 6 percent. She is the sole supporter of two brothers for whom she claims spousal equivalent and disability/caregiver tax credit amounts. Her payroll deductions include the family rate for medical premiums.

Ben Branjil, the second cook at Carnival Catering, has the same job responsibilities and wages as Sera Suflay. He is married but his wife earns a full-time salary. He pays the married medical insurance premium for his family and makes weekly RRSP contributions through payroll.

Sylvia Mellon works as one of three waiters for Carnival Catering. Her job is to help set up, serve food, and clean up at all catered events. She is paid bi-weekly at $10 per hour for regular work and $15 for overtime work, and vacation pay is calculated at 4 percent. She is single and self-supporting and pays the single rate for medical premiums. She also makes regular RRSP contributions through payroll and has elected to pay additional income tax.

Adrian Poppi, the second waiter, shares responsibilities with Sylvia Mellon and Aziz Atta. His wages and vacation pay are also the same as Mellon's. He is single and self-supporting and pays the single rate for medical premiums.

Aziz Atta is the third waiter and has the same job responsibilities and wages as Sylvia Mellon and Adrian Poppi. He is single and self-supporting and pays the single rate for medical premiums.

Additional Payroll Information

1. The owner, chef and sous chef are paid monthly, cooks are paid weekly and waiters are paid bi-weekly.
2. EI, CPP and income taxes withheld are remitted monthly to the Receiver General of Canada.
3. Medical payments are remitted monthly to the provincial Minister of Finance.
4. Participation in the Registered Retirement Savings Plan (RRSP) is voluntary.
5. The number of hours usually worked in each pay period is 40 hours per week for hourly paid employees and 150 hours per month for salaried employees.
6. The employer's contributions include
   - CPP contributions equal to employee contributions
   - EI factor of 1.4
   - WCB rate of 1.09

Accounting Procedures

The Goods and Services Tax: Remittances

Carnival Catering uses the regular method for remittance of the Goods and Services Tax. It records the GST collected from customers as a liability in *GST Charged on Services*. GST paid by vendors is recorded in *GST Paid on Purchases* as a decrease in the liability to Canada Customs and Revenue Agency. The GST quarterly refund or remittance is calculated automatically in the *GST Owing (Refund)* subgroup total account. You will see this balance when you display or print the Balance Sheet. Susie Sardinha files for a refund or remits the balance owing to the Receiver General of Canada by the last day of the month for the previous quarter.

notes

Bank and other financial institution services are exempt from GST charges in this application.

Food is zero rated with respect to GST. Vendors who supply food also sell taxable goods, therefore, the option to include them in GST reports is turned on so that the GST field is available when needed. You can enter GST Code 0 when the GST amount paid is zero or leave the GST code field blank.

PST

Provincial Sales Tax at 7 percent is charged on all food services provided. This amount is set up in the defaults for the company. However, because the Inventory Ledger is not set up, the program does not enter the PST rate automatically. You must type 7 in the PST field. Simply Accounting will then automatically calculate the amount of tax and credit *PST Payable*.

PST at the rate of 7 percent is also paid on non-food purchases.

Advances from Customers
Sardinha prepares sales quotes for new contracts. When clients sign the contract, they pay an advance of between 25 and 30 percent of the total contracted price, usually one to two weeks before the catered event. The advance is entered in the Receipts Journal as a customer deposit so that the entry will credit *Accounts Receivable* for the customer. When the catering services are performed, complete a Sales Journal entry by filling the sales quote for the full amount of the contract, with the appropriate taxes and revenue account. When the customer pays the balance of the invoice, mark the invoice for both the deposit and the full contract price as paid. In this way, the balance owing will match the amount of the cheque. Customers are expected to settle their accounts as soon as the catered event is finished. Thus, for each event, there are four transactions: a sales quote, a receipt entry for the advance, a sales invoice for the event (filling the quote) and a final payment.

Two sales quotes have already been accepted.

Because customers pay a non-refundable advance, the credit limit option is not used. The Bridge Club is the exception because it negotiated with Carnival Catering to provide hors d'oeuvres and beverages for its weekly bridge tournaments. The Bridge Club settles its accounts at the end of each month. This is a normal account customer.

notes

- Processing the advance through the Receipts Journal ensures that the advance will appear in the correct customer account in the Receivables Ledger. The other approach, a General Journal entry that debits the Bank account and credits Unearned Revenue, a liability account, does not show this customer link.
- We have omitted the step of converting the sales quote to a sales order in this application.

INSTRUCTIONS

1. Using the instructions for accessing data files on page 15, open the data files for Carnival Catering. Using Simply Accounting and the Chart of Accounts, Vendor, Customer and Employee Information, enter the transactions for the June 7 session date up to the payroll entries. (Refer to the keystroke instructions covered earlier in this workbook.)

   The procedures for entering each new transaction for this application are outlined step by step in the keystroke section following the source documents. These transactions have a ✔ in the check box and the page number where the keystrokes begin appears immediately below the check box.

2. After you have finished making your entries, print the reports and graphs marked on the printing form below. Keystrokes for payroll reports begin on page 251.

REPORTS

Lists
- [ ] Chart of Accounts
- [ ] Vendors
- [ ] Customers
- [x] Employees

Financials
- [ ] Balance Sheet
- [x] Income Statement
  from June 1 to June 30
- [x] Trial Balance
  date: June 30
- [x] General Ledger
  accounts: 2310 2320 2330 5300
  from June 1 to June 30
- [ ] Cash Flow Projection

GST
- [ ] GST Report

Payroll
- [x] Employee Summary
- [x] Employee Detail
  include all details for all employees
- [ ] T4 Slips
- [ ] Relevé 1 Slips

Journals
- [x] All Journals (by posting date)
  from June 1 to June 30
- [ ] General
- [ ] Purchases
- [ ] Payments
- [x] Sales (by posting date)
  from June 1 to June 30
- [ ] Receipts
- [x] Payroll (by posting date)
  from June 1 to June 30

Payables
- [ ] Vendor Aged
- [ ] Aged Overdue Payables
- [ ] Pending Purchase Orders

Receivables
- [ ] Customer Aged
- [ ] Aged Overdue Receivables
- [ ] Customer Statements

Management Reports
- [ ] Ledgers

Mailing Labels
- [ ] Labels

GRAPHS

- [ ] Payables by Aging Period
- [ ] Receivables by Aging Period
- [ ] Sales vs Receivables
- [ ] Revenues by Account
- [x] Expenses and Net Profit as % of Revenue
- [ ] Payables by Vendor
- [ ] Receivables by Customer
- [ ] Receivables Due vs Payables Due
- [ ] Expenses by Account
- [ ] Current Revenue vs Last Year

SOURCE DOCUMENTS

SESSION DATE – June 7

- [ ] Cash Receipt #CR-1
  Dated June 1/03
  From Ministry of Environment, cheque #1206 for $6 000 as deposit #1 in acceptance of sales contract.

- [ ] Cash Receipt #CR-2
  Dated June 1/03
  From Coastal Corporation, cheque #161 for $3 000 as deposit #2 in acceptance of sales contract.

> **notes**
>
> Remember that food purchases are exempt from both GST and PST.

- [ ] Purchase Invoice #RF-411
Dated June 1/03
From Reliable Food Supplies, $2 000 for delivery of basic grocery items for catering services. This is a weekly recurring purchase as agreed. Terms: n/15.

- [ ] Purchase Invoice #ESM-1712
Dated June 1/03
From European Smoked Meats, $1 000 for delivery of cheeses and deli meats for catering services. This is a weekly recurring purchase. Terms: n/15.

- [ ] Cheque Copy #11
Dated June 2/03
To Commercial Cutlery Ltd., $1 150 in full payment of account. Reference invoice #CC-4321.

- [ ] Purchase Invoice #DP-1793
Dated June 3/03
From David's Fresh Produce, $500 for delivery of fresh fruits and vegetables for catering services. This is a weekly recurring purchase. Terms: n/15.

- [ ] Purchase Invoice #CF-976
Dated June 3/03
From Coastal Fish Wholesalers, $1 000 for delivery of shrimp, lobster and assorted fresh fish for catering services. Terms: n/15.

- [ ] Cash Purchase Invoice #VP-11234
Dated June 5/03
From Valu Petroleum, $80 plus 7% GST for gas and oil change to delivery truck. Invoice total $85.60. Paid by cheque #12.

> **notes**
>
> Use only the numeric part of sales invoice numbers so that the program can update them. Choose GST Code 3 and type 7 in the PST rate field for purchases and sales to record the taxes.

- [ ] Sales Invoice #CC-121
Dated June 5/03
To Ministry of Environment, $20 000 plus 7% GST and 7% PST for catering contract completed. Invoice total $22 800. Terms: cash on receipt of invoice.

- [ ] Cash Receipt #CR-3
Dated June 6/03
From Ministry of Environment, cheque #1371 for $16 800 in full payment of account. Reference invoice #CC-121 and deposit #1.

> **notes**
>
> - [ ] Lisa Haskett is located at 555 Honeymooners Lane Victoria, BC V8T 4W2 Tel: (250) 882-7499 Charge PST & GST
>
> Refer to Accounting Procedures on page 226.
>
> We use the term delivery date for the catering quotes because it is more appropriate for services than shipping date.

- [ ] Sales Quote #1001
Dated June 6/03
Delivery date June 14/03
For Lisa Haskett (use Full Add), catering of wedding reception will cost $15 000 plus 7% GST and 7% PST. Total catering cost, $17 100. Terms: cash on receipt of invoice.

- [ ] Cash Receipt #CR-4
Dated June 6/03
From Lisa Haskett, cheque #271 for $4 500 (deposit #3) toward wedding reception and in acceptance of sales quote #1001.

- [ ] Sales Invoice #CC-122
Dated June 6/03
To Victoria Ladies Bridge Club, $500 plus 7% GST and 7% PST for weekly contracted catering services. Invoice total $570. Terms: net 30 days. Store this entry as a weekly recurring sale.

☐ Sales Invoice #CC-123
Dated June 7/03
To Coastal Corporation, $10 000 plus 7% GST and 7% PST for catering contract completed. Invoice total $11 400. Terms: cash on receipt of invoice.

notes

Refer to Keystrokes page 236.

EMPLOYEE TIME SUMMARY SHEET #1

(pay period ending June 7, 2003)

	Name of Employee	Regular Hours	Overtime Hours
☐ 236	Sera Suflay	40	2
☐	Ben Branjil	40	–

a. Using Employee Time Summary Sheet #1 and the Employee Information Sheet, complete payroll for weekly paid employees.
b. Sera Suflay will receive an advance of $240 for emergency car repairs. Her next four paycheques will each have $60 deducted to pay back the advance.
c. Issue cheques #13 and #14.

☐ Purchase Invoice #CS-9114
Dated June 7/03
From Caterers Suppliers, $200 plus 7% PST and 7% GST for regular weekly delivery of catering supplies. Invoice total $228. This is a weekly recurring purchase. Terms: net 30 days.

SESSION DATE – June 14

☐ 241 Memo #1
Dated June 8/03
From Manager: Adjust paycheque for Sera Suflay (cheque #13) to include 4 hours overtime. Suflay has returned the original cheque.

☐ Cash Receipt #CR-5
Dated June 8/03
From Coastal Corporation, cheque #194 for $8 400 in full payment of account. Reference invoice #CC-123 and deposit #2.

notes

Remember to use the stored entries for recurring purchases and sales.

☐ Purchase Invoice #RF-507
Dated June 8/03
From Reliable Food Supplies, $2 000 for regular weekly delivery of basic grocery items for catering services. Terms: n/15.

☐ Purchase Invoice #ESM-2027
Dated June 8/03
From European Smoked Meats, $1 000 for regular weekly delivery of cheeses and deli meats for catering services. Terms: n/15.

☐ Purchase Invoice #DP-1993
Dated June 10/03
From David's Fresh Produce, $500 for regular weekly delivery of fresh fruits and vegetables for catering services. Terms: n/15.

- [ ] Cheque Copy #15
  Dated June 10/03
  To Ideal Equipment, $5 300 in full payment of account. Reference invoice #IE-6374.

notes

Gloria Vitale is located at
88 Bridal Path
Victoria, BC V8P 9H4
Tel: (250) 893-7014
Fax: (250) 893-7711
Charge PST & GST

- [ ] Sales Quote #1002
  Dated June 10/03
  Delivery date June 21/03
  For Gloria Vitale (use Full Add), wedding catering will cost $12 000 plus 7% GST and 7% PST. Total cost will be $13 680. Terms: Cash on receipt of invoice.

- [ ] Cash Receipt #CR-6
  Dated June 10/03
  From Gloria Vitale, cheque #37 for $3 600 as deposit #4 toward wedding reception and in acceptance of sales quote #1002.

- [ ] Sales Invoice #CC-124
  Dated June 13/03
  To Victoria Ladies Bridge Club, $500 plus 7% GST and 7% PST for weekly contracted catering services. Invoice total $570. Terms: net 30 days.

- [ ] Purchase Invoice #CF-1211
  Dated June 13/03
  From Coastal Fish Wholesalers, $500 for fresh fish for wedding catering contract. Terms: n/15.

- [ ] Sales Invoice #CC-125
  Dated June 14/03
  To Lisa Haskett, to fill sales quote #1001, $15 000 plus 7% GST and 7% PST for completion of wedding catering contract. Invoice total $17 100. Terms: Cash on receipt of invoice.

notes

Sean O'Casey is located at
120 Wakefield Rd.
Victoria, BC V8E 6G9
Tel: (250) 895-7397
Fax: (250) 895-7399
Charge PST & GST

- [ ] Sales Quote #1003
  Dated June 14/03
  Delivery date June 17/03
  For Sean O'Casey (use Full Add), catering for wake will cost $4 000 plus 7% GST and 7% PST. Total cost will be $4 560. Terms: Cash on receipt of invoice.

- [ ] Cash Receipt #CR-7
  Dated June 14/03
  From Sean O'Casey, cheque #631 for $1 000 as deposit #5 in acceptance of sales quote #1003.

- [ ] Cash Purchase Invoice #HS-75200
  Dated June 14/03
  From House of Spirits, $1 500 for wine and liquor plus $105 GST. Invoice total $1 605. Terms: COD. Issued cheque #16.

- [ ] Purchase Invoice #CS-9327
  Dated June 14/03
  From Caterers Suppliers, $200 plus 7% PST and 7% GST for regular weekly delivery of catering supplies. Invoice total $228. Terms: net 30 days.

notes

Use the Paycheques Journal to enter Suflay's pay so you can recover the advance.

- [ ] Memo #2
  Dated June 14/03
  From Manager: Prepare paycheque for Sera Suflay (cheque #17) for 40 hours of regular pay and 2 hours of overtime. Recover $60 of the advance paid on June 7. Remember to change the amount in the Advance field from –$240 to –$60.

EMPLOYEE TIME SUMMARY SHEET #2

(pay period ending June 14, 2003)

	Name of Employee	Week 1 Hours	Week 2 Hours	Regular Hours	Overtime Hours
☑ 243	Aziz Atta	40	40	80	–
☑	Ben Branjil	N/A	40	40	–
☑	Sylvia Mellon	40	40	80	–
☑	Adrian Poppi	40	42	80	2

a. Using Employee Time Summary Sheet #2 and the Employee Information Sheet, complete payroll run for all other hourly employees.
b. Issue cheques #18 through #21.

SESSION DATE – June 21

☐ Cash Receipt #CR-8
Dated June 15/03
From Lisa Haskett, cheque #288 for $12 600 in full payment of account. Reference invoice #CC-125 and deposit #3.

☐ Purchase Invoice #RF-611
Dated June 15/03
From Reliable Food Supplies, $2 000 for regular weekly delivery of basic grocery items for catering services. Terms: n/15.

☐ Purchase Invoice #ESM-2410
Dated June 15/03
From European Smoked Meats, $1 000 for regular weekly delivery of cheeses and deli meats for catering services. Terms: n/15.

☐ Cheque Copy #22
Dated June 16/03
To Reliable Foods Supplies, $2 000 in payment of account. Reference invoice #RF-411.

☐ Cheque Copy #23
Dated June 16/03
To European Smoked Meats, $1 000 in payment of account. Reference invoice #ESM-1712.

☐ Purchase Invoice #DP-2114
Dated June 17/03
From David's Fresh Produce, $500 for regular weekly delivery of fresh fruits and vegetables for catering services. Terms: n/15.

☐ Sales Quote #1004
Dated June 17/03
Delivery date June 24/03
For Pringle Estate (use Full Add), catering for anniversary party will cost $8 000 plus 7% GST and 7% PST. Total cost will be $9 120. Terms: Cash on receipt of invoice.

notes

☐ Pringle Estate (contact Molly Pringle) is located at
1 Pringle Circle
Victoria, BC V9B 6F7
Tel: (250) 891-7492
Fax: (250) 891-7000
Charge PST & GST

- [ ] Cash Receipt #CR-9
Dated June 17/03
From Pringle Estate, cheque #5991 for $2 400 as deposit #6 on anniversary party catering contract. Acceptance of quote #1004.

- [ ] Sales Invoice #CC-126
Dated June 17/03
To Sean O'Casey, $4 000 plus 7% GST and 7% PST for catering services completed. Invoice total $4 560. Sales quote #1003 filled. Terms: Cash on receipt of invoice.

- [ ] Cheque Copy #24
Dated June 18/03
To David's Fresh Produce, $500 in payment of account. Reference invoice #DP-1793.

- [ ] Cash Receipt #CR-10
Dated June 18/03
From Sean O'Casey, cheque #649 for $3 560 in full payment of account. Reference invoice #CC-126 and deposit #5.

notes

- [ ] Pacific College (contact Alana Teutor) is located at 777 Scholars Rd. Victoria, BC V8N 4D1 Tel: (250) 885-8101 Fax: (250) 885-8800 Charge PST & GST

- [ ] Sales Quote #1005
Dated June 18/03
Delivery date June 28/03
For Pacific College (use Full Add), catering for retirement party will cost $8 000 plus 7% GST and 7% PST. Total cost will be $9 120. Terms: Cash on receipt of invoice.

- [ ] Cash Receipt #CR-11
Dated June 18/03
From Pacific College, cheque #4581 for $2 400 as deposit #7 on retirement catering contract and acceptance of sales quote #1005.

- [ ] Sales Invoice #CC-127
Dated June 20/03
To Victoria Ladies Bridge Club, $500 plus 7% GST and 7% PST for weekly contracted catering services. Invoice total $570. Terms: net 30 days.

- [ ] Cash Purchase Invoice #IM-6119
Dated June 20/03
From Island Motors (use Quick Add for new vendor), $400 plus 7% PST and 7% GST for new tires for delivery truck. Invoice total $456. Terms: Cash on receipt of invoice. Issued cheque #25. (Use Truck Expenses account.)

- [ ] Sales Invoice #CC-128
Dated June 21/03
To Gloria Vitale, $12 000 plus 7% GST and 7% PST for catering services completed as described in sales quote #1002. Invoice total $13 680. Terms: Cash on receipt of invoice.

- [ ] Purchase Invoice #CS-10107
Dated June 21/03
From Caterers Suppliers, $200 plus 7% PST and 7% GST for regular weekly delivery of catering supplies. Invoice total $228. Terms: net 30 days.

EMPLOYEE TIME SUMMARY SHEET #3

(pay period ending June 21, 2003)

	Name of Employee	Regular Hours	Overtime Hours
❑	Sera Suflay	40	2
❑	Ben Branjil	40	–

a. Using Employee Time Summary Sheet #3 and the Employee Information Sheet, complete payroll for weekly paid employees in the Paycheques Journal.
b. Recover $60 advance from Sera Suflay.
c. Issue cheques #26 and #27.

SESSION DATE – June 28

❑ Cash Receipt #CR-12
Dated June 22/03
From G. Vitale, cheque #61 for $10 080 in full payment of account. Reference invoice #CC-128 and deposit #4.

❑ Purchase Invoice #RF-724
Dated June 22/03
From Reliable Food Supplies, $2 000 for regular weekly delivery of basic grocery items for catering services. Terms: n/15.

❑ Purchase Invoice #ESM-2719
Dated June 22/03
From European Smoked Meats, $1 000 for regular weekly delivery of cheeses and deli meats for catering services. Terms: n/15.

❑ Cheque Copy #28
Dated June 22/03
To Reliable Food Supplies, $2 000 in payment of account. Reference invoice #RF-507.

❑ Cheque Copy #29
Dated June 22/03
To European Smoked Meats, $1 000 in payment of account. Reference invoice #ESM-2027.

❑ Cheque Copy #30
Dated June 23/03
To David's Fresh Produce, $500 in payment of account. Reference invoice #DP-1993.

notes

❑ Create new Group account for the labour expenses, 5280 Personnel Services Expense.

❑ Cash Purchase Invoice #KPS-4010
Dated June 23/03
From Kwik Personnel Services (use Quick Add for new vendor), $1 500 plus 7% GST (no PST) for labour supplied for catering contracts. Invoice total $1 605. Terms: Payment on completion of contract. Issued cheque #31.

❑ Purchase Invoice #DP-2302
Dated June 24/03
From David's Fresh Produce, $500 for regular weekly delivery of fresh fruits and vegetables for catering services. Terms: n/15.

- [ ] Purchase Invoice #IE-6931
Dated June 24/03
From Ideal Equipment, $2 500 for new appliances plus 7% PST and 7% GST. Invoice total $2 850. Terms: net 30 days.

- [ ] Sales Invoice #CC-129
Dated June 24/03
To Pringle Estate, $8 000 plus 7% GST and 7% PST for anniversary catering contract according to sales quote #1004 completed. Invoice total $9 120. Terms: Cash on receipt of invoice.

- [ ] Cash Purchase Invoice #HS-88620
Dated June 25/03
From House of Spirits, $1 200 for wine and liquor plus $84 GST. Invoice total $1 284. Terms: Cash. Issued cheque #32.

- [ ] Cash Receipt #CR-13
Dated June 27/03
From Pringle Estate, cheque #6113 for $6 720 in full payment of account. Reference invoice #CC-129 & deposit #6.

- [ ] Sales Invoice #CC-130
Dated June 27/03
To Victoria Ladies Bridge Club, $500 plus 7% GST and 7% PST for weekly contracted catering services. Invoice total $570. Terms: net 30 days.

notes

- [ ] Vancouver Island Cadets (contact Gunnel Cannon) are located at
48 Archer St.
Victoria, BC V8R 5B8
Tel: (250) 881-7014
Fax: (250) 881-6215
Charge PST & GST

- [ ] Sales Quote #1006
Dated June 27/03
Delivery date July 5/03
For Vancouver Island Cadets (use Full Add), catering for graduation ceremony will cost $10 000 plus 7% GST and 7% PST. Total cost will be $11 400. Terms: Cash on receipt of invoice.

- [ ] Cash Receipt #CR-14
Dated June 27/03
From Vancouver Island Cadets, cheque #721 for $3 000 as deposit #8 for graduation ceremony catering contract and acceptance of sales quote #1006.

- [ ] Sales Invoice #CC-131
Dated June 28/03
To Pacific College, $8 000 plus 7% GST and 7% PST for retirement catering contract as outlined in quote #1005 completed. Invoice total $9 120. Terms: Cash on receipt of invoice.

- [ ] Purchase Invoice #CS-11191
Dated June 28/03
From Caterers Suppliers, $200 plus 7% PST and 7% GST for regular weekly delivery of catering supplies. Invoice total $228. Terms: net 30 days.

notes

Use the Paycheques Journal to enter Suflay's pay so you can recover the advance.

- [ ] Memo #3
Dated June 28/03
From Manager: Prepare paycheque for Sera Suflay (cheque #33) for 40 hours of regular pay and 2 hours of overtime. Recover $60 of the advance paid on June 7.

EMPLOYEE TIME SUMMARY SHEET #4

(pay period ending June 28, 2003)

	Name of Employee	Week 3 Hours	Week 4 Hours	Regular Hours	Overtime Hours
❑	Aziz Atta	40	40	80	–
❑	Ben Branjil	N/A	40	40	–
❑	Sylvia Mellon	40	42	80	2
❑	Adrian Poppi	42	40	80	2

a. Using Employee Time Summary Sheet #4 and the Employee Information Sheet, complete payroll run for all other hourly employees.
b. Issue cheques #34 through #37.

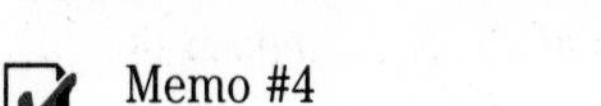

SESSION DATE – June 30

> **notes**
> Keystrokes for all entries resulting from the To-Do Lists begin on page 245.

☑ Memo #4
Dated June 29/03
245
From Owner: Check all To-Do Lists. Complete the following entries that are due:

☑ Sales Due: Cash Receipt #CR-15
From Pacific College, cheque #4688 for $6 720 in full payment of account. Reference invoice #CC-131 & deposit #7.

☑ Purchase Due: Cheque Copy #38
To Coastal Fish Wholesalers, $1 500 to settle account. Reference invoices #CF-976 & CF-1211.

☑ Purchase Due: Cheque Copy #39
To Reliable Food Supplies, $2 000 in payment of account. Reference invoice #RF-611.

☑ Purchase Due: Cheque Copy #40
To European Smoked Meats, $1 000 in payment of account. Reference invoice #ESM-2410.

☑ Recurring Purchase: Invoice #RF-863
From Reliable Foods, $2 000 for regular weekly delivery of basic grocery items for catering services. Terms: n/15.

☑ Recurring Purchase: Invoice #ESM-3162
From European Smoked Meats, $1 000 for regular weekly delivery of cheeses and deli meats for catering services. Terms: n/15.

☑ Memo #5
Date June 30/03
249
From Owner: Branjil is leaving Carnival Catering for employment elsewhere. He has worked 8 hours since his last paycheque. Issue cheque #41 as Branjil's final paycheque including all retained vacation pay.

notes

- Create two new Group accounts for the bank memo transaction:
  5140 Loan Interest
  5160 Mortgage Interest

- [ ] Bank Debit Memo PT-555111
  Dated June 30/03
  From Pacific Trust: authorized withdrawals
  $40 for monthly bank service charges
  $850 monthly loan payment, including $210 interest and $640 principal
  $2 250 monthly mortgage payment, including $2 025 interest and $225 principal

- [ ] Memo #6
  Dated June 30/03
  From Owner: Complete a payroll run to pay the owner and salaried employees, Susie Sardinha, Louie Perch and Peter Terkee. Issue cheques #42 to #44. Perch's commission for June is $790 and Terkee's is $395.

- [ ] Memo #7
  Dated June 30/03
  From Owner: Adjust the inventory and supplies accounts for amounts used in catering contracts for the month of June as follows:
  Charge $15 800 from Food Inventory to Food Used for Catering account.
  Charge $4 200 from Liquor & Wine Inventory to Liquor Used for Catering.
  Charge $890 from Catering Supplies to Catering Supplies Used.

KEYSTROKES

Entering Payroll Transactions

Payroll transactions are entered in the Payroll Journal indicated by the pointer on the Paycheques icon on the following screen:

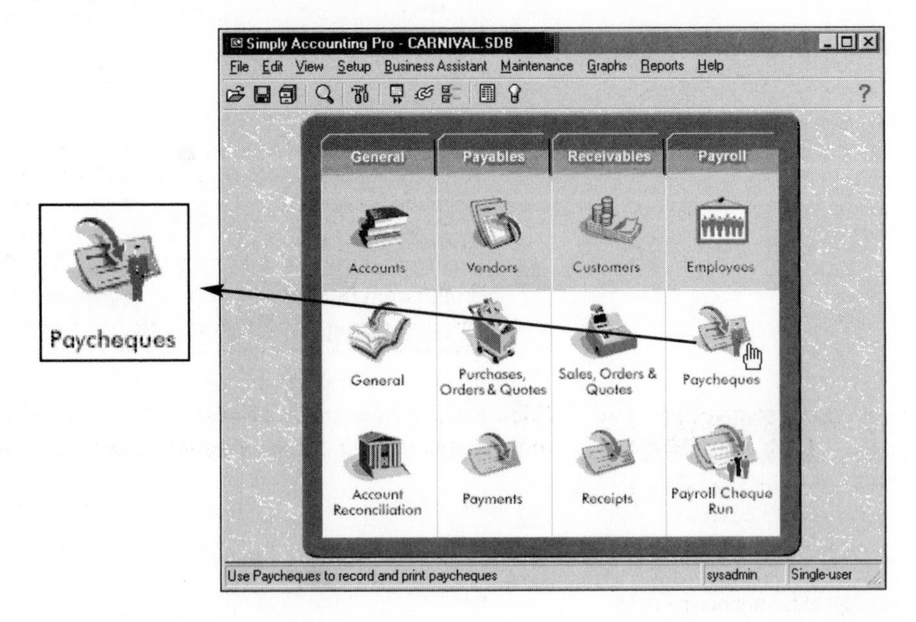

Click the **Paycheques icon** to open and display the Payroll Journal input form:

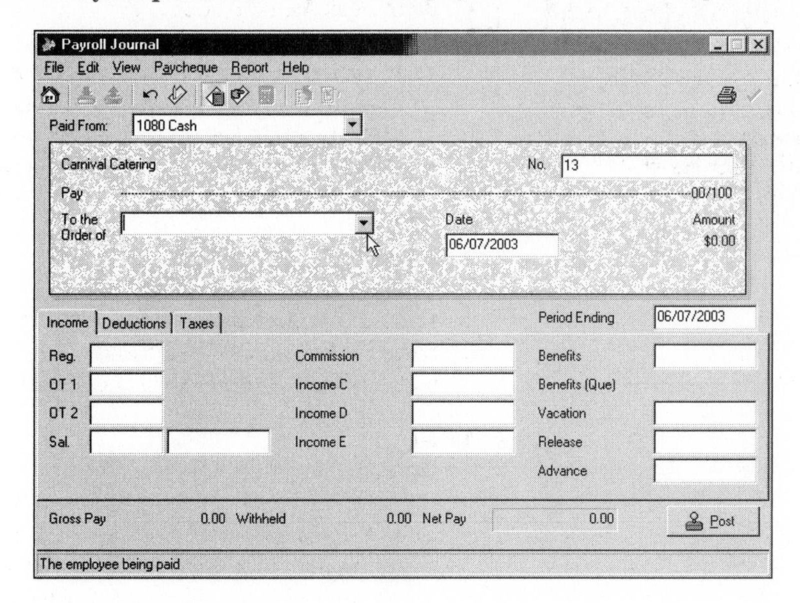

The cursor is in the Employee (To the Order of) field.

Click the **To the Order of (Employee) field arrow** to see the list of employees as follows:

notes

Four buttons on the tool bar relate specifically to the Payroll Journal — Calculate taxes automatically, Enter taxes manually, Recalculate taxes and, for Pro Version 8.5 only, Reset payroll information. The remaining buttons — Home window, Store, Recall, Undo, Adjust cheque, Refresh lists (Pro Version 8.5 only), Print and Allocate — are the same as those found in other journals.

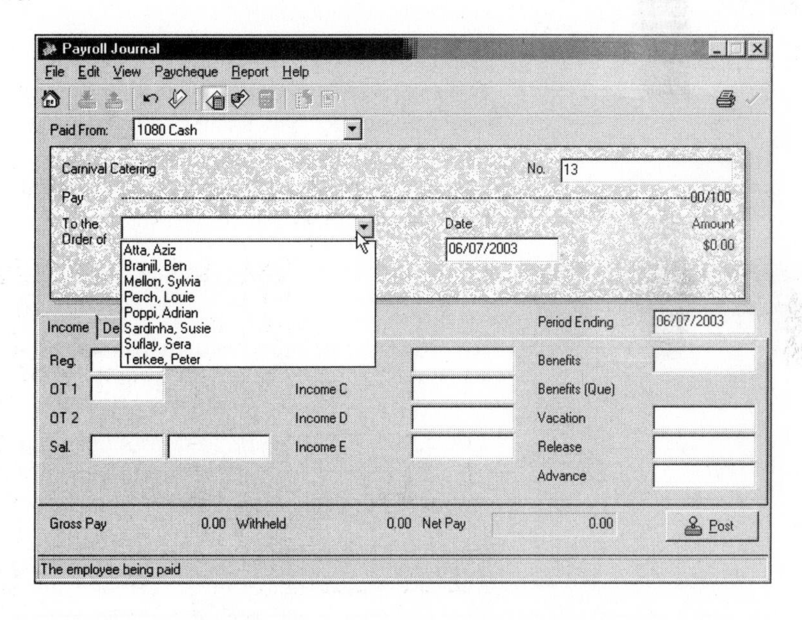

Click **Suflay, Sera** to select this employee and add her name to the input form. If you have not chosen correctly, return to the employee list and select again.

notes

To add new employees from the Payroll Journal, type the new name in the Name field and press *tab*. There is no Quick Add option for employees because complete details are required for income tax purposes.

Press tab to add the payroll details for the selected employee:

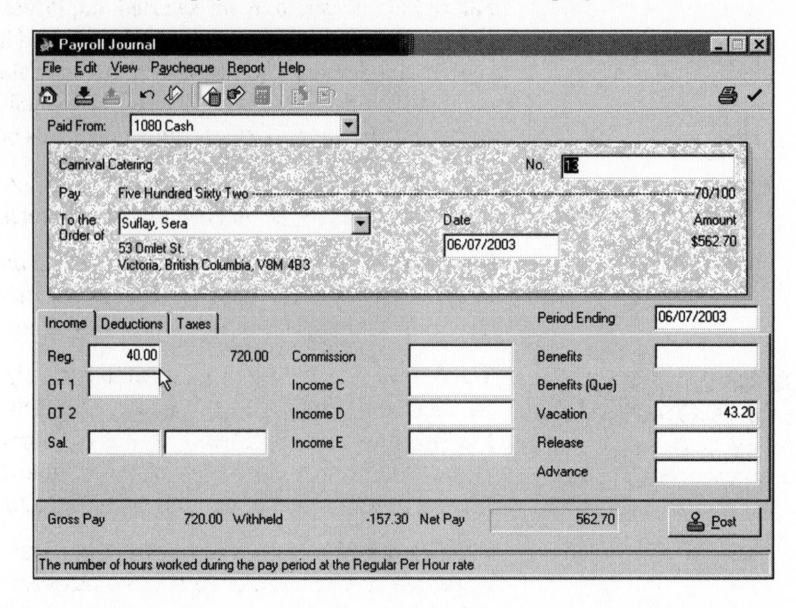

Most of the payroll form is completed automatically based on the ledger details for the employee. The cursor is now in the Cheque (No.) field. The employee's address has been added. The cheque number, 13, should be correct because we have set up the number to advance automatically. If the number is incorrect, you can change it.

There are two date fields. In the Date field, you should enter the date of payment. As usual, the session date, June 7, has been entered by default. Since the session date, June 7, is correct, you should accept this date. The Period Ending field refers to the last day of the pay period for the employee. It may be later or earlier than the cheque date. In this case, the session date is also the same as the pay period ending date, so you can accept the default date again.

notes

For salaried employees, you will skip the Regular and Overtime fields. The Salary amount is entered automatically.

The Regular hours (Reg.) field contains the number of regular hours an employee has worked for the regular pay rate during the pay period. You can edit this entry.

The Gross Pay amount is calculated and added to the bottom portion of the journal window. Overtime fields (O/T 1 and O/T 2) contain the number of overtime hours an employee has worked during the pay period. There are two overtime fields in case there are different overtime rates. For example, pay for evening overtime work may be less than the pay for Sundays or holidays. The second overtime rate is not set up, so the field is not available.

Click the **Taxes tab** to see that the tax amounts have been calculated automatically. You will see that the tax fields are not available for editing because we have chosen to let the program complete the tax calculations. If you need to edit the tax amounts, you can choose to calculate taxes manually.

Click the **Income tab** to continue with the payroll entry.

Click the **OT 1 field** to continue.

Type 2

Press tab

notes

Salaried employees receive their regular pay during their vacations instead of receiving vacation pay.

Notice that the Gross Pay and vacation pay are updated to include the additional pay. Notice, too, that the upper cheque portion of your input form window is updated continually as you add information. To see that tax amounts have also changed, click the Taxes tab. Click the Income tab again to continue with the payroll entry.

The Salary field and the next several fields apply to different types of income. The Salary field is used only for salaried employees. The Commission field is used for employees who earn a commission to be paid in this pay period. For employees who receive commissions, you will have to calculate manually the amount of the commission and enter it in this field. The additional income fields may be renamed and used for other special payments such as bonuses.

Sera Suflay is not a salaried employee and does not receive commissions, bonuses or other forms of pay, so you can skip these fields.

The Benefits field is used to enter the total amount of taxable benefits a business offers to its employees, such as health insurance or dental plans. Carnival Catering does not offer any employee benefits, so ignore this field.

notes

Vacation pay is released when employee takes a vacation or leaves the business.

The Simply Accounting program automatically calculates an amount in the Vacation pay field and displays it as a default. This default amount is calculated at the vacation pay rate of 6 percent entered for this employee and will be retained by the business (*Vacation Payable* account) until the employee takes a vacation or leaves the employ of the business. (See the Employee Information Sheet.) You should accept the default.

The Release field is used to release the accumulated vacation pay retained for an employee. The amount to be released appears as a default when you turn off the option to retain vacation in the employee ledger. (See page 249.)

Click the **Advance field** to move the cursor.

The Advance field is used to enter an amount advanced to an employee in addition to his or her normal pay from wages or salary. Advances are approved by management for emergencies and other personal reasons. An advance offered to an employee is shown as a positive amount. An advance recovered on a regular basis is indicated as a negative amount in this same field. An advance of $240 for Sera Suflay has been approved.

notes

If the amount of a deduction is incorrect, and it is not a one-time change, you can edit the employee record in the Payroll Ledger. The next time you open the payroll journal for the employee, the edited amount will be entered.

Type `240`

Press tab

The cheque portion of the journal is updated again. Advances do not affect the tax amounts or vacation pay.

The journal advances to the Deductions tab screen because Advance was the last field on the Income tab screen.

Notice that the medical deduction is entered automatically because the amounts were entered as part of the setup. If necessary, the amount can be edited.

notes

If you are using a different version of the Simply Accounting program, your tax amounts and amount withheld may be different from those shown because different tax tables are used. Your Gross Pay and Vacation amounts should always be the same as shown here.

version 8

Click the **Income tab** again. Your complete payroll form should look like the one shown below:

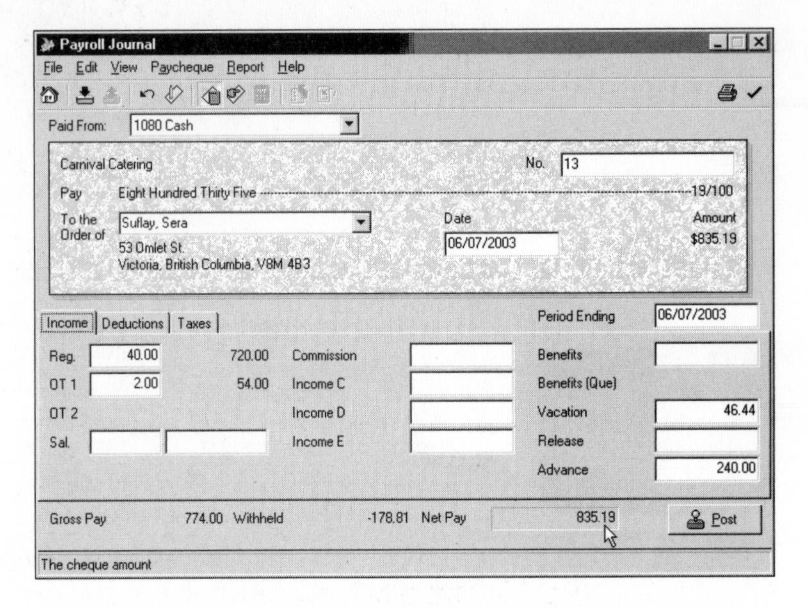

Reviewing the Payroll Journal Transaction

When you have entered all the information, you should review the completed transaction before posting.

Choose the **Report menu** and **click Display Payroll Journal Entry**. The transaction you have just completed appears as follows:

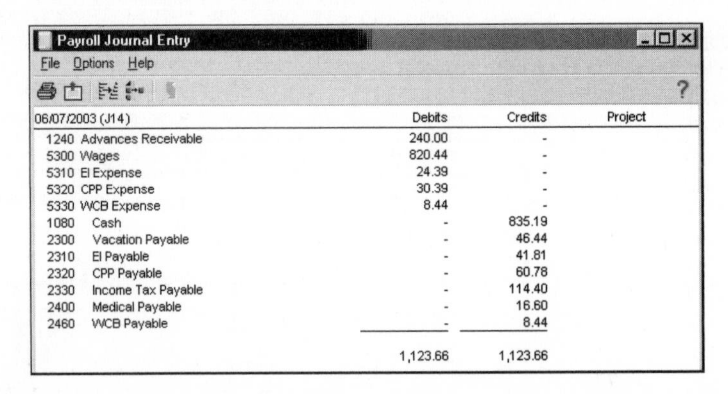

Payroll Journal Entry

06/07/2003 (J14)	Debits	Credits	Project
1240 Advances Receivable	240.00	-	
5300 Wages	820.44	-	
5310 EI Expense	24.39	-	
5320 CPP Expense	30.39	-	
5330 WCB Expense	8.44	-	
1080 Cash	-	835.19	
2300 Vacation Payable	-	46.44	
2310 EI Payable	-	41.81	
2320 CPP Payable	-	60.78	
2330 Income Tax Payable	-	114.40	
2400 Medical Payable	-	16.60	
2460 WCB Payable	-	8.44	
	1,123.66	1,123.66	

notes

Payroll expense accounts reflect the employer's share of payroll tax obligations. The liabilities reflect the amounts that the owner must remit to the appropriate agencies and include both the employer's share of these tax liabilities and the employee's share (deductions withheld). For example, CPP contributions by the employee are matched by the employer. Therefore, the CPP Expense (employer's share) is one-half of the CPP Payable amount (employee and employer's share). WCB is paid entirely by the employer (the expense amount is the same as the liability amount) while Medical is paid entirely by the employee so there is no expense amount. For EI, the employer's share is 1.4 times the employee's share. Vacation pay is part of the Wages expense.

Notice that all the relevant wage expense accounts have been debited. In addition, all the wage-related liability accounts and the *Cash* account have been updated automatically because the Payroll Ledger is linked to the General Ledger. The accounts shown in the journal entry have all been defined as linked accounts for the Payroll Ledger so you do not enter any account numbers directly.

Simply Accounting uses the Canada Customs and Revenue Agency (CCRA, formerly named Revenue Canada) tax formulas to calculate the deduction amounts for CPP, EI and income tax. These formulas are updated every six months. The remaining deductions are determined from Employee Ledger entries, if different rates apply to different employees (WCB, vacation pay rate and Medical), or from Payroll Ledger settings if the same rate applies to all employees (EI factor of 1.4).

Close the display to return to the Payroll Journal input screen.

CORRECTING THE PAYROLL JOURNAL ENTRY BEFORE POSTING

Move the cursor to the field that contains the error. **Press** tab to move forward through the fields or **press** shift and tab together to move back to a previous field. This will highlight the field information so that you can change it. **Type** the correct information and **press** tab to enter the change.

You can also use the mouse to point to a field and drag through the incorrect information to highlight it. **Type** the correct information. **Press** tab to save the corrections.

You can discard the entry by **clicking** [X] or [↶] or return to the employee list by **clicking** a different employee name. **Click** the name of the correct employee and **press** tab. When prompted, confirm that you want to discard the incorrect entry. **Click Yes**, and start again from the beginning.

Payroll Journal entries may be stored as recurring entries before posting. Follow the same steps as you would for recurring sales or purchases.

Posting

When all the information in your journal entry is correct,

Click Post [Post] to save your work.

The following caution is displayed when the dates of the transaction are different from the dates of the tax tables in your Simply Accounting program:

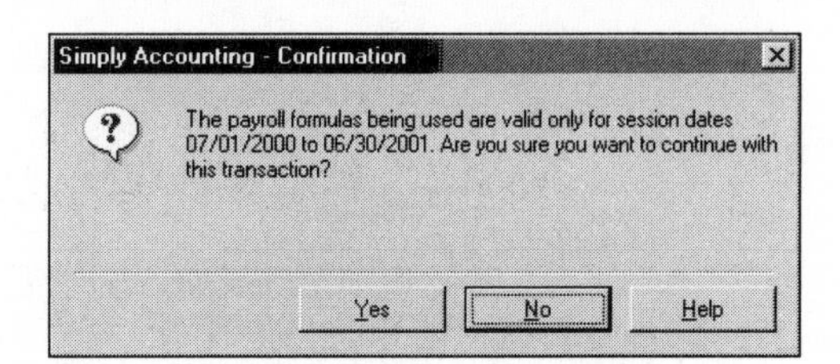

Click Yes, unless you have made a mistake. A new blank Payroll Journal input screen appears for you to enter the next payroll transaction.

Complete the payroll transaction for Branjil.

To complete transactions involving other ledgers, you must **close** the Payroll Journal input form window to return to the Home window.

Adjusting Payroll Entries

On June 8, Sera Suflay returned with her paycheque to ask for a correction because she worked four hours of overtime instead of the two she was paid for. Simply Accounting does not require reversing and correcting entries for situations like these. Instead you can complete a paycheque adjustment in the Payroll Journal, just as you make adjustments in the General, Purchases and Sales journals.

Click the **Paycheques icon** [Paycheques] to open the Payroll Journal.

Click the **Adjust Cheque button** on the Payroll Journal tool bar or choose the Paycheque menu and click Adjust Cheque to access the list of payroll entries posted:

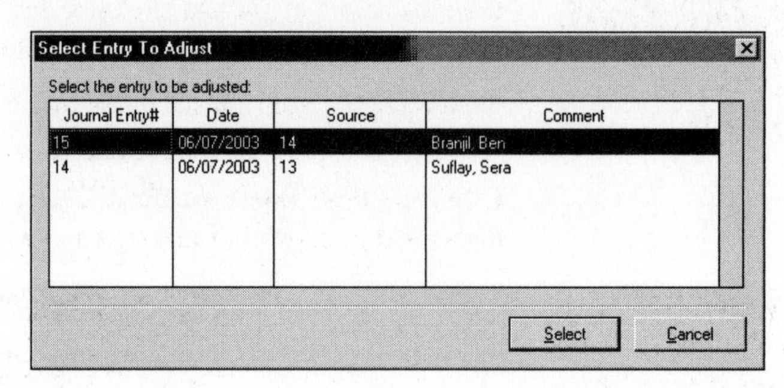

Click JE #14 Suflay, Sera to select the Payroll Journal entry for Suflay.

Click Select to display the entry that was posted. First, Simply Accounting offers the following reminder about recalculating taxes for an adjustment:

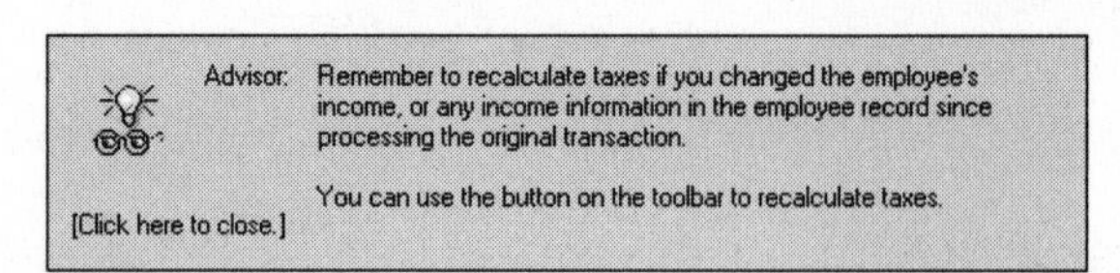

Advisor: Remember to recalculate taxes if you changed the employee's income, or any income information in the employee record since processing the original transaction.
You can use the button on the toolbar to recalculate taxes.
[Click here to close.]

The program is advising you that the tax recalculation will not be automatic if you change an amount on the payroll entry.

Click the **advisor icon** to close the warning and display the payroll journal entry:

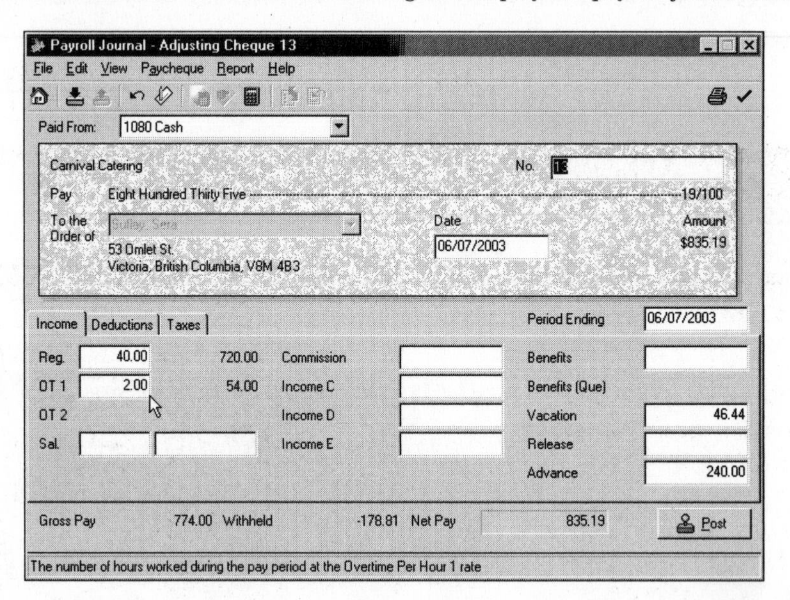

notes

If you want, you may change the date to June 8, the date for the new cheque. The reversing entry will retain the original posting date.

This is a duplicate of the payroll entry. All the fields can be edited with the exception of the employee name. The cheque number is highlighted because normally you would prepare a new cheque. However, Suflay has not cashed the cheque so we could use the same number. We need to change the number of overtime hours.

Double click the **OT 1 field** (Overtime hours) to highlight the current entry.

Type 4

Press *tab* to enter the change and update the gross pay.

The Vacation pay and Withheld amounts have not been updated for the new amount of gross pay. Compare the amounts with those in the screen display on page 240.

> **notes**
>
> Return to the Income tab screen to see that the Vacation amount has increased from $46.44 to $49.68.

Click the **Taxes tab**. The deduction amounts have not changed yet.

Click the **Recalculate taxes button** on the Payroll Journal tool bar or choose the Paycheque menu and click Recalculate Taxes. All the deduction amounts are updated for the additional wages for the extra overtime hours worked.

Review the Payroll Journal entry, and close the display when you have finished. Make corrections if necessary.

Click the **Post button** [Post] to save the adjustment. Simply Accounting displays the following warning when you do not change the cheque number:

> **version 8**
>
> Read the question in the warning carefully. The question in Version 8 is different and requires a different response. Click Yes to continue.

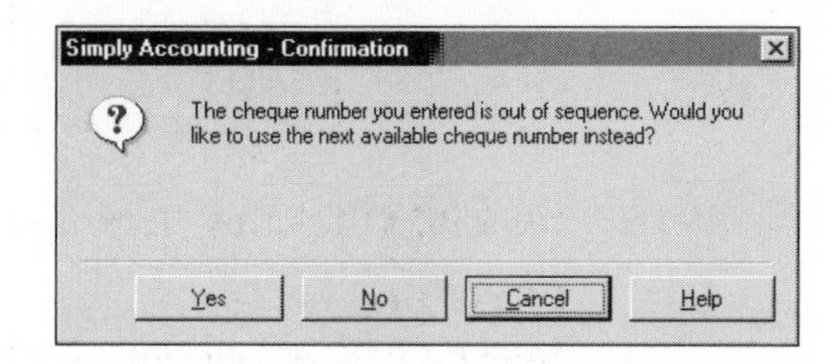

If you want to change the cheque number, click Yes, make the change, then post. If you want to proceed with the duplicate cheque number, because Suflay returned the original,

Click No to display the Payroll Journal input screen.

Close the Payroll Journal to return to the Home window.

When you display the Payroll Journal, you will see three journal entries for Suflay: the original entry, the reversing adjusting entry and the final correct entry.

> **notes**
>
> All three journal entries are posted with the original session date, unless you changed the date.

Completing a Payroll Cheque Run

If several employees are paid at the same time, you can complete a payroll cheque run to prepare all the cheques and journal entries in a single transaction from the Payroll Cheque Run Journal shown with the arrow pointer below:

> **notes**
>
> - If the pay run is different from the standard in any way (e.g., there are advances paid or recovered, or the deduction amounts have changed) you must complete a regular entry in the Paycheques Journal, as we did to issue and recover the advance from Suflay.
> - You cannot adjust paycheques from the Payroll Run Journal, although paycheques prepared here can be adjusted in the Paycheques Journal.

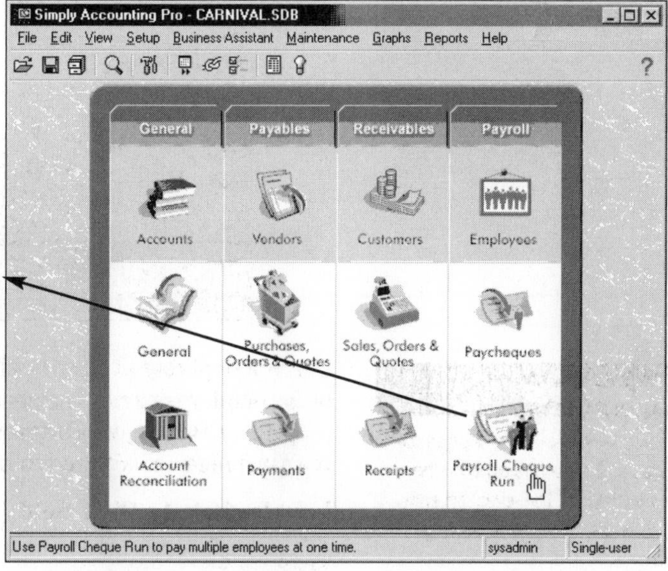

version 8

Click the **Payroll Cheque Run icon** to open the Payroll Run Journal:

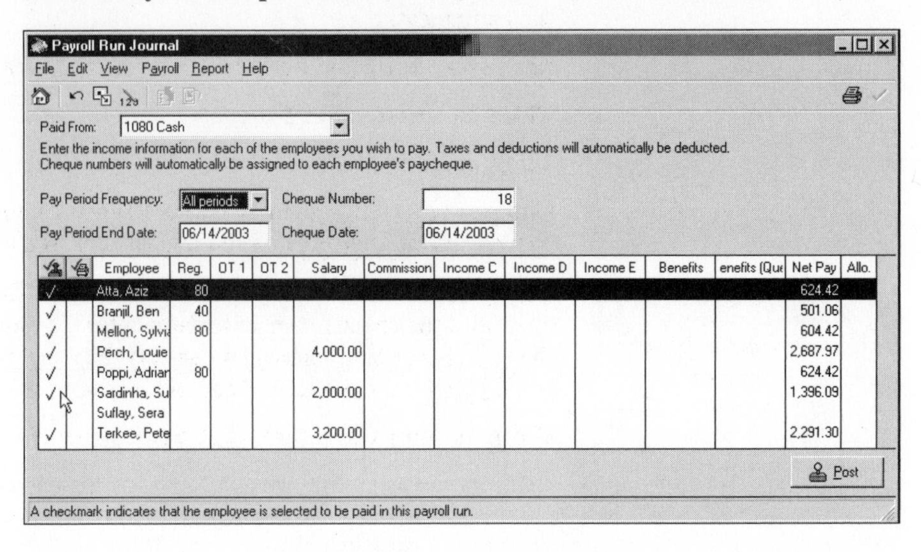

notes

The salaried employees on monthly pay cycles are selected because no paycheque has yet been issued for them. You can edit the number of hours worked or the salary amounts.

From this screen, you can pay all employees with a single transaction. Employees are listed in alphabetic order and checkmarks indicate that they will be paid in this payroll run. For hourly paid employees, you need to enter only the number of overtime hours worked. For salaried employees, the regular salary amount is entered by default, so you need to enter only additional sources of pay. Initially, the program selects all employees for inclusion if their pay cycle has ended. Suflay has already been paid so there is no ✓ beside her name. We want to pay only the four remaining hourly employees, that is, we will remove the salaried employees from the payroll run.

You can select a single pay period frequency for the cheque run from the Pay Period Frequency list or you can choose All periods, the default, to include more than one period. Since Branjil is paid weekly and the others are paid bi-weekly, we must include all periods. The cheque date and initial cheque number can also be edited if necessary.

Click the ✔ beside Perch, Louie to deselect the employee and remove the ✓.

Now deselect Sardinha and Terkee to remove their ✓.

Click the **OT 1 hours column beside Poppi**.

Type 2

Press *tab*

Warning!

The Cheque Date for the Payroll Run must be the same as the session date. If it is not, the transaction will be discarded and the journal will be opened again with the session date in the Cheque Date field.

The completed Payroll Run Journal form should look like the one shown here:

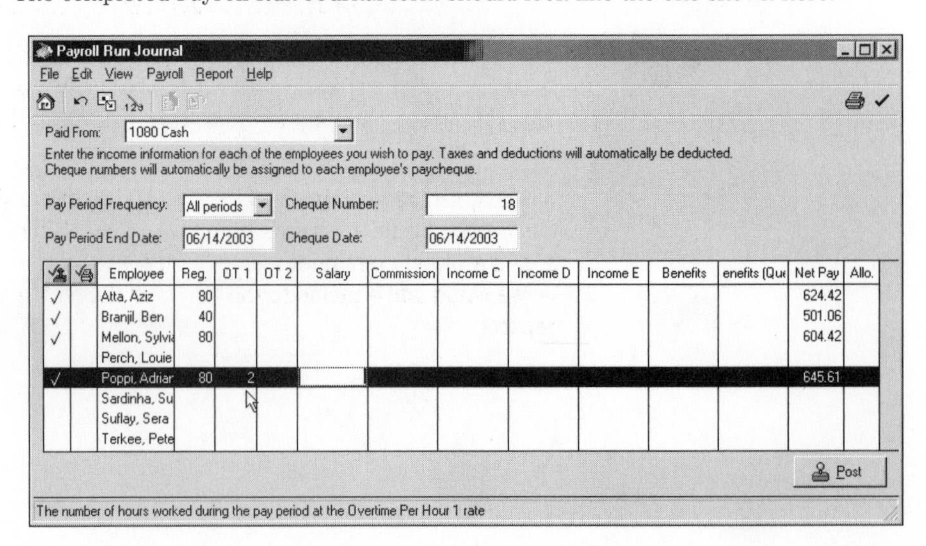

Choose the **Report menu** and **click Display Payroll Run Journal Entry** to review the journal entry.

Notice that there are four journal entries, one for each employee who was paid.

Close the display when finished.

Turn on your printer.

Choose the **Report menu** and **click Payroll Cheque Run Summary** to provide a printed record of the payroll run transactions. You cannot display this summary.

Click Post [Post] to save the transaction. The Payroll Run Journal remains open with the cheque number updated after the four cheques that were prepared in the payroll run. The Journal now selects the remaining three unpaid salaried employees for the next run. They will be paid at the end of the month.

Close the journal to return to the Home window.

Enter the remaining source documents up to Memo #4 for June 29.

Working from To-Do Lists

notes

You can show To-Do Lists automatically each time you advance the session date, each time you start the program or both. Choose the View menu, then choose User Preferences and To-Do Lists. Click the choice At Startup to add the checkmark. Repeat the procedure for After Changing Session Date to add a checkmark for this option too. Menu and tool bar access to the lists are always available from the Home window.

Simply Accounting helps a business to monitor its performance and cash flow through several of the reports that you have seen so far. It also keeps track of recurring transactions, and payments and receipts due in the form of To-Do Lists. These lists offer an additional method of internal control.

You must be in the Home window to access the To-Do Lists.

Click the **To-Do Lists button** or **choose** the **Business Assistant menu** and **click To-Do Lists** to see the following screen:

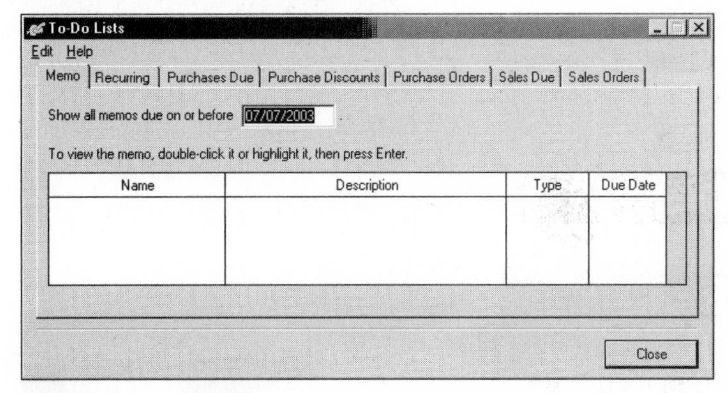

By default, Simply Accounting chooses a date that is one week past the current session date for its To-Do Lists. The date can be edited like any other date field by typing in a new date and pressing tab. The list will be updated to reflect the change in date.

Since there are no memos on file, the list is empty. Memos can be added to employee, customer or vendor records from the memo tab screens. For example, we could have added a weekly reminder memo to Suflay's record about recovering the advance paid, or we could add a memo to the Receiver General ledger with due dates for GST reports.

Click the **Sales Due tab** to see a list of Sales Invoices due within the next week:

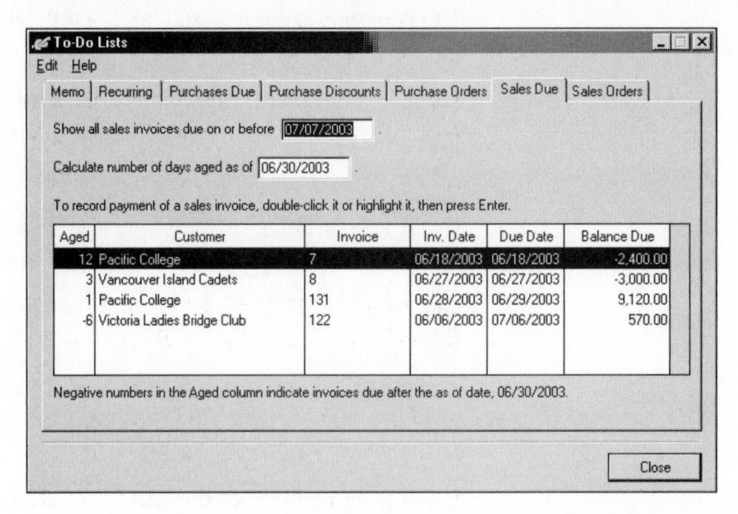

The columns of this list repeat journal information, including the customer, invoice number, invoice date and balance due. The due date is calculated from the posting date and the payment terms on the invoice. The Aged column shows the number of days remaining until the invoice is due, using the session date as the base for counting. Positive numbers show overdue invoices and negative numbers indicate the invoice is not yet due. Thus, on June 30, the invoice for Pacific College is overdue by one day and payment from Victoria Ladies Bridge Club is due in six days. The two customer deposits show as overdue. Because no terms are attached to these entries, they are interpreted by the program as net 0 days. The negative balance due indicates the customer's credit balance.

If you want to see invoices due in the next month, you can change the date in the upper date field — Show all sales invoices due on or before — to 07/30/2003. You can also change the base date for aging — the Calculate number of days aged as of field — to the current calendar date if that is different from the session date.

Invoices displayed on the Sales Due list can be matched against receipts on hand and paid directly from the To-Do Lists window. They can also be used to determine whether customers need to be reminded of outstanding debts. The payment from Pacific College is the next source document.

notes

To open the journal, you can double click any part of the line for the entry you want or click the line and press *enter*.

Double click the **first Pacific College journal line (Invoice/deposit #7)** to open the Receipts Journal with the invoices for the selected customer displayed:

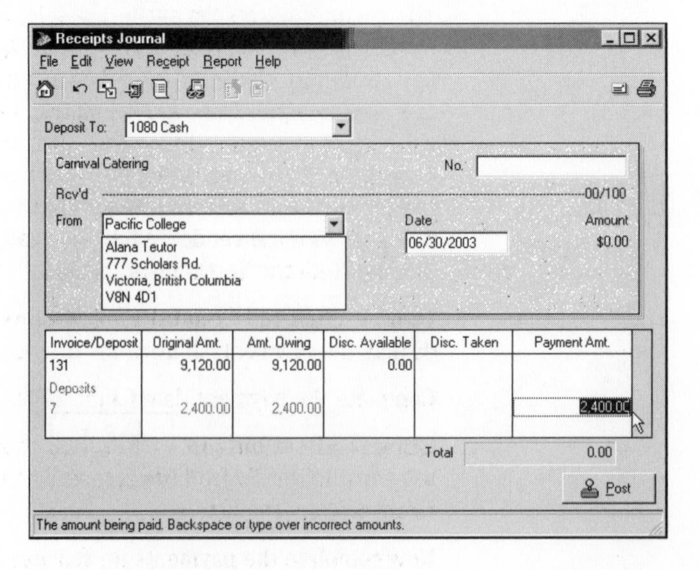

The deposit is selected for payment because we opened the journal from that entry. The payment amount is $6 720, the full balance, so we must mark both the invoice and the deposit as paid.

Click the **Payment Amt. field for invoice #131** and press tab. This will include both the invoice and the deposit in the payment.

Add the customer's cheque number (4688). Change the date of the cheque to June 29.

Display the journal entry to review your work and check that both the invoice and deposit are included. **Close** the display and make corrections if necessary.

Click Post Post to record the transaction. **Close** the Receipts journal to return to the To-Do Lists window. Both entries for Pacific College are removed from the list.

The next source documents describe cheques issued in payment for outstanding invoices from vendors. To be certain that all outstanding invoices are paid in a timely fashion, we can use the To-Do Lists.

Click the **Purchases Due tab** to see payments that are due within one week of the session date:

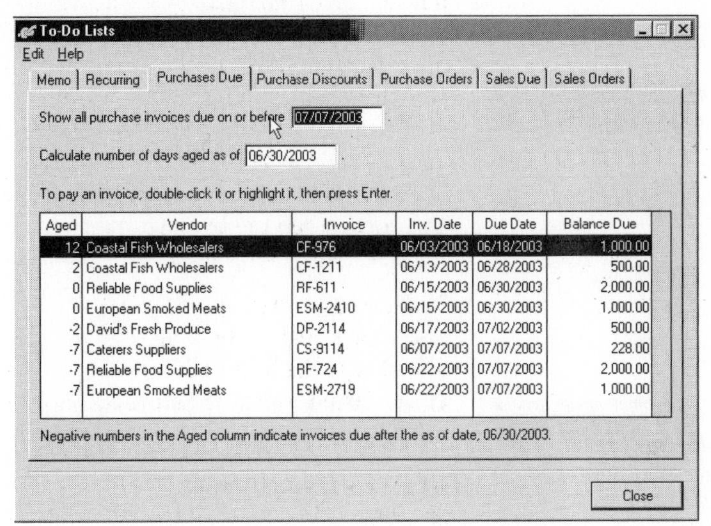

This list is the vendor equivalent of the Sales Due list. Again, if you want, you can change the date to display, for example, all invoices that should be paid within the next month. You might use this list to plan a payment schedule.

The columns of this list again repeat journal information, using the posting date and the payment terms on the invoice. The Aged column is calculated as the number of days from the current session date. Positive numbers in the Aged column indicate overdue accounts and negative numbers indicate that payment is due after the session date. You can see that the two invoices from Coastal Fish Wholesalers are overdue. Two other invoices are due now. Although there is no interest penalty for late payments, these invoices should be paid immediately to maintain good business relations with the vendor. Again, you can access the Payments Journal for a vendor directly from the To-Do Lists screen.

Double click the **Coastal Fish Wholesalers** entry that is selected or highlighted to display the Payments Journal for this vendor.

Complete the payment dated June 29 for $1 500 to cover both outstanding invoices.

Click the **Post button** Post to save the entry. **Close** the Payments Journal to return to the To-Do Lists screen. The Coastal Fish Wholesalers entries have been removed from the list.

Now complete the payments for Reliable Food Supplies and European Smoked Meats.

Close the Payments Journal to return to the To-Do Lists window. The two invoices just paid are removed from the list.

Click the **Recurring tab** to see the next list of transactions that we can process directly from To-Do Lists:

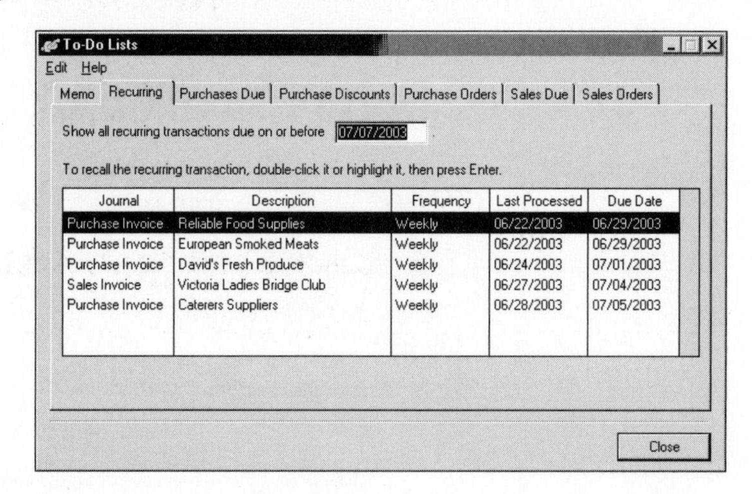

All recurring entries due on or before the date shown are listed with the original journal used for the entry, the entry name and its recurring frequency. The most recent posting date and the due date are also included. The entries are listed according to the due date, with the earliest date at the top of the list.

notes

An advantage to using To-Do lists is that the entries for all journals are listed. You can open a journal and recall a stored transaction in a single step.

You can see that two entries — the purchases from Reliable Food Supplies and European Smoked Meats — are due today, June 29. As indicated by the instructions on the screen above the list, you can open the journal for these entries directly from the To-Do List. Since these are the next two purchases in our source documents, we will complete the journal entries from the To-Do Lists screen.

notes

You can double click any part of the line for the entry you want to recall to open the journal.

Double click the **Reliable Food Supplies** entry that is selected or highlighted to display the Purchases Journal entry for this item.

Click the **Invoice field**.

Type `RF-863` (to enter the new invoice number from the source document to complete the journal entry)

Click the **Post button** [Post] to save the entry. **Close** the Purchases Journal to return to the To-Do Lists screen. You can now enter the purchase from European Smoked Meats.

Double click the **European Smoked Meats** entry. Complete this invoice by typing the new invoice number, ESM-3162. Post the entry and close the journal to return to the To-Do Lists screen. The remaining list items are not due before the end of the month, so we can proceed to the next part of the To-Do Lists.

Three more lists are available, **Purchase Discounts**, **Purchase Orders** and **Sales Orders**. To see outstanding items, click the corresponding tab. The Purchase Discounts list includes invoices that are eligible for discounts if paid on time. Purchase and Sales Orders lists show unfilled orders due within the next week. Again, the lists are aged and you can show more items by extending the dates. You can access the journal windows for items on these lists just as you did for purchases and sales due.

Currently none of Carnival Catering's vendors offers discounts for early payment, and there are no orders outstanding so these lists are blank. A business might use the Purchase Discounts list to plan payment schedules. For example, a business could choose to pass up a discount for a small amount to take advantage of larger discounts if there were insufficient cash for both payments.

Click [X] to return to the Home window.

Releasing Vacation Pay

When Branjil leaves Carnival Catering at the end of the month, he should receive his final paycheque plus the vacation pay that has been retained. Before releasing the vacation pay, you must change the setting in the employee ledger.

Click the **Employees icon** to open the Employees window:

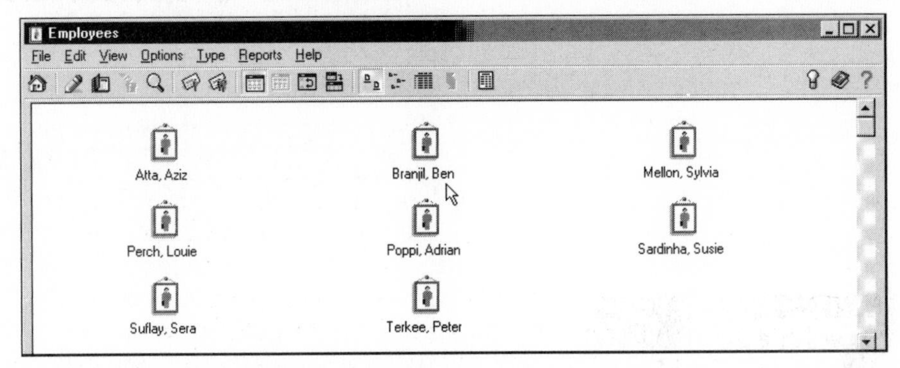

Double click the **icon for Ben Branjil** to open his ledger record:

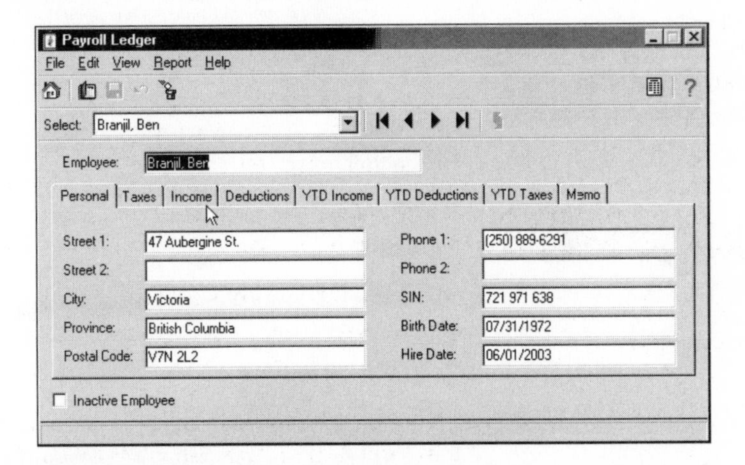

Click the **Income tab** to access the vacation pay settings:

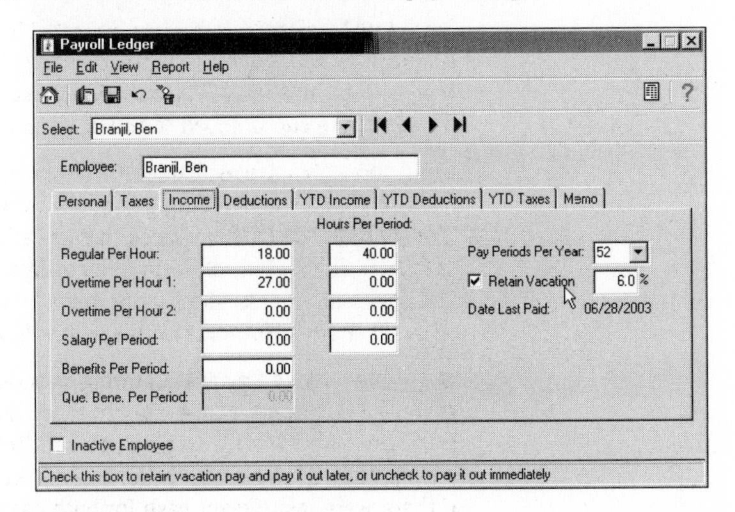

Click Retain Vacation to remove the checkmark.

Close the ledger window to return to the Employees window. Branjil's icon should still be selected.

notes

If Branjil's icon is not selected when you open the journal, no employee will be selected. Choose Branjil from the employee list and press tab to continue.

Click the **Payroll Journal icon** in the ledger window or choose the Type menu and select Payroll Journal to access the Payroll Journal with Branjil already selected as the employee:

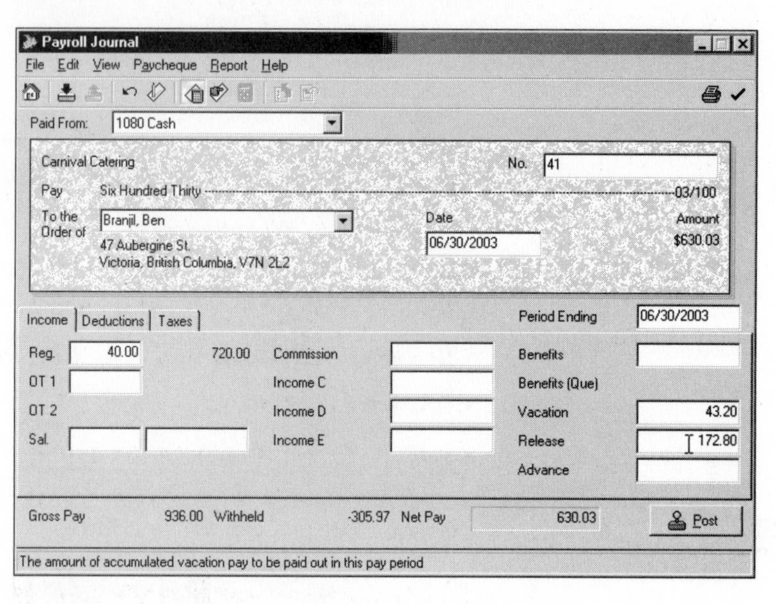

version 8

Notice that the accumulated vacation pay appears in the Release box. We need to change the number of hours worked.

Click 40.00 in the Reg. field.

Type 8

Press tab to update the amounts and complete the entry as shown:

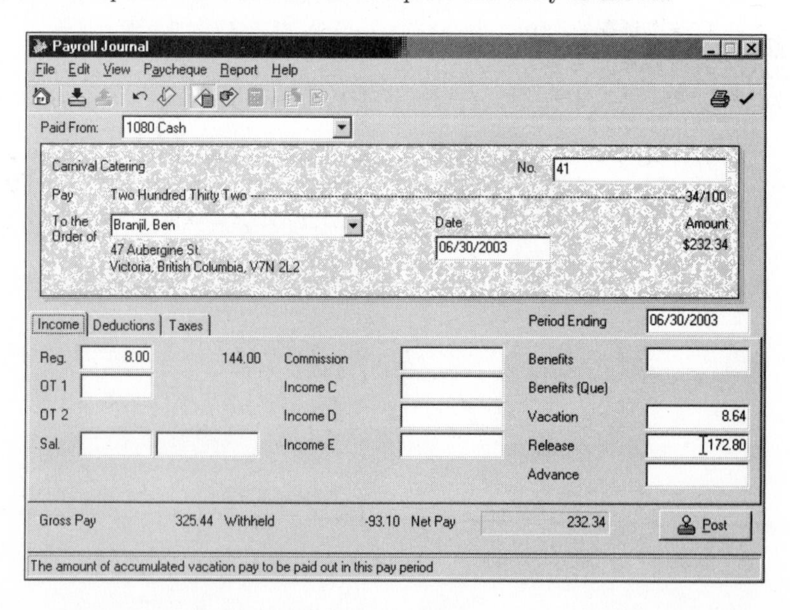

You should review the journal entry before posting.

Choose the **Report menu** and **click Display Payroll Journal Entry** to see the transaction:

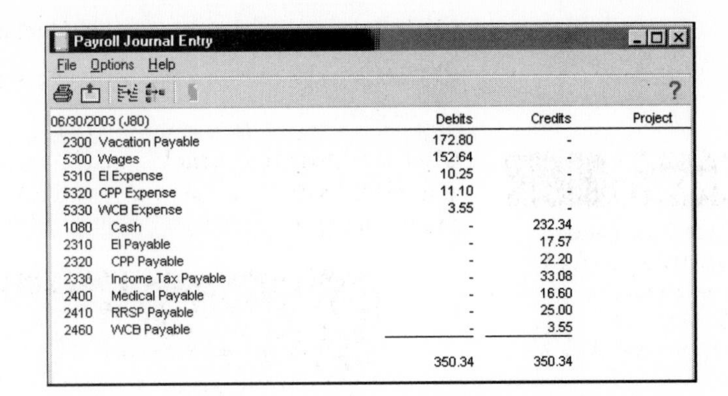

Payroll Journal Entry

File Options Help

06/30/2003 (J80)	Debits	Credits	Project
2300 Vacation Payable	172.80	-	
5300 Wages	152.64	-	
5310 EI Expense	10.25	-	
5320 CPP Expense	11.10	-	
5330 WCB Expense	3.55	-	
1080 Cash	-	232.34	
2310 EI Payable	-	17.57	
2320 CPP Payable	-	22.20	
2330 Income Tax Payable	-	33.08	
2400 Medical Payable	-	16.60	
2410 RRSP Payable	-	25.00	
2460 WCB Payable	-	3.55	
	350.34	350.34	

The released vacation pay shows as a debit (decrease) to *Vacation Payable* while the amount for the current paycheque is added to the Wages amount. The rest of the entry is the same as for other paycheques.

Close the display to return to the journal and make corrections if necessary.

Click Post Post to save the transaction.

Close the Payroll Journal.

Close the Employees window to return to the Home window.

Continue with the remaining entries for the June 30 session date.

Displaying Payroll Reports

You can access all payroll reports from the Reports menu in the Employees window. Double click the Employees icon to open the Employees window.

Displaying Employee Lists

You can drill down to Employee Detail Reports from Employee Lists. Sorting and filtering are not available for employee reports.

You should be in the Home window.

Right-click the **Employees icon** Employees to select it.

Click the **Display button** or choose the Reports menu, then choose Lists and click Employees. The report will display a list of all current employees, together with their addresses and telephone numbers.

Close the display when you have finished.

Displaying Employee Reports

You should be in the Home window.

Choose the **Reports menu**, then **choose Payroll** and **click Employee** to see the following Employee Report Options window:

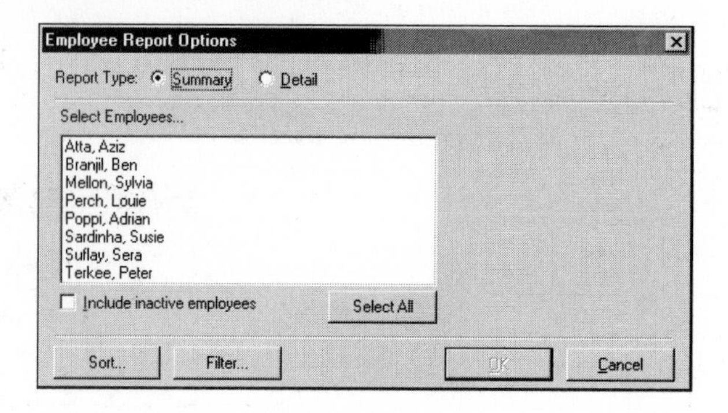

notes

You can drill down to the Detail Report from the Summary Report. From the Detail Report you can drill down to the Employee Ledger.

Press ctrl and **click** the **employees** for whom you want the report, or **click Select All** to include all employees in the report.

The **Summary** option allows you to see an employee's payroll report in summary form. The summary report will give accumulated totals for all deductions and payments, which are updated each pay period. Since summary reports are available only for the session date, you will not be able to see earlier summary reports unless you have a backup copy for that specific time period (i.e., session date) or a hard copy of the summary output.

If there are employees who are inactive (e.g., taking an unpaid leave of absence) you can include their names on the list by choosing to Include inactive employees.

Click Detail to choose from the following payroll items for the report:

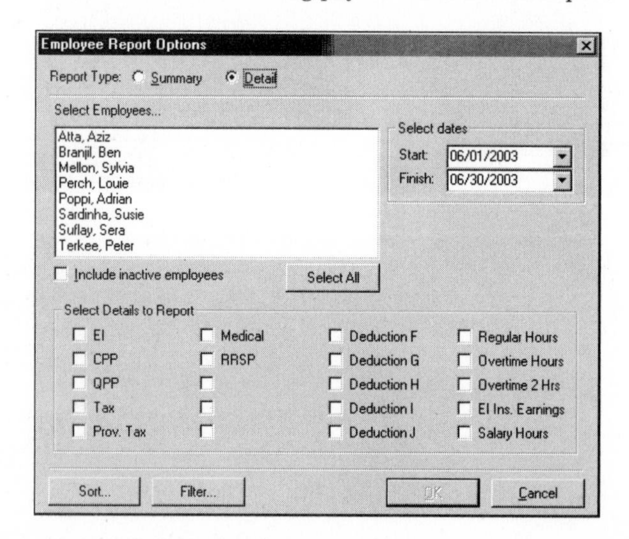

Type the beginning date for the report you want in the Start field and **press** tab

Type the ending date for the report.

Click all the details you want to include in the report. The amount for each detail you choose will be listed for each payroll period for the selected employees, with the totals for the period selected. Select the employees to include in the report.

Click OK

Close the display when you have finished.

Displaying the Payroll Journal

You should be in the Home window.

Right-click the **Paycheques icon** 

(or the Payroll Cheque Run Journal icon) to select it.

Click the **Display button** or choose the Reports menu, then choose Journal Entries and click Payroll. Your screen will display the following Payroll Journal Options window:

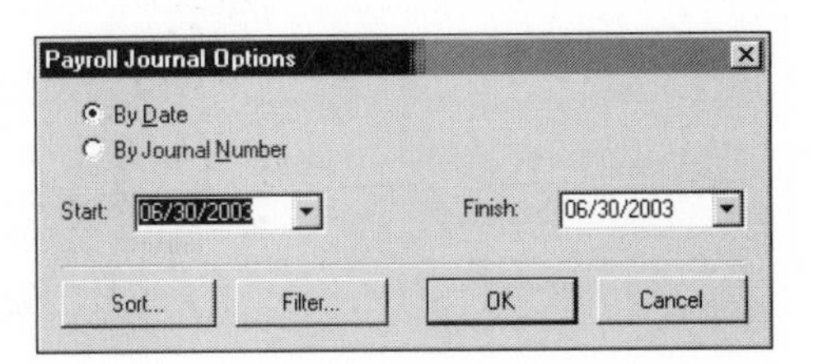

notes

- The Payroll Journal report includes all transactions from the Payroll Journal and the Payroll Cheque Run Journal.
- You can drill down to the Employee Detail Report and the General Ledger Report from the Payroll Journal.
- The usual sort and filter journal options are available for the Payroll Journal report.

By default, the By Date option is selected. This option is used for all reports in this application. Your latest session date appears by default in both the Start and Finish date fields. The start date is highlighted, ready for editing.

Type the beginning date for the report you want to see and **press** (tab).

Type the ending date for the report you want to see.

Click OK

Close the display when you have finished.

Management Reports for Payroll

Choose the **Reports menu**, then **choose Management Reports** and **click Payroll**:

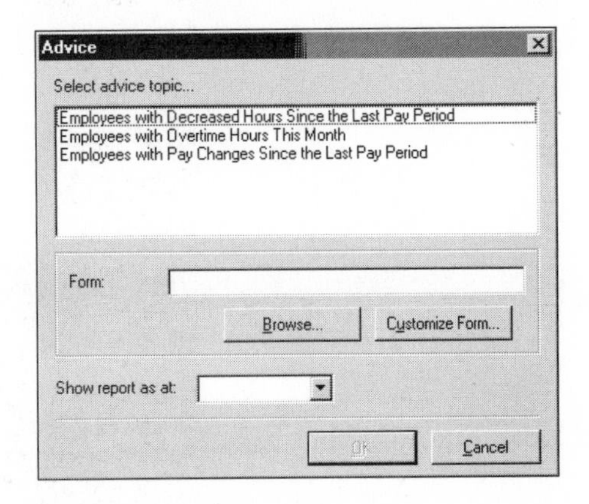

Click the topic for which you want the report.

Choose a month for the report on Employees with Overtime Hours This Month from the list in the Show report as at field. Choose a form, if appropriate.

Click OK to see the report. **Close** the display when you have finished.

Printing Payroll Reports

Display the report you want to print. **Choose** the **File menu** from the report window and **click Print**. **Close** the display when you have finished.

Printing T4s

> **notes**
>
> Relevé 1 slips are used only in Quebec. The report options are similar to those for the T4 Slips.

You can also print two reports that are not available for display: **T4 Slips** and **Relevé 1 Slips**. The **T4** option will allow you to print T4 slips, which are compulsory for employees filing income tax returns. You should have the proper tax statement forms from CCRA to take full advantage of this option. You should retain payroll information for employees who leave during the year so that you can prepare T4 slips to mail to them.

Choose the **Reports menu**, then **choose Payroll** and **click Print T4 Slips** (or **Print Relevé 1 Slips**) to display the following options:

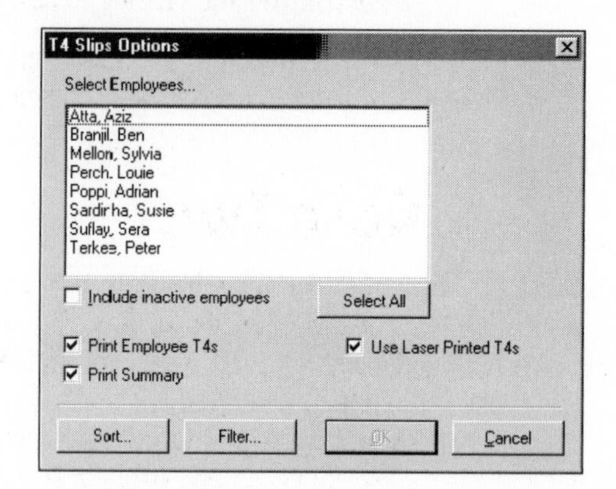

Click Select All or press ctrl and click the names of the employees for whom you want the report printed. Notice that you may use a laser printer for the forms and include a printed summary of the amounts on the T4. Again, you may include employees who are inactive.

Click OK

The T4 box options screen appears. You can choose a form box number for optional deduction amounts if these are related to income tax and should be included on the T4s.

Click OK to begin printing. Be sure that you have set up your printer correctly before you begin.

Print Employee Mailing Labels

Choose the **Reports menu**, then **choose Mailing Labels** and **click Employees** to display the list of employee names.

Press ctrl and **click** the **Employees' names** or **click Select All**.

Click OK to start printing.

CASE PROBLEMS

Case One

After several months of successful operation, Susie Sardinha realized how large a role her cooks play in the success of her catering business, so she decided to include a commission with their regular wages.

1. What must she do to the setup of the Simply Accounting program and in the regular Payroll Journal entries to add the commissions?
2. Before making the commitment to the employees, what information should she consider, and how should she determine the basis or amount of the commission?

Case Two

During the fall when her father was ill, Sardinha was away from Victoria for four weeks to take care of him. She left her chef in charge of the business. On her return, she was extremely pleased to learn that the business had run smoothly and the chef had successfully negotiated some new contracts with only minimal telephone assistance from Sardinha. She wanted to show her appreciation to the staff by adding a significant bonus to their next paycheques.

Sardinha knew that if she added the bonus directly in the next Payroll Journal entry, the taxes would be overpaid because the program assumes that the pay for the period selected is the regular rate of pay. She needed to turn off the automatic payroll deductions feature before she could edit the tax amounts that the program calculates automatically. However, she still needed to know how much tax should be deducted. In the manual approach, she would divide the bonus evenly over the entire year, calculate the amount of tax increase for each pay period, then multiply this amount by the number of pay periods. This way, the entire tax amount is paid at the time of the bonus, but the amount is based on the yearly increase in income.

Describe how Sardinha can use the software to perform these calculations.

CHAPTER NINE

OBJECTIVES

After completing this chapter, you should be able to

- *enter* inventory-related purchase transactions
- *enter* inventory-related sale transactions of goods and services
- *make* inventory adjustments
- *enter* sales to preferred customers
- *create* new foreign vendor records
- *enter* transactions with foreign vendors
- *transfer* funds to foreign currency accounts
- *understand* the integration of the Inventory Ledger with the Payables, Receivables and General Ledgers
- *enter* new inventory items
- *display* and *print* inventory reports

COMPANY INFORMATION

Company Profile

Meteor Mountain Bike Shop in Collingwood, Ontario, serves the cottage country area by selling bicycles and bicycle accessories, and by renting, servicing and repairing bicycles. The shop, owned and operated by Tom and Betsy Trycykel, carries a small inventory of popular bicycle models and basic accessories. In addition, the shop carries a few bicycles for rentals on a daily or weekly basis to individuals, clubs and resorts in the area. A few clubs and resorts that purchase regularly from Meteor Mountain Bike Shop have opened accounts. Some of these are given preferred customer reduced prices. The Trycykels recommend annual spring bicycle tune-ups to all their customers.

Based on the spring to fall season for biking and cottage use, the Trycykels decided to restrict their business to May through October each year. With this schedule, they are free to participate in the local opportunities for skiing in the winter.

Because the shop is small, the Trycykels are able to manage most of the work themselves. Occasionally, however, such as during summer long weekends, they engage the help of local students who work as needed on a casual hourly basis. One of these students helped Tom Trycykel convert the manual accounting records to Simply Accounting. On May 31, 2003, the books were closed and the following information was used to set up the Simply Accounting files:

- Chart of Accounts
- Post-Closing Trial Balance
- Vendor Information
- Customer Information
- Inventory Information
- Accounting Procedures

notes

USD is the abbreviation for United States dollars. The abbreviation for Canadian dollars is CAD.

METEOR MOUNTAIN BIKE SHOP
CHART OF ACCOUNTS

ASSETS
1080 Bank Account: Chequing
1090 Bank Account: Credit Cards
1100 Bank: USD
1200 Accounts Receivable
1220 Bicycle Repair Parts
1240 Prepaid Insurance
1260 Rental Bicycles
1280 Store Supplies
1300 Accessories
1320 Helmets
1340 Mountain Bicycles
1420 Cash Register
1440 Computers & Peripherals
1480 Display Fixtures
1500 Fax Machine
1520 Shop
1540 Tools & Equipment

LIABILITIES
2100 Bank Loan
2200 Accounts Payable
2300 Credit Cards Payable
2640 PST Payable
2650 GST Charged on Sales
2670 GST Paid on Purchases
2850 Mortgage Payable

EQUITY
3560 Trycykels, Capital
3580 Trycykels, Drawings
3600 Net Income

REVENUE
4020 Revenue from Sales
4030 Sales Allowances & Discounts
4040 Revenue from Services
4100 Sales Tax Compensation
4200 Freight Revenue

EXPENSES
5020 Advertising & Promotion
5030 Exchange Rate Differences
5040 Bank Charges
5050 Credit Card Fees
5060 Cost of Goods Sold
5080 Purchases Returns
5100 Damaged Inventory
5200 Freight Expense
5220 Interest Expense
5260 Telephone Expense
5300 Temporary Services

METEOR MOUNTAIN BIKE SHOP
POST-CLOSING TRIAL BALANCE

May 31, 2003

Account	Debit	Credit
1080 Bank Account: Chequing	$ 7 150.00	
1090 Bank Account: Credit Cards	1 100.00	
1100 Bank: USD	100.00	
1200 Accounts Receivable	460.00	
1220 Bicycle Repair Parts	2 000.00	
1240 Prepaid Insurance	500.00	
1260 Rental Bicycles	3 000.00	
1280 Store Supplies	200.00	
1300 Accessories	1 960.00	
1320 Helmets	830.00	
1340 Mountain Bicycles	15 700.00	
1420 Cash Register	1 000.00	
1440 Computers & Peripherals	2 800.00	
1480 Display Fixtures	1 200.00	
1500 Fax Machine	400.00	
1520 Shop	72 000.00	
1540 Tools & Equipment	2 400.00	
2100 Bank Loan		$ 5 000.00
2200 Accounts Payable		4 025.00
2640 PST Payable		1 280.00
2650 GST Charged on Sales		1 120.00
2670 GST Paid on Purchases	560.00	
2850 Mortgage Payable		60 000.00
3560 Trycykels, Capital		41 935.00
	$113 360.00	$113 360.00

METEOR MOUNTAIN BIKE SHOP
VENDOR INFORMATION

Vendor Name (Contact)	Address	Phone No. Fax No.	Terms
Bell Canada (Dessy Bell)	13 Sonic St. Collingwood, ON L9Y 8T2	Tel: (705) 711-7483 Fax: (705) 711-8100	Net 1
Cycling Equipment Inc. (Petal Spokes)	62 Cyclo Dr. North York, ON M9Y 7H3	Tel: (416) 488-6190 Fax: (416) 488-9000	Net 30
Global Cyclists (Norma Ryder)	710 Touring Cr. Toronto, ON M4P 2M9	Tel: (416) 932-7401 Fax: (416) 932-6222	Net 30
Minister of Finance	Box 620, 33 King St. W. Oshawa, ON L1H 8H5	Tel: (905) 965-8470	Net 1
Ontario Hydro (Atam Powers)	201 Generator Rd. Collingwood, ON L9Y 5B7	Tel: (705) 714-9733	Net 1
Receiver General of Canada	Sudbury Tax Services Offices PO Box 20004 Stn A Sudbury ON P3A 6B4	Tel: (705) 821-8186	Net 1
Trail Canada Accessories & Parts (Helmut Locke)	18 Woodlands Trail Waterloo, ON N2L 6F2	Tel: (519) 886-6321 Fax: (519) 886-7191	Net 30
Wheeler & Shield Co. (Lawrence Shields)	75 Raleigh Ct. Hamilton, ON L8H 4B8	Tel: (905) 522-6123 Fax: (905) 522-9210	Net 15

METEOR MOUNTAIN BIKE SHOP
OUTSTANDING VENDOR INVOICES

Vendor Name	Date	Inv/Chq No.	Terms	Amount	Total
Cycling Equipment Inc.	5/11/03	CE-714	Net 30	$575.00	$ 575.00
Global Cyclists	5/6/03	GC-1543	Net 30	$3 450.00	3 450.00
				Grand Total	$4 025.00

METEOR MOUNTAIN BIKE SHOP
CUSTOMER INFORMATION

Customer Name Status (Contact)	Address	Phone No. Fax No.	Credit Limit Terms
Bay Land Bikers (Kyle Wheeling)	72 Bayview Ave. Collingwood, ON L9Y 4D3	Tel: (705) 713-4567 Fax: (705) 713-6285	$4 000 2/10, Net 15
Blue Mountain Lodge Preferred customer (Ceram Potter)	95 Ridgewood Dr. Collingwood, ON L9Y 6V1	Tel: (705) 711-4723 Fax: (705) 711-4111	$4 000 2/10, Net 15
Lakeland Mountain Bike Club Preferred customer (Sylva Lake)	811 Highland Cr. Meaford, ON N4L 1E3	Tel: (519) 653-8016 Fax: (519) 653-9054	$4 000 2/10, Net 15
Teehani Summer Resort Preferred customer (Edward Bassige)	4 Seasons Rd. Meaford, ON N4L 1C8	Tel: (519) 655-3478 Fax: (519) 655-5522	$4 000 2/10, Net 15

Customer Status: Preferred customers receive special pricing on some products.

METEOR MOUNTAIN BIKE SHOP
OUTSTANDING CUSTOMER INVOICES

Customer Name	Date	Inv/Chq No.	Terms	Amount	Total
Blue Mountain Lodge	5/21/03	53	2/10, Net 15	$287.50	$287.50
Teehani Summer Resort	5/28/03	59	2/10, Net 15	$172.50	172.50
			Grand Total		$460.00

METEOR MOUNTAIN BIKE SHOP
INVENTORY INFORMATION

Code	Description	Reg Selling Price	(Preferred) (Price)	Qty on Hand	Amt (Cost)	Min Stock Level
Accessories						
ACC-BS1	Bell - steel	$ 6		10	$ 30	2
ACC-CL1	Cable Lock - heavy duty	30		15	150	3
ACC-LH1	Light - halogen clamp style	20		10	100	2
ACC-PA1	Pump - lightweight aluminum	20		10	100	2
ACC-SD1	Speedometer - digital deluxe	40		10	200	2
ACC-SD2	Speedometer - digital standard	30		10	150	2
ACC-SG1	Seat - gel extra cushioning	20		20	200	4
ACC-TK1	Toolkit - multi-function	40		10	100	2
ACC-TR1	Tires - 26" mountain	20		20	200	4
ACC-TR2	Tires - 24" mountain	16		20	160	4
ACC-TR3	Tires - 20" mountain	12		20	120	4
ACC-UL1	U-Lock - heavy duty	40		10	200	2
ACC-UL2	U-Lock - heavy duty, centre lock	50		10	250	2
					$1 960	
Helmets						
HMT-11A	Charm - 11 vent aerodynamic in-line	$25		10	$150	2
HMT-11B	Tuff - 11 vent super lock-tech	40		10	250	2
HMT-21A	Myti - 21 vent adjustable in-line	40		10	250	2
HMT-21B	Excel - 21 vent lightweight	30		10	180	2
					$830	
Mountain Bicycles (1-21 speed)						
MTB-A241	Brava - 18sp Shimano SIS alum alloy	$ 500	($450)	5	$ 1 500	1
MTB-A242	Brava - 18sp high tensile steel	250	(225)	5	700	1
MTB-A261	Maxim - 18sp Shimano alloy rim/hub	400	(360)	10	2 500	2
MTB-A262	Maxim - 15sp high tens steel hybrid	160	(144)	10	800	2
MTB-A263	Summit - 18sp STX Alvio A-frame	800	(720)	3	1 500	0
MTB-A264	Summit - 18sp Alvio drivetrain chr	600	(540)	10	4 000	2
MTB-A265	Summit - 21sp Shimano XT/LE Al. DB	1 600	(1 440	2	2 000	0
MTB-Y201	BMC - 1sp deluxe high tensile	150	(135)	5	400	1
MTB-Y202	Trac - 5sp chromoly hybrid	300	(270)	10	1 800	2
MTB-YU20	Trac - 5sp steel frame twist shift	200	(180)	5	500	1
					$15 700	
Services						
SRV-RTD	Daily rental per bicycle	$15/day		Apply PST		
SRV-RTW	Weekly rental per bicycle	50/wk		Apply PST		
SRV-TU	Tune-up per bicycle	30		Apply PST		

Accounting Procedures

notes

Refer to Chapter 2 and page 204 for further information about GST remittances.

The Goods and Services Tax: Remittances

Meteor Mountain Bike Shop uses the regular method for remittance of the Goods and Services Tax. GST collected from customers is recorded as a liability in *GST Charged on Sales*. GST paid to vendors is recorded in *GST Paid on Purchases* as a decrease in liability to Canada Customs and Revenue Agency. The Trycykels file their return to the Receiver General of Canada by the last day of the month for the previous quarter, either requesting a refund or remitting the balance owing.

GST remittances are recorded in the Payments Journal as Other Payments. Select the Receiver General as the vendor. Enter the GST charged as a **positive** amount in the

Amount field with *GST Charged on Sales* in the Account field. On the next line, enter the GST paid as a **negative** amount in the Amount field with *GST Paid on Purchases* in the Account field. This will debit the GST charged account and credit the GST paid account.

Provincial Sales Tax (PST)
Provincial Sales Tax of 8 percent is applied to all cash and credit sales of goods and services in Ontario and remitted monthly to the Minister of Finance. Set up a liability owing to the vendor, Minister of Finance, in the Payments Journal (Other Payment), using the General Ledger balance in *PST Payable* for the end of the previous month to determine the balance owing. A 5 percent sales tax compensation is earned for prompt payment and reduces the liability to the Minister of Finance.

PST at the rate of 8 percent is also paid on purchases that are not inventory items for resale. PST paid is not allocated to a separate account. It is charged to the asset or expense account associated with the purchase.

notes

We use the term cash sales and purchases to apply to payments by cash and by cheque.

Sales Invoices
Meteor allows customers to pay on account, or by cash, cheque and credit card. The keystrokes for cash and credit card inventory transactions are similar to those for account sales, except for the method of payment. The program will automatically debit the appropriate bank account instead of *Accounts Receivable*.

If you want to print sales invoices through the program, complete the Sales Journal transaction as you would otherwise. Before posting the transaction, choose the File menu and click Print or click the Print button. Printing will begin immediately, so be sure you have the correct forms for your printer before you begin. To e-mail an invoice, click the E-mail button.

Credit Card Sales and Purchases
Meteor has set up its accounts for credit card transactions for both sales and purchases. There are no discounts on credit card sales.

Freight Expenses and Charges
When a business purchases inventory items, the cost of any freight that cannot be directly allocated to a specific item must be charged to *Freight Expense*. This amount will be regarded as an expense rather than being charged to an inventory asset account. Freight or delivery charges to customers are allocated to *Freight Revenue*.

Discounts
Meteor offers its account customers a 2 percent discount on after-tax amounts if they pay their accounts within 10 days, to encourage customers to settle their accounts early. Discounts are calculated automatically in the Receipts Journal by the program when the payment terms are set up and the customer is eligible to receive the discount. Some vendors also offer discounts for early payments. All discounts are calculated on after-tax amounts. The discount terms and the settings for pre-tax or after-tax calculations are entered as defaults in the ledger records. There are no discounts on cash sales.

version 8

For Version 8.0, the preferred customer option is not available. Instead, you can edit the prices for these customers in the Sales Journal to create the same discounts.

Some customers have preferred customer status that entitles them to reduced prices on some products. These reduced prices are entered in the inventory ledger records.

INSTRUCTIONS

1. Using the Chart of Accounts, Trial Balance, Vendor Information, Customer Information and Inventory Information provided, record entries for the source documents for June 2003 using Simply Accounting. The procedures for entering

each new type of transaction are outlined step by step in the keystroke section that follows the source documents. These transactions have a ✔ in the check box, and the page number where the keystrokes begin is printed below the check box.

2. After finishing your entries, print the reports indicated on the following printing form. Instructions for printing inventory reports begin on page 290.

notes

For reports, you should Show Foreign Amounts whenever this option is available.

REPORTS

Lists
- ☐ Chart of Accounts
- ☐ Vendors
- ☐ Customers
- ☐ Inventory & Services

Financials
- ☑ Comparative Balance Sheet dates: June 1 and June 14 With Dollar Difference
- ☑ Income Statement from June 1 to June 14
- ☑ Trial Balance date: June 14
- ☑ General Ledger accounts: 1300 5060 from June 1 to June 14
- ☐ Cash Flow Projection

GST
- ☑ GST Detail Report date: June 14

Inventory
- ☐ Inventory
- ☑ Inventory Activity all details for Bags & Accessories
- ☑ Inventory Sales Detail for Accessories from June 1 to June 14
- ☑ Inventory Transaction Detail for Mountain Bikes from June 1 to June 14

Journals
- ☑ All Journals (by posting date) from June 1 to June 14
- ☐ General
- ☐ Purchases
- ☐ Payments
- ☐ Sales
- ☐ Receipts
- ☑ Adjustments (by posting date) from June 1 to June 14

Payables
- ☐ Vendor Aged
- ☐ Aged Overdue Payables
- ☑ Vendor Purchases Summary for all vendors, all items from June 1 to June 14
- ☐ Pending Purchase Orders

Receivables
- ☐ Customer Aged
- ☐ Aged Overdue Receivables
- ☐ Customer Sales
- ☐ Pending Sales Orders
- ☐ Customer Statements

Management Reports
- ☐ Ledger

Mailing Labels
- ☐ Labels

GRAPHS

- ☐ Payables by Aging Period
- ☐ Receivables by Aging Period
- ☐ Sales vs Receivables
- ☐ Revenues by Account
- ☐ Expenses and Net Profit as % of Revenue
- ☐ Payables by Vendor
- ☐ Receivables by Customer
- ☐ Receivables Due vs Payables Due
- ☐ Expenses by Account
- ☐ Current Revenue vs Last Year

SOURCE DOCUMENTS

SESSION DATE – June 7

notes

For inventory sales, we show unit selling prices in source documents.

269

Sales Invoice #61
Dated June 1/03
To Bay Land Bikers

two MTB-A261 Maxim - 18sp Shimano alloy rim/hub	$400 each
two MTB-Y202 Trac - 5sp chromoly hybrid	300 each
one MTB-A264 Summit - 18sp Alvio drivetrain chr	600
two HMT-21A Myti - 21 vent adjustable in-line	40 each
two ACC-UL1 U-Lock - heavy duty	40 each
three ACC-CL1 Cable Lock - heavy duty	30 each
Delivery charge	50
Goods & Services Tax	7%
Provincial Sales Tax	8%

Terms: 2/10, n/15.

notes

For inventory purchases, we show the total prices (amounts) in source documents.

273

Purchase Invoice #WS-1217
Dated June 1/03
From Wheeler & Shield Co.

five ACC-CL1 Cable Lock - heavy duty	$ 50.00
five ACC-UL1 U-Lock - heavy duty	100.00
five ACC-UL2 U-Lock - heavy duty, centre lock	125.00
GST Paid	19.25
Invoice Total	$294.25

Terms: n/15.

276

Memo #1
Dated June 2/03
From Owner: Adjust inventory records for one Speedometer - digital deluxe valued at $20. The speedometer was accidentally dropped and damaged beyond repair. Charge to Damaged Inventory account.

279

Memo #2 Re Purchase Invoice #SSB-8218
Dated June 2/03
In the Purchases Journal:

Add new vendor: Sedona Saddle & Bags
Add two new inventory records
Create new asset group account 1310 Bags

Code	Description	Reg. Price (Pref.)	Min.
BAG-N1	Saddle Bags - ballistic nylon light	$35 each ($30)	1
BAG-L1	Saddle Bags - leather split cowhide	$75 each ($65)	1

Asset account: 1310 Bags (New account)
Revenue account: 4020 Revenue from Sales
Expense account: 5060 Cost of Goods Sold

notes

Sedona Saddle & Bags (Contact JoAnn Baggett) is located at RR #3, Sedona, AZ 86336
Tel: (520) 821-6344
Fax: (520) 821-6211
Currency: USD
Vendor collects GST

279

Purchase Invoice #SSB-8218
Dated June 2/03
From Sedona Saddle & Bags (Use Full Add for the new USD vendor)

five BAG-N1 Saddle Bags - ballistic nylon light	$ 60.00 USD
five BAG-L1 Saddle Bags - leather split cowhide	120.00 USD
GST Paid	12.60 USD
Invoice Total	$192.60 USD

Terms: n/15. The exchange rate is 1.555.

version 8

Version 8.0 users should edit the sale prices for the bicycles to match the source document. Click the amount in the Price field and type the reduced price.

notes

- Use One-time customer for new cash and credit card customers. Type the customer's name in the Address text box.
- Note that there is no discount on cash or credit card sales.

☑ 285

Sales Invoice #62
Dated June 3/03
To Lakeland Mountain Bike Club (preferred customer)

two MTB-A241 Brava - 18sp Shimano SIS alum alloy	$ 450 each
two MTB-A261 Maxim - 18sp Shimano alloy rim/hub	360 each
four ACC-BS1 Bells - steel	6 each
four ACC-LH1 Lights - halogen clamp style	20 each
four ACC-SG1 Seats - gel extra cushioning	20 each
four ACC-SD2 Speedometers - digital standard	30 each
four HMT-11B Tuff - 11 vent super lock-tech	40 each
three SRV-TU Tune-ups	30 each
Delivery charge	50
Goods & Services Tax	7%
Provincial Sales Tax	8%

Terms: 2/10, n/15.

☐ Memo #3
Dated June 3/03
From Owner: Adjust the purchase invoice from Sedona Saddle & Bags to include $20 USD for freight charges plus 7% GST. Invoice total to increase by $21.40 to $214 USD.

☐ Credit Card Sales Invoice #63
Dated June 3/03
To Gus Farouk

one MTB-A263 Summit - 18sp STX Alvio A-frame	$800
one ACC-UL2 U-Lock - heavy duty, centre lock	50
one ACC-PA1 Pump - lightweight aluminum	20
one ACC-TK1 Toolkit - multi-function	40
Goods & Services Tax	7%
Provincial Sales Tax	8%

Paid by Visa #4504 5612 9118 7231

☑ 286

Cheque Copy #301
Dated June 4/03
To Sedona Saddle & Bags, $214 USD in full payment of account. Reference invoice #SSB-8218. The exchange rate is 1.585. Payment from USD bank account.

288

Memo #4
Dated June 4/03
From Owner: Transfer $200 in USD from Bank Account: Chequing to Bank: USD to cover cheque for Sedona Saddle & Bags. The exchange rate is 1.585.

Credit Card Sales Invoice #64
Dated June 4/03
To Chris Chihrin

one MTB-A265 Summit - 21sp Shimano XT/LE Al. DB	$1 600
Goods & Services Tax	7%
Provincial Sales Tax	8%

Paid by MasterCard #9215 4421 3361 7712

Cash Receipt #50
Dated June 4/03
From Blue Mountain Lodge, cheque #2994 for $287.50 in full payment of account. Reference invoice #53.

❑ Cash Sales Invoice #65
Dated June 4/03
To Vinoo Manga

one SRV-TU Tune-up	$30
one day SRV-RTD Daily rental	15
Goods & Services Tax	7%
Provincial Sales Tax	8%

Paid in cash.

notes

Use Quick Add for new cash purchase vendors. Enter the cash purchases in the Payments Journal as Other Payments.

❑ Cash Purchase Invoice #CG-662
Dated June 5/03
From Collingwood Graphics, $250 for business cards and flyers for business promotion, plus $17.50 GST (7%) and $20 PST (8%). Invoice total $287.50. Terms: Cash on receipt of invoice. Issued cheque #44 in payment.

❑ Cheque Copy #45
Dated June 5/03
To Global Cyclists, $3 450 in full payment of account. Reference invoice #GC-1543.

❑ Cash Sales Invoice #66
Dated June 6/03
To Ikuko Hashimi

two ACC-TR1 Tires - 26" mountain	$20 each
one BAG-L1 Saddle Bags - leather split cowhide	75
one HMT-21A Myti - 21 vent adjustable in-line	40
one SRV-TU Tune-up	30
Goods & Services Tax	7%
Provincial Sales Tax	8%

Paid by certified cheque #221.

notes

❑ Collingwood Kiwanis Youth Centre (Contact Amos Young) is a preferred customer located at
15 Springtime Ave.
Collingwood, ON L9Y 6F3
Tel: (705) 713-4928
Fax: (705) 713-7010
Terms: 2/10, n/15
Charge PST and GST
Credit Limit: $4 000

- Version 8.0 users should edit selling prices.

❑ Sales Invoice #67
Dated June 7/03
To Collingwood Kiwanis Youth Centre (use Full Add for preferred customer)

five MTB-Y202 Trac - 5sp chromoly hybrid	$270 each
five HMT-21B Excel - 21 vent lightweight	30 each
five ACC-CL1 Cable Lock - heavy duty	30 each
Delivery charge	50
Goods & Services Tax	7%
Provincial Sales Tax	8%

Terms: 2/10, n/15.

❑ Sales Invoice #68
Dated June 7/03
To Teehani Summer Resort

six SRV-RTW Weekly rentals	$50 each
Goods & Services Tax	7%
Provincial Sales Tax	8%

Terms: 2/10, n/15.

SESSION DATE – June 14

❑ Cash Receipt #51
Dated June 8/03
From Bay Land Bikers, cheque #411 for $2 588.18 in full payment of account, including $52.82 (2%) discount taken for early payment of account. Reference invoice #61.

notes

Refer to page 213 for assistance with looking up invoices.

- [ ] Memo # 5
Dated June 8/03
From Owner: Teehani Summer Resort has decided to rent 6 bicycles per week for the rest of the summer with an option to purchase at the end of the summer. Look up the original sales invoice #68 and store it as a weekly recurring entry.

- [ ] Purchase Invoice #TC-7141
Dated June 8/03
From Trail Canada Accessories & Parts, $150 for bicycle repair parts, plus $10.50 GST (7%) and $12 PST (8%). Invoice total $172.50. Terms: net 30 days.

- [ ] Credit Card Sales Invoice #69
Dated June 8/03
To Jasmine Traynor

two MTB-A242 Brava - 18sp high tensile steel	$250 each
two HMT-11B Tuff - 11 vent super lock-tech	40 each
two ACC-UL2 U-Lock - heavy duty, centre lock	50 each
Goods & Services Tax	7%
Provincial Sales Tax	8%

Paid by Visa #4510 7333 0022 1185

notes

Use the default terms for purchase orders and sales orders.

- [ ] Purchase Order #1
Dated June 8/03
Shipping date June 12/03
From Global Cyclists

five MTB-Y202 Trac - 5sp chromoly hybrid	$ 900.00
four MTB-A261 Maxim - 18sp Shimano alloy rim/hub	1 000.00
two MTB-A241 Brava - 18sp Shimano SIS alum alloy	600.00
two MTB-A264 Summit - 18sp Alvio drivetrain chr	800.00
GST Paid	231.00
Invoice total	$3 531.00

version 8

Users of Version 8.0 should edit selling prices.

- [ ] Sales Order #TSR 1068
Dated June 9/03
Delivery date June 18/03
From Teehani Summer Resort (preferred customer)

five MTB-A241 Brava - 18 sp Shimano SIS alum alloy	$450.00 each
five MTB - YU20 Trac - 5sp steel frame twist shift	180.00 each
ten ACC-CL1 Cable lock -heavy duty	30.00 each
Delivery Charge	50.00
Goods & Services Tax	7%
Provincial Sales Tax	8%

Teehani Summer Resort will purchase a set of bicycles to replace the rentals.

- [ ] Purchase Order #2
Dated June 9/03
Shipping date June 14/03
From Global Cyclists

five MTB-A241 Brava - 18 sp Shimano SIS alum alloy	$1 500.00
five MTB - YU20 Trac - 5sp steel frame twist shift	500.00
GST Paid	140.00
Invoice total	$2 140.00

- [ ] Cheque Copy #46
Dated June 9/03
To Cycling Equipment Inc., $575 in full payment of account. Reference invoice #CE-714.

notes

❑ Muskoka Seniors Club (Contact Hendrik Oude) is a preferred customer located at
4 Everyoung Circle
Collingwood, ON L9Y 3B9
Tel: (705) 711-4926
Fax: (705) 711-4998
Terms: 2/10, n/15
Charge PST and GST
Credit Limit: $4 000

- Version 8.0 users should edit the selling prices.

❑ Sales Invoice #70
Dated June 9/03
To Muskoka Seniors Club (use Full Add for preferred customer)

two MTB-A262 Maxim - 15sp high tens steel hybrid	$144 each
two HMT-11A Charm - 11 vent aerodynamic in-line	25 each
two ACC-SG1 Seats - gel extra cushioning	20 each
two BAG-N1 Saddle Bags - ballistic nylon light	30 each
Goods & Services Tax	7%
Provincial Sales Tax	8%

Terms: 2/10, n/15.

❑ Credit Card Sales Invoice #71
Dated June 10/03
To Grygori Ryder

one MTB-A264 Summit - 18sp Alvio drivetrain chr	$600
one ACC-SD1 Speedometer - digital deluxe	40
two ACC-TR2 Tires - 24" mountain	16 each
Goods & Services Tax	7%
Provincial Sales Tax	8%

Paid by Visa #4421 6499 7280 0375

notes

To enter the PST remittance

- Refer to previous end-of-month General Ledger balances for the exact amount of the liability for PST and GST.
- Choose Other Payments in the Payments Journal.
- Enter PST Payable as a positive amount (debit entry) and Sales Tax Compensation as a negative amount (credit entry).

To enter the GST remittance

- Enter GST Charged on Sales as a positive amount (debit entry) and GST Paid on Purchases as a negative amount (credit entry). (Refer to page 204 for further details.)

❑ Memo #6
Dated June 11/03
Record the PST Payable account balance for May 31, 2003, as a liability owing to the Minister of Finance. The liability must be reduced by the sales tax compensation of 5% on the PST Payable account balance ($1 280 x .05 = $64). Recognize $64 as the Sales Tax Compensation earned. Issue cheque #47 for $1 216 in payment.

❑ Memo #7
Dated June 11/03
Refer to the May 31 General Ledger balances to record the liability for GST to the Receiver General for May 2003. Issue cheque #48 for $560 in full payment.

❑ Credit Card Sales Invoice #72
Dated June 11/03
To Jon Ming

one MTB-YU20 Trac - 5sp steel frame twist shift	$200
Goods & Services Tax	7%
Provincial Sales Tax	8%

Paid by MasterCard #9123 6154 3491 6101

notes

Enter the payment to Jay Ruby as an Other Payment in the Payments Journal, rather than through the General Journal. This will maintain the proper cheque number sequence.

❑ Memo #8
Dated June 11/03
From Owner: Issue cheque #49 for $50 to Jay Ruby for assisting with sales in store for a few hours. Use Quick Add to create the new vendor. Charge expense to Temporary Services account.

❑ Cash Receipt #52
Dated June 11/03
From Teehani Summer Resort, cheque #34 for $510.60 in payment of account (including 2% discount taken on invoice #68). Reference invoices #59 and 68.

notes

- Edit the amount in the Purchases Journal for the helmets.
- ❑ Edit the Inventory Ledger for item HMT-21B to increase the selling price to $35.

❑ Purchase Invoice #CE-918
Dated June 12/03
From Cycling Equipment Inc.
Cycling Equipment included a notice of a price increase for Excel helmets.

five HMT-21B Excel - 21 vent lightweight	$ 100.00
five ACC-SG1 Seats - gel extra cushioning	50.00
five ACC-SD2 Speedometers - digital standard	75.00
GST Paid	15.75
Invoice total	$240.75

Terms: net 30 days.
Increase the regular selling price of Excel helmets (HMT-21B) to $35 in the Inventory Ledger.

❑ Credit Card Sales Invoice #73
Dated June 12/03
To Bonni Peddler

one MTB-Y201 BMC - 1sp deluxe high tensile	$150
one ACC-PA1 Pump - lightweight aluminum	20
one ACC-SD2 Speedometer - digital standard	30
one BAG-L1 Saddle Bags - leather split cowhide	75
Goods & Services Tax	7%
Provincial Sales Tax	8%

Paid by Visa #4503 6719 9670 0613

❑ Purchase Invoice #GC-1871
Dated June 12/03
Received from Global Cyclists to fill purchase order #1

five MTB-Y202 Trac - 5sp chromoly hybrid	$ 900.00
four MTB-A261 Maxim - 18sp Shimano alloy rim/hub	1 000.00
two MTB-A241 Brava - 18sp Shimano SIS alum alloy	600.00
two MTB-A264 Summit - 18sp Alvio drivetrain chr	800.00
GST Paid	231.00
Invoice total	$3 531.00

Terms: net 30 days.

❑ Memo #9
Dated June 13/03
From Owner: The following youth bicycles will be used for rental. For internal control purposes, prepare an inventory adjustment entry and debit the Rental Bicycles asset account instead of the default Damaged Inventory account.

one MTB-Y201 BMC - 1sp deluxe high tensile	$ 80
one MTB-YU20 Trac - 5sp steel frame twist shift	100

notes

Enter a negative quantity for the return.

❑ Purchase Return #GC-1871R
Dated June 13/03
To Global Cyclists

one MTB-Y202 Trac - 5sp chromoly hybrid	$180.00
GST Paid	12.60
Total Credit amount	$192.60

❑ Cash Receipt #53
Dated June 13/03
From Lakeland Mountain Bike Club, cheque #4272 for $2 502.53 in payment of account (including $51.07 discount taken). Reference invoice #62.

☐ Sales Invoice #74
Dated June 14/03
To Blue Mountain Lodge

five SRV-RTW Weekly rentals	$50 each
Goods & Services Tax	7%
Provincial Sales Tax	8%

Terms: 2/10, n/15.

☐ Sales Invoice #75
Dated June 14/03
To Teehani Summer Resort, $300 plus $24 PST and $21 GST for regular weekly rental of six bicycles as agreed. Invoice total $345. Terms: 2/10, n/15. Recall stored entry.

notes

☐ Create a new Group account, 5240 Hydro Expense.

☐ Cash Purchase Invoice #OH-5119
Dated June 14/03
From Ontario Hydro, $100 for hydro services plus $7 GST (7%). Invoice total $107. (PST is not charged on hydro in Ontario.) Issued cheque #50 in payment.

☐ Purchase Invoice #GC-1903
Dated June 14/03
From Global Cyclists to fill purchase order #2

five MTB-A241 Brava - 18 sp Shimano SIS alum alloy	$1 500.00
five MTB - YU20 Trac - 5sp steel frame twist shift	500.00
GST Paid	140.00
Invoice total	$2 140.00

Terms: net 30 days.

notes

Allow customer to exceed credit limit.

☐ Sales Invoice #76
Dated June 14/03
To Teehani Summer Resort, to fill sales order #TSR-1068

five MTB-A241 Brava - 18 sp Shimano SIS alum alloy	$450.00 each
five MTB - YU20 Trac - 5sp steel frame twist shift	180.00 each
ten ACC-CL1 Cable lock - heavy duty	30.00 each
Delivery Charge	50.00
Goods & Services Tax	7%
Provincial Sales Tax	8%

Terms: 2/10, n/15.

☐ Cash Purchase Invoice #BC-11008
Dated June 14/03
From Bell Canada, $80 for telephone services plus $5.60 GST (7%) and $6.40 PST (8%). Invoice total $92. Issued cheque #51 in payment.

KEYSTROKES

Accounting for Inventory Sales

The first transaction involves the sale of inventory items. Many of the steps are identical to those you used for sales in previous applications. You will be using the inventory database and all the Sales Invoice fields to complete this transaction.

Using the instructions for accessing data files in Chapter 1, page 15, open the files for Meteor Mountain Bike Shop.

Type `6 7 03` (or **type** `jun 7 03`)

notes

The Payroll and Project ledgers are hidden because they are not set up and are not used.

This will enter the session date June 7, 2003. The familiar Home window appears.

Click the **Sales Journal icon** 

to open and display the familiar Sales Journal input screen:

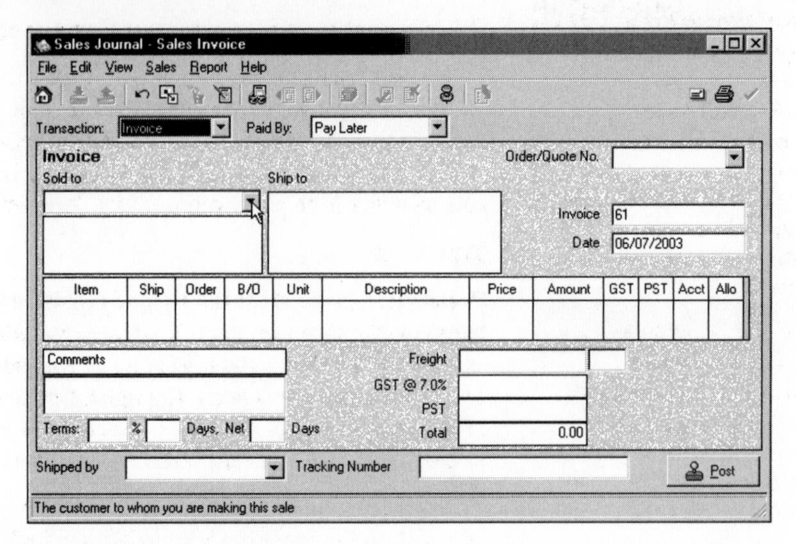

Invoice is selected as the type of transaction and Pay Later as the payment method. These default choices are correct.

Click the **Sold to (Customer) field list arrow** to display the list of customers.

Click Bay Land Bikers to enter the customer's name and address on the form. If you have selected an incorrect customer, return to the customer list and select again.

You can skip over the Ship to fields because the default information is correct and the Order/Quote No. is not used for invoices. The Invoice number is correct because the numeric invoice sequence has been set up in the defaults. If necessary, you can edit the invoice number. Payment terms are also added from the default settings and can be edited if necessary.

Double click the **Date field** to advance the cursor and highlight the contents. Enter the source document date because the default session date is incorrect.

Type `Jun 1`

Press *tab*

The cursor advances to the first line of the Item field. One line is used for each different inventory item or service sold by the business. A separate line would also be used to enter returns and allowances made.

Press *enter*

The following inventory list appears:

- Notice that you can add new inventory items from the Select Inventory/service screen.
- Sorting the inventory items by description or name, instead of by number, is an option that can be selected in the Setup for Inventory Settings.

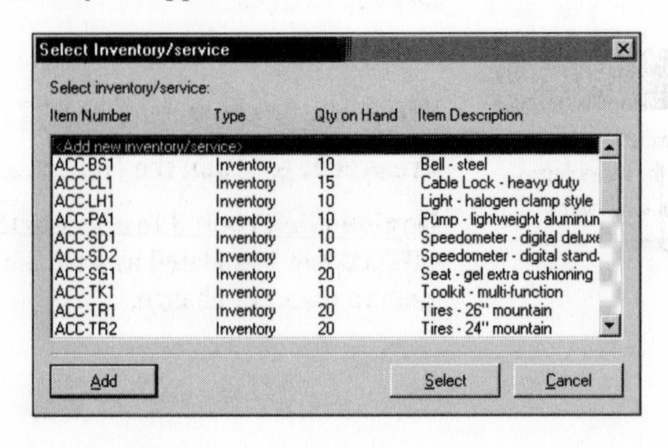

All inventory items the business offers are listed in order according to the item number or code. Quantities available are also included in this display for reference.

Click [▼] or **press** ⇩ to scroll down the list.

Click MTB-A261 Maxim - 18sp Shimano alloy rim/hub from the list.

Click Select to add the inventory item to your form.

The cursor moves to the Ship field for the quantity sold. If you try to enter a quantity greater than the available stock, the program warns you before you can continue. (You may want to continue with the order if the customer is purchasing inventory stock that is backordered.) If you have made an incorrect selection, return to the Item field and re-select from the inventory list. Then enter the number of units of this item sold.

Type 2

Press tab. Notice that the program adds information in each field automatically, based on the inventory record information. All the information except quantity and amount is added by default as soon as you enter the inventory item number. If you select a preferred customer, the default price is the preferred customer price instead of the regular selling price. (If you are using Version 8.0, you can edit the selling prices to match those for preferred customers.)

Since the default information is correct, you do not need to change it. You can edit or add GST code 3 from the Select GST screen if necessary. The PST rate, set up at 8 percent for the company, is also entered by default for inventory sales, unless the customer is marked as not paying PST. The rate can be edited if necessary, or deleted if the item is non-taxable. The rate is correct.

Click the **Item field on the second line**, because the default information based on the records is correct. If you need to change the selling price for a particular item or customer, you can edit the price. The program automatically calculates an amount based on the selling price per unit. This figure appears in the Amount field.

The default revenue account appears but can be accepted or changed. You would change the account for returns and allowances or unusual entries. Press enter while in the Account field to obtain a list of accounts. Accept the default revenue account for this sale.

You may now enter the second and remaining sale items using the same steps that you used to enter the first item. As you complete each line and advance to the next, the totals and tax amounts at the bottom of the form are updated to include the last item entered.

If there are no further items on your input form to enter, the next step is to enter the delivery or freight charges to the customer. There are two Freight fields, just below the section for inventory items. The first Freight field contains the amount of freight. The second field, the small box, contains the GST code that applies to freight charges.

Click the first Freight field where you should enter the amount of the freight or delivery charges.

Type 50

Press tab to advance to the GST code field.

Press enter to obtain the familiar list of GST code options.

Double click code 3 to add it to the return and update the totals. Notice that the GST amount is updated as well. Since there is no PST on freight in Ontario, the PST amount does not change.

notes

- Type the first letter or number of the inventory code to advance to the part of the list beginning with that letter or number, just as you do for account, vendor and customer lists. If the code begins with an upper case letter, you must type an upper case letter.
- You must change the Inventory Ledger settings to allow inventory to be oversold, that is, to allow the quantity on hand to go below zero. This option is explained in the setup for Hearth House.

notes

Services can be set up in the Inventory Ledger so that PST is applied by default, or omitted if the services do not have PST applied.

notes

- You can press tab repeatedly to advance to the next invoice line and update a previous line.
- Press tab in the Account field to add a new invoice line in the viewing space of the journal.

notes

To include more invoice lines on your screen, drag the lower frame of the Sales Journal window or maximize the window.

Your completed invoice should look like the one shown here:

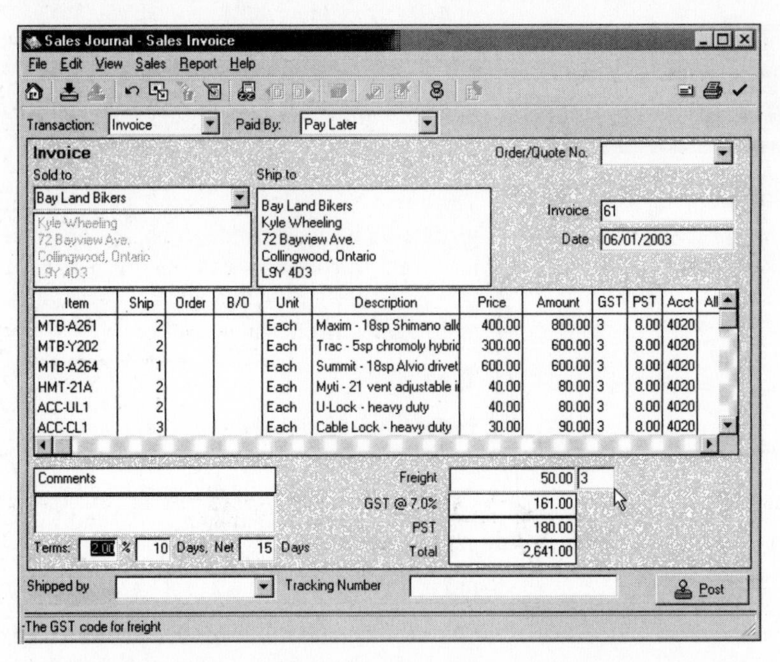

Item	Ship	Order	B/O	Unit	Description	Price	Amount	GST	PST	Acct
MTB-A261	2			Each	Maxim - 18sp Shimano all	400.00	800.00	3	8.00	4020
MTB-Y202	2			Each	Trac - 5sp chromoly hybri	300.00	600.00	3	8.00	4020
MTB-A264	1			Each	Summit - 18sp Alvio drivet	600.00	600.00	3	8.00	4020
HMT-21A	2			Each	Myti - 21 vent adjustable i	40.00	80.00	3	8.00	4020
ACC-UL1	2			Each	U-Lock - heavy duty	40.00	80.00	3	8.00	4020
ACC-CL1	3			Each	Cable Lock - heavy duty	30.00	90.00	3	8.00	4020

Reviewing the Inventory Sales Journal Transaction

Choose the **Report menu** and **click Display Sales Journal Entry**:

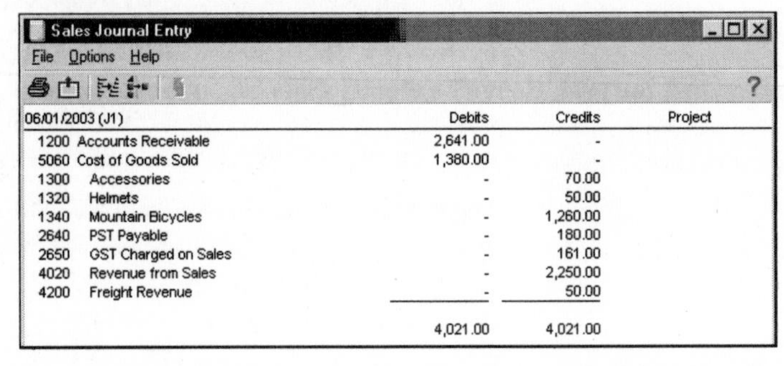

06/01/2003 (J1)	Debits	Credits	Project
1200 Accounts Receivable	2,641.00	-	
5060 Cost of Goods Sold	1,380.00	-	
1300 Accessories	-	70.00	
1320 Helmets	-	50.00	
1340 Mountain Bicycles	-	1,260.00	
2640 PST Payable	-	180.00	
2650 GST Charged on Sales	-	161.00	
4020 Revenue from Sales	-	2,250.00	
4200 Freight Revenue	-	50.00	
	4,021.00	4,021.00	

notes

The Simply Accounting program uses the average cost method in determining the cost of goods sold. If the stock for an inventory item were purchased at different times and prices, the average of these prices would be used as the cost of goods sold.

Warning!

Please be careful when reviewing your transaction to make sure you have entered the correct information.

Notice that all relevant accounts have been updated automatically because the Inventory and Receivables ledgers are linked to the General Ledger. Therefore, the linked asset, revenue and expense accounts defined for each inventory item have been debited or credited as required. In addition, the linked Receivables accounts we saw earlier — PST and GST liability accounts, *Accounts Receivable* and *Freight Revenue* — are used. The inventory database and customer record are also updated.

Close the display to return to the journal input screen.

CORRECTING THE INVENTORY SALES ENTRY BEFORE POSTING

To correct an item on the inventory line, **click** the incorrect field to move the cursor and highlight the field contents. **Press** *enter* to display the list of inventory items, GST codes or accounts. **Click** the correct selection to highlight it, then **click Select**. For the remaining fields, **type** the correct information. **Press** *tab* to enter the change. If you change the inventory item, you must re-enter the quantity sold and **press** *tab*. The totals will be updated correctly if you follow this procedure. If you have forgotten a complete line of the invoice, **click** the line below the one you have forgotten. **Choose** the **Edit menu** and **click Insert Line** to add a blank invoice line to your form. To remove a complete line, **click** the line you want to delete and **choose** the **Edit menu** and **click Remove Line**. For corrections of other details, refer to page 124.

notes

To correct errors after posting, use the Adjust invoice feature (tool button or Sales menu option).

Posting

If this is a recurring inventory sale, you can store it just like other sales.

When all the information in your journal entry is correct, you must post the transaction to save your work.

Click Post [Post] to save the transaction.

The next transaction is an inventory purchase, not a sale. **Close** the Sales Journal window to exit to the Home window.

Accounting for Inventory Purchases

The second transaction involves the purchase of inventory items. Many of the steps in completing this entry are the same as those you have been using for other credit purchase transactions. Now you will be completing all parts of this form, using the inventory database for the additional information.

Click the **Purchases Journal icon** [Purchases, Orders & Quotes] in the Home window to display the familiar Purchases Journal input form window:

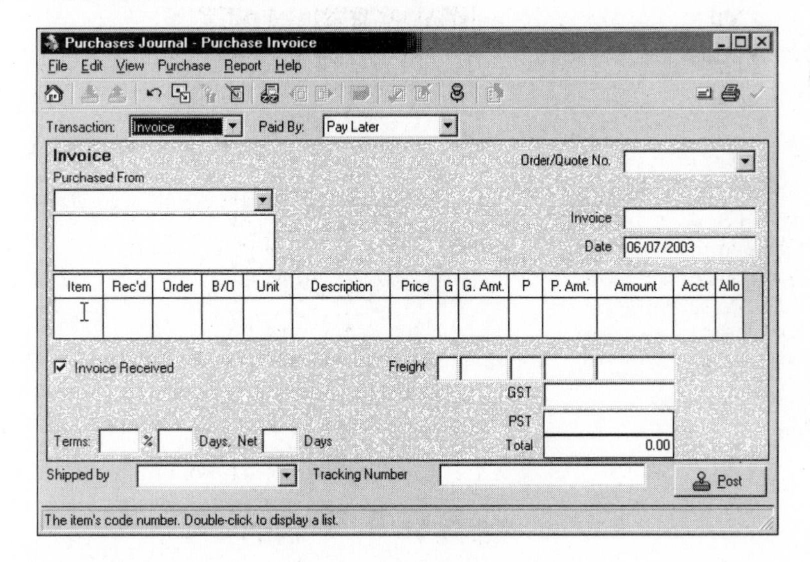

You are now ready to enter the second transaction. Invoice is correctly selected as the type of transaction, and Pay Later as the method of payment.

Click the **Vendor (Purchased From) field** to display the list of vendors.

Click Wheeler & Shield Co. from the list to add it to your input form. You now have the opportunity to check your selection. If you have selected an incorrect vendor, select again from the vendor list. If you have selected correctly, proceed by entering the invoice number.

Press *tab* twice to skip the Order/Quote No. field and advance to the Invoice field.

Type `WS-1217`

Press *tab*

The cursor advances to the Date field. Here you should enter the source document date, unless it is the same as the default session date.

Type `6-1` (or **type** `June 1`)

Press tab to advance the cursor to the Item field.

Press enter to see the list of inventory items.

Click **ACC-CL1 Cable Lock - heavy duty** from the list to highlight it.

Press enter

The cursor advances to the Rec'd field (quantity received). The Description field should now show the name, **Cable Lock - heavy duty**. If you have made an incorrect selection, return to the Item field and select again. The default price contained in the inventory records is entered automatically. Now enter the quantity for this item.

Type 5

Press tab

The cursor advances to the Unit field, skipping the Order and B/O (backorder) fields because this is not a purchase order or quote.

The Unit and Description are correct based on inventory ledger records.

The Price field records the unit price paid for the purchase of the inventory items. This amount should not include any GST paid that can be used as an input tax credit, or PST paid on the purchase. The default information, based on previous purchases, is correct so do not change it. If it is incorrect because the price has changed, you can edit the default amount.

The correct code is entered by default. If it is not, enter GST code 3 from the Select GST screen.

PST is not paid on inventory purchases so we must remove the default entry.

Click **8.00** in the P field to select it.

Press del to remove the default entry.

Press tab repeatedly to advance to the next line, with the cursor blinking in the Item field again. Notice that the Account field was skipped over, because you cannot change the entry for inventory purchases. The Asset account for the inventory purchase is defined in the inventory ledger as the linked account for purchases and sales. To change the account, you must edit the Inventory Ledger record.

Enter the remaining items from the source document, using the same steps that you used to record the first item.

The Freight fields are used to enter any freight charges that cannot be allocated to a specific item purchased and to enter the taxes paid on the freight charges. There are five Freight fields: GST code, GST amount, PST rate, PST amount and finally the base amount of the freight charge. Because GST is paid on freight you must enter GST information if the vendor charges freight. Click the first Freight field. **Press** enter to see the list of GST codes and select the correct one. You do not need to enter amounts for the taxes; they are calculated as soon as you enter the amount of freight charged. **Press** tab to advance to the PST rate field. If provincial taxes are applied to freight, enter the tax rate in the third Freight field. In the final Freight field, type the base amount of freight and **press** tab. Simply Accounting calculates the amount of GST and PST and updates all the totals.

notes

Notice again that you can add new inventory from the Select Inventory/services window.

notes

When purchasing new inventory, there is no price recorded. You should enter the total purchase amount in the Amount field. When you press tab to advance the cursor, Simply Accounting will calculate the price per unit.

There are no freight charges for this entry so you can skip the freight fields. Your input form is completed and should appear as follows:

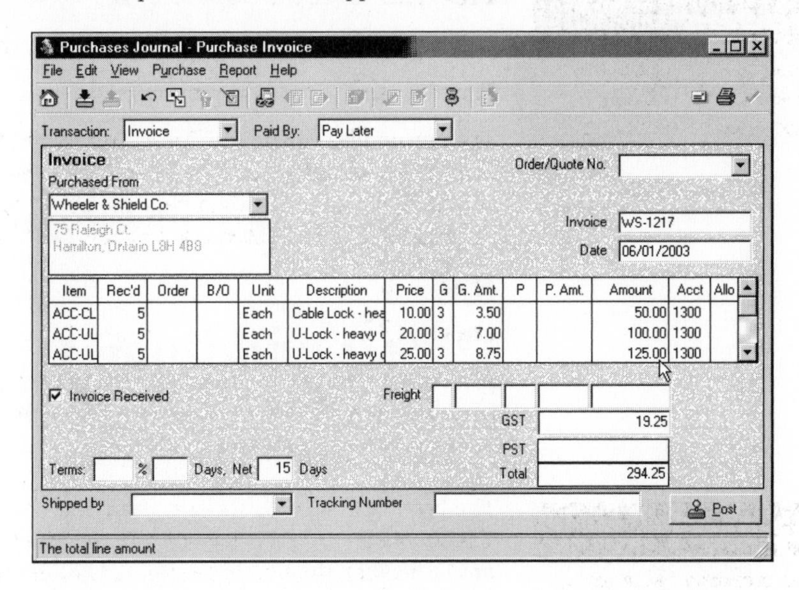

Reviewing the Inventory Purchase Transaction

Choose the **Report menu** and **click Display Purchases Journal Entry** to display the transaction you have entered, as shown:

Purchases Journal Entry

File Options Help

06/01/2003 (J2)	Debits	Credits	Project
1300 Accessories	275.00	-	
2670 GST Paid on Purchases	19.25	-	
2200 Accounts Payable	-	294.25	
	294.25	294.25	

Warning!

Please be careful when reviewing your transaction to make sure you have entered the correct information.

You can see that the Simply Accounting program has automatically updated all accounts relevant to this transaction. The appropriate inventory asset account (*Accessories*) and the *Accounts Payable* and *GST Paid on Purchases* accounts have been updated as required because the ledgers are linked. The inventory database and the vendor record are also updated.

Close the display to return to the Purchases Journal input screen.

CORRECTING THE INVENTORY PURCHASES JOURNAL ENTRY

If the inventory item is incorrect, re-select from the inventory list by pressing *enter* while in this field. **Click Select** to add the item to your form. **Type** the quantity purchased and **press** *tab* repeatedly to advance to the next line to update the totals. Remember to delete the PST rate again for the newly selected inventory item.

Account numbers cannot be changed on the purchase invoice for inventory items. They must be edited in the Inventory Ledger.

If you have forgotten a complete line of the invoice, **click** the line below the one you have forgotten. **Choose** the **Edit menu** and **click Insert Line** to add a blank invoice line to your form. To remove a complete line, **click** the line you want to delete, **choose** the **Edit menu** and **click Remove Line**.

For assistance with correcting other details, refer to page 82.

Posting

If this is a recurring purchase, you can store the entry, just like other recurring purchases.

When all the information in your journal entry is correct, you must post the transaction to save your work.

Click Post Post

The next transaction is an inventory adjustment. **Close** the Purchases Journal to exit to the Home window.

> **notes**
>
> To correct an inventory purchase after posting, use the Adjust invoice feature.

Orders and Quotes

Placing a purchase order or quote for inventory items is the same as a purchase order or quote for non-inventory items.

Choose the appropriate Transaction Type.

Enter the Order or Quote Number and Shipping Date. Quote numbers are updated automatically.

Then complete the selection of inventory items as you would for an inventory purchase. Instead of filling in the Rec'd field, however, you will complete the Order and B/O fields.

When the goods are received, fill the purchase order/quote. Refer to Chapter 4, page 87 if you need to review purchase orders and quotes.

Sales Orders and Quotes for inventory items are entered and filled in the same way as they are for non-inventory items, except, of course, for the addition of inventory item details.

Making Inventory Adjustments

Sometimes inventory is lost, stolen or damaged and adjusting entries are required to reflect the expenses. These inventory adjustments are made in the Adjustments Journal indicated in the Home window shown here:

> **notes**
>
> The Adjustments Journal is also used to record lost inventory that is recovered and inventory that is used by the business instead of sold to customers.

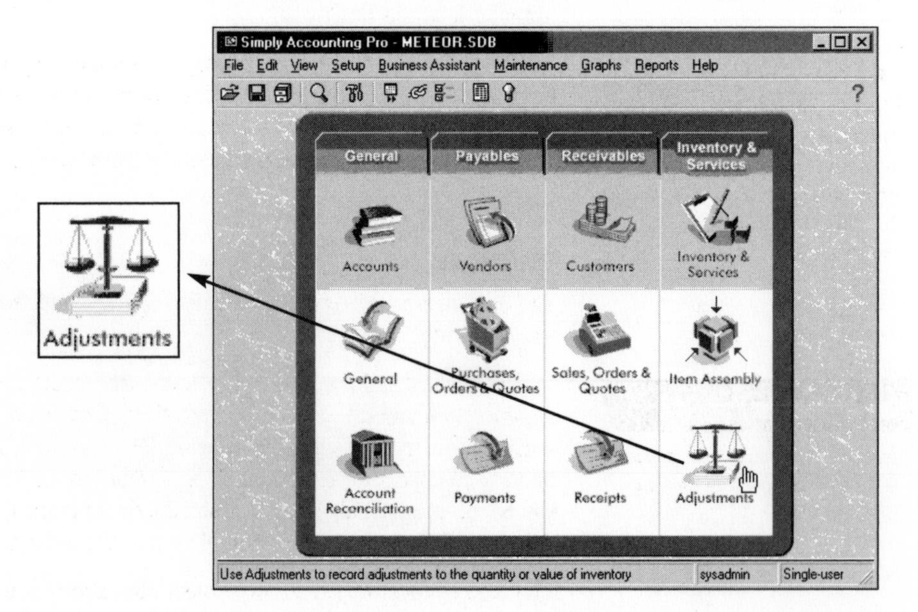

Click the **Adjustments Journal icon** to display the blank inventory Adjustments Journal input screen:

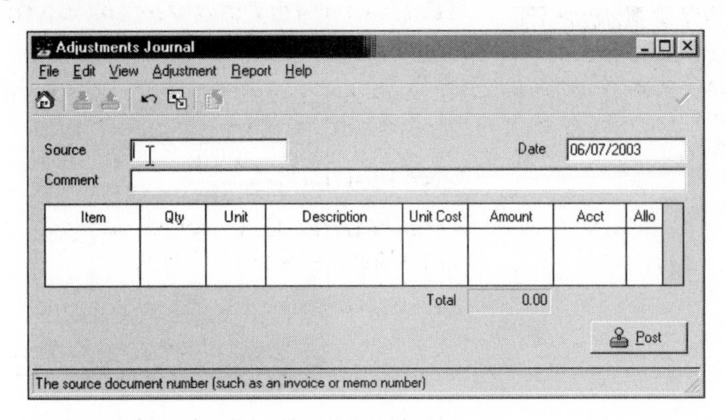

The cursor is in the Source field. The source for an adjustment will normally be a memo from a manager or owner.

Type `Memo 1`

Press *tab*

The cursor is now in the Date field, with the session date entered and highlighted as usual.

Type `06-02-03`

Press *tab*

The cursor is now in the Comment field, where you can enter a brief explanation for this transaction.

Type `Speedometer damaged beyond repair`

Press *tab*

The cursor is now in the Item field.

Press *enter* to display the familiar inventory list. Notice that the quantities have been updated to include the previous sale and purchase.

Double click ACC-SD1 Speedometer - digital deluxe from the list to select it and enter it onto the form.

notes

Remember always to enter a negative quantity when there is an inventory loss. If lost inventory is recovered later, enter the adjustment with a positive quantity.

The item name, *Speedometer - digital deluxe*, the unit, the unit cost and the account have been added automatically. The cursor advances to the Quantity field. You need to indicate that the inventory has been reduced because of the damaged item. You do this by typing a negative number in the field.

Type `-1`

Press *tab*

The cursor advances to the Unit field. The rest of the journal line is completed automatically.

notes

You can store Adjustments Journal entries just as you store entries in other journals.

In the Amount field, a negative amount, reflecting the inventory loss, automatically appears as a default. In the Account field, *Damaged Inventory*, the default linked account for inventory losses, appears for this entry. This is the correct account. If you need to choose another account, press *enter* to display the list of accounts and select the account as usual. You can also edit the amount if you know that the price of the unit was different from the default price, the average of all inventory in stock.

The Allo (allocation) field for project allocations is not used by Meteor Mountain Bike Shop, so ignore it. We will discuss it in a later application.

Your entry is complete as shown and you are ready to review it:

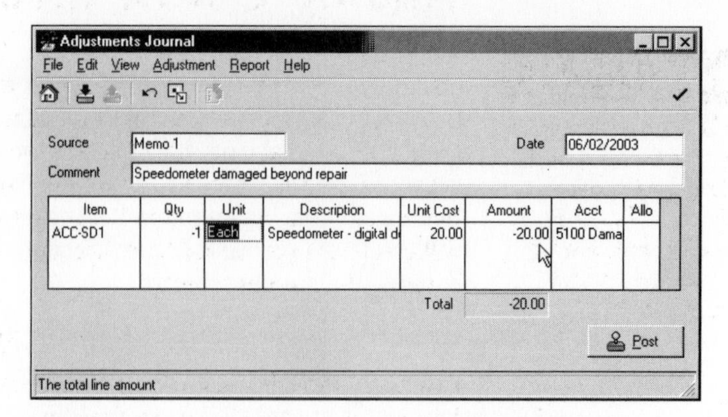

Reviewing the Adjustments Journal Entry

The other inventory ledger linked account is used for item assembly costs in the Item Assembly Journal. Item assembly is introduced in the Puretek application.

Choose the **Report** menu and **click Display Adjustments Journal Entry** to display the transaction you have entered as shown here:

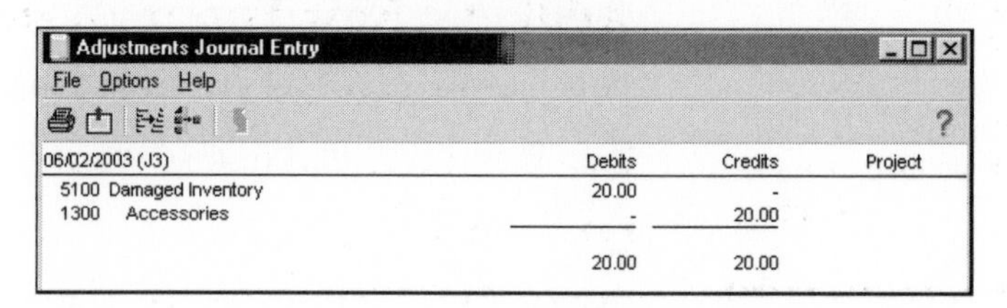

You can see that the Simply Accounting program has automatically updated all relevant accounts for this transaction. The appropriate inventory asset defined for this inventory item, *Accessories*, and the inventory database have also been reduced to reflect the loss. *Damaged Inventory*, the Inventory linked expense account that was defined for inventory losses or adjustments, has been debited or increased.

Close the display to return to the Adjustments Journal input screen.

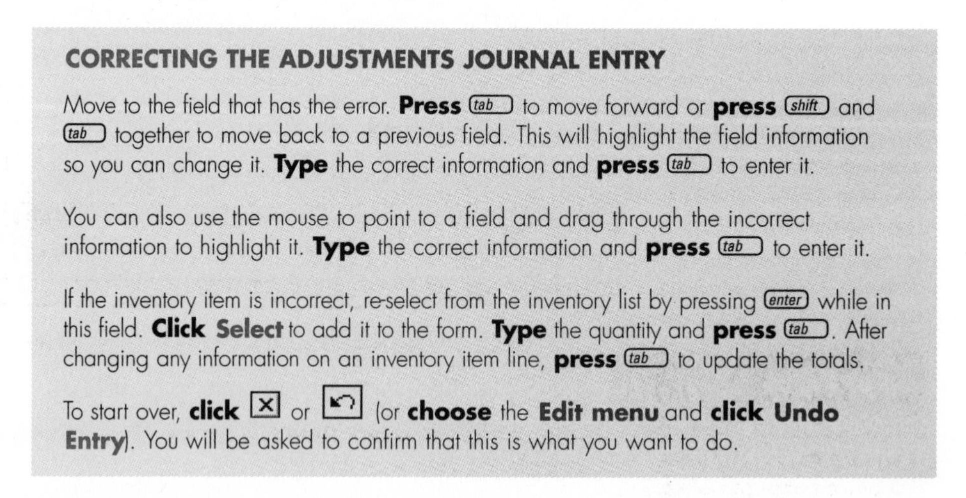

CORRECTING THE ADJUSTMENTS JOURNAL ENTRY

Move to the field that has the error. **Press** tab to move forward or **press** shift and tab together to move back to a previous field. This will highlight the field information so you can change it. **Type** the correct information and **press** tab to enter it.

You can also use the mouse to point to a field and drag through the incorrect information to highlight it. **Type** the correct information and **press** tab to enter it.

If the inventory item is incorrect, re-select from the inventory list by pressing enter while in this field. **Click Select** to add it to the form. **Type** the quantity and **press** tab. After changing any information on an inventory item line, **press** tab to update the totals.

To start over, **click** ☒ or ↶ (or **choose** the **Edit menu** and **click Undo Entry**). You will be asked to confirm that this is what you want to do.

Posting

When all the information in your journal entry is correct, you must post the transaction to save your work.

Click Post [Post]

Close the Adjustments Journal to return to the Home window. The next keystroke transaction is a purchase of new inventory items.

Adding a New Inventory Item

notes

You can add new accounts and vendors by accessing the ledgers from the Home window before opening the journal if you want. Refer to the CISV application for adding new accounts and the Maverick application for adding new vendors.

The source document, Memo #2, on June 2 requires you to add Saddle Bags as a new inventory item to the current list. When you check the Chart of Accounts, you can see that saddle bags do not belong in any of the existing inventory asset accounts. In the Purchases Journal, you cannot access the account list or the Wizard for adding a new account for inventory items. Therefore, you must create the account in the journal **before** selecting an inventory item or create the account in the Inventory Ledger. We will create the new Group asset account, **1310 Bags** in the Inventory Ledger while entering the inventory record.

Warning!

You must choose Full Add for the new vendor so that you can enter currency information correctly. The default currency selection, used with Quick Add, Continue and One-time vendors is CAD, Canadian dollars, the home currency.

Click the **Purchases Journal icon** to open the Purchases Journal with Invoice selected as the transaction type.

First we will add the new vendor.

Adding a New Foreign Vendor Record

Click the **Purchased From field** to move the cursor.

Type `Sedona Saddle & Bags`

Press *tab*

Choose **Full Add** and enter the address details.

notes

Do not forget to add the currency as USD (Options tab screen) for this new vendor.

version 8

Click the **Options tab** to open the next vendor information screen:

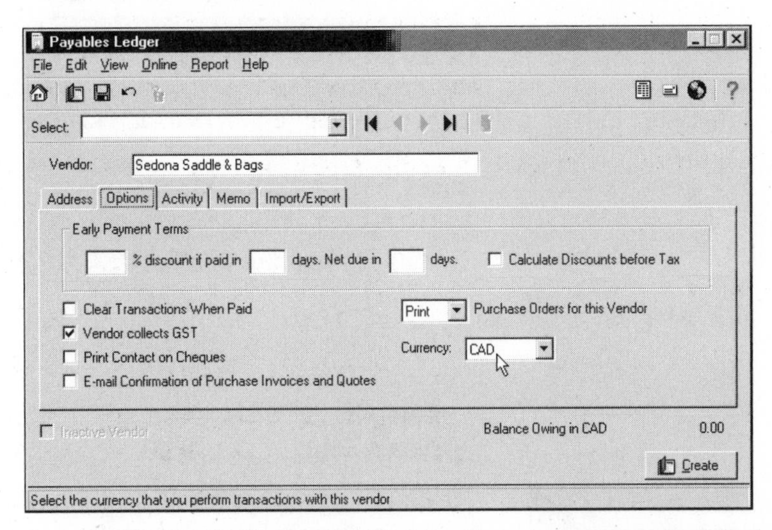

Type `15` (in the Net due in days field to enter the payment terms from the invoice)

Leave the checkmark for Vendor collects GST.

notes

Even though foreign vendors do not collect the GST themselves, the purchaser must pay GST on imported goods. The tax is collected with import duties as part of the customs/importing procedure and sent directly to CCRA. In this workbook, we will include the GST in the purchase invoice.

Click the **Currency field list arrow**. All currencies set up for the company will be on the list for this field.

Click **USD** (United States dollars) to select the foreign currency.

Click **Create** to save the information and return to the Purchases Journal. The journal now has the currency designated as USD and the Exchange Rate field is added.

Add the Invoice number, date and exchange rate to the journal.

Double click the **Item field** to access the Select Inventory list.

version 8

notes

- To edit an inventory item record, click the Home window button in a journal to return to the Home window. Click the Inventory & Services icon to open the Inventory window. Double click the icon or name of the inventory item that you need to change to see the item's ledger record. Highlight the information that is incorrect, and then type the correct information. Close the ledger window and the Inventory & Services window.
- From the Inventory & Services Ledger, use the Select list to find the ledger record.

Double click Add new inventory/service to access the Inventory Ledger as shown:

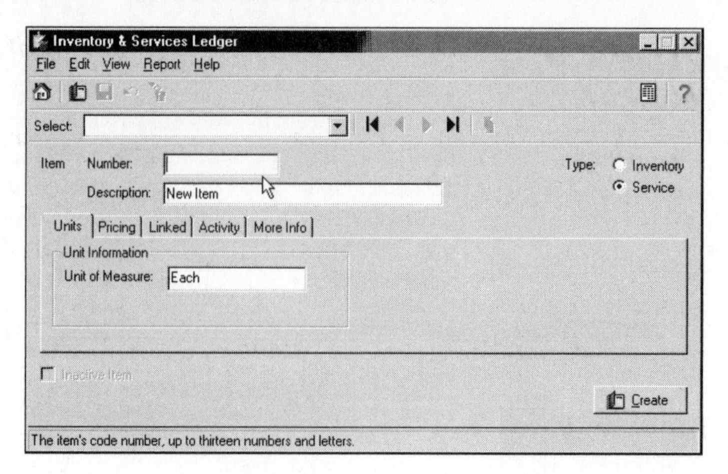

The Inventory Ledger is set for the entry of services because the last item entered was a service. Saddle bags are inventory rather than services.

Click Inventory in the Type section of the ledger window to change the input form:

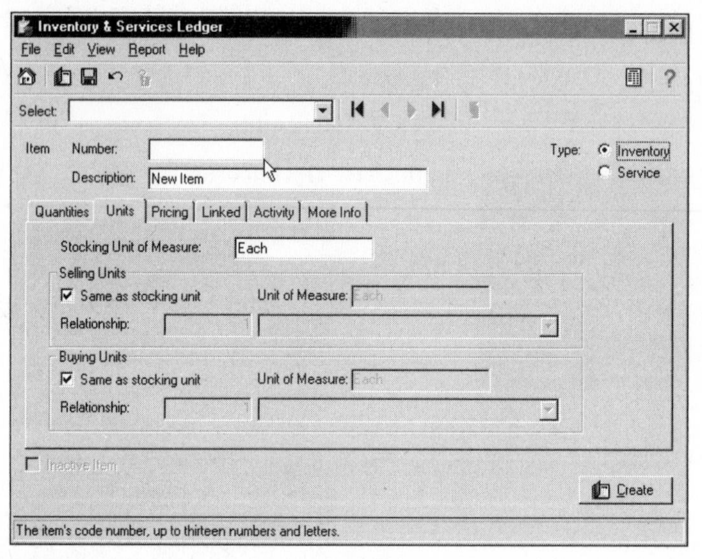

The fields needed for inventory items are added to the ledger window. The Units tab information is still displayed because for Services it is the first tab screen and it remains selected.

notes

The setup option chosen for inventory is to sort the items by code or number. Therefore, the number field is the first item field. When you choose to sort by description, the longer description field will come first. (See Chapter 13.)

From your source document information, you must enter the item code and description. The first Item field contains the code or number of the inventory item; the second Item field contains the description or item name.

Click the **Item Number field**.

Type `BAG-N1`

Press *tab* to advance to the Item Description field.

Type `Saddle Bags - ballistic nylon light`

We have already selected the type as inventory and the default entry for Stocking Unit of Measure is correct. Units show the way in which goods are stored, bought and sold (e.g., by the dozen, by the tonne or by the item). These units may be different if, for example, merchandise is purchased in bulk packages and sold in individual units. Meteor measures all units the same way and the default Unit information is correct.

Click the **Quantities tab**:

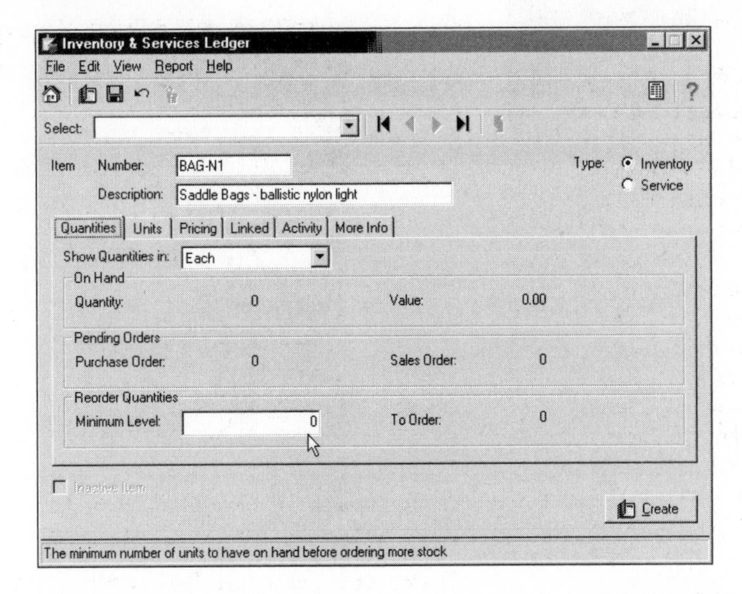

Click the **Minimum Level field** in the Reorder Quantities section. Here you must enter the stock level at which you want to reorder the item in question. When you print inventory reports, items that have fallen below the minimum level will be flagged.

Type 1

The remaining fields are dimmed because they are updated from journal entries. Before the Inventory Ledger history is finished, you can add this information as historical data.

This is the Pricing tab screen for Pro Version 8.5.

Click the **Pricing tab**:

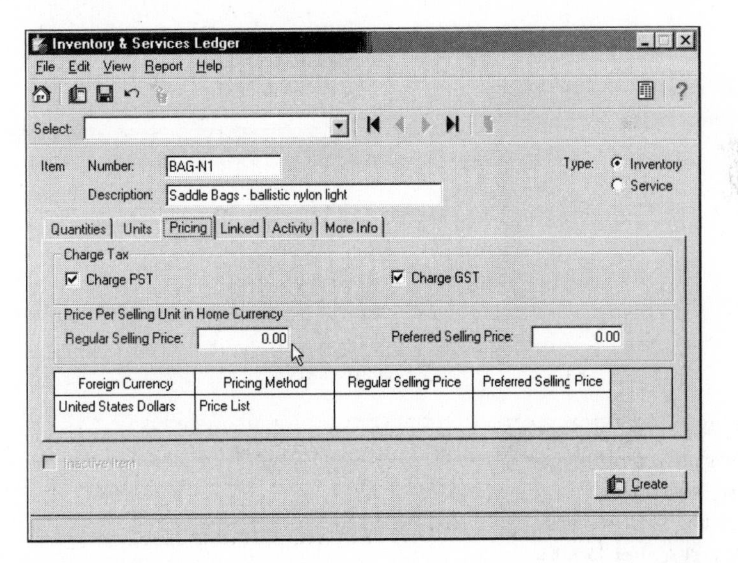

Several pricing options are available. PST and GST may be charged or omitted by default. Because most goods have these taxes applied to the sale, the default is to charge them. The default settings are correct.

version 8

In addition, each item may be assigned a regular price and a preferred selling price for customers who should be given discounted prices. Regular and preferred selling prices can also be entered for foreign customers in the foreign currencies. Pro Version 8.5 allows the use of multiple currencies so the Foreign currency pricing portion is of the ledger is in column form.

This is the Pricing tab screen for Version 8.5 (the regular non-Pro version).

Since Version 8.5 is a dual currency program, it has only one field for the regular foreign price and one for the preferred foreign price as in the following screen:

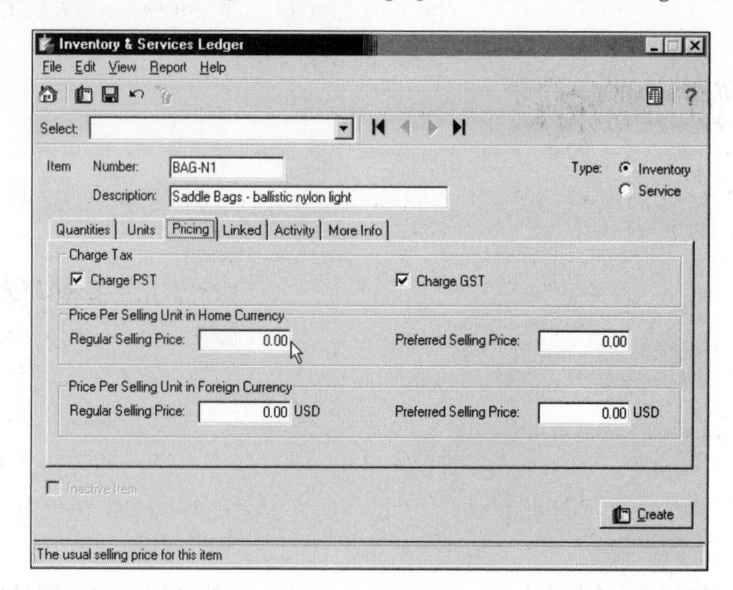

Click the **Regular Selling Price field** in the Home Currency section so you can enter the selling price of the item.

Type 35

Press tab to advance to the Preferred Selling Price field.

Type 30

We will skip the Foreign Currency pricing section because Meteor has no USD customers.

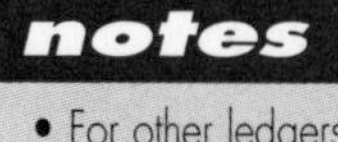

- For other ledgers, the linked accounts are defined for the entire ledger. For example, there is only one Accounts Receivable account.
- Only asset accounts are listed for the Asset field.
- Only revenue accounts are available for the Revenue field.
- Only expense accounts are available for the C.O.G.S. field and the Variance field.
- Variance accounts are used in the Hearth House application.

Click the **Linked tab** to access the linked accounts window for the inventory item:

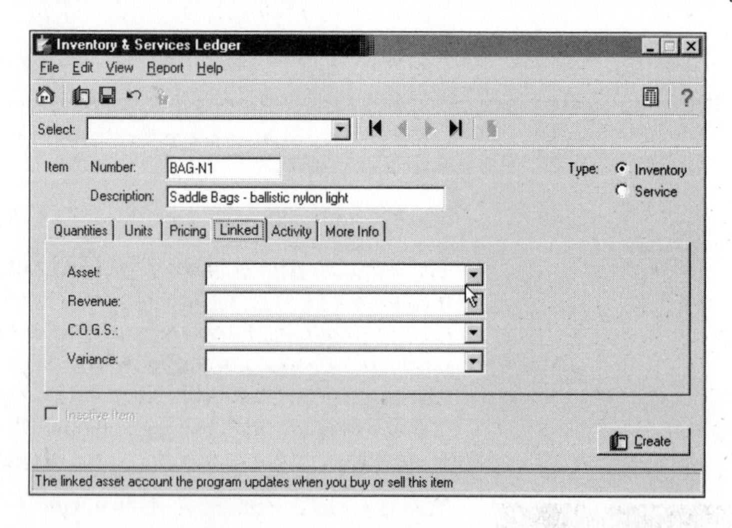

There are two sets of linked accounts for inventory, those that apply to the entire ledger such as the default account for inventory adjustments, and those that apply to specific inventory items. The ones in the ledger are item specific and are used as the default accounts whenever inventory items are sold or purchased. Linked accounts are defined for each item in the Inventory Ledger because each inventory item can be related to separate asset, revenue, expense and variance accounts.

In the Asset field, you must enter the number of the linked asset account affected by purchases and sales of this item. Because the account does not yet exist, we cannot choose it from the account list for the field.

Click the **Asset field**.

Type 1310

Press tab

Warning!

Check the linked account numbers carefully. If they are incorrect, corresponding journal entries will be posted incorrectly. If you discover the error when you are reviewing the journal entry, you should edit the Inventory Ledger record before posting.

You will see a screen advising you that the account does not exist and offering you the chance to create it:

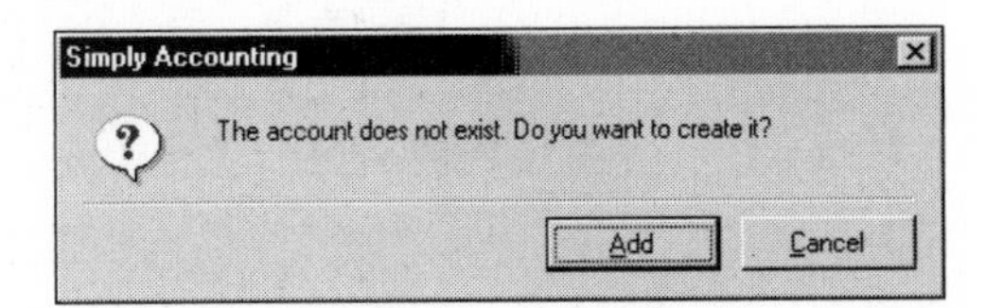

Click Add to proceed to the Add an account Wizard and finish creating the account.

After you click Finish, you will see another message advising you of an account class change for the linked account:

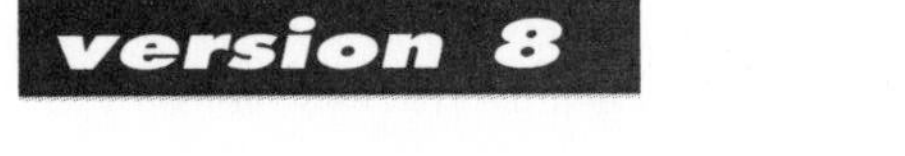

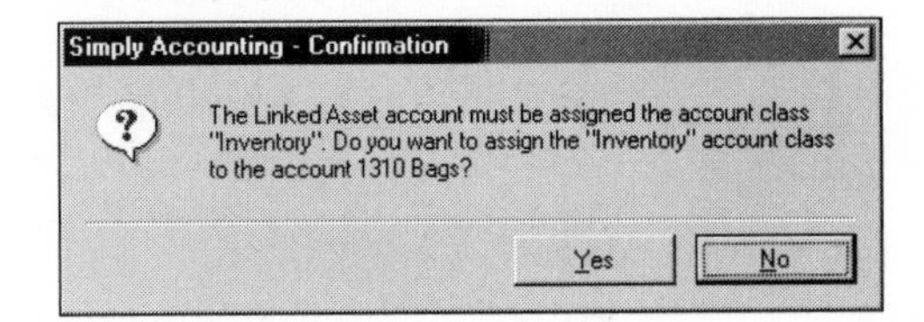

Click Yes to accept the change.

In the Revenue field, you must enter the linked revenue account that will be credited when this inventory item is sold. Again, you can type the account number or select from the list.

Click the **Revenue field list arrow** to see the revenue accounts available.

Click 4020 Revenue from Sales to enter it on your form.

Click the **C.O.G.S. (Expense) field list arrow** to see the expense accounts available. Here you must enter the linked expense account that will be debited when this inventory item is sold.

Click 5060 Cost of Goods Sold from the list.

The Variance field contains the linked variance expense account, used when the inventory sold is on order, before the goods are in stock. At the time of the sale, the *Cost of Goods Sold* account is debited for the average cost of the inventory on hand, based on previous purchases. When the goods are received, the actual purchase price may be different from this historical average cost. The price difference is charged to the variance account. Meteor does not allow inventory to be oversold so you should **leave the Variance account field blank**.

notes

Inventory Activity details are added to inventory tracking reports.

The next tab screen for Activity applies to historical data. Click the Activity tab to see these fields. Since this is a new inventory item, there are no previous sales and you should leave all entries at zero. The Date of Last Sale is the most recent date that this item was sold, using an accepted date format. The Year To Date section refers to historical information for the current fiscal period and the Last Year fields apply to the previous year because Simply Accounting stores two years of transactions.

The No. (number) of Transactions refers to the total number of times the item was sold. For example, if one customer bought the item on three separate dates, there would be three transactions. If four customers bought the item on one day, there would be four transactions. If one customer bought four of the same item at one time, there would be one transaction. The Units Sold counts the total number of items that were sold on all occasions to all customers in the relevant period. In the Amount Sold field you would enter the total sale price of all items sold in the period, and in the Cost of Goods Sold field, enter the total purchase price of all the items sold.

The final tab screen is also not needed. The More Info tab allows a more detailed description of the inventory item and a bitmap file name for a picture of the item.

Correct the information if necessary by returning to the field that contains the error. Click the appropriate tab to change information screens if necessary. Highlight the error and type the correct information. Press *tab* to enter the correction. When all the information is correct, you must save your information.

Click Create [Create] to save the new record and add it to your ledger list of inventory items.

You will return to the Purchases Journal with the new item added to the Item field. Complete the rest of the journal invoice line to record this purchase by entering the quantity received and the amount for the purchase.

Press *tab* to advance to the Rec'd field.

Type 5

The GST code and PST rate fields are blank by default because this is a foreign vendor. However, GST must be paid on imported goods.

notes

GST on imported goods is collected by CCRA at the same time as the import duties. This would require a separate cash payment to CCRA and the amount would not appear in GST reports. For the sake of simplicity, we indicate that foreign vendors collect GST.

Type 3 (in the G field to indicate that GST should be added to the price)

Click the **Amount field**.

Type 60

Press *tab*

Repeat the procedures above for the second new inventory item in the source document. Inventory should be selected as the Type by default and the Quantities tab screen is displayed first. Because Services do not have quantity information, the Unit tab screen was displayed first and remained selected when we changed the type to Inventory. You should use the same asset, revenue and expense accounts that you used for the first new inventory item. Create the record and return to the journal. Record the remaining purchase invoice details.

version 8

When you have finished, your journal entry should look like the one shown here:

Warning!

You cannot adjust invoices to correct for selecting the wrong vendor or customer. For these errors, you must complete a reversing entry. Refer to Appendix A.

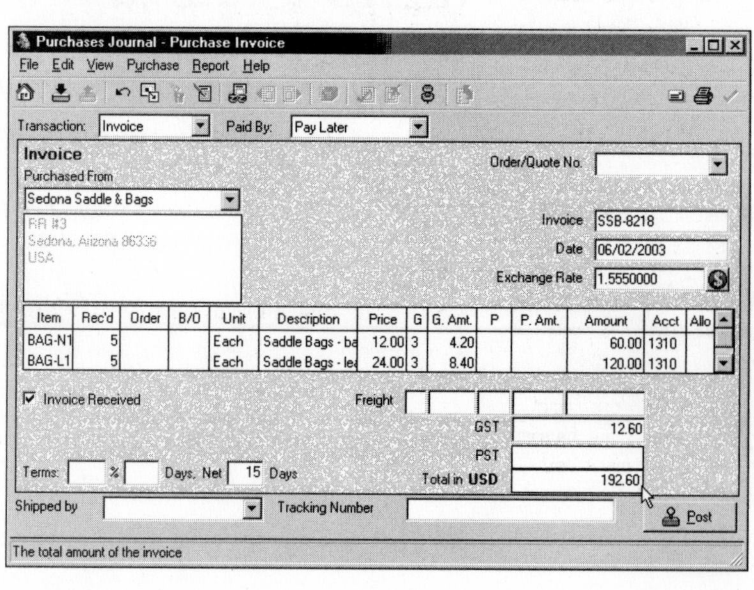

notes

To edit an Inventory Ledger record after creating it, return to the Home window. (If the journal is open, delete the journal line for the inventory item that has an error. Otherwise the fields for this ledger record will be dimmed and unavailable. Then click the Home window button.) Click the Inventory & Services icon and double click the inventory item name or icon. Click the tab you need to access the fields you need to edit.

Choose the **Report menu** and **click Display Purchases Journal Entry** to review the entry carefully:

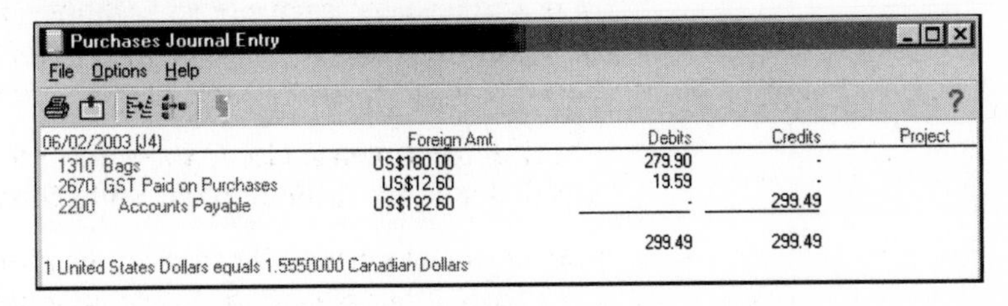

Notice that the entry shows amounts in both currencies, CAD and USD, as did the Sales Journal entry in Chapter 7. Otherwise, the transaction involves the same linked accounts as a purchase transaction in CAD, the home currency. Close the display when finished. If you find that one of the inventory item linked account numbers is incorrect, edit the inventory ledger record before posting. You cannot edit the inventory record while you are using it so you should delete the relevant journal line, edit the Inventory Ledger and then re-enter the item.

Close the display. Make corrections if necessary.

When the entry is correct, **post** it. **Close** the Purchases Journal.

Selling to Preferred Customers

New to Simply Accounting Version 8.5 is the ability to record separate inventory prices for preferred customers and to mark customers as preferred or regular to indicate which prices they will pay. Sales for both groups of customers are entered the same way since the program automatically brings up the correct price depending on the customer selected. Lakeland Mountain Bike Club is a preferred customer.

Click the **Sales Journal icon** 

to open the Sales Journal.

Invoice and Pay Later are the correct selections for this sale to Lakeland. The Invoice number is also correct by default.

Choose Lakeland Mountain Bike Club from the customer list.

Type `June 3` (in the Date field). **Press** *tab* to move to the Item field.

Press *enter* to see the inventory list.

Scroll down and then **double click MTB-A241 Brava - 18sp Shimano SIS alum alloy** to add it to the invoice and move the cursor to the Ship (quantity) field.

This adds the first item sold to the customer at the preferred customer price of $450 instead of $500, the regular price.

Type 2

Press *tab*

Enter the remaining items sold to this customer and the freight charges.

version 8

If you are using Version 8, the preferred customer feature is not available. Instead, you should edit the selling price to match the source document as follows:

- Choose MTB-A241, the first item sold to the customer.
- Type 2 in the Ship field.
- Click 500 in the Price field.
- Type 450 to edit the price.
- Press *tab* to update the taxes, Amount and Totals.
- Repeat this procedure for other items with different prices, substituting the appropriate prices.

When completed, your journal entry should should look the same as the one shown on the next page for Version 8.5.

Your finished journal entry should look like the one below:

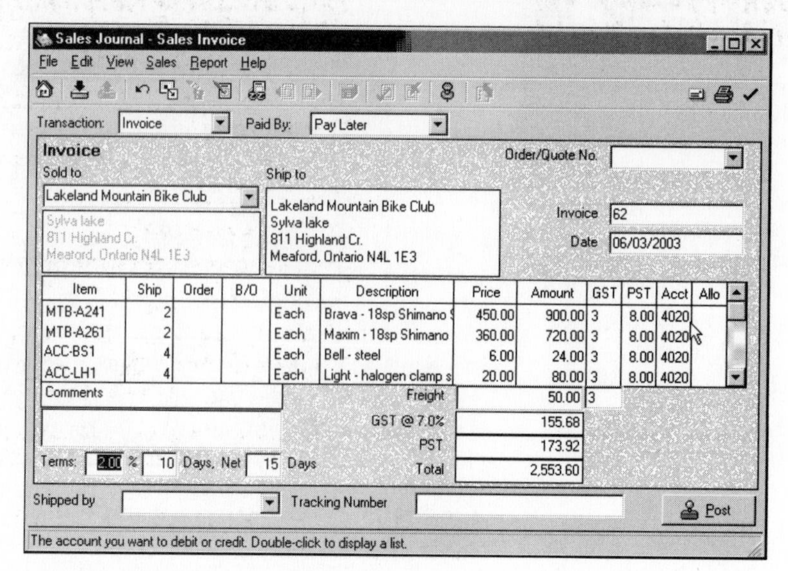

You should review the entry as usual.

Choose the **Report menu** and **click Display Sales Journal Entry**:

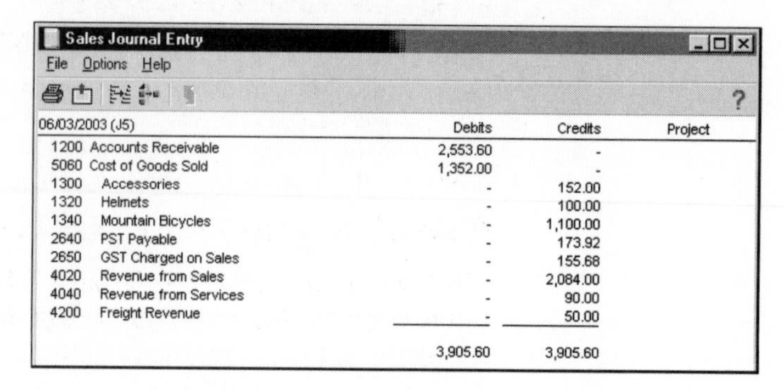

Notice that the entry is the same as a regular non-discounted sale. The revenue has been reduced because of the change in selling price but this change is not recorded as a discount.

Close the display when finished to return to the journal.

Make corrections if necessary and then **post** the entry. **Close** the Sales Journal.

Making Payments to Foreign Vendors

Payments to foreign vendors are the same as those for home currency vendors. Once the vendor is selected, the currency designation is added along with the exchange rate fields. You can pay foreign vendors from any Bank class account, although frequently a business will have a separate bank account in the foreign currency.

Click the **Payments Journal icon** [Payments] to open the Payments Journal.

Choose Sedona Saddle & Bags from the vendor list to view the outstanding invoice.

Click the **From list arrow** to see the available bank accounts as shown:

version 8

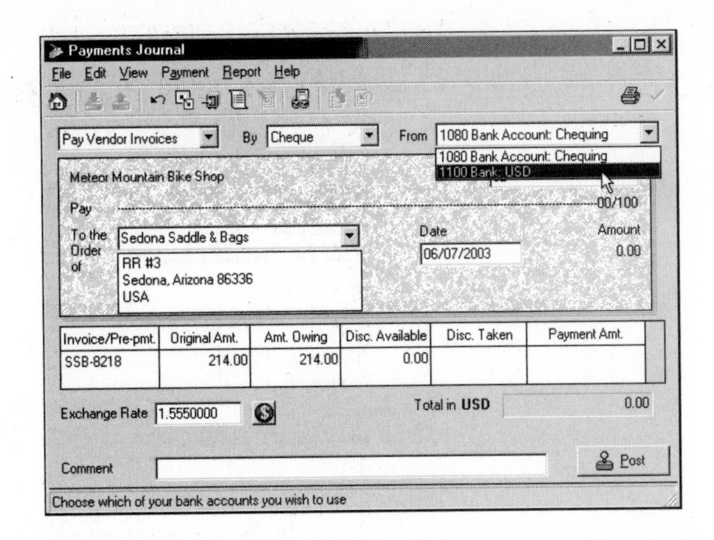

Click1100 Bank: USD to indicate that the money should be taken from the foreign currency account.

The cheque number changes to 301, the next cheque number for the USD bank account. Other than the Exchange Rate field and the Total in USD label for the total amount, the journal is the same as before. All amounts are automatically shown in United States dollars, the currency on record for this vendor.

Double click06/07/2003 , the session date in the Date field so that you can enter the date of the cheque.

Type `June 4`

Press (tab) to see the Exchange Rate screen.

The last rate we entered was for June 3. Since it is now one day old, you see the warning screen. The rate is selected for editing.

Type `1.585`

ClickMake this the default rate for 06/04/2001

ClickOK

Click the**Payment Amt. field** to enter the default payment amount.

Press (tab) to accept the full invoice amount as payment.

The journal entry is complete as shown:

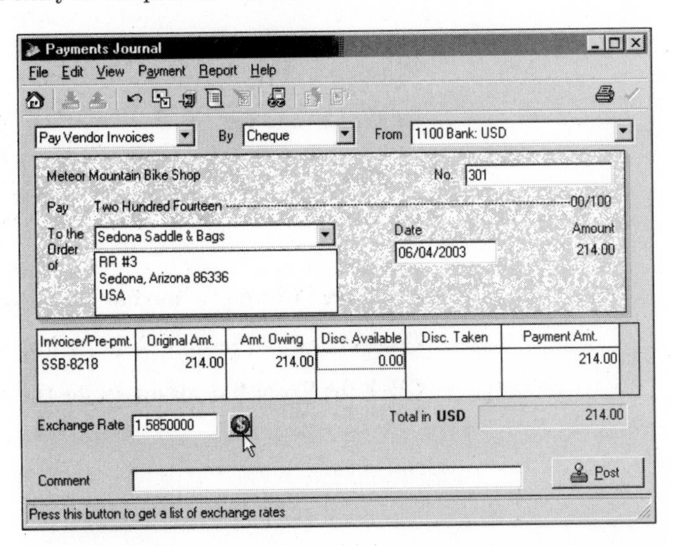

You are ready to review the transaction.

Choose the **Report menu** and **click Display Payments Journal Entry**:

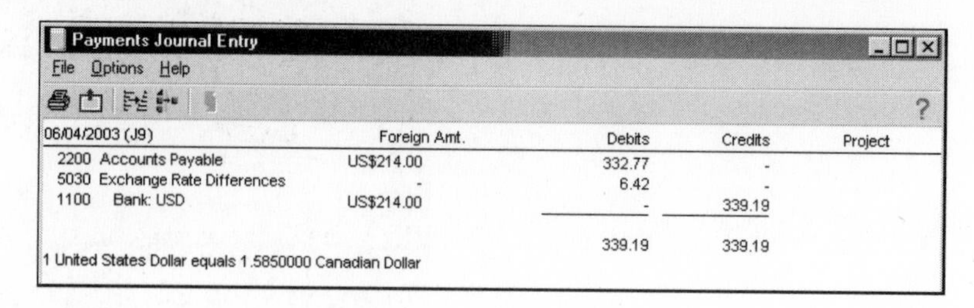

The usual linked accounts, a bank account (*Bank: USD*) and *Accounts Payable* are used for the entry. In addition, because the exchange rates at the time of payment and purchase were different, there is an entry to the *Exchange Rate Differences* account. The rate increased, creating an expense — the purchase was more expensive on the day of payment — so the linked expense account is debited for the difference.

Close the display and make corrections if necessary.

Post the transaction. If you did not change the bank account selection, you will see the following warning when you try to post the entry:

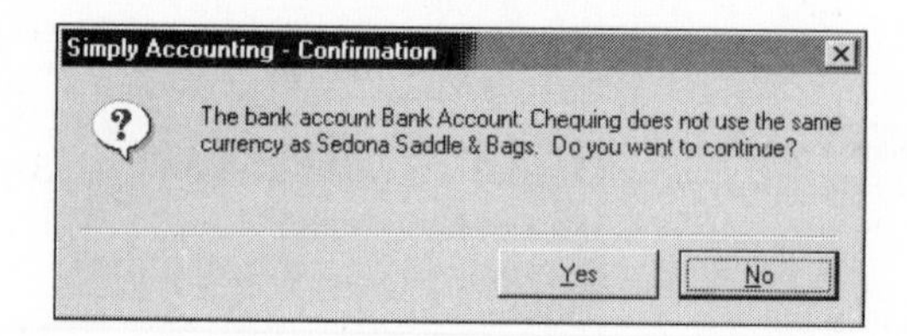

Each bank account has a currency identified for it. If that does not match the currency for the transaction, you will see this warning. **Click No** to cancel the transaction and return to the journal. Select the USD bank account and then post.

Close the Payments Journal.

Transferring Foreign Currency Funds

The USD bank account does not have sufficient funds to cover the cheque to Sedona Saddle & Bags, so a transfer of funds is required. The General Journal allows you to designate the currency for a transaction.

Click the **General Journal icon** [General] to open the General Journal. The cursor is in the Source field.

Type `Memo 4`

Press tab to advance to the Date field.

Type `06 04`

Press tab to advance to the Comment field.

Type `Transfer funds to USD account`

The next step is to select the appropriate currency.

Click the **Currency field list arrow** to see the options as shown:

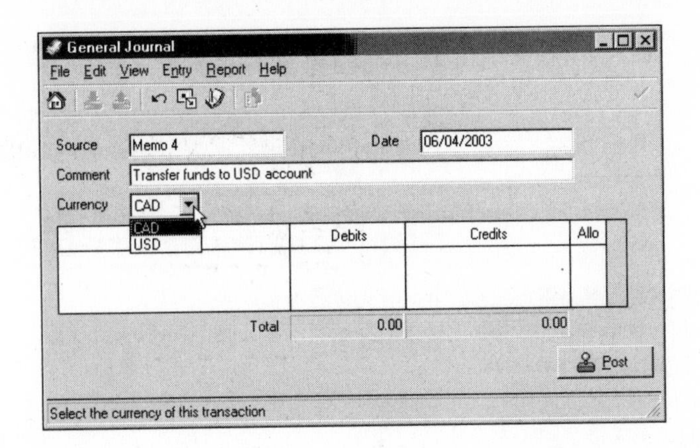

Warning!

To transfer funds to or from a foreign currency account, you must choose the foreign currency. If you choose the home currency, the foreign bank account will not be included in the Select Account list.

Click USD to select the foreign currency and open the Exchange Rate field with the most recent rate entered. The date is unchanged since we last entered the rate, so we can accept the amount.

Click the **Account field**.

Enter the rest of the transaction as usual, debiting the *Bank: USD* account for $200 and crediting *Bank: Chequing Account* for $200.

The completed entry should look like the one shown:

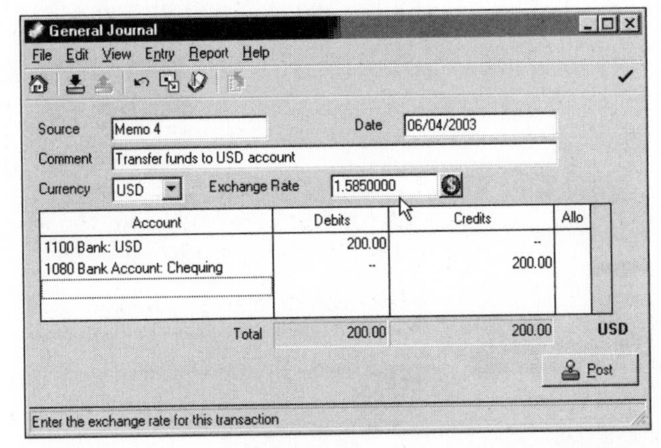

Choose the **Report menu** and **click Display General Journal Entry** to review the transaction:

06/04/2003 (J10)	Foreign Amt.	Debits	Credits	Project
1100 Bank: USD	US$200.00	317.00	-	
1080 Bank Account: Chequing	US$200.00	-	317.00	
		317.00	317.00	

1 United States Dollar equals 1.5850000 Canadian Dollar

The only difference from a regular journal entry is the additional column for foreign currency amounts and the listing of the exchange rate for the transaction.

Close the display when finished. Make corrections to the entry if necessary.

Post the transaction and then **close** the General Journal.

Displaying Inventory Reports

Most inventory reports can be displayed from the Reports menu in the Inventory & Services window.

Displaying Inventory Lists

notes

You can drill down to the Inventory Transaction Report and the General Ledger Report from Inventory Lists.

In the Home window,

Right-click the **Inventory & Services icon** to select it.

Click the **Display button** or choose the Reports menu and choose Lists, then click Inventory & Services. You will see the list immediately.

Close the display when you have finished.

Displaying the Adjustments Journal

notes

Inventory reports can be sorted and filtered. The criteria available are generally the same as the details that are included in the report.

In the Home window,

Right-click the **Adjustments Journal icon** to select it.

Click the **Display button** or choose the Reports menu, then choose Journal Entries and click Adjustments to see the familiar journal options screen:

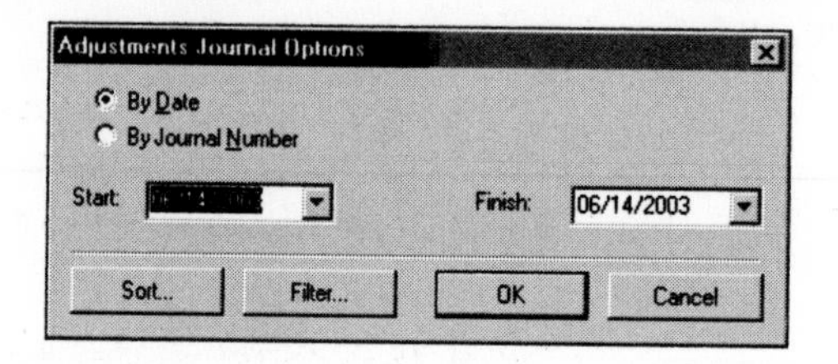

notes

You can drill down to the Vendor or Customer Aged Report, Invoice Lookup (if applicable) or the General Ledger reports from the Adjustments Journal.

As usual, the session date and the By Date option are provided by default.

Type the beginning date for the report you want.

Press tab

Type the ending date for the report.

Click **OK**

Close the display when you have finished.

Displaying Inventory Reports

notes

For all inventory reports, the sort and filter options include most of the fields that are also included in the reports.

Choose the **Reports menu**, **choose** **Inventory & Services** and then **click** **Inventory** to display the following report options:

notes

- Services are not included in the Inventory Report because there is no quantity or cost information for them.
- You can drill down to the Inventory Transaction Report from the Inventory Quantity or Synopsis Reports.

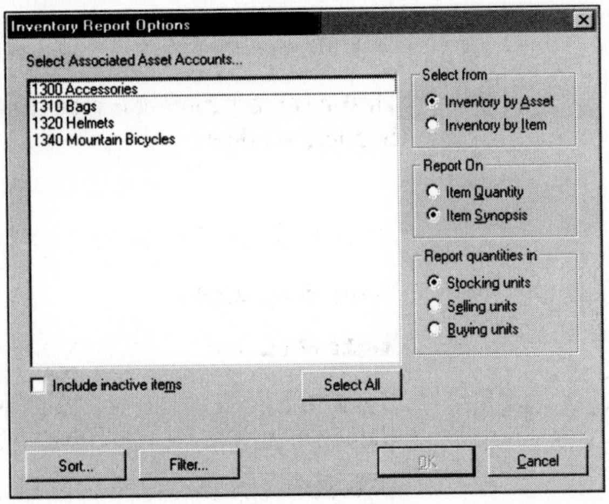

version 8

notes

To select multiple items, press *ctrl* and then click the items you want to add to the list.

Selecting the **Inventory by Asset** option will provide information for all inventory items in the asset group(s) chosen.

The **Inventory by Item** option will provide information for all the items selected. When you click Inventory by Item, the box lists all inventory items.

Clicking or selecting a single asset or item will provide a report for that item only. You can obtain information for all items by choosing **Select All**.

Inventory reports can be displayed with two types of information, **quantity** or **synopsis**.

The **Item Quantity** option provides current information for selected items about the quantity on hand, the minimum stock levels, whether the item has fallen below the minimum level and needs to be re-ordered, and outstanding purchase and sales orders.

The **Item Synopsis** option lists the selling price, the quantity on hand, the unit cost of the inventory, the total value or cost of inventory on hand, and the profit margin or markup for the items requested. The total value of the inventory in an asset group is also provided when you select **Inventory by Asset**.

Choose the options you need for your report.

Press *ctrl* and **click** the **names** of all the items or asset groups you want included in the report.

Click OK

Close the display when you are finished.

Displaying Inventory Management Reports

The management reports for the Inventory Ledger focus on potential problem items, such as listing the inventory items that are not profitable or that have low markups.

Choose the **Reports menu**, then **choose Management Reports** and **click Inventory & Services**:

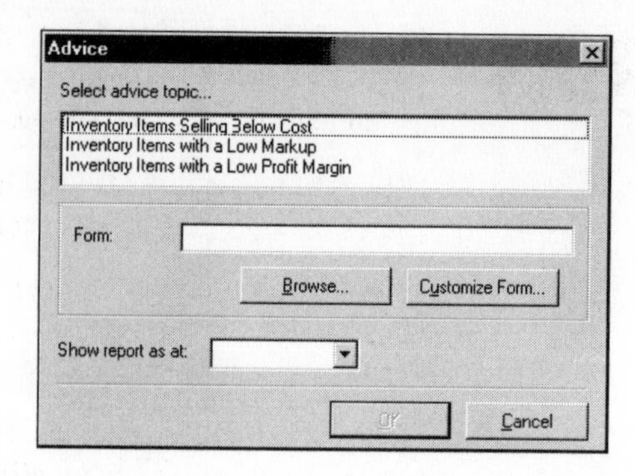

Select the report you want from the list and choose the report form you need.

Click OK to view the report.

Close the display when finished.

Displaying Inventory Tracking Reports

There are several reports that provide information about the turnover of inventory products.

Inventory Activity Reports

notes

You can drill down to the Inventory Sales Report from the Inventory Activity Report.

Choose the **Reports menu**, then **choose Inventory & Services** and **click Activity** to display the following report options:

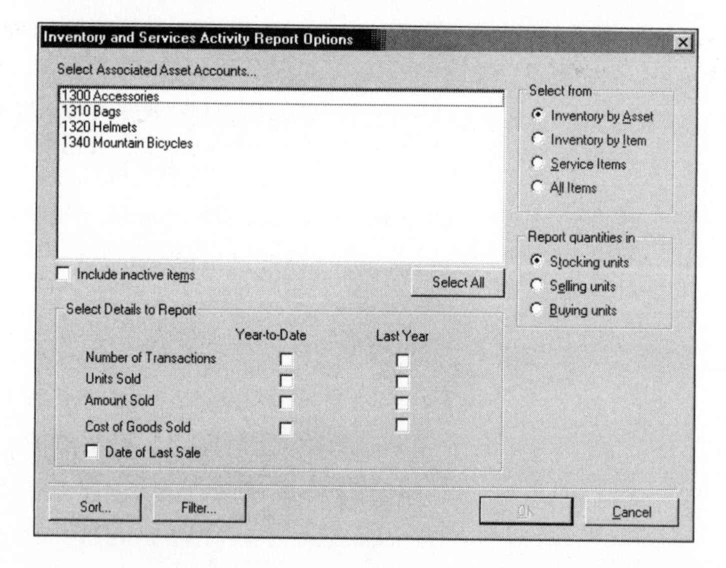

The Activity report has the summary of all transactions for the year to date and the previous year, the same historical information that is contained in the inventory ledger record. You can use the report to determine whether a large volume of sales of an item resulted from a single sale for a large quantity or from a large number of smaller sales.

notes

Simply Accounting uses the average cost method to calculate the cost of goods sold.

Clicking a detail will include it in the report for each selected item or asset group. There are five details that you can add to the report. The **Number of Transactions** refers to the number of separate sales invoices that included the inventory item. **Units Sold** reports on the total number of individual items of a kind that were sold in the period; the **Amount Sold** refers to the total sale price for all items sold, and the **Cost of Goods Sold** is the total purchase cost of all the items that were sold. The

Date of Last Sale, the date on which the item was most recently sold, can also be included in the report.

Press ctrl and **click one or more asset groups** to include them in the report, or **click Select All** to include all asset groups in the report. Selecting an asset group will include all the inventory items in that group in the report.

notes

To select multiple assets or items, press ctrl and then click the items you want to add to the list.

Click Inventory by Item to include individual inventory items in the report. Select one or more items for the report, or **click Select All** to include all inventory items.

Click Service Items to include individual services in the report. **Press** ctrl and **click one or more services** to include them, or **click Select All** to include all services in the report.

Click All Items to include both individual inventory items and individual services in the report. **Press** ctrl and **click one or more items and services** to include them in the report, or **click Select All** to include all items and services in the report.

The list of items will expand according to your selection and you can choose single or multiple items for inclusion.

Quantities can be reported in any of the units on record — the units for stocking the inventory, for buying and for selling — if these are different.

Choose the **items** you want in the report.

Choose the **details** for which you want the report.

Click OK to display the report.

Close the display when you are finished.

Inventory Sales Reports

Choose the **Reports menu**, then **choose Inventory & Services** and **click Sales** to display the following report options:

notes

You can drill down to the Inventory Detail Report from the Inventory Sales Summary Report. You can display the Customer Aged, Inventory Ledger, Journal Report and Invoice Lookup from the Inventory Sales Detail Report.

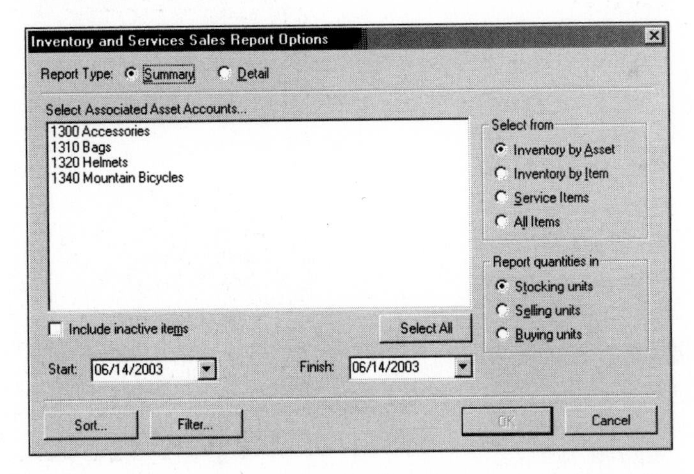

The **Summary** option, selected by default, includes totals for the selected inventory items organized by item. The **Detail** option provides the same information listed by individual journal entry, including the source document numbers and journal entry numbers. The report includes details on the number of transactions (Summary option only), the quantity of items sold, the revenue per item, the cost of goods sold and the profit on each sale transaction. Non-inventory sales are not included. **Click Detail** to choose the Detail option.

notes

The Inventory Sales report provides the same details as the Customer Sales report, but the Customer Sales report has the details organized by customer as well as by item. Customer Sales Reports also have the option to include non-inventory sales.

Quantities may be reported for the units recorded for stocking, buying or selling.

As usual, choosing **Select All** provides a report on all items that are in the list, and you can choose to report on inventory items, services or both. To report only on all services, **click Service Items** and then **Select All**. **Click All Items** to include both inventory and services. The list of items will expand accordingly, and you can choose single or multiple items for inclusion. Select All at this stage will provide a report on all inventory and service items.

Again, quantities may be reported in stocking, buying or selling units.

Type the starting date for the report in the Start field and the ending date for the report in the Finish field. By default, the latest session date appears in both fields.

Choose the **items** to include in the report.

Choose the **Summary** or **Detail** option.

Click OK

Close the display when you are finished.

Inventory Transaction Reports

The Transaction report shows the inventory activity summarized according to the journal used to record the transaction.

Choose the **Reports menu**, then **choose Inventory & Services** and **click Transaction** to display the following report options:

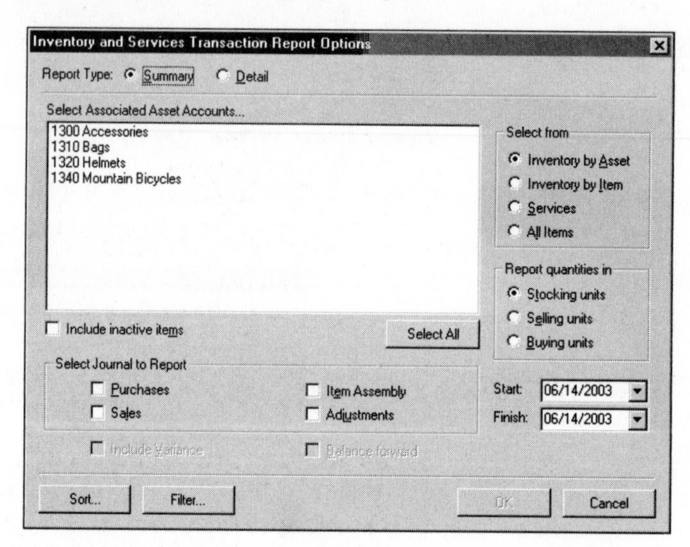

notes

You can drill down to the Transaction Detail Report from the Transaction Summary Report. You can display the Inventory Ledger and Journal Report from the Transaction Detail Report. You can also look up invoices from the Detail report.

The **Summary** option, selected by default, includes totals for the selected inventory items organized by item. The **Detail** option provides the same information listed by individual journal entry, including the source document numbers and journal entry numbers. The report includes details on the number of transactions (Summary option only), the Quantity In (increases to inventory from purchases, sales returns or recovery of lost items) and Out (decreases in inventory from sales, purchase returns or losses and adjustments) and the Amount In and Out (cost price) for each item chosen in each of the selected journals.

Click Detail to choose the Detail option.

As in the previous report, you can prepare a report for one or more asset groups, one or more inventory items, one or more service items or a combination of services and items (All Items). Clicking the appropriate button in the Select From list will expand the item list accordingly. Select All will automatically include any item that is displayed in the list box.

Quantities may be reported in stocking, buying or selling units.

Type the starting date for the report in the Start field and the ending date for the report in the Finish field. By default, the latest session date appears in both fields.

Click the journals to include in the report.

Click Balance Forward to include opening balances for each item.

Variances can also be added to the report when they are used.

Click OK

Close the display when you have finished.

Vendor Purchases Reports

The next two reports combine inventory information with vendor or customer details to show how purchases are spread among vendors and how sales are divided among customers. The Vendor Purchases and Customer Sales Reports also allow you to include information for non-inventory purchases or sales.

notes

You can drill down to the Inventory Purchases Detail Report from the Purchases Summary Report. You can look up invoices, or display the Vendor Aged and Journal Report from the Purchases Detail Report.

Choose the **Reports menu**, then **choose Payables** and **click Vendor Purchases** to display the following report options:

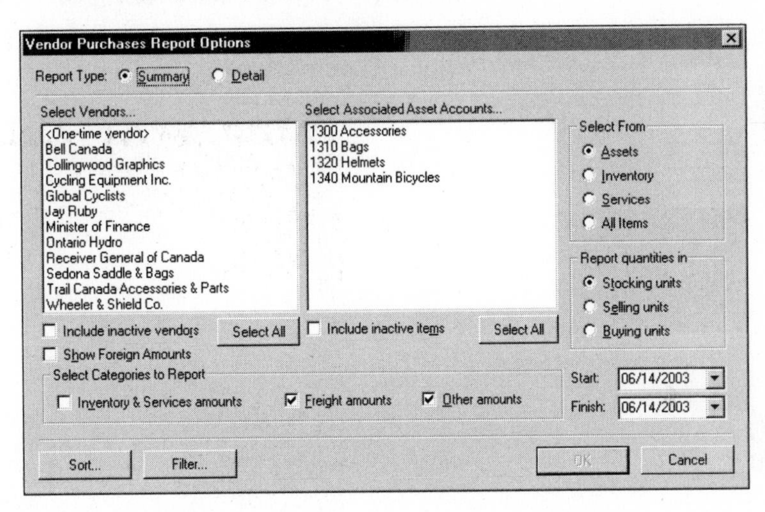

The **Summary** option, selected by default, includes totals for the selected categories and items or asset group, organized by vendor. The **Detail** option provides the same information by individual journal entry, including the source document numbers and journal entry numbers. The report includes details on the number of transactions (Summary option only), the quantity of items sold, the unit cost and the total cost of the purchase. Non-inventory purchases, such as telephone services, are listed as Other. **Click Detail** to choose the Detail option.

Amounts for foreign vendors may be shown in either the home currency or the foreign currency.

The selection of inventory, services or asset groups is the same as it was for the previous inventory report.

notes

To select multiple items, press ctrl and then click the items you want to add to the list.

Click the **assets, inventory items, or services** to include in the report, or **click Select All** to include all listed items in the report.

Click the **Vendor names** to include in the report, or **click** the **Select All** button below the Select Vendors list to include all Vendors in the report.

Type the starting date for the report in the Start field and the ending date for the report in the Finish field. By default, the latest session date appears in both fields.

Once a category is not selected you can click it again to select it.

By default, all categories will be included in the report. Click any category to remove the ✔ and deselect it. You can choose to include purchases of inventory items, non-inventory purchases (other) and freight charges for the selected vendor and item transactions.

Click OK. **Close** the display when finished.

Customer Sales Reports

notes

You can drill down to the Inventory Sales Detail Report from the Customer Sales Summary Report. You can drill down to the Customer Aged, Invoice Lookup and Journal Report from the Customer Sales Detail Report.

Choose the **Reports menu**, then **choose Receivables** and **click Customer Sales** to display the following report options:

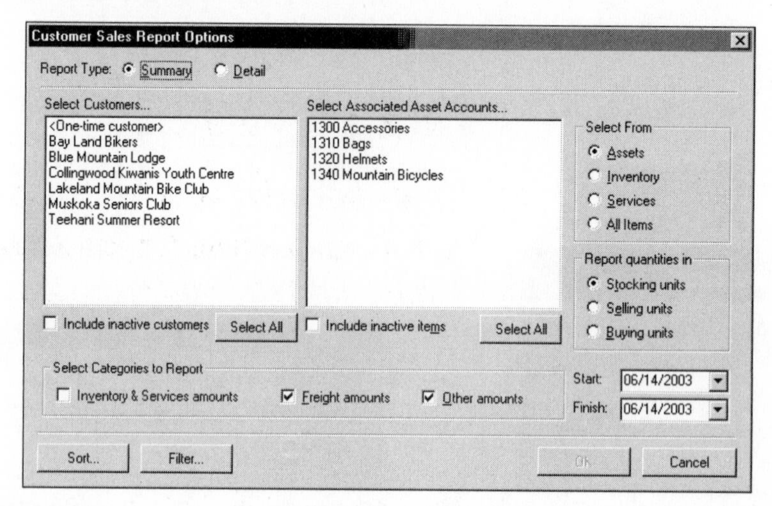

The **Summary** option, selected by default, includes totals for the selected categories and items or asset groups, organized by customer. The **Detail** option provides the same information listed by individual journal entry, including the source document numbers and journal entry numbers. The report includes details on the number of transactions (Summary option only), the quantity of items sold, the revenue per item, the cost of goods sold, and the profit on each sale transaction. Non-inventory sales, such as discounts, are listed as Other. **Click Detail** to choose the Detail option.

Select assets, inventory or services, customers, dates and categories as you do for Vendor Purchases reports.

Click OK. **Close** the display when you have finished.

Printing Inventory Reports

To print an inventory report, first display the report. Then, **choose** the **File menu** in the report window and **click Print**. **Close** the display.

CASE PROBLEM

Examine the sale of new items — saddle bags — and determine how successful they have been relative to other items. What information should Meteor Mountain Bike Shop use in deciding whether to continue selling these items?

How is the decision to continue providing a service different from the decision to carry inventory items? Why might a store continue to sell inventory items or provide a service even if they were not selling well?

CHAPTER TEN

OBJECTIVES

After completing this chapter, you should be able to

- *plan* and *design* an accounting system for a small business
- *prepare* procedures for converting from a manual system
- *understand* the objectives of a computerized system
- *create* company files
- *observe* and *understand* linked accounts
- *create* linked accounts
- *enter* settings for foreign currency transactions
- *set up* accounts in the General, Payables and Receivables Ledgers
- *enter* historical information for vendors and customers
- *set up* credit cards for receipts and payments
- *finish* entering history after entering journal transactions
- *enter* postdated transactions

COMPANY INFORMATION

Company Profile

notes

Maverick Micro Solutions is located at
17 Turbo Lane
Calgary, AB T3B 4U2
Business No.: 98233 2812

Maverick Micro Solutions is a sole proprietorship owned and run by James Maverick in Calgary, Alberta. Maverick graduated from the computer engineering program at Calgary College several years ago. After working as a computer technician for several years with a large computer company in Winnipeg, he returned to Calgary and started his own business in January 2003.

Maverick provides on-site service to a few large firms and colleges in the Calgary district. These account customers have a credit limit of $5 000, are offered a 1 percent discount for payment within five days and are requested to settle their accounts in

20 days. After 30 days, Maverick charges 1 percent interest per month on amounts overdue and accounts are aged accordingly. Customer statements are sent monthly.

Maverick designed, printed and distributed a promotional brochure at the beginning of the year. In it he described the variety of services that he offers to businesses that use computers as an integral part of their day-to-day operation. Currently, Maverick is able to set up new computer systems and networks, install memory chips, circuit boards, modems, backup drives and hard disks as equipment upgrades, install and test software protection and other programs, recover damaged or deleted data files and convert PC data files to TV format. Maverick also repairs computers, printers, monitors, digital cameras, projection panels and other related components. His fee for these services is always negotiated before he begins the work. In addition to these services, Maverick provides technical training in his machine shop to interested individuals. For training, he charges on an hourly basis.

By dealing with both the software and hardware needs of his clients, Maverick has been able to expand his customer base quickly. He estimates that in the near future, he will require a full-time assistant. For now, he works alone most of the time. Whenever he has a large contract with tight deadlines, he brings in as assistants some of the advanced students from the evening class he teaches at Calgary College.

Just last month, the editor of a popular computer magazine approached Maverick to ask him to contribute to their reviews and tests of new hardware and software. Even though he was already very busy with the other aspects of his work, he accepted because it would provide further opportunity for keeping up with the rapid changes in industry standards, and for increased recognition and professional credibility.

At the start of his business, Maverick also set up accounts with a few suppliers of computers and related equipment. Regular vendors, some of whom are in the United States, will be included as Maverick's vendor accounts. Vendor accounts are aged at 15-day intervals.

Maverick Micro Solutions has its bank account, bank loan and mortgage with Alberta Trust. As an incentive to new high-tech firms located in Calgary, the bank has provided a waiver on mortgage interest for the first six months on long-term mortgages. In July, Maverick will begin to make regular monthly mortgage payments of $1 550.

Although Maverick could have set up his business records in Simply Accounting at the beginning of January, he chose to wait until he had a more accurate picture of his ongoing accounting profile. He found the business guides in Simply Accounting helpful when he was organizing the accounts to prepare for computerization. After closing his books manually on March 31, he is ready to make the conversion from the manual system to the computerized accounting system for his next fiscal quarter beginning on April 1, 2003, using the following information:

- Business Information
- Chart of Accounts
- Income Statement
- Balance Sheet
- Post-Closing Trial Balance
- Vendor Information
- Customer Information
- Accounting Procedures

MAVERICK MICRO SOLUTIONS BUSINESS INFORMATION

Address: 17 Turbo Lane
Calgary Alberta T3B 4U2
Phone: (403) 672-9140
Fax: (403) 672-9100
Business No.: 98233 2812

Printers: Select printer for
Reports:
Cheques:
Invoices:
Labels:
Other:

User Preferences:
Use Accounting Terms
Open Ledgers & Journals with Single Click
Automatically save changes to records

General Settings: no changes

Sales Taxes:
GST 7%
PST 0%

Payables Settings:
Aging periods: 15, 30, 45 days
Discounts before tax: Yes

System Settings:
Store invoice lookup
Allow future transactions
Warn if more than 7 days in future
Warn if accounts not balanced
Backup Weekly

Receivables Settings:
Aging periods: 5, 20, 30 days
Interest charges: 1% after 30 days
Statements include invoices for 31 days
Payment terms: 1/5, n/20
Discounts before tax: Yes

Forms Settings (Next Number):
Sales Invoice No. 60
Sales Quote No. 82
Receipts No. del
Customer Deposit 18
Purchase Order No. 1001

Comments
Sales Invoice: Interest @ 1% per month charged on accounts over 30 days

Next Cheque No.:
Bank Account: Chequing 201
Bank Account: USD 100

Foreign Currency:
USD United States Dollars
Tracking Account: 5020
Exchange Rate on 04/01/03 1.554

Credit Card Information:
Card Accepted: VISA
Discount Fee: 3.5%
Expense Account: 5030
Asset Account: 1090

Card Used: VISA
Payable Account: 2150
Expense Account: 5030

View Settings:
Hide Modules: Payroll, Inventory & Services, Project
To-Do Lists: turn off
Checklists: turn off
Show Select Company Window at Startup

notes

The Chart of Accounts includes all accounts. Account types are marked for all subgroup Accounts [A], Subgroup totals [S], Heading accounts [H],Total accounts [T] and the type X account. All other accounts are postable Group accounts. The Group accounts are not marked.

MAVERICK MICRO SOLUTIONS
CHART OF ACCOUNTS

ASSETS
1000 CURRENT ASSETS [H]
1030 Test Balance Account
1080 Bank Account: Chequing [A]
1090 Bank Account: VISA [A]
1100 Bank Account: USD [A]
1110 Bank: Total [S]
1200 Accounts Receivable
1240 Parts Inventory
1300 Office Supplies
1390 TOTAL CURRENT ASSETS [T]
1400 PLANT & EQUIPMENT [H]
1420 Furniture & Fixtures
1460 Machinery & Equipment
1490 Machine Shop
1520 Motor Vehicles
1550 Specialty Tools
1590 TOTAL PLANT & EQUIPMENT [T]

LIABILITIES
2000 CURRENT LIABILITIES [H]
2100 Bank Loan
2150 Credit Card Payable
2200 Accounts Payable
2650 GST Charged on Services [A]
2670 GST Paid on Purchases [A]
2750 GST Owing (Refund) [S]
2790 TOTAL CURRENT LIABILITIES [T]
2800 LONG TERM DEBT [H]
2850 Mortgage Payable
2890 TOTAL LONG TERM DEBT [T]

EQUITY
3000 OWNER'S EQUITY [H]
3560 J. Maverick, Capital
3580 J. Maverick, Drawings
3600 Net Income [X]
3690 TOTAL OWNER'S EQUITY [T]

REVENUE
4000 REVENUE [H]
4020 Revenue from Services
4080 Revenue from Training
4100 Sales Discounts
4120 Interest Revenue
4390 TOTAL REVENUE

EXPENSE
5000 OPERATING EXPENSES [H]
5010 Bank Charges
5020 Exchange Rate Differences
5030 Credit Card Fees
5040 Hydro Expenses
5060 Purchase Discounts
5080 Damaged Inventory
5100 Delivery Expenses
5120 Parts Used
5140 Telephone Expenses
5160 Insurance Expense
5200 Temporary Services
5690 TOTAL OPERATING EXPENSES [T]

notes

- Accounts with zero balances are omitted from the Balance Sheet, Income Statement and Trial Balance.
- The Balance Sheet has pre-closing balances for equity accounts.

MAVERICK MICRO SOLUTIONS
BALANCE SHEET

March 31, 2003

Assets		
1000 CURRENT ASSETS		
1080 Bank Account: Chequing	$ 34 480.00	
1090 Bank Account: VISA	2 000.00	
1110 Bank: Total		$36 480.00
1200 Accounts Receivable		5 420.00
1240 Parts Inventory		3 000.00
1300 Office Supplies		200.00
1390 TOTAL CURRENT ASSETS		$ 45 100.00
1400 PLANT & EQUIPMENT		
1420 Furniture & Fixtures		1 800.00
1460 Machinery & Equipment		48 000.00
1490 Machine Shop		165 000.00
1520 Motor Vehicles		25 000.00
1550 Specialty Tools		20 000.00
1590 TOTAL PLANT & EQUIPMENT		$259 800.00
TOTAL ASSETS		$304 900.00
Liabilities		
2000 CURRENT LIABILITIES		
2100 Bank Loan		25 000.00
2200 Accounts Payable		4 480.00
2650 GST Charged on Services	840.00	
2670 GST Paid on Purchases	−420.00	
2750 GST Owing (Refund)		420.00
2790 TOTAL CURRENT LIABILITIES		$ 29 900.00
2800 LONG TERM DEBT		
2850 Mortgage Payable		150 000.00
2890 TOTAL LONG TERM DEBT		$150 000.00
TOTAL LIABILITIES		$179 900.00
Equity		
3000 OWNER'S EQUITY		
3560 J. Maverick, Capital		115 600.00
3600 Net Income		9 400.00
3690 TOTAL OWNER'S EQUITY		$125 000.00
TOTAL EQUITY		$125 000.00
LIABILITIES AND EQUITY		$304 900.00

MAVERICK MICRO SOLUTIONS
INCOME STATEMENT

For the Quarter Ending March 31, 2003

Revenue	
4000 REVENUE	
4020 Revenue from Services	$10 500.00
4080 Revenue from Training	560.00
4120 Interest Revenue	40.00
4390 TOTAL REVENUE	$11 100.00
TOTAL REVENUE	$11 100.00
Expense	
5000 OPERATING EXPENSES	
5010 Bank Charges	50.00
5040 Hydro Expenses	180.00
5080 Damaged Inventory	70.00
5100 Delivery Expenses	60.00
5120 Parts Used	770.00
5140 Telephone Expenses	65.00
5160 Insurance Expense	205.00
5200 Temporary Services	300.00
5690 TOTAL OPERATING EXPENSES	$ 1 700.00
TOTAL EXPENSE	$ 1 700.00
NET INCOME	$ 9 400.00

MAVERICK MICRO SOLUTIONS
POST-CLOSING TRIAL BALANCE

March 31, 2003

1080 Bank Account: Chequing	$ 34 480.00	
1090 Bank Account: VISA	2 000.00	
1200 Accounts Receivable	5 420.00	
1240 Parts Inventory	3 000.00	
1300 Office Supplies	200.00	
1420 Furniture & Fixtures	1 800.00	
1460 Machinery & Equipment	48 000.00	
1490 Machine Shop	165 000.00	
1520 Motor Vehicles	25 000.00	
1550 Specialty Tools	20 000.00	
2100 Bank Loan		$ 25 000.00
2200 Accounts Payable		4 480.00
2650 GST Charged on Services		840.00
2670 GST Paid on Purchases	420.00	
2850 Mortgage Payable		150 000.00
3560 J. Maverick, Capital		125 000.00
	$305 320.00	$305 320.00

MAVERICK MICRO SOLUTIONS VENDOR INFORMATION

Vendor Name (Contact)	Address	Phone No. Fax No.	E-mail Web Site	Terms Tax ID
Alberta Hydro (Nida Power)	49 Glowing Lights Rd. Calgary, AB T3P 4X2	Tel: (403) 771-8877 Fax: (403) 771-2900	npower@altahydro.ca www.altahydro.ca	Net 1 43685 2989
Alberta Telephone (Mora Noys)	344 A. G. Bell Way Calgary, AB T2T 7N8	Tel: (403) 775-6644 Fax: (403) 775-8102	mnoys@bell.ca www.bell.ca	Net 1 69102 2818
Cybertek Systems (Colm Peuter)	586 Pentium Alley Calgary, AB T2E 7D3	Tel: (403) 778-6188 Fax: (403) 778-6100	cp_3@netcom.com www.cybertek.com	2/5, n/20 (pre-tax) 21985 5544
Flextech Products (Mike Roechip)	42 Intell Blvd. Calgary, AB T1S 5C8	Tel: (403) 522-1817 Fax: (403) 522-1899	miker@istar.ca www.flextech.com	1/10, n/30 (pre-tax) 34100 2234
Microtek Corporation (Meg A. Herz)	486 Memory Lane Calgary, AB T3K 2H5	Tel: (403) 528-7365 Fax: (403) 528-7433	maherz@microtek.com www.microtek.com	Net 30 49218 3229
Receiver General of Canada	Summerside Tax Centre Summerside, PE C1N 6L2	Tel: (902) 821-8186	www.ccra-adrc.gc.ca	Net 1
Vision Technologies (Ram Sites) USD vendor	10 Nuview Cr. El Cerrito, California USA 94531	Tel: (510) 526-3921 Fax: (510) 526-3376	rsites@vision.com www.visiontech.com	Net 20

OUTSTANDING VENDOR INVOICES

Vendor Name	Date	Inv/Chq No.	Terms	Pretax Amount	Tax	Total
Cybertek Systems	03/28/03	CS-4211	2/5, n/20	$1 000	$70	$1 070
	03/28/03	Chq 189	Payment	–500		500
			Balance			$ 570
Flextech Products	03/24/03	FP-95	1/10, n/30	$3 000	$210	$3 210
	03/24/03	Chq 181	Payment	–1 000		1 000
			Balance			$2 210
Microtek Corporation	03/21/03	MC-721	Net 30			$1 600
				Grand Total		$4 380

MAVERICK MICRO SOLUTIONS CUSTOMER INFORMATION

Customer Name (Contact)	Address	Phone No. Fax No.	E-mail Web Site	Credit Limit Terms
Alberta Insurance Co. (Joel Careless)	571 Litty Gate Calgary, AB T2B 1A6	Tel: (403) 773-0208 Fax: (403) 773-0100	Joel_Careless@protec.com www.protec.com/altainsure	$5 000 1/5, n/20
Calgary College (Jan Booker)	54 University Ave. Calgary, AB T3D 6B1	Tel: (403) 525-4412 Fax: (403) 525-7100	jb@calcol.edu www.calcol.edu	$5 000 1/5, n/20
Performance Technical School (Arch I. Tektur)	19 Scholastic Rd. Calgary, AB T1W 4R1	Tel: (403) 774-8135 Fax: (403) 774-7200	archie@pts.edu www.pts.edu	$5 000 1/5, n/20
Prairie Finance Company (Andy Bluitt)	131 Bond St. Calgary, AB T2V 5F8	Tel: (403) 526-6101 Fax: (403) 526-1919	abluitt@flatland.ca www.flatland/pfc.ca	$5 000 1/5, n/20
Western Home Security (Marlie Safer)	9 Vigilance Blvd. Calgary, AB T1B 8R2	Tel: (403) 771-7711 Fax: (403) 771-6292	safer@homesafe.com www.homesafe.com	$5 000 1/5, n/20

OUTSTANDING CUSTOMER INVOICES

Customer Name	Date	Inv/Chq No.	Terms	Pretax Amount	Tax	Total
Calgary College	03/28/03	52	1/5, n/20	$4 000	$280	$4 280
	03/28/03	Chq#187	Payment	−1 000		1 000
			Balance			$3 280
Prairie Finance Company	03/25/03	49	1/5, n/20	$2 000	$140	$2 140
			Grand Total			$5 420

Accounting Procedures

Open-Invoice Accounting for Payables and Receivables

The open-invoice method of accounting for invoices allows the business to keep track of each individual invoice and any partial payments made against it. This is in contrast to methods that only keep track of the outstanding balance by combining all invoice balances owed to a vendor or by a customer. Simply Accounting uses the open-invoice method. When invoices are fully paid, they should be removed periodically after statements are received from the vendor or sent to the customers.

notes

- Provincial sales taxes are not levied in Alberta.
- Most bank and other financial institution services are exempt from GST collection.

The Goods and Services Tax: Remittances

Maverick Micro Solutions uses the regular method for remittance of the Goods and Services Tax. GST collected from customers is recorded as a liability in *GST Charged on Services*. GST paid to vendors is recorded in *GST Paid on Purchases* as a decrease in the liability. The balance, or request for refund, is remitted to the Receiver General of Canada by the last day of the month for the previous month.

Sales of Services

Maverick has accounts set up for several customers. He also prepares sales quotes on request and accepts sales orders from regular and new customers. In addition, some customers pay for their purchases immediately by cash, cheque or credit card. A separate bank account is set up for credit card deposits. Transactions for cash and credit card customers may be entered by choosing One-time customer from the customer list and typing the name of the customer in the address field or by typing the customer's name in the name field and choosing the Quick Add option.

For cash sales, the program will debit *Bank Account: Chequing* (or *Bank Account: VISA* for credit card payments) instead of the *Accounts Receivable* control account. All other accounts for this transaction will be appropriately debited and credited.

Purchases

Most of Maverick's regular vendors have given him credit terms, including some discounts for early payment. Purchase quotes and purchase orders are also a regular part of dealing with these vendors. Some purchases are accompanied by immediate payment, usually by cheque or credit card. Maverick prefers cheque payments because the cancelled cheques become part of his business records. Enter the cash transaction for purchases from new vendors in the Payments Journal as an Other Payment. Choose the appropriate "paid by" option; choose One-time vendor from the vendor list; type the vendor's name in the address field. You can also type the name in the vendor field and choose Quick Add.

For cash purchases paid by cash or cheque, the program will credit *Bank Account - Chequing* instead of the *Accounts Payable* control account. For credit card purchases, *Credit Card Payable* is credited. All other accounts for this transaction will be appropriately debited and credited. Maverick pays his credit card balance in full each month. Refer to Chapter 7, page 198, for further information about credit card payments.

> **notes**
>
> Discounts for customers and from vendors are all calculated on the amounts before taxes. To receive the discount, full payment must be made within the discount period.

Discounts

Maverick offers a 1 percent discount to his account customers if they settle their accounts within five days. Full payment is requested within 20 days. These payment terms are set up as defaults. When the receipt is entered, if the discount is still available, the program will show the amount of the discount and the net amount owing automatically. Discounts are not allowed on partial payments or on cash purchases paid by cheque or credit card. All discounts are calculated on before-tax amounts.

Some vendors also offer discounts for early settlement of accounts. Again, when the terms are entered for the vendor and full payment is made before the discount period expires, the program will display the pretax discount as available and automatically calculate a net balance owing. Payment terms vary from vendor to vendor.

INSTRUCTIONS

> **notes**
>
> If you prefer to enter the source documents before setting up the data files, you can use the MAVERICK.SDB file in the SETUP folder (inside the Data folder). In this way, you will become familiar with the account structure and the setup may be easier to complete.

1. Using the Business Information, Chart of Accounts, Balance Sheet, Income Statement, Trial Balance and Vendor and Customer Information provided above for March 31, 2003, set up the company accounts. Detailed instructions to assist you in setting up the company accounts follow. Source documents begin on page 341 after the setup instructions.
2. Using the Chart of Accounts, Vendor Information, Customer Information and Accounting Procedures, enter the transactions beginning on page 341 using Simply Accounting.
3. After you have completed your entries, print the reports and graphs indicated on the following printing form:

> **notes**
>
> Include foreign amounts in reports when the option is available.

REPORTS & GRAPHS

Lists
- ☐ List:...

Journals
- ☑ All Journals (by date) from April 1 to June 15 include foreign amounts

Financials
- ☑ Comparative Balance Sheet dates: April 1 and April 28 with dollar difference
- ☑ Income Statement from April 1 to April 28
- ☐ Trial Balance
- ☐ General Ledger
- ☐ Cash Flow Projection

Payables
- ☑ Vendor Aged Detail for all vendors
- ☐ Aged Overdue Payables
- ☐ Pending Purchase Orders

Receivables
- ☑ Customer Aged Detail for all customers
- ☐ Aged Overdue Receivables
- ☐ Customer Statements

GST
- ☑ GST Detail Report date: April 28

Labels
- ☐ Labels for:...

Management Reports
- ☐ Report on:...

GRAPHS
- ☑ Sales vs Receivables (all accounts)
- ☐ Other
- ☐ Other

KEYSTROKES FOR SETUP

Creating Company Files

notes

Save your work frequently and update your backup copy frequently as you work through the setup.

version 8

For Maverick Micro Solutions, we will create the company files from scratch rather than use one of the starter files. Once we create the files and define the defaults, we will add the accounts, define linked accounts for the General, Payables and Receivables Ledgers and create vendor and customer records.

Start the Simply Accounting program. You should see the Welcome to Simply Accounting Select Company window:

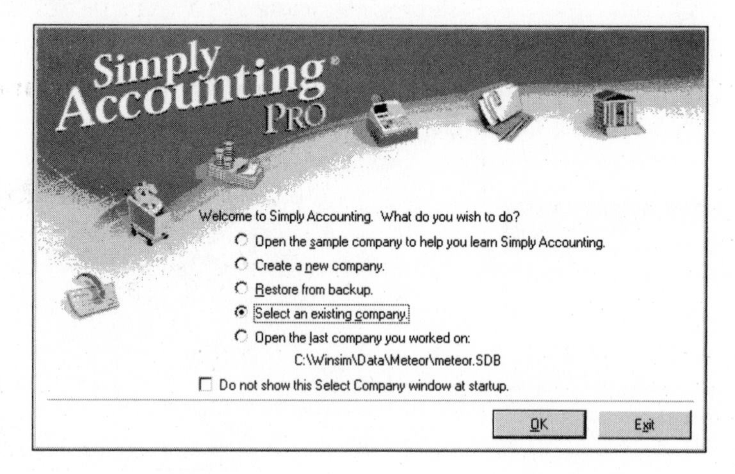

Click Create a new company.

Click OK

You will see the Setup wizard welcome screen:

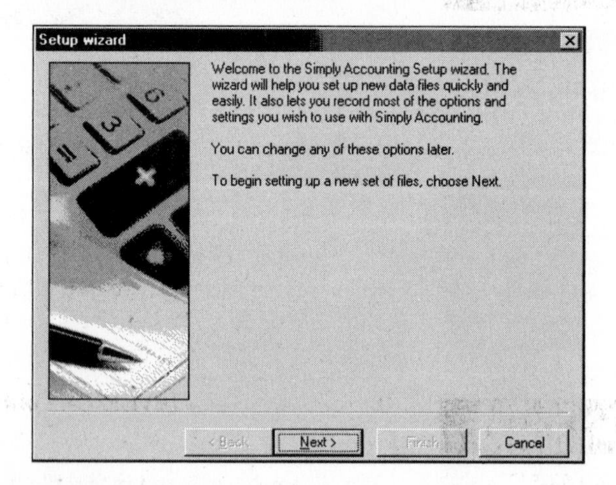

This screen is an invitation to use the Setup wizard to begin the company setup.

Click Next to continue:

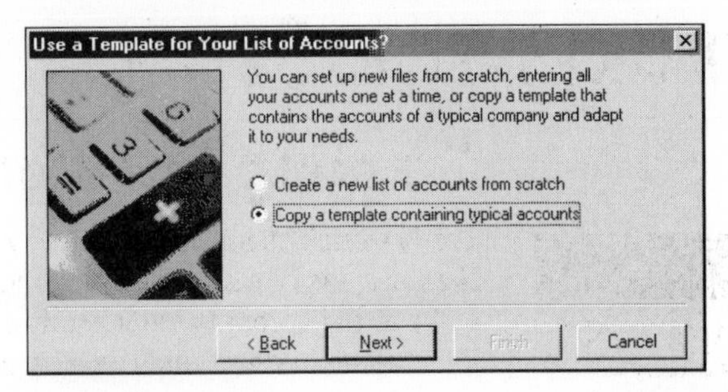

You can use one of the many templates that came with the program or start from scratch to create the data files. Because our setup is relatively small and we want to show all the stages of the setup, we will start from scratch. We also want to show all the options available for each stage.

Click Create a new list of accounts from scratch

Click Next to proceed:

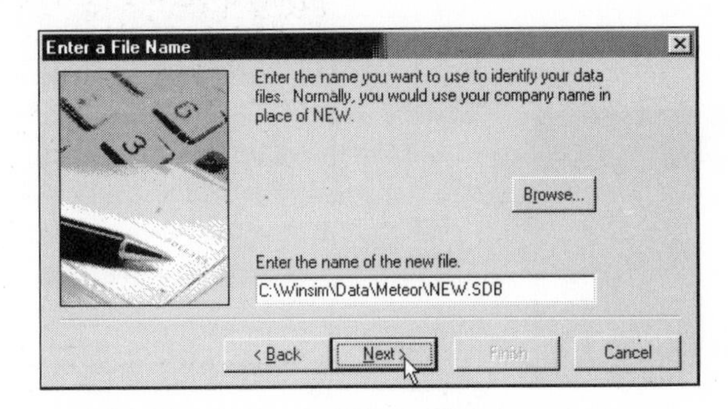

Now you must choose a folder to store the new data set.

Click Browse to select another folder. This will open the Create Company window:

notes

Change folders if necessary to access the one with your other data files. The last folder you used will be the default selection.

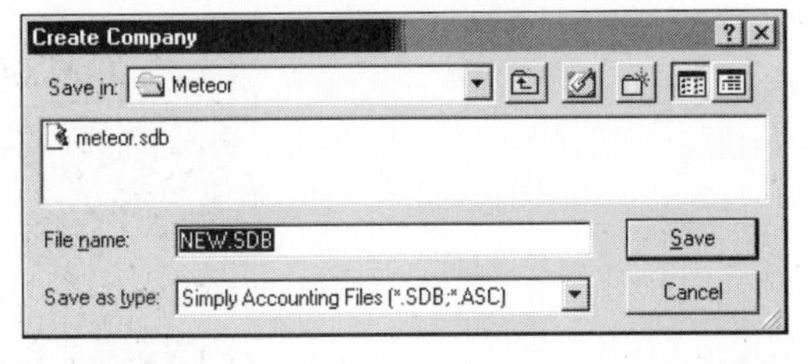

In the Create Company window, create a new folder called MAVERICK to contain the company files. You should create this folder inside the same DATA folder where your other Simply Accounting company data files are stored. Refer to Chapter 6, page 155 if you need further assistance.

Double click the **MAVERICK folder** you just created to select and open it, or click the folder to select it and click Open to open it.

notes

The Save button changes to Open when you select a folder.

No file names are listed in the file list box because the new folder is empty. The File name field contains the name NEW (or NEW.SDB if your computer is set up to show file extensions):

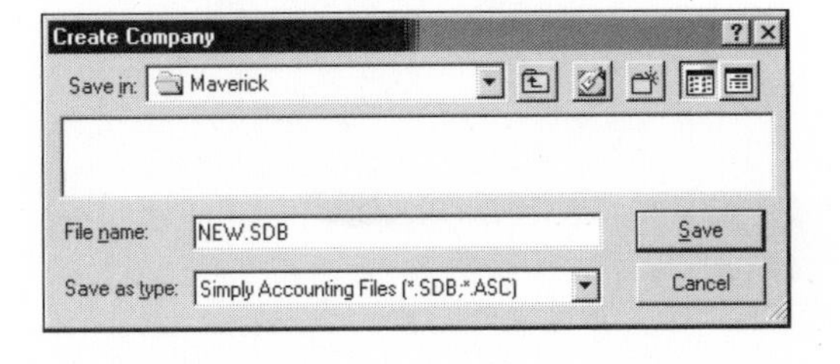

Double click NEW (or NEW.SDB) in the File name field to highlight the file name.

Type maverick (Do not type a file extension. The program adds it automatically.)

Click Save to return to the Wizard with the new file and folder named on the Enter a File Name screen.

Click Next to see the following company Dates window:

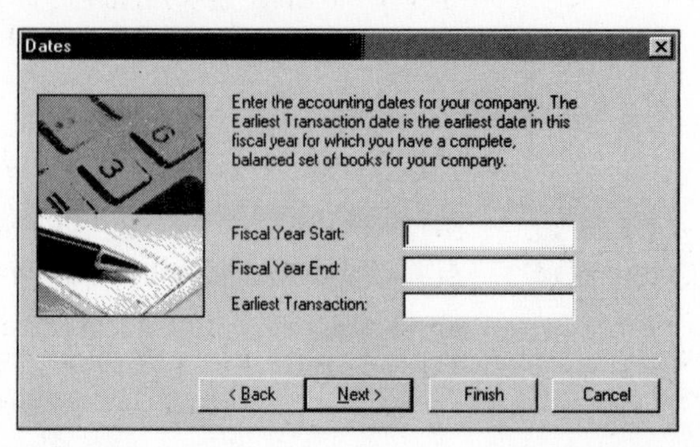

notes

Remember that you should type a four-digit year the first time you enter a date in the year 2000 or later to be certain that the year will be 2003 and not 1903.

These company fiscal dates are like the ones you entered for CISV (Chapter 6) as part of the Company Information setup. The cursor is in the Fiscal Start field. This is the date on which the business begins its fiscal year. For Maverick Micro Solutions, the fiscal start date is the same as the date the business is converting to Simply Accounting because the books were closed before the conversion.

Type 04-01-2003

Press tab

The cursor advances to the Fiscal End field for the date on which Maverick Micro Solutions ends its fiscal period. Maverick closes his books quarterly.

Type 06-30-2003

Press tab

The program now advances to the Earliest Transaction date field. This is the date on which the business is changing from a manual accounting system to a computerized accounting system — the earliest date for posting journal entries and the latest date for historical information.

Type 04-01-2003

Click Finish to save the date information. The program now requests confirmation that you do not want to continue using the Wizard for the setup:

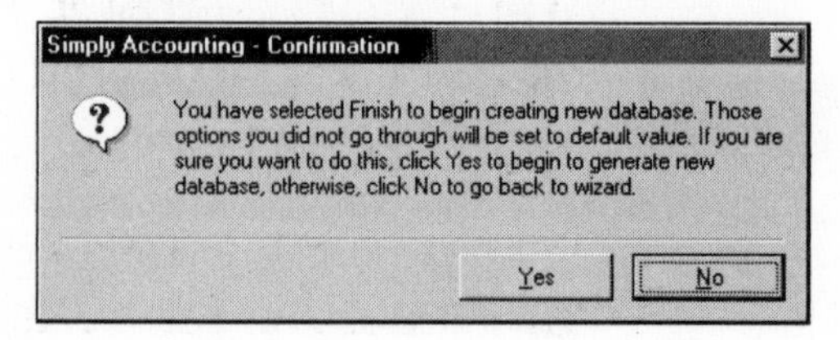

Click Yes to confirm.

notes

Miscellaneous Transactions is the non-accounting name of the General Journal. Vendors & Purchases replaces Payables and Customers & Sales replaces Receivables as module headings.

After a brief interval, the familiar Home window appears with the name Maverick in the title bar. Your default window colours may be different from the ones we show and non-accounting terms are selected initially, so the icons names will be different from the ones in previous applications. We will change these settings as part of the setup.

All the ledger icons have the open history quill pen icon because the ledgers are still open for entering historical information.

Display the Chart of Accounts. You will see that the only account provided by default is the type X account, the General Ledger linked account, *Current Earnings*.

Preparing the System

notes

- You may want to refer to keystrokes in the previous applications to assist you in completing the setup and the transactions for this application.
- If necessary refer to the CISV application for a review of formats of financial statements and the organization of the accounts on pages 164–168.

The next step is to enter the company information to customize the files for Maverick Micro Solutions. You begin by preparing the system and changing the defaults.

You should change the defaults to suit your own work environment if you have more than one printer or if you are using forms for cheques, invoices or statements. The instructions for computer-generated cheques, invoices and statements are provided.

Changing Defaults

Use the Business Information on page 299 to enter the defaults for Maverick Micro Solutions.

Changing Company Information

version 8

Choose the **Setup menu**, then **choose System Settings** and **click Company Information** to display the company information screen.

Notice that the name and address fields are blank and that the fiscal dates you entered in the previous stage are provided. You can edit these if you made a mistake.

The cursor is in the Name field.

Type `Maverick Micro Solutions` **Press** tab to enter the name.

Type `17 Turbo Lane` **Press** tab to enter the street address.

Press tab to skip the Street 2 field.

Type `Calgary` **Press** tab to enter the city.

Type `Alberta` **Press** tab to enter the province.

Type `t3b4u2` **Press** tab to enter the postal code.

Type `Canada` **Press** tab to enter the country.

Type `4036729140` **Press** tab to enter the phone number.

Press tab to skip the Phone 2 field.

Type `4036729100` **Press** tab to enter the fax number.

Type `98233 2812` (to enter the business number)

notes

If there are any postdated transactions in the file, they will show in the Latest Transaction Date, which will be later than the session date.

Check the information you have just entered and make any necessary corrections, including corrections to the fiscal dates. Notice that the fiscal start date appears as the session date on the Company Information screen.

Click OK to save the new information and return to the Home window.

You can return to the Company Information screen at any time to make changes. The program will set up defaults for the session date and for the city, province and country fields for customers and vendors based on the information you have just entered.

Changing the Printer Defaults

Choose the **Setup menu** and **click Reports & Forms**.

The printer setting options for reports are given. Notice that the defaults include adding to reports the computer system (calendar) date and information about whether the report is filtered. The default settings should be correct, but you may want to change the margins, font and font size for your reports. When all the settings are correct,

Click OK to save the new information, or **click Cancel** if you have not made any changes, and return to the Home window. You can change printer settings at any time.

Changing User Preferences

version 8

Choose the **Setup menu**, then **choose User Preferences** and **click Settings** to display the default settings.

Click Use Accounting Terms so that your on-screen terms will match the ones used in this workbook.

Click Automatically save changes to vendor, customer and other records so that you will not be prompted to save information each time you close a ledger after making a change.

Click OK to return to the Home window. You should now see the familiar accounting term labels for the ledger and journal icons.

Choose the **View menu**, then **choose User Preferences** and **To-Do Lists** and **click After Changing Session Date** to remove the ✓.

Choose the **View menu**, then **choose User Preferences** and **Checklists** and **click After Changing Session Date** to remove the ✓.

Choose the **View menu**, then **choose User Preferences** and **Modules** and **click Payroll** (then repeat for **Inventory** and **Project**) to hide the unused modules.

Changing System Defaults

version 8

notes

- If you choose Settings when a ledger icon is selected, you will display the settings for the selected ledger.
- If you click the Setup button when a ledger icon is selected, you will display the Settings for the selected ledger.
- If you click the Setup tool icon when no ledger or journal icon is selected, select a ledger from the list.

Choose the **Setup menu**, then **choose System Settings** and **click Settings**.

Most of the default settings are correct. Use Cash-Basis Accounting should be unchecked because Maverick uses the accrual basis of accounting. The option to Use Cheque No. as the source code can remain selected because Maverick does use cheques and may later choose to use account reconciliation. There is no previous year of data so this option is dimmed.

The Store Invoice Lookup option is correctly selected for Maverick Micro Solutions. The Lookup feature allows us to adjust or correct invoices already posted.

We want to post future transactions but receive a warning if the dates are more than seven days in the future. The defaults are correct.

Click Warn if accounts are not balanced when entering a new month. Since you can enter transactions before completing the history (formerly called setting the ledgers Ready) you should activate this warning to prevent mistakes. The warning makes you aware of errors or omissions before you proceed too far with transactions.

Choose Weekly as the Backup frequency.

Changing Sales Taxes Defaults

notes

You can also use the second GST rate for HST if you have business transactions with participating Atlantic provinces, as we did for Outset Media.

Click the **Sales Taxes tab** at the top of the Settings screen to display the default tax settings:

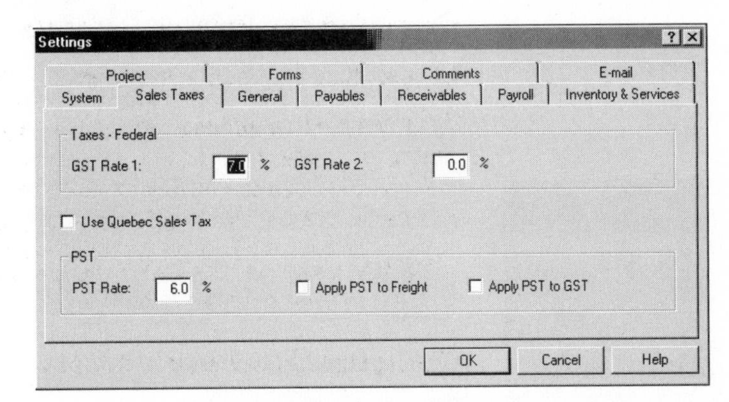

The GST Rates at 7% and 0% are correct. The GST Rate 2 field might be used in the future if different tax rates are applied to different types of goods or services. At present, however, there is no second rate for GST, so you can leave 0.0% unchanged. Since we do not need to use the Quebec Sales Tax, this default is also correctly set.

No PST is applied in Alberta so you must change the PST rate.

Click the **PST Rate field** to highlight the contents.

Type 0

Two other options concern the application of PST. Leave the boxes unchecked for Maverick Micro Solutions because PST is not applied to freight charges or on GST. For Prince Edward Island, you would choose to apply PST to GST. Some provinces, such as British Columbia, apply PST to freight as well. GST is always applied to freight. If at any time the regulations in a province change, you can return to this screen and change the settings.

The **General Ledger** settings are correct for Maverick Micro Solutions. For now, Maverick will not use the budgeting feature so you can skip this tab screen.

Payables Default Settings

version 8

Click the **Payables tab** on the Settings screen to display the default settings for the Payables Ledger:

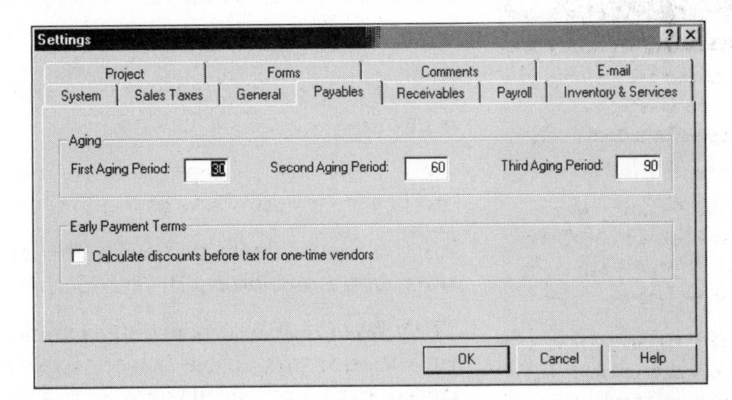

The option for the aging of accounts in the Payables Ledger is preset at 30, 60 and 90 days. We will change these for Maverick to reflect the payment terms most commonly used by Maverick's vendors.

> **notes**
>
> Double click the entry in a field to prepare it for editing if it is not already selected.

The First Aging Period field is selected so you can change this number.

Type `15`

Press *tab* to advance to the Second Aging Period field and select it.

Type `30`

Press *tab* to advance to the Third Aging Period field.

Type `45`

> **notes**
>
> Refer to Chapter 2 for further information about taxes and discounts. We will add discount terms to individual vendor records when we set up the Payables Ledger.

The second option determines how discounts are calculated. If the discount is taken only on the pretax total of the invoice, the discount is calculated before taxes. If the discount is applied to the entire invoice amount, including taxes, the discount is not calculated before taxes. For Maverick's vendors and customers, all discounts are calculated before taxes so you must change the setting.

Click Calculate discounts before tax for one-time vendors

Receivables Default Settings

Click the **Receivables tab** to display the following Receivables Ledger choices:

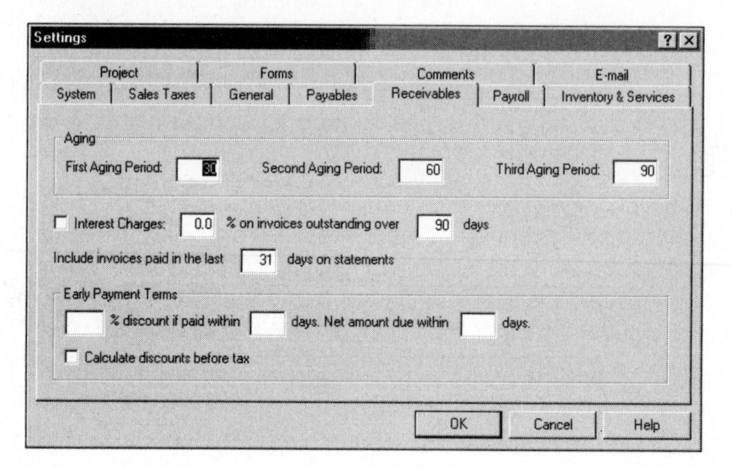

Maverick Micro Solutions offers a 1 percent discount if customers pay within 5 days, and expects full payment within 20 days. After 30 days, customers are charged 1 percent interest per month on the overdue accounts. Therefore, the aging periods are 5, 20 and 30 days and we must change the default settings. The First Aging Period field is selected for editing.

Type `5`

Press *tab* to advance to the Second Aging Period field.

Type `20`

Press *tab* to advance to the Third Aging Period field.

Type `30`

> **notes**
>
> You must create a Sales Journal entry for the amount of the interest charge. Simply Accounting calculates interest charges and prints them on the customer statements and management reports. The program does not create an invoice for the interest amount.

Click Interest Charges to select this feature.

Press *tab* to advance to and highlight the contents of the interest rate field for editing.

Type `1.0`

Press *tab* to advance to and highlight the contents of the days field for editing.

Type `30`

The next option relates to printing historical information on invoices. The maximum setting is 999 days. For Maverick Micro Solutions, the period should be 31 days because they send customer statements every month. Any invoices paid in the past 31 days will be included in the statements. Unpaid invoices are always included on statements. The default setting is correct. Next we must enter the payment terms for account customers: 1 percent discount if the account is paid in the first 5 days, and net payment due in 20 days.

Click the **first Early Payment Terms field**, the % field, to advance the cursor.

Type `1.0`

Press (tab) to advance to the days field.

Type `5`

Press (tab) to advance to the Net days field.

Type `20`

Click **Calculate discounts before tax** to turn on this option.

Simply Accounting adds the customer payment terms you just entered as a default for all customers. Individual customer records or invoices can still be modified if needed.

Changing Forms Default Settings

version 8

Click the **Forms tab** to display the Settings screen for Forms:

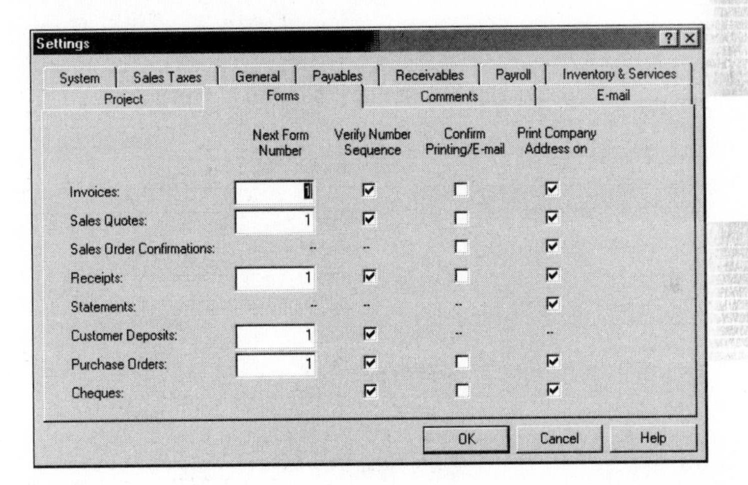

notes

- Since sales orders originate with customers and purchase quotes come from vendors, their numbers are not automatically updated.
- Cheque sequence numbers for bank accounts will be entered in the ledger record for the accounts (page 317).

This window allows you to set up the automatic numbering sequences for the business forms that are generated internally.

The Invoices number field is ready for editing.

Type `60`

Click the **Sales Quotes field** to highlight the contents.

Type `82`

Click the **Receipts field**. If you want to record receipt numbers for a business in the Receipts Journal, you can enter the next sequence number in this field. Maverick records the customer's cheque number instead, and this number cannot be updated by the program.

Press (del) to remove the entry. This will leave the Receipts field blank on the Receipts Journal so you can use the field for customer cheque numbers.

Click the **Customer Deposits field**. This entry will update the sequence number for deposits or advances from customers.

Type `18`

Click the **Purchase Orders field** to highlight the contents.

Type `1001`

notes

Click to add a ✔ to the check box and click again to remove a ✔ from the check box.

The column checklists on the Forms Settings screen allow you to verify sequence numbers and add reminders if you print invoices, quotes, purchase orders, and so forth. Verifying sequence numbers will provide a warning if you skip or duplicate a number and will give you a chance to make a correction if necessary before posting. Choosing to confirm will set up the program to remind you to print or e-mail the form if you try to post before printing since posting removes the form from the screen. You should add the confirmation if you print or e-mail regularly.

The final column allows you to add a company address to various forms that you print. If you have pre-printed forms that already include the address, remove the checkmarks to avoid double printing of this information. If you are using generic blank forms, leave the checkmarks so that the address is included.

Entering Default Comments for Sales Invoices

Click the **Comments tab** to open the screen for default comments:

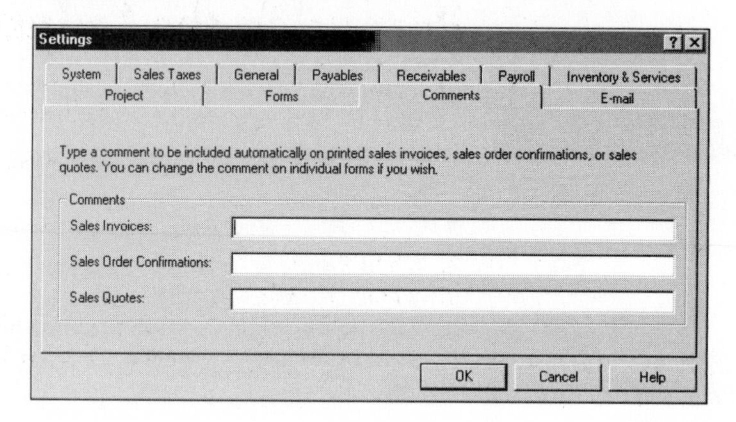

We want to add a default comment that will appear on every customer invoice. The comment may include payment terms, company motto, notice of an upcoming sale or, in this case, a warning about interest charges. Remember that you can change the default message any time you want. You can also edit it for a particular invoice when you are completing the invoice. The cursor should be in the Sales Invoices field. If not,

Click the **Sales Invoices field** to move the cursor.

Type `Interest at 1% per month charged on accounts over 30 days.`

You can enter the same comment for all sales forms (invoices, sales order confirmations and quotes) or you can add a unique comment for each. Remember that you can always edit the comment in the journal if necessary. Leave the remaining comment fields blank.

Entering Default Comments for E-mail

The next step is to add a default message to e-mail communications.

Click the **E-mail tab** to open the next Settings screen:

version 8

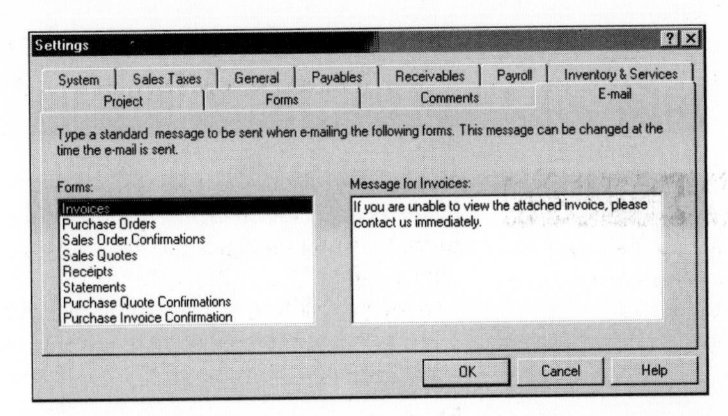

The left-hand list box contains the forms that you can e-mail to vendors or customers. The right-hand box contains the message that will be added to all e-mails of the form selected on the left. Click a form to select it and then type the message you want in the message box. You do not need to change any of the default messages.

Click OK to return to the Home window and save all the changes.

Preparing the Ledgers

The third stage in setting up an accounting system involves preparing each ledger for operation. This stage involves the following steps:

1. organizing all accounting reports and records (this step has already been completed for you)
2. modifying the *Current Earnings* account
3. creating new accounts
4. defining linked accounts
5. inserting vendor and customer information
6. entering historical account balances and invoices

Preparing the General Ledger

Accounts are organized by section, including Assets, Liabilities, Equity, Revenue and Expense. The account type, such as Heading (H), Subgroup total (S), Total (T), subgroup Account (A), Group account (G) and Current Earnings (X), is a method of classifying and organizing accounts within a section or subsection of a report.

The accounts follow the same pattern described previously:

- 1000–1999 Assets
- 2000–2999 Liabilities
- 3000–3999 Equity
- 4000–4999 Revenue
- 5000–5999 Expense

Use the Chart of Accounts, Income Statement and Balance Sheet to enter all the accounts you need to create. Remember to include all group headings, totals and subgroup totals in addition to the postable group and subgroup accounts. Remember to add the type of account and whether you want to omit printing accounts with zero balances.

Modifying Accounts in the General Ledger

The following keystrokes will modify the *Current Earnings* account in the General Ledger to match the account name defined in the Chart of Accounts.

In the Home window,

Click the Accounts icon  to open the Accounts window.

The accounts should be displayed in Type view, in numerical order, with names, account types and balances. If not, choose the Accounts window View menu and click Type.

Double click 3600 Current Earnings to display its ledger form.

Press tab to advance to the Account name field and highlight it.

Type `Net Income`

The account types are dimmed because the *Current Earnings* account type must remain as type X. Only the account number and account title can be edited. You cannot enter a balance because the program automatically calculates the amount as the net difference between the total revenue and expense account balances for the fiscal period.

Close the General Ledger account window. **Close** the Accounts icon window to return to the Home window unless you want to continue to the next step, which also involves working in the General Ledger.

notes

You can also open the ledger form by clicking the account to select it and then clicking the Edit button or choosing the Edit menu and then clicking Edit.

Creating New Accounts in the General Ledger

With the Accounts window open, or any account ledger window on display,

Click the **Create button** in the Accounts window or choose the File menu and then Create.

Enter account information for the accounts from page 300. Remember, you cannot use duplicate account numbers.

Type the account number.

Press tab

Type the account title or name.

Click the Account type for the account.

If this is a postable account, indicate whether you want to omit the account from financial statements if its balance is zero. Leave Allow Project Allocations unchecked.

You can skip the Opening Balance field for now. We will enter all account balances in the next stage.

When all the information is entered correctly, you must save your account.

Click Create Another Create Another to save the new account and advance to a new blank ledger account window.

Create the remaining accounts from the Chart of Accounts, Balance Sheet and Income Statement.

Close the General Ledger account window. **Close** the Accounts icon window to return to the Home window unless you want to continue to the next step, which also involves working in the General Ledger.

notes

We will enter account balances as a separate step so that you can enter all balances in a single session. This may help you to avoid leaving the data file with an incorrect Trial Balance.

notes

Remember that Bank: Total and GST Owing (Refund) are subgroup totals, following the subgroup bank and GST accounts respectively.

notes

Display or print your updated Chart of Accounts at this stage to check for accuracy.

Entering Opening Account Balances

notes

- Accounts that decrease the total in a group or section (e.g., GST Paid on Purchases) must be entered as negative numbers. These account balances are indicated with a (–) minus sign in the Balance Sheet.
- After entering all account balances, display or print your Balance Sheet and Trial Balance to check for accuracy.
- You may want to save your work and finish your session. This will give you a chance to read the next section.

The opening historical balances for Maverick Micro Solutions can be found in the Post-Closing Trial Balance dated March 31, 2003, on page 302. For headings, totals or subgroup totals (i.e., for the non-postable accounts), you cannot enter balances and the balance field is removed.

Remember to use the *Test Balance Account* for any adjustments that would leave the Trial Balance in a forced balance position before you are finished or if one of the remaining balances is incorrect. When you have finished entering all balances, the *Test Balance Account* should have a zero balance and you can remove it.

The Accounts window should be open.

Open the General Ledger account information window for the first account that has a balance, *1080 Bank Account: Chequing*. Notice the additional tabs on the ledger screen.

Click the **Opening Balance field** to highlight its contents.

Type the balance.

Correct the information if necessary by repeating the above steps.

Click the **Next button** in the ledger window to advance to the next account ledger record. Repeat the above procedures to enter the balances for the remaining accounts as indicated in the Trial Balance.

Close the General Ledger window to return to the Accounts window. You can check your work from the Trial Balance.

Choose the **Reports menu** and **click Trial Balance** to display the Trial Balance. Print the report. **Close** the display when finished and correct account balances if necessary.

Bank Class Accounts

Before proceeding, we must enter account class information for bank accounts. Account class is another way of organizing accounts into related groups. Each section may be divided into various classes. When you create a new account, the program assigns the section name (Asset, Liability, Equity, Revenue or Expense) to an account as its default class according to the first digit of the account number. For most accounts, you can accept this setting and the program will prompt you to change the class for special purpose accounts as needed. Bank accounts are not automatically reassigned by the program.

Chequing bank accounts, have additional information that must be entered in the ledger and therefore require that you change the class. You cannot select bank accounts for payments and receipts unless the Bank class is assigned. Bank class accounts must also be defined as such before you can select them as the default linked accounts for the Payables, Receivables and Payroll Ledgers. There are two chequing accounts that we must define as Bank class accounts.

You should be in the Accounts window. If not, click the Accounts icon.

Double click 1080 Bank Account: Chequing to open the ledger window.

Click the **Class Options tab** to see the current class setting — Asset:

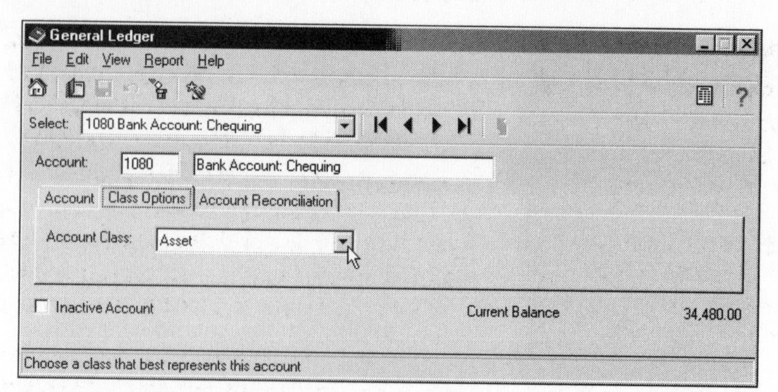

Click the **Account Class list arrow** to see the class options for asset accounts. Assets may subdivided into bank accounts, credit card accounts, receivables, inventory, and so on.

Click Bank from the list to open the bank-related fields:

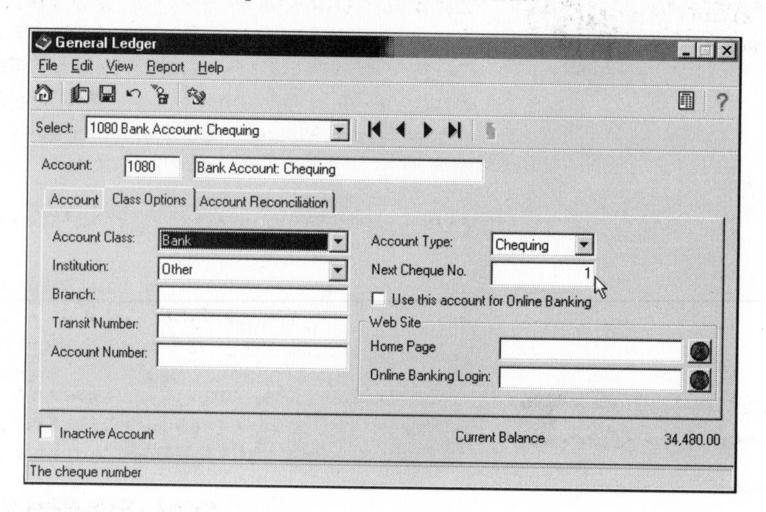

This screen allows you to define the type of bank account, enter a starting number for the cheque sequence and identify the bank for online banking access. We need to enter only the cheque number. Chequing as the the default Account Type is correct.

Click the **Next Cheque No. field** to select 1, the default number.

Type `201`

Click the **Next button** twice to skip the Credit Card account. The record for account *1100 Bank Account: USD* should be displayed.

> **notes**
>
> Although the Credit Card account is a bank account, it cannot be defined as a Bank class account because it will be used as the credit card linked account.

The Class Options tab should be displayed.

Choose Bank from the Account Class list.

Click the **Next Cheque No. field** to select 1, the default number.

Type `100`

We will identify the currency for the foreign bank account after setting up the foreign currency (page 325).

Close the ledger window.

Close the Accounts window to return to the Home window.

Linked Accounts

> **notes**
>
> The Integration Plus starter files have a full set of linked accounts already defined. Open the inteplus.sdb file from the Template folder and copy the file before changing any of the default information, as you did for CISV. You can delete and modify the linked accounts for the ledgers as needed rather than entering them from scratch.

Linked accounts are accounts in the General Ledger that are affected by changes resulting from entries in other journals. For example, an entry to record a credit sale in the Sales Journal will cause automatic changes in several General Ledger accounts. In the General Ledger, the *Accounts Receivable* [+], *Revenue from Sales* [+], *GST Charged on Sales* [+] and *PST Payable* [+] accounts will all be affected by the sale. The type of change, increase [+] or decrease [–], is indicated in the brackets. The program must know which account numbers are to be used for posting journal entries in any of the journals. It is this interconnection of account numbers and information between ledgers that makes Simply Accounting fully integrated.

Since the only linked account already defined is *Net Income*, the linked account for Current Earnings in the General Ledger, we must identify the remaining linked accounts for the General, Payables and Receivables Ledgers.

Setup Tool Button

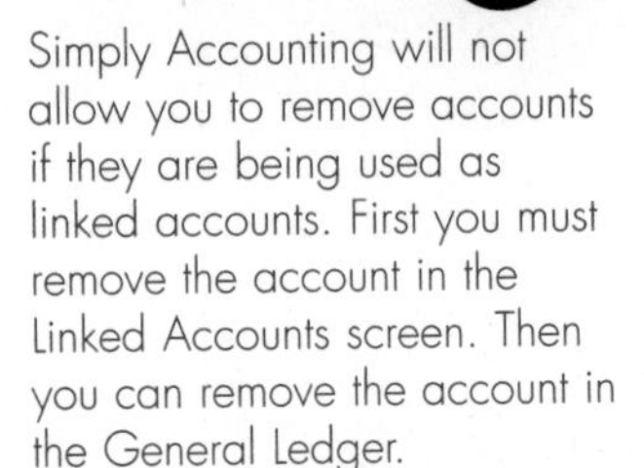

> **Warning!**
>
> Simply Accounting will not allow you to remove accounts if they are being used as linked accounts. First you must remove the account in the Linked Accounts screen. Then you can remove the account in the General Ledger.

The Setup button on the tool bar works very much like the Display button. Select a journal icon and click the Setup button to see the linked accounts window for the corresponding ledger. If no icon is selected, choose the journal name from the Setup button's list to display the linked accounts for the corresponding ledger. If a ledger icon is selected, clicking the Setup tool button displays the Settings window for that ledger.

Defining the General Linked Accounts

Right-click the **General Journal icon** in the Home window to select it. (Do not click because you do not want to open the journal.)

> **version 8**

Click the **Setup button** or **choose** the **Setup menu**, then **choose System Settings** and **Linked Accounts** and **click General** to display the General Linked Accounts window with the cursor in the Retained Earnings field:

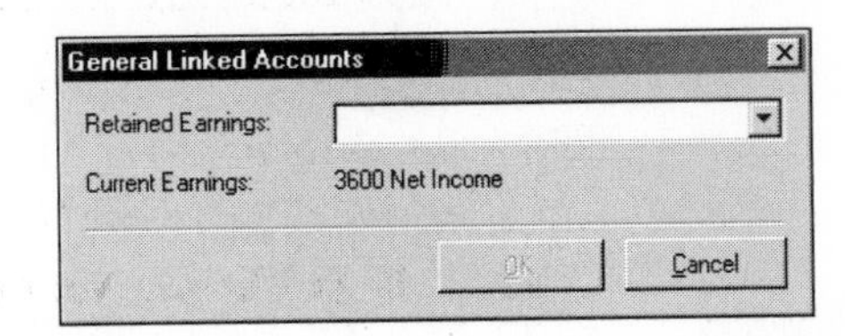

The Retained Earnings account is the Capital account to which expense and revenue accounts are closed at the end of the fiscal period.

Click the **list arrow beside the field**. All available postable capital accounts are listed.

Click 3560 J. Maverick, Capital

> **notes**
>
> You can also type account numbers directly in the linked account fields. Then press *tab* to complete the entry and advance to the next field.

The Current Earnings account is correctly defined and cannot be changed, although, as you saw earlier, you can modify the account number and account title.

Click OK. Simply Accounting shows a message about account class changes:

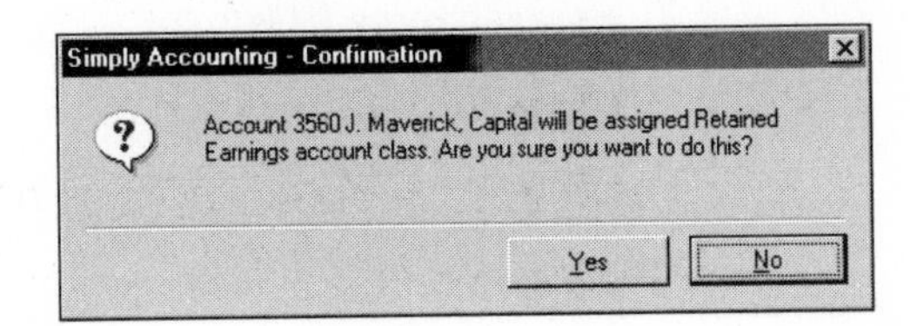

Many linked accounts must have the correct account class to be used as linked accounts. Normally, you can accept the account class definitions and changes assigned by the program. The exception is the Bank class accounts, which you must assign before you can use them as linked bank accounts.

Click Yes to accept the change and return to the Home window.

Defining the Payables Linked Accounts

To enter the Payables Ledger linked accounts,

Right-click the **Purchases** [Purchases, Orders & Quotes icon] or **Payments** [Payments icon] **Journal icon** in the Home window to select it.

version 8

Click the **Setup button** [Setup icon] or choose the Setup menu, then choose System Settings and Linked Accounts and click Payables to display the linked accounts window:

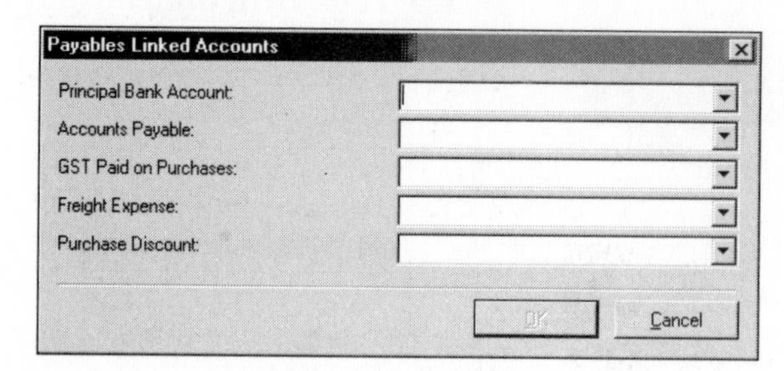

We need to identify the default General Ledger bank account used to make payments to vendors. Cash transactions in the Payments Journal will be posted to the bank account you select in the journal window. All Bank class accounts are available in the journals and the principal linked account is selected as the default.

You can see the list of accounts available for linking by clicking the drop-down list arrow for any linked account field. Only Bank class accounts may be used in the bank fields.

Maverick has two bank accounts for payments. The chequing account is the principal bank account.

Click the **list arrow for Principal Bank Account**.

Click 1080 Bank Account: Chequing

> **notes**
>
> When we create the files for Hearth House (Chapter 13), we will identify a linked bank account for foreign currency transactions.

Press *tab* to enter the account number. The cursor advances to the Accounts Payable field. This account is used to record the amounts owing to vendors whenever a credit Purchases Journal entry is completed. The balance in this account reflects the total owing to all vendors. You must use a liability account in this field.

Select 2200 Accounts Payable, the control account, from the drop-down list.

> **notes**
>
> In this workbook, GST accounts are defined as liability accounts because there is normally a balance owing to the Receiver General.

Press *tab* to enter the account number. The cursor advances to the GST Paid on Purchases field. This account records the totals of amounts entered in the GST field in the Purchases Journal whenever a purchase is made. You may choose an asset or a liability account.

Choose 2670 GST Paid on Purchases from the drop-down list.

Press *tab* to enter the account number. The cursor advances to the Freight Expense field. This account is used to record the delivery or freight charges associated with purchases. Only freight charged by the vendor should be entered using this account. Since Maverick's vendors do not charge for delivery, you should leave this field blank.

notes

You can add a linked account for Freight later if you need it.

Press (tab) to advance to the Purchase Discount field. This account is used to record any vendor discounts taken for early payments.

Choose 5060 Purchase Discounts from the drop-down list.

Press (tab)

Check the linked accounts carefully. To delete a linked account, click it to highlight it and press (del). To select a different account, highlight the one that is incorrect and type in the correct number, or select from the drop-down list.

Click OK to see the account class change confirmation for account 2200:

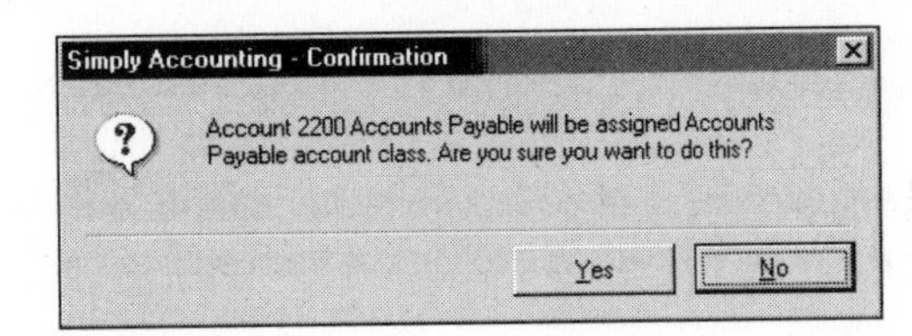

Click Yes to accept the class change, save the linked accounts and return to the Home window.

Defining the Receivables Linked Accounts

version 8

notes

Or, you can click the Sales or Receipts journal icon in the Home window and click the Setup button to display the linked accounts window.

To enter the Receivables Ledger linked accounts,

Choose the **Setup menu**, then **choose System Settings** and **Linked Accounts** and **click Receivables**:

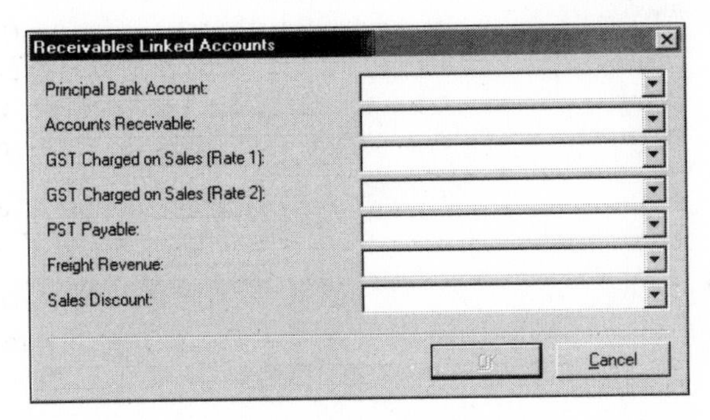

We need to identify the default General Ledger bank account used to receive payments from customers. Cash transactions in the Sales and Receipts Journals will be posted to the linked bank account you select in the journals. The linked account is the default but any Bank class account may be selected.

You can see the list of available bank accounts by clicking the drop-down list arrow. Maverick has two bank accounts, *Bank Account: Chequing* is the principal bank account and the *USD* account is the used for foreign currency transactions.

notes

Although most linked accounts may be used only once, one bank account can be linked to the Payables, Receivables and Payroll Ledgers.

Select 1080 Bank Account: Chequing from the list for Principal Bank Account.

Press (tab) to enter the account number. The cursor advances to the Accounts Receivable field. This account records the amounts owed to Maverick by its customers whenever a credit Sales Journal entry is completed. The balance in this account reflects the total owed by all customers. You must use an asset account in this field.

Select 1200 Accounts Receivable, the control account, from the drop-down list.

Press (tab) to enter the account number. The cursor advances to the GST Charged on Sales (Rate 1) field. This account records the totals of amounts entered in the GST field in the Sales Journal whenever a sale is made. You may use an asset or a liability account.

Choose 2650 GST Charged on Services from the drop-down list.

Since there is currently only one GST rate, leave the GST Charged on Sales (Rate 2) field blank. Similarly, the next two fields should be left blank. PST is not applied in Alberta and Maverick does not collect Freight Revenue because it does not charge for deliveries.

notes

Since Maverick does not use the Payroll or Inventory Ledgers, you do not need to define linked accounts for them.

Click the **Sales Discount field list arrow**. This field is used to record the discounts that customers receive for early settlement of their accounts.

Choose 4100 Sales Discounts from the drop-down list.

Press tab

Click OK to see the message about the account class change for account 1200:

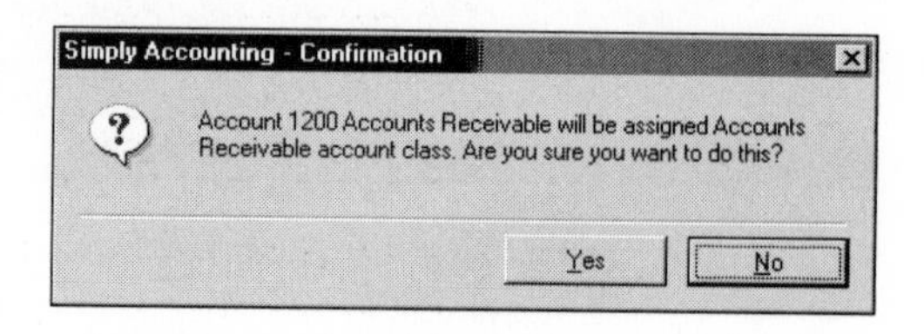

Click Yes to accept the change and return to the Home window.

Setting up Foreign Currencies

Warning!

You cannot change the currency for a vendor or customer after entering historical invoices so you must set up the currencies first.

Before entering Vendor and Customer records, we must define the currencies used by the company so that we can choose a currency when we create customer and vendor records. Maverick has vendors in the United States but no customers at this time.

You should be in the Home window.

Choose the **Setup menu**, then **choose System Settings** and **click Currencies** to see the **Currency Information window for Pro Version 8.5**:

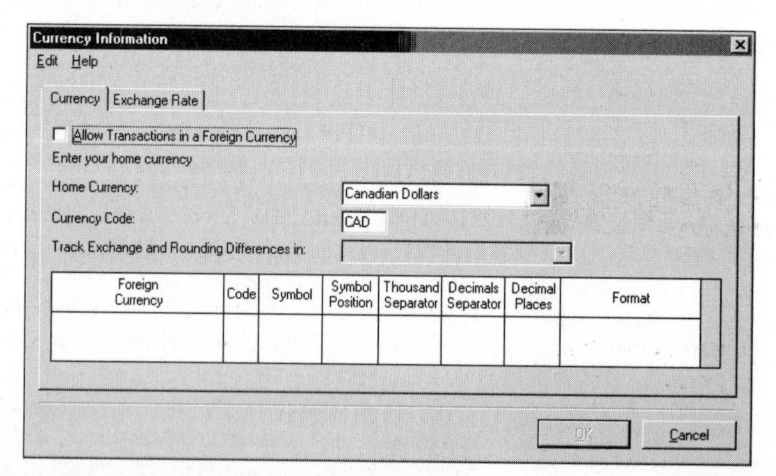

version 8

The **Version 8.5 Currency Information window** and the Version 8.0 window look like the following one:

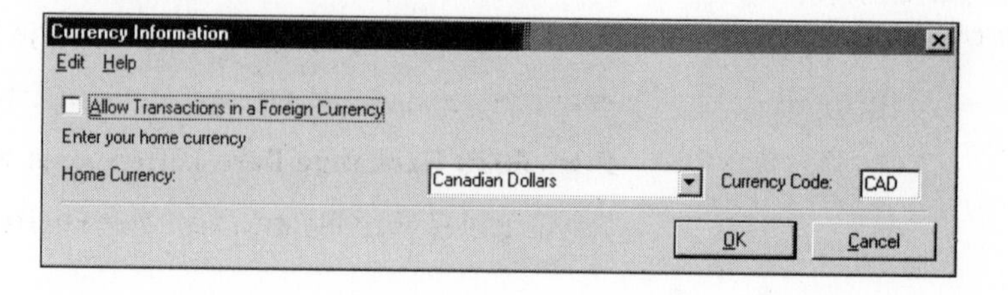

Click Allow Transactions in a Foreign Currency to activate the option and open the linked account tracking field in the **Pro Version 8.5 Currency Information** window:

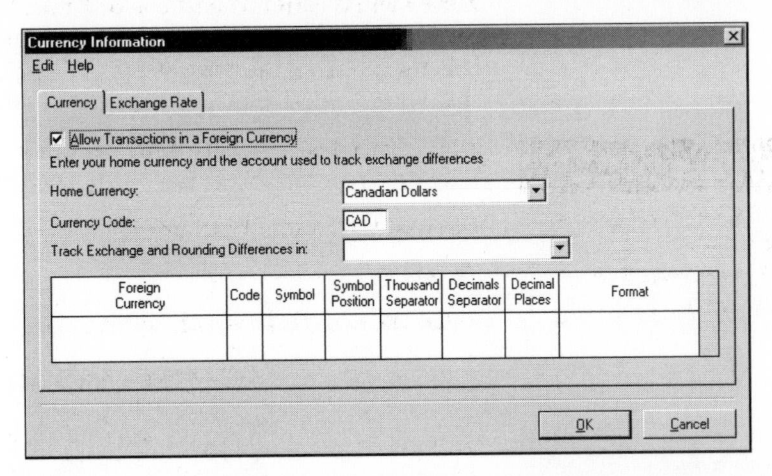

In **Version 8.5** (and in Version 8.0), the **Currency Information window** expands for the selection of the currency and the addition of exchange rates:

> **notes**
>
> The regular version of Simply Accounting 8.0 and 8.5 is a dual currency version, with one home currency and one foreign currency. Therefore, they require only one information screen for all the currency details. The Pro version of Simply Accounting accepts more than one foreign currency. Enter additional currencies in the same way as the first one.

Exchange rates vary from day to day and even within the day. When purchases and payments are made at different times, they are subject to different exchange rates. We have seen these differences in the Outset Media and Meteor Mountain Bike chapters. Exchange rate differences may result in a gain — if the exchange rate drops before a payment is made or if the rate increases before a payment is received from a customer — or a loss — if the rate increases before a payment is made or if the rate drops before a customer makes a payment. These differences are tracked in the linked account designated on this screen. Rounding differences may also result in gains and losses because the currency is recorded with two digits and the exchange rate may have several significant digits. The account for these differences may be an expense account or a revenue account. Maverick uses an expense account because there are no foreign customers, so the gain or loss is linked to business purchases or expenses.

Click the **list arrow for Track Exchange Rate and Rounding Differences in**.

Both revenue and expense accounts are displayed as available for linking.

Click 5020 Exchange Rate Differences to enter this as the linked account.

The next step is to identify the foreign currency.

Double click the **Foreign Currency field** (for **Pro Version 8.5**) to see the list of currencies available:

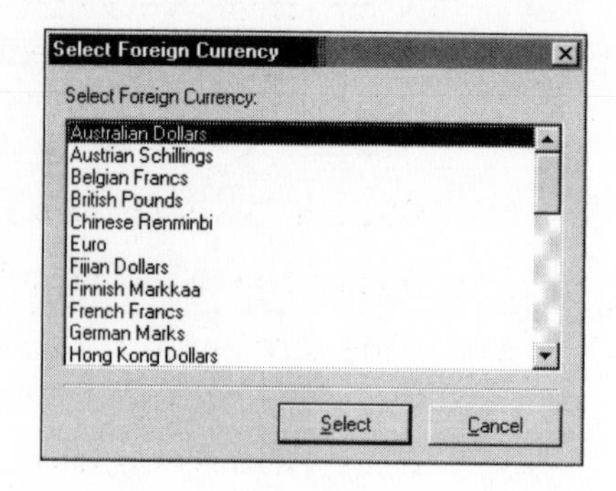

For **Version 8.5**, **click** the **Foreign Currency field list arrow**.

Type U (to advance the list to currencies beginning with U, then scroll down)

Click United State Dollars to add it to the Currency Information screen. The currency code and format are added for the selected currency. Accept the defaults.

Click the **Exchange Rate tab** (**Pro Version 8.5 only**) to access the next information screen:

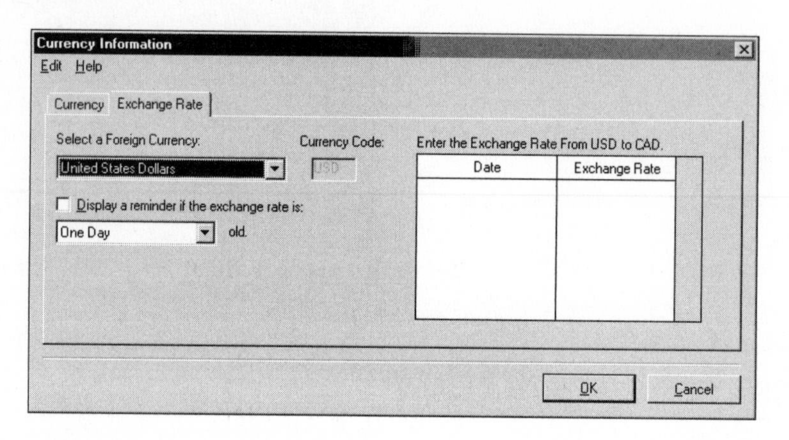

notes

After setting up a foreign currency, the linked accounts screens for the Receivables and Payable ledgers allow you to define a linked foreign bank account that will be selected by default for each foreign currency. You can select one account for each currency in Pro Version 8.5.

The foreign currency you just entered is selected and you can enter dates and exchange rates for it.

Click the **Date field**.

Type `04 01`

Press tab to advance to the Exchange Rate field.

Type `1.5554`

If you know the rates for other dates you can enter them as well. Otherwise, you can enter current rates in the journals as we did in the previous chapters.

notes

For the Pro version, all the currencies you entered will be in the Select Foreign Currency list and you can enter rates for each of them.

To be sure that you do not use an old exchange rate that is no longer accurate, you should turn on the reminder warning that the rate is out of date. A one-day period for updating should be sufficient.

Click Display a reminder if the exchange rate is field

Accept One Day as the time. In this way, every time you change the transaction date to one day past the previously used exchange rate entry, the program will warn you and give you an opportunity to change the rate. If the rate has not changed, you can accept the old rate.

Click OK to save the currency information and return to the Home window.

Setting Bank Accounts for Foreign Currencies

Before entering vendor and customer information, we will update the bank account ledgers to assign each one the correct currency. By default, all amounts are in the home currency, Canadian dollars or CAD. Therefore, the only account we need to change is the USD account used for foreign currency transactions.

Click the **Accounts icon** to open the Accounts window.

Double click 1100 Bank Account: USD to open its ledger window.

Notice that CAD has been added to the label for the Opening Balance field. Currencies are assigned from the Class Options tab screen.

Click the **Class Options tab** to access the currency field:

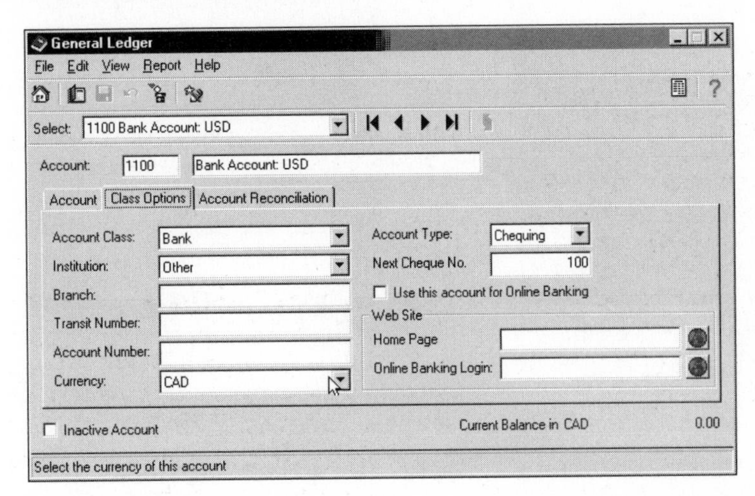

Click the **Currency field list arrow**. The two currencies, CAD and USD, are listed.

Click USD to change the currency.

Notice that the Current Balance amount is now displayed in both currencies.

Click the **Account tab**. There are also two Opening Balance fields now, one for each currency.

Close the ledger to return to the Accounts window. The Accounts window has an additional column for foreign currency amounts. **Close** the Accounts window to return to the Home window.

Entering Vendor Accounts in the Payables Ledger

Use the Vendor Information for Maverick Micro Solutions on page 303 to enter vendor details and historical invoices. The following keystrokes will enter the information for **Alberta Hydro**, a vendor of Maverick Micro Solutions.

Click the **Vendors icon** in the Home window to display the Vendors window:

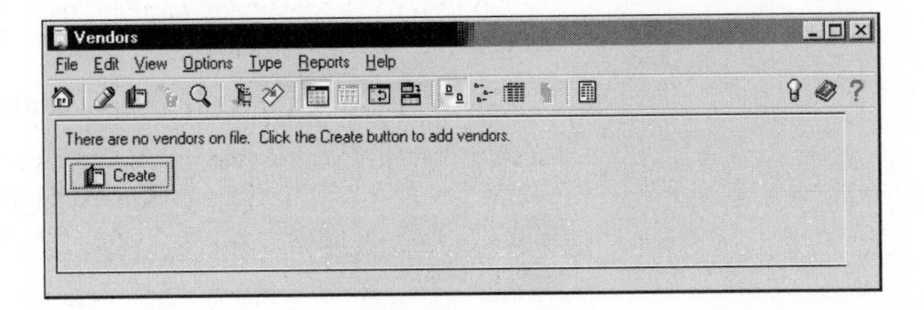

notes

- If you choose to skip the Vendors icon window from the View menu (User Preferences, Icon Windows) in the Home window, you will see this Payables Ledger window immediately when you click the Vendors icon.
- Vendor icons may be moved to a different position by dragging. New vendors are added to the end of the display, regardless of order. To restore the alphabetic order for icons, choose the Options menu and then Re-sort Icons.
- If you prefer to list the vendors by name in the Vendors window, choose the View menu and Name. The list will retain its alphabetic order, even when you add or remove vendors.

The window is empty because no vendors are on file for Maverick. Once we add the vendor accounts, this window contains an icon for each vendor that you can use to access the vendor's ledger record. The vendors may be displayed in icon form or by name by selecting from the View menu.

Click the **Create button** [Create] in the Vendors window or choose the File menu and click Create to display the following vendor input screen:

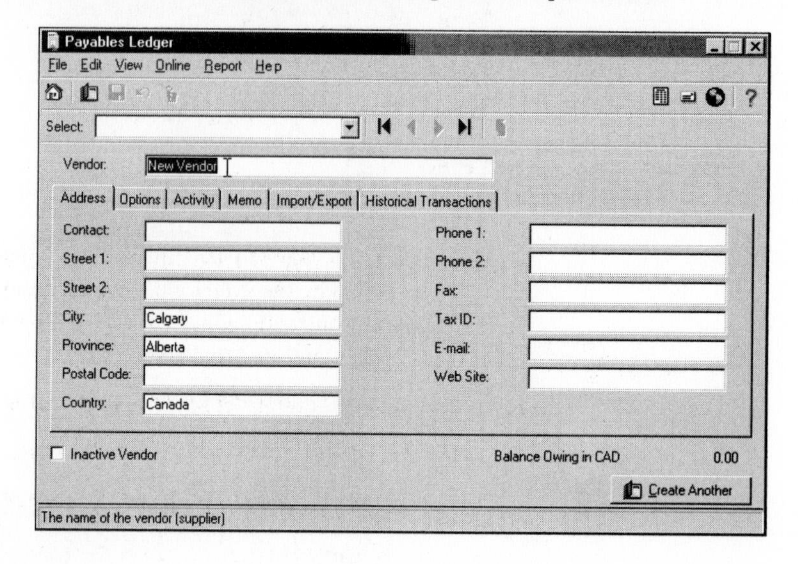

The Address tab screen is displayed first and the Vendor field is highlighted, ready for you to enter information.

version 8

Type `Alberta Hydro`

Press *tab*

The cursor advances to the Contact field. Here you should enter the name of the person (or department) at Alberta Hydro with whom Maverick Micro Solutions will be dealing. This information will enable a company to make inquiries more professionally and effectively. For a small business, the owner's name may appear in this field.

Type `Nida Power`

Press *tab*

The cursor advances to the Street 1 field.

Type `49 Glowing Lights Rd.`

There is no additional street address information for the Street 2 field. The program uses the Company Information entries as the defaults for the City, Province and Country fields. Therefore, Calgary has been entered in the City field because it is the city in which Maverick Micro Solutions is located. It is correct. The default Province and Country are also correct.

notes

You may skip any of the address tab fields if the information is missing for the vendor. Just click the next field for which you have information to move the cursor. To edit any field, drag to highlight the contents and type the correct information.

Click the **Postal Code field**.

Type `t3p4x2`

Click the **Phone 1 field**.

The program corrects the format of the postal code. (Only Canadian postal codes are reformatted.) You can enter phone and fax numbers with or without the area code.

Type `4037718877`

Click the **Fax field** because there is no second phone number. The program corrects the format of the phone number.

Type 4037712900

Press tab

The Tax ID field allows you to enter the vendor's tax ID or business number. The following two fields contain the e-mail and Web site address for the vendor. Enter them just as you would type them in your Internet and e-mail programs.

Type 43685 2989

Press tab

Type npower@altahydro.ca

Press tab

Type www.altahydro.ca

Notice that the vendor's account balance appears at the bottom of the ledger, along with the currency identification. A vendor may also be marked as Inactive if there are currently no transactions. Reports have the option to include or omit inactive vendors. All Maverick's vendors are active.

The remaining vendor details are entered from the other tab screens.

Click the **Options tab** to open the next screen:

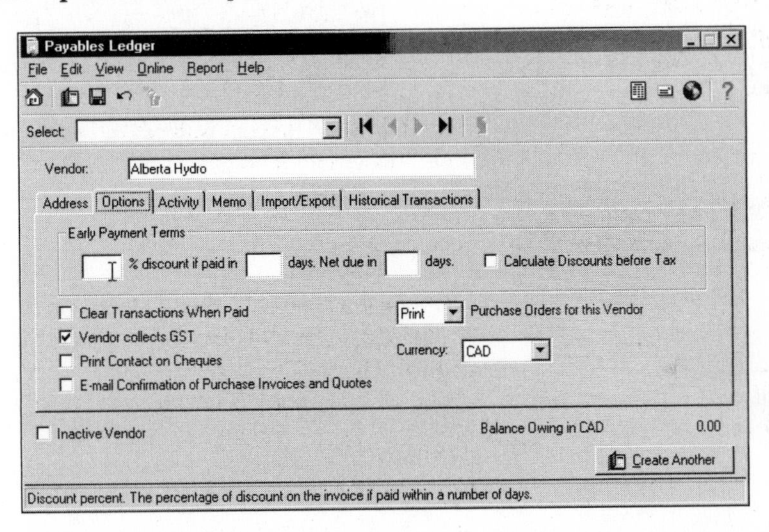

Warning!

Do not forget to choose USD as the currency for Vision Technologies.

If the vendor offers a discount for early payment or has a term for the net amount, you can enter these details on this screen. Alberta Hydro expects payment immediately on receipt of invoices, terms that we will enter as Net 1 Day. Since there is no discount, skip to the third Terms field.

Click the **Net amount due in ___ days field.**

Type 1

Since there is no discount, we can skip the discount before or after tax option.

Indicate that you want to retain all invoices for this vendor by leaving the box beside Clear Transactions When Paid unchecked. Do not turn on the option to Print Contact on Cheques because the contact field does not contain address information.

Indicate that this vendor collects GST, and purchases are eligible for GST input credits and should be included in GST reports by leaving this box checked. All vendors for Maverick Micro Solutions, except the Receiver General, collect GST. Vendors such as the Receiver General of Canada, who do not supply goods or services eligible for input tax credits, should not be included in GST reports.

notes

When you enter zero in the Net days field, the field remains blank and invoices will not show as overdue, therefore, 1 is entered instead. Payment terms may be changed in the journal for individual invoices.

notes

Unless you have checked Vendor collects GST, the GST codes will not be available in the Purchases Journal for that vendor.

If you e-mail purchase orders to a vendor, choose this option from the drop-down list to replace the default option to print purchase orders. Click E-mail Confirmation if you choose to e-mail purchase orders to be certain that the order is received. Even if you choose Print as the default, you can still e-mail the order from the Purchases Journal.

Currency is also defined on the Options tab screen. By default, vendors use the home currency, CAD. The currencies set up in the Currency Information screen are listed on the drop-down list in the currency field. After you enter historical transactions or journal transactions for a vendor in one currency, you cannot change the currency.

notes

Records for foreign vendors will have all amounts in both currencies.

Click the **Activity tab** to open the next information screen:

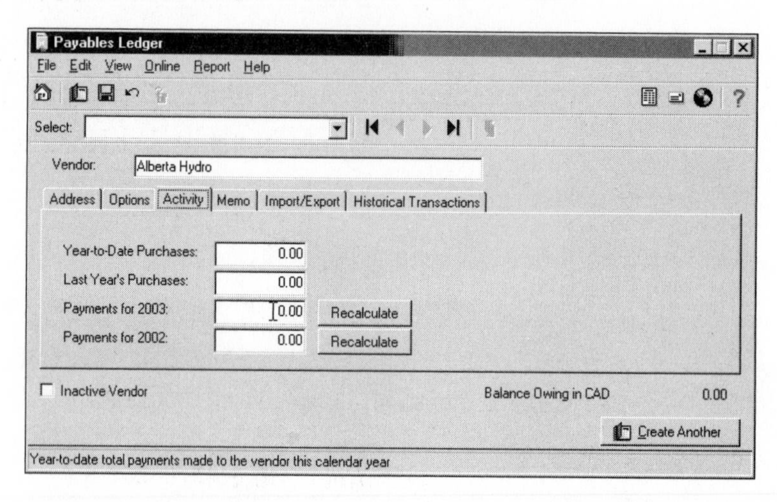

notes

The vendor's name appears at the top of each tab screen for reference. When the vendor uses a foreign currency, the activity summary information is presented for both currencies.

Maverick Micro Solutions will not enter the historical summary information of total purchases for the previous and current year. Maverick will enter only outstanding invoices and the balance field will be completed automatically by the program once you have entered these historical invoices in the following section. The remaining fields are also updated automatically from journal entries, but you can add a starting historical balance as well.

Click the **Memo tab** to advance to the next screen:

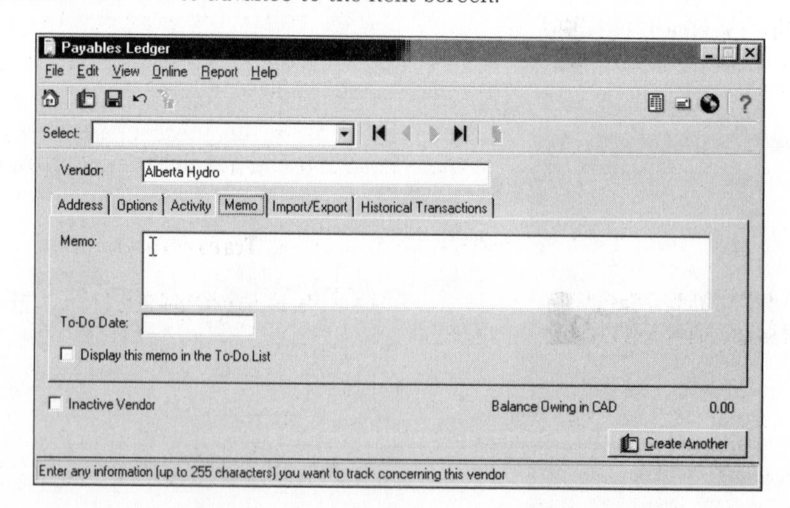

The Memo tab screen allows you to enter a message related to the vendor that is added to the to-do lists, the automatic reminder system.

Click the **Import/Export tab** to open the next information screen:

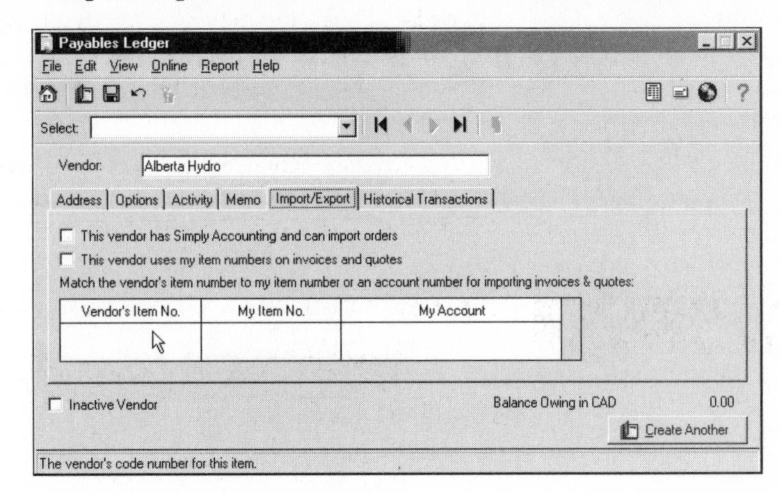

The Import/Export screen refers to inventory items. If the vendor also uses Simply Accounting, you can match the vendor's inventory item codes to your own for electronic transfers of information.

There are no outstanding invoices for Alberta Hydro so we can check the details.

Click the **Address tab**. Correct any errors by returning to the field with the mistake, highlighting the errors and entering the correct information. You can now save the record.

Click Create Another [Create Another] to save the vendor information and display a blank new vendor screen. When you return to the Vendors window, you will see that Simply Accounting has created a vendor icon for Alberta Hydro. The Create button has been removed. The Create tool button is still available.

Repeat these procedures to enter the next vendor, Alberta Telephone.

Entering Historical Vendor Information

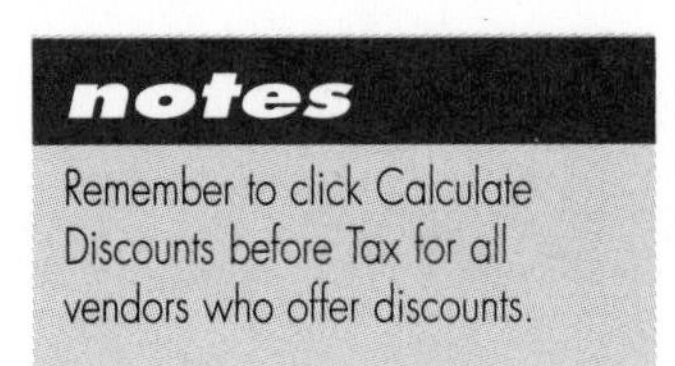

The following keystrokes will enter the historical information for Cybertek Systems, the first vendor with outstanding invoices from page 303. You should have a blank Payables Ledger window on-screen.

Cybertek Systems has an outstanding invoice so we must enter historical transaction details. Finish entering the Address and Options information, remembering to click Calculate Discounts before Tax.

Click the **Historical Transactions tab**:

Enter invoice details carefully. To correct a historical invoice amount, you must pay the invoice and then clear paid transactions (Maintenance menu). Then reset the historical payments for the year to zero (Payables Ledger, Activity tab screen) and re-enter the outstanding invoices.

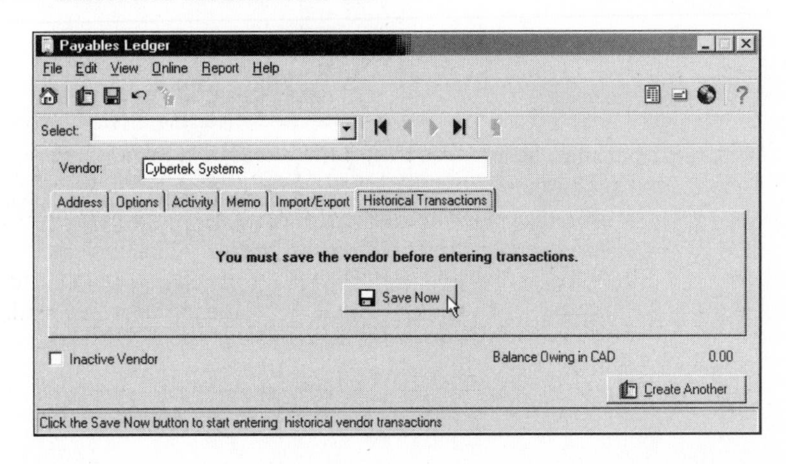

notes

You can also enter the address and options details for all vendors and then open the ledger to add historical information by clicking the Historical Transactions tab. Open the ledger for any vendor by double clicking the vendor's icon in the Vendors window.

You must save or create the vendor ledger record before adding historical invoices.

Click the **Save Now button** to modify the ledger screen:

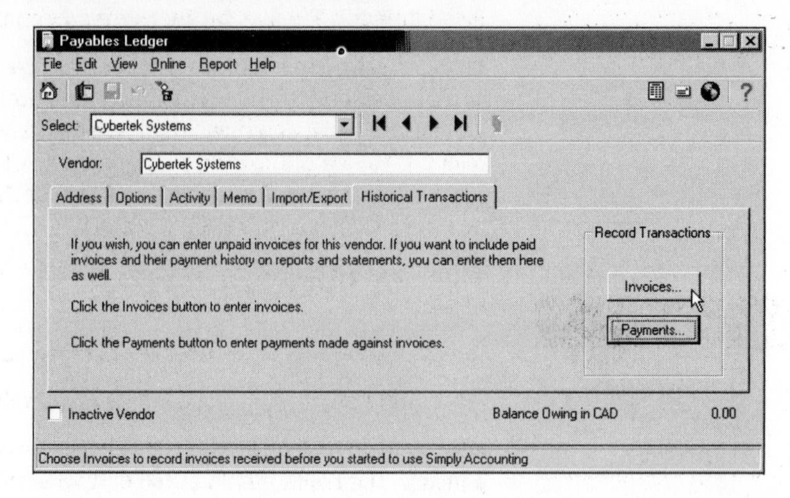

Notice that the screen has two new options: *Invoices* and *Payments*. You should select the **Invoices** option to record the outstanding invoices. Use the **Payments** option to record prior payments that you want to keep on record after entering the invoices.

Click Invoices to see the following input screen:

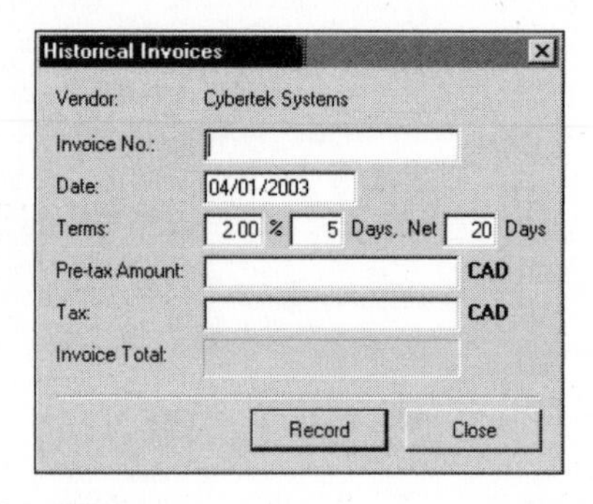

notes

USD vendors will have USD as the currency designation as well as a field for the exchange rate and the amount in the home currency.

The cursor is in the Invoice No. field so you can enter the first invoice number.

Type `CS-4211`

Press *tab*

The cursor advances to the Date field. Enter the invoice date for the first invoice to replace the default earliest transaction date. The invoice date must not be later than the earliest transaction date.

Type `03-28-03`

notes

The totals of the outstanding invoice and payment amounts must match the historical balance entered in the Accounts Payable control account in the General Ledger.

The Terms are entered from the Vendor record and are correct, although they can be edited if necessary. You should enter the amount for the first invoice. The amount is divided into a pretax and a tax amount so that Simply Accounting can correctly calculate the discount on the before-tax amount. When the option to calculate discounts before tax is not selected, a single amount field appears on the invoice for the full amount of the invoice with taxes included.

Click the **Pre-tax Amount field** to advance the cursor.

Type `1000`

Press *tab* to advance to the Tax amount field.

Type `70`

Press tab to update the Invoice Total field.

You may correct any errors by pressing tab to return to the field with the error and highlighting it. Then, enter the correct information.

Be sure that all the information is entered correctly before you save your vendor account balance. If you save incorrect invoice information and you want to change it, you must first pay the invoice, clear paid transactions (Home window, Maintenance menu, Clear Data, Clear Paid Transactions, Clear Paid Vendor Transactions), then reset the payments for 2003 to zero, and finally re-enter the invoice. Otherwise the historical information will be incorrect.

You must click Record and then Close to save the historical information correctly.

Click Record to save the information and to display another blank invoice for this vendor.

Repeat these procedures to enter additional invoices for the vendor if there are any.

When you have recorded all outstanding invoices for a vendor,

Click Close to return to the ledger. The invoice you have just entered has been added to the Balance field at the bottom of the ledger screen. Now you can enter the historical payment information for this vendor.

Click Payments to display the payments form:

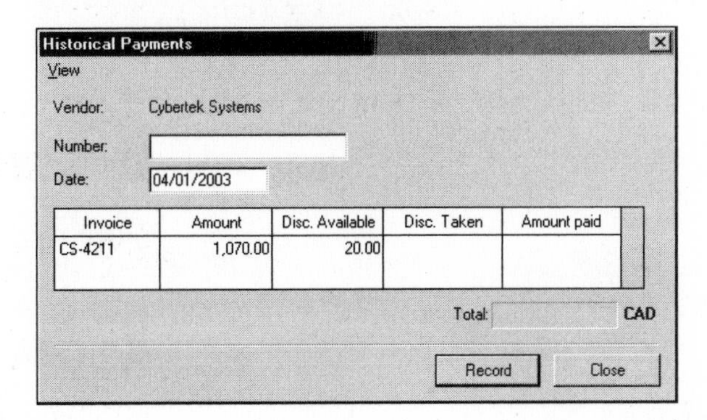

All outstanding invoices that you entered are displayed. Notice that the discount is $20, 2% of $1 000, the pretax amount. Entering historical payments is very much like entering current payments in the Payments Journal.

Click the **Number field** if necessary to move the cursor to the cheque number field.

Type 189

Press tab

The cursor advances to the Date field. Enter the cheque date for the first payment towards invoice #CS-4211 to replace the default earliest transaction date.

notes

The full amount of the discount will remain available until the five days have passed. If the balance is paid within that time, the full discount will be taken.

Type 03-28-03

Click the **Amount paid column on the line for invoice #CS-4211**. Because the full amount is not being paid, the discount does not apply.

The full invoice amount is displayed as the default and is highlighted so you can edit it.

Type 500

Press tab

If an amount appears in the Disc. Taken field, delete it before recording the payment.

Check your information carefully before you proceed and make corrections if necessary.

Click Record to save the information and to display another payment form for this vendor in case there are additional payments to record. Notice that the amount owing has been updated to include the payment entry just completed.

Repeat these procedures to enter any other payments to this vendor.

When you have recorded all outstanding payments to a vendor,

Click the **Address tab**.

Click Create Another 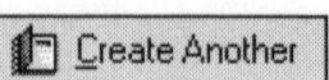

Click Close to return to the vendor information form. When you click the Activity tab, you will see that the payment you entered has been included to reduce the amount of the balance owing.

> **notes**
>
> Display or print your vendor list to check the accuracy of your address details. Display or print a Vendor Aged Detail Report including terms and historical differences to check the accuracy of the historical transactions.

Repeat these procedures to enter the remaining vendors and historical transactions.

Close the vendor ledger and Vendors icon window to return to the Home window.

Entering Customer Accounts in the Receivables Ledger

Use the Customer Information chart for Maverick Micro Solutions on page 303 to complete this step. The following keystrokes will enter the information for **Alberta Insurance Co.**, the first customer on the list for Maverick Micro Solutions.

Click the **Customers icon** in the Home window to display the Customers icon window. The window is empty because there are no customers on file yet for Maverick.

Click the **Create button** in the Customers window or choose the File menu and click Create to display the customer input screen:

> **notes**
>
> - If you choose to skip the Customers icon window from the Home window View menu, you will see this Receivables Ledger window immediately when you click the Customers icon.
> - Customer icons may be moved to a different position by dragging. New customers are added to the end of the display, regardless of order. To restore the alphabetic order for icons, choose the Options menu and then Re-sort Icons.
> - If you prefer to list the customers by name in the Customers window, choose the View menu and then Name. The list will retain its alphabetic order, even when you add or remove customers.

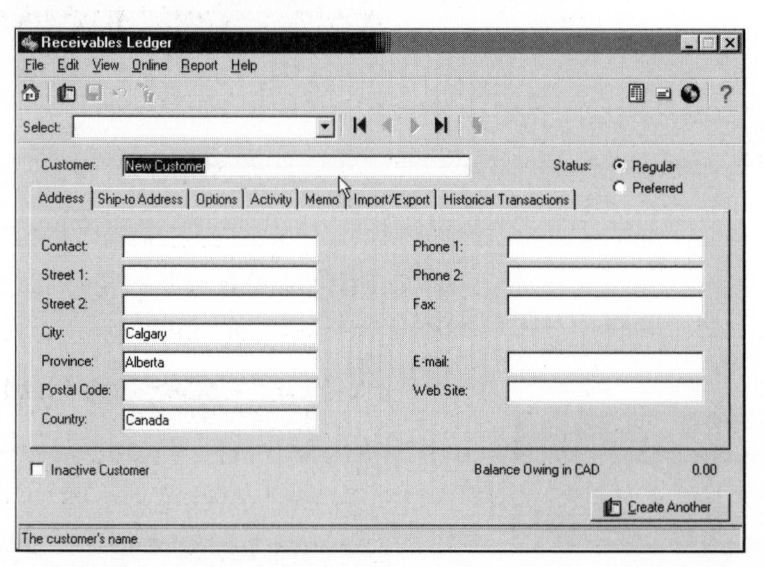

The Address tab screen is displayed initially and the Customer field is highlighted, ready for you to enter information. Regular customer status is selected as the default setting and this is correct for all Maverick customers since prices for individual contracts are negotiated with customers.

Type `Alberta Insurance Co.`

Click the **Contact field**. Enter the name of the primary person or department to be contacted by Maverick Micro Solutions about any sale.

notes

You may skip any of the address tab fields if the information is missing for the customer. Just click the next field for which you have information to move the cursor.

Type `Joel Careless`

Press tab to advance the cursor to the Street 1 field.

Type `571 Litty Gate`

The default City, Province and Country are correct so you should accept them.

Click the **Postal Code field**.

Type `t2b1a6`

Click the **Phone 1 field**. The program corrects the format of the postal code.

Type `4037730208`

Click the **Fax field**. The program corrects the format of the phone number. You should enter the customer's fax number if there is one.

Type `4037730100`

Press tab to move the cursor to the E-mail field.

Type `Joel_Careless@protec.com`

Press tab to move to the Web Site field.

Type `www.protec.com/altainsure`

The current balance and currency are noted at the bottom of the ledger window. Customers, like vendors and accounts, may be marked as inactive if they have not bought merchandise or services for some time. They can then be omitted from reports.

The Ship-to Address tab screen has room for a second address that is used when the customer wants merchandise to be shipped to a separate mailing address.

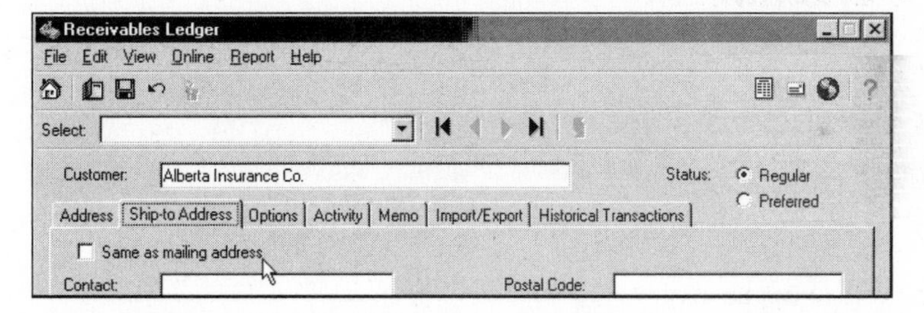

Click Same as mailing address since the customer has only one address.

Click the **Options tab** to see the payment and invoice options for the customer:

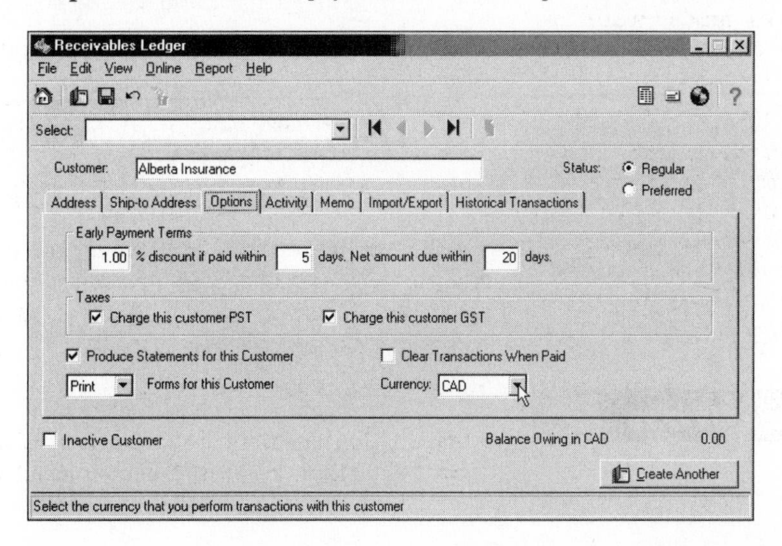

notes

Unless you check Charge this customer GST, the GST fields and codes will not be available in the Sales Journal for this customer.

notes

Records for foreign customers will have sales summary amounts and balances in both currencies.

Most of the default entries are correct. The payment terms are entered automatically from the Receivables Settings. Terms can be edited if necessary for individual customers and invoices in the Sales Journal. We want to retain paid transactions so that they will be available for statements and for adjustments. The customer pays GST and should be included in GST reports, so GST codes must be available. We want to be able to print statements for the customer and we will choose to print invoices rather than to e-mail them. The currency definition is correct as CAD, the home currency.

PST is not charged on sales in Alberta, so you should change this setting.

Click Charge this customer PST to remove the ✓.

Click the **Activity tab** to view the next set of customer details:

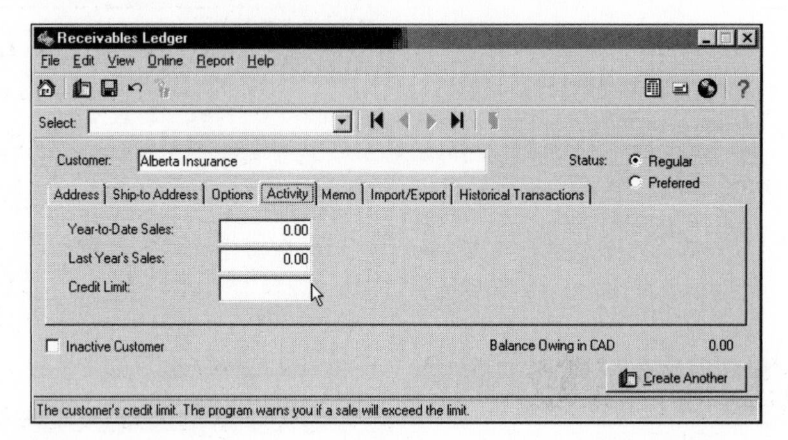

Skip the Year-to-Date Sales and Last Year's Sales fields because Maverick Micro Solutions has not kept this historical information on record. Balances will be included automatically once you provide the outstanding invoice information. Year-to-date sales are also updated from journal entries, but you can add a historical balance as well. When you have two years of data, there will be an amount for last year's sales, too.

You should enter the amount that the customer can purchase on account before payments are required. If the customer goes beyond this credit limit, the program will issue a warning when you attempt to post the invoice.

Click the **Credit Limit field**.

Type 5000

Click the **Memo tab** to view the memo detail screen. If you had a message that you wanted to display as a reminder, you could enter it here along with the reminder date. The program would display the message on the session date you provided.

Click the **Import/Export tab**. If the customer also uses Simply Accounting, you can match the customer's inventory codes to your own for electronic data transfers.

notes

You can correct address and options details at any time.

You may correct any errors by returning to the field with the error. Click the appropriate tab, highlight the error and enter the correct information. When all the information is entered correctly, you must save your customer information.

Click the **Address tab**.

Click Create Another 

to save the information and advance to the next new customer input screen. Simply Accounting has created an icon for Alberta Insurance Co. in the Customers window.

Entering Historical Customer Information

The following keystrokes will enter the information for the next customer, **Calgary College**, a customer with historical activity. Repeat the procedures above to enter the address, options and credit limit for the customer. You can now enter the historical invoices and payments from page 304.

Click the **Historical Transactions tab**:

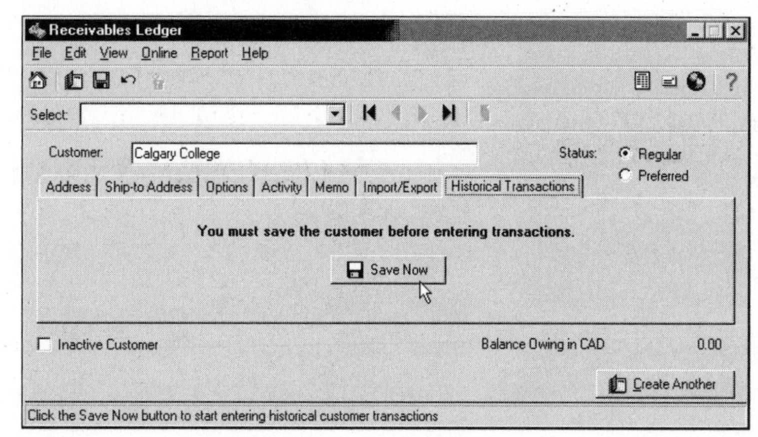

You must save or create the customer record before you can add historical invoices.

Click the **Save Now button**:

> **notes**
>
> If you prefer, you can enter address, options and credit limit details for all customers and then add the historical invoices and payments from the Historical Transactions tab screen. You can open a customer ledger record by double clicking the icon for the customer in the Customers window.

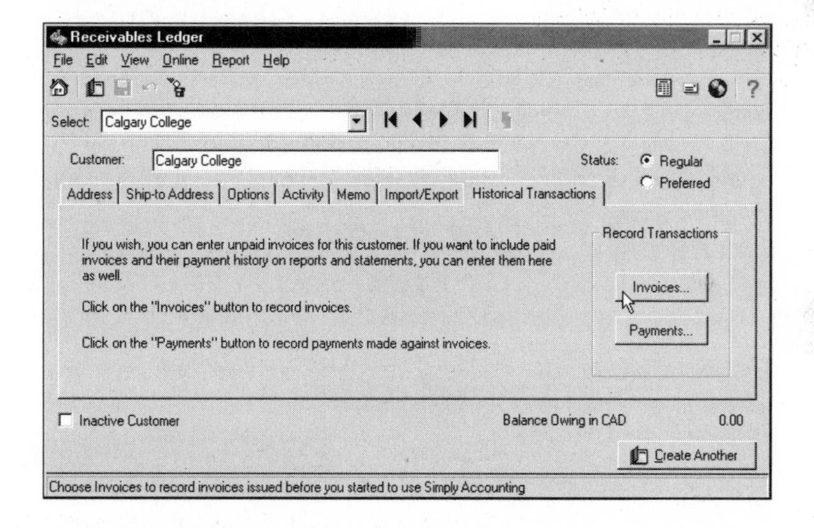

Just as in the Payables Ledger, you enter invoices and payments separately. You can use the Payments option to record any payments against previous invoices that you want to keep on record.

> **Warning!**
>
> Enter invoice details carefully. To correct a historical invoice amount, you must pay the invoice and then clear paid transactions (Maintenance menu). Then re-enter the outstanding invoices.

Click Invoices to display the following input form:

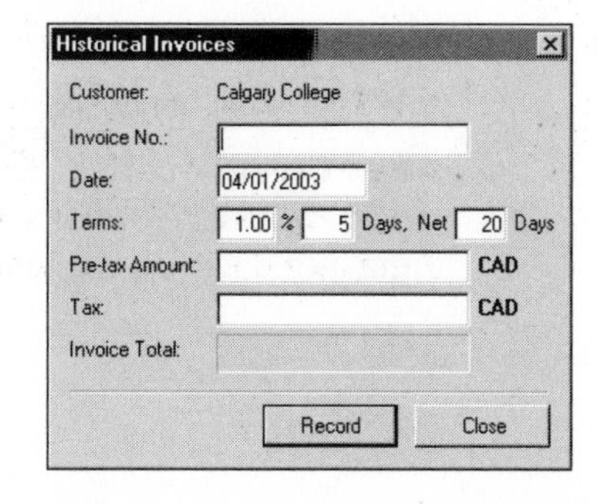

notes

When discounts are not calculated before tax, there is a single amount field for the total amount of the invoice.

notes

The totals of these outstanding invoices, after payments, must match the historical balance entered in the Accounts Receivable control account in the General Ledger.

notes

For foreign customers, amounts are in the foreign currency together with the exchange rate and the amount in the home currency.

The cursor is in the Invoice Number field so you can enter the first invoice number.

Type 52

Press tab

The cursor advances to the Date field, ready for you to replace the earliest transaction or session date with the date for the first invoice.

Type 03-28

Because the payment terms are correctly entered, we can skip them. Discounts are calculated before taxes and we must enter the invoice amount as a pretax total and a tax amount.

Click the **Pre-tax Amount field**.

Type 4000

Press tab to advance to the Tax amount field.

Type 280

Press tab to update the Invoice Total.

You may correct any errors by returning to the field with the error, highlighting the error and entering the correct information.

Check the information carefully before you save your customer account balance. Incorrect invoices can be changed only by paying the outstanding invoices, clearing paid transactions (Home window, Maintenance menu, Clear Data, Clear Paid Transactions, Clear Paid Customer Transactions) and then re-entering the invoices.

Click Record to save the invoice and to display a new blank invoice form for this customer.

Repeat these procedures to enter the remaining invoices for this customer, if any.

After all invoices for a customer have been entered,

Click Close to return to the customer's information window. Notice that the program has added the customer's balance in the ledger window. You are now ready to record the payment made by Calgary College against this invoice.

Click Payments to display the customer payments form:

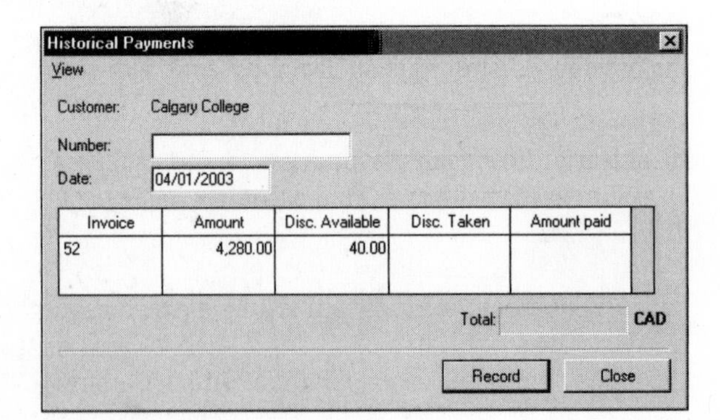

All outstanding invoices that you entered are displayed. Entering historical customer payments is very much like entering current receipts in the Receipts journal.

Click the **Number field** to move the cursor to the cheque number field if necessary.

Type 187

Press tab

The cursor advances to the Date field. Enter the date for the first cheque to replace the default earliest transaction date.

Type 03-28

notes

The full discount is available until the discount period has ended.

Discounts can be taken only when the full payment is made before the due date, so we must skip the Discount fields.

Click the **Amount paid column on the line for invoice #52**.

The full invoice amount is displayed as the default, and is highlighted so you can edit it.

Type 1000

Press tab

Warning!

If an amount appears in the Disc. Taken field, delete it before recording the payment.

Check your information carefully before you proceed and make corrections if necessary.

Click Record to save the information and to display another payment form for this customer in case there are additional payments to record. Notice that the amount owing in the ledger has been updated to include the payment entry just completed.

Repeat these procedures to enter other payments by this customer if there are any.

When you have recorded all outstanding payments by a customer,

Click Close to return to the customer information form.

notes

Display or print the Customer List to check the accuracy of your address information. Display or print a Customer Aged Detail Report including terms and historical differences to check the historical information for accuracy.

Click the **Address tab**.

Click Create Another [Create Another] to open a new ledger record window.

Repeat these procedures to enter the remaining customers and historical transactions.

Close the customer ledger and the Customers icon window to return to the Home window.

Setting up Credit Cards

Since Maverick accepts credit card payments from customers and uses credit cards in payment for purchases, we must set up the credit cards by naming them and identifying the linked accounts for deposits, payments and fees associated with the cards. Maverick accepts and uses VISA for credit card payments.

You should be in the Home window.

version 8

Choose the **Setup menu** then **choose System Settings** and **click Credit Cards** to see the Credit Card Information screen:

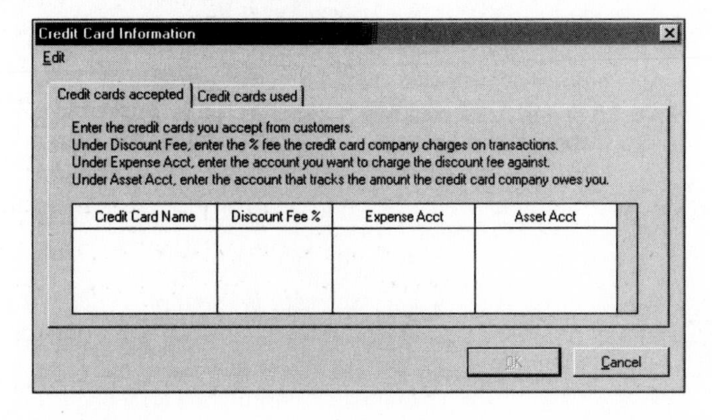

The first tab screen applies to credit cards accepted from customers in payment.

Each card accepted should be listed on a separate line. The cursor is in the Name field. All the cards you name here will appear on the Paid By list for Sales Invoices.

Type `VISA`

Press tab

The cursor advances to the Discount Fee % field. The discount fee is the amount that the card company withholds as a merchant transaction fee for use of the card. This expense is withheld from the total invoice amount that the card company deposits to the business bank account for each sale. Fees vary from one company to another and also for the type of business. For example, high-volume businesses pay a lower percentage than businesses with a smaller volume of sales.

Type `3.5`

Press tab

The cursor advances to the Expense Account field. This is the linked account that will be debited automatically for the discount fee for a credit card sale. The expense amount is the total invoice amount times the discount fee percentage.

Press enter to see the list of accounts available for linking.

Click 5030 to choose the account.

Click Select to add the account to the card information screen.

The cursor is in the Asset Account field, the linked account for deposits from the card company. Normally a bank account is set up for credit card deposits.

Press enter to see the list of accounts available for linking. Notice that Bank class accounts are not on this list.

notes

If you classify credit card accounts as Bank accounts, you cannot select them for linking to the credit card.

Click 1090 to choose the account.

Click Select to add the account to the card information screen.

If there are additional credit cards, the information for them is entered in the same way. First name the card, then enter the discount fee and the two linked accounts.

Cards used for payments to vendors are set up in the same way. The business may use and accept the same cards or different cards.

Click the **Credit cards used tab** to open the screen for the cards that the business uses:

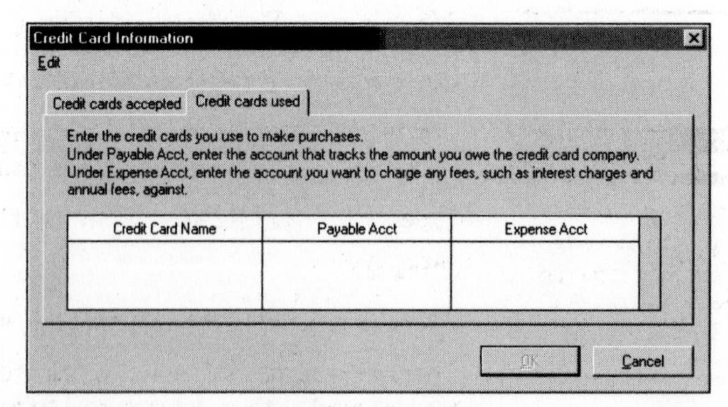

Again, each card is listed on a separate line with its associated linked accounts. Each card named on this screen will appear in the Purchases Journal in the Paid By list. There is no discount fee associated with individual purchases, although there may be an annual or monthly fee attached to the card usage.

Click the **Credit Card Name field**.

Type VISA

Press tab

The cursor moves to the Payable Account field. This account is the liability account that records the balance owing to the card company.

Press enter to see the list of available accounts.

Click 2150, the liability account for the card.

Click Select to add the account and move to the Expense Account field.

The Expense account records any monthly or annual fees paid to the card company for the privilege of using the card. Not all cards have user fees. Maverick uses the same expense account for all credit card-related expenses.

Press enter to see the account list.

Double click 5030

Click OK to see the message about account class changes:

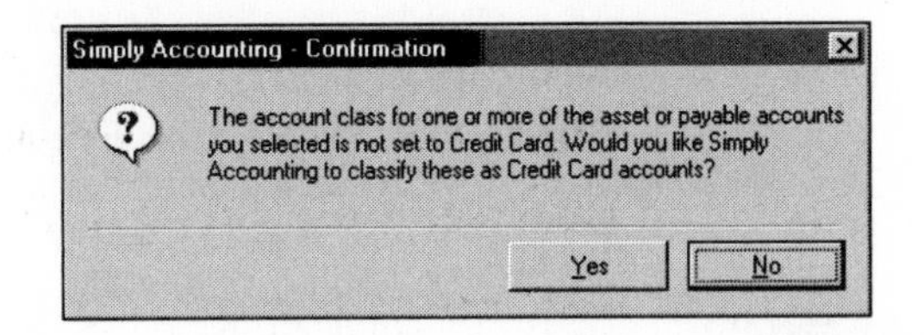

Click Yes to accept the change and return to the Home window.

Preparing for Journal Entries

Warning!

Make a backup copy before proceeding. This way, if you finish entering history and discover an incorrect amount, you can correct the error without re-entering all the information.

The last stage in setting up the accounting system involves closing off the historical entries, indicating that all historical data have been entered. You can proceed with journalizing before finishing the history, but you must complete this step before beginning the next fiscal period. Finishing history involves changing the status of each ledger from an open to a finished history state. In the open history state the ledgers are not integrated, so you can add or change historical information in one ledger without affecting any other ledger. It is easier to correct mistakes.

Making a Backup of the Company Files

Choose the **File menu** and **click Backup**.

notes

You can use a floppy disk for a backup but you can save only one backup on each floppy disk. Substitute the appropriate drive and folders for the location of your files.

Create a new folder called NF-MAVE in your data folder to store the not-finished version of your data files. In the File name field,

Type `C:\program files\winsim\data\nf-mave\nf-mave`

Click OK

Click Yes when prompted so that the program will create the new folder.

The "NF" designates files as not finished or open to distinguish them from the ones you will work with to enter journal transactions. Continue by following the backup instructions on-screen. You can use another name and location for your backup if you want. This will create a backup copy of the files for Maverick Micro Solutions.

Working with Unfinished History

Simply Accounting permits you to enter current journal transactions before the history is finished and balanced. In this way, you can keep the journal records current and enter the historical details later when there is time available to do so, or the setup may be completed later by a different individual.

There are, however, a number of elements that must be completed before you can make journal entries. The General Ledger accounts must be created and essential linked accounts must be defined before you can use the journals. Historical customer and vendor invoices must be entered before you can enter payments for them, and invoices must have the correct payment terms and dates. You do not need to enter General Ledger opening account balances. These may be added later from the Opening Balance field on the Account tab screen. The General Ledger also shows the current balance that changes as you post new journal entries. Your Trial Balance and Accounts window will display only current balances.

From a control point of view, it is preferable to enter all historical information first so that you do not confuse the historical and current data or work with accounts that are not correct in some way. You cannot change account numbers after the accounts are used in journal entries so some corrections may be difficult to make later. After you start journalizing, the balances for *Accounts Receivable* and *Accounts Payable* reflect all the entries made to date; there may be mistakes in journal entries as well as in the history. Therefore, it is more difficult to find the historical errors later.

notes

Account, vendor and customer names and address details can be corrected at any time.

There are a number of checks that you can perform to increase the accuracy of your work. You should compare your reports carefully with the charts given at the beginning of this application and make corrections. Pay particular attention to correct account numbers and historical invoices. Printing Vendor and Customer Aged Reports with historical differences can reveal errors in invoices or payments. The Accounts window has an Edit menu option and tool to check the validity of accounts. The Home window Maintenance menu has an option to check data integrity that looks for differences in balances between the subsidiary ledgers and the corresponding General Ledger control accounts. All these checks help point to mistakes that should be corrected before proceeding.

Choose the **Maintenance menu** and **click Check Data Integrity** to see the summary:

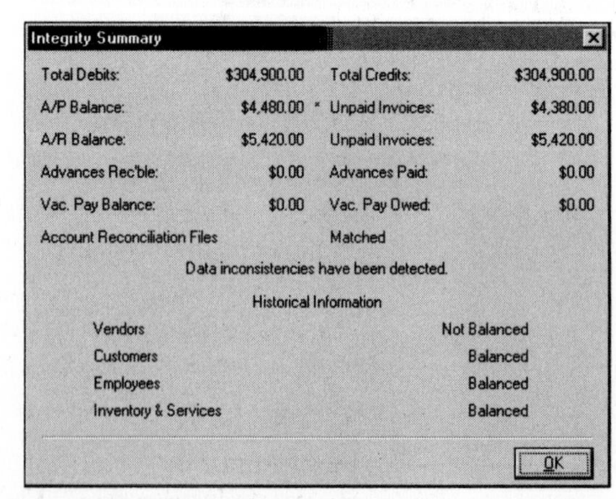

You can see that the vendor history is not correct. This error will prevent us from finishing the history.

Click OK to return to the Home window.

Choose the **History menu** and **click Finish Entering History**:

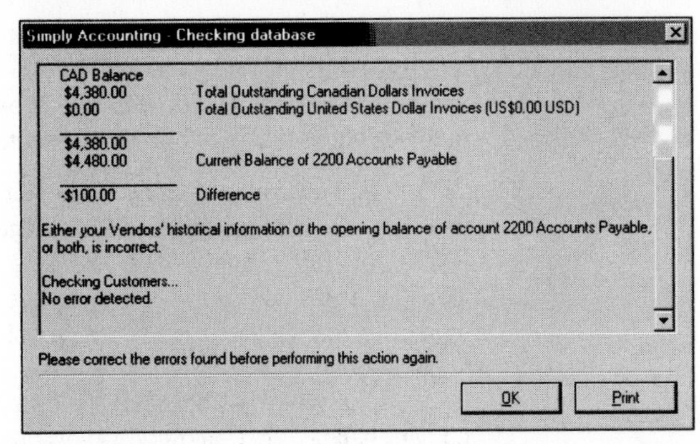

When all your essential linked accounts are defined and all the historical amounts balance, you will see the warning that this step cannot be reversed, as in Chapter 6, page 174. Otherwise, Simply Accounting warns you about errors that prevent you from finishing the history. For example, the accounts may be out of order if a subgroup total is missing after a set of subgroup accounts, or the Accounts Receivable ledger balances may not equal the control account balance. If you have omitted one of the essential linked accounts, that information will also be included on this screen. To help you correct the mistakes, print the message for reference by **clicking Print**.

We see the message that the Vendors or Accounts Payable history is not balanced. Since the Trial Balance is correct, we may be missing a historical Payables Ledger invoice as suggested from the data integrity check.

Click OK to return to the Home window.

We will proceed with entering the source documents and when the missing invoice surfaces, we can enter it and finish the history. You can proceed with journal entries until you start the next fiscal period. At that point, you must finish the history.

You can now exit the program or continue by entering the transactions that follow. Remember to advance the session date.

SOURCE DOCUMENTS

SESSION DATE – April 7

- ❑ Purchase Order #1001
  Dated April 2/03
  Shipping date April 5/03
  From Vision Technologies, $400 USD for a new projection panel circuit board (Parts Inventory), plus $28 GST paid. Invoice total $428 USD. Terms: net 20 days. The exchange rate is 1.555.

- ❑ Sales Invoice #60
  Dated April 2/03
  To Alberta Insurance Co., $3 000 for installation of new hard drives on company computers, plus $210 GST charged. Sales invoice total $3 210. Terms: 1/5, net 20 days.

notes

Remember that Maverick records the customer's cheque number in the Receipts Journal number field.

- ❑ Cash Receipt #101
  Dated April 2/03
  From Calgary College, cheque #209 for $3 240 in full payment of account including $40 discount (before tax) for early payment. Reference invoice #52.

- ❑ Cheque Copy #201
  Dated April 2/03
  To Cybertek Systems, $550 in payment of account including 2% discount (before tax) for early payment. Reference invoice #CS-4211.

- ❑ Cheque Copy #202
  Dated April 3/03
  To Flextech Products, $2 180 in full payment of account including 1% discount (before tax) for early payment. Reference invoice #FP-95.

- ❑ Sales Quote #82
  Dated April 4/03
  Delivery date: work to be completed by April 11/03
  To Performance Technical School, the repair, installation, and PC to TV conversion work will cost $2 000, plus $140 GST charged. Sales quote total $2 140. Terms: 1/5, net 20 days.

- ❑ Sales Quote #83
  Dated April 4/03
  Delivery date: work to be completed by April 17/03
  To Calgary College, $3 600 for memory upgrades on computers, and repairs to monitors and digital cameras, plus $252 GST charged. Sales quote total $3 852. Terms: 1/5, net 20 days.

- ❑ Sales Quote #84
  Dated April 4/03
  Delivery date: Work to be completed by April 27/03
  To Performance Technical School, $1 200 for installation of memory chips and new disk drives, plus $84 GST charged. Sales quote total $1 284. Terms: 1/5, net 20 days.

- ❑ Bank Debit Memo #142723
  Dated April 4/03
  From Alberta Trust, $48 for service charges.

- ❑ Purchase Invoice #VT-397
  Dated April 5/03
  From Vision Technologies, to fill Purchase Order #1001, $400 USD for a new projection panel circuit board (Parts Inventory), plus $28 GST paid. Purchase invoice total $428 USD. Terms: net 20 days. The board, a replacement part for a repair job, will be shipped express at Maverick's expense. The exchange rate is 1.556.

- ❑ Cash Purchase Invoice #UPS-1142
  Dated April 5/03
  From UPS Delivery (use Quick Add), $20 for delivery charges, plus $1.40 GST paid. Purchase invoice total $21.40. Terms: Cash on receipt. Paid by cheque #203.

notes

Although the owner's withdrawal is a cash purchase, you should create a vendor record for the owner because he will make further withdrawals. The owner does not collect GST. Record the withdrawal as a cash purchase.

❑ Memo #1
Dated April 6/03
From the owner: Withdrew $450 from the business for personal use. Paid by cheque #204.

SESSION DATE – April 14

❑ Sales Order #CC-559
Dated April 8/03
Convert sales quote #83 to a sales order.
From Calgary College, acceptance of quote #83 for $3 600 to upgrade memory on computers, and repair monitors and digital cameras, plus $252 GST charged. Sales order total $3 852. Terms: 1/5, net 20 days.

❑ Memo #2
Dated April 8/03
From the owner: 5 memory chips (Parts Inventory) were accidentally crushed and damaged beyond repair. Charge the $125 cost of the chips to the Damaged Inventory expense account.

notes

- Use Full Add for the two new insurance vendors so that you can indicate that they do not collect GST. Enter the insurance quotes as the amount for the first month.
- For other new vendors, use the Quick Add option.

❑ Purchase Quote #II-882
Dated April 9/03
Delivery date April 15/03
From Independent Insurers, $107 per month (no GST) for 12 months for a one-year policy for business property insurance. Computer equipment not included. Terms: first month payable in advance, balance in equal monthly payments.

❑ Purchase Quote #YIC-629
Dated April 9/03
Delivery date April 15/03
From Your Insurance Company, $160.50 per month (no GST) for 12 months for a one-year policy for comprehensive business property insurance including loss-of-use coverage for all equipment. Terms: first month payable in advance, balance in equal monthly payments.

❑ Purchase Invoice #FP-121
Dated April 9/03
From Flextech Products, $1 200 for data recovery equipment, plus $84 GST paid. Purchase invoice total $1 284. Terms: 1/10, net 30 days.

❑ Purchase Invoice #CS-4440
Dated April 10/03
From Cybertek Systems, $400 for a specialized microcomputer tool set, plus $28 GST. Purchase invoice total $428. Terms: 2/5, net 20 days.

❑ Sales Invoice #61
Dated April 11/03
To Performance Technical School, to fill sales quote #82, $2 000 for repairs, installation, and PC to TV conversion, plus $140 GST charged. Sales invoice total $2 140. Terms: 1/5, net 20 days.

notes

Add A and B to the original Bank Debit Memo number for the postdated transactions.

❑ Bank Debit Memo #142993
Dated April 14/03
From Alberta Trust, $1 200 for reduction of bank loan principal. Since this is a fixed payment, store it as a recurring monthly entry. Enter the bank loan payments for the remaining two months of the fiscal quarter as postdated entries. Recall the stored entry and post the transactions for May 14 and June 14.

- [ ] Cheque Copy #205
Dated April 14/03
To Cybertek Systems, $420 in payment of account including 2% discount (before tax) for early payment. Reference invoice #CS-4440.

notes

You can process the GST remittance as a cash purchase from the Receiver General.

- [ ] Memo #3
Dated April 14/03
From the owner: Remit GST payment to the Receiver General for the month of March. Refer to the April 1 General Ledger account balances to determine the amount owing, and issue cheque #206 in payment.

- [ ] Cash Receipt #102
Dated April 14/03
From Performance Technical School, cheque #2615 for $2 120 in full payment of account including $20 discount for early payment. Reference invoice #61.

SESSION DATE – April 21

- [ ] Cash Purchase Invoice #YIC-29101
Dated April 15/03
From Your Insurance Company, acceptance of quote #YIC-629 for insurance policy for one year. Pay $160.50 in advance for first month with cheque #207. Store as recurring monthly entry.

notes

Add A and B to the original purchase invoice numbers for the postdated payment entries.

- [ ] [ ] Memo #4
Dated April 15/03
From the owner: Recall the purchase invoice from Your Insurance Company and pay the insurance premium for the following month. Issue cheque #208 for $160.50 dated May 15. Recall the invoice again and postdate the payment for June 15 using cheque #209 for $160.50.

- [ ] Sales Invoice #62
Dated April 16/03
To Western Home Security, $800 for installation of software protection program and projection panel repair work, plus $56 GST charged. Sales invoice total $856. Terms: 1/5, net 20 days.

- [ ] Sales Invoice #63
Dated April 17/03
To Calgary College, to fill sales order #CC-559, $3 600 for memory upgrades on computers, and repairs to monitors and digital cameras, plus $252 GST charged. Sales invoice total $3 852. Terms: 1/5, net 20 days.

- [ ] Memo #5
Dated April 18/03
Prepare a series of postdated cheques (cheques #210, 211, 212 and 213) to pay the Microtek Corporation account. Four cheques for $400 each should be dated April 18, April 22, April 26 and April 30. Reference invoice #MC-721.

- [ ] Cheque Copy #214
Dated April 18/03
To Flextech Products, $1 272 in full payment of account including 1% discount (before tax) for early payment. Reference invoice #FP-121.

- [ ] Cash Sales Invoice #64
Dated April 19/03
To Michael Salerno (use Quick Add), $275 for personal training on computer technology, plus $19.25 GST charged. Sales invoice total $294.25. Received certified cheque #RB2742 for $294.25 in full payment. Remember to delete the discount.

notes

The payment to Jocelyn is a cash purchase (Payments Journal, Other Payment).

- [ ] Memo #6
Dated April 20/03
To Celine Jocelyn (use Quick Add), $200 for assistance in completing the work for Calgary College. Charge to Temporary Services expense account. Issue cheque #215.

- [ ] Cash Receipt #103
Dated April 21/03
From Calgary College, cheque #1104 for $3 816 in full payment of account including $36 discount for early payment. Reference invoice #63.

SESSION DATE – April 28

- [ ] Cash Receipt #104
Dated April 22/03
From Alberta Insurance Co., cheque #613 for $3 210 in full payment of account. Reference invoice #60.

- [ ] Cheque Copy #100
Dated April 23/03
To Vision Technologies, $428 USD in full payment of account. Reference invoice #VT-397. Paid from Bank Account: USD. The exchange rate is 1.557.

notes

Choose USD as the currency in the General Journal for the transfer of funds.

- [ ] Memo #7
Dated April 23/03
From Owner: Transfer $500 USD from Bank Account: Chequing to Bank Account: USD.

- [ ] Cash Purchase Invoice #AH-61421
Dated April 24/03
From Alberta Hydro, $100 for hydro services, plus $7 GST paid. Purchase invoice total $107. Terms: Cash on receipt. Paid by cheque #216.

notes

Enter only the current charges ($50 plus GST) in the purchase invoice. Refer to Memo #8 to add the outstanding balance.

- [ ] Purchase Invoice #AT-21417
Dated April 25/03
From Alberta Telephone, $50 charges for telephone services for the current month, plus $3.50 GST paid. The balance outstanding from invoice AT-19982 dated March 25 for service in the previous month is $100. (See Memo #8.) The total amount outstanding is $153.50. Terms: n/1.

notes

The outstanding telephone invoice covers the difference in balance between the Payables Ledger and the Accounts Payable account. Enter the balance for the previous month as a historical invoice for the vendor. Check the data integrity (Maintenance menu) after entering the historical invoice.

❑ Memo #8
Dated April 25/03
From Owner: The telephone bill (previous invoice) includes an outstanding amount from the previous month, which must be entered as a historical invoice. To enter the historical invoice, click the Vendors icon and open the ledger record for Alberta Telephone. From the Historical Transactions tab screen, select Invoices. Enter invoice #AT-19982 dated March 25, 2003, and $100 as the amount. Click Record and then click Close to save the invoice. Close the ledger window and the Vendors window to return to the Home window.

❑ Cheque Copy #217
Dated April 25/03
To Alberta Telephone, $153.50 in full payment of account. Reference invoices #AT-21417 and #AT-19982.

❑ Purchase Invoice #MC-912
Dated April 26/03
From Microtek Corporation, $500 for memory chips (Parts Inventory), plus $35 GST paid. Purchase invoice total $535. Terms: net 30 days.

❑ Sales Invoice #65
Dated April 27/03
To Performance Technical School, to fill sales quote #84, $1 200 for installation of memory chips and new disk drives, plus $84 GST charged. Sales invoice total $1 284. Terms: 1/5, net 20 days.

❑ Sales Invoice #66
Dated April 28/03
To Calgary College, $800 for repairs and maintenance to college computers, plus $56 GST charged. Sales invoice total $856. Terms: 1/5, net 20 days.

notes

Use Memo #9 as the invoice number, do not include GST on the sale and choose the Interest Revenue account.

❑ Memo #9
Dated April 28/03
The account from Prairie Finance Company is overdue. Prepare a sales invoice for the interest charges for one month for $21.40 (1% of $2 140).

❑ Memo #10
Dated April 28/03
From Owner: Charge $1 300 for parts used for customer repairs and installations from Parts Inventory supplies account to Parts Used expense account.

notes

Choose the History menu in the Home window and click Finish Entering History.

❑ Memo #11
Dated April 28/03
From Owner: Make a backup copy of the data files. Using the working copy of the files, finish entering history.

CASE PROBLEM

A new vendor for Maverick Micro Solutions routinely adds freight charges to the purchase invoices. However, Maverick does not have a Freight Expense account. How can Maverick enter the freight charges in the Purchases Journal? What must he do if he wants to use the Freight Expense linked account?

CHAPTER ELEVEN

OBJECTIVES

After completing this chapter, you should be able to

- *enter* transactions in all journals
- *allocate* revenues and expenses in the General, Sales, Purchases and Payroll Journals
- *create* new projects
- *assemble* or set aside inventory items to reserve them for projects
- *display* and *print* transactions with project details
- *display* and *print* project reports

COMPANY INFORMATION

Company Profile

Puretek Paving & Stoneworks operates in the Hamilton, Ontario, area, laying brick and stone walkways and driveways, building stone retaining walls for gardens, and paving driveways. Some concrete work is involved, but most customers use Puretek for their excellent stone work.

Rochi Stoanfayce, the owner, started Puretek four years ago, after an apprenticeship and several years of masonry experience. Since 90 percent of his business falls within the spring to autumn season, he decided to make the business a seasonal one, closing down each winter. In March, he purchased new inventory and supplies with the bank loan he secured and negotiated some contracts with new customers. In April, when he opens the store and brings back his staff, they can be fully employed immediately. Clients pay a 20 percent cash advance when they sign a contract, ensuring no cash flow problems for Stoanfayce. By mid-November, he starts to shut down for the winter and does not negotiate any new contracts to begin before the following spring.

Most projects take one to two weeks to complete, and employees are scheduled to work on projects in the most efficient way. Employees are not at the same project every day but are moved from job to job according to the PERT and CPM schedules that Stoanfayce and the field manager draw up each time a new project is negotiated, to minimize unnecessary delays. Weather, yet to be controlled or even accurately predicted, remains the principal cause of delays.

Stoanfayce also manages the store himself with the help of an assistant who sells store and yard inventory and has accounting and other clerical responsibilities. The rest of the staff are primarily occupied as stone workers on the construction projects under the supervision of the field manager who is an engineer by training. Although Stoanfayce is active in the business, he has chosen not to draw a regular salary, instead withdrawing money from the business as needed. His store assistant and manager are salaried, while the other five employees are paid on an hourly basis.

For each contract, a separate project is set up when the contract is signed. Project costs are allocated based on time spent and materials used as a percentage of the totals. The field manager keeps track of these breakdowns. In addition, the operation of the store is defined as an ongoing project.

As soon as a contract is signed, the necessary inventory is requisitioned and reserved. Other construction materials are requisitioned as needed, and records of the actual usage for each project are kept for accurate costing and inventory control.

Joanna Souto, a business teacher, and Mita Ashikaya, the accounting and store assistant for Puretek, have together compiled the following records and used them to set up the business in Simply Accounting:

- Chart of Accounts
- Post-Closing Trial Balance
- Vendor Information
- Customer Information
- Employee Information
- Employee Profiles and TD1 Information
- Inventory Information
- Project Information
- Accounting Procedures

PURETEK PAVING & STONEWORKS
CHART OF ACCOUNTS

ASSETS

Current Assets

1060 Bank: Chequing Account
1080 Bank: Visa
1090 Bank: MasterCard
1200 Accounts Receivable
1220 Advances Receivable
1240 Construction Materials
1260 Office Supplies

Inventory Assets

1360 Base Materials
1380 Cobble Pavestones
1400 Edging Stone Blocks
1420 Patio Stone Blocks
1440 Paver Slabs
1460 Stone Slabs
1480 Wall Building Blocks

Plant & Equipment

1760 Cash Register
1780 Computers & Peripherals
1820 Construction Equipment
1840 Delivery Truck
1860 Furniture & Fixtures
1880 Loading Equipment
1940 Warehouse
1960 Yard

LIABILITIES

Current Liabilities

2100 Bank Loan
2200 Accounts Payable
2300 Vacation Payable
2310 EI Payable
2320 CPP Payable
2330 Income Tax Payable
2390 EHT Payable
2400 CSB Plan Payable
2460 WSIB Payable
2640 PST Payable
2650 GST Charged on Sales
2670 GST Paid on Purchases

Long Term Liabilities

2850 Mortgage Payable

EQUITY

Owner's Equity

3560 R. Stoanfayce, Capital
3580 R. Stoanfayce, Drawings
3600 Current Earnings

REVENUE

Revenue

4020 Revenue from Store Sales
4040 Revenue from Contracting
4080 Sales Returns & Allowances
4100 Returns Policy Revenue
4150 Other Revenue

EXPENSES

Operating Expenses

5020 Advertising & Promotion
5040 Bank Charges & Card Fees
5060 Construction Materials Used
5080 Cost of Goods Sold
5100 Delivery Expense
5120 Freight Expense
5140 Hydro Expense
5150 Interest Expense - Loan
5160 Interest Expense - Mortgage
5180 Inventory Adjustment
5200 Legal Expenses
5220 Repairs & Maintenance
5260 Telephone Expense
5280 Item Assembly Costs

Payroll Expenses

5300 Wages
5310 EI Expense
5320 CPP Expense
5330 WSIB Expense
5360 EHT Expense

PURETEK PAVING & STONEWORKS
POST-CLOSING TRIAL BALANCE

March 31, 2003

Account	Debit	Credit
1060 Bank: Chequing Account	$44 600.00	
1080 Bank: Visa	445.00	
1090 Bank: MasterCard	350.00	
1240 Construction Materials	2 800.00	
1360 Base Materials	6 500.00	
1380 Cobble Pavestones	10 145.00	
1400 Edging Stone Blocks	1 950.00	
1420 Patio Stone Blocks	6 600.00	
1440 Paver Slabs	4 380.00	
1460 Stone Slabs	13 900.00	
1480 Wall Building Blocks	9 000.00	
1760 Cash Register	1 200.00	
1780 Computers & Peripherals	3 800.00	
1820 Construction Equipment	45 000.00	
1840 Delivery Truck	50 000.00	
1860 Furniture & Fixtures	3 000.00	
1880 Loading Equipment	25 000.00	
1940 Warehouse	150 000.00	
1960 Yard	100 000.00	
2100 Bank Loan		40 000.00
2200 Accounts Payable		20 330.00
2670 GST Paid on Purchases	1 330.00	
2850 Mortgage Payable		200 000.00
3560 R. Stoanfayce, Capital		219 670.00
	$480 000.00	$480 000.00

PURETEK PAVING & STONEWORKS
VENDOR INFORMATION

Vendor Name (Contact)	Address	Phone No. Fax No.	E-mail Web Site	Terms Tax ID
Bell Canada (Colin Yu)	88 Sounder Ave. Hamilton, ON L8M 9T3	Tel: (905) 525-6100 Fax: (905) 525-6000	colinyu@bell.ca www.bell.ca	Net 1
Castillo & Maturi, Lawyers (Vito Castillo)	44 Barton St. Hamilton, ON L9P 6F1	Tel: (905) 822-8320 Fax: (905) 822-8321	vito@legaleagles.ca www.legaleagles.ca	Net 10
Dundas Concrete Works (C. Mentor)	642 Dundas St. Dundas, ON L8P 7G9	Tel: (905) 592-7299 Fax: (905) 592-8234	cmentor@rocks.ca www.rocks.ca/dundas	Net 20 64181 4531
Groundfos Machinery (Max Groundfos)	96 Caterpillar Rd. Hamilton, ON L8R 4D7	Tel: (905) 524-8124 Fax: (905) 524-8221	mg@groundfos.com www.groundfos.com	Net 15 58024 6472
Hamilton Hydro (Electra Deau)	27 Utility St. Hamilton, ON L8T 3V7	Tel: (905) 788-9245 Fax: (905) 788-8101	www.hydro.ca	Net 1
Hamilton Mountain Quarry (Stoney Quartz)	RR #2 Hamilton, ON L9N 5S3	Tel: (905) 522-5724 Fax: (905) 522-6267	quartz@rocks.ca www.rocks.ca/hamilton	Net 20 73275 3853
Hamilton Spectator (Nuse Worthy)	5 Readers Den Hamilton, ON L8P 6H3	Tel: (905) 633-5839 Fax: (905) 633-5889	nw@spectator.com www.spectator.com	Net 30

PURETEK PAVING & STONEWORKS
VENDOR INFORMATION CONTINUED

Vendor Name (Contact)	Address	Phone No. Fax No.	E-mail Web Site	Terms Tax ID
Manitoulin Flagstone & Slate (Peter Cutter)	Mindemoya Manitoulin Island, ON P0P 1S0	Tel: (705) 736-8542 Fax: (705) 736-5377	pcutter@rocks.ca www.rocks.ca/manitoulin	Net 15 33424 4644
Receiver General of Canada	Summerside Tax Centre Summerside, PE C1N 6L2	Tel: (902) 821-8186	www.ccra-adrc.gc.ca	Net 1
Stoanfayce, R. Drawings	N/A			
Stoneycreek Cement Co. (Conn Kreat)	59 Sandfield Rd. Stoney Creek, ON L8J 5E1	Tel: (905) 664-6644 Fax: (905) 664-8993	ckreat@rocks.ca www.rocks.ca/stoneycreek	Net 30 76543 8641
Sudbury Granite (Jem Stone)	38 Blackstone Cr. Sudbury, ON P3A 7N2	Tel: (705) 594-7428 Fax: (705) 594-7654	jemstone@rocks.ca www.rocks.ca/sudbury	Net 30 55467 3992
Waterloo Pavestone Ltd. (Crystal Slater)	66 Rockcliff St. Waterloo, ON N2T 3V2	Tel: (519) 663-7373 Fax: (519) 663-7711	slater@rocks.ca www.rocks.ca/waterloo	Net 20 48951 3111

PURETEK PAVING & STONEWORKS
OUTSTANDING VENDOR INVOICES

Vendor Name	Terms	Date	Inv/Chq No.	Amount	Total
Dundas Concrete Works	Net 20	3/21/03	DC-1472	$2 140	$ 2 140
Groundfos Machinery	Net 15	3/18/03	GM-677	$10 700	10 700
Hamilton Mountain Quarry	Net 20	3/20/03	HMQ-614	$3 210	3 210
Waterloo Pavestone Ltd.	Net 20	3/21/03	WP-3124	$4 280	4 280
				Grand Total	$20 330

PURETEK PAVING & STONEWORKS
CUSTOMER INFORMATION

Customer Name	Address	Phone No. Fax No.	E-mail	Terms
Akonta, Wisdom	359 Forest Glen Blvd. Hamilton, ON L8N 5W2	Tel: (905) 788-8234	wiseman@hotmail.com	Net 1
MacGregor, Cameron	101 Chaplin Cres. Hamilton, ON L9R 2S6	Tel: (905) 622-7351 Fax: (905) 622-1199	allstar@netcom.ca	Net 1
Omand, Jim	222 Briar Hill Ave. Hamilton, ON L8P 4B8	Tel: (905) 488-6126 Fax: (905) 488-8221	omand@magi.com	Net 1
Payne, Mark	43 Sherwood Dr. Dundas, ON L9T 3E2	Tel: (905) 522-1369	wetblanket@home.ca	Net 1

PURETEK PAVING & STONEWORKS
OUTSTANDING SALES QUOTES

Customer Name	Quote Date	Quote No.	Completion Date	Amount	Terms
Akonta, Wisdom	3/27/03	1	April 30	$10 000 plus tax	net 1
MacGregor, Cameron	3/28/03	2	April 30	$15 000 plus tax	net 1
Omand, Jim	3/30/03	3	April 30	$10 000 plus tax	net 1
Payne, Mark	3/31/03	4	April 30	$12 500 plus tax	net 1

PURETEK PAVING & STONEWORKS
EMPLOYEE INFORMATION SHEET

	Alana Gascon	Michael Arturo	Hans Bekker	Dimitri Valios
Position	Field Engineer/Mgr	Stone Cutter	Bricklayer	Bricklayer
Social Insurance Number	593 821 648	621 534 965	499 634 525	512 523 549
Address & Telephone	12 Rockland Ave. Hamilton, ON L8W 3B7 (905) 583-1020	62 Stonegate Dr. Ancaster, ON L9G 3P3 (905) 413-6021	77 Rockcliffe Rd. Dundas, ON L9H 7H5 (905) 734-9209	6 Mountain Ave. Hamilton, ON L8P 4E9 (905) 522-8165
Date of Birth (dd-mm-yy)	21-6-58	15-3-63	11-11-52	10-8-54
Federal (Ontario) Tax Exemption - TD1				
Basic Personal	$7 412 (7 426)	$7 412 (7 426)	$7 412 (7 426)	$7 412 (7 426)
Spouse	$6 294 (6 306)	$6 294 (6 306)		
Total Exemptions	$13 706 (13 732)	$13 706 (13 732)	$7 412 (7 426)	$7 412 (7 426)
Employee Earnings				
Regular Wage Rate		$18.00	$18.00	$16.00
Overtime Wage Rate		$27.00	$27.00	$24.00
Regular Salary	$4 000/mo			
Hours per Period	150	80	80	80
Commission	2% (Contracts)			
Vacation	3 weeks	6%	6%	6%
Employee Deductions				
Canada Savings Bond (CSB)	$200	$100	$50	$50
EI, CPP & Income Tax	calculations built into Simply Accounting program			
Additional Federal Tax	$50	$25		

PURETEK PAVING & STONEWORKS
EMPLOYEE INFORMATION SHEET CONTINUED

	Mita Ashikaya	Evelyn Nicols	Max Matthias
Position	Clerk/Accountant	Part time	Part time
Social Insurance Number	477 527 691	514 825 637	412 645 962
Address & Telephone	58 Highridge Ave. Hamilton, ON L8E 2S2 (905) 889-3465	32 Stonecliffe Crt. Hamilton, ON L9C 7G3 (905) 421-8313	66 Mountain Brow Blvd. Hamilton, ON L8T 1A4 (905) 782-3429
Date of Birth (dd-mm-yy)	31-7-65	29-4-75	2-12-78
Federal (Ontario) Tax Exemption - TD1			
Basic Personal	$7 412 (7 426)	$7 412 (7 426)	$7 412 (7 426)
Spouse	$6 294 (6 306)		
Education & Tuition		$5 800 (5 840)	$4 800 (4 840)
Total Exemptions	$13 706 (13 732)	$13 212 (13 266)	$12 212 (12 266)
Employee Earnings			
Regular Wage Rate		$14.00	$12.00
Overtime Wage Rate		$21.00	$18.00
Regular Salary	$2 500/mo		
Hours per Period	150	40	40
Commission	1% (Sales - Returns)		
Vacation	3 weeks	4%	4%
Employee Deductions			
Canada Savings Bond (CSB)	$100		
EI, CPP & Income Tax	calculations built into Simply Accounting program		
Additional Federal Tax	$20		

Employee Profiles and TD1 Information

Alana Gascon, the field manager and engineer for Puretek, plans and designs the stonework for all projects, and schedules and oversees the field workers. She is single and supports her father, for whom she claims the spousal equivalent tax exemption. She contributes $200 to the Canada Savings Bond payroll deduction plan each month and has elected to have additional income tax deducted from her pay. Her monthly salary of $4 000, paid on the last day of each month, is supplemented by a commission of 2 percent of contract revenue. Gascon is entitled to three weeks' vacation with pay.

Michael Arturo is a stonecutter by training. He is married and fully supports his wife and 12-year-old child who have no income. Every two weeks he receives $18 per hour for the first 40 hours of work per week and $27 for each hour of overtime work. He makes bi-weekly payroll contributions of $100 to the Canada Savings Bond plan and has additional income tax deducted from each pay. Arturo's vacation pay, at the rate of 6 percent, is retained until he takes vacation time.

Hans Bekker is employed as a bricklayer and general handyperson. He is single and self-supporting and participates in the Canada Savings Bond plan, paying $50 every bi-weekly pay period. He earns $18 per hour for regular work and $27 for overtime hours. Bekker's vacation pay, at the rate of 6 percent, is retained until he takes vacation time.

Dimitri Valios assists with bricklaying and operates the machinery. He is single and self-supporting. He has chosen to participate in the payroll savings plan, deducting $50 for Canada Savings Bond purchases. He is paid bi-weekly, earning $16 per hour for regular work and $24 for overtime work. Valios' vacation pay, at the rate of 6 percent, is retained until he takes vacation time.

Mita Ashikaya works in the store, performing clerical, sales and accounting tasks. She is single and fully supports her younger sister. Since her sister has no income, Ashikaya is entitled to the spousal equivalent tax claim for her sister. She contributes $100 each month to purchase Canada Savings Bonds and pays additional income tax from her $2 500 monthly salary. As an additional incentive, she receives a commission of 1 percent of store sales, net of returns and taxes. Ashikaya receives three weeks vacation with pay each year.

Evelyn Nicols works wherever she is needed most, either in the store or on projects. Nicols is a single, self-supporting university student who claims her tuition fees and education deduction for the eight-month school year. She is paid weekly, earning $14 per hour for regular hours and $21 for overtime work, and she does not participate in the Canada Savings Bond plan. Her 4 percent vacation pay is retained. Nichols works part time during the school year and full time during the summers.

Max Matthias also assists as needed with project or store work. He too is single and self-supporting while he attends college. His tuition fees and his education deduction are claimed as tax exemptions. He earns $12 per hour for regular work and $18 for overtime work, receives his pay weekly, and does not participate in the Canada Savings Bond plan. His 4 percent vacation pay is retained. Matthias works full time during the summers and part time during the school year.

Additional Payroll Information

Employees have the following pay periods:
- salaried employees are paid on the last day of each month
- part-time employees are paid weekly
- the remaining full-time hourly workers are paid bi-weekly

Remember that WSIB is the name for WCB in Ontario.

The employer's contributions include the following:

- CPP contributions equal to employee contributions
- EI contributions at 1.4 times the employee contributions
- WSIB rate for Ashikaya is 1.52
  WSIB rate for all other employees is 7.87
- EHT rate is 0.98

notes

Preferred pricing is not used by Puretek. All customers pay the regular price for inventory.

PURETEK PAVING & STONEWORKS
INVENTORY INFORMATION

Code	Description	Selling Price /Unit	Qty on Hand	Amt (Cost)	Min Stock
Base materials					
BM-1	Base Material: Gravel 3/4 crushed	$30.00 /ton	100	$1 800	10
BM-2	Base Material: Gravel 3/4 smooth	32.00 /ton	100	2 000	10
BM-3	Base Material: Sand	25.00 /ton	100	1 500	10
BM-4	Base Material: Screening	22.00 /ton	100	1 200	10
				$6 500	
Cobble Pavestones					
CP-1	Cobblestone: Berlin circular 4x8	$1.80 /sqft	1 000	$ 1 000	100
CP-2	Cobblestone: Cordoba textured 4x8	1.60 /sqft	1 200	960	120
CP-3	Cobblestone: Goteberg random 4x8	1.60 /sqft	1 200	960	120
CP-4	Cobblestone: Haarlem octagonal 4x8	1.50 /sqft	1 000	750	100
CP-5	Cobblestone: Leeds texture reg. 4x8	1.40 /sqft	1 500	1 050	150
CP-6	Cobblestone: Madrid hexagon 4x8	1.40 /sqft	1 500	1 050	150
CP-7	Cobblestone: Verona classic 4x8	1.50 /sqft	1 500	1 125	150
CP-8	Cobblestone: Ypress Roman 9x18	3.95 each	500	1 250	50
CP-9	Cobblestone: Zurich grid 18x18	6.95 each	500	2 000	50
				$10 145	
Edging Stone Blocks					
ES-1	Edging Stone: Crv scalloped 2ft	$3.00 each	250	$ 450	25
ES-2	Edging Stone: Crv scalloped 3ft	4.50 each	250	750	25
ES-3	Edging Stone: Str scalloped 2ft	2.00 each	250	300	25
ES-4	Edging Stone: Str scalloped 3ft	3.00 each	250	450	25
				$1 950	
Patio Stone Blocks					
PTS-1	Patio Block: Deck concrete 24x24	$6.00 each	500	$2 000	50
PTS-2	Patio Block: Diamond natural 24x30	8.00 each	300	1 500	30
PTS-3	Patio Block: Diamond non-slip 18x18	3.00 each	300	600	30
PTS-4	Patio Block: Diamond non-slip 24x24	5.00 each	300	900	30
PTS-5	Patio Block: Red brick litewt 24x24	6.00 each	400	1 600	40
				$6 600	
Paver Slabs					
PVS-1	Paver Slab: Natural expose 18x16	$1.00 each	1 000	$ 500	100
PVS-2	Paver Slab: Natural pattern 18x16	1.50 each	800	800	80
PVS-3	Paver Slab: Red expose 18x16	1.20 each	800	640	80
PVS-4	Paver Slab: Red pattern 18x16	1.80 each	1 000	1 000	100
PVS-5	Paver Slab: Texture non-slip 12x12	2.00 each	1 200	1 440	80
				$4 380	
Stone Slabs					
SF-1	Stone Slab: Flagstone irregular	$160.00 /ton	25	$ 2 500	5
SF-2	Stone Slab: Flagstone prem. square	12.00 /sqft	300	2 400	30
SF-3	Stone Slab: Granite irregular	180.00 /ton	25	3 000	5
SF-4	Stone Slab: Granite premium square	14.00 /sqft	250	2 000	25
SF-5	Stone Slab: Slate irregular	140.00 /ton	25	2 000	5
SF-6	Stone Slab: Slate premium square	10.00 /sqft	400	2 000	40
				$13 900	
Wall Building Blocks					
WB-1	Wall Block: Retaining basic	$6.00 each	1 000	$4 000	100
WB-2	Wall Block: Retaining curvable	9.00 each	500	2 500	50
WB-3	Wall Block: Retaining step plus	8.00 each	500	2 500	50
				$9 000	

Project Information

Puretek uses a separate project for each new contract. At the beginning of April, there are four contracts to be set up as projects: Briar Hill, Chaplin Estates, Forest Glen and Sherwood. In addition, Store Operations is an ongoing project. The field manager keeps track of the percentage of time each worker spends on each project. Because these times vary from project to project and from week to week, the percentage allocation is included with each source document that follows. Revenue allocations are also included with the source documents.

Accounting Procedures

The Employer Health Tax (EHT)

The Employer Health Tax (EHT) is paid by all employers in Ontario. The EHT is based on the total annual remuneration paid to employees. The EHT rate ranges from 0.98 percent to 1.95 percent. The lowest rate (0.98 percent) applies if the employer's total remuneration is under $200 000. The highest rate (1.95 percent) applies to employers whose total remuneration exceeds $400 000.

Simply Accounting will calculate the employer's liability to the Ontario Minister of Finance automatically once the information is set up correctly in the payroll defaults and linked accounts. A later application, Hearth House, will provide you with the keystrokes necessary for setting up the EHT information. The EHT can be remitted monthly or quarterly, depending on the total payroll amount.

The Goods and Services Tax: Remittances

Puretek Paving & Stoneworks uses the regular method for remittance of the Goods and Services Tax. All vendors and customers, except the Receiver General, charge and pay GST, respectively. GST collected from customers is recorded as a liability in *GST Charged on Sales*. GST paid to vendors is recorded in *GST Paid on Purchases* as a decrease in liability to Canada Customs and Revenue Agency. The report is filed with the Receiver General of Canada by the last day of the month for the previous quarterly period, either including the balance owing or requesting a refund.

Normally the business makes GST remittances, and the Receiver General is listed as a vendor. However, since business purchases were made in March, before the business opened for the season, Puretek has a debit balance and will file for a refund in the month of April. GST refunds are processed through the Sales Journal. The Receiver General must be added as a customer and then selected to process the request for a refund. When the refund is received, it is processed as a customer receipt.

Customer Deposits on Projects: Sales Quotes and Orders

Sales quotes are prepared for new contract work. When a customer signs a contract, the quote is converted to an order and the customer pays a deposit of 20 percent of the negotiated price (before taxes). The deposit is entered in the Receipts Journal for the customer. *Accounts Receivable* will automatically be credited for the amount of the advance for the selected customer, and the selected linked bank account will be debited.

notes

Processing the deposit through the Receipts Journal ensures that the advance will appear in the correct customer account in the Receivables Ledger. The other approach, a General Journal entry that debits Bank Account: Chequing and credits Unearned Revenue, a liability account, does not show this link with the customer.

When the project is completed, make a Sales Journal entry for the full amount of the contract, including relevant taxes, by filling the Sales Order. Because the order was for the full contracted price, with labour and materials combined, you need to edit the sales invoice after filling the order. Change the contracted price to the charges for labour and add the reserved project inventory as the second line on the invoice. The total for the labour and inventory will equal the original total contracted price. When the customer settles the account, mark the invoices for both the deposit and the full invoice amount as paid. The balance in the Receipts Journal should then match the amount of the customer's cheque.

Four quotes given in March are on file for work to be completed in April. These are ready to be converted to orders because all customers have accepted the contracts.

notes

To be strictly correct, you should reverse the original cash sale entry so that revenue will not be overstated. If you created a customer record by using Quick Add, you can adjust the sales invoice by changing the method of payment from Cheque to Pay Later. You cannot change the payment method for One-time customers.

NSF Cheques

When a bank returns a customer's cheque because there were insufficient funds in the customer's bank account to cover the cheque, the payment must be reversed. If the payment was processed through the Receipts Journal, the reversal should also be processed through the Receipts Journal by including fully paid invoices on the screen. If the sale was a cash sale, the reversal must be processed through the Sales Journal. Create a customer record for the customer and process a credit sale for the amount of the NSF cheque. Choose Code 1 for GST and leave the PST field blank to indicate the amount is non-taxable because taxes for the sale were recorded at the time of the original sale. Enter the amount as a positive amount in the amount field and enter *Bank Account: Chequing* in the account field. On a separate invoice line, enter the amount of the handling charge for the NSF cheque in the amount field with *Other Revenue* in the account field. Again, the handling charge is non-taxable.

notes

The sales tax rules for credits, allowances and discounts are complex and may vary from province to province and for federal taxes. Adjusting General Journal entries may be required to adjust the amount of tax owing and calculate the tax remittance. Therefore, we have chosen to leave out the tax component for transactions of this type.

Returns

When customers return merchandise, they are charged a 20 percent handling charge. In the Sales Journal, enter the quantity returned with a **minus** sign at the full sale price with taxes, and enter *Sales Returns & Allowances* in the account field. The amounts will automatically be negative because of the minus sign in the quantity field, so that *Accounts Receivable* will be credited automatically as well. On a separate invoice line, enter the amount withheld — the handling charge — as a **positive** amount with no GST or PST and credit *Returns Policy Revenue*. Treat this revenue as non-taxable. *Accounts Receivable* will be debited automatically for the amount of the handling charge.

If the original sale was a credit sale, and the account is not yet paid, the return should also be entered as a credit sale so that *Accounts Receivable* will be credited. If the original sale was paid in cash, or the account has been paid, the return should be entered as a cash sale so that *Bank Account: Chequing* will be credited.

Reserved Inventory for Projects

When customers sign a contract, the inventory items needed to complete the project are set aside or reserved by transferring them through the software to a designated account. In this way, these items cannot be sold to other customers because the inventory quantities are already reduced. The minimum stock level for reserved inventory will be zero. Refer to the Keystrokes section, page 378.

notes

We use the term Cash Sales and Purchases for cash and cheque transactions.

Cash Sales and Purchases

Cash and credit card transactions for goods and services occur normally in most types of businesses. The Simply Accounting program handles these transactions through the Sales Journal by choosing the appropriate method of payment. Choose One-time customer from the customer list, and add the new customer's name in the Address field if this is not a regular customer. If payment is by cheque, a cheque number field opens. Puretek also accepts Visa and MasterCard from customers for store sales.

Enter the remainder of the transaction in the same way you would enter any account or Pay Later sale transaction.

The program will debit the appropriate bank account instead of the *Accounts Receivable* control account. All other accounts for this transaction will be appropriately debited or credited.

Similarly, for cash purchases, choose the vendor from the vendor list or add the vendor using Quick Add. Cash purchases may be entered in the Payments Journal as Other Payments or in the Purchases Journal. Choose the appropriate method of payment from the Paid By list. For cheque payments, a cheque number field opens with the next cheque number entered. Complete the remainder of the cash transaction in the same way you would enter a credit purchase transaction. Puretek does not make credit card purchases.

The program will debit *Bank Account: Chequing* instead of the *Accounts Payable* control account. All other accounts for this transaction will be appropriately debited or credited.

Freight Expense
When a business purchases inventory items, the cost of any freight that cannot be directly allocated to a specific item must be charged to the *Freight Expense* account. This amount will be regarded as an expense rather than being charged to any inventory asset account.

PST
In Ontario, PST is calculated on the base amount of the invoice, which does not include the GST. In this application, Provincial Sales Tax of 8 percent is applied to all sales of paving materials and to construction work. Customers pay PST on both direct sales and contract work. PST at 8 percent is also paid on purchases of non-inventory items that are not used in the construction work.

Printing Invoices, Orders and Quotes
If you want to print the invoices, purchase orders or sales quotes through the program, complete the journal transaction as you would otherwise. Before posting the transaction, choose the File menu and then Print or click the Print button on the tool bar for the invoice form. Printing will begin immediately, so be sure you have the correct forms for your printer before you begin. If you and the customer or vendor have e-mail, click the E-mail button to send the invoice or order.

Materials Summary Form
Construction materials are requisitioned for projects as needed. These requisition forms are summarized twice a month in a Materials Summary Form. When this form is completed, an adjusting entry must be made in the General Journal to reduce the *Construction Materials* asset account and increase the *Construction Materials Used* expense account.

INSTRUCTIONS

1. Using the Chart of Accounts, Trial Balance and other information, record entries for the source documents for April 2003 using Simply Accounting. The procedures for entering each new type of transaction are outlined step by step in the keystroke section that follows the source documents. A ✔ in the source document completion check box indicates that keystrokes are provided. The page number immediately below the check box indicates where these keystroke instructions begin. Keystroke instructions begin on page 371, after the source documents.
2. After you have finished making your entries, print the reports and graphs indicated on the following printing form.

REPORTS

Lists
- ☐ Chart of Accounts
- ☐ Vendors
- ☐ Customers
- ☐ Employees
- ☐ Inventory & Services
- ☐ Project

Journals
- ☑ All Journals (by posting date) from April 1 to April 30 with project allocations
- ☐ General
- ☐ Purchases
- ☐ Payments
- ☐ Sales
- ☐ Receipts
- ☐ Payroll
- ☑ Item Assembly (by posting date) from April 1 to April 30
- ☐ Adjustments

Financials
- ☑ Comparative Balance Sheet dates: April 1 and April 30 with percent difference
- ☑ Income Statement from April 1 to April 30
- ☑ Trial Balance date: April 30
- ☑ General Ledger accounts: 1380 4020 4040 from April 1 to April 30
- ☑ Cash Flow Projection Detail Report for account 1060 for 30 days

GST
- ☐ GST Report

Payables
- ☐ Vendor Aged
- ☐ Aged Overdue Payables
- ☐ Vendor Purchases
- ☐ Pending Purchase Orders

Receivables
- ☐ Customer Aged
- ☐ Aged Overdue Receivables
- ☐ Customer Sales
- ☐ Pending Sales Orders
- ☐ Customer Statements

Payroll
- ☑ Employee Summary for all employees
- ☐ T4 Slips

Inventory
- ☐ Inventory
- ☐ Inventory Activity
- ☑ Inventory Sales Summary for Base Materials from April 1 to April 30
- ☑ Inventory Transaction Summary for Patio Blocks, all journals from April 1 to April 30

Project
- ☑ Project Income Summary for all projects, all accounts from April 1 to April 30
- ☐ Project Allocation Report

Mailing Labels
- ☐ Labels

Management Reports
- ☐ Ledger

GRAPHS

- ☐ Payables by Aging Period
- ☐ Payables by Vendor
- ☐ Receivables by Aging Period
- ☐ Receivables by Customer
- ☐ Sales vs Receivables
- ☐ Receivables Due vs Payables Due
- ☐ Revenues by Account
- ☐ Expenses by Account
- ☑ Expenses and Net Profit as % of Revenue
- ☐ Current Revenue vs Last Year

SOURCE DOCUMENTS

SESSION DATE – April 7

notes

Keystrokes begin on page 371.

☑ 371

Project Setup
Dated April 1/03
Create the following projects for the store and the construction contracts:
Briar Hill Project
Chaplin Estates Project
Forest Glen Project
Sherwood Project
Store Operations

☑ 374

Legal Statement #CM-67
Dated April 1/03
From Castillo & Maturi, Lawyers, $200 to draw up contracts for clients, plus $14 GST. Purchase invoice total $214. Terms: net 10 days. Charge expense at 25% to each contract project, excluding Store Operations.

notes

Accept the account class change for the inventory asset account 1500 when prompted.

☑ 378

Reserved Inventory Form #RIF-1001
Dated April 1/03
Reserve inventory for Briar Hill Project with minimum level set at zero. Create a new inventory asset Group account, 1500 Reserved Inventory for Projects.
Create a new inventory record in the inventory ledger for the project:
Item Description: Briar Hill Project: reserved   Item Number: BH-1
Price = $2 415/project
Charge PST and GST
Asset Account: 1500   Revenue Account: 4040   C.O.G.S. Account: 5080

notes

Be very careful in making item Assembly entries. Because they are compound entries, they are difficult to reverse and there is no option to adjust them. Therefore, keystrokes are included for storing the entry so you will have a copy on record if a reversal is necessary.

Assemble the following as reserved inventory BH-1 at the cost price, $1 395.
10 tons Base Material: Gravel 3/4 crushed
5 tons Base Material: Sand
5 tons Base Material: Screening
60 sqft Stone Slabs: Flagstone prem. square
600 sqft Cobblestone: Cordoba textured 4x8
100 Edging Stones: Str scalloped 2ft

☐ Memo #1
Dated April 1/03
From Owner: Convert the four sales quotes on record to sales orders to confirm them. Retain the sales quote number as the sales order number.

☐ Cash Receipt #1
Dated April 1/03
From Wisdom Akonta, cheque #723 for $2 000 (deposit #1) to confirm sales order #1.

☐ Cash Receipt #2
Dated April 1/03
From Cameron MacGregor, cheque #109 for $3 000 (deposit #2) to confirm sales order #2.

☐ Cash Receipt #3
Dated April 1/03
From Jim Omand, cheque #64 for $2 000 (deposit #3) to confirm sales order #3.

❑ Cash Receipt #4
Dated April 1/03
From Mark Payne, cheque #35 for $2 500 (deposit #4) to confirm sales order #4.

notes

Enter a positive amount for GST Paid on Purchases in the Sales Journal to credit this account. Use Memo 2 as the invoice number. Refer to Accounting Procedures and Chapter 2 if you need more information about GST.

❑ Memo #2
Dated April 2/03
From Owner: File Goods and Services Tax return for March. Create a Customer record for the Receiver General and complete a Sales Journal entry to file for the refund of $1 330. Refer to General Ledger GST account balances for March 31.

❑ Cash Sales Invoice #100
Dated April 2/03
To Carol Jasenko (Choose One-time customer for cash sales)

100 Wall Blocks: Retaining basic	$6.00 each
Goods & Services Tax	7%
Provincial Sales Tax	8%

Paid by certified cheque #RB-6143. Allocate 100% of revenue and costs to Store Operations.

❑ Cheque Copy #55
Dated April 3/03
To Groundfos Machinery, $10 700 in full payment of account. Reference invoice #GM-677.

❑ Purchase Invoice #HS-6927
Dated April 3/03
From Hamilton Spectator, $400 for weekly ad in newspaper, plus $28 GST. Purchase invoice total $428. Terms: net 30 days. Charge expense at 20% to each project.

notes

Choose One-time customer for MasterCard and Visa sales. Enter the customer's name in the Address field.

❑ MasterCard Sales Invoice #101
Dated April 4/03
To Brian Wilkinson

400 Cobblestone: Berlin circular 4x8	$1.80 /sqft
200 Cobblestone: Verona classic 4x8	1.50 /sqft
25 Paver Slabs: Texture non-slip 12x12	2.00 each
Goods & Services Tax	7%
Provincial Sales Tax	8%

Paid by Master Card #7432 6634 9810 1231. Allocate 100% of revenue and costs to Store Operations.

notes

Remember to delete the PST on inventory purchases.

❑ Purchase Invoice #MFS-541
Dated April 4/03
From Manitoulin Flagstone & Slate

100 sqft Stone Slabs: Flagstone prem. square	$ 800.00
100 sqft Stone Slabs: Slate premium square	500.00
GST Paid	91.00
Invoice Total	$1 391.00

Terms: n/15.

❑ Cash Sales Invoice #102
Dated April 4/03
To Mergim Shena

10 Patio Blocks: Deck concrete 24x24	$6.00 each
10 Edging Stones: Crv scalloped 3ft	4.50 each
Goods & Services Tax	7%
Provincial Sales Tax	8%

Paid by cheque #44. Allocate 100% of revenue and costs to Store Operations.

❑ Purchase Invoice #MD-14171
Dated April 5/03
From Mohawk Office Depot (use Full Add), $100 for office supplies plus $7 GST. Invoice total $107. No PST charged as special promotional offer to new account customers. Terms: net 30.

> **notes**
> ❑ Mohawk Office Depot (Contact Joseph Beaucage) is located at
> 165 Mohawk Rd.
> Ancaster, ON L9G 3L9
> Tel: (905) 744-6288
> Fax: (905) 744-8111
> Tax ID: 89929 9399
> beaucage@natcan.ca

❑ Visa Sales Invoice #103
Dated April 5/03
To Elaine Sivcoski

5 tons Stone Slabs: Granite irregular	$180.00 /ton
50 sqft Stone Slabs: Granite premium square	14.00 /sqft
Goods & Services Tax	7%
Provincial Sales Tax	8%

Paid by Visa #4714 5531 9762 4453. Allocate 100% of revenue and costs to Store Operations.

❑ Bank Debit Memo #671431
Dated April 6/03
From National Bank, $120.75 for NSF cheque #44 from Mergim Shena. Reference invoice #102. Mr. Shena has been notified by owner about the outstanding balance plus a $15 charge for issuing the NSF cheque. Other Revenue is assigned to Store Operations.

> **notes**
> Create a customer record for Shena. Process the NSF cheque in the Sales Journal. (Use NSF-44 or memo number as the invoice number.) Refer to Accounting Procedures for further information.

❑ Cash Receipt #5
Dated April 7/03
From Mergim Shena, certified cheque #NB-1421 for $135.75 in full payment of account including $15 NSF handling charges. Reference invoice #102 and Bank Debit Memo #671431. Mr. Shena apologized for the error.

❑ Cash Refund Receipt #1
Dated April 7/03
To Carol Jasenko for return of 100 Wall Blocks: Retaining basic purchased on April 2/03. Invoice total was $690. Issued $552 cash and retained $138 as Returns Policy Revenue. Reference invoice #100. Allocate 100% of revenue and costs to Store Operations.

> **notes**
> Remember to use the Sales Returns & Allowances account for returns. Use Ret–100 as the invoice no. See Accounting Procedures.

> **notes**
> You may use the Payroll Journal or the Payroll Cheque Run Journal to complete payroll transactions.

EMPLOYEE TIME SUMMARY SHEET #1

(pay period ending April 7, 2003)

	Name of Employee	Regular Hours	Overtime Hours
❑	Matthias, Max	30	–
❑	Nicols, Evelyn	32	–

a. Using Employee Time Summary Sheet #1 and the Employee Information Sheet, complete payroll for weekly paid employees. Edit the default entries for number of hours worked.
b. Charge payroll expenses at 60% to Store Operations and 40% to Briar Hill project for both employees.
c. Issue cheques #56 and #57.

> **Warning!**
> Do not forget to allocate payroll transactions. The program does not provide the warning for incomplete allocations in the Payroll Cheque Run Journal.

notes

Freight expense amounts will not be allocated.

☐ Purchase Invoice #SG-1352
Dated April 7/03
From Sudbury Granite

20 tons Stone Slabs: Flagstone irregular	$2 000.00
150 sqft Stone Slabs: Flagstone prem. square	1 200.00
Freight	200.00
GST Paid	238.00
Invoice Total	$3 638.00

Terms: n/30.

SESSION DATE – April 14

☐ Reserved Inventory Form #RIF-1002
Dated April 8/03
Reserve inventory for Chaplin Estates Project
Create a new inventory record for the project in the inventory ledger:
Item Description: Chaplin Estates Project: reserved Item Number: CE-1
Price = $4 885/project
Asset Account: 1500 Revenue Account: 4040 C.O.G.S. Account: 5080

Assemble the following inventory at cost price ($3 000) as reserved inventory for Chaplin Estates (CE-1).
10 tons Stone Slabs: Flagstone irregular
100 sqft Stone Slabs: Flagstone prem. square
300 Cobblestone: Zurich grid 18x18

notes

After filling the Sales Order and before posting the Sales Invoice, edit the invoice. Reduce the price (amount) of the contracted service from $10 000 to $7 585 and add the inventory item. The total for both lines will be $10 000. Refer to Accounting Procedures.

☐ Sales Invoice #104
Dated April 8/03
To Jim Omand, fill Sales Order #3, completion of Briar Hill Project

1 Briar Hill Project: reserved	$2 415.00
1 contracting services	7 585.00
Goods & Services Tax	7%
Provincial Sales Tax	8%

Terms: Cash on receipt of invoice. Allocate 100% of revenue and costs to Briar Hill Project.

☐ Cash Receipt #6
Dated April 8/03
From Jim Omand, cheque #72 for $9 500 in full payment of account. Reference invoice #104 and deposit #3.

☐ Purchase Invoice #SC-1117
Dated April 8/03
From Stoneycreek Cement Co., $500 for bi-weekly delivery of construction materials plus $35 GST. Invoice total $535. Terms: net 30 days.
Store this purchase as a bi-weekly recurring entry.

☐ Cash Sales Invoice #105
Dated April 9/03
To Bruce McCallum

5 tons Base Material: Gravel 3/4 smooth	$32.00 /ton
5 tons Base Material: Sand	25.00 /ton
Goods & Services Tax	7%
Provincial Sales Tax	8%

Paid by certified cheque #TD-4321. Allocate 100% of revenue and costs to Store Operations.

❑ Cheque Copy #58
Dated April 9/03
To Hamilton Mountain Quarry, $3 210 in full payment of account. Reference invoice #HMQ-614.

❑ Purchase Invoice #HMQ-769
Dated April 10/03
From Hamilton Mountain Quarry

10 tons Base Material: Gravel 3/4 crushed	$180.00
10 tons Base Material: Gravel 3/4 smooth	200.00
10 tons Base Material: Sand	150.00
10 tons Base Material: Screening	120.00
Freight Expense	50.00
GST Paid	49.00
Invoice Total	$749.00

Terms: n/20.

❑ Visa Sales Invoice #106
Dated April 10/03
To Karen Afante

10 tons Base Material: Sand	$25.00 /ton
10 tons Base Material: Screening	22.00 /ton
200 Cobblestone: Ypress Roman 9x18	3.95 each
Goods & Services Tax	7%
Provincial Sales Tax	8%

Paid by Visa #4502 7531 2276 5566. Allocate 100% of revenue and costs to Store Operations.

❑ Cheque Copy #59
Dated April 11/03
To Waterloo Pavestone Ltd., $4 280 in full payment of account. Reference invoice #WP-3124.

❑ Cheque Copy #60
Dated April 12/03
To Castillo & Maturi, $214 in full payment of account. Reference invoice #CM-67.

notes

❑ Westdale Machinery (Contact Dale West) is located at
35 Sterling St.
Hamilton, ON L8S 4H6
Tel: (905) 528-6992
Fax: (905) 528-8921
Tax ID: 2646 58166

❑ Purchase Invoice #WM-1912
Dated April 12/03
From Westdale Machinery (use Full Add), $500 for repairs to machinery and equipment plus $35 GST and 8% PST. Invoice total $575. Terms: net 30 days. Charge repairs at 50% to Store Operations, 25% to Briar Hill Project and 25% to Chaplin Estates Project.

❑ Cash Sales Invoice #107
Dated April 13/03
To Mark Lyne

100 Wall Blocks: Retaining curvable	$ 9.00 each
10 tons Stone Slabs: Flagstone irregular	160.00 /ton
Goods & Services Tax	7%
Provincial Sales Tax	8%

Paid by cheque #465. Allocate 100% of revenue and costs to Store Operations.

❑ Cash Purchase Invoice #HH-42142
Dated April 13/03
To Hamilton Hydro, $200 for hydro services plus $14 GST. Invoice total $214. Issued cheque #61 in payment. Charge full hydro expense to Store Operations.

- [ ] Cash Purchase Invoice #BC-43179
Dated April 13/03
To Bell Canada, $80 for telephone services plus $5.60 GST and $6.40 PST. Invoice total $92. Issued cheque #62 in payment. Charge total telephone expense to Store Operations.

- [ ] Purchase Invoice #WP-3857
Dated April 14/03
From Waterloo Pavestone

400 sqft Cobblestone: Berlin circular 4x8	$ 400.00
400 sqft Cobblestone: Cordoba textured 4x8	320.00
400 sqft Cobblestone: Verona classic 4x8	300.00
400 sqft Cobblestone: Zurich grid 18x18	1 600.00
GST Paid	183.40
Invoice Total	$2 803.40

Terms: n/20.

EMPLOYEE TIME SUMMARY SHEET #2

(pay period ending April 14, 2003)

	Name of Employee	Week 1 Hours	Week 2 Hours	Regular Hours	Overtime Hours
❑	Arturo, Michael	40	42	80	2
❑	Bekker, Hans	40	40	80	–
❑	Matthias, Max	n/a	42	40	2
❑	Nicols, Evelyn	n/a	40	40	–
❑	Valios, Dimitri	40	42	80	2

a. Using Employee Time Summary Sheet #2 and the Employee Information Sheet, complete payroll for all hourly employees.
b. For Arturo, Bekker and Valios, charge payroll expenses at 50% to Briar Hill Project and 50% to Chaplin Estates Project.
c. For Matthias and Nicols, charge payroll expenses at 60% to Store Operations and 40% to Chaplin Estates Project.
d. Issue cheques #63 through #67.

SESSION DATE – April 21

- [ ] Materials Summary Form #1
Dated April 15/03
From Owner: Charge $1 000 to Construction Materials Used account and reduce the Construction Materials asset account for the mid-month adjustment. Charge 60% of the materials cost to the Briar Hill Project and 40% to the Chaplin Estates Project.

- [ ] Reserved Inventory Form #RIF-1003
Dated April 15/03
Reserve inventory for Forest Glen Project
Create a new inventory record for the project in the inventory ledger:
Item Description: Forest Glen Project: reserved   Item Number: FG-1
Price = $3 020/project
Asset Account: 1500   Revenue Account: 4040   C.O.G.S. Account: 5080

Assemble the following inventory at cost price ($1 690) as reserved inventory for Forest Glen (FG-1).
10 tons Base Material: Gravel 3/4 crushed
10 tons Base Material: Sand
10 tons Base Material: Screening
1000 sqft Cobblestone: Madrid hexagon 4x8
100 Edging Stones: Crv scalloped 3ft
200 Paver Slabs: Texture non-slip 12x12

notes

Remember to edit the journal entry to match the Sales Invoice after filling the Sales Order.

❑ Sales Invoice #108
Dated April 15/03
To Cameron MacGregor, fill Sales Order #2, completion of Chaplin Estates Project

1 CE-1 Chaplin Estates Project: reserved	$ 4 885.00
1 contracting services	10 115.00
Goods & Services Tax	7%
Provincial Sales Tax	8%

Terms: Cash on receipt of invoice. Allocate 100% of revenue and costs to Chaplin Estates Project.

❑ Cash Receipt #7
Dated April 15/03
From Cameron MacGregor, cheque #121 for $14 250 in full payment of account. Reference invoice #108 and deposit #2.

❑ Cheque Copy #68
Dated April 15/03
To Dundas Concrete Works, $2 140 in full payment of account. Reference invoice #DC-1472.

❑ Visa Sales Invoice #109
Dated April 16/03
To Lou Sialtsis

200 Wall Blocks: Retaining step plus	$ 8.00 each
5 tons Base Material: Gravel 3/4 smooth	32.00 /ton
Goods & Services Tax	7%
Provincial Sales Tax	8%

Paid by Visa #4510 3416 3097 3782. Allocate 100% of revenue and costs to Store Operations.

❑ Purchase Invoice #DC-2599
Dated April 16/03
From Dundas Concrete Works

100 Wall Blocks: Retaining basic	$ 400.00
100 Wall Blocks: Retaining curvable	500.00
100 Wall Blocks: Retaining step plus	500.00
GST Paid	98.00
Invoice Total	$1 498.00

Terms: n/20.

❑ Cheque Copy #69
Dated April 18/03
To Manitoulin Flagstone & Slate, $1 391 in full payment of account. Reference invoice #MFS-541.

❑ Purchase Invoice #GM-719
Dated April 18/03
From Groundfos Machinery, $8 500 for new loading machinery plus $595 GST. Purchase invoice total $9 095. Terms: net 15 days.

- MasterCard Sales Invoice #110
  Dated April 18/03
  To John Pissaris

50 sqft Stone Slabs: Granite premium square	$14.00 /sqft
Goods & Services Tax	7%
Provincial Sales Tax	8%

  Paid by Master Card #7430 7491 8752 2784. Allocate 100% of revenue and costs to Store Operations.

- Visa Sales Invoice #111
  Dated April 19/03
  To Elena Cannatelli

600 Cobblestone: Goteberg random 4x8	$1.60 /sqft
200 Paver Slabs: Red pattern 18x16	1.80 each
Goods & Services Tax	7%
Provincial Sales Tax	8%

  Paid by Visa #4514 6673 4612 8902. Allocate 100% of revenue and costs to Store Operations.

notes

- Niagara Transport (Contact Water Fallis) is located at 699 Niagara St. Hamilton, ON L8L 6A7 Tel: (905) 527-1353 Fax: (905) 527-5221 Tax ID: 38648 9254 fallis@carryitall.com www.carryitall.com

- Purchase Invoice #NT-611
  Dated April 20/03
  From Niagara Transport (use Full Add), $200 for emergency delivery to Forest Glen project plus $14 GST and $16 PST. Invoice total $230. Terms: n/15. Charge 100% of the cost to Forest Glen Project.

- Sales Invoice #112
  Dated April 21/03
  To Wisdom Akonta, fill Sales Order #1, completion of Forest Glen Project

1 FG-1 Forest Glen Project: reserved	$3 020.00
1 Contracting Services	6 980.00
Goods & Services Tax	7%
Provincial Sales Tax	8%

  Terms: Cash on receipt of invoice. Allocate 100% of revenue and costs to Forest Glen Project.

- Cash Receipt #8
  Dated April 21/03
  From Wisdom Akonta, certified cheque #SB-81214 for $9 500 in full payment of account. Reference invoice #112 and deposit #1.

EMPLOYEE TIME SUMMARY SHEET #3

(pay period ending April 21, 2003)

Name of Employee	Regular Hours	Overtime Hours
Matthias, Max	40	–
Nicols, Evelyn	40	–

a. Using Employee Time Summary Sheet #3 and the Employee Information Sheet, complete payroll for weekly paid employees.
b. Charge payroll expenses at 75% to Store Operations and 25% to Forest Glen Project for both employees.
c. Issue cheques #70 and #71.

SESSION DATE – April 28

❑ Reserved Inventory Form #RIF-1004
Dated April 22/03
Reserve inventory for Sherwood Project
Create a new inventory record for the project in the inventory ledger:
Item Description: Sherwood Project: reserved   Item Number: SH-1
Price = $3 910/project
Asset Account: 1500   Revenue Account: 4040   C.O.G.S. Account: 5080

Assemble the following inventory at cost price ($2 270) as reserved inventory for Sherwood (SH-1).
10 tons Base Material: Gravel 3/4 crushed
10 tons Base Material: Sand
10 tons Base Material: Screening
600 sqft Cobblestone: Leeds texture reg. 4x8
100 sqft Stone Slabs: Granite premium square
5 tons Stone Slabs: Granite irregular

❑ Purchase Invoice #SC-1194
Dated April 22/03
From Stoneycreek Cement Co., $500 for construction materials plus $35 GST. Purchase invoice total $535. Terms: net 30 days. Recall stored entry.

❑ Cash Sales Invoice #113
Dated April 23/03
To Karlene Mistry

50 Patio Blocks: Red brick litewt 24x24	$6.00 each
50 Paver Slabs: Red pattern 18x16	1.80 each
Goods & Services Tax	7%
Provincial Sales Tax	8%

Paid by certified cheque #TD-8918. Allocate 100% of revenue and costs to Store Operations.

notes

❑ McMaster Paintworks (Contact Art Paynter) is located at
42 McMaster Ave.
Dundas, ON L9H 4M7
Tel: (905) 588-7129
Fax: (905) 588-2101
Tax ID: 67767 2159
art@colourit.ca
www.colourit.ca

❑ Purchase Invoice #MP-614
Dated April 24/03
From McMaster Paintworks (use Full Add), $1 000 for painting logo on delivery truck plus $70 GST. Invoice total $1 070. Terms: net 30 days. Capitalize this cost to the Delivery Truck account.

❑ Purchase Invoice #WP-3996
Dated April 24/03
From Waterloo Pavestone Ltd.

400 sqft Cobblestone: Goteberg random 4x8	$320.00
400 sqft Cobblestone: Haarlem octagonal 4x8	300.00
400 sqft Cobblestone: Madrid hexagon 4x8	280.00
GST Paid	63.00
Invoice Total	$963.00

Terms: n/20.

❑ Cash Sales Invoice #114
Dated April 24/03
To Manek Singh

50 sqft Stone Slabs: Flagstone prem. square	$12.00 /sqft
Goods & Services Tax	7%
Provincial Sales Tax	8%

Paid by money order #RB-67214. Allocate 100% of revenue and costs to Store Operations.

notes

❑ Renaissance Renovations (Contact Renee Nova) is located at
58 Paradise Rd. N.
Hamilton, ON L8S 3T4
Tel: (905) 532-7456
Fax: (905) 532-7772
renova@improvements.ca
www.improvements.ca
Credit Limit: $5 000

❑ Sales Invoice #115
Dated April 24/03
To Renaissance Renovations (use Full Add)

10 tons Base Material: Gravel 3/4 smooth	$32.00 /ton
10 tons Base Material: Sand	25.00 /ton
10 tons Base Material: Screening	22.00 /ton
500 Cobblestone: Haarlem octagonal 4x8	1.50 /sqft
100 Patio Blocks: Diamond non-slip 24x24	5.00 each
Goods & Services Tax	7%
Provincial Sales Tax	8%

Terms: 2/10, n/15. Allocate 100% of revenue and costs to Store Operations.

❑ Visa Sales Invoice #116
Dated April 26/03
To Lori Christoffer

3 tons Base Material: Sand	$25.00 /ton
100 Cobblestone: Zurich grid 18x18	6.95 each
Goods & Services Tax	7%
Provincial Sales Tax	8%

Paid by Visa #4502 8123 6500 4893. Allocate 100% of revenue and costs to Store Operations.

notes

The inventory returned is shown here with a minus sign and should be entered in the Sales Journal as a negative quantity. Remember to use the Sales Returns & Allowances account.

❑ Sales Invoice #117
Dated April 27/03
To Renaissance Renovations (returns and exchange)

– 100 Patio Blocks: Diamond non-slip 24x24	$ 5.00 each
100 Patio Blocks: Diamond natural 24x30	8.00 each
Returns Policy handling charge (no GST or PST)	115.00
Goods & Services Tax	7%
Provincial Sales Tax	8%

Terms: 2/10, n/15. Allocate 100% of revenue and costs to Store Operations.

❑ Sales Invoice #118
Dated April 28/03
To Mark Payne, fill Sales Order #4, completion of Sherwood Project

SH-1 Sherwood Project: reserved	$3 910.00 /project
1 Contracting Services	8 590.00
Goods & Services Tax	7%
Provincial Sales Tax	8%

Terms: Cash on receipt of invoice. Allocate 100% of revenue and costs to Sherwood Project.

❑ Cash Receipt #9
Dated April 28/03
From Mark Payne, certified cheque #BM-54821 for $11 875 in full payment of account. Reference invoice #118 and deposit #4.

notes

❑ Nora Nesbitt is located at
677 Victoria Ave.
Hamilton, ON L8L 8B3
Tel: (905) 525-3745
noranesbitt@home.ca

❑ Sales Quote #5
Dated April 28/03
Project completion date May 29/03
To Nora Nesbitt (use Full Add), $10 000 plus 7% GST and 8% PST for stone walkways and driveway. Terms: 20% deposit on acceptance of contract and balance on completion of project.

EMPLOYEE TIME SUMMARY SHEET #4

(pay period ending April 28, 2003)

	Name of Employee	Week 1 Hours	Week 2 Hours	Regular Hours	Overtime Hours
❑	Arturo, Michael	42	40	80	2
❑	Bekker, Hans	42	40	80	2
❑	Matthias, Max	n/a	40	40	–
❑	Nicols, Evelyn	n/a	40	40	–
❑	Valios, Dimitri	42	40	80	2

a. Using Employee Time Summary Sheet #4 and the Employee Information Sheet, complete payroll for all hourly employees.
b. For Arturo, Bekker and Valios, charge payroll expenses at 50% to Forest Glen Project and 50% to Sherwood Project.
c. For Matthias and Nicols, charge payroll expenses at 75% to Store Operations and 25% to Sherwood Project.
d. Issue cheques #72 through #76.

SESSION DATE – April 30

❑❑ Cash Receipt #9
Dated April 29/03
From Nora Nesbitt, cheque #167 for $2 000 received in advance (deposit #5) on the negotiated Nesbitt House contract. Convert sales quote #5 to a sales order.

❑❑ Memo #3
Dated April 30/03
From Owner: Complete payroll for salaried employees. Issue cheques #77 and #78. Employee commissions of $950 (2% of Contracting Revenue) for Alana Gascon, and $147 (1% of Store Sales less Returns) for Mita Ashikaya should be included in their paycheques. Charge Gascon's payroll expenses at 20% to each project. Charge Ashikaya's payroll expenses fully to Store Operations project.

notes

Treat the withdrawal as a cash purchase by the owner (Other Payment). The Drawings account should be debited.

❑ Memo #4
Dated April 30/03
From Owner: For audit and internal control purposes, prepare journal entry for withdrawal of $2 000 from the business for owner's personal use. Issue cheque #79.

❑ Bank Debit Memo #924793
Dated April 30/03
From Royal Bank

Bank charges	$ 32.00
Interest on 3-yr bank loan	240.00
Bank loan principal reduced	160.00
Interest on mortgage	1 900.00
Mortgage principal reduced	100.00

Allocate 100% of costs to Store Operations.

❑ Cash Receipt #10
Dated April 30/03
From Receiver General of Canada, cheque #2114321 for $1 330 for GST refund filed earlier in the month.

- [ ] Materials Summary Form #2
  Dated April 30/03
  From Owner: Charge $1 200 to Construction Materials Used account and reduce the Construction Materials asset account for the end-of-month adjustment. Charge 50% of the materials cost to the Forest Glen Project and 50% to the Sherwood Project.

- [ ] Cheque Copy #80
  Dated April 30/03
  To Hamilton Mountain Quarry, $749 in full payment of account. Reference invoice #HMQ-769.

- [ ] Memo #5
  Dated April 30/03
  From Owner: Create a new project for the Nesbitt House work.

KEYSTROKES

Creating New Projects

notes

If you are unable to allocate an amount, check the ledger record for the account you are using to be sure that the option to Allow Project Allocations is selected.

Simply Accounting allows allocations for both Balance Sheet and Income Statement accounts. Each account ledger record has a check box to allow project allocations for the account. If this box is checked, the allocation option is available for that account in any journal entry. If it is not checked, you cannot allocate an amount for that account. For Puretek, only amounts for revenue and expense accounts will be allocated so that Income Statements can be generated for the projects. The option to allow allocations is already turned on for all these accounts in the file for Puretek.

Before entering any transactions with cost or revenue allocations, you should create the projects.

Open the files for Puretek Paving & Stoneworks. Advance the session date.

Type `04-07-03` (or **type** `apr 7 03`)

Click **OK** to enter the session date, April 7, 2003. The Home window appears.

Projects are created in the Project Ledger indicated with the pointer on the following screen:

notes

The name of the Project Ledger can be changed to Division or Department, or something else if these are more appropriate for a business. The new name will appear instead of Project in the Home window and on reports.

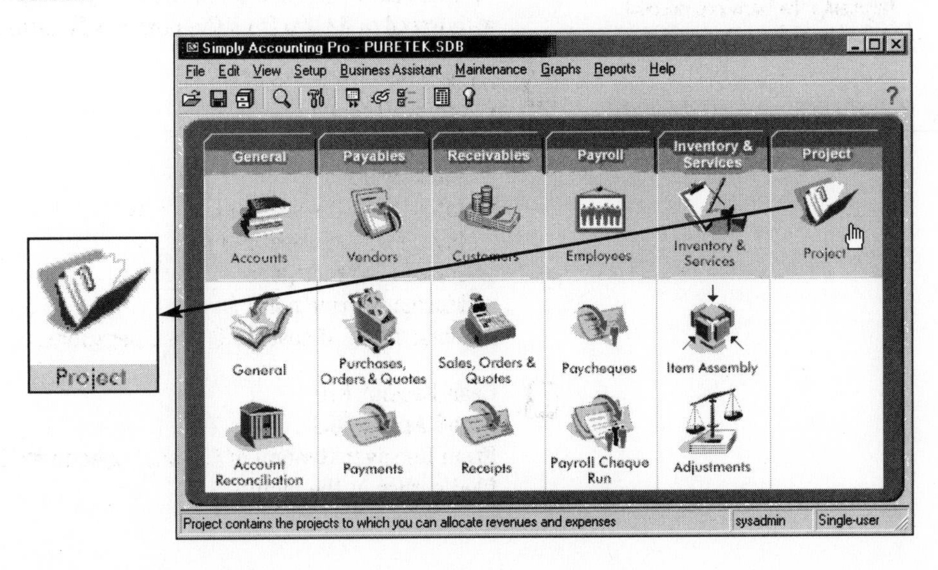

Click the **Project icon** to open the Project window:

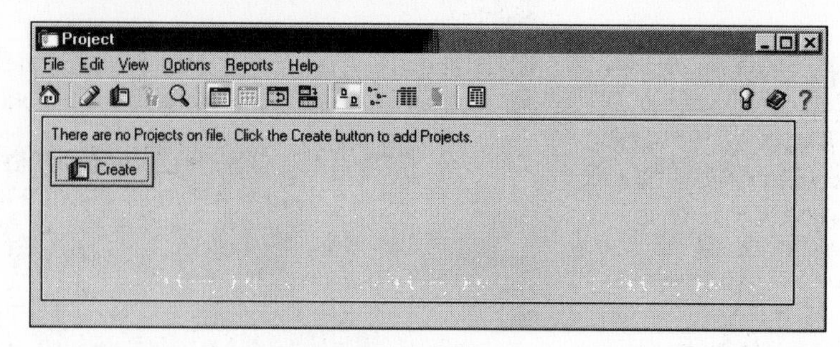

The Project window is empty because we have not yet created any projects.

Click the **Create button** Create in the Project window or choose the File menu and then Create. The following new Project Ledger screen appears:

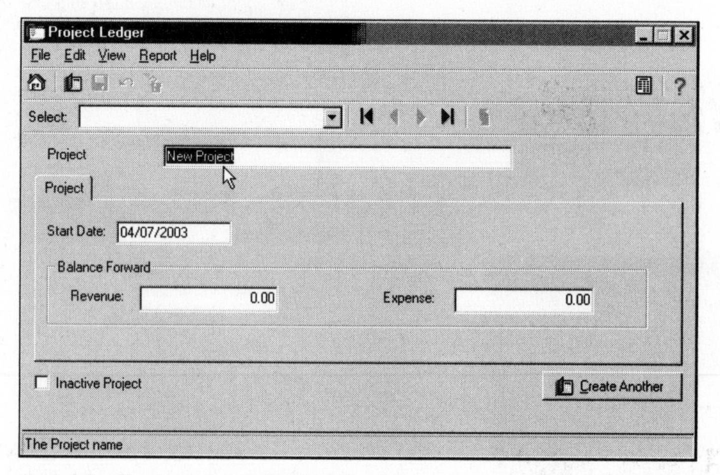

The cursor is in the Project name field with the contents highlighted, ready to be edited. You must enter the name of the first project.

Type `Briar Hill Project`

Press *tab*

The cursor moves to the Start Date field. Enter the date on which you want to begin recording project information, April 1, 2003. The session date appears automatically by default, ready to be accepted. You need to change the date.

Type `04-01`

Press *tab*

The cursor moves to the Revenue Balance Forward field. This field and the next, Expense Balance Forward, can be used to enter historical information for the project, the amount of revenue and expense generated by the project before the records were converted to Simply Accounting. The balances are zero for Puretek because a new fiscal year is just beginning. The project information is complete.

notes

You can re-sort the project icons if they are out of order by choosing the Options menu and Re-sort Icons. You can list the projects by name in the Project window by choosing the View menu and By Name.

Click Create Another Create Another to save the new project. Another blank project ledger appears for you to enter the next project on the list. Enter the remaining four projects, using the steps described above for the Briar Hill Project, and use the April 1, 2003, starting date.

When you have entered and saved all five projects,

Close the Project Ledger to return to the Project window. Notice that Simply Accounting has created an icon for each project.

Close the Project window to return to the Home window. Leave the Project icon selected.

Click the **Setup button** or choose the Setup menu, then choose System Settings and click Settings to display the Settings window as shown here:

version 8 notes

If the Project icon is not selected, choose Project from the Setup button drop-down list and click Select. Or choose the Setup menu, then choose System Settings and click Settings. Click the Project tab.

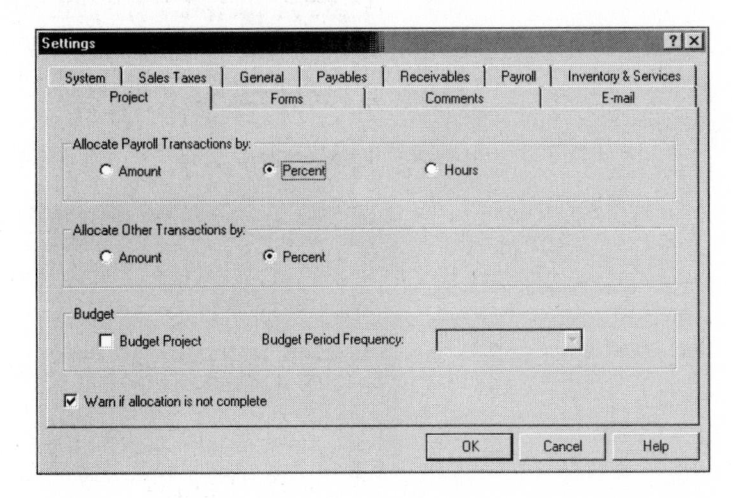

Warning!

The warning for incomplete allocations may not appear in the Payroll Cheque Run Journal, so you must remember to allocate payroll amounts. If you forget, adjust the journal entry after posting to add the allocation.

Because the Project icon was selected, you will see the Project Settings immediately.

Simply Accounting includes a warning for incomplete allocations. Because you must complete the allocation procedure even if 100% of the costs are allocated to a single project and you must allocate separately for each expense or revenue account listed in the journals, it is easy to miss an allocation. You will receive the warning if you try to post an entry that has not been fully allocated. If you are using the project module, you should always turn on the warning. The warning should be selected by default.

If this option is not already selected, **click Warn if allocation is not complete**. The remaining default settings, to allocate expenses by percentage, are correct.

notes

The option to allocate by amount requires you to enter the exact dollar amount for each project. Project work for payroll purposes is often recorded by time spent on the project and this is the third option for payroll allocations.

Puretek does not use the budgeting feature so this step is shown for information only. If you want to budget projects, click Budget Project and choose a budget frequency from the drop-down list. Project ledgers will have added a Budget tab. Then click Budget this Project on the Budget tab screen to access an input screen for entering budgeted revenue and expense amounts. For a quarterly budget, the input screen will look like the one shown below:

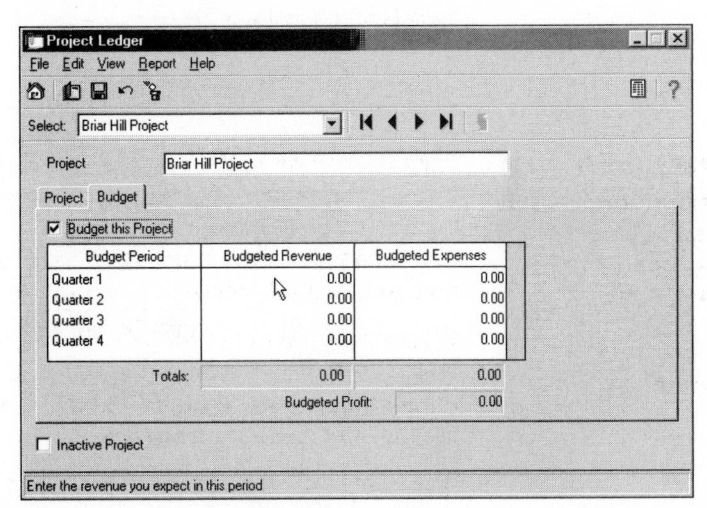

You would add a budgeted revenue and expense amount for each quarter. The program will calculate the budgeted profit amount as the difference.

Click OK to save the allocation settings.

Entering Cost Allocations

Costs or expenses and revenues are allocated after the regular journal entry is completed but before it is posted. In a journal entry, whenever you use an account for which you have allowed project allocations in the General Ledger, the allocation option is available. For Puretek, all revenue and expense accounts allow project allocations.

Click the **Purchases icon** (Purchases, Orders & Quotes) to open the Purchases Journal:

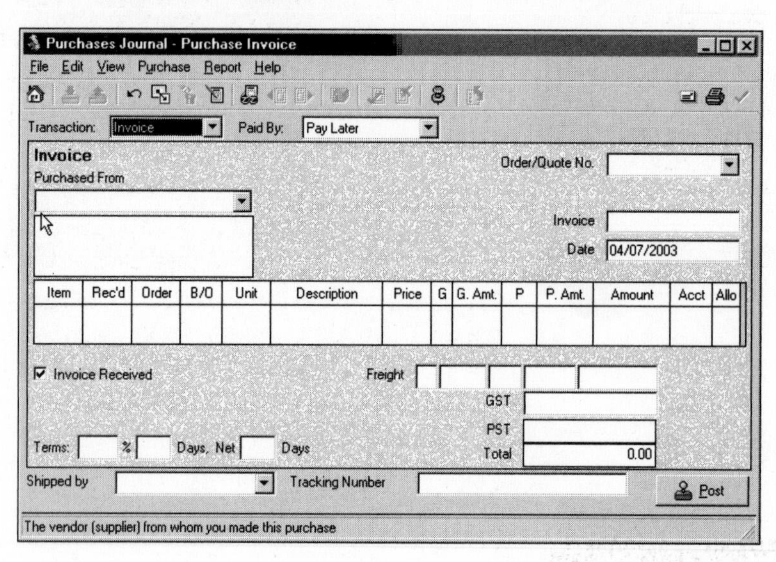

The first transaction does not involve the purchase of inventory items, so you will not use the inventory database to complete this transaction. Invoice is correct as the transaction type, and Pay Later is the correct payment method.

From the list of vendors,

Click Castillo & Maturi, Lawyers

Click the **Invoice field**

Type `CM-67`

Press tab

The cursor moves to the Date field. Enter the date on which the transaction took place, April 1, 2003. You need to change the default session date.

Type `apr 1`

Click the **G (GST code) field** and **press** enter to display the list of GST codes.

Double click 3 from the selection list to add the code to the input form.

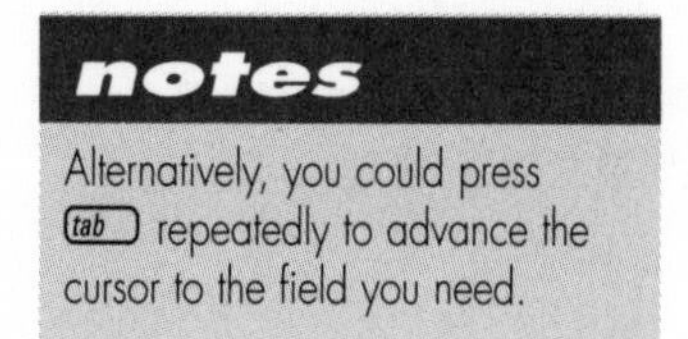

notes

Alternatively, you could press tab repeatedly to advance the cursor to the field you need.

Click the **Amount field** because there is no PST charged on the service. Enter the amount of the invoice, excluding any taxes.

Type `200`

Press tab

The cursor moves to the Account (Acct) field. When you are working in a subsidiary ledger, the *Accounts Payable* control account in the General Ledger will automatically be credited for purchases you enter. You must enter the expense or debit part of the entry.

Press enter to display the list of accounts.

Click 5200 Legal Expenses

Click Select to add the account to the input form.

Notice that the Allocate button is no longer dimmed.

Click the **Allocate button** or **double click** the **Allo column** beside the account to see the Project Allocation window for the Purchases Journal as follows:

notes

If the cursor has advanced to the next line of the invoice, the Allocate button will be dimmed and unavailable. Click the invoice line for the amount you want to allocate to activate the Allocate option. Only accounts that have selected the option to Allow Project Allocations will activate the Allocate button.

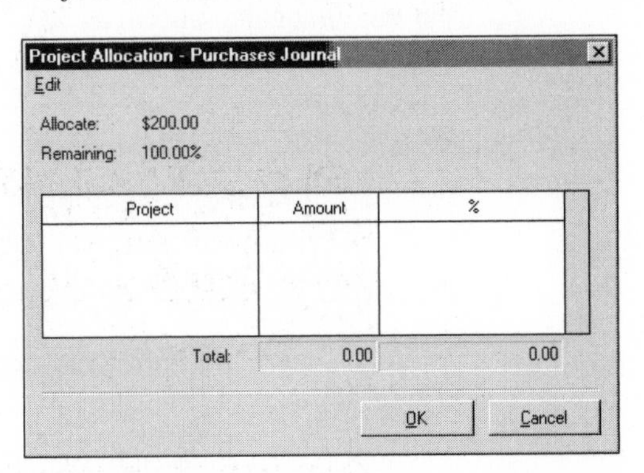

The cursor is in the Project field. The full amount to be allocated, $200, is shown at the top for reference together with the proportion remaining to be allocated, 100%. Amounts can be allocated by percentage or by actual amount. This choice is made in the Project Settings window shown on page 373 (choose the Setup menu, System Settings and then Settings and the Project tab). The setting can be changed as needed. Puretek uses the percentage allocation method as indicated in the Project Information.

Press *enter*

The following list of Projects is displayed in alphabetic order:

notes

- You must complete the allocation process even if 100 percent of the revenue or expense is assigned to a single project.
- You must complete the allocation process separately for each revenue and expense account or each invoice line on your input form.

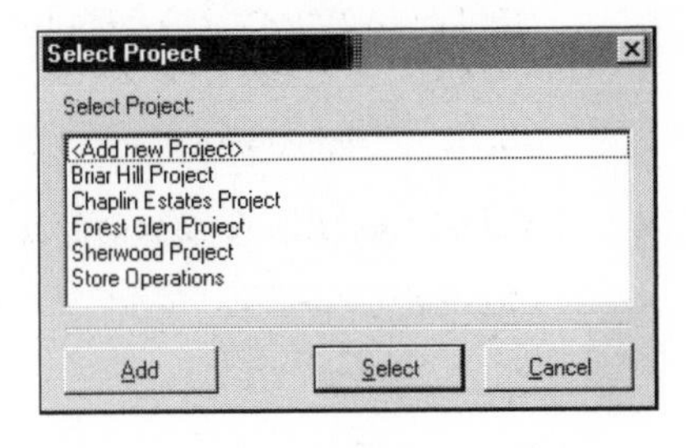

notes

Notice that you can add a new project from the Select Project window. Choosing Add will open a Project Ledger window for creating the new project.

The first project is Briar Hill, which incurs 25% of the total legal expense according to the source document information.

Click Briar Hill Project, the first one we need.

Click Select to enter it on your form.

The cursor advances to the percentage field because we selected this method of allocation. By default the unallocated portion is indicated in this field.

Type 25

Press *tab*

The program calculates the dollar amount for this project automatically based on the percentage entered. The percentage remaining at the top of the input form has been updated to 75%. The cursor moves to the next line in the Project field. Now you are ready to enter the amounts for the other projects, 25% each. You need to repeat the steps outlined above to allocate the remainder of the expense.

Press *enter*

Double click Chaplin Estates Project. The cursor is in the Percentage field again, with the default amount shown as 75%.

Type 25 **Press** tab to return to the Project field.

Press enter to display the list of projects.

Double click Forest Glen Project. The cursor is in the Percentage field again, with the default amount shown as 50%.

Type 25 **Press** tab to return to the Project field.

Double click the **Project field** to display the list of projects.

Double click Sherwood Project to add the final project for this transaction and advance to the percentage field. The final percentage is correct.

Press tab to enter it and complete the allocation as shown here:

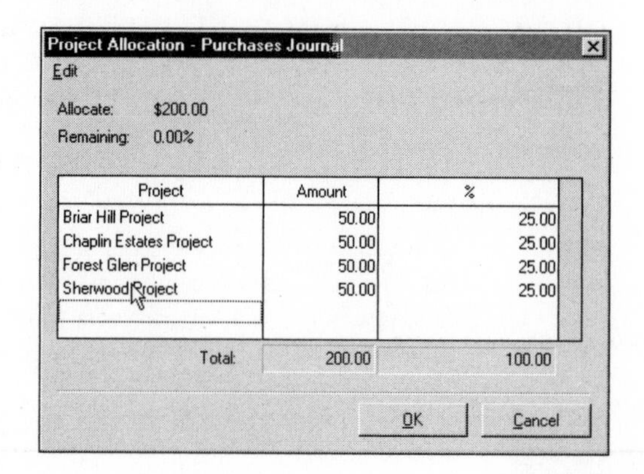

notes

- If this is a recurring entry, you can store it, complete with allocation details, by clicking the Store button, choosing a recurring frequency and clicking OK.
- To see the allocation again, double click the checkmark in the Allo column or click the Allocate button when the cursor is on the relevant line.

Click OK to return to the Purchases Journal. Your form is now complete as shown below, and you are ready to review your work:

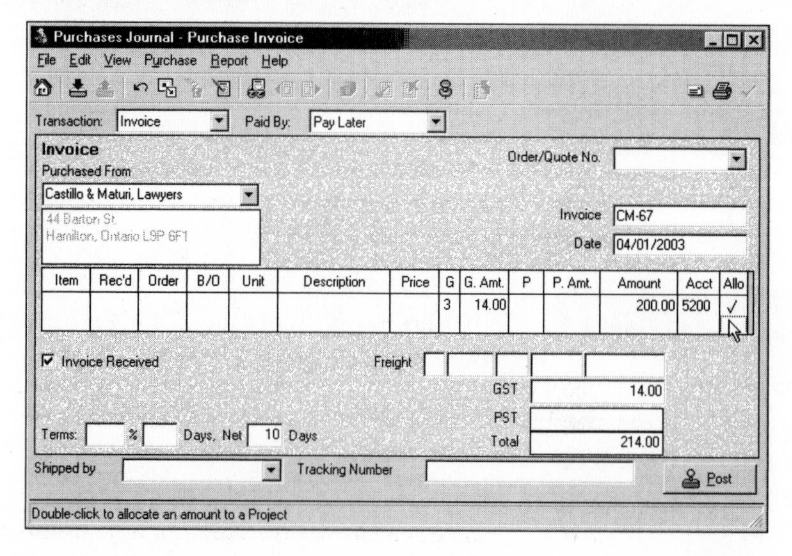

The journal appears unchanged, except for the ✔ in the Allo column indicating that the amount has been allocated.

Reviewing the Purchases Journal Allocation

notes

The amount for GST Paid is not allocated.

Choose the **Report menu** and **click Display Purchases Journal Entry** to display the transaction you have entered:

Purchases Journal Entry

File Options Help

04/01/2003 (J1)	Debits	Credits	Project
2670 GST Paid on Purchases	14.00	-	
5200 Legal Expenses	200.00	-	
- Briar Hill Project			50.00
- Chaplin Estates Project			50.00
- Forest Glen Project			50.00
- Sherwood Project			50.00
2200 Accounts Payable	-	214.00	
	214.00	214.00	

You may need to scroll to see all the information. Notice that the Simply Accounting program has automatically updated the *Accounts Payable* control account because the Payables and General ledgers are fully integrated. Notice also that the legal expense has been allocated among the four projects.

Close the display to return to the Purchases Journal input screen.

CORRECTING THE PURCHASES JOURNAL ENTRY ALLOCATION

Correct the Purchases Journal part of the entry as you would correct any other purchase invoice. Refer to page 82 if you need assistance.

If you have made an error in the allocation, **click** the **Allocate button** ✓ to return to the allocation window. **Click** the line for the amount being allocated to activate the Allocate button if necessary. Highlight an incorrect project by **clicking** it. **Press** *enter* to access the project list. **Click** the correct project and **click Select** to enter the change. **Click** an incorrect percentage and **type** the correct information. **Press** *tab* to save the correction. **Click OK** to return to the journal window.

Posting

When you are certain that you have entered all the information correctly,

Post the transaction to save it and **close** the Purchases Journal.

Allocating in Other Journals

notes

- In the Paycheque Journal, you must use the Allo tool.
- To correct allocations, click ✓ to re-open the allocation screen.
- In the setup for Payroll allocations, you can choose to allocate expenses according to the number of hours worked on each project.

Use the same principles outlined above to allocate revenues and expenses in the Sales Journal, General Journal, Adjustments Journal or the Payroll Journals to projects, departments or profit centres. You can change the setup to make allocations by dollar amounts or by percentage.

Once you have entered the journal information, the Allocate button will be available. Use it to enter the allocation information as you did for the Purchases Journal.

In the Payroll Cheque Run Journal, the Allocate button applies to the single employee who is selected from the list. You must allocate the pay for one employee at a time. There is no Allo column in the Paycheque Journal. To begin the allocation, click the Allo tool ✓ or choose the Paycheque menu and click Allocate.

In the Payroll Journals, the total payroll expense, including employer contributions such as EI, CPP, WSIB/WCB and EHT, not the net pay, is being allocated. When you review the journal entry, you will see that all the payroll-related expenses are divided among the projects according to the percentages you entered. They are shown under the Project column. You may have to scroll to see all the information.

Assembling Inventory Items

notes

Inventory item assembly is also used when you offer packages of two or more regular items for sale at a special price. The new inventory item, the special package, is priced at the sale price, and the cost is the sum of the original component costs.

Puretek uses the inventory Item Assembly Journal in Simply Accounting to ensure that the inventory to complete a project will be available when needed. The necessary items are taken out of their regular inventory account and transferred to a special reserve account. When requested under the usual inventory names, they appear not to be there because those quantities are reduced, but they will appear in the new account.

You must create the required new Group asset account, *1500 Reserved Inventory for Projects* and the inventory ledger item, *Briar Hill Project: reserved* (number: *BH-1)*, before beginning the transfer. Inventory ledgers and lists will appear with the inventory description before the number. Because we have not included inventory numbers in the source transactions, we have changed the inventory settings to sort inventory by description to make it easier to work through the source transactions.

Inventory assemblies or transfers are completed in the Item Assembly Journal:

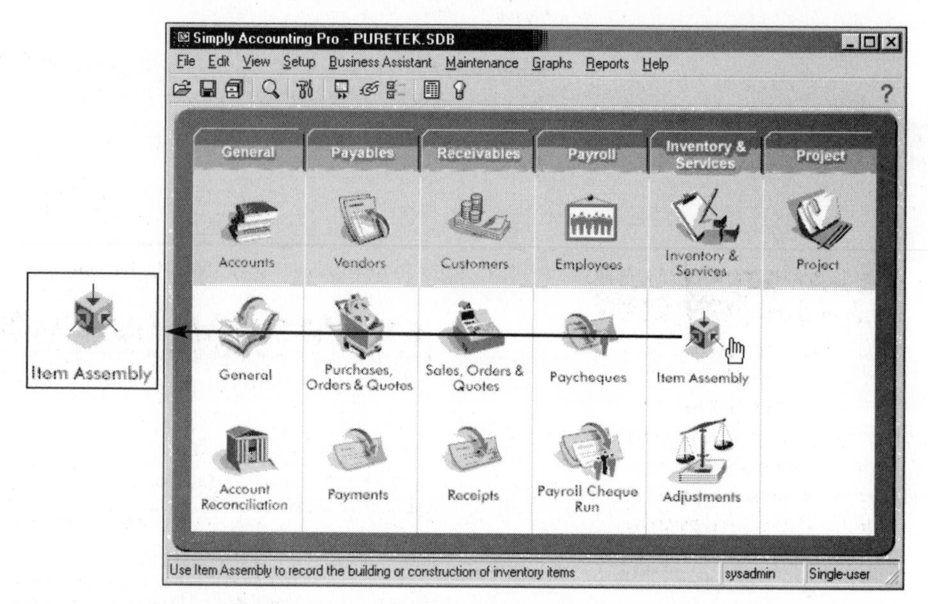

Click the **Item Assembly icon** to open the Item Assembly Journal as shown:

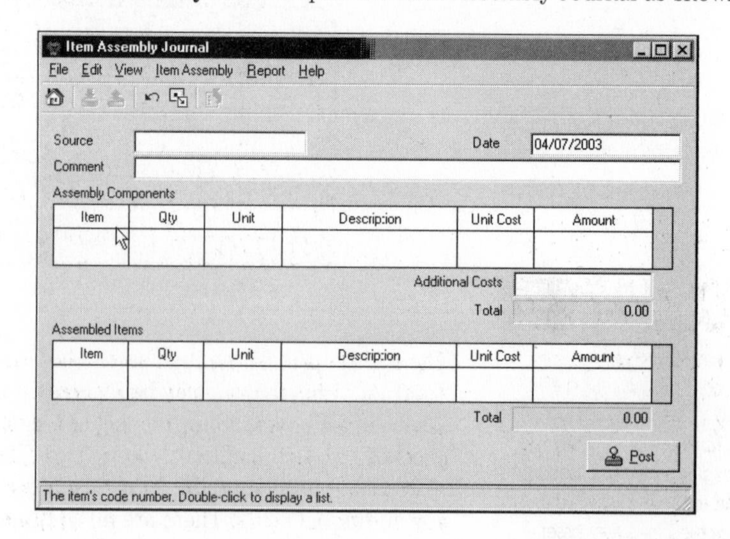

> **notes**
>
> You can drag the lower frame of the journal window to have more input lines on the screen and see your entire entry on the screen at the same time.

The cursor is in the Source field, where you should enter the invoice number.

Type `RIF-1001`

Press tab to advance to the Date field. Enter the date of the transfer.

Type `04-01-03`

Press tab to advance to the Comment field.

Type `Inventory required for Briar Hill`

Press tab to advance to the first line of the Item field in the Assembly Components section. This section refers to the items that are being removed from inventory, the "from" part of the transfer or assembly. These items are being reserved for the project.

> **notes**
>
> Notice that you can add new inventory items from the Select Inventory list in the Item Assembly Journal.

Press enter to display the familiar inventory selection list sorted by description.

Click Base Material: Gravel 3/4 crushed (BM-1) to select the first item needed for the Briar Hill Project.

Click Select to add the item to the item assembly form and advance to the Quantity (Qty) field.

Type `10`

Press tab to advance the cursor to the Unit field and to update the amount. The unit cost is correct but can be edited if necessary.

Click the **next line in the Item column**.

> **notes**
>
> The unit cost may be incorrect if inventory was purchased at different prices over time. For example, the cost of transferred items may be lower than the default if older stock is being transferred and it was purchased at a lower price. After entering the change in cost, press tab to update the amount.

Select the next inventory item to be transferred, enter the quantity and then continue to enter the remaining inventory for the Briar Hill Project.

At this stage, your screen should look like the one shown here:

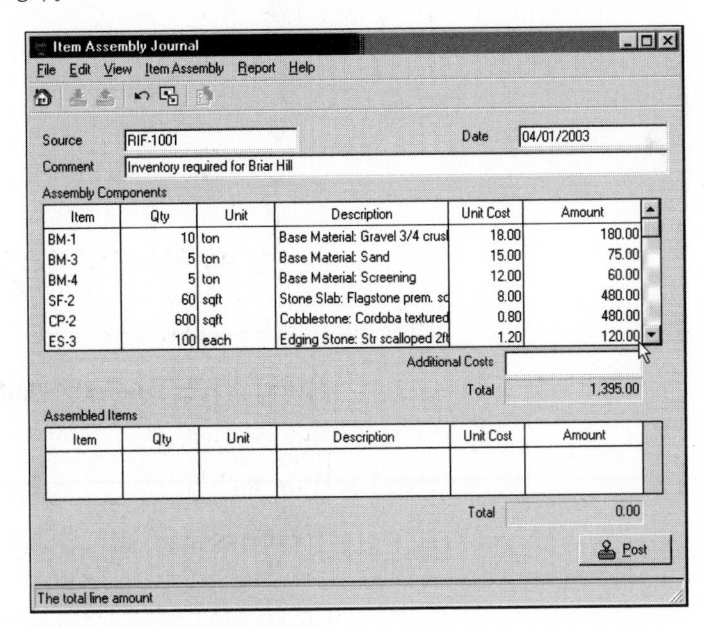

> **notes**
>
> Item Assembly costs (the Additional Costs), if any, are assigned to the linked account defined for these costs. They are contra-expense accounts because they add to the inventory value of the assembled inventory asset.

The middle part of the item assembly form contains two fields, Additional Costs and Total. Additional costs may be incurred if there are shipping or packaging costs involved with assembling, moving or transferring the inventory. These costs should be entered into the Additional Costs field. The Total is calculated automatically by Simply Accounting to include the individual costs of all items transferred or assembled plus any additional costs. There are no additional costs in this transaction.

Click the **first line in the Item column** of the Assembled Items section. This section refers to the new or reserved inventory, the item being assembled or the "to" part of the transfer.

Press (enter) to display the familiar inventory selection list.

Click Briar Hill Project: reserved (BH-1) to select the new inventory ledger item created for the Briar Hill Project.

Click Select to add the item to the item assembly form and advance to the Quantity (Qty) field. We will enter the reserved inventory as a group into the single ledger item or category.

Type `1`

Click the **Unit Cost field**. Because all items were transferred at cost and the quantity is one, the unit cost is the Total amount listed under the assembly components section.

Type `1395`

Press (tab) to enter the cost and update the amount. The Totals in the two parts of the transfer form should be the same. If they are not, you will be unable to post the entry. Your completed form should now resemble the following:

> **notes**
>
> If you forgot to add the new inventory item, open the ledger from the Select inventory/service screen by clicking Add. If you forgot to add the new account, type 1500 in the Linked Asset account field and press (tab). Use the Wizard to create the account.

> **notes**
>
> The unit cost of the assembled items is the total cost of the assembly components, including additional costs, divided by the quantity or number of units assembled. When a single type of item is assembled and the quantity is greater than one, it is simpler to enter the quantity and the amount (the total of the costs in the assembly components portion in the top half of the form) and then let Simply Accounting calculate the unit cost.

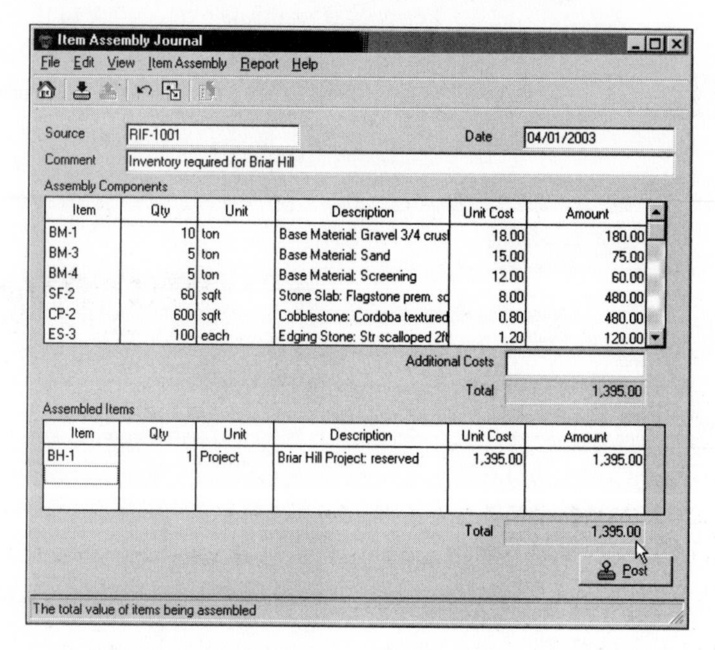

Reviewing the Item Assembly Journal Entry

Choose the **Report menu**, then **click Display Item Assembly Journal Entry** to display the transaction you have entered:

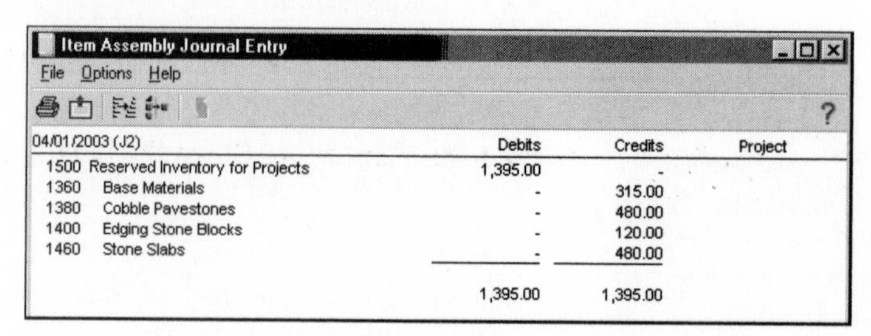

You may need to scroll to see all the information. Notice that the Simply Accounting program has moved the inventory items from their original asset account to the new reserved inventory asset account. When you display inventory selection lists or quantity reports, you will see that all the quantities for the items involved have been updated.

Close the display to return to the Item Assembly Journal input screen.

CORRECTING THE ITEM ASSEMBLY JOURNAL ENTRY

Move to the field that has the error. **Press** tab to move forward through the fields or **press** shift and tab together to move back to a previous field. This will highlight the field information so you can change it. **Type** the correct information and **press** tab to enter it. You must advance the cursor to the next invoice field to enter a change.

You can also use the mouse to point to a field and drag through the incorrect information to highlight it. **Type** the correct information and **press** tab to enter it.

If an inventory item is incorrect, **press** enter while the cursor is in the Item field to display the appropriate list. **Click** the correct selection to highlight it and **click Select** to enter the change. Re-enter the quantity and **press** tab to update the totals.

Because the item assembly is a complex transaction, it is very easy to make a mistake, so check your work carefully. You may also want to store the original entry. If you discover later that you have made an error, you can recall the entry and add a minus sign to each quantity and to the Additional Costs amount to create a reversing entry.

Click the **Store button** to display the familiar Store Recurring Transaction screen:

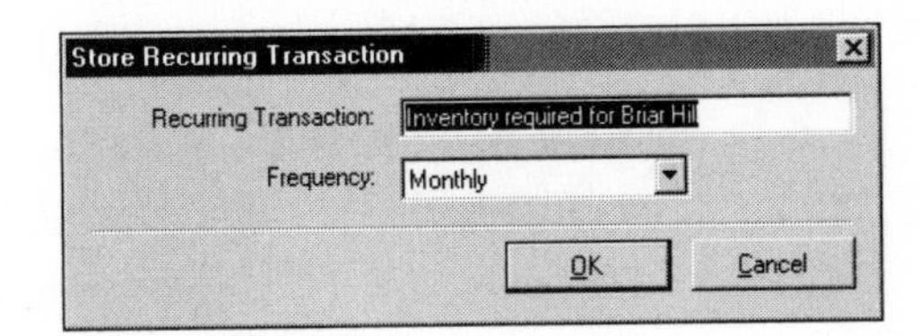

Because this is not a regular recurring transaction, we will use the Random frequency.

Click Monthly to display the Frequency options.

Scroll up until the Random frequency is in view.

Click Random to select this frequency.

Click OK to save the entry and return to the Item Assembly Journal. Notice that the Recall button is now active.

notes

Choosing the Random frequency for recurring entries enters the session date as the date when you recall the journal entry.

Posting

When you are certain that you have entered all the information correctly, you must post the transaction to save it.

Post the transaction. **Close** the Item Assembly Journal.

Displaying Project Reports

Displaying the Project List

notes

You can display the Project Detail Report from the Project List.

Right-click the **Project icon** to select it.

Click the **Display button** or choose the Reports menu, then choose Lists and click Projects.

Close the display when you have finished viewing it.

Adding Project Details to Journal Reports

When you have entered project information in a journal, you can add the allocation details to any journal report. The journal report options window will include a check box for project allocations as shown:

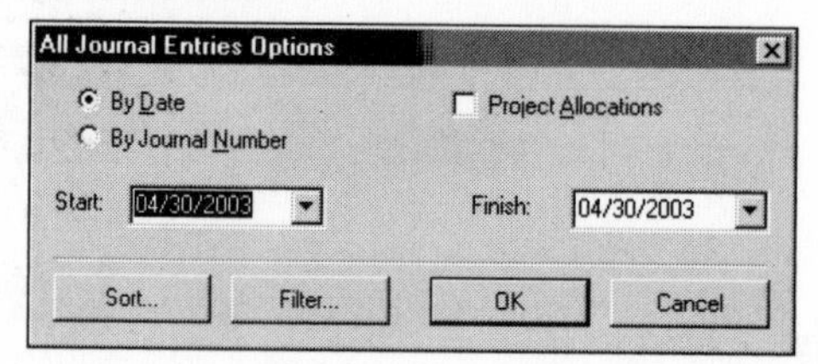

Click Project Allocations to include project information in journal reports. By default, journal reports do not have project details. **Type** the dates for the report and **click OK**. **Close** the display when finished.

Displaying Project Income Reports

Choose the **Reports menu**, then **choose Project** and **click Income** to display the following Project Reports Options window:

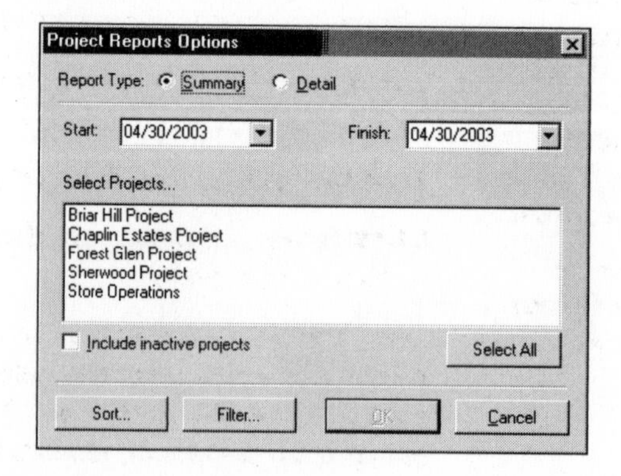

notes

You can sort and filter project reports by date, comment, source, journal number and amount per transaction.

As usual, the program gives the session date as the default.

Type the beginning date for the report you want.

Press *tab*

Type the ending date for the report.

Click Select All to include all of the projects in the report, or **press** *ctrl* and **click** the **individual projects** you want to include in the report.

> **notes**
>
> You can drill down to the Project Detail Report from the Project Summary Report. You can drill down to the Project Ledger, Journal Report, General Ledger, Invoice Lookup, Customer or Vendor Aged or Employee Report (if applicable) from the Project Detail Report.

Leave the **Summary** option, the one selected by default, if you want your report to show summary information (i.e., totals) for each account selected for each project. The **Detail** option provides complete journal information for each account for each project selected, including the names of all customers, vendors and employees, as well as the reference document number, journal entry number and date. Both options provide a calculation for revenue minus expense.

After you have indicated which options you want,

Click OK

The program then asks you to select the particular revenue or expense accounts that you want the report for, as in the following window:

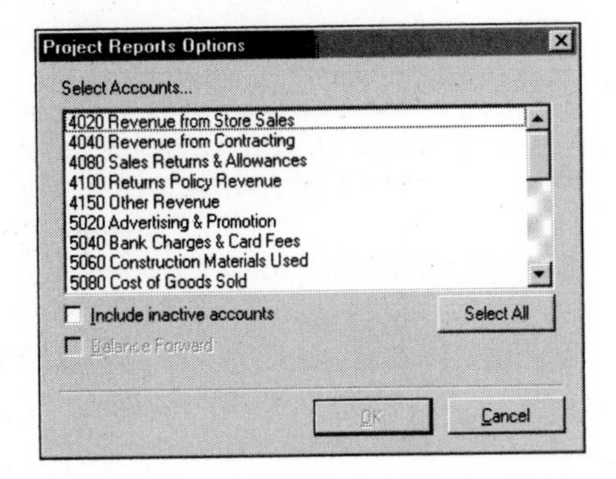

> **notes**
>
> Include multiple selections from a list by pressing and holding ctrl while clicking the items.

Click Select All or **press** ctrl and **click** the **individual accounts** you want.

Click OK to display the report.

Close the display when finished.

Displaying Project Allocation Reports

> **notes**
>
> - If you allow allocation for Balance Sheet accounts, they will be reported in the Project Allocation Report. The Project Income Report has only revenue and expense accounts.
> - Drill-down reports from the Allocation Report are the same as for the Project Income Report.

The project allocation report shows the breakdown of amounts for each project by accounts. It is similar to the project income report, but the total revenue and expense and the net project income are omitted.

Choose the **Reports menu**, then **choose Project** and **click Allocation** to display the Project Report Options window.

Type the start and end dates for the report.

Click Select All to include all projects in the report, or **press** ctrl and **click individual projects**.

Leave the **Summary** option, the one selected by default, if you want your report to show totals for each account selected for each project. The **Detail** option provides complete journal information for each account for each project selected, including the names of all customers, vendors and employees, as well as the reference document number, journal entry number and date.

After you have indicated which options you want,

Click OK

From the next screen, select the accounts you want to report on.

Click Select All or **press** ctrl and **click** the **specific accounts** you want.

Click OK to display the report.

Close the display when you have finished.

Displaying Project Management Reports

There are management reports for the Project Ledger, just as there are for every other ledger in Simply Accounting.

Choose the **Reports menu**, then **choose Management Reports** and **click Project** to see the report options window:

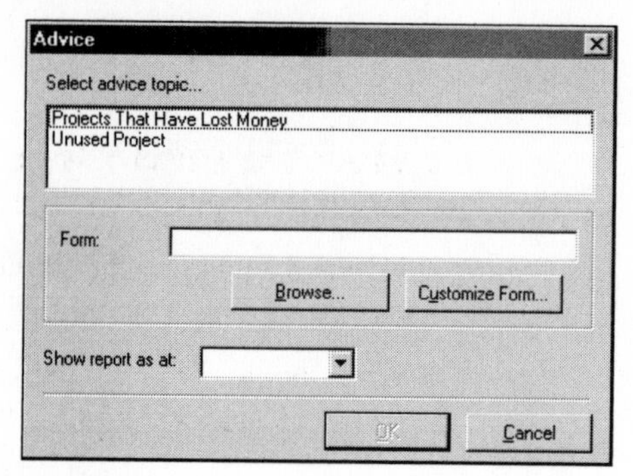

Click the **topic** for the report.

Click OK

Close the report when finished.

Displaying the Item Assembly Journal

Right-click the **Item Assembly icon** to select it.

Click the **Display button** or choose the Reports menu, then choose Journal Entries and click Item Assembly to display the report options:

- The Item Assembly Journal report does not have a project option because it does not allow allocations.
- You can display General Ledger reports and Invoice Lookup from the Item Assembly Journal Report.

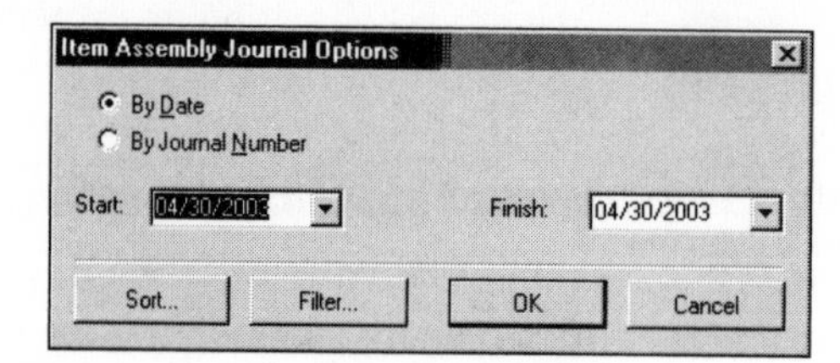

Again, the program gives the session date as the default.

Type the beginning date for the report you want.

Press tab

Type the ending date for the report.

Click OK to display the report.

Close the display when you have finished.

Printing Reports

Display the report you want on the screen by following the instructions above.

Choose the **File menu** and **click Print**. **Close** the display.

CASE PROBLEM

Puretek has been advised that the stock of several styles of cobblestone is being discontinued. Since they will be unable to replace the current stock when it runs out, they have decided to clear it at sale prices.

1. How should they record the sales of the items with reduced prices in the Sales Journal?
2. What changes should they make in the Inventory Ledger in the Simply Accounting program to build in the price changes?
3. If they decide to offer additional volume discounts, how should the changes be made in Simply Accounting?
4. What should they do if they decide to bundle several different kinds of cobblestones at special sale prices?

CHAPTER TWELVE

BONNIE BRIDES

BRIDAL GOWNS, FORMAL GOWNS & ACCESSORIES

OBJECTIVES

After completing this chapter, you should be able to

- *turn on* the budgeting feature in Simply Accounting
- *determine* budgeting periods and amounts
- *allocate* budget amounts to revenue and expense accounts
- *enter* transactions involving Quebec Sales Tax
- *enter* inventory adjustments
- *enter* import duty rates and amounts
- *remit* payments for import duties
- *display* and *print* income statements with budget comparisons
- *graph* budget reports
- *analyze* budget reports

COMPANY INFORMATION

Company Profile

Bonnie Brides, a small bridal boutique owned and operated by Bonnie Brioche, has been in business for about two years in Montreal. The store sells a small but carefully selected range of moderately priced designer bridal gowns and bridal accessories, as well as gowns for the other members of the bridal party, bridesmaids and mothers. Some of the attendants' gowns are specifically designed to complement the brides' gowns. The rest of the store's revenue comes from custom-made gowns whose designs are chosen from a specialized pattern catalogue or adapted from photographs in bridal magazines. The custom work is completed by Sylvie Couturier, Brioche's cousin. Couturier, who had previously worked from her home designing a variety of business and formal wear for women, joined the business in January after repeated inquiries from customers about such work. The change was a relatively easy one to make because the store already had sewing machines for alteration work.

notes

Bonnie Brides is located at Rue Simard, 1650 Montreal, QC H2H 2K8. Its tax ID business number is 58123 0458.

Since most weddings are planned for the summer, most brides choose their gowns at the beginning of the year, making January and February the busiest months. Although Brioche requests that customers pay for their gowns immediately, she offers to store them until just before the wedding when final fittings and alterations are made. As a service to her clients, Brioche provides free alterations on all regularly priced merchandise.

Custom-made gowns take about two weeks of full-time work to complete. Dress fabrics are purchased immediately after the dress is ordered and measurements are taken. Although a small supply of beads, pearls, buttons and lace is kept on hand at the store, most dresses require a special order of these items as well. Specialty fabrics are imported from Paris. Some accessory items are also imported and import duties are applied according to the rates set by Canada Customs and Revenue Agency (CCRA). Because the fabrics for custom gowns are specially ordered, customers pay a 25 percent non-refundable deposit to allow the store to purchase the necessary materials. The balance is paid when the dress is completed. Couturier is paid only a commission for her work, at the rate of 25 percent of revenue from design work.

Bonnie Brides keeps two sets of customer mailing lists. All custom-order customers are entered into the Simply Accounting program Receivables Ledger. Brioche maintains a second customer list in a mail merge program to send information about the store's new line of gowns or about promotions. Vendors who are regular suppliers are entered into the Payables Ledger in the Simply Accounting program.

Bonnie Brides entered all its manual accounting records into the Simply Accounting program at the end of December 2002 in preparation for the new fiscal year. Brioche has also decided to use the budgeting feature based on the previous year's Income Statement and projections for the new design part of the business. She set up the company files with the help of Lori Christoffer who studied with her at McGill University. They used the following information for the conversion:

- Chart of Accounts
- Income Statement
- Post-Closing Trial Balance
- Vendor Information
- Customer Information
- Employee Information
- Inventory Information
- Accounting Procedures

notes

The accounts PST Payable, CPP Payable and CPP Expense appear in the Chart of Accounts in the data files because they are necessary for the program to finish entering the history. They are not used in Quebec; their balances will remain at zero. CPP Expenses will therefore not be part of the budget.

BONNIE BRIDES
CHART OF ACCOUNTS

ASSETS
1060 Chequing Bank Account
1070 Visa Bank Account
1080 MasterCard Bank Account
1090 Bank: Foreign Currency Account
1100 Marketable Securities
1200 Accounts Receivable
1220 Fabrics
1240 Dressmaking Supplies
1260 Prepaid Insurance
1280 Store Supplies
1300 Accessories
1320 Bridal Gowns
1340 Bridesmaids' Gowns
1360 Hats and Veils
1380 Mothers' Gowns
1420 Cash Register
1440 Computers & Peripherals
1480 Display Fixtures
1500 Sewing Machines & Sergers
1520 Shop

LIABILITIES
2200 Accounts Payable
2240 Import Duties
2310 EI Payable
2330 Income Tax Payable
2350 QPP Payable
2360 Quebec Income Tax Payable
2370 QHSF Payable
2460 WCB Payable
2650 GST Charged on Sales
2670 GST Paid on Purchases
2800 Refundable QST Paid
2810 QST Charged on Sales
2950 Mortgage Payable

EQUITY
3560 Bonnie Brioche, Capital
3580 Bonnie Brioche, Drawings
3600 Current Earnings

REVENUE
4020 Revenue from Sales
4040 Sales Discount
4100 Revenue from Design
4200 Interest Revenue

EXPENSES
5020 Advertising & Promotion
5030 Exchange Rate Differences
5050 Bank Charges & Card Fees
5060 Cost of Goods Sold
5070 Fabrics Used
5080 Dressmaking Supplies Used
5100 Damaged Inventory
5150 Delivery Expense
5160 Freight Expense
5170 Hydro Expense
5180 Insurance Expense
5200 Interest Expense
5240 Store Supplies Used
5260 Telephone Expense
5300 Commissions
5310 EI Expense
5330 WCB Expense
5340 QPP Expense
5350 QHSF Expense
5380 Subcontractors' Fees

BONNIE BRIDES
INCOME STATEMENT

FOR THE YEAR ENDING DECEMBER 31, 2002

REVENUE		
4020 Revenue from Sales	$112 650.00	
4040 Sales Discount	- 1 179.00	
4080 Net Sales		$111 471.00
4200 Interest Revenue		7 500.00
TOTAL REVENUE		$118 971.00
EXPENSES		
5020 Advertising & Promotion		2 160.00
5050 Bank Charges & Card Fees		360.00
5060 Cost of Goods Sold		57 560.00
5070 Fabrics Used		500.00
5080 Dressmaking Supplies Used		300.00
5100 Damaged Inventory		955.00
5150 Delivery Expense		720.00
5160 Freight Expense		405.00
5170 Hydro Expense		1 283.40
5180 Insurance Expense		800.00
5200 Interest Expense		10 098.00
5240 Store Supplies Used		1 620.00
5260 Telephone Expense		872.76
TOTAL EXPENSE		$ 77 634.16
NET INCOME		$ 41 336.84

BONNIE BRIDES
POST-CLOSING TRIAL BALANCE

December 31, 2002

1060 Chequing Bank Account	$ 19 397.45	
1090 Bank: Foreign Currency Account	800.00	
1100 Marketable Securities	50 000.00	
1200 Accounts Receivable	1 139.55	
1220 Fabrics	3 000.00	
1240 Dressmaking Supplies	1 000.00	
1280 Store Supplies	650.00	
1300 Accessories	7 265.00	
1320 Bridal Gowns	28 950.00	
1340 Bridesmaids' Gowns	3 680.00	
1360 Hats and Veils	2 440.00	
1380 Mothers' Gowns	2 170.00	
1420 Cash Register	1 200.00	
1440 Computers & Peripherals	3 000.00	
1480 Display Fixtures	1 500.00	
1500 Sewing Machines & Sergers	7 200.00	
1520 Shop	100 000.00	
2200 Accounts Payable		$ 2 782.00
2650 GST Charged on Sales		2 450.00
2670 GST Paid on Purchases	840.00	
2950 Mortgage Payable		84 000.00
3560 Bonnie Brioche, Capital		145 000.00
	$234 232.00	$234 232.00

BONNIE BRIDES
VENDOR INFORMATION

Vendor Name (Contact)	Address	Phone No. Fax No.	Terms
Beads & Threads (Louise Fabricant)	10823 Rue Laperle Montreal, QC H2C 3C6	Tel: (514) 476-8109 Fax: (514) 476-8225	Net 10
Bell Quebec	8180 Rue Alouette Montreal, QC H9A 3G8	Tel: (514) 573-7102 Fax: (514) 573-7211	Net 1
Bridal Originals Ltd. (Yves Rodier)	505 Ch De Mariee Montreal, QC H3F 2S3	Tel: (514) 386-5199 Fax: (514) 385-2926	Net 20
Bridal Xpress Delivery	4021 Av Chamionnage Montreal, QC H1G 5B2	Tel: (514) 622-5372 Fax: (514) 622-5710	Net 10
Kristin Couture (Kristin Couture)	6022 Rue Carriere Montreal, QC H1B 3X5	Tel: (514) 782-7493 Fax: (514) 782-7408	Net 1
Ministre du Revenu du Québec	400 Boul De Maisonneuve E Montreal, QC H2L 5A1	Tel: (514) 829-6201 Fax: (514) 829-0900	Net 1
Quebec Hydro	300 Rue Fullum Montreal, QC H2K 4R4	Tel: (514) 566-8224 Fax: (514) 566-8210	Net 1
Receiver General of Canada	Summerside Tax Centre Summerside, PE C1N 6L2	Tel: (902) 821-8186	Net 1
Voiles de Paris (Emilie Paquin) (French Vendor)	117 rue Pierre Lescot 1st Arrondissement Paris, France 75001	Tel: (33-1) 8486 2365 Fax: (33-1) 8486 2309	Net 15

OUTSTANDING VENDOR INVOICES

Vendor Name	Date	Inv/Chq No.	Terms	Amount	Total
Bridal Originals Ltd.	12/15/02	BO-1347	Net 20	$2 140	$2 140
Voiles de Paris	12/20/02	VP-642	Net 15	F3 040 FRF	642 CAD
				Grand Total	$2 782

BONNIE BRIDES
CUSTOMER INFORMATION

Customer Name (Contact)	Address	Phone No. Fax No.	Credit Limit Terms
Josee Drouin	56 Rue Camille Montreal, QC H8R 1G4	Tel: (514) 622-6197	$5 000 Net 1

OUTSTANDING CUSTOMER INVOICES

Customer Name	Date	Inv/Chq No.	Terms	Amount	Total
Josee Drouin	12/29/02	169	Net 1	$1 139.55	$1 139.55

BONNIE BRIDES
EMPLOYEE INFORMATION SHEET

	Sylvie Couturier
Position	Designer/Dressmaker
Social Insurance Number	414 243 642
Address & Telephone	5020 Rue Carillon Dorval, QC H9A 2K5 (514) 687-2104
Date of Birth (dd-mm-yy)	21-04-69
Tax Exemption (TD1)	
Federal Claim	$7 412
Quebec Tax Claim	$5 900
Employee Earnings	
Commission	25% of Revenue from Design
Vacation	3 weeks
Employee Deductions	
EI, QPP and QHSF,	calculations built into Simply Accounting program
Quebec Tax and Income Tax	calculations built into Simply Accounting program
Additional Income Tax	

Employee Profile and TD1 Information

Sylvie Couturier began working for Bonnie Brides on January 1, 2003, as a designer and dressmaker. She is married and self-supporting. At the end of each month, she is paid a 25 percent commission based on the design revenue. She receives no vacation pay or employee benefits, but she expects to take about three weeks off during the less busy time of the year.

Additional Payroll Information

The employer's contributions include the following:

- QPP contributions equal to employee contributions
- EI factor of 1.4
- Workers Compensation Board (WCB) at the rate 3.82

notes

- The preferred customer pricing option is not used. All customers pay regular prices, although discounts are offered to some customers.
- Duty rates are entered only for items that are normally imported.

BONNIE BRIDES
INVENTORY INFORMATION

Code	Description	Sell Price /Unit	Qty on Hand	Amt (Cost)	Min Stock	Duty Rate
Accessories						
AC01	Capes: brocade full length	$700 each	2	$ 800	1	
AC02	Capes: velvet full length	800 each	2	900	1	
AC03	Earrings: diamond studs	200 /pair	10	1 000	2	6.5
AC04	Earrings: pearl studs	70 /pair	15	450	5	8.5
AC05	Earrings: pearl tear drop	110 /pair	10	500	2	8.5
AC06	Garters: blue, var designs S/M/L	30 each	12	240	6	
AC07	Muffs: imitation fur	60 each	4	120	1	15.5
AC08	Shoes: peau-de-soie/satin/leather	110 /pair	60	3 000	12	18.0
AC09	Stockings: sheer white/almnd/taupe	10 /pair	30	150	5	
AC10	Stockings: lace white/almond	15 /pair	15	105	3	
				$7 265		
Bridal Gowns: various sizes each						
BG01	Ari empire line antique ivory lace	$1 100 each	2	$ 1 100	1	
BG02	Arezzo peau-de-soie A-line fl lace	1 050 each	5	2 500	2	
BG03	Ferrucci embr silk satn sheer slv	1 500 each	5	3 750	2	
BG04	Lagar matte satn/halter top/roses	1 200 each	5	3 000	2	
BG05	Miyaki matte organza/chapel train	1 400 each	5	3 500	1	
BG06	Paolo poly-satn fit/flare prl clus	950 each	5	2 250	2	
BG07	Raffaelli full tulle/basque waist	1 000 each	5	2 500	2	
BG08	Rojas peau-de-soie slvless/prl bttn	800 each	5	2 000	1	
BG09	Shijo silk satn slvless/prl bodice	1 250 each	5	3 100	2	
BG10	Vasari silk satn roses/cathed train	2 500 each	1	1 250	1	
BG11	Vernet nat'l silk/lace/sweep train	1 600 each	4	4 000	1	
				$28 950		
Bridesmaids' Gowns: various colours and sizes						
BMG01	Ferrucci velvet/satn fit/flare	$250 each	4	$ 500	2	
BMG02	Lagar velvet/chiffon skirt/empire	225 each	8	900	2	
BMG03	Miyaki cut velvet/crepe flared skrt	200 each	8	800	2	
BMG04	Rojas poly-satn drop waist skirt	160 each	8	640	2	
BMG05	Shijo crepe sweetheart neckline	180 each	6	540	2	
BMG06	Vernet short floral pattern skirt	150 each	4	300	2	
				$3 680		
Hats and Veils						
HV01	Hats: ostrich w/chenille dot veil	$140 each	2	$ 140	0	12.5
HV02	Hats: sheer organza w/silk bow	150 each	2	150	1	12.5
HV03	Headband: silk satn rosettes	50 each	6	150	2	12.5
HV04	Veil: lace cath embroid w/sequins	200 each	4	400	1	20.0
HV05	Veil: lace chapel w/pearl bead edge	170 each	4	320	1	20.0
HV06	Veil: silk cathedral w/prl clusters	180 each	4	360	1	10.0
HV07	Veil: tulle full asymetric scallopd	150 each	8	600	2	20.0
HV08	Veil: tulle plain chapel length	80 each	8	320	2	20.0
				$2 440		
Mothers' Gowns: various sizes each						
MG01	Ari crepe sand 2pce suit	$200 each	3	$ 300	1	
MG02	Paolo ivory crepe empire line gown	140 each	4	280	1	
MG03	Raffaelli gold khaki gown w/lace	175 each	2	170	1	
MG04	Rojas 2pce suit w/lace overlay	225 each	4	440	1	
MG05	Vasari black satn w/gold embroid	210 each	3	300	1	
MG06	Vernet silk sarong w/gold bead	195 each	2	180	1	
MG07	Vezeley pink crepe w/cord lace jckt	190 each	5	500	1	
				$2 170		

Accounting Procedures

The Goods and Services Tax: Remittances

Bonnie Brides uses the regular method for remittance of the Goods and Services Tax. GST collected from customers is recorded as a liability in *GST Charged on Sales*. GST paid to vendors is recorded in *GST Paid on Purchases* as a decrease in the liability to Canada Customs and Revenue Agency. Brioche files her return to the Receiver General of Canada by the last day of the month for the previous quarterly period, either requesting a refund or remitting the balance owing.

notes

Both customer and vendor ledgers have the option to charge or collect QST. If this option is not selected, the QST fields are not available, similar to the option to charge or collect GST.

Quebec Sales Tax (QST)

Provincial sales tax (Quebec Sales Tax or QST) of 7.5 percent is applied to all cash and credit sales of goods and services in the province of Quebec. At the time this workbook was written, the Quebec Sales Tax applied to the amount of the invoice with GST included. This is often referred to as a "tax on a tax" or a "piggy-backed" tax. The defaults for this application are set so that the program will automatically calculate the QST on the amount with GST included. Accounting examples for sales taxes in different provinces are provided in Chapter 2.

Refundable and Non-refundable QST

Some purchases qualify for refundable QST credits to reduce the QST owing in much the same way as the GST owing is calculated. Generally QST is refundable if the purchase consists of inputs to the items sold, for example, the QST on fabrics that are used to make dresses for sale. QST on sales are similarly divided into refundable and non-refundable taxes. The codes for QST available in the QST field (press enter when the cursor is in the tax field), therefore, include refundable and non-refundable codes as follows:

notes

Refundable does not appear with the on-screen code descriptions. Codes D and F are refundable because they are not listed as non-refundable.

A - QST exempt
B - QST nontaxable
C - QST @ 0%
D - QST @ 7.5%, not included (refundable)
E - QST @ 7.5%, not included, non-refundable
F - QST @ 7.5%, included (refundable)
G - QST @ 7.5%, included, non-refundable

Only businesses qualify for refunds on QST paid. Since customers of Bonnie Brides purchase items for personal use, Code E is used for all sales — the QST is not included and is non-refundable. In this application, Codes D and E are used for purchases. Any purchases that qualify for the refundable tax credits are clearly indicated in the source documents.

QST owing (*QST Charged on Sales* less *Refundable QST Paid*) must be remitted quarterly to the ministre du Revenu du Québec.

When Quebec Sales Taxes are included in the company setup, the Reports menu item GST Reports is replaced by "Tax" because both GST and QST reports can be displayed and printed. Detail and summary forms are available.

notes

Processing the advance through the Receipts Journal ensures that the advance will appear in the correct customer account in the Receivables Ledger. The other approach, a General Journal entry that debits the bank account and credits Unearned Revenue, a liability account, does not show this link with the customer.

Deposits on Custom Orders

When customers order custom-made gowns, they place a sales order and pay an advance of 25 percent of the negotiated price (before taxes). The advance is entered in the Receipts Journal for the customer as a deposit. The *Accounts Receivable* ledger for the selected customer will be credited for the advance and *Chequing Bank Account* will be debited. When the work is completed, fill the Sales Order to make a Sales Journal entry for the full amount of the contract, including relevant taxes. When the customer settles the account, mark both the deposit and the full invoice amount as paid. The balance in the Receipts Journal should then match the amount of the customer's cheque.

Sales Discounts
Bonnie Brides occasionally offers customer discounts at the time of a cash sale. These discounts are like a negative invoice line attached to the original sales invoice. Discounts are recorded in the Sales Journal at the time of the sale as follows:

- Choose the customer, Invoice as the transaction and the appropriate method of payment. Enter the cheque number, if appropriate, and invoice number and date.
- Enter all items sold to the customer as usual, entering one item per invoice line.
- Click the discount field (%) in the Terms section at the bottom of the invoice.
- Enter the percentage discount and press *tab*.

The invoice total is reduced by the discount amount and the GST and QST are reduced.

Brioche has set up separate bank accounts with both Visa and MasterCard and will begin accepting payment by credit card beginning in January.

Freight Expenses
When a business purchases inventory items, the cost of freight that cannot be directly allocated to a specific item of purchase must be charged to *Freight Expense*. This amount will be regarded as an expense and will not be part of the costs of any inventory asset account.

Printing Sales Invoices
If you want to print sales invoices through the program, complete the Sales Journal transaction as you would otherwise. Before posting the transaction, click Print or choose the File menu and then Print. Printing will begin immediately, so be sure you have the correct forms for your printer before you begin. Brioche will not use the e-mail features of the program yet.

INSTRUCTIONS

1. Set up the budget for Bonnie Brides on January 1, 2003, using Simply Accounting. Detailed keystroke instructions to assist you begin on page 401 following the source documents.
2. Using the Chart of Accounts, the Trial Balance, Vendor, Customer, Payroll and Inventory information provided, enter the source documents for January 2003 in Simply Accounting.
3. Print the following reports and graphs:
   - Balance Sheet as at Jan. 31
   - Journal Entries for all journals by date from Jan. 1 to Jan. 31
   - Inventory Sales Detail Report for Bridal Gowns
   - Inventory Quantity Report for all items to check re-order requirements
   - Income Statement, Budget Percentage Difference Report for Jan. 1 to Jan. 31
   - Sales vs Budget graph for accounts 4020 and 4100
   - Expenses vs Budget graph for accounts 5060, 5070 and 5080

SOURCE DOCUMENTS

SESSION DATE – January 7

Memo #1
401
Dated Jan. 1/03
From Owner: Set up the budget for the coming year based on last year's income statements and projections for the year.

notes

F is the symbol for French francs. FRF is the code for French francs, comparable to the dollar sign ($) and CAD for the Canadian dollar.

Purchase Invoice #VP-793
407
Dated Jan. 2/03
From Voiles de Paris

No.	Item	Amount (FRF)	Duty %
2	Hats: ostrich w/chenille dot veil HV01	600.00 F	12.5%
2	Hats: sheer organza w/silk bow HV02	650.00 F	12.5%
2	Veil: lace cath embroid w/sequins HV04	900.00 F	20.0%
2	Veil: lace chapel w/pearl bead edge HV05	700.00 F	20.0%
2	Veil: silk cathedral w/prl clusters HV06	800.00 F	10.0%
2	Veil: tulle full asymetric scallopd HV07	670.00 F	20.0%
2	Veil: tulle plain chapel length HV08	350.00 F	20.0%
	GST Paid @ 7%	326.90 F	
	Invoice Total	4996.90 F	
	Import Duties	760.25 F	
	Freight included in item prices.		

Terms: net 15.
All amounts in French francs. The exchange rate is 0.2114.

notes

Enter the payment to the Receiver General as an Other Payment in the Payments Journal. Debit Import Duties account.

Memo #1
Dated Jan. 2/03
Issue cheque #100 for $160.72 to the Receiver General to pay the duty owing for purchase from Voiles de Paris (F760.25).

Cash Purchase Invoice #SL-43216
Dated Jan. 2/03
From Sunlife Insurance Co. (use Quick Add), $840 for a one-year insurance policy. Paid by cheque #101.

notes

Deanne Demarais is located at
450 Av. De L'Eglise
Montreal, QC H4E 1G3
Tel: (514) 583-5437
Fax: (514) 583-7501
Charge GST & QST
- Use QST Code E, QST @ 7.5%, not included, non-refundable for sales.

Sales Order #101
Dated Jan. 2/03
Completion date Jan. 15/03
From Deanne Demarais (use Full Add), order for custom-design silk and satin gown plus cathedral length train with floral lace and sequin embroidery details costing $8 000 plus GST and QST. Sales order total $9 202. Deposit of 25% required to confirm order. Balance to be paid on delivery. Credit Revenue from Design.

Cash Receipt #1
Dated Jan. 2/03
From Deanne Demarais cheque #45 for $2 000 for deposit #1 on custom gown to confirm sales order #101.

Cash Receipt #2
Dated Jan. 2/03
From Josee Drouin, cheque #32 for $1 139.55 in full payment of account. Reference invoice #169.

- [ ] Cheque Copy #102
Dated Jan. 3/03
To Bridal Originals Ltd., $2 140 in full payment of account. Reference invoice #BO-1347.

- [ ] MasterCard Sales Invoice #1001
Dated Jan. 3/03
To Jocelyn Carnot (One-time customer)

one Miyaki matte organza/chapel train BG05	$1 400
two Lagar velvet/chiffon skirt/empire BMG02	225 each
one Veil: lace chapel w/pearl bead edge HV05	170
one pr Earrings: diamond studs AC03	200
three pr Shoes: peau-de-soie AC08	110 /pair
Goods & Services Tax	7.0%
Non-refundable Quebec Sales Tax	7.5%

Paid by MasterCard #6453 9104 6832 4015.

notes

Use QST Code D, QST @ 7.5%, not included for QST refundable purchases.

- [ ] Purchase Invoice #BT-804
Dated Jan. 3/03
From Beads & Threads, $200 for lace, sequins and other supplies for Deanne Demarais gown plus $14 GST and $16.05 refundable QST. Purchase invoice total $230.05. Terms: net 10 days.

- [ ] Purchase Invoice #VP-891
Dated Jan. 3/03
From Voiles de Paris, F8 500 for silk and satin fabrics required for Deanne Demarais gown plus F595 GST. Purchase invoice total F9 095. Terms: net 15 days. The exchange rate is 0.21136. These fabrics are duty free. (Duty is 0%.)

notes

Remember to use QST Code E, QST @ 7.5%, not included, non-refundable for sales. You will need to edit the code if a different code was used for the previous purchase or sale.

- [ ] Visa Sales Invoice #1002
Dated Jan. 5/03
To Simone Villeneuve (One-time customer)

one Vernet nat'l silk/lace w/sweep train BG11	$1 600
one Headband: silk satn rosettes HV03	50
four Rojas poly-satn drop waist skirt BMG04	160 each
one pr Earrings: pearl studs AC04	70
one Garter: blue, M AC06	30
Goods & Services Tax	7.0%
Non-refundable Quebec Sales Tax	7.5%

Paid by Visa #4510 5649 6152 5962.

- [ ] Cheque Copy #351
Dated Jan. 5/03
To Voiles de Paris, F3 040 in payment of account. Paid from account 1090 Bank: Foreign Currency Account. Reference invoice #VP-642. The exchange rate is 0.21136.

- [ ] Memo #2
Dated Jan. 7/03
Adjust inventory for one HV03 Headband: silk satn rosettes ripped on the display fixtures and damaged beyond repair. Charge to Damaged Inventory account.

SESSION DATE – January 14

> **notes**
> In the Add account wizard, click Yes for the option to budget the new account and enter $100 for each month.

- [ ] Cash Purchase Invoice #MS-314
Dated Jan. 8/03
From Montreal Sewing Centre (use Quick Add), $120 for servicing sewing machines and sergers plus $8.40 GST and $9.63 non-refundable QST (code E). Purchase invoice total $138.03. Paid by cheque #103. Create a new Group account, 5220 Maintenance & Repairs. Budget $100 per month for this expense.

> **notes**
> Allow inventory to drop below re-order point.

- [ ] Visa Sales Invoice #1003
Dated Jan. 8/03
To Renee Gilles (One-time customer)

one Ferrucci embr silk satn sheer slv BG03	$1 500
three Ferrucci velvet/satn fit/flare BMG01	250 each
one Rojas 2pce suit w/lace overlay MG04	225
one Garter: blue, S AC06	30
one Veil: tulle full asymetric scallopd HV07	150
Goods & Services Tax	7.0%
Non-refundable Quebec Sales Tax	7.5%

Paid by Visa #4502 3299 5373 2418.

- [ ] Cash Purchase Invoice #WB-13121
Dated Jan. 10/03
From Wedding Bells Magazine (use Quick Add), $200 for promotional ads plus $14 GST and $16.05 non-refundable QST. Purchase invoice total $230.05. Paid by cheque #104.

> **notes**
> Enter 10 in the Discount % field of the Terms section of the invoice. Refer to the Accounting Procedures for the Sales Discount.

- [ ] Visa Sales Invoice #1004
Dated Jan. 12/03
To Julie Therieaux (One-time customer)

one Ari empire line antique ivory lace BG01	$1 100
two Vernet short floral pattern skirt BMG06	150 each
one Vezeley pink crepe w/cord lace jckt MG07	190
three pr Shoes: leather AC08	110 /pair
three pr Stockings: lace almond AC10	15 /pair
Sales Discount	10.0%
Goods & Services Tax	7.0%
Non-refundable Quebec Sales Tax	7.5%

Paid by Visa #4610 8261 4577 3981.

- [ ] Cash Purchase Invoice #QH-67120
Dated Jan. 13/03
From Quebec Hydro, $100 for hydro service in store plus $7 GST and $8.03 non-refundable QST. Purchase invoice total $115.03. Paid by cheque #105.

- [ ] Cheque Copy #106
Dated Jan. 13/03
To Beads & Threads, $230.05 in full payment of account. Reference invoice #BT-804.

- [ ] Cheque Copy #352
Dated Jan. 13/03
To Voiles de Paris, F14 091.90 in full payment of account. Reference invoices #VP-793 and VP-891. Paid from account 1090. The exchange rate is 0.2114.

- [ ] Memo #3
Dated Jan. 13/03
Transfer F20 000 from Chequing Bank Account to Foreign Currency Account.

☐ Sales Invoice #1005
Dated Jan. 14/03
To Deanne Demarais, to fill sales order #101, $8 000 for completion of custom bridal gown, plus $560 GST and $642 QST. Sales invoice total $9 202. Terms: cash on receipt.

☐ Cash Receipt #3
Dated Jan. 14/03
From Deanne Demarais, cheque #58 for $7 202 in full payment of account. Reference invoice #1005 and deposit #1.

notes

Enter the payment for subcontracting work as an other payment.

☐ Memo #4
Dated Jan. 14/03
Paid cheque #107 for $500 to Kristin Couture for subcontracting work on Deanne Demarais gown.

SESSION DATE – January 21

☐ Purchase Invoice #BX-956
Dated Jan. 15/03
From Bridal Xpress Delivery, $60 for delivery of gowns and other inventory to customers, plus $4.20 GST and $4.82 non-refundable QST. Purchase invoice total $69.02. Terms: net 10 days.

notes

☐ Catherine Rothchild
is located at
62 Place De La Capricieuse
Montreal, QC H4J 6D2
Tel: (514) 838-3896
Fax: (514) 838-4021
Charge GST & QST

☐ Sales Order #102
Dated Jan. 15/03
Completion date Jan. 31/03
From Catherine Rothchild (use Full Add), custom-design full lace and organza gown with genuine pearl buttons and bead embroidery costing $10 000. Sales order total $11 502.50. Deposit of 25% required to confirm order. Balance to be paid on delivery.

☐ Cash Receipt #4
Dated Jan. 15/03
From Catherine Rothchild, cheque #385 for $2 500 for deposit #2 on custom-design gown to confirm sales order #102.

☐ Cash Purchase Invoice #BQ-13459
Dated Jan. 16/03
From Bell Quebec, $68 for telephone services plus $4.76 GST and $5.46 non-refundable QST. Purchase invoice total $78.22. Issued cheque #108.

☐ Purchase Invoice #BT-1022
Dated Jan. 16/03
From Beads & Threads, $250 for pearls, beads and other supplies for Catherine Rothchild gown, plus $17.50 GST and $20.06 refundable QST. Purchase Invoice total $287.56. Terms: net 10 days.

☐ Purchase Invoice #VP-1205
Dated Jan. 18/03
From Voiles de Paris, F11 350 for organza and lace fabrics required for Catherine Rothchild gown, plus F794.50 GST. Purchase invoice total F12 144.50. Terms: net 15 days. These fabrics are duty free. The exchange rate is 0.21133.

❑ MasterCard Sales Invoice #1006
Dated Jan. 19/03
To Genevieve Thibault (One-time customer)

one Vasari silk satn roses/cathed train BG10	$2 500
one Veil: lace cath embroid w/sequins HV04	200
one pr Shoes: satin AC08	110
one pr Earrings: diamond studs AC03	200
one Cape: velvet full length AC02	800
Goods & Services Tax	7.0%
Non-refundable Quebec Sales Tax	7.5%

Paid by MasterCard #5319 6492 3880 4765.

❑ Visa Sales Invoice #1007
Dated Jan. 20/03
To Monique Ranier (One-time customer)

one Shijo silk satn slvless/prl bodice BG09	$1 250
four Shijo crepe sweetheart neckline BMG05	180 each
four pr Shoes: leather AC08	110 /pair
four pr Earrings: pearl tear drop AC05	110 /pair
four pr Stockings: sheer white AC09	10 /pair
Goods & Services Tax	7.0%
Non-refundable Quebec Sales Tax	7.5%

Paid by Visa #4300 7332 1591 8386.

SESSION DATE – January 28

❑ Visa Sales Invoice #1008
Dated Jan. 25/03
To Andree Villone (One-time customer)

one Raffaelli full tulle/basque waist BG07	$1 000
four Rojas poly-satn drop waist skirt BMG04	160 each
one Raffaelli gold khaki gown w/lace MG03	175
five pr Shoes: peau de soie AC08	110 /pair
one Hat: sheer organza w/silk bow HV02	150
Goods & Services Tax	7.0%
Non-refundable Quebec Sales Tax	7.5%

Paid by Visa #4510 4117 1281 5137.

❑ Cheque Copy #109
Dated Jan. 25/03
To Bridal Xpress Delivery, $69.02 in full payment of account. Reference invoice #BX-956.

❑ Sales Invoice #1009
Dated Jan. 28/03
To Catherine Rothchild, to fill sales order #102, $10 000 for completion of custom bridal gown, plus $700 GST and $802.50 QST. Sales invoice total $11 502.50. Terms: cash on receipt.

❑ Cash Receipt #5
Dated Jan. 28/03
From Catherine Rothchild, cheque #481 for $9 002.50 in full payment of account. Reference invoice #1009 and deposit #2.

- [ ] Purchase Invoice #VP-1793
Dated Jan. 28/03
From Voiles de Paris

No.	Item	Amount (FRF)	Duty %
6	Muffs: imitation fur AC07	760.00 F	15.5%
	GST Paid @ 7%	53.20 F	
	Invoice Total	813.20 F	
	Import Duties	117.80 F	
	Freight included in item prices.		

Terms: net 15.
All amounts in French francs. The exchange rate is 0.21137.

- [ ] Memo #5
Dated Jan. 28/03
Issue cheque #110 for $24.90 to the Receiver General to pay the duty owing for purchase from Voiles de Paris (F117.80).

SESSION DATE – January 31

- [ ] Purchase Invoice #BX-1021
Dated Jan. 29/03
From Bridal Xpress Delivery, $60 for delivery of gowns and other inventory to customers, plus $4.20 GST and $4.82 non-refundable QST. Purchase invoice total $69.02. Terms: net 10 days.

notes

Enter the payment for subcontracting work as a cash purchase.

- [ ] Memo #6
Dated Jan. 30/03
Paid cheque #111 for $500 to Kamala Srivina (use Quick Add) for subcontracting work on Catherine Rothchild gown.

- [ ] Bank Debit Memo #6432193
Dated Jan. 31/03
For monthly bank service charges on chequing account, $30.

- [ ] Bank Debit Memo #6432194
Dated Jan. 31/03
For mortgage payment, $850 withdrawn from chequing account, including $765 for interest and $85 for reduction of principal.

- [ ] Bank Credit Memo #3214721
Dated Jan. 31/03
For interest on bank account and securities, $625 deposited to chequing account.

- [ ] Memo #7
Dated Jan. 31/03
Prepare payroll for Sylvie Couturier. Couturier earned $4 500 in commissions for custom design and tailoring work. Issue cheque #112.

- [ ] Memo #8
Dated Jan. 31/03
Prepare adjusting entry for $70 prepaid insurance expired in January.

- [ ] Memo #9
Dated Jan. 31/03
From owner: Make entries to record the following adjustments:
Physical count shows the following inventory on hand

Fabrics	$2 800
Dressmaking Supplies	$800
Store Supplies	$500

notes

Refer to Updating Budgets in the Keystrokes section on page 406.

- [x] Memo #7 **406**
Dated Jan. 31/03
From owner: Increase all revenue budget amounts by 10% to allow for expected increases in sales as a result of the closing of a nearby competitor.

KEYSTROKES

Setting up Budgets

It is important for a business to gauge its performance against some standards. These standards can be provided through comparisons with other companies that are in the same kind of business or by comparing the same company over several time periods. It is common for a business to set goals for future performance based on the past. For example, there may be an expectation that profits will increase by 10 percent over the previous year or that expenses will be reduced because of the introduction of new cost-reduction methods. If a business waits until the end of the year to assess its progress towards its goals, it may be too late to make necessary corrections if things are not proceeding according to plan. Budgets serve this purpose of offering a realistic financial plan for the future that can be used as a standard for assessing performance.

Before analyzing a budget report, you must turn on the option and enter the budget amounts for the relevant accounts.

Turning on the Budgeting Feature

Open the data files for Bonnie Brides. Do not advance the session date until you have finished the budget setup.

version 8

Choose the **Setup menu**, then **choose System Settings** and **click Settings**.

Click the **General tab** in the Settings window to display the following setup options for the General Ledger:

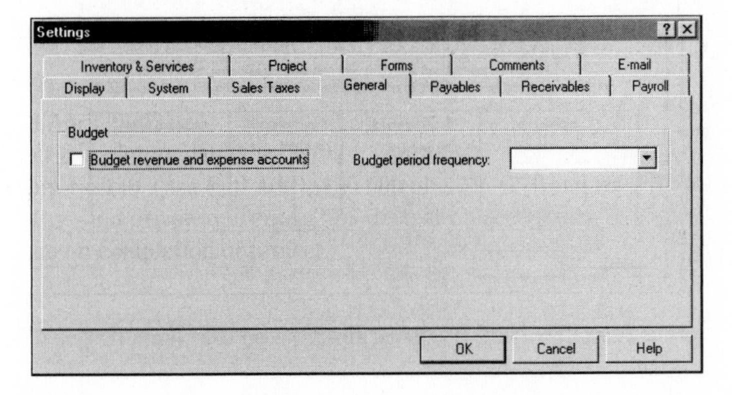

Click Budget revenue and expense accounts to turn on the budgeting feature.

The first decision after choosing the budgeting feature involves a budget period. Whether a business chooses to budget amounts on a yearly, quarterly or monthly basis depends on the needs and nature of the business. Monthly budget reports will be appropriate if the business cycle of buying and selling is short but not appropriate if long-term projects are involved. The period chosen must provide meaningful feedback about performance. If the periods are too short, there may be insufficient information to judge performance; if the periods are too long, there may be no opportunity to correct problems because they are not detected soon enough. Bonnie Brides will use monthly budget periods, at least initially, because Bonnie Brioche wants frequent progress reports.

Click the **Budget period frequency field** to see the period options:

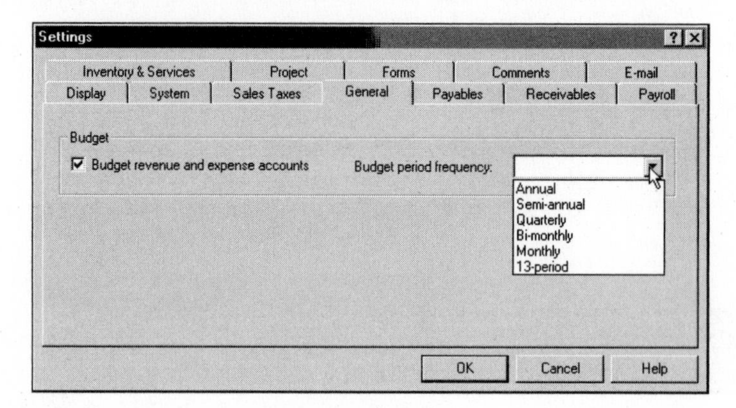

Click Monthly

Click OK to return to the Home window and save the settings.

Setting a Budget

The next step is to enter the budget amounts for all expense and revenue accounts.

Budgets can be determined in several different ways. The most common methods are zero-based and incremental budgeting. With the zero-based method, a forecast is made for each revenue and expense account based on expectations about specific planned activities and expenditures. Each budget item must usually be justified. More commonly, last year's budgets and income statements are used as the starting point and a specific percentage change is included. Thus, a company might expect to improve its performance over last year by 5 percent, either by increasing sales or by decreasing expenses. Planned special events such as annual month-long sales, new customer drives, peak holiday periods or slow periods for the product can be built into the changes in budgeted amounts from one period to the next. Whatever method is used, it is important that the budget be realistic.

Bonnie Brioche's approach is to examine her previous income statements and business practices to see where she can make improvements and get a realistic forecast. She has observed that her business is growing at about 10 percent per year. The corresponding expenses, sales discounts, cost of goods sold, and so on will also increase by the same amount. Sales are not divided evenly throughout the 12-month period. Most brides purchase their gowns about six months before the wedding date, and spring and summer are the most popular choices for weddings. This results in January and February being the busiest months for the shop, followed by March through June in preparation for fall through holiday season weddings.

This pattern has led Brioche to expect 15 percent of her year's sales to occur each month in January and February, 10 percent each month in March through June, and 5 percent each month in July through December. Her addition of custom-design dresses is based on her best guess, taking into account the seasonal pattern. Her estimate of 12 gowns per year is a conservative one, but she does not want to promise her cousin work that she cannot deliver. During the busiest months, she expects to use assistants to complete the work in a timely fashion.

Her detailed forecast is presented in the following chart:

BONNIE BRIDES
BUDGET FORECAST FOR 2003

	12 Months	Jan–Feb each month	Mar–Jun each month	Jul–Dec each month
Revenue				
Revenue from Sales	$122 000	$18 300	$12 200	$ 6 100
Sales Discount	−1 220	−183	−122	−61
Revenue from Design	108 000	16 200	10 800	5 400
Interest Revenue	7 500	625	625	625
Total Revenue	$236 280	$34 942	$23 503	$12 064
Expenses				
Advertising & Promotion	$ 2 400	$ 200	$ 200	$ 200
Exchange Rate Differences	0	0	0	0
Bank Charges & Card Fees	600	50	50	50
Cost of Goods Sold	61 000	9 150	6 100	3 050
Fabrics Used	27 000	4 050	2 700	1 350
Dressmaking Supplies Used	5 400	810	540	270
Damaged Inventory	1 220	183	122	61
Delivery Expense	600	90	60	30
Freight Expense	600	90	60	30
Hydro Expense	1 320	110	110	110
Insurance Expense	840	70	70	70
Interest Expense	9 600	800	800	800
Store Supplies Used	1 500	125	125	125
Telephone Expense	900	75	75	75
Commissions	27 000	4 050	2 700	1 350
EI Expense	800	120	80	40
WCB Expense	1 040	156	104	52
QPP Expense	850	127	86	42
QHSF Expense	1 200	180	120	60
Subcontractors' Fees	1 600	800	0	0
Total Expense	$145 470	$21 236	$14 102	$ 7 765
Net Income	$ 90 810	$13 706	$ 9 401	$ 4 299

She has based these amounts on the following estimates for the year's activities:

Sales: January 15% of sales, February 15%, March 10%, April 10%, May 10%, June 10%, July 5%, August 5%, September 5%, October 5%, November 5%, December 5%
Sales Revenue: increase by 10% over previous year
Sales Discount: expect about 1% on average, most sales are not discounted
Revenue from Design: make 12 dresses at an average price of $9 000
Interest Revenue: constant monthly income, same as previous year
Cost of Goods Sold: 50% of net sales
Damaged Inventory: 2% of Cost of Goods Sold

Delivery and Freight: average at about 1% of sales
Fabrics Used: mostly for custom-made gowns — estimated at 25% of finished price
Dressmaking Supplies Used: some for alterations, most for custom-made gowns — estimated at 5% of finished price of gowns (Revenue from Design)
Commissions: pay 25% of finished price of gowns (Revenue from Design)
EI, QPP, WCB and QHSF: straight percentage of commissions
Subcontractors' Fees: assistance with four gowns at $400 each, Jan. and Feb. only
Interest Expense: small decrease each year as loan principal is reduced
Bank Charges & Card Fees: increase over last year for credit card fees
Exchange Rate Differences: these are expected to cancel each other over time
Other Expenses: constant each month, no change over last year

notes

Remember that QPP replaces CPP for Quebec.

Entering Budget Amounts in the General Ledger

Click the **Find record button** in the Home window to open the Select Record Type window with Accounts selected as the record type:

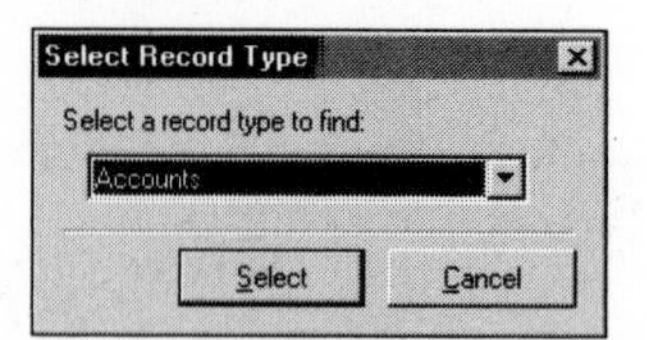

notes

- You can also click the Accounts icon in the Home window and then double click the account to open the ledger record.
- If a ledger is selected when you click the Find button, the list of records for that ledger will be displayed immediately.

Click **Select** to open the list of accounts in the General Ledger:

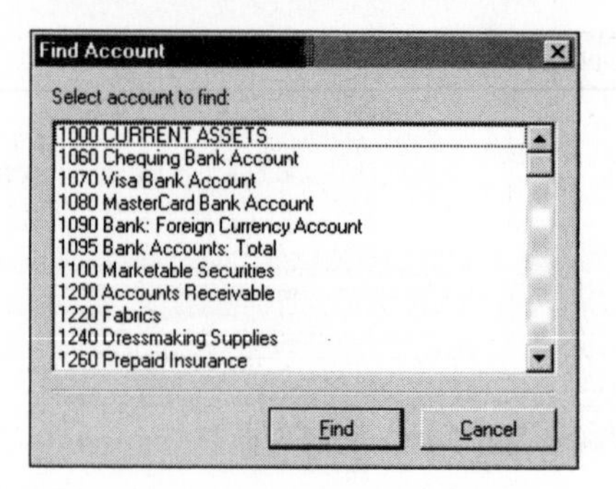

Scroll down the list to see the 4000-level Revenue accounts.

Click **4020 Revenue from Sales** to highlight this first postable revenue account.

Click **Find** to open the account ledger window as shown:

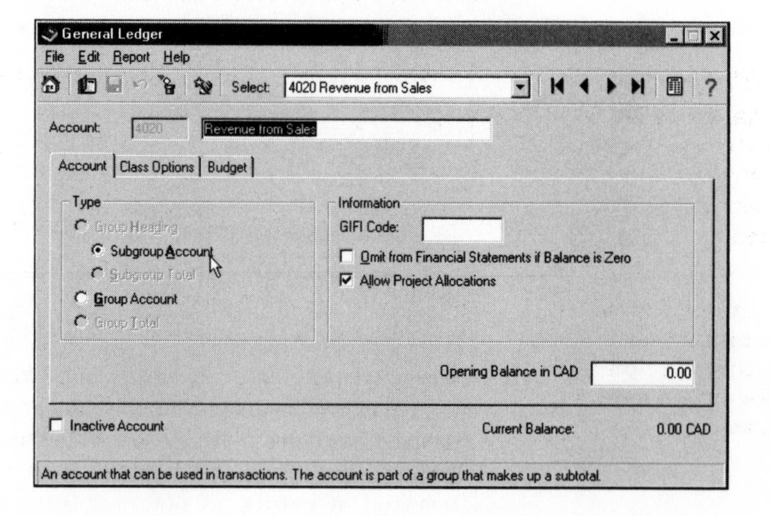

Because we turned on the Budgeting feature in the General Settings window, a tab has been added for budgeting. This tab will appear only for postable revenue and expense accounts.

notes

- Refer to the chart on page 403 for budget amounts.
- For each revenue and expense, you may choose to add budget amounts or not. Of course, the most meaningful budget reports come from including budget details for all accounts.

Click the **Budget tab** to reveal the Budget option button as shown:

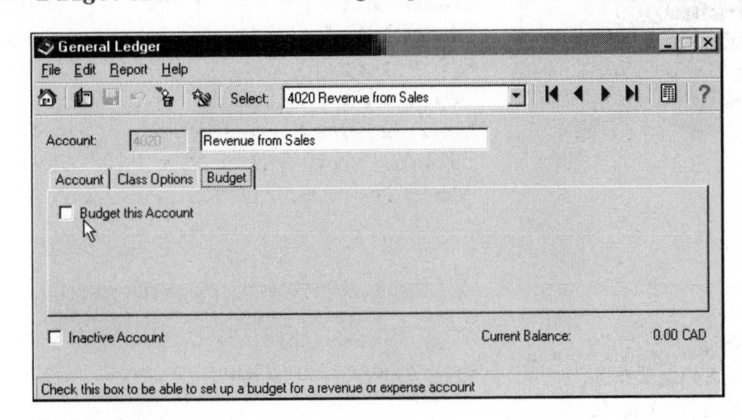

notes

You can change the budget frequency at any time in the General Settings window. The program will re-allocate the previously budgeted amounts proportionately for the new periods after warning you that this will be done and giving you a chance to confirm that you want to proceed.

Click **Budget this Account** to open the Budget amount fields as shown:

General Ledger
File Edit Report Help
Select: 4020 Revenue from Sales
Account: 4020 Revenue from Sales
Account | Class Options | Budget
Budget this Account — Total budgeted amount: 0.00 — Allocate

January	0.00	May	0.00	September	0.00
February	0.00	June	0.00	October	0.00
March	0.00	July	0.00	November	0.00
April	0.00	August	0.00	December	0.00

Inactive Account — Current Balance: 0.00 CAD
The revenue or expense you expect for the indicated period

The budget periods displayed at this stage match the period frequency selected in the setup stage. Because we selected Monthly, a 12-month calendar is given, beginning with the first month of the fiscal year as entered in the company setup window. If we had selected Quarterly, four input fields would be provided. You can enter the budget amounts for one period or for more, if the information is available. For Bonnie Brides, we will enter the amounts for each month as determined earlier.

notes

- Remember to enter negative budget amounts for accounts that decrease the total in a Group or Section (e.g., Sales Discount).
- You can use the copy and paste commands (Edit menu) to copy amounts from one field to another and save some data entry time.

Click the **January field** to select the amount.

Type 18300

Press *tab*

The cursor advances to the February field and highlights the entry for editing.

Enter the amounts for the remaining 11 months according to the budget forecast on page 403 by typing the amount and pressing *tab* to move to the next month. The Total budgeted amount is updated continually as you enter amounts for each period.

If the amounts for each period are equal, you can enter the Total budgeted amount and then click Allocate to divide the amounts evenly among all budget periods. For example, for Interest Revenue, enter 7500 as the Total budgeted amount, and click Allocate to have 625 entered as the budget amount for each month.

notes

When you enter the individual monthly amounts, use the Total budgeted amount to check your work. It should equal the budget amount for 12 months.

When you have entered the amounts for each month,

Click the **Next button** ▶ to advance to the next revenue account in the budget tab screen.

Budget amounts can be updated if needed based on feedback from earlier budget reports. They should not, of course, be changed without good reason.

Continue to enter budget information for the remaining revenue and expense accounts by following the steps outlined above. Use the amounts determined previously for each account in the chart on page 403.

Close the account information window.

Updating Budget Amounts

If you discover that your budget forecasts are incorrect, you can update the amounts in two ways:

1. editing the amounts individually for each account, repeating the process described above for entering initial budget amounts
2. globally updating all amounts by a fixed percentage

To update the amounts globally, **choose** the **Maintenance menu** in the Home window and **click Update Budget Amounts**. You will see the following Update Budget window:

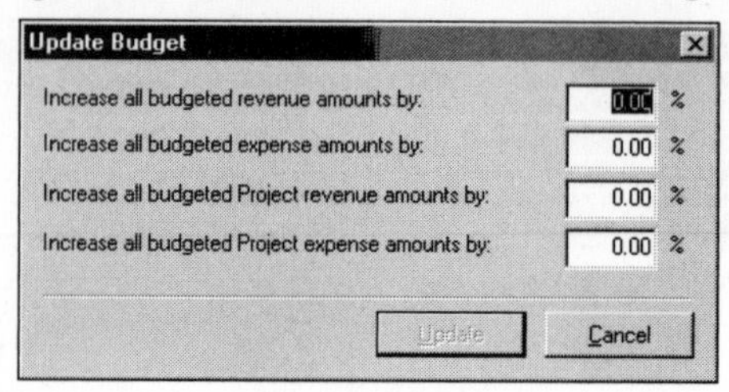

You can change the budgets for revenue and expense accounts separately. **Type** the **percentage change** that you want to apply, typing a negative number for decreases. You can change project revenue and expense amounts by a different percentage. **Click Update** to apply the change. The screen that follows asks you to confirm that you want to update the budget. **Click Yes** to apply the changes and return to the Home window. When you review the account's budget information in the account ledger, you will see that the change has been applied.

You can also change the budget frequency in the General Ledger Settings screen. For example, to change the period from monthly to quarterly, **choose** the **Setup menu**, then **choose System Settings** and **click Settings**. **Click** the **General tab**. Then **choose Quarterly** from the frequency drop-down list and **click OK**.

notes

When you have a quarterly budget with different amounts for each quarter and you change the frequency to monthly, each month will have the same budget amount, the total for the four quarters divided by 12. You must edit the amounts if these are incorrect.

Before applying the new budget settings, Simply Accounting shows you the following warning each time you change a budget frequency:

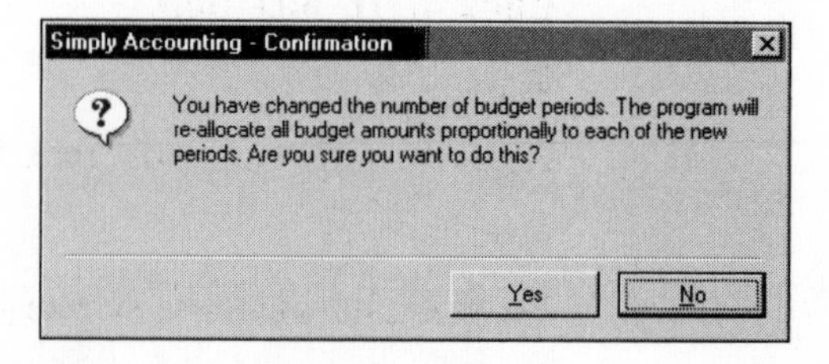

The statement warns that previous budget amounts will be reallocated evenly among the new number of periods. Thus each quarter will have the same budget amount.

Click No to cancel the change.

Import Duties on Foreign Purchases

Import duties are usually applied by governments to encourage the local economy by raising the price of imported goods. Duty rates or tariffs vary from one type of item to another. The duty is collected by Canada Customs and Revenue Agency when the goods enter Canada, before they are released to the buyer.

notes

GST on imported goods is collected by CCRA at the same time as the import duties. This would require a separate cash payment to CCRA and the amount would not appear in GST reports. For the sake of simplicity, we indicate that foreign vendors collect GST.

In Simply Accounting, before you can enter duty amounts with the purchase, you must set up the company files for charging and tracking import duties. You must also indicate in the foreign vendor's record that duty is applied to purchases from that vendor. In the inventory ledger records, you can enter the duty applied as a percentage, or enter the rates in the Purchases Journal.

The first purchase invoice from a foreign vendor has import duties applied because Canada does not have a free trade agreement with France. The data files for Bonnie Brides already contain these changes.

Change the session date to January 7 if you have not already done so.

Click the **Purchases Journal icon** Purchases, Orders & Quotes to open the Purchases Journal.

Choose **Voiles de Paris** from the list of vendors to see the modified journal:

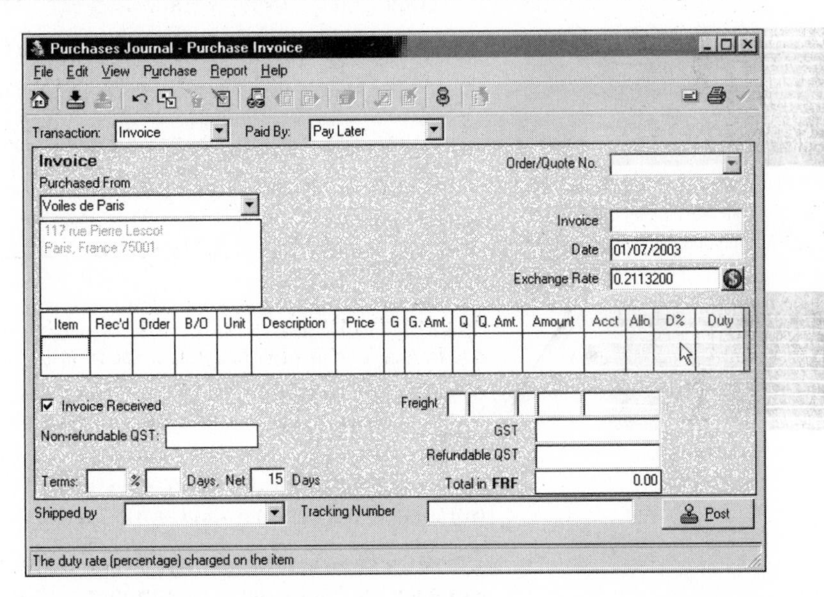

In addition to the exchange rate field and the indication that French franc (FRF) is the currency for this vendor, two new columns appear in the journal to the right of the Allo column — one for the duty percentage and one for the amount. You may need to scroll to the right to see these columns, or drag the right-hand side invoice frame.

Click the **Invoice field**.

Type `VP-793`

Press tab to move to the Date field.

Type `1 2`

Press tab to open the Exchange Rate screen with the most recent rate highlighted.

Type `0.2114`

Click **Make this the default rate for 01/02/2003**

Click **OK** to return to the journal.

notes

Notice that the inventory list is sorted by item description rather than by item number for Bonnie Brides.

version 8

Double click the **Item field** to open the Select Inventory & Services screen.

Double click Hats: ostrich w/chenille dot veil to add this item to the invoice as shown:

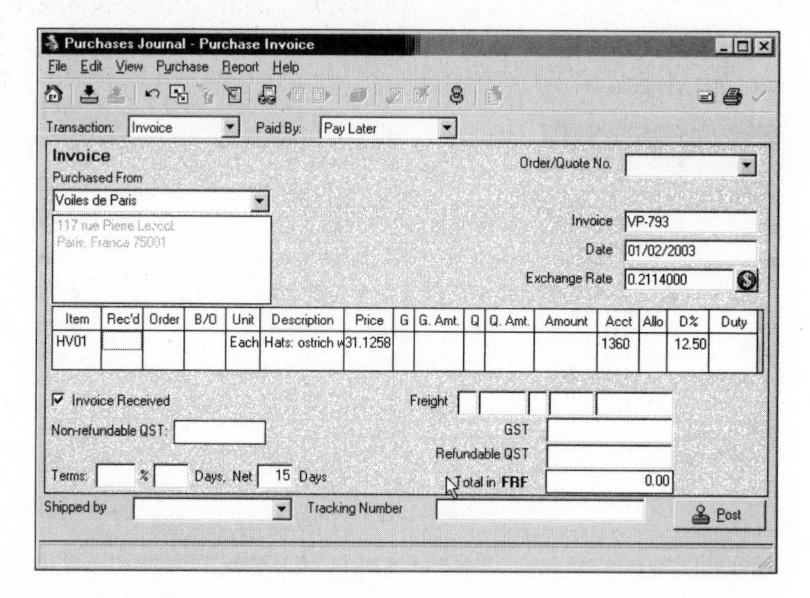

notes

For non-inventory purchases that have duty applied, click the D% field and type the duty rate as a percentage directly in the journal on the appropriate invoice line. If no duty is charged, leave the duty fields blank.

Notice that the D% field has 12.50 as its entry. This information is stored in the ledger record as the percentage duty that is applied to these kinds of products. The rate will be multiplied by the Amount to determine the duty amount. You can edit the rate, or if the field is blank because the rate is not stored with the inventory ledger, you can enter the correct rate directly in the journal. The cursor should be in the Rec'd field.

Type 2

Press *tab* to add the Amount for the item based on cost information on record, and the Duty amount. We need to add the GST code because GST is applied to the purchase. We also need to change the amount.

Click the **G field**.

Type 3

All amounts are entered in French francs. The default amount is incorrect for this purchase so you should change it.

Click the **Amount field**.

Type 600

Press *tab* to update the totals and the duty amounts.

Enter the remaining items purchased. You can maximize the journal window to create space for more invoice lines, or you can drag the lower frame of the journal down to lengthen the invoice window so that you can see all the items purchased at the same time. As you enter the items, notice that the duty rates vary for the different items. These different rates are stored in the inventory ledger records.

When you have entered all the items, your finished journal should look like the following:

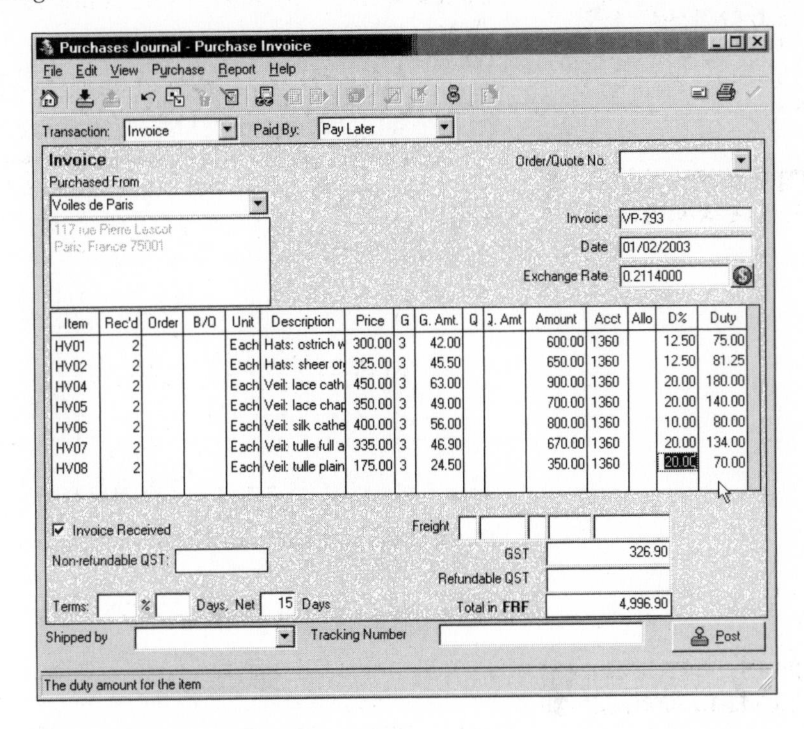

You should review the journal entry before proceeding.

Choose the **Report menu** and **click Display Purchases Journal Entry**:

Purchases Journal Entry

01/02/2003 (J1)	Foreign Amt.	Debits	Credits	Project
1360 Hats and Veils	F5,430.32	1,147.97	-	
2670 GST Paid On Purchases	F326.90	69.11	-	
2200 Accounts Payable	F4,996.90	-	1,056.34	
2240 Import Duties	F760.25	-	160.72	
5030 Exchange Rate Differences	-	-	0.02	
		1,217.08	1,217.08	

1 French Franc equals 0.2114000 Canadian Dollar

notes

The Exchange Rate Difference linked account tracks rounding errors as well as differences arising from fluctuating exchange rates between the time of purchase and payment. Refer to page 322 to see the screen for defining and setting up this linked account.

The journal entry differs from the standard purchase in several important details. The journal shows amounts in both Canadian dollars and French francs. The linked *Exchange Rate Differences* account has an amount because of rounding off from the exchange rate's four or more decimals to two for the actual dollar amount. The total duty amount for all items is credited to the *Import Duties* linked account. This liability account is credited because the amount of the duty is added (debited) to the inventory asset amount and the duty amount must be paid to the Receiver General. The total of the Amounts on the invoice is F4 670. The debit to the linked Hats and Veils account, F5 430 includes the import duties — F4 670 plus F760 (with an allowance for rounding differences). The amount owing to the vendor and credited to *Accounts Payable* does not include the amount for import duties because duties are collected by CCRA and not by the vendor.

Close the display when you have finished to return to the journal.

Make corrections if necessary.

Post the entry when it is correct. **Close** the Purchases Journal.

Enter the payment of import duties to the Receiver General in the Payments Journal.

Budget Reports

The effective use of budget reports involves more than merely observing whether budgeted targets were met or not. Sometimes more information is gained when targets are not met, because the differences can lead to asking important questions:

- Were the targets realistic? What items were not on target and why?
- If performance exceeds the targets, how can we repeat the success?
- If performance did not meet the targets, were there factors that we failed to anticipate?
- Should we revise future budgets based on the new information?

In other words, the problem-solving cycle is set in motion. Even an Income Statement that is on target should be reviewed carefully. There may be room for improvements if the budget was a conservative estimate. There may be new information that will affect future performance that was unknown when the budget was drawn up.

Displaying Budget Reports

Choose the **Reports menu** in the Home window, then **choose Financials** and **click Income Statement** to display the Income Statement options window.

Click the **Report Type field**:

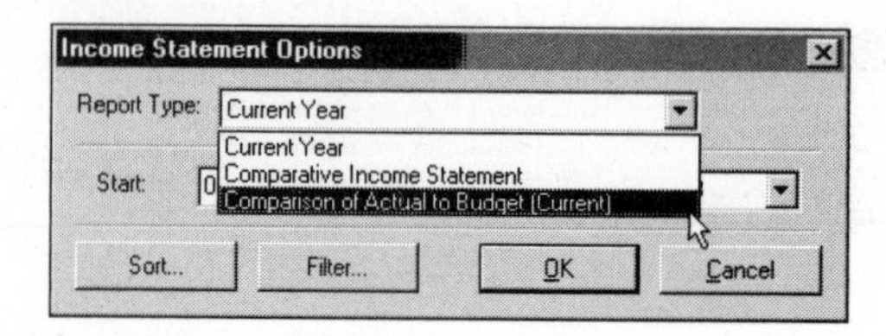

A budget-related option has been added in the Report Type drop-down list.

Click Comparison of Actual to Budget to select this option and open the Report on list of reports with budget reports added.

Click the **Report on field** to show the types of budget reports in the drop-down list as follows:

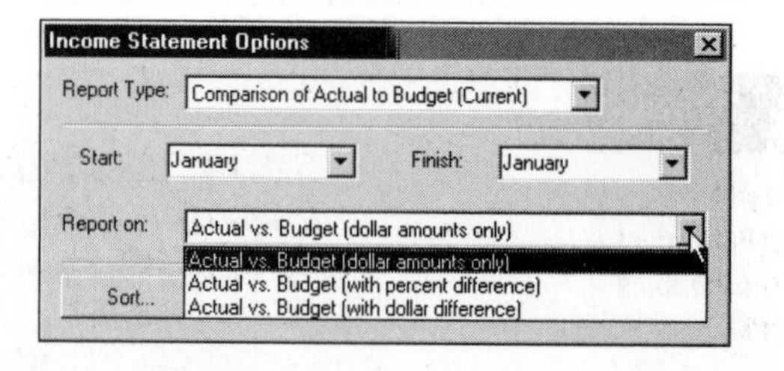

notes

Cost of Goods Sold will increase directly with sales, so positive differences can mean either improved sales or higher costs.

Three types of reports are available. The first, Actual vs. Budget (dollar amounts only), lists the amounts that were budgeted for the revenue and expense accounts for the period indicated and the revenues and expenses actually obtained for the same period. The second, Actual vs. Budget (with percent difference), gives these two amounts as well as the percentage that the actual amount is above or below the budgeted amount. The third option, Actual vs. Budget (with dollar difference) provides the same two base amounts, budget and actual, as well as the difference between them as a dollar amount.

For the dollar difference and the percent difference reports, a positive difference means that the budget was exceeded, a negative difference indicates that the results came in under budget. Remember that for revenues, a positive difference means results were better than expected, but for expenses, a positive difference means that results were poorer than expected (expenses were higher than budgeted).

Click the **budget report** you want.

Close the display when finished.

Printing Budget Reports

Display the report you want to print.

Choose the **File menu** in the report window and **click Print**.

Close the displayed report when you are finished.

Graphing Budget Reports

When the Budgeting option is activated and set up, two additional graphs are available from the Graphs menu, Sales vs Budget and Expenses vs Budget.

Sales vs Budget Graphs

Choose the **Graphs menu** in the Home window and **click Sales vs Budget** to display the set of revenue accounts:

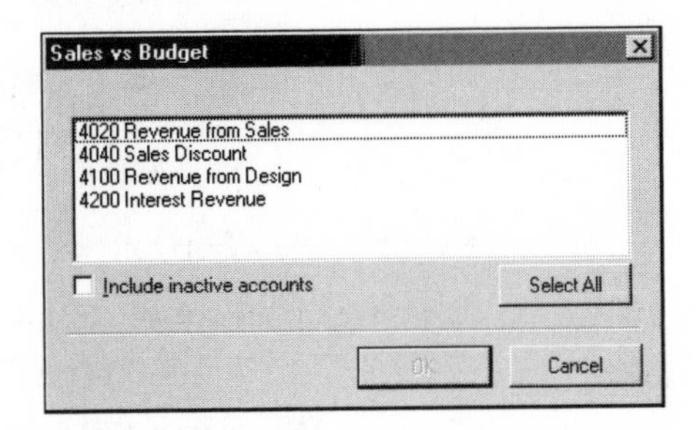

Press ctrl and **click** the **accounts** you want to include in the graph or **click Select All**.

Click OK to display the bar chart graph:

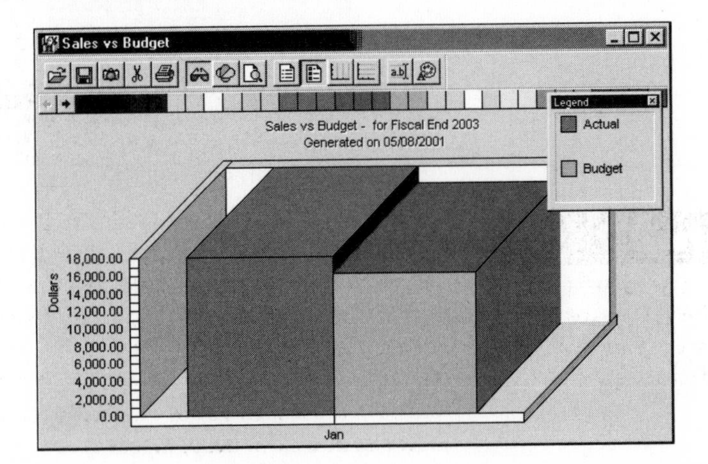

notes

The options for displaying, editing, printing, copying budget graphs, and so on, are the same as those for other graphs.

The displayed graph includes the *Revenue from Sales* and the *Revenue from Design* accounts before the 10 percent budget increase at the end of the January. The amounts for the two revenue accounts are added together in the single bar labelled

Actual. The other bar represents the budgeted amount for the two accounts together. Revenue was higher than expected, suggesting improved performance.

Close the displayed graph when you have finished.

Expenses vs Budget Graphs

Choose the **Graphs menu** in the Home window and **click Expenses vs Budget** to display the set of expense accounts:

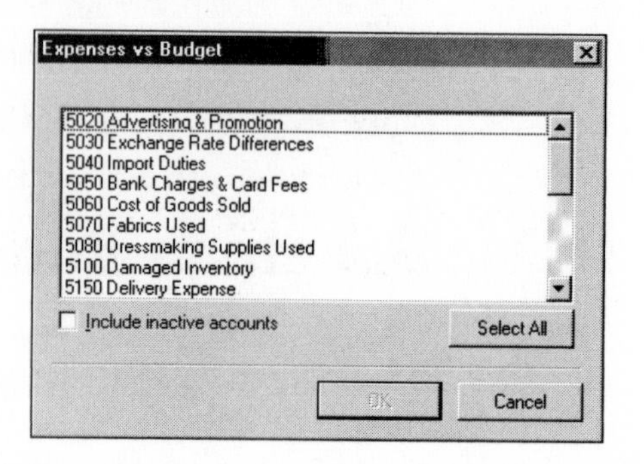

Press ctrl and **click** the **accounts** you want to include in the graph or **click Select All**.

Click OK to display the bar chart graph:

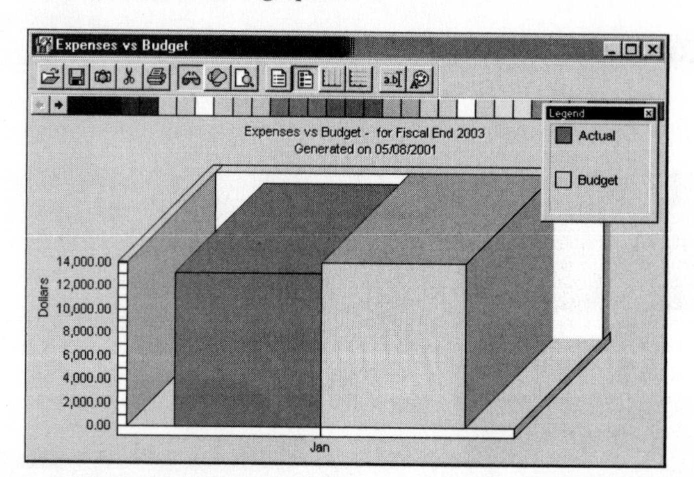

The displayed graph includes three expense accounts, *Cost of Goods Sold*, *Fabrics Used* and *Dressmaking Supplies Used*, at the end of January. The expense accounts are added together in the bar labelled Actual. The second bar represents the budgeted amount for the three accounts. The graph shows that expenses were lower than expected, supporting the trend in revenue graph for better performance.

Close the displayed graph when finished.

CASE PROBLEMS

Case One

At the end of February, a custom-made gown costing $8 000 was completed but not picked up by the customer. Inquiries revealed that she had cancelled her wedding plans and did not intend to take possession of her dress, even though the store reminded her that her $2 000 deposit was not refundable.

1. How should the store record the accounting transactions for this situation?
2. How should Brioche process the inventory setup for the special item?
3. What factors should Brioche consider in setting the selling price for the special-order gown? For example, would the dress size and style of the gown influence the pricing decision in any way?

Case Two

At the end of February, Bonnie Brioche printed her monthly Income Statement. Individual items that differed by more than 10 percent from her updated budget forecasts are shown in the following Income Statement. Items that did not differ from the forecast are combined into the Other Expenses category. (All amounts are rounded to the nearest $10.)

SUMMARY OF EXCEPTIONAL BUDGET ITEMS – FEBRUARY 2003

	Actual	Budget
Revenue		
Revenue from Sales	$24 000	$20 130
Sales Discount	-50	-200
Revenue from Design	27 500	17 820
Interest Revenue	430	690
Total Revenue	$51 880	$38 440
Operating Expenses		
Bank Charges & Card Fees	$ 850	$ 50
Cost of Goods Sold	14 400	9 150
Fabrics Used	6 750	4 050
Dressmaking Supplies Used	1 400	810
Delivery Expense	240	90
Commissions	6 880	4 050
Other Payroll Expenses	940	580
Subcontractors' Fees	1 620	800
Other Expenses	1 760	1 740
Total Expenses	$34 840	$21 320
Net Income	$17 040	$17 120

Explain some of the reasons why these differences may have occurred. You may want to review the rationale notes for the preliminary budget on pages 403–404.

CHAPTER THIRTEEN

Hearth House

OBJECTIVES

After completing this chapter, you should be able to

- *plan* and *design* an accounting system for a small business
- *prepare* procedures for converting from a manual system
- *understand* the objectives of a computerized system
- *create* company files
- *set up* company accounts
- *prepare* files for foreign currency transactions and importing goods
- *identify* preferred customers for reduced prices
- *enter* preferred customer prices and import duty rates for inventory
- *finish* entering the accounting history for all modules
- *insert* new accounts, vendors, customers and employees as required
- *create* new projects as required
- *export* reports
- *use* spreadsheets for analyzing, planning and decision making
- *enter* transactions that result in inventory variances
- *enter* end-of-accounting-period adjustments
- *perform* end-of-accounting-period closing routines
- *analyze* and *interpret* case studies
- *develop* further group interpersonal skills
- *develop* further oral and written skills

INTRODUCTION

This application provides a complete accounting cycle for a merchandising business. It is a comprehensive application covering a three-month fiscal period. You will use Simply Accounting to convert a manual accounting system to a computerized accounting system and then enter transactions for each month. The routines in this application are part of the demands of many small businesses, so you should find them useful. The information in this application reflects the business realities in Ontario in 2001.

You may substitute information relevant to other provinces or the latest payroll and tax regulations wherever it is appropriate to do so. Rules for the application of the federal Goods and Services Tax (GST), provincial sales taxes and payroll may vary from one province to another.

Because of the length of the application, instructions for working with the source documents are presented with those documents, on page 469.

notes

Because of the length of the Hearth House application, group work is encouraged in setting up error-free company files and completing the transactions.

COMPANY INFORMATION

Company Profile

Hearth House, owned by Amber Ashe, is situated in the Beaches area of Toronto. Ashe has built up her business steadily since graduating from Ryerson, beginning with freelance contract work installing and renovating all types of fireplaces. She opened her retail business two years ago, selling a variety of fireplaces and related products and providing design consultation and installation services for her customers.

Most of the customers for Hearth House own homes and are adding a fireplace or want to replace existing woodburning fireplaces with the newer, cleaner, more efficient gas-burning units. People frequently install more than one fireplace in their homes. These homeowners pay cash on delivery of the fireplace or on completion of the installation. In addition, Hearth House installs fireplaces in the lobbies and lounges of clubs, apartment buildings and other businesses. These customers, who have accounts with Hearth House, can take a 1 percent discount if they settle their account within five days. Full payment is requested in 10 days. Those who are preferred customers pay discounted prices for goods as well.

notes

Hearth House is located at
44 Warmley Road
Toronto, Ontario M6R 2P6
Phone: (416) 589-9121
Fax: (416) 589-9000
Business No.: 20736 5818

Hearth House has credit accounts with several suppliers of fireplaces, related products and other business supplies. Some of these suppliers offer discounts for early payment. Other vendors that Hearth House deals with on a regular cash basis are also included in the list of vendors.

Amber Ashe has three full-time employees to assist her: the manager helps with contract negotiations and supervises store sales and installation work; the installer, an experienced gas-fitter, completes most of the installation work and is assisted by the manager on difficult projects; the store assistant handles store sales and accounting work. Ashe is still active in her business but mostly with design consultation, purchases and contract negotiations. If there is additional work that the current staff cannot complete or that requires special skills, Hearth House will subcontract to another installer, a former employee who now works independently.

Ashe wanted to computerize her accounting records and asked the manager and store assistant to research the available software. They recommended Simply Accounting for Windows, outlining their reasons in the following report.

MANAGER'S REPORT

1. Using Simply Accounting would allow the business to process all source documents in a timely fashion. It would automatically prepare both single-period and comparative accounting reports for planning, making decisions and controlling operations within the business.
2. The software would eliminate some of the time-consuming clerical functions that are performed manually. For example, it can automatically prepare invoices, cheques and statements, and it can perform all the necessary arithmetic calculations. Being freed from these chores, the accountant could extend his or her role to assume a much higher level of responsibility. For example, the accountant would have more time to spend analyzing reports with the owner and could work more directly with the owner in making business decisions.
3. Simply Accounting can easily export reports to spreadsheets for further analysis or link with the Internet, with other software programs and with vendors and customers for interactive data exchange. When combined with the graphing, account reconciliation and budgeting features, these reports would permit the owner to analyze past trends and to make better predictions about the future behaviour of the business.
4. As the business grows, the manager could divide work more meaningfully among new accounting personnel. Since Simply Accounting provides subsidiary ledgers that are linked to control accounts in the General Ledger, it could automatically coordinate accounting work performed by different individuals. Customizable window backgrounds could even accommodate mood changes of the different users.
5. It would allow the owner to exercise business controls in a number of areas:

In General

- Access to confidential accounting records and editing capability can be restricted to authorized personnel by using passwords.
- Mechanical errors can be virtually eliminated, since journal transactions with unequal debits and credits cannot be posted. Customer, vendor, employee, inventory and jobcost names appear in full on the journal entry input forms, making errors less likely.
- The ability to store recurring entries and look up posted invoices makes it possible to double check invoices in response to customer and vendor inquiries.
- Errors in Sales, Purchases and Payroll Journal entries can be corrected as adjustments. The software automatically creates and posts the reversing entries.
- Simply Accounting provides an audit trail for all journals.
- Bank accounts, customer, vendor and inventory records can be set up to calculate many foreign currency transactions automatically, including import duties.
- To-Do Lists and Checklists provide reminders of upcoming discounts and recurring entries.
- Business guides, accounting advice, and management reports and advice all provide helpful information for running the business.

General Ledger

- The software provides a directory of accounts used by the business, including all the linked accounts for the other ledgers in Simply Accounting. The information in these accounts can be used to prepare and analyze financial reports such as the Balance Sheet and Income Statement.

Receivables Ledger

- Simply Accounting provides a directory of customers and mailing labels.
- Credit limit entries for each customer should reduce the losses from non-payment of accounts. Customers with poor payment histories can have their credit limits reduced or their credit purchase privileges removed.
- Preferred customers can be marked so that they automatically receive lower prices.
- Sales Quote and Order entries result in automatic Sales Journal entries when the quotes or orders are filled.
- Accounts receivable can be aged, and each customer's payment behaviour can be analyzed. This allows for the accurate calculation of provisions for bad debts.

Payables Ledger

- Simply Accounting provides a directory of vendors and mailing labels.
- The information from the review of transactions with vendors and from the accounts payable aged analysis can be combined with detailed cash flow reports to make payment decisions. Simply Accounting helps to predict short-term cash needs in order to establish priorities for making payments and to schedule payments to vendors.
- The GST remittance or refund is calculated automatically because of the linked GST accounts in the Payables and Receivables ledgers.
- Simply Accounting Purchase Quote and Order entries result in automatic Purchases Journal entries when quotes or orders are filled.

Payroll Ledger

- Simply Accounting maintains employee records with both personal and payment information for personnel files.
- Paycheques for several employees can be processed in a single entry.
- Once the information has been set up, the program automatically withholds several employee deductions including income tax, CPP (Canada Pension Plan) and EI (Employment Insurance) and is therefore less prone to error. These payroll deductions are updated regularly by ACCPAC INTERNATIONAL, INC. in later versions of the software.
- Summaries of employer contributions, such as EHT (Employer Health Tax), WSIB (Workplace Safety and Insurance Board), EI and CPP, permit easy analysis of payroll expenses for compulsory and optional benefits.
- Simply Accounting automatically links payroll with control accounts in the General Ledger to keep a cumulative record of amounts owing to various agencies for monthly or quarterly remittance.

Inventory Ledger

- The software provides an inventory summary or database of all inventory items.
- Inventory reports flag items that need to be re-ordered and the reports can be used to make purchase decisions.
- Import duty rates and preferred customer prices in home and foreign currencies can be set up in the ledger so that they appear automatically in the journals.
- Inventory codes can be matched to the codes used by vendors and customers so that common order forms are created automatically.
- The software automatically calculates inventory variance costs when the inventory sold is out of stock and is later purchased at different prices.
- Simply Accounting automatically updates inventory records when inventory is purchased, sold, transferred, lost, recovered or returned. It warns you when you try to oversell inventory.
- Inventory tracking reports can monitor sales and purchase activity on individual inventory items to see which ones are selling well and which are not. These reports can be used to determine optimum inventory buying patterns to reduce storage costs.

6. In summation, Simply Accounting provides an integrated management accounting information system.

The manager found an application called Artistic Interiors in an older Simply Accounting textbook. It appeared similar in complexity and structure to Hearth House and even included complete instructions for setting up a computerized accounting system in Simply Accounting. She and the store assistant used this for practice before converting the books for Hearth House. They printed all the relevant business guide information and then prepared the following reports to assist with the conversion:

- Business Information
- Income Statement
- Post-Closing Trial Balance
- Customer Information
- Inventory Information
- Chart of Accounts
- Balance Sheet
- Vendor Information
- Employee Information
- Accounting Procedures

HEARTH HOUSE BUSINESS INFORMATION

Address: 44 Warmley Road
Toronto, Ontario M6R 2P6
Phone: (416) 589-9121
Fax: (416) 589-9000
Business No.: 20736 5818

Printers:
Reports & Graphs:
Cheques:
Invoices
Labels:
Other:

Names Settings:
Tax GST
Income A Salary
Income B Commission
Income C – E not used
Prov. Tax not applicable

Deduction A RRSP
Deduction B CSB Plan
Deduction C Gp Insurance
Deduction D – J not used
Project Title Project

User Preference Settings:
Use Accounting Terms
Show Select Company window at startup
Automatically save changes to records

System Settings:
Store invoice lookup
Allow future transactions
Warn if history not balanced
Backup Weekly

General Settings: no changes

Sales Taxes:
GST 7%
PST 8%

Receivables Settings:
Aging periods: 5, 10, 30 days
Interest charges: 1.5% after 30 days
Statements include invoices for 31 days
Payment terms: 1/5, n/10
Discounts before tax: No

Payables Settings:
Aging periods: 15, 30, 45 days
Discounts before tax: No

Payroll Settings:
EI factor 1.4
Salary taxable yes
Other Income taxable yes
EHT factor 0.98

RRSP before-tax deduction
CSB Plan after-tax deduction
Gp Insurance after-tax deduction

Inventory Settings:
Profit evaluation: markup
Sort Inventory: by description
Allow inventory levels to go below zero: yes

Comments
Sales Invoice: Interest @ 1.5% per month on accounts over 30 days

Forms Settings — Next number on:
Sales Invoice No. 120
Receipts No. del
Purchase Order No. 101

Sales Quotes No. 82
Customer Deposits No. 38

Bank Class Accounts:
1060 Bank Account: Chequing
Currency: Canadian Dollars (CAD)
Next cheque no.: 300

1090 Bank: Foreign Funds GBP
Currency: British Pounds (GBP)
Next cheque no.: 125

Credit Card Accepted:
Visa 3.5% fee Accts: 5020, 1080

Credit Cards Used:
Visa Accts: 2150, 5020

Currency:
Foreign Currency: British Pounds (GBP)
10/01/2003 Exchange Rate: 2.2424
Account: 5030

Track Import Duties:
Account: 2360

HEARTH HOUSE
CHART OF ACCOUNTS

ASSETS
1000 CURRENT ASSETS [H]
1060 Bank Account: Chequing [A]
1080 Bank Account: Credit Card [A]
1090 Bank: Foreign Funds GBP [A]
1100 Bank: Total [S]
1200 Accounts Receivable [A]
1220 Allowance for Doubtful Accounts [A]
1240 Advances Receivable [A]
1260 Interest Receivable [A]
1270 Net Receivables [S]
1280 Prepaid Advertising
1300 Prepaid Insurance
1320 Supplies: Office
1340 Supplies: Insulation
1360 Supplies: Fireplace Hardware
1380 TOTAL CURRENT ASSETS [T]

1390 INVENTORY ASSETS [H]
1400 Accessories & Tools
1410 Ceramic Gas Logs
1420 Glass Doors
1430 Grills
1440 Fireplaces and Inserts
1450 Mantels and Surrounds
1460 Remote Control Units
1470 Space Heaters
1490 TOTAL INVENTORY ASSETS [T]

1500 PLANT & EQUIPMENT [H]
1510 Computers [A]
1520 Accum Deprec: Computers [A]
1525 Net Computers [S]
1530 Installation Equipment [A]
1540 Accum Deprec: Install Equip [A]
1545 Net Install Equipment [S]
1560 Shop Centre [A]
1570 Accum Deprec: Shop Centre [A]
1575 Net Shop Centre [S]
1590 Transport Vehicles [A]
1600 Accum Deprec: Trans Vehicles [A]
1610 Net Transport Vehicles [S]
1690 TOTAL PLANT & EQUIPMENT [T]

LIABILITIES
2000 CURRENT LIABILITIES [H]
2100 Bank Loan
2150 Credit Card Payable
2200 Accounts Payable
2300 Vacation Payable
2310 EI Payable [A]
2320 CPP Payable [A]
2330 Income Tax Payable [A]
2340 Receiver General Payable [S]
2360 Import Duties
2390 EHT Payable
2400 RRSP Payable
2410 CSB Plan Payable
2420 Group Insurance Payable
2460 WSIB Payable
2500 Business Income Tax Payable
2640 PST Payable
2650 GST Charged on Sales [A]
2670 GST Paid on Purchases [A]
2690 GST Payroll Deductions [A]
2710 GST Adjustments [A]
2730 ITC Adjustments [A]
2750 GST Owing (Refund) [S]
2790 TOTAL CURRENT LIABILITIES [T]

2800 LONG TERM LIABILITIES [H]
2850 Mortgage Payable
2890 TOTAL LONG TERM LIABILITIES [T]

EQUITY
3000 OWNER'S EQUITY [H]
3100 Test Balance
3560 AA, Capital
3600 Current Earnings [X]
3690 UPDATED CAPITAL [T]

REVENUE
4000 GENERAL REVENUE [H]
4020 Revenue from Sales [A]
4040 Revenue from Services [A]
4060 Sales Returns & Allowances [A]
4070 Sales Discount [A]
4080 Net Sales [S]
4100 Interest Revenue
4120 Sales Tax Compensation
4390 TOTAL GENERAL REVENUE [T]

EXPENSES
5000 OPERATING EXPENSES [H]
5010 Advertising & Promotion
5020 Bank Charges & Card Fees
5030 Exchange Rate Differences
5050 Cost of Goods Sold [A]
5055 Variance Costs [A]
5060 Purchase Discounts [A]
5070 Purchases Returns & Allowances [A]
5075 Damaged Inventory [A]
5080 Net Cost of Goods Sold [S]
5085 Depreciation: Computers
5090 Depreciation: Install Equip
5095 Depreciation: Shop Centre
5100 Depreciation: Transport Vehicles
5110 Delivery Expenses
5120 Freight Expense
5130 Hydro Expense
5150 Insurance Expense
5160 Interest on Loan
5165 Interest on Mortgage
5170 Maintenance and Repairs
5180 Property Taxes
5200 Supplies Used: Office
5230 Supplies Used: Insulation
5240 Supplies Used: FP Hardware
5250 Telephone Expense
5260 Uncollectable Accounts Expense
5290 TOTAL OPERATING EXPENSES [T]

5295 PAYROLL EXPENSES [H]
5300 Wages
5310 EI Expense
5320 CPP Expense
5330 WSIB Expense
5360 EHT Expense
5390 TOTAL PAYROLL EXPENSES [T]

5500 INCOME TAX EXPENSE [H]
5540 Business Income Tax Expense
5590 TOTAL INCOME TAX EXPENSE [T]

ACCOUNT TYPES
[H] Heading
[A] Subgroup Account
[S] Subgroup Total
[T] Total
[X] Current Earnings
Group accounts are unmarked

notes

- In the Income Statement and Balance Sheet, the subgroup accounts have a separate column for account balances to the left of the group account balances. They are followed by a subgroup total whose balance is in the right column with the group account balances. All headings and totals are numbered and printed in uppercase letters (e.g., 4000 GENERAL REVENUE).
- Accounts with zero balances are omitted from all financial reports.

HEARTH HOUSE
INCOME STATEMENT

For the quarter ending September 30, 2003

REVENUE		
4000 GENERAL REVENUE		
4020 Revenue from Sales	$157 500.00	
4040 Revenue from Services	22 500.00	
4080 Net Sales		$180 000.00
4100 Interest Revenue		340.00
4120 Sales Tax Compensation		480.00
4390 TOTAL GENERAL REVENUE		$180 820.00
TOTAL REVENUE		$180 820.00
EXPENSE		
5000 OPERATING EXPENSES		
5010 Advertising & Promotion		$ 235.00
5020 Bank Charges & Card Fees		75.00
5030 Exchange Rate Differences		15.00
5050 Cost of Goods Sold	$94 650.00	
5060 Purchase Discounts	−300.00	
5080 Net Cost of Goods Sold		94 350.00
5085 Depreciation: Computers		500.00
5090 Depreciation: Install Equip		250.00
5095 Depreciation: Shop Centre		3 000.00
5100 Depreciation: Transport Vehicles		1 000.00
5110 Delivery Expenses		800.00
5120 Freight Expense		300.00
5130 Hydro Expense		360.00
5150 Insurance Expense		300.00
5160 Interest on Loan		800.00
5165 Interest on Mortgage		6 100.00
5170 Maintenance and Repairs		250.00
5180 Property Taxes		750.00
5200 Supplies Used: Office		150.00
5230 Supplies Used: Insulation		1 200.00
5240 Supplies Used: FP Hardware		300.00
5250 Telephone Expense		160.00
5260 Uncollectable Accounts Expense		900.00
5290 TOTAL OPERATING EXPENSES		$111 795.00
5295 PAYROLL EXPENSES		
5300 Wages		33 772.00
5310 EI Expense		1032.19
5320 CPP Expense		1006.98
5330 WSIB Expense		889.52
5360 EHT Expense		324.38
5390 TOTAL PAYROLL EXPENSES		$ 37 025.07
5500 INCOME TAX EXPENSE		
5540 Business Income Tax Expense		7 500.00
5590 TOTAL INCOME TAX EXPENSE		$ 7 500.00
TOTAL EXPENSE		$156 320.07
NET INCOME		$ 24 499.93

notes

- The Balance Sheet is shown with pre-closing balances for Equity accounts.
- £ is the symbol for British pounds and GBP is the code for British pounds, the foreign currency used by Hearth House for foreign purchases.

HEARTH HOUSE
BALANCE SHEET

September 30, 2003

ASSETS		
1000 CURRENT ASSETS		
1060 Bank Account: Chequing	$39 670.10	
1080 Bank Account: Credit Card	150.00	
1090 Bank: Foreign Funds GBP (£245)	550.00	
1100 Bank: Total		$ 40 370.10
1200 Accounts Receivable	9 200.00	
1220 Allowance for Doubtful Accounts	–900.00	
1240 Advances Receivable	200.00	
1260 Interest Receivable	340.00	
1270 Net Receivables		8 840.00
1280 Prepaid Advertising		250.00
1300 Prepaid Insurance		1 500.00
1320 Supplies: Office		200.00
1340 Supplies: Insulation		600.00
1360 Supplies: Fireplace Hardware		500.00
1380 TOTAL CURRENT ASSETS		$ 52 260.10
1390 INVENTORY ASSETS		
1400 Accessories & Tools		4 490.00
1410 Ceramic Gas Logs		4 374.00
1420 Glass Doors		5 640.00
1430 Grills		2 880.00
1440 Fireplaces and Inserts		30 180.00
1450 Mantels and Surrounds		5 760.00
1460 Remote Control Units		900.00
1470 Space Heaters		5 040.00
1490 TOTAL INVENTORY ASSETS		$ 59 264.00
1500 PLANT & EQUIPMENT		
1510 Computers	6 000.00	
1520 Accum Deprec: Computers	–1 500.00	
1525 Net Computers		4 500.00
1530 Installation Equipment	15 000.00	
1540 Accum Deprec: Install Equip	–750.00	
1545 Net Install Equipment		14 250.00
1560 Shop Centre	300 000.00	
1570 Accum Deprec: Shop Centre	–9 000.00	
1575 Net Shop Centre		291 000.00
1590 Transport Vehicles	40 000.00	
1600 Accum Deprec: Trans Vehicles	–3 000.00	
1610 Net Transport Vehicles		37 000.00
1690 TOTAL PLANT & EQUIPMENT		$346 750.00
TOTAL ASSETS		$458 274.10

continued...

HEARTH HOUSE
BALANCE SHEET CONTINUED

September 30, 2003

LIABILITIES

2000 CURRENT LIABILITIES		
2100 Bank Loan		$ 75 000.00
2150 Credit Card Payable		150.00
2200 Accounts Payable		9 309.00
2300 Vacation Payable		1 860.00
2310 EI Payable	$ 531.07	
2320 CPP Payable	473.40	
2330 Income Tax Payable	1 691.80	
2340 Receiver General Payable		2 696.27
2390 EHT Payable		324.38
2400 RRSP Payable		450.00
2410 CSB Plan Payable		450.00
2420 Group Insurance Payable		35.00
2460 WSIB Payable		889.52
2640 PST Payable		4 800.00
2650 GST Charged on Sales	4 200.00	
2670 GST Paid on Purchases	-2 520.00	
2750 GST Owing (Refund)		1 680.00
2790 TOTAL CURRENT LIABILITIES		$ 97 644.17
2800 LONG TERM LIABILITIES		
2850 Mortgage Payable		248 800.00
2890 TOTAL LONG TERM LIABILITIES		$248 800.00
TOTAL LIABILITIES		$346 444.17

EQUITY

3000 OWNER'S EQUITY		
3560 AA, Capital		$ 87 330.00
3600 Current Earnings		24 499.93
3690 UPDATED CAPITAL		$111 829.93
TOTAL EQUITY		$111 829.93
LIABILITIES AND EQUITY		$458 274.10

HEARTH HOUSE
POST-CLOSING TRIAL BALANCE

September 30, 2003

Account	Debit	Credit
1060 Bank Account: Chequing	$39 670.10	
1080 Bank Account: Credit Card	150.00	
1090 Bank: Foreign Funds GBP (£245)	550.00	
1200 Accounts Receivable	9 200.00	
1220 Allowance for Doubtful Accounts		$ 900.00
1240 Advances Receivable	200.00	
1260 Interest Receivable	340.00	
1280 Prepaid Advertising	250.00	
1300 Prepaid Insurance	1 500.00	
1320 Supplies: Office	200.00	
1340 Supplies: Insulation	600.00	
1360 Supplies: Fireplace Hardware	500.00	
1400 Accessories & Tools	4 490.00	
1410 Ceramic Gas Logs	4 374.00	
1420 Glass Doors	5 640.00	
1430 Grills	2 880.00	
1440 Fireplaces and Inserts	30 180.00	
1450 Mantels and Surrounds	5 760.00	
1460 Remote Control Units	900.00	
1470 Space Heaters	5 040.00	
1510 Computers	6 000.00	
1520 Accum Deprec: Computers		1 500.00
1530 Installation Equipment	15 000.00	
1540 Accum Deprec: Install Equip		750.00
1560 Shop Centre	300 000.00	
1570 Accum Deprec: Shop Centre		9 000.00
1590 Transport Vehicles	40 000.00	
1600 Accum Deprec: Trans Vehicles		3 000.00
2100 Bank Loan		75 000.00
2150 Credit Card Payable		150.00
2200 Accounts Payable		9 309.00
2300 Vacation Payable		1 860.00
2310 EI Payable		531.07
2320 CPP Payable		473.40
2330 Income Tax Payable		1 691.80
2390 EHT Payable		324.38
2400 RRSP Payable		450.00
2410 CSB Plan Payable		450.00
2420 Group Insurance Payable		35.00
2460 WSIB Payable		889.52
2640 PST Payable		4 800.00
2650 GST Charged on Sales		4 200.00
2670 GST Paid on Purchases	2 520.00	
2850 Mortgage Payable		248 800.00
3560 AA, Capital		111 829.93
	$475 944.10	$475 944.10

HEARTH HOUSE
VENDOR INFORMATION

Vendor Name (Contact)	Address	Phone No. Fax No.	E-mail Web Site	Terms Tax ID
Bell Canada (Maisie Speaker)	88 Holler St. Toronto, ON M6R 3F2	Tel: (416) 588-7290 Fax: (416) 588-9001	www.bell.ca	Net 1
Cambridge Castings (Blackie Smith) Currency: GBP	210 Ironside Rd. Cambridge, United Kingdom CB5 8PA	Tel: (44 223) 241-447 Fax: (44 223) 241-411	bs@cambridge.com www.cambridge.com	2/10, n/15 after tax
City Treasurer (Business Dept.)	100 Queen St. W. Toronto, ON M5H 2N1	Tel: (416) 393-6101 Fax: (416) 393-1000	www.city.toronto.on.ca	End of Month (15 days)
Matchless Flame (Ashleigh Burns)	552 Igniter Ct. Hamilton, ON L8V 5N8	Tel: (905) 525-6774 Fax: (905) 525-8108	ashes@matchless.com www.matchless.com	Net 15 22877 5201
Minister of Finance	Box 620, 33 King St. W. Oshawa, ON L1H 8H5	Tel: (905) 965-8470	www.gov.on.ca/FIN	Net 1
Overload Office Supplies (Nellie Stapler)	48 Paper Ave. Toronto, ON M4T 2W1	Tel: (416) 788-1074 Fax: (416) 788-6198	www.OOSupplies.com	Net 10 49926 6322
Penguin Insulating Co. (Rob Warme)	386 Vermiculite St. Mississauga, ON L6B 3D5	Tel: (905) 773-5924 Fax: (905) 773-6111	RW@keepwarm.com www.keepwarm.com	Net 15 38649 1665
Power Hardware (Shaina Toole)	92 Power St. North York, ON M3H 7E9	Tel: (416) 748-7291 Fax: (416) 748-8282	SToole@power.com www.power.com	Net 10
Receiver General of Canada	Sudbury Tax Services Office PO Box 20004, Station A Sudbury, ON P3A 6B4	Tel: (705) 821-8186	www.ccra-adrc.gc.ca	Net 1
Standard Insurance Co. (Nevva Smoke)	234 Carefree Blvd. Toronto, ON M3G 5X5	Tel: (416) 489-2935 Fax: (416) 489-2900	NSmoke@life.com	Net 1
Starfire Fireplaces (Cindy Heatlie)	355 Sparks St. Scarborough, ON M2F 6C4	Tel: (416) 529-6185 Fax: (416) 529-8100		Net 20 48865 3122
Telecompute Computers (N. T. Windows)	95 Processor Ave. Etobicoke, ON M8B 2W6	Tel: (416) 630- 6291 Fax: (416) 633-6222	www.telecompute.com	Net 15
Therma Glow (Margo Flamer)	183 Bright St. Windsor, ON N8N 5F4	Tel: (519) 422-4587 Fax: (519) 423-9464		2/10, n/20 after tax 33445 5661
Toronto Hydro	14 Carlton St. Toronto, ON M5B 1K5	Tel: (416) 599-0735 Fax: (416) 599-6000	www.torontohydro.com	Net 1
Toronto Star	1 Yonge St. Toronto, ON M5E 1E6	Tel: (416) 368-3611 Fax: (416) 368-1000	www.thestar.com	Net 1
Transcend Investment Co. (Rich Better)	10 Stocks St. Toronto, ON M6H 4R7	Tel: (416) 663-7401 Fax: (416) 663-7400	rich@transcend.com www.transcend.com	Net 1 53276 9824
Vulcan Stove Co. (Bryan Stokes) Currency: GBP	45 Firestone Cr. London, United Kingdom EC1R 4TY	Tel: (44 207) 278-3111 Fax: (44 207) 278-3000	www.vulcan.com	Net 30
Workplace Safety & Insurance Board	1033 Bay St. Toronto, ON M5T 1D3	Tel: (416) 925-7176 Fax: (416) 925-7222	www.wsib.on.ca	Net 1

HEARTH HOUSE
OUTSTANDING VENDOR INVOICES

Vendor Name	Date	Inv/Chq No.	Terms	CAD Amount	(GBP Amt)	Total
Cambridge Castings	09/24/03	CC-818	2/10, n/15	$4 237.20	£1 890	$4 237.20
Matchless Flame	09/24/03	MF-1201	Net 15	$3 210.00		
	09/24/03	CHQ#281	Payment	–1 070.00		
			Balance			2 140.00
Penguin Insulating Co.	09/30/03	PI-901	Net 15	$428.00		428.00
Therma Glow	09/28/03	TG-1421	2/10, n/20	$1 797.60		1 797.60
Vulcan Stove Co.	09/27/03	VS-699	Net 30	$706.20	£315	706.20
				Grand Total		$9 309.00

HEARTH HOUSE
CUSTOMER INFORMATION

Customer Name (Contact)	Address	Phone No. Fax No.	E-mail Web Site	Credit Limit Terms
Brookhaven Funeral Home (Grim Reaper)	11 Spirits Ave. Toronto, ON M6F 3K2	Tel: (416) 838-5757 Fax: (416) 838-0903	greaper@enders.com www.brookhaven.com	$10 000 1/5, n/10
Lakeshore Condos (Liv Intown) *Preferred Customer	550 Beach Ave. Toronto, ON M7H 4L4	Tel: (416) 363-6336 Fax: (416) 366-5554	intown@condos.com	$10 000 1/5, n/10
Rosedale Estates (Dale Rosewood)	75 Crescent Rd. Toronto, ON M1B 3X9	Tel: (416) 488-3939 Fax: (416) 488-9211	rosewood@istar.ca	$10 000 1/5, n/10
Scarlett Road Condos (Rhett Butler)	450 O'Hara Rd. Toronto, ON M7T 2F5	Tel: (416) 784-5632 Fax: (416) 784-6021	butler@condos.com	$15 000 1/5, n/10
University Alumni House (Izzy Dunskule)	540 Spadina Ave. Toronto, ON M5J 4E3	Tel: (416) 528-8642 Fax: (416) 528-7201	izzy@uah.ca www.uah.ca	$15 000 1/5, n/10
Walden Apartments (E. Thoreau)	488 Walden Pond Rd. Toronto, ON M4S 7N2	Tel: (416) 393-0987 Fax: (416) 393-9731	thoreau@walden.ca www.walden.ca	$10 000 1/5, n/10
York Seniors' Club (Nonny Genarian) *Preferred Customer	129 York Blvd. Toronto, ON M8B 2R3	Tel: (416) 528-5522 Fax: (416) 528-6001	nonny@oldyork.ca www.oldyork.ca	$10 000 1/5, n/10

HEARTH HOUSE
OUTSTANDING CUSTOMER INVOICES

Customer Name	Date	Inv/Chq No.	Terms	Amount	Total
Brookhaven Funeral Home	09/21/03	HH-110	1/5, n/10	$4 600	
	09/21/03	CHQ#51	Payment	–1 150	
			Balance		$3 450
Rosedale Estates	09/27/03	HH-115	1/5, n/10	$3 680	3 680
University Alumni House	09/28/03	HH-117	1/5, n/10	$2 070	2 070
				Grand Total	$9 200

HEARTH HOUSE
EMPLOYEE INFORMATION SHEET

	Ella Cinder	Kris Kindl	Dana Damper
Position	Manager	Installer	Store Assistant
Social Insurance Number	494 663 487	482 876 349	442 552 774
Address & Telephone	921 Fireside Dr. Scarborough, ON M1B 2C9 (416) 578-7291	82 Mantle St. Toronto, ON M5B 6D1 (416) 779-7299	588 Hotspur Rd. North York, ON M6A 1X6 (416) 482-6234
Date of Birth (mm-dd-yy)	12-25-74	02-14-71	04-01-81
Date of Hire (mm-dd-yy)	01-01-03	01-12-03	01-01-03
Federal (Ontario) Tax Claim - TD1			
Basic Personal	$7 412 (7 426)	$7 412 (7 426)	$7 412 (7 426)
Spouse/Equivalent	$6 294 (6 306)	$6 294 (6 306)	$6 294 (6 306)
Other			$3 619 (3 626)
Total Claim Amount	$13 706 (13 732)	$13 706 (13 732)	$17 325 (17 358)
Additional Federal Tax		$20	
Employee Income			
Regular Wage Rate		$20.00	
Overtime Wage Rate		$30.00	
Regular Salary	$4 500		$1 400
Hours per Period	150	80	75
Vacation	4 weeks	6%	3 weeks
Employee Deductions			
Registered Retirement Savings Plan (RRSP)	$200	$50	$50
Canada Savings Bond (CSB)	$200	$50	$50
Group Insurance	$10	$5	$5
EI, CPP and Income Tax	calculations built into Simply Accounting program		
Historical Income			
Regular		$30 400.00	
Overtime		600.00	
Salary	$40 500.00		$25 200.00
Vacation Pay Paid			
Vacation Pay Owed		1 860.00	
Advances Paid		200.00	
EI Ins Earnings	39 000.00	31 000.00	25 200.00
Gross Pay	$40 500.00	$31 000.00	$25 200.00
Historical Deductions & Taxes			
RRSP	$ 1 800.00	$ 950.00	$ 900.00
CSB	1 800.00	950.00	900.00
Group Insurance	90.00	95.00	90.00
Income Tax	7 778.79	5 046.10	2 421.27
EI	936.00	740.16	604.80
CPP	1 329.90	1 100.43	880.47
Withheld	$13 734.69	$ 8 881.69	$ 5 796.54
Net Pay	$26 765.31	$22 118.31	$19 403.46

Employee Profiles and TD1 Information

Ella Cinder, the manager at Hearth House, manages the day-to-day store operations, schedules and manages installation projects, assists with difficult installations and assists the owner in decision making. She is married and fully supports her husband and two children under 12. Her salary, $4 500 per month for a normal month of 150 hours, is paid at the end of each month. She is entitled to four weeks' vacation with pay each year. Through payroll deductions, she contributes to a Registered Retirement Savings Plan, a Canada Savings Bond Plan and a Group Insurance Plan that provides a basic level of term life insurance. There are no company benefits. She began working for Hearth House on January 1, 2003.

Kris Kindl installs fireplaces for Hearth House and is responsible for shipping and receiving. He is married and fully supports his wife but has no other dependents. Kindl is paid every two weeks (26 pay periods) and earns $20 per hour. After 40 hours in the week he receives $30 per hour as his overtime wage rate. His vacation pay, at the rate of 6 percent, is retained. Kindl has not yet taken vacation time this year. He makes regular payroll contributions to a Registered Retirement Savings Plan, a Canada Savings Bond Plan and a Group Insurance Plan. He has received $200 as advances, which will be paid back over the next two pay periods at $100 each period. He started working for Hearth House on January 12, 2003.

Dana Damper works in the store as salesperson and office/accounting assistant. Damper is single and fully supports her father, for whom she claims spousal equivalence as well as the age deductions because he is over 65. Her salary of $1 400 is paid semi-monthly (24 pay periods of 75 hours each), and she takes three weeks' vacation each year with pay. She contributes to a Registered Retirement Savings Plan, a Canada Savings Bond Plan and a Group Insurance Plan. There are no company benefits. She began working for Hearth House on January 1, 2003.

Additional Payroll Information

The CSB Plan is administered by Transcend Investment Co., and the RRSP and Group Insurance Plan are administered by Standard Insurance Co. Deductions withheld from employee paycheques are remitted monthly to the proper agencies.

The employer's contributions include the following:

- CPP contributions equal to employee contributions
- EI factor of 1.4
- EHT rate of .98
- Workplace Safety & Insurance Board (WSIB) rates for this type of business:
  4.97 for employees who complete installations – Kindl and Cinder
  1.52 for store salesworker – Damper

Inventory Information

Linked Accounts for Inventory Items

- Each inventory item is listed under its asset account name (e.g., *Accessories and Tools*, *Ceramic Gas Logs*, etc.)
- *Revenue from Sales*, *Cost of Goods Sold* and *Variance Costs* are the linked Revenue, C.O.G.S. and Variance linked accounts for all items.
- *Revenue from Services* and *Cost of Goods Sold* are the linked Revenue and Expense accounts for all services.

Preferred selling prices are provided in brackets beside the regular prices.

Duty rates are provided only for those items that are imported.

HEARTH HOUSE
INVENTORY INFORMATION

Code	Description	Min Stock	Price/Unit Regular	(Preferred)	Qty on Hand	Amt (Cost)	Duty Rate
Accessories & Tools							
AC01	Andirons: cast iron	1	$100	(90) /set	5	$ 250	8.0%
AC02	Firescreen: brass accent rect	1	200	(180) each	3	300	8.0%
AC03	Firescreen: brass arch shape	1	250	(225) each	3	375	8.0%
AC04	Firescreen: iron black accent rect	1	150	(135) each	3	225	8.0%
AC05	Grate: cast iron black	1	150	(135) each	4	240	8.0%
AC06	Thermostat: standard	1	140	(125) each	6	420	
AC07	Toolset: brass handle solid	1	300	(270) /set	4	720	8.0%
AC08	Toolset: cast iron/black enamel	1	200	(180) /set	5	600	8.0%
AC09	Toolset: glass handle/cast iron	1	400	(360) /set	4	960	8.0%
AC10	Woodholder: oak/mhg/walnut	2	80	(75) each	10	400	8.0%
						$4 490	
Ceramic Gas Logs							
CL01	Ceram Log: Algonquin Maple AMF5	0	$500	(450) /set	3	$ 900	
CL02	Ceram Log: Birdseye Maple BMF5	0	550	(500) /set	3	1 050	
CL03	Ceram Log: Georgian Oak GOF4	0	450	(410) /set	3	810	
CL04	Ceram Log: Laurentian Birch LBF4	0	400	(360) /set	3	750	
CL05	Ceram Log: Tobermory Ash TAF5	0	480	(440) /set	3	864	
		0				$4 374	
Fireplaces and Inserts							
FI01	CC: Fireplace coal CC200FS	0	$1 800	(1 650) each	2	$ 2 160	0.0%
FI02	CC: Fireplace free-std gas DV30DVT	0	3 000	(2 700) each	2	3 600	0.0%
FI03	CC: Fireplace gas ins DV32HET	0	2 800	(2 500) each	2	3 360	0.0%
FI04	CC: Fireplace wood WC100FS	0	1 800	(1 650) each	2	2 160	0.0%
FI05	MF: Fireplace gas ins DV27TVT	0	1 950	(1 750) each	2	2 340	
FI06	MF: Fireplace gas ins DV30HE	0	2 000	(1 800) each	2	2 400	
FI07	MF: Fireplace gas ins slim DV20SL	0	1 200	(1 100) each	2	1 440	
FI08	SF: Fireplace gas ins bay DV30BWT	0	1 800	(1 650) each	2	2 160	
FI09	SF: Fireplace gas ins tp-vnt DV30TV	0	1 500	(1 350) each	2	1 800	
FI10	TG: Fireplace gas ins bay BVDV30T	0	2 300	(2 100) each	2	2 760	
FI11	TG: Fireplace gas ins multi MSDV45T	0	2 800	(2 500) each	2	3 360	0.0%
FI12	VS: Fireplace pellet stove VPS1000	0	2 200	(2 000) each	2	2 640	0.0%
						$30 180	
Glass Doors							
GD01	Door: Apparition w/damper 2.5wf	0	$ 800	(725) each	2	$ 960	
GD02	Door: Charade w/damper 1wf	0	600	(550) each	2	720	
GD03	Door: Mirage w/damper 2.75wf	0	900	(810) each	2	1 080	
GD04	Door: Pinnacle Arch w/damper 2wf	0	1 000	(900) each	2	1 200	
GD05	Door: Quest w/damper custom 2wf	0	750	(675) each	2	900	
GD06	Door: Viewzone w/damper 1.5wf	0	650	(590) each	2	780	
						$5 640	
Grills (Barbecue)							
GR01	Grill: mobile/side burner DL-60	0	$1 100	(1 000) each	2	$1 320	
GR02	Grill: rotisserie & spit DX80	0	1 300	(1 175) each	2	1 560	
						$2 880	

continued...

HEARTH HOUSE
INVENTORY INFORMATION CONTINUED

Code	Description	Min Stock	Price/Unit Regular	(Preferred)	Qty on Hand	Amt (Cost)	Duty Rate
Mantels & Surrounds							
MS01	Mantel: cherry MC-DVT40 kit	0	$1 200	(1 075) /kit	2	$1 440	9.5%
MS02	Mantel: marble MM-DVT40 kit	0	1 800	(1 600) /kit	2	2 160	9.5%
MS03	Mantel: oak MO-DVT30 kit	0	1 000	(900) /kit	2	1 200	9.5%
MS04	Mantel: tile MT-DVT30 kit	0	800	(725) /kit	2	960	9.5%
						$5 760	
Remote Control Units							
RC01	Remote control: economy RCE-100	1	$120	(110) each	6	$360	
RC02	Remote control: luxury RCL-1000	1	180	(160) each	6	540	
						$900	
Space Heaters							
SH01	Heater: vintage 20,000BTU ADVSH-20	1	$500	(450) each	4	$1 200	
SH02	Heater: vintage 30,000BTU ADVSH-30	1	750	(675) each	4	1 800	
SH03	Heater: vintage 50,000BTU ADVSH-50	1	850	(775) each	4	2 040	
						$5 040	
Services							
SV01	Basic installation		$450 /job		Charge PST	Charge GST	
SV02	Basic installation - plus		500 /job		Charge PST	Charge GST	
SV03	Customizing inserts		300 /job		Charge PST	Charge GST	
SV04	Insulating chimney		100 /job		Charge PST	Charge GST	

Accounting Procedures

The Goods and Service Tax

GST at the rate of 7 percent is applied to all goods and services offered by Hearth House. Hearth House uses the regular method for remittance of the Goods and Services Tax. GST collected from customers is recorded as a liability in *GST Charged on Sales*. GST paid to vendors is recorded in *GST Paid on Purchases* as a decrease in liability to Canada Customs and Revenue Agency (CCRA).

Two additional GST accounts, *GST Adjustments* and *ITC (Input Tax Credit) Adjustments*, are used to adjust for changes in GST owing, for example, as a result of bad debts. When a bad debt is written off, the GST liability should be reduced because GST was part of the original invoice. Remove the GST portion of the invoice from GST owing by debiting *GST Adjustments* for this amount. If the debt is later recovered, the GST liability should be restored as well. Record the recovery of GST as a credit to *ITC Adjustments*.

notes

In previous applications, only the GST Charged on Sales and GST Paid on Purchases accounts were set up and all transactions were processed through them. Although the net effect is the same, the GST report submitted to CCRA includes the other categories as well. Refer to Chapter 2 for more details.

A fifth postable GST account, *Payroll Adjustments*, is used to record the GST portion of taxable employee benefits that the employer withholds. Although there are currently no payroll benefits, the account will be created for future use.

These five postable accounts are added together in the subgroup total account, *GST Owing (Refund)*. The balance of GST to be remitted or the request for a refund is sent to the Receiver General of Canada by the last day of the current month for the previous month.

notes

Only customers and vendors for whom the charge or collect GST box was checked will be included in GST reports.

Only the GST transactions entered through the Sales Journal, Purchases and Payments Journals are included in the GST report available from the **Reports menu**. GST-related transactions completed in the General Journal will not be included. Therefore, the amounts shown in the GST report may differ from the balances in the General Ledger GST accounts, which include all GST transactions. Use the General Ledger accounts to verify the balance owing (or refund due) and make adjustments to the report manually as necessary.

After the report is filed, clear the GST report (**choose** the **Maintenance menu**, then **Clear Data** and **click** **Clear GST Report**). Enter the last day of the previous month as the date for clearing. Always back up your files before clearing the GST report.

notes

- Provincial taxes will be levied for all sales in this application.
- Adjustments for bad debts may also be required for PST remittances, similar to those for GST. We do not cover these adjustments in this text.

Provincial Sales Tax (PST)

Provincial Sales Tax of 8 percent is applied to all sales of goods and services provided by Hearth House. It is applied to the amount of the sale without GST included and is not applied to freight. The PST collected must be remitted monthly to the Minister of Finance. Provincial Sales Taxes to be remitted must be set up as a liability owing to the vendor, Minister of Finance, in the Purchases Journal. The General Ledger balance for *PST Payable* for the last day of the previous month will provide the total owing. You may display or print this account for reference. A 5 percent sales tax compensation is earned for prompt payment. Remittance must be made by the 23rd of the current month for the previous month.

Business Income Tax

Hearth House pays income tax in quarterly instalments to the Receiver General based on its previous year's net income.

The Employer Health Tax (EHT)

The Employer Health Tax (EHT) is paid by all employers permanently established in Ontario to provide Ontario Health Insurance Plan (OHIP) coverage for all eligible Ontario residents. The EHT is based on the total annual remuneration paid to employees. The EHT rate ranges from 0.98 percent to 1.95 percent. The lowest rate (0.98) is used when the employer's total remuneration is less than $200 000. The highest rate (1.95) is used when the employer's total remuneration exceeds $400 000.

In this application, EHT Payable will be remitted quarterly. The EHT Payable account must be set up as a liability owing to the vendor, the Minister of Finance. The account balance in the General Ledger for the last day of the previous three months will provide you with the liability owing to the Minister of Finance.

Aging of Accounts

Hearth House uses aging periods that reflect the payment terms that it provides to customers and that it receives from vendors. For customers, this will be 5, 10 and 30 days, and for vendors, 15, 30 and 45 days. Interest at 1.5% is charged on accounts over 30 days. Regular customer statements show interest amounts, and invoices are then prepared to add the interest to the amount owing in the ledger record.

notes

To-Do Lists are helpful for making sure that you take advantage of available discounts.

Discounts

Hearth House offers a 1 percent discount to regular account customers if they settle their accounts within five days. Full payment is requested within 10 days. These payment terms are set up as defaults. When the receipt is entered and the discount is still available, the program will show the amount of the discount and the net amount owing automatically. No discounts are given on cash or credit card sales.

version 8

The preferred customer pricing option is not available in Version 8.0.

Some customers receive preferred customer prices, approximately 10 percent below the regular prices. These customers are identified in the ledger records and the preferred prices are set up in the inventory ledger records.

Some vendors also offer discounts for early settlement of accounts. Again, when the terms are entered for the vendor and payment is made before the discount period expires, the program will display the discount as available and automatically calculate a net balance owing. Payment terms vary from vendor to vendor. All discounts are calculated on after-tax amounts.

Freight Expense

When a business purchases inventory items, the cost of any freight that cannot be directly allocated to a specific item must be charged to *Freight Expense*. This amount will be regarded as a general expense rather than being charged to the costs of any inventory asset account. Customers are not charged for delivery.

Imported Inventory

Some inventory items are imported from Great Britain. The bank accounts, vendor records and inventory records are modified to accommodate the foreign currency transactions and import duties automatically.

Purchase Returns and Allowances

A business will sometimes return inventory items to vendors because of damage, poor quality or shipment of the wrong items. Usually a business records these returns after it receives a credit note from a vendor. The return of inventory is entered in the Purchases Journal as an inventory purchase:

- Select the item in the Item field and enter the quantity returned as a **negative** amount in the Quantity field. The program will automatically calculate a negative amount as a default in the Amount field. You cannot change the account number.
- Accept the default amount and enter other items returned to the vendor.
- When there are no further items, enter any freight charges as a **negative** amount.
- Enter the appropriate GST codes and PST rates for each item returned and for freight.

The program will create a negative invoice to reduce the balance owing to the vendor and will reduce the applicable inventory asset accounts, the freight accounts, *GST Paid on Purchases* and the quantity of items in the Inventory Ledger database.

Purchase allowances for damaged merchandise that is not returned are entered as non-inventory negative purchase invoices. Enter the amount of the allowance as a **negative** amount in the Amount field and leave the tax fields blank (i.e., treat it as non-taxable). Enter *Purchases Returns and Allowances* in the Account field.

notes

The sales tax rules for credits, allowances and discounts are complex and may vary from province to province and for federal taxes. Adjusting General Journal entries may be required to adjust the amount of tax owing and calculate the tax remittance. We have chosen to leave out the tax component for transactions of this type. Refer to Chapter 2 for more information about sales taxes.

Sales Returns and Allowances

Sometimes customers will return inventory items. Usually a business records the return after it has issued a credit note. The return is entered in the Sales Journal as a negative inventory sale for the customer:

- Select the appropriate item in the Item field.
- Enter the quantity returned with a **negative** number in the Quantity field.
- The price of the item appears as a positive number in the Price field, and the Amount field is calculated automatically as a negative amount that should be correct. If it is not, you can change it.
- Enter the applicable GST code, PST rate and the account number for *Sales Returns & Allowances*.
- If there were freight charges, enter them as **negative** amounts with the appropriate GST code.

The program will create a negative invoice to reduce the balance owing by the customer, *Cost of Goods Sold*, *GST Charged on Sales* and *PST Payable*. The applicable inventory asset accounts and the quantity of items in the Inventory Ledger database will be increased.

Sales allowances are entered as non-taxable, non-inventory negative sales invoices, creating a debit entry for *Sales Returns & Allowances* and a credit for *Accounts Receivable*. If the allowance is paid by cheque, enter the allowance in the Payments Journal as an other payment paid by cheque.

GST Adjustments for Bad Debt

Most businesses set up an allowance for doubtful accounts or bad debts, knowing that some of their customers will fail to pay. When the allowance is set up, a bad debts or uncollectable accounts expense account is debited. When a business is certain that a customer will not pay its account, the debt should be written off. In the past, the business would do this by crediting *Accounts Receivable* and debiting *Allowance for Doubtful Accounts*. When GST applies, an extra step is required. Part of the original sales invoice was entered as a credit (increase) to *GST Charged on Sales*. The amount of the GST liability can be reduced by the portion of the unpaid debt that was GST. A special GST account, *GST Adjustments*, is used to record the GST for this transaction. The procedure for entering the transaction in Simply Accounting is to record the write-off of the debt in the Sales Journal using the following steps:

- Select the customer whose debt will not be paid.
- Enter a source document number to identify the transaction (e.g., memo).
- Enter a **negative** amount for the unpaid invoice **minus GST** in the Amount field.
- Enter *Allowance for Doubtful Accounts* in the Account field.
- Advance to the next line of the invoice.
- Enter the amount of GST that was charged on the invoice in the Amount field as a **negative** amount.
- Enter *GST Adjustments* in the Account field.

Review the transaction. The *Accounts Receivable* account is credited (reduced) by the full amount of the invoice to remove the balance owing by this customer. *Allowance for Doubtful Accounts* has been debited (reduced) by the amount of the invoice minus GST. *GST Adjustments* has been debited for the GST portion of the invoice to reduce the liability to the Receiver General.

notes

After recording the write-off, "pay" both the original invoice and the write-off in the Receipts Journal. The balance will be zero and there will be no journal entry. This step removes the items from the journal for the customer so that you can clear the paid transactions and later remove the customer's record.

Manually you would complete the entry as follows:

1. Set up the Allowance for Bad Debts.

Date	Particulars	Debit	Credit
xx/xx	Uncollectable Accounts Expense	1 000.00	
	Allowance for Doubtful Accounts		1 000.00

2. Customer G. Bell declares bankruptcy. Write off outstanding balance, $214, including GST.

Date	Particulars	Debit	Credit
xx/xx	Allowance for Doubtful Accounts	200.00	
	GST Adjustments	14.00	
	Accounts Receivable, G. Bell		214.00

Occasionally, a bad debt is recovered after it has been written off. When this occurs, the above procedure is reversed and the GST liability must also be restored. Another special GST account, *ITC Adjustments*, is used to record the increase in the liability to the Receiver General. The recovery is entered as a non-inventory sale in the Sales Journal using the following steps:

- Select the customer and enter the date and source document number.
- Type an appropriate comment such as "Debt recovered" in the Description field.
- Enter a **positive** amount for the invoice **minus GST** in the Amount field.
- Enter *Allowance for Doubtful Accounts* in the Account field.
- Advance to the next line of the invoice.
- Enter the amount of GST that was charged on the original invoice as a **positive** amount in the Amount field.

- Enter *ITC Adjustments* in the Account field.

Review the transaction. You will see that *Accounts Receivable* has been debited for the full amount of the invoice. *Allowance for Doubtful Accounts* has been credited for the amount of the invoice minus GST. *ITC Adjustments* has been credited for the amount of the GST to record the increase in the liability to the Receiver General.

As the final step, record the customer's payment using the Receipts Journal as you would record any other customer payment.

NSF Cheques

If a cheque is deposited from an account that does not have enough money to cover it, the bank returns it to the depositor as NSF (non-sufficient funds). If the cheque was in payment for a cash sale, you must process the NSF cheque through the Sales Journal because there was no Receipts Journal entry. Create a customer record if necessary and enter a **positive** amount for the amount of the cheque. Choose *Bank Account: Chequing* as the account. If the customer is expected to pay the bank charges, enter these on the second invoice line as a **positive** amount and select the appropriate revenue account.

Hardware and Insulation Supplies

Insulation materials and fireplace hardware supplies are requested as needed for contracts by completing a Materials Request Form. Based on these forms, the inventory used is charged to the appropriate expense accounts each month.

Remittances

The Receiver General of Canada:

- Monthly EI, CPP and Income Tax deductions withheld from employees must be paid by the 15th of each month for the previous month.
- Monthly GST owing or requests for refunds must be filed by the end of each month for the previous month. The General Ledger GST accounts will provide you with the balance.
- Business Income Tax is paid in quarterly installments.

notes

Normally a business would make these tax remittances to different federal and provincial tax offices. In this case, you could set up separate vendor accounts for each remittance. For this application, one vendor account and address has been used for the Receiver General and one for the Minister of Finance to reduce the length of the vendor list.

The Minister of Finance:

- Quarterly Employer Health Tax (EHT) deductions must be paid by the 15th of April, July, October and January for the previous quarter.
- Monthly Provincial Sales Taxes (PST) on revenue from sales must be paid by the 23rd of the month for the previous month. A 5 percent sales tax compensation is earned for prompt payment of PST.

The Standard Insurance Company:

- Monthly Registered Retirement Savings Plan (RRSP) deductions withheld from employees must be paid by the 15th of the month for the previous month.
- Group insurance contributions withheld from employees must be paid by the 15th of the month for the previous month.

The Transcend Investment Corporation:

- Monthly Canada Savings Bond Plan (CSB Plan) deductions withheld from employees must be paid by the 15th of the month for the previous month.

The Workplace Safety and Insurance Board:

- Quarterly Workplace Safety and Insurance Board (WSIB) assessment for employees must be paid by the 15th of the month for the previous quarter.

SPECIAL DATA FILES

Detailed keystroke instructions are included for you to set up the Hearth House application files. However, the Data CD also includes files for this application so that you can complete segments of the application rather than having to work through it entirely. Each file stands alone so you can omit any month at your discretion.

To Enter	For (Period Covered)	Use (File name on Data CD)
Transactions:	Oct. 1–Oct. 31	setup\hearth\hh-oct.sdb
Transactions:	Nov. 1–Nov. 30	setup\hearth\hh-nov.sdb
Transactions:	Dec. 1–Dec. 31	setup\hearth\hh-dec.sdb

INSTRUCTIONS FOR SETUP

Using the Business Information, Chart of Accounts, Balance Sheet, Income Statement, Post-Closing Trial Balance and Vendor, Customer, Employee and Inventory Information provided above for September 30, 2003, set up the company accounts. Instructions to assist you in setting up the company accounts follow. The setup of the Payroll and Inventory Ledgers is given in detail. Abbreviated instructions are included for the remaining steps. Refer to the CISV and the Maverick Micro Solutions applications if you need more detailed explanations.

KEYSTROKES FOR SETUP

Creating Company Files

notes

Save your work frequently and update your backup copy frequently as you work through the setup.

For Hearth House, we will create the company files from scratch. Once we create the files and define the defaults, we will add the accounts, define linked accounts for all ledgers, create vendor, customer, employee and inventory records and add historical data.

Start the Simply Accounting program. You should see the Select Company window.

Click Create a new company

Click OK

You will see the Setup wizard welcome screen.

Click Next

Click Create a new set of accounts from scratch

Click Next

notes

- If you are using an alternative location for your company files, substitute the appropriate path, folder or drive in the example.
- You can also type the complete path in the File name field after creating the new folder — Type c:\program files\winsim\data\hearth\hearth

Click Browse to select a folder location for your new data files. You should place the new folder inside the same Data folder that contains your other Simply Accounting company data files.

Create a new folder named **Hearth**.

Double click the **HEARTH folder** you just created to open it.

Double click NEW (or NEW.SDB) in the File name field to highlight the file name.

Type `hearth`

Click Save. Check your file name and change it if necessary.

notes

- If you need to change the file name, click Browse again and repeat the steps that follow.
- To be certain that you have the correct year, type four digits for the year.

Click Next to see the company Dates window. The cursor is in the Fiscal Start field, the date on which the business begins its fiscal year. Hearth House closes its books quarterly and is beginning a new quarter in October.

Enter the fiscal dates as follows:

- Fiscal Start: October 1, 2003
- Fiscal End: December 31, 2003
- Earliest Transaction date: October 1, 2003

Click Finish to save the date information and bypass the remaining wizard steps.

Click Yes to confirm that you want to leave the Setup wizard. (Close the reminder about payroll updates if it appears.) The familiar Home window appears with the name Hearth at the top of the window and non-accounting term labels for icons.

Preparing the System

The next step involves changing the defaults. Change the defaults to suit your own work environment if you have more than one printer or if you are using forms for cheques, invoices or statements. The keystroke instructions are given for computer-generated cheques, invoices and statements. Refer to the Business Information Chart on page 418 for the company default settings.

Changing Defaults

Changing Company Information

version 8

notes

- Use the Backup feature frequently while setting up your files to update your backup copy.
- Save your work frequently by choosing the Save command. You will also save your work by finishing your session properly. You may finish your session at any time while completing the setup. Simply open the data file, accept the session date and continue from where you left off.

Choose the **Setup menu**, then **choose System Settings** and **click Company Information**.

The cursor is flashing in the Name field.

Type `Hearth House` **Press** tab to advance to the Street 1 address field.

Type `44 Warmley Road` **Press** tab **twice** to skip the Street 2 field.

Type `Toronto` **Press** tab

Type `Ontario` **Press** tab

Type `m6r2p6` **Press** tab

Type `Canada` **Press** tab

Type `4165899121` **Press** tab **twice** to skip the Phone 2 field.

Type `4165899000` **Press** tab

Type `207365818`

Check the information you have just entered and correct any errors. Remember that you can correct company dates only before finishing the history. Company name and address information can be changed at any time.

Click OK to save the new information and return to the Home window. The program will automatically set up defaults for the session date and for the city, province and country fields for customers, vendors and employees based on the information you have just entered.

Changing Default Names

version 8

Choose the **Setup menu**, then **choose System Settings** and **click Names** to display the following screen showing the preset payroll and tax field names:

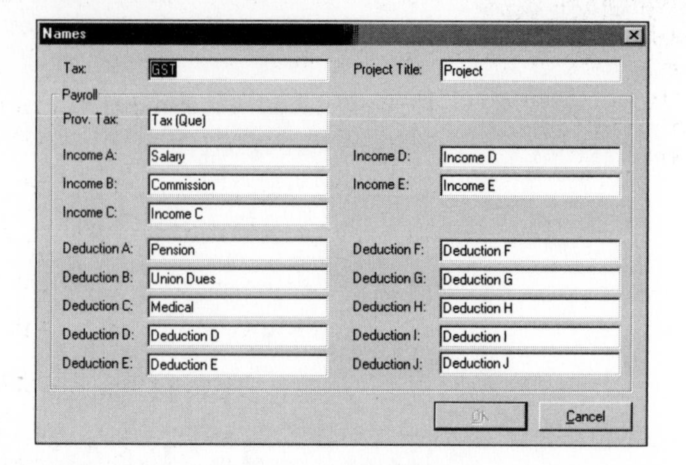

notes

For Grandeur Graphics, the Tax name was changed to HST so that the relevant tax fields and reports were all labelled as HST.

Some of the default names are already correct so you do not need to redefine them. Tax is correctly named GST for Ontario. You can leave Income A and Income B, labelled "Salary" and "Commission," unchanged because Hearth House has salaried employees and is considering paying sales commissions to store employees.

The Prov. Tax field is used for Quebec payroll taxes. Since we will not choose Quebec as the province, the program will automatically skip the related payroll fields. The Project Ledger will not be used initially so you can leave it unchanged. The Project name you enter in this window will appear in the Home window as the icon label.

Double click the **Deduction A field**. Each deduction field name may have up to 12 characters. Hearth House will use this field for Registered Retirement Savings Plan contributions.

Type `RRSP`

Press *tab* to advance to the next field.

The Deduction B field will be used for the Canada Savings Bond Plan that Hearth House offers its employees.

Type `CSB Plan`

Press *tab*

The Deduction C field will be used for the Group Insurance Plan that Hearth House offers its employees.

Type `Gp Insurance`

Press *tab* to highlight the contents of the next field.

notes

To copy N/A from one field to another, double click it and press *ctrl* + C to copy it. Press *tab* to move to the next field where you want to type N/A next and press *ctrl* + V to paste it. (Double clicking a field will select only the single word in that field.)

You can ignore the remaining name fields because Hearth House does not have other payroll deductions. To indicate that each of these fields is not applicable, you may leave the default entries, delete the default contents or change them to N/A.

Type `N/A` (or press *del*) **Press** *tab* to select the next field. Continue in this way until you have changed the entries for Prov. Tax, income and deductions that are not used by Hearth House.

Click OK to save the new name settings and to return to the Home window.

You should now enter the information about printers you are using.

Changing Printer Settings

Choose the **Setup menu** and **click Reports & Forms.**

The printer setting options for reports are given. Choose the printer you will be using for reports. Change the margins if necessary. Choose a suitable font and type size from the lists available.

notes

Once you set up a printer for one type of report or form, the settings will apply to reports of that type in all your Simply Accounting data files.

Click Setup to set the options for your particular printer if you need to change the paper size and location.

Click OK to save your settings and return to the previous Printer setting screen.

To set the printer options for cheques, invoices or other forms,

Click the tab for the type of output you are setting up.

Click the **Invoices tab** to see the settings for printing invoices:

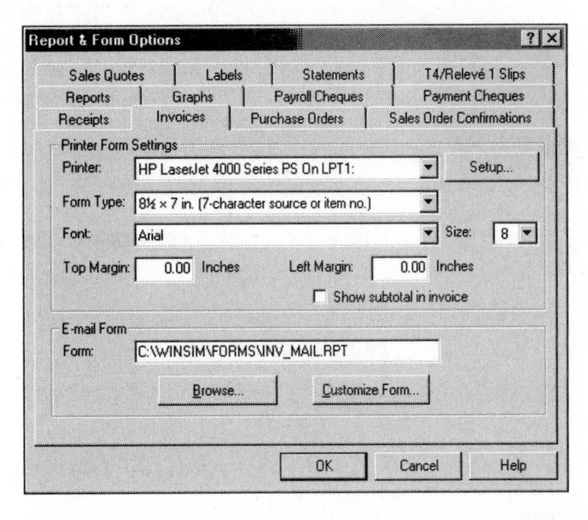

notes

You may want to choose 8.5x11 in. paper as the Form Type if you are using standard printer paper. You should show subtotals in invoices.

Unless you have the programs to create or modify forms, you should accept the default form type. These forms were included as part of the program installation. As you did for reports, select the printer, set the margins, font and type size to match the forms you are using.

Click Setup and complete the setting of options if necessary.

Click OK to save the information.

For printing labels, you need to include the size of the labels and the number that are placed across the page. These fields will become available when you choose the Labels tab.

To set the printer options for cheques or other forms,

Click the tab for the type of output you want and make the necessary changes.

Click OK to save the information when all the settings are correct and to return to the Home window. You can change printer settings at any time.

Warning!

Do not skip any ledger icon windows before completing the setup.

version 8

Changing the User Preference Settings

You should make the following changes to the User Preferences from the View menu and the Setup menu. Refer to Chapter 6, page 161, for assistance if necessary.

Since all modules are used, you should not hide any of them.

From the View menu User Preferences, turn off To-Do lists and Checklists at startup and after changing the session date.

Leave the option to show the Select Company Window at Startup selected.

notes

Notice that ledger and journal icons in the Home window have accounting term labels after you change these settings.

Choose the **Setup menu**, then **choose User Preferences** and **click Settings**.

Click Use Accounting Terms

Click Automatically save changes to vendor, customer and other records

Click OK to save the settings and return to the Home window. The preference settings can be modified at any time by repeating these steps.

Changing System Defaults

version 8

notes

Invoice Lookup (introduced in the Outset Media Corp. application) allows you to view and adjust invoices that have been posted, and to track shipments.

Choose the **Setup menu**, then **choose System Settings** and **click Settings** to display the default settings for the System. The following settings should be used:

- Store invoice lookup details
- Use Cheque No. as the source code for cash purchases and sales
- Allow transactions in the future
- Warn if transactions are more than 7 days in the future
- Warn if accounts are not balanced when entering a new month
- Weekly backup frequency

These settings can be modified at any time by returning to this screen.

Changing Sales Taxes Defaults

Click the **Sales Taxes tab** to display the default Sales Taxes settings. The GST rates are correct and PST is not applied to GST or to freight in Ontario. The only setting that you must change is the PST rate for Ontario.

Click the **PST field** to highlight the contents.

Type 8

Changing General Ledger Defaults

No changes are required for General Ledger settings because budgeting is not used.

notes

Click OK at any time to save the settings and close the Settings window. To continue later, you can use the Setup tool to access Settings. If a ledger icon is selected in the Home window, you will display the Settings for that ledger when you click the Setup button. If no ledger icon is highlighted, you can click the Setup tool and select the ledger from the list to display the Settings for the ledger.

Changing Payables Defaults

Click the **Payables tab**. (The tab label is Vendors & Purchases if you use non-accounting terms.)

For the Payables Ledger, you should change the settings for the aging of accounts.

Set the aging intervals at 15, 30 and 45 days since some vendors ask for payment within 15 days. Discounts from one-time vendors are calculated on after-tax amounts.

Changing Receivables Defaults

Click the **Receivables tab** to display the defaults for the Receivables Ledger. (The tab label is Customers & Sales if you use non-accounting terms.)

You can also decide whether to charge interest on overdue accounts, how long to provide historical information about paid invoices on customer statements, payment terms and aging intervals.

Hearth House offers its account customers a 1 percent after-tax discount in the first five days; full payment is due in 10 days. Interest charges are 1.5% for accounts over 30 days. We will use terms to set the aging intervals.

Enter 5, 10 and 30 days as the aging periods.

Including paid invoices for 31 days is appropriate for the monthly statements.

Click Interest Charges to turn on the calculation.

Click the **% field** for Interest Charges.

Type 1.5

Press tab

Type 30 (to enter the interest charges)

Click the **% field** of the Early Payment Terms section.

Type 1

Press tab

Type 5

Press tab

Type 10

Changing Default Comments

Click the **Comments tab**.

You may add a comment or notice to all your invoices, quotes and order confirmations. You could use this feature to include payment terms, a company motto, or notice of an upcoming sale. Remember that you can change the default message any time you want. You can also edit it for a particular sale or quote when you are completing the invoice.

Click the **Sales Invoices field**.

Type `Interest @ 1.5% per month on accounts over 30 days.`

Repeat this procedure if you want to enter comments for the other forms.

Setting Defaults for Payroll

Use the Payroll Settings from the Business Information Chart on page 418 to complete this step.

Click the **Payroll tab** to display the Payroll Ledger settings:

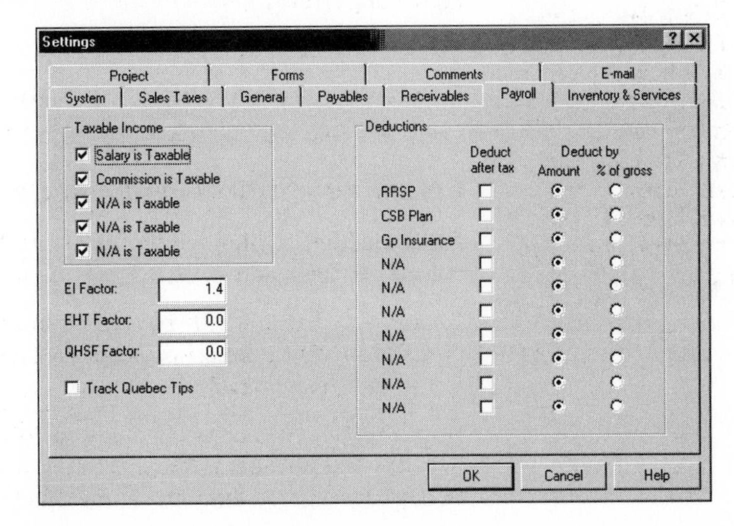

Notice that the names for deductions and incomes that you entered earlier appear on the screen. Again, most of the information is correct. All types of income from Hearth House are taxable so the default settings are correct.

notes

EI (Employment Insurance) was previously named UI or Unemployment Insurance.

The next two fields refer to the rate at which employer tax obligations are calculated. The factor for Employment Insurance (EI Factor) is correct at 1.4. The employer's contribution is set at 1.4 times the employee's contribution.

Click the **EHT factor field**. This field shows the percentage of payroll costs that the employer contributes to the provincial health plan. Based on the total payroll costs per year, the percentage for Hearth House is 0.98 percent.

Type .98

QHSF (Quebec Health Services Fund) is similar to EHT but applies to payroll in Quebec, so we do not need to enter the employer's contribution rate. Similarly, the option to track tips received as pay applies only to Quebec.

notes

You can calculate deductions as a percentage of the gross pay or as a fixed amount.

All deductions are set by default as pretax. For RRSP, this is correct (after tax is not turned on or checked). This means that RRSP contributions qualify as tax deductions and will be subtracted from gross income before income tax is calculated.

CSB Plan and Group Insurance are after-tax deductions, meaning that they are subtracted from income after income tax has been deducted.

Click the **Deduct after tax check box for CSB Plan** to change the setting to after tax.

Click the **Deduct after tax check box for Gp Insurance** to change this setting too.

The remaining deduction fields are not used so you can leave them as they are.

You have now finished setting the Payroll defaults.

Setting Defaults for Inventory & Services

notes

- If you choose to sort inventory ledger items by description, the product name field will appear first in the inventory ledger input forms and inventory selection lists, before the product number.
- After you add a foreign currency, the option to take foreign prices for sales from the inventory ledger or from the exchange rate is added to the ledger settings screen.

Click the **Inventory & Services tab** to see the options for this ledger:

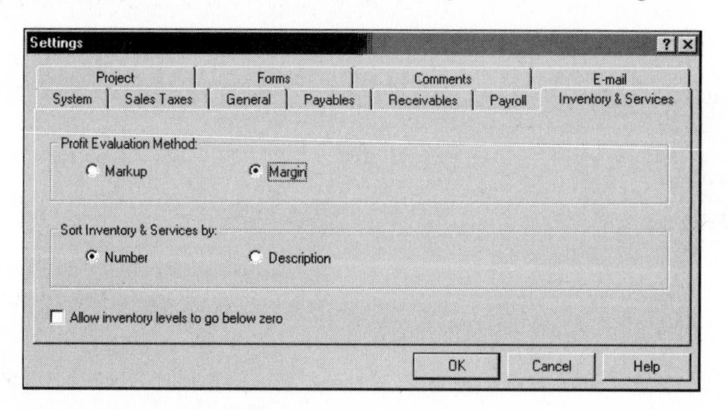

Hearth House uses the markup method of evaluating the profit on inventory sales. Markup is calculated as follows:

Markup = 100% x (Selling Price – Cost Price)/Cost Price

notes

The formula for profit evaluation by Margin is:

$$\frac{\text{Selling Price} - \text{Cost}}{\text{Selling Price}} \times 100\%$$

Click Markup to change the calculation method. You can change the setting at any time so you can prepare reports using both evaluation methods.

Click Description (in the Sort Inventory & Services by section) to change the setting. Because we do not include item numbers in source transactions, this setting will make it easier for you to complete the transactions because it places the inventory item name or description first in inventory selection lists.

The final option is to allow inventory levels to go below zero. Hearth House will choose this option in order to permit customer sales for inventory that is back-ordered.

Click Allow inventory levels to go below zero to select the option.

Setting Defaults for Allocations

Click the **Project tab** to display the Project settings:

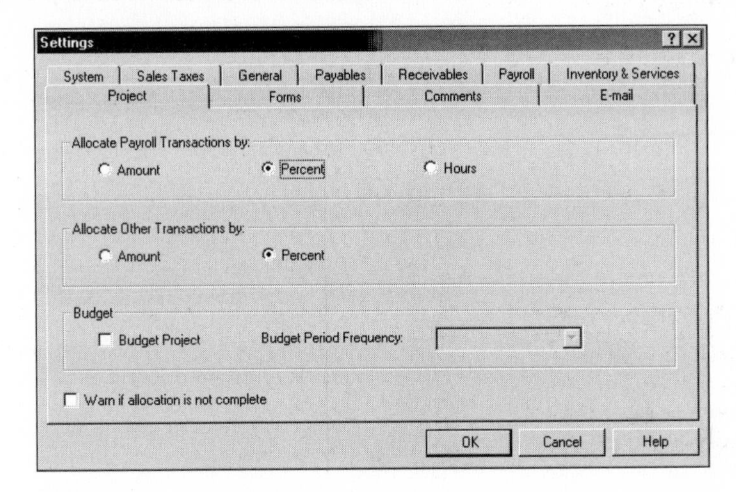

Since Hearth House does not use project costing until December, you do not need to change these settings at this time. You can see that the alternative ways of allocating costs are by percentage (as used in the Puretek application) and by amount. For payroll, the costs may also be distributed according to the number of hours worked. You can also apply budgeting to projects. If you are using job costing allocations, you should turn on the warning for incomplete allocations by clicking its box.

Changing Default Settings for Forms

Click the **Forms tab** to display the defaults.

The Forms options relate to the automatic numbering and printing of all cheques and invoices. They apply only to numerical invoices and are very useful for most businesses. Many invoices include the alpha portion of the invoice number on the preprinted invoice form. You could then enter the next number from the numeric portion in the Invoice number field. Alphanumeric invoice numbers cannot be increased automatically by the computer.

notes

Using the automatic numbering reduces the opportunity to type an incorrect invoice or cheque number even when you are not printing cheques and invoices.

If you want to use automatic invoice numbering, type the next number from the source documents so the automatic numbering system can take over from the manual system. For Hearth House, the next invoice is #HH-120.

The Invoices number field entry is already highlighted, ready to be changed.

Type `120`

Click the **Sales Quotes number field**.

Type `82`

Click the **Receipts number field**.

Press del to leave this field blank. It will be used for customer cheque numbers.

Click the **Customer Deposits number field**.

Type `38`

Click the **Purchase Orders number field**.

Type `101`

Leave selected the option to verify number sequences for all forms.

If you are printing invoices and cheques through the computer, you should turn on the option to confirm printing. The program will then warn you to print before posting a transaction. Remember that if a cheque is printed in error, an appropriate entry or comment should be recorded to explain the discarded cheque or the missing number.

When printing invoices, statements or cheques, you should include the company address, unless it is already printed on your forms.

A ✓ in the appropriate boxes will add this feature.

Click OK to save your new settings and to return to the Home window.

Entering Users and Security Passwords

Simply Accounting allows you to set up passwords for different users. The password for the system administrator (sysadmin) controls access to the system or program. Others control viewing and editing privileges for different ledgers. For example, if different employees work with different accounting records, they should use different passwords.

We strongly advise you not to set passwords for applications used for tutorial purposes. If you set them and forget them, you will be locked out of your data files.

If you want to set passwords, refer to Appendix B and your Simply Accounting manuals before you begin.

Preparing the Ledgers

notes

You can save your work and finish your session at any time. This will give you an opportunity to read the next section.

The third stage in setting up an accounting system involves preparing each ledger for operation. This stage involves

1. organizing all accounting reports and records (this step has already been completed for you)
2. creating new accounts
3. identifying linked accounts for all ledgers
4. inserting vendor, customer, employee and inventory information
5. entering historical startup information
6. printing reports to check the accuracy of your records

Creating New Accounts

notes

- Refer to Linked Accounts (pages 319–322) and Format of Financial Statements (Pages 164–167) for a review of these topics if needed.
- Maximize the Accounts window and drag the ledger account window to a position on the screen so that the Accounts window is still visible. In this way, you should be able to see both the Accounts window and the ledger account window.

Current Earnings is the only pre-defined account and you do not need to edit it. The next step is to create the remaining accounts, including the non-postable accounts. Remember to add the type of account. For postable accounts you should also indicate whether you want to omit accounts with zero balances from financial statements. Again, you need to refer to the company Chart of Accounts, Balance Sheet and Income Statement, pages 419–422, to complete this step.

Refer to the instructions in the CISV application, page 169, if you need help with creating accounts.

Click the **Accounts icon** Accounts to open the Accounts window. If the accounts are not displayed by name or by type, you should change the view. Click the Display by type tool or choose the View menu and click Type.

Click the **Create button** in the Accounts window or choose the File menu and click Create.

Type the account number. **Press** tab and **type** the name for the first account.

Click the **correct account type**. Remember subgroup accounts (A) have the balance in the left column of the group and must be followed by a subgroup total (S).

Click Omit from Financial Statements if Balance is Zero to turn on this option.

Click Allow Project Allocations for all postable revenue and expense accounts.

You will enter the account balances in the next stage.

When all the information is correct, you must save your account.

Click Create Another [Create Another] to save the new account and advance to a blank ledger account window.

Repeat these procedures to create the other accounts.

Close the General Ledger window when you have entered all the accounts on page 419, or when you want to end your session. After entering all the accounts, you should check them for mistakes in type and order.

Click [✓] or **choose** the **Edit menu** and **click Check the validity of accounts** for errors in account sequence such as missing subgroup totals, headings or totals. The first error is reported.

Correct the error and check the validity again. When the accounts are in logical order, **close** the Accounts window to return to the Home window.

You may want to finish your session.

notes

Remember to create the Test Balance account.

notes

Display or print your updated Chart of Accounts at this stage to check for accuracy.

Entering Historical Account Balances

The opening historical balances for Hearth House can be found in the Post-Closing Trial Balance dated September 30, 2003 (page 423). All Income Statement accounts have zero balances because the books were closed at the end of the first quarter. Headings, totals and subgroup totals (i.e., the non-postable accounts) do not have balances. Remember to put any forced balance amounts into the *Test Balance* account.

Open the account information window for *1060 Bank Account: Chequing*, the first account requiring a balance.

Click the **Opening Balance field**.

Type the balance.

Correct the information if necessary by repeating the above steps.

Click the **Next button** [▶] to advance to the next ledger account window.

Repeat the above procedures to enter the balances for the remaining accounts in the Post-Closing Trial Balance on page 423. The *Test Balance* account should have a zero balance.

Close the ledger account window and then the Accounts window when you want to finish your session and return to the Home window.

notes

Accounts that decrease the total in a group or section (e.g., Allowance for Doubtful Accounts, Accumulated Depreciation, GST Paid on Purchases, etc.) have their balances entered as negative numbers. These account balances are indicated with a minus sign (–) in the Balance Sheet.

notes

Display or print your Trial Balance after entering all account balances to check it for accuracy.

Adding a Foreign Currency

Hearth House purchases some inventory items from vendors in the United Kingdom and must set up the company files to allow transactions in £, Great Britain pounds (GBP). You must set up the currency before modifying the bank accounts so that you can identify the currency for the bank accounts and vendors.

Choose the **Setup menu**, then **choose System Settings** and **click Currencies** to open the Currency Information screen.

version 8

Click Allow Transactions in a Foreign Currency to open the required fields. Next you must enter the linked account to track exchange rate differences and rounding differences that result from working with only two decimal places for amounts.

Choose 5030 Exchange Rate Differences from the drop-down list.

For Pro Version 8.5, double click the **Foreign Currency field** to see the list of currencies.

notes

In the Version 8.0 and 8.5 of Simply Accounting, you can identify only one foreign currency and exchange rates for it, Therefore the Currency Information screen does not have the option for additional currencies that appears in Pro Version 8.5.

Click British Pounds

Click Select to add the remaining details for this currency.

Click the **Exchange Rate tab**.

(**For Version 8.5** and **for Version 8.0**, you need only to **choose British Pounds** from the drop-down list.)

Click the **Date column**.

Type `10-01-03`

Press tab to advance to the Exchange Rate field for this currency and date.

Type `2.2424`

Click Display a reminder if the exchange rate is One day old to turn on the warning.

Click OK to return to the Home window. You are now ready to add all the bank account details.

Defining Bank Class Accounts

Defining bank accounts involves changing the account class to Bank and indicating the currency for the accounts and the cheque number sequence.

notes

If you use online banking, you must also enter the remaining bank information, including bank name, account numbers and Web site.

Click the **Accounts icon** Accounts to open the Accounts window.

Double click 1060 Bank Account: Chequing to open the Ledger window.

Click the **Class Options tab**.

Choose Bank from the drop-down list of account classes.

Click the **Next Cheque No. field**.

Type `300`

CAD is the correct currency for this account.

Click the **Next account button** **twice** to open the ledger for *1090 Bank: Foreign Funds GBP*.

Choose Bank as the account class.

Type `125` (to enter the next cheque number)

Choose GBP from the Currency field list.

version 8

Close the ledger window. Simply Accounting shows a warning message:

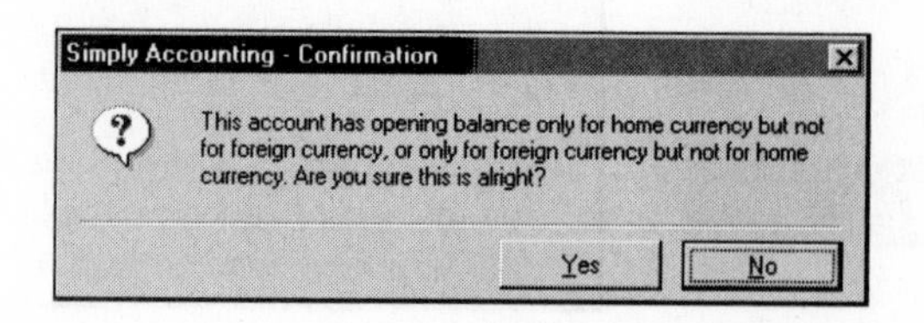

We entered a balance for the foreign account only in Canadian dollars because only one balance field was available. We can now add the balance in GBP.

Click No to return to the Ledger window.

Click the **Account tab** to access the Opening Balance field. There are now two balance fields, one for each currency.

Click the **GBP Opening Balance field**.

Type `245`

Close the Ledger window. **Close** the Accounts window to return to the Home window.

Linked Accounts

notes

Refer to page 319 for a review of linked accounts. Refer to page 166 for a review of the Current Earnings Account.

Linked Accounts are General Ledger accounts that are affected by entries in other journals. For example, recording an inventory purchase will update the Inventory Ledger, several General Ledger accounts and the balance owing to the vendor.

Identifying General Linked Accounts

The *Current Earnings* capital account records the changes in net income resulting from sales and expenses. At the end of the fiscal period, the net income, the balance from *Current Earnings*, is transferred to the *Retained Earnings* capital account and income and expense accounts are reset to zero to prepare for the new fiscal period.

There are two linked accounts for the General Ledger. Both must be capital accounts.

General Linked Accounts	
Retained Earnings	3560 AA, Capital
Current Earnings	3600 Current Earnings

To enter the linked accounts,

Right-click the **General Journal icon** (General) in the Home window to select it.

version 8

Click the **Setup button** or choose the Setup menu, then choose System Settings and Linked Accounts and click General.

You can type in the account number or select the account from the drop-down list.

Click OK to save the new account settings.

Click Yes to accept the account class change for account *3560* and return to the Home window.

Identifying Linked Accounts for the Payables Ledger

Hearth House has one principal bank account, *Bank Account: Chequing*, that is linked to the subsidiary Payables, Receivables and Payroll ledgers and used for all home currency bank transactions.

notes

In Version 8.0 and Version 8.5, enter the linked account for foreign currency transactions in the field for Principal Bank Account for GBP. In Pro Version 8.5, enter the foreign currency account on the Foreign bank account tab screen in the Bank account to use column, beside British Pounds.

Payables	
Principal Bank Account for CAD	1060 Bank Account: Chequing
Accounts Payable	2200 Accounts Payable
GST Paid on Purchases	2670 GST Paid on Purchases
Freight Expense	5120 Freight Expense
Purchase Discount	5060 Purchase Discounts
Foreign Bank Account for GBP (Principal Bank Account for GBP)	1090 Bank: Foreign Funds GBP

To add the Payables Ledger linked accounts,

Right-click the **Purchases** 

or the **Payments Journal icon** 

in the Home window to select it.

Click the **Setup button** or choose the Setup menu, then choose System Settings and Linked Accounts and click Payables.

You can type in the account number or select the account from the drop-down list.

For Pro Version 8.5, the first set of linked accounts are on the General tab screen. There is a second tab screen for foreign bank accounts.

Click the **Foreign bank account tab** to access the screen for entering the GBP linked account:

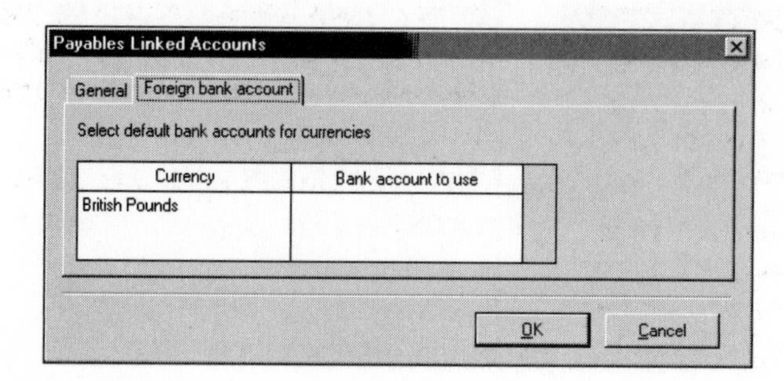

Double click the **Bank account to use field** for British Pounds.

Double click 1090 Bank: Foreign Funds GBP

Click OK to save the new account settings.

Click Yes to accept the account class change for *Accounts Payable* and return to the Home window.

Receivables Linked Accounts

The following accounts are required as linked accounts for the Receivables Ledger.

Receivables Linked Accounts

Principal Bank Account for CAD	1060 Bank Account: Chequing
Accounts Receivable	1200 Accounts Receivable
GST Charged on Sales (Rate 1)	2650 GST Charged on Sales
GST (Rate 2)	not used
PST Payable	2640 PST Payable
Freight Revenue	not used
Sales Discount	4070 Sales Discount
Foreign Bank Account for GBP (Principal Bank Account for GBP)	1090 Bank: Foreign Funds GBP

Right-click the **Sales** or the **Receipts Journal icon** 

in the Home window to select it.

Click the **Setup button** or choose the Setup menu, then choose System Settings and Linked Accounts and click Receivables.

You can type in the account number or select the account from the drop-down list.

> **notes**
>
> - If a journal icon is selected in the Home window, you will display the Linked Accounts for the corresponding ledger when you click the Setup button.
> - If no icon is highlighted, you can click the Setup button and select the journal from the pop-up list to display the ledger's Linked Accounts.
> - When Quebec taxes apply, there will be additional linked accounts for QST in the Receivables and Payables Ledgers.

For **Pro Version 8.5**, after entering the linked accounts on the General tab screen, you should enter the linked foreign bank account for the Receivables Ledger.

Click the **Foreign bank account tab** to access the screen for entering the GBP linked account.

Double click the **Bank account to use field** for British Pounds.

Double click **1090 Bank: Foreign Funds GBP**

Click **OK** to save the new account settings.

Click **Yes** to accept the account class change for *Accounts Receivable* and return to the Home window.

Identifying the Payroll Linked Accounts

notes

- If no icon is selected, you can use the Setup tool icon pop-up list and choose Paycheques.
- If another Home window icon is already highlighted, you can use the appropriate arrow keys to select the Paycheques icon.

There are many linked accounts for payroll because each type of income, deduction and expense that is used must be linked to a General Ledger account. The following linked accounts are used by Hearth House for the Payroll Ledger.

Payroll Linked Accounts Used		Not used
Principal Bank	1060 Bank Account: Chequing	Wages – OT 2
Vacation	2300 Vacation Payable	Wages – NA (Income C)
Advances	1240 Advances Receivable	Wages – NA (Income D)
Wages – Reg	5300 Wages	Wages – NA (Income E)
Wages – OT1	5300 Wages	
Wages – Salary	5300 Wages	NA (Deduction D Payable
Wages – Commission	5300 Wages	NA (Deduction E Payable)
Wages – Vacation Pay	5300 Wages	NA (Deduction F Payable)
RRSP	2400 RRSP Payable	NA (Deduction G Payable)
CSB Plan	2410 CSB Plan Payable	NA (Deduction H Payable)
Gp Insurance	2420 Gp Insurance Payable	NA (Deduction I Payable)
EI Payable	2310 EI Payable	NA (Deduction J Payable)
CPP Payable	2320 CPP Payable	Tax (Que.) Payable
Tax Payable	2330 Income Tax Payable	QPP Payable
WCB Payable	2460 WSIB Payable	QHSF Expense
EHT Payable	2390 EHT Payable	QPP Expense
EI Expense	5310 EI Expense	QHSF Expense
CPP Expense	5320 CPP Expense	
WCB Expense	5330 WSIB Expense	
EHT Expense	5360 EHT Expense	

Right-click the **Paycheques Journal icon** 

in the Home window.

notes

If you deleted the unused income and deduction names, they will not appear on the screens for linked accounts.

Click the **Setup button** or choose the Setup menu, then choose System Settings and Linked Accounts and click Payroll to display the Payroll Linked Accounts for Income:

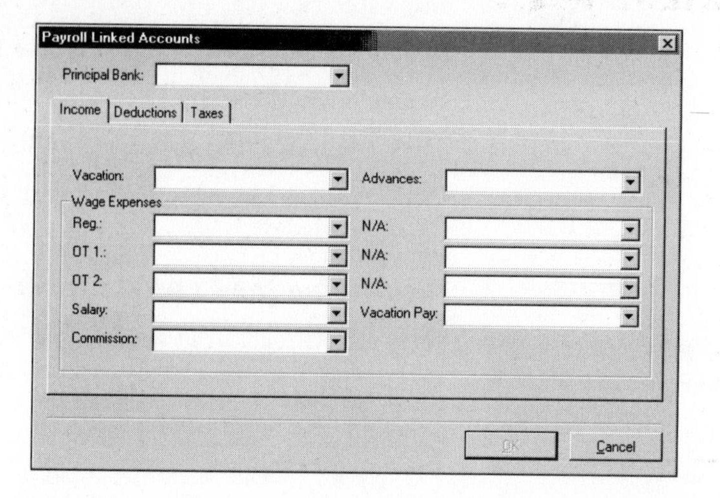

notes

If you can use an account for more than one link, the account will be available in the drop-down list. Otherwise, once an account is selected as a linked account, it is removed from the list.

The linked accounts for all types of income appear together on this first tab screen. Even though Hearth House records all wage expenses in a single *Wages* account, you must identify this as the account for all types of employee payments used by the company. Once the Payroll bank account is identified as the same one used for Payables, the program will apply a single sequence of cheque numbers for all cheques prepared from the Payables and Payroll Journals.

You can type in the account number or select the account from the drop-down list.

Choose 1060 Bank Account: Chequing for the Principal Bank field.

Choose 2300 Vacation Payable for the Vacation field.

Choose 1240 Advances Receivable for the Advances field.

Choose 5300 Wages for all Income fields used.

notes

The names here are the ones you entered in the Names window from the Setup menu. If you deleted a name in the Names window, there will be no name beside the field.

Click the **Deductions tab** to see the next set of Payroll linked accounts:

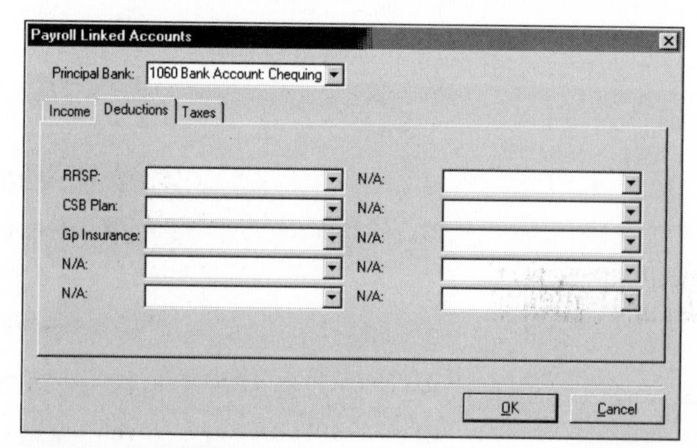

Again you should enter the linked payable accounts for RRSP, CSB Plan and Group Insurance from the chart on page 447.

Click the **Taxes tab** to see the final set of Payroll linked accounts:

Warning!

Simply Accounting will not allow you to remove an account while it is being used as a linked account. Click OK in the warning window to return to the Accounts window. First, turn the linking function off by deleting the account in the linked accounts window. Then remove the account in the Accounts window. You cannot remove an account if it has a balance or if journal entries have been posted to it.

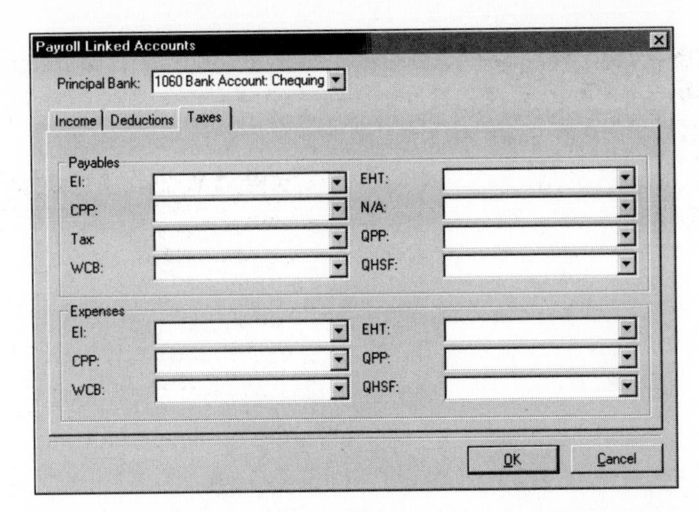

Enter the final set of linked accounts for EI, CPP, Tax, WCB (WSIB) and EHT in both the Payables and the Expenses sections.

Check the linked payroll accounts against the chart on page 447 before proceeding. Click the tabs to see the different linked account screens.

Click OK to save the new account settings and return to the Home window.

Inventory Items Linked Accounts

Hearth House currently uses only one linked account for inventory, the one for damaged merchandise. The linked accounts for the Inventory Ledger are:

Inventory

Item Assembly Costs	not used
Adjustment Write-off	5075 Damaged Inventory

Click the **Item Assembly** or the **Adjustments Journal icon** 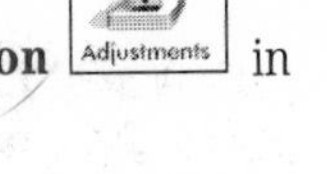 in the Home window to select it.

Click the **Setup button** or choose the Setup menu, then choose System Setting and Linked Accounts and click Inventory Items to open the Inventory Linked Accounts window:

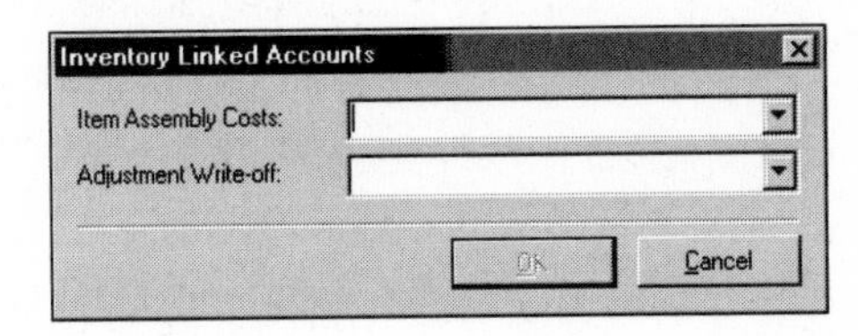

Warning!

Check your work carefully. Although you can change the designated linked accounts at any time, the journal entries will be posted incorrectly if you do not have the correct linked accounts.

You can type in the account number or select the account from the drop-down list.

Choose 5075 Damaged Inventory as the Adjsutment Write-off linked account.

Click OK to save the new account settings and return to the Home window.

Setting up Import Duties

Some goods imported from England are subject to tariffs or import duties. You must activate the duty option before creating vendor records so that you can indicate in the vendor records which vendors supply goods on which duty is charged. Without these two steps, the duty fields in the Purchases Journal will be unavailable.

version 8

Choose the **Setup menu**, then **choose System Settings** and **click Import Duty Information** to access the information screen:

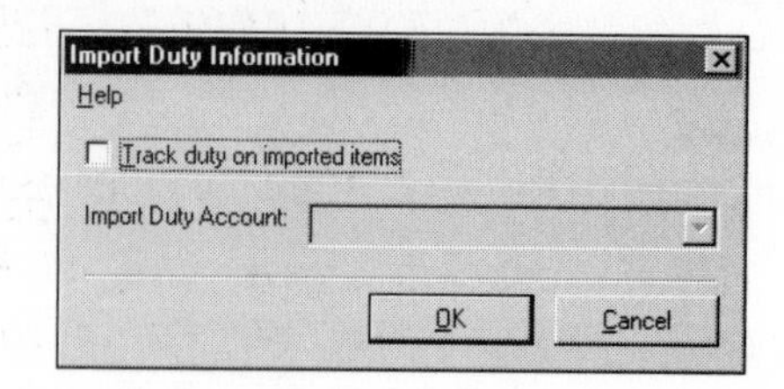

notes

A Payables account is used for import duties because it is a liability to the Receiver General.

Click Track duty on imported items to use the feature.

Click 2360 Import Duties from the Import Duty Account drop-down list.

Click OK to return to the Home window.

Setting up Credit Cards

Hearth House accepts Visa credit card payments from customers and uses a Visa card in payment for purchases. Setting up credit cards includes naming them, identifying the linked accounts and entering fees associated with the cards.

You should be in the Home window.

version 8

Choose the **Setup menu**, then **choose System Settings** and **click Credit Cards** to see the Credit Card Information screen. The cursor is in the Name field.

Type VISA

Press tab to advance to the Discount Fee % field.

Type 3.5

Press tab to advance to the Expense Account field.

Press enter to see the list of accounts available for linking.

Double click 5020 to choose and enter the account. The cursor advances to the Asset Account field.

Press enter to see the list of accounts available for linking.

Double click 1080 to choose and add the credit card bank account.

Click the **Credit cards used tab** to open the screen for the cards that the business uses. Hearth House uses Visa for occasional purchases.

Click the **Name field**.

Type VISA

Press tab to move to the Payable Account field.

Press enter to see the list of available accounts.

Double click 2150 to add the account and move to the Expense Account field.

Press enter to see the account list.

Double click 5020

Click OK to save the information.

Click Yes to accept the account class changes and return to the Home window.

Preparing the Payables Ledger

Use Hearth House's Vendor Information on page 424 to create the vendor records and add the outstanding historical invoices.

Entering Vendor Accounts

Click the **Vendors icon** [Vendors] in the Home window to open the Vendors window.

Click the **Create button** [Create] or choose the File menu and click Create. The Vendor field is highlighted in the Payables Ledger window, ready for you to enter information.

Type the vendor's name. On the Address tab screen, enter the contact, address, phone, fax and tax ID numbers, and the e-mail and Web site addresses from page 424.

Click the **Options tab**.

In the Terms fields, enter the discounts, if there are any, and the number of days in which the net amount is due. All discounts are after tax (leave the box unchecked).

Indicate that you want to retain all invoices for this vendor by leaving the box beside Clear Transactions When Paid unchecked. Check the Print Contact on Cheques option if the contact field contains address information.

version 8

Indicate that the vendor collects GST (purchases from this vendor are eligible for GST input credits) by leaving this box checked. Remember that vendors such as the City Treasurer, Transcend Investment Co., and others who do not supply goods or services eligible for input tax credits do not collect GST.

Identifying Foreign Vendors

For Cambridge Castings and Vulcan Stove, the Options tab screen requires additional information to identify these as foreign vendors.

Warning!

You cannot change a vendor's currency after adding historical transactions. You will need to pay the invoices, clear paid transactions and then remove the vendor record. You cannot access the duty fields in the Purchases Journal unless Charge Duty on Items Purchases is checked in the vendor's ledger.

The Options tab screen for Cambridge Castings is shown here:

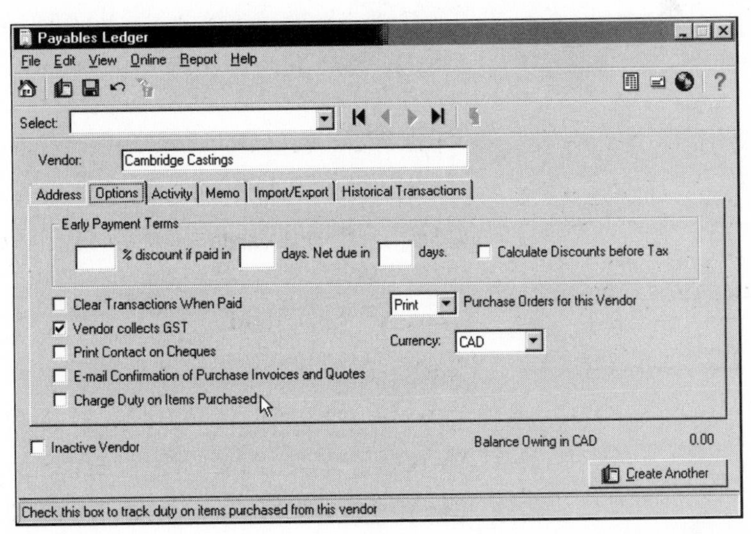

Enter 2% in 10 days, net 15 days as the Early Payment Terms for the vendor.

Click the **Currency field list arrow**.

Click GBP

Click Charge Duty on Items Purchased

Skip the Activity, Memo and Import/Export tab screens. The Balance Owing will be entered automatically by the program once you have entered historical invoices.

Correct any errors by returning to the field with the mistake, highlighting the errors and entering the correct information.

If the vendor has historical transactions, continue by entering historical transactions. If not, **click Create Another** to save the record and open a blank Payables Ledger window. **Click** the **Address tab** to begin entering the next vendor record.

Entering Historical Vendor Transactions

The chart on page 425 provides the information you need to complete this stage.

Click the **Historical Transactions tab**.

Click Save Now

Click Invoices

> **notes**
>
> You can edit the payment terms for individual invoices if needed. Because all discounts are calculated after taxes, there are no separate fields for pretax and tax invoice amounts.

Invoices for Foreign Vendors

The Historical Invoices input screen for foreign vendors has additional fields to accommodate the second currency information, as shown here for Cambridge Castings:

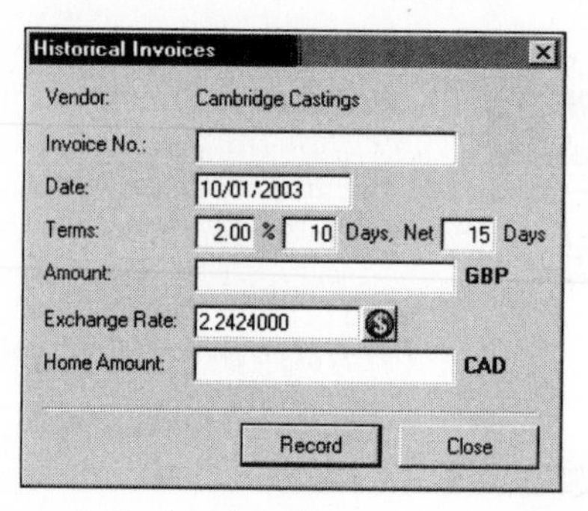

Enter the Invoice Number and the invoice Date.

Press *tab* to see the Exchange Rate screen.

Click Cancel. We will enter the amounts in both currencies and allow the program to calculate the exchange rate.

> **Warning!**
>
> If you save an incorrect invoice amount, you must pay the invoice, clear paid invoices for the vendor (Home window, Maintenance menu), reset the payments for the year to zero (vendor's ledger, Activity tab) and re-enter the outstanding invoices.

Click the **Amount field for GBP**.

Type `1890`

Click the **Home Amount field CAD**.

Type `4237.20` **Press** *tab*

The exchange rate is entered automatically as determined by these two amounts.

Click Record

When you have recorded all outstanding invoices for a vendor,

Click Close to save the invoice and return to the Historical Transactions tab screen. The invoices you have just entered have been added to the Balance fields. Balances are displayed in both currencies. Continue by entering historical payments to this vendor if there are any, or proceed to the next vendor with outstanding invoices.

Invoices for Other Vendors

Enter the Invoice Number, Date and Amount for the first invoice. The default terms should be correct.

Press (tab) to advance to the next field after entering each piece of information.

When all the information is entered correctly, you must save your vendor invoice.

Click Record to save the information and to display another blank invoice for this vendor.

Repeat these procedures to enter the remaining invoices for the vendor.

Click Close to return to the Payables Ledger when you have recorded all outstanding invoices for the vendor.

Historical Payments

notes

Enter historical payments to foreign vendors in the same way as historical payment to other vendors, except that you must enter an exchange rate for the payment.

Click Payments

Click the **Number field**.

Enter the cheque number for the first payment.

Press (tab) and enter the payment date for the first payment. Skip the Discount fields because discounts are taken only when the early payment is a full payment.

Click the **Amount paid column** (on the line for the invoice being paid).

Enter the payment amount or accept the default.

Press (tab) to advance to the next invoice if there is one. Delete any amounts or discounts that are not included in the payment.

Click Record to save the information and to display an updated statement for this vendor.

Repeat these procedures to enter the remaining payments for the vendor.

When you have recorded all outstanding payments for a vendor,

Click Close to return to the Payables Ledger form for the vendor. Notice that the payments you have just entered have been added to the Balance field.

Click Create Another [Create Another] to save the vendor information and display a new blank Payables Ledger screen.

Click the **Address tab**.

Repeat these procedures to enter the remaining vendors and their historical transactions.

Close the vendor ledger and the Vendors icon window to return to the Home window.

notes

Display or print the Vendor List and the Vendor Aged Detail Report, including terms and historical differences, to check the accuracy of your work.

Preparing the Receivables Ledger

Use Hearth House's Customer Information on page 425 to create the customer records and add the outstanding historical invoices. All the current customers are in the Home country.

Entering Customer Accounts

Click the **Customers icon** [Customers] in the Home window to open the Customers window.

Click the **Create button** [Create] or choose the File menu and then click Create. The Customer field in the Receivables Ledger window is highlighted, ready for you to enter information.

notes

You can edit the payment terms for individual customers or for individual historical invoices if necessary.

Type the customer's name. On the Address tab screen, enter the contact, address, phone and fax numbers, and the e-mail and Web site addresses according to page 425.

Remember to **click Preferred Customer** for **Lakeshore Condos** and for **York Seniors' Club** to change the status for these two customers.

Click the **Ship-to Address tab**.

Click Same as mailing address to have the same address apply to both fields on invoices, orders and quotes.

The default entries on the Options tab screen are correct. The payment terms are entered from the default Receivables settings. All invoices will be retained, all customers pay GST (the GST fields will be available in the Sales Journal and GST paid by this customer will be included in the detailed GST reports), and statements should be printed for this customer. All customers are home currency customers.

Click the **Activity tab**.

In the Credit Limit field, type in the amount that the customer can purchase on account before payments are required. If the customer goes beyond the credit limit, the program will issue a warning before posting an invoice.

The balance owing will be included automatically once you have provided the outstanding invoice information. If the customer has outstanding transactions, proceed to the next section on historical information. Otherwise,

Click Create Another [Create Another] to save the information and advance to the next new Receivables Ledger input screen. **Click** the **Address Tab**.

Entering Historical Customer Information

The chart on page 425 provides the information you need to complete this stage.

Click the **Historical Transactions tab**.

Click Save Now

Click Invoices

Warning!

If you save an incorrect invoice amount, you must pay the incorrect invoice, clear paid transactions for the customer, then re-enter the customer's outstanding invoices.

Enter the invoice number, date and amount for the first invoice. The default terms should be correct.

Press tab to advance to the next field after entering each piece of information.

When all the information is entered correctly, you must save your customer invoice.

Click Record to save the information and to display another blank invoice for this customer.

Repeat these procedures to enter the remaining invoices for the customer, if there are any.

When you have recorded all outstanding invoices for a customer,

Click Close to return to the Receivables Ledger window for the customer. The invoices you have just entered have been added to the Balance field. Continue by entering payments received from this customer, if there are any, or proceed to enter the next customer.

Click Payments

Click the **Number field**.

Type the cheque number for the first payment.

Press tab and enter the payment date for the first payment. Again, discounts apply only to full payments made before the due dates, so you can skip the Discount fields.

Click the **Amount paid column** (on the line for the invoice being paid).

Type the payment amount.

Press tab to advance to the next amount if there are other invoices. Delete any amounts or discounts that will not be included in the payment.

Click Record to save the information and to display an updated statement for this customer.

Repeat these procedures to enter the remaining payments for the customer.

When you have recorded all outstanding receipts from a customer,

Display or print the Customer List and the Customer Aged Detail Report, including terms and historical differences, to check the accuracy of your work.

Click Close to return to the Receivables Ledger window for the customer. The payments you have just entered have been added to the customer's Balance field.

Click Create Another Create Another to save the information and advance to the next new Receivables Ledger input screen.

Click the **Address tab**. After entering all customer records and historical data,

Close the customer ledger and Customers window to return to the Home window.

Preparing the Payroll Ledger

Use the Hearth House Employee Information Sheet, Employee Profiles and Additional Payroll Information on pages 426–427 to create the employee records and add historical information.

The following keystrokes will enter the information for Hearth House employee **Ella Cinder**.

Click the **Employees icon** Employees in the Home window to open the Employees window:

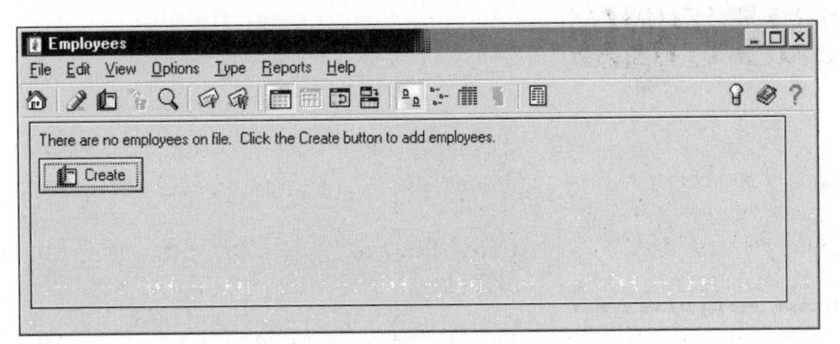

The Employees icon window is blank because no employees are on file at this stage.

Click the **Create button** Create or choose the File menu and click Create.

Entering Personal Details for Employees

notes

If you skip the Employees icon window in the View menu (User Preferences), you will see the Payroll Ledger window immediately when you click the Employees icon.

The following Payroll Ledger new employee information form opens at the Personal information tab screen:

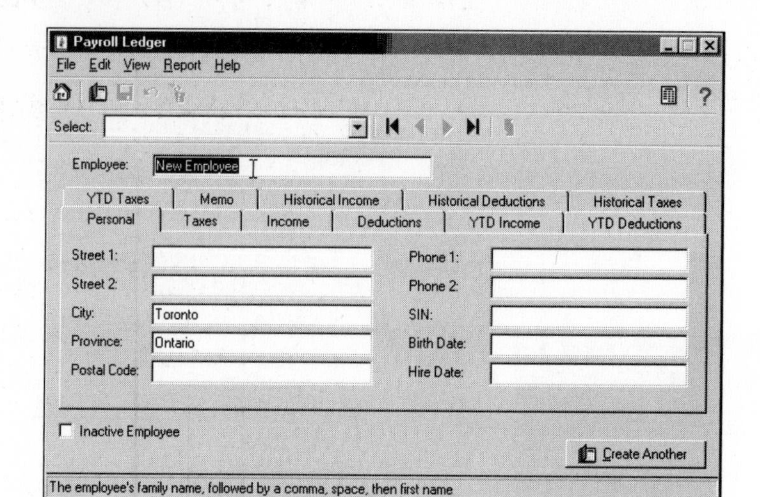

notes

By entering the surname first, your employee lists will be in correct alphabetic order.

The Employee field is highlighted, ready for you to enter information.

Type `Cinder, Ella`

Press *tab*

The cursor advances to the Street 1 field.

Type `921 Fireside Dr.`

Press *tab*

Double click the **City field**.

Type `Scarborough`

Ontario is the correct entry in the Province field.

Click the **Postal Code field**.

Type `m1b2c9`

Press *tab*

The program corrects the postal code format and advances the cursor to the Phone 1 field.

Type `4165787291`

Click the **Social Insurance Number (SIN) field**. The program corrects the telephone number format. You must use a valid SIN number.

Type `494663487`

Press *tab*

The cursor advances to the Birth Date field. Enter the month, day and year using any accepted date format.

Type `12-25-74`

Press *tab*

The cursor moves to the Hire Date field, which should contain the date when the employee began working for Hearth House.

Type `1-1-03`

The final option designates the employee as active or inactive. All employees at Hearth House are active, so the default selection is correct.

Entering Employee Tax Information

version 8

Click the **Taxes tab** to advance to the next set of employee details:

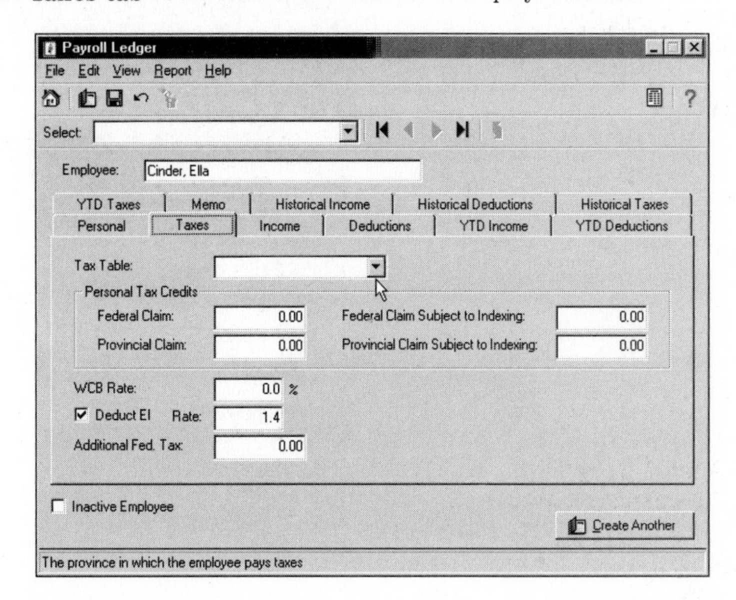

This window allows you to enter income tax-related information for the employee.

version 8

notes

Starting in 2001, different provinces have different rates for personal income tax. This option is not available in Version 8 because the program was released before the tax change and updated to Version 8.5 after.

Click the **Tax Table list arrow**. A list of provinces appears on the screen.

Click Ontario, the province of taxation for Hearth House for income tax purposes.

Press tab

The cursor advances to the Federal Claim field, which holds the total claim for personal tax credits.

Type `13706`

Press tab to advance to the Federal Claim Subject to Indexing. This is the amount of personal claim minus pension and tuition/education contributions.

Type `13706`

Press tab to advance to the Provincial Claim field. Provincial taxes are no longer calculated as a percentage of the federal taxes so separate provincial claim amounts are needed.

Type `13732`

Press tab

Type `13732` (to enter the provincial claim amount subject to indexing)

Press tab

notes

WCB has been renamed WSIB (Workplace Safety and Insurance Board) in Ontario to emphasize safety rather than compensation for accidents.

The cursor advances to the WCB Rate field. Here you should enter the applicable rate for the Workplace Safety and Insurance Board.

Type `4.97`

If an employee is insurable by EI, you must leave the box for Deduct EI checked. The default EI contribution factor, 1.4, for Hearth House is correct. We entered it in the Payroll Settings window.

If an employee has chosen to have additional federal income tax deducted from each paycheque, you can enter the amount of the deduction in the Additional Fed. Tax field. Employees might make this choice if they receive regular additional income from which no tax is deducted. By making this choice, they avoid paying a large amount of tax at the end of the year and possible interest penalties.

Entering Income Amounts for Employees

Click the **Income tab** to open the next screen of employee details:

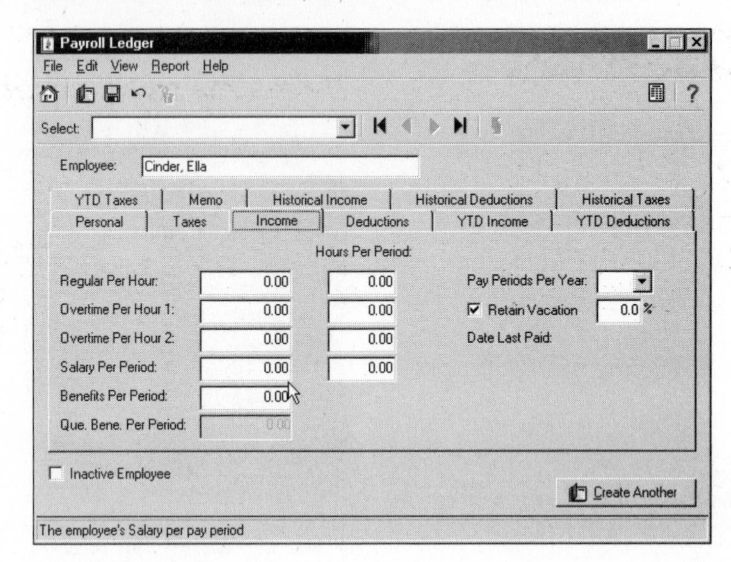

In the Regular Per Hour field you would enter the regular per hour wage for an employee. The number of hours usually worked in the pay period is entered beside the rate. These fields apply to Kindl but you should skip them for salaried employees.

In the Overtime Per Hour 1 field, enter the per hour overtime earnings for the employee. Again, skip this field since Cinder is a salaried employee.

If there are two different overtime rates, enter the second rate in the Overtime Per Hour 2 field.

Click the **Salary Per Period field** where you can enter the salary Cinder receives every pay period.

Type 4500

Press tab

The cursor moves to the Salary Hours Per Period field where you can enter the number of hours the employee normally works in each pay period (e.g., 35 hours per week or 140 hours per month).

Type 150

Pay Periods Per Year refer to the number of times the employee is paid, or the pay cycle.

Click the **list arrow** beside the field for Pay Periods Per Year.

Click 12

Retaining vacation pay is normal for full-time hourly paid employees. Part-time and casual workers often receive their vacation pay with each paycheque because of the uncertainty of their work schedule. You will turn the option to retain vacation off when an employee receives the vacation pay, either when taking a vacation or when

notes

Employees may be paid yearly (1), semi-annually (2), monthly for 10 months (10), monthly (12), every four weeks (13), every two weeks for a 10-month year (22) twice a month (24), every two weeks (26) or weekly (52).

leaving the company. If the employee is salaried and does not receive vacation pay, the option should also be turned off. Cinder is salaried.

Click Retain Vacation to remove the ✔ for Cinder.

For Kindl or for any employee who receives vacation pay, leave the option to Retain Vacation checked and type the vacation pay rate in the % field.

Entering Default Payroll Deduction Amounts

> **notes**
>
> If you choose to calculate deductions as a percent of gross pay in the Payroll Settings, the deduction fields will have % beside them so you can enter a percentage instead of a fixed amount.

Click the **Deductions tab** to open the screen for entering payroll deductions:

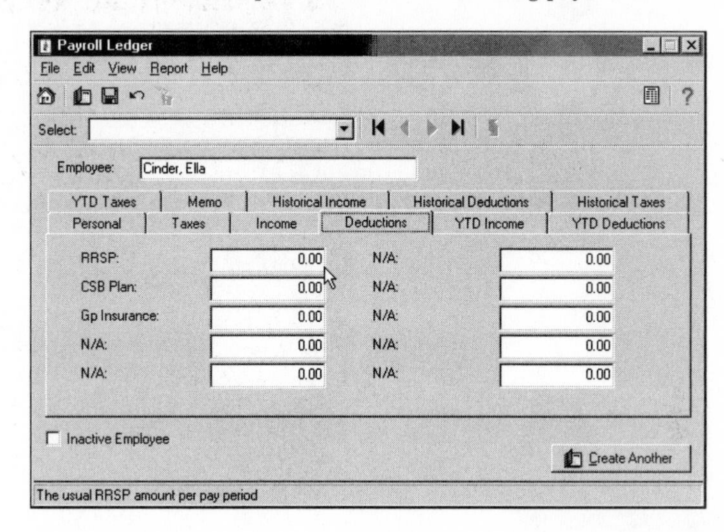

> **notes**
>
> For one-time changes, you can edit deduction amounts in the Paycheques Journal on the Deductions tab screen. You cannot edit these deduction amounts in the Payroll Cheque Run Journal.

You have the option of entering the deductions here, so that they are included automatically on the Payroll Journal input forms, or entering them manually in the Journal for each pay period. Since all three employees have chosen to participate in these plans, you can enter the information here so that the deductions are made automatically. You should make permanent changes by editing the employee ledger record.

Click the **RRSP field**. You should enter the amount that is to be withheld in each pay period.

Type `200`

Press tab to advance the cursor to the CSB Plan field. Enter the amount that is to be withheld in each pay period.

Type `200`

Press tab to advance the cursor to the Gp Insurance field. Enter the amount that is to be withheld in each pay period.

Type `10`

The remaining deductions, labelled N/A, are not used by Hearth House, so you can skip them.

> **Warning!**
>
> Enter employee historical payroll details carefully. You will be unable to edit these fields after finishing the history or once you begin to make Payroll Journal entries for the employee.

Entering Historical Income Amounts

The next step in setting up the Payroll Ledger for employees is to enter the historical data, the income and deductions for the year to date. Because there are yearly maximum amounts for CPP and EI contributions, these historical details are needed so that tax and deductions can be calculated correctly. Totals for optional deductions are also retained in the employee record.

Click the **Historical Income tab** to open the information window:

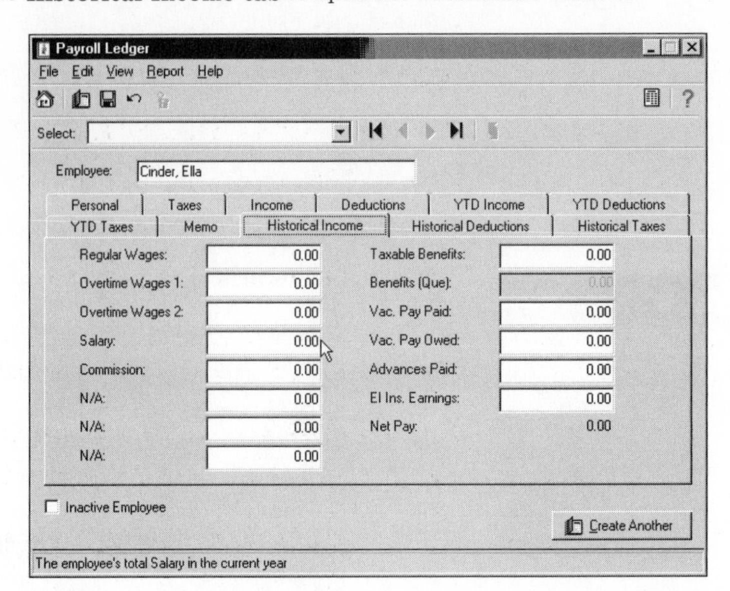

Warning!

The totals for all employees for advances paid and vacation pay owing must match the corresponding General Ledger account balances before you can finish entering the history.

The Regular Wages and the Overtime Wages fields apply to hourly paid employees. They do not apply to Cinder because she is a salaried employee.

Double click the **Salary field**.

Type 40500

notes

For Kindl, or any employees who are owed vacation pay, enter the amount in the Vac. Pay Owed field. If they have received vacation pay, enter this amount in the Vac. Pay Paid field. Any advances paid to the employees and not yet repaid are recorded in the Advances Paid field.

The Commission field, other income fields, taxable benefits and vacation pay fields are not applicable. Cinder does not receive a sales commission or company benefits. She takes time off work with pay instead of receiving vacation pay. She has no advances outstanding. Once all the information is added, the program will update the Net Pay.

In the EI Insurable Earnings field, you should enter the total salary received to date that is EI insurable. The program will update this total every time you make payroll entries until the maximum salary on which EI is calculated has been reached. At that time, no further EI premiums will be deducted.

Double click the **EI Ins. Earnings field**.

Type 39000

Entering Historical Employee Deductions

Click the **Historical Deductions tab** to open the next information window:

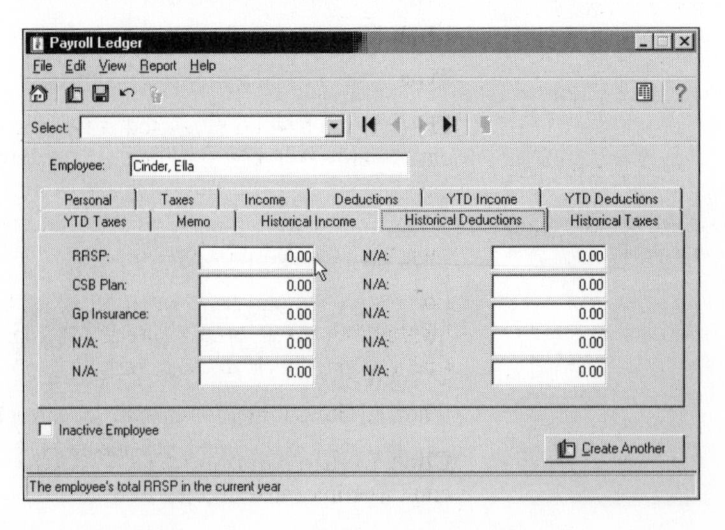

Click the **RRSP field**.

Type 1800

Press tab

The cursor advances to the CSB Plan field.

Type 1800

Press tab

The cursor advances to the Gp Insurance field.

Type 90

The remaining deduction fields are not used.

Entering Historical Tax Amounts

Click the **Historical Taxes tab** to open the next screen we need to complete:

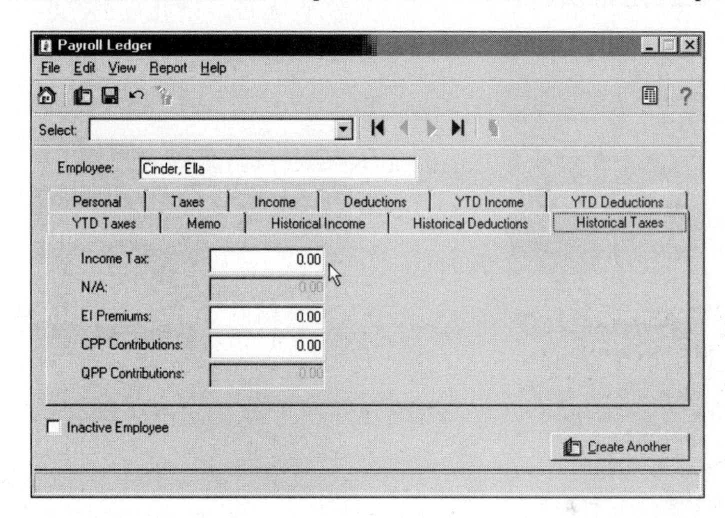

Click the **Income Tax field**.

Type 7778.79

Press tab

The cursor advances to the EI Premiums field. Enter the amount of EI paid to date.

Type 936

Press tab to move to the CPP Contributions field.

Type 1329.90

The Memo tab will not be used at this time. You could enter a note with a reminder date to appear in the To-Do Lists, for example, a reminder to issue vacation paycheques on a specific date. The three YTD tab screens contain the Year-To-Date totals for the employee which are updated initially from the historical information and then from current payroll entries.

Correct any employee information errors by returning to the field with the error, highlighting the error and entering the correct information. Click each tab in turn so that you can check all the information.

When all the information is entered correctly, you must save your employee record.

Click Create Another [Create Another] to save the record and to open a new blank employee information form.

notes

- The program automatically calculates net earnings. You can confirm the accuracy of this amount with your input form.
- The program updates YTD amounts automatically from the historical data you enter and from current payroll journal entries.

notes

When you have finished, display or print the Employee List and the Employee Summary Report to check the accuracy of your work.

Click the **Personal tab**.

Repeat these procedures to enter other employee records.

Close the employee ledger and Employees window to return to the Home window.

Preparing the Inventory Ledger

Use the Hearth House Inventory Information and chart on pages 427–429 to record details about the inventory items on hand.

Entering Inventory Records

The following keystrokes will enter the information for Hearth House's first inventory item, **Andirons: cast iron**.

Click the **Inventory & Services icon** [Inventory & Services] in the Home window. Again, with no inventory items on file, the icon window is empty.

notes

If you skip the Inventory icon window (View menu, User Preferences), you will see this Inventory Ledger when you click the Inventory icon.

Click the **Create button** [Create] or choose the File menu and click Create to display the Inventory Ledger — the new inventory item input screen that follows:

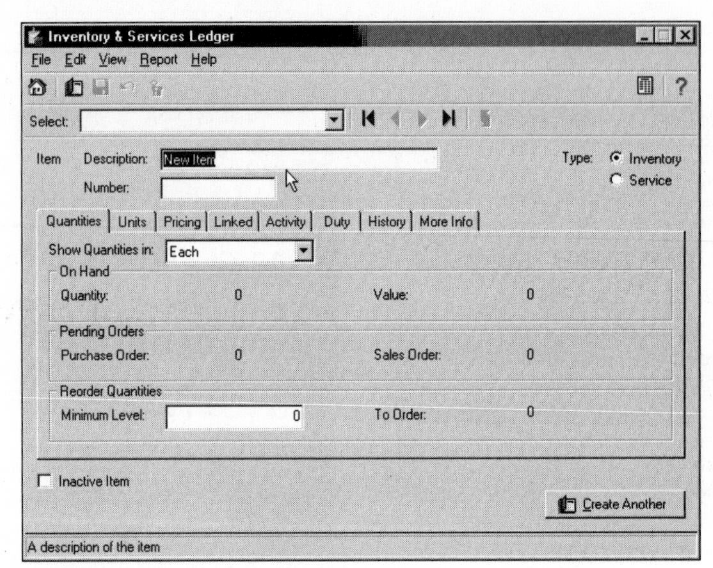

Warning!

Enter inventory details very carefully. You cannot remove an inventory record or change the Type if there is a quantity on hand. You must edit the History fields to reduce the quantity and value to zero. Then remove the item and re-enter all the details correctly. To change the Type, close the ledger to save the changes in history. When you open the ledger again, you may edit the Type.

The Item Description field is selected. Use this field for the name or description for the first item.

Type `Andirons: cast iron`

Press *tab* to advance to the Item Number field where you should enter the inventory number or code.

version 8

notes

When you sort inventory by number, the two item fields shown here are reversed. The Number field appears first.

Type `AC01`

The Type is set correctly for this item as Inventory rather than Service.

The **Show quantities in field** allows you to select the units displayed in the ledger. If you have entered different units for stocking, selling and buying, these will be available from the drop-down list.

notes

The Quantity On Hand and Value fields are updated by the program as are the Purchase Orders and Sales Orders Pending.

Click the **Minimum Level field**. Here you should enter the minimum stock level or re-order point for this inventory item.

Type `1`

notes

For some kinds of items, the units for buying, stocking and selling may differ and you can enter different units.

Click the **Units tab** to see the next information screen:

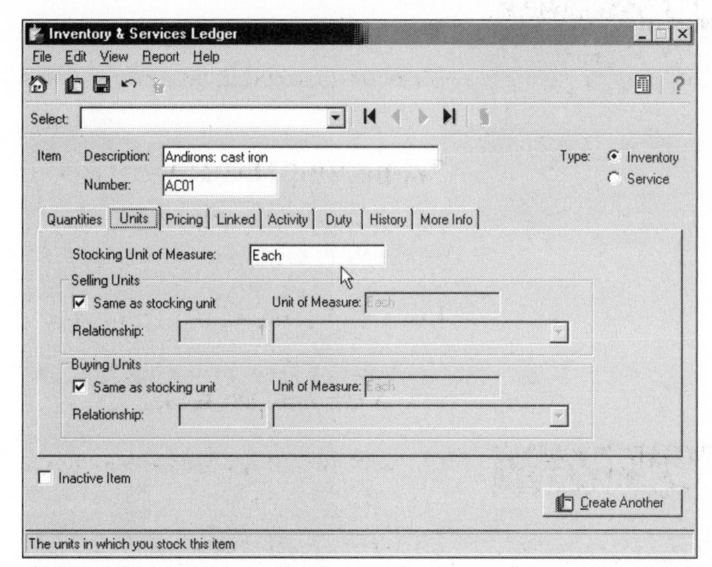

Hearth House uses the same units for all its transactions, so the checkmarks for Same as stocking unit are correct. If you click these check boxes, the unit fields will open and you can enter a different unit of measure and the relationship between units. For example, if items are purchased in dozens and stocked individually, the relationship is 12 to 1. The Stocking unit must be changed.

Double click the default entry **Each** for the Stocking Unit of Measure.

Type `Set`

notes

- For Version 8.0 and Version 8.5, there is only one Regular Foreign Selling Price field.
- Foreign price fields are available only if you indicate that inventory prices should be taken from the inventory ledger and not calculated using the exchange rate. This is the default setting for Version 8.5, so we do not need to change the settings for the ledger. The pricing option appears on the Inventory Settings screen only after you enter foreign currency information. Therefore, the Settings screen on page 440 does not show the foreign pricing options.

Click the **Pricing tab** to open the next group of inventory record fields:

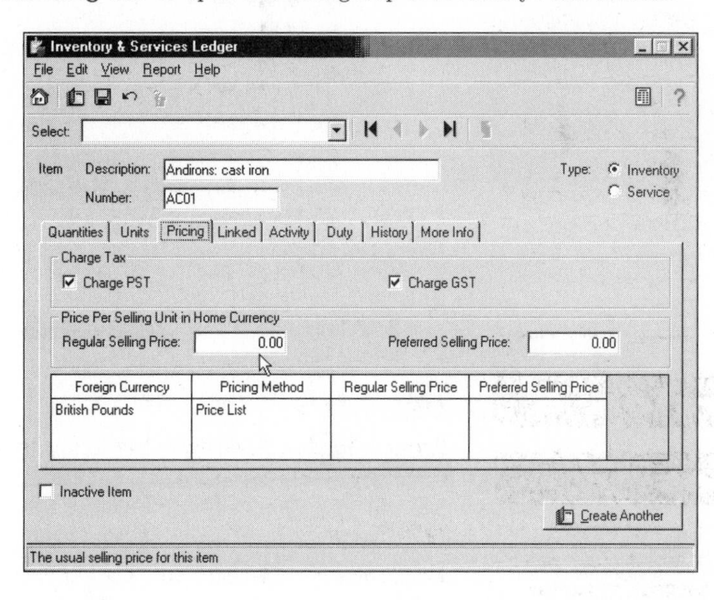

On the pricing tab screen, you can indicate whether the item is taxable for both provincial and federal sales taxes, and you can enter regular and preferred prices in the currencies that you have set up. Because there are no foreign customers, you can skip the Foreign Currency pricing section.

Click the **Regular Selling Price field**. Here you should enter the selling price for this inventory item.

Type `100`

Press tab to advance to the Preferred selling Price field.

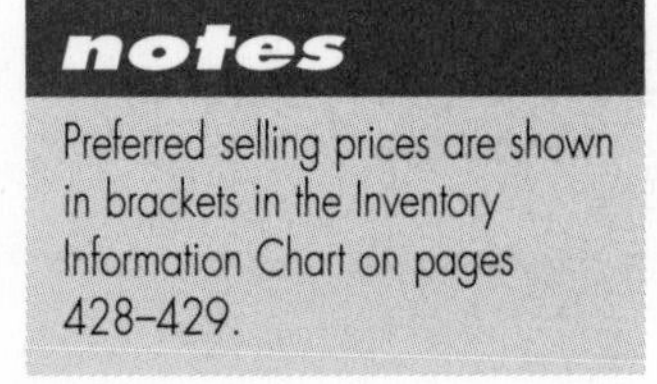

Preferred selling prices are shown in brackets in the Inventory Information Chart on pages 428–429.

Type 90

Click the **Linked tab** to open the linked accounts screen for the item:

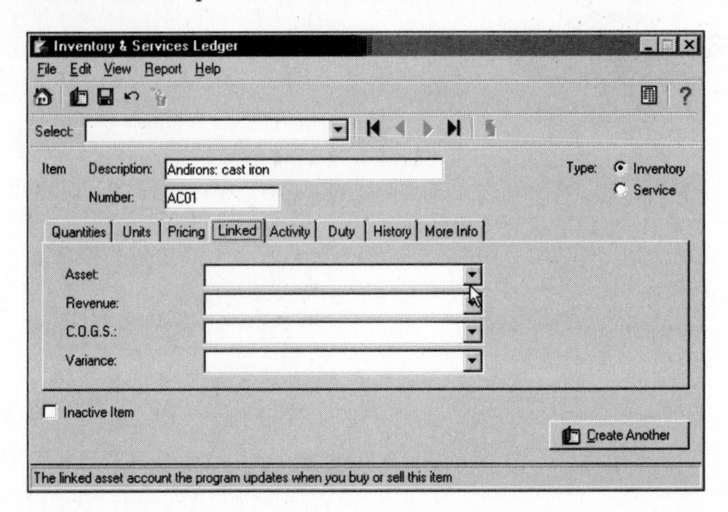

Click the **Asset field list arrow**. Here you must enter the asset account associated with the sale or purchase of this inventory item. Refer to the Chart of Accounts on page 419 to find the account number for the inventory asset category *Accessories & Tools*. All available asset accounts are in the displayed list.

If you type a new account number you have the option to create the new account and, because the history is not finished, you can add the Opening Balance using the Add an Account wizard.

Click 1400

Press tab

The program asks you to confirm the account class change for account *1400*:

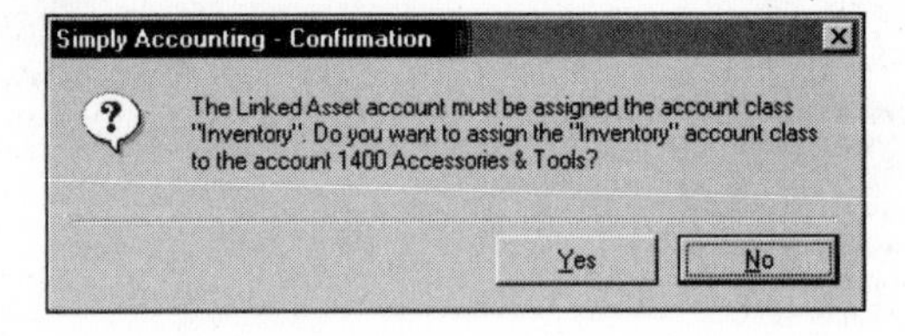

Click Yes to accept the change.

The cursor advances to the Revenue field. Here you must enter the revenue account that will be credited with the sale of this inventory item. Again, you can display the list of revenue accounts by clicking the list arrow.

Click 4020

Press tab

The cursor advances to the C.O.G.S. field. Here you must enter the expense account to be debited with the sale of this inventory item, normally the *Cost of Goods Sold* account. If a company wanted to keep track of each inventory category separately, it could set up different expense accounts for each category and enter them in this field. The appropriate expense account would then be updated automatically when an inventory item was sold. Click the list arrow beside the field to display the list of available expense accounts.

Click 5050

Press tab

Click Yes to accept the account class change for *5050* and advance to the Variance field.

notes

If there are no items on hand at the time of the sale, the average cost is zero and the entire purchase price becomes the variance.

Simply Accounting uses the variance linked account when sales are made of items that are not in stock. If there is a difference between the historical average cost of goods remaining in stock and the actual cost when the new merchandise is received, the price difference is charged to the variance expense account at the time of the purchase. If you have not indicated a variance account, the program will ask you to identify one when you are entering the purchase. Click the list arrow.

Click 5055 and **click Yes** to accept the account class change.

Click the **Activity tab**:

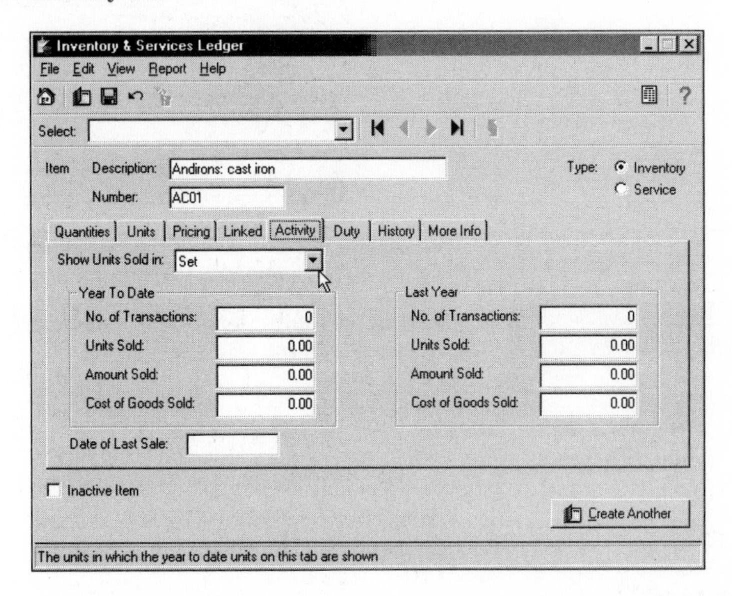

If you have historical information about the sale of the product, you could enter it on this tab screen. It would then be added to the inventory tracking information for reports.

The first activity field, the Date of Last Sale, refers to the last date on which the item was sold. The next two sections contain information for the Year To Date and the previous year. Since Hearth House has not kept this information, you can skip these fields. Refer to the description of new inventory items on pages 283–284 in the Meteor Mountain Bike application for a more detailed description of these historical fields.

Click the **Duty tab** to see the next information screen for inventory items:

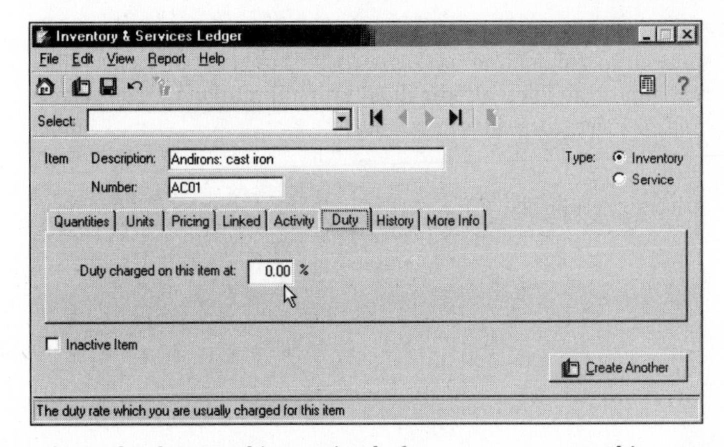

You must activate the duty tracking option before you can access this screen.

Click the **Duty charged on this item at field**.

Type 8

Click the **History tab** to see the next information screen for inventory items:

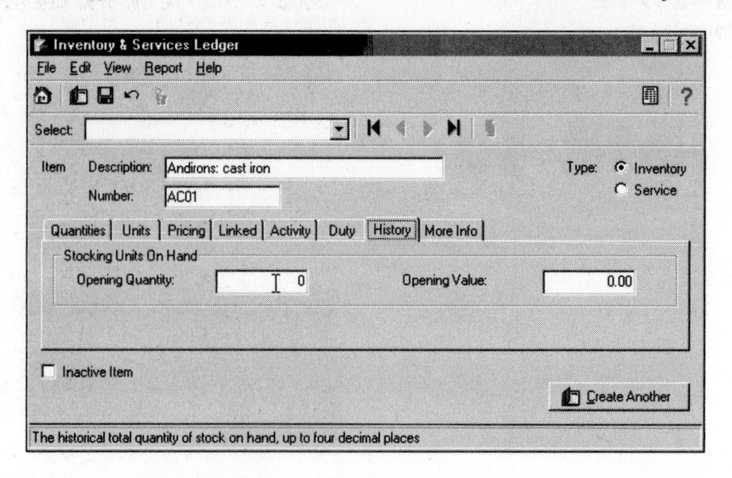

This screen has information about the starting quantities for the item at the time of conversion to Simply Accounting.

Warning!

The total opening value amounts for all items in an asset group must match the General Ledger asset account balance before you can finish entering the history.

Click the **Opening Quantity field** to enter the opening level of inventory — the actual number of items available for sale. These opening quantities are added to the quantity on hand in the Quantities tab screen.

Type 5 **Press** tab

The cursor advances to the Opening Value field, where you should enter the actual total cost of the inventory on hand.

Type 250

More Info, the final tab, allows you to add a longer description for the item and even a picture file.

Correct any errors by returning to the field with the mistake. Highlight the error and enter the correct information. Click the different tabs to see all the information that you entered.

When all the information is entered correctly, you must save your inventory record.

notes

Display or print the Inventory List, Synopsis and Quantity reports to check them for accuracy. You may want to sort inventory by number (Setup menu, System Settings, Settings, Inventory tab screen) before printing the inventory reports. Your reports will then be easier to check against the ones we show. Change the settings again to sort by description for entering source documents.

Click Create Another Create Another to save the record and advance to a new input screen.

Click the **Quantities tab**.

Repeat these procedures to enter other inventory records.

Entering Inventory Services

The final items on the inventory chart are services that Hearth House provides on a regular basis. Entering service items is similar to entering inventory, but there are fewer details to enter.

You should have a blank Inventory & Services Ledger window open at the Quantities tab screen.

Click Service to change the Type in the upper right section of the screen.

version 8

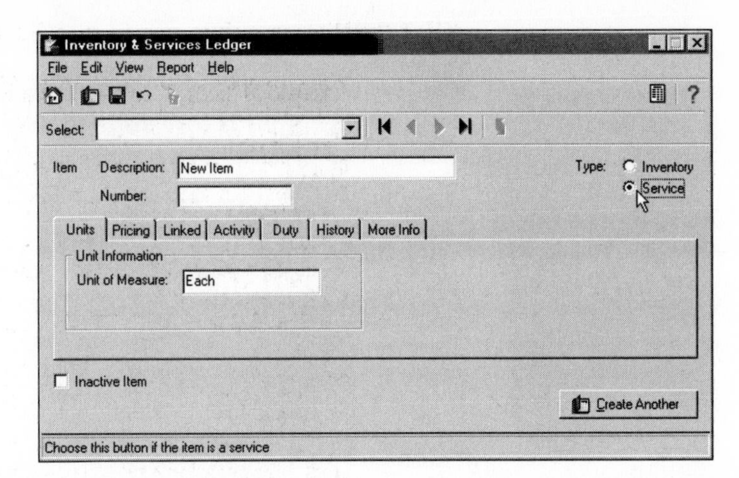

There are fewer tabs and fields for services because some of the item details are not applicable. The Unit of Measure and Selling Price have the same meaning for services as they do for inventory items. There is no minimum quantity because service items are not purchased or kept in stock. Thus the History tab fields are removed.

Some services are subject to Provincial Sales Taxes and others are not. These rules also vary from one province to another. Therefore, you should indicate in the ledger record whether the service should have PST charged. If you choose not to apply PST, the PST fields in the Sales Journal will be unavailable. Customers are charged PST for all services offered by Hearth House, so you should click Charge PST to add a ✓.

Only expense and revenue accounts are linked for services. The other two linked account fields are removed for services.

Close the inventory information window to return to the Home window.

notes

Remember to use Revenue from Services as the linked account for inventory services.

Finishing the History

The last stage in setting up the accounting system involves confirming that the history for each ledger is finished. Before proceeding, you should check the data integrity (Home window, Maintenance menu) to see whether there are any out-of-balance ledgers that will prevent you from proceeding. Correct these errors and then make a backup copy of the files.

Warning!

Before you finish entering the history, make a backup copy of Hearth House company files. This is necessary if you decide later that you want to change some of the historical information. Remember, once you finish entering the history, you cannot add information for any period before the earliest transaction date.

Making a Backup of the Company Files

With the Hearth House files open, use the File menu Backup command to create a backup. Instead, you may want to create a complete working copy of the not-finished files.

Choose the **File menu** and **click Save As**.

Choose the data folder you want for the not-finished version of the data file.

Make a new folder, NFHEARTH, and open it.

Double click the **File name field**.

Type `nfhearth`

Click Save

This command will create a copy of all the files for Hearth House. The "NF" designates files as not finished to distinguish them from the ones you will work with to enter journal transactions. Remember to return to your working copy of the file before finishing the history. (Close the nfhearth file and open the hearth file.)

notes

If you are using a different location for your files, substitute the file name and path for your setup.

Changing the History Status of Ledgers to Finished

Choose the **History menu** and **click Finish Entering History** to display the familiar warning. If you have made errors, you will not see the warning message. Instead you will see a list of errors.

Click Print so that you can refer to the list for making corrections.

Click OK to return to the Home window. Make the corrections, then try again.

Click Proceed when there are no errors and you have already backed up your files.

The Hearth House files are now ready for you to enter transactions. Notice that all the Home window icons appear without the open history icons. Congratulations on reaching this stage! This is a good time to take a break.

Finish your session. This gives you the opportunity to read the next section and the instructions before starting the source document transactions.

notes

Only unhidden modules are set as finished. If modules are hidden and then later unhidden, they will appear with the open history quill pen icon. When you choose the History menu, open or unfinished modules will be listed individually so you can set them as finished one at a time.

Exporting Reports

Simply Accounting allows you to export reports to a specified drive and path. The files created by the program may then be used by a spreadsheet or wordprocessing program. File formats available for export purposes include Text for a wordprocessing format file, Lotus Versions 1 and 2, Symphony, Excel Versions 97 and 2.1, Supercalc and Comma separated.

notes

Integration with other software is described further in Appendix D.

Exporting files will allow you to manipulate and interpret data for reporting purposes. This process of integrating Simply Accounting files with other software is an important step in making the accounting process meaningful.

The following keystrokes will export the opening Balance Sheet for Hearth House to a Lotus Version 2 file.

Display the Balance Sheet or the report you want to export.

Choose the **File menu** and **click Export** to display the following screen:

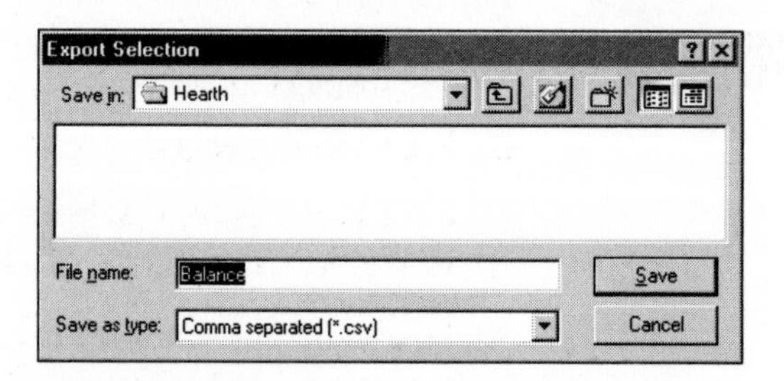

Click Lotus 1-2-3 v2 as the type for the Balance Sheet in the Save as type field. Use the field list arrow to display the file type options if necessary.

Choose the location for your exported file. By default your working folder is selected.

Click the **list arrow for the Save in field** to access the drive and folder you want.

For example, **click 31/2 Floppy (A:)** from the list to select Drive A. (Be sure that you have formatted disk in Drive A.) Then double click the folder you want to use to store your file or create a new folder.

notes

To create an Excel spreadsheet, click Microsoft Excel 97 (or 2.1 if your version is older than Excel 97). To generate a file that you can use with wordprocessing software, click Text.

Accept the default file name, or type the name you want for your file. The program assigns an extension to the file name so that Lotus will recognize the new file as a Lotus file.

Click Save

Using the Exported Files with Other Software

notes

Some spreadsheet programs can open and convert a file that was saved in the format of a different program. For example, Microsoft Excel can open (or save) text files or Lotus 1-2-3 files. Simply choose the alternative file type in your Open File (or Save File) window.

Finish the session using Simply Accounting. Start the software program you want to use with the exported file, referring to the program manuals if necessary. When the blank document or spreadsheet screen appears,

Choose the File menu and **click** Open if this is a Windows program. Change folders if necessary to locate and then select the exported file. Be sure that the selected file type also matches the format of your exported file (e.g., .txt for a text file, or .xls for Excel).

Click OK. Your exported file should replace the blank document screen.

Once you have exported a financial statement as a text file, you can include it in a written report prepared with any wordprocessing program. You can then use the features of the wordprocessing software to enhance the appearance of the statement using format styles that are consistent with the remainder of the report. If you have exported a spreadsheet file, you can use the spreadsheet program to perform additional calculations. Then you can save the modified report as a text file to be incorporated in a wordprocessing report.

When working with a spreadsheet program such as Lotus 1-2-3 or Microsoft Excel, you can use the calculation capabilities of the spreadsheet program to make comparisons between statements from different financial periods. You might also want to use the charting or graphing features to prepare presentation materials.

Exporting reports offers advantages over re-creating the statements. Not only do you save the time of retyping, but you also ensure greater accuracy by avoiding errors made while retyping the numbers and accounts.

INSTRUCTIONS FOR SOURCE DOCUMENTS

Instructions for October

1. Using the Chart of Accounts and other information provided, enter the transactions for October.
2. Print the following:
   a. Journal Entries (All Journals) for October
   b. the Customer Aged Detail report for all customers for October
   c. the General Ledger account reports for
      - Bank Account: Chequing
      - Revenue from Sales
      - Sales Returns and Allowances
   d. Vendor Purchases Summary for Cambridge Castings, all categories, for October
3. Export the Balance Sheet as at October 31, 2003, to a spreadsheet application.
4. Calculate the following key ratios in your spreadsheet:
   a. current ratio
   b. quick ratio
5. Based on expenses and revenues for October, set up a budget for use in November and December.

Instructions for November

1. Using the Chart of Accounts and other information provided, enter the transactions for November.
2. Print the following reports:

   a. Journal Entries (All Journals) for November
   b. the Vendor Aged Detail Report for all vendors for November
   c. the Employee Summary report for all employees for the pay period ending November 30, 2003
   d. the Inventory Synopsis Report (observe and report items that have not sold well over the two-month period)
   e. Customer Sales Summary (all customers, items and categories) for November

3. Export the Comparative Balance Sheet for October 31 and November 30, 2003, to a spreadsheet application. You will use these at the end of the year for three-month comparisons.
4. Compare November's performance against October's budget forecast.

Instructions for December

1. Using the Chart of Accounts and other information provided, enter the transactions for December.
2. Print the following reports:

   a. Journal Entries (All Journals) for December
   b. Trial Balance, Balance Sheet and Income Statement on December 31
   c. Project Income Summary report for Highlife Townhouse (all accounts) for December
   d. Inventory Activity report for Fireplaces and Inserts (all journals) for December

3. Export the Balance Sheet and Income Statement to a spreadsheet application. Combine the Balance Sheet with the comparative one for October and November. Compare first- and second-quarter figures, item by item, to assess the performance of Hearth House.
4. Print T4 slips and the cumulative year-to-date 2003 payroll information for each employee.
5. Make a backup copy of your Data Disk before you proceed with this step. Advance the session date to January 1, 2002. Print the Trial Balance, Balance Sheet and Income Statement for January 1, 2002. Compare the end of December and the first of January statements and note the changes that result from Simply Accounting closing the books for the new fiscal period.

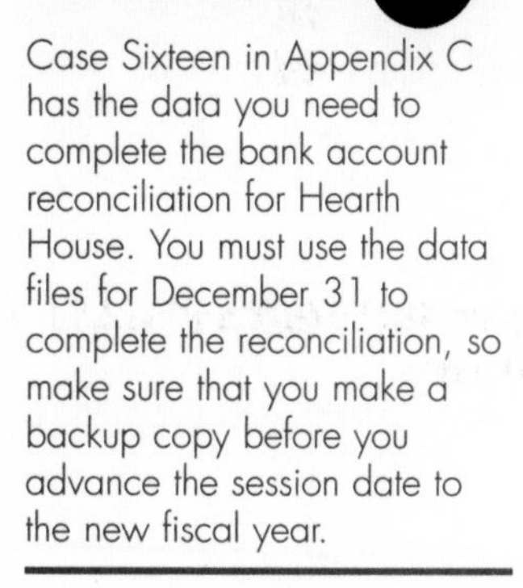

Warning!

Case Sixteen in Appendix C has the data you need to complete the bank account reconciliation for Hearth House. You must use the data files for December 31 to complete the reconciliation, so make sure that you make a backup copy before you advance the session date to the new fiscal year.

SOURCE DOCUMENTS

SESSION DATE – October 7

> **notes**
>
> If your inventory list is sorted by number, change the settings for the Inventory Ledger to sort items by description. Refer to page 440 for assistance.

❑ Visa Sales Invoice #HH-120
Dated Oct. 2/03
To L. Gien (One-time customer)

1 Ceram Log set: Laurentian Birch LBF4	$ 400
1 Firescreen: brass arch shape	250
1 Door: Pinnacle Arch w/damper 2wf	1 000
Goods & Services Tax	7%
Provincial Sales Tax	8%

Paid by Visa #4518 6722 8821 8375.

❑ Cash Receipt #100
Dated Oct. 3/03
From University Alumni House, cheque #337 for $2 049.30 in full payment of account including $20.70 discount for early payment. Reference invoice #HH-117.

❑ Cheque Copy #125
Dated Oct. 3/03
To Cambridge Castings, £1 852.20 (GBP) in full payment of account, including £37.80 (GBP) discount taken for early payment. Reference invoice #CC-818. The exchange rate is 2.2421.

❑ Memo #1
Dated Oct. 3/03
Transfer £2 000 from Bank Account: Chequing to Bank: Foreign Funds GBP. The exchange rate is 2.2421.

> **notes**
>
> ❑ Stacie's Sports Bar (contact Stacie Ball) is located at:
> 6 Raptor Cres.
> Toronto, ON M4E 3Y6
> Tel: (416) 923-6719
> Fax: (416) 923-9911
> stacie@netball.com
> Credit Limit: $10 000

❑ Sales Invoice #HH-121
Dated Oct. 3/03
To Stacie's Sports Bar (use Full Add)

1 CC: Fireplace gas ins DV32HET	$2 800
1 SF: Fireplace gas ins tp-vnt DV30TV	1 500
2 Basic installation jobs	450 /job
2 Insulating chimney jobs	100 /job
Goods & Services Tax	7%
Provincial Sales Tax	8%

Terms: 1/5, n/10.

❑ Purchase Invoice #OS-6431
Dated Oct. 4/03
From Overload Office Supplies, $150 for supplies plus $10.50 GST and $12.00 PST. Purchase invoice total $172.50. Terms: net 10 days.

> **notes**
>
> Choose One-time customer for Visa and cash sales. Add the customer's name to the address field.

❑ Visa Sales Invoice #HH-122
Dated Oct. 5/03
To Arlene Hope

1 VS: Fireplace pellet stove VPS1000	$2 200
1 Basic installation job	450
1 Insulating chimney job	100
Goods & Services Tax	7%
Provincial Sales Tax	8%

Paid by Visa #5623 7765 7109 3411.

☐ Memo #2
Dated Oct. 5/03
From Manager to Store Assistant: Adjust inventory records for one Thermostat: standard valued at $70 and broken beyond repair. Charge to account 5075 Damaged Inventory.

notes

Use Quick Add for new customers unless full details are available. Remember to add the PST rate for the sale.

☐ Sales Order #Fuller
Dated Oct. 5/03
Delivery date Oct. 21/03
To Terry Fuller

1 MF: Fireplace gas ins DV27TVT	$1 950
1 Mantel: cherry MC-DVT40 kit	1 200
1 Heater: vintage 50,000BTU ADVSH-50	850
3 Basic installation jobs	450 /job
1 Customizing inserts job	300
Goods & Services Tax	7%
Provincial Sales Tax	8%

Terms: payment on delivery. (There is no discount.)

☐ Cash Receipt #101
Dated Oct. 7/03
From Rosedale Estates, cheque #31 for $3 680 in full payment of account. Reference invoice #HH-115.

☐ Purchase Quote #QTS-31432
Dated Oct. 7/03
Delivery date Oct. 20/03
From Toronto Star $400 for advertising over 20 weeks plus $28 GST and $32 PST. Purchase invoice total $460. Terms: cash on receipt.

☐ Purchase Quote #QSUN-2199
Dated Oct. 7/03
Delivery date Oct. 20/03
From Toronto Sun $500 for advertising over 20 weeks plus $35 GST and $40 PST. Purchase invoice total $575. Terms: net 30 days.

SESSION DATE – October 14

☐ Cheque Copy #300
Dated Oct. 8/03
To Therma Glow, $1 761.65 in full payment of account including $35.95 discount taken for early payment. Reference invoice #TG-1421.

☐ Cheque Copy #301
Dated Oct. 9/03
To Matchless Flame, $2 140 in full payment of account. Reference invoice #MF-1201.

version 8

Remember to edit the prices.

☐ Sales Invoice #HH-123
Dated Oct. 10/03
To Lakeshore Condos (preferred customer)

1 CC: Fireplace free-std gas DV30DVT	$2 700
1 TG: Fireplace gas ins bay BVDV30T	2 100
1 Mantel: marble MM-DVT40 kit	1 600
2 Basic installation jobs	450 /job
Goods & Services Tax	7%
Provincial Sales Tax	8%

Terms: 1/5, n/10.

❑ Sales Invoice #HH-124
Dated Oct. 12/03
To University Alumni House

3 Remote controls: economy RCE-100	$ 120 each
3 MF: Fireplaces gas ins DV30HE	2 000 each
3 Mantels: oak MO-DVT30 kit	1 000 /kit
3 Basic installation - plus jobs	500 /job
3 Customizing inserts jobs	300 /job
Goods & Services Tax	7%
Provincial Sales Tax	8%

Terms: 1/5, n/10.

❑ Cash Receipt #102
Dated Oct. 13/03
From Stacie's Sports Bar, cheque #103 for $6 210 in full payment of account. Reference invoice #HH-121.

notes

- Remember to edit the Amount field for the Gas Fireplaces (DV30HE) in Purchase Order #101 and for the Oak Mantels in Purchase Order #102.
- Accept the default terms for purchase orders.

❑ Purchase Order #101
Dated Oct. 13/03
Shipping date October 22, 2003
From Matchless Flame

1 MF: Fireplace gas ins slim DV20SL	$ 720.00
2 MF: Fireplace gas ins DV30HE	2 500.00
1 MF: Fireplace gas ins DV27TVT	1 170.00
1 Door: Mirage w/damper 2.75wf	540.00
1 Door: Pinnacle Arch w/damper 2wf	600.00
Goods & Services Tax	387.10
	$5 917.10

notes

- Remember to edit amounts for purchases from foreign vendors.
- Import duties are applied at the time of purchase, not at the time of placing an order.

❑ Purchase Order #102
Dated Oct. 13/03
Shipping date October 20, 2003
From Vulcan Stove (British vendor)

1 VS: Fireplace pellet stove VPS1000	£ 550.00
2 Mantels: marble MM-DVT40 kits	900.00
3 Mantels: oak MO-DVT30 kits	750.00
Freight	100.00
Goods & Services Tax	161.00
	£2 461.00

The exchange rate is 2.25.

❑ Cheque Copy #302
Dated Oct. 13/03
To Overload Office Supplies, $172.50 in full payment of account. Reference invoice #OS-6431.

EMPLOYEE TIME SUMMARY SHEET #20

(pay period ending October 14, 2003)

	Name of Employee	Week 41 Hours	Week 42 Hours	Regular Hours	Overtime Hours
❑	Kris Kindl	40	40	80	-

Using Employee Time Summary Sheet #20 and the Employee Information Sheet, complete payroll for hourly employee. Recover $100 advance. Issue cheque #303.

SESSION DATE – October 21

❑ Cheque Copy #304
Dated Oct. 15/03
To Penguin Insulating Co., $428 in payment of account. Reference invoice #PI-901.

❑ Memo #3
Dated Oct. 15/03
From Manager: Using the Employee Information Sheet, prepare payroll for Dana Damper, the store assistant, for the pay period ending October 15, 2003. Damper will receive an advance of $200; $50 will be recovered from each of the next four paycheques. Issue cheque #305.

Memo #4
Dated Oct. 15/03
From Manager: Refer to September 30 General Ledger balances. For audit and internal control purposes:

❑ Record GST Owing for September as a liability owing to the Receiver General of Canada and issue cheque #306 for $1 680 in payment.

❑ Record EI, CPP and Income Tax Payable for September as a liability owing to the Receiver General of Canada and issue cheque #307 for $2 696.27 in payment.

❑ Record EHT Payable for the past three months as a liability owing to the Minister of Finance and issue cheque #308 for $324.38 in payment.

❑ Record PST Payable for September as a liability owing to the Minister of Finance and issue cheque #309 for $4 560 in payment. Remember to reduce PST by 5% sales tax compensation.

❑ Record RRSP Payable for September as a liability owing to Standard Insurance Co. and issue cheque #310 for $450 in payment.

❑ Record CSB Plan Payable for September as a liability owing to Transcend Investment Co. and issue cheque #311 for $450 in payment.

❑ Record Group Insurance Payable for September as a liability owing to Standard Insurance Co. and issue cheque #312 for $35 in payment.

❑ Record WSIB Payable for the past three months as a liability owing to the Workplace Safety & Insurance Board and issue cheque #313 for $889.52 in payment.

notes

- Record these payments in the Payments Journals as other payments.
- You can use the September 30 Balance Sheet to check the amounts for these liabilities.
- Use Memo 4A, 4B, and so on, as the source document numbers.

❑ Purchase Invoice #PI-1082
Dated Oct. 16/03
From Penguin Insulating Co., $300 for insulation supplies plus $21 GST. Purchase invoice total $321. Store this entry because it is a standing monthly order. Terms: net 15 days.

❑ Sales Invoice #HH-125
Dated Oct. 16/03
To Max Polisena (use Full add for new preferred customer)

1 TG: Fireplace gas ins multi MSDV45T	$2 500
1 CC: Fireplace gas ins DV32HET	2 500
1 Mantel: marble MM-DVT40 kit	1 600
1 Mantel: tile MT-DVT30 kit	725
2 Remote controls: luxury RCL-1000	160 each
2 Basic installation - plus jobs	500 /job
Goods & Services Tax	7%
Provincial Sales Tax	8%

Terms: 1/5, n/10.

notes

❑ Max Polisena (Preferred customer) is located at:
45 Fieldstone Rd.
Toronto, ON M3F 4S2
Tel: (416) 662-7165
Fax: (416) 662-6611
madmax@hotmail.com
Credit Limit: $12 000

version 8

Remember to edit the prices.

❑ Cash Receipt #103
Dated Oct. 17/03
From University Alumni House, cheque #378 for $13 388.76 in payment of account including $135.24 discount for early payment. Reference invoice #HH-124.

❑ Visa Sales Invoice #HH-126
Dated Oct. 17/03
To Maria Andersson

1 CC: Fireplace coal CC200FS	$1 800
1 Mantel: cherry MC-DVT40 kit	1 200
1 Toolset: glass handle/cast iron	400
1 Grate: cast iron black	150
1 Basic installation job	450
Goods & Services Tax	7%
Provincial Sales Tax	8%

Paid by Visa #4104 6127 1195 8825.

❑ Visa Purchase Invoice #TS-31432
Dated Oct. 18/03
From Toronto Star, to fill purchase quote #QTS-31432, $400 for advertising over the next 20 weeks plus $28 GST and $32 PST. Purchase invoice total $460. Terms: payment on receipt. Paid by Visa.

❑ Cash Receipt #104
Dated Oct. 20/03
From Lakeshore Condos, cheque #167 for $8 395 in full payment of account. Reference invoice #HH-123.

notes

Remember to add the 8% PST to the sales invoice for Fuller. It is not entered automatically when the Quick Add option is selected.

❑ Cash Sales Invoice #HH-127
Dated Oct. 21/03
To Terry Fuller, to fill sales order #Fuller

1 MF: Fireplace gas ins DV27TVT	$1 950
1 Mantel: cherry MC-DVT40 kit	1 200
1 Heater: vintage 50,000BTU ADVSH-50	850
3 Basic installation jobs	450 /job
1 Customizing inserts job	300
Goods & Services Tax	7%
Provincial Sales Tax	8%

Paid by certified cheque #SB-6712. (There is no discount.)

❑ Purchase Invoice #MF-1283
Dated Oct. 21/03
Received from Matchless Flame to fill purchase order #101

1 MF: Fireplace gas ins slim DV20SL	$ 720.00
2 MF: Fireplace gas ins DV30HE	2 500.00
1 MF: Fireplace gas ins DV27TVT	1 170.00
1 Door: Mirage w/damper 2.75wf	540.00
1 Door: Pinnacle Arch w/damper 2wf	600.00
Goods & Services Tax	387.10
	$5 917.10

Terms: net 15 days.

❑ Cash Purchase Invoice #TH-6392
Dated Oct. 21/03
From Toronto Hydro, $110 for hydro services plus $7.70 GST. Purchase invoice total $117.70. Terms: cash on receipt. Issued cheque #314 in payment.

SESSION DATE – October 28

❑ Cash Sales Invoice #HH-128
Dated Oct. 22/03
To Nicole Harbon

1 Ceram Log: Birdseye Maple set BMF5	$ 550
1 Door: Mirage w/damper 2.75wf	900
1 Toolset: brass handle solid	300
1 Grill: rotisserie & spit DX-80	1 300
1 Thermostat: standard	140
1 Woodholder: mhg	80
Goods & Services Tax	7%
Provincial Sales Tax	8%

Paid by cash.

❑ Cash Purchase Invoice #BC-43293
Dated Oct. 22/03
From Bell Canada, $80 for telephone services plus $5.60 GST and $6.40 PST. Purchase invoice total $92. Terms: cash on receipt. Issued cheque #315 in payment.

notes

The $610 balance in the journal is the General Ledger balance, not the statement balance. Refer to page 198 if you need help with the Visa payment.

❑ Visa Statement #Oct-03
Dated Oct. 22/03
Visa Statement balance is $162. This includes $150 for purchases made before Oct. 15 and $12 for annual fee (Additional Fees amount). To avoid interest charges, payment of statement balance is due by Nov. 1. Issue cheque #316 for $162. (Do not pay the $610 balance showing in the Payments Journal because this includes $460 in purchases that will appear on the November statement.)

❑ Purchase Invoice #VS-813
Dated Oct. 22/03
Received from Vulcan Stove to fill purchase order #102

1 VS: Fireplace pellet stove VPS1000	£ 550.00
2 Mantels: marble MM-DVT40 kits	900.00
3 Mantels: oak MO-DVT30 kits	750.00
Freight	100.00
Goods & Services Tax	161.00
	£2 461.00
Import Duties	£ 156.75

Terms: net 30 days. The exchange rate is 2.255.

❑ Memo #5
Dated Oct. 22/03
Pay Import Duties owing to Receiver General. Issue cheque #317 for $353.47. Reference invoice #VS-813. The exchange rate is 2.255.

❑ Realty Tax Bill #T2003-4
Dated Oct. 23/03
From City Treasurer, $750 for quarterly property tax assessment. Terms: Due in 3 instalments of $250 on October 28, November 28 and December 28.

❑ Cash Receipt #105
Dated Oct. 25/03
From Max Polisena, cheque #208 for $9 941.75 in full payment of account. Reference invoice #HH-125.

- [ ] Cash Sales Invoice #HH-129
Dated Oct. 25/03
To Irene Mota

1 Grill: mobile/side burner DL-60	$1 100
1 Firescreen: brass accent rect	200
2 Andiron sets: cast iron set	100 /set
1 CC: Fireplace wood WC100FS	1 800
1 Toolset: glass handle/cast iron	400
Goods & Services Tax	7%
Provincial Sales Tax	8%

Paid by cheque #39 (certified).

- [ ] Sales Quote #82
Dated Oct. 25/03
Delivery date Nov. 7/03
To Scarlett Road Condos

4 CC: Fireplace gas ins DV32HET	$2 800 each
4 Basic installation jobs	450 /job
4 Insulating chimney jobs	100 /job
Goods & Services Tax	7%
Provincial Sales Tax	8%

Terms: 1/5, net 10 days.

- [ ] Cheque Copy #126
Dated Oct. 26/03
To Vulcan Stove Co., £315 in payment of account. Reference invoice #VS-699. The exchange rate is 2.266.

notes

Be sure that you select Bank Account: Chequing for the property tax payments.

- [ ] Cheque Copy #318
Dated Oct. 27/03
To City Treasurer, $250 in payment of property tax assessment. Reference realty bill #T2003-4.

- [ ] Cheque Copy #319
Dated Nov. 27/03
To City Treasurer, $250 in payment of property tax assessment. Reference realty bill #T2003-4. Enter a postdated payment.

- [ ] Cheque Copy #320
Dated Dec. 27/03
To City Treasurer, $250 in payment of property tax assessment. Reference realty bill #T2003-4. Enter a postdated payment.

- [ ] Purchase Invoice #TG-1447
Dated Oct. 28/03
From Therma Glow

1 TG: Fireplace gas ins bay BVDV30T	$1 380.00
1 TG: Fireplace gas ins multi MSDV45T	1 680.00
Goods & Services Tax	214.20
	$3 274.20

Terms: 2/10, net 20 days.

- [ ] Visa Sales Invoice #HH-130
Dated Oct. 28/03
To Polly Sekhon

1 SF: Fireplace gas ins bay DV30BWT	$1 800
1 MF: Fireplace gas ins slim DV20SL	1 200
2 Basic installation - plus jobs	500 /job
2 Customizing inserts jobs	300 /job
2 Insulating chimney jobs	100 /job
Goods & Services Tax	7%
Provincial Sales Tax	8%

Paid by Visa #4620 6154 2829 4914.

notes

These items are duty free.

- [ ] Purchase Invoice #CC-960
Dated Oct. 28/03
From Cambridge Castings

1 CC: Fireplace coal CC200FS	£ 450.00
1 CC: Fireplace free-std gas DV30DVT	800.00
2 CC: Fireplace gas ins DV32HET	1 500.00
1 CC: Fireplace wood WC100FS	475.00
1 Ceram Log: Birdseye Maple set BMF5	150.00
1 Ceram Log: Georgian Oak set GOF4	120.00
2 Ceram Log: Laurentian Birch sets LBF4	220.00
Freight	100.00
Goods & Services Tax	267.05
	£4 082.05

Terms: 2/10, net 15 days. The exchange rate is 2.27.

EMPLOYEE TIME SUMMARY SHEET #21

(pay period ending October 28, 2003)

	Name of Employee	Week 43 Hours	Week 44 Hours	Regular Hours	Overtime Hours
❑	Kris Kindl	42	40	80	2

Using Employee Time Summary Sheet #21 and the Employee Information Sheet, complete payroll for Kindl. Recover $100 advance. Issue cheque #321.

SESSION DATE – October 31

- [ ] Visa Sales Invoice #HH-131
Dated Oct. 29/03
To Siva Lingam

1 Ceram Log: Georgian Oak set GOF4	$450
1 Ceram Log: Laurentian Birch set LBF4	400
1 Door: Apparition w/damper 2.5wf	800
1 Door: Viewzone w/damper 1.5wf	650
2 Thermostats: standard	140 each
Goods & Services Tax	7%
Provincial Sales Tax	8%

Paid by Visa #4502 6129 5138 2114.

- [ ] Cheque Copy #322
Dated Oct. 30/03
To Penguin Insulating, $321 in payment of account. Reference invoice #PI-1082.

notes

Treat the allowance as a cash purchase (other payment) using Sales Returns & Allowances as the account. This will credit Bank Account: Chequing.

❑ Credit Invoice #HH-127C
Dated Oct. 30/03
To Terry Fuller, $100 allowance for scratched cherry mantel kit. Issued cheque #323.

❑ Bank Debit Memo #6343172
Dated Oct. 30/03
From Royal Bank, for $2 500. This amount includes $250 for the reduction of principal on mortgage and $2 250 interest.

❑ Bank Debit Memo #6343173
Dated Oct. 30/03
From Royal Bank, for $2 400. This amount includes $2 100 for the reduction of principal on bank loan and $300 interest.

❑ Purchase Invoice #SF-927
Dated Oct. 30/03
From Starfire Fireplaces

1 SF: Fireplace gas ins bay DV30BWT	$1 080.00
1 SF: Fireplace gas ins tp-vnt DV30TV	900.00
1 Grill: mobile/side burner DL-60	660.00
1 Grill: rotisserie & spit DX-80	780.00
Goods & Services Tax	239.40
	$3 659.40

Terms: net 20 days.

❑❑ Memo #6
Dated Oct. 31/03
Using the Employee Information Sheet, prepare payroll for salaried employees, Damper and Cinder, the store assistant and manager, for the pay period ending October 31. Recover $50 advance from Damper. Issue cheques #324 and #325.

❑ Materials Summary Form #10
Dated Oct. 31/03
Re: Insulation and Hardware supplies: A physical count of materials inventory used for job orders indicated the following:

Insulation used	$150
Fireplace Hardware used	$75

Make the necessary asset adjustments and expense charges.

notes

Remember that taxes are not applied to interest charges and there is no discount. Credit the interest charges to Interest Revenue.

❑ Memo #7
Dated Oct. 31/03
Prepare customer statements and prepare invoices for interest charges. Create invoice Int-memo7 for Brookhaven Funeral Home to charge $51.75 interest for overdue account. Terms net 30 days.

SESSION DATE – November 7

❑ Visa Sales Invoice #HH-132
Dated Nov. 2/03
To Crystal Waters

1 Ceram Log: Birdseye Maple set BMF5	$ 550
1 Door: Pinnacle Arch w/damper 2wf	1 000
1 Toolset: brass handle solid	300
1 Thermostat: standard	140
Goods & Services Tax	7%
Provincial Sales Tax	8%

Paid by Visa #4398 6101 3725 1846.

❑ Visa Sales Invoice #HH-133
Dated Nov. 3/03
To Joanna Severino

1 VS: Fireplace pellet stove VPS1000	$2 200
1 Toolset: glass handle/cast iron	400
1 Ceram Log: Tobermory Ash set TAF5	480
1 Door: Apparition w/damper 2.5wf	800
1 Mantel: marble MM-DVT40 kit	1 800
1 Basic installation job	450
Goods & Services Tax	7%
Provincial Sales Tax	8%

Paid by Visa #4164 7279 6571 6741.

notes

❑ Railside Equipment (Contact Ray Bannister) is located at
444 Railside Drive
East York, ON M7T 3V2
Tel: (416) 772-7210
Fax: (416) 772-7100
Tax ID: 641816517

❑ Purchase Invoice #RE-947
Dated Nov. 4/03
From Railside Equipment (use Full Add), $1 000 for new installation equipment plus $70 GST and $80 PST. Purchase invoice total $1 150. Terms: net 30 days.

❑ Purchase Invoice #CC-1005
Dated Nov. 5/03
From Cambridge Castings

4 CC: Fireplace gas ins DV32HET	£3 000.00
Freight	100.00
Goods & Services Tax	217.00
	£3 317.00

Terms: 2/10, net 15 days. The exchange rate is 2.258.

❑ Cheque Copy #326
Dated Nov. 6/03
To Matchless Flame, $5 917.10 in full payment of account. Reference invoice #MF-1283.

notes

Read the advice messages and then proceed with the sale. Brookhaven has always been a customer in good standing and there is every reason to expect that it will settle the account shortly.

❑ Sales Invoice #HH-134
Dated Nov. 6/03
To Brookhaven Funeral Home

1 TG: Fireplace gas ins multi MSDV45T	$2 800
1 SF: Fireplace gas ins bay DV30BWT	1 800
2 Remote controls: luxury RCL-1000	180 each
2 Basic installation jobs	450 /job
2 Customizing inserts jobs	300 /job
2 Insulating chimney jobs	100 /job
Goods & Services Tax	7%
Provincial Sales Tax	8%

Terms: 1/5, net 10 days.

❑ Sales Invoice #HH-135
Dated Nov. 7/03
To Scarlett Road Condos, to fill Sales Quote #82

4 CC: Fireplace gas ins DV32HET	$2 800 each
4 Basic installation jobs	450 /job
4 Insulating chimney jobs	100 /job
Goods & Services Tax	7%
Provincial Sales Tax	8%

Terms: 1/5, net 10 days.

- [ ] Cheque Copy #127
  Dated Nov. 7/03
  To Cambridge Castings, £4 000.41 in payment of account including £81.64 discount taken for early payment. Reference invoice #CC-960. The exchange rate is 2.249.

- [ ] Memo #8
  Dated Nov. 7/03
  Transfer £5 000 from Bank Account: Chequing to Bank: Foreign Funds GBP. The exchange rate is 2.249.

SESSION DATE – November 15

- [ ] Create the following new inventory records:

Number	Item Description	Reg	(Pref) Price/unit	Min Qty
GR03	Grill: stainless steel deluxe M700	$1 400	(1 250) each	0
GR04	Grill: stainless stl built-in M900	1 750	(1 600) each	0

  Asset account: 1430 Revenue account: 4020 C.O.G.S. account: 5050
  Variance account: 5055

notes

- [ ] Hickory Grills (Contact Barb Eekew) is located at:
  445 Nutley St.
  Toronto, ON M6G 2B6
  Tel: (416) 781-5284
  Fax: (416) 788-6666
  Tax ID: 539977453
  BBQ@hickory.com
  www.hickory.com

- [ ] Purchase Invoice #HG-751
  Dated Nov. 9/03
  From Hickory Grills (use Full Add)

1 Grill: stainless steel deluxe M700	$1 000.00
1 Grill: stainless stl built-in M900	1 250.00
Goods & Services Tax	157.50
	$2 407.50

  Terms: 2/5, net 10 days.

- [ ] Cash Receipt #106
  Dated Nov. 10/03
  From Brookhaven Funeral Home, cheque #123 for $11 084.16 in full payment of account, including $76.59 discount for early payment. Reference invoices #HH-110, #HH-134 and Int-Memo7.

notes

To issue vacation pay, turn off the Retain Vacation setting in the Payroll Ledger (Income tab screen) for Kindl before preparing the paycheque (see page 249). Remember to delete the default entries for Reg. hours and all deductions. Turn the Retain setting on again so that future vacation pay will be retained.

EMPLOYEE TIME SUMMARY SHEET #22

(pay period ending November 11, 2003)

Name of Employee	Week 45 Hours	Week 46 Hours	Regular Hours	Overtime Hours
Kris Kindl	40	40	80	–

- [ ] a. Using Employee Time Summary Sheet #22 and the Employee Information Sheet, complete payroll for hourly employee. Issue cheque #327.
- [ ] b. Kindl will take a two-week vacation and his vacation pay should be released. Issue a separate cheque for the vacation pay. A new employee will be hired immediately to replace him during vacation and to help with the increasing workload after his return. Issue cheque #328.

❑ Memo #9
Dated Nov. 11/03
From Manager: Add a new employee record for MyTee Strong

Ms. Strong lives at	454 Merlin Cres.
	Toronto, ON M7T 3R1
Telephone	(416) 569-5612
SIN	499 312 767
Birthdate	Feb. 3, 1962
WSIB (WCB) rate:	4.97
EI Factor:	1.4

MyTee Strong, an experienced gas-fitter and installer, is single and self-supporting. Her federal claim amount is $7 412 and provincial amount is $7 426 (full amounts subject to indexing). She will begin work immediately, replacing Kindl who is on vacation, and will continue working for the store after Kindl returns, since Hearth House expects to be successful in its present bid for work on a new building complex to be completed in December. She will begin working at $18 per hour for regular hours and $27 for overtime work, receiving her pay every two weeks. Her salary will be reviewed after a six-month probationary period. Vacation pay at the rate of 6% will be retained until she takes vacation time off. Strong has chosen to participate in the savings and insurance plans that Hearth House offers, paying $50 each pay period for RRSP contributions, $50 to the CSB Plan and $5 per period for group insurance.

❑ Cheque Copy #329
Dated Nov. 14/03
To Hickory Grills, $2 359.35 in full payment of account, taking advantage of the $48.15 discount for early payment. Reference invoice #HG-751.

❑ Cash Sales Invoice #HH-136
Dated Nov. 15/03
To Oskar Werner

1 Grill: stainless stl built-in M900	$1 750
1 Ceram Log: Algonquin Maple set AMF5	500
1 Door: Viewzone w/damper 1.5wf	650
Goods & Services Tax	7%
Provincial Sales Tax	8%

Paid by cheque #373.

❑ Memo #10
Dated Nov. 15/03
From Manager: Using the Employee Information Sheet, prepare payroll for Damper for the pay period ending November 15. Issue cheque #330. Recover $50 advance.

Memo #11
Dated Nov. 15/03
From Manager: Refer to previous end-of-month (October 31) General Ledger account balances to record liabilities and payments to the following agencies.

❑ Issue cheque #331 for GST owing to the Receiver General of Canada.
❑ Issue cheque #332 for EI, CPP and Income Tax Payable owing to the Receiver General of Canada.
❑ Issue cheque #333 for PST Payable owing to the Minister of Finance. Remember to take the 5% sales tax compensation.
❑ Issue cheque #334 for RRSP Payable owing to Standard Insurance Co.
❑ Issue cheque #335 for CSB Plan Payable owing to Transcend Investment Co.
❑ Issue cheque #336 for Group Insurance Payable to Standard Insurance Co.

notes

- You may use the October 31 Balance Sheet to check the amounts for these liabilities.
- Use Memo 11A, 11B, and so on, as the source document numbers.

❑ Cheque Copy #128
Dated Nov. 15/03
To Cambridge Castings, £3 250.66 in full payment of account including £66.34 discount for early payment. Reference invoice #CC-1005. The exchange rate is 2.2544.

❑ Memo #12
Dated Nov. 15/03
Transfer £5 000 from Bank Account: Chequing to Bank: Foreign Funds GBP. The exchange rate is 2.2544.

SESSION DATE – November 22

❑ Purchase Invoice #PI-1139
Dated Nov. 16/03
From Penguin Insulating Co., $350 for insulation supplies plus $24.50 GST. Purchase invoice total $374.50. Recall and edit the stored entry. Store the new invoice because future purchases will also be for the larger quantity.
Terms: net 15 days.

❑ Purchase Invoice #MF-1291
Dated Nov. 17/03
From Matchless Flame

3 MF: Fireplace gas ins slim DV20SL	$2 160.00
Goods & Services Tax	151.20
	$2 311.20

Terms: net 15 days.

❑ Sales Invoice #HH-137
Dated Nov. 17/03
To Walden Apartments

3 MF: Fireplace gas ins slim DV20SL	$1 200 each
3 Basic installation jobs	450 /job
3 Customizing inserts jobs	300 /job
3 Insulating chimney jobs	100 /job
Goods & Services Tax	7%
Provincial Sales Tax	8%

Terms: 1/5, net 10 days.

❑ Cheque Copy #337
Dated Nov. 18/03
To Therma Glow, $3 274.20 in payment of account. Reference invoice #TG-1447.

❑ Cheque Copy #338
Dated Nov. 19/03
To Starfire Fireplaces, $3 659.40 in full payment of account. Reference invoice #SF-927.

❑ Cash Purchase Invoice #BC-51239
Dated Nov. 19/03
From Bell Canada, $80 for telephone services plus $5.60 GST and $6.40 PST. Purchase invoice total $92. Issued cheque #339 in payment.

❑ Cash Purchase Invoice #TH-8497
Dated Nov. 21/03
From Toronto Hydro, $100 for hydro services plus $7 GST. Purchase invoice total $107. Issued cheque #340 in payment.

- [ ] Cheque Copy #129
  Dated Nov. 21/03
  To Vulcan Stove, £2 461 in payment of account. Reference invoice #VS-813. The exchange rate is 2.257.

- [ ] Visa Sales Invoice #HH-138
  Dated Nov. 22/03
  To Veronica England

1 MF: Fireplace gas ins DV27TVT	$1 950
1 Mantel: oak MO-DVT30 kit	1 000
1 Customizing inserts job	300
1 Basic installation - plus job	500
Goods & Services Tax	7%
Provincial Sales Tax	8%

  Paid by Visa #4502 3661 2291 6242.

- [ ] Visa Statement #Nov. 03
  Dated Nov. 22/03
  Visa statement balance is $460 for purchases made before Nov. 15. To avoid interest charges, payment of total statement balance is due by Dec. 1. Issue cheque #341 for $460.

SESSION DATE – November 30

- [ ] Visa Purchase Invoice #PH-36914
  Dated Nov. 23/03
  From Power Hardware, $150 for hardware supplies plus $10.50 GST. Purchase invoice total $160.50. Paid by Visa.

- [ ] Cash Receipt #107
  Dated Nov. 23/03
  From Walden Apartments, certified cheque #RB-69912 for $7 072.50 in full payment of account. Reference invoice #HH-137.

- [ ] Cash Sales Invoice #HH-139
  Dated Nov. 23/03
  To Trevor Bullen

1 Mantel: marble MM-DVT40 kit	$1 800
1 Ceram Log: Algonquin Maple set AMF5	500
1 Door: Quest w/damper custom 2wf	750
1 Insulating chimney job	100
1 Grill: rotisserie & spit DX80	1 300
Goods & Services Tax	7%
Provincial Sales Tax	8%

  Paid by certified cheque #RB-7726.

- [ ] Cash Sales Invoice #HH-140
  Dated Nov. 24/03
  To Gary Tsumura

1 CC: Fireplace coal CC200FS	$1 800
1 Mantel: oak MO-DVT30 kit	1 000
1 Heater: vintage 30,000BTU ADVSH-30	750
1 Firescreen: iron black accent rect	150
Goods & Services Tax	7%
Provincial Sales Tax	8%

  Paid by certified cheque #SB-19962.

notes

❑ Rudy's Sunoco (Contact Rudy Mekkanik) is located at
21 Oiler St.
Toronto, ON M4H 3F9
Tel: (416) 822-8101
Tax ID: 331122655
RudyMekk@golden.net

❑ Visa Purchase Invoice #RS-574
Dated Nov. 24/03
From Rudy's Sunoco (use Full Add), $200 for repairs and maintenance on vehicles plus $14 GST and $16 PST. Purchase invoice total $230 paid by Visa. Create new Group account 5270 Vehicle Expenses and allow allocations.

EMPLOYEE TIME SUMMARY SHEET #23

(pay period ending November 25, 2003)

	Name of Employee	Week 47 Hours	Week 48 Hours	Regular Hours	Overtime Hours
❑	MyTee Strong	40	40	80	-

a. Using Employee Time Summary Sheet #23 and the Employee Information Sheet, complete payroll for hourly employee.
b. Issue cheque #342.

❑ Purchase Invoice #VS-914
Dated Nov. 25/03
From Vulcan Stove

1 VS: Fireplace pellet stove VPS1000	£ 500.00
2 Mantels: cherry MC-DVT40 kits	610.00
2 Mantels: marble MM-DVT40 kits	900.00
2 Mantels: oak MO-DVT30 kits	500.00
Goods & Services Tax	175.70
	£2 685.70
Import Duties	£ 190.95

Terms: net 30 days. The exchange rate is 2.258.

❑ Memo #13
Dated Nov. 25/03
Pay Import Duties owing to Receiver General. Issue cheque #343 for $431.17. Reference invoice #VS-914. The exchange rate is 2.258.

notes

Revenue for subcontracting work should be credited to Revenue from Services.

❑ Visa Sales Invoice #HH-141
Dated Nov. 26/03
To Shereen Ahmed

1 TG: Fireplace gas ins bay BVDV30T	$2 300
1 Heater: vintage 20,000BTU ADVSH-20	500
1 Mantel: marble MM-DVT40 kit	1 800
1 Basic installation job	450
1 Customizing inserts job	300
Subcontracting work on marble	250
Goods & Services Tax	7%
Provincial Sales Tax	8%

Paid by Visa #4110 6396 3502 1808.

notes

- ☐ Missoni Marbleworks (Contact Petra Missoni) is located at 67 Stonehenge Ave. Toronto, ON M8D 1C7 Tel: (416) 923-6291 Fax: (416) 923-0011 www.beststonework.com
- ☐ Create new Group account 5380 Subcontracting Fees Allow project allocations for this account.

☐ Cash Purchase Invoice #MM-1347
Dated Nov. 27/03
From Missoni Marbleworks (use Full Add), $250 for marble work completed for Shereen Ahmed plus $17.50 GST and $20 PST. Purchase invoice total $287.50. Terms: cash on receipt. Issued cheque #344 in payment.

☐ Purchase Invoice #CC-1320
Dated Nov. 28/03
From Cambridge Castings

1 CC: Fireplace coal CC200FS	$ 450.00
1 CC: Fireplace free-std gas DV30DVT	800.00
2 Ceram Log: Birdseye Maple sets BMF5	300.00
2 Ceram Log: Georgian Oak sets GOF4	240.00
2 Ceram Log: Laurentian Birch sets LBF4	220.00
2 Firescreens: brass accent rect	80.00
Freight	100.00
Goods & Services Tax	153.30
	$2 343.30
Import Duty	$ 6.40

Terms: 2/10, net 15 days. The exchange rate is 2.26.

☐ Memo #14
Dated Nov. 28/03
Pay Import Duties owing to Receiver General. Issue cheque #345 for $14.46. The exchange rate is 2.26.

☐ Purchase Invoice #MF-1401
Dated Nov. 28/03
From Matchless Flame

1 MF: Fireplace gas ins DV27TVT	$1 170.00
2 Doors: Apparition w/damper 2.5wf	960.00
1 Door: Charade w/damper 1wf	360.00
1 Door: Pinnacle Arch w/damper 2wf	600.00
1 Door: Quest w/damper custom 2wf	450.00
2 Doors: Viewzone w/damper 1.5wf	780.00
Goods & Services Tax	302.40
	$4 622.40

Terms: net 15 days.

☐ Purchase Invoice #TG-1601
Dated Nov. 29/03
From Therma Glow

1 TG: Fireplace gas ins bay BVDV30T	$1 380.00
1 TG: Fireplace gas ins multi MSDV45T	1 680.00
Goods & Services Tax	214.20
	$3 274.20

Terms: 2/10, net 20 days.

☐ Purchase Invoice #SF-1009
Dated Nov. 30/03
From Starfire Fireplaces

1 SF: Fireplace gas ins bay DV30BWT	$1 080.00
1 Grill: mobile/side burner DL-60	660.00
1 Grill: rotisserie & spit DX80	780.00
Goods & Services Tax	176.40
	$2 696.40

Terms: net 20 days.

❑ Bank Debit Memo #7214153
Dated Nov. 30/03
From Royal Bank, for $2 400. This amount includes $2 125 for the reduction of principal on bank loan and $275 interest.

❑ Bank Debit Memo #7214154
Dated Nov. 30/03
From Royal Bank, for $2 500. This amount includes $275 for the reduction of principal on mortgage and $2 225 interest.

❑ Visa Sales Invoice #HH-142
Dated Nov. 30/03
To Kevin O'Casey

1 Mantel: cherry MC-DVT40 kit	$1 200
1 CC: Fireplace free-std gas DV30DVT	3 000
1 Grill: mobile/side burner DL-60	1 100
Goods & Services Tax	7%
Provincial Sales Tax	8%

Paid by Visa #4516 7179 5553 2627.

❑❑ Memo #15
Dated Nov. 30/03
From Manager: Using the Employee Information Sheet, prepare payroll for the salaried employees, Damper and Cinder, for the pay period ending November 30. Recover $50 advance from Damper. Issue cheques #346 and #347.

❑ Materials Summary Form #11
Dated Nov. 30/03
Re: Insulation and Hardware supplies: A physical count of materials inventory used for job orders indicated the following:

Insulation used	$500
Fireplace Hardware used	$100

Make the necessary asset adjustments and expense charges.

❑ Cheque Copy #348
Dated Nov. 30/03
To Penguin Insulating, $374.50 in full payment of account. Reference invoice #PI-1139.

notes

The default setting, distributing amounts by percentage, is correct. Remember to turn on the warning for incomplete distributions in the Allocations Settings. Refer to page 373 if you need further assistance.

❑ Memo #16
Dated Nov. 30/03
The manger of Hearth House has negotiated a project with the management at Highlife Townhouses to install 10 fireplaces in the 10 townhouse units. The work will be completed over two weeks in December.
After some discussion, the owner and manager decided to record the revenue and costs of this project separately from the general sales from the store. Create the two projects that are needed for December's revenue and costs:

- General Sales Project for regular store sales and services to customers
- Highlife Townhouse Project for the large contract just negotiated

In addition to the preferred customer price, a special discount of 5 percent was agreed on as an incentive to get the Highlife contract. A credit invoice will be issued with each sales invoice (one sales invoice per week) to account for the discount. All revenue and costs will be allocated as indicated in the source document transactions.

version 8

Edit the price for Highlife.

notes

- [ ] Highlife Townhouses (Preferred customer) Contact: Marcel Hauteville is located at 999 Skyview Rd. Toronto, ON M6R 3F3 Tel: (416) 882-0123 Fax: (416) 882-8888 www.highlife.com Credit Limit: $20 000

- [ ] Sales Order #Highlife
Dated Nov. 30/03
Delivery Date Dec. 7/03
To Highlife Townhouses (use Full Add for new preferred customer)

10 MF: Fireplace gas ins DV30HE	$1 800 each
10 Basic installation - plus jobs	500 /job
Goods & Services Tax	7%
Provincial Sales Tax	8%

Terms: 5% discount, cash on receipt of invoice. (There is no allocation for sales orders.)

SESSION DATE – December 7

- [ ] Purchase Invoice #MF-1439
Dated Dec. 1/03
From Matchless Flame

10 MF: Fireplace gas ins DV30HE	$12 500.00
Goods & Services Tax	875.00
	$13 375.00

Terms: net 15 days.

- [ ] Cheque Copy #349
Dated Dec. 2/03
To Matchless Flame, $2 311.20 in payment of account. Reference invoice #MF-1291.

- [ ] Cheque Copy #350
Dated Dec. 4/03
To Railside Equipment, $1 150 in payment of account. Reference invoice #RE-947.

version 8

Edit the prices for the preferred customer for the sales invoice and the credit invoice.

- [ ] Sales Invoice #HH-143
Dated Dec. 5/03
To York Seniors' Club

1 SF: Fireplace gas ins bay DV30BWT	$1 650
1 TG: Fireplace gas ins bay BVDV30T	2 100
2 Mantels: oak MO-DVT30 kits	900 /kit
2 Basic installation jobs	450 /job
2 Woodholders: mhg	75 each
Goods & Services Tax	7%
Provincial Sales Tax	8%

Terms: 1/5, net 10 days.
Allocate 100% of revenue and costs to General Sales Project.

notes

Use the Revenue from Sales account because this is not a return. You may enter this transaction as a negative sale for the two items or as a Sales Adjusting Entry.

- [ ] Credit Invoice #HH-143C
Dated Dec. 6/03
To York Seniors' Club

–2 Woodholders: mhg	$75 each
Goods & Services Tax	7%
Provincial Sales Tax	8%

The customer did not purchase these items (woodholders are not required for gas fireplaces). They were incorrectly included in invoice. Allocate 100% of costs to General Sales Project. Terms: net 30.

- [ ] Cheque Copy #130
Dated Dec. 6/03
To Cambridge Castings, £2 296.43 in full payment of account including £46.87 discount. Reference invoice #CC-1320. The exchange rate is 2.262.

❑ Memo #17
Dated Dec. 6/03
Transfer £2 500 from Bank Account: Chequing to Bank: Foreign Funds GBP. The exchange rate is 2.262.

notes

Edit the quantity received for the five units delivered on Dec. 7. The remaining part of the order is filled on Dec. 14.

❑ Sales Invoice #HH-144
Dated Dec. 7/03
To Highlife Townhouses to fill first half of sales order #Highlife

5 MF: Fireplace gas ins DV30HE	$1 800 each
5 Basic installation - plus jobs	500 /job
Goods & Services Tax	7%
Provincial Sales Tax	8%

Terms: 5% discount, cash on receipt of invoice.
Allocate 100% of revenue and costs to Highlife Townhouse Project.

SESSION DATE – December 14

❑ Cash Receipt #108
Dated Dec. 8/03
From Highlife Townhouses, certified cheque #NT-37124 for $12 563.75 in full payment of account, including $661.25 discount. Reference Invoice #HH-144.

❑ Cash Receipt #109
Dated Dec. 8/03
From York Seniors' Club, cheque #229 for $7 341.60 in payment of account including $75.90 discount. Reference invoices #HH-143 and HH-143C. The full discount is allowed on the original invoice out of courtesy to the customer.

EMPLOYEE TIME SUMMARY SHEET #24

(pay period ending December 9, 2003)

	Name of Employee	Week 48 Hours	Week 49 Hours	Regular Hours	Overtime Hours
❑	Kris Kindl	40	40	80	–
❑	MyTee Strong	40	40	80	–

a. Using Employee Time Summary Sheet #24 and the Employee Information Sheet, complete payroll for hourly employees.
b. Give Kindl $100 advance and issue cheques #351 and #352.
c. Allocate 50% of costs to General Sales Project and 50% to Highlife Townhouse Project for each employee.

❑ Cash Sales Invoice #HH-145
Dated Dec. 10/03
To The Irish Pub

1 TG: Fireplace gas ins multi MSDV45T	$2 800
1 CC: Fireplace free-std gas DV30DVT	3 000
1 Mantel: marble MM-DVT40 kit	1 800
2 Basic installation - plus jobs	500 /job
2 Remote controls: economy RCE-100	120 each
Goods & Services Tax	7%
Provincial Sales Tax	8%

Paid by certified cheque #BM-321431.
Allocate 100% of revenue and costs to General Sales Project.

❑ Purchase Order #103
Dated Dec. 11/03
Shipping Date Dec. 31/03
From Cambridge Castings

2 CC: Fireplace free-std gas DV30DVT	£1 600.00
1 CC: Fireplace gas ins DV32HET	750.00
Freight	75.00
Goods & Services Tax	169.75
	£2 594.75

Terms: 2/10, net 15 days. The exchange rate is 2.254.

❑ Purchase Order #104
Dated Dec. 11/03
Shipping Date Dec. 20/03
From Vulcan Stove

1 Mantel: cherry MC-DVT40 kit	£ 305.00
3 Mantels: marble MM-DVT40 kits	1 350.00
2 Mantels: oak MO-DVT30 kits	500.00
1 Mantel: tile MT-DVT30 kit	200.00
1 VS: Fireplace pellet stove VPS1000	500.00
Freight	100.00
Goods & Services Tax	206.85
	£3 161.85

Terms: net 30 days. The exchange rate is 2.254.

❑ Visa Purchase Invoice #ST-239
Dated Dec. 11/03
From Speedy Transport (use Quick Add), $50 for emergency delivery of gas fireplace inserts to Highlife Townhouses plus $3.50 GST and $4.00 PST. Purchase invoice total $57.50. Terms: cash on receipt of invoice. Paid by Visa. Charge 100% of delivery expense to Highlife Townhouse Project.

❑ Cheque Copy #353
Dated Dec. 13/03
To Matchless Flame, $4 622.40 in partial payment. Reference invoice #MF-1401.

❑ Sales Invoice #HH-146
Dated Dec. 14/03
To Highlife Townhouses to complete sales order #Highlife

5 MF: Fireplace gas ins DV30HE	$1 800 each
5 Basic installation - plus jobs	500 /job
Goods & Services Tax	7%
Provincial Sales Tax	8%

Terms: 5% discount, cash on receipt of invoice.
Allocate 100% of revenue and costs to Highlife Townhouse Project.

SESSION DATE – December 21

❑ Memo #18
Dated Dec. 15/03
From Manager: Using the Employee Information Sheet, prepare payroll for Damper for the pay period ending December 15. Allocate 100% of payroll costs to General Sales Project. Recover the final $50 of the advance. Issue cheque #354.

❑ Cash Receipt #110
Dated Dec. 15/03
From Highlife Townhouses, certified cheque #NT-38991 for $12 563.75 in full payment of account, including $661.25 discount. Reference Invoice #HH-146.

❑ Memo #19
Dated Dec. 15/03
Issue to the Receiver General of Canada cheque #355 for $7 500 to pay quarterly Business Income Tax installment. Allocate 100% to General Sales Project.

Memo #20
Dated Dec. 15/03
From Manager: Refer to previous end-of-month (November) General Ledger account balances to record liabilities and payments to the following agencies.

❑ Issue cheque #356 for GST owing to the Receiver General of Canada.

❑ Issue cheque #357 for EI, CPP and Income Tax Payable owing to the Receiver General of Canada.

❑ Issue cheque #358 for PST Payable owing to the Minister of Finance. Remember to take the 5% sales tax compensation.

❑ Issue cheque #359 for RRSP Payable owing to Standard Insurance Co.

❑ Issue cheque #360 for CSB Plan Payable owing to Transcend Investment Co.

❑ Issue cheque #361 for Group Insurance Payable to Standard Insurance Co.

notes

- Use Memo 20A, Memo 20B, and so on, as the source document numbers.
- Allocate 100% of the sales tax compensation to the General Sales Project.

❑ Memo #21
Dated Dec. 15/03
Prepare sales invoice for Scarlett Road Condos to charge $231.15 interest on overdue account (1.5% interest on $15 410). Allocate 100% of the interest revenue to the General Sales Project. Terms: net 30 days.

notes

Use Int-Memo21 as the source document number.

❑ Visa Sales Invoice #HH-147
Dated Dec. 16/03
To Arend Versteeg

1 MF: Fireplace gas ins DV27TVT	$1 950
1 Heater: vintage 50,000BTU ADVSH-50	850
1 Basic installation - plus job	500
Goods & Services Tax	7%
Provincial Sales Tax	8%

Paid by Visa #5297 5261 2835 5521.
Allocate 100% of revenue and costs to General Sales Project.

❑ Purchase Invoice #PI-1321
Dated Dec. 16/03
From Penguin Insulating Co., $350 for insulation supplies plus $24.50 GST. Purchase invoice total $374.50. Recall the stored entry. Terms: net 15 days.

❑ Cheque Copy #362
Dated Dec. 16/03
To Matchless Flame, $13 375 in full payment of account. Reference invoice #MF-1439.

❑ Cheque Copy #363
Dated Dec. 18/03
To Therma Glow, $3 274.20 in payment of account. Reference invoice #TG-1601.

❑ Cash Receipt #111
Dated Dec. 18/03
From Scarlett Road Condos, certified cheque #CIB6431 for $15 641.15 in full payment of account. Reference invoices #HH-135 and Int-Memo21.

Purchase Invoice #VS-1002
Dated Dec. 18/03
From Vulcan Stove

2 Toolsets: brass handle solid	£150.00
2 Toolsets: cast iron/black enamel	100.00
2 Toolsets: glass handle/cast iron	200.00
Freight	25.00
Goods & Services Tax	33.25
	£508.25
Import Duty	£ 36.00

Terms: net 30 days. The exchange rate is 2.252.

Memo #22
Dated Dec. 18/03
Pay Import Duties owing to Receiver General. Issue cheque #364 for $81.07. Reference invoice #VS-1002. The exchange rate is 2.252.

Visa Sales Invoice #HH-148
Dated Dec. 18/03
To Maria's Bed & Breakfast

1 VS: Fireplace pellet stove VPS1000	$2 200
1 CC: Fireplace free-std gas DV30DVT	3 000
2 Basic installation - plus jobs	500 /job
2 Insulating chimney jobs	100 /job
Goods & Services Tax	7%
Provincial Sales Tax	8%

Paid by Visa #4102 3731 6749 8716.
Allocate 100% of revenue and costs to General Sales Project.

notes

Remember to enter a negative amount.

Purchase Invoice #VS-1002C
Dated Dec. 18/03
From Vulcan Stove, £50 allowance for damaged Toolset: glass handle/cast iron valued at £100. Reference invoice #VS-1002. Allocate 100% of allowance to General Sales Project. The exchange rate is 2.252.

Cheque Copy #365
Dated Dec. 19/03
To Starfire Fireplaces, $2 696.40 in full payment of account. Reference invoice #SF-1009.

Cheque Copy #131
Dated Dec. 19/03
To Vulcan Stove Co., £2 685.70 in payment of account. Reference invoice #VS-914. The exchange rate is 2.258.

Memo #23
Dated Dec. 19/03
Transfer £3 000 from Bank Account: Chequing to Bank: Foreign Funds GBP. The exchange rate is 2.258.

Purchase Invoice #MM-1392
Dated Dec. 20/03
From Missoni Marbleworks, $250 for marble work completed for Adrian Lee plus $17.50 GST and $20 PST. Purchase invoice total $287.50. Terms: cash on receipt. Allocate 100% of expense to General Sales Project.

- [ ] Cheque Copy #366
Dated Dec. 20/03
To Missoni Marbleworks, $287.50 in full payment of account. Reference invoice #MM-1392.

- [ ] Visa Sales Invoice #HH-149
Dated Dec. 20/03
To Adrian Lee

1 CC: Fireplace gas ins DV32HET	$2 800
1 Mantel: marble MM-DVT40 kit	1 800
1 Basic installation - plus job	500
Subcontracting work on marble	250
Goods & Services Tax	7%
Provincial Sales Tax	8%

Paid by Visa #4591 5281 4567 2345.
Allocate 100% of revenue and costs to General Sales Project.

notes

Process the purchase invoice without allocating the amount for variance costs.

- [ ] Purchase Invoice #VS-1007
Dated Dec. 20/03
From Vulcan Stove to fill Purchase Order #104

1 Mantel: cherry MC-DVT40 kit	£ 305.00
3 Mantels: marble MM-DVT40 kits	1 350.00
2 Mantels: oak MO-DVT30 kits	500.00
1 Mantel: tile MT-DVT30 kit	200.00
1 VS: Fireplace pellet stove VPS1000	500.00
Freight	100.00
Goods & Services Tax	206.85
	£3 161.85
Import Duty	£ 223.73

Terms: net 30 days. The exchange rate is 2.255.

- [ ] Memo #23
Dated Dec. 20/03
Pay Import Duties owing to Receiver General. Issue cheque #367 for $504.51. Reference invoice #VS-1007. The exchange rate is 2.255.

SESSION DATE – December 28

- [ ] Cash Purchase Invoice #TH-11073
Dated Dec. 22/03
From Toronto Hydro, $110 for hydro services plus $7.70 GST. Purchase invoice total $117.70. Issued cheque #368 in payment. Allocate 100% of expense to General Sales Project.

- [ ] Cash Purchase Invoice #BC-52147
Dated Dec. 22/03
From Bell Canada, $90 for telephone services plus $6.30 GST and $7.20 PST. Purchase invoice total $103.50. Issued cheque #369 in payment. Allocate 100% of expense to General Sales Project.

- [ ] Visa Statement #Dec-03
Dated Dec. 22/03
Visa statement balance is $390.50 for purchases made before Dec. 10. To avoid interest charges, payment of total statement balance is due by Jan. 2. Issue cheque #370 for $390.50.

❑ Cash Sales Invoice #HH-150
Dated Dec. 22/03
To Sal Rigger

1 set Andirons: cast iron	$100
Goods & Services Tax	7%
Provincial Sales Tax	8%

Paid by cheque #49. In the rush of pre-holiday sales fever, no credit check was completed. Allocate 100% of revenue and costs to General Sales Project.

notes

Remember to edit the price of the damaged inventory in the Price field to record the reduced sale price.

❑ Cash Sales Invoice #HH-151
Dated Dec. 23/03
To Amir Husein

1 Toolset: glass handle/cast iron (Damaged)	$ 200
1 Ceram Log: Birdseye Maple set BMF5	550
1 Door: Pinnacle Arch w/damper 2wf	1 000
1 Grill: rotisserie & spit DX80	1 300
Goods & Services Tax	7%
Provincial Sales Tax	8%

Paid by certified cheque #CB-43228.
Allocate 100% of revenue and costs to General Sales Project.

notes

To issue a bonus cheque, open the Payroll Journal. Select the employee. Delete the default salary amounts, hours and vacation pay. Click the Enter taxes manually button to turn off the automatic payroll deductions. All the deduction amount fields should now be available for editing. Prepare the paycheque by entering the bonus in the Bonus field in the Payroll Journal. Enter the income tax amount (10% of the bonus) to replace the amount in the Income Tax field. Delete all default amounts in the other deduction fields (Deductions and Taxes tabs). Remember to click the Calculate taxes automatically button to turn on the automatic payroll deductions immediately when preparing the next paycheques.

Memo #24
Dated Dec. 23/03
From owner to accountant: All employees will receive a holiday bonus in addition to their final paycheques for 2003. Add Bonus as a type of income (Home window, Setup menu, System Settings, Names, change the name of Income C to Bonus). The amounts of the bonuses will be as follows:

❑ Cinder (Manager)	$800
❑ Damper (Store Assistant)	$500
❑ Kindl (Installer)	$600
❑ Strong (New Installer)	$100

The minimum income tax of 10% should be withheld. Delete the other deductions in the Payroll Journal. (WSIB and EHT expenses cannot be deleted and will still appear in the journal.)
Allocate 100% of the cost of the bonus to the General Sales Project for Cinder, Kindl and Damper. Allocate 100% of the bonus for Strong to the Highlife Townhouse Project. Issue cheques #371 through #374 for the bonuses.

Warning!

Increase the wage rate in the employee record for Strong (Employees icon) before completing the payroll entry.

EMPLOYEE TIME SUMMARY SHEET #25

(pay period ending December 23, 2003)

	Name of Employee	Week 50 Hours	Week 51 Hours	Regular Hours	Overtime Hours
❑	Kris Kindl	42	40	80	2
❑	MyTee Strong	42	40	80	2

a. Strong's work has been excellent and the manager is concerned that she may leave because her pay is less than Kindl's. Therefore, Strong will receive a wage increase with this pay. Her new rate is $20 for regular hours and $30 for overtime.
b. Using Employee Time Summary Sheet #25 and the Employee Information Sheet, complete payroll for hourly employees.
c. Recover $50 advance from Kindl and issue cheques #375 and #376.
d. Allocate 50% of payroll costs to General Sales Project and 50% to Highlife Townhouse Project for each employee.

- [ ] Cash Sales Invoice #HH-152
  Dated Dec. 27/03
  To Brian Ames

1 Mantel: cherry MC-DVT40 kit	$1 200
1 Ceram Log: Algonquin Maple set AMF5	500
1 Door: Mirage w/damper 2.75wf	900
1 Woodholder: walnut	80
Goods & Services Tax	7%
Provincial Sales Tax	8%

  Paid by cash.
  Allocate 100% of revenue and costs to General Sales Project.

SESSION DATE – December 31

> **notes**
>
> - [ ] Sal Rigger is located at
>   696 Alias Drive
>   Toronto, ON M4G 2K8
>   Tel: (416) 482-1938
> - [ ] Create new Group account: 4200 Other Revenue and allow project allocations.
>
> Refer to Accounting Procedures for the two transactions relating to Sal Rigger.

- [ ] Bank Debit Memo #831214
  Dated Dec. 29/03
  From Royal Bank, $115 for NSF cheque from Sal Rigger, plus bank service charge of $20 to handle NSF cheque. Set up a customer record for Sal Rigger and charge the full amount to his account. Reference invoice #HH-150 and cheque #49. Allocate 100% of Other Revenue to General Sales Project. Delete the terms and the discount.

- [ ] Purchase Invoice #CC-1504
  Dated Dec. 29/03
  From Cambridge Castings to fill purchase order #103

2 CC: Fireplace free-std gas DV30DVT	£1 600.00
1 CC: Fireplace gas ins DV32HET	750.00
Freight	75.00
Goods & Services Tax	169.75
	£2 594.75

  Terms: 2/10, net 15 days. The exchange rate is 2.258.

> **notes**
>
> Remember to write off the account in the Receipts Journal as well by making a payment for these entries. No journal entry results from this receipt transaction because the amount is zero.

- [ ] Memo #25
  Dated Dec. 30/03
  From Manager: Write off the Sal Rigger account because we are unable to collect. His phone number and address are incorrect and attempts to notify him were unsuccessful. Remember to complete credit checks for all customers in future. The amount allocated to the GST Adjustment account is $7. Remove the payment terms.

- [ ] Bank Debit Memo #831419
  Dated Dec. 30/03
  From Royal Bank, for $2 400. This amount includes $2 150 for the reduction of principal on bank loan and $250 interest. Allocate 100% of expense to General Sales Project.

- [ ] Bank Debit Memo #831420
  Dated Dec. 30/03
  From Royal Bank, for $2 500. This amount includes $300 for the reduction of principal on mortgage and $2 200 interest. Allocate 100% of expense to General Sales Project.

- [ ] Bank Debit Memo #831421
  Dated Dec. 30/03
  From Royal Bank, for $75 in bank service charges, including NSF charges. Allocate 100% of expense to General Sales Project.

Bank Credit Memo #142341
Dated Dec. 31/03
From Royal Bank, for $712 for semi-annual interest on bank account. Remember that $340, Interest Receivable, was entered as revenue in the previous quarter. Allocate 100% of revenue to General Sales Project.

Cheque Copy #377
Dated Dec. 31/03
To Penguin Insulating Co., $374.50 in full payment of account. Reference invoice #PI-1321.

Memo #26
Dated Dec. 31/03
From Manager: Using the Employee Information Sheet, prepare payroll for Damper and Cinder for the pay period ending December 31. Issue cheques #378 and #379. Allocate 100% of payroll expense for Damper to General Sales Project. Allocate 70% of payroll expense for Cinder to the General Sales Project and 30% to the Highlife Townhouse Project.

Materials Summary Form #12
Dated Dec. 31/03
Re: Insulation and Hardware supplies: A physical count of materials inventory used for job orders indicated the following:

		Allocations	
		General Sales	Highlife Townhouse
Insulation used	$300	90%	10%
Fireplace Hardware used	$180	50%	50%

Make the necessary asset adjustments and expense charges.

Memo #27
Dated Dec. 31/03
From Manager: The following year-end adjustments are required:

notes

Use Memo 27A, 27B, and so on as source numbers.

Depreciation for the fiscal quarter ending December 31, 2003:

		Allocations	
		General Sales	Highlife Townhouse
Computers	$ 500	100%	
Installation Equipment	250	90%	10%
Shop Centre	3 000	100%	
Transport Vehicles	1 000	90%	10%

The amount of office supplies on hand based on a physical count is $160. Allocate 100% of expense to General Sales Project.

Payroll liability accrued for hourly employees on December 31, 2003:

Kindl	$ 800
Strong	800
	$1 600

A new Group account, 2240 Accrued Payroll is required.
Allocate 100% of expense to General Sales Project.

The following amounts of prepaid expenses have expired on December 31:

Prepaid Advertising	$480
Prepaid Insurance	$450

Allocate 100% of expenses to General Sales Project.

- [ ] Memo #28
  Dated Dec. 31/03
  Transfer $50 000 from Bank Account: Credit Card to Bank Account: Chequing.

- [ ] Memo #29
  Dated Dec. 31/03
  From Manager: Access the Canada Customs and Revenue Agency Web site and find the revised Federal Claims for basic personal and spousal amounts (search for TD1). Update all employee records with new amounts to prepare for the new year.

CASE PROBLEMS

1. Amber Ashe, the owner, wants to reorganize the Chart of Accounts for Hearth House. The first change is to include *Freight Expense* as part of the subtotal for Net Cost of Goods Sold. However, because the account has journal entries posted to it, the account number cannot be changed so that it is placed before the subtotal account. How can she resolve this problem?

   Ashe has also decided that she would prefer to have separate costs for each inventory category, a total for the cost of all inventory goods sold, and another total for all costs related to the goods sold (i.e., including cost of inventory, discounts and allowances, etc.). Describe in detail the procedures for making these changes. What are the advantages of the more detailed accounting for costs? Are there any disadvantages?

2. Hearth House has an opportunity to purchase an adjacent property for its store expansion. Before proceeding, Ashe wants an analysis of how she can include other projects or divisions for the distribution of costs.

   a. What kinds of divisions or projects could a business like Hearth House use?
   b. What advantages are offered by adding project information?
   c. How might the allocation of revenue and expenses be determined for the different projects you are proposing?

3. How does Simply Accounting assist a business that sells inventory items with inventory control? What additional inventory controls can a business put into place to ensure that costs and losses are minimal?

4. How can a business like Hearth House assess the profitability of the service side of its operations separately from the profitability of its retail or product sales? What factors should a business take into account in pricing its services or in the decision to continue to offer them?

5. Evaluate the profitability of the Highlife Project. Review all the allocations for December and determine whether they were fair and reasonable.

CHAPTER FOURTEEN

After completing this chapter, you should be able to

OBJECTIVES

- *print* the General Ledger report for the bank account
- *observe* the differences between a bank statement and the General Ledger report
- *turn on* the account reconciliation feature
- *create* new accounts for reconciliation
- *link* the new reconciliation accounts
- *set up* the account reconciliation information
- *reconcile* the bank account statement with the General Ledger
- *display* and *print* account reconciliation reports
- *clear* journal entries and paid invoices

COMPANY INFORMATION

Company Profile

notes

Although many schools have a school store, the details presented here may be different from the ways other stores operate or set prices.

HSC School Store is located on the ground floor of the High School of Commerce in Toronto, Ontario. It operates for the convenience of the students, who can buy their stationery and school supplies at reasonable prices. Markups on all store goods are very small because the store is not set up to make a profit. The teachers may also buy from the store. They usually do so to provide a service to their students, buying items that the students are required to have and then reselling them to the students at the same price. This helps to reduce lineups at the store. As representatives of a school department, teachers are allowed to buy on credit and customer accounts have been set up for them. The head of each department is the store's contact, but individual teachers are expected to settle their accounts within 15 days. Students pay for all their purchases in cash.

Although supervised by a business department teacher, the store is managed and operated by students in the school, who may earn partial credits toward a business course that they are currently taking.

To help the store get started in the fall, the school board provides an interest-free loan because margins on goods sold are too small to build up a bank account balance large enough to purchase inventory. The store repays the loan at the end of the school year.

September is the busiest month for the school store, followed by October and then February, the beginning of the second semester. Store hours are set accordingly. The store is open every day for the first two weeks of September, three days per week until the middle of October and the first four weeks of the winter term, and two days per week for the rest of the year. During exam periods and holidays, the store is closed. The hours of operation, one hour before and after school and during lunch, avoid all conflicts with scheduled classes and make employment in the store equally accessible to all students.

In previous years, all the record keeping has been performed manually. At the end of August, in keeping with the gift of a used computer and the business department offering Simply Accounting courses, the accounts were set up in Simply Accounting. The following information is available to complete the transactions for October:

- Chart of Accounts
- Trial Balance as at September 30, 2003
- Vendor Information
- Customer Information
- Inventory Information
- Accounting Procedures

notes

The account 2670 GST Paid on Purchases is required as a linked account for the software to work properly. It is not used in transactions and will maintain a zero balance.

HSC SCHOOL STORE
CHART OF ACCOUNTS

ASSETS
1080 Cash in Bank
1200 Accounts Receivable
1300 Merchandise Inventory
1400 Computers & Peripherals
1450 Cash Register

LIABILITIES
2100 Loan from Administration
2200 Accounts Payable
2640 PST Payable
2650 GST Charged on Sales
2670 GST Paid on Purchases

EQUITY
3560 School Store Surplus
3600 Current Earnings

REVENUE
4020 Revenue from Sales
4100 Revenue from Textbooks

EXPENSES
5060 Cost of Goods Sold
5100 Damages and Losses
5140 General Expenses

HSC SCHOOL STORE
TRIAL BALANCE

September 30, 2003

Account	Debit	Credit
1080 Cash in Bank	$ 4 987.51	
1200 Accounts Receivable	642.00	
1300 Merchandise Inventory	7 890.05	
1400 Computers & Peripherals	500.00	
1450 Cash Register	200.00	
2100 Loan from Administration		$ 8 000.00
2200 Accounts Payable		1 921.00
2640 PST Payable		284.21
2650 GST Charged on Sales		441.05
3560 School Store Surplus		2 423.50
4020 Revenue from Sales		3 552.65
4100 Revenue from Textbooks		2 748.00
5060 Cost of Goods Sold	5 150.85	
	$19 370.41	$19 370.41

HSC SCHOOL STORE
VENDOR INFORMATION

Vendor Name (Contact)	Address	Phone No. Fax No.	Terms
A.W. Publishers (Wesley Addison)	PO Box 580 Toronto, ON M3C 2T8	Tel: (416) 447-5101	Net 15
Asian Clothing Co.	93 Spadina Ave. Toronto, ON M4R 1K3	Tel: (416) 923-5411	Net 15
Ling Mfg. Co. (Mi Ling)	395 Queen St. E. Toronto, ON M2P 2T2	Tel: (416) 778-2972	Net 30
Metro Bookstore (Rhonda Reading)	349 Parliament St. Toronto, ON M3G 6F2	Tel: (416) 672-6219	Net 30
T.O. School Suppliers (Tori Osborne)	555 Dundas St. W. Toronto, ON M6L 1N4	Tel: (416) 882-7219	Net 15
Tudor Lock Co. (Mary Q. Scott)	33 Jarvis St. Toronto, ON M4R 1B1	Tel: (416) 528-5119	Net 20

HSC SCHOOL STORE
OUTSTANDING VENDOR INVOICES

Vendor Name	Date	Inv/Chq No.	Terms	Amount	Total
A.W. Publishers	8/30/03	AW-334	Net 15	$ 600	
	9/10/03	100		– 600	
	9/30/03	AW-619	Net 15	1 680	
			Balance owing		$1 680
T.O. School Suppliers	8/30/03	TSS-642	Net 15	$ 550	
	9/12/03	101		– 550	
	9/30/03	TSS-991	Net 15	91	
			Balance owing		91
Tudor Lock Co.	8/30/03	TLC-497	Net 20	$ 450	
	9/15/03	102		– 450	
	9/30/03	TLC-632		150	
			Balance owing		150
			Grand Total		$1 921

HSC SCHOOL STORE
CUSTOMERS AND OUTSTANDING INVOICES

Customer Name (Contact)	Date	Invoice No.	Terms	Amount	Balance Owing
Accounting Dept. (S. Gallo)	9/3/03	EC-1	Net 15	$299.00	
	9/10/03	Chq 38		–299.00	
	9/11/03	EC-8	Net 15	192.60	
	9/26/03	Chq 103		–192.60	
	9/22/03	EC-12	Net 15	642.00	$642.00
Data Processing Dept. (M. Musta)	9/3/03	EC-2	Net 15	$ 69.00	
	9/18/03	Chq 11		–69.00	
	9/4/03	EC-4	Net 15	69.00	
	9/20/03	Chq 23		–69.00	
	9/19/03	EC-11	Net 15	82.80	
	9/28/03	Chq 29		–82.80	
English Dept. (H. Garber)					
Geography Dept. (D. Little)					
History Dept. (S. Halloran)					
Keyboarding Dept. (C. Chihrin)	9/5/03	EC-5	Net 15	$ 10.35	
	9/16/03	Chq 15		–10.35	
	9/5/03	EC-6	Net 15	57.50	
	9/21/03	Chq 62		–57.50	
Math Dept. (W. Erdman)	9/14/03	EC-9	Net 15	$ 46.00	
	9/25/03	Chq 33		–46.00	
Phys. Ed. Dept. (L. Sialtsis)	9/4/03	EC-3	Net 15	$331.20	
	9/16/03	Chq 31		–331.20	
Science Dept. (H. Heinola)					
			Grand Total		$642.00

HSC SCHOOL STORE
INVENTORY INFORMATION

Code	Description	Selling Price /Unit	Qty on Hand	Amt (Cost)	Min Stock
010	ACCO 3 Ring Binder 1″ spine	$ 1.00 each	30	$ 24.00	10
020	ACCO 3 Ring Binder 2″ spine	3.00 each	30	75.00	10
030	Accounting Paper - 25 sheets	.75/pkg	20	12.00	5
040	Binder - Blue 3 Ring 2″ spine	1.50 each	25	31.25	5
050	Calculator - Basic Math	10.00 each	30	240.00	5
060	Calculator - Scientific	20.00 each	30	480.00	5
070	Clipboard - Acrylic Letter	7.00 each	20	120.00	5
080	Clipboard - Hardwood Letter	1.50 each	40	40.00	10
090	Clipboard - Hardwood Legal	2.00 each	20	30.00	5
100No PST	Dictionary - Pocket Cant/Eng	12.00 each	21	210.00	10
110No PST	Dictionary - Pocket Eng	12.00 each	39	390.00	10
120No PST	Dictionary - Pocket Fr/Eng	12.00 each	14	140.00	2
130No PST	Dictionary - Pocket Punj/Eng	12.00 each	20	200.00	2
140No PST	Dictionary - Pocket Viet/Eng	12.00 each	27	270.00	2
150	Diskettes - DSHD 3.5″	1.00 each	65	32.50	20
160	Dividers - 5 pack	.65/pkg	20	12.00	5
170	Duo Tang Folder	.35 each	30	9.00	5
180	Duo Tang Folders - 4 pack	1.20/pkg	10	10.00	2
190	Eraser	.20 each	50	7.50	10
200	Executive Secretary	3.30 each	10	30.00	2
210	Exercise Book - 4 pack	2.00/pkg	60	105.00	10
220	Glue Stick	1.30 each	50	57.50	5
230	Glue Sticks - 3 pack	4.50/pkg	10	40.00	2
240	Graph Paper - 50 sheets	1.00/pkg	50	40.00	5
250	Gym Bag - HSC Logo	16.00 each	20	240.00	5
260	Index Cards	1.50/pkg	20	25.00	5
270	Knapsack - HSC Logo	20.00 each	20	300.00	5
280	Lock - Combination	4.00 each	80	240.00	30
290	Markers - Self-stick 4 pack	2.00/pkg	20	35.00	2
300	Math Set	5.00/set	40	160.00	5
310	Paper - Blank 50 refill sheets	.60/pkg	50	22.50	10
320	Paper - Lined 200 refill sheets	2.00/pkg	30	48.00	5
330	Paper - Typing 50 full sheets	.65/pkg	40	22.00	5
340	Paper - Typing 50 half sheets	.50/pkg	20	8.00	3
350	Pen - Blue/red	.20 each	50	8.00	10
360	Pen - Blue/red 12 pack	1.20/pkg	10	10.00	2
370	Pen - Solo Cross	10.00 each	10	80.00	2
380	Pencil	.15 each	40	4.80	10
390	Pencil Crayons - 8 pack	1.40/pkg	40	48.00	10
400	Pencil Crayons - 20 pack	2.50/pkg	30	60.00	5
410	Post-it notes - 3x3	.60/pad	30	15.00	5
420	Post-it notes - 3x5	.80/pad	10	6.00	2
430	Portfolio	.30 each	10	2.00	2
440	Reinforcements - Gummed	.40/pkg	20	6.00	2
450	Ruler - 15 cm.	.40 each	20	6.00	5
460	Ruler - 30 cm.	.50 each	20	8.00	2
470	Scissors - 5″	4.00 each	20	60.00	2
480	Scissors - 7″	6.00 each	20	90.00	2
490	Shorthand Coil Notebook	3.00 each	10	20.00	2

continued...

HSC SCHOOL STORE
INVENTORY INFORMATION CONTINUED

Code	Description	Selling Price /Unit	Qty on Hand	Amt (Cost)	Min Stock
500	Sweatpants - HSC Logo	25.00 each	20	$ 400.00	5
510	Sweatshirt - HSC Logo	24.00 each	20	360.00	5
520	Template - Flowchart	1.20 each	10	10.00	2
530No PST	Workbook - Accounting D'Amico	18.00 each	20	300.00	10
540No PST	Workbook - Accounting Palmer	18.00 each	30	450.00	10
550No PST	Workbook - Simply Version 7 Purbhoo	30.00 each	40	1 120.00	10
560No PST	Workbook - Simply Version 8 Purbhoo	30.00 each	40	1 120.00	10
				$7 890.05	

Accounting Procedures

notes

Remember to delete PST from purchases of inventory items.

PST

PST at 8 percent for Ontario is charged on all goods sold by the store, excepts books (workbooks and dictionaries). All books in inventory have "No PST" included as part of the item code as an additional reminder to the students working in the store not to charge PST on books. That is, they should delete the default entry of 8 percent in the PST field. The School Board makes PST remittances centrally based on the store's total sales. Revenue from books is separated to make tax calculations easier.

notes

Vendors are set up not to collect GST so that only codes 0 and 1 should be available. If an entry for GST appears, delete the GST code and amount from the purchase invoices.

GST

GST at 7 percent is charged on all goods sold by the store, including books. Again, remittances are handled centrally by the School Board based on total sales. However, educational institutions providing mainly tax-exempt services (similar to financial institutions) are not allowed to deduct the GST paid on goods they purchase from the GST charged on sales to calculate the GST owing. They pay all the GST they collect directly to the Receiver General. Therefore, the GST paid account is not used and GST paid on purchases is added to the purchase price as part of the cost of goods sold.

Cash Sales Summary

Most store sales are for small amounts. Therefore, individual sales are recorded on a printed inventory list as they occur. Twice a week, the summaries of these transactions are entered into the accounting program. This saves time because entries for each individual sale are not required. Bank deposits are also made twice a week.

NSF Cheques

If a cheque is deposited from an account that does not have enough money to cover it, the bank returns it to the depositor as NSF (non-sufficient funds). To record the NSF cheque, first reverse the receipt in the Receipts Journal. Turn on the option to Include Fully Paid Invoices and enter a **negative** payment amount. Then enter a Sales Journal invoice for the amount of the handling charge. Refer to Chapter 5, page 135, if you need more help.

If the paid invoices have been cleared, or if the sale was a cash sale, you must process the NSF cheque through the Sales Journal because there is no Receipts Journal entry. Create a customer record if necessary and enter a **positive** amount for the amount of the cheque. Choose *Cash in Bank* as the account. *Cash in Bank* will be credited and *Accounts Receivable* will be debited. If the customer is expected to pay the bank charges, enter these on the second invoice line as a **positive** amount and select the appropriate revenue account. No taxes are charged on these amounts.

INSTRUCTIONS

1. Using the Chart of Accounts, the Trial Balance, Vendor, Customer and Inventory information provided, and using the Keystrokes that follow as a guide, set up and complete the account reconciliation for HSC School Store for September. The journal transactions for September have been completed for you.
2. Enter the source documents for October including the account reconciliation. The source documents begin on page 524.
3. After completing your entries, print the reports indicated on the chart below.

REPORTS

Lists
- ☐ Chart of Accounts
- ☐ Vendors
- ☐ Customers
- ☐ Inventory & Services

Financials
- ☑ Comparative Balance Sheet
  dates: September 30 and October 31
  with dollar difference
- ☑ Income Statement
  from September 1 to October 31
- ☐ Trial Balance
- ☑ General Ledger
  accounts: 4020 4100
  from September 1 to October 31
- ☐ Cash Flow Projection

GST
- ☐ GST Report

Account Reconciliation
- ☑ Account Reconciliation Status Summary
  from September 1 to September 30
- ☑ Account Reconciliation Status Detail
  from October 1 to October 31

Mailing Labels
- ☐ Labels

Management Reports
- ☐ Ledger

Journals
- ☐ All Journals
- ☐ General
- ☐ Purchases
- ☐ Payments
- ☑ Sales (by posting date)
  from October 1 to October 31
- ☐ Receipts
- ☐ Item Assembly
- ☐ Adjustments
- ☑ Account Reconciliation
  (by posting date)
  from September 1 to October 31

Payables
- ☐ Vendor Aged
- ☐ Aged Overdue Payables
- ☐ Vendor Purchases
- ☐ Pending Purchase Orders

Receivables
- ☑ Customer Aged Detail
  for all customers
- ☐ Aged Overdue Receivables
- ☐ Customer Sales
- ☐ Pending Sales Orders
- ☐ Customer Statements

Inventory
- ☐ Inventory
- ☐ Inventory Activity
- ☐ Inventory Sales
- ☐ Inventory Transaction

KEYSTROKES FOR ACCOUNT RECONCILIATION

Account Reconciliation

Warning!

Make a backup copy of your data files before you set up the account reconciliation feature.

For any bank account, the timing of monthly statements is usually not perfectly matched with the accounting entry of the corresponding transaction. Usually some of the cheques written do not appear on the statement, and interest earned on the account or bank charges are not yet recorded because they may be unknown until receipt of the statement. Thus the balance of the bank statement most likely does not match the balance in the cash account. The process of identifying the differences to achieve a match is the process of account reconciliation.

You can apply account reconciliation to any Balance Sheet account for which you have regular statements, including credit card payable accounts. For each account you want to reconcile, you must complete the setup procedure.

The keystrokes that follow will set up account reconciliation for the bank account for the HSC School Store.

Creating Linking Accounts for Reconciliation

notes

You can save your work and exit at any time. Any changes you have made will be saved and you can continue from where you left off when you are ready.

Most bank statements include monthly bank charges, loan or mortgage payments and interest on deposits. That is, there are usually some regular sources of income and expense. Normally the only source document for these bank account transactions is the bank statement. To use Simply Accounting's account reconciliation feature, you must first create the accounts that link to these regular bank account transactions. When you examine the September Bank Statement for HSC School Store on page 509, you can see that there is an interest deposit and a withdrawal for service charges. The store does not currently have accounts for either of these items, so you must create them. In addition, you will need an account to enter adjustments related to the reconciliation. The exact role of these accounts will be further explained as we proceed with the account reconciliation setup.

Open the data files for HSC with September 30 as the session date and open the Accounts window.

Create the following new Group accounts.

- *Revenue from Interest* *4160*
- *Bank Charges* *5020*
- *Reconciliation Adjustment* *5170*

These are the accounts that will be linked to the Account Reconciliation process to identify the bank account-related expenses and income.

Before completing the reconciliation procedure, the General Ledger accounts that will be reconciled must be identified and modified.

You should remain in the Accounts window.

notes

Remember that you can print the General Ledger from the Reports menu in the Accounts window.

Print the General Ledger for the *Cash in Bank* account from September 1 to September 30, the period covering all transactions after the last bank statement. You will need the ledger report at the next stage to compare with the bank statement. In an ongoing business, print the Ledger report beginning on the date of the oldest outstanding item from your previous bank statement up to the date of the most recent statement.

Turning on the Account Reconciliation Feature

Double click the account **1080 Cash in Bank** to open its ledger window:

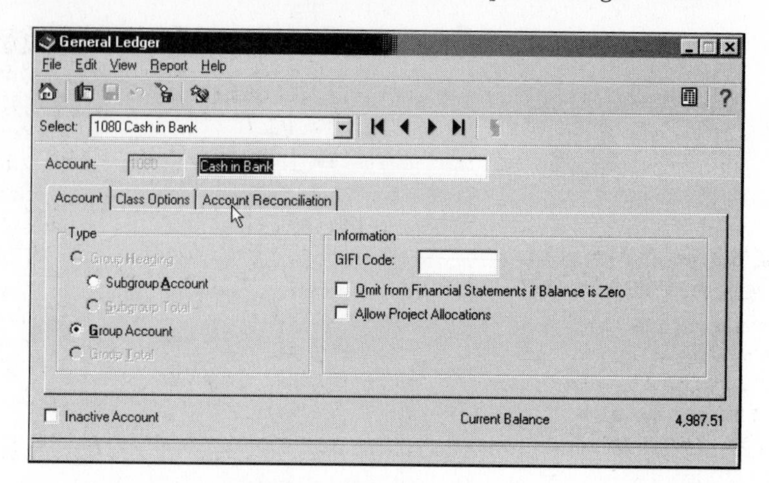

Click the **Account Reconciliation tab**:

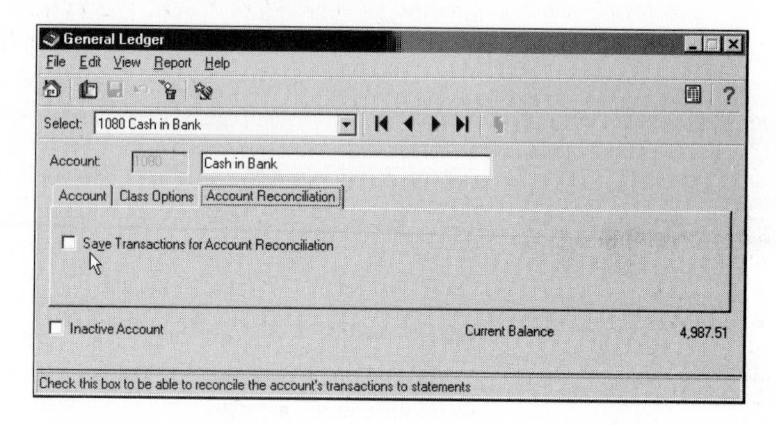

notes

All Balance Sheet accounts have an account reconciliation tab. You can reconcile any accounts for which you have regular statements. Usually these are the bank accounts or Credit Card Payable accounts.

Click Save Transactions for Account Reconciliation to display the additional option buttons shown in the following screen:

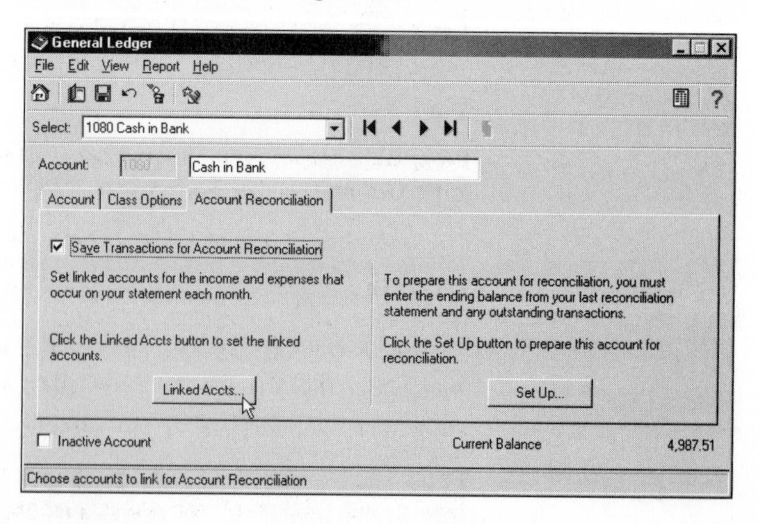

Naming and Linking Reconciliation Accounts

Click Linked Accts to display the following screen:

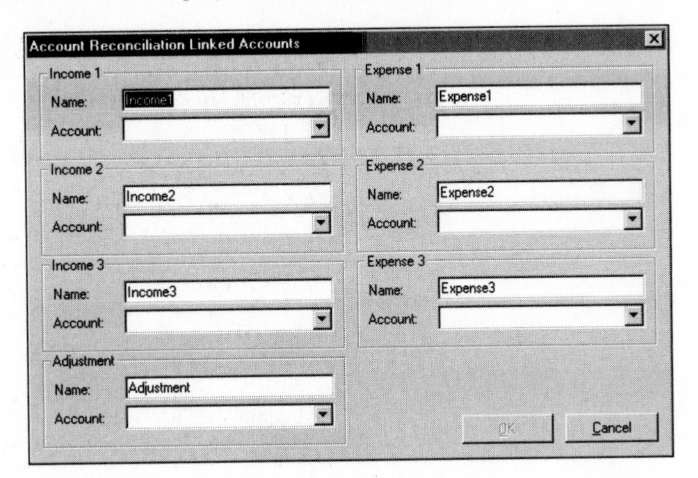

notes

The name fields on this form cannot be left blank. You can leave the default names as they are or enter "n/a" for not applicable if they are not needed.

The fields on this Account Reconciliation Linked Accounts form will be used to identify the appropriate General Ledger accounts for income (interest received) from bank deposits; for expenses associated with the bank account, such as bank charges or interest paid on bank loans; and for adjustments — small discrepancies between the accounting entries and the bank statements, such as for amounts entered incorrectly in journal transactions. You can identify up to three sources of income, three types of expenses and one adjustment account for each bank account.

notes

You can edit these names and accounts at any time and you can add new sources of income or expense later if they are needed.

The first Income Name field is highlighted, ready for editing. The only source of income for this account that is not accounted for elsewhere is interest income. You can use up to 10 characters for each name.

Type `Bank Int`

Click the **list arrow for the Account field** for Income 1 to list the revenue accounts that are available.

Click 4160 Revenue from Interest, the account you created earlier as part of the reconciliation setup.

Press tab to advance to the next Income field. This field and the third Income field are not needed, so you will indicate that they are not applicable.

Type `n/a`

Press tab twice to skip the Account field and advance to the third Income field. Indicate that it too is not applicable.

Leave the default name for adjustments unchanged.

Click the **Adjustment Account field list arrow** to display the list of eligible accounts. Either an expense or a revenue account can be used for adjustments because they can increase or decrease the account balance. HSC School Store will use the expense account created for this purpose.

Click 5170 Reconciliation Adjustments

Press tab to advance to and highlight the first Expense Name field. The School Store has one automatic bank account-related expense, bank charges.

Type `Bk Charges`

Click the **Account field list arrow** for Expense 1 to display the list of expense accounts.

Select 5020 Bank Charges for this expense account.

Press tab to advance to and highlight the second Expense Name field.

Type `n/a`

Press tab twice to skip the Account field and advance to the third Expense field. Indicate that it is not needed.

Check your work carefully. When you are certain that all the names and accounts are correct,

Click OK to save the new information and return to the *Cash in Bank* General Ledger window.

Setting up for Reconciliation

We are now ready to compare the bank statement with the General Ledger report for the bank account. The General Ledger and September bank statement for the HSC School Store follow:

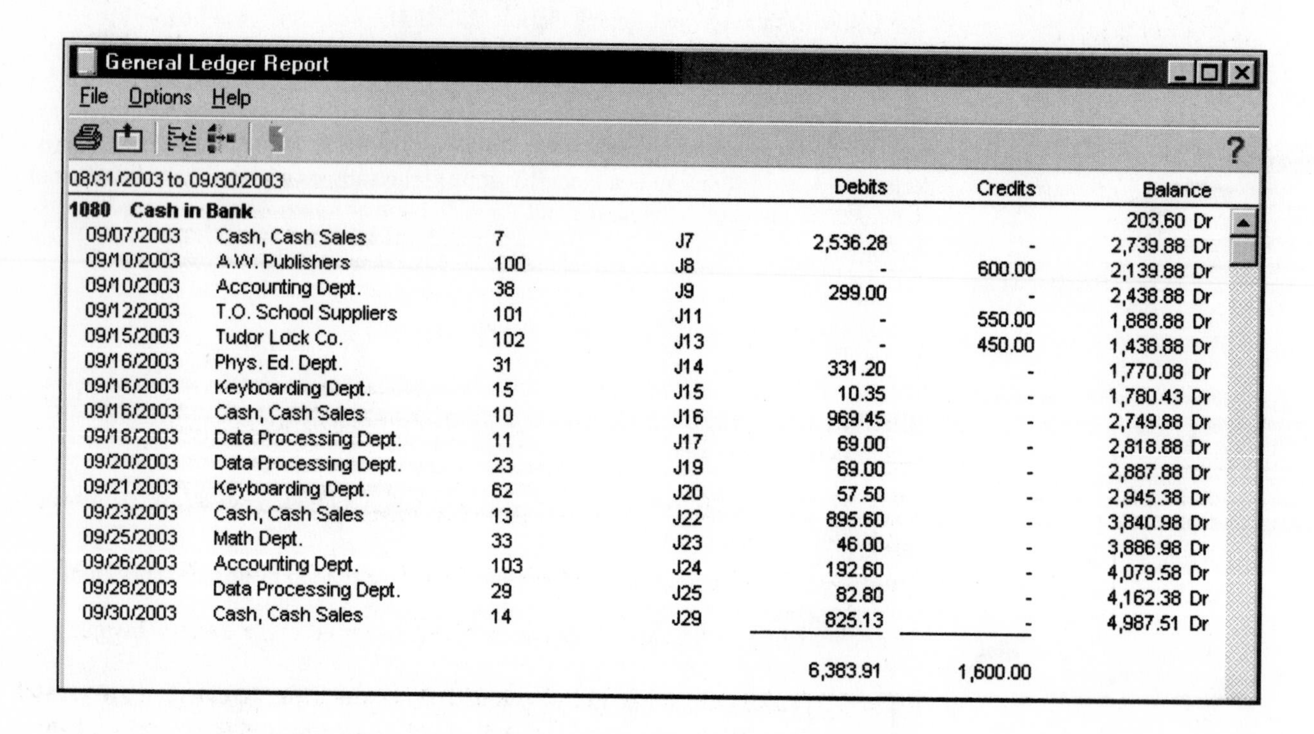

General Ledger Report

File Options Help

08/31/2003 to 09/30/2003

				Debits	Credits	Balance
1080 Cash in Bank						203.60 Dr
09/07/2003	Cash, Cash Sales	7	J7	2,536.28	-	2,739.88 Dr
09/10/2003	A.W. Publishers	100	J8	-	600.00	2,139.88 Dr
09/10/2003	Accounting Dept.	38	J9	299.00	-	2,438.88 Dr
09/12/2003	T.O. School Suppliers	101	J11	-	550.00	1,888.88 Dr
09/15/2003	Tudor Lock Co.	102	J13	-	450.00	1,438.88 Dr
09/16/2003	Phys. Ed. Dept.	31	J14	331.20	-	1,770.08 Dr
09/16/2003	Keyboarding Dept.	15	J15	10.35	-	1,780.43 Dr
09/16/2003	Cash, Cash Sales	10	J16	969.45	-	2,749.88 Dr
09/18/2003	Data Processing Dept.	11	J17	69.00	-	2,818.88 Dr
09/20/2003	Data Processing Dept.	23	J19	69.00	-	2,887.88 Dr
09/21/2003	Keyboarding Dept.	62	J20	57.50	-	2,945.38 Dr
09/23/2003	Cash, Cash Sales	13	J22	895.60	-	3,840.98 Dr
09/25/2003	Math Dept.	33	J23	46.00	-	3,886.98 Dr
09/26/2003	Accounting Dept.	103	J24	192.60	-	4,079.58 Dr
09/28/2003	Data Processing Dept.	29	J25	82.80	-	4,162.38 Dr
09/30/2003	Cash, Cash Sales	14	J29	825.13	-	4,987.51 Dr
				6,383.91	1,600.00	

U Can Trust Co.
5621 Honesty Way
Toronto, Ontario
M2Y 3E4

Transit #61290
Account # 003 77238-2

September 30, 2003

HSC School Store
16 Phin Ave.
Toronto, Ontario M3B 9J2

Date	Transaction	Deposits	Withdrawals	Balance
08/31/03	Balance Fwd.			203.60
09/10/03	Deposit	2,536.28		2,739.88
09/10/03	Deposit	299.00		3,038.88
09/12/03	CHQ #100		600.00	2,438.88
09/15/03	CHQ #101		550.00	1,888.88
09/16/03	Deposit	1,311.00		3,199.88
09/19/03	CHQ #102		450.00	2,749.88
	Deposit	69.00		2,818.88
09/20/03	Deposit	69.00		2,887.88
09/21/03	Deposit	57.50		2,945.38
09/23/03	Deposit	895.60		3,840.98
09/26/03	Deposit	238.60		4,079.58
09/28/03	Deposit	82.80		4,162.38
09/30/03	Interest	4.35		4,166.73
	Service Fee		11.50	4,155.23
09/30/03	Closing Balance			4,155.23
Total Deposits		5,563.13		
Total Withdrawals			1,611.50	

notes

The deposit on September 16 includes the cash deposit for $969.45 and two cheques for $10.35 and $331.20. The September 26 deposit includes two cheques for $46.00 and $192.60. Notice that the deposit dates are not always the same as the journal entry dates.

When you compare this statement with the General Ledger Report, you will notice these differences:

- One deposit for $825.13 in the General Ledger Report at the end of the month is not listed on the bank statement.
- Interest of $4.35 received on the deposit account does not appear in the General Ledger Report.
- Monthly bank charges of $11.50 have not been recorded in the General Ledger Report.
- Two of the deposits, for $1 311.00 and $238.60 on the bank statement, do not match any journal entry in the General Ledger because they were multiple deposits (see notes in margin).

Sometimes items that appear in the General Ledger report were part of the previous month's bank statement, as when bank charges are recorded as General Journal entries.

All these items must be accounted for in order to have the bank statement match the bank balance on the Balance Sheet.

notes

If the ledger for Cash in Bank is not open, open it by clicking the Accounts icon in the Home window and double clicking the account 1080 Cash in Bank.

The next step involves identifying all transactions for the account that have not appeared on previous bank statements, that is, they have not been reconciled and were outstanding at the time of the previous statement.

Your Ledger window for *Cash in Bank* should still be open at the Account Reconciliation tab window.

Click Set Up to display the following advisory screen:

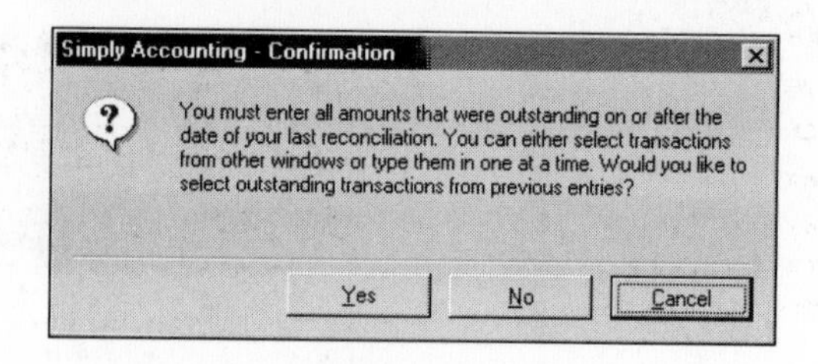

notes

If you finish your session and continue with the setup later, choose No when asked to enter outstanding transactions. Otherwise you will enter all the transactions twice and you will have to delete the second set of transactions. You can also restore your backup and begin again.

You are being asked to enter amounts that were outstanding at the previous reconciliation.

Click Yes to display the following dialogue box:

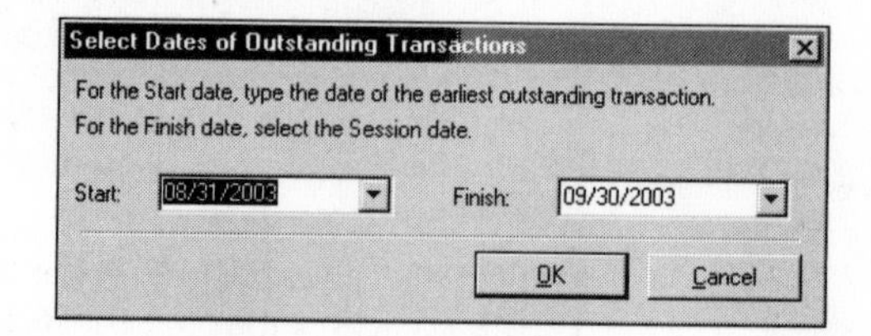

This screen asks you for the dates of the earliest and latest journal entries that have not yet been reconciled on your previous bank statement, usually for the previous month. For HSC School Store, these will include the journal entries made during September that followed the August bank statement. The default start and finish dates are correct, so do not change them.

Click OK to display these outstanding transactions, as shown here:

Select Outstanding Amounts

Select all transactions that were outstanding on or after the date of your last reconciliation by highlighting the line.

Transactions with a checkmark have already been selected for reconciliation and do not need to be selected again.

Source	Comment	Date	Debits	Credits	S
7	Cash, Cash Sales	09/07/2003	2,536.28	--	
100	A.W. Publishers	09/10/2003	--	600.00	
38	Accounting Dept.	09/10/2003	299.00	--	
101	T.O. School Suppliers	09/12/2003	--	550.00	
102	Tudor Lock Co.	09/15/2003	--	450.00	
31	Phys. Ed. Dept.	09/16/2003	331.20	--	
15	Keyboarding Dept.	09/16/2003	10.35	--	
10	Cash, Cash Sales	09/16/2003	969.45	--	
11	Data Processing Dept.	09/18/2003	69.00	--	
23	Data Processing Dept.	09/20/2003	69.00	--	
		Selected Total:	0.00	0.00	

OK | Cancel | Select All | Help

notes

You can also click each item or line individually to complete the selection. If you include an entry by mistake, click it again to deselect it. If all items are selected, clicking Select All again will undo the selection.

Click Select All to select all the journal entries because they are all outstanding.

If any items on the list of journal entries were in fact part of the previous bank statement, such as bank charges or interest from the previous statement, you should deselect them by clicking the lines that contain these items. This action will leave all other items selected while the ones you click will not be selected. The unselected items are not outstanding according to the August bank statement.

notes

- If you have duplicated transactions by entering the outstanding ones twice, you can remove the duplicates. For each duplicate, click to select it then choose the Edit menu and click Remove Line.
- If you have forgotten to include a transaction, you can type it into this screen by inserting the line in its correct sequence using the Edit menu, Insert Line option.
- If you need to add items, for example, historical transactions that do not appear in the General Ledger, you can enter them by inserting lines (Edit menu) where needed and typing the missing information.

Click OK to advance to the next step and screen:

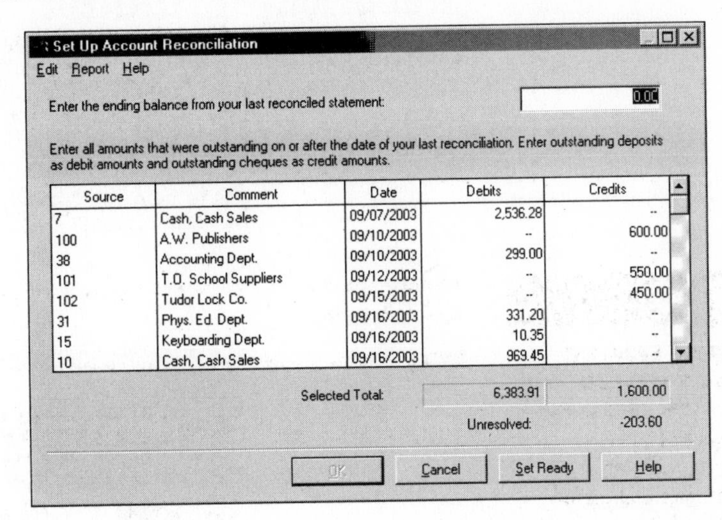

At this point you must enter the opening balance from the current bank statement as the Ending balance from your last reconciled statement. For the School Store, this is the September opening *Cash in Bank* account balance from the bank statement (or from the General Ledger statement minus any not-outstanding items for the previous month, if there are any).

notes

This balance should be the amount that will offset the unresolved amount displayed at the bottom of the screen.

The field for Entering the ending balance from your last reconciled statement is highlighted, ready to be changed.

Type `203.60`

Press tab to set the unresolved amount to zero. Account reconciliation can now be set ready for the account.

Click Set Ready. A cautionary message appears on the screen:

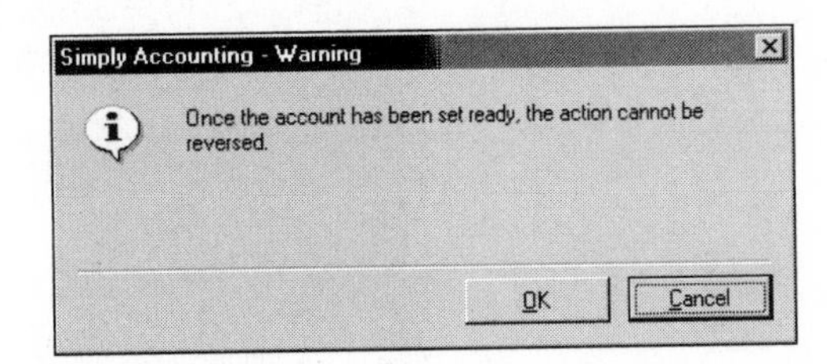

Simply Accounting is advising you that this step cannot be reversed. If you have not yet made a backup, click Cancel in the Warning screen. Then click OK to close the Set Up window and make a backup before proceeding. Remember not to include outstanding amounts this time.

notes

The Linked Accts button remains available because you can add and change linked accounts.

Click OK to continue. You will return to the bank account information window. The Set Up button has been removed because the setup is complete.

Close the *Cash in Bank* ledger account information window.

Close the Accounts window to return to the Home window.

notes

The account reconciliation status detail report lists all individual journal entries and their status as outstanding.

To see what you have done so far, **choose** the **Reports menu**, then **choose Account Reconciliation** and **click Account Reconciliation Status Report**. **Choose** the **Summary** option, **select 1080 Cash in Bank** and **click OK**. All the current month's journal transactions are still outstanding, but you have adjusted the report for the correct opening balance.

Close the displayed report when you are finished and return to the Home window. You are now ready to begin reconciling the current bank statement.

Reconciling the Bank Statement

The account reconciliation procedure consists of three steps to update the General Ledger. First, you record the new ending balance from the bank statement for the account. Next, you identify all the deposits and withdrawals that have been processed by the bank. Finally, you must complete journal entries for any transactions for which the bank statement is the source document. The result should be a match between the bank balances in the two statements.

All three steps are completed in the Account Reconciliation Journal indicated by the pointer:

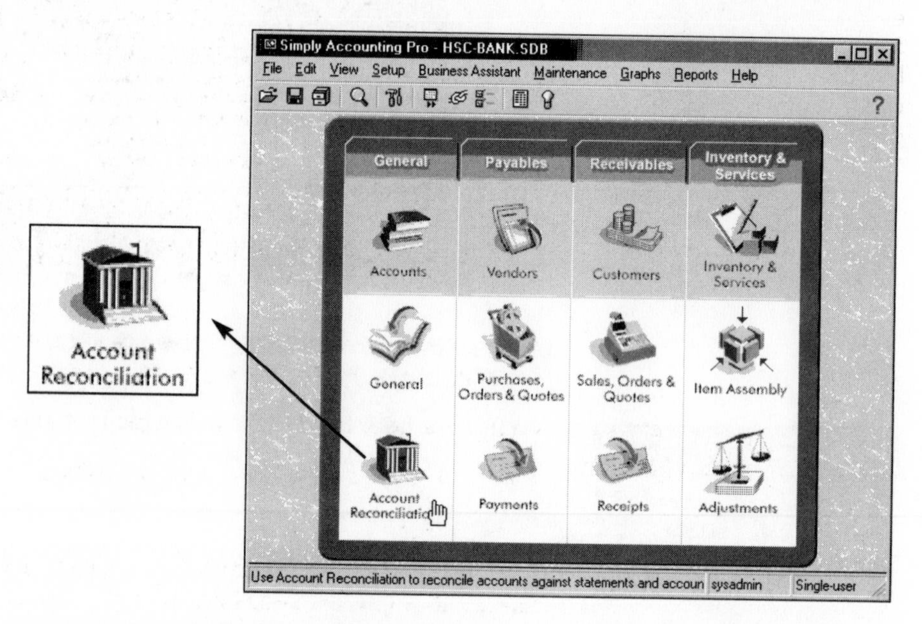

Click the **Account Reconciliation Journal icon** in the Home window. The Account Reconciliation Journal entry form is shown:

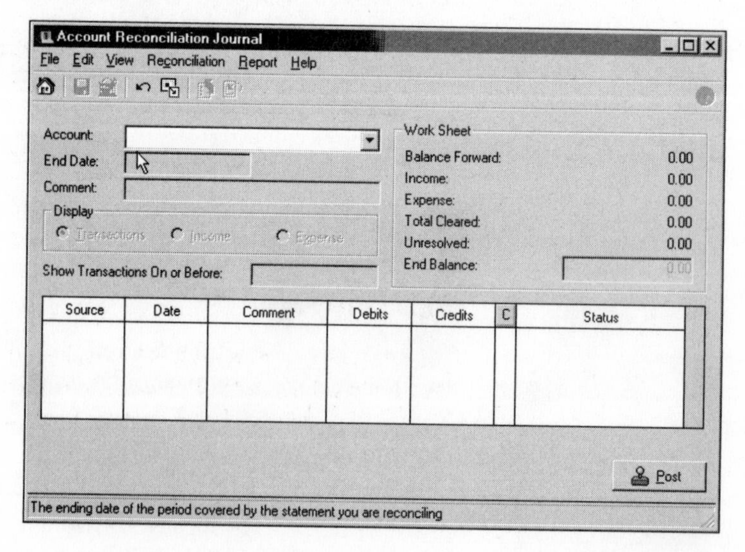

Click the **Account field list arrow** to display the available accounts for reconciliation. The list displays the single bank account because it was the only one that was set up for account reconciliation.

Select 1080 Cash in Bank to display the reconciliation information for this bank account:

Do not post the account reconciliation journal transaction until the unresolved amount is zero (or a small discrepancy that you can explain). You can click the Save button to save your work before posting, exit the journal and return later to find the error and make corrections.

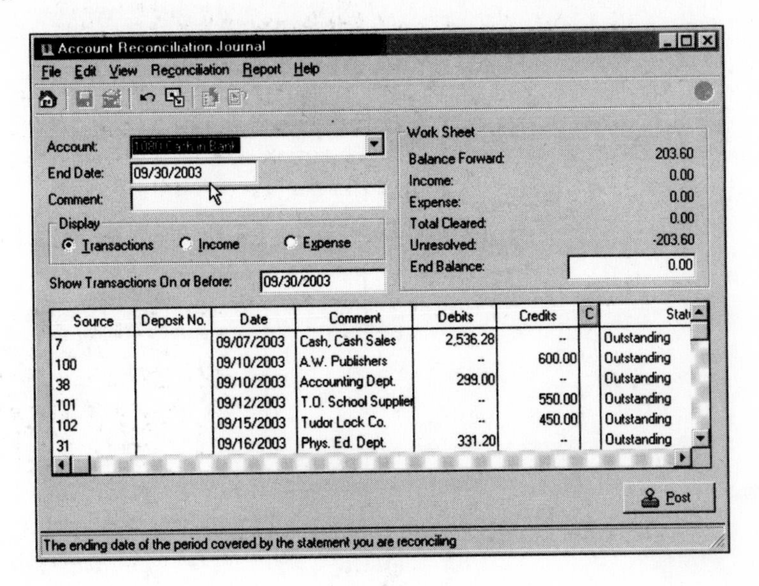

The account is entered in the Account field and the session date is entered automatically in the End Date field. The date is correct so do not change it.

Press tab twice to advance to the Comment field.

Type `September Bank Reconciliation`

Press tab

The cursor moves to the Transactions option in the Display box at the left side of the screen. All outstanding transactions for the account are listed on the screen.

Press tab to move to the second date field. The default is to show all transactions that occurred on or before the session date. Unless you are reconciling for a different period, the default should be correct.

Press tab again to move to the End Balance field in the Work Sheet area at the right side of the screen. This field will be used for the closing bank balance as it appears on the bank statement.

Type `4155.23`

Press tab

notes

The End Date will advance by one month once you have finished reconciling the bank account for the current month.

notes

If you have several bank statements to reconcile, it is easier to show transactions for only the month that corresponds to the bank statement. When you complete the second month's reconciliation, show transactions for that month.

Marking Journal Entries as Cleared

You are now ready to begin processing individual journal entries to indicate whether they have been cleared in this bank statement. That is, you must indicate whether the bank has processed the items and the amounts have been withdrawn from or deposited to the account.

notes

Drag the lower frame of the journal window or maximize the journal window to include more transactions on your screen at the same time.

Your screen should now resemble the following:

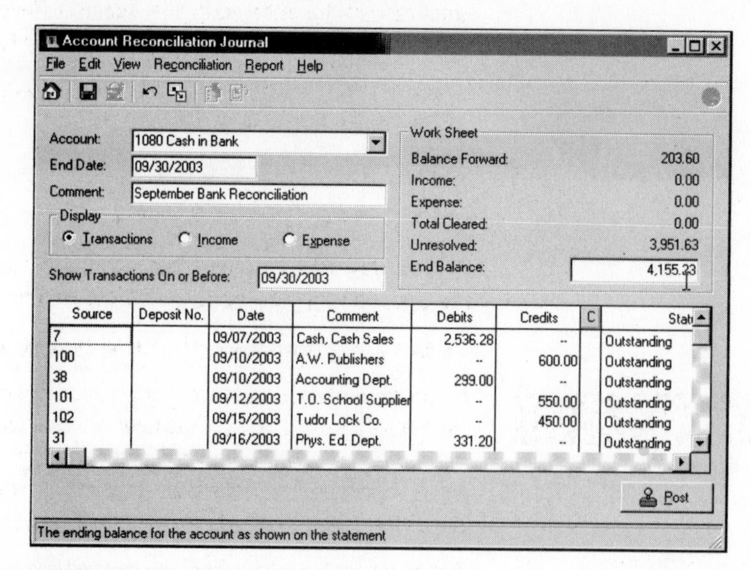

All outstanding items for the month are listed. These are the items that were left as outstanding during the setup stage. In addition, the unresolved amount has changed to reflect the new balance, the difference between the previous and current balances.

Sometimes several cheques are deposited as a group, as they were by the HSC School Store on September 16 and September 26. Each of these group deposits can also be cleared as a group. Refer to the bank statement on page 509.

notes

To be certain that you choose the correct transaction for the group deposit, click the transaction in the Source column (click 31) and then press (tab) to move to the Deposit No. field.

Click the **Deposit No. column beside the entry for Cheque #31**.

Type 1

Press ⬇ to advance to the next line in the Deposit No. column for Cheque #15.

Type 1

Press ⬇ to advance to the next line in the Deposit No. column.

Mark Cheque #10 as belonging in Group One as well so that all three items that were deposited at the same time have the same group number.

With one item in the group still selected, point to the C (cleared) column.

Click the **C at the top of the column**. Your transactions list appears as follows:

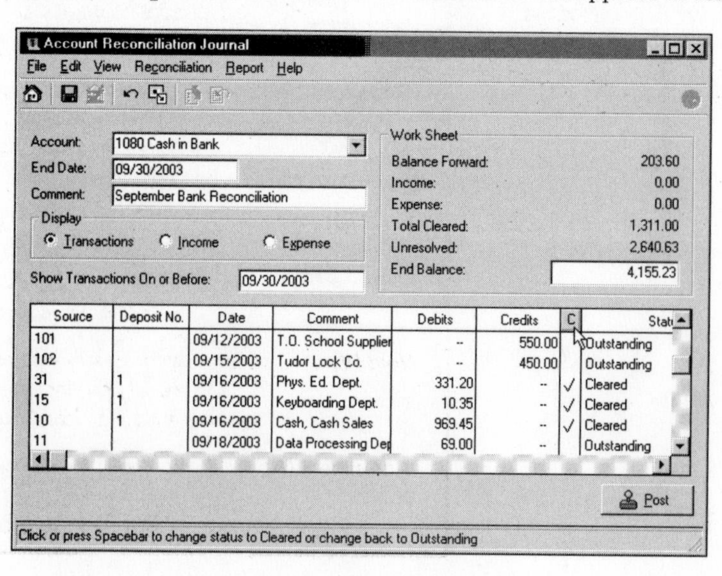

All items in the group have their status changed to cleared at the same time. Deposit numbers can be entered in the Account Reconciliation Journal at the time of the deposit and then saved until you are ready to reconcile the bank statement.

Beside the two cheques that were deposited together on September 26 (Cheque #33 for $46.00 and Cheque #103 for $192.60),

Type 2

Click the **C at the top of the column**.

You are now ready to mark the remaining transactions that have been cleared, that is, the ones that appear on the bank statement.

Click the **C column for the first transaction on the list**.

A checkmark appears in this column and the Status has been changed from Outstanding to Cleared. Continue to clear the remaining journal entries that appear on the bank statement and scroll as necessary to display additional items. You should leave only the last item as outstanding — the deposit that was not yet processed by the end of the month. As you clear each item, the unresolved amount is updated.

notes

- If you mark an item as Cleared by mistake, click the C column again to return the status to Outstanding.
- Remember not to clear the deposit for $825.13.
- After clearing all transactions from the bank statement, the unresolved amount should be -7.15.

The next section describes the procedure for clearing transactions that are different in some way, like NSF cheques. By marking their status correctly, you will have a more accurate picture of your business transactions. Read the following section. You will use it to mark the NSF cheque for the October bank reconciliation.

Marking NSF Cheques

For some items, you may want to add further information, in particular NSF cheques and their reversing entries. The available status alternatives are explained in the Status Options chart below.

STATUS OPTIONS

Cleared (C)	for deposits and cheques that have been processed correctly.
Deposit Error (D)	for the adjusting journal entry to account for the difference between the amount of a deposit that was recorded incorrectly and the bank statement amount for that deposit. Assign the Cleared status to the original entry for the deposit.
Payment Error (P)	for the adjusting entry to account for a difference between the amount of a cheque recorded incorrectly and the bank statement amount for that cheque. Assign the Cleared status to the original entry for the cheque.
NSF (N)	for customer cheques returned by the bank because there was not enough money in the customer's account. Assign the Adjustment status to the adjusting entry that reverses the NSF cheque.
Reversed (R)	for the entry for cheques that are cancelled by posting a reversing transaction entry to the bank account or the Sales or Purchases Journals. Assign the Adjustment status to the reversing entry that cancels the cheque.
Void (V)	for the entry for cheques that are cancelled because of damage during printing. Assign the Adjustment status to the reversing entry that voids the cheque.
Adjustment (A)	for the adjusting or reversing entries that are made to cancel NSF, void or reversed cheques. (See the explanations for NSF, Void and Reversed above.)

To mark a cheque as NSF,

Click the word **Cleared** in the Status column for the NSF cheque.

Press *enter* to display the alternatives available for the Status of a journal entry as shown here:

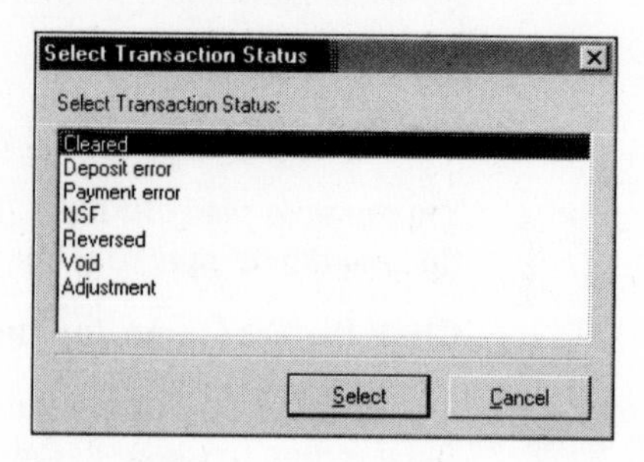

Click **NSF** to highlight this alternative.

Click **Select** to enter it. The word Cleared changes to NSF for this item.

The last step is to change the status of the entry that reverses the payment or NSF cheque to Adjustment. The final cheque received in payment is cleared normally.

Adding Account Statement Journal Entries

notes

If you display your journal entry at this stage, you will see a credit to Cash in Bank and a debit to Reconciliation Adjustments for $7.15, the unresolved amount at this stage. The journal entries for income and expenses will remove the unresolved amount.

Click **Income** in the **Display** portion of the window to begin entering the journal information for income to this account. Bank Int, the income source we named earlier, is selected in the Income group list. The Account Reconciliation Journal now includes a journal entry form for this income transaction as shown here:

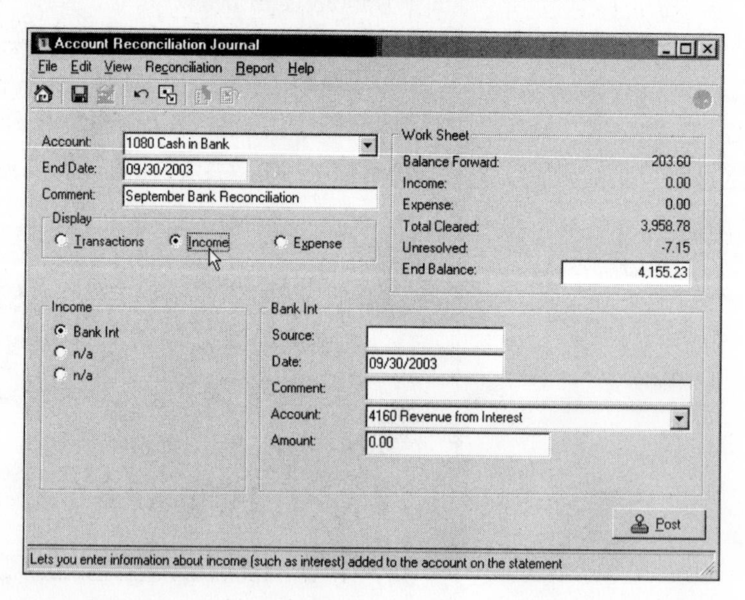

notes

You can edit these journal entries or transaction status entries at any time before posting. Choosing Save will save the work you have completed so far and still permit you to make changes later.

Click the **Source field** to advance the cursor.

Type `Bk-Stmt`

Press *tab*

The session date is highlighted and can be changed. Since it matches the bank statement entry date for interest paid on the account, it is correct.

Press *tab* to advance to the Comment field.

Type `Interest Earned on Bank Deposits`

Press tab twice to skip over the correctly entered Account number and advance to the Amount field. You can select a different account if needed. The amount is highlighted, ready for editing. Check the bank statement for the correct amount.

Type `4.35`

Press tab. Notice that the unresolved amount now matches the service fee amount.

If there are other income categories, click the income name in the Income group list to the left of the journal information. A new journal form will appear for this income.

notes

Duplicate source document codes are allowed in this journal.

Click Expense in the **Display** portion of the window. The expense, Bk Charges, is selected on the left side of the screen, and its journal form appears on the right-hand side.

Click the **Source field**.

Type `Bk-Stmt`

Press tab twice to advance to the Comment field, accepting the date as entered because it is correct.

Type `Bank Charges and Service Fee`

Press tab twice to skip over the correctly entered account number and advance to the Amount field. The bank statement contains the amounts for this expense.

notes

- You may combine the regular service charges with the charges for other specific or unusual services such as stopping a payment on a cheque or returning an NSF cheque. Or you may make separate journal entries for them by choosing n/a or another expense category. You can use the same account for more than one journal entry. You cannot choose the same expense or income category twice.
- There is no allocation option in the Account Reconciliation Journal.

Type `11.50`

Press tab

If there are other expense categories, click the expense name in the list to the left of the journal information. A new journal form will appear for this expense.

At this stage, the unresolved amount should be zero if everything is reconciled. If the unreconciled amount is not zero, check your journal entries to see whether you have made an error. Click each option in the Display box to show your work for the corresponding part of the reconciliation procedure. Make corrections if necessary.

You should also review the reconciliation journal entry before proceeding.

Choose the **Report menu** and **click Display Account Reconciliation Journal Entry**. Your journal entry should appear as follows:

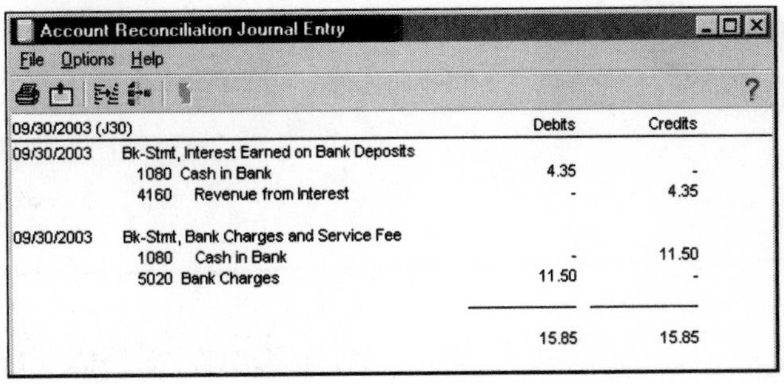

Account Reconciliation Journal Entry

File Options Help

09/30/2003 (J30)		Debits	Credits
09/30/2003	Bk-Stmt, Interest Earned on Bank Deposits		
	1080 Cash in Bank	4.35	-
	4160 Revenue from Interest	-	4.35
09/30/2003	Bk-Stmt, Bank Charges and Service Fee		
	1080 Cash in Bank	-	11.50
	5020 Bank Charges	11.50	-
		15.85	15.85

notes

If you have an unresolved amount, save the entry without posting and return later to try to determine whether you made a mistake or whether there was an error on the bank statement.

The income and expense journal entries are listed. In addition, an adjustment entry will be displayed if there is any unresolved amount.

Close the report window when you have finished.

Any discrepancy or unresolved amount will be posted as an adjustment to the reconciliation adjustments expense account created earlier. This account should be used only for small amounts not significant enough to warrant a separate journal entry.

Click the **Save button**. **Click** ☒ to close the journal without posting.

Make a backup copy. Open the Account Reconciliation Journal, select account *1080 Cash in Bank* and resume your work.

Click the **Post button** [Post].

The program will warn you before posting an unresolved amount, giving you a chance to correct any mistakes you may have made before posting the journal entries.

A blank journal window appears.

Close the Account Reconciliation Journal to return to the Home window to complete the transactions for October.

Displaying Account Reconciliation Reports

Account Reconciliation Journal

notes

You can display the Account Reconciliation Journal from the Reports menu. Choose the Reports menu, then choose Journal Entries and click Account Reconciliation.

Right-click the **Account Reconciliation icon** [Account Reconciliation] and then **click** [icon] (the **Display button**) in the Home window. You will see the report options screen:

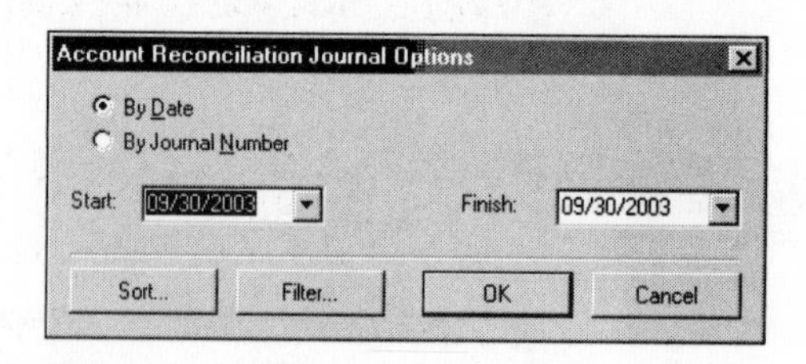

notes

You can display the General Ledger Report, Invoice Lookup, Vendor/Customer Aged or Employee Reports (if applicable) from the Account Reconciliation Journal. The usual sort and filter options for journals are available.

The journal can be prepared by journal entry numbers or by date. By default, the report uses posting dates. Enter the starting and ending dates or journal numbers for the report you want. The usual sort and filter options are available.

Click OK

Close the display when you have finished.

Account Reconciliation Report

notes

- You can display Journal Reports, Invoice Lookup, and Vendor or Customer Aged or Employee Reports (if applicable) from the Account Reconciliation Detail Report.
- The status reports cannot be sorted or filtered.

Choose the **Reports menu**, then **choose Account Reconciliation** and **click Account Reconciliation Status Report** to display the following report options:

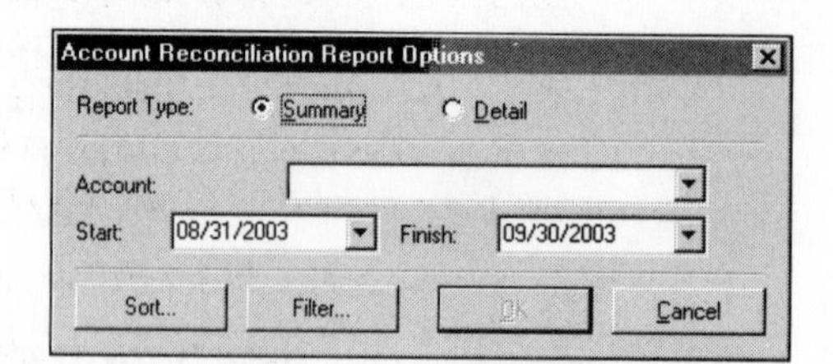

Type `1080` (to enter the bank account number in the Account field) or choose the account from the drop-down list for the Account field.

Type the start and end dates. Usually these dates will coincide with the bank statement period. The Summary report provides totals for each type of Status, totals for income and expense categories and outstanding amounts that will reconcile the bank statement with the General Ledger account balance.

Click Detail

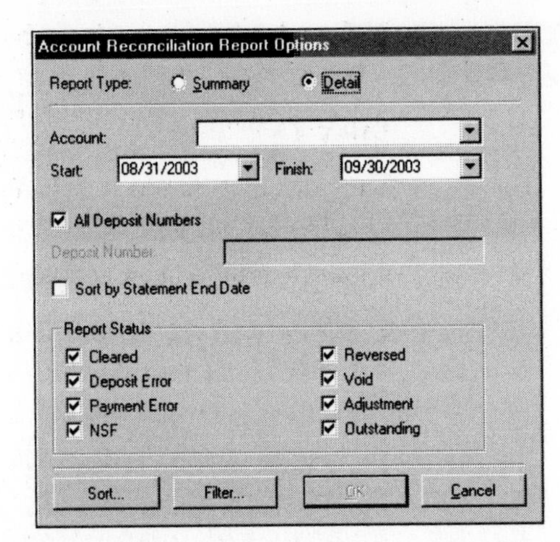

The **Detail** report lists all journal entries with their status. You can even prepare the Detail report for a specific Deposit Number. Choose the Status categories to include in your reports. By default, all are included. Clicking a category will remove the ✔ from the check box and omit this category from your report.

Close the displayed report when you have finished.

Printing Account Reconciliation Reports

Display the report you want to print.

Choose the **File menu** and **click Print** to print the displayed report.

Close the report window when finished.

End-of-Month Procedures

There are accounting activities that should be completed at the end of regular accounting periods. Normally a business will print all journal transactions at the end of each business day; statements and financial reports will be printed at the end of each month and all reports, including T4s, should be printed at the end of the fiscal period.

Periodically, a business will clear old information from its accounting files to make space. In the manual system, it might store the details in archives or on microfiche to keep the current files manageable in size. Computerized systems should be similarly maintained by making backups of the data files and then clearing the information that is not required. These periodic procedures include clearing journal entries for prior periods, removing paid invoices from customer and vendor records, and removing vendors and customers who no longer do business with the company.

Simply Accounting's checklists can assist with these routine procedures.

You should be in the Home window.

Choose the **Business Assistant menu** and **click Checklists** to see the available lists.

version 8

Click Month-End Procedures to select it and then **click Modify** to see the list:

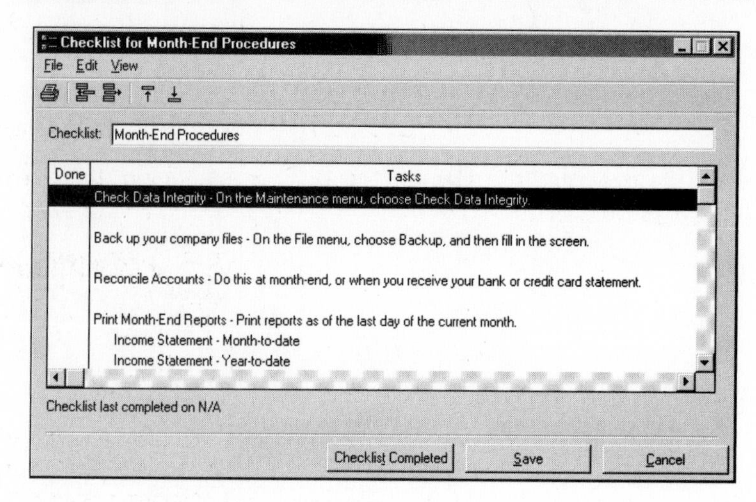

Read the task list. You have already completed some tasks on this list.

Click the **Done column** beside the two tasks that are completed — Back up and Reconcile Accounts. We will complete the remaining tasks before marking them.

Click Save to return to the main checklists window. A ✓ appears in the Task in Progress column beside Month-End Procedures.

Click Close to leave the opening checklists window and return to the Home window.

Choose the **Maintenance menu** and **click Check Data Integrity**. You should see the message "Data OK." If you do not, make a note of any data inconsistencies and return to your most recent backup copy of the file.

Click OK to close the Integrity Summary window

Warning!

You must make a backup copy of your data files and print all reports before clearing any information. Once the journals and invoices are cleared, they cannot be recovered. We recommend making a separate copy of the data file if you want to practise clearing data.

Clearing Journal Entries

Back up the data files before proceeding and print all relevant available reports: journals, vendor and customer detail reports, inventory tracking reports, and the other reports listed in the month-end checklist.

You should be in the Home window.

Choose the **Maintenance menu**, then **choose Clear Data** and **click Clear Journal Entries** to display the following dialogue box:

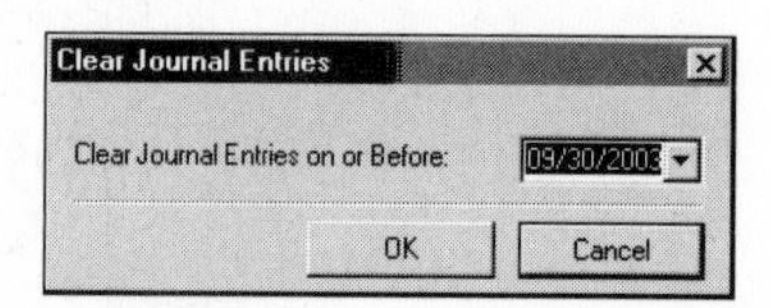

You must enter the date **before** the first journal entry that you want to keep. For HSC, September 30 is correct, so accept the date.

Click OK. The following warning is shown:

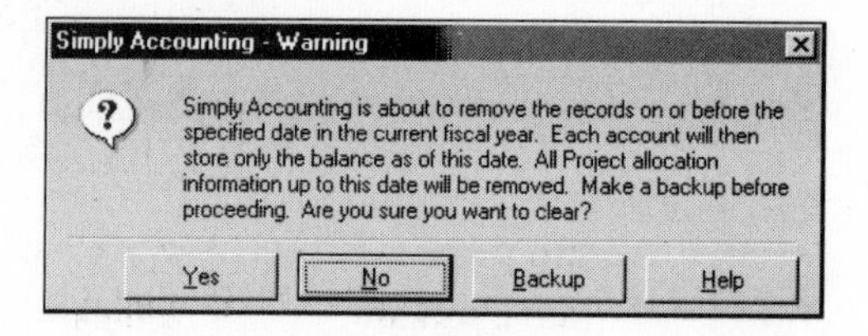

version 8

notes

Simply Accounting does not remove information without a warning. This allows you to reconsider, make backups or just confirm that you have selected the option or entry you want. Always read the warning carefully.

Click No to stop without deleting any information. Continue if you have made a backup.

Click Yes to remove the journal entries and return to the Home window.

Clearing Paid Vendor Transactions

version 8

Choose the **Maintenance menu**, then **choose Clear Data** and **Clear Paid Transactions** and **click Clear Paid Vendor Transactions** to display the following:

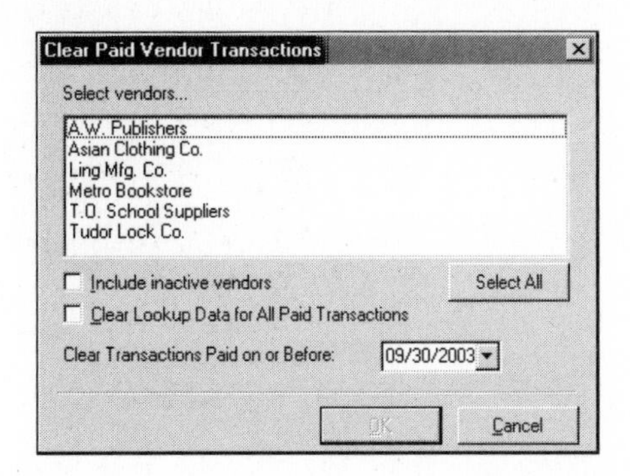

You can clear invoices for one or more vendors at the same time. Unpaid invoices are always retained.

Type the last date for which you want to remove invoices. September 30 is correct.

Click Select All (To select individual vendors, press ctrl and click their names.) We also have stored lookup details and do not need to keep that information.

Click Clear Lookup Data for All Paid Transactions

Click OK. Again, Simply Accounting presents the warning shown here:

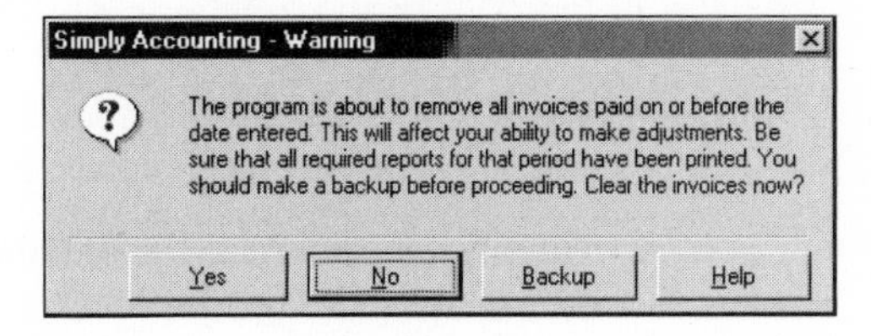

If you have selected correctly and are ready to proceed,

Click Yes. When you choose to clear lookup data, you will see this additional warning:

Again, if you are certain that you should continue,

Click Yes. If you see this additional information screen:

notes

If you cleared the lookup data before clearing the invoices, you will see this message that there is no lookup data to clear. There is a separate menu option for clearing lookup data.

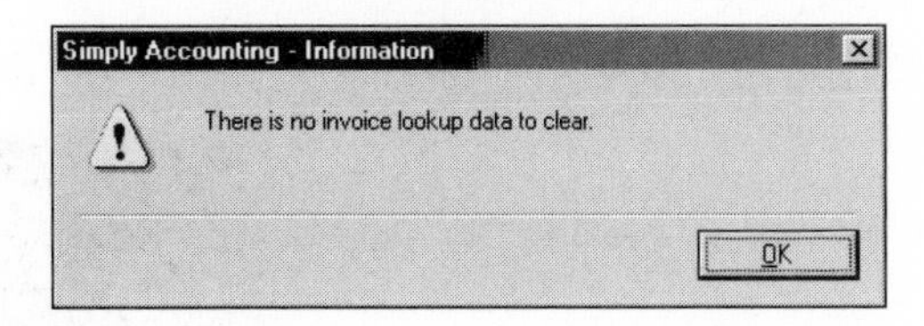

Click OK to continue. The information will be removed, and you will return to the Home window.

Clearing Paid Customer Transactions

Clearing customer invoices is similar to clearing vendor invoices.

version 8

Choose the **Maintenance menu**, then **choose Clear Data** and **Clear Paid Transactions** and **click Clear Paid Customer Transactions** to display the following dialogue box:

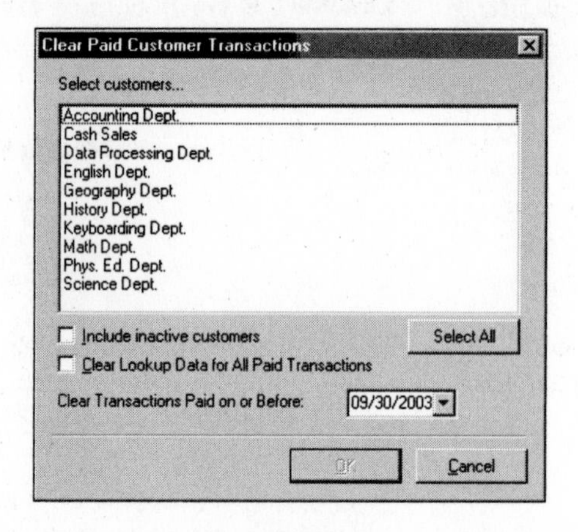

Again, you should accept the date because we will begin entering new transactions in October. We will clear the invoices for a single customer, the Data Processing Dept.

You can clear paid invoices for all customers by clicking Select All.

Click Data Processing Dept. We also have stored lookup details that we do not need to keep.

Click Clear Lookup Data for All Paid Transactions

Click OK

The next warning is the same as the one we saw for removing vendor invoices. If you are ready, you should proceed.

Click Yes. Again, the additional warning for lookup data is shown. If you are certain that you want to continue,

Click Yes to return to the Home window. The requested information has been removed.

Clearing Inventory Tracking Data

version 8

Choose the **Maintenance menu**, then **choose Clear Data** and **click Clear Inventory Tracking Data** to display the following dialogue box:

You need to enter the date. Entries on and before the date you enter will be removed. You can accept September 30.

Click OK. Again, you see the warning before any data is removed:

If you are certain that you want to proceed,

Click Yes to delete the requested information and return to the Home window.

Clearing Invoice Lookup Data

version 8

notes

From this menu option, you can choose to clear invoice lookup data either for vendors or for customers or for both. If you choose only customers or vendors, you can choose from lists the ones for whom you want to remove lookup data.

Choose the **Maintenance menu**, then **choose** **Clear Data** and **Clear Invoice Lookup Data** and **click** **Clear Vendor & Customer Invoice Lookup Data** to display the following:

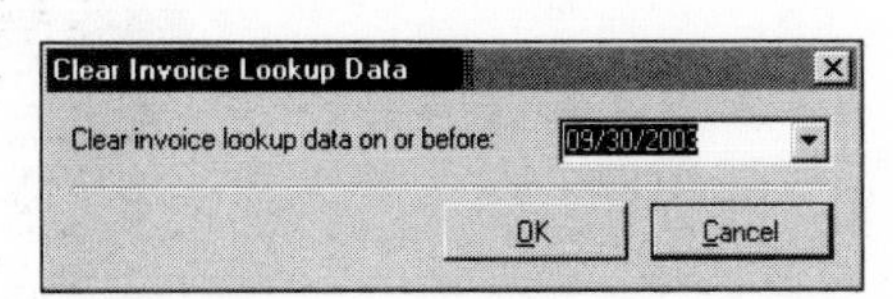

You need to enter the date. Entries on and before the date you enter will be removed. September 30 is correct, so you can accept it.

Click OK

Once again, you see the warning before any data is removed. If you are certain that you want to proceed,

Click Yes. You may see the message that there is no lookup data. **Click** OK to continue.

The requested information is deleted and you will return to the Home window.

Removing Vendor and Customer Records

Sometimes you know that you will not be doing business with a customer or vendor again. Removing their records reduces the length of the displays to scroll through for journal entries and saves on mailing costs. Vendors are removed from the Vendors window. Customers are removed from the Customers window. We will remove the customer History Dept. because it will not be purchasing from the school store in the near future.

Click the **Customers icon** to open the Customers window.

Click the **History Dept. icon** to highlight this customer.

Click the **Remove button** or choose the File menu and click Remove to display the warning:

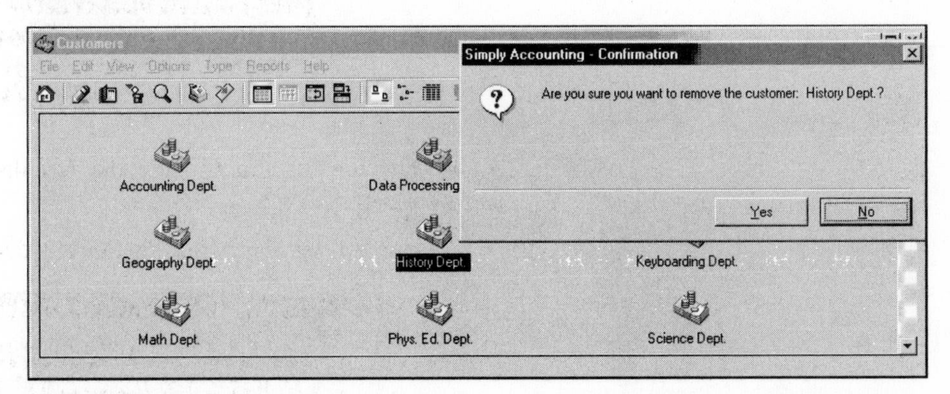

Again, you should check that you have selected the customer you want before continuing.

Click Yes if you have selected correctly.

You may see an additional warning about removing invoice lookup data. **Click** Yes to close the warning and continue.

If you see the message that there is no lookup data, **click** OK to continue.

If you have selected a customer (or vendor) for whom the invoices have not been cleared, Simply Accounting will not permit you to remove the customer (or vendor). You will see the following warning:

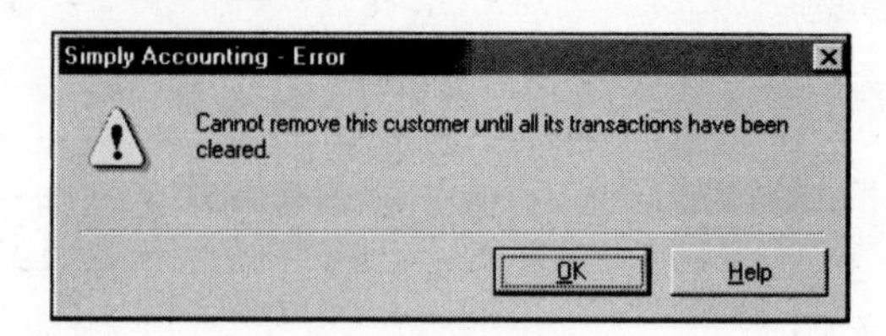

Click OK to return to the Customers window. Clear the details, if appropriate, and then remove the customer's record.

Close the Customers window to return to the Home window. We will now return to the checklist and mark the remaining tasks as done.

Completing the Month-End Checklist

We will now continue with the month-end checklist. The tasks relating to budgeting, do not apply so we can delete them from the list, thus customizing the list for HSC.

version 8

notes

You can also add tasks to customize the list even further. Just click on the list where you want to add a task, choose the Edit menu and click Insert line (or click the Insert line tool). Then type the task description.

Choose the **Business Assistant menu** and **click** **Checklists** to see the available lists.

Double click **Month-End Procedures** to open this list.

Scroll down the list to the budget-related tasks.

Click **Check your budget** to select this line.

Choose the **Edit menu** and **click** **Remove** or click the Remove item tool 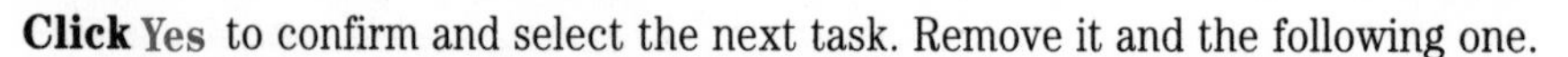.

Click Yes to confirm and select the next task. Remove it and the following one.

Click the **Done column** for the remaining tasks.

Click **Checklist Completed** to return to the opening checklist window. For reference, the session date appears as the Date Last Completed beside Month-End Procedures.

Click Close to return to the Home window. Proceed with the journal transactions.

Source Documents

notes

Remember to delete the PST for all books that are sold — those items that have No PST as part of the item number. You may prefer to sort inventory by description for these transactions (Inventory Settings).

SESSION DATE – October 7

Sales Invoice #EC-15
Dated Oct. 2/03
To Accounting Dept.

10 Workbooks - Simply Version 7 Purbhoo	$30.00	each
10 Workbooks - Simply Version 8 Purbhoo	30.00	each
GST	7 %	

Terms: Net 15 days.

- [ ] Cash Receipt #10
Dated Oct. 2/03
From Accounting Dept., cheque #52 for $642 in payment of account. Reference invoice #EC-12.

- [ ] [ ] Sales Invoice #EC-16
Dated Oct. 2/03
To Math Dept., notification of NSF cheque #33 for $46 plus $20 handling charges. Mr. Farouk was notified of the outstanding balance still owing.

- [ ] Cash Receipt #11
Dated Oct. 4/03
From Math Dept. (Mr. Farouk) money order #64321 for $66 in full payment of account. Reference invoices #EC-16, EC-9 and bank statement. Mr. Farouk added a note of apology.

- [ ] Cash Sales Summary #EC-17
Dated Oct. 4/03

No.	Item	Quantity Sold
010	ACCO 3 Ring Binder 1" spine	3
030	Accounting Paper - 25 sheets	4
050	Calculator - Basic Math	2
070	Clipboard - Acrylic Letter	1
110No PST	Dictionary - Pocket Eng	10
130No PST	Dictionary - Pocket Punj/Eng	1
140No PST	Dictionary - Pocket Viet/Eng	2
190	Eraser	3
220	Glue Stick	1
250	Gym Bag - HSC Logo	6
280	Lock - Combination	6
320	Paper - Lined 200 refill sheets	2
350	Pen - Blue/red	2
400	Pencil Crayons - 20 pack	2
510	Sweatshirt - HSC Logo	9
520	Template - Flowchart	1
560No PST	Workbook - Simply Version 8 Purbhoo	2

- [ ] Cash Sales Summary #EC-18
Dated Oct. 7/03

No.	Item	Quantity Sold
020	ACCO 3 Ring Binder 2" spine	2
040	Binder - Blue 3 Ring 2" spine	2
060	Calculator - Scientific	1
100No PST	Dictionary - Pocket Cant/Eng	8
120No PST	Dictionary - Pocket Fr/Eng	3
150	Diskettes - DSHD 3.5"	12
270	Knapsack - HSC Logo	8
290	Markers - Self-stick 4 pack	1
330	Paper - Typing 50 full sheets	1
380	Pencil	2
500	Sweatpants - HSC Logo	7
550No PST	Workbook - Simply Version 7 Purbhoo	5

notes

- [ ] Create new Group account, 4200 Handling Charges.

- Reverse the Receipts Journal entry and enter a sales invoice for handling charges in the Sales Journal. If you have cleared the paid transactions, use the Sales Journal to enter both parts. See Accounting Procedures.
- The bank charges expense will be recorded as part of the account reconciliation at the end of the month.

notes

- Choose Cash Sales as the customer for Cash Sales Summary entries.
- Remember to accept the default selling prices and to remove the PST for sales of books.

SESSION DATE – October 14

Memo #1
Dated Oct. 9/03
From S. Gallo, Accounting Dept. Head: One scientific calculator in the store was damaged beyond repair. Write it off to the Damages and Losses account.

notes

Allow inventory to drop below re-order point.

Sales Invoice #EC-19
Dated Oct. 9/03
To Keyboarding Dept.,

50 Diskettes - DSHD 3.5″	$1.00 each
GST	7%
PST	8%

Terms: net 15 days.

Cash Receipt #12
Dated Oct. 11/03
From Accounting Dept., cheque #59 for $642 in payment of account. Reference invoice #EC-15.

Cheque Copy #103
Dated Oct. 11/03
To A.W. Publishers, $1 680 in payment of account. Reference invoice #AW-619.

Cash Sales Summary #EC-20
Dated Oct. 11/03

No.	Item	Quantity Sold
040	Binder - Blue 3 Ring 2″ spine	4
060	Calculator - Scientific	2
110No PST	Dictionary - Pocket Eng	7
140No PST	Dictionary - Pocket Viet/Eng	1
240	Graph Paper - 50 sheets	3
260	Index Cards	1
280	Lock - Combination	8
340	Paper - Typing 50 half sheets	1
380	Pencil	2
410	Post-it Notes - 3x3	2
450	Ruler - 15 cm.	1
510	Sweatshirt - HSC Logo	3
550No PST	Workbook - Simply Version 7 Purbhoo	5

- [ ] Cash Sales Summary #EC-21
Dated Oct. 14/03

No.	Item	Quantity Sold
050	Calculator - Basic Math	2
070	Clipboard - Acrylic Letter	2
100No PST	Dictionary - Pocket Cant/Eng	7
170	Duo Tang Folder	1
250	Gym Bag - HSC Logo	8
270	Knapsack - HSC Logo	4
310	Paper - Blank 50 refill sheets	2
350	Pen - Blue/red	4
390	Pencil Crayons - 8 pack	1
420	Post-it Notes - 3x5	1
500	Sweatpants - HSC Logo	6
530No PST	Workbook - Accounting D'Amico	1
560No PST	Workbook - Simply Version 8 Purbhoo	4

SESSION DATE – October 21

- [ ] Sales Invoice #EC-22
Dated Oct. 16/03
To Phys. Ed. Dept.

6 Sweatpants - HSC Logo	$25 each
6 Sweatshirts - HSC Logo	24 each
GST	7%
PST	8%

Terms: net 15 days.

- [ ] Cash Receipt #13
Dated Oct. 18/03
From Keyboarding Dept., cheque #68 for $57.50 in payment of account. Reference invoice #EC-19.

- [ ] Cheque Copy #104
Dated Oct. 18/03
To T.O. School Suppliers, $91 in full payment of account. Reference invoice #TSS-991.

- [ ] Cheque Copy #105
Dated Oct. 18/03
To Tudor Lock Company, $150 in full payment of account. Reference invoice #TLC-632.

- [ ] Purchase Invoice #TSS-1414
Dated Oct. 18/03
From T.O. School Suppliers

50 Diskettes - DSHD 3.5"	$25.00
GST included in price	

Terms: net 15 days.

- [ ] Purchase Invoice #LM-6123
Dated Oct. 18/03
From Ling Mfg. Co.

20 Gym Bags - HSC Logo	$240.00
GST included	

Terms: net 30 days.

notes

For all purchases, skip the tax fields and include the full invoice amount in the Amount field because GST Paid is not refundable. Vendors are set up to "Not collect GST" so that the GST codes are not available.

Purchase Invoice #ACC-75110
Dated Oct. 18/03
From Asian Clothing Co.

20 Sweatpants - HSC Logo	$400.00
20 Sweatshirts - HSC Logo	360.00
Total (GST included)	$760.00

Terms: net 15 days.

Purchase Invoice #MBS-4100
Dated Oct. 18/03
From Metro Bookstore

15 Dictionaries - Pocket Cant/Eng	$150.00
GST included	

Terms: net 30 days.

Cash Sales Summary #EC-23
Dated Oct. 18/03

No.	Item	Quantity Sold
010	ACCO 3 Ring Binder 1" spine	2
080	Clipboard - Hardwood Letter	3
110No PST	Dictionary - Pocket Eng	8
150	Diskettes - DSHD 3.5"	6
210	Exercise Book - 4 pack	1
230	Glue Sticks - 3 pack	1
270	Knapsack - HSC Logo	1
290	Markers - Self-stick 4 pack	1
330	Paper - Typing 50 full sheets	1
380	Pencil	2
440	Reinforcements - Gummed	1
550No PST	Workbook - Simply Version 7 Purbhoo	2

Cash Sales Summary #EC-24
Dated Oct. 21/03

No.	Item	Quantity Sold
050	Calculator - Basic Math	1
090	Clipboard - Hardwood Legal	1
100No PST	Dictionary - Pocket Cant/Eng	7
150	Diskettes - DSHD 3.5"	1
220	Glue Stick	2
250	Gym Bag - HSC Logo	7
280	Lock - Combination	3
320	Paper - Lined 200 refill sheets	2
370	Pen - Solo Cross	1
400	Pencil Crayons - 20 pack	2
470	Scissors - 5"	1
560No PST	Workbook - Simply Version 8 Purbhoo	5

SESSION DATE – October 28

- [ ] Sales Invoice #EC-25
Dated Oct. 23/03
To Math Dept.

10 Math Sets	$5.00 each
GST	7%
PST	8%

Terms: net 15 days.

- [ ] Cash Receipt #14
Dated Oct. 23/03
From L. Sialtsis in the Phys. Ed. Dept., cheque #39 for $338.10 in payment of account. Reference invoice #EC-22.

- [ ] Cash Purchase #PR-223
Dated Oct. 25/03
To Patris Restaurant, cheque #106 for $150 to pay for school store staff and student luncheon. Choose Continue for the new vendor.

- [ ] Cash Sales Summary #EC-26
Dated Oct. 25/03

No.	Item	Quantity Sold
020	ACCO 3 Ring Binder 2" spine	1
080	Clipboard - Hardwood Letter	1
100No PST	Dictionary - Pocket Cant/Eng	5
180	Duo Tang Folders - 4 pack	1
210	Exercise Book - 4 pack	2
250	Gym Bag - HSC Logo	2
270	Knapsack - HSC Logo	5
290	Markers - Self-stick 4 pack	1
310	Paper - Blank 50 refill sheets	2
360	Pen - Blue/red 12 pack	1
390	Pencil Crayons - 8 pack	1
420	Post-it notes - 3x5	1
480	Scissors - 7"	1
490	Shorthand Coil Notebook	4
510	Sweatshirt - HSC Logo	2
520	Template - Flowchart	1
550No PST	Workbook - Simply Version 7 Purbhoo	2

Cash Sales Summary #EC-27
Dated Oct. 28/03

No.	Item	Quantity Sold
050	Calculator - Basic Math	1
110No PST	Dictionary - Pocket Eng	6
150	Diskettes - DSHD 3.5"	8
190	Eraser	2
240	Graph Paper - 50 sheets	1
260	Index Cards	1
280	Lock - Combination	5
300	Math Set	1
340	Paper - Typing 50 half sheets	1
380	Pencil	2
410	Post-it notes - 3x3	1
460	Ruler - 30 cm.	1
500	Sweatpants - HSC Logo	2
530No PST	Workbook - Accounting D'Amico	1

SESSION DATE – October 31

Cheque Copy #107
Dated Oct. 30/03
To T.O. School Suppliers, $25 in full payment of account. Reference invoice #TSS-1414.

Cheque Copy #108
Dated Oct. 30/03
To Asian Clothing Co., $760 in full payment of account. Reference invoice #ACC-75110.

notes

- Refer to the keystrokes beginning on page 512 if you need help with reconciling the bank statement.
- Remember to create an entry for the NSF charges. You can combine this with other bank charges or create a separate journal entry by choosing n/a as the expense category to open a new journal form. Use 5020 as the expense account but add a unique comment.

notes

There are two group deposits — one on Oct. 12 for $1 085.65 ($642 + $443.65) and one on Oct. 19 for $273.12 ($57.50 + $215.62).

❑ Memo # 2
Dated Oct. 31/03
Reconcile the following Bank Statement for October.

U Can Trust Co.
5621 Honesty Way
Toronto, Ontario
M2Y 3E4

Transit #61290
Account # 003 77238-2

October 31, 2003

HSC School Store
16 Phin Ave.
Toronto, Ontario M3B 9J2

Date	Transaction	Deposits	Withdrawals	Balance
09/30/03	Balance Fwd.			4,155.23
10/03/03	Deposit	825.13		4,980.36
10/02/03	Deposit	642.00		5,622.36
10/02/03	NSF CHQ #33		46.00	5,576.36
	NSF Charges		20.00	5.556.36
10/05/03	Deposit	66.00		5,622.36
10/05/03	Deposit	669.85		6,292.21
10/07/03	Deposit	737.54		7,029.75
10/12/03	Deposit	1,085.65		8,115.40
10/14/03	CHQ #103		1,680.00	6,435.40
10/15/03	Deposit	693.57		7,128.97
10/19/03	Deposit	273.12		7,402.09
10/21/03	Deposit	437.37		7,839.46
10/21/03	CHQ #105		150.00	7,689.46
10/22/03	CHQ #104		91.00	7,598.46
10/24/03	Deposit	338.10		7,936.56
10/26/03	Deposit	376.23		8,312.79
10/28/03	CHQ #106		150.00	8,162.79
10/28/03	Deposit	208.77		8,371.56
10/31/03	Interest	13.10		8,384.66
	Service Fee		11.50	8,373.16
10/31/03	Closing Balance			8,373.16
Total Deposits		6,366.43		
Total Withdrawals			2,148.50	

CASE PROBLEM

The bank statement for November listed a deposit for $188 but the journal entry shows that the amount deposited was $198.

1. How could you trace back to find the source of the error?
2. How can the bank help in finding the source of the error?
3. How would you complete the account reconciliation journal for this entry?

CHAPTER FIFTEEN

OBJECTIVES

After completing this chapter, you should be able to

- *plan* and *design* an accounting system for a small business
- *prepare* a conversion procedure from manual records
- *understand* the objectives of a computerized accounting system
- *create* company files
- *set up* company accounts
- *finish* entering historical data to prepare for journal entries
- *enter* accounting transactions from realistic source documents
- *display* and *print* reports
- *analyze* and *interpret* case studies
- *develop* further group interpersonal skills
- *develop* further oral and written skills

COMPANY INFORMATION

Company Profile

Serene Sailing and Boating is located just outside Baysville, Ontario. Situated in the heart of the Lake of Bays cottage and tourist region, Serene earns its revenue from renting out its canoes, kayaks and small sailboats at daily or weekly rates. Individuals and small groups often use Serene's equipment for short-term guided camping trips, booking on their own or through clubs at which they have memberships. Most of these clubs have opened accounts with Serene and are located in Toronto or other southern Ontario cities.

notes

Serene Sailing and Boating is located at RR #5
Baysville, Ontario
P0B 1A0
Tel: (705) 682-1021
Fax: (705) 682-1000
Business number: 12365 4987

Serene Sailing and Boating has available for its patrons a comfortable lounge area that serves beverages, snacks and light meals. Most of these sales are credit card transactions for which Serene Sailing pays a 3.5% fee. The business is seasonal, and Serene closes down each year at the end of September, re-opening in May.

Serene has set up accounts for its regular vendors, who supply food for the lounge area and boats and other supplies and equipment for the marina.

The owner, Alicia Nemo, has chosen not to be involved in the day-to-day aspects of running her business. She leaves that to Sid Surfer, the manager, who supervises the other three employees, performs the full range of management duties and pilots the cruise yacht during the three-hour cruise around the Lake of Bays. Nemo handles the promotion and marketing aspects of the business, looking for new clients at the yacht clubs in cities where she has connections, and negotiating prices and terms with vendors. The remaining three employees provide sailing, kayaking and canoeing lessons to clients. They also inspect and maintain all the boating equipment, performing minor repairs to ensure client safety, and they work in the lounge on a rotating schedule.

Although Nemo leaves the operating side of the business to her manager, she has chosen to do the accounting herself as a way of keeping track of the business. She has always enjoyed accounting work and excelled in her business studies, which included a course in Simply Accounting. She especially finds the reports that are so easy to prepare in Simply Accounting very informative, and uses them as the basis for her weekly planning meetings with her manager. In preparing for the conversion of her manual records, Nemo and Surfer have gathered the following information:

- Chart of Accounts
- Post-Closing Trial Balance
- Vendor Information
- Customer Information
- Employee Information and Profiles

notes

Use appropriate account numbers and add subgroup totals, headings and totals to organize your Chart of Accounts as necessary. Remember to add a test balance account for the setup.

SERENE SAILING AND BOATING
CHART OF ACCOUNTS

ASSETS
Bank Account: Chequing
Bank Account: Visa
Accounts Receivable
Food Inventory
Marine Hardware
Marine Supplies
Safety Gear
Boats and Canoes
Cruise Yacht
Kayaks
Dock & Marina
Dry Dock & Office
Computers & Peripherals
Fax/Scanner
Vehicles

LIABILITIES
Bank Loan
Accounts Payable
Vacation Payable
EI Payable
CPP Payable
Income Tax Payable
EHT Payable
WSIB Payable
PST Payable
GST Charged on Services
GST Paid on Purchases
Mortgage Payable

EQUITY
Alicia Nemo, Capital
Alicia Nemo, Drawings
Current Earnings

REVENUE
Charter and Cruise Services
Instructional Services
Leisure & Hospitality Services
Rental Services

EXPENSES
Advertising & Promotion
Bank Charges & Credit Card Fees
General Expenses
Hydro Expense
Maintenance & Repairs
Telephone Expense
Wages
EI Expense
CPP Expense
WSIB Expense
EHT Expense

SERENE SAILING AND BOATING
POST-CLOSING TRIAL BALANCE

June 30, 2003

Bank Account: Chequing	$ 55 041.25	
Bank Account: Visa	550.00	
Accounts Receivable	1 150.00	
Food Inventory	2 000.00	
Marine Hardware	1 500.00	
Marine Supplies	2 000.00	
Safety Gear	1 000.00	
Boats and Canoes	14 000.00	
Cruise Yacht	75 000.00	
Kayaks	10 000.00	
Dock & Marina	150 000.00	
Dry Dock & Office	150 000.00	
Computers & Peripherals	3 500.00	
Fax/Scanner	500.00	
Vehicles	18 000.00	
Bank Loan		$ 24 000.00
Accounts Payable		1 380.00
Vacation Payable		0.00
EI Payable		806.18
CPP Payable		595.66
Income Tax Payable		2 660.17
EHT Payable		115.02
WSIB Payable		364.22
PST Payable		3 200.00
GST Charged on Services		2 800.00
GST Paid on Purchases	1 680.00	
Mortgage Payable		200 000.00
Alicia Nemo, Capital		250 000.00
	$485 921.25	$485 921.25

SERENE SAILING AND BOATING
VENDOR INFORMATION

Vendor Name (Contact)	Address	Phone No. Fax No.	Terms
Bell Canada (Gabby Feast)	2 Call Ave. Huntsville, ON P1H 2A4	Tel: (705) 412-7108 Fax: (705) 412-7777	Net 1
Minister of Finance	Box 620, 33 King St. W. Oshawa, ON L1H 8H5	Tel: (905) 965-8470	Net 1
Neptune Yacht Outfitters (Roy Poseidon)	142 Safety Ave. Bracebridge, ON P1L 1A4	Tel: (705) 699-0234 Fax: (705) 699-0220	Net 5
Ontario Hydro (S. Erge)	33 Power Ave. Huntsville, ON P1H 1A4	Tel: (705) 412-5323 Fax: (705) 412-6333	Net 1
Pirate Marina (John Silver)	RR #5 Baysville, ON P0B 1A0	Tel: (705) 639-6503 Fax: (705) 639-7181	Net 10
Pisces Nautical (Ryan Fish)	100 Lakeshore Rd. Dorset, ON P0A 1E0	Tel: (705) 834-7195 Fax: (705) 834-7100	Net 10

SERENE SAILING AND BOATING
VENDOR INFORMATION CONTINUED

Vendor Name (Contact)	Address	Phone No. Fax No.	Terms
Pride Foods (Sherry Spicer)	33 Root Ave. Huntsville, ON P1H 1A3	Tel: (705) 523-8622 Fax: (705) 523-7155	Net 15
Receiver General of Canada	Summerside Tax Centre Summerside, PE C1N 6L2	Tel: (902) 821-8186	Net 1
Sharkey's Marine House (Len Sharkey)	43 Dwight Bay Rd. Dwight, ON P0A 1B0	Tel: (705) 721-6345 Fax: (705) 721-8246	Net 5

SERENE SAILING AND BOATING
OUTSTANDING VENDOR INVOICES

Vendor Name	Date	Inv/Chq No.	Terms	Amount	Total
Neptune Yacht Outfitters	6/26/03	NY-347	Net 5	$460	$ 460
Pisces Nautical	6/27/03	PN-411	Net 10	$920	920
				Grand Total	$1 380

SERENE SAILING AND BOATING
CUSTOMER INFORMATION

Customer Name (Contact)	Address	Phone No. Fax No.	Credit Limit Terms
Burlington Sail Club (Sara Sayles)	650 Dundas St. Burlington, ON L7W 2J2	Tel: (905) 792-4710 Fax: (905) 792-5271	$4 000 Net 10
CEO Rowers (Keith Sorenson)	50 Bay Street Toronto, ON M4R 1K3	Tel: (416) 592-6252 Fax: (416) 592-0568	$4 000 Net 10
City College Rowing Club (Ellis Tranner)	255 King St. E. Hamilton, ON L9H 2E4	Tel: (905) 523-8883 Fax: (905) 523-6858	$4 000 Net 10
Guelph Seniors' Canoe Club (Jason Warren)	612 Woolrich Rd. Guelph, ON N1H 2G2	Tel: (519) 822-7109 Fax: (519) 822-6179	$4 000 Net 10
Scarborough Sailing School (Tracey Mullen)	55 Rift Rd. Scarborough, ON M7L 2N3	Tel: (416) 596-7265 Fax: (416) 596-8821	$4 000 Net 10
Varsity Kayak Team (John Stamos)	33 St. George St. Toronto, ON M4R 2J2	Tel: (416) 923-8653 Fax: (416) 923-7192	$4 000 Net 10

SERENE SAILING AND BOATING
OUTSTANDING CUSTOMER INVOICES

Customer Name	Date	Inv/Chq No.	Terms	Amount	Total
Scarborough Sailing School	6/23/03	SS-78	Net 10	$1 150	$1 150

SERENE SAILING AND BOATING
EMPLOYEE INFORMATION SHEET

	Sid Surfer	Jennifer Charybdis	Joseph Mara	Scylla Siren
Position	General Manager	Assistant	Assistant	Assistant
Social Insurance Number	412 666 232	373 821 149	271 832 149	634 279 145
Address & Telephone	500 Fairy Lake Dr. Huntsville, ON P1H 1C3 (705) 412-4589	35 Whirlpool Circle Huntsville, ON P1H 1B1 (705) 632-4190	89 Seashore Blvd. Huntsville, ON P1H 1E3 (705) 412-9023	61 Alarm Rd. Huntsville, ON P1H 1B5 (705) 632-7521
Date of Birth (mm-dd-yy)	07-04-66	08-08-78	05-21-77	03-02-79
Federal Tax (Ontario) Exemption				
Basic Personal	$7 412 (7 426)	$7 412 (7 426)	$7 412 (7 426)	$7 412 (7 426)
Education & Tuition		$4 600 (4 640)	$4 600 (4 640)	$4 600 (4 640)
Other				
Total Exemptions	$7 412 (7 426)	$12 012 (12 066)	$12 012 (12 066)	$12 012 (12 066)
Employee Earnings				
Regular Wage Rate		$16.00	$16.00	$16.00
Overtime Wage Rate		$24.00	$24.00	$24.00
Regular Salary	$3 600			
Hours Per Period	160	80	80	80
Vacation	2 weeks	4%	4%	4%
Employee Deductions				
EI, CPP, Income Tax	calculations built into Simply Accounting program			
Additional Income Tax				

SERENE SAILING AND BOATING
HISTORICAL PAYROLL INFORMATION

Pay Period Ending June 30, 2003

	Sid Surfer	Jennifer Charybdis	Joseph Mara	Scylla Siren
Regular		$2 560.00	$2 560.00	$2 560.00
Overtime		48.00	48.00	48.00
Salary	$3 600.00			
Commission				
Benefit				
Vacation Pay Paid		104.32	104.32	104.32
Vacation Pay Owed				
Advance Paid				
EI Ins Earnings	3 600.00	2 608.00	2 608.00	2 608.00
Gross	$3 600.00	$2 712.32	$2 712.32	$2 712.32
Income Tax	$ 955.81	$ 568.12	$ 568.12	$ 568.12
EI	95.88	80.01	80.01	80.01
CPP	92.63	68.40	68.40	68.40
Withheld	$1 144.32	$ 716.53	$ 716.53	$ 716.53
Net Pay	$2 455.68	$1 995.79	$1 995.79	$1 995.79

Employee Profiles

Sid Surfer, as manager, oversees all aspects of the day-to-day business, including developing a balanced and fair rotating schedule of work for the three summer students. Surfer is married but does not claim his partner as a dependent for tax purposes. He has worked for Serene Sailing since May 1, 1997, and now receives a monthly salary of $3 600. At the end of each work season, he receives an additional two weeks of salary as vacation pay. There are no company benefits or other deductions.

Jennifer Charybdis, **Joseph Mara** and **Scylla Siren** are Physical Education students at the college in Huntsville. Since they were all hired on May 1, 2002, this is their second summer working at Serene. Together they perform the variety of tasks that Serene requires, dividing their time between instruction, guided cruise tours, serving and preparing food in the lounge, and maintenance work. All three have life guard, first aid and CPR training. They are all single and self-supporting but have their college tuition and education deduction as additional TD1 claims. In addition to an hourly wage of $16 and $24 for each hour of overtime work after 40 hours, they receive 4 percent vacation pay with their bi-weekly paycheque. That is, vacation pay is not retained. There are no company benefits or other deductions.

Additional Payroll Information

notes

Remember that WSIB is the name for WCB in Ontario.

Employer contributions include:

- WSIB rate at 3.103
- EHT factor of 0.98
- CPP contributions equal to employee contributions
- EI contributions at 1.4 times the rate of employee contributions

The full federal and provincial claim amounts are subject to indexing.

The salaried employee is paid monthly, hourly employees are paid every two weeks, and vacation pay is included with each paycheque.

INSTRUCTIONS

Warning!

Save your work and make backups frequently.

Warning!

Remember to use a test balance account to check the trial balance before finishing the history for the General Ledger. Print the appropriate reports to check your work as you enter the company data.

1. Use all the information presented in this application to set up the company accounts for Serene Sailing and Boating in Simply Accounting using the following steps:

   a. **create** company files in a new data folder for storing the company records
   b. **enter** the company information, starting a new fiscal period on July 1, 2003, and finishing the period on Sept. 30, 2003
   c. **enter** names and printer information
   d. **prepare** the settings by changing the default settings as necessary
   e. **organize** the Balance Sheet and Income Statement accounts
   f. **create** accounts to correspond to your Balance Sheet and Income Statement
   g. **change** the bank account class and set up the cheque sequence
   h. **enter** linked accounts for the ledgers and credit cards accepted
   i. **enter** customer, vendor and employee information
   j. **enter** historical balances in all ledgers
   k. **back up** your files
   l. **finish** entering the history for all ledgers and finish your session

2. Using the information provided, record entries for the source documents using Simply Accounting.

3. After you have completed your entries, print the following reports:

   a. Journal Entries (All Journals) from July 1 to July 14, 2003
   b. the Vendor Aged Detail Report for all vendors on July 14, 2003
   c. the Customer Aged Detail Report for all customers on July 14, 2003
   d. the Employee Summary (all employees) for the pay period ending July 14, 2003
   e. the Income Statement for the period ending July 14, 2003

SOURCE DOCUMENTS

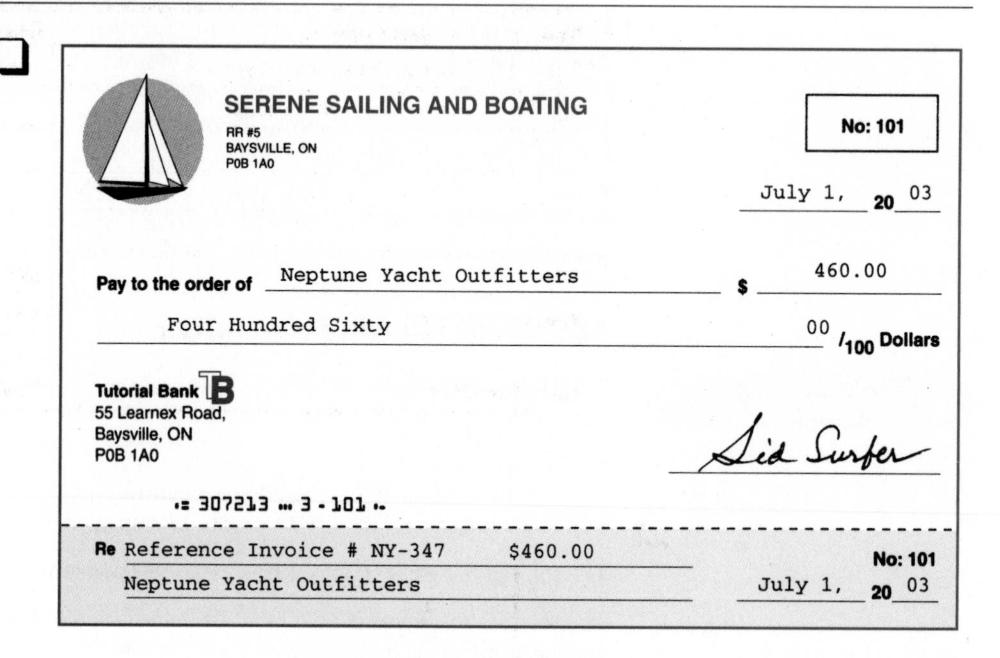
SERENE SAILING AND BOATING
RR #5
BAYSVILLE, ON
P0B 1A0

No: 101

July 1, 20 03

Pay to the order of Neptune Yacht Outfitters $ 460.00

Four Hundred Sixty 00 /100 Dollars

Tutorial Bank TB
55 Learnex Road,
Baysville, ON
P0B 1A0

Sid Surfer

⑈ 307213 ⑉ 3 - 101 ⑈

Re Reference Invoice # NY-347 $460.00
Neptune Yacht Outfitters

No: 101
July 1, 20 03

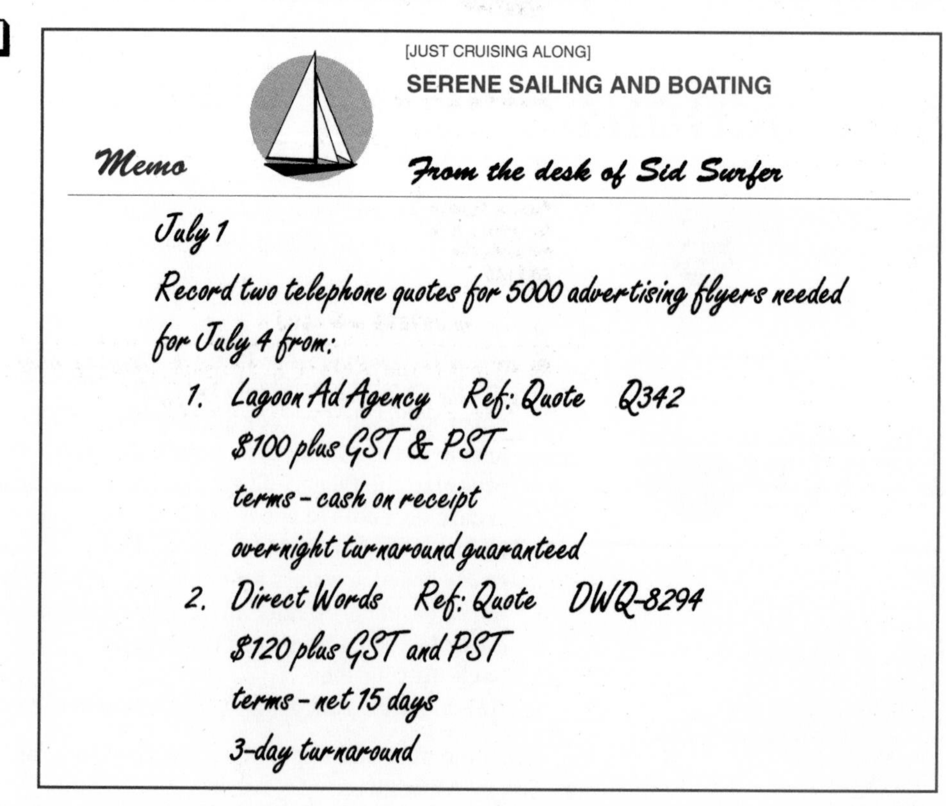
[JUST CRUISING ALONG]
SERENE SAILING AND BOATING

Memo From the desk of Sid Surfer

July 1

Record two telephone quotes for 5000 advertising flyers needed for July 4 from:

1. Lagoon Ad Agency Ref: Quote Q342
   $100 plus GST & PST
   terms - cash on receipt
   overnight turnaround guaranteed
2. Direct Words Ref: Quote DWQ-8294
   $120 plus GST and PST
   terms - net 15 days
   3-day turnaround

❑

Lagoon Ad Agency
33 Muskoka Rd.
Huntsville, ON
P1H 1A2

LAA-691

NAME: Serene Sailing and Boating
ADDRESS: RR#5
Baysville, ON
P0B 1A0

phone: 705-412-8002
fax : 705-412-7909

Date	Description	Charges		Amount	
July 2/03	Advertising Flyers	100	00	100	00
	Ref: quote # Q342				
		GST		7	00
Terms: Cash on Receipt		PST		8	00
GST # 345279128		Total		115	00

❑

SERENE SAILING AND BOATING
RR #5
BAYSVILLE, ON
P0B 1A0

No: 102

July 2, 20 03

Pay to the order of Lagoon Ad Agency $ 115.00

One Hundred Fifteen 00/100 Dollars

Tutorial Bank

55 Learnex Road,
Baysville, ON
P0B 1A0

Sid Surfer

⑆ 307213 ⑈ 3 - 102 ⑈

Re Advertising Flyers Reference Invoice #LAA-691 — No: 102

Lagoon Ad Agency $115.00 — July 2, 20 03

❑

[JUST CRUISING ALONG]

SERENE SAILING AND BOATING

RR #5
Baysville, ON
P0B 1A0

PO # 12638

Date: July 2, 2003
Expected delivery: July 7, 2003

Ordered from: Sharkey's Marine House

#	Item	Price		Amount	
2	Canoes	400	00	800	00
2	Kayaks	300	00	600	00
		GST		98	00
		PST		112	00
		Total		1610	00

Authorization: Sid Surfer

Date: July 2/03

❑

Metro Trust
33 Redway Rd.
Scarborough, ON
M7L 2N9

No: 139

July 3, 20 03

Pay to the order of Serene Sailing and Boating **$** 1,150.00

One Thousand One Hundred Fifty 00/100 **Dollars**

SCARBOROUGH SAILING SCHOOL
55 Rift Road,
Scarborough, ON
M7L 2N3

Tracey Mullen
Treasurer

⑈ 2022 ⑆ 045 - 139 ⑈

Re Reference Invoice #SS-78 $1,150.00
Serene Sailing and Boating

No: 139
July 3, 20 03

❑

[JUST CRUISING ALONG]

SERENE SAILING AND BOATING

RR #5
Baysville, ON
P0B 1A0

Phone for reservations (705) 682-1021
Fax for reservations (705) 682-1000

GST # 123654987

QUOTE # 9421

RENTALS:		RATE PER PERSON:
CRUISES	☐	$75 / Day
BOATS & CANOES	☐	$50 / Day
KAYAKS	☐	$40 / Day
INSTRUCTION	☐	$100 / Day

EQUIPMENT INCLUDED IN CHARGES.

NAME: Burlington Sail Club
ADDRESS: 650 Dundas Street
Burlington, ON
L7W 2J2

Details	Rate/Person		Amount	
Kayaks and Equipment Rental for party of				
8 for 3 days	40	00	960	00
Full Day Instruction for 4 persons	100	00	400	00
Terms: net 10 days				
Signature: Sid Surfer	**Goods & Services Tax**		95	20
Date: July 4/03	**Provincial Sales Tax**		108	80
Quotes remain valid for 30 days	**Total**		1564	00

❑

[JUST CRUISING ALONG]

SERENE SAILING AND BOATING

RR #5
Baysville, ON
P0B 1A0

Phone for reservations (705) 682-1021
Fax for reservations (705) 682-1000

SS-101

GST # 123654987

CUSTOMER STATEMENT

RENTALS:		RATE PER PERSON:
CRUISES	☐	$75 / Day
BOATS & CANOES	☑	$50 / Day
KAYAKS	☐	$40 / Day
INSTRUCTION	☐	$100 / Day

EQUIPMENT INCLUDED IN CHARGES.

NAME: Guelph Seniors' Canoe Club
ADDRESS: 612 Woolrich Rd.
Guelph, Ontario
N1H 2G2

#	Item	Rate/Person		Amount	
July 4/03	Canoe & Equipment Rental for				
	party of 10 for 2 days	50	00	1000	00
	Terms: net 10 days				

Signature: Jason Warren			**Goods & Services Tax**	70	00
Paid by:	**Visa**	**M-C**	**Provincial Sales Tax**	80	00
Cash	**Cheque**	**Other**	**Amount Owing**	1150	00

notes

Use August 3, the last day the the quote remains in effect, as the shipping date.

[JUST CRUISING ALONG]

SERENE SAILING AND BOATING

Memo *From the desk of Sid Surfer*

July 5

Record two sales orders confirmed by telephone

1. *Convert sales quote 9421 for Burlington Sail Club to sales order #9421 for July 10 delivery*

2. *Enter new sales order 2898 for Scarborough Sailing School for 1 day kayak rentals for 25 @$40 each - total $1000 plus GST & PST (net 10) delivery date July 14*

Serene Sailing and Boating
RR #5
Baysville, ON
P0B 1A0

WE TAKE PRIDE

Pride Foods

33 Root Ave.
Huntsville, ON
P1H 1A3
(705) 523-8622
(705) 523-7155 [Fax]

Billing Date: July 5/03

Customer No: P4293

CUSTOMER COPY

PF-3312

Date	Description	Charges		Payments		Amount	
July 5/01	Smoked Meats	200	00			200	00
	Prepared Foods (taxable)	500	00			500	00
	Fresh Fruits & Veg.	200	00			200	00
	Dry Goods	100	00			100	00
				SUBTOTAL		1000	00
Terms: net 15 days				GST	7%	35	00
GST # 267212432				PST	8%	40	00
Signature *Sid Surfer*				OWING		1075	00

Overdue accounts are subject to 18% interest per year.

ONTARIO HYDRO

33 POWER AVENUE, HUNTSVILLE, ON P1H 1A4

SERVICE NAME AND ADDRESS

Serene Sailing and Boating
RR #5
Baysville, ON
P0B 1A0

Invoice Date: July 5, 2003
No: 4017 09428 01
Invoice No: 432174

CUSTOMER COPY

Months	Reading	Description	Net Amount	
1	63538	Commercial Consumption 5000kwh	200	00
1		Flat Rate Energy Charge-Water Heater	60	00
1		Water Heater Rental 3 (Tanks)	40	00

Average Daily kwh Consumption		Before	GST	7%	21	00
Same Period Last Year	This Bill	July 15/03				
197	176	Pay This Amount ☞	Total		321	00
GST # 367432432		After July 15/03	Pay		351	00

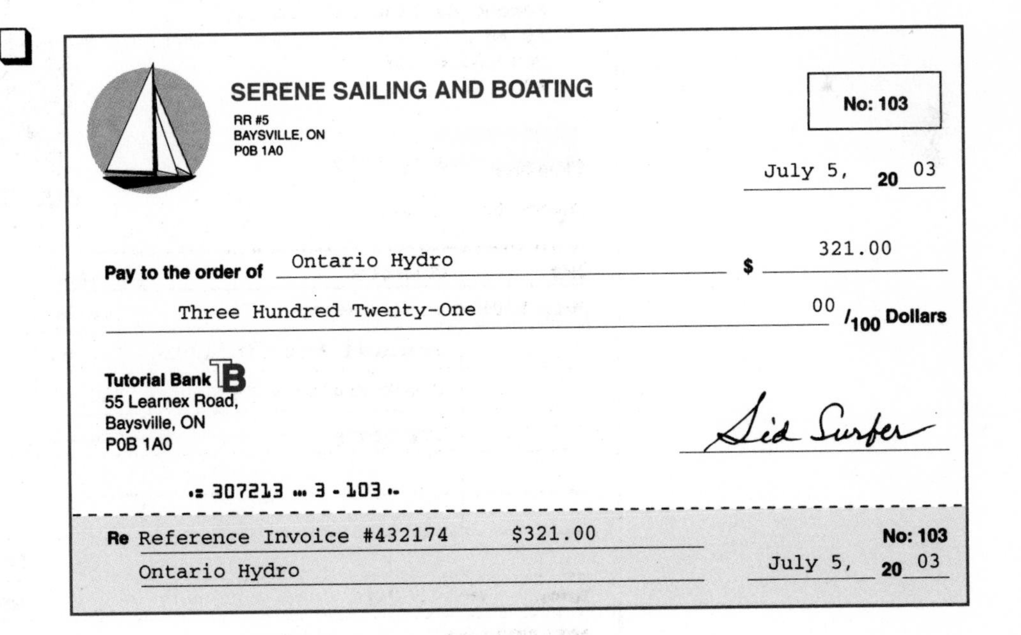

SERENE SAILING AND BOATING
RR #5
BAYSVILLE, ON
P0B 1A0

No: 103

July 5, 20 03

Pay to the order of Ontario Hydro $ 321.00

Three Hundred Twenty-One 00/100 Dollars

Tutorial Bank TB
55 Learnex Road,
Baysville, ON
P0B 1A0

Sid Surfer

⑆ 307213 ⑈ 3 - 103 ⑆

Re Reference Invoice #432174 $321.00
Ontario Hydro

No: 103
July 5, 20 03

❑

[JUST CRUISING ALONG]

SERENE SAILING AND BOATING

RR #5
Baysville, ON
P0B 1A0

Phone for reservations (705) 682-1021
Fax for reservations (705) 682-1000

SS-102

GST # 123654987

CUSTOMER STATEMENT

RENTALS:		RATE PER PERSON:
CRUISES	☐	$75 / Day
BOATS & CANOES	☑	$50 / Day
KAYAKS	☑	$40 / Day
INSTRUCTION	☑	$100 / Day

EQUIPMENT INCLUDED IN CHARGES.

NAME: CEO Rowers
ADDRESS: 50 Bay Street,
Toronto, ON
M4R 1K3

Date	Transaction	Rate/Person		Amount	
July 6/03	Canoes for 4 persons for 3 days	50	00	600	00
	Kayaks for 2 persons for 3 days	40	00	240	00
	Full Day Instruction for 2 persons	100	00	200	00
	Terms: net 10 days				

Signature: Keith Sorenson			**Goods & Services Tax**	72	80
Paid by:	**Visa**	**M-C**	**Provincial Sales Tax**	83	20
Cash	**Cheque**	**Other**	**Amount Owing**	1196	00

❑

FIT FOR SAILING
Neptune Yacht Outfitters
142 Safety Avenue, Bracebridge, ON P1L 1A4

INVOICE NO 232

Date: July 7/03

Phone 699-0234
Fax 699-0220

To
Serene Sailing and Boating
RR #5
Baysville, ON
P0B 1A0

Stock Code	Qty	Description	Price		Amount	
LJ-153	6	Life-jackets	40	00	240	00
WO-192	6	Pairs of wooden oars	60	00	360	00
			GROSS		600	00
CUSTOMER COPY		**Terms on Account:** net 5 days	**GST**	**7%**	42	00
Method of Payment		**On account** ✓ / **C.O.D.** / **Credit Cards**	**PST**	**8%**	48	00
GST # 4 2 1 3 2 7 1 6 7			**TOTAL**		690	00

☐

Sharkey's Marine House FOR PASSIONATE SAILORS

NO: 673

43 Dwight Bay Road, Dwight, ON P0A 1B0

Date: July 7/2003

Phone 721-6345
Fax 721-8246

Sold To:
Serene Sailing and Boating
RR #5
Baysville, ON
P0B 1A0

Product Code	Qty and Description	Price		Amount	
CN-XZ250	2 Canoes	400	00	800	00
KY-AF100	2 Kayaks	300	00	600	00
	Ref: PO # 12638				
		GST		98	00
Signature	Terms: net 5 days	PST		112	00
Sid Surfer	GST # 3 8 3 1 2 3 4 5 6	AMOUNT OWING		1610	00

☐

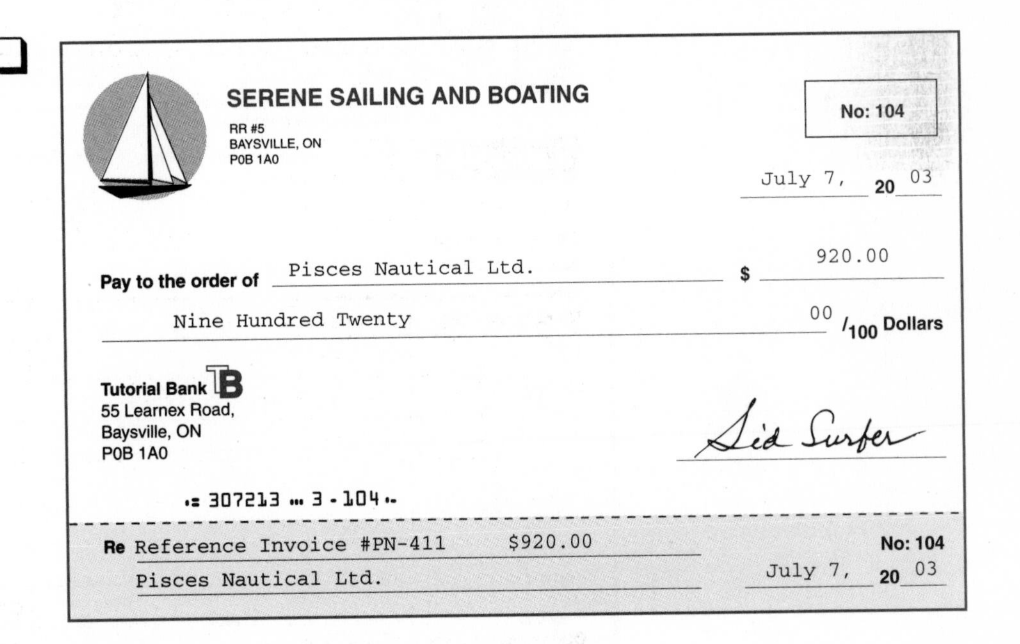

SERENE SAILING AND BOATING
RR #5
BAYSVILLE, ON
P0B 1A0

No: 104

July 7, 20 03

Pay to the order of Pisces Nautical Ltd. $ 920.00

Nine Hundred Twenty 00/100 Dollars

Tutorial Bank TB
55 Learnex Road,
Baysville, ON
P0B 1A0

Sid Surfer

⑆307213⑈3-104⑈

Re Reference Invoice #PN-411 $920.00 No: 104
Pisces Nautical Ltd. July 7, 20 03

☐

[JUST CRUISING ALONG]

SERENE SAILING AND BOATING
RR #5
Baysville, ON
P0B 1A0

SALES SUMMARY STATEMENT

NO: 5

CRUISES ☑
HOSPITALITY SERVICES ☑

Week	Transaction	Rate/Person		Amount	
July 1-7	30 Cruises # 121-150	75	00	2250	00
	Hospitality Services Receipts				
	#1093-1428			1250	00
	Visa Sales				
	SUBTOTAL			3500	00
Approved: *Sid Surfer*	GST			245	00
	PST			280	00
GST # 123654987	Amount Deposited in Bank			4025	00

☐

[JUST CRUISING ALONG]
SERENE SAILING AND BOATING
RR #5
Baysville, ON
P0B 1A0
Phone for reservations (705) 682-1021
Fax for reservations (705) 682-1000

SS-103

GST # 123654987

CUSTOMER STATEMENT

NAME: City College Rowing Club
ADDRESS: 255 King East
Hamilton, ON
L9H 2E4

RENTALS:		RATE PER PERSON:
CRUISES	☐	$75 / Day
BOATS & CANOES	☑	$50 / Day
KAYAKS	☐	$40 / Day
INSTRUCTION	☑	$100 / Day

EQUIPMENT INCLUDED IN CHARGES.

Date	Transaction	Rate/Person		Amount	
July 8/03	Canoes for 6 persons for 1 day	50	00	300	00
	Full Day Instruction for 1 person	100	00	100	00
	Terms: net 10 days				

Signature: *Ellis Trainer*			**Goods & Services Tax**	28	00
Paid by:	**Visa**	**M-C**	**Provincial Sales Tax**	32	00
Cash	**Cheque**	**Other**	**Amount Owing**	460	00

notes

Choose One-time customer for the Visa sales summary.

❑

BELL CANADA
2 CALL AVENUE
HUNTSVILLE ON
P1H 2A4

CUSTOMER COPY

July 9, 2003

Call 412-7108 for enquiries about this bill.

Telephone : (705) 682-1021

Account: Serene Sailing and Boating
Address: RR #5
Baysville, ON
P0B 1A0

SUMMARY				
	Service		120	00
	Equipment Rental		80	00
	Tax-Fed.	14.00	14	00
	Tax-Prov.	16.00	16	00
	Chargeable Calls			
	Tax-Fed	0.00		
	Tax-Prov.	0.00		
GST #412379129				
INVOICE NO: BC-1411	PLEASE PAY THIS AMOUNT UPON RECEIPT		$230	00

❑

SERENE SAILING AND BOATING
RR #5
BAYSVILLE, ON
P0B 1A0

No: 105

July 9, 20 03

Pay to the order of Bell Canada $ 230.00

Two Hundred Thirty 00/100 Dollars

Tutorial Bank
55 Learnex Road,
Baysville, ON
P0B 1A0

Sid Surfer

⑆ 307213 ⑈ 3 - 105 ⑈

Re Reference Invoice BC-1411 $230.00
Bell Canada

No: 105
July 9, 20 03

☐

WATERWORKS CLOTHING
64 Lake Road
Huntsville, ON P1H 2A1
IN MUSKOKA SINCE 1947

INVOICE NO: 5524
Phone: 705-699-2218

CUSTOMER
Serene Sailing and Boating
RR #5
Baysville, ON
P0B 1A0

Date: July 10/2003

GST # 5 1 2 4 2 3 1 2 9

CODE	Description	Qty	Price		Amount	
DS-1422	Deck shoes	3	40	00	120	00
			GST		8	40
Signature	Terms: net 30 days		PST		9	60
Sid Surfer	Overdue accounts subject to 2% interest penalty per month		TOTAL		138	00

☐

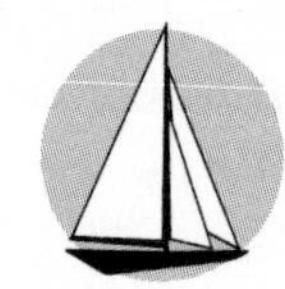

[JUST CRUISING ALONG]
SERENE SAILING AND BOATING
RR #5
Baysville, ON
P0B 1A0
Phone for reservations (705) 682-1021
Fax for reservations (705) 682-1000

SS-104
GST # 123654987

CUSTOMER STATEMENT

RENTALS:		RATE PER PERSON:
CRUISES	☐	$75 / Day
BOATS & CANOES	☐	$50 / Day
KAYAKS	☑	$40 / Day
INSTRUCTION	☑	$100 / Day

EQUIPMENT INCLUDED IN CHARGES.

NAME: Burlington Sail Club
ADDRESS: 650 Dundas Street
Burlington, ON
L7W 2J2

Date	Transaction	Rate/Person		Amount	
July 10/03	Kayaks and Equipment Rental for				
	party of 8 for 3 days	40	00	960	00
	Full Day Instruction for 4 persons	100	00	400	00
	Ref: order # 9421				
	Visa# 4510 692 181 022				
	Terms:				

Signature:			Goods & Services Tax	95	20
Paid by:	Visa ✓	M-C	Provincial Sales Tax	108	80
Cash	Cheque	Other	Amount Owing	1564	00

❑

GST # 2 7 9 1 2 4 3 2 7

Invoice No: 451

Date: July 11/2003

Serene Sailing and Boating
RR #5
Baysville, ON
P0B 1A0

QUALITY PARTS AND SERVICE

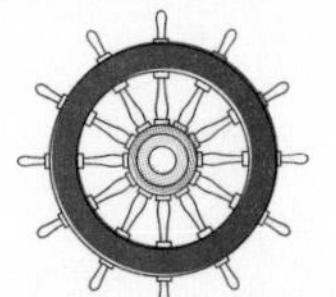

PIRATE MARINA
RR #5, Baysville, ON
P0B 1A0
Tel: 705-639-6503
Fax: 705-639-7181

CODE	Description	Price		Amount	
RPM-AWL	Repairs & maintenance and				
	overhaul of engines	800	00	800	00
		GST		56	00
APPROVAL:	Terms: net 10 days	PST		64	00
Sid Surfer	CASH: / ON ACCOUNT: ✓ / CREDIT CARD:	OWING		920	00

❑

SERENE SAILING AND BOATING
RR #5
BAYSVILLE, ON
P0B 1A0

No: 106

July 12, 20 03

Pay to the order of Neptune Yacht Outfitters $ 690.00

Six Hundred Ninety 00/100 Dollars

Tutorial Bank TB
55 Learnex Road,
Baysville, ON
P0B 1A0

Sid Surfer

⑆ 307213 ⑈ 3 - 106 ⑆

Re Reference Invoice #232 $690.00
Neptune Yacht Outfitters

No: 106
July 12, 20 03

☐

SERENE SAILING AND BOATING
RR #5
BAYSVILLE, ON
P0B 1A0

No: 107

July 12, **20** 03

Pay to the order of Sharkey's Marine House **$** 1610.00

Sixteen Hundred Ten 00 /100 **Dollars**

Tutorial Bank TB
55 Learnex Road,
Baysville, ON
P0B 1A0

Sid Surfer

⑆ 307213 ⑈ 3 - 107 ⑈

Re Reference Invoice #673 $1610
Sharkey's Marine House

No: 107
July 12, **20** 03

☐

PISCES NAUTICAL
100 Lakeshore Road
Dorset, ON P0A 1E0

Invoice: PN413

CUSTOMER
Serene Sailing and Boating
RR #5
Baysville, ON
P0B 1A0

GST # 167279142

Telephone: (705) 834-7195

Date	Transaction			Amount	
July 12/03	1 Sailboat	300	00	300	00
	1 Sail	100	00	100	00
		Federal Tax		28	00
Signature:	Sid Surfer	Provincial Tax		32	00
Paid by:	on account	Amount Due		$460	00
Terms: net 10 days					

❑

[JUST CRUISING ALONG]

SERENE SAILING AND BOATING

RR #5
Baysville, ON
P0B 1A0

Phone for reservations (705) 682-1021
Fax for reservations (705) 682-1000

SS-105

GST # 123654987

CUSTOMER STATEMENT

NAME: Varsity Kayak Team
ADDRESS: 33 St. George St., Toronto, ON M4R 2J2

RENTALS:		RATE PER PERSON:
CRUISES	☐	$75 / Day
BOATS & CANOES	☐	$50 / Day
KAYAKS	☑	$40 / Day
INSTRUCTION	☐	$100 / Day

EQUIPMENT INCLUDED IN CHARGES.

Date	Transaction	Rate/Person	Amount
July 12/03	Kayaks and Equipment Rental for		
	party of 8 for 3 days	40 00	960 00

PAID IN CASH

Terms:

Signature: John Stamos			Goods & Services Tax	67 20
Paid by:	Visa	M-C	Provincial Sales Tax	76 80
Cash ✓	Cheque	Other	Amount Owing	1104 00

❑

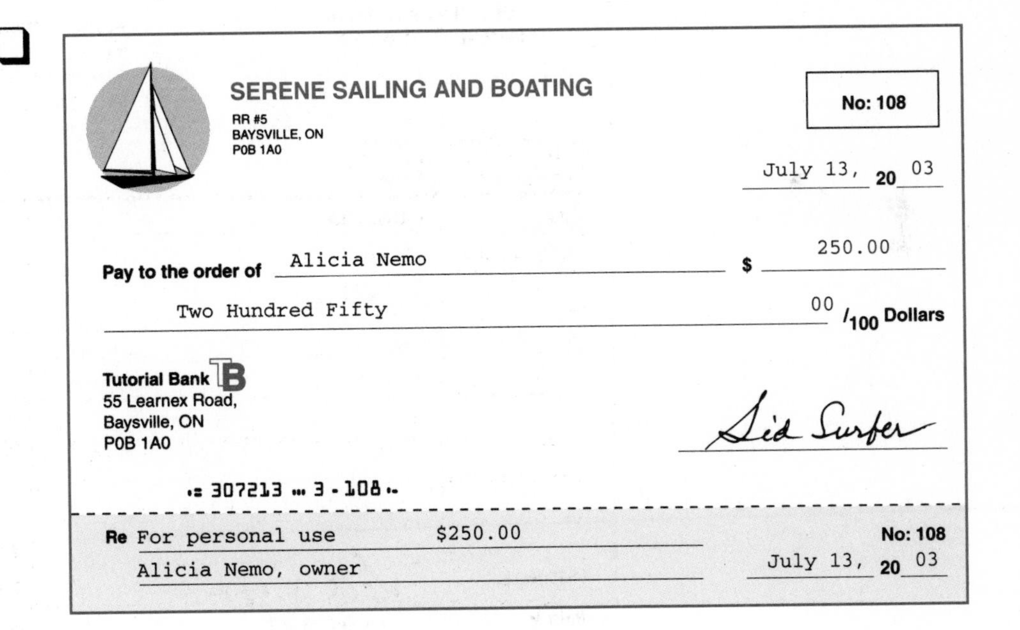

SERENE SAILING AND BOATING
RR #5
BAYSVILLE, ON
P0B 1A0

No: 108

July 13, 20 03

Pay to the order of Alicia Nemo $ 250.00

Two Hundred Fifty 00/100 Dollars

Tutorial Bank
55 Learnex Road,
Baysville, ON
P0B 1A0

Sid Surfer

⑆307213⑈3-108⑈

Re For personal use $250.00
Alicia Nemo, owner

No: 108
July 13, 20 03

❑

Guelph Seniors' Canoe Club

No: 43

July 13, 20 03

Pay to the order of Serene Sailing and Boating $ 1,150.00

One Thousand One Hundred Fifty 00/100 Dollars

NB National Bank
40 CLARK AVE.
GUELPH, ON
N1G 1X7

Klas Vanderwaet
Manager

⑈ 3014 ⑆ 2 - 43 ⑈

Re Reference Invoice #SS-101
Serene Sailing Re: Rentals $1150

No: 43
July 13, 20 03

❑

CEO ROWERS

No: 124

July 13, 20 03

Pay to the order of Serene Sailing and Boating $ 1,196.00

One Thousand One Hundred Ninety-Six 00/100 Dollars

Toronto Trust
61 Bay Street
Toronto, Ont.
M4R 1K3

Rick Solway
ASSISTANT: FINANCE DEPT

⑈ 41414 ⑆ 4 - 124 ⑈

Re Reference Invoice #SS-102
Serene Sailing and Boating $1196.00

No: 124
July 13, 20 03

☐

[JUST CRUISING ALONG]

SERENE SAILING AND BOATING
RR #5
Baysville, ON
P0B 1A0
Phone for reservations (705) 682-1021
Fax for reservations (705) 682-1000

SS-106

GST # 123654987

CUSTOMER STATEMENT

RENTALS:		RATE PER PERSON:
CRUISES	☐	$75 / Day
BOATS & CANOES	☐	$50 / Day
KAYAKS	☑	$40 / Day
INSTRUCTION	☐	$100 / Day

EQUIPMENT INCLUDED IN CHARGES.

NAME: Scarborough Sailing School
ADDRESS: 55 Rift Road
Scarborough, ON
M7L 2N3

Date	Transaction	Rate/Person		Amount	
July 14/03	Kayaks and Equipment Rental for				
	party of 25 for 1 day	40	00	1000	00
	Ref: order # 2898				
	Terms: net 10 days				

Signature:	Tracey Mullen		**Goods & Services Tax**	70	00
Paid by:	**Visa**	**M-C**	**Provincial Sales Tax**	80	00
Cash	**Cheque**	**Other**	**Amount Owing**	$1150	00

☐

July 14, 2003

ACCOUNT NO.:	307213	**ADVICE TO ACCOUNT HOLDER**	**DEBIT MEMO**	
CODE:	12		3246721	

PARTICULARS	AMOUNT
Bank Charges and Services	34.95

ISSUED BY:	LK	**VERIFIED BY:**	NTM

MAIL TO
Serene Sailing and Boating
RR #5
Baysville, ON
P0B 1A0

TB
TUTORIAL BANK
55 Learnex Road
Baysville, ON
P0B 1A0

☐

July 14, 2003

ACCOUNT NO.:	307213	ADVICE TO ACCOUNT HOLDER	CREDIT MEMO
CODE:	14		2143217

PARTICULARS	AMOUNT
Semi-Annual Interest on Bank Account	365.00

ISSUED BY:	LK	VERIFIED BY:	NTM

MAIL TO

Serene Sailing and Boating
RR #5
Baysville, ON
P0B 1A0

TUTORIAL BANK
55 Learnex Road
Baysville, ON
P0B 1A0

☐

[JUST CRUISING ALONG]

SALES SUMMARY STATEMENT

SERENE SAILING AND BOATING
RR #5
Baysville, ON
P0B 1A0

NO: 6

CRUISES ☑
HOSPITALITY SERVICES ☑

Week	Transaction	Rate/Person		Amount	
July 8-14	35 Cruises # 151-185	75	00	2625	00
	Hospitality Services Receipts				
	#1429-1802			1400	00
	Visa Sales				
	SUBTOTAL			4025	00
Approved: Sid Surfer	GST			281	75
	PST			322	00
GST # 123654987	Amount Deposited in Bank			4628	75

Employee Time Sheet

[JUST CRUISING ALONG]

SERENE SAILING AND BOATING
RR #5
Baysville, ON
P0B 1A0

NAME JENNIFER CHARYBDIS

EMPLOYEE NUMBER 1

SOCIAL INSURANCE NUMBER 373821149 **PAY PERIOD ENDING** 07-14-03

Day	Week 1 July 1 - July 7		Week 2 July 8 - July 14	
	Hours		Hours	
	Reg	Ovt	Reg	Ovt
Mon			8	
Tues	8		8	2
Wed	8			
Thurs	8	2	8	
Fri			8	
Sat	8		8	
Sun	8			
Total hours	40	2	40	2

Employee Time Sheet

[JUST CRUISING ALONG]

SERENE SAILING AND BOATING
RR #5
Baysville, ON
P0B 1A0

NAME JOSEPH MARA

EMPLOYEE NUMBER 2

SOCIAL INSURANCE NUMBER 271832149 **PAY PERIOD ENDING** 07-14-03

Day	Week 1 July 1 - July 7		Week 2 July 8 - July 14	
	Hours		Hours	
	Reg	Ovt	Reg	Ovt
Mon	8			
Tues	8	2		
Wed			8	
Thurs	8		8	
Fri	8		8	
Sat	8		8	
Sun			8	
Total hours	40	2	40	0

❑

[JUST CRUISING ALONG]

SERENE SAILING AND BOATiNG

RR #5
Baysville, ON
P0B 1A0

Employee Time Sheet

NAME S C Y L L A S I R E N

EMPLOYEE NUMBER 3

SOCIAL INSURANCE NUMBER 6 3 4 2 7 9 1 4 5

PAY PERIOD ENDING 0 7 - 14 - 0 3

Day	Week 1 July 1 - July 7		Week 2 July 8 - July 14	
	Hours		Hours	
	Reg	Ovt	Reg	Ovt
Mon	8			
Tues	8		8	
Wed	8		8	
Thurs			8	
Fri	8	2	8	
Sat			8	
Sun	8			
Total hours	40	2	40	0

❑

[JUST CRUISING ALONG]

SERENE SAILING AND BOATING

Memo *From the desk of Sid Surfer*

July 14

For month ending June 30:

Remit to Receiver General of Canada

A) GST

B) EI

CPP

Income Tax

Remit to Minister of Finance

C) PST less <u>5%</u> Sales Tax Compensation.

CASE PROBLEM

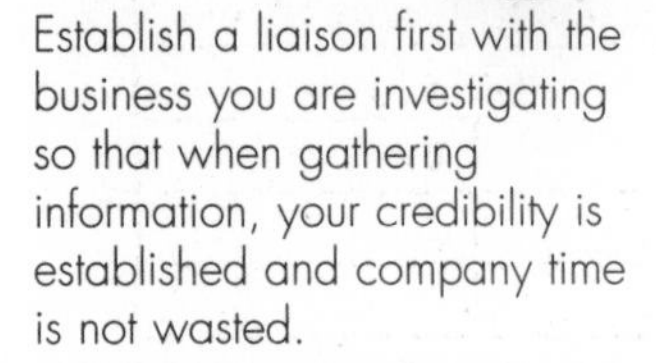

Establish a liaison first with the business you are investigating so that when gathering information, your credibility is established and company time is not wasted.

Some small businesses in your neighbourhood probably still maintain their accounting records manually, often relying on independent accountants to keep their records, prepare the required statements and file returns with Canada Customs and Revenue Agency.

Take a survey of about 10 to 15 small businesses in your neighbourhood, including both service and retail types of business, to find out what accounting methods or systems they use. Prepare your questions ahead of time and keep them short and simple. Always maintain a professional, businesslike and courteous manner with the businesses you are surveying.

Choose one of the businesses that is using manual accounting methods. Assume that you are their consultant and prepare a proposal for the conversion to Simply Accounting. Your report for them should include the following:

1. a description of the tasks involved in converting their accounting records and implementing the new system for the business
2. a time frame for completing each task
3. your rationale or decision-making criteria for each task and time estimates
4. an estimate of the training required to familiarize the owner/accountant with the new methods (assume they have no previous experience with computers)
5. a description of the problems they can expect to encounter in using the new system and any limitations of the new system

To prepare your answer, you should visit the business to investigate its methods of operation. Use this information to guide your discussion of the conversion process. (Your instructor will tell you whether you should investigate an actual business as part of the case problem, or whether your proposal should be theoretical only.)

You may want to work in groups. If so, suggest a plan by which members within your group could be given specific duties in helping to assess the needs of the business and to implement the computerized accounting system. Your group should decide the following in advance:

1. What information will you gather?
2. Who will gather the information?
3. How much time will you allow for each stage?
4. How will you coordinate the work of the different team members?
5. How will you implement the conversion for the business?
6. How will the group members be accountable to one another?

Part Three

Using Simply Accounting V 8.0

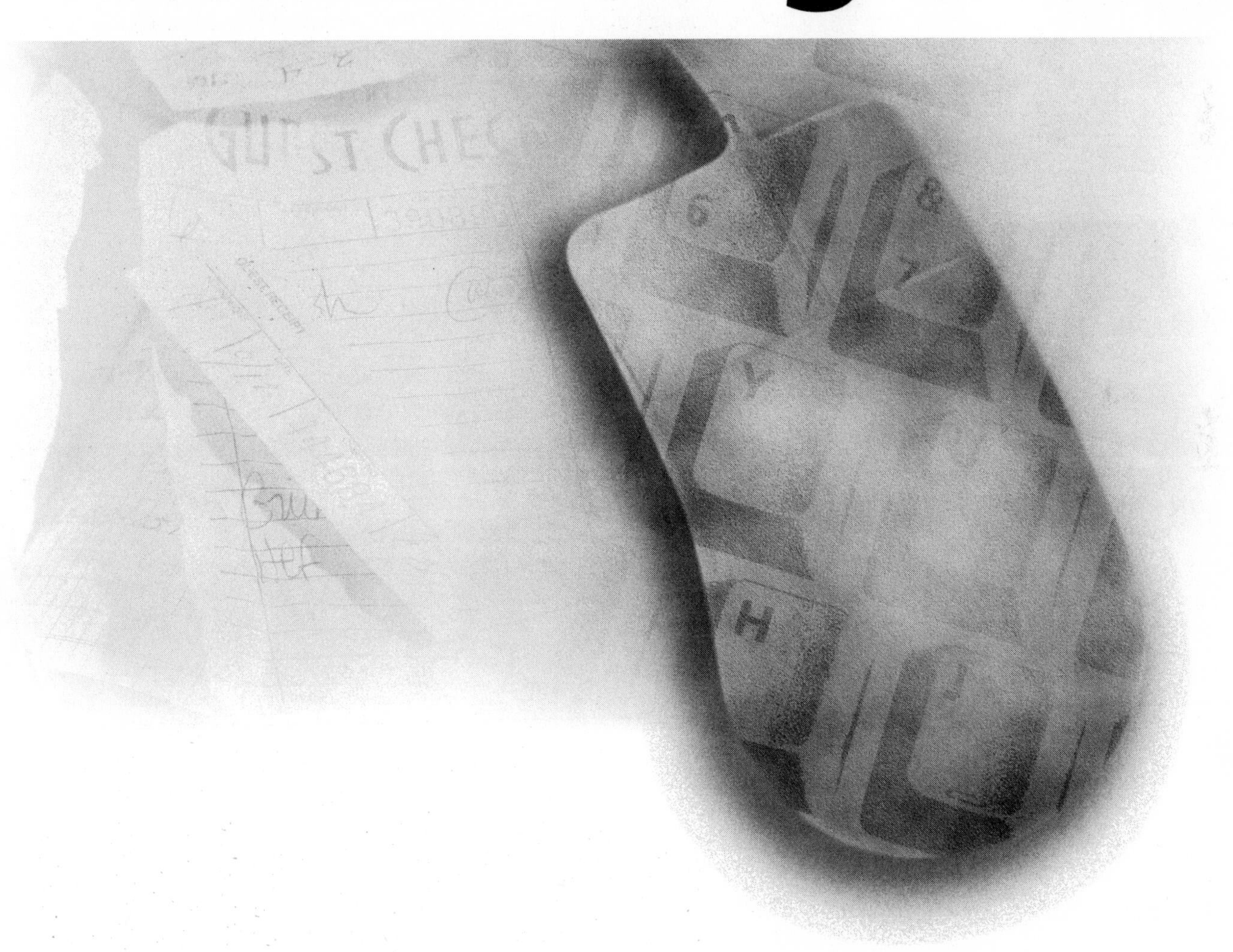

Version 8.0 Using Simply Accounting V 8.0

Most screens and procedures are the same for Versions 8.0 and 8.5. This section outlines the changes between Version 8.0 and 8.5 by showing the keystrokes and screens that are different for the two versions of the software.

This section is organized on a chapter-by-chapter basis with page numbers referring to the text position of the Version 8.5 keystrokes. Further cross-referencing is provided in the text by the Version 8.0 sidebar note headings that direct you to this part of the book, where we provide the detailed information about how Version 8.0 and 8.5 differ.

If you are using Version 8.0, we recommend reading this part of the book before starting so that you gain an overall picture of the kinds of differences involved. In many cases, you may not even need to refer back to this section because the differences are minor. In our efforts to be thorough, we have included as many of these differences as possible.

CHAPTER 1

page 13

To **install the data** files for Version 8.0,

Run Load80 from the CD. All other instructions are the same. You will install the data files that are compatible with Simply Accounting Version 8.0.

page 15

When you start Simply Accounting, the **Select Company window** in Version 8.0 has different graphics from Version 8.5 as shown:

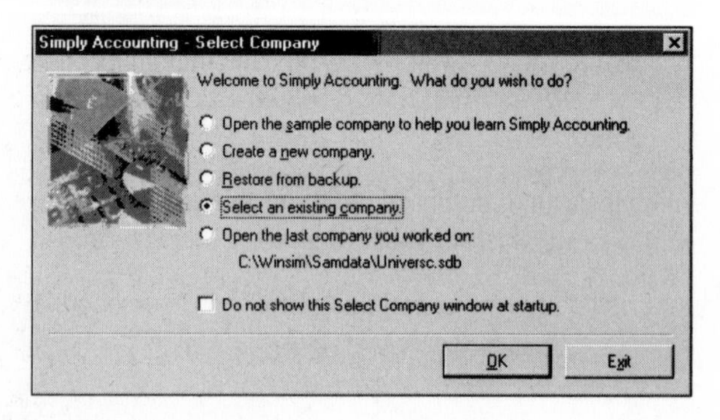

The options on this screen are the same in both versions.

page 17

The **Home window** will not have **Pro** in the title with Simply Accounting and the status bar will not show the **sysadmin** and **Single-user** information tags.

page 18

Turn off (and on) the status bar from the View menu. There is no User Preferences submenu.

page 21

Turn off (and on) the automatic advice from the View menu. There is no User Preferences submenu.

CHAPTER 3

page 39

Entering the year is optional for the **opening session date screen** in Version 8.0. The default entry for the year is provided by the company information on fiscal dates.

page 40

The **Home window** in Version 8.0 does not have **sysadmin** (the name of the current user) in the status bar right-hand corner. As is the case for the non-pro Version 8.5, **Single-user** is not shown on the status bar and **Pro** is not included in the title bar.

page 43

In Version 8.0, you can **use each account only once** in a General Journal entry. After choosing an account for part of the transaction, that account will not appear in the Select Account list. When you scroll through the Select Account list, you will see that 1360 is not listed because it has been used already in the transaction. If you have a compound entry (an account has more than one debit or credit), add all amounts for the account and enter a net debit or credit amount, or use separate journal entries.

page 45

The **Display Journal Entry screen** and all report screens do not have a tool bar:

General Journal Entry

File Options Help

07/02/2003 (J1)	Debits	Credits	Project
1360 Supplies: Roofing	850.00	-	
2670 GST Paid on Purchases	59.50	-	
2160 A/P - Dominion Building Supplies	-	909.50	
	909.50	909.50	

You must use the menu options instead.

Choose the **File menu** and **click Print** to print a displayed report.

Exporting is also started from the File menu. To **Sort** or **Filter**, use the buttons in the Report Options window or use the Options menu in the displayed report. Access **Help** from the Help menu. There is no refresh icon or menu selection for it.

page 46

The **Modify Accounts Wizard** for adding new accounts from a journal does not have the **logo** on the right-hand side of the information screens.

The fields and sequence are the same with one exception. The screen for **account reconciliation** is not present in Version 8.0. After the option to omit an account with a zero balance from financial statements, the wizard proceeds to the Finish screen.

page 48

When you click the **Adjust a posted entry** tool, the **first screen** you will see is the Select Entry to Adjust. You will **skip** the **Adjust an Entry date/source** screen.

page 50

The Home window **Maintenance menu options** are different. The Change Session Date option is unchanged but several Clear options from Version 8.0 are combined under the Version 8.5 submenu Clear Data. The menu for Version 8.0 is shown:

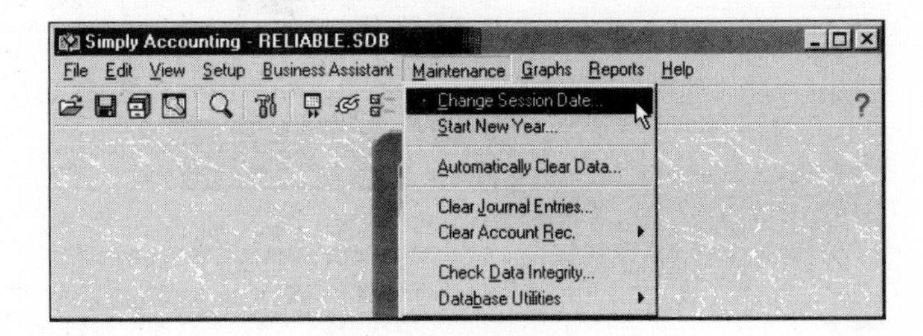

Clear Data menu options are used in Chapter 14.

page 56

When you start the **report filtering** procedure, you will proceed directly to the screen with the filter fields for inputting your choices. You will **skip** the screen with the check box for **Use your filtering specifications**.

CHAPTER 4

page 89

The **Payables Ledger window** is shown here for Version 8.0:

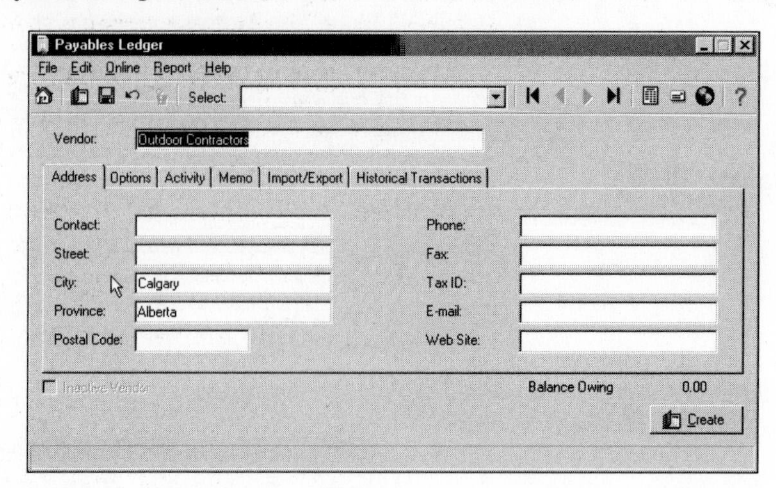

There are a few minor differences from Version 8.5. The **Select vendor** drop-down list is on the tool bar line instead of below it.

There is only **one Street field**. If you need a second address line, use the Contact field. Choose Print Contact on Cheques on the Options tab screen if the Contact field has address information.

There is **no Country field** in Version 8.0.

There is only **one Phone field** in Version 8.0.

page 90

The **Options tab screen** uses a different field label. **Include in GST Report** is used in Version 8.0 instead of Vendor collects GST. The results of making these selections are the same — the vendor is included in GST reports and all GST codes are available for the vendor in the Payables journals. The Version 8.0 screen is shown:

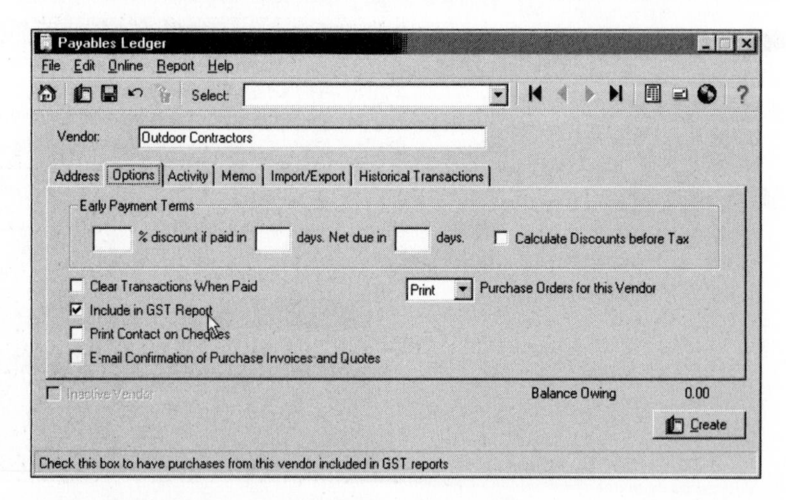

Click Include in GST Report instead of Vendor collects GST throughout the book. As in Version 8.5, the option is selected as the default.

page 106

There is no print tool for printing displayed reports.

Choose the **File menu** and **click print** to print the displayed report. This change applies to all reports.

CHAPTER 5

page 129

Many of the changes in the Receivables Ledger screens are parallel to those in the Payables Ledger. The **Address screen** is shown here:

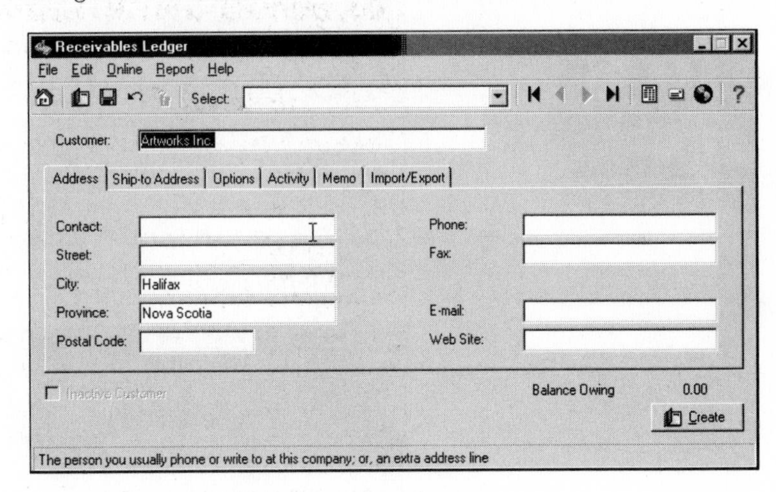

The **Select customer** drop-down list is on the tool bar line.

There is only **one Street address line**. If you need an additional address line, use the Contact field. Pressing (tab) after typing Street information places the cursor in the City field.

There is **no Country field**.

There is only **one Phone field**.

The option to select a **preferred or a regular customer** is not available in Version 8.0.

page 130

The **Options tab screen** is also different in Version 8.0:

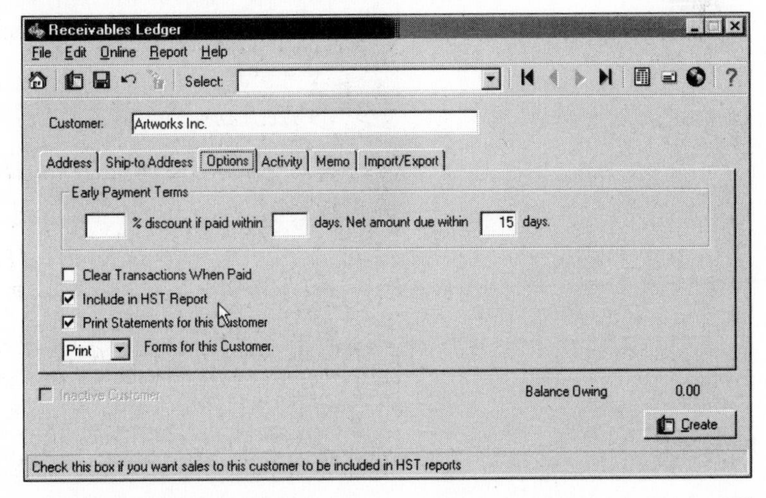

The label **Include in HST (GST) Report** is used in Version 8.0 instead of Charge this customer HST (GST). The results of making these selections are identical. Sales to the customer will be added to the HST/GST report and all the GST codes will be accessible in the Sales Journal.

The option to **Charge this customer PST** is **not available** in Version 8.0. The PST fields are always accessible in Version 8.0 if PST rates are entered for the business.

page 142

Version 8.0 does not include a **Statement of Cash Flows**.

page 143

Because there is no tool bar in any report windows, **choose** the **File menu** and **click Print** to print reports.

CHAPTER 6

page 156

In Version 8.0, some of the Home window main menu options are organized differently from the options in Version 8.5. Version 8.5 uses more submenus to group similar features and to reduce the length of the menu lists.

The Version 8.0 **Setup menu** is shown here:

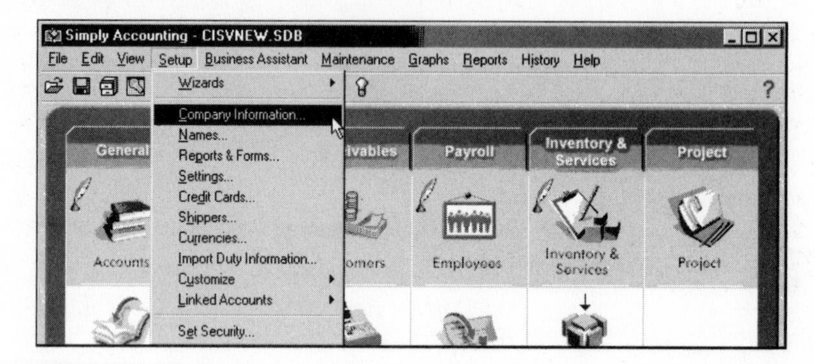

The submenu System Settings is not used in Version 8.0. Instead, the options that are under System Settings in Version 8.5 — Company Information, Names, Settings, Credit Cards, Shippers, Currencies, Import Duty Information and Linked Accounts — are located directly under the Setup menu.

The **View menu** for Version 8.0 is shown here:

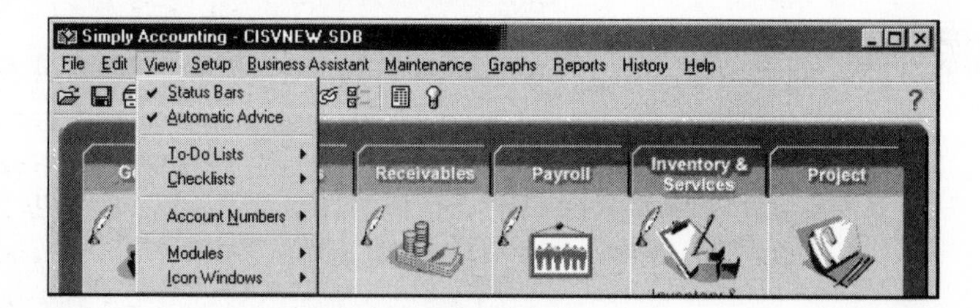

The View menu options in 8.0 have been moved to the System Settings and User Preferences submenus that are in Version 8.5.

The following chart summarizes these key menu differences.

SUMMARY OF MENU DIFFERENCES BETWEEN VERSION 8.0 AND VERSION 8.5

To Set up or Change...	In Version 8.0, Go to...	In Version 8.5, Go to...
Company Information	Setup menu	Setup menu, System Settings
Names	Setup menu	Setup menu, System Settings
Reports & Forms	Setup menu	Setup menu
Settings	Setup menu	Setup menu, System Settings
Credit Cards	Setup menu	Setup menu, System Settings
Shippers	Setup menu	Setup menu, System Settings
Currencies	Setup menu	Setup menu, System Settings
Import Duty Information	Setup menu	Setup menu, System Settings
Customize (Colours)	Setup menu, Customize, Appearance	Setup menu, User Preferences, Colour Scheme
Customize (Journals)	Setup menu, Customize, Journals	View menu, System Settings, Customize Journals
Linked Accounts	Setup menu	Setup menu, System Settings
Set Security	Setup menu	Setup menu, Set Up Users
Use Accounting Terms	Setup menu, Settings, Display tab	Setup menu, User Preferences, Settings
Single Click to open...	Setup menu, Settings, Display tab	Setup menu, User Preferences, Settings
Automatically save...	Setup menu, Settings, Display tab	Setup menu, User Preferences, Settings
Show Select Company...	Setup menu, Settings, Display tab	View menu
Status Bars	View menu	View menu, User Preferences
Automatic Advice	View menu	View menu, User Preferences
To-Do Lists	View menu	View menu, User Preferences
Checklists	View menu	View menu, User Preferences
Account Numbers	View menu	View menu, System Settings
Modules	View menu	View menu, User Preferences
Icon Windows	View menu	View menu, User Preferences

page 156

To enter the **Company Information**,

Choose the **Setup menu** and **click Company Information**. The Company Information screen in Version 8.0 has fewer information fields:

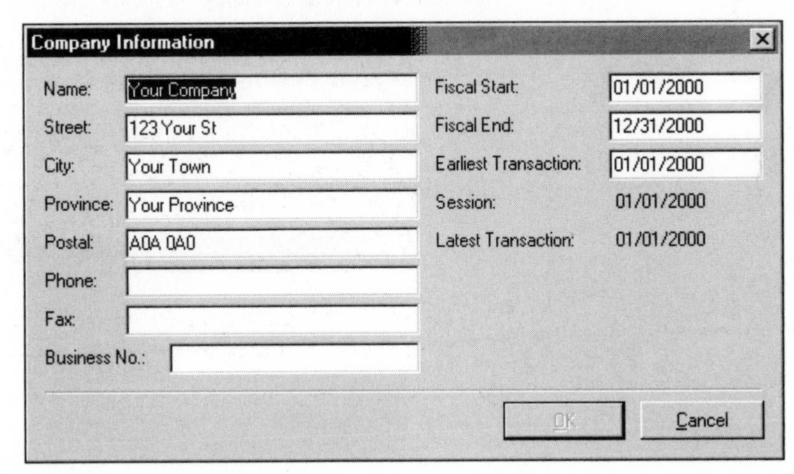

Version 8.0 has only **one Street** address field, **one Phone** number field and **no Country** field.

After typing the company name, press *tab* to advance to the Street field.

Type `North Toronto PO Box 38172` (Enter the complete street address in the Street field.)

Press *tab* to advance to the City field.

Type `Toronto`

Press tab to advance to the Province field.

Type `Ontario`

Press tab to advance to the Postal code field.

Type `m5n3a8`

Press tab to advance to the Phone field.

Type `4164887711`

Press tab to advance to the Fax field. Continue by typing the Fax number and the Business Number.

page 158

The **printer settings** for Reports & Graphs are combined in one tab screen in Version 8.0 instead of separated as in Version 8.5:

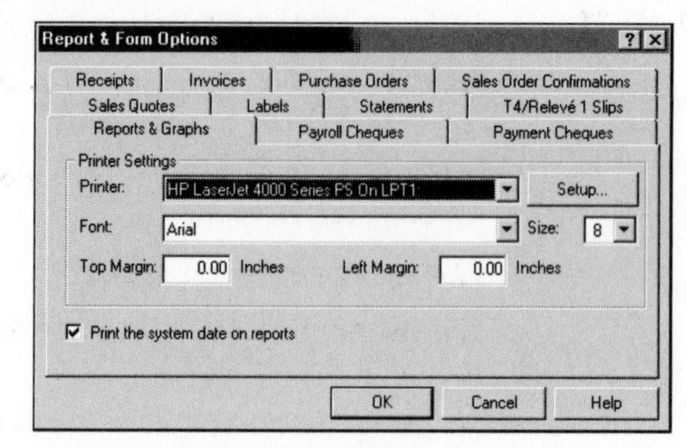

In Version 8.0, you choose a **single font and size** for all components of the report. The option to **show if a report is filtered** is not available.

page 159

To change the **System Settings**,

Choose the **Setup menu** and **click Settings**. Then **click** the **System tab**. In Version 8.0, Display settings are displayed first when you open the Settings screen. In Version 8.5, Display settings are moved to the User Preferences submenu under the Setup menu (see chart on page 565).

page 161

Change the **User Setting Defaults** from the Settings screen. Do not close the General Settings screen. (If you have already closed the Settings window, choose the Setup menu and click Settings.) After viewing the General Settings screen,

Click the **Display tab**:

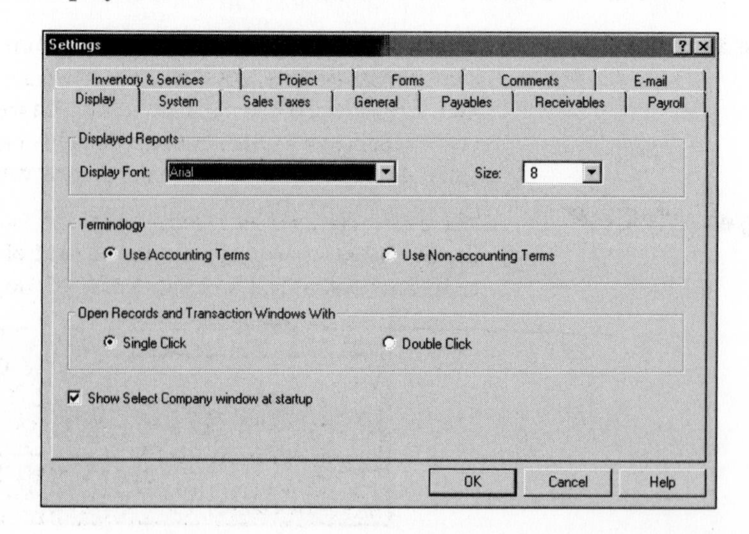

Most Setup menu User Preferences Settings in Version 8.5 are included with other Settings in Version 8.0 on the Display tab screen. The default settings are correct. The Show Select Company window at startup option is under the View menu in Version 8.5.

Click OK to return to the Home window.

page 162

To control whether account numbers are used in transactions and reports, choose the View menu, then choose Account Numbers and click In Reports or In Transactions. The default setting includes account numbers.

To **customize journals**,

Choose the **Setup menu** and then **choose Customize** and **click Journals**.

The View menu options under User Preferences in Version 8.5 are under the View menu directly in Version 8.0 (see the chart on page 565).

page 163

To **turn off the To-Do Lists** and **Checklists**,

Choose the **View menu**, then **choose To-Do Lists** and **click After Changing Session Dates**.

Choose the **View menu**, then **choose Checklists** and **click After Changing Session Dates**.

To **hide the unused modules**,

Choose the **View menu**, then **choose Modules** and **click Payables**. Repeat this step for the remaining modules.

To change the colour scheme in Version 8.0, choose the Setup menu, then choose Customize and click Appearance.

page 172

In Version 8.0, when you create a new account, the opening ledger screen has an **account number** already **entered** and selected. The default number is mid-way between the account you had selected before creating the new account and the one immediately above it in the Accounts window. The account type selected will be the one most likely to maintain the logical order of accounts.

Type the new number to replace the selected default entry.

CHAPTER 7

page 192

To enter Memo 48, you should complete **four separate journal entries** for the bank account transfers because you can use an account only once in a transaction. *Bank Account: Chequing* is used for all four transfers and involves both debit and credit entries. Separate journal entries will help ensure that you transfer the correct amounts and make it easier to check your work.

page 207

The **Sales Journal** for foreign customers looks slightly different — the **USD label for** the **Total** amount appears to the right of the amount in Version 8.0 not to the left as in Version 8.5. The relevant portion of the journal is shown here:

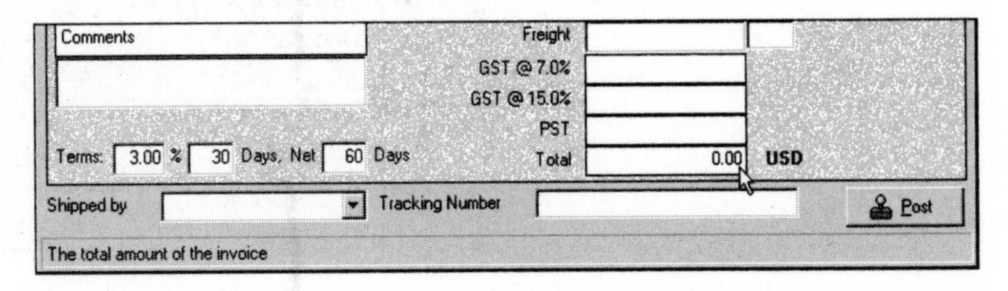

page 211 In the **Receipts Journal**, the **foreign currency code**, **USD**, appears to the right of the Total amount field, not to the left.

page 216 In the **Checklists** window, the **Edit button** is used in Version 8.0 instead of Modify:

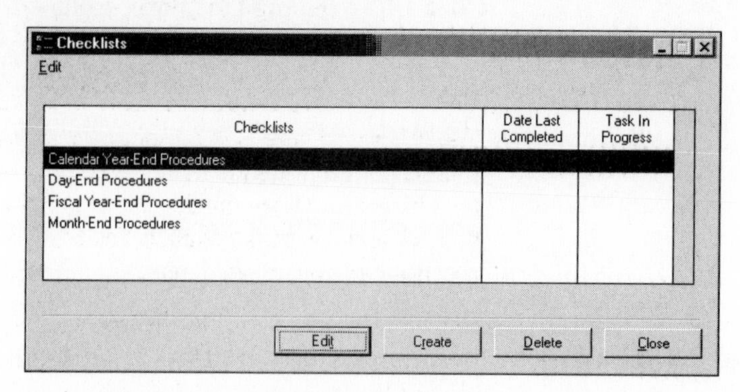

page 217 In the **Fiscal Year-End Procedures** checklist window, the **button label Task Completed** is used instead of Checklist Completed:

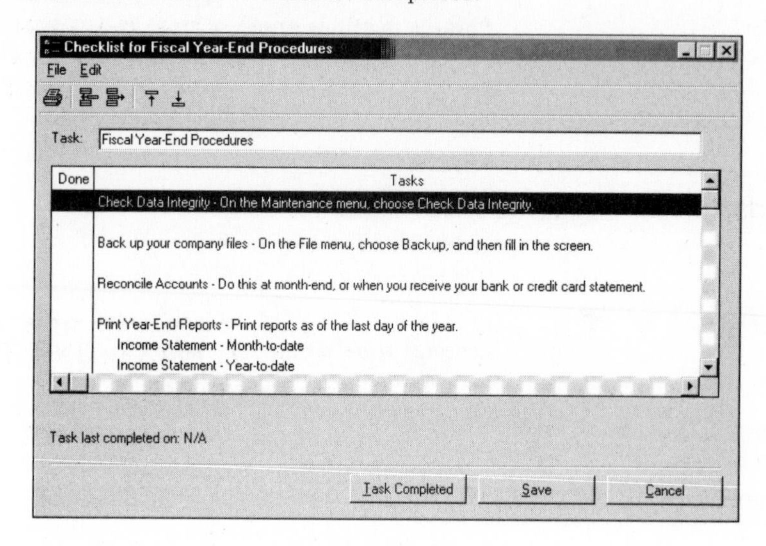

CHAPTER 8

page 240 In all **Payroll Journal entry screens** and **Payroll Journal Entry display screens**, your **payroll tax amounts**, and therefore, your net pay amounts, will likely be different in Version 8.0 than in Version 8.5 because different tax tables with different rates are used in later versions of the program. Since 2000, the income tax and EI premium rates have decreased, while CPP rates have increased. However, since we do not know which tax tables your version of Simply Accounting has, we do not show the screen for these amounts.

page 243 When you **adjust a paycheque** and post using the same cheque number as in the original entry, the program warns you. The **warning** for Version 8.0 is shown here:

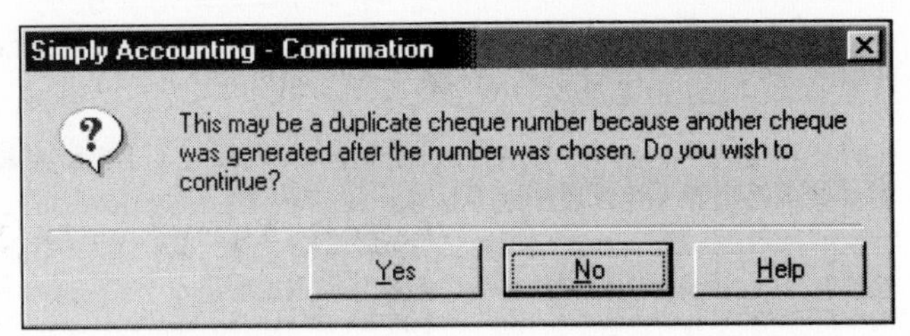

The difference here is important because the **question has changed**. Version 8.5 warns about the cheque number sequence and you must choose No to avoid updating the cheque sequence number. Version 8.0 warns about the possible duplicate cheque number and you **must choose Yes to continue** by posting the transaction and accepting the old cheque number.

Choose Yes to accept the cheque number and post the payroll transaction. If you choose No, you will return to the Journal.

page 244

In the **Payroll Run Journal**, the **Net Pay amounts** will likely be different from the ones in the text because of changes in tax rates for income tax, EI and CPP.

page 250

In the **Payroll Journal screens** and **Payroll Journal Entry display** on page 251, the **tax amounts** and the **Net Pay amounts** will likely be different because of changes in tax rates for income tax, EI and CPP.

CHAPTER 9

page 264

Version 8.0 does not have a customer status setting for preferred or regular customers. Therefore, you must enter sales to preferred customers by editing the sales prices in the Sales Journal.

Click the default selling price in the **Price field**.

Type the preferred customer price to replace it.

page 266

Edit the selling prices in the Sales Journal for the preferred customer.

page 279

The changes in the Payables Ledger were discussed in Chapter 4 of this section (see page 562). On the Options tab screen, the label **Include in GST Report** is used instead of Vendor collects GST.

page 280

The **Inventory & Services Ledge**r has **fewer tabs** in Version 8.0 and correspondingly fewer data fields. When you first open the ledger for adding the new item, you will see this screen:

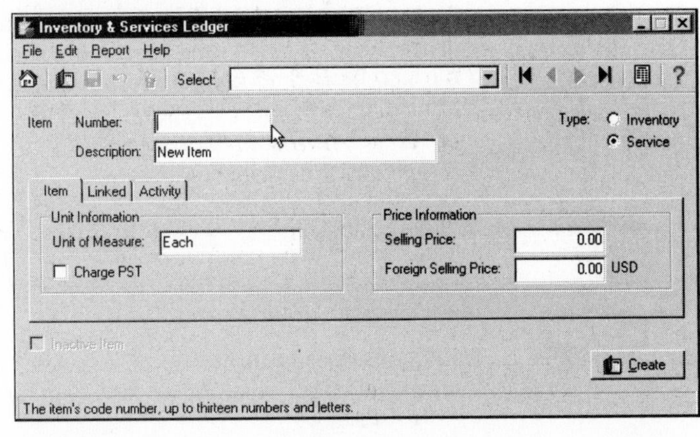

In Version 8.0, the Item tab screen for Services has both units and pricing information.

Click Inventory to open the data fields for inventory items rather than for Service items. The following screen appears:

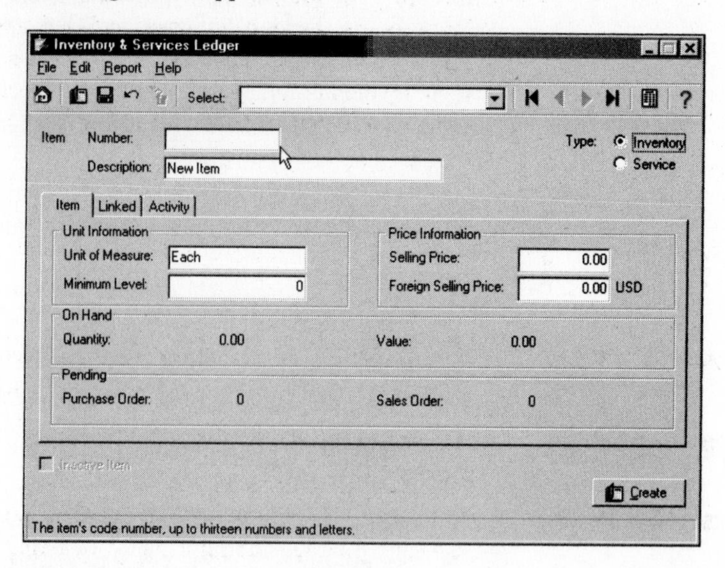

The **Item tab screen** combines the details about **Pricing**, **Units** and **Quantity** that are on separate tab screens in Version 8.5. Version 8.0 does not have a More Info tab screen.

Use the following steps to enter the units and pricing details.

Type `BAG-N1` (the item number)

Type `Saddle Bags - ballistic nylon light` (the item description)

Click the **Minimum Level field**.

Type `1`

Press tab to move to the Selling Price field.

Type `35`

Foreign prices are not used.

Click the **Linked tab** to access the linked account fields.

The **Charge PST and Charge GST** options (on the Pricing tab screen in Version 8.5) are **not available** in Version 8.0. Add taxes as needed in the Sales Journal. By default, both will be entered when they are set up (Sales Taxes Settings). There is a single unit of measure.

page 281

Version 8.0 does not have an option to store **preferred customer prices**. Instead, you should **edit the price in the Sales Journal** at the time of sale (or quote or order). Just click the default price to select it and type the new price. The program will automatically calculate the Amount as the quantity (Ship field) times the price.

page 283

Create the new asset account and then choose the linked revenue and expense accounts from the lists. You will see the **message about changing the account class** for *1310 Bags* when you click the Create button, not when you advance to the Revenue field.

page 284

In the **Purchases Journal**, the **currency code** appears to the right of the amount, not the left.

page 287

In the **Payments Journal**, the **currency code** appears to the right of the amount, not the left.

page 291

Version 8.0 records a **single unit of measure** for inventory items. Therefore, in inventory reports (Inventory, Inventory Activity, Inventory Sales, Inventory Transactions, Vendor Purchases and Customer Sales Reports), the report options screens allow you to show the units of measure in the reports, the single unit for the item. By default, units are included in reports. Separate unit information for stocking, selling and buying that is used in Version 8.5 is not available in Version 8.0.

CHAPTER 10

page 306

The **Select Company window** has different graphics in Version 8.0, but the choices on it are the same as in Version 8.5 (see page 560).

page 309

To enter company information, **choose** the **Setup menu** and **click Company Information**.

page 310

Enter **User Preferences** from the **View menu** and from the **Setup menu**. Refer to the chart on page 565 for a complete listing of the menu differences.

Choose the **View menu**, then **choose To-Do Lists** and **click After Changing Session Dates**.

Choose the **View menu**, then **choose Checklists** and **click After Changing Session Dates**.

Choose the **View menu**, then **choose Modules** and **click Payroll**. Repeat this step for the Inventory & Services and Project modules.

Enter the remaining **user preferences** from the Setup menu.

Choose the **Setup menu** and **click Settings** to see the Display Settings screen:

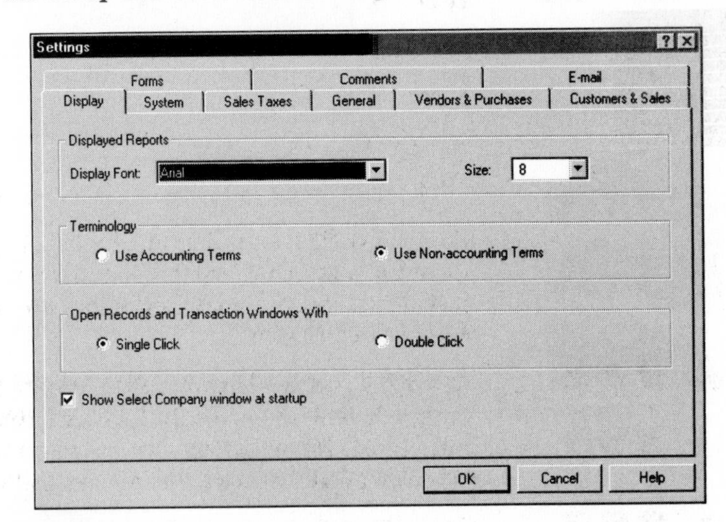

Non-accounting terms are in effect because we have not yet changed them. The non-accounting term tab label for the Payables Ledger is Vendors & Purchases. For the Receivables Ledger, the tab label is Customers & Sales. Since we are changing the terminology on this screen, the labels will not change until we save the new settings after exiting the Settings windows.

Click Use Accounting Terms to change the setting.

Click OK to save the change. The Home window now has accounting term labels for the ledgers.

page 310

To change system defaults, **choose** the **Settings menu** and **click Settings**.

Click the **System tab**. The accounting term labels, Payables and Receivables are now in effect.

Click Automatically save changes to vendor customer and other records.

The remaining System settings are the same for both versions.

The settings for Sales Taxes, Payables and Receivables are the same for both versions.

page 311

The **Payables** and **Receivables tab labels** should have changed (from Vendors & Purchases and Customers & Sales) if you followed the sequence we gave above.

If the non-accounting term labels still appear, **click** the **Display tab** and **click Use Accounting Terms**. **Click OK** to save the change. **Choose** the **Setup menu** and **click Settings**. **Click** the **tab** you need.

page 313

The **Forms tab screen** is organized differently in Version 8.0:

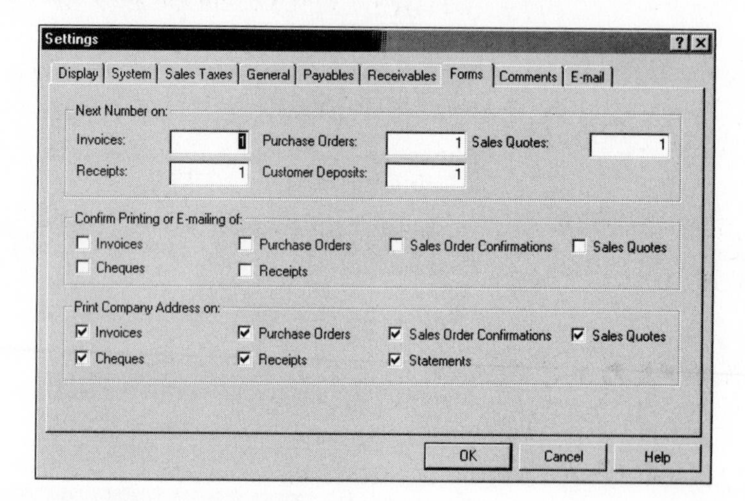

The Next Number fields are in a **different order** (Purchase Orders follows Invoices in Version 8.0 instead of all the other customer-related forms in Version 8.5). Version 8.0 does not have the column for **verifying the number sequences**. Number sequences are verified automatically.

page 315

There is **no default message** for e-mail messages in Version 8.0. You can add one if you want.

page 319

To access the General Linked Accounts screen from the menu, **choose Setup**, then **choose Linked Accounts** and **click General**.

page 320

To access the Payables Linked Accounts screen from the menu, **choose Setup**, then **choose Linked Accounts** and **click Payables**.

page 321

To enter **Receivables Ledger linked accounts**,

Choose the **Setup menu**, then **choose Linked Accounts** and **click Receivables**.

page 322

To set up **foreign currency transactions**, follow the instructions for Version 8.5 (not Pro Version 8.5).

page 326

The differences for the **Payables Ledger** were described for Chapter 4 (see page 562). They will be summarized here briefly.

On the **Address tab screen**:

- only one Street address field
- only one Phone field
- no Country field

On the **Options tab screen**:
- Include in GST Report is used instead of Vendor collects GST

page 332

The differences for the **Receivables Ledger** were described for Chapter 5 (see page 563). They are summarized here.

On the **Address tab screen**:
- only one Street address field
- only one Phone field
- no Country field
- no setting for Regular vs. Preferred customer status

On the **Options tab screen**:
- Include in GST Report is used instead of Charge this customer GST
- no setting for Charge this customer PST

page 337

To **set up credit cards**,

Choose the **Setup menu** and **click Credit Cards**.

CHAPTER 11

page 373

To enter **Project settings** from the menu, **choose** the **Setup menu**, then **click Settings** (if necessary, **click** the **Project tab**).

CHAPTER 12

page 401

Access the **Budget Setup** from the General Ledger Settings screen.

Choose the **Setup menu** and **click Settings**. Then **click** the **General tab**.

page 408

When you enter **purchases** from **foreign vendors**, the **price** is **not entered** automatically.

After you select the inventory item, the journal looks like the following:

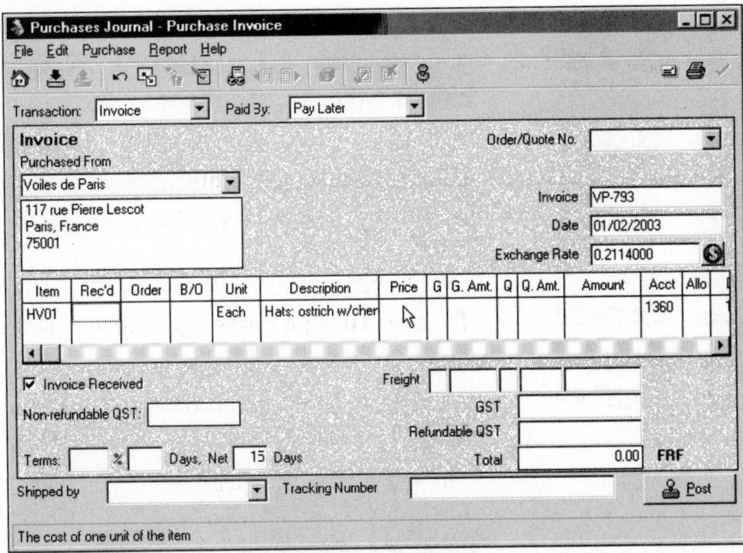

As soon as you enter the quantity (Rec'd) and the Amount, the price is calculated and entered so there is nothing you need to do differently for these purchases.

CHAPTER 13

page 435

To change **Company Information**,

Choose the **Setup menu** and **click Company Information**. **Click** the appropriate field and type the address details. There is no Country field and only one field for Street and one for Phone number.

page 436

To access the **Names** screen,

Choose the **Setup menu** and **click Names**. (Refer to page 565 in this section to see the complete list of menu changes for setup information.)

page 437

To change user preferences,

Choose the **View menu**, then **choose To-Do Lists** and **click After Changing Session Dates.**

Choose the **View menu**, then **choose Checklists** and **click After Changing Session Dates**.

Choose the **Setup menu** and **click Settings** to see the Display settings screen.

Click Use Accounting Terms

Click OK to switch to using the accounting terms for the rest of the settings changes.

page 438

To begin changing the default settings,

Choose the **Setup menu**, then **choose Settings** and **click** the **System tab**.

Click Automatically save changes to vendor, customer and other records

Changes for the remaining settings for all ledgers are the same as for Version 8.5.

page 443

To access **Currency information**, **choose** the **Setup menu** and **click Currencies**.

page 444

When you set up the **foreign currency bank account**, there is **no warning** about the missing currency balance. **You must enter the foreign balance amount before you close the ledger**.

page 445

To access linked account screens from the menu, **choose** the **Setup menu**, then **choose Linked Accounts** and **click** the ledger name. The Linked Accounts screens for Version 8.0 are the same as those for Version 8.5 (not Pro Version 8.5).

page 450

To enter **import duties**, **choose** the **Setup menu** and **click Import Duty Information**.

page 450

To enter **credit cards**, **choose** the **Setup menu** and **click Credit Cards**.

page 451

The vendors and customers **Options tab** screen uses the label **Include in GST Report**.

page 456

Version 8.0 has one Street field and one Phone field for employees in the Personal tab screen.

page 457

Because Version 8.0 was available before provincial tax claims were introduced, the fields for provincial claim amounts are not included. There is a **single Federal Claim field** for income taxes. Before January 2001, provincial taxes were calculated as a percentage of federal taxes (except in Quebec) so a single claim amount was required. The fields for claim amounts subject to indexing are also not included in Version 8.0.

The **Taxes tab screen** in the **Payroll Ledger** has fewer fields in Version 8.0 as shown:

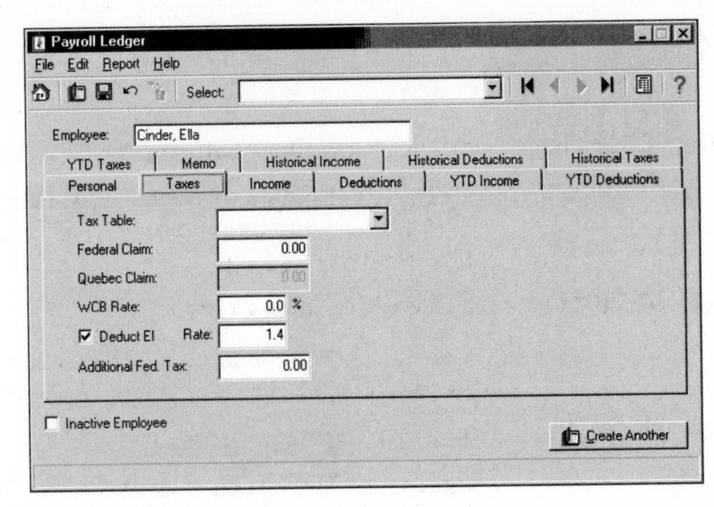

page 457

For Hearth House employees, enter the federal claim amount from the Employee Information Chart. This is the first figure, not the one in brackets.

For Cinder, **click** the **Federal Claim field**.

Type `13706`

Click the **WCB field** and continue.

page 462

The **Inventory Ledger** in Version 8.0 has units and pricing information on the Item tab screen:

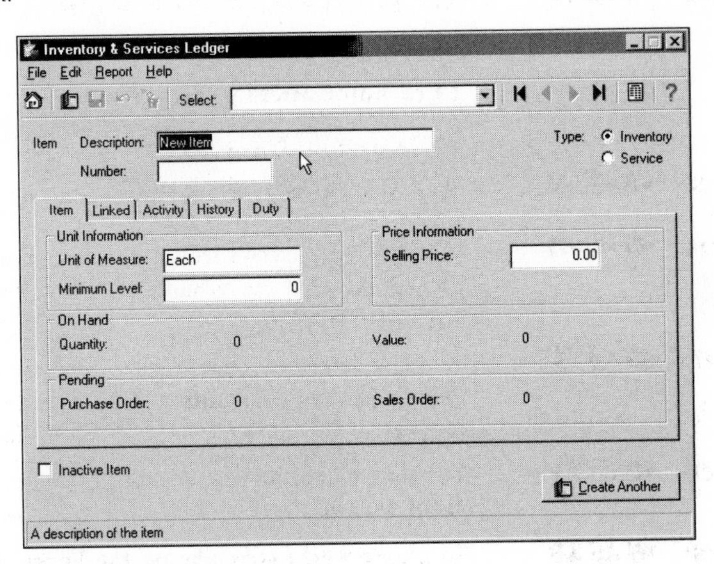

Enter the item description and number.

Click the **Minimum Level field**.

Type `1`

Double click Each (in the Unit of Measure field).

Type `Set`

Click the **Selling Price field**.

Type `100`

Continue by adding the Linked Accounts, Duty and History details.

notes

The foreign price option does not appear on the Settings screen until after you set up a foreign currency. In Version 8.0, the default setting is to calculate prices using the exchange rate.

There is no Foreign Selling Price field displayed because the default **Inventory Ledger setting** is to **calculate foreign prices using the exchange rate**. The ledger Settings screen is shown here:

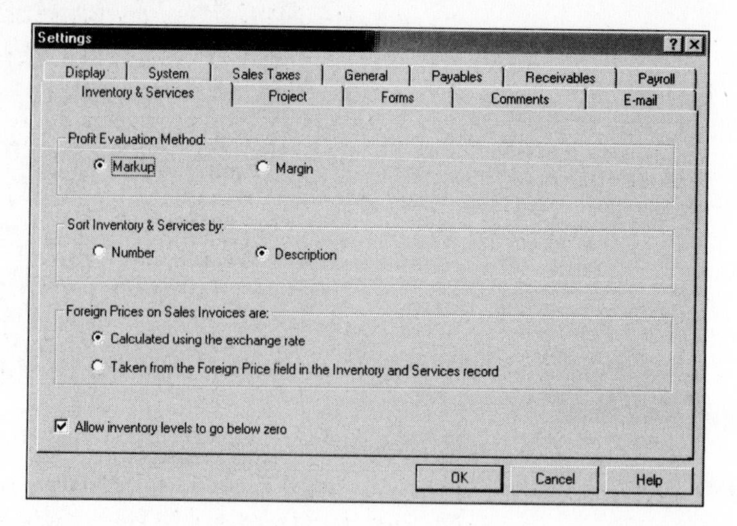

You do not need to change this setting because Hearth House has no foreign customers. If you want to change the setting, finish entering the inventory item and then close the Ledger and Inventory & Services window to return to the Home window. Choose the Setup menu and click Settings. Then click the Inventory tab. Click Taken from the Foreign Price field in the Inventory and Services record. Click OK to save the changes. When you create the next inventory item, your opening ledger Item tab screen will look like the following one:

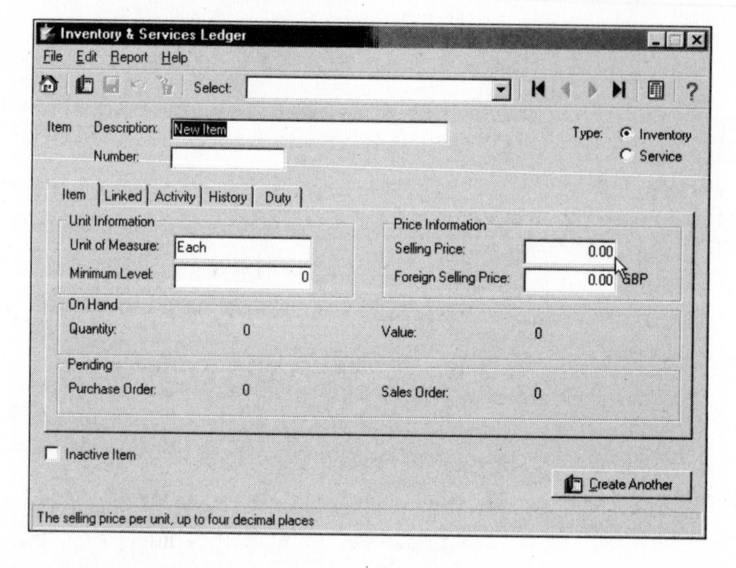

You can add foreign selling prices later if needed by editing the inventory records.

page 467

In Version 8.0, the ledger window for **inventory services** look like the following:

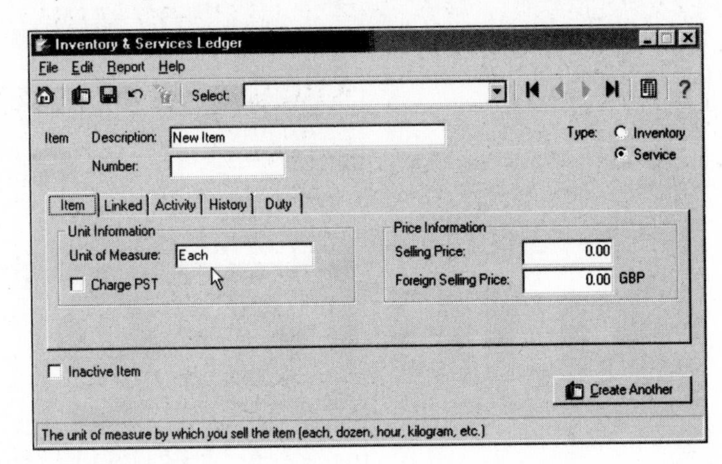

Units and pricing details are entered on the **Item tab screen**.

page 472

To enter sales to preferred customers in Version 8.0, you must edit the selling prices. You must also edit the selling prices to the preferred customers on pages 474 and 488.

CHAPTER 14

page 520

In the main **Checklists window**, the label **Edit** is used in Version 8.0 instead of Modify.

Click **Month-End Procedures** and then **click** Edit.

In the **Month-End Procedures checklist window**, the label **Task Completed** is used in Version 8.0 instead of Checklist Completed.

page 520

In Version 8.0, several **data-clearing** options are separate under the Maintenance menu rather than combined under the submenu Clear Data in Version 8.5.

To **clear journal entries**,

Choose the **Maintenance menu** and **click** **Clear Journal Entries**.

page 521

To **clear paid vendor transactions**,

Choose the **Maintenance menu**, then **choose** **Clear Paid Transactions** and **click** **Clear Paid Vendor Transactions**.

page 522

To **clear paid customer transactions**,

Choose the **Maintenance menu** and **click** **Clear Paid Transactions** and **click** **Clear Paid Customer Transactions**.

page 522

To **clear inventory tracking data**,

Choose the **Maintenance menu** and **click** **Clear Inventory Tracking Data**.

page 523

To **clear invoice lookup data**,

Choose the **Maintenance menu** and **click** **Clear Invoice Lookup Data**.

page 524

In the **Checklist window** for Month-End Procedures, **Delete** is used instead of Remove for deleting or removing an item from the checklist. Similarly, the **tool** button label is **Delete item** in Version 8.0 instead of Remove item.

The Edit menu is shown here:

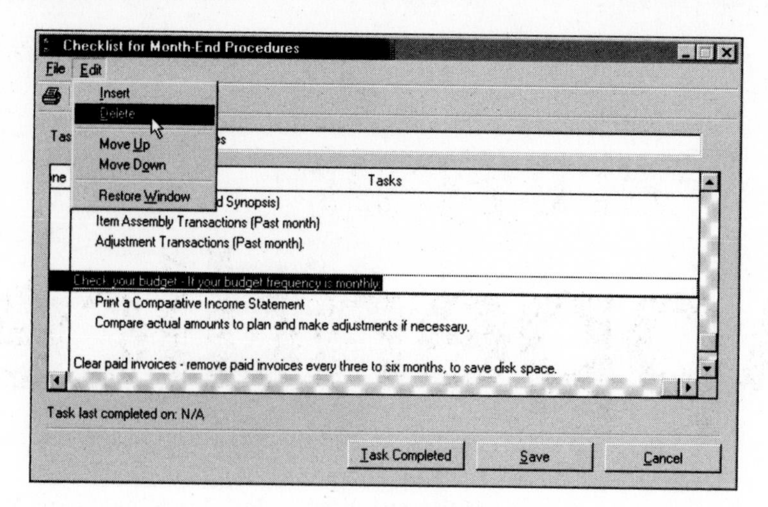

APPENDICES

page 590

To **set up users**, **choose** the **Setup menu** and **click Set Security**.

Set Security replaces Set up Users as the screen heading in all screens.

The button labels are also different. In Version 8.0, **Edit** is used as the button label instead of Modify for changing passwords and rights; **Add** is used instead of Add User and **Delete** is used instead of Remove User. The Version 8.0 screen is shown here:

page 605

The File menu does not have **Import/Export** as a submenu. Instead, all the import and export options (Export to MicroSoft Access, Export GIFI, Import Online Statements and Import General Journal Entries) are listed directly under the File menu, as shown. **Choose** the **File menu** and **click** an import or export option.

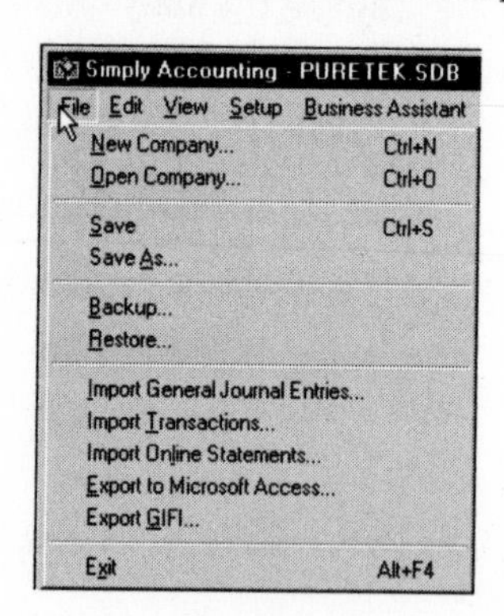

Part Four
Appendices

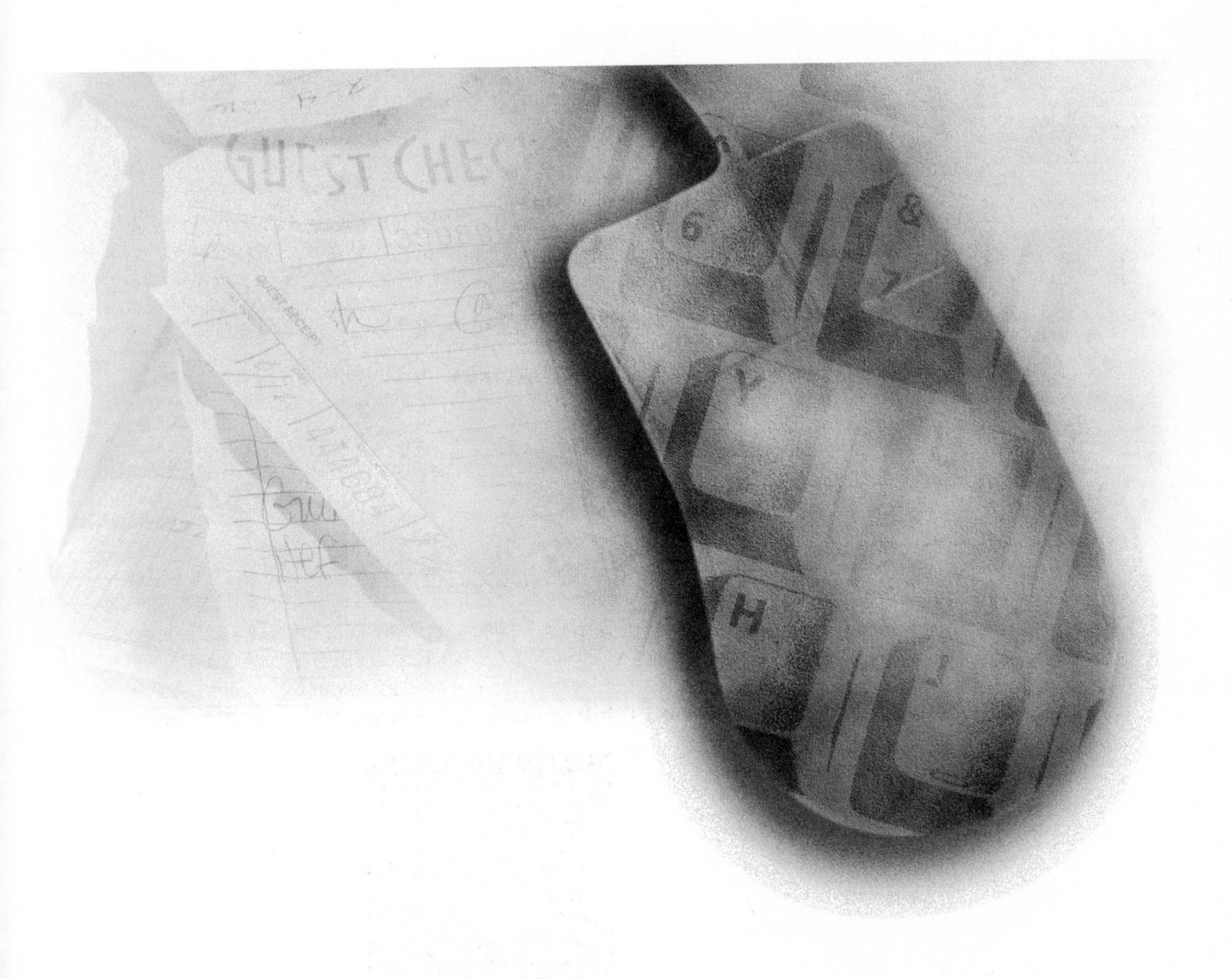

APPENDIX A Correcting Errors After Posting

We all make mistakes. This appendix outlines briefly the procedures you need to follow for those rare occasions when you have posted a journal entry incorrectly and you cannot use the adjust journal entry feature.

Obviously, you should try to detect errors before posting. Reviewing the journal entry should become routine practice. The software has built in a number of safeguards that help you avoid mistakes. For example, outstanding invoices cannot be overpaid, employee wages and payroll deductions are calculated automatically, and so on. Furthermore, names of accounts, customers, vendors, employees and inventory items appear in full, so that you may check your journal information easily.

Before making a reversing entry, consider the consequences of not correcting the error. For example, misspelled customer names may not be desirable, but they will not influence the financial statements. After making the correction in the ledger, the newly printed statement will be correct (the journal will retain the original spelling). Sometimes, however, the mistake is more serious. Financial statements will be incorrect if amounts or accounts are wrong. Payroll tax deductions will be incorrect if the wage amount is incorrect. GST and PST remittances may be incorrect as a result of incorrect sales or purchase amounts. Discounts will be incorrectly calculated if an invoice or payment date is incorrect. Some errors also originate from outside sources. For example, purchase items may be incorrectly priced by the vendor.

notes

You cannot adjust a posted invoice to correct for selecting the wrong customer, vendor or employee. In these cases, you must complete a reversing entry.

For audit purposes, prepare a memo explaining the error and the correction procedure. A complete reversing entry is often the simplest way to make the corrections for a straightforward audit trail. With Simply Accounting's recall and lookup features, a reversing entry is made easier because you can see an exact copy of the original incorrect entry. With invoice lookup turned on, you can automatically reverse and correct Sales and Purchases journal entries by adjusting the original entry. Choose Adjust Invoice from the pull-down menu under Sale or Purchase, or click the Adjust invoice button in the journal (page 99). General Journal and Payroll entries can be reversed and corrected in the journal by choosing Adjust Entry or Cheque menu item, or clicking the appropriate Adjust tool button (pages 48 and 241, respectively). Under all circumstances, Generally Accepted Accounting Principles should be followed.

Reversing entries in all journals have several common elements. In each case, you should use an appropriate source number that identifies the entry as reversing (e.g., add ADJ or REV to the original source number). You should use the original posting date and add a comment. Make the reversing entry as illustrated on the following pages. Display the journal entry, review it carefully and, when you are certain it is correct, post it. Next you must enter the correct version of the transaction as a new journal entry with an appropriate identifying source number, (e.g., add COR to the original source number).

Reversing entries are presented for each journal. Only the transaction portion of each screen is shown because the remaining parts of the journal screen do not change. The original and the reversing entry screens and most of the corresponding journal displays are included. Explanatory notes appear beside each set of entries.

GENERAL JOURNAL: Original Entry

Account	Debits	Credits	Allo
1360 Supplies: Roofing	850.00	--	
2670 GST Paid on Purchases	59.50	--	
2160 A/P - Dominion Building Supplies	--	909.50	
Total	909.50	909.50	

Reversing Entry

Account	Debits	Credits	Allo
2160 A/P - Dominion Building Supplies	909.50	--	
2670 GST Paid on Purchases	--	59.50	
1360 Supplies: Roofing	--	850.00	
Total	909.50	909.50	

notes

GENERAL JOURNAL

- Use the same accounts and amounts in the reversing entry as in the original entry.
- Accounts that were debited should be credited and accounts that were credited originally should be debited.
- The General Journal display is not shown because it basically looks the same as the journal input form.
- You can use the Adjust entry feature instead. See page 48.

PURCHASES JOURNAL (NON-INVENTORY): Original Entry

Item	Rec'd	Order	B/O	Unit	Description	Price	G	G. Amt.	P	P. Amt.	Amount	Acct	Allo
					advertising flyers		3	28.00	8.00	32.00	400.00	5020	✓

☑ Invoice Received

Freight

GST	28.00
PST	32.00
Total	460.00

Terms: % Days, Net 30 Days

04/07/2003 (J12)	Debits	Credits	Project
2670 GST Paid on Purchases	28.00	-	
5020 Advertising & Promotion	432.00	-	
- Briar Hill Project			108.00
- Chaplin Estates Project			108.00
- Store Operations			216.00
2200 Accounts Payable	-	460.00	
	460.00	460.00	

Reversing Entry

Item	Rec'd	Order	B/O	Unit	Description	Price	G	G. Amt.	P	P. Amt.	Amount	Acct	Allo
					Reverse advertising		3	-28.00	8.00	-32.00	-400.00	5020	✓

☑ Invoice Received

Freight

GST	-28.00
PST	-32.00
Total	-460.00

Terms: % Days, Net 30 Days

04/07/2003 (J13)	Debits	Credits	Project
2200 Accounts Payable	460.00	-	
2670 GST Paid on Purchases	-	28.00	
5020 Advertising & Promotion	-	432.00	
- Briar Hill Project			-108.00
- Chaplin Estates Project			-108.00
- Store Operations			-216.00
	460.00	460.00	

notes

PURCHASES JOURNAL

- The only change you must make is that positive amounts in the original entry become negative amounts in the reversing entry (place a minus sign before the amount in the Amount field).
- Similarly, negative amounts, such as for GST Paid in GST remittances, must be changed to positive amounts (remove the minus sign).
- If freight was charged, enter the amount of freight with a minus sign.
- Use the same accounts and amounts in the reversing entry as in the original entry. Tax amounts change automatically.
- Repeat the allocation with the original percentages.
- If you have invoice lookup turned on, you can use the Adjust Invoice option instead (page 99).

PAYMENTS JOURNAL — OTHER PAYMENTS: Original Entry

Acct	Description	Amount	G	G. Amt.	P	P. Amt.	Allo
5260 Telephone Expe	phone service	140.00	3	9.80	8.00	11.20	✓
						Total	161.00

04/08/2003 (J11)	Debits	Credits	Project
2670 GST Paid on Purchases	9.80	-	
5260 Telephone Expense	151.20	-	
- Briar Hill Project			30.24
- Chaplin Estates Project			30.24
- Store Operations			90.72
1060 Bank: Chequing Account	-	161.00	
	161.00	161.00	

notes

OTHER PAYMENTS

- The only change you must make is that positive amounts in the original entry become negative amounts in the reversing entry (place a minus sign before the amount in the Amount field).
- Similarly, negative amounts, such as for GST Paid in GST remittances, must be changed to positive amounts (remove the minus sign).
- Use the same accounts and amounts in the reversing entry as in the original entry. Tax amounts change automatically.
- Repeat the allocation with the original percentages.
- If you have invoice lookup turned on, you can use the Adjust Invoice option instead (page 99).

Reversing Entry

Acct	Description	Amount	G	G. Amt.	P	P. Amt.	Allo
5260 Telephone Expe	reverse phone entry	-140.00	3	-9.80	8.00	-11.20	✓
						Total	-161.00

04/08/2003 (J12)	Debits	Credits	Project
1060 Bank: Chequing Account	161.00	-	
2670 GST Paid on Purchases	-	9.80	
5260 Telephone Expense	-	151.20	
- Briar Hill Project			-30.24
- Chaplin Estates Project			-30.24
- Store Operations			-90.72
	161.00	161.00	

PAYMENTS: Original Entry

Invoice/Pre-pmt.	Original Amt.	Amt. Owing	Disc. Available	Disc. Taken	Payment Amt.
DC-3490	1,605.00	1,605.00	32.10	32.10	1,572.90
				Total	1,572.90

04/10/2003 (J7)	Debits	Credits	Project
2200 Accounts Payable	1,605.00	-	
1060 Bank: Chequing Account	-	1,572.90	
5110 Purchase Discounts	-	32.10	
	1,605.00	1,605.00	

notes

PAYMENTS

- Click the Include Fully Paid Invoices tool button.
- The only change you must make is that positive amounts in the original entry become negative amounts in the reversing entry.
- In the Payment Amt. field, click the invoice line for the payment being reversed.
- Type a minus sign and the amount.
- If a discount was taken, type the discount amount with a minus sign in the Disc. Taken field.

continued...

Reversing Entry

Invoice/Pre-pmt.	Original Amt.	Amt. Owing	Disc. Available	Disc. Taken	Payment Amt.
DC-3490	1,605.00	0.00	0.00	-32.10	-1,572.90
				Total	-1,572.90

04/10/2003 (J8)	Debits	Credits	Project
1060 Bank: Chequing Account	1,572.90	-	
5110 Purchase Discounts	32.10	-	
2200 Accounts Payable	-	1,605.00	
	1,605.00	1,605.00	

notes

PAYMENTS CONTINUED

- This will restore the original balance owing for the invoice. Refer to page 135.
- If you have already cleared the paid invoice, prepare a new Purchases Journal entry for the amount of the payment (non-taxable) to restore the balance owing. Enter a positive amount in the Amount field for the amount of the cheque and the Bank account in the Account field. On the next line, enter the discount amount (positive) with the Purchase Discounts account in the Account field. This will debit the Bank and Purchase Discounts accounts and credit Accounts Payable.

CREDIT CARD PAYMENTS: Original Entry

Credit Card Payable Account Balance:	460.00
Additional Fees and Interest:	30.00
Payment Amount:	270.00

04/15/2003 (J28)	Debits	Credits	Project
2150 Credit Card Payable	240.00	-	
5020 Bank Charges & Card Fees	30.00	-	
1060 Bank Account: Chequing	-	270.00	
	270.00	270.00	

notes

CREDIT CARD PAYMENT

- Enter the same amounts as in the original entry.
- Add a minus sign to the Additional Fees and Interest Amount and to the Payment Amount in the reversing entry.

Reversing Entry

Credit Card Payable Account Balance:	220.00
Additional Fees and Interest:	-30.00
Payment Amount:	-270.00

04/15/2003 (J29)	Debits	Credits	Project
1060 Bank Account: Chequing	270.00	-	
2150 Credit Card Payable	-	240.00	
5020 Bank Charges & Card Fees	-	30.00	
	270.00	270.00	

INVENTORY PURCHASES: Original Entry

notes

INVENTORY PURCHASE

- Change positive quantities in the original entry to negative ones in the reversing entry (place a minus sign before the quantity in the Rec'd field).
- Similarly, change negative quantities, such as for returns, to positive ones (remove the minus sign).
- Add a minus sign to the freight amount if freight is charged.
- Use the same accounts and amounts in the reversing entry as in the original entry. Tax amounts are corrected automatically.
- Repeat the allocation using the original percentages.
- If you have invoice lookup turned on, you can use the Adjust Invoice option instead (page 99).

Item	Rec'd	Order	B/O	Unit	Description	Price	G	G. Amt.	P	P. Amt.	Amount	Acct	Allo
PTS-2	300			each	Patio Block: Diamo	5.00	3	105.00	8.00	120.00	1,500.00	1420	

☑ Invoice Received

Freight 3 | 3.50 | | | 50.00

GST 108.50

PST 120.00

Terms: 2.00 % 10 Days, Net 20 Days

Total 1,778.50

04/10/2003 (J14)	Debits	Credits	Project
1420 Patio Stone Blocks	1,620.00	-	
2670 GST Paid on Purchases	108.50	-	
5120 Freight Expense	50.00	-	
2200 Accounts Payable	-	1,778.50	
	1,778.50	1,778.50	

Reversing Entry

Item	Rec'd	Order	B/O	Unit	Description	Price	G	G. Amt.	P	P. Amt.	Amount	Acct	Allo
PTS-2	-300			each	Patio Block: Diamo	5.00	3	-105.00	8.00	-120.00	-1,500.00	1420	

☑ Invoice Received

Freight 3 | -3.50 | | | -50.00

GST -108.50

PST -120.00

Terms: 2.00 % 10 Days, Net 20 Days

Total -1,778.50

04/10/2003 (J15)	Debits	Credits	Project
2200 Accounts Payable	1,778.50	-	
1420 Patio Stone Blocks	-	1,620.00	
2670 GST Paid on Purchases	-	108.50	
5120 Freight Expense	-	50.00	
	1,778.50	1,778.50	

SALES JOURNAL (INVENTORY AND NON-INVENTORY): Original Entry

Item	Ship	Order	B/O	Unit	Description	Price	Amount	GST	PST	Acct	Allo
PVS-4	200			each	Paver Slab: Red patter	1.80	360.00	3	8.00	4020	✓
BH-1	1			Project	Briar Hill Project: reserv	2,415.00	2,415.00	3	8.00	4040	✓
					contract labour		7,585.00	3	8.00	4040	✓

Comments

Terms: % Days, Net 1 Days

Freight	50.00	3
GST @ 7.0%	728.70	
PST	828.80	
Total	11,967.50	

04/14/2003 (J14)	Debits	Credits	Project
1200 Accounts Receivable	11,967.50	-	
5080 Cost of Goods Sold	1,595.00	-	
- Store Operations			200.00
- Briar Hill Project			1,395.00
1440 Paver Slabs	-	200.00	
1500 Reserved Inventory for Projects	-	1,395.00	
2640 PST Payable	-	828.80	
2650 GST Charged on Sales	-	728.70	
4020 Revenue from Store Sales	-	360.00	
- Store Operations			360.00
4040 Revenue from Contracting	-	10,000.00	
- Briar Hill Project			10,000.00
4200 Freight Revenue	-	50.00	
	13,562.50	13,562.50	

Reversing Entry

Item	Ship	Order	B/O	Unit	Description	Price	Amount	GST	PST	Acct	Allo
PVS-4	-200			each	Paver Slab: Red patter	1.80	-360.00	3	8.00	4020	✓
BH-1	-1			Project	Briar Hill Project: reserv	2,415.00	-2,415.00	3	8.00	4040	✓
					contract labour		-7,585.00	3	8.00	4040	✓

Comments

Terms: % Days, Net 1 Days

Freight	-50.00	3
GST @ 7.0%	-728.70	
PST	-828.80	
Total	-11,967.50	

04/14/2003 (J15)	Debits	Credits	Project
1440 Paver Slabs	200.00	-	
1500 Reserved Inventory for Projects	1,395.00	-	
2640 PST Payable	828.80	-	
2650 GST Charged on Sales	728.70	-	
4020 Revenue from Store Sales	360.00	-	
- Store Operations			-360.00
4040 Revenue from Contracting	10,000.00	-	
- Briar Hill Project			-10,000.00
4200 Freight Revenue	50.00	-	
1200 Accounts Receivable	-	11,967.50	
5080 Cost of Goods Sold	-	1,595.00	
- Store Operations			-200.00
- Briar Hill Project			-1,395.00
	13,562.50	13,562.50	

notes

SALES

- For inventory sales, change positive quantities in the original entry to negative ones in the reversing entry (place a minus sign before the quantity in the Ship field). Similarly, change negative quantities, such as for returns, to positive ones (remove the minus sign).
- For non-inventory sales, change positive amounts in the original entry to negative amounts in the reversing entry (place a minus sign before the amount in the Amount column).
- Add a minus sign to the freight amount if freight is charged.
- Use the same accounts and amounts in the reversing entry as in the original entry.
- Repeat the allocation using the original percentages.
- If invoice lookup is turned on, you can use the Adjust Invoice option instead (page 124).

notes

DEPOSITS

- Enter the same amount as in the original entry.
- Add a minus sign to the Deposit Amount in the reversing entry.
- Change the Deposit Reference No. and Cheque number by adding REV.

DEPOSITS: Original Entry

Deposit Reference No.	3	Deposit Amount	2,000.00
		Total	2,000.00

04/15/2003 (J21)	Debits	Credits	Project
1060 Bank: Chequing Account	2,000.00	-	
1200 Accounts Receivable	-	2,000.00	
	2,000.00	2,000.00	

Reversing Entry

Deposit Reference No.	Rev-3	Deposit Amount	-2,000.00
		Total	-2,000.00

04/15/2003 (J22)	Debits	Credits	Project
1200 Accounts Receivable	2,000.00	-	
1060 Bank: Chequing Account	-	2,000.00	
	2,000.00	2,000.00	

notes

RECEIPTS

- Click the Include Fully Paid Invoices tool.
- Change positive amounts in the original entry to negative amounts in the reversing entry.
- In the Payment Amt. field, click the invoice or deposit line for the payment being reversed.
- Type a minus sign and the amount for invoices and deposits.
- If a discount was taken, type the discount amount with a minus sign in the Disc. Taken field.
- This will restore the original balance owing for the invoice. Refer to page 135.
- If you have already cleared the invoice, make a new Sales Journal entry for the payment amount (non-taxable) to restore the balance owing. Enter both the cheque and discount amounts as positive amounts to credit the Bank and Sales Discounts accounts.

RECEIPTS WITH DEPOSITS: Original Entry

Invoice/Deposit	Original Amt.	Amt. Owing	Disc. Available	Disc. Taken	Payment Amt.
104	11,500.00	11,500.00	0.00		11,500.00
Deposits					
3	2,000.00	2,000.00			2,000.00
				Total	9,500.00

04/15/2003 (J23)	Debits	Credits	Project
1060 Bank: Chequing Account	9,500.00	-	
1200 Accounts Receivable	-	9,500.00	
	9,500.00	9,500.00	

Reversing Entry

Invoice/Deposit	Original Amt.	Amt. Owing	Disc. Available	Disc. Taken	Payment Amt.
104	11,500.00	0.00	0.00		-11,500.00
Deposits					
3	2,000.00	0.00			-2,000.00
				Total	-9,500.00

04/15/2003 (J24)	Debits	Credits	Project
1200 Accounts Receivable	9,500.00	-	
1060 Bank: Chequing Account	-	9,500.00	
	9,500.00	9,500.00	

notes

PAYROLL JOURNAL

- Redo the original incorrect entry but DO NOT POST IT!
- Click the Enter taxes manually button to open all the deduction fields for editing.
- Type a minus sign in front of the number of hours (regular and overtime) or in front of the Salary and Commission amounts. Press tab to update the amounts, including vacation pay (i.e., change them to negative amounts).
- For the Advance field, change the sign for the amount. Advances should have a minus sign in the reversing entry and advances recovered should be positive amounts.
- Click the Deductions tab and edit each deduction amount by typing a minus sign in front of it.
- Click the Taxes tab. Check the amounts for CPP, EI and Tax with the original journal entry because these amounts may be incorrect (the employee may have reached the maximum contribution since the original entry, or may have entered a different tax bracket). Change the amounts to match the original entry if necessary. The Employee Detail Report will provide the amounts entered for each paycheque.
- Repeat the allocation with the original percentages.
- Remember to click the Calculate taxes automatically button before you make the correct payroll entry.
- You can use the Adjust Cheque option instead to reverse and correct the Payroll Journal entry (see page 241).

PAYROLL JOURNAL: Original Entry

Income | Deductions | Taxes

Period Ending 04/15/2003

Reg. 40.00 640.00 | Commission | Benefits
OT 1 | Income C | Benefits (Que)
OT 2 | Income D | Vacation 38.40
Sal. | Income E | Release
Advance 100.00

Gross Pay 640.00 Withheld -156.87 Net Pay 583.13 Post

Income | Deductions | Taxes

CSB Plan 50.00

Income | Deductions | Taxes

EI 14.40
CPP/QPP 21.73
Tax 70.74
Prov. Tax

04/15/2003 (J11)	Debits	Credits	Project
1220 Advances Receivable	100.00	-	
5300 Wages	678.40	-	
5310 EI Expense	20.16	-	
5320 CPP Expense	21.73	-	
5330 WSIB Expense	50.37	-	
5360 EHT Expense	6.27	-	
1060 Bank: Chequing Account	-	583.13	
2300 Vacation Payable	-	38.40	
2310 EI Payable	-	34.56	
2320 CPP Payable	-	43.46	
2330 Income Tax Payable	-	70.74	
2390 EHT Payable	-	6.27	
2400 CSB Plan Payable	-	50.00	
2460 WSIB Payable	-	50.37	
	876.93	876.93	

Reversing Entry

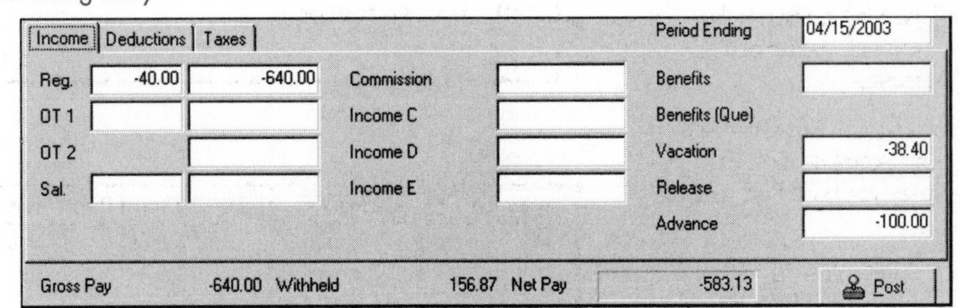

Income | Deductions | Taxes

CSB Plan -50.00

Income | Deductions | Taxes

EI -14.40
CPP/QPP -21.73
Tax -70.74
Prov. Tax

04/15/2003 (J12)	Debits	Credits	Project
1060 Bank: Chequing Account	583.13	-	
2300 Vacation Payable	38.40	-	
2310 EI Payable	34.56	-	
2320 CPP Payable	43.46	-	
2330 Income Tax Payable	70.74	-	
2390 EHT Payable	6.27	-	
2400 CSB Plan Payable	50.00	-	
2460 WSIB Payable	50.37	-	
1220 Advances Receivable	-	100.00	
5300 Wages	-	678.40	
5310 EI Expense	-	20.16	
5320 CPP Expense	-	21.73	
5330 WSIB Expense	-	50.37	
5360 EHT Expense	-	6.27	
	876.93	876.93	

ITEM ASSEMBLY JOURNAL: Original Entry

> **notes**
>
> **ITEM ASSEMBLY JOURNAL**
> - Re-enter the assembly as you did originally.
> - Type a minus sign in front of each quantity in the Qty field in both the Assembly Components and Assembled Items sections.
> - Also type a minus sign in front of the amount for Additional Costs.

Assembly Components

Item	Qty	Unit	Description	Unit Cost	Amount
CP-1	50	sqft	Cobblestone: Berlin circular 4x8	1.00	50.00
ES-1	50	each	Edging Stone: Crv scalloped 2f	1.80	90.00
PTS-1	50	each	Patio Block: Deck concrete 24	4.00	200.00

Additional Costs 50.00

Total 390.00

Assembled Items

Item	Qty	Unit	Description	Unit Cost	Amount
Promo-1	5	Each	Promotional Package Offer	78.00	390.00

Total 390.00

04/20/2003 (J16)	Debits	Credits	Project
1510 Special Offers	390.00	-	
1380 Cobble Pavestones	-	50.00	
1400 Edging Stone Blocks	-	90.00	
1420 Patio Stone Blocks	-	200.00	
5280 Item Assembly Costs	-	50.00	
	390.00	390.00	

Reversing Entry

Assembly Components

Item	Qty	Unit	Description	Unit Cost	Amount
CP-1	-50	sqft	Cobblestone: Berlin circular 4x8	1.00	-50.00
ES-1	-50	each	Edging Stone: Crv scalloped 2f	1.80	-90.00
PTS-1	-50	each	Patio Block: Deck concrete 24	4.00	-200.00

Additional Costs -50.00

Total -390.00

Assembled Items

Item	Qty	Unit	Description	Unit Cost	Amount
Promo-1	-5	Each	Promotional Package Offer	78.00	-390.00

Total -390.00

04/20/2003 (J17)	Debits	Credits	Project
1380 Cobble Pavestones	50.00	-	
1400 Edging Stone Blocks	90.00	-	
1420 Patio Stone Blocks	200.00	-	
5280 Item Assembly Costs	50.00	-	
1510 Special Offers	-	390.00	
	390.00	390.00	

notes

ADJUSTMENTS JOURNAL

- Change the sign for the quantity in the Qty field (positive to negative or negative to positive).
- Repeat the allocation using the original percentages.

ADJUSTMENTS JOURNAL: Original Entry

Item	Qty	Unit	Description	Unit Cost	Amount	Acct	Allo
SF-2	-100	sqft	Stone Slab: Flagstone	8.00	-800.00	5180 Inven	✓
				Total	-800.00		

04/25/2003 (J18)	Debits	Credits	Project
5180 Inventory Adjustment	800.00	-	
- Store Operations			800.00
1460 Stone Slabs	-	800.00	
	800.00	800.00	

Reversing Entry

Item	Qty	Unit	Description	Unit Cost	Amount	Acct	Allo
SF-2	100	sqft	Stone Slab: Flagstone	8.00	800.00	5180 Inven	✓
				Total	800.00		

04/25/2003 (J19)	Debits	Credits	Project
1460 Stone Slabs	800.00	-	
5180 Inventory Adjustment	-	800.00	
- Store Operations			-800.00
	800.00	800.00	

APPENDIX B Setting up Users and Security

ENTERING USERS AND PASSWORDS

In Chapter 13, we introduced system security and passwords. Passwords may be needed when a company's computer is shared and files can be accessed easily by any of the users. It is very easy to remove and modify data in Simply Accounting, although it is not easy to do it by accident because of the built-in warnings. Nonetheless, security of confidential information is always important, and Simply Accounting's passwords offer protection from unauthorized access or alteration.

Pro Version 8.5 is a multi-user program that allows more than one user to access or share the data files at the same time. When more than one user is set up, the refresh tool that updates the data file becomes available in the journal and ledger windows. In Version 8.5 and Version 8.0, you can set up the program for multiple users but only one user can access the data files at any one time. The steps for entering users and passwords are the same in the three versions of Simply Accounting, as are the methods of using the program to enter transactions and records and prepare reports.

Users and passwords are entered from the Home window.

Warning!

If you have forgotten your password, you will be unable to open the files. For this reason, you should
- keep the code in a safe place
- choose a code that is unique for you but easy for you to remember
- keep a backup copy of the unprotected files in a safe place

Choose the **Setup menu** and **click Set Up Users** to display the control window:

This user maintenance window lists all users currently set up with the data files. Initially, the only user is sysadmin (system administrator). The highest level of access comes with the sysadmin password that allows the user to enter, use or modify any part of the data files, including the passwords. The sysadmin password must be set before any other passwords can be set, so this user is selected initially. You can set up passwords for many additional users to allow them access to different parts of the program. Begin by adding a password for sysadmin.

Click Modify to open the password entry screen:

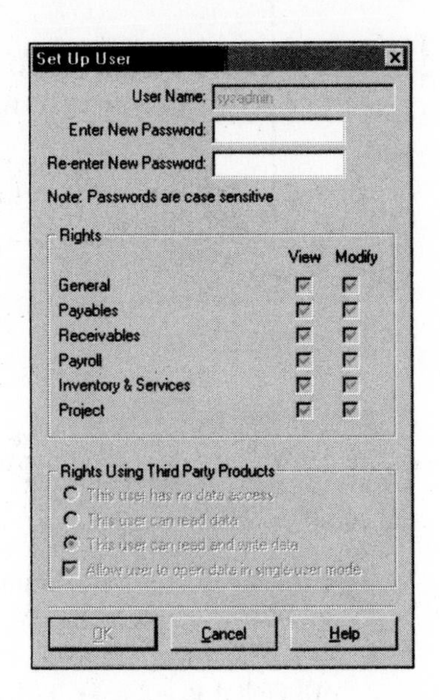

You cannot modify access privileges for the sysadmin because someone (the system administrator) must have full access to the data. All the rights options are dimmed. The cursor is in the Enter New Password field.

Type the word or code that you want as your password. You can use up to seven letters and/or numbers as the code. Passwords are case-sensitive. If you enter a password with an uppercase (capital) letter, you must use an uppercase letter each time.

Press *tab* to advance to the next field, Re-enter New Password. For security reasons, the password never shows on the screen — you will see an asterisk (*) for each letter or number that you typed. As an additional precaution, Simply Accounting requires you to enter the code twice in exactly the same way.

Type the password or code again.

notes

For practice, choose a simple password such as your first name or your initials.

If the two entries do not match, Simply Accounting will warn you that they do not match and you can try re-entering the code again. It is possible that you mistyped the first entry, so if you still do not have a match, go back to the Enter New Password field and type in the code. Then re-enter the password in the Re-enter New Password field.

Click OK when you have entered the code twice. You will return to the Set Up Users - Maintenance screen.

If you return to the Home window now, there will be one password for the data files, the one for sysadmin. You can now set up additional users with passwords.

Click Add User to open the Set Up User screen again:

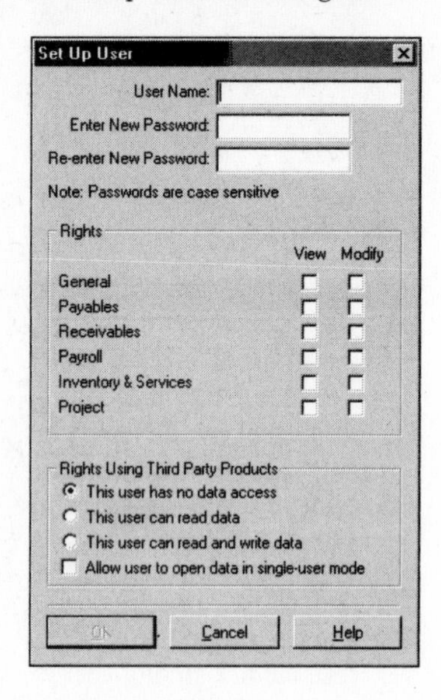

For each ledger, you can allow viewing only, modifying (editing) or no access. Each user may have different access rights. Viewing access permits the users to see the reports and previous entries but not to add to or change information. Editing access allows the user to make journal entries and ledger changes but not to view reports.

Warning!

Restricting access by setting passwords is different from hiding ledgers using the View menu. Since the View menu itself is not restricted, these hidden ledgers can be restored at any time. Ledgers hidden by restricted access passwords can be accessed and restored only by opening the files with the sysadmin password.

Each user must have a unique name and password. The passwords must be different to serve their purpose of restricting access. The cursor is in the User Name field.

Type the name of the first user.

Press tab to advance to the Enter New Password screen.

Type the word or code that you want as your restricted usage password. You can use up to seven letters and/or numbers as the code.

Press tab to advance to the next field, Re-enter New Password.

Type the password or code again.

When the two entries match, you can define access rights for the first user.

To allow access, click the check box beside the ledger in the appropriate column. For example, to allow viewing access only for the General Ledger, click the box beside General in the View column. To allow no access, leave the check boxes empty.

Similarly, you can restrict access to third-party information for each user.

notes

Passwords would not serve their purpose if the user could not view reports in Simply Accounting but could access and modify those reports in another program.

Click OK to save the user information and return to the user maintenance screen.

After you have entered all the users, you can return to the Home window to save all the changes.

Click Close. Nothing has changed yet. However, the next time you open the file, the following dialogue box will appear and you will be required to enter the password before you can display the Home window:

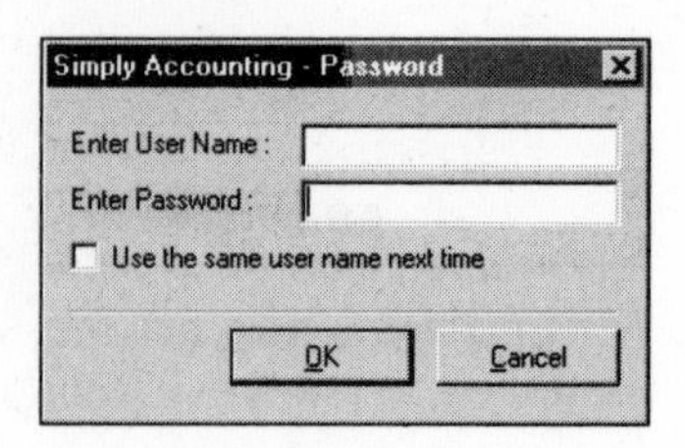

Type the user name, either sysadmin or another user name.

Press tab

Type the password or code for this user.

Click OK

In the Pro Version, the Password screen has the extra option of working in single-user or multi-user mode. The differences are explained below the options, as shown here:

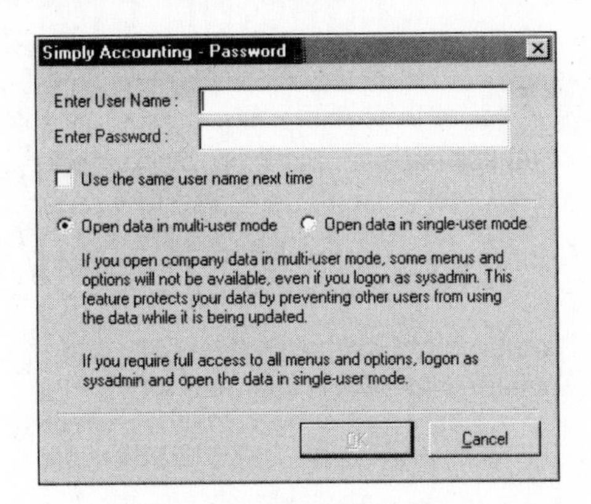

Again, you must type the user name and password to gain access to the data set.

If you enter an incorrect code, nothing happens — the Password dialogue box remains open. If you enter the system password, you will have full access to all parts of the program, including the security settings. If you have set passwords, you must enter the program with the system password in order to change the security settings.

If you enter as a user other than the sysadmin, you will be shown a restricted view of the Home window similar to the following one:

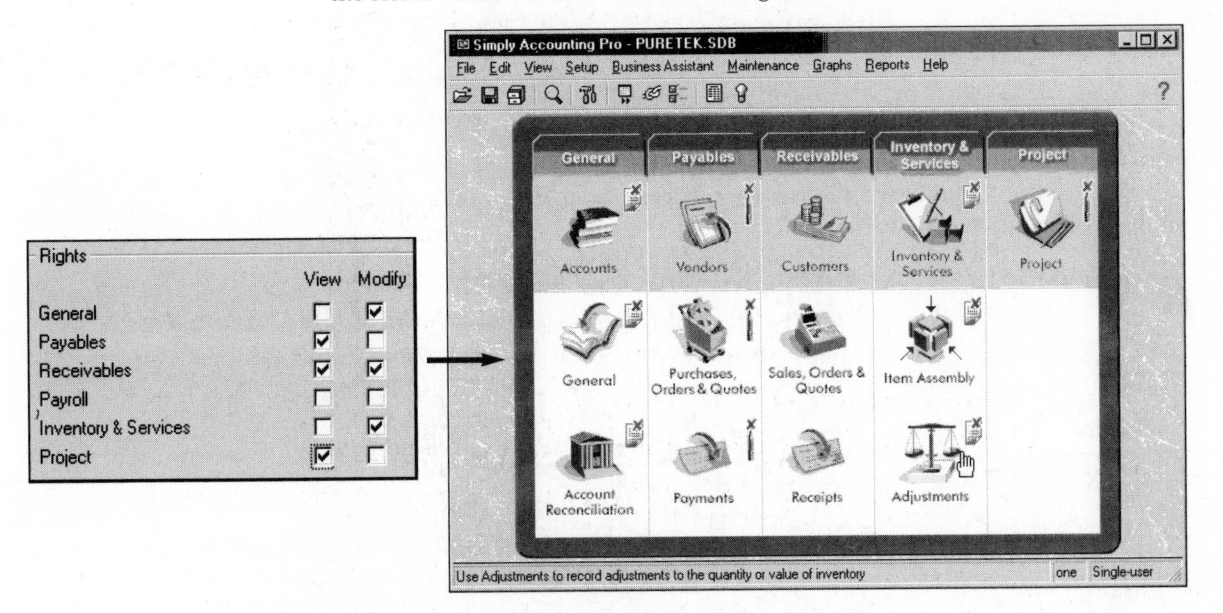

The Home window shown above has restricted access settings. There is no access to the Payroll Ledgers or Journals — these icons do not appear (no checkmarks for the ledger). Full access to the Receivables Ledgers and Journals is available because these icons are shown in their normal manner (checkmarks in View and Modify columns).

The **x** on the report icon, , for the General and Inventory Ledgers shows that they can be edited and accessed for journal entries, but reports cannot be viewed (checkmark only in the Modify column).

The **x** above the pencil icons, , for the Payables and Project Ledgers and Journals shows that they can be viewed but not edited (checkmark only in the View column). Several of the main menu options are also restricted, including the Set Up Users option. Only the sysadmin has access to this menu option after passwords are set.

Changing and Removing Passwords

notes

To change access privileges, choose the User name, then click Modify to see the rights for that user. Click the view and edit check boxes you want. You can also change a user's name.

To change or remove passwords, access the restricted files using the system password. To change a password, access the files as the sysadmin with the correct password.

Choose the **Setup menu** and **click Set Up Users**.

Click the **User's name**.

Click Modify to access the Set Up User screen.

Type a new code or password in the Enter New Password field. Re-enter the same code in the Re-enter New Password field. To change other passwords, select the user whose password you want to change. Click Modify and repeat the step of entering the new code in the two password fields. You can also change access rights by clicking a check box to add a restriction or to remove one if it is already in place.

Click OK and then **click Close** to save the changes and return to the Home window.

You can remove one or more users or all users. To remove a single user, start in the Home window.

Choose the **Setup menu** and **click Set Up Users**.

Click the **User's name**.

Click Remove User to see the warning confirmation message:

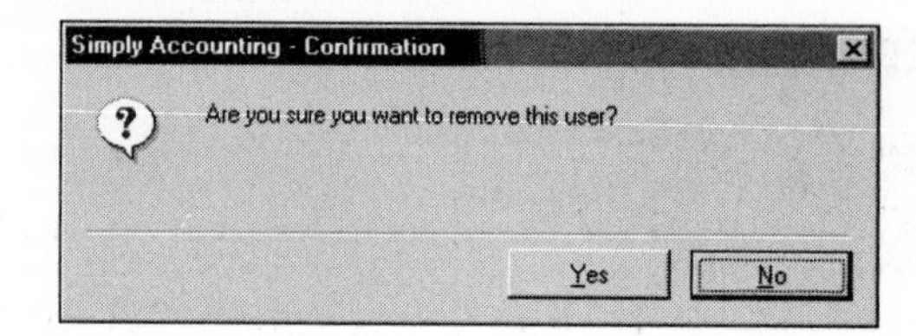

Click Yes to proceed.

You can also remove all passwords and users in a single step from the User Maintenance window.

Click Clear

You will see the warning that all passwords will be removed and all users except the sysadmin will also be removed:

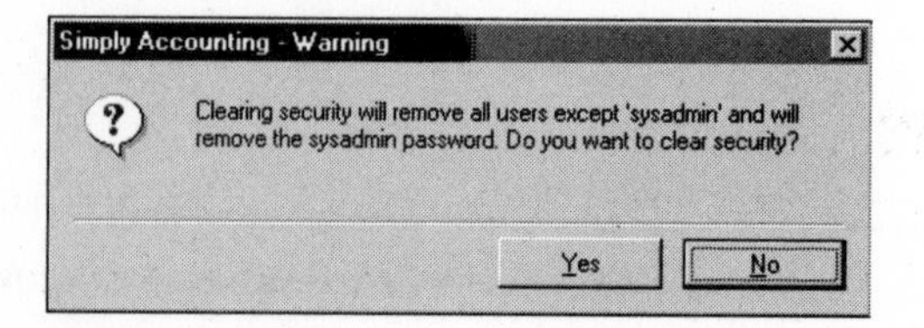

Click Yes to proceed.

Click Close to return to the Home window. You should now be able to access your data files without a password.

APPENDIX C Supplementary Case Problems

CASE ONE

To be completed: after Reliable Roofing
Data used: Reliable Roofing

Complete the following purchase in the General Journal.

❑ Purchase Invoice #ID-67113
Dated July 31, 2003
From InfraRed Diagnostics, $200 for rental of diagnostic equipment, plus $14 GST. Invoice total $214. Terms: net 30 days. Charge to Consultation Expense.

After posting the above transaction, you realize that the expense should be charged to an equipment rental account.

Change the name of the Scaffolding Rentals account to Equipment Rentals and make the corrections necessary to reflect this expense accurately.

Why is it important to make the correction even though the income will not change on the income statement?

CASE TWO

To be completed: after Outset Media

Grandeur Graphics would like to keep track of credit card sales separately from other cash sales without sorting through all the sales invoices manually. Grandeur wants to determine whether to continue to pay the fees attached to the different kinds of cards. How can Grandeur set up the Receivables Ledger to track this information? How and why might she accept credit card payments even if it is relatively more costly than cash?

CASE THREE

To be completed: after Grandeur Graphics

Why might a business choose to set up customer records for all customers, including cash or one-time customers? Do the same arguments apply to setting up vendor records?

CASE FOUR

To be completed: after Grandeur Graphics

The credit limit information in Simply Accounting can be very helpful. Discuss an optimum strategy for setting up customer credit limits so that the program warnings will be helpful.

CASE FIVE

To be completed: after Carnival Catering
Data used: Carnival Catering

Complete a Payroll Journal entry dated July 12 to pay Sylvia Mellon for 50 hours of work.

When you issue the cheque to Mellon, she points out that the number of hours for the two-week period should be 70 hours. Adjust the initial payroll entry. What difference will it make whether you go through the reversing entry (adjust paycheque) procedure or just complete an additional entry for the difference in hours?

CASE SIX

To be completed: after Meteor Mountain Bike Shop

At the end of the season, the Trycykels want to reduce their in-store inventory to a minimum for winter storage. Therefore, they are offering a 10-percent storewide discount and no taxes on the sale price.

Describe the accounting procedures for entering sales transactions for the reduced-price merchandise. Remember that although the customer pays no taxes, the store is still required to pay the sales taxes to the provincial and federal governments.

How would you record these sales in different provinces with their different tax policies? (Refer to Chapter 2 for information about provincial taxes.)

How would discounted sales like this be recorded using the quick method for GST administration?

CASE SEVEN

To be completed: after Meteor Mountain Bike Shop

Meteor Mountain Bike Shop is adding five styles of youth bicycles to its inventory line and wants to set up a separate inventory category for these new bikes. The other youth bikes that are already in the inventory ledger should be part of the new Youth Bike category. Advise the Trycykels on how to make these inventory changes.

CASE EIGHT

To be completed: after Meteor Mountain Bike Shop
Data used: Outset Media

Manga would like to use the Inventory Ledger to record and track sales, both to individual retail customers and to stores (wholesale). He sells the following versions of the game:

- The All Canadian Trivia Board Game (Original Edition — OE)
- The All Canadian Trivia Board Game Junior Edition (JE)
- The All Canadian Trivia Board Game Millennium Edition (ME)
- D'un Océan à l'Autre (French Edition — FE)
- Supplementary Question Set for Original Edition (SQS)

notes

In 2001, Outset Media Corp. had more games than are listed here. Refer to the Web sites, <www.CanadianTrivia.com> and <www.outsetmedia.com>, for additional information about the company and its board games.

Version	Unit Cost	Selling Price	Wholesale Price
OE	$16.50	$39.99/game	$252.00/carton
JE	$15.50	$34.99/game	$242.00/carton
ME	$17.50	$39.99/game	$252.00/carton
FE	$17.50	$39.99/game	$252.00/carton
SQS	$ 9.00	$24.99/game	$132.00/carton

Individual customers usually buy one or two games. Stores buy cartons of 12 games.

Describe the inventory records you would create for Outset Media.

CASE NINE

To be completed: after Meteor Mountain Bike Shop

The Trycykels have expanded their customer base to include some individuals in the United States. In addition they would like to offer preferred prices to some select customers. Modify the inventory ledger records to add these prices. USD prices should be set at 60% of the CAD prices and preferred customers will pay 10% less than the regular prices.

CASE TEN

To be completed: after Bonnie Brides

In the fall, when Brioche is purchasing new gowns for her upcoming busy months, she realizes that several classic style gowns that she has been selling for two years have increased in price since she last purchased them. This means that her own prices will have to increase to maintain her profit margins. She knows that Simply Accounting determines the cost of goods sold on an average cost basis so that the lower-cost gowns still in stock will be combined with the new higher-priced gowns in determining cost. She prefers to use the FIFO (first-in first-out) method to assess the cost of goods sold.

Describe how she can modify her accounts and inventory ledger so that she can use the FIFO cost calculation method.

CASE ELEVEN

To be completed: after Puretek Paving & Stoneworks

At the end of a project in May, 20 percent of the reserved inventory for the project was unused because of last-minute changes in the design of a walkway. Since Simply Accounting allows fractional quantities, the customer was billed for only the inventory materials actually used. This was entered as .80 in the quantity field of the Sales Journal. The remaining 20 percent (quantity .20) should be transferred back to the regular inventory stock. Describe the procedures for making this transfer.

CASE TWELVE

To be completed: after HSC School Store

The school store wants to offer "Be Prepared Student Packs" for its next fall season. These packages would include an assortment of items needed on a day-to-day basis, such as a dictionary, math set, lock, paper, pens, and so on.

Examine the inventory list and develop a strategy for bundling items in this way, including selling price. Describe the procedure for implementing the package offers.

CASE THIRTEEN

To be completed: after HSC School Store
Data used: HSC School Store

During the October sales transactions, the advisory message appeared that some inventory items had fallen below the re-order point. Export the appropriate inventory report (for the end of October) to a spreadsheet program so that you can prepare order information. Print a list of all items that have fallen below the minimum stock level. Print another list of all items that are very close to the minimum level and that should be re-ordered soon.

CASE FOURTEEN

To be completed: after Hearth House
Data used: Java Jean's

Java Jean's currently uses only the Payables and General Ledgers because all sales are cash and payroll is looked after by the bank.

Set up the Receivables Ledger for Java Jean's. Can this be done without having any customer names? How? What will be the advantages for the Emporium to using the Receivables Ledger? (In other words, is it worth the time that it would take to do this?)

Next, set up the Payroll Ledger for four part-time employees. Use yourself and three people you know as the employees to provide the information required, including deduction amounts.

CASE FIFTEEN

To be completed: after Hearth House

Hearth House has set up users with passwords for access to its computer accounting records. Wanting to maintain the confidentiality of their payroll records, they have one sysadmin password and one password that allows access to all parts of the system except payroll. This second password therefore permits access to all the accounting information for entering the day-to-day business transactions.

One day, the employee in charge of payroll, the system administrator — the only person with the system-level password who could access the payroll journal and ledger — suddenly became seriously ill and was unable to complete the payroll or even to give the password to someone else.

Now that this situation already exists, is there any way to overcome the problem in order to complete the immediate payroll (pay the staff), prepare year-end T4s and submit the payroll deductions to the Receiver General? What precautions should be in place to prevent a situation like this from disrupting a business? It could have just as easily been the Sales Journal that was inoperative. (Have you ever gone into a bank and been told that there was nothing they could do for you because the computer system was down?)

CASE SIXTEEN

To be completed: after HSC School Store
Data used: Hearth House

1. Use the December 31 backup data files, after completing all the source document transactions and before advancing the session date to the new fiscal year. Make a new working copy of the data files before proceeding.
2. Complete a reversing entry for three months of bank charges and interest (December 30) so that these amounts can be entered on a monthly basis in the Account Reconciliation Journal. (Hint: debit *Interest Revenue* $372, credit *Bank Charges & Card Fees* $75, credit *Bank Account: Chequing* $297. We will skip the adjustment for the *Interest Receivable* portion.)
3. Create a new Group account, *5025 Reconciliation Adjustments.*
4. Use the following names and linked accounts for all bank accounts:
   - Income: Interest *4100 Interest Revenue*
   - Expense: Bk Charges *5020 Bank Charges & Card Fees*
   - Adjustment: Adjustment *5025 Reconciliation Adjustments*

   For all accounts, all transactions are outstanding for the setup stage.
5. a) Set up *1060 Bank Account: Chequing* for account reconciliation. The ending bank account balance from the last reconciled statement is $39 670.10.

   b) Set up *1080 Bank Account: Credit Card* for account reconciliation. The ending bank account balance from the last reconciled statement is $150.00.

   c) Set up *1090 Bank: Foreign Funds GBP* for account reconciliation. The ending bank account balance from the last reconciled statement is £245.00.

notes

Refer to the keystrokes beginning on page 505 for assistance with the account reconciliation setup and process.

6. The October, November and December bank statements for Hearth House follow. Using the Account Reconciliation Journal, reconcile the bank statements, one month at a time. For each month, use the statement date as the end date and show only the transactions on or before the statement date.

7. Print the Reconciliation Summary Reports for all three bank accounts for October 31, November 30 and December 31.

Royal Bank Transit #55442
10000 Richest Way
Toronto, Ontario M4Y 3F4

Account # 44 389 388 (Chequing)
Hearth House
44 Warmley Road
Toronto, Ontario M6R 2P6

Statement Date: October 31, 2003

Date	Transaction	Deposits	Withdrawals	Balance
09-30-03	Balance Fwd.			39,670.10
10-03-03	Deposit	2,049.30		41,719.40
10-03-03	Transfer		4,484.20	37,235.20
10-07-03	Deposit	3,680.00		40,915.20
10-09-03	300		1,761.65	39,153.55
10-11-03	301		2,140.00	37,013.55
10-13-03	Deposit	6,210.00		43,223.55
10-15-03	302		172.50	43,051.05
10-15-03	303		1,036.13	42,014.92
10-17-03	Deposit	13,388.76		55,403.68
10-17-03	305		1,283.05	54,120.63
10-19-03	304		428.00	53,692.63
10-21-03	306		1,680.00	52,012.63
10-21-03	307		2,696.27	49,316.36
10-20-03	308		324.38	48,991.98
10-22-03	309		4,560.00	44,431.98
10-19-03	310		450.00	43,981.98
10-19-03	311		450.00	43,531.98
10-19-03	312		35.00	43,496.98
10-22-03	Deposit	18,653.00		62,149.98
10-23-03	313		889.52	61,260.46
10-23-03	314		117.70	61,142.76
10-24-03	315		92.00	61,050.76
10-24-03	316		162.00	60,888.76
10-25-03	Deposit	14,196.75		75,085.51
10-30-03	Mortgage		2,500.00	72,585.51
10-30-03	Loan payment		2,400.00	70,185.51
10-30-03	317		353.47	69,832.04
10-31-03	318		250.00	69,582.04
10-31-03	Interest	88.00		69,670.04
10-31-03	Service Fee		15.00	69,655.04
10-31-03	Closing Balance			69,655.04
Total Deposits		58,265.81		
Total Withdrawals			28,280.87	

notes

- Two group deposits were made: on Oct. 22 for $18 653 (8 395 + 6 497.50 + 3 760.50) and on Oct. 25 for $14 196.75 (9 941.75 + 4 255).
- Your payroll cheque or payroll remittance amounts may be different from the ones shown on these bank statements if you are using a different version of the program with different tax tables. Accept these differences as reconciliation adjustments. As described in Chapter 8, Version 8.0 will have different paycheque amounts.

notes

There is one group deposit on Nov. 24 for $16 445 (7 072.50 + 5 117.50 + 4 255).

Royal Bank
10000 Richest Way
Toronto, Ontario M4Y 3F4

Transit #55442

Account # 44 389 388 (Chequing)
Hearth House
44 Warmley Road
Toronto, Ontario M6R 2P6

Statement Date: November 30, 2003

Date	Transaction	Deposits	Withdrawals	Balance
10-31-03	Balance Fwd.			69,655.04
11-02-03	321		1,073.46	68,581.58
11-02-03	322		321.00	68,260.58
11-02-03	323		100.00	68,160.58
11-02-03	324		3,109.62	65,050.96
11-02-03	325		1,033.05	64,017.91
11-07-03	Transfer		11,245.00	52,772.91
11-10-03	326		5,917.10	46,855.81
11-11-03	Deposit	11,084.16		57,939.97
11-13-03	327		1,136.13	56,803.84
11-13-03	328		1,589.08	55,214.76
11-15-03	Transfer		11,272.00	43,942.76
11-15-03	Deposit	3,335.00		47,277.76
11-16-03	330		1,033.05	46,244.71
11-16-03	329		2,359.35	43,885.36
11-18-03	334		400.00	43,485.36
11-18-03	335		400.00	43,085.36
11-19-03	336		30.00	43,055.36
11-21-03	337		3,274.20	39,781.16
11-21-03	338		3,659.40	36,121.76
11-21-03	339		92.00	36,029.76
11-23-03	333		4,674.38	31,355.38
11-24-03	Deposit	16,445.00		47,800.38
11-24-03	331		2,422.59	45,377.79
11-21-03	340		107.00	45,270.79
11-24-03	332		2,738.54	42,532.25
11-26-03	342		1,002.21	41,530.04
11-26-03	341		460.00	41,070.04
11-29-03	344		287.50	40,782.54
11-29-03	343		431.17	40,351.37
11-30-03	Loan payment		2,400.00	37,951.37
11-30-03	Mortgage		2,500.00	35,451.37
11-30-03	Interest	72.00		35,523.37
11-30-03	Service Fees		15.00	35,508.37
11-30-03	Closing Balance			35,508.37
Total Deposits		30,936.16		
Total Withdrawals			65,082.83	

Royal Bank Transit #55442
10000 Richest Way
Toronto, Ontario M4Y 3F4

Account # 44 389 388 (Chequing)
Hearth House
44 Warmley Road
Toronto, Ontario M6R 2P6

Statement Date: December 31, 2003

Date	Transaction	Deposits	Withdrawals	Balance
11-30-03	Balance Fwd.			35,508.37
12-02-03	319		250.00	35,258.37
12-02-03	345		14.46	35,243.91
12-02-03	347		1,033.05	34,210.86
12-02-03	346		3,276.12	30,934.74
12-03-03	348		374.50	30,560.24
12-05-03	349		2,311.20	28,249.04
12-05-03	350		1,150.00	27,099.04
12-06-03	Transfer		5,655.00	21,444.04
12-08-03	Deposit	19,905.35		41,349.39
12-10-03	351		1,272.13	40,077.26
12-11-03	352		1,002.21	39,075.05
12-14-03	Deposit	10,166.00		49,241.05
12-13-03	353		4,622.40	44,618.65
12-14-03	Deposit	12,563.75		57,182.40
12-16-03	354		1,033.05	56,149.35
12-17-03	355		7,500.00	48,649.35
12-18-03	Deposit	15,641.15		64,290.50
12-18-03	361		30.00	64,260.50
12-19-03	Transfer		6,774.00	57,486.50
12-19-03	359		400.00	57,086.50
12-19-03	360		400.00	56,686.50
12-19-03	363		3,274.20	53,412.30
12-20-03	356		1,818.12	51,594.18
12-20-03	357		3,028.84	48,565.34
12-20-03	358		4,562.28	44,003.06
12-20-03	362		13,375.00	30,628.06
12-21-03	364		81.07	30,546.99
12-21-03	365		2,696.40	27,850.59
12-21-03	366		287.50	27,563.09
12-22-03	Deposit	115.00		27,678.09
12-22-03	367		504.51	27,173.58
12-23-03	Deposit	3,507.50		30,681.08
12-23-03	373		540.00	30,141.08
12-23-03	374		90.00	30,051.08
12-23-03	375		1,171.78	28,879.30
12-23-03	376		1,139.69	27,739.61
12-24-03	Deposit	3,082.00		30,821.61
12-24-03	369		103.50	30,718.11
12-24-03	368		117.70	30,600.41
12-24-03	370		390.50	30,209.91
12-24-03	371		720.00	29,489.91
12-24-03	372		450.00	29,039.91
12-29-03	NSF		115.00	28,924.91
12-29-03	319		250.00	28,674.91
12-30-03	Loan payment		2,400.00	26,274.91
12-30-03	Mortgage		2,500.00	23,774.91
12-30-03	Interest	52.00		23,826.91
12-30-03	Service Fees		45.00	23,781.91
12-31-03	Transfer	50,000.00		73,781.91
2003-12-31	Closing Balance			73,781.91
Total Deposits		115,032.75		
Total Withdrawals			76,759.21	

notes

- Remember to mark the deposit on Dec. 23 for $115 as NSF, and then mark the reversing entry on Dec. 28 as an Adjustment.
- There is one group deposit on Dec. 8 for $19 905.35 (12 563.75 + 7 341.60).

notes

This bank statement is for the Bank Account: Credit Card account.

Royal Bank
10000 Richest Way
Toronto, Ontario M4Y 3F4

Transit #55442

Account # 502 764 647 (VISA)
Hearth House
44 Warmley Road
Toronto, Ontario M6R 2P6

Statement Date: October 31, 2003

Date	Transaction	Deposits	Withdrawals	Balance
09-30-03	Balance Fwd.			150.00
10-02-03	Deposit	1,831.09		1,981.09
10-03-03	Deposit	3,051.81		5,032.90
10-17-03	Deposit	4,439.00		9,471.90
10-28-03	Deposit	5,326.80		14,798.70
10-29-03	Deposit	2,863.15		17,661.85
10-31-03	Interest	22.00		17,683.85
10-31-03	Closing Balance			17,683.85
Total Deposits		17,533.85		
Total Withdrawals			0.00	

Statement Date: November 30, 2003

Date	Transaction	Deposits	Withdrawals	Balance
10-31-03	Balance Fwd.			17,683.85
11-02-03	Deposit	2,208.40		19,892.25
11-03-03	Deposit	6,802.77		26,695.02
11-22-03	Deposit	4,161.56		30,856.58
11-26-03	Deposit	6,214.60		37,071.18
11-30-03	Interest	46.00		37,117.18
11-30-03	Closing Balance			37,117.18
Total Deposits		19,433.33		
Total Withdrawals			0.00	

Statement Date: December 31, 2003

Date	Transaction	Deposits	Withdrawals	Balance
11-30-03	Balance Fwd.			37,117.18
12-01-03	Deposit	5,881.67		42,998.85
12-16-03	Deposit	3,662.17		46,661.02
12-18-03	Deposit	7,102.40		53,763.42
12-20-03	Deposit	5,937.16		59,700.58
12-31-03	Transfer		50,000.00	9,700.58
12-31-03	Interest	86.00		9,786.58
11-30-03	Closing Balance			9,786.58
Total Deposits		22,669.40		
Total Withdrawals			50,000.00	

notes

Use the following exchange rates for the interest deposits

Oct. 31 – 2.27
Nov. 30 – 2.26
Dec. 31 – 2.258

Royal Bank
10000 Richest Way
Toronto, Ontario M4Y 3F4

Transit #55442

Account # 11-7753-652 (GBP)
Hearth House
44 Warmley Road
Toronto, Ontario M6R 2P6

Statement Date: October 31, 2003

All amounts in British pounds (£)

Date	Transaction	Deposits	Withdrawals	Balance
09-30-03	Balance Fwd.			245.00
10-03-03	Transfer	2,000.00		2,245.00
10-08-03	125		1,852.20	392.80
10-31-03	126		315.00	77.80
10-31-03	Interest	2.00		79.80
10-31-03	Closing Balance			79.80
Total Deposits		2,002.00		
Total Withdrawals			2,167.20	

Statement Date: November 30, 2003

Date	Transaction	Deposits	Withdrawals	Balance
10-31-03	Balance Fwd.			79.80
11-07-03	Transfer	5,000.00		5,079.80
11-11-03	127		4,000.41	1,079.39
11-15-03	Transfer	5,000.00		6,079.39
11-19-03	128		3,250.66	2,828.73
11-24-03	129		2,461.00	367.73
11-30-03	Interest	6.00		373.73
11-30-03	Closing Balance			373.73
Total Deposits		10,006.00		
Total Withdrawals			9,712.07	

Statement Date: December 31, 2003

Date	Transaction	Deposits	Withdrawals	Balance
11-30-03	Balance Fwd.			373.73
12-06-03	Transfer	2,500.00		2,873.73
12-11-03	130		2,296.43	577.30
12-19-03	Transfer	3,000.00		3,577.30
12-24-03	131		2,685.70	891.60
12-31-03	Interest	8.00		899.60
11-30-03	Closing Balance			899.60
Total Deposits		5,508.00		
Total Withdrawals			4,982.13	

APPENDIX D

Integration with Other Software

EXPORTING DATA AND REPORTS

Simply Accounting includes a large number and variety of reports and graphs as part of the standard package. However, there may still be times when you want to work with the financial data of your company in ways that cannot be accommodated by the accounting software. Simply Accounting allows any report or graph that you can display to be exported to other kinds of software. Exporting is the ability to transfer information from one software application to another. These exported reports may then be used with a spreadsheet or wordprocessing application.

Simply Accounting allows files to be exported to the file and folder you specify. Exporting report files to other software applications allows you to perform additional calculations and interpret reports for management decision making. Thus, integration is an important step in making the accounting process meaningful.

Integrated files can be used by businesses in several different ways as decision support tools. They include sales forecasting, determining implications of new taxes and tax increases and ratio analysis of financial statements. Reports gathered from Simply Accounting and spreadsheet applications can be brought together in a wordprocessing or presentation package to prepare comprehensive final documents.

Exporting Reports from a Display

Any report that you can display and print, you can also export to another software application. The procedure for exporting displayed reports was described in Chapter 13, page 468.

Exporting Data to MS Access

You can export reports to Microsoft Excel or you can export other parts of your data set directly to a Microsoft Access database. Since you do not have to choose a report, you can export a wide range of data in this way. To begin the export to MS Access,

version 8

Choose the **File menu** in the Home window, then **choose Import/Export** and **click Export to Microsoft Access**.

The introductory wizard window appears:

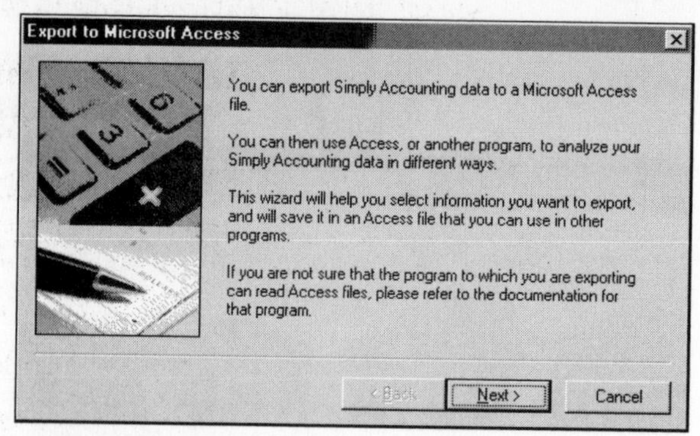

Click Next to proceed:

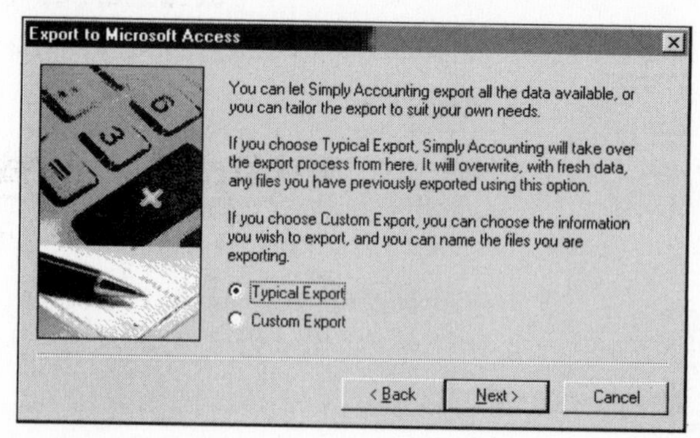

At this stage, you can choose whether to export the entire data set (Typical Export) or only the parts that you select. The custom export option will display all the data elements from which you may choose for the MS Access file. You can select one or more or all the data from the file, and you can change the name of the exported file. The wizard guides you through the steps of making these selections.

Leave the typical export option selected.

Click Next to continue:

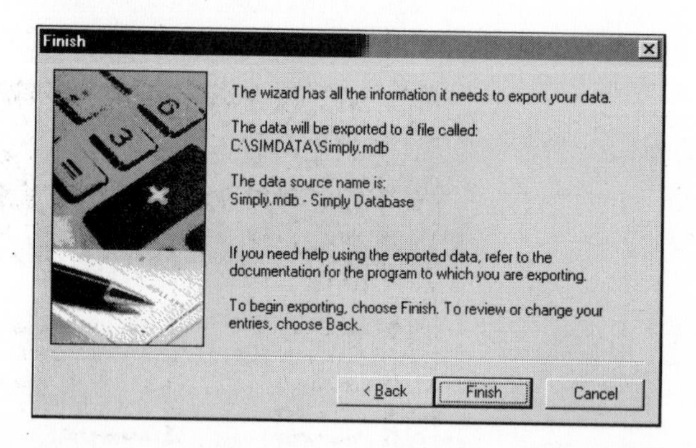

The file name and location are displayed for your reference.

Click Finish to begin exporting the file. The Home window reappears when the file is completed.

Close the Simply Accounting program.

Open the **Microsoft Access program** and open the file you just created (C:\SIMDATA\Simply.mdb).

If your version of Access is newer than the one used to create the database, you will see the following screen offering to convert the file:

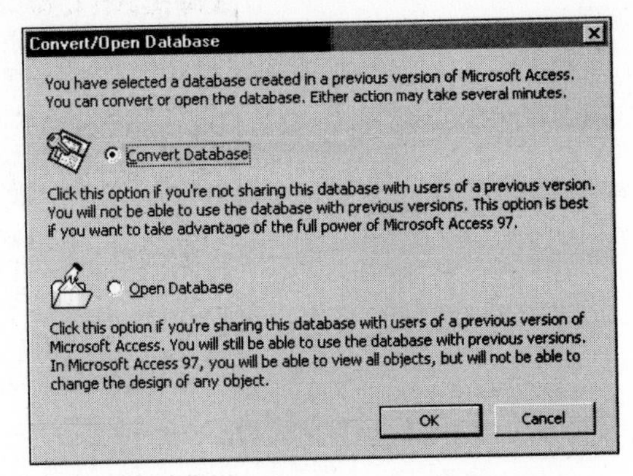

You should convert (update) the database, the default selection.

Click OK

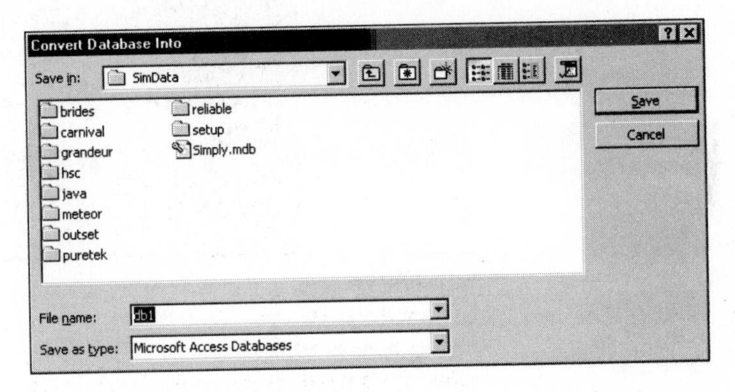

Type `Simply1` (in the highlighted File name field. You must use a different name from the original file name.)

Click Save

You will see the parts of the database that you can now modify as needed:

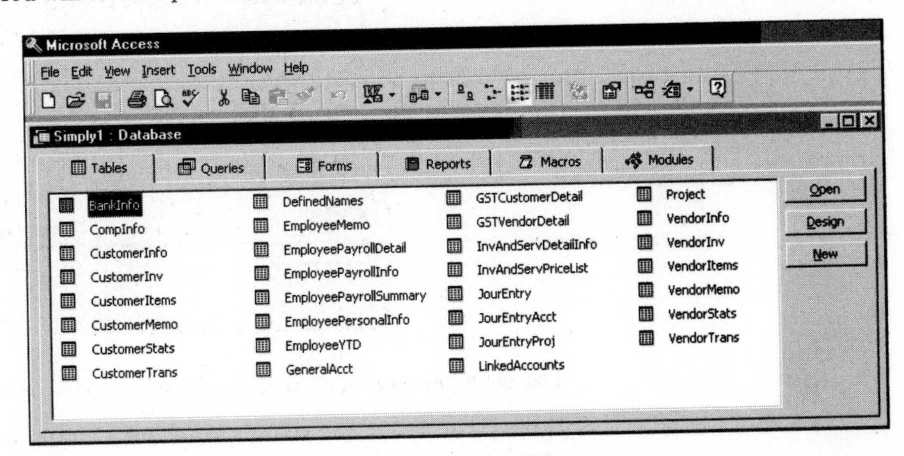

Data from all the ledgers are included, as well as budget details and data for the previous year, if these are part of your data files.

notes

Once you are in the MS Access program, you have full MS Access database-modifying and report-generating capabilities.

Click JourEntry and **click Open** to see the journal report in table format (Puretek is illustrated without the project allocations):

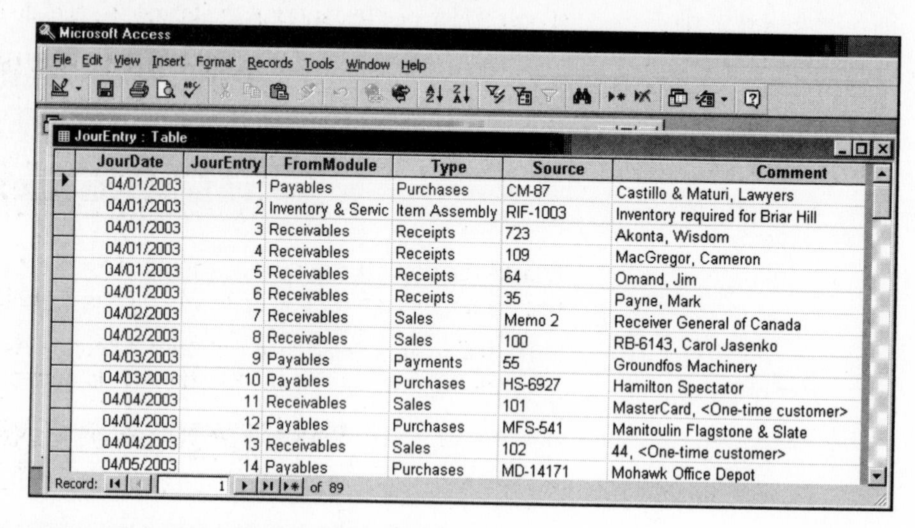

Microsoft Access — JourEntry : Table

JourDate	JourEntry	FromModule	Type	Source	Comment
04/01/2003	1	Payables	Purchases	CM-87	Castillo & Maturi, Lawyers
04/01/2003	2	Inventory & Servic	Item Assembly	RIF-1003	Inventory required for Briar Hill
04/01/2003	3	Receivables	Receipts	723	Akonta, Wisdom
04/01/2003	4	Receivables	Receipts	109	MacGregor, Cameron
04/01/2003	5	Receivables	Receipts	64	Omand, Jim
04/01/2003	6	Receivables	Receipts	35	Payne, Mark
04/02/2003	7	Receivables	Sales	Memo 2	Receiver General of Canada
04/02/2003	8	Receivables	Sales	100	RB-6143, Carol Jasenko
04/03/2003	9	Payables	Payments	55	Groundfos Machinery
04/03/2003	10	Payables	Purchases	HS-6927	Hamilton Spectator
04/04/2003	11	Receivables	Sales	101	MasterCard, <One-time customer>
04/04/2003	12	Payables	Purchases	MFS-541	Manitoulin Flagstone & Slate
04/04/2003	13	Receivables	Sales	102	44, <One-time customer>
04/05/2003	14	Payables	Purchases	MD-14171	Mohawk Office Depot

Record: 1 of 89

Close the database files and MS Access when you have finished.

Warning!

You must enter GIFI codes in all General Ledger account records before attempting to export GIFI reports. If you do not, you will see error messages when you export the data.

Exporting GIFI Reports

When you add the GIFI (General Index of Financial Information) codes to the General Ledger account records, you can export financial statements that use these codes to organize the reports. These are the account numbers or codes required for businesses filing their tax returns electronically with Canada Customs and Revenue Agency. You can obtain more information about GIFI from the CCRA Web site at <www.ccra-adrc.gc.ca>.

The following chart shows the GIFI codes that correspond to some of the accounts for Hearth House:

HEARTH HOUSE ACCOUNTS	GIFI ACCOUNT CODES
Assets	
1080 Cash in Bank	1000 Cash and deposits
1200 Accounts Receivable	1060 Accounts Receivable
1300 Prepaid Insurance	1484 Prepaid Expenses
1510 Computers	1774 Computer equipment/software
1520 Accum Deprec: Computer	1775 Accumulated amortization of Computer equipment/software
1530 Installation Equipment	1740 Machinery, equipment, furniture and fixtures
1550 Accum Deprec: Install Equip	1741 Accumulated Amortization of machinery equipment, furniture & fixtures
Liabilities	
2200 Accounts Payable	2621 Trade payables
2650 GST Charged on Services	2680 Taxes payable
2670 GST Paid on Purchases	2680 Taxes payable
2850 Mortgage Payable	3141 Mortgages
Equity	
3100 AA, Capital	3600 Retained earnings/deficit
3600 Current Earnings	3680 Net Income/loss
Revenue	
4020 Revenue from Sales	8000 Trade sales of goods and services (net of discounts, returns, etc.)
Expense	
5050 Cost of Goods Sold	8320 Cost of Purchases (net of discounts)
5180 Hydro Expense	8812 Office Utilities (or 9221 Electricity)
5200 Maintenance and Repairs	8961 Repairs and maintenance - buildings
5300 Wages	8320 Direct wages (included in cost of sales)

Choose the **File menu** in the Home window then **choose Import/Export** and **click Export GIFI**. If you have data for the current and the previous fiscal period, you may choose which one to export in the following dialogue box:

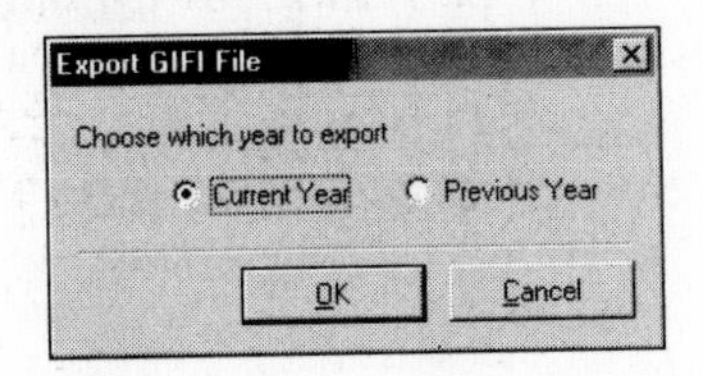

Choose the data set you want to export: the current year or the previous fiscal year. Usually tax returns are prepared after a fiscal year has ended.

Click OK to open the Export Selection screen. If you have only data for the current year, you will see the Export Selection window directly when you choose Export GIFI:

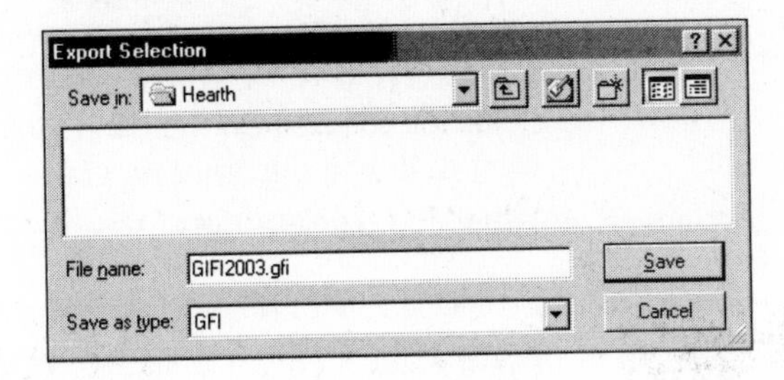

At this stage, you can rename the exported file and choose a destination folder. You should not change the file extension because it indicates the required format for this database.

Click Save to save the file and return to the Home window.

You can now open the newly created data file with a database program and print the report, or send the file electronically directly to Canada Customs and Revenue Agency.

DDE (Dynamic Data Exchange)

All the exported reports described so far provide a single or static file that you can integrate with other software programs. DDE interacts dynamically or interactively with your data files, as the name suggests. As you make changes in Simply Accounting by entering transactions or changing records, the corresponding information in the linked file in the other program is also updated with the current information.

Data from each ledger must be exported separately, although you can easily combine information from two ledgers into a single external file by repeating the DDE selection process. We will add a list of vendors and the balance owing, to a WordPerfect file.

Choose the **Edit menu** in the Home window, then **choose DDE** and **click Vendors** to see the data selection screen:

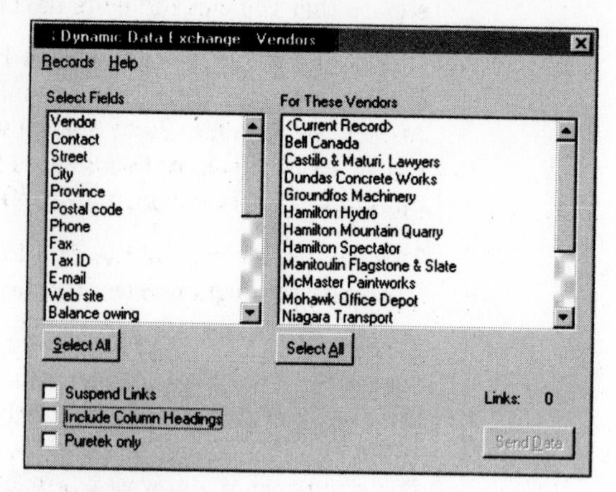

The data to be selected include a set of fields and records. You can select one or more fields for one or more vendors. First, select the fields, the kind of information you want to link to the other program.

Click Vendor in the Select Fields list.

Press ctrl and **click Balance owing** in the Select Fields list.

Click Select All below the For These Vendors list to include all vendors. You can include only one or several of the vendor names individually.

There are three options in the DDE screen.

Click Suspend Links. With this option, Simply Accounting will not update the linked program references until you have finished entering transactions. This speeds up the processing of data because the linked program is not updated continually as you work. Continual updating would have some pieces of information changed more than once in a work session because the link is dynamic, rather like the automatic re-calculation in spreadsheets. If you have a large amount of data, frequent updating can slow down the program.

Click Include Column Headings to add column headings to the data, making it easier to distinguish fields of information that may look similar.

Click Puretek only (your own file name will be substituted for Puretek). If you have data for more than one company, you should include only the current file — the one that is open — in the DDE linkage. This will prevent the DDE link from updating references to other company files that you may have created elsewhere.

Click Send Data. After a brief delay, you will see the confirmation message:

The message advises you of the size of the data table you are linking. The one we selected contains all vendors in Column One with the balance owing to each vendor in Column Two.

Click OK to close the message and return to the DDE screen.

Close the DDE window.

Open the **WordPerfect** program (or another Windows wordprocessing program). You may want to leave the Simply Accounting program open in the background for this step so that you can add more data links.

Choose the **Edit menu** and **click Paste Special** (or Paste Link). Do not use the Paste command as this will copy only the contents and not the link with the Simply Accounting data file. Paste Special will maintain the link. You may see an intermediate screen advising you of the format of the data you are pasting. **Choose Paste Link** at this stage if this is an option. **Click OK** (or the appropriate command button) to continue.

This will place a copy of the data from the Simply Accounting program into your WordPerfect program. Save this file when you have finished working with it.

Now when you add a new purchase invoice or make a payment to one of these vendors, the WordPerfect file will also remain current. If you add a new vendor, however, you must repeat the DDE procedure for the new vendor to add the new link. (From the DDE screen in Simply Accounting, choose the Vendor and Balance Owing fields and click the new vendor name. Click Send Data. Start WordPerfect and open the data file that contains the previous vendor information. Place the cursor in the WordPerfect file where you want to add the new vendor. Choose Edit and Paste Special and then Paste Link.)

Although a link may contain several fields and several records, each link will be treated as a single block of information. It is generally easier to manage the linked data if each link contains one piece of information. It may take longer to set up, but the end result is a more flexible file.

Although DDE takes more effort than exporting a report, you need to complete the setup only once and your end document will contain current information automatically whenever you need it. In addition, with DDE you can combine information from different ledgers or reports into a single document. For example, you can create form letters advising employees of their payroll deduction amounts, or send a letter to all customers including an inventory list containing only item names and prices.

Importing Data

The other half of integration with other software programs involves bringing data into Simply Accounting. Some of these connections — Web linkages to vendor and customer sites, e-mail capabilities for sales quotes and purchase orders and tracking of shipments — were introduced in Chapter 7.

Importing Bank Statements

When you import online bank statements into Simply Accounting by downloading from your financial institution's Web site, Simply Accounting automates the matching and clearing process. Simply Accounting changes the status of matched transactions to Cleared in the Account Reconciliation window by using the source number (such as the cheque number) and the amount to match transactions on your downloaded statement with transactions in your Simply Accounting records.

To import online statements, you must set up your bank account to use online banking on the Class Options tab screen in the account's ledger record.

Open the **ledger record for the bank account**.

notes

Your bank must be able to download statements in OFX (Open Financial Exchange) format, the file format used by Simply Accounting. Not all financial institutions supported this format at the time of writing this text.

notes

If your bank requires you to enter a unique identifier instead of the bank's transit number in the Transit Number field, you can include the transit number at the beginning of the Account Number field. Contact your bank for more information.

Click the **Class Options tab** to access the bank information as shown:

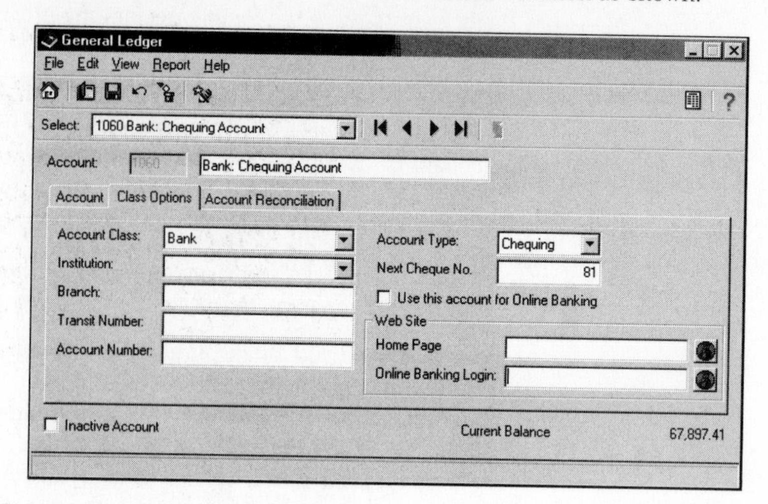

Choose your bank from the Institution list.

Type the Branch, Transit Number and bank Account Number in the appropriate files.

Click Use this account for Online Banking

Type the bank's Web site address and login information.

Close the ledger and Accounts windows to return to the Home window.

Choose the **File menu**, then **choose Import/Export** and **click Import Online Statements** to begin the downloading procedure:

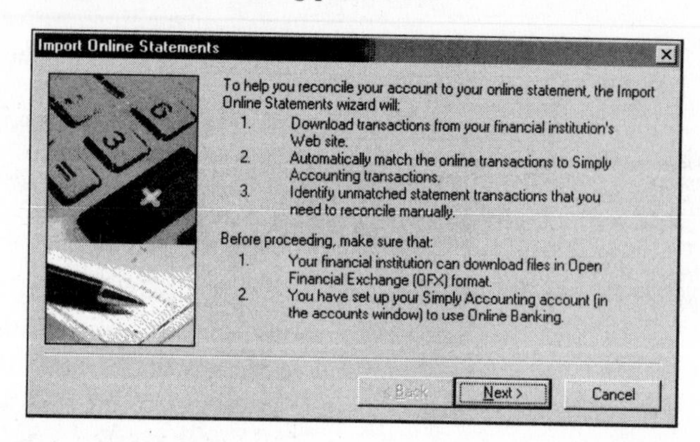

The opening screen advises you of what the program will do and the information you need to obtain.

Click Next

The following screen asks if you have previously downloaded statements:

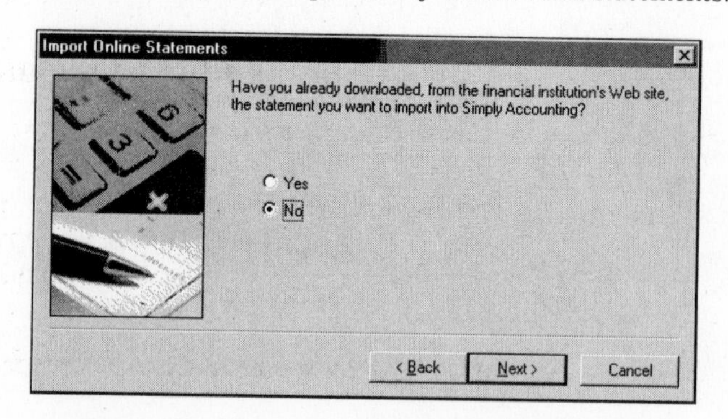

Click No if this is the first download.

Click Next to proceed to the Web connecting screen:

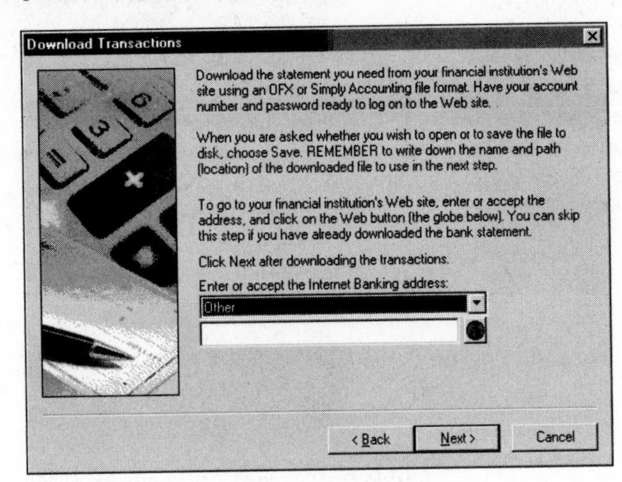

On this screen, you must enter the bank name and its Web address. The drop-down list includes some banks, and their Web sites will be added automatically.

Enter the necessary details.

Click the **Web tool** to access the bank's Web site. Remember that if you have a network connection for your Internet access, you must open your Internet connection before clicking the Web tool. After downloading your statements,

Click Next

The following screen asks for the location of the files you have just downloaded:

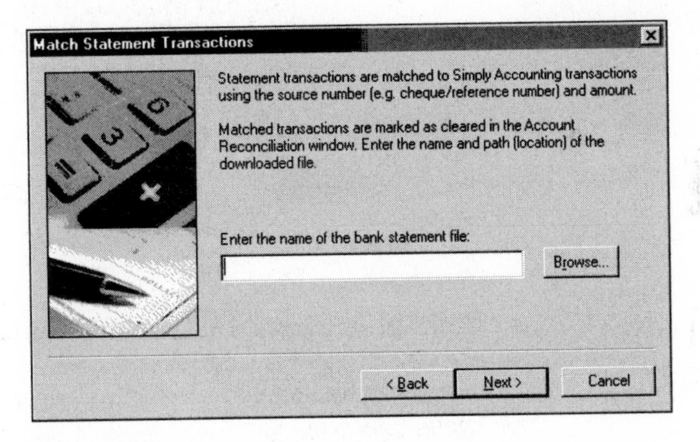

Choose the **file** that contains the downloaded information.

Click Next and follow the steps outlined in each screen to continue.

Importing Vendor and Customer Transactions

Vendors and Customers can e-mail you their sales invoices, sales quotes or purchase orders. When you import these transactions directly into Simply Accounting, your records are updated automatically. You can recall the imported quote or order to fill it. Similarly, you can e-mail (export) purchase orders, sales invoices or sales quotes to vendors and customers. First you should enter the Import/Export tab information in the vendor/customer record.

notes

Because the procedure for setting up and working with vendor and customer importing/exporting information is the same, we will show only vendor information.

Open the **ledger record** for the vendor (or customer) you want to e-mail.

notes

- Both you and your vendors or customers must use Simply Accounting Version 7 or later and have MAPI-compatible e-mail programs (such as Lotus Domino or Microsoft Outlook Express) to use this feature.
- Your vendor or customer must also identify you in their records as a Simply Accounting user.

Click the **Import/Export tab** to open this information screen:

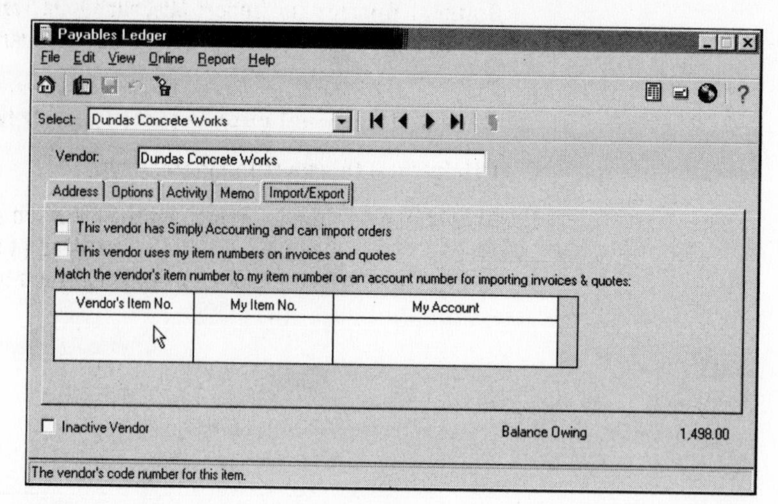

Click This vendor (or customer) has Simply Accounting and can import orders

If you and the vendor use the same inventory item numbers, click this option. The inventory matching boxes will be removed from the screen because they are not needed. If you do not use the same numbers, you can enter the matching information item by item. You may also do the matching when you import the transaction.

notes

A sales invoice or sales quote from a vendor becomes a purchase invoice or purchase quote, respectively. A purchase order from a customer becomes a sales order when imported.

Close the ledger window and the Vendors (Customers) window.

Exit the **Simply Accounting program** before you attempt to import a form.

Open your **e-mail program**.

Open the **e-mail message** containing the Simply Accounting attachment. Then either

notes

If the vendor or customer does not exist in your system, choose to Add a new record to your company files.

Save the **attached IMP file for later use**

Or, **double click** the **IMP file** to use it immediately.

Choose to **Open the file** rather than to save it.

Enter the **name** (including the path or location) of your company file, or click Browse to select your company file.

Click OK

Open the transaction window for the transaction you imported. Use the Invoice Lookup feature to display the invoice, order or quote. Correct the details if necessary. Inform your vendor or customer if you make any changes. Proceed just as you do for other Simply Accounting transactions.

Importing General Journal Transactions

Simply Accounting can also import General Journal transactions (Miscellaneous Transactions) from another program, such as a spreadsheet program. However, there are some limitations. You can import only transactions that you would normally enter in the General Journal. No linked Accounts Receivable, Accounts Payable, Payroll Advances, Vacation Payable or Inventory accounts may be used in the transactions after you have finished entering the history. Other modules are not updated as a result of the imported transactions. The file must be in text format and the data must be organized in a very specific order and format. Refer to the Simply Accounting Help topic **Importing miscellaneous transactions** for details about the required text format.

Begin importing the transactions from the Simply Accounting Home window.

Choose the **File menu**, then **choose Import/Export** and **click Import General Journal Entries** (or Import Miscellaneous Transactions if you are using non-accounting terms). An open file window appears for you to choose the file from which to import the transactions.

Choose the **journal entries text file**. Only text files are listed in this window.

Click Open to import the journal entries.

Simply Accounting will report on the errors in the format of the text files, if there are any, so that you can correct them and attempt the import again. The imported transactions will be included in your journal reports.

APPENDIX E Non-Accounting Terms

ACCOUNTING VS. NON-ACCOUNTING TERMS

We have chosen to use the accounting terms in this workbook because they are familiar to students of accounting, and because we needed to provide a consistent language for the book. The most frequently used non-accounting terms are included here for reference and comparison, in case you want to leave the non-accounting terms selected (Home window, Setup menu, User Preferences and Settings).

SUMMARY OF MAJOR EQUIVALENT TERMS

Accounting Terms	Non-Accounting Terms
General Journal	Miscellaneous Transactions
Journal Entries	Transaction Details
Payables	Vendors & Purchases
Receivables	Customers & Sales
Post	Process

DETAILED LIST OF EQUIVALENT TERMS

Location	Accounting Terms	Non-Accounting Terms
Home window icon	General (Journal)	Miscellaneous Transactions
File menu – Import/Export...	General Journal Entries	Miscellaneous Transactions
Maintenance menu – Clear Data	Clear Journal Entries	Clear Transaction Details
Setup menu, System Settings – Linked Accounts	Payables	Vendors & Purchases
	Receivables	Customers & Sales
View menu, User Preferences – Modules	Payables	Vendors & Purchases
	Receivables	Customers & Sales
Graphs menu	Payables	Unpaid Purchases
	Receivables	Unpaid Sales
Reports menu – Financials	General Ledger	Transactions by Account
Reports menu	Payables	Vendors & Purchases
	Receivables	Customers & Sales
Reports menu	Journal Entries — General	Transaction Details — Miscellaneous
Reports menu – Management Reports	Payables	Vendors & Purchases
	Receivables	Customers & Sales
Settings screen tabs	Payables	Vendors & Purchases
	Receivables	Customers & Sales
All Icon window menus	Type	Transactions
Accounts window — menu	Type — General	Transactions — Miscellaneous Transactions
Accounts ledger window	General Ledger	Chart of Accounts Records
Vendors ledger window	Payables Ledger	Vendor Records
Customers ledger window	Receivables Ledger	Customer Records
All journals (button and menu)	Post	Process

Index